Labor Relations Law

Labor Relations Law

Cases and Materials

FOURTEENTH EDITION

Charles B. Craver
Freda H. Alverson Professor of Law
The George Washington University

Marion G. Crain
Wiley B. Rutledge Professor of Law
Washington University in St. Louis

Grant M. Hayden
Professor of Law
SMU-Dedman School of Law

Carolina Academic Press
Durham, North Carolina

Copyright © 2021
Carolina Academic Press, LLC
All Rights Reserved

ISBN   978-1-5310-2033-0
e-ISBN   978-1-5310-2034-7
LCCN   2021934090

Carolina Academic Press
700 Kent Street
Durham, NC 27701
Telephone (919) 489-7486
Fax (919) 493-5668
www.cap-press.com

Printed in the United States of America

Contents

Table of Cases	xvii
Preface to the Fourteenth Edition	xliii

Part 1 • Introduction and Historical Background   3

Union Relevance in the 21st Century   3
    Charles B. Craver, *Why Labor Unions Must (and Can) Survive*   3
    Marion Crain & Ken Matheny, *Labor's Identity Crisis*   7
Section I. Historical Background   10
  A. The Pre-Civil War Period   10
    1. Early Development of Labor Unions   10
    2. The "Criminal Conspiracy" Doctrine   10
      Philadelphia Cordwainers' Case [Commonwealth v. Pullis]   11
  B. The Post-Civil War Era   12
    1. The Growth of National Unions and Labor Unrest   12
    2. Judicial Reaction and the Labor Injunction   14
    3. Labor Unions from 1900 to 1933   14
  C. The Period Since 1933   14
    1. The Initial New Deal Labor Policies   14
    2. The National Labor Relations Act (Wagner Act), 1935   15
      NLRB v. Jones & Laughlin Steel Corp.   15
    3. Union Growth under the Wagner Act: The CIO and Industrial Unions   16
    4. The Labor Management Relations Act (Taft-Hartley Act), 1947   18
    5. The Labor-Management Reporting and Disclosure Act (Landrum-Griffin Act), 1959   19
    6. Organized Labor from the 1970s to the Present   20
      Steven Greenhouse, Beaten Down, Worked Up: The Past, Present, and Future of American Labor   20
      Robert B. Reich, Saving Capitalism   21
Section II. Introductory Materials   24
  A. Coverage of the National Labor Relations Act   24
    1. Scope of the Concept "Affecting Commerce"   24
    2. NLRB Exercise of Its Jurisdiction   25
      NLRB, A Guide to Basic Law and Procedures Under the National Labor Relations Act   25
    3. Exclusions from Coverage   27

a. Independent Contractors	27
House Committee on Education and Labor	28
b. Supervisory Employees	30
c. Managerial Employees	32
d. Confidential Employees	33
e. Other Exclusions	33
i. Agricultural Laborers and Domestic Servants	33
ii. Residents, Interns, and Other Students	34
iii. Undocumented Workers	34
iv. Employees at Religious Schools and Health Care Institutions	35
v. Employees of Businesses Operated by Native American Tribes	36
Problems	36
B. Organization and Procedure of the National Labor Relations Board	38
1. Organization of the Board and the General Counsel	38
2. NLRB Procedures	39
C. NLRB Rule-Making Authority	42

Part 2 • The Right of Self-Organization and Protection against Employer Unfair Labor Practices — 45

SEMINAR ON FREE SPEECH AND PREELECTION CONDUCT, SOUTHWESTERN LEGAL FOUNDATION, LABOR LAW DEVELOPMENTS, PROCEEDINGS OF THE ELEVENTH ANNUAL INSTITUTE ON LABOR LAW	45
BERNARD KARSH, DIARY OF A STRIKE	46
Section I. Employer Interference, Restraint, or Coercion	47
A. Limiting Organizational Activities on Employer's Premises	48
Lechmere, Inc. v. NLRB	48
Notes	57
NLRB v. United Steelworkers [Nutone, Inc.]	63
Note	65
Problem	66
B. Anti-Union Speeches and Publications	67
Notes	69
NLRB v. Gissel Packing Co.	71
Notes	75
Problems	76
C. Interrogation	78
Blue Flash Express, Inc.	78
Notes	82
Problems	83
D. Economic Coercion and Inducement	84
NLRB v. Exchange Parts Co.	84
Notes	86
Problem	87
E. Violence and Intimidation, Espionage and Surveillance, and Economic Coercion	88

F. Employer Responsibility for Anti-Union Conduct of Subordinates and Others	90
Section II. Employer Domination or Support	91
Michael C. Harper, *The Continuing Relevance of Section 8(a)(2) to the Contemporary Workplace*	95
Problem	96
International Ladies' Garment Workers' Union v. NLRB [Bernhard-Altmann Texas Corp.]	97
Notes	101
Section III. Employer Discrimination	103
A. Discrimination to Discourage Union Activity	103
Edward G. Budd Mfg. Co. v. NLRB	103
Notes	106
Problems	112
B. Discrimination to Encourage Union Membership	113
1. Hiring Halls and Other Practices	113
International Brotherhood of Teamsters, Local 357 v. NLRB	113
Notes	118
2. Union Security Under Federal Legislation	121
Statutory References	121
NLRB v. General Motors Corp.	123
Marquez v. Screen Actors Guild	127
Notes	128
3. The First Amendment and the Free Rider Problem	131
Ellis v. Brotherhood of Railway, Airline & Steamship Clerks	131
Notes	141
4. State "Right-to-Work" Legislation	144
Statutory Reference	144
Retail Clerks, Local 1625 v. Schermerhorn	145
Retail Clerks International Ass'n, Local 1625 v. Schermerhorn	147
Note	147
C. Which Activities Are Protected Under Section 7?	148
1. Concerted Activity on Social Media	149
2. Employer Work Rules and Policies Potentially Restricting §7 Activity	151
Problems	153
3. Arbitration Clauses Prohibiting Class Actions in the Nonunion Setting	154
Epic Systems Corp. v. Lewis	155
Note	156
4. Constructive Concerted Activity	157
NLRB v. City Disposal Systems	157
Notes	163
Problem	165
5. *Weingarten* Rights	166

NLRB v. J. Weingarten, Inc.	166
Notes	167
6. Loss of Protection Due to Unlawful Objective, Unlawful Means, or Means against Public Policy	169
Elk Lumber Co.	172
Notes	174
Problem	179
Mastro Plastics Corp. v. NLRB	180
Notes	186
7. Use of Replacement Workers during Strikes	187
NLRB v. Mackay Radio & Telegraph Co.	187
Notes	188
8. Inducements to Strike Crossovers and New Hires	194
9. Proof of Motive in Cases Involving Violations of Sections 8(a)(3) and (1)	197
NLRB v. Great Dane Trailers, Inc.	197
Note	198
Problem	198
D. Lockouts, Plant Closings, and "Runaway Shops"	199
NLRB v. Truck Drivers, Local 449, International Brotherhood of Teamsters [Buffalo Linen Case]	199
NLRB v. Brown	200
Notes	206
American Ship Building Co. v. NLRB	206
Notes	217
Problem	219
Textile Workers Union v. Darlington Mfg. Co.	220
Notes	227
Problem	230
E. Remedial Problems	230
Phelps Dodge Corp. v. NLRB	230
Notes	231
Part 3 • Representation Questions	**235**
John Logan, *Consultants, Lawyers, and the "Union Free" Movement in the USA Since the 1970s*	235
Section I. Establishing Representative Status through NLRB Elections	238
Statutory References	238
NLRB, Twenty-Sixth Annual Report	238
NLRB, Forty-Sixth Annual Report	239
Notes	240
A. Bars to Conducting an Election	240
NLRB, Thirty-Seventh Annual Report	240
Notes	241
B. Defining the Appropriate Unit	243

Blue Man Vegas, LLC v. NLRB	243
Notes	251
1. Multiple Plant Units	255
NLRB, Seventeenth Annual Report	255
Note	256
2. Multiemployer Units	256
NLRB, Twenty-Third Annual Report	256
Charles D. Bonanno Linen Service, Inc. v. NLRB	257
Notes	259
Problem	259
C. The Conduct of Representation Elections	260
NLRB, Thirty-First Annual Report	260
Note	261
NLRB, Thirty-First Annual Report	262
Notes	263
Problem	272
D. Court Review of Representation Proceedings	273
Leedom v. Kyne	273
Notes	277
Section II. Establishing Representative Status through Unfair Labor Practice Proceedings	278
NLRB v. Gissel Packing Co.	279
Notes	289
Linden Lumber Division, Summer & Co. v. NLRB	292
Note	298
Section III. Duration of the Duty to Bargain	298
Brooks v. NLRB	298
Notes	302
Auciello Iron Works, Inc. v. NLRB	304
Notes	308
NLRB v. Curtin Matheson Scientific, Inc.	309
Notes	318
American Seating Co.	319
Note	321
International Ladies' Garment Workers' Union Local 57 v. NLRB [Garwin Corp.]	322
Problems	322
Part 4 • Union Collective Action	**325**
Neil W. Chamberlain, *The Philosophy of American Management Toward Labor,* in Labor in a Changing America	325
Lloyd G. Reynolds, Stanley H. Masters & Colletta H. Moser, Labor Economics and Labor Relations	325
Section I. Introduction	326
A. Collective Action at Common Law	326

B. Anti-Injunction Statutes	326
Marine Cooks & Stewards v. Panama S.S. Co.	327
Notes	328
Section II. Union Discipline	330
NLRB v. Allis-Chalmers Mfg. Co.	330
Notes	337
NLRB v. Boeing Co.	339
Note	340
Pattern Makers' League of North America v. NLRB	340
Notes	351
Problem	352
Section III. Organizational and Recognitional Picketing	353
NLRB v. Drivers, Chauffeurs, Helpers, Local 639 [Curtis Bros.]	353
Note	355
International HOD Carriers Local 840 [Blinne Construction Co.]	356
Note	364
Smitley, d/b/a Crown Cafeteria v. NLRB	365
Notes	368
Houston Building & Construction Trades Council [Claude Everett Construction Co.]	369
Note	371
Problems	372
Section IV. Secondary Pressure	374
A. Primary-Secondary Distinction	376
NLRB v. International Rice Milling Co.	376
Notes	378
B. Common Situs Problems	380
Sailors' Union of the Pacific & Moore Dry Dock Co.	380
Notes	382
Problem	383
NLRB v. Denver Building & Construction Trades Council	384
Note	389
International Union of Electrical, Radio & Machine Workers, Local 761, AFL-CIO v. NLRB [General Electric Co.]	389
Notes	395
Problems	396
C. The Ally Doctrine	398
NLRB v. Business Machine & Office Appliance Mechanics Conference Board, IUE, Local 459 [Royal Typewriter Co.]	398
Notes	402
Problems	402
D. Consumer Picketing	404
NLRB v. Retail Clerks, Local 1001 [Safeco Title Insurance Co.]	404
Note	412
Problem	413

E. Threats and Coercion of Secondary Employers	414
Notes	414
Edward J. DeBartolo Corp. v. Florida Gulf Coast Building Trades Council	415
Note	422
Problem	423
F. Hot Cargo Agreements	424
United Brotherhood of Carpenters & Joiners, Local 1976 v. NLRB [Sand Door]	424
Notes	427
Connell Construction Co. v. Plumbers Local 100	429
Note	440
Labor and Antitrust	440
Amalgamated Meat Cutters & Butcher Workmen Local 189 v. Jewel Tea Co.	441
United Mine Workers v. Pennington	442
Note	442
National Woodwork Manufacturers Ass'n v. NLRB	443
NLRB v. International Longshoremen's Ass'n	450
Notes	453
Problem	454
G. Damages for Unlawful Secondary Activity	455
United Mine Workers, District 28 v. Patton	455
Notes	456
Section V. Jurisdictional Disputes	457
NLRB, THIRTY-SEVENTH ANNUAL REPORT	457
NLRB v. Radio & Television Broadcast Engineers Local 1212 (CBS)	458
Notes	459
Section VI. "Featherbedding"	461
American Newspaper Publishers Ass'n v. NLRB	461
NLRB v. Gamble Enterprises, Inc.	462
Section VII. National Labor Relations Act Preemption	463
A. *Garmon* Preemption	464
San Diego Building Trades Council v. Garmon	464
Notes	466
Amalgamated Ass'n of Street, Electric Railway & Motor Coach Employees of America v. Lockridge	468
Notes	476
Sears, Roebuck & Co. v. San Diego County Dist. Council of Carpenters	477
Notes	479
International Brotherhood of Teamsters, Local 24 v. Oliver	480
B. *Machinists* Preemption	481
Lodge 76, Int'l Ass'n of Machinists & Aerospace Workers v. Wisconsin Employment Relations Commission	481

Chamber of Commerce of the United States v. Brown	482
Notes	482
Metropolitan Life Ins. Co. v. Massachusetts	483
Notes	484
C. Comparing *Garmon* Preemption and *Machinists* Preemption	486
Belknap, Inc. v. Hale	486
Notes	497
Problem	499

Part 5 • Collective Bargaining — 501

ALBERT REES, THE ECONOMICS OF TRADE UNIONS	501
Freeman & Medoff, *The Two Faces of Unionism*, in THE PUBLIC INTEREST	502
Notes	504
Section I. Exclusive Representation and Majority Rule	507
J. I. Case Co. v. NLRB	507
Notes	509
Problems	511
Emporium Capwell Co. v. Western Addition Community Organization	511
Notes	518
Molly S. McUsic & Michael Selmi, *Postmodern Unions: Identity Politics in the Workplace*	520
Marion Crain & Ken Matheny, *"Labor's Divided Ranks": Privilege and the United Front Ideology*	521
Notes	522
Section II. Fair Representation and Individual Contract Rights	526
Archibald Cox, *The Duty of Fair Representation*	526
Clyde W. Summers, *Individual Rights in Collective Agreements and Arbitration*	526
A. Judicial Enforcement of Fair Representation	527
Steele v. Louisville & Nashville Railroad	527
Notes	530
Problem	530
1. Defining the Duty	531
Vaca v. Sipes	531
Notes	539
Air Line Pilots Ass'n, Int'l v. O'Neill	542
Notes	542
Problems	546
2. Relationship to Contract Breach	547
Hines v. Anchor Motor Freight, Inc.	547
Notes	551
Clayton v. International Union, United Automobile Workers	553
Notes	553

Glover v. St. Louis-San Francisco R. Co.	554
Notes	554
B. Unfair Representation as an Unfair Labor Practice	555
Teamsters (Ind.) Local 553 (Miranda Fuel Co., Inc.)	555
Notes	555
Problem	559
Section III. Union Representation and Antidiscrimination Law	560
A. An Overview of Title VII	560
B. The Age Discrimination in Employment Act (ADEA)	561
C. The Americans with Disabilities Act (ADA)	561
D. Areas of Tension between Labor Law and Antidiscrimination Law	562
1. Sexual and Racial Harassment by Coworkers	562
2. Individual Requests for Accommodation Under the ADA	565
Problem	567
E. Union Waiver of Individual Statutory Forum Rights	567
Alexander v. Gardner-Denver Co.	567
Notes	569
Gilmer v. Interstate/Johnson Lane Corp.	571
Notes	571
Wright v. Universal Maritime Serv. Corp.	573
14 Penn Plaza LLC v. Pyett	574
Notes	585
Section IV. The Nature of the Duty to Bargain	588
A. Good Faith	590
LABOR STUDY GROUP, THE PUBLIC INTEREST IN NATIONAL LABOR POLICY	590
General Electric Co.	591
Note	594
NLRB v. General Electric Co.	595
Notes	600
Problems	604
NLRB v. American National Insurance Co.	605
Problem	610
NLRB v. Insurance Agents' International Union	611
General Electric Co. v. NLRB	611
Notes	612
Problem	614
Charles D. Bonanno Linen Service, Inc. v. NLRB	614
Notes	615
B. Bargaining Remedies	615
H. K. Porter Co. v. NLRB	615
Notes	620
Ex-Cell-O Corp.	621
Notes	628
C. Unilateral Action	634

NLRB v. Katz	634
Notes	637
Problems	646
D. Supplying Information	646
NLRB v. Truitt Manufacturing Co.	646
NLRB v. Acme Indus. Co.	648
Notes	649
Problems	658
Section V. The Subject Matter of Collective Bargaining	659
NLRB v. Wooster Division of Borg-Warner Corp.	659
Notes	663
Problems	667
Allied Chemical & Alkali Workers Local 1 v. Pittsburgh Plate Glass Co.	669
Notes	674
Problem	679
Fibreboard Paper Products Corp. v. NLRB	679
Notes	685
First National Maintenance Corp. v. NLRB	688
Dubuque Packing Co.	697
Notes	698
Problems	702
Section VI. The Duty to Bargain during a Contract's Term	704
The Jacobs Manufacturing Co.	704
Notes	710
NLRB v. Lion Oil Co.	713
Notes	714
Problem	714
Part 6 • The Collective Agreement	**717**
Section I. The Legal Status of the Collective Agreement	717
Section II. Enforcement of the Collective Agreement through the Grievance and Arbitration Process	719
Labor Study Group, The Public Interest in National Labor Policy	719
A. The Grievance Procedure	720
B. Voluntary Arbitration	720
1. Interest Arbitration	722
2. Grievance Arbitration	724
C. Arbitration Under the Railway Labor Act	726
Section III. Judicial Enforcement of the Collective Agreement	727
A. Federal Oversight: Section 301 of the Labor Management Relations Act	727
Textile Workers Union v. Lincoln Mills	727

  Teamsters, Chauffeurs, Warehousemen & Helpers, Local 174 v.
    Lucas Flour Co.   732
   Notes   735
  Retail Clerks International Ass'n v. Lion Dry Goods, Inc.   737
   Note   737
 B. Arbitrability   738
  United Steelworkers v. Warrior & Gulf Navigation Co.   738
  United Steelworkers v. American Mfg. Co.   745
   Note   745
  AT&T Technologies, Inc. v. Communications Workers of America   746
  Granite Rock Co. v. Int'l Bhd. of Teamsters   747
   Notes   749
 C. Arbitration Under Lapsed Collective Bargaining Agreements   751
  Nolde Bros. v. Bakery & Confectionery Workers Local 358   751
   Notes   751
 D. Judicial Enforcement of Arbitration Awards   754
  United Steelworkers v. Enterprise Wheel & Car Corp.   754
   Note   755
  Major League Baseball Players Ass'n v. Garvey   756
   Notes   757
 E. The Public Policy Exception   762
  United Paperworkers International Union v. Misco, Inc.   762
   Notes   764
  Eastern Associated Coal Corp. v. United Mine Workers District 17   765
   Note   770
   Problem   771
Section IV. The Enforcement of Strike Bans and the Effect of Norris-La
 Guardia   772
  Boys Markets, Inc. v. Retail Clerks Local 770   772
   Notes   778
   Problem   781
  Buffalo Forge Co. v. United Steelworkers   782
   Notes   789
   Problem   790
  Complete Auto Transit, Inc. v. Reis   791
   Notes   792
Section V. Section 301 Preemption and State Claims   795
  Lingle v. Norge Division of Magic Chef, Inc.   795
   Notes   800
   Problem   804
  Lividas v. Bradshaw   805
   Notes   807
   Problem   809
Section VI. Contract Rights and Statutory Rights — Overlapping Law
 and Forums   809

A. Unilateral Contract Modification Cases — Bargaining during the Term of the Agreement	810
NLRB v. C & C Plywood Corp.	810
Notes	814
Milwaukee Spring Division of Illinois Coil Spring Co.	816
Note	822
B. Deference to Arbitration	822
Collyer Insulated Wire	823
Notes	830
Problem	835
C. Deferral Where Labor Board Has Primary Jurisdiction — Representational Issues	836
Notes	836
Smith v. Evening News Ass'n	837
Notes	838
D. Contract Rejection in Bankruptcy	838
Notes	838
Section VII. Successor Employers' Contractual and Bargaining Obligations	841
John Wiley & Sons, Inc. v. Livingston	841
Notes	842
NLRB v. Burns International Security Services, Inc.	842
Howard Johnson Co. v. Detroit Local Joint Executive Board	849
Notes	850
Problem	857
Fall River Dyeing & Finishing Corp. v. NLRB	858
Notes	869
Part 7 • Internal Union Affairs	**873**
Archibald Cox, *Internal Affairs of Labor Unions Under the Labor Reform Act of 1959*	873
Section I. The Bill of Rights	875
Clyde W. Summers, *The Impact of Landrum-Griffin in State Courts*, in N.Y.U. Thirteenth Annual Conference on Labor	876
Directors Guild of America, Inc. v. Superior Court of Los Angeles County	876
Section II. Reporting and Disclosure Provisions	877
House Committee on Education and Labor	877
Section III. Trusteeships and Parent-Local Relations	880
Section IV. The Regulation of Racketeering and Communist Activity	881
Index	**885**

Table of Cases

14 Penn Plaza LLC v. Pyett, 574, 585, 586
3750 Orange Place L.P. v. NLRB, 870
520 S. Mich. Ave. Assocs., Ltd. v. Shannon, 485
A. R. Barnes & Co. v. Berry, 718
Abdullayeva v. Attending Homecare Servs., LLC, 586
Abood v. Detroit Board of Education, 133, 135, 139, 140, 141, 143
Ace Elec. Contrs. v. IBEW, Local Union 292, 762
Acrylic Indus. v. NLRB, 192
Action Elec., Inc. v. Local Union No. 292, International Brotherhood of Electrical Workers, 615
Adcock v. Freightliner LLC, 101, 678, 881
Addington v. U.S. Air Line Pilots Ass'n, Int'l, 544
Adkins v. Times-World Corp., 746
Adorno v. Crowley Towing & Transp. Co., 552
Adtranz ABB Daimler-Benz Transp., N.A. v. NLRB, 60
Advanced Disposal Services East, Inc. v. NLRB, 266
Aero. Workers v. AK Steel Corp., 749
Aeronautical Indus. Dist. Lodge 91 v. United Techs. Corp., 780
AFL v. NLRB, 274
AFL-CIO Joint Negotiating Committee for Phelps Dodge v. NLRB, 613
AFL-CIO v. Chao, 879
AFL-CIO v. NLRB, 264
AFTRA v. NLRB, 602
Agri Processor Co. v. NLRB, 34, 245
Aguilera v. Pirelli Armstrong Tire Corp., 802
Aguinaga v. United Food & Commercial Workers Int'l Union, 543, 544
Air Line Pilots Ass'n, Int'l v. Northwest Airlines, Inc., 587
Air Line Pilots Ass'n, Int'l v. O'Neill, 542
Air Methods Corp. v. Office & Prof'l Emps., 760
Air Transport Ass'n. v. National Mediation Board, 271
Airport Shuttle-Cincinnati, Inc. v. NLRB, 302
Aka v. Washington Hosp. Ctr., 566
Akers Nat'l Roll Co. v. United Steel, Paper and Forestry, Rubber, Mfg., Energy, Allied Indus. & Serv. Workers Int'l Union, 759, 856
Akins v. USW, Local 187, 552
Albertson's, Inc. v. NLRB, 58
Alday v. Raytheon Co., 676
Aleem v. General Felt Industries, Inc., 570
Aleman v. Chugach Support Servs., Inc., 586
Alexander v. Anthony Int'l, L.P., 572
Alexander v. Choate, 562
Alexander v. Gardner-Denver Co., 516, 567, 569, 575, 578, 579, 581, 582, 583, 798
Alexander v. Local 496, Laborers' Int'l Union, 792

Algoma Plywood & Veneer Co. v. Wisconsin Employment Relations Board, 125, 148
Alkire v. NLRB, 856
Allen Bradley Co. v. Electrical Workers, 431, 437, 438
Allen v. McWane Inc., 711
Allen-Bradley Local v. Wisconsin Employment Relations Board, 467
Allentown Mack Sales & Serv. v. NLRB, 318, 854
Allied Chemical Workers v. Pittsburgh Plate Glass Co., 515, 669, 691, 694
Allied Sys. Ltd. v. Teamsters Nat'l Auto. Transporters Indus. Negotiating Comm., Local Union 327, 779
Allis-Chalmers Corp. v. Lueck, 795, 796, 798, 806
Am. Steel Erectors v. Local Union No. 7, 428
Amalgamated Ass'n of Street, Electric Railway & Motor Coach Employees of America v. Lockridge, 468
Amalgamated Clothing Workers v. NLRB, 70
Amalgamated Clothing Workers v. Richman Bros., 467
America v. Enterprise Wheel & Car Corp., 363 U.S. , 569
American Boiler Mfrs. Ass'n v. NLRB, 454
American Bread Co. v. NLRB, 411
American Broadcasting Cos. v. Writers Guild of Am., W., 339
American Cyanamid Co. v. NLRB, 192
American Federation of Television & Radio Artists v. NLRB, 402
American Hospital Association v. NLRB, 251
American Newspaper Publishers Ass'n v. NLRB, 461
American Radio Ass'n v. Mobile S.S. Ass'n, 407
American Ship Building Co. v. NLRB, 203, 206
American Smelting & Refining Co. v. NLRB, 664
American Steel Foundries v. Tri-City Central Trades Council, 16
American Tel. & Tel. Co. v. Communications Workers of America, 779
Americare Pine Lodge Nursing & Rehabilitation Ctr. v. NLRB, 603
AmeriSteel Corp. v. Int'l Bhd. of Teamsters, 854
Amoco Petroleum Additives Co., In re, 801
Ampersand Publishing LLC v. NLRB, 179
AMTRAK v. Transp. Workers Union, 790
Anheuser-Busch, Inc. v. Beer Drivers, Local 744, Int'l Bhd. of Teamsters, 759
Anheuser-Busch, Inc. v. NLRB, 168
AP Parts Co. v. International Union, United Auto. Aerospace & Agricultural Implement Workers, 761
Apex Hosiery Co. v. Leader, 426, 436
Aqua-Chem, Inc., Cleaver-Brooks Div. v. NLRB, 196
Architectural Glass & Metal Co. v. NLRB, 109
Arnold v. Air Midwest, 551, 793
Aro, Inc. v. NLRB, 159
Arriaga-Zayasv v. International Ladies' Garment Workers' Union-Puerto Rico Council, 553
ASARCO LLC v. United Steel, Paper and Forestry, Rubber, Mfg., Energy, Allied Ind'l and Serv. Workers Int'l Union, 757
Ashland Facility Operations LLC v. NLRB, 270

Ashwander v. TVA, 134
Associated Builders & Contractors of Texas v. NLRB, 264
Associated Builders. & Contrs. v. Local 302, IBEW, 807
Associated Rubber Co. v. NLRB, 268
Association of Westinghouse Salaried Employees v. Westinghouse Corp., 729, 731, 735
AT&T Technologies, Inc. v. Communications Workers of America, 746, 748
Atchison, T. & S. F. R. Co. v. Buell, 799
Atlantic-Pacific Constr. Co. v. NLRB, 148
Atlas Life Ins. Co. v. NLRB, 78
Atrium of Princeton, LLC v. NLRB, 641
Auciello Iron Works, Inc. v. NLRB, 304
Auto Workers Local 3047 v. Hardin County, 145
Automotive, Petroleum, Local 618 v. NLRB, 394
Avco Corp. v. Aero Lodge No. 735, 773, 806
Aviation Corp. v. NLRB, 59, 64, 117, 215, 222

Babbitt v. Farm Workers, 419
Badkin v. Lockheed Martin Corp., 540
Baker v. Farmers Elec. Coop., 800
Baker v. General Motors Corp., 483
Bakery Drivers Local v. Wohl, 409
Bakery Sales Drivers, Local 33 v. Wagshal, 329
Baldracchi v. Pratt & Whitney Aircraft Div., United Technologies Corp., 799
Bally's Park Place, Inc. v. NLRB, 107
Barnes v. Stone Container Corp., 808
Barnhart v. Sigmon Coal Co., 579
Barrentine v. Arkansas-Best Freight System, Inc., 484, 570, 583, 584, 798

Barton v. Constellium Rolled Products, 645
Barton v. House of Raeford Farms, Inc., 803
Bath Marine Draftsmen's Ass'n v. NLRB, 713
Baxter v. United Paperworkers Int'l Union, Local 7370, 540
BE&K Constr. Co. v. NLRB, 89
Beals v. Kiewit Pacific Co., 802
Beck v. UFCW, Local 99, 540, 563
Becton v. Detroit Terminal of Consol. Freightways, 570
Belknap, Inc. v. Hale, 486
Bell Aerospace Co. Div. of Textron, Inc. v. NLRB, 43
Bell v. DaimlerChrysler Corp., 554
Bellagio, LLC v. NLRB, 167, 254
Benson v. Northwest Airlines, 566
Berger v. Iron Workers Reinforced Rodmen Local 201, 793
Bernard v. Air Line Pilots Ass'n, Int'l, 545
Bernard v. IBP, Inc., 570
Beth Israel Hosp. v. NLRB, 61
Beverly Enterprises in Beverly Health & Rehab. Servs. v. NLRB, 233
Beverly Farm Found. v. NLRB, 638
Beverly Health & Rehabilitation Servs. v. Feinstein, 40
Bidlack v. Wheelabrator Corp., 676
Bill Johnson's Restaurants, Inc. v. NLRB, 89
Bishop v. ALPA, Int'l, 543
BIW Deceived v. Local S6, Indus. Union of Marine & Shipbuilding Workers, 803
Black v. Ryder/P.I.E. Nationwide, 552
Black-Clawson Co. Paper Machine Div. v. International Ass'n of Machinists, 540
Bldg. & Constr. Trades Council v. Associated Builders & Contrs., 497
Bldg. Trades Emplrs. Educ. Ass'n v. McGowan, 498

Blesedell v. Chillicothe Telephone Co., 541
Bliesner v. Commun. Workers of Am., 551
Blue Man Vegas, LLC v. NLRB, 243
Board of Commissioners v. United States, 730
Bob Evans Farms v. NLRB, 149
Boeing Airplane Co. v. NLRB, 714
Boeing Co. v. International Ass'n of Machinists & Aerospace Workers, 850
Boersig v. Union Elec. Co., 566
Boire v. Greyhound Corp., 278
Boisdore's Heirs, United States v., 183
Bonnell/Tredegar Indus. v. NLRB, 643
Bonwit Teller, Inc. v. NLRB, 65
Bostock v. Clayton County, 560
Boston Med. Ctr. v. SEIU, Local 285, 770
Bourne v. NLRB, 83
Bowen v. United States Postal Service, 541
Boxhorn's Big Muskego Gun Club, Inc. v. Electrical Workers Local 494, 423
Boys Markets, Inc. v. Retail Clerks Local 770, 772, 783
Bratten v. SSI Servs., Inc., 586
Breda v. Scott, 793
Breininger v. Sheet Metal Workers Int'l Ass'n Local 6, 542
Brenner v. United Bhd. of Carpenters & Joiners, 792
Brentwood Med. Assocs. v. UMW, 758
Brockway Motor Trucks, Div. of Mack Trucks, Inc. v. NLRB, 687, 691, 696
Brooks v. NLRB, 99, 298, 307
Bro-Tech Corp. v. NLRB, 271
Brotherhood of Electrical Workers, Local 387 v. NLRB, 193
Brotherhood of R. Trainmen v. Toledo, P. & W. Railroad, 781
Brotherhood of R.R. Trainmen v. Chicago River & Ind. R.R., 776, 781
Brown & Pipkins, LLC v. SEIU, 750
Brown & Root, Inc. v. NLRB, 853
Brown Shoe Co. v. NLRB, 658
Brown v. Board of Educ., 519
Brown v. Hotel & Restaurant Employees & Bartenders International Union Local 54, 483
Browning-Ferris Industries of Calif. v. NLRB, 253
Brownlee v. Yellow Freight System, Inc., 552
Buffalo Forge Co. v. United Steelworkers, 782
Buford v. Laborers' Int'l Union Local 269, 562
Burger King Corp. v. NLRB, 61
Burkevich v. Air Line Pilots Ass'n, Int'l, 543
Burlington N. R.R. Co. v. Brotherhood of Maintenance of Way Employees, 379
Burns Int'l Sec. Servs. v. NLRB, 830
Burnside v. Kiewit Pac. Corp., 808

Cal. Grocers Ass'n v. City of Los Angeles, 485
Calatrello ex rel. v. "Automatic" Sprinkler Corp. of Am., 687
Califano v. Yamasaki, 134
California Brewers Assn. v. Bryant, 768
California ex rel. Brown v. Safeway, Inc., 442
California Grocers' Ass'n v. City of Los Angeles, 857
Cantrell v. International Bhd. of Elec. Workers, Local 2021, 736, 737
Capital Service, Inc. v. NLRB, 467
Carbon Fuel Co. v. United Mine Workers, 792
Carey Salt Co. v. NLRB, 602, 639
Carey v. Westinghouse Corp., 812, 836

Carino v. Stefan, 793
Carlson v. Arrowhead Concrete Works, Inc., 801
Carpet Service Int'l. v. Chicago Reg'l Council of Carpenters, 383
Carrier Air Conditioning Co. v. NLRB, 454
Carroll College, Inc. v. NLRB, 35
Casino Pauma v. NLRB, 36
Caterpillar Logistics, Inc. v. NLRB, 89
Caterpillar, Inc. v. Williams, 509, 801
Cavallaro v. UMass Mem'l Healthcare, Inc., 586
CBOCS West, Inc. v. Humphries, 582
Cedar Coal Co. v. United Mine Workers, 790
CenterPoint Energy Res. Corp. v. Gas Workers Union, Local No. 340, 757, 760
Central Hardware Co. v. NLRB, 51, 53, 55
Centralia Bldg. & Constr. Trades Council v. NLRB, 371
Cephas v. MVM, Inc., 552
Ceridian Corp. v. NLRB, 612
Chamber of Commerce of the United States v. Brown, 482
Chamber of Commerce of the United States v. Reich, 190
Chamber of Commerce of U.S. v. NLRB, 43
Charles D. Bonanno Linen Service, Inc. v. NLRB, 257, 614
Charles Dowd Box Co. v. Courtney, 474, 733, 735
Charleston & West. Carolina R. Co. v. Varnville Furniture Co., 465
Chauffeurs, Teamsters & Helpers, Local 391 v. Terry, 552
Cheney California Lumber Co. v. NLRB, 714
Chester ex rel. NLRB v. Grane Healthcare Co., 630
Chi. Dist. Council of Carpenters Pension Fund v. K & I Constr., 779

Chicago & N.W.R. Co. v. Transportation Union, 695
Chicago Dist. Council of Carpenters Pension Fund v. Reinke Insulation Co., 480
Chicago Tribune Co. v. NLRB, 643, 658, 713
Children's Hosp. Med. Ctr. v. Cal. Nurses Ass'n, 193, 790
Ciba-Geigy Pharmaceuticals Div. v. NLRB, 814
Cintas Corp. v. NLRB, 151
Circuit City Stores, Inc. v. Adams, 571, 572, 576, 578
Circuit City Stores, Inc. v. Mantor, 572
CITGO Asphalt Ref. Co. v. Paper, Allied-Industrial, Chem., & Energy Workers Int'l Union Local 2-991, 761
CitiSteel USA v. NLRB, 869
Clayton v. International Union, United Automobile Workers, 553
Clear Channel Outdoor, Inc. v. Int'l Unions of Painters & Allied Trades, Local 770, 760
Clearfield Trust Co. v. United States, 730
Clearwater Paper Corp., 152
Cleveland Real Estate Partners v. NLRB, 58
Cleveland v. Porca Co., 542
Cmty. Hosps. of Cent. Cal. v. NLRB, 869
CNH Am. LLC v. Int'l Union, United Auto., Aerospace & Agr. Implement Workers of Am. (UAW), 801
Coastal Derby Refining Co. v. NLRB, 870
Cole v. Burns Int'l Sec. Servs., 572
Cole v. Int'l Union, UAW, 551
Coleman v. Donahoe, 570
Colgate-Palmolive-Peet Co. v. NLRB, 298

Collins v. N.Y. City Transit Auth., 569
Colony Materials, Inc. v. Rothman, 363
Colorado Fire Sprinkler, Inc. v. NLRB, 102
Comau, Inc. v. NLRB, 642
Commonwealth Edison Co. v. IBEW, Local Union No. 15, 857
Commonwealth v. Hunt, 11
Communications Workers of Am. v. Beck, 127, 128, 141
Communications Workers v. American Tel. & Tel. Co., 736
Complete Auto Transit, Inc. v. Reis, 791
ConAgra, Inc. v. NLRB, 651
Conair Corp. v. NLRB, 291
Connell Construction Co. v. Plumbers Local 100, 429
Consolidated Edison Co. v. Public Service Commission, 409
Consolidation Coal Co. v. Local 1702 United Mine Workers, 793
Cont'l Airlines, Inc. v. Air Line Pilots Ass'n, Int'l, 770
Contemporary Cars, Inc. v. NLRB, 89
Cooper v. Honeywell International, Inc., 676
Cooper v. Nutley Sun Printing Co., 477
Coronet Foods, Inc. v. NLRB, 229
Country Ford Trucks, Inc. v. NLRB, 245, 246, 250
Crawford Mfg. Co. v. NLRB, 281
Creative Vision Resources, LLC v. NLRB, 870
Crowell v. Benson, 134
Crown Cafeteria v. NLRB, 327 F.2d 351 (1964), 365
Crown Central Petroleum Corp. v. NLRB, 161
Crown Cork & Seal Co. v. International Ass'n of Machinists and Aero. Workers, 753
Cruz v. Local 3 of the IBEW, 540

Ctr. Constr. Co. v. NLRB, 89, 289
Cummings v. John Morrell & Co., 736
Cunningham v. Air Line Pilots' Ass'n., 546
Cut Stone Co. v. Journeymen Stone Cutters' Ass'n, 327, 446
Czosek v. O'Mara, 541

D.R Horton, Inc. v. NLRB, 155
DaimlerChrysler Corp. v. NLRB, 832
Daniel Constr. Co. v. NLRB, 70
Danylchuk v. Des Moines Register & Tribune Co., 542
Darrington v. Milton Hershey School, 586
Daugherty v. City of El Paso, 566
Davis v. Florida Power & Light Co., 566
Dayton Hudson Dep't Store Co. v. NLRB, 269
Dayton Newspapers, Inc. v. NLRB, 217
De Veau v. Braisted, 882
Dean Transp. v. NLRB, 869
DeCoe v. GMC, 800
Delaware Coca-Cola Bottling Co. v. General Teamster Local Union 326, 779
DelCostello v. Int'l Bhd. of Teamsters, 552, 736
Delta Air Lines, Inc. v. Air Line Pilots Ass'n, International, 764
Demitris v. Transport Workers Union, 544
Derwin v. General Dynamics Corp., 736
Detabali v. St. Luke's Hospital, 809
Detroit Edison Co. v. NLRB, 653
Detroit Newspaper Publishers Ass'n v. NLRB, 259
Detroit Typographical Union No. 18 v. NLRB, 640
Detroit Typographical Union, Local 18 v. Detroit Newspaper Agency, 752

Diesel Co. v. NLRB, 60
Directors Guild of America, Inc. v. Superior Court of Los Angeles County, 876
Dish Network Corp. v. NLRB, 639
District No. 1-Marine Eng'rs Benefit Ass'n v. GFC Crane Consultants, Inc., 754
Dodge of Naperville, Inc. v. NLRB, 701
Doerfer Eng'g v. NLRB, 832
Donnelly v. United Fruit Co., 539
Dorsey Trailers, Inc. v. NLRB, 700
Double Eagle Hotel & Casino v. NLRB, 151
Douds v. Architects, Engineers, Chemists & Technicians, Local 231, 400, 446
Dowd v. United Steelworkers of Am., Local No. 286, 563
Drake Bakeries, Inc. v. American Bakery & Confectionery Workers International, 793
Drivers' Union v. Lake Valley Co., 776
Drum, United States v., 672
Duffy Tool & Stamping, L.L.C. v. NLRB, 640
Dunbar Armored, Inc. v. NLRB, 246
Duplex Printing Press Co. v. Deering, 327, 438, 446
Duquesne Univ. of the Holy Spirit v. NLRB, 35

E.I. du Pont de Nemours & Co. v. NLRB, 639, 640
East Chicago Rehabilitation Center v. NLRB, 518
Eastern Associated Coal Corp. v. Mine Workers, 765
Eastex, Inc. v. NLRB, 161, 165
Eatz v. DME Unit of Local 3, 27
Eckles v. CONRAIL, 565
Edward G. Budd Mfg. Co. v. NLRB, 103
Edward J. DeBartolo Corp. v. Florida Gulf Coast Building Trades Council, 415
Edward J. DeBartolo Corp. v. NLRB, 417, 419
Edward S. Quirk Co. v. NLRB, 641
Eisenmann Corp. v. Sheet Metal Workers Int'l Ass'n Local 24, 761
El Paso Elec. Co. v. NLRB, 701
Electrical Workers v. NLRB, 407
Electrical Workers, Local 761 v. NLRB, 214
Electromation v. NLRB, 93
Elevator Mfrs' Ass'n v. International Union of Elevator Constructors, 779
Eliserio v. USW, Local 310, 563
Eller v. National Football Players Ass'n, 677
Ellis v. Brotherhood of Railway, Airline & Steamship Clerks, 131
Ellison v. Brady, 564
Emmanuel v. Int'l Bhd. of Teamsters, Local 25, 540
Employers Ass'n v. United Steelworkers, 497
Emporium Capwell Co. v. Western Addition Community Organization, 172, 511, 580
Engine Div. v. United Auto., Aero. & Agric. Implement Workers, 736
Enloe Med. Ctr. v. NLRB, 713
Entergy Operations, Inc. v. United Gov't Sec. Officers of Am. Int'l Union, 770
Epic Systems Corp. v. Lewis, 155
Epilepsy Found. v. NLRB, 169
Equitable Res., Inc. v. United Steel, Local 8-512, 855
Erie R. Co. v. Tompkins, 770
Essex County & Vicinity Dist. Council of Carpenters v. NLRB, 429
Evergreen Am. Corp. v. NLRB, 289
Ewing v. NLRB, 163

Ex-Cell-O Corp. v. NLRB, 631
Exelon Generation Co., LLC v. Local 15, 677
Exxel/Atmos, Inc. v. NLRB, 302
Exxon Chem. Co. v. NLRB, 842
Exxon Corp. v. Esso Workers' Union, Inc., 766

F.L. Thorpe & Co. v. NLRB, 192
Fall River Dyeing & Finishing Corp. v. NLRB, 305, 307, 310, 316, 858
Fallbrook Hosp. Corp. v. NLRB, 620
Family Serv. Agency San Francisco v. NLRB, 270
Fansteel Metallurgical Corp., 170
Farmer v. United Brotherhood of Carpenters & Joiners, 479, 488, 493
Fashion Valley Mall, LLC v. National Labor Relations Bd., 59
Fay v. Douds, 278
Federation of Musicians v. Carroll, 431
FedEx Home Delivery v. NLRB, 29
Felice v. Sever, 793
Ferriso v. NLRB, 144
Fibreboard Corp. v. NLRB, 221, 448, 671, 672, 679, 691, 692, 693
Fidelity Interior Constr. Inc. v. Southwestern Carpenters Reg'l Council, 383
Fieldcrest Cannon v. NLRB, 632
Figueroa v. Foster, 804
Finley Hospital v. NLRB, 644
Firestone v. S. Cal. Gas Co., 802
First Healthcare Corp. v. NLRB, 62
First National Maintenance Corp. v. NLRB, 688, 817
First Student, Inc. v. NLRB, 851
Five Star Transp., Inc. v. NLRB, 177
Flight Attendants in Reunion v. Am. Airlines, Inc., 546
Florida Dept. of Revenue v. Piccadilly Cafeterias, Inc., 579
Florida Power & Light Co. v. International Brotherhood of Elec. Workers, Local 641, 339
Florida Power Corp. v. International Brotherhood of Electrical Workers, etc., Local Union 433, 764
Food & Allied Workers Local 721 v. Needham Packing Co., 794
Food Employees v. Logan Valley Plaza, Inc., 51
Food Store Employees Union, etc. v. NLRB, 633
Ford Motor Co. (Chicago Stamping Plant) v. NLRB, 664, 675, 692
Ford Motor Co. v. Huffman, 515, 530, 532, 536
Ford Motor Co. v. NLRB, 347
Forest Products Co. v. NLRB, 198
Fort Halifax Packing Co. v. Coyne, 484, 799
Foy v. Giant Food, Inc., 800
Frandsen v. Brotherhood of Ry., etc., 553
Frankl ex rel. NLRB v. HTH Corp., 633
Franks Bros. Co. v. NLRB, 865
Freight Handling Co. v. Solien, 329
Frenchtown Acquisition Co. v. NLRB, 32
Freund Baking Co. v. NLRB, 268
Fry v. Airline Pilots Ass'n, 793
Furniture Rentors of Am. v. NLRB, 699

Ga. Power Co. v. NLRB, 666
Garity v. APWU Nat'l Labor Org., 564
Garment Workers v. NLRB, 307
Garner v. Teamsters, 125, 465, 466
Gates v. Arizona Brewing Co., 720
Gateway Coal Co. v. Mine Workers, 748, 779, 783, 786
Gatliff Coal Co. v. NLRB, 164
Gen. Dynamics Land Sys. v. Cline, 561
Gen. Indus. Emples. Union, Local 42 v. NLRB, 192

General Drivers, Local Union No. 509 v. Ethyl Corp., 750
General Electric Co. v. Local Union 191, 773
General Electric Co. v. NLRB, 611
General Motors Corp. v. Mendicki, 480
George A. Hormel & Co. v. NLRB, 175
Gestamp S.C., LLC v. NLRB, 108
Getreu v. Bartenders and Hotel & Restaurant Employees Union Local 58, 367
GGNSC Springfield LLC v. NLRB, 32
Giacalone v. NLRB, 41
Gilmer v. Interstate/Johnson Lane Corp., 571, 576, 577
Globe Cotton Mills v. NLRB, 589
Glover v. St. Louis-San Francisco R. Co., 554
Golden State Bottling Co. v. NLRB, 234, 851, 861, 862, 864
Golden State Transit Corp. v. Los Angeles, 498
Gonzalez v. Prestress Engineering Corp., 797
Good Samaritan Med. Ctr. v. NLRB, 150
Goodman v. Lukens Steel Co., 563
Graham v. Brotherhood of Firemen, 731
Granite Rock Co. v. Int'l Bhd. of Teamsters, 747, 749
Green v. Am. Fed'n of Teachers/Ill. Fed. of Teachers Local 604, 564
Greenier v. Pace, Local No. 1188, 563
Groves v. Ring Screw Works, Ferndale Fastener Div., 555
Gullett Gin Co. v. NLRB, 363
Guss v. Utah Labor Relations Bd., 476

H. Blum & Co. v. Landau, 718
H. K. Porter Co. v. NLRB, 615, 617, 622, 845
Haggins v. Verizon New England Inc., 800
Hammontree v. NLRB, 834
Hanna Mining Co. v. District 2, Marine Engineers Beneficial Ass'n, 477
Harmon v. Brucker, 276
Harnischfeger Corp. v. NLRB, 172
Harris v. Forklift Sys., 561
Harter Tomato Prods. Co. v. NLRB, 854
Hartman Bros. Heating & Air Conditioning, Inc. v. NLRB, 110
Hawaii Teamsters and Allied Workers Union, Local 996 v. UPS, 758
Hays v. National Electrical Contractors Ass'n, 119
Health Care v. NLRB, 59
Healthcare Emps. Union, Local 399 v. NLRB, 228
Heartland Plymouth Court MI, LLC v. NLRB, 633
Henderson v. Bluefield Hosp. Co., 630
Hertz Corp. v. NLRB, 656
Hill v. Florida, 483
Hines v. Anchor Motor Freight, Inc., 547
Hirsch v. Dorsey Trailers, Inc., 687
Hobet Mining v. Local 5817, United Mine Workers, 792
Hoffman ex rel. NLRB v. Cement Masons Local 337, 406
Hoffman Plastic Compounds, Inc. v. NLRB, 232
Hoffman v. Inn Credible Caterers, Ltd., 630
Holly Farms Corp. v. NLRB, 33
Holy Trinity Church v. United States, 445
Hooters of Am., Inc. v. Phillips, 572
Hoover Co. v. NLRB, 170, 175
Horton v. Miller Chemical Co., 797
Hotel Emples. & Rest. Emples. Union, Local 57 v. Sage Hospitality Res., LLC, 101, 678, 881

Houston Texas R. Co. v. United States, 730
Howard Johnson Co. v. Detroit Local Joint Executive Board, 849, 863, 867
Howard Johnson Co. v. NLRB, 32
Howard v. Int'l Molders & Allied Workers Union, etc., Local No. 100, 564
HTH Corp. v. NLRB, 633
Hudgens v. NLRB, 51, 53, 55, 479
Hughes v. Superior Court, 419
Humble v. Boeing Co., 808
Humphrey v. Moore, 474, 475, 532, 536, 575
Hurd v. Hodge, 770
Hutcheson, United States v., 776

IATSE Local 666, International Alliance of Theatrical Stage Employees etc. v. NLRB, 666
Ibarra v. United Parcel Serv., 586
IBEW Local 1395 v. NLRB, 193
IBEW Local 2150 v. NextEra Energy Point Breach, LLC, 745
IBEW, AFL-CIO Local 1245 v. Citizens Telcoms. Co., 677
IBEW, Local 501 v. NLRB, 391, 445
IBEW, Local 71 v. Trafftech, Inc., 750, 836
ILA v. Davis, 467
ILWU, Local 32 v. Pacific Maritime Ass'n, 460
In re (see name of party)
Indiana Metal Products Corp. v. NLRB, 109
Industrial Acoustics Co. v. NLRB, 271
Inechien v. Nichols Aluminum, LLC, 540
Ingle v. Circuit City Stores, Inc., 572
Inland Steel Co. v. NLRB, 663
Inland Trucking Co. v. NLRB, 218
Inlandboatmen's Union of the Pac. v. Dutra Group, 746

In-N-Out Burger, Inc. v. NLRB, 61
Int'l Ass'n of Machinists & Aero. Workers, Local Lodge 964 v. BF Goodrich Aero. Aerostructures Group, 882
Int'l Ass'n of Machinists and Aero. Workers Local Lodge 2121 v. Goodrich Corp., 677
Int'l Ass'n of Machinists v. Howmet Corp., 854
Int'l Chem. Workers Union Council v. NLRB, 652
Int'l Union of Electrical, etc. v. Ingram Mfg. Co., 736
Int'l Union of Operating Eng'rs, Local 150 v. NLRB, 110
Int'l Union, United Auto Workers v. Yard-Man, Inc., 675
Int'l Union, United Auto. v. Textron, Inc., 735
Int'l. Union, United Automobile v. NLRB, 541
International Ass'n of Machinists & Aero. Workers v. NLRB, 144
International Ass'n of Machinists & Aerospace Workers v. Lubbers, 40
International Assn. of Machinists v. Allen, 130
International Bhd. of Boilermakers v. NLRB, 110
International Bhd. of Elec. Workers v. Hechler, 803
International Bhd. of Teamsters, Local 245 v. Kansas City Piggy Back, 736
International Bhd. of Teamsters, Local 371 v. Logistics Support Group, 750
International Brotherhood of Electrical Workers v. Foust, 552
International Brotherhood of Electrical Workers v. NLRB, 170
International Brotherhood of Electrical Workers, Local No. 4 v. KTVI-TV, Inc., 750

International Brotherhood of Teamsters v. NLRB, 402
International Brotherhood of Teamsters, Local 24 v. Oliver, 480
International Brotherhood of Teamsters, Local 357 v. NLRB, 113, 222, 226
International Brotherhood v. W. L. Mead, Inc., 731
International Ladies' Garment Workers' Union v. NLRB [Bernhard-Altmann Texas Corp.], 97
International Longshore & Warehouse Union v. NLRB, 842
International Longshoremen's & Warehousemen's Union v. Juneau Spruce Corp., 457
International Longshoremen's & Warehousemen's Union, Local 14 v. NLRB, 460
International Longshoremen's & Warehousemen's Union, Local 62-B v. NLRB, 460
International Longshoremen's Ass'n v. Allied Int'l, 457
International Longshoremen's Ass'n v. Cataneo, Inc., 736
International Paper Co. v. NLRB, 219
International Transp. Serv. v. NLRB, 364
International Union of Elec., Salaried, Mach. & Furniture Workers v. Statham, 793
International Union of Electrical, Radio & Machine Workers, Local 761, AFL-CIO v. NLRB [General Electric Co.], 389, 446, 449, 450
International Union of Operating Eng'rs v. Flair Builders, Inc., 842
International Union of United Ass'n of Journeymen & Apprentices of Plumbing & Pipefitting Industry v. NLRB, 147

International Union, United Auto. Workers, Local 449 v. NLRB, 352
International Union, United Auto., Aerospace & Agricultural Implement Workers v. NLRB, 42
International Union, United Auto., etc. v. Dole, 879
International Union, United Auto., etc. v. NLRB, 631
International Wire v. International Brotherhood of Electrical Workers Local 38, 457
Ionosphere Clubs, In re, 839
Iron Moulders Union v. Allis-Chalmers Co., 401
Iron Workers Dist. Council of Pacific Northwest v. NLRB, 440
Iron Workers v. Perko, 472, 473, 477, 538
Irving Air Chute Co. v. NLRB, 70
Island Architectural Woodwork, Inc. v. NLRB, 856
Island Creek Coal Co. v. District 28, United Mine Workers, 760
ITT Industries v. NLRB, 58, 63
Ivaldi v. NLRB, 620

J. I. Case Co. v. NLRB, 488, 491, 507, 718
J. P. Stevens & Co. v. NLRB, 70, 232, 632
J.P. Stevens & Co., Gulistan Div. v. NLRB, 291
Jacksonville Bulk Terminals, Inc. v. International Longshoremen's Ass'n, 328, 790
Jacoby v. NLRB, 119, 120, 558
Janus v. AFSCME, Council 31, 143, 510
Jays Foods, Inc. v. NLRB, 224
Jeffreys v. Communication Workers, 544
Jerome v. United States, 730
Jim Walter Res., Inc. v. United Mine Workers of Am. Local 2397, 794

Joanna Cotton Mills Co. v. NLRB, 149
John Wiley & Sons, Inc. v. Livingston, 224, 841, 845
Johns-Manville Prods. Corp. v. NLRB, 219
Johnson v. Graphic Communications Int'l Union, 552
Johnson v. Humphreys, 800
Jolliff v. NLRB, 177
Jones v. Does 1-10 & SCO Silver Care Ops., LLC, 807
Joy Silk Mills, Inc. v. NLRB, 87

Kaiser v. Price-Fewell, Inc., 148
Kazolias v. IBEWLU 363, 877
Kelly v. Honeywell Int'l, 676
Kelsay v. Motorola, Inc., 795, 797
Kempf v. Carpenters & Joiners Local 1273, 477
KI (USA) Corp. v. NLRB, 270
Kidwell v. Transportation Communications Int'l Union, 144
Kiewit Power Constructors Co. v. NLRB, 177
King Soopers, Inc. v. NLRB, 231
Kinney Drugs v. NLRB, 289
K-Mart Corp. v. NLRB, 601
Kraft Foods, Inc. v. Office & Professional Employees Int'l Union, Local 1295, 758
Kravar v. Triangle Servs., 585
Kroger Co. v. NLRB, 413

L.A. Water Treatment, Div. of Chromalloy American Corp. v. NLRB, 191
L.O. Koven & Bro., Inc. v. United Steelworkers of America, 746
Labor Board v. Tex-Tan, Inc., 210
Laborers Dist. Council of Minnesota & N. Dakota v. NLRB, 415
Laborers' Int'l Union, Local 578 v. NLRB, 130
Lakeland Bus Lines, Inc. v. NLRB, 651
Landgrebe Motor Transp. Inc. v. Dist. 72, International Ass'n of Machinists & Aerospace Workers, 379
Lane v. NLRB, 218
Laughon v. Int'l Alliance of Theatrical Stage Emples., 792
Laurel Bay Health & Rehab. Ctr. v. NLRB, 639
Lechmere, Inc. v. NLRB, 48
Leedom v. Kyne, 273
Lemoyne-Owen College v. NLRB, 250
Letter Carriers Branch 496 v. Austin, 480
LID Elec., Inc. v. IBEW, Local 134, 761
Light & Power Co. v. Local Union 204 of International Brotherhood of Electrical Workers, 764
Lincourt v. NLRB, 40
Linden Lumber Division, Summer & Co. v. NLRB, 292
Lineback v. SMI/Div'n of DCX-CHOL Enters., Inc., 871
Lingle v. Norge Division of Magic Chef, Inc., 795, 806, 807
Linn v. Plant Guard Workers, 474, 479, 493, 494
Litton Fin. Printing Div. v. NLRB, 644
Lividas v. Bradshaw, 805
Local 1976, United Brotherhood of Carpenters and Joiners of America, AFL et al. (Sand Door & Plywood Co.) v. N.L.R.B., 356, 374, 391, 424, 428, 445, 446, 447
Local 324 Pension Fund v. Bourdow Contracting, Inc., 856
Local 348-S, UFCW, AFL-CIO v. Meridian Mgmt. Corp., 850
Local 38N Graphic Communs. Conference/IBT v. St. Louis Post-Dispatch, LLC, 750, 752
Local 46 v. NLRB, 402
Local 512, Warehouse & Office Workers' Union v. NLRB, 34

Local 560 of Int'l Bhd. of Teamsters, United States v., 882
Local 58, Intl. Broth. of Elect. Workers v. NLRB, 129
Local 702, Int'l. Union of Electrical Wkrs. v. NLRB, 170
Local 884, United Rubber, Cork, Linoleum & Plastic Workers v. Bridgestone/Firestone, 780
Local Joint Exec. Bd. of Las Vegas v. NLRB, 644
Local Joint Exec. Bd. v. Mirage Casino-Hotel, Inc., 749
Local Joint Exec. Bd. v. NLRB, 89
Local Joint Executive Bd., etc., Local 226 v. Royal Center, Inc., 855
Local Joint Executive Board v. NLRB, 147
Local No. 880 v. NLRB, 58
Local Union 501, International Brotherhood of Electrical Workers v. NLRB, 383
Local Union No. 12, United Rubber Workers of America v. NLRB, 516, 556
Local Union No. 6 v. NLRB, 665
Locke v. Karass, 142
Lodge 76, Int'l Ass'n of Machinists & Aerospace Workers v. Wisconsin Employment Relations Commission, 481, 488, 496, 498
Loewen Group Int'l v. Haberichter, 802
Lone Star Steel Co. v. NLRB, 855
Loral Defense Systems-Akron v. NLRB, 640
Louis Dreyfus Negoce S.A. v. Blystad Shipping & Trading, Inc., 746
Loyola University of Chicago v. Illinois Human Rights Comm'n, 797
Lucile Salter Packard-Children's Hosp. v. NLRB, 57
Luden's Inc. v. Local 6 of the Bakery, Confectionery & Tobacco Workers Int'l Union, 752
Lydon v. Electrical Workers IBEW Local 103, 558
Lyng v. Automobile Workers, 314

M & M Supermarkets, Inc. v. NLRB, 269
M&G Polymers USA, LLC v. Tackett, 674, 675, 676
M&M Backhoe Serv. v. NLRB, 319
Maalik v. Int'l Union of Elevator Constructors, Local 2, 563
Machinists & Aerospace Workers v. NLRB, 342, 347
Machinists v. Gonzales, 464, 469, 472
Machinists v. Street, 131, 133, 135, 138, 139, 333
Macy's, Inc. v. NLRB, 252
Mail Contrs. of Am. v. NLRB, 641
Maisel v. Sigman, 718
Maislin Industries, U.S., Inc. v. Primary Steel, Inc., 52
Major League Baseball Players Ass'n v. Garvey, 756
Manimark Corp. v. NLRB, 164
Margetta v. Pam Corp., 550
Marine Cooks & Stewards v. Panama S.S. Co., 327
Marquez v. Screen Actors Guild, 127, 580
Marranzano v. Riggs Nat'l Bank, 718
Marshall Field & Co. v. NLRB, 60
Masiongale Electrical-Mechanical v. NLRB, 109
Mass. Carpenters Cent. Collection Agency v. A.A. Bldg. Erectors, Inc., 856
Mass. Soc'y for the Prevention of Cruelty to Children v. NLRB, 256
Mastro Plastics Corp. v. NLRB, 162, 180, 363, 492, 673, 714, 776, 813
Matson Terminals v. NLRB, 109
Matson v. United Parcel Serv., Inc., 801
Matthews v. Milwaukee Area Local Postal Workers Union, AFL-CIO, 541

Maui Trucking v. Operating Eng'rs Local Union 3, 454
May Department Stores v. NLRB, 635
McCarroll v. Los Angeles County Dist. Council of Carpenters, 775
McClatchy Newspapers v. NLRB, 640
McCulloch v. Sociedad Nacional de Marineros de Honduras, 278
McDonald v. West Branch, 584
McGuire v. Humble Oil & Refining Co., 854
McIntyre v. Longwood Cent. Sch. Dist., 563
McKinney v. Creative Vision Res., LLC, 233
McKinney v. Southern Bakeries, LLC, 630
McKnight v. Dresser Inc., 801
McNamara-Blad v. Ass'n of Prof'l Flight Attendants, 545
Meade Elec. Co. v. Hagberg, 123
Meat Cutters v. Jewel Tea Co., 431, 432, 437, 441, 673
Medco Health Solutions of Las Vegas, Inc. v. NLRB, 61
Medeco Sec. Locks v. NLRB, 164
Medical Soc. of Mobile Cty. v. Walker, 347
Medo Corp. v. Labor Board, 635, 661, 663
Meijer, Inc. v. NLRB, 61
Meritor Sav. Bank, FSB v. Vinson, 561
Merritt v. Int'l Ass'n of Machinists & Aero. Workers, 544
Metropolitan Edison Co. v. NLRB, 186
Metropolitan Life Ins. Co. v. Massachusetts, 483
Metropolitan Milwaukee Ass'n of Commerce v. Milwaukee County, 498
Mich. Family Res., Inc. v. SEIU Local 517M, 759
Midgett v. Sackett-Chicago, Inc., 795, 797
Mid-South Bottling Co. v. NLRB, 229

Midwest Division-MMC, LLC v. NLRB, 167
Midwest Motor Express v. Int'l Bhd. of Teamsters Local 120, 497
Mike-Sell's Potato Chip Co. v. NLRB, 644
Milk Drivers' Union v. Lake Valley Farm Products, 27
Miller Electric Mfg. Co. v. NLRB, 106
Miller v. California Pac. Medical Ctr., 329
Milton v. Scrivner, Inc., 566
Mine Workers v. Pennington, 431, 432, 437, 442
Minn. Licensed Practical Nurses Ass'n v. NLRB, 179
Mitchell v. JCG Indus., Inc., 712
Mitchell v. Los Angeles Unified School Dist., 144
Mitsubishi Motors Corp. v. Soler Chrysler-Plymouth, Inc., 576, 579
Monmouth Care Ctr. v. NLRB, 657
Monongahela Valley Hosp. Inc. v. United Steel Paper and Forestry Rubber Mfg. Allied Indus. and Serv. Workers Int'l Union AFL-CIO, 759
Monroe v. International Union, UAW, 553
Montague v. NLRB, 101
Montplaisir v. Leighton, 793
Moore v. Local 569 of Int'l Bhd. of Elec. Workers, 794
MPC Restaurant Corp. v. NLRB, 112
Mt. Clemens Gen. Hosp. v. NLRB, 61, 179
Mulhall v. UNITE/HERE Local 355, 101, 678, 881
Multimedia KSDK, Inc. v. NLRB, 32
Mulvihill v. Top-Flite Golf Co., 564
Murray v. UFCW Int'l Union, Local 400, 572

Nat'l Ass'n of Letter Carriers, AFL-CIO, Branch 3126 v. NLRB, 559

Nat'l Ass'n of Mfrs. v. NLRB, 43
National Federation of Independent Business v. Perez, 880
National Gypsum Co. v. Oil, Chem., & Atomic Workers Int'l Union, 755
National Labor Relations Board v. Condenser Corp., 105
National Licorice Co. v. NLRB, 508
National Metropolitan Bank v. United States, 730
National Postal Mail Handlers Union v. Am. Postal Workers Union, 757
National Rejectors Indus. v. United Steelworkers, 779
National Steel & Shipbuilding Co. v. NLRB, 89
Nephi Rubber Prods. Corp. v. NLRB, 870
Nestle Ice Cream Co. v. NLRB, 268
New Alaska Development Corp. v. NLRB, 290
New Eng. Health Care Emps. Union, Dist. 1199 v. NLRB, 190
New Negro Alliance v. Sanitary Grocery Co., 328
New Orleans S.S. Ass'n v. General Longshore Workers, 789
New Process Steel, L.P. v. NLRB, 38
New River Industries, Inc. v. NLRB, 178
New York & Presbyterian Hosp. v. NLRB, 657
New York Shipping Ass'n v. FMC, 453
New York Tel. Co. v. New York State Dep't of Labor, 482
New York Times Co. v. Sullivan, 73, 480
New York-New York, LLC v. NLRB, 63
Newspaper Guild of St. Louis v. St. Louis Post Dispatch, 677
Newspaper Guild/CWA of Albany v. Hearst Corp., 753
Niagara Hooker Employees Union v. Occidental Chemical Corp., 780
Nielsen v. International Ass'n of Machinists & Aerospace Workers, Local Lodge 2569, 128
Niro v. Fearn International, Inc., 746
NLRB v. [International] Rice Milling Co., 181
NLRB v. A & S Electronic Die Corp., 112
NLRB v. Acme Indus. Co., 648, 653
NLRB v. Action Auto., Inc., 245
NLRB v. Adkins Transfer Co., 228
NLRB v. Advanced Stretchforming Int'l, Inc., 853
NLRB v. Advertisers Mfg. Co., 32
NLRB v. Affiliated Midwest Hospital, Inc., 269
NLRB v. Allcoast Transfer, Inc., 856
NLRB v. Allis-Chalmers Mfg. Co., 330, 339, 342, 343
NLRB v. Allison & Co., 636
NLRB v. Aluminum Casting & Eng'g Co., 87
NLRB v. American Cable Systems, Inc., 290
NLRB v. American Nat'l Can Co., 655
NLRB v. American National Insurance Co., 118, 605, 618, 660, 661, 681, 683
NLRB v. American Tube Bending Co., 68
NLRB v. Ancor Concepts, 217, 219
NLRB v. Auto Warehousers, Inc., 120
NLRB v. Babcock & Wilcox Co., 50, 261, 478
NLRB v. Bank of Am., 224
NLRB v. Baptist Hospital, Inc., 61
NLRB v. Bell Aerospace Co. Div. of Textron, Inc., 32, 43
NLRB v. Bildisco & Bildisco, 838
NLRB v. Bingham-Willamette Co., 196
NLRB v. Bluefield Hosp. Co., LLC, 38
NLRB v. Boeing Co., 339, 343
NLRB v. Boss Mfg. Co., 588

NLRB v. Bradford Dyeing Ass'n, 25
NLRB v. Brookshire Grocery Co., 170
NLRB v. Brown, 200, 208, 212, 673, 882
NLRB v. Burns International Security Services, Inc., 305, 842, 860, 863, 866, 868
NLRB v. Burnup & Sims, Inc., 198, 215
NLRB v. Business Machine & Office Appliance Mechanics Conference Board, IUE, Local 459 [Royal Typewriter Co.], 398, 446
NLRB v. C & C Plywood, 163, 711, 810
NLRB v. Cabot Carbon Co., 92
NLRB v. Catholic Bishop of Chicago, 35
NLRB v. Caval Tool Div., Chromalloy Gas Turbine Corp., 164
NLRB v. Certified Grocers of California, Ltd., 167
NLRB v. City Disposal Systems, Inc., 155, 157, 342
NLRB v. CJC Holdings, 656
NLRB v. CNN America, 853
NLRB v. Compact Video Servs., 702
NLRB v. Crompton-Highland Mills, 635, 636
NLRB v. Curtin Matheson Scientific, Inc., 305, 306, 309
NLRB v. CWI of Maryland, 109
NLRB v. Dahlstrom Metallic Door Co., 296
NLRB v. Deena Artware, Inc., 224
NLRB v. Delta-Macon Brick & Tile Co., 196
NLRB v. Denver Building & Construction Trades Council, 384, 394, 433, 445, 450
NLRB v. Deutsche Post Global Mail, Ltd., 870
NLRB v. District 50, U.M.W., 100
NLRB v. Draper Corp., 172
NLRB v. Drivers Local Union, 117

NLRB v. Drivers, Chauffeurs, Helpers, Local 639 [Curtis Bros.], 353
NLRB v. English Bros. Pattern & Foundry, 292
NLRB v. Erie Resistor Corp., 162, 194, 202, 205, 208, 209, 216
NLRB v. Exchange Parts Co., 84
NLRB v. F. W. Woolworth Co., 65
NLRB v. Federal Sec., 176
NLRB v. Ferguson Elec. Co., 110
NLRB v. Financial Institution Employees, 306
NLRB v. Fleetwood Trailer Co., 491
NLRB v. Fluor Daniel, Inc., 106
NLRB v. Ford Motor Co., 161
NLRB v. Ford, 47
NLRB v. Fruit Packers (Tree Fruits), 405, 407, 408, 409, 410, 447
NLRB v. Gamble Enterprises, Inc., 462, 463
NLRB v. General Electric Co., 595
NLRB v. General Motors Corp., 123
NLRB v. General Teamsters Local 439, 352
NLRB v. General Truck Drivers, Local 315 (Atchison, Topeka & Santa Fe Ry.), 396
NLRB v. George P. Pilling & Son Co., 596
NLRB v. Gimrock Constr., Inc., 630
NLRB v. Gissel Packing Co., 71, 279, 292, 293, 294, 296, 297, 844
NLRB v. Glass Bottle Blowers Ass'n, 556
NLRB v. Great Dane Trailers, Inc., 197
NLRB v. Greensburg Coca-Cola Bottling Co., 663
NLRB v. Grower-Shipper Vegetable Ass'n, 89
NLRB v. Gullett Gin Co., 231
NLRB v. Hanna Boys Center, 35
NLRB v. Hardesty Co., 602
NLRB v. Hartman & Tyner, Inc., 41, 630

NLRB v. Hartman, 259
NLRB v. Health Care & Retirement Corp. of Am., 31
NLRB v. Hearst Publs., 27, 28
NLRB v. Hendricks County Rural Elec. Membership Corp., 33
NLRB v. Herbert Halperin Distributing Corp., 270
NLRB v. Herman Wilson Lumber Co., 75
NLRB v. Holcombe, 475
NLRB v. Houston Maritime Ass'n, 119
NLRB v. Hub Plastics, 269
NLRB v. Huttig Sash & Door Co., 814
NLRB v. IAB Local 229, 396
NLRB v. IBEW, Local Union 16, 120
NLRB v. Illinois Dep't of Employment Sec., 231
NLRB v. Industrial Union of Marine & Shipbuilding Workers, 338, 347
NLRB v. Insurance Agents' Union, AFL-CIO (Prudential Ins. Co.), 297, 591, 596, 598, 611, 618, 634
NLRB v. Int'l. Bhd. of Teamsters Local 251, 453
NLRB v. International Ass'n of Bridge (Iron Workers Local 103), 368
NLRB v. International Bhd. of Elec. Workers, Local 340, 339
NLRB v. International Longshoremen's Ass'n, 453
NLRB v. International Rice Milling Co., 376, 391, 393, 446
NLRB v. International Van Lines, 190
NLRB v. J. P. Stevens & Co., 233
NLRB v. J.H. Allison & Co., 812
NLRB v. Jacobs Mfg. Co., 647, 710
NLRB v. Jeffries Lithograph Co., 862
NLRB v. Jones & Laughlin Steel Corp., 15, 515, 617, 618, 681, 730
NLRB v. Katz, 287, 598, 634, 690, 848
NLRB v. Kelly & Picerne, Inc., 224
NLRB v. Kentucky River Cmty. Care, Inc., 31

NLRB v. Knight Morley Corp., 714
NLRB v. Kobritz, 300
NLRB v. Kolkka, 240
NLRB v. Kropp Forge Co., 69
NLRB v. Ky. Tenn. Clay Co., 268
NLRB v. L. B. Foster Co., 290
NLRB v. L. G. Everist, Inc., 193
NLRB v. Laborers' International Union, 234
NLRB v. Lake Superior Lumber Corp., 53
NLRB v. Lampi LLC, 108
NLRB v. Laredo Coca Cola Bottling Co., 492
NLRB v. Lily Transp. Corp., 871
NLRB v. Lion Oil Co., 713
NLRB v. Living & Learning Centers, Inc., 256
NLRB v. Local 3, International Bhd. of Electrical Workers, 367
NLRB v. Local 334, Laborers Int'l Union of N. Am., 120
NLRB v. Local 449, Teamsters, 297
NLRB v. Local 73, Sheet Metal Workers' International Ass'n, 352
NLRB v. Local Union No. 1229, IBEW [Jefferson Standard], 176, 514
NLRB v. Local Union No. 46, Metallic Lathers & Reinforcing Iron Workers, 234
NLRB v. Logan Packing Co., 281, 288
NLRB v. Lorben Corp., 83
NLRB v. Lundy Packing Co. (Lundy II), 245, 247
NLRB v. Mackay Radio & Telegraph Co., 187, 205, 314
NLRB v. Magnavox Co., 576
NLRB v. Majestic Weaving Co., 101
NLRB v. Martin A. Gleason, Inc., 206
NLRB v. Metro. Life Ins. Co., 246
NLRB v. Mexia Textile Mills, Inc., 300
NLRB v. Milk Drivers & Dairy Employees, etc., 120

NLRB v. Mining Specialists, Inc., 663
NLRB v. Miscellaneous Drivers & Helpers Union Local 610 [Sears, Roebuck & Co.], 329
NLRB v. Mississippi Products, Inc., 91
NLRB v. Missouri Transit Co., 225
NLRB v. Modern Carpet Industries, Inc., 165
NLRB v. Montgomery Ward & Co., 173, 175, 302, 602
NLRB v. Nash-Finch Co., 467, 488, 711
NLRB v. National Garment Co., 224
NLRB v. National Maritime Union, 663
NLRB v. New Madrid Mfg. Co., 223
NLRB v. Noel Canning, 613
NLRB v. Norma Mining Corp., 224
NLRB v. Northern Metal Co., 159
NLRB v. Ohio Masonic Home, 62
NLRB v. Oregon Steel Mills, 191
NLRB v. Otis Elevator Co., 650
NLRB v. Overnite Transp. Co., 603
NLRB v. P. Lorillard Co., 287
NLRB v. Pacific Erectors, Inc., 102
NLRB v. Pecheur Lozenge Co., 192
NLRB v. Peninsula Gen. Hosp. Medical Ctr., 93
NLRB v. Pennsylvania Greyhound Lines, Inc., 92, 100
NLRB v. Pipefitters, 451
NLRB v. Pizza Crust Co., 62
NLRB v. Plainville Ready Mix Concrete Co., 643
NLRB v. Plasterers' Local Union 79, 460
NLRB v. Preston Feed Corp., 224
NLRB v. R. C. Mahon Co., 224
NLRB v. Radio & Television Broadcast Engineers Local 1212 (CBS), 458
NLRB v. Rapid Bindery, Inc., 228
NLRB v. Reed & Prince Mfg. Co., 596, 599

NLRB v. Retail Clerks, Local 1001 [Safeco Title Insurance Co.], 404, 419
NLRB v. River Togs, Inc., 74
NLRB v. Roll & Hold Warehouse & Distrib. Corp., 712
NLRB v. S & H Grossinger's Inc., 54
NLRB v. S.R.D.C., Inc., 240
NLRB v. Savair Mfg. Co., 267
NLRB v. Savoy Laundry, 225
NLRB v. Sehon Stevenson & Co., Inc., 281
NLRB v. Servette, Inc., 414, 420, 447
NLRB v. Seven-Up Bottling Co., 301, 683, 684
NLRB v. Somerset Classics, Inc., 215
NLRB v. Somerset Shoe Co., 215
NLRB v. Southern Stevedoring & Contracting Co., 119
NLRB v. St. George Warehouse, Inc., 231
NLRB v. Steelworkers, 347
NLRB v. Stremel, 215, 224
NLRB v. Strong, 815
NLRB v. Suffield Acad., 603
NLRB v. Sunbeam Lighting Co., 172
NLRB v. Super Toys, Inc., 82
NLRB v. Superior Forwarding, Inc., 840
NLRB v. SW General, Inc., 39
NLRB v. Tanner Motor Livery, Ltd., 476
NLRB v. Teamsters Local 294, 391, 392
NLRB v. Television & Radio Broadcasting Studio Employees, 130
NLRB v. Textile Workers, 342, 344, 347, 349, 351
NLRB v. Thompson Ramo Wooldridge, Inc., 92
NLRB v. Tito Contractors, Inc., 252
NLRB v. Town & Country Elec., 109
NLRB v. Transportation Mgt. Corp., 107

NLRB v. Truck Drivers Union, 199, 203, 215, 216, 442
NLRB v. Truitt Mfg. Co., 592, 598, 646
NLRB v. United Food & Commercial Workers Union, Local 23, 40
NLRB v. United States Postal Serv., 713
NLRB v. United Steelworkers [Nutone, Inc.], 63, 214, 222, 261
NLRB v. USA Polymer Corp., 290
NLRB v. USPS, 653
NLRB v. V & S Schuler Eng'g, Inc., 87
NLRB v. Virginia Electric & Power Co., 67, 227
NLRB v. Vitronic Div. of Penn Corp., 192
NLRB v. VSA, 267
NLRB v. Vulcan Forging Co., 298
NLRB v. W. C. McQuaide, Inc., 194
NLRB v. Wachter Constr., 655
NLRB v. Wallick, 224
NLRB v. Washington Aluminum Co., 148
NLRB v. Waterman S.S. Corp., 224
NLRB v. Waymouth Farms, Inc., 657
NLRB v. Weingarten, Inc., 342
NLRB v. Wemyss, 92
NLRB v. Wine, Liquor & Distillery Workers Union, 387
NLRB v. Winn-Dixie Stores, Inc., 690
NLRB v. Wooster Division of Borg-Warner Corp., 659, 672, 690, 692
NLRB v. Wright Motors, Inc., 601
NLRB v. Wyman-Gordon Co., 42, 261
NLRB v. Yeshiva University, 32
Noel Canning v. NLRB, 645
Nolde Bros. v. Bakery & Confectionery Workers Local 358, 751
Norelli v. Fremont-Rideout Health Group, 233
North River Energy Corp. v. United Mine Workers, 793
Northern States Power Co. v. Int'l Bhd. of Elec. Workers, Local 160, 761
Northern Wire Corp. v. NLRB, 192
Northwest Airlines Corp. v. Ass'n of Flight Attendants-CWA (In re Northwest Airlines Corp.), 840
Northwest Airlines, Inc. v. Air Line Pilots Ass'n, International, 764
Northwestern Ohio Adm'rs, Inc. v. Walcher & Fox, Inc., 793
Novelis Corp. v. NLRB, 290

O'Connor v. Consolidated Coin Caterers Corp., 561
Oakwood Hosp. v. NLRB, 58
Oberkramer v. IBEW-NECA Serv. Ctr., 808
Ohio State Bar Ass'n v. Burdzinski, Brinkman, Czarzasty & Landwehr, Inc., 498
Oil, Chem. & Atomic Workers Int'l Union v. NLRB, 780
Oil, Chem. & Atomic Workers Local Union No. 6-418 v. NLRB, 655
Oil, Chemical & Atomic Workers Int'l Union, Local 2-286 v. Amoco Oil Co., 780
Oncale v. Sundowner Offshore Servs., 561
Operating Eng'rs Local 3 v. Newmont Mining Corp., 752
Order of R. Telegraphers v. Railway Express Agency, Inc., 509, 528, 609
Order of Railroad Telegraphers v. Chicago & N.W.R. Co., 681, 695
Otis Elevator Co. v. Int'l Union of Elevator Constructors, Local 4, 778
Overnite Transp. Co. v. NLRB, 255, 271, 290
Oxford Health Plans, LLC v. Sutter, 573

Pa. Transformer Tech., Inc. v. NLRB, 869
Pac. 9 Transp., Inc., NLRB Div. of Advice, 29
Pac. Mar. Ass'n v. NLRB, 278

Pace Indus. v. NLRB, 853
Pacheco v. Honeywell International, Inc., 675
Pacific Maritime Ass'n v. International Longshoremen's & Warehousemen's Union, 790
Packard Motor Car Co. v. NLRB, 30
Pall Corp. v. NLRB, 678
Paper, Allied-Industrial, Chem. & Energy Workers Int'l Union, Local 5-0550 v. Air Products & Chems., Inc., 837
Paramount Transport Systems v. Chauffeurs, Teamsters & Helpers Local 150, 457
Parsons Elec., LLC v. NLRB, 638
Part Time Faculty Ass'n at Columbia Coll. Chicago v. Columbia Coll., 837
Pattern Makers' League of North America v. NLRB, 340
Paul v. Kaiser Found. Health Plan of Ohio, 808
Pauley v. CF Entm't, 540
Pawlowski v. Northeast Ill. Reg'l Commuter R.R. Corp., 169
Pedro's, Inc. v. NLRB, 87
Peeples v. City of Detroit, 564
Pennsylvania R. Co. v. Public Service Comm., 733
Periodical Drivers' & Helpers Local 921 v. San Francisco Newspaper Agency, 780
Peters v. NLRB, 851
Peterson v. Kennedy, 793
Phelps Dodge Corp. v. NLRB, 230, 301, 683
Phoenix Newspapers, Inc. v. Phoenix Mailers Union Local 752, Int'l Bhd. of Teamsters, 761
Pirelli Cable Corp. v. NLRB, 191
Pittsburgh Press Co. v. NLRB, 120
Pittsburgh S.S. Co. v. NLRB, 91, 109
Pleasantview Nursing Home, Inc. v. NLRB, 642

Plumbers Union v. Borden, 472, 473
Plumbers v. Plumbers Local 334, 737
Plumbers' Pension Fund, Local 130 v. Domas Mechanical Contractors, Inc., 736
Pol. Spring Corp. v. UFCW, 761
Police Department of Chicago v. Mosley, 408
Polycon Indus., Inc. v. NLRB, 309
Posadas De Puerto Rico Assocs. v. NLRB, 643, 664
PPG Indus. v. Int'l Chem. Workers Union Council of the United Food & Commer. Workers, 758
Premium Foods, Inc. v. NLRB, 864, 868
Price v. International Union, United Autoworkers etc., 144
Prill v. NLRB, 163
Prime Healthcare Services-Encino LLC v. NLRB, 644
Production & Maintenance Laborers Union Local 383 v. NLRB, 429
Production Workers Union, Local 707 v. NLRB, 379
Progressive Elec., Inc. v. NLRB, 75
Providence Hosp. v. NLRB, 702
Providence Journal Co. v. Providence Newspaper Guild, 753
PSC Custom, LP v. Steelworkers, 760
Public Serv. Co. v. NLRB, 601
Public Service Co. of New Mexico v. NLRB, 656
Publi-Inversiones de P.R., Inc. v. NLRB, 851, 869
Publishers' Ass'n of New York City v. NLRB, 259

Radio Officers' Union v. NLRB, 116, 126, 202, 205, 209, 210, 215, 222, 468, 476
Railway Clerks v. Allen, 133, 135, 139, 141

Railway Employees' Department v. Hanson, 132, 135, 139, 140
Ramey v. Dist. 141 Int'l Ass'n of Machinists & Aerospace Workers, 545
Raven Servs. Corp. v. NLRB, 641
Raymond Interior Systems, Inc. v. NLRB, 129, 218
Red Cross Line v. Atlantic Fruit Co., 729
Reece v. Houston Lighting & Power Co., 808
Reed v. Roumell, 358
Reef Industries, Inc. v. NLRB, 178
Reichard ex rel. NLRB v. Foster Poultry Farms, 233
Republic Steel Corp. v. Maddox, 534, 537
Retail Clerks International Ass'n v. Lion Dry Goods, Inc., 737
Retail Clerks International Ass'n, Local 1625 v. Schermerhorn, 147
Retail Clerks International Ass'n v. Schermerhorn, 127, 145
Retail Clerks Union v. Alfred M. Lewis, Inc., 735
Reyco Granning LLC v. Teamsters Local 245, 759
Rhino Northwest, LLC v. NLRB, 252
Rhode Island Hospitality Ass'n v. City of Providence, 485, 857
Richards v. United States, 776
Rite Aid of Pennsylvania, Inc. v. UFCW, Local 1776, 753
Robert P. Scott, Inc. v. Rothman, 363
Robinson v. Jacksonville Shipyards, Inc., 564
Rock-Tenn Co. v. NLRB, 699
Rollins v. Cmty. Hosp. of San Bernardino, 540
Rosetto v. Pabst Brewing Co., 677
Roundy's Inc. v. NLRB, 59
Rupcich v. Food & Commercial Workers Local 881, 541
Ryder Truck Lines, Inc. v. Teamsters Freight Local Union 480, 779

S & F Mkt. St. Healthcare LLC v. NLRB, 851
S. Cal. Painters & Allied Trades v. Rodin & Co., Inc., 857
S. Nuclear Operating Co. v. NLRB, 645, 677
S. Ocean Med. Ctr., 38
S.D. Warren Co., Div. of Scott Paper Co. v. United Paperworkers' International Union, Local 1069, 764
Saks & Co. v. NLRB, 864
Sales Drivers v. NLRB, 392
Salt River Valley Water Users' Ass'n v. NLRB, 164
San Antonio Community Hosp. v. Southern Cal. Dist. Council of Carpenters, 328
San Diego Building Trades Council v. Garmon, 430, 464, 468, 471, 472, 477, 487, 488, 495, 531, 532, 732, 733
Sandifer v. U.S. Steel Corp., 712
Sara Lee Bakery Group, Inc. v. NLRB, 657
Saunders v. Ford Motor Co., 540
Sayre v. United Steelworkers, 803
Schaub v. Detroit Newspaper Agency, 631
Schnuck Markets, Inc. v. NLRB, 31
School of Magnetic Healing v. McAnnulty, 276
Schwegmann Bros. v. Calvert Distillers Corp., 448
Scofield v. NLRB, 337, 339, 342, 343, 347, 351, 646
Scott ex rel. NLRB v Stephen Dunn & Assocs., 291
SDBC Holdings, Inc. v. NLRB, 651
Seafarers Int'l Union v. NLRB, 382, 392

Sears, Roebuck & Co. v. Carpenters, 488, 493
Sears, Roebuck & Co. v. San Diego County Dist. Council of Carpenters, 51, 53, 54, 477, 479
Seeler v. Trading Port, Inc., 291
SEIU v. Nat'l Union of Healthcare Workers, 793
SEIU v. St. Vincent Med. Ctr., 837
SEIU, United Healthcare Workers-West v. NLRB, 179
Serramonte Oldsmobile, Inc. v. NLRB, 246
Service Employees Int'l Union Local 36 v. City Cleaning Co., 736
Shea v. McCarthy, 793
Sheet Metal Div. v. Local 38, Sheet Metal Workers Int'l Ass'n, 453
Sheet Metal Workers Local 27 v. E.P. Donnelly, Inc., 460
Sidhu v. Flecto Co., 751
Sidney Wanzer & Sons, Inc. v. Milk Drivers Union, etc., 794
Silverman ex rel. NLRB v. Major League Baseball Player Relations Comm., 667
Siu de Puerto Rico, Caribe Y Latinoamerica v. Virgin Islands Port Auth., 736
Smith v. Evening News, 473, 533, 537, 539, 735, 837
Smith v. Transport Workers Union of Am., 749
Soaring Eagle Casino & Resort v. NLRB, 36
Soft Drink Workers Union Local12, Int'l Brotherhood of Teamsters v. NLRB, 368
South Cent. Power Co. v. IBEW, Local 2359, 752
Southern New England Telephone Co. v. NLRB, 61
Southern S.S. Co. v. NLRB, 170
Sparks Nugget, Inc. v. NLRB, 58, 601

Sperry v. Denver Building Trades Council, 385
Spurlino Materials, LLC v. NLRB, 192, 686
Square D Co. v. NLRB, 814
St. Margaret Mercy Healthcare Centers v. NLRB, 61
Stafford v. Ford Motor Co., 553
Starcon Int'l, Inc. v. NLRB, 110
Stark v. Wickard, 276
Std. Concrete Prods. v. General Truck Drivers, Office, Food & Warehouse Union, Local 952, 790
Steele v. Louisville & N. R. Co., 515, 527, 532
Steelworkers v. American Mfg. Co., 534
Stephens Institute v. NLRB, 33
Stevens Constr. Corp. v. Chi. Reg'l Council of Carpenters, 753
Stokely-Van Camp, Inc. v. NLRB, 198
Stotter Div. of Graduate Plastics Co. v. District 65, United Auto Workers, 854
Straight Creek Mining v. NLRB, 870
Sure-Tan, Inc. v. NLRB, 231
Surprenant Mfg. Co. v. NLRB, 70
Sutter East Bay Hospitals v. NLRB, 61
Sweeney v. Pence, 145
Switchmen's Union of North America v. National Mediation Board, 276, 277
Synergy Gas Co. v. Sasso, 760
Syres v. Oil Workers Int'l Union, 530, 532, 731
Sysco Grant Rapids, LLC v. NLRB, 632
Systems Mgt. v. NLRB, 869

T. Equip. Corp. v. Massachusetts Laborers' Dist. Council, 460
Taggart v. Weinacker's, Inc., 475
Taha v. Teamsters Local 781, 541
Teamsters Cannery Local 670 v. NLRB, 351

TABLE OF CASES

Teamsters Local Union 480 v. UPS, 750
Teamsters Local Union No. 783 v. Anheuser-Busch, Inc., 746
Teamsters Local Union No. 89 v. Kroger Co., 746
Teamsters Nat'l United Parcel Serv. Negotiating Comm. v. NLRB, 102
Teamsters Union v. Oliver, 672, 682
Teamsters Union v. Vogt, Inc., 407
Teamsters, Chauffeurs, Warehousemen & Helpers Local, etc. v. NLRB, 396
Teamsters, Chauffeurs, Warehousemen & Helpers, Local 174 v. Lucas Flour Co., 732, 796, 806
Terminal Railroad Ass'n v. Brotherhood of Railroad Trainmen, 812
Texas & N. O. R. Co. v. Brotherhood of R. & S.S. Clerks, 275, 276
Textile Workers Union v. American Thread Co., 728
Textile Workers Union v. Darlington Mfg. Co., 74, 220, 686, 691, 694
Textile Workers Union v. Lincoln Mills, 727, 733, 740, 796, 806
Thomas v. Collins, 68
Thompson v. Public Service Co., 480
Thorn v. Amalgamated Transit Union, 562
Three D, LLC v. NLRB, 150
Tierney v. Toledo, 144
Time-O-Matic, Inc. v. NLRB, 47
Timken Co. v. NLRB, 88
Timken Roller Bearing Co. v. NLRB, 814
Tipler v. E. I. Du Pont de Nemours & Co., 570
TNS, Inc. v. NLRB, 780
Tobacco Workers and Grain Millers, Int'l Union AFL-CIO v. Kellogg Co., 745
Trafford Distrib. Ctr. v. NLRB, 856
Trail v. Local 2850 UAW United Def. Workers of Am., 877
Trans Penn Wax Corp. v. McCandless, 802
Triangle Constr. & Maint. Corp. v. Our V.I. Labor Union, 781
Trident Seafoods, Inc. v. NLRB, 245
Trinidad Corp. v. National Maritime Union, Dist. No. 4, 752
Trs. of the Twin City Bricklayers Fringe Benefit Funds v. Superior Waterproofing, Inc., 803
Truck Drivers & Helpers, Teamsters Local 568 v. NLRB, 556
Truck Drivers Local 807, etc. v. Carey Transp., Inc., 839
Trump Entertainment Resorts, Unite Here Local 54, In re, 840
TruServ Corp. v. NLRB, 639
Tubari, Ltd. v. NLRB, 231
Tunstall v. Brotherhood of Locomotive Firemen, 532
TWA v. Independent Federation of Flight Attendants, 195, 196

U.S. Soccer Fed'n, Inc. v. U.S. Nat'l Soccer Team Players Ass'n, 759
U.S.A. Inc. v. Natural Resources Defense Council, Inc., 56
UAW v. Hoosier Cardinal Corp., 736
UAW v. Russell, 466, 470, 474
UAW v. WERB, 172, 465, 466, 471, 481
UC Health v. NLRB, 38
UFCW, AFL-CIO, Local 540 v. NLRB, 701
UFCW, Local 204 v. NLRB, 75
UMWA v. Rag Am. Coal Co., 855
Unbelievable, Inc. v. NLRB, 633
Union of Operating Engineers v. NLRB, 82
Union-Tribune Publishing Co. v. NLRB, 106
Unite Here Local 1 v. Hyatt Corp., 760

Unite Here Local 217 v. Sage Hospitality Res., 745, 750
Unite Here Local 355 v. Mulhall, 678, 881
Unite Here v. NLRB, 664
United Ass'n of Journeymen & Apprentices of Plumbing & Pipefitting Industry, etc., Local No. 198 v. NLRB, 119
United Brick & Clay Workers v. Deena Artware, Inc., 457
United Constr. Workers v. Laburnum Constr. Corp., 456, 466
United Exposition Service Co. v. NLRB, 32
United Food & Commer. Workers Union Local 751 v. Brown Group, 702
United Food & Commercial Workers Dist. Union Local One v. NLRB, 130
United Mine Workers 1974 Pension v. Pittston Co., 701
United Mine Workers v. NLRB, 714
United Mine Workers, District 28 v. Patton, 455
United Nurses Assn. of Calif. v. NLRB, 31
United Packinghouse Workers Union v. NLRB, 514, 557
United Parcel Serv. v. NLRB, 61
United Postal Service v. National Ass'n of Letter Carriers, 764
United Rentals Highway Techs., Inc. v. Indiana Constructors, Inc., 440
United Shoe Workers v. Brooks Shoe Mfg. Co., 794
United States Postal Serv. v. American Postal Workers Union, 757
United States Postal Service v. National Ass'n of Letter Carriers, 764
United States Postal Service v. NLRB, 168
United States Steel Corp. v. United Mine Workers, 790
United States Testing Co. v. NLRB, 652
United Steel Workers Local 850L v. Cont'l Tire North Am., Inc., 753
United Steel Workers, Etc. v. U.S. Steel Corp., 693
United Steel, Paper & Forestry, Rubber, Mfg., Energy, Allied Indus. & Serv. Workers Int'l Union v. NLRB, 190
United Steel, Paper and Forestry, Rubber, Mfg., Energy, Allied Indus. & Serv. Workers Int'l Union v. Trimas Corp., 753
United Steelworkers of Am. v. Reliance Universal, Inc., 854
United Steelworkers of America v. NLRB (Carrier Corp.), 395
United Steelworkers of America v. Rawson, 540, 804
United Steelworkers of America v. Warrior & Gulf Navigation Co., 718, 720, 721, 734, 738, 806, 818
United Steelworkers v. American Mfg. Co., 745
United Steelworkers v. Connors Steel Co., 794
United Steelworkers v. Cookson Am., Inc., 677
United Steelworkers v. Enterprise Wheel & Car Corp., 754, 766, 783, 789
United Steelworkers v. Ft. Pitt Steel Casting Division-Conval-Penn, Inc., 754
United Steelworkers v. NLRB, 394, 616, 618, 619, 794
United Steelworkers v. St. Gabriel's Hosp., 857
United Steelworkers v. Warrior & Gulf Nav. Co., 682
Univ. of Great Falls v. NLRB, 35
Univ. of Livonia, MI, LLC, 233, 631

Universal Camera Corp. v. NLRB, 42, 111, 227
Universal Camera Corp. v. NLRB, 515
University of Southern Calif. v. NLRB, 33
Uradnik v. Inter Faculty Association, 510
US Airways, Inc. v. Barnett, 566
US Ecology, Inc. v. NLRB, 269
USW, AFL-CIO-CLC v. Duluth Clinic, Ltd., 746

Va. Mason Hosp. v. Wash. State Nurses Ass'n, 770
Va. Mason Med. Ctr. v. NLRB, 302
Vaca v. Sipes, 474, 475, 531, 580
Van Pamel v. TRW Vehicle Safety Sys., Inc., 677
Vaughn v. Air Line Pilots, Ass'n, Int'l, 544
Vegelahn v. Guntner, 167 Mass. 92, 14
Veritas Health Services Inc. v. NLRB, 266
Vico Prods. Co. v. NLRB, 700
Virginia Pharmacy Bd. v. Virginia Citizens Consumer Council, Inc., 418
Virginian R. Co. v. System Federation, 276, 528, 588, 731
Visiting Nurse Servs. v. NLRB, 640

W. Penn Power Co. v. NLRB, 657
W.R. Grace & Co. v. Rubber Workers, 763, 767, 769
Wackenhut Corp. v. Int'l Union, United Plant Guard Workers, 854
Wallace Corp. v. NLRB, 515
Walls Mfg. Co. v. NLRB, 475
Wal-Mart Stores, Inc. v. NLRB, 61
Ward v. Circus Casinos, Inc., 804
Warehousemen's Union v. NLRB, 460
Wash. State Nurses Ass'n v. NLRB, 61

Washington Gas Light Co. v. Lansden, 456
Waterbury Hosp. v. NLRB, 196
Waterbury Hotel Mgmt., LLC v. NLRB, 852
Waterman v. Transport Workers' Union Local 100, 793
Watts v. United Parcel Serv., Inc., 809
Wausau Steel Corp. v. NLRB, 75
Weber v. AnheuserBusch, Inc., 465, 470
Weingarten v. NLRB, 159, 166
Wellington Mill Div., West Point Mfg. Co. v. NLRB, 70
Westmoreland Coal Co. v. International Union, United Mine Workers, 789
Wheelabrator Envirotech Operating Servs. v. Massachusetts Laborers Dist. Council Local 1144, 855
Wheeling-Pittsburgh Steel Corp. v. United Steelworkers, 839
Whirlpool Corp. v. Marshall, 165
Wilko v. Swan, 740
William E. Arnold Co. v. Carpenters Dist. Council, 838
Williams Motor Co. v. NLRB, 224
Williams v. NLRB, 130
Willis v. Pac. Mar. Ass'n, 566
Wilson v. NLRB, 131
Wisconsin Dep't of Indus., Labor & Human Relations v. Gould, Inc., 497
Woelke & Romero Framing v. NLRB, 440
Woods v. Graphic Communications, 563
Workers of America, Local 5008 v. NLRB, 169
Workers Union v. Darlington Mfg. Co., 867
Workers v. Beck, 575, 580
Workers v. Ingalls Shipbuilding Div., Litton Systems, Inc., 780

Wright v. Universal Maritime Serv. Corp., 573, 574, 576, 577, 578, 583

Wynn v. AC Rochester, 801

Yazoo & M. V. R. Co. v. Sideboard, 718

Youngdahl v. Rainfair, 466, 467

Zady Natey, Inc. v. United Food & Commercial Workers Int'l Union, Local 27, Workers Int'l Union, Local 27, 855

Preface to the Fourteenth Edition

The last several decades have seen explosive growth in the law governing the workplace. Even the name of the subject has changed at some schools from Labor Relations Law to Labor and Employment Law or Work Law to reflect the expanding governmental regulation of employer-employee relations, as distinct from traditional union-management relations. Although some professors still try to include both labor relations law and employment law within the same course, most law schools have created separate courses covering Employment Discrimination Law, Individual Employment Rights, and Employee Benefits or ERISA. We agree with this trend, because we believe there is a substantial risk of superficiality and a lack of focus if someone tries to include all of these areas in a single three- or four-hour offering. We also think that those two almost unique American institutions—the representative labor union and the collective bargaining process as they have evolved in this country—deserve study in a setting in which they occupy the center stage.

The fourteenth edition brings new authorship. We are excited to welcome Grant Hayden as coauthor. Grant brings fresh eyes and has been instrumental in thinking through the book's next evolution. We are forever indebted to Ted St. Antoine for his instrumental role in shaping the book's basic philosophy and structure, which endures. Like its predecessors, the fourteenth edition of this casebook is designed for an intensive examination of the union-management relationship throughout its major phases. We begin with a focus on the right of employees to join together for organizational purposes, regulation of the union organizing process including the use of economic weapons, development of bargaining relationships, the negotiation of collective agreements, and the enforcement of those agreements. A brief section addressing the law governing internal union affairs follows.

As in the past, we have tried to respond generously to the most significant current developments in the field, while simultaneously providing a set of materials that will be truly manageable in the usual three- or four-hour courses. We have included more than 60 new hypothetical problems designed to test students' knowledge of existing doctrines and push them to explore issues that don't admit of ready answers. And we will continue our practice of publishing a biennial supplement to keep the book up-to-date.

Finally, we express our appreciation to Drew Schendt, whose capable and conscientious research assistance contributed substantially to this revision; Rachel Mance, for her expert technical assistance with past editions; and Hallie Dunlap, for her essential logistical support. Biz Ebben at Carolina Academic Press makes the publishing experience a pleasure; this book owes its continued existence to her editorial expertise.

CHARLES B. CRAVER
Washington, D.C.

MARION G. CRAIN
St. Louis, Missouri

GRANT M. HAYDEN
Dallas, Texas

Labor Relations Law

Part 1

Introduction and Historical Background

Union Relevance in the 21st Century
Charles B. Craver, *Why Labor Unions Must (and Can) Survive*
1 U. Pa. J. Lab. & Emp. L. 15, 17–23 (1998)*

Every year thousands of unrepresented American employees are discharged without good cause. Several million are laid off by companies that transfer their production jobs to lower-wage facilities in the South, in Mexico, or in other developing countries. When workers at firms like Greyhound, Eastern Airlines, and Caterpillar walk out to protest wage and benefit reductions or to seek enhanced employment conditions, they are permanently replaced, and their representative labor organizations are greatly undermined. Senior personnel who participate in strikes against firms like Trans-World Airlines have their hard-earned positions filled by replacement workers and less senior coworkers who cross the picket lines during the labor dispute. Individuals who strike technologically advanced corporations like AT&T discover that their employers are able to maintain basic operations without the assistance of their regular employees. Other diversified corporations can relocate production from striking plants to non-striking facilities in other areas of the world. The declining economic power of organized labor makes it increasingly difficult for unionized employees to maintain beneficial compensation levels and preserve long-term employment security. Most unorganized workers enjoy no real job security and exercise no meaningful control over the fundamental terms of their employment.

During the past two decades, deregulation and government budget reductions have led to a decrease in the enforcement of health and safety laws, wage and hour statutes, pension guarantee provisions, and other employee protection legislation. As a result, thousands of American workers are seriously injured each year in industrial accidents that could be prevented through mandated safety inspections. Many more workers are underpaid or deprived of earned overtime compensation, and others are denied the protection of laws designed to enhance employment

---

* Copyright © 1998 by the University of Pennsylvania. Reprinted by permission.

conditions. The presence of conscientious union representatives would substantially diminish the likelihood of such violations continuing unabated.

. . . .

Many people believe that labor organizations are outmoded institutions providing representational services no longer needed by individuals employed by enlightened business enterprises. The unconscionable sweatshop conditions that were pervasive in the early twentieth century have been mainly eliminated, and the labor movement has directly or indirectly caused significantly enhanced employment conditions for most workers. . . .

Changing demographic, industrial, and technological conditions have also undermined the cohesiveness and effectiveness of unions. During the past few decades, the face of labor has changed dramatically. The participation rate for women, traditionally employed in unorganized lower-wage occupations, has significantly expanded. The labor force participation rate for minority persons has also increased, and is expected to continue to do so in the coming decades. Historically, labor organizations have not been responsive to the needs of female and minority employees, and will have to change their image if they hope to appeal effectively to these new labor force entrants. Due to the aging of the post-war baby boom generation, the number of older labor force participants will grow over the next two decades. As a result of this phenomenon, unions will have to address issues of interest to more senior employees.

. . . .

The introduction of new technologies in the workplace has substantially modified the structure of the American economy. The substitution of capital for labor in the manufacturing sector has caused the displacement of many organized blue-collar personnel and has generated a concomitant increase in nonunion white-collar positions. The service sector has experienced similar growth, and labor unions have discovered that organizing campaigns that used to appeal to traditional blue-collar workers are not well received by white-collar and service personnel.

The technological developments that have altered the structure of the American economy have also contributed to the internationalization of the global business system. By the twenty-first century, several hundred multinational corporations will dominate world trade. The developed nations provide the capital-intensive technologies, while the developing countries provide low-cost labor. The proliferation of low-cost "export platforms" has caused the exporting of many blue-collar jobs. If labor organizations hope to meaningfully influence the employment of international business enterprises, they must coordinate their efforts with trade unions located in the other countries in which those firms operate.

. . . .

When Congress enacted the NLRA in 1935, it acknowledged in section 1 "[t]he inequality of bargaining power between employees who do not possess full freedom of association . . . and employers who are organized in the corporate [form] . . . ." It declared the policy of the United States to alleviate this economic power imbalance "by encouraging the practice and procedure of collective bargaining and by protecting the exercise by workers of full freedom of association, self-organization, and designation of representatives of their own choosing, for the purpose of negotiating the terms and conditions of their employment. . . ."

. . . .

Empirical evidence demonstrates that workers who have selected bargaining agents have enhanced their individual economic benefits.[1] Their wage rates have improved, and they have obtained health care coverage, pension programs, supplemental unemployment benefits, day-care centers, and other important fringe benefits. Similar studies indicate that unorganized personnel have received indirect financial gain from the labor movement, as their employers have provided them with wage and benefit packages competitive with those enjoyed by unionized employees. If these business firms did not fear the possible unionization of their own employees, many would show little concern about their employment terms. It is thus clear that labor unions have directly advanced the economic interests of the employees they have represented, and have indirectly enhanced the economic benefits received by unorganized workers.

Labor organizations do not merely advance the economic interests of their members. Through the "collective voice" exerted by united groups, workers have also advanced important noneconomic interests.[2] Collective bargaining agreements generally preclude worker discipline except for "just cause." This protection contrasts with the traditional "employment-at-will" doctrine, under which employers are authorized to discharge employees for good cause, bad cause, or no cause at all. Other contractual provisions typically establish orderly layoff and recall procedures, and require the application of relatively objective criteria to promotional opportunities.

When employees are not satisfied with the way in which contractual terms are applied, they may invoke grievance-arbitration procedures. During grievance-adjustment sessions, labor and management representatives are usually able to negotiate mutually acceptable solutions for their outstanding contractual disputes. When no mutual accords are achieved, the dissatisfied parties may ask neutral arbitrators to determine the contractual issues. Grievance-arbitration procedures prevent arbitrary employer action and provide workers with access to impartial determinations of controversies concerning the interpretation and application of contractual terms. Without the rights and protections contained in bargaining agreements, individual employees could rarely challenge questionable employer decisions. They would be required to either accept the actions of their employers or seek work elsewhere.

---

1. [16] *See generally* Richard B. Freeman & James L. Medoff, What Do Unions Do? 43–77 (1984).
2. [18] *See id.* at 94–110.

Business firms depend upon the input of three fundamental groups for their success: investors, managers, and workers. Shareholders provide the necessary capital; managers provide the requisite managerial skills; and employees create the commercial goods or provide the business services. As each of these groups competes for a greater share of company profits and a more significant degree of control over corporate decision making, individual employees are at a distinct disadvantage. Companies seeking investment capital must provide prospective stock or bondholders with detailed information regarding the proposed venture. Shareholders have the right to vote on significant corporate issues, and they can limit their exposure to particular firm financial difficulties through diversified investment strategies. When investors become disenchanted with the performance of specific corporations, they can sell their shares in that firm and invest the proceeds elsewhere.

Professional managers may similarly protect their own interests. Those with relatively unique personal skills can negotiate long-term employment contracts that may provide them with "golden parachutes" in the event the business relationship is terminated prematurely. High-level executives have access to confidential financial information, apprising them of their firm's economic well-being. They are usually well-connected at the upper levels of other business entities, and can use those contacts to locate other employment when they decide to leave their current positions.

Rank-and-file employees do not enjoy any of these privileges. They are fortunate to have one or two job opportunities at any one time. Employers feel no need to give job applicants detailed information regarding firm affairs. Once they accept employment with a specific company, workers enjoy minimal mobility. They possess limited information about other job openings, and the transaction costs associated with relocation may be substantial. To change jobs, they may lose some or all of their pension rights. They may also be forced to forfeit accrued seniority and to start at the bottom of the ladder in their new work environment, greatly jeopardizing their future employment security.

It is ironic that the individuals who possess the least mobility normally exercise only marginal control over their employment destiny. Unorganized workers are generally powerless to negotiate with their corporate employers over their wages, hours, and working conditions. They must accept the terms unilaterally offered or else look for alternative employment. If they are directed to submit to drug testing or to engage in particularly arduous tasks, they have no real choice but to comply. This loss of personal freedom results directly from the considerable inequality of bargaining power that exists between individual employees and corporate managers.

The labor movement was initiated to provide individual workers with a collective voice that could effectively counter the aggregate power possessed by corporate enterprises. Without organizational strength, there is no broad-based institution to represent the interests of rank-and-file employees. A lack of such power would render workers one of the few groups in America without a collective voice. Business firms have organizations like the National Chamber of Commerce and the National

Association of Manufacturers to represent their interests.... Workers who think it would be "unprofessional" or "lower class" to join labor organizations should remember that their employers are all affiliated with business "unions" that effectively advance their economic interests. It is hypocritical for these business enterprises to tell their employees that they do not need a collective voice to further their employment interests.

. . . .

The United States prides itself on being one of the world's great democracies.... The importance of democratic employment environments was recognized by Senator Robert Wagner, the principal author of the NLRA:

> [W]e must have democracy in industry as well as in government.... [D]emocracy in industry means fair participation by those who work in the decisions vitally affecting their lives and livelihood; and ... the workers in our great mass production industries can enjoy this participation only if allowed to organize and bargain collectively through representatives of their own choosing.

Marion Crain & Ken Matheny, *Labor's Identity Crisis*
89 Cal. L. Rev. 1767, 1779–81, 1820–21, 1828–29 (2001)*

... The ideology of the American labor movement since World War II, called "business unionism," has been described as follows:

> [U]nions exist in order to address the immediate and practical concerns of unionized workers. The objective of unions is to protect their members economically, primarily by negotiating and enforcing the union contract. Unions are seen essentially as service organizations, whose task is to insure fair wages, increase job security, protect against victimization, improve the conditions of work, and provide additional economic benefits.... In the arena of politics, unions are concerned only with those issues that have a direct or indirect impact on unions, their members, and the industries in which they function.[3]

This philosophy stemmed from an ideological stance that defended and espoused the virtues of capitalism, seeking to "make the world safe for U.S. business." Unions came to see themselves as allied with business and with government rather than as opposed to capitalist interests. The economic security of union members depended upon "shared prosperity"; "a rising tide lifts all boats." Business unionism explains

---

* Copyright © 2001 by the California Law Review. Reprinted by permission of the Regents of the University of California, Berkeley.

3. [78] Gregory Mantsios, *What Does Labor Stand For?*, in A New Labor Movement for the New Century 44, 46 (Gregory Mantsios ed., 1998).

labor's stance on issues ranging from immigration to its historical support for the Vietnam War.

Business unionism combines elements of both job consciousness and class consciousness. Although protectionist strategies still heavily influence AFL-CIO policies on, for example, the North American Free Trade Agreement (NAFTA), immigrant labor, and workfare issues, class consciousness is plainly visible in labor's recognition that political action is necessary to protect and extend gains won at the bargaining table. Some of labor's direct appeals to the public have contained indicia of a more class-conscious solidarity as well. Finally, organized labor has actively supported employment legislation that benefits workers generally.

. . . .

A narrow vision of unionism that assumes that white workers lack interest in discrimination issues is risky for unions seeking to survive in the new millennium. Clinging to a unidimensional vision of labor's role as guardian of workers' economic interests is poor strategy in an increasingly diverse workforce. The "new working class" is a mix of pink collar, white collar female, African American, Asian American, and Latino/a workers. Whites will decline precipitously to 64% of the labor force in 2025, down from 74% in 1998 and 82% in 1980. Women are projected to increase their share of the labor force, moving from 46.3% to 48% during the period between 1998 and 2015. For this workforce, racial, ethnic, and gender equality issues that intersect with class oppression or are expressed as economic harms will likely eclipse "pure" class concerns. In order to attract and mobilize these workers, the labor movement must evolve to address their concerns.

Exciting new research indicates that workforce diversity presents growth opportunities for unions, as Blacks and women have the highest union organizability rates. But these same workers are also the most likely to look to antidiscrimination statutes for protection against workplace practices that disadvantage them on the basis of their racial, ethnic, or gender identities. If unions' role in advocating for these workers is narrowly circumscribed, the EEOC, the courts, and nonlabor social justice groups will usurp this role, and policies respecting wages, hours, and working conditions that affect labor's traditional membership (white male workers) will be established without labor's input. Thus, labor's continued isolation from social justice issues will compromise its ability to represent the interests of its traditional white male membership.

We recognize that emphasizing race, ethnicity, and gender in union organizing and representation risks alienating labor's historical membership base. Pragmatic concerns nonetheless militate in this direction. For unions to be effective in the next century, they must not only continue to strive to attract new membership from the diverse workforce, but also demonstrate to other progressive social justice groups the depth of their commitment to issues that are important to those groups. Unions cannot reverse their decline unilaterally. Civil rights organizations, community-based social justice organizations, and other similar groups can be powerful allies. Such alliances will be forged only if unions move race, ethnicity, and gender equality issues from the periphery to the heart of their mission. Doing so may cost unions the loyalty of some of their traditional membership base, but we doubt that this cost will be unacceptably high. The economic benefits of union membership are significant, and a stronger labor movement would make these benefits even more significant. Even if some conservative white male members disagree with the new labor movement's focus, most will prioritize economic self-interest over political ideology. Hopefully, as they experience the benefits of labor's growth and enhanced political power, they will acknowledge the wisdom of a social justice focus.

. . . .

Until very recently, organized labor pursued a job-conscious strategy with regard to immigrant labor, actively seeking to exclude immigrants from the United States in order to preserve American jobs for American workers. In 1986, for example, the AFL-CIO supported the passage of the Immigration Reform and Control Act, which imposes sanctions on employers who hire immigrant workers. Recently, however, pragmatic concerns have prompted the AFL-CIO to alter its position on immigrant workers. Projections of increasing diversity of the workforce attributable to immigration leave labor little choice but to organize immigrants, particularly Latino/as. In 1998, Latino/as constituted 10.4% of the labor force, and they are projected to make up 17.2% of the workforce by 2025. Immigrants are also heavily concentrated in areas of labor market growth, specifically the light manufacturing and service sector areas of the economy. Labor's altered perception of immigrant workers as a population ripe for organizing and as a potential base for rebuilding union strength combined with an aggressive INS workplace enforcement program that provided employers a weapon against nascent union organizing of immigrant workers to cause a shift in the AFL-CIO's internal politics. In October of 1999, the AFL-CIO National Convention adopted a resolution opposing the INS enforcement program and calling for a repeal of employer sanctions for hiring immigrant workers. In February 2000, the AFL-CIO Executive Council unanimously approved a resolution supporting a new program providing amnesty to undocumented immigrants and an altered system of employer verification of eligibility to work in the U.S.

Labor's ambivalence about pursuing a strategy of inclusion remains, however. Other commentators have noted that the Executive Council's resolution, distinguishes between immigrant workers and undocumented workers, according immigrant workers full workplace rights but seemingly affording a lesser set of protections to undocumented workers. This stance leaves labor vulnerable to wage undercutting by employer exploitation of the undocumented. The resolution thus preserves the core of business unionism, favoring a reduction in undocumented immigration and seeking to maintain a partnership with business that preserves jobs for American workers.

Section I. Historical Background

A. The Pre-Civil War Period

1. Early Development of Labor Unions

In the early years of this country's history there were comparatively few free workers. The great majority of laborers were either enslaved people from Africa or indentured servants who, to secure passage to America, had bound themselves in servitude for a term of years. As trade and commerce increased, however, there was an increased demand for free workers. The skilled craftsmen, as they began to open small shops and use helpers, soon found it to their advantage to employ free workers whom they could dismiss when business was poor and for whose maintenance they had no responsibility.

In these times the master worked side by side with his journeymen and apprentices, and there was as yet no well-defined distinction between the interests of master and workmen. There were labor organizations of a sort in America as early as the seventeenth century, but they were not trade unions in the modern sense — that is, permanent organizations of workers created to achieve, by concerted action, improvements in wages, hours, and other terms and conditions of employment. Rather, they were primarily guilds of artisans who marketed their own products. They sought to maintain working standards by regulation of apprenticeship requirements and exertion of control over wage rates and prices. The few so-called "strikes" that occurred in the colonial period were not strikes by workers against their masters for increased wages, but for the most part were protests by master craftsmen against local government regulations relaxing apprenticeship requirements or setting ceilings on prices.

2. The "Criminal Conspiracy" Doctrine

Judicial reaction to these early attempts of labor to organize in order to improve working conditions was highly unfavorable. The courts began to condemn the concerted activities of workers' associations as "criminal conspiracies." The following case, digested from the full report that appears in the monumental documentary history compiled by John R. Commons and associates, is a classic in the history of labor law. It is fully analyzed in its social setting in Nelles, *The First American Labor Case*, 41 YALE L.J. 165 (1931).

Philadelphia Cordwainers' Case [Commonwealth v. Pullis]

Philadelphia Mayor's Court (1806)
3 Doc. Hist. of Am. Ind. Soc. 59 (2d ed. Commons 1910)

Indictment for common law conspiracy, tried before a jury consisting of two innkeepers, a tavern-keeper, three grocers, a merchant, a hatter, a tobacconist, a watchmaker, a tailor, a bottler.

The indictment charged in substance: (1) That defendants conspired and agreed that none of them would work at the shoemaking craft except at certain specified prices higher than prices which had theretofore customarily been paid; (2) that defendants conspired and agreed that they would endeavor to prevent "by threats, menaces, and other unlawful means" other craftsmen from working except at said specified rates; and (3) that defendants, having formed themselves into an association, conspired and agreed that none of them would work for any master who should employ a cordwainer who had broken any rule or bylaw of the association, and that defendants, in accordance with such agreement refused to work at the usual rates and prices.

. . . .

Recorder Levy, in his charge to the jury, made the following statements, among others:

> It is proper to consider, is such a combination consistent with the principles of our law, and injurious to the public welfare? The usual means by which the prices of work are regulated, are the demand for the article and the excellence of its fabric. Where the work is well done, and the demand is considerable, the prices will necessarily be high. Where the work is ill done, and the demand is inconsiderable, they will unquestionably be low. . . . These are the means by which prices are regulated in the natural course of things. To make an artificial regulation, is not to regard the excellence of the work or quality of the material, but to fix a positive and arbitrary price, governed by no standard, controlled by no impartial person, but dependent on the will of the few who are interested; this is the unnatural way of raising the price of goods or work. This is independent of the number who are to do the work. It is an unnatural, artificial means of raising the price of work beyond its standard, and taking an undue advantage of the public. . . .
>
> What is the case now before us? . . . A combination of workmen to raise their wages may be considered in a twofold point of view; one is to benefit themselves . . . the other is to injure those who do not join their society. The rule of law condemns both. . . .

The defendants were found guilty and were fined eight dollars each plus costs.

It wasn't until the decision in *Commonwealth v. Hunt*, 45 Mass. (4 Met.) 111, 38 Am. Dec. 346 (1842), that the first break in the doctrine of criminal conspiracy occurred, enabling labor to shift its emphasis from political action towards "business unionism" (which seeks improvement through collective bargaining). In that case certain workmen had been found guilty of criminal conspiracy. On appeal, however, the conviction was reversed. The opinion of Chief Justice Shaw indicated that a conspiracy to impoverish another worker, who was alleged to have lost his employment because he was not a union member, was not in itself unlawful, and that illegality would depend upon the means used. "If it is to be carried into effect by fair or honorable and lawful means, it is, to say the least, innocent; if by falsehood or force, it may be stamped with the character of conspiracy." For a detailed examination of the case, see Nelles, *Commonwealth v. Hunt*, 32 COLUM. L. REV. 1128 (1932).

B. The Post-Civil War Era

1. The Growth of National Unions and Labor Unrest

In 1866 the National Labor Union was formed under the leadership of William H. Silvis, a leader in the iron molders' union. This was a loosely built federation of national trades unions, city trades assemblies, local trades unions, and reform organizations of various kinds. Among the contributions of this union to the development of the trade union movement in the United States was its leadership in the movement for an eight-hour day, its insistence upon organization of women and black workers, and its emphasis upon equal pay for equal work for these two categories of workers most frequently and flagrantly discriminated against. By 1872 it had virtually disappeared.

One of the two important survivors among the labor unions of the depression years of 1873–1879 was the Noble Order of the Knights of Labor, which was organized in 1869 by the tailors of Philadelphia. The sponsors of this union conceived that the weaknesses that the trade unions had shown during the depression period were in part attributable to lack of unity, and that strength would come from a consolidation in one organization of all labor groups, including the unskilled as well as the skilled. They therefore welcomed into their ranks all who worked, even some employers and members of the professions.

The general aims of the organization were to oppose the accumulation of wealth in the hands of a few and in other ways to secure for workers a fuller enjoyment of the wealth they created. These aims were to be achieved by legislation and education rather than by strikes and other forms of economic action.

This idealistic program for a cooperative society found its most ardent supporter in Terence V. Powderly, who became president (Master Workman) of the Knights in 1878. But despite the philosophy that was written into the Preamble of the Order and was referred to as the "First Principles"—that improvement of the worker's condition should be sought through political action and not by means of the militant methods of industrial warfare—a more pragmatic element in the union ultimately got control and turned to typical economic action in an effort to achieve immediate results. Threats of strikes became common and the fear of a general strike made even such a powerful capitalist as Jay Gould seek terms with the union. In 1885, strikes had been called on Gould-controlled railroads because of a reduction in wages. These strikes were successful largely because engineers, firemen, brakemen, and conductors all along the lines joined with the strikers. Shortly thereafter another strike was called because of a reduction in the labor force on one of the roads. Even though the operating employees did not support the strikers this time, Gould, fearing a general strike, held a conference with members of the executive board of the Order and the receivers of his railroads, at which time he threw his influence in favor of the union. This was the first time a great capitalist had discussed the workers' problems with a labor organization.

The year 1886 has sometimes been called the period of "the great upheaval." It was a period of nationwide strikes, sympathetic strikes that were set in motion on the least provocation, violence, and turbulence — including the famous "Haymarket" riots in Chicago, the widespread use of the boycott, and the rise of a strong feeling of labor class consciousness, particularly among the unskilled.

The ideology of the Knights of Labor was in direct contrast with that of the trade unions, one of which was the Cigar Makers' International Union. Both Adolph Strasser, president of this union in 1877, and Samuel Gompers, then president of its New York local, who had been influenced by men trained in the Marxist school, were leaders in the cigar makers' unions in New York. Both Strasser and Gompers eventually turned away from the philosophies of the more radical element in the union in support of a program that they believed would bring more immediate benefits to the worker. "The philosophy which these new leaders developed might be termed a philosophy of pure wage consciousness. It signified a labor movement reduced to an opportunistic basis, accepting the existence of capitalism and having for its object the enlarging of the bargaining power of the wage earner in the sale of his labor." S. PERLMAN, A HISTORY OF TRADE UNIONISM IN THE UNITED STATES 78 (1937).

Gompers and other leaders also stood for craft union autonomy and accused the Knights of Labor of trying to make the craft unions subservient to the interests of the less skilled workers. This bitter rivalry eventually led to the reorganization of the Federation of Organized Trades and Labor Unions, which had been impotent since its birth in 1881. The reorganization occurred in 1886, at which time the name of the organization was changed to "The American Federation of Labor." The AFL placed its emphasis upon business unionism rather than upon reform through legislation, relegating to subordinate state federations its legislative interests.

Employers began to adopt numerous new anti-union tactics. During the depression of 1907, they disregarded collective agreements made when business had been good and labor had been in demand. "Scientific management" and "efficiency" (speed-up) systems were introduced in plants that forced the workers to work harder and faster for the same wages. Vigilante groups and citizens' committees were fostered by employers to resist union activities. Employer associations took a hand.

The National Founders' Association and the National Metal Trades Association, for example, each maintained a "labor bureau," which kept a card index of every man in the employ of its members, and facilitated the use of the "black list" against unionists. These associations also furnished workers when needed, so that resort to the unions for employees was unnecessary, and they furnished strikebreakers upon request.

2. Judicial Reaction and the Labor Injunction

Opposition to the trade union movement came not only from employers. The courts began to issue injunctions against strikes and picketing. *See, e.g., Vegelahn v. Guntner*, 167 Mass. 92, 44 N.E. 1077 (1896). This form of remedy, with its obvious advantages of speed and flexibility, especially when issued ex parte, quickly became standard in this country almost to the exclusion of criminal prosecutions.

3. Labor Unions from 1900 to 1933

During the early part of the twentieth century, the membership of the AFL increased considerably and by 1913 it was almost 2,000,000. There was extensive organization in previously unorganized trades, as well as expansion into the South and West, with continued concentration on the skilled and semiskilled groups. For a time, some competition came from the Industrial Workers of the World (IWW), or "Wobblies," a movement of militant syndicalists that aimed at bringing all workers, without regard to craft or skill, into "One Big Union." Although the IWW was never a serious rival of the AFL, its espousal of the cause of the unskilled brought these workers' problems to the attention of the federation's leaders, who were finally forced to alter the organizational structure of the AFL so as to give the unskilled at least limited recognition.

C. The Period Since 1933

1. The Initial New Deal Labor Policies

The Roosevelt administration attempted to make effective a national labor policy favorable to trade unionism. An effort in this direction was made in the ill-starred National Industrial Recovery Act (NIRA), 48 Stat. 198 (1933), § 7a of which provided as follows:

> Every code of fair competition, agreement, and license approved, prescribed, or issued under this title shall contain the following conditions: (1) That employees shall have the right to organize and bargain collectively through representatives of their own choosing, and shall be free from the interference, restraint, or coercion of employers of labor, or their agents, in the designation of such representatives or in self-organization or in other concerted activities for the purpose of collective bargaining; (2) that no employee and no one seeking employment shall be required as a condition

of employment to join any company union or to refrain from joining, organizing, or assisting a labor organization of his own choosing; and (3) that employers shall comply with the maximum hours of labor, minimum rates of pay, and other conditions of employment, approved or prescribed by the President.

2. The National Labor Relations Act (Wagner Act), 1935

Senator Wagner, the Chairman of the National Labor Board under the NIRA, was determined that the labor relations policies, at least, of the NIRA should not be sacrificed but, indeed, should be reinforced, if possible. In little more than two months following the demise of the NIRA, the original National Labor Relations Act was enacted on July 5, 1935. This statute declared it to be "the policy of the United States" to encourage the practice of collective bargaining and full freedom of worker self-organization, as a means of facilitating the free flow of interstate commerce. Employees covered by the act were given the "right" to organize and to bargain collectively and this right was made effective by proscribing as "unfair labor practices" five kinds of employer conduct vis-à-vis unionism. The principle of "majority rule" among employees in selecting union representatives was adopted, and a three-member National Labor Relations Board was created with authority to settle representation questions and to prosecute violations of the unfair labor practice provisions of the act, 49 Stat. 449 (1935), 29 U.S.C. §§ 151–68. This Board, in accordance with the then-prevailing vogue as to administrative agencies, combined the functions of prosecutor and judge, although its orders had no binding force until "enforced" by a circuit court of appeals upon petition. All employers whose labor practices might "affect" interstate commerce were subject to the act, with the exception of those covered by the Railway Labor Act, and the United States and states or political subdivisions thereof. *See* Casebeer, *Drafting Wagner's Act: Leon Keyserling and the Precommittee Drafts of the Labor Disputes Act and the National Labor Relations Act*, 11 INDUS. REL. L.J. 73 (1989).

NLRB v. Jones & Laughlin Steel Corp., 301 U.S. 1, 57 S. Ct. 615, 81 L. Ed. 893 (1937). The corporation was engaged in the manufacture of steel in Pennsylvania, importing iron ore from Michigan and Minnesota and shipping steel products to many states. The NLRB found that the corporation had committed an unfair labor practice by discharging 10 men because of their union activities. The court of appeals declined to enforce the Board's order to cease and desist. The Supreme Court granted certiorari and, in a divided 5-4 decision, sustained the constitutionality of the NLRA and the authority of the NLRB to regulate local disputes that affected interstate commerce.

> . . . We think it clear that the National Labor Relations Act may be construed so as to operate within the sphere of constitutional authority. . . . The grant of authority to the Board does not purport to extend to the relationship between all industrial employees and employers. Its terms do not impose

collective bargaining upon all industry regardless of effects upon interstate or foreign commerce. It purports to reach only what may be deemed to burden or obstruct that commerce and, thus qualified, it must be construed as contemplating the exercise of control within constitutional bounds. It is a familiar principle that acts which directly burden or obstruct interstate or foreign commerce, or its free flow, are within the reach of the congressional power. Acts having that effect are not rendered immune because they grow out of labor disputes. . . .

[I]n its present application, the statute goes no further than to safeguard the right of employees to self-organization and to select representatives of their own choosing for collective bargaining or other mutual protection without restraint or coercion by their employer.

That is a fundamental right. Employees have as clear a right to organize and select their representatives for lawful purposes as the respondent has to organize its business and select its own officers and agents. Discrimination and coercion to prevent free exercise of the right of employees to self-organization and representation is a proper subject for condemnation by competent legislative authority. Long ago we stated the reason for labor organizations. We said that they were organized out of the necessities of the situation; that a single employee was helpless in dealing with an employer; that he was dependent ordinarily on his daily wage for the maintenance of himself and family; that if the employer refused to pay him the wages that he thought fair, he was nevertheless unable to leave the employ and resist arbitrary and unfair treatment; that union was essential to give laborers opportunity to deal on an equality with their employer. *American Steel Foundries v. Tri-City Central Trades Council*, 257 U.S. 184, 209 (1921). . . .

Experience has abundantly demonstrated that the recognition of the right of employees to self-organization and to have representatives of their own choosing for the purpose of collective bargaining is often an essential condition of industrial peace. Refusal to confer and negotiate has been one of the most prolific causes of strife. . . .

3. Union Growth under the Wagner Act: The CIO and Industrial Unions

Both the NIRA and the NLRA, with their guarantees of the right to self-organization without employer interference, gave a tremendous impetus to the organization of the millions of unskilled and semiskilled workers in the mass production industries. As a result, there came to a head within the AFL the issue of industrial unionism, which had been all but forgotten since the demise of the Knights of Labor in the 1890s. The AFL Convention of 1934 recognized that these potential new recruits to the ranks of organized labor would not fit very well into the traditional pattern of craft unionism, but took an equivocal stand as to just what was to be done.

In the 1934 convention, a resolution to organize new industrial-type unions within the AFL was decisively defeated. The leading craft unionists took the position that the problem could be handled by using local federal unions within plants already partially organized by craft unions and by enlarging the jurisdiction of the established craft unions. Chartering industrial-type unions would have precluded the expansion of the craft unions into certain industries, and the Carpenters, Teamsters, Machinists, Plumbers, and other unions could not face this result with equanimity, nor could they, in fact, easily have resolved the competitive problems that would have attended an attempt to enlarge their respective jurisdictions so as to bring in groups of previously unorganized employees. On the other hand, the industrial union partisans maintained that to split up workers within an industry among the various craft unions would weaken the bargaining position of such workers by preventing timely and concerted action.

Certain of the federation's affiliates — such as the United Mine Workers, the Ladies Garment Workers and the Amalgamated Clothing Workers — had become very strong and had successfully used the industrial type of organization. Few of the affiliated craft unions had done so well in rate or extent of growth and the successful pro-industrialist union leaders were impatient with the craft unionists who were dominant in high federation councils. Finally, the industrial union protagonists decided to undertake organizing campaigns in mass production industries on their own, and in November 1935, the presidents of eight AFL unions created the Committee for Industrial Organization, the purpose of which was stated to be "encouragement and promotion of organization of unorganized workers in mass production and other industries on an industrial basis." John L. Lewis was chosen chairman.

In June 1936, a drive was undertaken by this group through the "Steelworkers Organizing Committee" to organize the iron and steel industry. It met with great success the following year when the United States Steel Corporation capitulated and entered into an agreement with the committee. Many other steel companies followed suit. There were also important membership gains in other fields, especially in the automobile, electrical manufacturing, and textile industries.

The Committee for Industrial Organization had stated its purpose was purely "educational" and "advisory" to convince the rank and file of the federation of the need of organizing the millions of workers in the mass production industries. However, the Executive Committee of the AFL considered the committee a "dual" organization and ordered its dissolution. When the ultimatum was disregarded, the member unions of the committee were suspended from the federation.

In November 1938, the various groups then forming the Committee for Industrial Organization broke away completely from the AFL and changed the name of the organization to the "Congress of Industrial Organizations" (CIO). Its avowed purpose was to promote union organization, to extend the benefits of collective bargaining, and to obtain legislation safeguarding the economic security and social welfare of the workers of America. John L. Lewis was the organization's first president. When he resigned in 1940, Philip Murray, president of the CIO's United Steelworkers and a vice president of the CIO, became president. For years he had handled difficult organizational assignments, and he was welcomed to the presidency of the CIO as a brilliant organizer and a skillful negotiator. Both the CIO and the AFL had undertaken very active organizational campaigns that were accompanied by an unprecedented number of strikes. By 1937, union membership rose to more than 7,000,000.

The period following the passage of the NLRA was not one of tranquility in labor relations. Coupled with the AFL-CIO rift was the fact that countless employers, who had neither the desire nor the experience that makes for successful collective bargaining, were forced to deal with unions. And the fact that many of them had to negotiate with young, militant, and inexperienced unions did not improve the opportunity for good relations. The result was a sharp increase, over the previous decade, in the number of strikes and in the number of production man-days lost as a result of labor disputes. *See* 62 MONTHLY LAB. REV. 720 (1946).

4. The Labor Management Relations Act (Taft-Hartley Act), 1947

The process of reconversion during late 1945 and 1946 from a wartime to a peacetime economy was accompanied by a wave of strikes in many vital industries, including steel, coal, oil, automobiles, meat packing, and electrical products. In contrast to the post-World War I situation, the unions, particularly in the mass production industries, demonstrated their cohesiveness and strength of organization. The strikes involved a loss of 116,000,000 worker-days — an all-time record. A reaction to this showing of union power became evident in 1947 when the Eightieth Congress enacted the Labor Management Relations Act (Taft-Hartley Act), 61 Stat. 136 (1947), 29 U.S.C. §§ 141–97, over President Truman's veto.

In § 7, a basic change in emphasis can be seen in the addition of the right to refrain from organization and concerted activities. This was implemented in § 8(b)(1) by the prohibition of union restraint and coercion against employees exercising such rights.

In § 8(a), the various employer unfair labor practices were retained, but § 8(c) made it clear that employers may express their opinions about unionism unless they threaten reprisal or wrongfully promise benefits. Under § 8(a)(3), the closed shop was no longer authorized and the union shop was subjected to limitations.

Most important, the Taft-Hartley Act noted in § 1 that certain union practices obstruct commerce, and § 8(b) outlawed a number of them, including secondary boycotts (§ 8(b)(4)(A) and (B)) and jurisdictional strikes (§ 8(b)(4)(D)).

The changes in § 9 placed various restrictions on the NLRB in conducting representation proceedings, and those in § 10 tightened up procedures in unfair labor practice cases.

The NLRB was increased from three to five members, and the final authority to investigate charges, issue complaints, and present them before the Board was placed in the hands of the General Counsel, in order to avoid casting the Board in the role of both prosecutor and judge.

In addition to these and many other amendments to the Wagner Act, the Taft-Hartley Act contained much entirely new material. In Title II, the Federal Mediation and Conciliation Service was set up as an independent agency, and an elaborate procedure was outlined for the handling of national emergency disputes. Various important matters were dealt with in Title III of the LMRA, including a provision for suits in federal courts to enforce collective agreements (§ 301), restrictions on payments to employee representatives and on health and welfare funds (§ 302), damage suits in federal courts for secondary boycotts (§ 303), restrictions on political contributions (§ 304), and the outlawing of strikes by government employees (§ 305).

5. The Labor-Management Reporting and Disclosure Act (Landrum-Griffin Act), 1959

Beginning in 1957, the Senate Select Committee on Improper Activities in the Labor or Management Field (McClellan Committee) held a series of hearings lasting more than two years, in the course of which instances were brought into public view of misuse of union funds; lack of democratic procedures in internal union affairs; improper imposition of trusteeships over locals by parent unions; collusive dealings between management and union officials, resulting in "sweetheart" contracts and payoffs to union officials; improper use of "middlemen" to discourage genuine union organization; infiltration of certain unions by gangsters and racketeers; laxity in local law enforcement dealing with violence and racketeering; misuse of picketing and secondary boycotting as an instrument of power, sometimes for extortion; and the existence of a "no-man's land," under which employers and employees were without either a federal or a state forum to hear and determine their complaints.

The 1959 labor reform legislation implements the recommendations of the McClellan Committee by establishing a "bill of rights" for union members; requiring periodic financial and other reports from unions and their officers and employees, employers, and labor relations consultants; regulating trusteeships over local unions; regulating union election procedures; regulating misappropriation of union funds and loans from union treasuries; and prohibiting Communists and persons convicted of certain crimes within the preceding five years from holding union office.

In addition, a number of important amendments were made to the Labor Management Relations Act of 1947 (Taft-Hartley Act): in order to fill the "no-man's land," states were permitted to handle cases declined by the NLRB, but the Board was prohibited from further restricting its jurisdiction; economic strikers, though permanently replaced, were given limited voting rights in NLRB elections; the secondary boycott prohibitions of the Taft-Hartley Act were tightened up so as to prevent direct pressure upon secondary employers; hot cargo clauses were outlawed, with certain exceptions for the garment and construction industries; and organizational and recognition picketing were placed under explicit restrictions.

6. Organized Labor from the 1970s to the Present

STEVEN GREENHOUSE, BEATEN DOWN, WORKED UP: THE PAST, PRESENT, AND FUTURE OF AMERICAN LABOR
xi-xii, 328 (Alfred A. Knopf 2019)*

Now . . . labor unions are far weaker. The decline of unions, and of worker bargaining power in general, has taken a toll on our nation. It has contributed to many of the country's major problems: increased income inequality, wage stagnation, declining mobility, the high number of low-wage jobs, and the skewing of our politics in favor of corporations and wealthy campaign donors.

. . . .

Labor unions and their ability to create a powerful collective voice for workers, played a huge role in building the world's largest, richest middleclass. The success of American business of course played a major part as well, but it was unions' strikes, and the millions of workers who took to the streets, that pressured companies to share their profits more fairly after World Wat II.

. . . .

[J]ust 6.4 percent of private-sector workers are union members, and just 10.5 percent of the workforce overall. By far the biggest obstacle to unions' growth is fierce employer opposition, which is encouraged by the extraordinarily weak penalties that companies face when they break the law battling unions . . . [T]he main penalty that employers often face for such lawbreaking is having to post a notice on the bulletin board admitting they broke the law and promising not to do it again. Researchers have found that nearly 20 percent of rank-and-file union activists are fired during organizing drives, a percentage that is so high because the punishment is so puny. It is almost foolhardy for antiunion companies not to fire the two or three workers heading an organizing drive.

---

* Excerpt(s) from BEATEN DOWN, WORKED UP: THE PAST, PRESENT, AND FUTURE OF AMERICAN LABOR by Steven Greenhouse, copyright © 2019 by Steven Greenhouse. Used by permission of Alfred A. Knopf, an imprint of the Knopf Doubleday Publishing Group, a division of Penguin Random House LLC. All rights reserved.

Robert B. Reich, Saving Capitalism
126–127 (Alfred A. Knopf 2015)*

A third driving force behind the declining power of the middle class has been the demise of unions. Fifty years ago, when General Motors was the largest employer in America, the typical worker earned $35.00 an hour in today's dollars. By 2014, America's largest employer was Walmart, and the average hourly wage of Walmart workers was $11.22. This does not mean that the typical GM employee was "worth" more than three times what the typical Walmart employee in 2014 was worth. The GM worker was not better educated or more motivated than the Walmart worker. The real difference was that GM workers a half century ago had a strong union behind them that summoned the collective bargaining power of all autoworkers to get a substantial share of company revenues for its members. And because more than a third of workers across American belonged to a labor union, the bargains those unions struck with employers raised the wages and benefits of nonunionized workers as well. Nonunion firms knew they would be unionized if they did not come close to matching the union contracts.

Another significant factor with respect to the decline of union membership concerns the impact of technology on traditional unionized jobs. See generally Daniel Susskind, *A World Without Work* (2020). Many manufacturing jobs have been automated, many service positions are being replaced by robots, and within the next few years several million truck driver and taxi/Uber/Lift driver jobs will be taken over by autonomous vehicles. If unions are to expand in future years, they will have to determine how to organize individuals working in positions that have not been entirely taken over by artificial intelligence.

Union membership in the United States exceeded 19 million in 1970, much of the growth in recent years coming in the public sector. However, the workforce expanded faster than unionization; the proportion of the nonagricultural workforce comprised of union members declined from a high of 35% in 1953 to 27.3% in 1970, 23% in 1980, and 16.1% in 1990. Unions that had won 70–86% of NLRB representation elections during the 1940s and 60–75% of elections during the 1950s prevailed in less than half of Labor Board elections conducted during the late 1980s. Much of this decline has resulted from the shift in employment from industrial production, the traditional center of union strength, to white-collar and service work, the substitution of new technology for manufacturing workers, and the migration of millions of jobs from unionized north eastern and north central states to less unionized

---

* Excerpt(s) from SAVING CAPITALISM: FOR THE MANY, NOT THE FEW by Robert B. Reich, copyright © 2015 by Robert B. Reich. Used by permission of Alfred A. Knopf, an imprint of the Knopf Doubleday Publishing Group, a division of Penguin Random House LLC. All rights reserved.

southern and southwestern states and to low-wage foreign countries. *See generally* C. Craver, Can Unions Survive? (1993); M. Goldfield, The Decline of Organized Labor in the United States (1987); D. Montgomery, The Fall of the House of Labor (1987).

By the end of 2020, union membership had declined to 14,300,000 individuals, comprising 10.8% of the nonagricultural workforce. While union members currently comprise 34.8% of government workers, private sector union membership constitutes a mere 6.3% of workforce participants. This decline helps explain the fact that labor's share of national income has decreased by six percent since the 1970s. Kristal, *The Capitalist Machine: Computerization, Workers' Power, and the Decline in Labor's Share Within U.S. Industries*, 78 Amer. Sociological Rev. 361 (2013). If the downward trend of the past two decades continues, labor organizations will only represent five percent of private sector workers by the end of this decade. Union membership is much higher among public sector workers than among private sector employees, due in large part to greater private sector employer opposition.

Managerial opposition [to unions] takes on two, often interrelated but at least conceptually distinct, forms. One form is union substitution—employer policies that match or exceed wages and working practices found in union settings that thereby reduce worker motivation to organize... [F]irms that have an explicit union avoidance strategy and implement workplace innovations including employee participation and non-union grievance procedures are almost immune from successful union organizing... The second form of management opposition—union suppression through direct opposition in organizing drives—has been shown to have increased substantially from the 1960s through to the present time, if measured either by the rise in employer unfair labour practices or by the number of workers illegally fired for engaging in union organizing activities. Numerous studies have shown management opposition significantly reduces union organizing and first contract success rates. The most recent study has shown that employer unfair labour practices were associated with a 50 per cent decline in the probability that a union organizing drive was successful in getting a first contract. Indeed, unions had only a 20 per cent overall chance of making it through the organising process and less than 10 per cent if unfair labour practices were present.

Clearly, the increase in management opposition and the ineffectiveness of American labour law in redressing illegal employer behavior account for a substantial portion of union decline.

Kochan, *Collective Bargaining: Crisis and Its Consequences for American Society*, 43 Indus. Rel. J. 302, 304 (2012). *See* S. Greenhouse, Beaten Down, Worked Up: The Past, Present, and Future of American Labor (2019); Martinez & Fiorito, *General Feelings Toward Unions and Employers as Predictors of Union Voting Intent*, 30 J. Lab. Res. 120 (2009). Another critical factor concerning the decline of union membership is the impact of technology on traditional union jobs, as many of those positions have been automated. *See* D. Susskind, A World without Work (2020). *See also* R. Reich, Saving Capitalism (2015).

[Margin note: Automation has also ↓ union membership by eliminating traditional union jobs]

If the labor movement is to remain an established and powerful force in American society, unions will have to adapt to the challenge of changed conditions. The traditional goal of achieving bigger bargaining "gains" may have to be supplemented with new goals concerned with greater job security and improved quality of life, both on the job and in the communities surrounding the workplace. These broader goals may be pursued in a number of ways. Andrias, for example, has promoted the rise of "social bargaining," which locates "decisions about basic standards of employment at the sectoral, industrial, and regional levels, rather than at the level of the individual worksite or employer." Under this view, unions become more like political actors, looking out for workers more generally and attempting to involve the state as a more active participant in support of goals such as a higher minimum wage and greater workplace protections. Kate Andrias, *The New Labor Law*, 126 Yale L.J. 2 (2016). Others have called for greater worker involvement by making them more active participants in firm decisionmaking through the mechanisms of corporate governance. *See, e.g.*, D. Webber, The Rise of the Working-Class Shareholder (2018) (calling for workers to use their capital in the form of pension funds to pursue more worker-friendly policies in the corporate boardroom); G. Hayden & M. Bodie, Reconstructing the Corporation: From Shareholder Primacy to Shared Governance (2020) (arguing for a system of codetermination, where both shareholders and employers have representatives on corporate boards).

A study conducted by Professors Richard Freeman and Joel Rogers in the late 1990s found that 87% of private sector workers would like some form of collective voice to influence employer decisions that affect their job security and employment conditions, but they fear employer reprisals if they openly support unionization. R. Freeman & J. Rogers, What Workers Want 147 Exhibit 7.2 (1999). About half of these respondents favored traditional independent union representation, while the other half preferred less independent and more cooperative forms of representation. The Employee Free Choice Act, considered by Congress in 2009 and 2010, would have amended the National Labor Relations Act to enable unions to obtain Labor Board certification as bargaining agents through demonstrations of majority support among targeted workers based upon signed authorization cards indicating their desire for representation instead of through secret ballot Labor Board elections, which usually take six to eight weeks to conduct following union petitions for such elections. Such a practice would have returned to the way Labor Board certifications could be carried out from 1935, when the original NLRA was enacted, until the 1947 Taft-Hartley Act amendments requiring secret ballot elections, and it would have significantly shortened the time employers could campaign against unionization. Do you think that such options should be available to employees who indicate a clear desire for representation? *See* Gould, *The Employee Free Choice Act* of 2009, Labor Law Reform, and What Can Be Done About the Broken System of Labor-Management Relations Law in the United States*, 43 U.S.F. L. Rev. 291 (2008); Craver, *How to Make the Much Needed Employee Free Choice Act Politically Acceptable*, 60 Lab. L.J. 82 (2009). More recently, the House of Representatives passed the Protecting the Right to Organize Act, which, among other things, would impose monetary penalties on employers found to have committed unfair labor practices, make it easier for workers to be classified as employees rather than independent contractors, prevent the use of permanent replacement workers, and weaken right-to-work laws in states that allow employees to avoid paying union dues. That bill, however, has drawn vociferous opposition from business and industry groups, and faces significant hurdles on its path to be enacted into law. *See* Rosenberg, *House Passes Bill to Rewrite Labor Laws and Strengthen Unions*, Wash. Post, Feb. 6, 2020.

Two contrasting trends seem apparent: (1) a hardening of the adversarial position by some employers, including a willingness to operate during strikes and to employ consultants in an effort to preserve or obtain "union-free" environments; and (2) a movement in the direction of greater cooperation between some managements and some unions in the effort to improve productivity. There has been some reflection in the United States, although still very limited, of a worldwide trend toward greater worker participation in managerial decisions. *See* Craver, *The American Worker: Junior Partner in Success and Senior Partner in Failure*, 37 U.S.F. L. Rev. 587 (2003); Craver, *Mandatory Worker Participation Is Required in a Declining Union Environment to Provide Employees with Meaningful Industrial Democracy*, 66 Geo. Wash. L. Rev. 135 (1997); Merrifield, *Worker Participation in Decisions Within Undertakings*, 5 Comp. Lab. L.J. 1 (1982); Weiler, *Promises to Keep: Securing Workers' Rights to Self-Organization Under the NLRA*, 96 Harv. L. Rev. 1769 (1983) ("Contemporary American labor law more and more resembles an elegant tombstone for a dying institution.").

Section II. Introductory Materials

A. Coverage of the National Labor Relations Act

1. Scope of the Concept "Affecting Commerce"

In the *Jones & Laughlin* case, the Supreme Court approved the interpretation by the NLRB (*see* First Annual Report 195 (1936)) that Congress had given the Board jurisdiction coextensive with congressional power to legislate under the commerce clause of the Constitution. As stated in §10(a) of the National Labor Relations Act, the NLRB is empowered "to prevent any person from engaging in any unfair labor practice (listed in §8) affecting commerce."

A long series of later cases have made it clear that federal power (and hence the jurisdiction of the NLRB) over industries in which a labor dispute would "affect commerce" is very broad.

In general, the NLRA applies to:

(a) employers producing goods which are destined directly or indirectly to go out into interstate commerce;

(b) employers receiving goods from out-of-state, directly or indirectly, so that a labor dispute would tend to slow down the flow of goods in interstate commerce;

(c) employers engaged in commerce — communications, transportation, etc. — or performing services for such industries, so that a labor dispute would interfere with the movement of commerce.

The company need not do a majority of its business across state lines, and the company may do a very small percentage of the total business in its industry. It is immaterial whether the same goods or services could be obtained from another company in the event of a labor dispute. *NLRB v. Bradford Dyeing Ass'n*, 310 U.S. 318 (1940).

2. NLRB Exercise of Its Jurisdiction

NLRB, A Guide to Basic Law and Procedures Under the National Labor Relations Act
41–43 (1987)

Although the National Labor Relations Board could exercise its powers to enforce the Act in all cases involving enterprises whose operations affect commerce, the Board does not act in all such cases. In its discretion it limits the exercise of its power to cases involving enterprises whose effect on commerce is substantial. The Board's requirements for exercising its power or jurisdiction are called "jurisdictional standards." These standards are based on the yearly amount of business done by the enterprise, or on the yearly amount of its sales or of its purchases. They are stated in terms of total dollar volume of business and are different for different kinds of enterprises. The amounts have not been adjusted for inflation, which makes them increasingly outdated. The Board's standards in effect since July 1, 1976, are as follows:

1. *Nonretail business:* Direct sales of goods to consumers in other States, or indirect sales through others (called outflow), of at least $50,000 a year; or direct purchases of goods from suppliers in other States, or indirect purchases through others (called inflow), of at least $50,000 a year.

2. *Office buildings:* Total annual revenue of $100,000 of which $25,000 or more is derived from organizations which meet any of the standards except the indirect outflow and indirect inflow standards established for nonretail enterprises.

3. *Retail enterprises:* At least $500,000 total annual volume of business.

4. *Public utilities:* At least $250,000 total annual volume of business, or $50,000 direct or indirect outflow or inflow.

5. *Newspapers:* At least $200,000 total annual volume of business.

6. *Radio, telegraph, television, and telephone enterprises:* At least $100,000 total annual volume of business.

7. *Hotels, motels, and residential apartment houses:* At least $500,000 total annual volume of business.

8. *Privately operated health care institutions:* At least $250,000 total annual volume of business for hospitals; at least $100,000 for nursing homes, visiting nurses associations, and related facilities; at least $250,000 for all other types of private health care institutions defined in the 1974 amendments to the Act. The statutory definition includes: "any hospital, convalescent hospital, health maintenance organization, health clinic, nursing home, extended care facility, or other institution devoted to the care of the sick, infirm, or aged person." Public hospitals are excluded from NLRB jurisdiction by Section 2(2) of the Act.

9. *Transportation enterprises, links and channels of interstate commerce:* At least $50,000 total annual income from furnishing interstate passenger and freight transportation services; also performing services valued at $50,000 or more for businesses which meet any of the jurisdictional standards except the indirect outflow and indirect inflow standards established for nonretail enterprises.

10. *Transit systems:* At least $250,000 total annual volume of business.

11. *Taxicab companies:* At least $500,000 total annual volume of business.

12. *Associations:* These are regarded as a single employer in that the annual business of all association members is totaled to determine whether any of the standards apply.

13. *Enterprises in the Territories and the District of Columbia:* The jurisdictional standards apply in the Territories; all businesses in the District of Columbia come under NLRB jurisdiction.

14. *National defense:* Jurisdiction is asserted over all enterprises affecting commerce when their operations have a substantial impact on national defense, whether or not the enterprises satisfy any other standard.

15. *Private universities and colleges:* At least $1 million gross annual revenue from all sources (excluding contributions not available for operating expenses because of limitations imposed by the grantor).

16. *Symphony orchestras:* At least $1 million gross annual revenue from all sources (excluding contributions not available for operating expenses because of limitations imposed by the grantor).

17. *Law firms and legal assistance programs:* At least $250,000 gross annual revenues.

18. *Employers that provide social services:* At least $250,000 gross annual revenues.

19. *Lawful gambling casinos:* At least $500,000 gross annual revenues.

Through enactment of the Postal Reorganization Act of 1970, NLRA coverage was extended to U.S. Postal Service personnel, but Post Office employees are expressly denied the right to strike.

Enterprises that satisfy the Board's monetary standards are ordinarily engaged in activities that "affect" commerce. The NLRB must find, however, based on evidence, that each enterprise does in fact "affect" commerce. When an employer whose operations "affect" commerce refuses to supply the Board with information concerning total annual business, etc., the Board generally dispenses with the monetary requirement and asserts jurisdiction.

Finally, §14(c)(1) authorizes the Board, in its discretion, to decline to exercise jurisdiction over any class or category of employers where a labor dispute involving those firms is not sufficiently substantial to warrant the exercise of jurisdiction, but it cannot refuse to exercise jurisdiction over any labor dispute over which it would have asserted jurisdiction under the standards it had in effect on August 1, 1959. In accordance with this provision, the Board has declined to exercise jurisdiction over racetracks, owners, breeders, and trainers of racehorses, and real estate brokers. State substantive law governs disputes pertaining to industries over which the NLRB refuses to assert jurisdiction. *See Eatz v. DME Unit of Local 3*, 973 F.2d 64 (2d Cir. 1992).

3. Exclusions from Coverage

a. Independent Contractors

The Wagner Act did not contain any specific exclusion of independent contractors, and the Supreme Court in *NLRB v. Hearst Publs.*, 322 U.S. 111, 126–28 (1944), sustained the NLRB in its finding that the newsmen selling papers at fixed spots on the streets were employees entitled to the protection of the act. The Court reasoned:

> The mischief at which the Act is aimed and the remedies it offers are not confined exclusively to "employees" within the traditional legal distinctions separating them from "independent contractors." . . .

> Unless the common-law tests are to be imported and made exclusively controlling, without regard to the statute's purposes, it cannot be irrelevant that the particular workers in these cases are subject, as a matter of economic fact, to the evils the statute was designed to eradicate and that the remedies it affords are appropriate for preventing them or curing their harmful effects in the special situation. Interruption of commerce through strikes and unrest may stem as well from labor disputes between some who, for other purposes, are technically "independent contractors" and their employers as from disputes between persons who, for those purposes, are "employees" and their employers. *Cf. Milk Drivers' Union v. Lake Valley Farm Products*, 311 U.S. 91. Inequality of bargaining power in controversies over wages, hours and working conditions may as well characterize the status of the one group as of the other. The former, when acting alone, may

be as "helpless in dealing with an employer," as "dependent . . . on his daily wage" and as "unable to leave the employ and to resist arbitrary and unfair treatment" as the latter. For each, "union . . . [may be] essential to give . . . opportunity to deal on equality with their employer." And for each, collective bargaining may be appropriate and effective for the "friendly adjustment of industrial disputes arising out of differences as to wages, hours, or other working conditions." 49 Stat. 449. In short, when the particular situation of employment combines these characteristics, so that the economic facts of the relation make it more nearly one of employment than of independent business enterprise with respect to the ends sought to be accomplished by the legislation, those characteristics may outweigh technical legal classification for purposes unrelated to the statute's objectives and bring the relation within its protections.

House Committee on Education and Labor
H.R. Rep. No. 245 on H.R. 3020, 80th Cong., 1st Sess. 18 (1947)

An "employee," according to all standard dictionaries, according to the law as the courts have stated it, and according to the understanding of almost everyone, with the exception of members of the National Labor Relations Board, means someone who works for another for hire. But in the case of *NLRB v. Hearst Publications, Inc.*, 322 U.S. 111 (1944), the Board expanded the definition of the term "employee" beyond anything that it ever had included before, and the Supreme Court, relying upon the theoretic "expertness" of the Board, upheld the Board. In this case, the Board held independent merchants who bought newspapers from the publisher and hired people to sell them to be "employees." The people the merchants hired to sell the papers were "employees" of the merchants, but holding the merchants to be "employees" of the publisher of the papers was most far reaching. It must be presumed that when Congress passed the Labor Act, it intended words it used to have the meanings that they had when Congress passed the Act, not new meanings that, nine years later, the Labor Board might think up. In the law there always has been a difference, and a big difference, between "employees" and "independent contractors." "Employees" work for wages or salaries under direct supervision. "Independent contractors" undertake to do a job for a price, decide how the work will be done, usually hire others to do the work, and depend for their income not upon wages, but upon the difference between what they pay for goods, materials, and labor and what they receive for the end result, that is, upon profits. It is inconceivable that Congress, when it passed the Act, authorized the Board to give to every word in the Act whatever meaning it wished. On the contrary, Congress intended then, and it intends now, the Board to give to words not farfetched meanings but ordinary meanings. To correct what the Board has done, and what the Supreme Court, putting misplaced reliance upon the Board's expertness, has approved, the bill excludes "independent contractors" from the definition of "employee."

The NLRB subsequently explained its understanding of the distinction as follows:

> The Board has consistently held that the act requires that the question whether an individual is an independent contractor be determined by applying the "right-of-control" test. Under this test an independent contractor relationship will be found where the record shows that the person for whom services are performed reserves control only as to the result sought. On the other hand, where the record shows that control is retained over the manner and means by which the result is to be accomplished, an employer-employee relationship will be found.

NLRB, Twenty-Third Annual Report 40 (1958).

The Board and courts have continued to struggle over the correct classification of many workers. In *FedEx Home Delivery v. NLRB*, 563 F.3d 492 (D.C. Cir. 2009), for example, the court reversed a Labor Board finding of "employee" status for truck drivers. Although the court recognized the applicability of the traditional "right to control" test, it emphasized the need to ask whether the individuals in question have "significant entrepreneurial opportunity for gain or loss." Since the drivers could contract to serve multiple routes, could hire their own employees, and could assign or sell the contractual rights to their routes, providing them with entrepreneurial opportunities, the court found them to be independent contractors. *Accord FedEx Home Delivery v. NLRB*, 849 F.3d 1123 (D.C. Cir. 2014).

However, in *Lancaster Symphony Orchestra*, 361 N.L.R.B. No. 101 (2014), the Board ruled that a group of orchestra musicians working for a small orchestra were employees covered by the NLRA, even though they were free to accept or reject opportunities to play in seasonal programs, were contracted for only a year at a time, provided their own instruments and performance outfits, and were free to perform or teach elsewhere while under contract with the orchestra. Applying the common law agency test, the Board reasoned that the orchestra controlled the manner and means of the musicians' work: once the musicians agreed to perform, the orchestra dictated the number of rehearsals and performances, imposed prohibitions on personal mannerisms and habits, and enforced a strict dress code.

Many employers have been working to classify workers as independent contractors or as employees of outside entities. One scholar recently predicted that by 2020 up to 40% of workers will fall into one of these categories and lose their protection under various labor and employment laws unless courts adopt a modern approach to determining which party really controls and benefits from the work of such persons. *See* Cunningham-Parmeter, *From Amazon to Uber: Defining Employment in the Modern Economy*, 96 B.U. Law Rev. 1673 (2016). This effort by employers also raises the question of whether an employer's misclassification of workers as independent contractors rather than employees itself violates the NLRA where it is designed to block union organizing efforts. Although the NLRB's General Counsel previously suggested that it could be a violation in *Pac. 9 Transp., Inc.*, NLRB Div. of Advice, No. 21-CA-150875 (released Aug. 26, 2016), the Labor Board rejected this perspective in *Velox Express, Inc.*, 368 N.L.R.B. No. 61 (2019). The Board found that such a misclassification does not communicate to workers that organizing or other protected activities would be futile, nor does it threaten workers for reprisal if they engage in such activities.

b. Supervisory Employees

The status of supervisory employees presented one of the most troublesome problems to confront the NLRB under the original NLRA. The question was to what extent, if at all, supervisory groups were to be accorded the rights of "employees" under the statute. It was early and consistently held by the Board with judicial support that supervisory employees were protected against acts of discrimination under § 8(3) of the act.

The next question was whether, as employees protected in some respects under the act, supervisors also had bargaining rights and, if so, in what form of bargaining unit. After considerable difference of opinion among members of the NLRB, the Board certified the Foreman's Association of America as representative of a bargaining unit of foremen, and the Supreme Court enforced an order to bargain in *Packard Motor Car Co. v. NLRB*, 330 U.S. 485 (1947). In *Jones & Laughlin Steel Corp. (Pittsburgh, Pa.)*, 66 N.L.R.B. 386 (1946), the Board held that District 50 of the United Mine Workers could represent mine foremen even though the UMW also represented the rank-and-file miners.

The Board's policy of according to supervisory personnel the full status of employees under the original act was the subject of bitter attack by employers, with the result that in the Taft-Hartley Act of 1947 Congress expressly excluded from the definition of "employee" "any individual employed as a supervisor" (§ 2(3)), and adopted an apparently broad definition of "supervisors" (§ 2(11)). At the same time, it was provided in § 14(a) that "[n]othing herein shall prohibit any individual employed as a supervisor from becoming or remaining a member of a labor organization, but no employer subject to this act shall be compelled to deem individuals defined herein as supervisors as employees for the purpose of any law, either national or local, relating to collective bargaining." While the act thus established a new national policy with respect to the status of such employees, the debate on the merits will doubtless continue, especially since supervisors remain free of any legislative prohibition against unionization.

The NLRB has commented:

> The supervisory status of an employee under the act depends on whether he possesses authority to act in the interest of his employer in the matters and the manner specified in Section 2(11) which defines the term "supervisors." Generally, it is the existence rather than the exercise of authority within the meaning of Section 2(11) that determines an employee's supervisory status.
>
> In determining the existence of supervisory authority in contested cases, the Board has continued to take into consideration such record facts as the

ratio of supervisory to supervised employees in the particular department or plant.... Manner and rate of pay is also considered relevant in ascertaining the status of employees.

Employees who possess some supervisory authority may be included in a bargaining unit if the exercise of their supervisory functions is only sporadic or occasional. On the other hand, employees who substitute regularly and periodically for their superior during his absence are generally excluded from bargaining units.

NLRB Twenty-Third Annual Report 40–41 (1958).

Overruling a long line of precedent, the Labor Board held that "system supervisors" who responsibly "direct" employees are supervisors within the meaning of the NLRA even though they do not hire, fire, transfer, lay off, recall, or promote, etc. It is enough to establish "any one of the statutory criteria listed, regardless of the frequency of its use." *Big Rivers Elec. Corp.*, 266 N.L.R.B. 618 (1983). *But cf. Anamag*, 284 N.L.R.B. 621 (1987) (leaders of cooperative work teams not supervisors when decisions regarding individual group members made by entire team). In *Schnuck Markets, Inc. v. NLRB*, 961 F.2d 700 (8th Cir. 1992), the court reversed the Board and held that a night manager who spent 30 to 40% of his time on manual work was a "supervisor," since he was the highest-ranking person on duty at night and had complete authority to manage the store.

Because of the unique relationships among registered nurses, practical nurses, nurse's aides, and patients, the Labor Board and the courts have had a difficult time determining when registered nurses and practical nurses who can direct the work of nurse's aides constitute excluded "supervisors." These cases have also been the source of much of the law on who counts as a "supervisor." In *NLRB v. Health Care & Retirement Corp. of Am.*, 511 U.S. 571 (1994), the Supreme Court tried to clarify this area. The Board had held that "a nurse's direction of less-skilled employees, in the exercise of professional judgment incidental to the treatment of patients, is not authority exercised 'in the interest of the employer'" thus rendering those nurses "employees" under the Act. The Court rejected this approach, and held that nurses who exercise independent judgment of more than a routine nature when they direct the work of less-skilled employees are acting "in the interest of the employer" under § 2(11) and are supervisory personnel. Nonetheless, in *Providence Hosp.*, 320 N.L.R.B. 717 (1996), *enforced*, 121 F.3d 548 (9th Cir. 1997), the Board held that charge nurses who served as lead employees in a hospital department were not supervisors, because it found end-of-shift reporting to be clerical in nature and the monitoring of lower-level personnel skills to be routine. *See also United Nurses Assn. of Calif. v. NLRB*, 871 F.3d 767 (9th Cir. 2017) (finding that a hospital violated the NLRA when it promoted a pro-union employee to a supervisory position and then terminated him because of his prior organizing activities).

In *NLRB v. Kentucky River Cmty. Care, Inc.*, 532 U.S. 706 (2001), the Labor Board held that registered nurses who use "ordinary professional or technical judgment" to direct the work of less skilled employees are not "supervisors," since such work does not involve the exercise of "independent judgment." Although the Supreme Court agreed with the Board that parties seeking to exclude individuals from NLRA coverage based upon their alleged supervisory status have the burden to establish the factors necessary for exclusion, the Court refused to accept the Board's claim that the professional direction of others does not usually involve "independent judgment." So long as the directive work of the nurses is not merely of a routine nature and requires the use of independent discretion, they must be excluded as supervisory personnel. Courts have extended the *Kentucky River* reasoning to other situations involving the direction of less skilled workers by professional personnel. *See, e.g., Multimedia KSDK, Inc. v. NLRB*, 303 F.3d 896 (8th Cir. 2002).

In *Frenchtown Acquisition Co. v. NLRB*, 683 F.3d 298 (6th Cir. 2012), the court sustained a Labor Board finding that charge nurses at a Michigan nursing home were covered employees instead of excluded supervisors. It found that the nursing home failed to demonstrate that the charge nurses had the authority to perform supervisory functions using independent judgment. The court also noted that if the charge nurses were considered supervisors, the nursing home's supervisory staff would outnumber the rank-and-file nursing aides. On the other hand, in *GGNSC Springfield LLC v. NLRB*, 721 F.3d 403 (6th Cir. 2013), the court refused to enforce the Board's ruling that registered nurses who functioned as charge nurses were covered employees, finding that they were supervisory personnel responsible for exercising independent judgment to issue discipline in the employer's progressive disciplinary process.

Although supervisors are no longer directly protected by the NLRA, they may gain the benefit of Labor Board remedial orders if employer action against them has adversely affected *employee* rights. *See, e.g., NLRB v. Advertisers Mfg. Co.*, 823 F.2d 1086 (7th Cir. 1987) (supervisor reinstated when discharged because of her son's union activity); *Howard Johnson Co. v. NLRB*, 702 F.2d 1 (1st Cir. 1983) (supervisor reinstated when fired for refusing to spy on employees); *United Exposition Service Co. v. NLRB*, 945 F.2d 1057 (8th Cir. 1991) (denial of supervisory position because of employee's prior strike activities unlawful since related to his conduct as an employee). *Compare Parker-Robb Chevrolet, Inc.*, 262 N.L.R.B. 402 (1982), *review denied*, 711 F.2d 383 (D.C. Cir. 1983) (supervisor not protected merely because allied with rank-and-file employees).

c. Managerial Employees

Managerial employees (those who are in a position to formulate and effectuate management policies) are excluded from the coverage of the Act, even though they are not supervisors or persons involved with labor relations policies. *NLRB v. Bell Aerospace Co. Div. of Textron, Inc.*, 416 U.S. 267 (1974). In *NLRB v. Yeshiva University*, 444 U.S. 672 (1980), the U.S. Supreme Court held that the faculty of a "mature" private university are more than simply professional employees. The Court held that they are "managerial employees" and thus excluded from the coverage of the Act because of their significant role in formulating and implementing university policy. The Ninth Circuit, however, in *Stephens Institute v. NLRB*, 620 F.2d 720 (9th Cir.), *cert. denied*, 449 U.S. 953 (1980), declined to apply *Yeshiva* concepts where the institution involved was not found to be a "mature" university. The employer's claim was unpersuasive where faculty members had no input on policy matters, no duties of a supervisory nature, and fit easily within the normal definition of "employees" under the Act. *Accord Bradford College*, 261 N.L.R.B. 565 (1982) (faculty, departmental chairmen, and librarians not "managerial" employees). More recently, in *University of Southern Calif.*, 365 N.L.R.B. No. 89 (2016), the Board held that non-tenure track faculty members are not "managerial" employees and are thus eligible to vote in a representational election, due to their lack of meaningful control over academic programs, finances, and other areas of university governance. On appeal, the D.C. Circuit upheld the general rule applied by the Labor Board to determine whether faculty members constituted excluded "managerial" personnel, but held that the Board had focused too rigidly on the number of faculty members on basic university committees. The Court indicated that whether a particular faculty subgroup is in the majority or minority of university committees is a relevant issue, but one that should not be applied in a determinative manner. The Board had to consider other factors that might be relevant to the degree to which the academics in question influence basic university policies. *University of Southern Calif. v. NLRB*, 918 F.3d 126 (D.C. Cir. 2019).

d. Confidential Employees

Confidential employees (those who assist and act in a confidential capacity to persons who formulate and effectuate management labor relations policies) are also excluded from NLRA coverage. Nonetheless, in *NLRB v. Hendricks County Rural Elec. Membership Corp.*, 454 U.S. 170 (1981), the Supreme Court sustained the Labor Board, holding that the personal secretary to the chief executive officer of a rural cooperative was covered by the NLRA, because she did not act in a confidential capacity with respect to labor relations matters, even though she had access to other confidential business information.

e. Other Exclusions

i. Agricultural Laborers and Domestic Servants

Other categories of persons who are excluded from the coverage of the Taft-Hartley Act by virtue of the definition of "employee" in §2(3) include agricultural laborers and domestic servants. In *Holly Farms Corp. v. NLRB*, 517 U.S. 392 (1996), a closely divided Supreme Court held that the Labor Board could reasonably determine that "live-haul" crews, consisting of chicken catchers, forklift operators, and truck drivers employed by integrated poultry producers, who collect chickens raised by independent contract growers and transport them to a processing plant, are "employees" rather than exempt agricultural workers. *See also Olaa Sugar Co., Ltd.*, 118 N.L.R.B. 1442 (1957) ("employees who perform any regular amounts of non-agricultural work are covered by the Act with respect to the portion of the work that is non-agricultural" despite their performance of other agricultural work). Under the §2(2) definition of "employer," federal, state, and local governments and employers subject to the Railway Labor Act are also excluded from NLRA coverage.

ii. Residents, Interns, and Other Students

The Taft-Hartley exemption for nonprofit hospitals was removed in 1974, which meant the Board had to confront workers who appeared to be both students and employees in teaching hospitals and universities. In *Cedars-Sinai Medical Center*, 223 N.L.R.B. 251 (1976), the NLRB held that interns and residents are primarily students and not employees, because they participate in intern and resident programs not for the purpose of making a living, but to satisfy the requirements for entry into the medical profession. In *Boston Med. Ctr. Corp.*, 330 N.L.R.B. 152 (1999), the Board overruled *Cedars-Sinai Medical Center* and held that interns, residents, and fellows at private hospitals are covered "employees." They spend 80% of their time providing direct patient care. The fact they also continue their medical education while working in these positions does not detract from their primary function as employees of the hospitals involved.

Following the *Boston Medical Center* rationale, the Labor Board held in *New York Univ.*, 332 N.L.R.B. 1205 (2000), that graduate teaching assistants (GTAs) who are paid to teach college courses are covered "employees," rather than uncovered students. Although many GTAs perform teaching duties in furtherance of their degrees, the Board emphasized the fact that they perform teaching functions under university control, they are remunerated for their services, and their teaching duties are not primarily educational. Since then, however, the Board has reversed itself several times on the issue. In *Brown Univ.*, 342 N.L.R.B. 483 (2004), a closely divided Labor Board overruled *New York University*, and held that graduate teaching assistants and graduate research assistants are primarily students and are thus not "employees" under the NRLA. Later, in *Columbia University*, 364 N.L.R.B. No. 90 (2016), the Labor Board overturned the *Brown Univ.* decision and held that graduate teaching assistants and research assistants are "employees" under the NLRA and can unionize for bargaining purposes. How far could this be extended? Should undergraduate resident advisers be considered "employees" for purposes of union representation and bargaining? After a change in administrations, however, the Board withdrew the proposed rule in early 2021.

iii. Undocumented Workers

The Board and courts have recognized that undocumented aliens are entitled to employee status under §2(3) of the Act, and share a sufficient "community of interest" to be included in bargaining units and to vote in NLRB elections. *See Agri Processor Co. v. NLRB*, 514 F.3d 1 (D.C. Cir.), *cert. denied*, 550 U.S. 1031 (2008); *Local 512, Warehouse & Office Workers' Union v. NLRB*, 795 F.2d 705 (9th Cir. 1986).

iv. Employees at Religious Schools and Health Care Institutions

The Supreme Court held (5-4) that the NLRB's assertion of jurisdiction over secondary schools operated by the Roman Catholic Church was not authorized by the NLRA, thus avoiding a First Amendment question concerning the separation of church and state. *NLRB v. Catholic Bishop of Chicago*, 440 U.S. 490 (1979). The Labor Board has extended the Supreme Court's *Catholic Bishop* decision in two respects. First, concerns about risks to freedom of religion under the First Amendment through the exercise of Board jurisdiction are not limited to parochial elementary and secondary schools, but apply to church-operated colleges and universities as well. *Trustee of St. Joseph's College*, 282 N.L.R.B. 65 (1986). Second, even when a school is not church-operated, the Board considers itself precluded from asserting jurisdiction when the purpose and function of the educational institution are, in substantial part, the propagation of a religious faith. *Jewish Day School, Inc.*, 283 N.L.R.B. 757 (1987). *See also Carroll College, Inc. v. NLRB*, 558 F.3d 568 (D.C. Cir. 2009); *Univ. of Great Falls v. NLRB*, 278 F.3d 1335 (D.C. Cir. 2002) (educational institutions exempt from NLRA jurisdiction if they: (1) hold themselves out to students, faculty, and the community as providing religious educational environments; (2) are organized as nonprofit entities; and (3) are affiliated with recognized religious organizations). *Compare NLRB v. Hanna Boys Center*, 940 F.2d 1295 (9th Cir. 1991), *cert. denied*, 504 U.S. 985 (1992) (sustaining exercise of jurisdiction over *non-teaching* parochial school employees not significantly involved with institution's religious mission).

In *Pacific Lutheran Univ.*, 361 N.L.R.B. 1404 (2014), the Labor Board decided to modify the standards established by the Supreme Court in the *Catholic Bishop of Chicago* case with respect to when teachers at religious schools should be excluded from NLRA coverage. This case involved a group of contingent faculty members who were not eligible for tenure who sought union representation. The three-member Board majority decided to apply a two-stage analysis. First, does the educational institution hold itself out as providing a religious educational environment? If the answer is affirmative, can the institution demonstrate that the faculty members sought to be represented perform a specific role in creating or maintaining the religious environment? If the answer to the second question is negative, the Board will assert jurisdiction over their organizing endeavors, as it did in this case. In 2018, the Labor Board ordered Duquesne University of the Holy Spirit to bargain with a union that represented adjunct faculty members even though the college is a religious entity, on the ground the adjunct teachers did not carry out any religious functions. Nonetheless, on appeal the D.C. Circuit Court vacated the Board's decision. It held that under the Supreme Court's *NLRB v. Catholic Bishop of Chicago* decision, the Board could not assert jurisdiction over even lay teachers at religious schools since such action would create a "significant risk" of a First Amendment violation. *Duquesne Univ. of the Holy Spirit v. NLRB*, 947 F.3d 824 (D.C. Cir. 2020).

The Senate's rejection of an amendment that would have excluded church-run hospitals from coverage and the addition of § 19 to the Act has convinced the Board that Congress intended to extend NLRA coverage to religious health care institutions. The Board thus determined that its assertion of jurisdiction over a hospital owned by a Roman Catholic religious order would not violate the First Amendment, since there would be no "excessive entanglement" with the Catholic religion. *St. Elizabeth Community Hospital*, 259 N.L.R.B. 1135 (1982), *enforced*, 708 F.2d 1436 (9th Cir. 1983).

v. Employees of Businesses Operated by Native American Tribes

In *San Manuel Indian Bingo & Casino*, 341 N.L.R.B. 1055 (2004), the Board held that it will exercise jurisdiction over businesses operated by Native American tribes on land owned by the tribes unless doing so would touch on "purely intramural matters" or abrogate treaty rights. In *Chickasaw Nation d/b/a Winstar World Casino*, 362 N.L.R.B. 942 (2015), the Board ruled that the Chickasaw Nation's tribal sovereignty pursuant to a treaty specific to the Choctaw and Chickasaw Nations prevented the NLRB from asserting jurisdiction over unfair labor practice charges filed against a tribe-controlled casino. On the other hand, in *Little River Band of Ottawa Indians Tribal Government v. NLRB*, 361 N.L.R.B. 436 (2014), *enforced*, 788 F.3d 537 (6th Cir. 2015), the Board concluded that a Native American-operated casino must adhere to the NLRA where no treaty rights were abrogated, there was no legislative history preventing application of the NLRA to the tribe, and the majority of the employees were not enrolled members of the band nor Native American. *See also Soaring Eagle Casino & Resort v. NLRB*, 791 F.3d 648 (6th Cir. 2015) (applying *Little River Band of Ottawa Indians* to uphold Board's jurisdiction over employment practices in an Indian tribe's casino); *Casino Pauma v. NLRB*, 888 F.3d 1066 (9th Cir. 2018), *cert. denied*, 139 S. Ct. 2614 (2019) (upholding the NLRB's exercise of jurisdiction over the Pauma Band of Mission Indians' Pauma Casino).

Problems

1. A meal delivery company uses a smart phone application that allows consumers to order food from participating restaurants and have it picked up and delivered by one of the company's drivers. Upon receiving an order, the company confirms the order with the restaurant and offers the delivery job through the app to a driver in the restaurant's vicinity. The driver can accept or reject the trip, and if rejected, the job is offered to other drivers in succession until someone accepts it. The delivery company tracks the ride by GPS, and uses the distance traveled, in combination with base fare amounts and time charges, to calculate the total delivery fee. The customer pays that fee through the app, and the delivery company retains a percentage of the fee and remits the remaining amount to the driver.

Drivers provide their own cars, and are responsible for all gas, maintenance, and expenses. The delivery company requires its drivers to keep up the outside appearance of their cars, maintain a professional appearance, and complete a 45-minute training video that covers everything from appropriate communications with restaurant workers and customers to competent navigation and driving. Many drivers also work for competing food delivery and ride share companies.

With a surge in business brought on by the COVID-19 pandemic, the delivery company found it difficult to maintain its high level of reliability. In order to ensure that it had a sufficient number of drivers, the company lowered its percentage take of the delivery fee and modified its algorithms in a way that disfavored drivers who declined delivery jobs. The company also began offering drivers an additional flat rate to remain "on call" during its busiest times — drivers who are on call must pick up orders in their vicinity or risk having their driver privileges suspended for one month.

Are the drivers covered employees under the NLRA?

2. The associates at a medium-sized law firm, fed up with their long hours and below-market salaries, are thinking of organizing. The associates typically work as part of larger departmental teams, which include other associates, paralegals, and legal assistants. Each team is overseen by one or more of the law firm's partners. The associates are given a fair amount of autonomy as they complete their team assignments, and are able to give cite-checking and photocopying projects to the paralegals and legal assistants on their team. While they do not have the authority to discipline these other workers on their teams, they are asked to provide yearly evaluations of them that are used in compensation, promotion, and termination decisions. Those decisions, though, are ultimately in the hands of the partners. Are the associates covered employees?

3. The men's basketball players for a large private university have decided to organize. The team has 13 scholarship players and three walk-ons. The scholarship players are identified and recruited for their basketball prowess and not because of their academic achievement in high school. They each receive a grant-in-aid scholarship worth about $65,000 per year. It pays for tuition, room and board, and books, and the funds are directly applied to those expenses. The walk-on players do not receive any scholarship money, but are able to make use of the athletic facilities and academic support services available only to the athletes. Last year, the basketball program generated some $30 million in revenue from ticket sales, broadcast contracts, and merchandise sales, though the program also incurred close to $18 million in expenses.

The players are full-time students, but they also spend a substantial amount of time on basketball. During the season, which lasts from October through March, they are expected to devote 40 to 50 hours per week to basketball-related activities, including travel to and from their games. On days when they do not have games and are not traveling, they typically attend classes in the morning, practice from 1:00 to 5:00, attend a team meal, and then attend a mandatory study hall followed by either a film session or strength and conditioning session. Although they receive no academic credit for their basketball activities, some players believe they learn valuable life lessons from the game and their coaches. None of the coaches, however, teach courses or belong to the academic faculty.

All of the players are required to be enrolled as full-time students, make adequate progress toward obtaining a degree, and maintain a minimum GPA. They must also follow a number of team rules that do not apply to regular students. For example, if players want to obtain outside employment, they must first secure permission from the athletic department. All players are required to abide by a strict social media policy, which restricts what they can post on the internet and allows the athletic department unfettered access to their content. They are prohibited from profiting from their names or likenesses; indeed, they are required to sign a contract allowing the university and athletic conference to utilize their names, likenesses, and images for any purpose. Violations of any of these or other team rules may result in dismissal from the team and the loss of the scholarship.

Are the players covered employees?

4. If the professors at your law school decide to go on strike, would the dispute be covered by the NLRA? What else would you need to know to answer this question?

B. Organization and Procedure of the National Labor Relations Board

1. Organization of the Board and the General Counsel

The functions of the NLRB in implementing the general policy of the NLRA are mainly twofold: (1) the prevention of unfair labor practices, known as complaint or "C" proceedings; and (2) the settling of representation questions, including the conduct of elections, known as representation or "R" proceedings. The Board's procedure in representation cases will be discussed later.

The Board, located in Washington, D.C., consists of five members, appointed by the President for staggered five-year terms. When it decides cases, it may sit in panels of three. Each Board member has a sizable staff of legal assistants. If the Labor Board assigns a case to a three-member panel and one member has to recuse himself or herself, the other two may still resolve the matter since the panel began with a statutory quorum of three. *S. Ocean Med. Ctr.*, 22-CA-223734, 2020 NLRB LEXIS 8 (2020). On the other hand, if three Board seats become vacant, the remaining two members may no longer resolve cases, even if given such authority by their departing colleagues, due to the absence of the three-member quorum required under § 3(b). *New Process Steel, L.P. v. NLRB*, 560 U.S. 674 (2010). But even during a period when the Board lacks a quorum and cannot conduct business on its own, Regional Directors continue to possess the authority to supervise and conduct representation elections because that authority had been delegated to them when the Board had a quorum. *UC Health v. NLRB*, 803 F.3d 669 (D.C. Cir. 2015); *accord NLRB v. Bluefield Hosp. Co., LLC*, 821 F.3d 534 (4th Cir. 2016).

The Administrative Law Judges (ALJs), also located in Washington, with local offices in San Francisco, New York, and Atlanta, travel throughout the country to hold hearings. Although selected by the Board, they are independent and may not be removed except for cause after a hearing by the Civil Service Commission. The ALJs were called Trial Examiners until 1972.

The General Counsel, appointed by the President for a four-year term, has final authority, under § 3(d) of the NLRA, over the investigation and prosecution of unfair labor practice charges. The 40-odd regional and sub-regional offices of the NLRB are under the supervision of the General Counsel. Each regional office is under the direction of a Regional Director, assisted by a Regional Attorney. Field examiners investigate charges and conduct elections, and field attorneys prosecute complaints before the ALJs.

The 1998 Federal Vacancies Reform Act requires almost all persons serving in an acting capacity to step aside once they have been nominated for the permanent position in question while the Senate is deciding whether to confirm their permanent appointment. 5 U.S.C. § 3345(b)(1). In 2010, President Obama put Lafe Solomon in the position of Acting General Counsel to the Labor Board, and seven months later nominated him for a four-year term as General Counsel. Although the Senate never acted on his nomination, he continued to serve as Acting General Counsel until November of 2013. In *NLRB v. SW General, Inc.*, 137 S. Ct. 929 (2017), the Supreme Court held that this action violated § 3345(b)1) and was thus invalid.

2. NLRB Procedures

Our attention will be focused on the difficult, controversial cases that go to the Board and the courts. Consequently, it is important to take note of the fact that the vast majority of cases are disposed of at the regional office level—most without any formal proceedings. In recent years, a little more than 30% of unfair labor practice charges are withdrawn before complaints are issued, about 25% are administratively dismissed prior to the issuance of complaints, and close to 40% are settled or adjusted before issuance of administrative law judge decisions. Only about two percent of the cases closed are decided by the Board in contested cases, and fewer than one percent reach the court of appeals via petitions for enforcement or review. *See Reports: Disposition of Unfair Labor Practice Charges Per FY*, NATIONAL LABOR RELATIONS BOARD, https://www.nlrb.gov/reports/nlrb-case-activity-reports/unfair-labor-practice-cases/disposition-of-unfair-labor-practice (last visited Aug. 26, 2020); *Reports: Appellate Court Decisions (10 Years)*, NATIONAL LABOR RELATIONS BOARD, https://www.nlrb.gov/reports/nlrb-case-activity-reports/unfair-labor-practice-cases/litigation/appellate-court (last visited Aug. 26, 2020).

An unfair labor practice case begins when some person writes or visits an NLRB Regional Office and makes a charge against an employer or a union. The Board has no power to commence proceedings on its own. Indeed, the charging party may elect, when both the employer and the union are involved in an alleged unfair practice, to bring a charge against either or both.

The Act contains a six-month statute of limitations, requiring the filing of a charge within six months of the date on which the alleged unfair practice occurred. When an individual is terminated, the §10(b) statutory period begins to run on the date the employee is notified of the impending discharge, and not on the date the termination is effectuated. *See United States Postal Serv. Marina Mail Processing Ctr.*, 271 N.L.R.B. 397 (1984).

Under §10(*l*) and (m) of the NLRA, as amended by the Labor-Management Reporting and Disclosure Act of 1959, priority handling must be given to cases involving secondary boycotts, hot cargo contracts, organizational or recognition picketing, and discrimination against individual employees.

After the case is assigned to a Board agent in the Regional Office, the charging party is usually asked to submit whatever evidence it has to support the charge, including the names and addresses of witnesses. The charged party is then asked to submit its version of the facts and circumstances surrounding the alleged unfair labor practices. The Board agent makes an investigation, interviews witnesses, and prepares a report with recommendations. The Regional Director decides whether to issue a complaint.

Short of issuance of a complaint, a charge may be disposed of in three ways: (1) withdrawal (sometimes pursuant to a non-Board settlement between the charging party and the charged party); (2) dismissal; or (3) settlement or adjustment. An adjustment means that the Regional Office has reached a settlement of the case, accomplishing the purposes of the act. It may be either *informal*, in which the charged party agrees to remedy its unfair practices, or *formal*, in which a consent decree is issued by the NLRB and a U.S. court of appeals. A decision by the General Counsel to accept an informal settlement after issuance of a complaint but before commencement of a hearing, over the objection of the charging party, is not subject to NLRB review and does not constitute a final Board order that is subject to judicial review. *NLRB v. United Food & Commercial Workers Union, Local 23*, 484 U.S. 112 (1987); *Sheet Metal Workers Int'l Ass'n, Local Union 28, etc.*, 306 N.L.R.B. 981 (1992). In *Pottsville Bleaching & Dyeing Co.*, 301 N.L.R.B. 1095 (1991), the Board indicated that it will no longer permit the inclusion of non-admission clauses in NLRB notices that must be posted as part of informal or formal Board settlement agreements.

If the Regional Director decides to dismiss the charge, an appeal may be taken to the General Counsel (not the Board) in Washington. The General Counsel's decision whether to issue a complaint is final, and is not subject to judicial review. *Beverly Health & Rehabilitation Servs. v. Feinstein*, 103 F.3d 151 (D.C. Cir. 1996), *cert. denied*, 522 U.S. 816 (1997); *Lincourt v. NLRB*, 170 F.2d 306 (1st Cir. 1948). The nonreviewability of the General Counsel's discretionary decisions also applies to withdrawal of a previously issued complaint. *International Ass'n of Machinists & Aerospace Workers v. Lubbers*, 681 F.2d 598 (9th Cir. 1982), *cert. denied*, 459 U.S. 1201 (1983).

After the formal complaint has been issued, the Board has the power, under §10(j) of the act, to seek a temporary injunction or restraining order against the unfair labor practice in a U.S. district court, but this is seldom done. Courts generally grant requested relief under § 10(j) only where there is "reasonable cause" to believe an unfair labor practice has occurred and the requested relief is "just and proper." *See, e.g., NLRB v. Hartman & Tyner, Inc.*, 714 F.3d 1244 (11th Cir. 2013). Section 10(*l*) requires that an injunction be sought where there is reasonable cause to believe that a charge of certain union unfair labor practices is true.

The respondent is given time to file an answer to the complaint, and then the case proceeds to a hearing before an ALJ. The case is presented by an attorney from the Regional Office, representing the General Counsel. The respondent may cross-examine witnesses, and may obtain, for this purpose, copies of any written pretrial statements given to Board investigators by such witnesses. *Ra-Rich Mfg. Corp.*, 121 N.L.R.B. 700 (1958). The charging party is also permitted to participate in the hearing.

The Administrative Law Judge (ALJ) is fully responsible for the conduct of hearings, ruling upon applications for subpoenas and depositions and other motions. He or she may call witnesses and cross-examine witnesses of the parties. Under § 10(b), the ALJ is required to conduct the proceedings in accordance with the rules of evidence applicable in the U.S. district courts, so far as practicable.

Parties may make an oral argument at the conclusion of the testimony and may file a brief with the ALJ. The ALJ then returns to his or her office with a transcript of the record and prepares the decision, which includes findings of fact, conclusions of law, and recommended order.

After receiving a copy of the ALJ's decision, parties are given an opportunity to file exceptions with the Board within 20 days. An alleged discriminatee who chose not to participate as a party in an unfair labor practice hearing does not have the right to file exceptions to the ALJ's order recommending dismissal of the complaint. *Giacalone v. NLRB*, 682 F.2d 427 (3d Cir. 1982). If no exceptions are filed, the Board adopts the decision of the ALJ as its own. If exceptions are filed, parties may file briefs in support of their exceptions, and the Board will consider the case on the record. Application may be made for oral argument before the NLRB in Washington, but it is seldom granted except where the Board wishes to examine or reexamine a basic policy question.

When a case goes to the Board, the Executive Secretary assigns the case to one of the five Board members, and the record is read and analyzed by one of his or her legal assistants. This assistant meets with his or her supervisor and the chief counsel of the Board member, and if the case is a simple one, an affirmance of the ALJ's decision is prepared for the approval of the three Board members on the panel. If more difficult questions are involved, the matter goes to a "sub-panel," consisting of the chief counsels of the Board members on the panel, who meet with the legal assistant and his or her supervisor and analyze the case. A draft decision and order then goes to the three Board members for approval of changes. When necessary, the Board members hold a conference on it.

If the case involves novel issues or important questions of policy, it is sent to an "agenda" of the full Board. The legal assistant assigned to the case prepares a full memorandum for the consideration of the Board, and he or she attends the session. After discussion, a tentative decision is reached, and the legal assistant prepares a draft of the Board's decision. This is circulated to the members for approval or modification, and it may be discussed further at a later agenda. Finally, the decision is approved and issued by the Board.

When the Board finds, upon a "preponderance of the testimony" (§10(c)), that an unfair labor practice had been committed, it makes findings of fact and issues a cease and desist order that may be accompanied by an order for affirmative action, such as reinstatement. If the Board finds a violation, it must issue a remedial order, even though it believes an order would serve no useful purpose. *International Union, United Auto., Aerospace & Agricultural Implement Workers v. NLRB*, 427 F.2d 1330 (6th Cir. 1970).

If the party against whom the order is issued does not comply, the Board can seek an enforcement order from a U.S. court of appeals. An aggrieved party need not wait for Board enforcement; it may ask the appropriate court of appeals to review the Board's order. In either case, the test for judicial review of factual questions is whether the Board's findings are supported by "substantial evidence on the record considered as a whole" (§10(e)). If the party against whom the court's enforcement order is issued does not comply, it runs the risk of being held in contempt of court. The existence of multiple potential venues for the enforcement of Board orders under §10(e) and (f) creates the possibility of inter-circuit disagreements over governing NLRA law. The NLRB has a history of nonacquiescence, both intra-circuit and inter-circuit, to press for its preferred statutory interpretation despite contrary judicial precedent. *See* Davies, *Remedial Nonacquiescence*, 89 Iowa L. Rev. 65 (2003).

The final possibility for review is to the U.S. Supreme Court upon petition for writ of certiorari, but the Supreme Court has warned: "Whether on the record as a whole there is substantial evidence to support agency findings is a question which Congress has placed in the Courts of Appeals. This Court will intervene only in what ought to be the rare instance when the standard appears to have been misapprehended or grossly misapplied." *Universal Camera Corp. v. NLRB*, 340 U.S. 474, 491 (1951).

C. NLRB Rule-Making Authority

The NLRB generally adjudicates on a case-by-case basis, only occasionally exercising its rule-making authority—usually in setting guidelines for representation elections. In *NLRB v. Wyman-Gordon Co.*, 394 U.S. 759 (1969), the Supreme Court declared that the Board had promulgated a rule in violation of the rule-making requirements of the Administrative Procedure Act, 5 U.S.C. §1, when it decided a case by announcing a rule for prospective application only. Since the rule was not applied to the parties immediately involved, the Board's decision was held not to be an "adjudication," which would have made it exempt from the procedural requirements of the APA. Relying on *Wyman-Gordon*, a court of appeals held that the Board must proceed by rulemaking, not adjudication, when it proposes to "reverse a long-standing and oft-repeated policy" in representation cases. *Bell Aerospace Co. Div. of Textron, Inc. v. NLRB*, 475 F.2d 485 (2d Cir. 1973). The Supreme Court, however, held that the Board has the discretion to proceed either by adjudication or by rulemaking in effecting a change in policy, so long as the Board's holding does not amount to an abuse of discretion. Adjudication was found to be especially appropriate where the multiplicity and variety of possible applications made it "doubtful whether any generalized standard could be framed which would have more than marginal utility." *NLRB v. Bell Aerospace Co. Div. of Textron, Inc.*, 416 U.S. 267 (1974).

More recently, the Labor Board began exercising its rule-making authority more frequently, but with mixed results. In 2011, for example, the Board published a rule that required employers covered by the NLRA to post notices informing employees of their rights under that statute. But that rule was later struck down when the D.C. Circuit found that the notice posting rule contravened the First Amendment rights of employers as well as §8(c) of the NLRA, which "precludes the Board from finding noncoercive employer speech to be an unfair labor practice, or evidence of an unfair labor practice." *Nat'l Ass'n of Mfrs. v. NLRB*, 717 F.3d 947 (D.C. Cir.), *rehearing en banc denied*, 2013 U.S. App. LEXIS 18566 (D.C. Cir. Sept. 4, 2013); *see also Chamber of Commerce of U.S. v. NLRB*, 721 F.3d 152 (4th Cir. 2013) (addressing the same arguments and concluding that neither the plain language nor the structure of the NLRA authorized the Board to issue the notice-posting rule).

In another 2011 rule-making attempt, the Board proposed new election procedures that would have streamlined representation cases in a number of ways. But a federal district court struck down the rule because the Board lacked a quorum for its final vote on it. *Chamber of Commerce v. NLRB*, 879 F. Supp. 2d 18 (D.D.C. 2012). In 2014, a newly constituted Board with a full complement of members adopted a new version of the election rules by a 3-2 vote. 79 Fed. Reg. 74318. The Senate and the House voted to disapprove the NLRB's regulatory action, but President Obama vetoed their Congressional Review Act resolution, and the new rule went into effect on April 14, 2015. Daily Lab. Rep. (BNA) No. 71, Apr. 14, 2015, at A-1. That rule was short-lived, however, as the Trump Board soon promulgated a new rule revising those election procedures. Representation-Case Procedures, 84 Fed. Reg. 69,524 (Dec. 18, 2019) (to be codified at 29 C.F.R. pt. 102). The new Board has also issued or proposed rules on a number of other topics, including the standard for determining joint-employer status, the standard for determining whether graduate teaching and research assistants are "employees" under the Act, and further regulations on representation elections. *See About NLRB: National Labor Relations Board Rulemaking*, NATIONAL LABOR RELATIONS BOARD, https://www.nlrb.gov/about-nlrb/what-we-do/national-labor-relations-board-rulemaking (last visited Aug. 26, 2020). At the time this book went to press, however, the Biden administration had already withdrawn several of these proposed rules.

Part 2

The Right of Self-Organization and Protection against Employer Unfair Labor Practices

Seminar on Free Speech and Preelection Conduct, Southwestern Legal Foundation, Labor Law Developments, Proceedings of the Eleventh Annual Institute on Labor Law
239–46 (1965)

A Management Lawyer: [T]he limitation of free speech in this area of the National Labor Relations Act primarily restricts the employer. Especially is this true of the inexperienced employer who finds out, frequently too late, that speech which comes instinctively is not permitted and, therefore, not free as far as he understands that term. His frustration is aggravated when he discovers the election process bears little resemblance to the democratic process which he understands as a fundamental part of American society.

Thus, the inexperienced employer is astounded to find that his employees are rugged and intelligent enough in a bitter presidential campaign to cast a ballot freely, based on their own judgment — or utter lack of it — for the man who in the next four years will have a life and death atomic choice over their destinies. Yet, the same employees' judgment must be protected by an untrammeled free choice, akin to "laboratory conditions," in the election determining whether or not he wants a union to represent him in dealing with his employer.

Also — and I cannot emphasize this point too much as we get into the area of the so-called great debate — the employer quickly discovers the basic fundamental that probably is the main issue in most elections: "Promise of future benefits" cannot be discussed by him but can be discussed by the union. Picture what would happen if, in the presidential campaign, they could take away all promises of future benefits. . . .

A Union Lawyer: [E]mployee fear . . . takes this whole question completely outside the area with which we are used to dealing in political elections. . . . Think of a man whose whole livelihood is dependent upon a particular job. That is the loss he faces. This factor may vary. I can imagine that in the city of Pittsburgh an employer could make a certain kind of speech, using the language a lawyer has taken out of a book as being approved in past NLRB elections. He might not cause the least bit of fear in the employees listening to that speech.... But there are other places in our country where the identical speech would have a totally different impact. Out on the Great Plains, for example, you can get into a little town where one proprietary employer holds sway as economic emperor. In that little town the banker, the newspaper, the sheriff, and the entire community dance to the tune that employer calls. There, fear can be pervasive....

A much different problem is presented when you are trying to give everyone "equal time" and are trying to provide, as the union people urge, for a fair balance in the right to communicate with the employees.... We are not now talking about employee fear; we are talking about a chance to get your point of view across. Here the political analogy holds very well. As far as the unions are concerned, it is almost as if the Republican or the Democratic Party owned the television networks and prevented the opposition from appearing on them to address the voters....

BERNARD KARSH, DIARY OF A STRIKE
47, 117, 119–20 (1958)

A UNION ORGANIZER: I organized a union and I ran a strike. When you have a job to do, you do it. If anyone tells you that there's a fixed way of running a strike, that you can plan it, they're insane. You build it from day to day, just like you build a union from day to day. There's nothing you can plan ahead. Sure, you can plan pickets, you can plan picket signs and songs, you can plan a kitchen and benefits. But your behavior, it varies from moment to moment according to the needs of the situation, and the important thing is to be there and be ready to do it, whatever it is, and go ahead and do it.

AN EMPLOYER: The management of this Company does not want a union, because we feel that our employees will not benefit by belonging to the union.... With the cooperation of our employees and without the interference of any outsiders, we have made the _____ Company a good place in which to work. Our wages, hours and working conditions compare favorably with those of other plants in this area and with the plants of others with whom we are in competition. You have received the benefits of this high standard without having to pay initiation fees, union dues and various special union assessments....

What the intervention of these strangers would mean in our relationship, no one can foretell. All of us know that unions engage in business interruptions and strikes and that frequently these cause substantial financial loss to the employees and their families....

AN EMPLOYEE: I was for it, but at the same time I didn't feel good about it. I had worked there so long, and I felt it wasn't right to strike. The Company had been very nice to me, and sometimes when I didn't feel well, they would let me come to work any time I felt like it and I appreciated that. But I felt we had to strike. We just weren't treated right in a lot of ways. I voted for the strike in the end.

Labor relations law deals with legal rights and duties. At the same time, students should not overlook the fact that we are dealing with a phase of human relations in which the parties—management and organized labor—through force of circumstances have an established relationship that implies responsibilities greatly transcending those minimum standards imposed by the law. The labor union that establishes itself firmly in a plant acquires a status that, even without legal recognition, necessitates important changes in management's conception of its function. Even accepting the narrowest definition of this function, it must be obvious that the presence of a union possessing the power both to interfere with and to promote the processes of production, calls for the adoption of management policies that will enlist the union's interest in continuous and efficient plant operation. The keynote of a desirable relationship between the parties will be their mutual acceptance of the fact that each has a status in the enterprise. When they have accepted this elemental fact, the rudimentary legal obligations that the law may impose upon them will be of minor significance. Just as in the case of the citizen in the community, or the spouse in the family, so here the necessity of continuing relations calls for a code of conduct much above and beyond the call of legal duty.

This conception of management-union relations presupposes the existence of an established union and management acceptance of the "right" of employee self-organization. As shown in Part One, however, and as might be expected in a land in which much emphasis has been placed upon individual initiative and self-determination, unionism has had to struggle hard against management resistance to gain a place for itself. In this part, we will survey the statutory provisions that have given unions and workers legal protection against employer anti-union tactics.

Section I. Employer Interference, Restraint, or Coercion

Section 8(a)(1) of the National Labor Relations Act is a broad, general provision. It may be violated by conduct that is contrary to any of the four following subsections (i.e., a "derivative" § 8(a)(1) violation). For example, a discharge on account of union activity would violate both §§ 8(a)(1) and 8(a)(3).

We shall deal first, however, with employer conduct that violates § 8(a)(1) independently of any other specific unfair labor practice. Such conduct ranges all the way from the crude and obvious to the ingenious and subtle.

It is not necessary, for proof of a violation, to show by direct evidence that any particular persons were in fact successfully restrained or coerced; it is enough if it is shown that the employer's conduct has a natural tendency to do so. *Time-O-Matic, Inc. v. NLRB*, 264 F.2d 96 (7th Cir. 1959); *NLRB v. Ford*, 170 F.2d 735 (6th Cir. 1948).

The Railway Labor Act, in §2 (Third and Fourth), also makes it unlawful for a carrier to interfere with, influence, or coerce employees in organizing. Since the RLA does not provide an administrative procedure for the prevention of such practices, enforcement must be had through either criminal proceedings or petition for injunctive relief in the courts. *Virginian R. Co. v. System Federation*, 300 U.S. 515 (1937); *Texas & N. O. R. Co. v. Brotherhood of R. & S.S. Clerks*, 281 U.S. 548 (1930). There has been very little litigation under these provisions of the RLA, probably because unionism had reached a fairly mature state in the railroad industry by the time these provisions were written into the law.

A. Limiting Organizational Activities on Employer's Premises

Lechmere, Inc. v. NLRB
Supreme Court of the United States
502 U.S. 527, 112 S. Ct. 841, 117 L. Ed. 2d 79 (1992)

JUSTICE THOMAS delivered the opinion of the Court.

This case requires us to clarify the relationship between the rights of employees under §7 of the National Labor Relations Act . . . and the property rights of their employers.

I

This case stems from the efforts of Local 919 of the United Food and Commercial Workers Union, AFL-CIO, to organize employees at a retail store in Newington, Connecticut, owned and operated by petitioner Lechmere, Inc. The store is located in the Lechmere Shopping Plaza, which occupies a roughly rectangular tract measuring approximately 880 feet from north to south and 740 feet from east to west. Lechmere's store is situated at the Plaza's south end, with the main parking lot to its north. A strip of 13 smaller "satellite stores" not owned by Lechmere runs along the west side of the Plaza, facing the parking lot. To the Plaza's east (where the main entrance is located) runs the Berlin Turnpike, a four-lane divided highway. The parking lot, however, does not abut the Turnpike; they are separated by a 46-foot-wide grassy strip, broken only by the Plaza's entrance. The parking lot is owned jointly by Lechmere and the developer of the satellite stores. The grassy strip is public property (except for a four-foot-wide band adjoining the parking lot, which belongs to Lechmere).

The union began its campaign to organize the store's 200 employees, none of whom was represented by a union, in June 1987. After a full-page advertisement in a local newspaper drew little response, nonemployee union organizers entered Lechmere's parking lot and began placing handbills on the windshields of cars parked in a corner of the lot used mostly by employees. Lechmere's manager immediately confronted the organizers, informed them that Lechmere prohibited solicitation or handbill distribution of any kind on its property,[1] and asked them to leave. They did so, and Lechmere personnel removed the handbills. The union organizers renewed this handbilling effort in the parking lot on several subsequent occasions; each time they were asked to leave and the handbills were removed. The organizers then relocated to the public grassy strip, from where they attempted to pass out handbills to cars entering the lot during hours (before opening and after closing) when the drivers were assumed to be primarily store employees. For one month, the union organizers returned daily to the grassy strip to picket Lechmere; after that, they picketed intermittently for another six months. They also recorded the license plate numbers of cars parked in the employee parking area; with the cooperation of the Connecticut Department of Motor Vehicles, they thus secured the names and addresses of some 41 nonsupervisory employees (roughly 20% of the store's total). The union sent four mailings to these employees; it also made some attempts to contact them by phone or home visits. These mailings and visits resulted in one signed union authorization card.

Alleging that Lechmere had violated the National Labor Relations Act by barring the nonemployee organizers from its property, the union filed an unfair labor practice charge with respondent National Labor Relations Board (Board). Applying the criteria set forth by the Board in *Fairmont Hotel Co.*, 282 N.L.R.B. 139 (1986), an administrative law judge (ALJ) ruled in the union's favor. . . . He recommended that Lechmere be ordered, among other things, to cease and desist from barring the union organizers from the parking lot and to post in conspicuous places in the store signs proclaiming in part:

> WE WILL NOT prohibit representatives of Local 919, United Food and Commercial Workers, AFL-CIO ("the Union") or any other labor organization, from distributing union literature to our employees in the parking lot adjacent to our store in Newington, Connecticut, nor will we attempt to cause them to be removed from our parking lot for attempting to do so. . . .

The Board affirmed the ALJ's judgment and adopted the recommended order, applying the analysis set forth in its opinion in *Jean Country*, 291 N.L.R.B. 11 (1988), which had by then replaced the short-lived *Fairmont Hotel* approach. . . . A divided panel of the United States Court of Appeals for the First Circuit denied Lechmere's petition for review and enforced the Board's order. 914 F.2d 313 (1990). This Court granted certiorari. . . .

---

1. [1] Lechmere had established this policy several years prior to the union's organizing efforts. The store's official policy statement provided, in relevant part: "Non-associates [*i.e.*, nonemployees] are prohibited from soliciting and distributing literature at all times anywhere on Company property, including parking lots. Non-associates have no right of access to the non-working areas and only to the public and selling areas of the store in connection with its public use." Brief for Petitioner 7. On each door to the store Lechmere had posted a 6 in. by 8 in. sign reading: "TO THE PUBLIC. No Soliciting, Canvassing, Distribution of Literature or Trespassing by Non-Employees in or on Premises." Lechmere consistently enforced this policy inside the store as well as on the parking lot (against, among others, the Salvation Army and the Girl Scouts).

II

A

... By its plain terms ... the NLRA confers rights only on *employees*, not on unions or their nonemployee organizers. In *NLRB v. Babcock & Wilcox Co.*, 351 U.S. 105 (1956), however, we recognized that insofar as the employees' "right of self-organization depends in some measure on [their] ability ... to learn the advantages of self-organization from others," *id.*, at 113, §7 of the NLRA may, in certain limited circumstances, restrict an employer's right to exclude nonemployee union organizers from his property. It is the nature of those circumstances that we explore today.

Babcock arose out of union attempts to organize employees at a factory located on an isolated 100-acre tract. The company had a policy against solicitation and distribution of literature on its property, which it enforced against all groups. About 40% of the company's employees lived in a town of some 21,000 persons near the factory; the remainder were scattered over a 30-mile radius. Almost all employees drove to work in private cars and parked in a company lot that adjoined the fenced-in plant area. The parking lot could be reached only by a 100yard-long driveway connecting it to a public highway. This driveway was mostly on company-owned land, except where it crossed a 31-foot-wide public right-of-way adjoining the highway. Union organizers attempted to distribute literature from this right-of-way. The union also secured the names and addresses of some 100 employees (20% of the total), and sent them three mailings. Still other employees were contacted by telephone or home visit.

The union successfully challenged the company's refusal to allow nonemployee organizers onto its property before the Board. While acknowledging that there were alternative, nontrespassory means whereby the union could communicate with employees, the Board held that contact at the workplace was preferable. *The Babcock & Wilcox Co.*, 109 N.L.R.B. 485, 493–494 (1954).... Concluding that traffic on the highway made it unsafe for the union organizers to distribute leaflets from the right-of-way, and that contacts through the mails, on the streets, at employees' homes, and over the telephone would be ineffective, the Board ordered the company to allow the organizers to distribute literature on its parking lot and exterior walkways.

The Court of Appeals for the Fifth Circuit refused to enforce the Board's order, *NLRB v. Babcock & Wilcox Co.*, 222 F.2d 316 (1955), and this Court affirmed.... [W]e explained that the Board had erred by failing to make the critical distinction between the organizing activities of employees (to whom §7 guarantees the right of self-organization) and nonemployees (to whom §7 applies only derivatively). Thus, while "[n]o restriction may be placed on the employees' right to discuss self-organization *among themselves*, unless the employer can demonstrate that a restriction is necessary to maintain production or discipline," 351 U.S., at 13 (emphasis added) (citing *Republic Aviation Corp. v. NLRB*, 324 U.S. 793, 803 (1945)), "no such obligation is owed nonemployee organizers," 351 U.S., at 113. As a rule, then, an employer cannot be compelled to allow distribution of union literature by nonemployee organizers on his property. As with many other rules, however, we recognized an exception. Where "the location of a plant and the living quarters of the employees place the employees beyond the reach of reasonable union efforts to communicate with them," *ibid.*, employers' property rights may be "required to yield to the extent needed to permit communication of information on the right to organize," *id.*, at 112.

Although we have not had occasion to apply *Babcock*'s analysis in the ensuing decades, we have described it in cases arising in related contexts. Two such cases, *Central Hardware Co. v. NLRB*, 407 U.S. 539 (1972), and *Hudgens v. NLRB*, 424 U.S. 507 (1976), involved activity by union supporters on employer-owned property. The principal issue in both cases was whether, based upon *Food Employees v. Logan Valley Plaza, Inc.*, 391 U.S. 308 (1968), the First Amendment protected such activities. In both cases we rejected the First Amendment claims, and in *Hudgens* we made it clear that *Logan Valley* was overruled. Having decided the cases on constitutional grounds, we remanded them to the Board for consideration of the union supporters' §7 claims under *Babcock*. In both cases, we quoted approvingly *Babcock*'s admonition that accommodation between employees' §7 rights and employers' property rights "must be obtained with as little destruction of the one as is consistent with the maintenance of the other," 351 U.S., at 112. There is no hint in *Hudgens* and *Central Hardware*, however, that our invocation of *Babcock*'s language of "accommodation" was intended to repudiate or modify *Babcock*'s holding that an employer need not accommodate non-employee organizers unless the employees are otherwise inaccessible. Indeed, in *Central Hardware* we expressly noted that nonemployee organizers cannot claim even a limited right of access to a nonconsenting employer's property until "[a]fter the requisite need for access to the employer's property has been shown." 407 U.S., at 545.

If there was any question whether *Central Hardware* and *Hudgens* changed §7 law, it should have been laid to rest by *Sears, Roebuck & Co. v. San Diego County District Council of Carpenters*, 436 U.S. 180 (1978). As in *Central Hardware* and *Hudgens*, the substantive §7 issue in *Sears* was a subsidiary one; the case's primary focus was on the circumstances under which the NLRA preempts state law. Among other things, we held in *Sears* that arguable §7 claims do not pre-empt state trespass law, in large part because the trespasses of nonemployee union organizers are "far more likely to be unprotected than protected," 436 U.S., at 205; permitting state courts to evaluate such claims, therefore, does not "create an unacceptable risk of interference with conduct which the Board, and a court reviewing the Board's decision, would find protected," *ibid.* . . .

We further noted that, in practice, nonemployee organizational trespassing had generally been prohibited except where "unique obstacles" prevented nontrespassory methods of communication with the employees. *Id.*, at 205–206, n. 41.

B

Jean Country, as noted above, represents the Board's latest attempt to implement the rights guaranteed by § 7. It sets forth a three-factor balancing test:

> [I]n all access cases our essential concern will be [1] the degree of impairment of the § 7 right if access should be denied, as it balances against [2] the degree of impairment of the private property right if access should be granted. We view the consideration of [3] the availability of reasonably effective alternative means as especially significant in this balancing process. [291 N.L.R.B., at 14.]

The Board conceded that this analysis was unlikely to foster certainty and predictability in this corner of the law, but declared that "as with other legal questions involving multiple factors, the 'nature of the problem, as revealed by unfolding variant situations, inevitably involves an evolutionary process for its rational response, not a quick, definitive formula as a comprehensive answer.'" Ibid. (quoting *Electrical Workers v. NLRB*, 366 U.S. 667, 674 (1961))....

Like other administrative agencies, the NLRB is entitled to judicial deference when it interprets an ambiguous provision of a statute that it administers....

Before we reach any issue of deference to the Board, however, we must first determine whether *Jean Country*—at least as applied to nonemployee organizational trespassing—is consistent with our past interpretation of § 7. "Once we have determined a statute's clear meaning, we adhere to that determination under the doctrine of *stare decisis*, and we judge an agency's later interpretation of the statute against our prior determination of the statute's meaning." *Maislin Industries, U.S., Inc. v. Primary Steel, Inc.*, 497 U.S. 116, 131.

In *Babcock*, as explained above, we held that the Act drew a distinction "of substance," 351 U.S., at 113, between the union activities of employees and nonemployees. In cases involving *employee* activities, we noted with approval, the Board "balanced the conflicting interests of employees to receive information on self-organization on the company's property from fellow employees during nonworking time, with the employer's right to control the use of his property." *Id.*, at 109–110. In cases involving *nonemployee* activities (like those at issue in *Babcock* itself), however, the Board was not permitted to engage in that same balancing (and we reversed the Board for having done so). By reversing the Board's interpretation of the statute for failing to distinguish between the organizing activities of employees and nonemployees, we were saying ... that § 7 speaks to the issue of nonemployee access to an employer's property. *Babcock*'s teaching is straightforward: § 7 simply does not protect nonemployee union organizers *except* in the rare case where "the inaccessibility of employees makes ineffective the reasonable attempts by nonemployees to communicate with them through the usual channels," 351 U.S., at 112. Our reference to "reasonable" attempts was nothing more than a common-sense recognition that unions need not engage in extraordinary feats to communicate with inaccessible employees—*not* an endorsement of the view (which we expressly rejected) that the

Act protects "reasonable" trespasses. Where reasonable alternative means of access exist, §7's guarantees do not authorize trespasses by nonemployee organizers, even (as we noted in *Babcock, id.*, at 112) "under . . . reasonable regulations" established by the Board.

Jean Country, which applies broadly to "all access cases," 291 N.L.R.B., at 14, misapprehends this critical point. Its principal inspiration derives not from *Babcock*, but from the following sentence in *Hudgens*: "[T]he locus of th[e] accommodation [between §7 rights and private property rights] may fall at differing points along the spectrum depending on the nature and strength of the respective §7 rights and private property rights asserted in any given context." 424 U.S., at 522. From this sentence the Board concluded that it was appropriate to approach every case by balancing §7 rights against property rights, with alternative means of access thrown in as nothing more than an "especially significant" consideration. As explained above, however, *Hudgens* did not purport to modify *Babcock*, much less to alter it fundamentally in the way *Jean Country* suggests. To say that our cases require accommodation between employees' and employers' rights is a true but incomplete statement, for the cases also go far in establishing the locus of that accommodation where nonemployee organizing is at issue. So long as nonemployee union organizers have reasonable access to employees outside an employer's property, the requisite accommodation has taken place. It is only where such access is infeasible that it becomes necessary and proper to take the accommodation inquiry to a second level, balancing the employees' and employers' rights as described in the *Hudgens* dictum. See *Sears*, 436 U.S., at 205; *Central Hardware*, 407 U.S., at 545. At least as applied to nonemployees, *Jean Country* impermissibly conflates these two stages of the inquiry — thereby significantly eroding *Babcock*'s general rule that "an employer may validly post his property against nonemployee distribution of union literature," 351 U.S., at 112. We reaffirm that general rule today, and reject the Board's attempt to recast it as a multifactor balancing test.

C

The threshold inquiry in this case, then, is whether the facts here justify application of *Babcock*'s inaccessibility exception. The ALJ below observed that "the facts herein convince me that reasonable alternative means [of communicating with Lechmere's employees] were available to the Union." . . . Reviewing the ALJ's decision under *Jean Country*, however, the Board reached a different conclusion on this point, asserting that "there was no reasonable, effective alternative means available for the Union to communicate its message to [Lechmere's] employees." . . .

We cannot accept the Board's conclusion. . . . As we have explained, the exception to *Babcock*'s rule is a narrow one. It does not apply wherever nontrespassory access to employees may be cumbersome or less-than-ideally effective, but only where "the *location of a plant and the living quarters of the employees* place the employees *beyond the reach* of reasonable union efforts to communicate with them," 351 U.S., at 113 (emphasis added). Classic examples include logging camps, see *NLRB v. Lake Superior Lumber Corp.*, 167 F.2d 147 (CA6 1948); mining camps, see *Alaska Barite*

Co., 197 N.L.R.B. 1023 (1972), *enforced mem.*, 83 LRRM 2992 (CA9), *cert. denied*, 414 U.S. 1025 (1973); and mountain resort hotels, see *NLRB v. S & H Grossinger's Inc.*, 372 F.2d 26 (CA2 1967). *Babcock*'s exception was crafted precisely to protect the §7 rights of those employees who, by virtue of their employment, are isolated from the ordinary flow of information that characterizes our society. The union's burden of establishing such isolation is, as we have explained, "a heavy one," *Sears, supra*, 436 U.S., at 205, and one not satisfied by mere conjecture or the expression of doubts concerning the effectiveness of nontrespassory means of communication.

The Board's conclusion in this case that the union had no reasonable means short of trespass to make Lechmere's employees aware of its organizational efforts is based on a misunderstanding of the limited scope of this exception. Because the employees do not reside on Lechmere's property, they are presumptively not "beyond the reach," *Babcock, supra*, 351 U.S., at 113, of the union's message. Although the employees live in a large metropolitan area (Greater Hartford), that fact does not in itself render them "inaccessible" in the sense contemplated by *Babcock*. See *Monogram Models, Inc.*, 192 N.L.R.B. 705, 706 (1971). Their accessibility is suggested by the union's success in contacting a substantial percentage of them directly, via mailings, phone calls, and home visits. Such direct contact, of course, is not a necessary element of "reasonably effective" communication; signs or advertising also may suffice. In this case, the union tried advertising in local newspapers; the Board said that this was not reasonably effective because it was expensive and might not reach the employees.... Whatever the merits of that conclusion, other alternative means of communication were readily available. Thus, signs (displayed, for example, from the public grassy strip adjoining Lechmere's parking lot) would have informed the employees about the union's organizational efforts. (Indeed, union organizers picketed the shopping center's main entrance for months as employees came and went every day.) *Access* to employees, not *success* in winning them over, is the critical issue—although success, or lack thereof, may be relevant in determining whether reasonable access exists. Because the union in this case failed to establish the existence of any "unique obstacles," *Sears*, 436 U.S., at 205–206, n. 41, that frustrated access to Lechmere's employees, the Board erred in concluding that Lechmere committed an unfair labor practice by barring the nonemployee organizers from its property.

. . . .

The judgment of the First Circuit is therefore reversed, and enforcement of the Board's order denied.

It is so ordered.

JUSTICE WHITE, with whom JUSTICE BLACKMUN joins, dissenting. . . .

In the case before us, the Court holds that *Babcock* itself stated the correct accommodation between property and organizational rights; it interprets that case as construing §§7 and 8(a)(1) of the National Labor Relations Act to contain a general rule forbidding third-party access, subject only to a limited exception where the union demonstrates that the location of the employer's place of business and the living quarters of the employees place the employees beyond the reach of reasonable efforts to communicate with them. The Court refuses to enforce the Board's order in this case, which rested on its prior decision in *Jean Country*, 291 N.L.R.B. 11 (1988), because, in the Court's view, *Jean Country* revealed that the Board misunderstood the basic holding in *Babcock*, as well as the narrowness of the exception to the general rule announced in that case.

For several reasons, the Court errs in this case. First, that *Babcock* stated that inaccessibility would be a reason to grant access does not indicate that there would be no other circumstance that would warrant entry to the employer's parking lot and would satisfy the Court's admonition that accommodation must be made with as little destruction of property rights as is consistent with the right of employees to learn the advantages of self-organization from others. Of course the union must show that its "reasonable efforts," without access, will not permit proper communication with employees. But I cannot believe that the Court in *Babcock* intended to confine the reach of such general considerations to the single circumstance that the Court now seizes upon. If the Court in *Babcock* indicated that non-employee access to a logging camp would be required, it did not say that only in such situations could non-employee access be permitted. Nor did *Babcock* require the Board to ignore the substantial difference between the entirely private parking lot of a secluded manufacturing plant and a shopping center lot which is open to the public without substantial limitation. Nor indeed did *Babcock* indicate that the Board could not consider the fact that employees' residences are scattered throughout a major metropolitan area; *Babcock* itself relied on the fact that the employees in that case lived in a compact area which made them easily accessible.

Moreover, the Court in *Babcock* recognized that actual communication with nonemployee organizers, not mere notice that an organizing campaign exists, is necessary to vindicate §7 rights. . . . If employees are entitled to learn from others the advantages of self-organization, . . . it is singularly unpersuasive to suggest that the union has sufficient access for this purpose by being able to hold up signs from a public grassy strip adjacent to the highway leading to the parking lot.

Second, the Court's reading of *Babcock* is not the reading of that case reflected in later opinions of the Court. We have consistently declined to define the principle of *Babcock* as a general rule subject to narrow exceptions, and have instead repeatedly reaffirmed that the standard is a neutral and flexible rule of accommodation. In *Central Hardware Co. v. NLRB*, 407 U.S. 539, 544 (1972), we explicitly stated that the "guiding principle" for adjusting conflicts between §7 rights and property rights enunciated in *Babcock* is that contained in its neutral "accommodation" language. *Hudgens v. NLRB*, 424 U.S. 507 (1976), gave this Court the occasion to provide direct guidance to the NLRB on this issue. In that case, we emphasized *Babcock*'s necessity-to-accommodate admonition, pointed out the differences between *Babcock* and *Hudgens*, and left the balance to be struck by the Board. . . . *Hudgens* did not purport to modify *Babcock* and surely indicates that *Babcock* announced a more flexible rule than the narrow, iron-clad rule that the Court now extracts from that case. If *Babcock* means what the Court says it means, there is no doubt tension between that case and *Hudgens*. If that is so, *Hudgens* as the later pronouncement on the question, issued as a directive to the Board, should be controlling.

The majority today asserts that "[i]t is *only* where [reasonable alternative] access is infeasible that it becomes necessary and proper to take the accommodation inquiry to a second level, balancing the employees' and employers' rights." . . . Our cases, however, are more consistent with the *Jean Country* view that reasonable alternatives are an important factor in finding the least destructive accommodation between §7 and property rights. The majority's assertion to this effect notwithstanding, our cases do not require a prior showing regarding reasonable alternatives as a precondition to any inquiry balancing the two rights. The majority can hardly fault the Board for a decision which "conflates . . . two stages of the inquiry," . . . when no two-stage inquiry has been set forth by this Court.

> [margin note: General rule advanced by majority is also from a time b4 Chevron deference & shd be revised on that ground]

Third, and more fundamentally, *Babcock* is at odds with modern concepts of deference to an administrative agency charged with administering a statute. See *Chevron U.S.A. Inc. v. Natural Resources Defense Council, Inc.*, 467 U.S. 837 (1984). When reviewing an agency's construction of a statute, we ask first whether Congress has spoken to the precise question at issue. . . . If it has not, we do not simply impose our own construction on the statute; rather, we determine if the agency's view is based on a permissible construction of the statute. . . . *Babcock* did not ask if Congress had specifically spoken to the issue of access by third parties and did not purport to explain how the NLRA specifically dealt with what the access rule should be where third parties are concerned. If it had made such an inquiry, the only basis for finding statutory language that settled the issue would have been the language of §7, which speaks only of the rights of employees; *i.e.*, the Court might have found that §7 extends no access rights at all to union representatives. But *Babcock* itself recognized that employees have a right to learn from others about self-organization . . . and itself recognized that in some circumstances, §§7 and 8 required the employer to grant the union access to parking lots. So have later Courts and so does the Court today.

That being the case, the *Babcock* Court should have recognized that the Board's construction of the statute was a permissible one and deferred to its judgment. Instead, the Court simply announced that as far as access is concerned, third parties must be treated less favorably than employees. Furthermore, after issuing a construction of the statute different from that of the Board, rather than remanding to the Board to determine how third parties should be dealt with, the *Babcock* Court essentially took over the agency's job, not only by detailing how union organizer access should be determined but also by announcing that the records before it did not contain facts that would satisfy the newly coined access rule.

Had a case like *Babcock* been first presented for decision under the law governing in 1991, I am quite sure that we would have deferred to the Board, or at least attempted to find sounder ground for not doing so. Furthermore, had the Board ruled that third parties must be treated differently than employees and held them to the standard that the Court now says *Babcock* mandated, it is clear enough that we also would have accepted that construction of the statute. But it is also clear, at least to me, that if the Board later reworked that rule in the manner of *Jean Country*, we would also accept the Board's change of mind. . . .

As it is, the Court's decision fails to recognize that *Babcock* is at odds with the current law of deference to administrative agencies and compounds that error by adopting the substantive approach *Babcock* applied lock, stock, and barrel. And unnecessarily so, for, as indicated above, *Babcock* certainly does not require the reading the Court gives it today, and in any event later cases have put a gloss on *Babcock* that the Court should recognize.

Finally, the majority commits a concluding error in its application of the outdated standard of *Babcock* to review the Board's conclusion that there were no reasonable alternative means available to the union. Unless the Court today proposes to turn back time in the law of judicial deference to administrative agencies, the proper standard for judicial review of the Board's rulings is no longer for "'erroneous legal foundations,'" *ante* at —, but for rationality and consistency with the statute. . . . The Board's conclusion as to reasonable alternatives in this case was supported by evidence in the record. Even if the majority cannot defer to that application, because of the depth of its objections to the rule applied by the NLRB, it should remand to the Board for a decision under the rule it arrives at today, rather than sitting in the place Congress has assigned to the Board.

[margin note: Majority applied improper standard for deference question]

The more basic legal error of the majority today, like that of the Court of Appeals in *Chevron*, is to adopt a static judicial construction of the statute when Congress has not commanded that construction. . . . By leaving open the question of how §7 and private property rights were to be accommodated under the NLRA, Congress delegated authority over that issue to the Board, and a court should not substitute its own judgment for a reasonable construction by the Board. . . .

[margin note: Majority substituted its own construction of §7 for Board's]

Under the law that governs today, it is *Babcock* that rests on questionable legal foundations. The Board's decision in *Jean Country*, by contrast, is both rational and consistent with the governing statute. The Court should therefore defer to the Board, rather than resurrecting and extending the reach of a decision which embodies principles which the law has long since passed by. . . .

[The dissenting opinion of JUSTICE STEVENS is omitted.]

Notes

1. *Discrimination* — When an employer has a written policy banning all solicitation, but only enforces the policy against unions, allowing solicitation by nonemployee groups such as the Camp Fire Girls and Boys, the Boy Scouts, and the Salvation Army, does it violate § 8(a)(1)? Initially the Labor Board held that failure to enforce a no-solicitation rule in an even-handed way across various groups was unlawful. See, e.g., *Lucile Salter Packard-Children's Hosp. v. NLRB*, 97 F.3d 583 (D.C. Cir. 1996)

(enforcing Board's order finding selective enforcement unlawful). Some circuit courts, however, interpreted the prohibition on discrimination differently. *Compare ITT Industries v. NLRB*, 251 F.3d 995 (D.C. Cir. 2001) (finding discriminatory enforcement of such a rule unlawful) *with Albertson's, Inc. v. NLRB*, 301 F.3d 441 (6th Cir. 2002) (finding no violation since no distinction between groups seeking to solicit employees with pro- or anti-union messages) *and Cleveland Real Estate Partners v. NLRB*, 95 F.3d 457 (6th Cir. 1996) (interpreting prohibition on discrimination as applicable only to rules that favor one union over another or allow employer-related information while barring union-related information). More recently, the Labor Board embraced the Sixth Circuit's narrower interpretation, holding that an employer that allowed several charitable organizations to solicit on its property had the right to prohibit solicitation in its parking lots by nonemployee union organizers because the activities were not similar in nature. According to the Board, similarity in nature is evaluated by considering not only the physical context but also the purpose of the solicitation. *Kroger*, 368 N.L.R.B. No. 64 (2019).

In *Brigadier Indus. Corp.*, 271 N.L.R.B. 656 (1984), *review denied*, 776 F.2d 365 (D.C. Cir. 1985), the Board indicated that an employer that does not act with anti-union animus may adopt an otherwise valid no-solicitation rule even after the commencement of a union organizing campaign:

> When faced with a union organizing campaign an employer may not for *union* reasons promulgate a no-solicitation and/or no-distribution rule or place other restrictions on employees. Nonetheless, during the union campaign, an employer maintains a legitimate interest in preserving production and discipline. When an employer adopts a rule during a union campaign, it does not automatically follow that the rule is invalid. If the employer has acted for legitimate business interests — rather than for union reasons — its promulgation of a rule cannot be deemed unlawful.

Compare Dillon Cos., 340 N.L.R.B. 1260 (2003) (employer violated NLRA when it resurrected facially valid no-solicitation rule it had not applied for many years directly in response to union organizing drive, where no showing rule needed to maintain production or discipline).

2. *Public Use Areas*—In cases applying *Lechmere*, the Board had historically treated employer-owned spaces open to the public (such as cafeterias) differently, allowing access to nonemployee union organizers as long as they acted non-disruptively and used the space in a fashion consistent with its intended use. *See, e.g., Montgomery Ward*, 256 N.L.R.B. 800 (1981), *enforced*, 692 F.2d 1115 (7th Cir. 1982). The circuit courts, on the other hand, have frequently applied *Lechmere* to deny union agents access to areas open to public use. *See, e.g., United Food & Commercial Workers, Local No. 880 v. NLRB*, 74 F.3d 292 (D.C. Cir.), *cert. denied*, 519 U.S. 809 (1996) (sustaining ban on consumer picketing of Sears, Roebuck stores at different shopping malls); *Sparks Nugget, Inc. v. NLRB*, 968 F.2d 991 (9th Cir. 1992) (hotel/casino may prohibit handbilling and picketing by nonemployee union agents where tour buses arrive); *Oakwood Hosp. v. NLRB*, 983 F.2d 698 (6th Cir. 1993) (hospital may

ban union organizer seeking to solicit employees in cafeteria). *But see North Memorial Health Care v. NLRB*, 860 F.3d 639 (8th Cir. 2017) (affirming Board finding that employer violated the NLRA when it refused to allow nonemployee union representatives access to facility cafeteria open to the general public). In *UMPC*, 368 N.L.R.B. No. 2 (2019), the Board, joining several of these courts, overturned its previous stance and held that employers may ban nonemployee union representatives from promoting union issues in public spaces within employer facilities, so long as they apply the practice in a nondiscriminatory manner by prohibiting other nonemployees from engaging in similar activity.

On the other hand, when state law modifies common law trespass rules by authorizing public access to shopping mall premises, it violates the NLRA for a mall owner to maintain a rule denying access to nonemployee union organizers. *See Equitable Life Assurance Soc'y*, 343 N.L.R.B. 438 (2004), *enforced*, 524 F.3d 1378 (D.C. Cir.), *cert. denied*, 555 U.S. 819 (2008). *See also Fashion Valley Mall, LLC v. National Labor Relations Bd.*, 42 Cal. 4th 850, 172 P.3d 742 (2007), *cert. denied*, 555 U.S. 819 (2008) (responding to certified question from D.C. Circuit indicating that California Constitution treats shopping malls as "public forums" open to access by individuals wishing to express public opinions); *Roundy's Inc. v. NLRB*, 674 F.3d 638 (7th Cir. 2012) (an employer violated the NLRA when it prohibited union handbilling in common areas of a shopping center where the firm enjoyed a nonexclusive easement permitting its use of that area, since the store did not have a sufficient property interest in that area to support its restriction). *See generally* Hirsch, *Taking State Property Rights out of Federal Labor Law*, 47 B.C. L. Rev. 891 (2006).

Of course, employers may not prohibit union representatives from soliciting or distributing union materials on public property. For example, in *Image FIRST Uniform Rental Service, Inc.*, 365 N.L.R.B. No. 132 2017 (2017), the Board held that an employer unlawfully prohibited union representatives from distributing union literature on a road adjacent to the firm's facility, tried to remove them, and summoned the police, where the distributors were standing on the shoulder and not on the employer's property.

3. *Employees*—*Lechmere* dealt with the rights on non-employee union organizers. Different rules apply to employees who organize on employer property—Why?

The law as to nondiscriminatory employer rules against solicitation and distribution of literature on company property by employees, as well as rules on union paraphernalia and the use of email, may be summarized as follows:

a. *Solicitation*:

(1) *During Working Time*—No-solicitation rules are enforceable; no violation of § 8(a)(1). *Peyton Packing Co., Inc.*, 49 N.L.R.B. 828, 843 (1943), *enforced*, 142 F.2d 1009 (5th Cir.), *cert. denied*, 323 U.S. 730 (1944);

(2) *During Nonworking Time*—No-solicitation rules are not enforceable, *Republic Aviation Corp. v. NLRB*, 324 U.S. 793 (1945), unless employer can show some

special circumstances that make rules necessary to maintain production or discipline. *Compare Adtranz ABB Daimler-Benz Transp., N.A. v. NLRB*, 253 F.3d 19 (D.C. Cir. 2001) (allowing application of handbook rule generally prohibiting abusive or threatening language by employees to abusive union solicitation), *with Consolidated Diesel Co. v. NLRB*, 263 F.3d 345 (4th Cir. 2001) (sustaining § 8(a)(1) finding where employer disciplined employees for "talking up" union to coworkers who complained they were "harassed" by such conduct since such application of policy would prohibit any concerted activity that might be considered offensive to anyone).

The Board distinguishes between rules banning solicitation and distribution during "working time" (presumptively valid) and those phrased in terms of "working hours" (presumptively invalid), since the latter phrase is susceptible to an interpretation covering all paid time, including meal periods and breaktime. *See Our Way, Inc.*, 268 N.L.R.B. 394 (1983).

In Labor Board jurisprudence, "solicitation" by a union historically referred to asking a coworker to join the union by signing an authorization card. Brief conversations about unionization or providing information to a coworker—even during working time—are not considered solicitation because they do not present the same potential for disruption of productivity that are created by presenting a card, which prompts the recipient for an immediate response. *See, e.g., Wal-Mart Stores*, 340 N.L.R.B. 637, 639 (2003); *Conagra Foods, Inc.*, 361 N.L.R.B. 944, 945 (2014). The Trump Board recently expanded the definition of solicitation, however, to include "the act of encouraging employees to vote for or against union representation," shifting away from its previous focus on interference with productivity. *See Wynn Las Vegas, LLC*, 369 N.L.R.B. No. 91 (2020) (upholding discipline of employee who engaged a coworker in three-minute discussion on working time encouraging a pro-union vote in an upcoming election).

b. *Distribution of Literature:*

(1) *In Working Areas*—no-solicitation rules are enforceable; no violation of § 8(a)(1). An employer may usually ban distribution in working areas of the plant even during nonworking time, because of its legitimate interest in keeping the plant free of litter.

(2) *In Nonworking Areas*—an employer may not ban employee distribution in nonworking areas without a showing of special circumstances. *Stoddard-Quirk Mfg. Co.*, 138 N.L.R.B. 615 (1962). However, an employer may prevent the distribution of literature that occurs in a manner that actually causes litter, even in nonworking areas. *Litton Industries, Inc., Erie Marine, Inc. Div.*, 192 N.L.R.B. 793 (1971), *enforced*, 465 F.2d 104 (3d Cir. 1972); *Genesee Merchants Bank & Trust Co.*, 206 N.L.R.B. 274 (1973).

Retail stores may generally ban solicitation and distribution in the *selling areas* even during employees' nonworking time, in order to avoid customer confusion. *Marshall Field & Co. v. NLRB*, 200 F.2d 375 (7th Cir. 1952); *Famous-Barr Co.*, 59 N.L.R.B. 976 (1944), *enforced*, 154 F.2d 533 (8th Cir), *cert. denied*, 329 U.S. 725 (1946).

Health care facilities are generally permitted to prohibit employee solicitation and distribution at all times in *immediate patient care areas*, including locations in which patients receive treatment. However, proscriptions that preclude such activities in nonpatient care areas during nonworking time contravene § 8(a)(1). *See NLRB v. Baptist Hospital, Inc.*, 442 U.S. 773 (1979) (sustaining legality of no-solicitation rule to extent it applied to hospital corridors and sitting rooms on floors containing patient rooms, but striking down rule to extent it covered cafeterias, gift shops, and first floor corridors, since employer failed to demonstrate that solicitation in such areas would significantly affect patient care); *Sutter East Bay Hospitals v. NLRB*, 687 F.3d 424 (D.C. Cir. 2012) (§ 8(a)(1) violation to ban solicitation and distribution in hospital cafeteria); *St. Margaret Mercy Healthcare Centers v. NLRB*, 519 F.3d 373 (7th Cir. 2008) (hospital violated § 8(a)(1) by applying no-solicitation/no-distribution rule to employee breakrooms even though such rooms were proximate to patient care areas). *See also Beth Israel Hosp. v. NLRB*, 437 U.S. 483 (1978).

c. *Buttons and Other Union Paraphernalia*—Absent "special circumstances based on legitimate production or safety reasons," an employer may generally not prohibit the wearing of union buttons or insignia by employees. *See USF Red Star, Inc.*, 339 N.L.R.B. 389 (2003); *Meijer, Inc. v. NLRB*, 130 F.3d 1209 (6th Cir. 1997). *See also Mt. Clemens Gen. Hosp. v.* NLRB, 328 F.3d 837 (6th Cir. 2003) (allowing wearing of union buttons by hospital employees since no showing of interference with patient care); *In-N-Out Burger, Inc. v. NLRB*, 894 F.3d 707 (5th Cir. 2018), *cert. denied*, 139 S. Ct. 1259 (2019) (upholding right of employees to wear "Fight for $15" button supporting campaign to increase minimum wage, where the firm failed to establish special circumstances indicating that such activity would negatively affect its public image).

In *Burger King Corp. v. NLRB*, 725 F.2d 1053 (6th Cir. 1984), however, the court held that a fast-food chain could lawfully ban the wearing of union buttons on employer-supplied uniforms by employees who had regular contact with the public. The rule was enforced in a nondiscriminatory manner, and the court found that the employer had the right "to project a clean, professional image to the public." *Accord United Parcel Serv. v. NLRB*, 41 F.3d 1068 (6th Cir. 1994). *Compare Wal-Mart Stores, Inc. v. NLRB*, 400 F.3d 1093 (8th Cir. 2005) (firm violated NLRA when it refused to allow off-duty employee to wear pro-union T-shirt in its retail store, since activity did not interfere with work of on-duty employees), *with Medco Health Solutions of Las Vegas, Inc. v. NLRB*, 701 F.3d 710 (D.C. Cir. 2012) (no § 8(a)(1) violation where employer required employee to remove T-shirt mocking firm's recognition program for worker achievements). *Compare Wash. State Nurses Ass'n v. NLRB*, 526 F.3d 577 (9th Cir, 2008) (ban on nurses wearing button stating that "RNs Demand Safe Staffing" where they might encounter patients or patient families unlawful, despite hospital claim buttons might induce patients or their relatives to think hospital maintained unsafe staffing levels), *with Southern New England Telephone Co. v. NLRB*, 793 F.3d 93 (D.C. Cir. 2015) (phone company did not violate § 8(a)(1) when it prohibited employees who made home service calls from wearing white T-shirt in support of union bargaining position stating "Inmate No. __" on front and "Prisoner of AT&T" on back, due to AT&T's reasonable belief message could harm customer relationships), *and Pathmark Stores, Inc.*, 342 N.L.R.B. 378 (2004) (employer had "special circumstances" warranting ban on retail employees wearing T-shirts saying "Don't Cheat About the Meat," since customers might not realize that employee complaint concerned sale of prepackaged meats and believe there was something wrong with the meats being sold).

d. *Employee Use of Company Email Systems* — Most employees work for firms that have on-line communication systems. They are usually permitted to use these email systems for personal reasons to communicate with friends and family members, and to access nonbusiness sites.

In *Purple Communications, Inc.*, 361 N.L.R.B. 1050 (2014), a closely divided NLRB noted that email systems have become a basic means of communication for twenty-first-century workers and held that it would "presume that employees who have rightful access to their employer's email system in the course of their work have a right to use the email system to engage in Section 7 protected communications on nonworking time." The majority further indicated that an employer could only justify a total ban on employee use of email if it could show that "special circumstances" make the ban necessary to maintain production or discipline. Employers would be allowed to monitor the use of email for valid business purposes. The two dissenting members asserted that the Labor Board had never previously held that employees have the right to use an employer's communication system simply because it exists, so long as no significant imbalances in communication opportunities exist.

But the Labor Board changed course in *Caesars Entertainment Inc.*, 368 N.L.R.B. No. 143 (2019), where it held that employers may lawfully ban employees from using company email systems during organizing campaigns. Workers "do not have a statutory right to use employers' email and other information-technology (IT) resources to engage in non-work related communications.... Rather, employers have the right to control the use of their equipment, including their email and other IT systems, and they may lawfully exercise that right to restrict the uses to which those systems are put, provided that in doing so, they do not discriminate" against union-related communications.

e. *Off-Duty Employees* — A rule denying off-duty employees access to the employer's premises is valid only if it (1) limits access solely with respect to the interior of the plant and other working areas, (2) is clearly disseminated to all employees, and (3) applies to off-duty employees seeking access to the plant for any purpose and not just to those employees engaging in union activity. Unless justified by business reasons, a rule that denies off-duty employees entry to parking lots, gates, and other outside nonworking areas is invalid. *Tri-County Medical Center, Inc.*, 222 N.L.R.B. 1089 (1976). *Accord NLRB v. Ohio Masonic Home*, 892 F.2d 449 (6th Cir. 1989); *NLRB v. Pizza Crust Co.*, 862 F.2d 49 (3d Cir. 1988). *See also First Healthcare Corp. v. NLRB*, 344 F.3d 523 (6th Cir. 2003) (employees assigned to off-site work locations may not be prohibited from access to external, nonworking areas of employer's main facility to reach other employees during their nonworking time); *J.W. Marriott Los Angeles at L.A. Live*, 359 N.L.R.B. 144 (2012) (employer operating hotel violated § 8(a)(1) when it maintained rule prohibiting employee access to interior areas of hotel more than 15 minutes before or after their shifts without the prior permission of their manager, since rule gave managers unlimited discretion to grant exceptions and employees could reasonably construe rule to prohibit protected concerted activity). The Trump Board signaled its intention to revisit this holding, however, under its *Boeing Company* framework applicable to workplace rules. *See The Boeing Company*, 365 N.L.R.B. No. 154, n. 54 (2017).

Suppose that the off-duty employees are employees who don't regularly work at that site, or are employees of a contractor doing work on that site. Do the same rules apply? In *ITT Indus. v. NLRB*, 413 F.3d 64 (D.C. Cir. 2005), the court found that an employer violated the NLRA when it denied employees who worked at another location the right to enter its parking lot during their nonwork hours to hand out union literature. The court concluded that the statutory rights of the off-site employees outweighed the property security interests of their employer, since these off-site workers were not strangers to that firm. *See also New York-New York, LLC v. NLRB*, 676 F.3d 193 (D.C. Cir. 2012), *cert. denied*, 568 U.S. 1244 (2013) (employer violated NLRA when it barred off-duty employees of on-site contractor from distributing handbills on employer's property, since such employees of subcontractor working on employer's property have same access rights as regular "employees" rather than the limited rights enjoyed by non-employees). However, in *Bexar County Performing Arts Foundation*, 368 N.L.R.B. No. 46 (2019), the Board ruled that the Bexar County Performing Arts Center Foundation lawfully prevented union musicians who worked for a symphony that leased space and performed at the auditorium from protesting a ballet company's use of recorded music inside the arts center. The Board significantly curtailed access rights for such employees, holding that an employer may exclude off-duty employees of one of its licensees from using its property to engage in Section 7 activity unless (1) those employees work both "regularly" and "exclusively" on the property, and (2) the property owner cannot show that the licensee's employees have at least one reasonably non-trespassory means to communicate their message.

NLRB v. United Steelworkers [Nutone, Inc.]

Supreme Court of the United States
357 U.S. 357, 78 S. Ct. 1268, 2 L. Ed. 2d 1383 (1958)

[The Supreme Court's discussion of a companion case involving Avondale Mills has not been included in this excerpt from the Court's opinion.]

Mr. Justice Frankfurter delivered the opinion of the Court.

In April of 1953 the respondent Steelworkers instituted a campaign to organize the employees of respondent NuTone, Inc., a manufacturer of electrical devices.... In June the company began to distribute, through its supervisory personnel, literature that, although not coercive, was clearly anti-union in tenor. In August, while continuing to distribute such material, the company announced its intention of enforcing its rule against employees posting signs or distributing literature on company property or soliciting or campaigning on company time. The rule, according to these posted announcements, applied to "all employees—whether they are for or against the union."....

In a proceeding before the Board commenced at the instance of the Steelworkers, the company was charged with a number of violations of the Act... including the discriminatory application of the no-solicitation rule.... The Board dismissed the allegation that the company had discriminatorily enforced its no-solicitation rule. 112 N.L.R.B. 1153. The Steelworkers sought review of this dismissal in the United States Court of Appeals for the District of Columbia Circuit.... The Court of Appeals concluded that it was an unfair labor practice for the company to prohibit the distribution of organizational literature on company property during working hours while the company was itself distributing antiunion literature....

Employer rules prohibiting organizational solicitation are not in and of themselves violative of the Act, for they may duly serve production, order and discipline. *See Republic Aviation Corp. v. NLRB*, 324 U.S. 793 (1945); *NLRB v. Babcock & Wilcox Co.*, 351 U.S. 105 (1956). In neither of the cases before us did the party attacking the enforcement of the no-solicitation rule contest its validity. Nor is the claim made that an employer may not, under proper circumstances, engage in noncoercive antiunion solicitation; indeed, his right to do so is protected by the so-called "employer free speech" provision of §8(c) of the Act. Contrariwise, as both cases before us show, coercive antiunion solicitation and other similar conduct run afoul of the Act and constitute unfair labor practices irrespective of the bearing of such practices on enforcement of a no-solicitation rule. The very narrow and almost abstract question here derives from the claim that, when the employer himself engages in antiunion solicitation that if engaged in by employees would constitute a violation of the rule—particularly when his solicitation is coercive or accompanied by other unfair labor practices—his enforcement of an otherwise valid no-solicitation rule against the employees is itself an unfair labor practice. We are asked to rule that the coincidence of these circumstances necessarily violates the Act, regardless of the way in which the particular controversy arose or whether the employer's conduct to any considerable degree created an imbalance in the opportunities for organizational communication. For us to lay down such a rule of law would show indifference to the responsibilities imposed by the Act primarily on the Board to appraise carefully the interests of both sides of any labor-management controversy in the diverse circumstances of particular cases and in light of the Board's special understanding of these industrial situations....

No attempt was made in either of these cases to make a showing that the no-solicitation rules truly diminished the ability of the labor organizations involved to carry their message to the employees. Just as that is a vital consideration in determining the validity of a no-solicitation rule, *see Republic Aviation Corp. v. NLRB*, supra at 797–798; *NLRB v. Babcock & Wilcox Co.*, supra at 112, it is highly relevant in determining whether a valid rule has been fairly applied. Of course the rules had the effect of closing off one channel of communication; but the Taft-Hartley Act does not command that labor organizations as a matter of abstract law, under all circumstances, be protected in the use of every possible means of reaching the minds of individual workers, nor that they are entitled to use a medium of communication simply because the employer is using it. *Cf. Bonwit Teller, Inc. v. NLRB*, 197 F.2d 640, 646 (2d Cir. 1952); *NLRB v. F. W. Woolworth Co.*, 214 F.2d 78, 84 (6th Cir. 1954) (concurring opinion). No such mechanical answers will avail for the solution of this non-mechanical, complex problem in labor-management relations. If, by virtue of the location of the plant and of the facilities and resources available to the union, the opportunities for effectively reaching the employees with a pro-union message, in spite of a no-solicitation rule, is at least as great as the employer's ability to promote the legally authorized expression of his antiunion message, there is no basis for invalidating these "otherwise valid" rules. The Board, in determining whether or not the enforcement of such a rule in the circumstances of an individual case is an unfair labor practice, may find relevant alternative channels available for communications on the right to organize. When this important issue is not even raised before the Board and no evidence bearing on it adduced, the concrete basis for appraising the significance of the employer's conduct is wanting.

We do not at all imply that the enforcement of a valid no-solicitation rule by an employer who is at the same time engaging in antiunion solicitation may not constitute an unfair labor practice. All we hold is that there must be some basis, in the actualities of industrial relations, for such a finding....

CHIEF JUSTICE WARREN... concurring in part.

... In *United Steelworkers*, I concur in the result. The National Labor Relations Board declined to hold that the enforcement of an employer's no-distribution rule against a union was an unfair labor practice even though it was coupled with an antiunion campaign. The Court of Appeals reversed the Board on this point, modifying the Board's order accordingly. This Court sustains the Board. It is conceded that the enforcement of this no-distribution rule against the union is not by itself an unfair labor practice. The Board determined that the employer's expressions of his antiunion views were noncoercive in nature.... Being noncoercive in nature, the employer's expressions were protected by § 8(c) of the National Labor Relations Act and so cannot be used to show that the contemporaneous enforcement of the no-distribution rule was an unfair labor practice.

JUSTICES BLACK and DOUGLAS dissented for the reasons set forth in the opinion of the Court of Appeals.

Note

Nutone makes clear that employers are not required to offer their employees the same kind of opportunities to communicate with their fellow employees that the employers themselves have with their employees. The resulting differential in the ability of unions to communicate with workers has been the subject of a substantial amount of criticism. For example, Cynthia Estlund noted:

> A frequent target of criticism has been the law's failure to afford unions physical access to the workplace during an organizing campaign. Unions have argued that their supposedly equivalent opportunity to reach employees in their homes or at union halls has become increasingly impracticable in an age of urban sprawl, especially for overextended working parents. At the same time, employers' property rights — and particularly their right to exclude others from property that has been opened to workers, customers, or the public — have been severely eroded by the antidiscrimination laws and regulatory regimes put in place since the 1950s. Yet efforts to legislate even limited union access to non-work areas of the workplace have failed.

Estlund, *The Ossification of American Labor Law*, 102 COLUM. L. REV. 1527, 1537–38 (2002). In what kinds of cases does the reasoning in *Babcock & Wilcox, Lechmere*, and *NuTone* require the NLRB to find that "reasonable efforts by the union through other available channels of communication will not enable it to reach the employees with its message" or that the employer's conduct has "created an imbalance in opportunities for organizational communication" or "truly diminished the ability of the labor organizations involved to carry their message to the employees"?

Problem

5. The Beaumont Bobcats, a professional women's soccer team, has finished in the bottom of its league standings for years. With a new season on the horizon, the Bobcats' owner, Redd Gumms, thought he needed to make some changes. The team usually has a 10-week off-season training camp at their regular facilities. But Redd believes that the booming town of Beaumont presents too many distractions for his players; they need to concentrate on their soccer. So he bought 500 acres in rural Texas — about two hours outside of Beaumont — and built a complete, state-of-the-art practice facility. The new complex has everything: regulation soccer fields, a weight room, whirlpools, and, in addition, a set of beautiful suites and a full-service cafeteria for the coaches and players so they never had to leave the premises.

Redd informed the coaches and players that they would have their training camp at the new facility, so they all moved in and began training. Their days were filled with long, hard practice sessions. Coaches didn't allow the players to use their phones during the day, but the phone restriction was lifted in the evenings. The players were allowed to leave the facility in the evenings and on weekends, but, with Beaumont so far away, most of the players just stayed at the facility relaxing and recovering. On some of the weekends, a few of the players drove back to Beaumont for a night, but otherwise, everybody stayed put.

A couple weeks into the training camp, a players' union decided that it wanted to organize the Bobcats before the start of the regular season. Upon hearing of the organizing drive, the owner posted a sign at the entrance to the property that read

"PRIVATE PROPERTY: NO SOLICITATION." When some of the union organizers drove out to the practice facility and started distributing handbills, Redd kicked them out, explaining that it was private property. Despite the sign, though, Redd continued to allow Girl Scouts selling cookies and "Born Again" Christians selling God (the players preferred the cookies).

The union was able to contact some of the players who had more public social media accounts. One of those players took up the cause, and began a group text with some of the other players about the benefits of joining the union. All of their texting went on during the evenings. When one of the players told an assistant coach about this, the coach asked who was on the text and made those players run extra laps the next day for engaging in "behavior detrimental to the team." He also told Redd which player started the text, and Redd responded by suspending that player from the team's first two matches.

Did the Beaumont Bobcats commit any unfair labor practices?

B. Anti-Union Speeches and Publications

In a broad sense, any expression of anti-union opinion by the employer has a tendency to "interfere with, restrain or coerce" employees in the exercise of their right of self-organization. The attitude of the NLRB in the early days of the Wagner Act was that the employer should remain neutral so that the employees could exercise a free choice as to organization.

> An employer's "opinion" about unionism expressed to his employees is not the same as his opinion on what doctor to use or about the international situation. . . . When an employer addresses his antagonism toward unionism, however devoid his words may be of direct threats, there is always implicit the threat of economic compulsion if his wishes are not heeded. . . . Freedom of speech is possible only among those who approximate each other in equality of position.

J. ROSENFARB, THE NATIONAL LABOR POLICY AND HOW IT WORKS 79 (1940). Against these considerations must be weighed the public policy—indeed the constitutional right—of freedom of speech. In *NLRB v. Virginia Electric & Power Co.*, 314 U.S. 469 (1941), the Supreme Court established the proposition that an employer's statements of opinion about unions should not be regarded as, or be evidence of, unfair labor practices unless, viewed against the "totality of conduct" of the employer, they appeared to be coercive.

The NLRB did not appear to construe the Supreme Court's *Virginia Electric* decision as requiring a marked departure from the Board's previous position with respect to employer publications. In *American Tube Bending Co., Inc.*, 44 N.L.R.B. 121 (1942), the publications consisted of letters sent to each employee and a speech made by the president to employees who were assembled for the purpose in the plant during working hours. There was no attempt to vilify the union, but the company did make clear that it thought the best interests of the employees would be served by voting against the union in the impending election. The "no union" choice received 280 out of 413 votes counted. On petition of the losing AFL union, the Board held that the company had interfered with rights guaranteed to employees by §7 of the Act, even though the case involved no other alleged unfair labor practices.

> Because of the relationship existing between the author of the utterances and the employees, as well as the circumstances under which the communications were delivered, they attained a force stronger than their intrinsic connotation, and beyond that of persuasion. They achieved a coercive effect that could not possibly be dissipated by the deft suggestion of Jones [the Company President] that the election would be "conducted in a fair and impartial manner . . . give you absolute freedom to express your choice without any coercion."

Enforcement of the Board's order was refused on the authority of the *Virginia Electric* case. *NLRB v. American Tube Bending Co.*, 134 F.2d 993 (2d Cir.), *cert. denied*, 320 U.S. 768 (1943).

In 1947, House and Senate bills containing provisions designed to preserve the free speech rights of employers and labor organizations were introduced. They culminated in the addition of § 8(c) to the NLRA.

The Senate Bill (S. 1126) contained the following provision:

> The Board shall not base any finding of unfair labor practice upon any statement of views or arguments, either written or oral, if such statement contains under all the circumstances no threat, express or implied, of reprisal or force, or offer, express or implied, of benefit.

The Senate Committee on Labor and Public Welfare explained the intent of this provision:

> Section 8(c): Another amendment to this section would insure both to employers and labor organizations full freedom to express their views to employees on labor matters, refrain from threats of violence, intimation of economic reprisal, or offers of benefit [*sic*]. The Supreme Court in Thomas v. Collins (323 U.S. 516) held, contrary to some earlier decisions of the Labor Board, that the Constitution guarantees freedom of speech on either side in labor controversies and approved the doctrine of the *American Tube Bending* case.
>
> The Board has placed a limited construction upon these decisions by holding such speeches by employers to be coercive if the employer was found guilty of some other unfair labor practice even though severable or unrelated (Monumental Life Insurance, 69 N.L.R.B. 247) or if the speech was made in the plant on working time (Clark Brothers, 70 N.L.R.B. 60). The committee believes these decisions to be too restrictive and, in this section, provides that if, under all the circumstances, there is neither an expressed

or implied threat of reprisal, force, or offer of benefit, the Board shall not predicate any finding of unfair labor practice upon the statement. The Board, of course, will not be precluded from considering such statements as evidence. [S. Rep. No. 105, 80th Cong., 1st Sess. 23 (1947).]

Section 8(d) of the House Bill (H.R. 3020) contained the following provision:

The following shall not constitute or be evidence of unfair labor practice under any of the provisions of the Act:

(1) Expressing any views, argument, or opinion, or the dissemination thereof, whether in written, printed, graphic, or visual form, if it does not by its own terms threaten force or economic reprisal. . . .

With reference to this provision, the House Committee on Education and Labor said:

Section 8(d)(1). — This guarantees free speech to employers, to employees, and to unions. Although the Labor Board says it does not limit free speech, its decisions show that it uses against people what the Constitution says they can say freely. Thus, if an employer criticizes a union, and later a foreman discharges a union official for gross misconduct, the Board may say that the official's misconduct warranted his being discharged, but "infer," from what the employer said, perhaps long before, that the discharge was for union activity, and reinstate the official with back pay. It has similarly abused the right of free speech in abolishing and penalizing unions of which it disapproved but which workers wished as their bargaining agents. The bill corrects this, providing that nothing that anyone says shall constitute or be evidence of an unfair labor practice unless it, by its own express terms, threatens force or economic reprisal. This means that a statement may not be used against the person making it unless it, standing alone, is unfair within the express terms of Sections 7 and 8 of the amended act. [H.R. Rep. No. 245, 80th Cong., 1st Sess. 33 (1947).]

Notes

1. *Speech in its Broader Context* — In light of this legislative history, did Congress intend the coercive nature of an employer's communication to its employees to be judged "on the face" of the communication or as viewed in the "totality of conduct of the employer"? In *NLRB v. Kropp Forge Co.*, 178 F.2d 822 (7th Cir. 1949), *cert. denied*, 340 U.S. 810 (1950), the Seventh Circuit addressed this issue:

It . . . seems clear to us that in considering whether such statements or expressions are protected by Section 8(c) of the Act, they cannot be considered as isolated words cut off from the relevant circumstances and background in which they are spoken. A statement considered only as to the words it contains might seem a perfectly innocent statement, including neither a threat nor a promise. But, when the same statement is made by an employer to his employees, and we consider the relation of the parties, the surrounding circumstances, related statements and events and the background of the employer's actions, we may find that the statement is part of a general pattern which discloses action by the employer so coercive as to entirely destroy his employees' freedom of choice and action. To permit statements or expressions to be so used on the theory that they are protected either by the First Amendment or by Section 8(c) of the Act, would be in violation of Section 7 and contrary to the expressed purpose of the Act. Therefore, in determining whether such statements and expressions constitute, or are evidence of unfair labor practice, they must be considered in connection with the positions of the parties, with the background and circumstances under which they are made, and with the general conduct of the parties. If, when so considered, such statements form a part of a general pattern or course of conduct which constitutes coercion and deprives the employees of their free choice guaranteed by Section 7, such statements must still be considered as a basis for a finding of unfair labor practice. To hold otherwise, would nullify the guaranty of employees' freedom of action and choice which Section 7 of the Act expressly provides. Congress, in enacting Section 8(c), could not have intended that result.

Accord Irving Air Chute Co. v. NLRB, 350 F.2d 176 (2d Cir. 1965). In a similar vein, the court in *Daniel Constr. Co. v. NLRB*, 341 F.2d 805, 811 (4th Cir.), *cert. denied*, 382 U.S. 831 (1965), said that "[e]ven if we assume that each of the key statements in the Daniel speeches considered separately would be lawful . . . it still does not follow that we must accept the position pressed upon us by the company [that the whole cannot be greater than the sum of its parts]. Daniel may have accurately stated an accepted rule of mathematics, but words and speech are not governed entirely by mechanical mathematical concepts. Words and phrases, each lawful when considered alone, can be united in such a fashion as to yield an improper end product."

In *J. P. Stevens & Co. v. NLRB*, 380 F.2d 292 (2d Cir.), *cert. denied*, 389 U.S. 1005 (1967), the court considered an employer statement that "if this Union were to get in here, it would not work to your benefit but, in the long run, would itself operate to your serious harm." The court found that this statement was made in a context of "massive" unfair labor practices.

> Apparently the Board has frequently characterized a substantially similar notice as an instrument of coercion. *E.g., Greensboro Hosiery Mills, Inc.*, 162 N.L.R.B. 1275 (1967); *White Oak Acres, Inc.*, 134 N.L.R.B. 1145, 1149–50 (1961). However, the Fourth and Sixth Circuits have disagreed with the Board, *see Wellington Mill Div., West Point Mfg. Co. v. NLRB*, 330 F.2d 579, 583 (4th Cir.), *cert. denied*, 379 U.S. 882 (1964); *Surprenant Mfg. Co. v. NLRB*, 341 F.2d 756, 758–60 (6th Cir. 1965). So has the Court of Appeals for the District of Columbia, with the important qualification that the notice may take a different coloration by virtue of the accompanying circumstances, *Amalgamated Clothing Workers v. NLRB*, 365 F.2d 898, 909–10 (D.C. Cir.

1966) (2–1 decision)... . There can hardly be disagreement with the view of the District of Columbia Court of Appeals that the words of a notice should not be so regarded [*in vacuo*], but may take on a darker hue when viewed in the perspective of the particular setting.

The court concluded that the setting in the *J.P. Stevens* case was of a sufficiently dark hue to warrant finding the "serious harm" statement as coercive under § 8(a)(1).

2. *The Role of Intent*—*Ralph's Toys, Hobbies, Cards & Gifts, Inc.*, 272 N.L.R.B. 164 (1984), involved an employer that left a letter threatening to discharge a primary union organizer in a folder. The letter was discovered by a coworker during the course of her duties, read by her, and disseminated to other employees. A violation was found, even though the employer did not intend to disclose the letter to any of the employees.

NLRB v. Gissel Packing Co.

Supreme Court of the United States
395 U.S. 575, 89 S. Ct. 1918, 23 L. Ed. 2d 547 (1969)

[The main part of the opinion in this case, dealing with the validity of bargaining orders based on authorization cards, is set out, *infra*. However, one of the four employers whose cases were consolidated before the Supreme Court—the Sinclair Company—raised the issue of "employer free speech," and the portion of the Court's opinion which passed upon that point is reproduced below.]

Mr. Chief Justice Warren delivered the opinion of the Court.

... The petitioner, a producer of mill rolls, wire, and related products at two plants in Holyoke, Massachusetts, was shut down for some three months in 1952 as the result of a strike over contract negotiations with the American Wire Weavers Protective Association (AWWPA), the representative of petitioner's journeymen and apprentice wire weavers from 1933 to 1952. The Company subsequently reopened without a union contract, and its employees remained unrepresented through 1964, when the Company was acquired by an Ohio corporation, with the Company's former president continuing as head of the Holyoke, Massachusetts, division. In July 1965, the International Brotherhood of Teamsters, Local Union No. 404, began an organizing campaign among petitioner's Holyoke employees and by the end of the summer had obtained authorization cards from 11 of the Company's 14 journeymen wire weavers choosing the Union as their bargaining agent. On September 20, the Union notified petitioner that it represented a majority of its wire weavers, requested that the Company bargain with it, and offered to submit the signed cards to a neutral third party for authentication. After petitioner's president declined the Union's request a week later, claiming, *inter alia*, that he had a good faith doubt of majority status because of the cards' inherent unreliability, the Union petitioned, on November 8, for an election that was ultimately set for December 8.

When petitioner's president first learned of the Union's drive in July, he talked with all of his employees in an effort to dissuade them from joining a union. He particularly emphasized the results of the long 1952 strike, which he claimed "almost put our company out of business," and expressed worry that the employees were forgetting the "lessons of the past." He emphasized secondly that the Company was still on "thin ice" financially, that the Union's "only weapon is to strike," and that a strike "could lead to closing the plant," since the parent company had ample manufacturing facilities elsewhere. He noted thirdly that because of their age and the limited usefulness of their skills outside their craft, the employees might not be able to find re-employment if they lost their jobs as a result of a strike. Finally, he warned those who did not believe that the plant could go out of business to "look around Holyoke and see a lot of them out of business." The president sent letters to the same effect to the employees in early November, emphasizing that the parent company had no reason to stay in Massachusetts if profits went down.

During the two or three weeks immediately prior to the election on December 9, the president sent the employees a pamphlet captioned "Do you want another 13-week strike?" stating, *inter alia*, that "We have no doubt that the Teamsters Union can again close the Wire Weaving Department and the entire plant by a strike. We have no hopes that the Teamsters Union bosses will not call a strike.... The Teamsters Union is a strike happy outfit." Similar communications followed in late November, including one stressing the Teamsters' "hoodlum control." Two days before the election, the Company sent out another pamphlet that was entitled "Let's Look at the Record," and that purported to be an obituary of companies in the Holyoke-Springfield, Massachusetts, area that had allegedly gone out of business because of union demands, eliminating some 3,500 jobs; the first page carried a large cartoon showing the preparation of a grave for the Sinclair Company and other headstones containing the names of other plants allegedly victimized by the unions. Finally, on the day before the election, the president made another personal appeal to his employees to reject the Union. He repeated that the Company's financial condition was precarious; that a possible strike would jeopardize the continued operation of the plant; and that age and lack of education would make re-employment difficult. The Union lost the election 7-6, and then filed both objections to the election and unfair labor practice charges which were consolidated for hearing before the trial examiner.

The Board agreed with the trial examiner that the president's communications with the employees, when considered as a whole, "reasonably tended to convey to the employees the belief or impression that selection of the Union in the forthcoming election could lead [the Company] to close its plant, or to the transfer of the weaving production, with the resultant loss of jobs to the wire weavers." Thus, the Board found that under the "totality of the circumstances" petitioner's activities constituted a violation of § 8(a)(1) of the Act.

On appeal, the Court of Appeals for the First Circuit sustained the Board's findings and conclusions and enforced its order in full. 397 F.2d 157. . . .

We consider finally petitioner Sinclair's First Amendment challenge to the holding of the Board and the Court of Appeals for the First Circuit. At the outset we note that the question raised here most often arises in the context of a nascent union organizational drive, where employers must be careful in waging their antiunion campaign. As to conduct generally, the above noted gradations of unfair labor practices, with their varying consequences, create certain hazards for employers when they seek to estimate or resist unionization efforts. But so long as the differences involve conduct easily avoided, such as discharge, surveillance, and coercive interrogation, we do not think that employers can complain that the distinctions are unreasonably difficult to follow. Where an employer's antiunion efforts consist of speech alone, however, the difficulties raised are not so easily resolved. The Board has eliminated some of the problem areas by no longer requiring an employer to show affirmative reasons for insisting on an election and by permitting him to make reasonable inquiries. We do not decide, of course, whether these allowances are mandatory. But we do note that an employer's free speech right to communicate his views to his employees is firmly established and cannot be infringed by a union or the Board. Thus, § 8(c) . . . merely implements the First Amendment. . . .

Any assessment of the precise scope of employer expression, of course, must be made in the context of its labor relations setting. Thus, an employer's rights cannot outweigh the equal rights of the employees to associate freely, as those rights are embodied in § 7 and protected by § 8(a)(1) and the proviso to § 8(c). And any balancing of those rights must take into account the economic dependence of the employees on their employers, and the necessary tendency of the former, because of that relationship, to pick up intended implications of the latter that might be more readily dismissed by a more disinterested ear. Stating these obvious principles is but another way of recognizing that what is basically at stake is the establishment of a nonpermanent, limited relationship between the employer, his economically dependent employee and his union agent, not the election of legislators or the enactment of legislation whereby that relationship is ultimately defined and where the independent voter may be freer to listen more objectively and employers as a class freer to talk. Compare *New York Times Co. v. Sullivan*, 376 U.S. 254 (1964).

Within this framework, we must reject the Company's challenge to the decision below and the findings of the Board on which it was based. The standards used below for evaluating the impact of an employer's statements are not seriously questioned by petitioner and we see no need to tamper with them here. Thus, an employer is free to communicate to his employees any of his general views about unionism or any of his specific views about a particular union, so long as the communications do not contain a "threat of reprisal or force or promise of benefit." He may even make a prediction as to the precise effects he believes unionization will have on his company. In such a case, however, the prediction must be carefully phrased on the basis of objective fact to convey an employer's belief as to demonstrably probable consequences beyond his control or to convey a management decision already arrived at to close the plant in case of unionization. See *Textile Workers v. Darlington Mfg.*

Co., 380 U.S. 263, 274, n.20 (1965). If there is any implication that an employer may or may not take action solely on his own initiative for reasons unrelated to economic necessities and known only to him, the statement is no longer a reasonable prediction based on available facts but a threat of retaliation based on misrepresentation and coercion, and as such without the protection of the First Amendment. We therefore agree with the court below that "conveyance of the employer's belief, even though sincere, that unionization will or may result in the closing of the plant is not a statement of fact unless, which is most improbable, the eventuality of closing is capable of proof." 397 F.2d, at 160. As stated elsewhere, an employer is free only to tell "what he reasonably believes will be the likely economic consequences of unionization that are outside his control," and not "threats of economic reprisal to be taken solely on his own volition." *NLRB v. River Togs, Inc.*, 382 F.2d 198, 202 (2d Cir. 1967)....

Equally valid was the finding by the court and the Board that petitioner's statements and communications were not cast as a prediction of "demonstrable economic consequences," 397 F.2d, at 160, but rather as a threat of retaliatory action. The Board found that petitioner's speeches, pamphlets, leaflets, and letters conveyed the following message: that the company was in a precarious financial condition; that the "strike-happy" union would in all likelihood have to obtain its potentially unreasonable demands by striking, the probable result of which would be a plant shut-down, as the past history of labor relations in the area indicated; and that the employees in such a case would have great difficulty finding employment elsewhere. In carrying out its duty to focus on the question "what did the speaker intend and the listener understand," Cox, Law and the National Labor Policy 44 (1960), the Board could reasonably conclude that the intended and understood import of that message was not to predict that unionization would inevitably cause the plant to close but to threaten to throw employees out of work regardless of the economic realities. In this connection, we need go no further than to point out: (1) that petitioner had no support for his basic assumption that the union, which had not yet even presented any demands, would have to strike to be heard, and that he admitted at the hearing that he had no basis for attributing other plant closings in the area to unionism; and (2) that the Board has often found that employees, who are particularly sensitive to rumors of plant closings, take such hints as coercive threats rather than honest forecasts.

Petitioner argues that the line between so-called permitted predictions and proscribed threats is too vague to stand up under traditional First Amendment analysis and that the Board's discretion to curtail free speech rights is correspondingly too uncontrolled. It is true that a reviewing court must recognize the Board's competence in the first instance to judge the impact of utterances made in the context of the employer-employee relationship, *see NLRB v. Virginia Elec. & Power Co.*, 314 U.S. 469, 479 (1941). But an employer, who has control over that relationship and therefore knows it best, cannot be heard to complain that he is without an adequate guide for his behavior. He can easily make his views known without engaging in "'brinkmanship'" when it becomes all too easy to "overstep and tumble into the brink," *Wausau Steel Corp. v. NLRB*, 377 F.2d 369, 372 (7th Cir. 1967). At the least he can avoid coercive speech simply by avoiding conscious overstatements he has reason to believe will mislead his employees.

For the foregoing reasons, we affirm the judgment of the Court of Appeals for the First Circuit.

Notes

1. *Distinguishing Threats from Predictions* — The line between a permissible prediction or statement of legal position and an illegal threat has been a difficult one for the Board and the courts to draw.

In *NLRB v. Herman Wilson Lumber Co.*, 355 F.2d 426 (8th Cir. 1966), the employer's speeches included the following remarks: "I will fight the Union in every legal way possible.... If the Union calls an economic strike, you place your job on the line. You can be permanently replaced. You can lose your job.... In dealing with the Union I'll deal hard with it — I'll deal cold with it — I'll deal at arm's length with it." The NLRB held that these statements violated § 8(a)(1), but the court of appeals denied enforcement.

The NLRB found no unfair labor practice when an employer referred to the lower wages being paid at unionized plants and suggested that the organization of its employees might result in similarly lower wages (*International Paper Co.*, 273 N.L.R.B. 615 (1984)) or when an employer told workers that wages and benefits are typically "frozen" during bargaining with a union, which could go on for more than a year (*Mantrose-Haeuser Co.*, 306 N.L.R.B. 377 (1992)). On the other hand, unlawful threats were found when an employer made a slide presentation showing rental trucks replacing employee-driven trucks after the union won an election at another company (*Coronet Foods, Inc.*, 305 N.L.R.B. 79 (1991), *enforced*, 981 F.2d 1284 (D.C. Cir. 1993)).

In *Dallas & Mavis Specialized Carrier Co.*, 346 N.L.R.B. 253 (2006), the Board found that an employer violated § 8(a)(1) when its general manager told an employee involved in union organizing that if the employees went union it would have to ask customers for more money and suggested that the company may "have to close the doors," where these statements were not based upon objective facts and did not refer to demonstrably probable consequences beyond the employer's control. *See also Progressive Elec., Inc. v. NLRB*, 453 F.3d 538 (D.C. Cir. 2006), (finding that an employer violated the NLRA when a supervisor told employees that a union organizer was trying to "cost all you guys your jobs ... and that's why we have to put a stop to it," since the employees could reasonably perceive a direct connection between the union organizing and the possible loss of their jobs). *Compare UFCW, Local 204 v. NLRB*, 506 F.3d 1078 (D.C. Cir. 2007) (no violation where employer stated that three other companies had previously operated the plant, that the union had organized the plant each time, and that each company ultimately shut down the plant; because the managers "carefully avoided linking the previous plant closures directly to the union," the statements were simply "relevant, factual information about the union's history at the facility" rather than threats); *Werthan Packaging, Inc.*, 345 N.L.R.B. 343 (2005) (no violation when manager suggested to employee that voting against the union would be in her family's "best interest," where remark not accompanied by threats and was too vague to support claim that manager had threatened or coerced employee).

At the margins, the Board's political makeup tends to drive the results. For example, a trucking company president's "opinion" that a major customer might withdraw its business if drivers unionized, placing the business in jeopardy, constituted an unlawful threat of closure. Even though the president told his employees that the customer always asked about unionization before selecting a motor carrier, suggesting that it did not wish to operate in a union environment, the Board majority found the statement to be mere speculation about what the customer might do in response to unionization, which did not satisfy the *Gissel* standard. *Hogan Transports, Inc.*, 363 N.L.R.B. No. 196 (2016). In *Stern Produce Co.*, 368 N.L.R.B. No. 31 (2019), however, a divided Board held that an employer did not violate the NLRA when a consultant told workers prior to a certification election that the company president "can lock the door on all of you" as a pressure tactic to force the union to agree to terms at the bargaining table, despite the fact that the employer had engaged in other "extensive" and "egregious" violations, since these actions were separate from the lockout statement.

2. *Anti-Union Speech in Representation Cases*—The NLRB has indicated that § 8(c) is limited to unfair labor practice cases and has no application in representation cases. "Conduct that creates an atmosphere which renders improbable a free choice will sometimes warrant invalidating an election even though the conduct may not constitute an unfair labor practice." *General Shoe Corp. (Nashville, Tenn.)*, 77 N.L.R.B. 124 (1948), *enforced*, 192 F.2d 504 (6th Cir. 1951), *cert. denied*, 343 U.S. 904 (1952). Thus, employer statements not constituting a "threat of reprisal" under § 8(c) may sufficiently cloud the atmosphere to warrant the setting aside of an election. This will be taken up in greater detail in the next part on representation.

Problems

6. A waitress at a restaurant called Shenanigans began organizing her fellow employees. The company soon found out about the organizing drive, and one of the owners made a speech to the assembled workers in which he told them that the restaurant business was highly competitive, and that:

> Unions do not work in restaurants — the balance is not there. If the union exists at Shenanigans, Shenanigans will fail. That is it in a nutshell. I won't be here if there is a Union within this particular restaurant. I am not making a

threat. I am making a statement of fact. I respect anyone who wants to join the Union in another workplace if that business can afford to pay Union wages. We can't in the restaurant business. Shenanigans can possibly exist with labor problems for a period of time. But in the long run we won't make it. The cancer will eat us up, and we will fall by the wayside.

He went on to say that the only restaurant in town that was unionized was struggling, and if Shenanigans had to raise its prices in order to pay union wages, its customers would probably switch to the nonunion restaurants with lower prices.

Was the owner's speech an unfair labor practice? What more would you like to know about the situation that could help you resolve this question?

7. A union began an organizing drive at a Hendrickson Springs, a company that manufactured suspensions for heavy trucks. Soon afterward, one of the company's managers had a meeting with the assembled employees. During the meeting, she pointed out how great management-employee relationships were at the facility, extolled the value of management's open-door policy, and praised the company's practice of working directly with employees to listen to and address their concerns.

A few days later, another manager sent a letter to "Hendrickson Employees & Family." The letter stated that "it has always been our goal as an Employer to provide a workplace with benefits, opportunities, and freedoms." It went on to detail its pension system and current fringe benefits package that included medical and dental coverage, basic life insurance, and disability insurance. The letter continued, "Some of you may feel that Union representation will preserve job security, lead to greater benefits, or enhanced compensation. The fact of the matter is that a Union cannot promise you, as a valued employee of Hendrickson, anything. If our plant were to be unionized, and the collective bargaining process to begin, none of the benefits, compensation, or job security that you currently enjoy would be guaranteed. The Company and the Union would begin the negotiating process from scratch."

Finally, the two managers played a PowerPoint presentation for the employees entitled "Hendrickson Springs: A Great Place to Work." The presentation highlighted the virtues of Hendrickson as an employer and the value of direct employer-employee relationships (without the union). It addressed numerous negative characteristics of unions, and negative consequences for employees and their families if they signed union cards and selected unionization. The presentation gave examples of what would be lost with a union, including "loss of our direct relationship" and "your right to speak for and represent yourself." The presentation concluded with the claim that, with a union in place, "The culture will definitely change."

Did the managers' speech, letter, or presentation constitute an unfair labor practice?

C. Interrogation

Blue Flash Express, Inc.
National Labor Relations Board
109 N.L.R.B. 591 (1954)

[Respondent, an interstate motor carrier, received a letter on May 19, 1953, from the union stating that it represented a majority of respondent's employees, that it was prepared to submit proof thereof, and that it desired to enter into collective bargaining negotiations. Before replying, respondent's general manager, Golden, interviewed each employee individually in his office, stating that he had received a letter from the union and that it was immaterial to him whether or not employees were union members, but that he desired to know whether they had joined so that he might know how to answer the letter. Each employee denied to Golden that he had signed any union card, although a majority of them had done so, designating the union as their representative, on or about May 17, 1953. Golden testified that this was the entire conversation. Several employees testified that Golden also stated on this occasion that the company was too small to operate with a union and that it would be impelled to sell out or reduce operations should the business be unionized. The Trial Examiner found that, since the witnesses appeared to be equally credible, the General Counsel had failed to establish the alleged threats of shutdown by a preponderance of the evidence and that the facts as to the interviews were as testified to by Golden.]

... [W]e are ... of the opinion that Golden's interrogation of the employees was not violative of the Act. At the time of the interrogation, the Respondent had just received a communication from the Union claiming majority status and the right to represent the Respondent's employees in collective bargaining. Golden so informed the employees. He further gave them assurances that the Respondent would not resort to economic reprisals and advised them that he wished to know whether they had signed union authorization cards in order to enable him to reply to the Union's request for collective bargaining. As found above, there is no credible evidence that the Respondent at any time made any threats or promises violative of the Act, resorted to any reprisals, or exhibited any antiunion animus. Although the employees who had signed union authorization cards gave false answers to Golden's inquiries, the Respondent did nothing to afford them a reasonable basis for believing that the Respondent might resort to reprisals because of their union membership or activity. The facts here are similar to those presented in *Atlas Life Ins. Co. v. NLRB*, 195 F.2d 136 (10th Cir. 1952), where the Employer tried to find out whether a union represented a majority of the employees so that he would know whether he was obligated to bargain with the union. In that case, the Court of Appeals for the Tenth Circuit held that such interrogation was proper. When such interrogation is conducted under proper safeguards, as was the situation in the instant case, the fact that the interrogation is systematic does not, in itself, impart a coercive character to the interrogation. The purpose of such interrogation could not be achieved without systematic inquiry.

Contrary to the assertion of our dissenting colleagues, we are not holding in this decision that interrogation must be accompanied by other unfair labor practices before it can violate the Act. We are merely holding that interrogation of employees by an employer as to such matters as their union membership or union activities, which, when viewed in the context in which the interrogation occurred, falls short of interference or coercion, is not unlawful.

Our dissenting colleagues rely upon the rationale of *Standard-Coosa-Thatcher*, 85 N.L.R.B. 1358, in which the Board held that interrogation *per se* is unlawful. They appear to overlook cases, for the most part of recent date, in which the courts of at least six circuits have explicitly or by necessary implication condemned the rationale of *Standard-Coosa-Thatcher*. We hereby repudiate the notion that interrogation *per se* is unlawful and overrule *Standard-Coosa-Thatcher* and the line of cases following it to the extent that they are inconsistent with our decision today.

In our view, the test is whether, under all the circumstances, the interrogation reasonably tends to restrain or interfere with the employees in the exercise of rights guaranteed by the Act. The fact that the employees gave false answers when questioned, although relevant, is not controlling. The Respondent communicated its purpose in questioning the employees — a purpose which was legitimate in nature — to the employees and assured them that no reprisal would take place. Moreover, the questioning occurred in a background free of employer hostility to union organization. These circumstances convince us that the Respondent's interrogation did not reasonably lead the employees to believe that economic reprisal might be visited upon them by Respondent.

The instant case is thus distinguishable from such cases as *Syracuse Color Press*, 103 N.L.R.B. 377, *enforced* by the Court of Appeals for the Second Circuit, 209 F.2d 596 (2d Cir. 1954), where the employer called the employees to the superintendent's office a week before a scheduled Board election, advocated adherence to 1 of 2 rival unions, and questioned them concerning their union membership and activities, as well as the membership and activities of other employees, without giving any legitimate explanation for the interrogation or any assurance against reprisal. In such cases, unlike the situation in the instant case, the surrounding circumstances together with the nature of the interrogation itself imparted a coercive character to the interrogation.

This decision does not by any means grant employers a license to engage in interrogation of their employees as to union affiliation or activity. We agree with and adopt the test laid down by the Court of Appeals for the Second Circuit in the *Syracuse Color Press* case which we construe to be that the answer to whether particular interrogation interferes with, restrains, and coerces employees must be found in the record as a whole. And, as the court states "The time, the place, the personnel involved, the information sought and the employer's conceded preference [as in that case] must be considered. . . ." Members of the majority have participated in a number of recent decisions in which we have joined in holding that certain acts of interrogation were violative of the Act, and we reaffirm that position here. Therefore, any employer who engages in interrogation does so with notice that he risks a finding of unfair labor practices if the circumstances are such that his interrogation restrains or interferes with employees in the exercise of their rights under the Act.

The rule which we adopt will require the Trial Examiners and the Board to carefully weigh and evaluate the evidence in such case, but that is what we believe the statute requires us to do. The only alternatives, both of which we reject, are either to find all interrogation *per se* unlawful, or to find that interrogation under all circumstances is permissible under the statute.

Our dissenting colleagues express disagreement with our decision, but do not make it clear precisely what rule they would follow. There is the strong implication that the dissenting members would hold interrogation to be coercive *per se*, which, of course, means wholly without regard to the circumstances in which it occurs. This would mean that a casual, friendly, isolated instance of interrogation by a minor supervisor would subject the employer to a finding that he had committed an unfair labor practice and result in the issuance of a cease and desist order, which, if enforced by the court, would subject the employer to punishment for contempt of court if the same or another minor supervisor repeated the question to the same or another employee. If this is not the position of our colleagues, and they agree that the Board is required to determine the significance of particular acts of interrogation in the light of the entire record in the case, the difference between their view and ours merely reflects disagreement as to the conclusion to be drawn from the particular facts of the case.

Hence, we conclude that the Respondent's interrogation of the employees under the circumstances of this case did not carry an implied threat of reprisal or in any other way interfere with, restrain, or coerce the employees in the exercise of the rights guaranteed in § 7 of the Act. Accordingly, we find that such conduct is not violative of § 8(a)(1) of the Act....

MEMBERS MURDOCK and PETERSON, dissenting:

The exact meaning and extent of the majority decision is not certain. Apparently, however, the majority has decided that interrogation unaccompanied by other unfair labor practices is not conduct which violates the Act. We cannot agree.

From the very beginning of the administration of this Act the Board has, with court approval, found that interrogation by an employer prevents employees from exercising freely their right to engage in concerted activities. After a substantial period of administrative experience and after amendment of the Act, the Board reaffirmed its position that when an employer questions his employees concerning any aspect of concerted activity he violates § 8(a)(1) of the Act. We believe that the carefully considered position on interrogation taken by the Board in previous cases is well founded, and we are aware of no recent development which warrants a departure from such precedent.

The rationale for finding interrogation violative of the Act is simple.... Employees can exercise fully their right to engage in or refrain from self-organizational and other concerted activities only if they are free from employer prying and investigation. When an employer inquires into organizational activity whether by espionage, surveillance, polling, or direct questioning, he invades the privacy in which employees are entitled to exercise the rights given them by the Act. When he questions an employee about union organization or any concerted activities he forces the employee to take a stand on such issues whether or not the employee desires to take a position or has had full opportunity to consider the various arguments offered on the subject. And the employer compels the employee to take this stand alone, without the anonymity and support of group action. Moreover, employer interrogation tends to implant in the mind of the employee the apprehension that the employer is seeking information in order to affect his job security and the fear that economic reprisal will follow the questioning. The fear induced by an employer's questions is illustrated by the fact that employees, as in this case, often give untruthful or evasive answers to such questions. The many cases in the Board's experience in which interrogation was the prelude to discrimination demonstrate the reasonableness of such fear. Interrogation thus serves as an implied threat or a warning to employees of the adverse consequences of organization and dissuades them from participating in concerted activity. It thereby undermines the bargaining agent chosen by the employees, thwarts self-organization, and frustrates employee attempts to bargain collectively. Such conduct tends to interfere with, restrain, or coerce employees in the exercise of the rights guaranteed by § 7 as prohibited by § 8(a)(1). Board condemnation of interrogation, which we believe is required by the Act, protects the right of employees to privacy in their organizational activities, removes the restraint and coercion resulting from the threat implicit in interrogation, and deters the commission of further unfair labor practices.

For these reasons the Board in its expert judgment and in the light of its administrative experience is warranted in concluding, as it has in the past, that interrogation generally inhibits employee self-organization and is violative of § 8(a)(1) whether or not other unfair labor practices are committed. This does not mean that all interrogation is automatically unlawful or requires remedial action by the Board. There are, of course, instances of interrogation which can be properly regarded as isolated, casual, and too inconsequential in their impact to constitute a violation of the Act or to warrant a Board remedy. In such situations we have participated in dismissing the allegations of illegal interrogation.

. . . .

Several approved methods of determining whether a labor organization represents a majority of his employees are available to an employer. He may ask the labor organization to offer proof of its majority; he may request the organization to file a petition for a Board determination by election; or he may file a similar petition himself. He may agree with the labor organization to submit authorization cards to an impartial third party for a check; and we note that in making its bargaining request the Union here stated its willingness to agree to such a check. Finally, if an employer has a *genuine* doubt as to the labor organization's majority status, he may simply refuse to recognize the organization, and his good-faith doubt is a defense to a charge of a violation of the duty to bargain. With all these avenues open to an employer, plainly there is no need for him to utilize interrogation, with its coercive effect, in order to reply to a union's request for recognition, and the Board should not approve such conduct. . . .

Notes

1. *Employer Polling*—In response to a directive from the D.C. Circuit in *International Union of Operating Engineers v. NLRB*, 353 F.2d 852 (D.C. Cir. 1965), the Board revised the *Blue Flash* tests and announced standards to be used to determine whether an employer "poll" is lawful:

> Absent unusual circumstances, the polling of employees by an employer will be violative of § 8(a)(1) of the Act unless the following safeguards are observed: (1) the purpose of the poll is to determine the truth of a union's claim of majority; (2) this purpose is communicated to the employees; (3) assurances against reprisal are given; (4) *the employees are polled by secret ballot* [emphasis added]; and (5) the employer has not engaged in unfair labor practices or otherwise created a coercive atmosphere.
>
> The purpose of the polling in these circumstances is clearly relevant to an issue raised by a union's claim for recognition and is therefore lawful. The requirement that the lawful purpose be communicated to the employees, along with assurances against reprisal, is designed to allay any fear of discrimination which might otherwise arise from the polling, and any tendency to interfere with employees' § 7 rights. Secrecy of the ballot will give further assurance that reprisals cannot be taken against employees because the views of each individual will not be known. And the absence of employer unfair labor practices or other conduct creating coercive atmosphere will serve as a further warranty to the employees that the poll does not have some unlawful object, contrary to the lawful purpose stated by the employer. In accord with presumptive rules applied by the Board with court approval in other situations, this rule is designed to effectuate the purposes of the Act by maintaining a reasonable balance between the protection of employee rights and legitimate interests of employers.
>
> On the other hand, a poll taken while a petition for a Board election is pending does not, in our view, serve any legitimate interest of the employer that would not be better served by the forthcoming Board election. In accord with long-established Board policy, therefore, such polls will continue to be found violative of § 8(a)(1) of the Act.

Struksnes Constr. Co., 165 N.L.R.B. 1062 (1967). The *Struksnes* standards have generally been followed by the Board (*Northeastern Dye Works, Inc.*, 203 N.L.R.B. 1222 (1973)) and by courts of appeals (*NLRB v. Super Toys, Inc.*, 458 F.2d 180 (9th Cir.

1972)). Nonetheless, in *Bushnell's Kitchens, Inc.*, 222 N.L.R.B. 110 (1976), where the employer's polling was done at a meeting of the employees upon the suggestion of the union business agent, no violation was found. The Board said that the *Struksnes* requirements are "not a straitjacket to be applied in any and all circumstances." See also *NLRB v. Lorben Corp.*, 345 F.2d 346 (2d Cir. 1965) (coercion may not be inferred simply from the employer's failure (1) to explain the purpose of a poll and (2) to assure employees against reprisal).

2. *Non-Polling Questioning*—*Bourne v. NLRB*, 332 F.2d 47, 48 (2d Cir. 1964), articulated the standards to be used to determine the legality of non-polling questioning of employees:

> Under our decisions, interrogation, not itself threatening, is not held to be an unfair labor practice unless it meets certain fairly severe standards. . . . These include: (1) The background, *i.e.*, is there a history of employer hostility and discrimination? (2) The nature of the information sought, *e.g.*, did the interrogator appear to be seeking information on which to base taking action against individual employees? (3) The identity of the questioner, *i.e.*, how high was he in the company hierarchy? (4) Place and method of interrogation, *e.g.*, was employee called from work to the boss's office? Was there an atmosphere of 'unnatural formality'? (5) Truthfulness of the reply.

In *Rossmore House*, 269 N.L.R.B. 1176 (1984), *affirmed*, 760 F.2d 1006 (9th Cir. 1985), the NLRB overruled recent decisions indicating that employer interrogation of employees regarding protected activities would generally violate §8(a)(1) and adopted the *Bourne* totality-of-the-circumstances approach. The Board concluded that the non-coercive questioning of an open and active union supporter by both the manager and one of the owners did not violate the Act.

Although a supervisor may ask "casual" questions regarding the union sympathies of an employee who is not an open union adherent, so long as under the "totality of the circumstances" no coercion is found (*Sunnyvale Medical Clinic, Inc.*, 277 N.L.R.B. 1217 (1985)), it is impermissible to ask such employees questions of a "probing, inquisitive and focused nature" (*Raytheon Missile System Div., Raytheon Co.*, 279 N.L.R.B. 245 (1986)).

Problems

8. A union started organizing the employees at Fresh & Easy, a supermarket specializing in organic food. After a few weeks, the union presented the employer with a petition, signed by a majority of employees, claiming that the union represented the employees. The employer refused to recognize the union, saying that it would insist on a government-supervised, secret ballot election.

Instead of filing a petition for an election, the union took to the streets and, among other things, handed out leaflets at the store entrance. The leaflets implored customers to act: "Tell Fresh & Easy: Let Your Workers Freely Choose a Union." The employer decided to counter the activity by distributing its own flyer, along with a $5 store coupon. The employer's flyer had three bullet points:

- The protestors are not our employees and have been hired by an outside union.
- We've told the union this is a decision only our employees can make. They have not made this choice.
- We offer good pay and affordable benefits to all our employees, and take pride in being a great place to work.

The employer then did what it always did when it came to such promotions: it asked its employees whether any of them wanted to work parts of their shift outside handing out coupons. This time, however, they would be handing out the flyer along with the coupon. Some of the employees volunteered for the task and spent the afternoon handing out the flyers and coupons in front of the store.

Did the employer commit an unfair labor practice in asking its employees whether they wanted to hand out the promotional materials? Would your answer change if the employer had ordered the employees to do so?

9. A union began organizing the employees of Redhook, a large construction company. One of the construction workers, Claudio, asked his supervisor, David, for a few days off to visit his ailing mother. On the way out of town, Claudio visited the union offices and signed a union authorization card. When he didn't show up to work on the day he was supposed to return, David texted Claudio "U work for redhook or u working for the union?" Claudio responded "Not today, can I return tomorrow?" David responded "Not right now! I filled your spot tomorrow. Come meet with me." Claudio never told David or any other supervisor that he had signed a union card, visited the union office, or supported the union.

Did Redhook commit an unfair labor practice?

D. Economic Coercion and Inducement

NLRB v. Exchange Parts Co.
Supreme Court of the United States
375 U.S. 405, 84 S. Ct. 457, 11 L. Ed. 2d 435 (1964)

[Respondent was engaged in the business of rebuilding automobiles and its employees were not represented by a union prior to 1959. On November 9, 1959, the Boilermakers Union announced that it was conducting an organizational campaign and on November 16 it petitioned the Board for a representation election which was ordered for March 18, 1960.]

Mr. Justice Harlan delivered the opinion of the Court.

This case presents a question concerning the limitations which § 8(a)(1) of the National Labor Relations Act, 49 Stat. 452 (1935), as amended, 29 U.S.C. § 158(a)(1), places on the right of an employer to confer economic benefits on his employees shortly before a representation election. The precise issue is whether that section prohibits the conferral of such benefits, without more, where the employer's purpose is to affect the outcome of the election. . . .

At two meetings on November 4 and 5, 1959, C. V. McDonald, the Vice President and General Manager of Exchange Parts, announced to the employees that their "floating holiday" in 1959 would fall on December 26 and that there would be an additional "floating holiday" in 1960. On February 25, six days after the Board issued its election order, Exchange Parts held a dinner for employees at which Vice-President McDonald told the employees that they could decide whether the extra day of vacation in 1960 would be a "floating holiday" or would be taken on their birthdays. The employees voted for the latter. McDonald also referred to the forthcoming representation election as one in which, in the words of the trial examiner, the employees would "determine whether . . . [they] wished to hand over their right to speak and act for themselves." He stated that the union had distorted some of the facts and pointed out the benefits obtained by the employees without a union. He urged all the employees to vote in the election.

On March 4 Exchange Parts sent its employees a letter which spoke of "the *Empty Promises* of the Union" and "the *fact* that *it is the Company that puts things in your envelope.* . . ." After mentioning a number of benefits, the letter said: "The Union can't put any of those things in your envelope — *only the Company can do that.*" [The italics appear in the original letter.] Further on, the letter stated: ". . . [I]t didn't take a Union to get any of those things and . . . it won't take a Union to get additional improvements in the future." Accompanying the letter was a detailed statement of the benefits granted by the company since 1949 and an estimate of the monetary value of such benefits to the employees. Included in the statement of benefits granted by the company for 1960 were the birthday holiday, a new system for computing overtime during holiday weeks which had the effect of increasing wages for those weeks, and a new vacation schedule which enabled employees to extend their vacations by sandwiching them between two weekends. Although Exchange Parts asserts that the policy behind the latter two benefits was established earlier, it is clear that the letter of March 4 was the first general announcement of the changes to the employees. In the ensuing election the union lost.

The Board, affirming the findings of the trial examiner, found that the announcement of the birthday holiday and the grant and announcement of overtime and vacation benefits were arranged by Exchange Parts with the intention of inducing the employees to vote against the union. It found that this conduct violated § 8(a)(1) of the National Labor Relations Act and issued an appropriate order. On the Board's petition for enforcement of the order, the Court of Appeals rejected the finding that the announcement of the birthday holiday was timed to influence the outcome of the election. It accepted the Board's findings with respect to the overtime and vacation benefits, and the propriety of those findings is not in controversy here. However, noting that "the benefits were put into effect unconditionally on a permanent basis, and no one has suggested that there was any implication the benefits would be withdrawn if the workers voted for the union," 304 F.2d 368, 375, the court denied enforcement of the Board's order. It believed that it was not an unfair labor practice under §8(a)(1) for an employer to grant benefits to its employees in these circumstances.

... We think the Court of Appeals was mistaken in concluding that the conferral of employee benefits while a representation election is pending, for the purpose of inducing employees to vote against the union, does not "interfere with" the protected right to organize.

... The danger inherent in well-timed increases in benefits is the suggestion of a fist inside the velvet glove. Employees are not likely to miss the inference that the source of benefits now conferred is also the source from which future benefits must flow and which may dry up if it is not obliged. The danger may be diminished if, as in this case, the benefits are conferred permanently and unconditionally. But the absence of conditions or threats pertaining to the particular benefits conferred would be of controlling significance only if it could be presumed that no question of additional benefits or renegotiation of existing benefits would arise in the future; and, of course, no such presumption is tenable.

... Other unlawful conduct may often be an indication of the motive behind a grant of benefits while an election is pending, and to that extent it is relevant to the legality of the grant; but when as here the motive is otherwise established, an employer is not free to violate §8(a)(1) by conferring benefits simply because it refrains from other, more obvious violations. We cannot agree with the Court of Appeals that enforcement of the Board's order will have the "ironic" result of "discouraging benefits for labor." 304 F.2d, at 376. The beneficence of an employer is likely to be ephemeral if prompted by a threat of unionization which is subsequently removed. Insulating the right of collective organization from calculated good will of this sort deprives employees of little that has lasting value.

Reversed.

Notes

1. *Remedies*—The pertinent part of the Board's order in the *Exchange Parts* case reads:

> Cease and desist from interfering with, restraining, or coercing its employees in the exercise of rights guaranteed in §7 of the Act by granting them economic benefits or by changing the terms and conditions of their employment; provided, however, that *nothing in this recommended order shall be construed as requiring the Respondent to vary or abandon any economic benefit or any term or condition of employment which it has heretofore established.*

131 N.L.R.B. 806, 807 (1961) (emphasis added). Such a rollback would probably contravene the anti-retaliation proscription in §8(a)(4). If the remedy doesn't include a retraction of the unlawful benefit, what is the point of the unfair labor practice charge?

2. *Predetermined or Customary Benefits*—The implementation of a health insurance plan during a union organizational effort was not a violation of § 8(a)(1), when preparations for the plan had begun nine months before the organizing campaign. *Pedro's, Inc. v. NLRB*, 652 F.2d 1005 (D.C. Cir. 1981). However, in *ManorCare Health Services*, 362 N.L.R.B. 644 (2015), the Labor Board found that an employer engaged in objectionable conduct that warranted the setting aside of a representation election when, during the critical period prior to the election, it announced to its nursing assistants the specific amount of a pay increase, informed certain nursing assistants they would receive lump sum payments, and issued paychecks reflecting these payments, even though the employer had notified the nursing assistants they would be receiving an unspecified increase under a "market adjustment" prior to the time the labor organization had filed a petition for a Board election, where the timing of these events had the tendency to interfere with employee free choice.

What if an employer customarily increases compensation levels at the same time each year, and a union organizing campaign is going on at that time? One court noted that such an employer confronts a "damned if you do, damned if you don't" situation in either granting or withholding a predetermined benefit prior to an election, since an employer that *withholds* a customary wage increase before an election may well be found in violation of § 8(a)(1). *NLRB v. Aluminum Casting & Eng'g Co.*, 230 F.3d 286 (7th Cir. 2000). *See also Pleasant Travel Servs.*, 317 N.L.R.B. 996 (1995) (employer did not interfere with representation election when it announced it would not disclose amount of semiannual pay increase until after election, since it wished to avoid appearance of improper influence over election).

3. *Promises of Benefits*—Employer statements containing threats of reprisals or promises of benefits constitute unlawful interference, restraint, and coercion. If the employer actually effectuates such reprisals or benefits for the purpose of defeating unionization, this constitutes a separate unfair labor practice. "The Act does not preclude an employer from introducing benefits during an organizational period. But when an employer uses proposed benefits as an inducement not to join the union, his activity bears no shield of privilege." *Joy Silk Mills, Inc. v. NLRB*, 185 F.2d 732, 739 (D.C. Cir. 1950), *cert. denied*, 341 U.S. 914 (1951). Employers that solicit employee grievances during organizing campaigns with the implicit promise to remedy those issues if the workers vote against unionization are usually found in violation of the Act. *See NLRB v. V & S Schuler Eng'g, Inc.*, 309 F.3d 362 (6th Cir. 2002).

Problem

10. The employees at Lavalamps Unlimited were fed up. For years, they had put up with substandard wages, terrible working conditions, and the cruel 1970s jokes that came with working at a lavalamp factory. Some of the employees decided to organize, and have been assisted in that effort by an electrical workers' union. Lavalamps Unlimited soon learned of the activity, and instituted a vigorous anti-union campaign.

First, the president of Lavalamps gave a speech to his employees saying, among other things, "Unions are vile. Unions are evil. Unions killed disco. We are adamantly opposed to this effort to unionize, and believe you are better off without one." Second, early in the campaign, the Lavalamps Unlimited personnel department, worried that it might appear to be "buying off" the workers, placed a notice in the October company newsletter stating that Lavalamps Unlimited's traditional gift of a frozen Thanksgiving turkey to every employee would be suspended this year. The week of Thanksgiving, though, the personnel department decided that it made a mistake, and handed out a frozen turkey to every employee. Finally, a few days before the election, the president gathered the employees together and promised them the "biggest party since the '70s" if they rejected the union.

Did Lavalamps commit any unfair labor practices?

E. Violence and Intimidation, Espionage and Surveillance, and Economic Coercion

(1) *Violence and Intimidation* — Violence and threats of violence to deter union organization are clearly unlawful. Examples were fairly common during the early days of the Wagner Act: an overseer offered to buy an employee a gallon of whiskey if he would "stamp the hell out of" a union organizer (*Mansfield Mills, Inc.*, 3 N.L.R.B. 901 (1937)); a supervisor supplemented her attempt to dissuade employees from accepting union pamphlets by suggesting, with reference to the union organizer, "What do you say, girls, we give her a beating?" (*Tiny Town Togs, Inc.*, 7 N.L.R.B. 54 (1938)); a reign of terror was conducted by an employer association, of which the company was a member, with union organizers ordered out of the county at gunpoint by private police hired by the association (*Clover Fork Coal Co.*, 4 N.L.R.B. 202 (1937), *enforced*, 97 F.2d 331 (6th Cir. 1938)).

The Byrnes Act, 18 U.S.C. §1231, makes unlawful and criminal the interstate transportation of persons employed for the purpose of obstructing, by force or threats, "(1) peaceful picketing by employees during any labor controversy affecting wages, hours or conditions of labor; or (2) the exercise by employees of any of the rights of self-organization, or collective bargaining."

(2) *Espionage and Surveillance* — In the period before the Wagner Act, the use of labor spies, often hired from detective agencies, to infiltrate unions and report on the "ringleaders" who were then discharged and blacklisted, received considerable publicity, and such practices were obviously included in the abuses aimed at in §8(1). *See, e.g., Baldwin Locomotive Works*, 20 N.L.R.B. 1100 (1940), *enforced as modified*, 128 F.2d 39 (3d Cir. 1942). More recently, while the use of labor spies is not unheard of, surveillance often takes other forms. For example, employers who photograph or videotape employees engaged in protected concerted activities during organizing campaigns will be found in violation of §8(a)(1), unless they can demonstrate special circumstances warranting such action. *See Timken Co. v. NLRB*, 2002 U.S. App. LEXIS 2059 (6th Cir. Feb. 4, 2002). Nonetheless, management's routine observation

of employees engaged in organizing activity on company property does not violate § 8(a)(1), unless it is "out of the ordinary" and "coercive." *Local Joint Exec. Bd. v. NLRB*, 515 F.3d 942 (2008).

It is not necessary to prove that employees knew they were being spied upon, since even surreptitious spying on protected activities is unlawful. *NLRB v. Grower-Shipper Vegetable Ass'n*, 122 F.2d 368 (9th Cir. 1941). *See also Ctr. Constr. Co. v. NLRB*, 482 F.3d 425 (6th Cir. 2006) (employer photographing of picketers violated § 8(a)(1)); *National Steel & Shipbuilding Co. v. NLRB*, 156 F.3d 1268 (D.C. Cir. 1998) (videotaping of union rallies held outside main shipyard entrance to enhance worker bargaining position violated § 8(a)(1)). Furthermore, if employers merely give employees *the impression* they have been subject to improper surveillance, a violation will usually be found. *Contemporary Cars, Inc. v. NLRB*, 814 F.3d 859 (7th Cir. 2016); *Caterpillar Logistics, Inc. v. NLRB*, 835 F.3d 536 (6th Cir. 2016).

(3) *Economic Coercion*—A unanimous Supreme Court ruled that the First Amendment petition clause precluded a Board order seeking to halt an employer's state court defamation action against employees, even if the suit was in retaliation for their filing of unfair labor practice charges, so long as the lawsuit did not lack a reasonable basis in fact or law. The Court stated, however, that if the employer lost in the state proceeding, the Board could consider the matter further. If it determined the lawsuit was brought with retaliatory intent, the Board could find a violation of § 8(a)(1) and (4) of the NLRA. *Bill Johnson's Restaurants, Inc. v. NLRB*, 461 U.S. 731 (1983).

In *BE&K Constr. Co. v. NLRB*, 536 U.S. 516 (2002), the Supreme Court reconsidered the degree to which the Labor Board may regulate retaliatory litigation. It discussed the expansive protection given to most lawsuits under the petition clause of the First Amendment, and concluded that NLRB regulation of lawsuits that may chill the exercise of protected rights should be narrowly permitted.

> In *Professional Real Estate Investors [v. Columbia Pictures Industries, Inc.*, 508 U.S.49 (1993)], we adopted a two-part definition of sham antitrust litigation: first, it "must be objectively baseless in the sense that no reasonable litigant could realistically expect success on the merits"; second, the litigant's subjective motivation must "concea[l] an attempt to interfere *directly* with the business relationships of a competitor ... through the use [of] the government process ... as an anticompetitive weapon." ... For a suit to violate the antitrust laws, then, it must be a sham *both* objectively and subjectively.

The *BE&K* Court decided to extend this doctrine to suits challenged as retaliatory under the NLRA, requiring the Labor Board to find *both* an objectively baseless lawsuit *and* a subjectively retaliatory motivation before it could normally subject a litigant to unfair labor practice liability. The Court did intimate, however, that the NLRB might also "declare unlawful any unsuccessful but reasonably based suits that would not have been filed but for a motive to impose the costs of the litigation process, regardless of the outcome, in retaliation for NRLA protected activity." How strong would the evidence of retaliatory motive have to be before the Labor Board could find an unsuccessful, but reasonably based, lawsuit unlawful?

On remand from the Supreme Court, the Labor Board held that BE&K Construction did not violate the NLRA when it prosecuted a § 303 suit against a union for allegedly secondary activity, even though the suit was at least partially motivated by retaliation against protected conduct. *Compare H.W. Barss Co.*, 296 N.L.R.B. 1286 (1989) (employer's "baseless" retaliatory defamation action violated § 8(a)(1)); *International Union of Operating Eng'rs, Local 520*, 309 N.L.R.B. 1199 (1992) (union violated § 8(b)(1)(A) by filing meritless defamation action against member who filed charges with NLRB).

F. Employer Responsibility for Anti-Union Conduct of Subordinates and Others

The Wagner Act contained no test or standard of employer responsibility except that the term "employer" was defined in § 2(2) to include "any person acting in the interest of an employer, directly or indirectly."

Section 2(2), as amended, substituted the language of agency for "interest" in defining "employer." According to the House Committee, it was intended by the change in § 2(2) to make "employers responsible for what people say and do only when it is within the *actual* or *apparent* scope of their authority" and thus to make the "ordinary rules of the law of agency equally applicable to employers and to unions." H.R. Rep. No. 245, 80th Cong., 1st Sess. 11 (1947). The dissenters on the committee objected to this change. "It would make necessary proof that an employer had specifically authorized his foremen or superintendents to engage in unfair labor practices; matters which are easily concealed. In modern industrial enterprises foremen and superintendents *are* management to the workers under them and employers should be held responsible for their actions." H.R. Rep. No. 245, 80th Cong., 1st Sess. 68 (1947). Later the conference report recommended both the change proposed in the House bill *and* a new provision, § 2(13), providing: "In determining whether any person is acting as an 'agent' of another person so as to make such other person responsible for his acts, the question of whether the specific acts performed were actually authorized or subsequently ratified shall not be controlling." According to the report, this means that "both employers and labor organizations will be responsible for the acts of their agents in accordance with the ordinary common law rules of agency (and only ordinary evidence will be required to establish the agent's authority)." H.R. Conf. Rep. No. 510, 80th Cong., 1st Sess. 36 (1947).

(1) *Supervisors*—An employer is generally held responsible for the statements and acts of supervisors, since it can usually be said that they have apparent authority to speak for the employer. Even when the employer has instructed its supervisors not to interfere with the employees' organizational activities, it may still be responsible if it has not communicated these instructions to the rank-and-file employees. *Broyhill Furniture Co.*, 94 N.L.R.B. 1452 (1951).

Isolated or sporadic instances of coercive statements by a supervisor do not give rise to employer responsibility when the circumstances indicate no employer authorization. *Pittsburgh S.S. Co. v. NLRB*, 180 F.2d 731 (6th Cir. 1950), *aff'd*, 340 U.S. 498 (1951).

(2) *Non-Supervisory Employees* — An employer is held responsible for the acts of its nonsupervisory employees when the employees act as agents of the employer. This may be shown when the employees are acting within the general scope of their employment, regardless of whether the specific acts have been authorized or even forbidden. *National Paper Co.*, 102 N.L.R.B. 1569 (1953), *enforcement denied*, 216 F.2d 859 (5th Cir. 1954) (armed guard made threatening and abusive phone calls to the union secretary, in a context of other coercive conduct by the employer).

When non-supervisory employees are clothed with apparent authority to speak for the employer, the employer is held responsible for their acts. *NLRB v. Mississippi Products, Inc.*, 213 F.2d 670 (5th Cir. 1954). The necessary agency relationship may also be found on the basis of implied authority or implicit ratification when the employer condones or affirms violence by rank-and-file employees. *See, e.g., Jewell, J. D., Inc.*, 99 N.L.R.B. 61 (1952).

(3) *Non-Employees* — Whether an employer will be held responsible for threatening speeches and publications of local business people and town officials depends on evidence of an agency relationship, such as employer instigation, participation, express, implied, or apparent authority, or express or implied ratification. *Southland Mfg. Co.*, 94 N.L.R.B. 813 (1951) (a supervisor urged employees to attend a meeting addressed by the mayor and a bank official, was present at the meeting and failed to disavow threats). But when the employer refrains from "aiding, abetting, assisting, or co-operating" with the local citizens, coercive statements and conduct by them are not unfair labor practices. *Clarke Mills*, 109 N.L.R.B. 666 (1954).

Note that the NLRB may set an election aside, without proof of agency, when community citizens have so inflamed the atmosphere with threats and appeals to passion and prejudice that employee free choice is prevented. *Universal Mfg. Corp.*, 156 N.L.R.B. 1459 (1966).

Section II. Employer Domination or Support

During the 1920s and the early 1930s, "company unions" or "employee representation plans" flourished. *See* H. PELLING, AMERICAN LABOR 146, 160 (1960). With the Railway Labor Act as a precedent, prohibiting in § 2, Fourth, a carrier from interfering with the organization of its employees or using its funds in maintaining or assisting any labor organization, the "Wagner Act" Congress in 1935 attacked the company union problem by making it an unfair labor practice for an employer to dominate or interfere with the formation or administration of any labor organization or to contribute financial or other support to it. The prohibition is now embodied in § 8(a)(2) of the NLRA.

During the early days of the NLRB, there was substantial litigation against company unions. *See, e.g., NLRB v. Pennsylvania Greyhound Lines, Inc.*, 303 U.S. 261 (1938), wherein the Supreme Court sustained the Board's unfair labor practice findings, based on evidence that company representatives were active in promoting the plan, in urging employees to join, in the preparation of the details of organization, including the bylaws, in presiding over organization meetings, and in selecting the employee representatives of the organization.

Remedies for (a) Domination or (b) Illegal Assistance or Support Not Amounting to Domination. During the Wagner Act period, the NLRB tended to order unaffiliated dominated unions disestablished, but, in the case of affiliated dominated unions, to merely order the employer to withdraw recognition until the affiliated union's majority status could be established by a secret Board election. The "Taft-Hartley" Congress amended § 10(c) of the Act to put an end to this disparate treatment. Although the NLRB believed that affiliated unions could probably eradicate the effects of illegal employer support, Congress thought this distinction was unfair to independent unions, which might also free themselves from employer control.

After examining this legislative history, the Board concluded in *Carpenter Steel Co.*, 76 N.L.R.B. 670 (1948), that it may no longer concern itself with the affiliation of a union, or lack thereof, in framing a remedy for violations of § 8(a)(2). Dominated unions will still be disestablished, with cease and desist orders being used for unlawfully supported unions. Domination is found only when the employer has interfered with the formation of the organization and has assisted and supported its administration to such an extent that it must be regarded as its own creation and subject to his control. Cases often refuse to find domination, but find the lesser offense of assistance and support. *NLRB v. Wemyss*, 212 F.2d 465 (9th Cir. 1954).

Employee Participation Programs. During World War II, in order to increase efficiency and productivity, the War Labor Board encouraged the formation of employee committees, which also handled grievances in plants without unions. The employer paid the expenses of these committees. After the War Labor Board authorization ceased, some of these committees continued. The Supreme Court held in *NLRB v. Cabot Carbon Co.*, 360 U.S. 203 (1959), that such committees were "labor organizations," within the meaning of § 8(a)(2), that the employer must disestablish, if they "deal with him concerning grievances." See § 2(5). Presentation to management of employee "views" and information, without specific recommendations as to what action is needed to accommodate those views, constitutes dealing with management under § 2(5) — if the purpose of the management-employee discussion is the correction of grievances. *NLRB v. Thompson Ramo Wooldridge, Inc.*, 305 F.2d 807 (7th Cir. 1962).

Electromation, Inc., 309 N.L.R.B. 990 (1992), *aff'd*, 35 F.3d 1148 (7th Cir. 1994), concerned a firm that established, in response to worker complaints, Action Committees comprised of employees and management representatives. The committees discussed various issues, including absenteeism, attendance bonuses, pay progression, and a no-smoking policy. Committee members could propose new policies regarding these matters, but management representatives retained final authority with respect to any recommendations. The NLRB found these committees to be "labor organizations" under § 2(5), since they acted in a representative capacity and "dealt with the employer" regarding basic terms of employment. Electromation defined the committee goals, determined how many employees would serve on each, and appointed the management participants. The Board decided that this significant involvement constituted unlawful domination. The Seventh Circuit affirmed the Board's decision. *Electromation v. NLRB*, 35 F.3d 1148, 1170–71 (7th Cir. 1994):

> [T]he principal distinction between an independent labor organization and an employer-dominated organization lies in the unfettered power of the independent organization to determine its own actions.... The Electromation action committees, which were wholly created by the employer, whose continued existence depended upon the employer, and whose functions were essentially determined by the employer, lacked the independence of action and free choice guaranteed by Section 7. This is not to suggest that ... management representatives were anti-union or had devious intentions in proposing the creation of the committees. But, even assuming they acted from good intentions, their procedure in establishing the committees, their control of the subject matters to be considered or excluded, their membership and participation on the committees, and their financial support of the committees all combined to make the committees labor organizations dominated by the employer in violation of the Act.

E. I. Du Pont de Nemours & Co., 311 N.L.R.B. 893 (1993), involved a unionized company that created six employee-management safety committees and one joint fitness committee to discuss safety and fitness issues and to submit recommendations to management officials regarding those topics. The Board decided that these committees constituted "labor organizations," because they "dealt with" Du Pont regarding important working conditions. Since Du Pont determined the number of employee participants, decided which employee volunteers would be selected if an excessive number sought the available positions, and reserved the right to abolish any committee at will, unlawful employer domination was found. On the other hand, the Board found no § 8(a)(2) violation with respect to safety conferences conducted by company officials with employees. These "brainstorming" sessions simply enhanced employee-management communication and elicited worker input. The employee participants were not "dealing with" management with regard to discussed safety matters, and company officials openly acknowledged the role of union representatives concerning these topics.

NLRB v. Peninsula Gen. Hosp. Medical Ctr., 36 F.3d 1262 (4th Cir. 1994), concerned the propriety of a nurses' committee that had been formed in 1968 as a forum for nurses to discuss practice issues. In 1989, the Vice President of Nursing, a member of the nurses' committee, encouraged the committee to communicate "major concerns" regarding weekend differential pay and the clinical ladder directly to management officials. When the committee communicated to management a list of concerns regarding wages, benefits, and working conditions, the Vice President indicated that the hospital had taken steps to deal with some. Although the Labor Board found this committee to constitute a management-dominated "labor organization," the Fourth Circuit rejected this conclusion. The court noted that while the § 2(5) "dealing with" language encompasses more than collective bargaining, it does not cover all employee committee communications to management concerning working conditions. The "dealing with" requirement is only satisfied when there is a pattern or practice over time of committee proposals and management responses. Isolated instances of committee proposals and management responses are insufficient to satisfy the "dealing with" prerequisite. When committees exist primarily to provide management with information with respect to employee concerns, they do not *ipso facto* contravene § 8(a)(2).

Crown Cork & Seal Co., 334 N.L.R.B. 699 (2001), involved an employer that had established four employee committees that made and implemented decisions on production, product quality, training, attendance, safety, maintenance, and discipline, and that possessed the authority to make decisions by consensus. The committees were part of an employee management program known as the "Socio-Tech" system, which delegates to employees substantial authority to operate the plant through their participation on committees. There was no union organizing activity at the time the committees were established or when the unfair labor practice charges were filed. Because these groups did not "deal with" management, but rather exercised authority to operate the plant comparable to that of a front-line supervisor in a traditional setting, which was rarely overruled by the plant manager, the Board found that these committees did not constitute "labor organizations" within the meaning of § 2(5).

As an alternative to employer-sponsored employee involvement programs, some supporters of the labor movement have expressed support for a mandatory worker participation statute, which would create an institutional basis for localized employee involvement committees in the absence of high union density. The idea of mandatory worker participation is based on the European system of works councils, where a number of countries have adopted legislation mandating direct worker input at the shop level. Charles Craver has proposed a statute that would require every employer with at least 15 to 25 employees to create a minimum number of worker involvement committees. These committees would have the right to review relevant financial information and would enjoy consultation rights regarding significant changes affecting employee interests. In addition, his proposal would afford rank-and-file employees the right to elect a percentage of corporate board members. Craver argues that these committees could replace traditionally adversarial labor-management relationships by allowing employees to better understand the competitive pressures facing their employers, empowering employees to oversee the enforcement of safety and health legislation and wage and hour laws, and even affording the committees the power to grant employers waivers from federal and state regulation in exchange for such representation. *See* Craver, *Mandatory Worker*

Participation Is Required in a Declining Union Environment to Provide Employees with Meaningful Industrial Democracy, 66 GEO. WASH. L. REV. 135 (1997–1998). See also Befort, *A New Voice for the Workplace: A Proposal for an American Works Councils Act*, 69 MO. L. REV. 607 (2004) (arguing that works councils provide the best option for reinvigorating employee voice at work); Estlund, *Rebuilding the Law of the Workplace in an Era of Self-Regulation*, 105 COLUM. L. REV. 319 (2005) (suggesting that outside monitors might work in tandem with employees who serve in "essential supporting roles as whistleblowers, informants, and watchdogs" in a system of monitored self-regulation); C. ESTLUND, REGOVERNING THE WORKPLACE: FROM SELF-REGULATION TO CO-REGULATION (2010).

Michael C. Harper, *The Continuing Relevance of Section 8(a)(2) to the Contemporary Workplace*
96 MICH. L. REV. 2322, 2338–39 (1998)*

... [C]ritics of section 8(a)(2) claim that, in contrast to the period during which section 8(a)(2) was enacted, employers today most often establish committees to facilitate the communication of employees' views to management not to discourage employees from choosing independent unions, or more generally to weaken employee autonomy, but rather to increase the employees' productivity by deepening their commitment to the production enterprise and by utilizing employees' insights on how production can be most efficient and consistent. My survey of the modern economy suggests that this contrast is overdrawn. Modern employers in America continue to utilize involvement programs to discourage unions and employee autonomy, often in more sophisticated and effective ways than the employers of the thirties. Moreover, the industrial relations theory that management-controlled employee-involvement programs can enhance the productivity of workers by deepening their commitment and loyalty to the goals of the firm for which they work antedates the NLRA and was rejected as a rationale for narrowing section 8(a)(2).

More important, the modern use of employee-involvement programs often represents an application of a "human relations" personnel theory for how management can obtain greater control over workers' time, which was first articulated before passage of the NLRA and which has been further developed in the last two decades to assist in the implementation of the much heralded Japanese "lean production" system. This system, far from offering American workers greater control over their work and enriched jobs, provides management with the tools to obtain minute control over every movement of front-line workers and to demand from them more intense and stressful performance. Utilization of some of these tools, however, depends upon the extraction of both front-line employee commitment and knowledge about the production process. Management-controlled employee-involvement programs, therefore, may be attractive to employers, not only to help

---

* Copyright © 1998 Michigan Law Review Association. Reprinted with permission.

avert independent unions, but also to avert other forms of employee resistance to the implementation of a system that ultimately makes work more difficult for employees. Far from offering employees half of the loaf of independent unions, management-controlled programs thus may threaten to place employees in a position worse than that of having no formal representational system....

The best preliminary evidence, some of it from outside the United States, ... indicates that the use of employee committees for skill enhancement and real worker job control is much more likely where strong, independent unions have been able to convince management to employ new technology for these purposes. Retaining a viable section 8(a)(2) to help protect the development of unions thus is likely to encourage, rather than discourage, new forms of worker empowerment. Furthermore, the narrowly framed section 8(a)(2) described above allows nonunion employers to transfer real decisionmaking authority to their employees, while only inhibiting illusory and manipulative participation programs designed to facilitate implementation of the more oppressive forms of the Japanese lean production system.

Problem

11. BankUSA decided to tackle some of its long-standing problems with the hiring and promotion of underrepresented groups in the banking industry, including women and racial and ethnic minorities. To this end, the CEO announced the creation of the BankUSA Diversity and Inclusion Council. The Council is co-chaired by the Vice President for Human Resources and the Chief Diversity Officer. The co-chairs, in turn, selected the remaining members of the Council from among employees who expressed an interest in participating and who secured approval from their supervisors. Care was taken to ensure that these additional members reflected the different business areas of the bank as well as a range of positions, including investment analysts, bank tellers, secretaries, and custodians.

The mission of the Council is to foster an environment that attracts the best talent, values diversity of life experiences and perspectives, and encourages innovation in pursuit of the company's mission. More specifically, the Council has the following responsibilities:

- Conduct a scan of the literature to identify the best diversity and inclusion practices supported by research

- Create opportunities for employees to provide feedback to executive staff about organizational climate and culture (i.e., climate assessments, anonymous satisfaction surveys, focus group sessions, etc.)

- Provide feedback and insight to executive staff on issues of culture, climate, equity, inclusion, and diversity in the workplace, including recommendations and support regarding short- and long-term strategies to meet the organization's current and future workforce needs (i.e., unbiased recruitment, hiring, and retention practices)

- Formulate recommendations for the development or modification of policies and practices that negatively impact diversity, inclusivity, and equity efforts
- Identify opportunities for the organization to engage with its broader communities to promote equity, social justice, and inclusion (i.e., community volunteer activities, corporate social responsibility initiatives, etc.)

Within the first year of its operation, the Council had made a number of recommendations to the CEO, including creating a blind system of reviewing resumes so that the hiring supervisor cannot see the "demographic characteristics" of the applicants; strengthening the bank's existing harassment policy and reporting procedures; setting aside dedicated nursing rooms for mothers; and offering "floating holidays" to accommodate the religious preferences of all employees. The CEO, in consultation with the co-chairs of the Council, has accepted and moved forward on a number of these recommendations, though several, including the nursing rooms, were rejected because they were considered too costly.

Has BankUSA engaged in any unfair labor practices? If so, how can BankUSA rework its approach to improving workplace diversity in a way that doesn't run afoul of the NLRA?

International Ladies' Garment Workers' Union v. NLRB [Bernhard-Altmann Texas Corp.]

Supreme Court of the United States
366 U.S. 731, 81 S. Ct. 1603, 6 L. Ed. 2d 762 (1961)

Mr. Justice Clark delivered the opinion of the Court.

We are asked to decide in this case whether it was an unfair labor practice for both an employer and a union to enter into an agreement under which the employer recognized the union as exclusive bargaining representative of certain of his employees, although in fact only a minority of those employees had authorized the union to represent their interests. The Board found that by extending such recognition, even though done in the good-faith belief that the union had the consent of a majority of employees in the appropriate bargaining unit, the employer interfered with the organizational rights of his employees in violation of § 8(a)(1) of the National Labor Relations Act and that such recognition also constituted unlawful support to a labor organization in violation of § 8(a)(2). In addition, the Board found that the union violated § 8(b)(1)(A) by its acceptance of exclusive bargaining authority at a time when in fact it did not have the support of a majority of the employees, and this in spite of its bona fide belief that it did. Accordingly, the Board ordered the unfair labor practices discontinued and directed the holding of a representation election. The Court of Appeals, by a divided vote, granted enforcement, 280 F.2d 616, 108 U.S. App. D.C. 68. We granted certiorari. 364 U.S. 811. We agree with the Board and the Court of Appeals that such extension and acceptance of recognition constitute unfair labor practices, and that the remedy provided was appropriate.

In October 1956 the petitioner union initiated an organizational campaign at Bernhard-Altmann Texas Corporation's knitwear manufacturing plant in San Antonio, Texas. No other labor organization was similarly engaged at that time. During the course of that campaign, on July 29, 1957, certain of the company's Topping Department employees went on strike in protest against a wage reduction. That dispute was in no way related to the union campaign, however, and the organizational efforts were continued during the strike. Some of the striking employees had signed authorization cards solicited by the union during its drive, and, while the strike was in progress, the union entered upon a course of negotiations with the employer. As a result of those negotiations, held in New York City where the home offices of both were located, on August 30, 1957, the employer and union signed a "memorandum of understanding." In that memorandum the company recognized the union as exclusive bargaining representative of "all production and shipping employees." The union representative asserted that the union's comparison of the employee authorization cards in its possession with the number of eligible employees representatives of the company furnished it indicated that the union had in fact secured such cards from a majority of employees in the unit. Neither employer nor union made any effort at that time to check the cards in the union's possession against the employee roll, or otherwise, to ascertain with any degree of certainty that the union's assertion, later found by the Board to be erroneous, was founded on fact rather than upon good-faith assumption. The agreement, containing no union security provisions, called for the ending of the strike and for certain improved wages and conditions of employment. It also provided that a "formal agreement containing these terms" would "be promptly drafted . . . and signed by both parties within the next two weeks."

Thereafter, on October 10, 1957, a formal collective bargaining agreement, embodying the terms of the August 30 memorandum, was signed by the parties. The bargaining unit description set out in the formal contract, although more specific, conformed to that contained in the prior memorandum. It is not disputed that as of execution of the formal contract the union in fact represented a clear majority of employees in the appropriate unit. In upholding the complaints filed against the employer and union by the General Counsel, the Board decided that the employer's good-faith belief that the union in fact represented a majority of employees in the unit on the critical date of the memorandum of understanding was not a defense, "particularly where, as here, the Company made no effort to check the authorization cards against its payroll records." 122 N.L.R.B. 1289, 1292. Noting that the union was "actively seeking recognition at the time such recognition was granted," and that "the Union was [not] the passive recipient of an unsolicited gift bestowed by the Company," the Board found that the union's execution of the August 30 agreement was a "direct deprivation" of the nonconsenting majority employees' organizational and bargaining rights. At pp. 1292, 1293, note 9. Accordingly, the Board ordered the employer to withhold all recognition from the union and to cease giving effect to agreements entered into with the union; the union was ordered to cease acting as bargaining representative of any of the employees until such time as a Board-conducted election demonstrated its majority status, and to refrain from seeking to enforce the agreements previously entered. . . .

At the outset, we reject as without relevance to our decision the fact that, as of the execution date of the formal agreement on October 10, petitioner represented a majority of the employees. As the Court of Appeals indicated, the recognition of the minority union on August 30, 1957, was "a *fait accompli* depriving the majority of the employees of their guaranteed right to choose their own representative." 280 F.2d, at 621. It is, therefore, of no consequence that petitioner may have acquired by October 10 the necessary majority if, during the interim, it was acting unlawfully. Indeed, such acquisition of majority status itself might indicate that the recognition secured by the August 30 agreement afforded petitioner a deceptive cloak of authority with which to persuasively elicit additional employee support.

Nor does this case directly involve a strike. The strike which occurred was in protest against a wage reduction and had nothing to do with petitioner's quest for recognition. Likewise, no question of picketing is presented. Lastly, the violation which the Board found was the grant by the employer of exclusive representation status to a minority union, as distinguished from an employer's bargaining with a minority union for its members only. Therefore, the exclusive representation provision is the vice in the agreement, and discussion of "collective bargaining," as distinguished from "exclusive recognition," is pointless. Moreover, the insistence that we hold the agreement valid and enforceable as to those employees who consented to it must be rejected. On the facts shown, the agreement must fail in its entirety. It was obtained under the erroneous claim of majority representation. Perhaps the employer would not have entered into it if he had known the facts. Quite apart from other conceivable situations, the unlawful genesis of this agreement precludes its partial validity.

In their selection of a bargaining representative, § 9(a) of the Wagner Act guarantees employees freedom of choice and majority rule. *J. I. Case Co. v. NLRB*, 321 U.S. 332, 339 (1944). In short, as we said in *Brooks v. NLRB*, 348 U.S. 96, 103 (1954), the Act placed "a nonconsenting minority under the bargaining responsibility of an agency selected by a majority of the workers." Here, however, the reverse has been shown to be the case. Bernhard-Altmann granted exclusive bargaining status to an agency selected by a minority of its employees, thereby impressing that agent upon the nonconsenting majority. There could be no clearer abridgement of § 7 of the Act, assuring employees the right "to bargain collectively through representatives of their own choosing" or "to refrain from" such activity. It follows, without need of further demonstration, that the employer activity found present here violated § 8(a)(1) of the Act which prohibits employer interference with, and restraint of, employee exercise of § 7 rights. Section 8(a)(2) of the Act makes it an unfair labor practice for an employer to "contribute . . . support" to a labor organization. The law has long been settled that a grant of exclusive recognition to a minority union constitutes unlawful support in violation of that section, because the union so favored is given "a marked advantage over any other in securing the adherence of employees,"

NLRB v. Pennsylvania Greyhound Lines, 303 U.S. 261, 267 (1938). In the Taft-Hartley Law, Congress added § 8(b)(1)(A) to the Wagner Act, prohibiting, as the Court of Appeals held, "unions from invading the rights of employees under § 7 in a fashion comparable to the activities of employers prohibited under § 8(a)(1)." 280 F.2d at 620. It was the intent of Congress to impose upon unions the same restrictions which the Wagner Act imposed on employers with respect to violations of employee rights.

The petitioner, while taking no issue with the fact of its minority status on the critical date, maintains that both Bernhard-Altmann's and its own good-faith beliefs in petitioner's majority status are a complete defense. To countenance such an excuse would place in permissibly careless employer and union hands the power to completely frustrate employee realization of the premise of the Act—that its prohibitions will go far to assure freedom of choice and majority rule in employee selection of representatives. We find nothing in the statutory language prescribing *scienter* as an element of the unfair labor practices here involved. The act made unlawful by § 8(a)(2) is employer support of a minority union. Here that support is an accomplished fact. More need not be shown, for, even if mistakenly, the employees' rights have been invaded. It follows that prohibited conduct cannot be excused by a showing of good faith.

This conclusion, while giving the employee only the protection assured him by the Act, places no particular hardship on the employer or the union. It merely requires that recognition be withheld until the Board-conducted election results in majority selection of a representative. The Board's order here, as we might infer from the employer's failure to resist its enforcement, would apparently result in similarly slight hardship upon it. We do not share petitioner's apprehension that holding such conduct unlawful will somehow induce a breakdown, or seriously impede the progress of collective bargaining. If an employer takes reasonable steps to verify union claims, themselves advanced only after careful estimate—precisely what Bernhard-Altmann and petitioner failed to do here—he can readily ascertain their validity and obviate a Board election. We fail to see any onerous burden involved in requiring responsible negotiators to be careful, by cross-checking, for example, well-analyzed employer records with union listings or authorization cards. Individual and collective employee rights may not be trampled upon merely because it is inconvenient to avoid doing so. Moreover, no penalty is attached to the violation. Assuming that an employer in good faith accepts or rejects a union claim of majority status, the validity of his decision may be tested in an unfair labor practice proceeding. If he is found to have erred in extending or withholding recognition, he is subject only to a remedial order requiring him to conform his conduct to the norms set out in the Act, as was the case here. No further penalty results. We believe the Board's remedial order is the proper one in such cases. *NLRB v. District 50, U.M.W.*, 355 U.S. 453 (1958).

Affirmed.

[**Mr. Justice Douglas** and **Mr. Justice Black** dissented in part.]

Notes

1. *Conditional Agreements* — Suppose the employer negotiates with a minority union an agreement purporting to bind all employees that is conditioned upon the union's attainment of majority status before the contract becomes effective. Such an agreement was found unlawful in *Majestic Weaving Co., Inc. of New York*, 147 N.L.R.B. 859 (1964). Although the Second Circuit denied enforcement on a procedural ground, Judge Friendly noted "that 'the premature grant of exclusive bargaining status to a union,' even if conditioned on attainment of a majority before execution of a contract, is similar to formal recognition 'with respect to the deleterious effect upon employee rights.'" *NLRB v. Majestic Weaving Co.*, 355 F.2d 854, 859–61 (2d Cir. 1966).

Compare the *Majestic Weaving Co.* decision with *Montague v. NLRB*, 698 F.3d 307 (6th Cir. 2012), in which the court enforced the Board's ruling in *Dana Corp.*, 356 N.L.R.B. 256 (2010), finding no violation of §8(a)(2) where the employer and organizing union executed a letter of agreement setting forth general principles to be included in labor contracts if the union were to win a representation election or obtain majority status based upon a card count evaluated by a neutral third party. The Board reasoned that the letter was conditioned upon the union winning the election and merely set forth a framework that would require substantial postelection negotiations before it could become a formal bargaining agreement. Thus, it did not amount to unlawful support or assistance of the union.

Mulhall v. UNITE/HERE Local 355, 667 F.3d 1211 (11th Cir. 2012), involved an agreement between UNITE/HERE and a dog track owner under which the employer promised to: (1) provide union representatives with access to nonpublic premises to engage in organizing activities during employee nonwork time; (2) provide union representatives with the names, classifications, and addresses of employees; and (3) remain neutral during the organizing campaign. In return for these promises, the union agreed to lend financial support for a ballot initiative regarding casino gaming, for which it spent more than $100,000. The union also agreed that it would refrain from picketing, boycotting, or striking the employer. An employee brought a lawsuit under §302 of the LMRA, which makes it unlawful for an employer to pay, lend, or deliver money or any other thing of value to a labor organization. In *Adcock v. Freightliner LLC*, 550 F.3d 369 (4th Cir. 2008), and *Hotel Emples. & Rest. Emples. Union, Local 57 v. Sage Hospitality Res., LLC*, 390 F.3d 206 (3d Cir. 2004), the courts had found such neutrality agreements not to constitute a "thing of value" under §302. Nonetheless, the *Mulhall* court held that such neutrality agreements may constitute a "thing of value" and contravene that provision. Although the Supreme Court granted a petition for certiorari to resolve the split among circuit courts, 570 U.S. 915 (2013), it subsequently found that the writ had been improvidently granted and dismissed the appeal. 571 U.S. 83 (2013).

2. *Adding Employees to Existing Bargaining Units* — When an employer and a labor organization agree to accrete to an existing bargaining unit a group of employees

who have historically remained unorganized, they will be found in violation of § 8(a)(2) in the absence of evidence demonstrating that a majority of the nonunion personnel currently desire representation. *Teamsters Nat'l United Parcel Serv. Negotiating Comm. v. NLRB*, 17 F.3d 1518 (D.C. Cir. 1994), *cert. denied*, 513 U.S. 1076 (1995).

Some unionized retail establishments with stores at different locations sign "after acquired" store clauses waiving their right to demand secret ballot Labor Board representation elections at new locations and agreeing to extend recognition to the representative labor organization at new stores once the union demonstrates that a majority of employees at that location have signed authorization cards. In *Shaw's Supermarkets*, 343 N.L.R.B. 963 (2004), the Labor Board remanded a representation case to the regional director for consideration of whether policy considerations outweigh the right of employers to waive the right of employees to have secret ballot elections before union recognition is extended to new facilities based solely upon authorization cards. Should employers be precluded from granting recognition to labor organizations that claim to have authorization cards signed by a majority of employees in an appropriate bargaining unit? Do employees in such a unit who might question the validity of those cards have the right to demand a secret ballot Labor Board election even if the employer has agreed to forgo that procedure? *See generally* Brudney, *Neutrality Agreements and Card Check Recognition: Prospects for Changing Paradigms*, 90 Iowa L. Rev. 819 (2005).

More recently, the Trump Board's General Counsel signaled that such neutrality agreements might violate § 8(a)(2). *See* Robb, *Guidance Memorandum on Employer Assistance in Union Organizing, Memorandum* GC 20-13, Sept. 4, 2020 (acknowledging that pre-recognition neutrality agreements are generally lawful, but opining that employers that agree to provide more than ministerial aid to unions during organizing campaigns, including allowing union organizers access to private employer property before or after work or during break times to facilitate solicitation of employees to sign union authorization cards, allowing employees to conduct union solicitation during working time, or providing contact information for employees to the union, violate § 8(a)(2)).

3. *Section 8(f) Pre-Hire Agreements*—In the construction industry, an employer does not violate § 8(a)(2) by making a "pre-hire" agreement with an unassisted union. Under § 8(f), such agreements are not illegal simply because "the majority status of such labor organization has not been established under the provisions of § 9 of this Act prior to the making of such agreement." If the employer hires on a job-by-job basis, its duty to honor the contract is contingent on the union's attaining majority support at the various construction sites. There is a rebuttable presumption of majority support when a union security agreement results in majority union membership on a project to which a § 8(f) pre-hire agreement applies. *See NLRB v. Pacific Erectors, Inc.*, 718 F.2d 1459 (9th Cir. 1983); *see also Colorado Fire Sprinkler, Inc. v. NLRB*, 891 F.3d 1031 (D.C. Cir. 2018) (requiring clear evidence that a majority of current employees support such a relationship before recognition is granted).

Section III. Employer Discrimination

The classic unfair labor practice is an employer's discharge of an employee for supporting a union or engaging in other §7 protected activity. More broadly, §8(a)(3) prohibits employers from committing acts of discrimination that encourage or discourage union membership. At the same time, 8(a)(1) requires employers to refrain from engaging in any activity that restrains or coerces employees in their right to engage in other forms of concerted activity. We begin this section with situations involving discrimination that discourages union membership.

A. Discrimination to Discourage Union Activity

Edward G. Budd Mfg. Co. v. NLRB
United States Court of Appeals for the Third Circuit
138 F.2d 86 (1943)

BIGGS, Circuit Judge.

On charges filed by International Union, United Automobile, Aircraft and Agricultural Workers of America, an affiliate of the Congress of Industrial Organizations, with the National Labor Relations Board, a complaint issued dated November 26, 1941, alleging that the petitioner was engaging in unfair labor practices within the meaning of Section 8(1), (2), (3) of the National Labor Relations Act.... The complaint, as subsequently amended, alleges that the petitioner, in September, 1933, created and foisted a labor organization, known as the Budd Employee Representation Association, upon its employees and thereafter contributed financial support to the Association and dominated its activities. The amended complaint also alleges that in July, 1941, the petitioner discharged an employee, Walter Weigand, because of his activities on behalf of the union, and in October of that year refused to reinstate another employee, Milton Davis, for similar reasons. The petitioner denies these charges as does the Association which was permitted to intervene. After extensive hearings before a trial examiner the Board on June 10, 1942 issued its decision and order, requiring the disestablishment of the Association and the reinstatement of Weigand and Davis.

Until the creation of the Association in 1933 no labor organization had existed in the petitioner's Philadelphia plant. Upon the passage of the National Industrial Recovery Act of June 16, 1933, 48 Stat. 195, some of the petitioner's employees desired to form a labor organization. Alminde, who worked in the petitioner's shipping department, tried to get a charter from the American Federation of Labor for a union to be composed of shipping department employees. This was refused. Thereupon he and some other members of the shipping department decided to form a labor organization. To facilitate this purpose Alminde went to Sullivan who was an assistant works-manager and requested a meeting with Harder, the works-manager. On August 24, 1933, Sullivan, Harder, McIlvain, the chief personnel officer, and Mahan, another assistant works-manager, met with Alminde and his committee from the petitioner's shipping department. At Alminde's request Sullivan produced a plan for employees representation which with some substantial modifications remains in effect today.... A notice of the proposal was posted in the plant on September 1, 1933. On September 5th the management caused to be placed in the time card rack of each employee the following: a pamphlet entitled "Proposed Plan of Employee Representation", a folder entitled "Preliminary Announcement of the Establishment of a Budd Employee Representation Association" signed by President Edward G. Budd, and a ballot to be used for nominating employee representatives. On September 7th the election was held and nineteen employee representatives were elected. The expenses of this election were paid by the petitioner and it was held on company time and on company property.

. . . .

Meetings of the representatives were held from time to time; the committees which had been appointed functioned actively. The management adopted a most cooperative attitude toward the Association. This was to be expected. What had happened was that the management had found a group of its own employees who desired to create a labor organization and the company had sponsored and created the Association at their request. The petitioner's attitude toward its employees seems to have been one of friendly interest. Nevertheless, we entertain no doubt that the plan and the Association were in fact sponsored, largely created and supported by the petitioner. The Association could not have continued to exist had the Budd Company withdrawn its support.

. . . .

Another indication of the dependent nature of the Association should be referred to. We think it is symptomatic. The petitioner treated the employee representatives with extraordinary leniency. The testimony shows to what very great lengths the employer went in its parental treatment of the Association and its officers. The petitioner permitted the employee representatives to conduct themselves about as they wished. They left the plant at will whether on personal business or on the business of the Association. Some of them did very little or no work but they received full pay. It is clear that some of them, Walter Weigand for example, were not disciplined because they were representatives. We can scarcely believe that the petitioner would have displayed such an attitude toward officers of an undominated "adversary" labor organization.

In our opinion the decision of the Board to the effect that the Association was and is subject to the petitioner's domination and control is amply supported by the evidence.

As to the decision of the Board requiring the reinstatement of Milton T. Davis, we find there is sufficient evidence to support the conclusion that this employee was discriminated against because of his connection with the CIO affiliate which filed the charge with the Board.

The case of Walter Weigand is extraordinary. If ever a workman deserved summary discharge it was he. He was under the influence of liquor while on duty. He came to work when he chose and he left the plant and his shift as he pleased. In fact, a foreman on one occasion was agreeably surprised to find Weigand at work and commented upon it. Weigand amiably stated that he was enjoying it. He brought a woman (apparently generally known as the "Duchess") to the rear of the plant yard and introduced some of the employees to her. He took another employee to visit her and when this man got too drunk to be able to go home, punched his time-card for him and put him on the table in the representatives' meeting room in the plant in order to sleep off his intoxication. Weigand's immediate superiors demanded again and again that he be discharged, but each time higher officials intervened on Weigand's behalf because as was naively stated he was "a representative." In return for not working at the job for which he was hired, the petitioner gave him full pay and on five separate occasions raised his wages. One of these raises was general; that is to say, Weigand profited by a general wage increase throughout the plant, but the other four raises were given Weigand at times when other employees in the plant did not receive wage increases.

The petitioner contends that Weigand was discharged because of cumulative grievances against him. But about the time of the discharge it was suspected by some of the representatives that Weigand had joined the complaining CIO union. One of the representatives taxed him with this fact and Weigand offered to bet a hundred dollars that it could not be proved. On July 22, 1941 Weigand did disclose his union membership to the vice-chairman (Rattigan) of the Association and to another representative (Mullen) and apparently tried to persuade them to support the union. Weigand asserts that the next day he with Rattigan and Mullen, were seen talking to CIO organizer Reichwein on a street corner. The following day, according to Weigand's testimony, Mullen came to Weigand at the plant and stated that Weigand, Rattigan and himself had been seen talking to Reichwein and that he, Mullen, had just had an interview with Personnel Director McIlvain and Plant Manager Mahan. According to Weigand, Mullen said to him, "Maybe you didn't get me in a jam." And, "We were seen down there." The following day Weigand was discharged.

As this court stated in *National Labor Relations Board v. Condenser Corp.*, *supra*, 3 Cir., 128 F.2d at page 75, an employer may discharge an employee for a good reason, a poor reason or no reason at all so long as the provisions of the National Labor Relations Act are not violated. It is, of course, a violation to discharge an employee because he has engaged in activities on behalf of a union. Conversely an employer may retain an employee for a good reason, a bad reason or no reason at all and the reason is not a concern of the Board. But it is certainly too great a strain on our credulity to assert, as does the petitioner, that Weigand was discharged for an accumulation of offenses. We think that he was discharged because his work on behalf of the CIO had become known to the plant manager. That ended his sinecure at the

Budd plant. The Board found that he was discharged because of his activities on behalf of the union. The record shows that the Board's finding was based on sufficient evidence.

The order of the Board will be enforced.

Notes

1. *Burden of Proof and the Effect of "For Cause" Provision of the Taft-Hartley Act, § 10(c)* — As in *Edward G. Budd Mfg. Co.*, cases brought under § 8(a)(3) usually turn on a central question: what was the employer's real reason for the discharge? Before the Board may find a violation of the act, it must find, under § 10(c), that a preponderance of the testimony taken shows that the employer committed an unfair labor practice by discharging the employee. And in order for the Board to award reinstatement or back pay as a remedy, the General Counsel must establish that the individual was not discharged for cause. NLRB General Counsel Robert N. Denham explained the impact of the "for cause" provision in a November 3, 1947 address before the St. Louis Bar Ass'n (21 L.R.R.M. 55):

> As I see it, "good cause," as the basis of a discharge, must be just as good under the provisions of this Act as it ever has been. . . . If a man is entitled to be discharged and the offenses he has committed are not offenses that customarily have been condoned in other employees, that constitutes good cause. On the other hand, where the offenses are relatively minor and are of a character that have been more or less common within the plant and have been passed over without disciplinary action, but the employee involved is one who has been an active union leader in an atmosphere of some degree of antagonism on the part of the employer, everyone is entitled to look at such a discharge with much questioning. We still are not only entitled, but are obligated to, weigh the bona fides of the so-called "good cause" and to reject the "good cause" theory if it has all the earmarks of nothing but a subterfuge.

Since the General Counsel is the moving party, he or she has the burden of proving a violation of the Act. *Miller Electric Mfg. Co. v. NLRB*, 265 F.2d 225 (7th Cir. 1959).

2. *Proof Structures*

   a. *Pretext Plus Cases* — Suppose the employer testifies that its real reason for discharging an employee was an infraction of company rules. What proof would be required to demonstrate that its real reason was to discourage union activity? In *Union-Tribune Publishing Co. v. NLRB*, 1 F.3d 486 (7th Cir. 1993), the court indicated that the mere finding that the reasons offered by a company to justify its discharge of a union official were pretextual does not *ipso facto* establish a § 8(a)(3) violation. Some additional evidence of anti-union animus must usually be provided. *See also NLRB v. Fluor Daniel, Inc.*, 102 F.3d 818 (6th Cir. 1996) (despite employer's anti-union animus in refusing to hire applicant, no § 8(a)(3) violation unless there was actually job vacancy for which applicant was qualified). *See generally* White,

Modern Discrimination Theory and the National Labor Relations Act, 39 Wm. & Mary L. Rev. 99 (1997).

b. *Mixed Motive Cases*—*NLRB v. Transportation Mgt. Corp.*, 462 U.S. 393 (1983), involved a bus driver, Santillo, who was fired by his employer, Transportation Management Corp., shortly after he distributed union authorization cards. He was told that he was discharged for leaving his keys in the bus and for taking unauthorized breaks. Santillo filed a charge with the NLRB, alleging that he was discharged because of his union activities. The NLRB applied the test used in "dual motive" cases that was formulated in *Wright Line, A Div. of Wright Line, Inc.*, 251 N.L.R.B. 1083 (1980). Under *Wright Line*, once the General Counsel proves by a preponderance of the evidence that the employer's action was based in whole or in part on anti-union animus, the employer will be found in violation—unless it can prove as an affirmative defense that the adverse action would have been taken even if the employee had not been involved in protected activities. The NLRB found that Transportation Management Corp. had failed to establish that Santillo's discharge would have taken place in the absence of the driver's protected activities.

The question before the Supreme Court was whether the burden placed on the employer under the *Wright Line* test is consistent with §8(a)(1) and (3), as well as with §10(c) of the NLRA, which provides that the Board must prove an unlawful labor practice by a "preponderance of the evidence." The Court held the *Wright Line* allocation was proper under the Act. The Court reasoned that the Board has consistently held that a violation of the Act consists of an adverse action based in whole or in part on anti-union animus. This requires that the employee's protected conduct have been a substantial or motivating factor in the adverse decision. The General Counsel is required by §10(c) to prove this by a preponderance of the evidence. The Court stated that the Board's construction of the NLRA permits an employer to avoid being held in violation of the statute by showing that it would have taken the same action regardless of the employee's protected conduct. This does not change or add to the elements the General Counsel must prove, but merely extends to the employer what the Board considers to be an affirmative defense. While the Board's construction is not mandated by the Act, the Court concluded, it is permissible and entitled to deference.

In *Bally's Park Place, Inc. v. NLRB*, 646 F.3d 929 (D.C. Cir. 2011), the court enforced the Board's ruling that an employer failed to carry its burden under *Wright Line* and thus violated §§ 8(a)(1) and 8(a)(3). The Board's General Counsel produced evidence of a discriminatory motive where the employer discharged a casino table dealer who was an outspoken union supporter for violating a "zero tolerance policy" against Family and Medical Leave Act abuse when he used 20 minutes of FMLA leave to attend a union rally. The employer had previously prohibited the dealer from discussing unionization on the casino floor, threatened to terminate him, and implicitly promised to remedy other dealers' grievances if they withdrew support from the union. Moreover, the disciplinary provisions in the casino's employee handbook were inconsistent with a zero tolerance policy, suggesting a progressive disciplinary process where less severe infractions were not punished by discharge. *See also The Fund for the Public Interest*, 360 N.L.R.B. 877 (2014) (employer that unlawfully discharged employee for engaging in protected union activity could not avoid reinstatement obligation simply because individual had told local newspaper reporter after his termination that his prior employer was operating a "Ponzi scheme," since this action would not render him unfit to return to his former position).

Classic dual motive cases involve employees with deteriorating work performance who support union organizing drives. Even if their employers consider their protected activities when deciding to terminate them, no § 8(a)(3) violations will be found if their employers can demonstrate that they would have been discharged anyway because of their poor performance. *See NLRB v. Lampi LLC*, 240 F.3d 931 (11th Cir. 2001); *Rockwell Automation/Dodge*, 330 N.L.R.B. 547 (2000).

3. *The Role of Employer Knowledge* — Suppose the employer denies that it knew that the discharged employee had been engaging in union activities. What kind of proof is needed to overcome this statement? *See* NLRB, Sixteenth Annual Report 163 (1952); *Long Island Airport Limousine Service Corp.*, 191 N.L.R.B. 94 (1971), *enforced*, 468 F.2d 292 (2d Cir. 1972).

In order to establish a violation of § 8(a)(3) under *Wright Line* for discharging an individual active in the union, the Board must prove that the employer representative responsible for the decision to discharge was aware of the employee's union activity. Thus, even where the discharged employees served on the union organizing committee and several supervisors knew they were active in the union effort, no violation was established where there existed a legitimate reason for discharge and the Human Resources director who made the decision was unaware of the employees' union activity. *Gestamp S.C., LLC v. NLRB*, 769 F.3d 254 (4th Cir. 2014).

In *Parexel International LLC*, 356 N.L.R.B. 516 (2011), the Labor Board held that an employer violated § 8(a)(1) when it discharged an employee it thought was going to discuss employment issues with her coworkers as a "pre-emptive strike" to prevent her from engaging in the anticipated protected concerted activity, even though she had not yet engaged in any such activity. *See also K-Air Corp.*, 360 N.L.R.B. 143 (2014) (employer violated § 8(a)(3) when it discharged recently hired employee after learning of union activity person had engaged in prior to his employment with this firm).

4. *Employer Anti-Union Statements as Evidence* — In the light of § 8(c), may an anti-union statement of an employer be used as evidence that its reason for discharging an employee was to discourage union activity? In this connection, note the following exchange in Congress in the debate on the act (93 Cong. Rec. 6604 (1947)):

> *Senator Pepper.* . . . If an employer were to say on Monday, 'I hate labor unions, and I think they are a menace to this country,' and if he fired a man on Thursday and the question was whether that man was fired for cause or fired because he was agitating for a union in the plant, would the statement made on Monday . . . be admissible in evidence as bearing on the question of the reason for the discharge?

Senator Taft. It would depend upon the facts. Under the facts generally stated by the Senator, I think that statement would not be evidence of any threat. There would have to be some other circumstances to tie in with the act of the employer. If the act of discharging is illegal and an unfair labor practice, consideration of such a statement would be proper. But it would not be proper to consider as evidence in such a case a speech which in itself contained no threat express or implied.

See also Pittsburgh S.S. Co. v. NLRB, 180 F.2d 731, 735 (6th Cir. 1950), *aff'd*, 340 U.S. 498 (1951), *and Indiana Metal Products Corp. v. NLRB*, 202 F.2d 613 (7th Cir. 1953), in which it was held that unless employer anti-union statements contained threats of reprisal or promises of benefit, they were not admissible as evidence of wrongful motivation regarding a discharge. *See generally* White, *The Statutory and Constitutional Limits of Using Protected Speech as Evidence of Unlawful Motive Under the National Labor Relations Act*, 53 Ohio St. L.J. 1 (1992).

5. *What Constitutes an Act of Discrimination?* — Various employment decisions may contravene § 8(a)(3) when motivated by anti-union considerations. *See, e.g., Yellow Enter. Sys.*, 342 N.L.R.B. 804 (2004) (employer constructively discharged union supporter when assigned day shift worker to night shift knowing that it would cause him to resign due to child care responsibilities); *NLRB v. CWI of Maryland*, 127 F.3d 319 (4th Cir. 1997) (relocation of reporting site of union supporter to new location 100 miles away constituted discriminatory constructive discharge); *Matson Terminals v. NLRB*, 114 F.3d 300 (D.C. Cir. 1997) (*promotion* of bargaining unit members into supervisory positions violated Act when purpose was to deny them organizing rights).

6. *Union Salts* — In *NLRB v. Town & Country Elec.*, 516 U.S. 85 (1995), the Supreme Court unanimously held that full-time, paid union organizers constitute "employees" under the NLRA and that an employer violates § 8(a)(3) if it refuses to hire such individuals or terminates them once it learns of their union relationship. The Court cited § 226 of the *Restatement (Second) of Agency* to the effect that a "person may be the servant of two masters . . . at one time as to one act, if the service to one does not involve abandonment of the service to the other." The Court countered the employer's argument that the union was trying to "salt" nonunion companies with paid union organizers who might harm the firms by observing that "nothing in this record suggests that such acts of disloyalty were present, in kind or degree, to the point where the company might lose control over the worker's normal workplace tasks."

The Labor Board has not been receptive to employer strategies for combating union "salting" campaigns. *See, e.g., Tualatin Elec.*, 319 N.L.R.B. 1237 (1995) (employer unlawfully prohibited employees from receiving compensation from any source other than the employer itself); *Masiongale Electrical-Mechanical v. NLRB*, 323 F.3d 546 (7th Cir. 2003) (employer reliance on policy of not hiring applicants with history of earning higher wages pretext for refusal to hire union-affiliated applicants). *Compare Architectural Glass & Metal Co. v. NLRB*, 107 F.3d 426 (6th Cir. 1997) (employer did not have to hire full-time, paid union organizer when it had a nondiscriminatory general rule against dual full-time employment); *Int'l Union of Operating Eng'rs, Local 150 v. NLRB*, 325 F.3d 818 (7th Cir. 2003) (employer policy of giving hiring preference to former employees and referrals from trusted sources over walk-in applicants valid justification for refusing to hire union "salts"). In *H.B. Zachry Co.*, 319 N.L.R.B. 967 (1995), the Board held that an employer with a policy of disqualifying job applications that contained "nonresponsive information" unlawfully refused to consider applicants who wrote on their applications that they were "volunteer union organizers." Since the Eleventh Circuit found that the H.B. Zachry Company had applied its policy in a nondiscriminatory manner, it denied enforcement of the Board's decision. *International Bhd. of Boilermakers v. NLRB*, 127 F.3d 1300 (11th Cir. 1997).

If paid union organizers lie on employment applications about their "salt" status in order to obtain positions with firms being organized, may the employers defend § 8(a)(3) charges by claiming they would have discharged these workers because of their application falsifications? In *Hartman Bros. Heating & Air Conditioning, Inc. v. NLRB*, 280 F.3d 1110 (7th Cir. 2002), the court held no on the ground that such union status misrepresentations were not relevant to legitimate job qualifications.

In *FES (a Division of Thermo Power)*, 331 N.L.R.B. 9 (2000), *enforced*, 301 F.3d 83 (3d Cir. 2002), the Board held that once the General Counsel establishes that an employer *refused to consider* union salts for positions the firm was thinking of filling because of their union membership, § 8(a)(3) violations will be found, even if the company actually hires no applicants. If the General Counsel seeks an affirmative instatement order and back pay, however, the Board will require additional proof that openings actually existed for the alleged discriminatees. *See also NLRB v. Ferguson Elec. Co.*, 242 F.3d 426 (2d Cir. 2001) (union organizer discriminatorily denied position entitled to full back pay with no deduction for amounts received during same period from union, since union pay constituted secondary earnings, not interim earnings that would normally be deducted from back pay owed). *See generally* Borger, *Should Non-Genuine Applicants Be Treated as Employees Under the NLRA?*, 77 U. Cin. L. Rev. 1247 (2009); Howlett, *"Salt" in the Wound? Making a Case and Formulating a Remedy When an Employer Refuses to Hire Union Organizers*, 81 Wash. U. L.Q. 201 (2003).

When it appears that union salts applied for positions for the purpose of generating discriminatory employer refusals to hire, back pay will only be ordered in favor of such discriminatees if their union can show that they would have accepted the positions had they been offered. *See Starcon Int'l, Inc. v. NLRB*, 450 F.3d 276 (7th Cir. 2006). In *Toering Elec. Co.*, 351 N.L.R.B. 225 (2007), *reconsideration denied*, 352 N.L.R.B. 814 (2008), a closely divided Labor Board went one step further and held that § 8(a)(3) only protects job applicants who have a "genuine interest" in employment. As a result, if union salts have no desire to obtain employment but merely apply with the hope they will be rejected and be able to file unfair labor practice charges, they will no longer be entitled to statutory protection.

The traditional NLRB remedy for discriminatory refusals to hire has included back pay from the hiring denial until the employer offer of employment. In *Oil Capitol Sheet Metal, Inc.*, 349 N.L.R.B. 1348 (2007), however, a closely divided Board decided that application of this remedial presumption in favor of discriminatee salts was inconsistent with the reality of union salting. The three-member Board majority indicated that salts generally remain on their new jobs only until they succeed in their organizational efforts or realize that their organizing efforts will be unsuccessful. If salts seek back pay for a longer period, the burden will be on their labor organization to demonstrate that they planned to remain in their new positions beyond the period of their organizing campaign.

For a good discussion of how labor organizations recruit individuals to serve as union "salts" during organizing campaigns, see J.D. Walsh, Playing Against the House: The Dramatic World of an Undercover Union Organizer (2016).

7. *Scope of Judicial Review* — Prior to the Taft-Hartley Act, the findings of fact of the Board (on such issues as the employer's real reason for a discharge) were conclusive if supported "by evidence," and this was construed by the courts to mean "substantial evidence." The Taft-Hartley Act substituted the language "substantial evidence on the record considered as a whole."

The authoritative case in which the Supreme Court dealt with the scope of judicial review under the National Labor Relations Act was *Universal Camera Corp. v. NLRB*, 340 U.S. 474 (1951). On the point of immediate interest here, Justice Frankfurter said:

> To be sure, the requirement for canvassing "the whole record" in order to ascertain substantiality does not furnish a calculus of value by which a reviewing court can assess the evidence. Nor was it intended to negative the function of the Labor Board as one of those agencies presumably equipped or informed by experience to deal with a specialized field of knowledge, whose findings within that field carry the authority of an expertness which courts do not possess and therefore must respect. Nor does it mean that even as to matters not requiring expertise a court may displace the Board's choice between two fairly conflicting views, even though the court would justifiably have made a different choice had the matter been before it *de novo*. Congress has merely made it clear that a reviewing court is not barred from setting aside a Board decision when it cannot conscientiously find that the evidence supporting that decision is substantial, when viewed in the light of evidence that the record in its entirety furnishes, including the body of evidence opposed to the Board's view.

Justice Frankfurter also addressed the situation in which the NLRB disagrees with the factual findings of the Administrative Law Judge (Trial Examiner):

> The "substantial evidence" standard is not modified in any way when the Board and its examiner disagree. We intend only to recognize that evidence

supporting a conclusion may be less substantial when an impartial, experienced examiner who has observed the witnesses and lived with the case has drawn conclusions different from the Board's than when he has reached the same conclusion.

When reviewing discrimination cases, courts of appeals ordinarily give great weight to the Administrative Law Judge's findings on credibility. *MPC Restaurant Corp. v. NLRB*, 481 F.2d 75 (2d Cir. 1973); *NLRB v. A & S Electronic Die Corp.*, 423 F.2d 218 (2d Cir.), *cert. denied*, 400 U.S. 833 (1970).

Problems

Put yourself in the position of the Administrative Law Judge as you read the following problem cases and think about what factors seem most significant in deciding the employer's real reason for the discharges. Almost every year, more than half of the unfair labor practice charges filed against employers allege unlawful discrimination.

12. Mr. White was a trucker for a large trucking company and had 30 years of unblemished service. Late last year, however, his performance at his position became somewhat erratic. He began arriving at work a little late, and leaving work a little early. He also began to pick up hitchhikers along his truck route, thereby violating a seldom enforced regulation of the company. His supervisor, Mr. Rodriguez, expressed displeasure with Mr. White's tardiness on several occasions, but dismissal was never recommended because of Mr. White's excellent record and because the infractions appeared to be minor and easily remedied by docking Mr. White's pay.

Last week, Mr. White began to wear a rather inconspicuous union button to work and pasted a union decal onto the cab window of the truck he regularly drove, again contrary to a seldom enforced regulation against decals on trucks. Mr. Rodriguez noticed the button and decal and called Mr. White into his office for a talk. There, Mr. Rodriguez asked Mr. White to remove the decal from his truck, but Mr. White refused, countering with the argument that all the drivers had decals on their truck windows. Mr. Rodriguez insisted on the point, and also criticized Mr. White's tardiness, concluding with a threat of firing if the situation did not improve. Mr. White replied that he could not be fired because he was working with a union and was thereby protected against any discharge.

The next day, Mr. White was told by Mr. Rodriguez that he was immediately discharged and that his pay would be forwarded to him at the end of the pay period. The reasons for the discharge were given as repeated infractions of the company regulations, chronic tardiness, and insubordination.

13. Ms. Larson was a probationary employee for a large manufacturing company engaged in interstate commerce, and as such had the lowest seniority in her 42-worker plant section. Last month, Ms. Larson began to actively advocate unionization of the plant among the other employees during lunch breaks. Mr. Miller, the supervisor, was told of Ms. Larson's organizational activities by a Mr. Sydney, an employee who had been specially recruited by Mr. Miller to keep management informed of such activities. Mr. Miller consequently called Ms. Larson into his office to review the latter's probationary period report, which was, by all accounts, unsatisfactory. Mr. Miller also lectured Ms. Larson on the evils of unionization, but asked Ms. Larson no questions about her own union activities.

Two weeks ago, without any prior warnings, Ms. Larson was told by Mr. Miller that she need not report in the next morning because the company was being forced to cut back on employees due to an economic slowdown and Ms. Larson, having the least seniority, would be the first employee laid off. Ms. Larson complained that her probationary period was not yet over, and then accused Mr. Miller of anti-union bias in the discharge, to which Mr. Miller replied only that "I have my orders."

The company retained all other employees, including several other union advocates. Proof was later offered that tended to show that last month was a very poor month, but that business in the months both before and after was above the normal. A new employee was hired yesterday to perform substantially the same job as Ms. Larson had performed.

B. Discrimination to Encourage Union Membership

It's easy to imagine why an employer might discriminate against an employee in order to discourage union membership. But why would an employer ever try to *encourage* union membership? We've already seen one set of situations where this might happen: as part of an employer's effort to dominate or assist a particular labor organization in violation of §8(a)(2). We now examine other situations where this might occur and how they are handled under the NLRA.

1. Hiring Halls and Other Practices

International Brotherhood of Teamsters, Local 357 v. NLRB

Supreme Court of the United States
365 U.S. 667, 81 S. Ct. 835, 6 L. Ed. 2d 11 (1961)

Mr. Justice Douglas delivered the opinion of the Court.

Petitioner union (along with the International Brotherhood of Teamsters and a number of other affiliated local unions) executed a three-year collective bargaining agreement with California Trucking Associations which represented a group of motor truck operators in California. The provisions of the contract relating to hiring of casual or temporary employees were as follows:

> Casual employees shall, wherever the Union maintains a dispatching service, be employed only on a seniority basis in the Industry whenever such senior employees are available. An available list with seniority status will be kept by the Unions, and employees requested will be dispatched upon call to any employer who is a party to this Agreement. Seniority rating of

such employees shall begin with a minimum of three months service in the Industry, *irrespective of whether such employee is or is not a member of the Union.*

Discharge of any employee by any employer shall be grounds for removal of any employee from seniority status. No casual employee shall be employed by any employer who is a party to this Agreement in violation of seniority status if such employees are available and if the dispatching service for such employees is available. The employer shall first call the Union or the dispatching hall designated by the Union for such help. In the event the employer is notified that such help is not available, or in the event the employees called for do not appear for work at the time designated by the employer, the employer may hire from any other available source. (Emphasis added.)

Accordingly the union maintained a hiring hall for casual employees. One Slater was a member of the union and had customarily used the hiring hall. But in August 1955 he obtained casual employment with an employer who was a party to the hiring-hall agreement without being dispatched by the union. He worked until sometime in November of that year, when he was discharged by the employer on complaint of the union that he had not been referred through the hiring-hall arrangement.

Slater made charges against the union and the employer. Though, as plain from the terms of the contract, there was an express provision that employees would not be discriminated against because they were or were not union members, the Board found that the hiring-hall provision was unlawful *per se* and that the discharge of Slater on the union's request constituted a violation by the employer of § 8(a)(1) and § 8(a)(3) and a violation by the union of § 8(b)(2) and § 8(b)(1)(A) of the National Labor Relations Act, as amended by the Taft-Hartley Act, 61 Stat. 140–141, as amended, 29 U.S.C. § 158. The Board ordered, *inter alia*, that the company and the union cease giving any effect to the hiring-hall agreement; that they jointly and severally reimburse Slater for any loss sustained by him as a result of his discharge; and that they jointly and severally reimburse all casual employees for fees and dues paid by them to the union beginning six months prior to the date of the filing of the charge. 121 N.L.R.B. 1629.

The union petitioned the Court of Appeals for review of the Board's action, and the Board made a cross-application for enforcement. That court set aside the portion of the order requiring a general reimbursement of dues and fees. By a divided vote it upheld the Board in ruling that the hiring-hall agreement was illegal *per se.* 107 App. D.C. 188, 275 F.2d 646 (1960). Those rulings are here on certiorari, 363 U.S. 837, one on the petition of the union, the other on petition of the Board.

Our decision in *Carpenters Locals 60 v. NLRB,* decided this day, *supra* at 651, is dispositive of the petition of the Board that asks us to direct enforcement of the order of reimbursement. The judgment of the Court of Appeals on that phase of the matter is affirmed.

The other aspect of the case goes back to the Board's ruling in *Mountain Pacific Chapter*, 119 N.L.R.B. 883. That decision, rendered in 1958, departed from earlier rulings and held, Abe Murdock dissenting, that the hiring-hall agreement, despite the inclusion of a nondiscrimination clause, was illegal, *per se*:

> Here the very grant of work at all depends solely upon union sponsorship, and it is reasonable to infer that the arrangement displays and enhances the Union's power and control over the employment status. Here all that appears is unilateral union determination and subservient employer action with no above-board explanation as to the reason for it, and it is reasonable to infer that the Union will be guided in its concession by an eye towards winning compliance with a membership obligation or union fealty in some other respect. The Employers here have surrendered all hiring authority to the Union and have given advance notice via the established hiring hall to the world at large that the Union is arbitrary master and is contractually guaranteed to remain so. From the final authority over hiring vested in the Respondent Union by the three AGC chapters, the inference of the encouragement of union membership is inescapable. [*Id.* 896].

The Board went on to say that a hiring-hall arrangement to be lawful must contain protective provisions. Its views were stated as follows:

> We believe, however, that the inherent and unlawful encouragement of union membership that stems from unfettered union control over the hiring process would be negated, and we would find an agreement to be nondiscriminatory on its face, only if the agreement explicitly provided that:
>
> (1) Selection of applicants for referral to jobs shall be on a nondiscriminatory basis and shall not be based on, or in any way affected by, union membership, bylaws, rules, regulations, constitutional provisions, or any other aspect or obligation of union membership, policies, or requirements.
>
> (2) The employer retains the right to reject any job applicant referred by the union.
>
> (3) The parties to the agreement post in places where notices to employees and applicants for employment are customarily posted, all provisions relating to the functioning of the hiring arrangement, including the safeguards that we deem essential to the legality of an exclusive hiring agreement. [*Id.* 897].

The Board recognizes that the hiring hall came into being "to eliminate wasteful, time-consuming, and repetitive scouting for jobs by individual workmen and haphazard uneconomical searches by employers." *Id.* 896, note 8. The hiring hall at times has been a useful adjunct to the closed shop. But Congress may have thought that it need not serve that cause, that in fact it has served well both labor and management—particularly in the maritime field and in the building and construction industry. In the latter the contractor who frequently is a stranger to the area where the work is done requires a "central source" for his employment needs; and a man looking for a job finds in the hiring hall "at least a minimum guarantee of continued employment."

Congress has not outlawed the hiring hall, though it has outlawed the closed shop except within the limits prescribed in the *provisos* to §8(a)(3). Senator Taft made clear his views that hiring halls are useful, that they are not illegal *per se*, that unions should be able to operate them so long as they are not used to create a closed shop:

> In order to make clear the real intention of Congress, it should be clearly stated that the hiring hall is not necessarily illegal. The employer should be able to make a contract with the union as an employment agency. The union frequently is the best employment agency. The employer should be able to give notice of vacancies, and in the normal course of events to accept men sent to him by the hiring hall. He should not be able to bind himself, however, to reject nonunion men if they apply to him; nor should he be able to contract to accept men on a rotary-hiring basis. . . .
>
> . . . The National Labor Relations Board and the courts did not find hiring halls as such illegal, but merely certain practices under them. The Board and the court found that the manner in which the hiring halls operated created in effect a closed shop in violation of the law. Neither the law nor these decisions forbid hiring halls, even hiring halls operated by the unions as long as they are not so operated as to create a closed shop with all of the abuses possible under such arrangement, including discrimination against employees, prospective employees, members of union minority groups, and operation of a closed union. [S. Rep. No. 1827, 81st Cong., 2d Sess., pp. 13, 14].

There being no express ban of hiring halls in any provisions of the Act, those who add one, whether it be the Board or the courts, engage in a legislative act. The Act deals with discrimination either by the employers or unions that encourages or discourages union membership. As respects §8(a)(3) we said in *Radio Officers' Union v. NLRB*, 347 U.S. 17, 42, 43 (1954):

> The language of §8(a)(3) is not ambiguous. The unfair labor practice is for an employer to encourage or discourage membership by means of discrimination. Thus this section does not outlaw all encouragement or discouragement of membership in labor organizations; only such as is accomplished by discrimination is prohibited. Nor does this section outlaw discrimination in employment as such; only such discrimination as encourages or discourages membership in a labor organization is proscribed.

It is the "true purpose" or "real motive" in hiring or firing that constitutes the test. *Id.* 347 U.S. 43. Some conduct may by its very nature contain the implications of the required intent; the natural foreseeable consequences of certain action may warrant the inference. *Id.* 347 U.S. 45. And see *Republic Aviation Corp. v. NLRB*,

324 U.S. 793 (1945). The existence of discrimination may at times be inferred by the Board, for "it is permissible to draw on experience in factual inquiries." *Radio Officers' Union v. NLRB, supra*, 49.

But surely discrimination cannot be inferred from the face of the instrument when the instrument specifically provides that there will be no discrimination against "casual employees" because of the presence or absence of union membership. The only complaint in the case was by Slater, a union member, who sought to circumvent the hiring-hall agreement. When an employer and the union enforce the agreement against union members, we cannot say without more that either indulges in the kind of discrimination to which the Act is addressed.

It may be that the very existence of the hiring hall encourages union membership. We may assume that it does. The very existence of the union has the same influence. When a union engages in collective bargaining and obtains increased wages and improved working conditions, its prestige doubtless rises and, one may assume, more workers are drawn to it. When a union negotiates collective bargaining agreements that include arbitration clauses and supervises the functioning of those provisions so as to get equitable adjustments of grievances, union membership may also be encouraged. The truth is that the union is a service agency that probably encourages membership whenever it does its job well. But as we said in *Radio Officers' Union v. NLRB, supra*, the only encouragement or discouragement of union membership banned by the Act is that which is "accomplished by discrimination." P. 43.

Nothing is inferable from the present hiring-hall provision except that employer and union alike sought to route "casual employees" through the union hiring hall and required a union member who circumvented it to adhere to it.

It may be that hiring halls need more regulation than the Act presently affords. As we have seen, the Act aims at every practice, act, source or institution which in fact is used to encourage and discourage union membership by discrimination in regard to hire or tenure, term or condition of employment. Perhaps the conditions which the Board attaches to hiring-hall arrangements will in time appeal to the Congress. Yet where Congress has adopted a selective system for dealing with evils, the Board is confined to that system. *NLRB v. Drivers Local Union*, 362 U.S. 274, 284–290 (1960). Where, as here, Congress has aimed its sanctions only at specific discriminatory practices, the Board cannot go farther and establish a broader, more pervasive regulatory scheme.

The present agreement for a union hiring hall has a protective clause in it, as we have said; and there is no evidence that it was in fact used unlawfully. We cannot assume that a union conducts its operations in violation of law or that the parties to this contract did not intend to adhere to its express language. Yet we would have to make those assumptions to agree with the Board that it is reasonable to infer the union will act discriminatorily.

Moreover, the hiring hall, under the law as it stands, is a matter of negotiation between the parties. The Board has no power to compel directly or indirectly that the hiring hall be included or excluded in collective agreements. *Cf. NLRB v. American Nat. Ins. Co.*, 343 U.S. 395, 404 (1952). Its power, so far as here relevant, is restricted to the elimination of discrimination. Since the present agreement contains such a prohibition, the Board is confined to determining whether discrimination has in fact been practiced. If hiring halls are to be subjected to regulation that is less selective and more pervasive, Congress not the Board is the agency to do it.

Affirmed in part and reversed in part.

MR. JUSTICE FRANKFURTER took no part in the consideration or decision of this case.

[The concurring opinion of MR. JUSTICE HARLAN, joined in by MR. JUSTICE STEWART, and the dissenting opinion of MR. JUSTICE CLARK, joined in by MR. JUSTICE WHITTAKER, are omitted.]

Notes

1. *General Considerations* — In the leading *Radio Officers'* case, cited in the principal case, the Supreme Court held the following to constitute unlawful encouragement of union membership by discrimination: (a) reducing a truck driver's seniority standing because he did not keep up his union dues; (b) causing a ship's radio officer to be refused employment because he did not obtain union clearance, where there was no valid hiring-hall agreement; (c) granting a retroactive wage increase to union members and refusing such benefits to other employees because they were not union members.

In *Radio Officers'*, the Court discussed several evidentiary considerations:

Necessity for Proving Employer's Motive

The language of § 8(a)(3) is not ambiguous. The unfair labor practice is for an employer to encourage or discourage membership by means of discrimination. Thus this section does not outlaw all encouragement or discouragement of membership in labor organizations; only such as is accomplished by discrimination is prohibited. Nor does this section outlaw discrimination in employment as such; only such discrimination as encourages or discourages membership in a labor organization is proscribed.

The relevance of the motivation of the employer in such discrimination has been consistently recognized under both § 8(a)(3) and its predecessor. . . .

That Congress intended the employer's purpose in discriminating to be controlling is clear. The Senate Report on the Wagner Act said: "Of course nothing in the bill prevents an employer from discharging a man for incompetence; from advancing him for special aptitude; or from demoting him for failure to perform. . . ."

Proof of Motive

But it is also clear that specific evidence of intent to encourage or discourage is not an indispensable element of proof of violation of § 8(a)(3).... [A]n employer's protestation that he did not intend to encourage or discourage must be unavailing where a natural consequence of his action was such encouragement or discouragement. Concluding that encouragement or discouragement will result, it is presumed that he intended such consequence. In such circumstances intent to encourage is sufficiently established....

Power of Board to Draw Inferences

There is nothing in the language of the amendment itself that suggests denial to the Board of power to draw reasonable inferences. It is inconceivable that the authors of the reports intended such a result for a fact-finding body must have some power to decide which inferences to draw and which to reject. We therefore conclude that insofar as the power to draw reasonable inferences is concerned, Taft-Hartley did not alter prior law.

2. *Hiring Halls* — Under a facially valid hiring-hall agreement, what kind of evidence would be required to prove that it actually functioned to encourage union membership by discrimination? *See United Ass'n of Journeymen & Apprentices of Plumbing & Pipefitting Industry, etc., Local No. 198 v. NLRB*, 747 F.2d 326 (5th Cir. 1984) (union gave lower referral priority to members of other locals); *NLRB v. Southern Stevedoring & Contracting Co.*, 332 F.2d 1017 (5th Cir. 1964) (union hiring hall gave direct preference to ILA members over IBL members); *NLRB v. Houston Maritime Ass'n*, 337 F.2d 333 (5th Cir. 1964) (union hiring hall selected members first and referred nonmembers only if members were not available). On the other hand, in *Hays v. National Electrical Contractors Ass'n*, 781 F.2d 1321 (9th Cir. 1986), the court found that a labor organization did not act unlawfully when it adopted a rule that restricted preferential-work referral status to those individuals who resided within 40 miles of the hiring hall. Such action disenfranchised few persons, and it constituted a legitimate exercise of union discretion.

When a labor organization operates an exclusive hiring hall, does it breach the duty of fair representation unions owe to all members if it negligently refers lower-priority candidates to job opportunities ahead of a higher-priority candidate? In *Steamfitters Local Union No. 342*, 329 N.L.R.B. 688 (1999), the Labor Board held no, noting that mere negligence with respect to the representation of bargaining unit personnel does not normally constitute a fair representation breach. Some evidence of personal hostility or capricious conduct is required. On appeal, the D.C. Circuit concluded that unions operating exclusive hiring halls owe a higher duty of care to members than is owed during the usual representational function. *Jacoby v. NLRB*, 233 F.3d 611 (D.C. Cir. 2000) (*Jacoby I*). On remand, the Board again found no fair representation breach, and the D.C. Circuit sustained this finding in light of the absence of any evidence of "ill will, discrimination, unlawful favoritism, [or] any other obviously unreasonable business practice." *Jacoby v. NLRB*, 325 F.3d 301 (D.C. Cir. 2003) (*Jacoby II*).

Unions may charge nonmembers reasonable "service fees" when they use hiring halls, but organizations charging excessive fees violate §8(b)(1)(A). See *Pittsburgh Press Co. v. NLRB*, 977 F.2d 652 (D.C. Cir. 1992). Unions may not refuse to refer members who are in arrearage with respect to their monthly dues, since labor organizations may not use hiring halls to enforce membership obligations. *NLRB v. IBEW, Local Union 16*, 425 F.3d 1035 (7th Cir. 2005).

A union operating a *nonexclusive* hiring hall may lawfully refuse to refer nonmembers to jobs. See *United Bhd. of Carpenters & Joiners, Local 537*, 303 N.L.R.B. 419 (1991). It may not, however, procure the discharge of individuals who obtain employment without going through the nonexclusive hiring hall, since employers may hire persons through other avenues. *Kvaerner Songer, Inc.*, 343 N.L.R.B. 1343 (2004), *enforced*, 481 F.3d 875 (6th Cir. 2007). See also *NLRB v. Local 334, Laborers Int'l Union of N. Am.*, 481 F.3d 875 (6th Cir. 2007) (union may not prevent employer from hiring individuals who have not been dispatched through nonexclusive hiring hall).

3. *Shop Stewards* — A union operating a hiring hall may lawfully refer an employee it wants as steward at a job site ahead of another person who is higher on the out-of-work referral list. See *Plumbers & Pipefitters Local Union No. 520, etc.*, 282 N.L.R.B. 1228 (1987). And contractual provisions granting shop stewards superseniority for purpose of *layoff* and *recall* are presumptively valid to ensure that there will be someone at the workplace to handle grievances and administer the bargaining agreement. Provisions granting such superseniority to stewards for other purposes, such as choice of lucrative delivery routes, are generally improper. See *NLRB v. Milk Drivers & Dairy Employees, etc.*, 531 F.2d 1162 (2d Cir. 1976); *Mechanics Educational Soc., Local 56*, 287 N.L.R.B. 935 (1987). But cf. *NLRB v. Auto Warehousers, Inc.*, 571 F.2d 860 (5th Cir. 1978) (holding that a contract clause permitting union stewards to exercise superseniority for purposes beyond layoff and recall is not *per se* invalid). In *Gulton Electro-Voice, Inc.*, 266 N.L.R.B. 406 (1983), *enforced*, 727 F.2d 1184 (D.C. Cir. 1984), the Board held that the grant of superseniority for layoff and recall purposes to union officials who do not handle grievances or exercise other on-the-job contract administrative responsibilities will be considered unlawful union-related discrimination. See also *IBEW, Local 48*, 342 N.L.R.B. 101 (2004) (unlawful for union to give preferential dispatching treatment to "salts" who will be used to organize target firm, since such preference unrelated to union's representative function). See generally Note, *New Limits on Superseniority: Ignoring the Importance of Efficient Union Operations*, 86 Colum. L. Rev. 631 (1986).

4. *Remedies* — In *United Brotherhood of Carpenters & Joiners Local 60 v. NLRB*, 365 U.S. 651 (1961), a company and a union maintained an illegal closed-shop hiring system. Two job applicants were denied employment by the company because they could not obtain referrals from the union. The Labor Board included, among other

relief, its so-called *"Brown-Olds"* remedy (*see* 115 N.L.R.B. 594 (1956)), requiring the reimbursement to *all* employees of all dues and fees collected by the union under the illegal contract during the six-month period prior to the filing of the charges. The Supreme Court rejected the Board's refund order:

> [T]he power of the Board "to command affirmative action is remedial, not punitive...." Where no membership in the union was shown to be influenced or compelled by reason of any unfair practice, no "consequences of violation" are removed by the order compelling the union to return all dues and fees collected from the members.

2. Union Security Under Federal Legislation

Statutory References

RLA § 2, Fourth, Fifth, and Eleventh
NLRA §§ 8(a)(3), 8(b)(2), 8(b)(5), 8(f), 9(e)

Unions ordinarily seek to make membership 100 percent in occupational groups that they represent. To accomplish this, they may employ persuasion or economic pressure. They may also try to obtain so-called "union security" agreements from employers. The most common types of union security agreements are the following:

Closed Shop

From the union point of view, the most effective form of union security provision is the "closed shop." A closed shop agreement makes union membership a condition of employment, giving the union the power to both restrict access to jobs by limiting its membership, and to use its control over jobs to discipline union members. A standard version would read:

> The employer hereby agrees to employ only members in good standing of the Union.

Prior to the 1947 Taft-Hartley amendments that prohibited closed shop agreements, such provisions were quite common, especially in such industries as construction, printing, hosiery, clothing, baking, brewing, and trucking, where a majority of the workers covered by collective agreements were under closed shop contracts.

Union Shop

The "union shop" contract does not require the employer to hire only union members, but does require nonunion employees to become members of the union within a prescribed period after their initial employment. A typical clause would provide:

> Each employee covered by this agreement shall, as a condition of continued employment, become and remain a member of the Union on and after the

thirtieth day following the beginning of his or her employment or following the effective date of this agreement, whichever is the later.

Next to the closed shop, an agreement of this kind is the most favored by unions as a security device. Even though the Taft-Hartley amendments technically proscribed union shop provisions, many collective contracts continue to contain language that appears to require new employees to become actual union members within the first 30 days of their employment.

Agency Shop

In deference to the religious scruples or ethical principles of some employees, or in response to certain state statutes, or the express language of the Taft-Hartley amendments, some labor contracts expressly provide for a so-called "agency shop" instead of a union shop. Under an agency shop provision, employees do not have to become formal union members, but any employees electing not to join must pay to the union amounts equal to the customary initiation fee and the periodic dues required of regular members.

Maintenance of Membership

A maintenance of membership agreement requires employees who are members of the union to remain members in good standing, usually for the duration of the collective bargaining agreement. Maintenance of membership gained wide use as a form of union security during World War II, largely because it was employed by the National War Labor Board as a formula for compromising the demands of unions for the closed shop and the demands of employers for the maintenance of the status quo in their plants during the war. A typical maintenance of membership clause, as directed by the WLB, follows:

> All members who, 15 days after the date of the Directive Order of the National War Labor Board in this case, are members of the Union in good standing in accordance with the constitution and bylaws of the Union, and those employees who may thereafter become members, shall, as a condition of employment, remain members of the Union in good standing during the life of the agreement.

Checkoff

Another contractual arrangement is regarded as a form of union security, although it does not itself condition employment on union membership. This is the "checkoff," under which workers authorize the employer to deduct union dues from employee wages and to transmit those amounts directly to the union. This is a great aid in keeping members in financial good standing. Sometimes unions have been satisfied with the checkoff as the sole security provision. More often, however, the checkoff has been used together with some type of provision conditioning employment on union membership. (Section 302(c)(4) of the LMRA requires written authorizations from employees before an employer can check off their dues.)

NLRB v. General Motors Corp.

Supreme Court of the United States
373 U.S. 734, 83 S. Ct. 1453, 10 L. Ed. 2d 670 (1963)

Mr. Justice White delivered the opinion of the Court.

The issue here is whether an employer commits an unfair labor practice, National Labor Relations Act § 8(a)(5), when it refuses to bargain with a certified union over the union's proposal for the adoption of the "agency shop." More narrowly, since the employer is not obliged to bargain over a proposal that he commit an unfair labor practice, the question is whether the agency shop is an unfair labor practice under § 8(a)(3) of the Act or else is exempted from the prohibitions of that section by the proviso thereto. We have concluded that this type of arrangement does not constitute an unfair labor practice and that it is not prohibited by § 8.

Respondent's employees are represented by the United Automobile, Aerospace and Agricultural Implement Workers of America, UAW, in a single, multi-plant, company-wide unit. The 1958 agreement between union and company provides for maintenance of membership and the union shop. These provisions were not operative, however, in such states as Indiana where state law prohibited making union membership a condition of employment.

In June 1959, the Indiana intermediate appellate court held that an agency shop arrangement would not violate the state right-to-work law. *Meade Elec. Co. v. Hagberg*, 129 Ind. App. 631, 159 N.E.2d 408 (1959). As defined in that opinion, the term "agency shop" applies to an arrangement under which all employees are required as a condition of employment to pay dues to the union and pay the union's initiation fee, but they need not actually become union members. The union thereafter sent respondent a letter proposing the negotiation of a contractual provision covering Indiana plants "generally similar to that set forth" in the *Meade* case. Continued employment in the Indiana plants would be conditioned upon the payment of sums equal to the initiation fee and regular monthly dues paid by the union members. The intent of the proposal, the NLRB concluded, was not to require membership but to make membership available at the employees' option and on nondiscriminatory terms. Employees choosing not to join would make the required payments and, in accordance with union custom, would share in union expenditures for strike benefits, educational and retired member benefits, and union publications and promotional activities, but they would not be entitled to attend union meetings, vote upon ratification of agreements negotiated by the union, or have a voice in the internal affairs of the union. The respondent made no counterproposal, but replied to the union's letter that the proposed agreement would violate the National Labor Relations Act and that respondent must therefore "respectfully decline to comply with your request for a meeting" to bargain over the proposal.

The union thereupon filed a complaint with the NLRB against respondent for its alleged refusal to bargain in good faith. In the Board's view of the record, "the union was not seeking to bargain over a clause requiring nonmember employees to pay sums equal to dues and fees as a condition of employment while at the same time maintaining a closed-union policy with respect to applicants for membership," since the proposal contemplated an arrangement in which "all employees are *given the option* of becoming, or refraining from becoming, members of the union." Proceeding on this basis and putting aside the consequences of a closed-union policy upon the legality of the agency shop, the Board assessed the union's proposal as comporting fully with the congressional declaration of policy in favor of union-security contracts and therefore a mandatory subject as to which the Act obliged respondent to bargain in good faith. At the same time, it stated that it had "no doubt that an agency-shop agreement is a permissible form of union-security within the meaning of §§ 7 and 8(a)(3) of the Act." Accordingly, the Board ruled that respondents had committed an unfair labor practice by refusing to bargain in good faith with the certified bargaining representative of its employees, and it ordered respondent to bargain with the union over the proposed arrangement; no back-pay award is involved in this case. 133 N.L.R.B. 451.

Respondent petitioned for review in the Court of Appeals, and the Board cross-petitioned for enforcement. The Court of Appeals set the order aside on the grounds that the Act tolerates only "an agreement requiring membership in a labor organization as a condition of employment" when such agreements do not violate state right-to-work laws, and that the Act does not authorize agreements requiring payment of membership dues to a union, in lieu of membership, as a condition of employment. It held that the proposed agency shop agreement would violate §§ 7, 8(a)(1), and 8(a)(3) of the Act and that the employer was therefore not obliged to bargain over it. 303 F.2d 428 (6th Cir. 1962). We granted certiorari ... and now reverse the decision of the Court of Appeals.

Section 8(3) under the Wagner Act was the predecessor to § 8(a)(3) of the present law. Like § 8(a)(3), § 8(3) forbade employers to discriminate against employees to compel them to join a union. Because it was feared that § 8(3) and § 7, if nothing were added to qualify them, might be held to outlaw union-security arrangements such as the closed shop, see 79 Cong. Rec. 7570 (statement of Senator Wagner), 7674 (statement of Senator Walsh); H.R. Rep. No. 972, at 17; H.R. Rep. No. 1147, at 19, the proviso to § 8(3) was added expressly declaring:

> "*Provided*, That nothing in this Act ... or in any other statute of the United States, shall preclude an employer from making an agreement with a labor organization ... to require as a condition of employment membership therein, if such labor organization is the representative of the employees as provided in section 9(a)...."

The prevailing administrative and judicial view under the Wagner Act was or came to be that the proviso to § 8(3) covered both the closed and union shop, as well as less onerous union security arrangements, if they were otherwise legal. The NLRB construed the proviso as shielding from an unfair labor practice charge less severe forms of union-security arrangements than the closed or the union shop, including an arrangement in *Public Service Co. of Colorado*, 89 N.L.R.B. 418, requiring nonunion members to pay to the union $2 a month "for the support of the bargaining unit." And in *Algoma Plywood & Veneer Co. v. Wisconsin Employment Relations Board*, 336 U.S. 301, 307 (1949), which involved a maintenance of membership agreement, the Court, in commenting on petitioner's contention that the proviso of § 8(3) affirmatively protected arrangements within its scope, *cf. Garner v. Teamsters Union*, 346 U.S. 485 (1953), said of its purpose: "The short answer is that § 8(3) merely disclaims a national policy hostile to the closed shop *or other forms of union-security agreement*." (Emphasis added.)

When Congress enacted the Taft-Hartley Act, it added . . . to the language of the original proviso to § 8(3). . . . These additions were intended to accomplish twin purposes. On the one hand, the most serious abuses of compulsory unionism were eliminated by abolishing the closed shop. On the other hand, Congress recognized that in the absence of a union-security provision "many employees sharing the benefits of what unions are able to accomplish, like collective bargaining, will refuse to pay their share of the cost." S. Rep. No. 105, 80th Cong., 1st Sess., at 6, 1 Leg. Hist. L.M.R.A. 412. Consequently, under the new law "employers would still be permitted to enter into agreements requiring all employees in a given bargaining unit to become members thirty days after being hired" but "expulsion from a union cannot be a ground of compulsory discharge if the worker is not delinquent in paying his initiation fees or dues." S. Rep. No. 105, at 7, 1 Leg. Hist. L.M.R.A. 413. The amendments were intended only to "remedy the most serious abuses of compulsory union membership and yet give employers and unions who feel that such agreements promoted stability by eliminating 'free riders' the right to continue such arrangements." *Ibid.* As far as the federal law was concerned, all employees could be required to pay their way. The bill "abolishes the closed shop but permits voluntary agreements for requiring such forms of compulsory membership as the union shop or maintenance of membership. . . ." S. Rep. No. 105, at 3, 1 Leg. Hist. L.M.R.A. 409.

We find nothing in the legislative history of the Act indicating that Congress intended the amended proviso to § 8(a)(3) to validate only the union shop and simultaneously to abolish, in addition to the closed shop, all other union-security arrangements permissible under state law. There is much to be said for the Board's view that, if Congress desired in the Wagner Act to permit a closed or union shop and in the Taft-Hartley Act the union shop, then it also intended to preserve the status of less vigorous, less compulsory contracts, which demanded less adherence to the union.

Respondent, however, relies upon the express words of the proviso which allow employment to be conditioned upon "membership": since the union's proposal here does not require actual membership but demands only initiation fees and monthly dues it is not saved by the proviso. This position, of course, would reject administrative decisions concerning the scope of § 8(3) of the Wagner Act, *e.g.*, *Public Service Co. of Colorado, supra*, reaffirmed by the Board under the Taft-Hartley amendments, *American Seating Co.*, 98 N.L.R.B. 800. Moreover, the 1947 amendments not only abolished the closed shop but also made significant alterations in the meaning of "membership" for the purposes of union security contracts. Under the second proviso to § 8(a)(3), the burdens of membership upon which employment may be conditioned are expressly limited to the payment of initiation fees and monthly dues. It is permissible to condition employment upon membership, but membership, insofar as it has significance to employment rights, may in turn be conditioned only upon payment of fees and dues. "Membership" as a condition of employment is whittled down to its financial core. This Court has said as much before in *Radio Officers' Union v. NLRB*, 347 U.S. 17, 41 (1954):

> ... This legislative history clearly indicates that Congress intended to prevent utilization of union security agreements for any purpose other than to compel payment of union dues and fees. Thus, Congress recognized the validity of unions' concern about 'free riders,' *i.e.*, employees who receive the benefits of union representation but are unwilling to contribute their fair share of financial support to such union, and gave the unions the power to contract to meet that problem while withholding from unions the power to cause the discharge of employees for any other reason. ...

We are therefore confident that the proposal made by the union here conditioned employment upon the practical equivalent of union "membership," as Congress used that term in the proviso to § 8(a)(3). The proposal for requiring the payment of dues and fees imposes no burdens not imposed by a permissible union shop contract and compels the performance of only those duties of membership which are enforceable by discharge under a union shop arrangement. If an employee in a union shop unit refuses to respect any union-imposed obligations other than the duty to pay dues and fees, and membership in the union is therefore denied or terminated, the condition of "membership" for § 8(a)(3) purposes is nevertheless satisfied and the employee may not be discharged for nonmembership even though he is not a formal member. Of course, if the union chooses to extend membership even though the employee will meet only the minimum financial burden, and refuses to support or "join" the union in any other affirmative way, the employee may have to become a "member" under a union shop contract, in the sense that the union may be able to place him on its rolls. The agency shop arrangement proposed here removes that choice from the union and places the option of membership in the employee while still requiring the same monetary support as does the union shop. Such a difference between the union and agency shop may be of great importance in some contexts, but for present purposes it is more formal than real. To the extent that it has any significance at all, it serves rather than violates, the desire of Congress to reduce the evils of compulsory unionism while allowing financial support for the bargaining agent.[2]

---

2. [12] Also wide of the mark is respondent's further suggestion that Congress contemplated the obligation to pay fees and dues to be imposed only in connection with actual membership in the union, so as to insure the enjoyment of all union benefits and rights by those from whom money

In short, the employer categorically refused to bargain with the union over a proposal for an agreement within the proviso to § 8(a)(3) and as such, lawful, for the purposes of this case. By the same token, § 7, and derivatively § 8(a)(1), cannot be deemed to forbid the employer to enter such agreements, since it too is expressly limited by the § 8(a)(3) proviso. We hold that the employer was not excused from his duty to bargain over the proposal on the theory that his acceding to it would necessarily involve him in an unfair labor practice. Whether a different result obtains in States which have declared such arrangements unlawful is an issue still to be resolved in *Retail Clerks Union v. Schermerhorn*, 373 U.S. 746 (1963), and one which is of no relevance here because Indiana law does not forbid the present contract proposal. In the context of this case, then, the employer cannot justify his refusal to bargain. He violated § 8(a)(5), and the Board properly ordered him to return to the bargaining table.

Reversed and remanded.

Mr. Justice Goldberg took no part in the consideration or decision of this case.

Marquez v. Screen Actors Guild, 525 U.S. 33, 119 S. Ct. 292, 142 L. Ed. 2d 242 (1998). The Screen Actors Guild (SAG) negotiated a bargaining agreement with Lakeside Productions, a movie producer. The contract contained a union security clause requiring each employee with 30 days of employment in the motion picture industry to become "a member of the Union in good standing." Since Marquez had previously been employed in the industry for more than 30 days, SAG insisted that she become a member as a condition of employment on a one-day job with Lakeside. When she failed to join, Lakeside hired another performer. Marquez filed suit alleging that SAG had breached its duty of fair representation by negotiating and enforcing a union security clause that required "membership" in SAG without expressly indicating that under *General Motors* employees need only become "financial core" members, by failing to explicitly apprise employees of their right to object to dues expenditures for reasons unrelated to collective bargaining, contract administration, and grievance handling under *Communications Workers of Am. v. Beck*, 487 U.S. 735 (1988), *infra*, and by requiring individuals with 30 days of employment in the motion picture industry to become SAG members as soon as they accept employment with any production company.

The Supreme Court unanimously held that the mere negotiation of a union security clause tracking the language of the proviso to § 8(a)(3) requiring "membership" in the union does not itself constitute a breach of the duty of fair representation. A

---

is extracted. Congress, it is said, had no desire to open the door to compulsory contracts which extract money but exclude the contributing employees from union membership. But, as analyzed by the Board and as the case comes to us, there is no closed-union aspect to the present proposal by the union. Membership remains optional with the employee and the significance of desired, but unavailable, union membership, or the benefits of membership, in terms of permissible § 8(a)(3) security contracts, we leave for another case....

plaintiff must provide additional information from which a court could find that the union in negotiating this language acted arbitrarily, discriminatorily, or in bad faith. To prevail on such a claim, a plaintiff would have to establish that the union had used the language in question in a bad faith effort to mislead employees. Marquez did not claim that SAG had used dues money to support inappropriate expenditures under *Beck*, thus no fair representation claim could be maintained with respect to this issue. The Court declined to decide whether the failure of a representative labor organization to notify bargaining unit members in a non-bargaining agreement publication of their right to become "financial core" members and their right to challenge improper expenditures under *Beck* might constitute a fair representation breach, because the lower appellate court had properly decided to remand this question to the district court for further proceedings.

The Supreme Court finally held that the challenge to the 30-day-in-the-industry provision did not raise an independent fair representation question but merely raised unfair labor practice issues under § 8(a)(3) and (b)(2) that are within the primary jurisdiction of the NLRB. As a result, neither a federal court nor a state court had jurisdiction to determine this question.

Notes

1. *Duty to Inform Employees of Union Security Rights/Obligations* — Does a union retain a significant practical advantage in being able to include union shop, rather than agency shop, language in a collective agreement? The Labor Board thinks so, and in *California Saw & Knife Works*, 320 N.L.R.B. 224 (1995), *enforced*, 133 F.3d 1012 (7th Cir. 1998), it held that: (1) fair representation principles apply to the writing of union-security agreements under the NLRA; and (2) a union must inform all bargaining unit employees, including both union members and nonmembers, of their rights under *General Motors* to become and remain "financial core members" and under *Communications Workers of Am. v. Beck*, 487 U.S. 735 (1988), to pay only for the support of union activities germane to collective bargaining. Should these obligations be imposed under the union security proviso to § 8(a)(3) to extend similar duties to both labor organizations *and* employers that enter into collective agreements containing union security clauses? Should the Labor Board adopt a rule requiring employers to post notices generally describing the rights and obligations of employees under the NLRA, including those arising under §7 and under the union security proviso to § 8(a)(3)?

In *Nielsen v. International Ass'n of Machinists & Aerospace Workers, Local Lodge 2569*, 94 F.3d 1107 (7th Cir. 1996), *cert. denied*, 520 U.S. 1165 (1997), the court held that a union security clause was not facially invalid because it failed to inform members of their *Beck* rights. Enforcement did not violate the union's duty of fair representation, since the union newspaper had provided a well-marked notice about *Beck* rights. *See also USW*, 329 N.L.R.B. 145 (1999) (union that annually apprises bargaining unit members of *Beck* rights not obliged to provide contemporaneous notice of those rights when individuals resign from union).

An employer gave unlawful assistance to a labor organization when it told new employees that they had to join the representative union "that day" if they wanted to keep their jobs, and the union violated the Act by failing to notify employees of their right to decline full membership and seek dues reductions for money spent on activities not germane to collective bargaining. *Raymond Interior Systems, Inc. v. NLRB*, 812 F.3d 168 (D.C. Cir. 2016).

Where a labor organization had a policy requiring individuals who wished to opt out of union membership to show up at the union office in person with photo identifications and provide written requests specifically indicating their intent to opt out, the Labor Board found such rigid procedures unreasonably limited the right of members to resign. Although the union claimed that these were merely procedural rules, the D.C. Circuit agreed with the Board that they unreasonably burdened the right of members to resign. *Local 58, Intl. Broth. of Elect. Workers v. NLRB*, 888 F.3d 1313 (D.C. Cir. 2018).

2. *Discharge for Reasons Other than Nonpayment of Dues*—Is there any practical difference between the "union shop" and the "agency shop"? In *Grain Processors, Local 1 (Union Starch & Refining Co.)*, 87 N.L.R.B. 779 (1949), *enforced*, 186 F.2d 1008 (7th Cir.), *cert. denied*, 342 U.S. 815 (1951), the Labor Board held employees could not lawfully be discharged so long as they tendered their initiation fees and dues, even though they refused to comply with a union rule requiring all applicants to attend a union meeting and to take a membership oath. Similarly, workers meet the "membership" requirement as long as they continue to pay union dues, despite their formal resignation from the union ("financial core members"). *Marlin Rockwell Corp. (Automobile Workers, Local 197) (AFL-CIO)*, 114 N.L.R.B. 553 (1955).

A union or agency shop provision may not be used to enforce membership obligations not relating to dues payments. Thus, for example, a discharge for failure to pay a union fine is an unfair labor practice. *Electric Auto Lite Co. (Toledo, Ohio)*, 92 N.L.R.B. 1073 (1950), *enforced per curiam*, 196 F.2d 500 (6th Cir.), *cert. denied*, 344 U.S. 823 (1952). In *Transportation Workers Union*, 326 N.L.R.B. 8 (1998), the Board held that a union that had lawfully and permanently expelled a member for circulating a petition seeking to replace the incumbent union with a rival could not invoke the union security clause against him if he stopped paying his dues. Carefully distinguished was *International Bhd. of Boilermakers*, 312 N.L.R.B. 218 (1993), *aff'd*, 56 F.3d 1438 (D.C. Cir. 1995), *cert. denied*, 516 U.S. 1171 (1996), in which the Board had held that a labor organization that merely suspended members from union activities could continue to enforce union security clause obligations against those individuals. The Board's *Transportation Workers Local 525* holding relied on the portion of the § 8(a)(3) union security proviso indicating that "no employer shall justify any discrimination against an employee for non-membership in a labor organization ... if he has reasonable grounds for believing that membership was denied or terminated for reasons other than the failure of the employee to tender the periodic dues."

Although unions may refund a portion of monthly dues to members who attend union meetings, requiring those who do not attend to pay the full amount (*Pulp,

Sulphite & Paper Mill Workers, Local 171 (Boise Cascade Corp.), 165 N.L.R.B. 971 (1967)), they may not impose higher dues as a penalty on those who do not attend meetings (*Electric Auto Lite Co. (Toledo, Ohio)*, 92 N.L.R.B. 1073 (1950), *enforced*, 196 F.2d 500 (6th Cir.), *cert. denied*, 344 U.S. 823 (1952)).

3. *Notice of Dues Obligation Prior to Discharge* — Before a labor organization seeks the termination of employees delinquent in their dues payments, it must notify those persons of the amounts due, provide them with a reasonable deadline for payment, and indicate that their failure to comply with this request could result in their loss of employment. *Laborers' Int'l Union, Local 578 v. NLRB*, 594 F.3d 732 (10th Cir. 2010). *See also General Motors Corp. (Local 717, Int'l Union of Elec. Workers or IUE)*, 134 N.L.R.B. 1107 (1961), wherein the Labor Board held that employees expelled from a union for dues delinquency may lawfully be discharged even though they make a belated tender of all back dues after their discharge has been requested but before it actually occurs.

4. *Dues Checkoff Authorizations* — An employee who resigns from a union may still be subject to a dues checkoff unless there is a timely revocation of the checkoff authorization. *Schweizer Local 1752 (UAW)*, 320 N.L.R.B. 528 (1995), *aff'd*, 105 F.3d 787 (2d Cir. 1996); *Williams v. NLRB*, 105 F.3d 787 (2d Cir. 1996). In *United Food & Commercial Workers Dist. Union Local One v. NLRB*, 975 F.2d 40 (2d Cir. 1992), the court held that in the absence of express language forbidding the partial revocation of dues checkoff agreements, employees could partially revoke their checkoff authorizations to prevent the deduction of money to support union organizing campaigns. *See also JBM, Inc.*, 349 N.L.R.B. 866 (2007) (employees may not be required to execute dues checkoff authorizations as condition of continued employment).

In *Valley Hospital Medical Ctr.*, 368 N.L.R.B. No. 139 (2019), the Labor Board held that employers have the right to unilaterally cease deducting union dues from employee paychecks once existing bargaining agreements have expired.

In *International Assn. of Machinists v. Allen*, 904 F.3d 490 (7th Cir. 2018), *cert. dismissed*, 139 S. Ct. 1599 (2019), the court held that a provision in the Wisconsin right-to-work law that allowed employees to revoke dues checkoff agreements with just 30 days' notice was preempted by Section 302(c)(4) of the LMRA, which allows such agreements to continue in force for up to one year.

In *Comau Inc.*, 358 N.L.R.B. 593 (2012), the Board held that an employer violated § 8(a)(1) when it threatened employees with discipline if they did not execute dues checkoff authorizations, based upon the fact that the execution of such agreements is entirely within the discretion of employees.

5. *Excessive Initiation Fees* — In the first court case to arise under § 8(b)(5), which makes it unlawful to "require of employees covered by an agreement authorized under subsection (a)(3) the payment, as a condition precedent to becoming a member of such organization, of a fee in an amount which the Board finds excessive or discriminatory under all the circumstances," the Third Circuit in *NLRB v. Television & Radio Broadcasting Studio Employees*, 315 F.2d 398 (3d Cir. 1963), upheld the

Board's finding that a union's increase of its initiation fee from $50 to $500 was excessive, discriminatory, and violative of the Act.

The Board has held that a union can lawfully charge members who have become delinquent in their dues payments a "reinstatement fee" in excess of the initiation fee charged to new members. *See Machinists (AFL-CIO) Local Lodge 504 (Food Machinery & Chemical Corp.)*, 99 N.L.R.B. 1430 (1952).

6. *Religious Accommodation* — Section 19 of the NLRA was amended in 1980 to extend special protection to persons with religious scruples against "joining or financially supporting labor organizations." Such individuals may be required to contribute amounts equal to the initiation fees and periodic dues to non-labor, non-religious charitable organizations, and they may be charged the reasonable cost of grievance processing if they invoke contractual grievance procedures. The Sixth Circuit has found that §19 unconstitutionally discriminates among religions, since it only protects members of "bona fide" religious organizations that have "traditional tenets" precluding financial support of unions. *Wilson v. NLRB*, 920 F.2d 1282 (6th Cir. 1990), *cert. denied*, 505 U.S. 1218 (1992).

3. The First Amendment and the Free Rider Problem

Once selected as the exclusive representative for a particular bargaining unit, the union is obligated to represent all members in the unit. Union security devices like the closed shop and the union shop ensured that all employees in the unit would contribute financially to the union's support, but raised significant issues in the public sector and in the Railway Labor Act context (where state action was present) for employees who objected on First Amendment grounds to mandatory membership or to the use of their funds for political causes. On the other hand, exempting objectors from payment of dues or their equivalent raised the specter of the "free rider," an employee who reaped the benefits of the collective bargaining agreement by virtue of her inclusion in the bargaining unit, but paid nothing for it. In a series of cases, the Court struggled to find an accommodation that respected both the First Amendment rights of individuals and the union's need for financial support from its members.

Ellis v. Brotherhood of Railway, Airline & Steamship Clerks
Supreme Court of the United States
466 U.S. 435, 104 S. Ct. 1883, 80 L. Ed. 2d 428 (1984)

JUSTICE WHITE delivered the opinion of the Court.

In 1951, Congress amended the Railway Labor Act (the Act or RLA) to permit what it had previously prohibited — the union shop. Section 2, Eleventh of the Act permits a union and an employer to require all employees in the relevant bargaining unit to join the union as a condition of continued employment. 45 U.S.C. §152, Eleventh. In *Machinists v. Street*, 367 U.S. 740 (1960), the Court held that the Act does not authorize a union to spend an objecting employee's money to support political causes. The use of employee funds for such ends is unrelated to Congress' desire to eliminate "free riders" and the resentment they provoked. *Id.*, at 768–769. The Court did not express a view as to "expenditures for activities in the area between the costs which led directly to the complaint as to 'free riders,' and the expenditures to support union political activities." *Id.*, at 769–770 and n. 18. Petitioners challenge just such expenditures.

I

> [margin note: Defs had agency shop agmt]

In 1971, respondent Brotherhood of Railway, Airline and Steamship Clerks (the union or BRAC) and Western Airlines implemented a previously negotiated agreement requiring that all Western's clerical employees join the union within 60 days of commencing employment. As the agreement has been interpreted, employees need not become formal members of the union, but must pay agency fees equal to members' dues. Petitioners are present or former clerical employees of Western who objected to the use of their compelled dues for specified union activities. They do not contest the legality of the union shop as such, nor could they. *See Railway Employees' Department v. Hanson*, 351 U.S. 225 (1956). They do contend, however, that they can be compelled to contribute no more than their pro rata share of the expenses of negotiating agreements and settling grievances with Western Airlines. Respondents — the national union, its board of adjustment, and three locals — concede that the statutory authorization of the union shop does not permit the use of petitioners' contributions for union political or ideological activities, *see Machinists v. Street, supra,* and have adopted a rebate program covering such expenditures. The parties disagree about the adequacy of the rebate scheme, and about the legality of burdening objecting employees with six specific union expenses that fall between the extremes identified in *Hanson* and *Street*: the quadrennial Grand Lodge convention, litigation not involving the negotiation of agreements or agreements of settlement of grievances, union publications, social activities, death benefits for employees, and general organizing efforts.

The District Court for the Southern District of California granted summary judgment to petitioners on the question of liability. Relying entirely on *Street*, it found that the six expenses at issue here, among others, were all "non-collective bargaining activities" that could not be supported by dues collected from protesting employees. After a trial on damages, the court concluded that with regard to political and ideological activities, the union's existing rebate program, under which objecting employees were ultimately reimbursed for their share of union expenditures on behalf of political and charitable causes, was a good faith effort to comply with legal requirements and adequately protected employees' rights. Relying on exhibits presented by respondents, the court ordered refunds of approximately 40% of dues paid for the expenditures at issue here. It also required that protesting employees' annual dues thereafter be reduced by the amount spent on activities not chargeable to them during the prior year. The court seems to have envisioned that this scheme would supplant the already-existing rebate scheme, for it included political expenditures among those to be figured into the dues reduction.

The Court of Appeals for the Ninth Circuit affirmed in part and reversed in part. 685 F.2d 1065 (1982). It held that the union's rebate plan was adequate even though it allowed the union to collect the full amount of a protesting employee's dues, use part of the dues for objectionable purposes, and only pay the rebate a year later. It found suggestions in this Court's cases that such a method would be acceptable, and had itself approved the rebate approach in an earlier case. The opinion did not address the dues reduction scheme imposed by the District Court. *Id.*, at 1069–1070. Turning to the question of permissible expenditures, the Court of Appeals framed "the relevant inquiry [a]s whether a particular challenged expenditure is germane to the union's work in the realm of collective bargaining. . . . [That is, whether it] can be seen to promote, support or maintain the union as an effective collective bargaining agent." *Id.*, at 1072, 1074–1075. The court found that each of the challenged activities strengthened the union as a whole and helped it to run more smoothly, thus making it better able to negotiate and administer agreements. Because the six activities ultimately benefited the union's collective bargaining efforts, the union was free to finance them with dues collected from objecting employees. One judge dissented, arguing that these were all "institutional expenses" that objecting employees cannot be forced to pay. *Id.*, at 1075–1076.

Petitioners sought review of the Court of Appeals' ruling on permissible expenses and the adequacy of the rebate scheme. We granted certiorari. We hold that the union's rebate scheme was inadequate and that the Court of Appeals erred in finding that the RLA authorizes a union to spend compelled dues for its general litigation and organizing efforts.

II

. . . As the Court of Appeals pointed out, there is language in this Court's cases to support the validity of a rebate program. *Street* suggested "restitution to each individual employee of that portion of his money which the union expended, despite his notification, for the political causes to which he had advised the union he was opposed." 367 U.S., at 775. See also *Abood v. Detroit Board of Education*, 431 U.S. 209, 238 (1977). On the other hand, we suggested a more precise advance reduction scheme in *Railway Clerks v. Allen*, 373 U.S. 113, 122 (1963), where we described a "practical decree" comprising a refund of exacted funds in the proportion that union political expenditures bore to total union expenditures and the reduction of future exactions by the same proportion. Those opinions did not, nor did they purport to, pass upon the statutory or constitutional adequacy of the suggested remedies. Doing so now, we hold that the pure rebate approach is inadequate.

By exacting and using full dues, then refunding months later the portion that it was not allowed to exact in the first place, the union effectively charges the employees for activities that are outside the scope of the statutory authorization. The cost to the employee is, of course, much less than if the money was never returned, but this is a difference of degree only. The harm would be reduced were the union to pay interest on the amount refunded, but respondents did not do so. Even then the union obtains an involuntary loan for purposes to which the employee objects.

The only justification for this union borrowing would be administrative convenience. But there are readily available alternatives, such as advance reduction of dues and/or interest-bearing escrow accounts, that place only the slightest additional burden, if any on the union. Given the existence of acceptable alternatives, the union cannot be allowed to commit dissenters' funds to improper uses even temporarily. A rebate scheme reduces but does not eliminate the statutory violation.

III

Petitioners' primary submission is that the use of their fees to finance the challenged activities violated the First Amendment. This argument assumes that the Act allows these allegedly unconstitutional exactions. When the constitutionality of a statute is challenged, this Court first ascertains whether the statute can be reasonably construed to avoid the constitutional difficulty. *E.g., Califano v. Yamasaki*, 442 U.S. 682, 692–693 (1979); *Ashwander v. TVA*, 297 U.S. 288, 347 (1936) (concurring opinion); *Crowell v. Benson*, 285 U.S. 22, 62 (1932)....

IV

Section 2, Eleventh contains only one explicit limitation to the scope of the union shop agreement: objecting employees may not be required to tender "fines and penalties" normally required of union members. 45 U.S.C. §152, Eleventh. If there were nothing else, an inference could be drawn from this limited exception that all other payments obtained from voluntary members can also be required of those whose membership is forced upon them. Indeed, several witnesses appearing before the congressional committees objected to the absence of any explicit limitation on the scope or amount of fees or dues that could be compelled. That Congress enacted the provision over these objections arguably indicates that it was willing to tolerate broad exactions from objecting employees.

Furthermore, Congress was well aware of the broad scope of traditional union activities. The hearing witnesses referred in general terms to the costs of "[a]ctivities of labor organizations resulting in the procurement of employee benefits," Hearings on H.R. 7789 before the House Committee on Interstate and Foreign Commerce, 81st Cong., 2d Sess., 10 (1950) (testimony of George Harrison), and the "policies and activities of labor unions," *id.*, at 50 (testimony of George Weaver). Indeed, it was pointed out that not only was the "securing and maintaining of a collective bargaining agreement . . . an expensive undertaking . . . , there are many other programs of a union" that require the financial and moral support of the workers. *Id.*, at 275; Hearings on S. 3295 before a Subcommittee of the Senate Committee on Labor and Public Welfare, 81st Cong., 2d Sess., 236 (1950) (statement of Theodore Brown). In short, Congress was adequately informed about the broad scope of union activities aimed at benefiting union members, and, in light of the absence of express limitations in §2, Eleventh it could be plausibly argued that Congress purported to authorize the collection from involuntary members of the same dues paid by regular members. This view, however, was squarely rejected in *Street*, over the dissents of three Justices, and the cases that followed it.

In *Street*, the Court observed that the purpose of § 2, Eleventh was to make it possible to require all members of a bargaining unit to pay their fair share of the costs of performing the function of exclusive bargaining agent. The union shop would eliminate "free riders," employees who obtained the benefit of the union's participation in the machinery of the Act without financially supporting the union. That purpose, the Court held, Congress intended to be achieved without "vesting the unions with unlimited power to spend exacted money." 367 U.S., at 768. Undoubtedly, the union could collect from all employees what it needed to defray the expenses entailed in negotiating and administering a collective agreement and in adjusting grievances and disputes. The Court had so held in *Railway Employees Department v. Hanson*, 351 U.S. 225 (1936). But the authority to impose dues and fees was restricted at least to the "extent of denying the union the right, over the employee's objection, to use his money to support political causes which he opposes," 367 U.S., at 768, even though Congress was well aware that unions had historically expended funds in support of political candidates and issues. Employees could be required to become "members" of the union, but those who objected could not be burdened with any part of the union's expenditures in support of political or ideological causes. The Court expressed no view on other union expenses not directly involved in negotiating and administering the contract and in settling grievances.

Railway Clerks v. Allen, 373 U.S. 113 (1963), reaffirmed the approach taken in *Street*, and described the union expenditures that could fairly be charged to all employees as those "germane to collective bargaining." *Id.*, at 121, 122. Still later, in *Abood v. Board of Education*, 431 U.S. 209 (1977), we found no constitutional barrier to an agency shop agreement between a municipality and a teachers' union insofar as the agreement required every employee in the unit to pay a service fee to defray the costs of collective bargaining, contract administration, and grievance adjustment. The union, however, could not, consistently with the Constitution, collect from dissenting employees any sums for the support of ideological causes not germane to its duties as collective-bargaining agent. In neither *Allen* nor *Abood*, however, did the Court find it necessary further to define the line between union expenditures that all employees must help defray and those that are not sufficiently related to collective bargaining to justify their being imposed on dissenters.

We remain convinced that Congress' essential justification for authorizing the union shop was the desire to eliminate free riders — employees in the bargaining unit on whose behalf the union was obliged to perform its statutory functions, but who refused to contribute to the cost thereof. Only a union that is certified as the exclusive bargaining agent is authorized to negotiate a contract requiring all employees to become members of or to make contributions to the union. Until such a contract is executed, no dues or fees may be collected from objecting employees who are not members of the union; and by the same token, any obligatory payments required by a contract authorized by § 2, Eleventh terminate if the union ceases to be the exclusive bargaining agent. Hence, when employees such as petitioners object to being burdened with particular union expenditures, the test must be whether the challenged expenditures are necessarily or reasonably incurred for the purpose of performing the duties of an exclusive representative of the employees in dealing with the employer on labor-management issues. Under this standard, objecting employees may be compelled to pay their fair share of not only the direct costs of negotiating and administering a collective-bargaining contract and of settling grievances and disputes, but also the expenses of activities or undertakings normally or reasonably employed to implement or effectuate the duties of the union as exclusive representative of the employees in the bargaining unit.

With these considerations in mind, we turn to the particular expenditures for which petitioners insist they may not be charged.

V

1. *Conventions.* Every four years, BRAC holds a national convention at which the members elect officers, establish bargaining goals and priorities, and formulate overall union policy. We have very little trouble in holding that petitioners must help defray the costs of these conventions. Surely if a union is to perform its statutory functions, it must maintain its corporate or associational existence, must elect officers to manage and carry on its affairs, and may consult its members about overall bargaining goals and policy. Conventions such as those at issue here are normal events about which Congress was thoroughly informed and seem to us to be essential to the union's discharge of its duties as bargaining agent. As the Court of Appeals pointed out, convention "activities guide the union's approach to collective bargaining and are directly related to its effectiveness in negotiating labor agreements." 685 F.2d at 1073. In fact, like all national unions, BRAC is required to hold either a referendum or a convention at least every five years for the election of officers. 29 U.S.C. § 481(a). We cannot fault it for choosing to elect its officers at a convention rather than by referendum.

2. *Social Activities.* Approximately .7% of Grand Lodge expenditures go toward purchasing refreshments for union business meetings and occasional social activities. 685 F.2d, at 1074. These activities are formally open to nonmember employees. Petitioners insist that these expenditures are entirely unrelated to the union's function as collective-bargaining representative and therefore could not be charged to them. While these affairs are not central to collective bargaining, they are sufficiently related to it to be charged to all employees. As the Court of Appeals noted, "[t]hese small expenditures are important to the union's members because they bring about harmonious working relationships, promote closer ties among employees, and create a more pleasant environment for union meetings." *Ibid.*

We cannot say that these *de minimis* expenses are beyond the scope of the Act. Like conventions, social activities at union meetings are a standard feature of union operations. In a revealing statement, Senator Thomas, Chairman of the Senate Subcommittee, made clear his disinclination to have Congress define precisely what normal, minor union expenses could be charged to objectors; he did not want the bill to say "that the unions ... must not have any of the ... kinds of little dues that they take up for giving a party, or something of that nature." Senate Hearings, *supra*, at 173–174. There is no indication that other Members of Congress were any more inclined to scrutinize the minor incidental expenses incurred by the union in running its operations.

3. *Publications.* The Grand Lodge puts out a monthly magazine, the *Railway Clerk/interchange*, paid for out of the union treasury. The magazine's contents are varied and include articles about negotiations, contract demands, strikes, unemployment and health benefits, proposed or recently enacted legislation, general news, products the union is boycotting, and recreational and social activities. See 685 F.2d at 1074.... The Court of Appeals found that the magazine "is the union's primary means of communicating information concerning collective bargaining, contract administration, and employees' rights to employees represented by BRAC." 685 F.2d, at 1074. Under the union's rebate policy, objecting employees are not charged for that portion of the magazine devoted to "political causes." The rebate is figured by calculating the number of lines that are devoted to political issues as a proportion of the total number of lines.

The union must have a channel for communicating with the employees, including the objecting ones, about its activities. Congress can be assumed to have known that union funds go toward union publications; it is an accepted and basic union activity. The costs of "worker education" were specifically mentioned during the hearings. House Hearings, *supra*, at 275; Senate Hearings, *supra*, at 236. The magazine is important to the union in carrying out its representational obligations and a reasonable way of reporting to its constituents.

Respondents' limitation on the publication costs charged objecting employees is an important one, however. If the union cannot spend dissenters' funds for a particular activity, it has no justification for spending their funds for writing about that activity.[3]

By the same token, the Act surely allows it to charge objecting employees for reporting to them about those activities it can charge them for doing.

4. *Organizing.* The Court of Appeals found that organizing expenses could be charged to objecting employees because organizing efforts are aimed toward a stronger union, which in turn would be more successful at the bargaining table. Despite this attenuated connection with collective bargaining, we think such expenditures are outside Congress' authorization. Several considerations support this conclusion.

First, the notion that § 2, Eleventh would be a tool for the expansion of overall union power appears nowhere in the legislative history. To the contrary, BRAC's president expressly disclaimed that the union shop was sought in order to strengthen the bargaining power of unions. "Nor was any claim seriously advanced that the

---

3. [11] Given our holding that objecting employees cannot be charged for union organizing or litigation, they cannot be charged for the expense of reporting those activities to the membership.

union shop was necessary to hold or increase union membership." *Street*, 367 U.S., at 763. Thus, organizational efforts were not what Congress aimed to enhance by authorizing the union shop.

Second, where a union shop provision is in place and enforced, all employees in the relevant unit are already organized. By definition, therefore, organizing expenses are spent on employees outside the collective-bargaining unit already represented. Using dues exacted from an objecting employee to recruit members among workers outside the bargaining unit can afford only the most attenuated benefits to collective bargaining on behalf of the dues payer.

Third, the free-rider rationale does not extend this far. The image of the smug, self-satisfied nonmember, stirring up resentment by enjoying benefits earned through other employees' time and money, is completely out of place when it comes to the union's overall organizing efforts. If one accepts that what is good for the union is good for the employees, a proposition petitioners would strenuously deny, then it may be that employees will ultimately ride for free on the union's organizing efforts outside the bargaining unit. But the free rider Congress had in mind was the employee the union was required to represent and from whom it could not withhold benefits obtained for its members. Non-bargaining unit organizing is not directed at that employee. Organizing money is spent on people who are not union members, and only in the most distant way works to the benefit of those already paying dues. Any free-rider problem here is roughly comparable to that resulting from union contributions to pro-labor political candidates. As we observed in *Street*, that is a far cry from the free-rider problem with which Congress was concerned.

5. *Litigation.* The expenses of litigation incident to negotiating and administering the contract or to settling grievances and disputes arising in the bargaining unit are clearly chargeable to petitioners as a normal incident of the duties of the exclusive representative. The same is true of fair representation litigation arising within the unit, of jurisdictional disputes with other unions, and of any other litigation before agencies or in the courts that concerns bargaining unit employees and is normally conducted by the exclusive representative. The expenses of litigation not having such a connection with the bargaining unit are not to be charged to objecting employees. Contrary to the view of the Court of Appeals, therefore, unless the Western Airlines bargaining unit is directly concerned, objecting employees need not share the costs of the union's challenge to the legality of the airline industry mutual aid pact; of litigation seeking to protect the rights of airline employees generally during bankruptcy proceedings; or of defending suits alleging violation of the non-discrimination requirements of Title VII.

6. *Death benefits.* BRAC pays from its general funds a $300 death benefit to the designated beneficiary of any member or nonmember required to pay dues to the union. In *Street*, the Court did not adjudicate the legality under § 2, Eleventh of compelled participation in a death benefit program, citing it as an example of an expenditure in the area between the costs which led directly to the complaint as to "free riders," and the expenditures to support union political activities. 367 U.S., at

769–770 and n. 18. In *Allen*, the state trial court, like the District Court in this case, found that compelled payments to support BRAC's death benefit system were not reasonably necessary or related to collective bargaining and could not be charged to objecting employees. *See* 373 U.S., at 117. We found it unnecessary to reach the correctness of that conclusion.

Here, the Court of Appeals said that death benefits have historically played an important role in labor organizations, that insurance benefits are a mandatory subject of bargaining, and that by providing such benefits itself rather than seeking them from the employer, BRAC is in a better position to negotiate for additional benefits or higher wages. The court added that "the provision of a death benefits plan, which tends to strengthen the employee's ties to the union, is germane to the work of the union within the realm of collective bargaining." 685 F.2d, at 1074. . . .

We find it unnecessary to rule on this question. Because the union is no longer the exclusive bargaining agent and petitioners are no longer involved in the death benefits system, the only issue is whether petitioners are entitled to a refund of their past contributions. We think that they are not so entitled, even if they had the right to an injunction to prevent future collections from them for death benefits. Although they objected to the use of their funds to support the benefits plan, they remained entitled to the benefits of the plan as long as they paid their dues; they thus enjoyed a form of insurance for which the union collected a premium. We doubt that the equities call for a refund of those payments.

VI

Petitioners' primary argument is that for the union to compel their financial support of these six activities violates the First Amendment. We need only address this contention with regard to the three activities for which, we have held, the RLA allows the union to use their contributions. We perceive no constitutional barrier.

The First Amendment does limit the uses to which the union can put funds obtained from dissenting employees. *See generally Abood*, 431 U.S. 209. But by allowing the union shop at all, we have already countenanced a significant impingement on First Amendment rights. The dissenting employee is forced to support financially an organization with whose principles and demands he may disagree. "To be required to help finance the union as a collective bargaining agent might well be thought . . . to interfere in some way with the employee's freedom to associate for the advancement of ideas, or to refrain from doing so, as he sees fit." *Id.*, at 222. It has long been settled that such interference with First Amendment rights is justified by the governmental interest in industrial peace. *Ibid.*; *Street*, 367 U.S., at 776, 778 (Douglas, J., concurring); *Hanson*, 351 U.S., at 238. At a minimum, the union may constitutionally "expend uniform exactions under the union-shop agreement in support of activities germane to collective bargaining." *Railway Clerks v. Allen*, 373 U.S., at 122. The issue is whether these expenses involve additional interference with the First Amendment interests of objecting employees, and, if so, whether they are nonetheless adequately supported by a governmental interest.

Petitioners do not explicitly contend that union social activities implicate serious First Amendment interests. We need not determine whether contributing money to such affairs is an act triggering First Amendment protection. To the extent it is, the communicative content is not inherent in the act, but stems from the union's involvement in it. The objection is that these are *union* social hours. Therefore, the fact that the employee is forced to contribute does not increase the infringement of his First Amendment rights already resulting from the compelled contribution to the union. Petitioners may feel that their money is not being well-spent, but that does not mean they have a First Amendment complaint.

The First Amendment concerns with regard to publications and conventions are more serious; both have direct communicative content and involve the expression of ideas. Nonetheless, we perceive little additional infringement of First Amendment rights beyond that already accepted, and none that is not justified by the governmental interests behind the union shop itself. As the discussion of these expenses indicated, they "relat[e] to the work of the union in the realm of collective bargaining." *Hanson*, 351 U.S., at 235. The very nature of the free-rider problem and the governmental interest in overcoming it require that the union have a certain flexibility in its use of compelled funds. "The furtherance of the common cause leaves some leeway for the leadership of the group." *Abood*, 431 U.S., at 222, quoting *Street*, 367 U.S., at 778 (Douglas, J., concurring). These expenses are well within the acceptable range.

VII

The Court of Appeals erred in holding that respondents were entitled to charge petitioners for their pro rata share of the union's organizing and litigating expenses, and that the former rebate scheme adequately protected the objecting employees from the misuse of their contributions. The decision of the Court of Appeals is affirmed in part and reversed in part and the case remanded for further proceedings consistent with this opinion.

It is so ordered.

JUSTICE POWELL, concurring in part and dissenting in part.

I am in accord with Parts I, II, III and IV of the Court's opinion, and with all of Part V except for Subsection 1, which addresses the "convention" issue. I also do not agree with the Court's analysis in Part VI in which petitioners' First Amendment arguments are disposed of summarily.

... I agree that conventions are necessary to elect officers, to determine union policy with respect to major issues of collective bargaining, and generally to enable the national union to perform its essential functions as the exclusive bargaining representative of employees. But, it is not seriously questioned that conventions also afford opportunities — that often are fully exploited — to further political objectives of unions generally and of the particular union in convention.

The District Court's findings in this case were based on the record with respect to the 25th quadrennial convention of BRAC. Its cost to the Union was approximately

$1,802,000. The minutes of the convention indicate that a number of major addresses were made by prominent politicians, including Senators Humphrey, Kennedy, Hartke, and Schweiker, the Mayor of Washington, D.C., and four congressmen. The Union has not shown how this major participation of politicians contributed even remotely to collective bargaining. Before a union may compel dissenting employees to defray the cost of union expenses, it must meet its burden of showing that those expenses were "necessarily or reasonably incurred for the purpose of performing the duties of an exclusive [collective bargaining] representative." See *Railway Clerks v. Allen*, 373 U.S., at 122. Apparently no effort was made by the Union in this case to identify expenses fairly attributable to these and other political activities, and to make appropriate deductions from the dues of objecting employees. I do not suggest that such an allocation can be made with mathematical exactitude. But reasonable estimates surely could have been made. See *id*. The Union properly felt a responsibility to allocate expenses where political material was carried in union publications.

In view of the foregoing, I do not understand how the Court can make the judgment today that all the expenses of the 25th quadrennial meeting of BRAC qualify under the Court's new standard as "necessarily or reasonably incurred for the purpose of performing the duties of an exclusive [collective-bargaining] representative." . . .

. . . I have expressed my disagreement with the Court's apparent determination that the Railway Labor Act permits the use of compulsory dues to help defray the costs of political activities incurred at the quadrennial conventions. Under that interpretation of the Act, it would be unnecessary to reach the constitutional question in this case. Even if Congress had intended the Act to permit such use of compulsory dues, it is clear that the First Amendment would not. Where funds are used to further political causes with which non-members may disagree, the decisions of this Court are explicit that non-member employees may not be compelled to bear such expenditures. The Court's conclusory disposition of petitioners' argument ignores the force of these decisions. See *Abood*, 431 U.S., at 234; *Street*, 376 U.S., at 777–778 (Douglas, J., concurring).

Notes

1. *Dues Expenditures Under the NLRA* — The Railway Labor Act's union security authorization provision presented a potential constitutional question because of the governmental action involved in the overriding of contrary state laws. Unlike the RLA, the NLRA contains an anti-preemption provision in §14(b), allowing state "right-to-work" laws to prohibit union security agreements despite the federal authorization for them. Thus, unions argued that the Supreme Court "need not strain to avoid the plain meaning" of the NLRA, which imposes no express restrictions on the spending of dues money. Nevertheless, in *Communications Workers of Am. v. Beck*, 487 U.S. 735 (1988), the Court held (5-3) that §8(a)(3) of the NLRA, like §2, Eleventh of the RLA, should be interpreted as forbidding union use of compulsory fees collected from objecting nonmember employees to fund activities unrelated to collective bargaining. Although the Court declared that the NLRB had primary jurisdiction over the § 8(a)(3) claim, it concluded a federal court could decide the merits of that claim insofar as it was necessary to resolve the employees' further challenge that the union had breached its duty of fair representation by its expenditures. The Court observed that the "same concern over the resentment spawned by 'free riders' in the railroad industry prompted Congress, four years after the passage of the Taft-Hartley Act, to amend the RLA," and that, in those circumstances, "Congress intended the same language to have the same meaning in both statutes." *See* Dau-Schmidt, *Union Security Agreements Under the National Labor Relations Act: The Statute, the Constitution, and the Court's Opinion in* Beck, 27 HARV. J. ON LEGIS. 51 (1990).

Although the Supreme Court held in *Ellis* that union organizing expenditures pertaining to bargaining units of other employers are not chargeable to objecting nonmembers, the Labor Board has limited that ruling to Railway Labor Act cases and held that NLRA unions may expend objector dues to organize the employees of competitor firms because of the union interest in limiting competition based on labor cost differentials and the direct relationship between wage levels of union-represented workers and the degree of unionization of employees in the same competitive market. *UFCW, Locals 951, 7 & 1036 (Meijer, Inc.)*, 329 N.L.R.B. 730 (1999), *enforced*, 284 F.3d 1099 (9th Cir.) (*en banc*), *amended*, 307 F.3d 760 (9th Cir), *cert. denied*, 537 U.S. 1024 (2002). In *Teamsters Local 75*, 349 N.L.R.B. 77 (2007), *enforced in relevant part*, 522 F.3d 423 (D.C. Cir. 2008), the Board indicated that unions wishing to rely upon this narrow exception must be able to demonstrate that the target firms within the same industry have a meaningful impact on the employment terms of individuals in the bargaining units whose dues money is being expended to support such organizing efforts.

The *Ellis* decision seemed to suggest that labor organizations could not use the dues money paid by financial core objectors to cover the litigation expenses incurred in lawsuits not pertaining to their own bargaining unit. In *Locke v. Karass*, 555 U.S. 207 (2009), however, the Court held that dues money paid by such objectors could be spent for non-unit litigation costs where the union imposes a reciprocal obligation on other locals to support litigation involving the unit of these employees if such litigation becomes necessary.

> In this case, a local union charges nonmembers a service fee that (among other things) reflects an affiliation fee that the local union pays to its national union organization. We focus upon one portion of that fee, a portion that the national union uses to pay for litigation expenses incurred in large part on behalf of *other* local units. We ask whether a local's charge to nonmembers that reflects that element is consistent with the First Amendment. And we conclude that under our precedent the Constitution permits including this element in the local's charge to nonmembers as long as (1) the subject matter of the (extra-local) litigation is of a kind that would be chargeable if the litigation were local, *e.g.*, litigation appropriately related to

collective bargaining rather than political activities, and (2) the litigation charge is reciprocal in nature, *i.e.*, the contributing local reasonably expects other locals to contribute similarly to the national's resources used for costs of similar litigation on behalf of the contributing local if and when it takes place.

More recently, the Labor Board has reaffirmed that private sector unions may not spend "agency fees" paid by nonmembers to fund lobbying efforts, since they may only charge nonmembers such fees for collective bargaining expenses and other nonpolitical activities. *United Nurses & Allied Professionals*, 367 N.L.R.B. No. 94 (2019).

2. *Public Sector Unions*—The public sector agency fee arrangements authorized by the Court in *Abood v. Detroit Bd. of Education*, 431 U.S. 209 (1977), cited and discussed in *Ellis*, were overruled in *Janus v. AFSCME, Council 31*, 138 S. Ct. 2448 (2018), in which the Supreme Court held that a state law requiring public sector employees who were not members of representative labor organizations to subsidize union representation activities violated the First Amendment free speech rights of those persons. The imposition of agency fees, according to the Court, forced individuals to endorse ideas about critically important matters of public concern, including the state's budget crisis, taxes, and collective bargaining issues related to education, child welfare, healthcare, and minority rights. This constraint on core free speech rights led the Court to apply heightened scrutiny to the agency fee system, a standard under which both of *Abood's* justifications were found to be lacking. The Court found that the agency fees could not be justified on the ground that they promoted labor peace, citing the millions of unionized employees working for the federal government and in states where agency fees are already prohibited. Further, the court found that avoiding free riders was not a compelling state interest and, in any case, could be overcome by less restrictive means than the imposition of agency fees.

While *Janus* was a major blow to union coffers and the progressive causes historically supported by labor, some scholars have argued that it should prompt a reexamination of what labor solidarity really means. The Court's agency fee doctrine in *Abood* backed unions into the position of identifying as narrow economic actors—service organizations dealing with a limited number of economic subjects in a transactional relationship with workers—which in turn reinforced the public perception of unions as special interest groups. Against this doctrinal backdrop, unions were forced to make the argument in *Janus* that they are merely economic agents, not political actors with a larger social justice agenda, in a vain attempt to salvage the dues equivalents from non-members. While this argument may make sense at a legal level, in the long run it may behoove unions to embrace their political identities rather than avoid them. *See* Crain & Matheny, *Labor Unions, Solidarity, and Money*, 22 Emp. Rts & Employ. Pol'y J. 259, 261–263 (2018).

3. *Voluntary Union Members*—A court of appeals ruled that voluntary union members, as distinguished from nonmembers who are contractually required to

pay agency shop fees, have no right under either the Railway Labor Act or the First Amendment to refuse to pay the costs of legitimate union activities even though they are unrelated to collective bargaining. *Kidwell v. Transportation Communications Int'l Union*, 946 F.2d 283 (4th Cir. 1991), *cert. denied*, 503 U.S. 1005 (1992). Another court found no First Amendment violation when a union insisted that nonmember employees who failed to respond within 30 days to two written notices informing them of their right to object to paying for the union's nonrepresentational activities had to pay an agency shop fee equal to full union dues. *Mitchell v. Los Angeles Unified School Dist.*, 963 F.2d 258 (9th Cir.), *cert. denied*, 506 U.S. 940 (1992).

4. *Information Requirements* — A labor organization has to supply agency-fee payers with sufficient financial data to enable them to decide whether to object to any portion of their dues being expended for inappropriate purposes. Although one court has ruled that a union may reasonably assume for accounting purposes that the allocation between chargeable and nonchargeable expenditures for the international organization is equal to the allocation for each local union (*Price v. International Union, United Autoworkers etc.*, 927 F.2d 88 (2d Cir. 1991)), another court has held that agency-fee payers are entitled to the disclosure of sufficient information to apprise them of the actual use being made by the international entity of their dues money (*Tierney v. Toledo*, 917 F.2d 927 (6th Cir. 1990)). *See also Teamsters, Local Union No. 579*, 350 N.L.R.B. 1166 (2007) (requiring labor organization to provide objector with financial information regarding its own expenditures and detailed information regarding expenditures of affiliate entities with which it shares dues receipts).

Must a labor organization provide nonmember objectors with financial information that has been verified by an independent auditor or may they rely on their own internal auditors? *Compare International Ass'n of Machinists & Aero. Workers v. NLRB*, 133 F.3d 1012 (7th Cir.), *cert. denied*, 525 U.S. 813 (1998) (internal union auditor sufficient), *with Ferriso v. NLRB*, 125 F.3d 865 (D.C. Cir. 1997) (requiring independent auditor).

4. State "Right-to-Work" Legislation

Statutory Reference

NLRA § 14(b)

Twenty-seven states (Alabama, Arizona, Arkansas, Florida, Georgia, Idaho, Indiana, Iowa, Kansas, Kentucky, Louisiana, Michigan, Mississippi, Nebraska, Nevada, North Carolina, North Dakota, Oklahoma, South Carolina, South Dakota, Tennessee, Texas, Utah, Virginia, West Virginia, Wisconsin, and Wyoming, see Lab. Rel. Rep. LRX 730:319) have "right-to-work" laws, which consist of constitutional or statutory prohibitions of union security arrangements. These laws take a variety of forms. Some merely forbid making union "membership" (or "nonmembership") a condition of employment. Such narrowly worded laws have invariably been interpreted by state courts or state attorneys general as reaching the agency shop as well as the union shop. Other statutes expressly prohibit conditioning employment on the payment of "dues, fees, or other charges of any kind" to a union. Several right-to-work laws go further, proscribing any "employment monopoly," or sanctioning individual bargaining despite the presence of a majority union. Enforcement provisions also vary widely. Most laws allow damages to persons injured by a violation, and many authorize injunctions. About half prescribe criminal penalties. In *Sweeney v. Pence*, 767 F.3d 654 (7th Cir. 2014), the court sustained the validity of the Indiana right-to-work law, finding that 14(b) is not limited to state laws prohibiting actual union membership as a condition of employment, but also allows laws proscribing agency shop provisions, and rejecting a claim that such laws conflict with the equal protection principles.

Right-to-work ordinances have been proposed or enacted in several cities and counties in states where passage of statewide right-to-work laws would be politically infeasible. Labor organizations have challenged these laws, claiming that they are preempted by the NLRA, since § 14(b) only allows a "State or Territory" to enact such legislation. The cities and counties involved claim that the 14(b) grant of authority extends to political subdivisions. How do you think this issue should be resolved? In *Auto Workers Local 3047 v. Hardin County*, 842 F.3d 407 (6th Cir. 2016), *cert. denied*, 138 S. Ct. 130 (2017), the court held that states and *state subdivisions*, including counties and municipalities, may enact such laws pertaining to their jurisdictions.

Retail Clerks, Local 1625 v. Schermerhorn

Supreme Court of the United States
373 U.S. 746, 83 S. Ct. 1461, 10 L. Ed. 2d 678 (1963)

[A collective bargaining agreement provided that employees who chose not to join the union would be required, as a condition of employment, to pay "service fees" to the union equal to the regular initiation fee and membership dues. Four nonunion employees sued to enjoin enforcement of this so-called agency shop clause on the ground it violated Florida's right-to-work law, which forbade denying a person the right to work on account of "membership or nonmembership" in a labor union. The Florida Supreme Court held its state law valid and applicable.]

MR. JUSTICE WHITE delivered the opinion of the Court.

... As is immediately apparent from its language, § 14(b) was designed to prevent other sections of the Act from completely extinguishing state power over certain union-security arrangements. And it was the proviso to § 8(a)(3), expressly permitting agreements conditioning employment upon membership in a labor union, which Congress feared might have this result. It was desired to "make certain" that § 8(a)(3) could not "be said to authorize arrangements of this sort in States where such arrangements were contrary to the State policy." H.R. Conf. Rep. No. 510, 80th Cong., 1st Sess. 60, 1 Leg. Hist. L.M.R.A. 564.

The connection between the § 8(a)(3) proviso and § 14(b) is clear. Whether they are perfectly coincident, we need not now decide, but unquestionably they overlap to some extent. At the very least, the agreements requiring "membership" in a labor union which are expressly permitted by the proviso are the same "membership" agreements expressly placed within the reach of state law by § 14(b). It follows that the *General Motors* case rules this one, for we there held that the "agency shop" arrangement involved here — which imposes on employees the only membership obligation enforceable under § 8(a)(3) by discharge, namely, the obligation to pay initiation fees and regular dues — is the "practical equivalent" of an "agreement requiring membership in a labor organization as a condition of employment." Whatever may be the status of less stringent union-security arrangements, the agency shop is within § 14(b). At least to that extent did Congress intend § 8(a)(3) and § 14(b) to coincide.

Petitioners, belatedly, would now distinguish the contract involved here from the agency shop contract dealt with in the *General Motors* case on the basis of allegedly distinctive features which are said to require a different result. Article 19 provides for nonmember payments to the union "for the purpose of aiding the Union in defraying costs in connection with its legal obligations and responsibilities as the exclusive bargaining agent of the employees in the appropriate bargaining unit," a provision which petitioners say confines the use of nonmember payments to collective bargaining purposes alone and forbids their use by the union for institutional purposes unrelated to its exclusive agency functions, all in sharp contrast, it is argued, to the *General Motors* situation where the nonmember contributions are available to the union without restriction.

We are wholly unpersuaded. There is before us little more than a complaint with its exhibits. The agency shop clause of the contract is, at best, ambiguous on its face and it should not, in the present posture of the case, be construed against respondent to raise a substantial difference between this and the *General Motors* case. There is no ironclad restriction imposed upon the use of nonmember fees, for the clause merely describes the payments as being for "the purpose of aiding the Union" in meeting collective bargaining expenses. The alleged restriction would not be breached if the service fee was used for both collective bargaining and other expenses, for the union would be "aided" in meeting its agency obligations, not only by the part spent for bargaining purposes but also by the part spent for institutional items, since an equivalent amount of other union income would thereby be freed to pay the costs of bargaining agency functions.

But even if all collections from nonmembers must be directly committed to paying bargaining costs, this fact is of bookkeeping significance only rather than a matter of real substance. It must be remembered that the service fee is admittedly the exact equal of membership initiation fees and monthly dues, . . . and that, as the union says in its brief, dues collected from members may be used for a "variety of purposes, in addition to meeting the union's costs of collective bargaining." Unions "rather typically" use their membership dues "to do those things which the members authorize the union to do in their interest and on their behalf." If the union's total budget is divided between collective bargaining and institutional expenses and if nonmember payments, equal to those of a member, go entirely for collective bargaining costs, the nonmember will pay more of these expenses than his pro rata share. The member will pay less and to that extent a portion of his fees and dues is available to pay institutional expenses. The union's budget is balanced. By paying a larger share of collective bargaining costs the nonmember subsidizes the union's institutional activities. In over-all effect, economically, and we think for the purposes of §14(b), the contract here is the same as the *General Motors* agency shop arrangement. Petitioners' argument, if accepted, would lead to the anomalous result of permitting Florida to invalidate the agency shop but forbidding it to ban the present service fee arrangement under which collective bargaining services cost the nonmember more than the member. . . .

Retail Clerks International Ass'n, Local 1625 v. Schermerhorn, 375 U.S. 96, 84 S. Ct. 219, 11 L. Ed. 2d 179 (1963). On reargument, it was held that §14(b) allows the states not only to prohibit the execution and application of union security agreements, but also to enforce their laws by appropriate sanctions:

> On the other hand, picketing in order to get an employer to execute an agreement to hire all-union labor in violation of a state union-security statute lies exclusively in the federal domain . . . because state power, recognized by §14(b), begins *only with the actual negotiation and execution of the type of agreement described by §14(b)*. [Emphasis in the original.]

Note

In *Local Joint Executive Board v. NLRB*, 657 F.3d 865 (9th Cir. 2011), the court held that dues checkoff provisions remain mandatory subjects for bargaining even in right-to-work states, since §14(b) only provides states with the authority to prohibit union security provisions, but does not give them the authority to regulate dues checkoff arrangements.

In *Albertson's/Max Food Warehouse*, 329 N.L.R.B. 410 (1999), the Labor Board held that the portion of the Colorado Labor Peace Act, which places greater limits than does federal law on the ability of employees covered by union security arrangements to seek deauthorization elections, transcends the authority granted states under §14(b).

Could a state prohibit a requirement that nonunion employees pay a "service fee" to cover the pro rata share of the union's expenses in negotiating and administering the collective-bargaining agreement? A divided panel of the D.C. Circuit held that a union violated §8(b)(3) of the NLRA when it insisted to impasse on a provision requiring nonunion employees to pay a "representation fee," covering the union's pro rata costs of "enforcing and servicing" its collective bargaining agreement once it was in effect, in a state whose right-to-work law prohibited the requirement of such fees. *International Union of United Ass'n of Journeymen & Apprentices of Plumbing & Pipefitting Industry v. NLRB*, 675 F.2d 1257 (D.C. Cir. 1982), *cert. denied*, 459 U.S. 1171 (1983). In *Cone v. Nev. Serv. Emples. Union/SEIU Local 1107*, 116 Nev.

473, 998 P.2d 1178 (2000), however, the court held that the Nevada right-to-work law authorizes unions to charge nonmembers fees for their representation in grievance handling. Does § 14(b) grant states the authority to regulate this aspect of the union-bargaining unit member relationship?

Some right-to-work laws, by their terms or through interpretation, purport to outlaw the exclusive hiring hall. *See, e.g.,* WYO. LAWS c. 39, § 5; *Kaiser v. Price-Fewell, Inc.*, 235 Ark. 295, 359 S.W.2d 449 (1962), *cert. denied*, 371 U.S. 955 (1963). The NLRB, however, holds that nondiscriminatory hiring halls are not a form of union security subject to state regulation under § 14(b). *Houston Chapter, Associated General Contractors of America, Inc. (Local 18, Hod Carriers)*, 143 N.L.R.B. 409 (1963), *enforced*, 349 F.2d 449 (5th Cir. 1965).

In *Algoma Plywood & Veneer Co. v. Wisconsin Empl. Rels. Bd.*, 336 U.S. 301 (1949), the Supreme Court upheld a state statute that did not absolutely prohibit union security agreements, but that regulated them by requiring a two-thirds employee vote for authorization.

C. Which Activities Are Protected Under Section 7?

To support a finding that §§ 8(a)(1) or 8(a)(3) has been violated, the record in the case must show that the complaining employees were engaged in activities that are protected under § 7. Clearly, employer retaliation or discrimination against workers because of their union membership falls within the protection of the Act.

Section 7 of the Act not only protects the right of employees to join (or refrain from joining) unions, but also their right to engage in other concerted activities for the purpose of mutual aid or protection. Employers that discriminate against employees for engaging in those kinds of activities may not have violated 8(a)(3), but they very well might have interfered with, restrained, or coerced employees in the exercise of these broader § 7 rights in violation of 8(a)(1). And the principal issue in these cases is very often whether the employee behavior being discouraged is, in fact, protected concerted activity under the Act.

Some concerted activities such as striking for higher wages are obviously protected by § 7 against employer reprisal. (*See* the *Mackay Radio* case in this section.) But even informal action without union organization may be protected, as long as it is "concerted" and "for mutual aid and protection." For example, in *NLRB v. Washington Aluminum Co.*, 370 U.S. 9 (1962), the action of seven employees who walked off their jobs to protest cold working conditions was found protected, and in *Ohio Oil Co.*, 92 N.L.R.B. 1597 (1951), an informal protest against the elimination of overtime work was held protected, although the participating employees had no authorization from other workers. Similarly, the Labor Board found that a slaughterhouse violated the NLRA when it discharged kill floor and boning room employees who walked off the job to protest a coworker's termination, since they were engaged in protected concerted activity. *Cent. Valley Meat Co.*, 346 N.L.R.B. 1078 (2006). *See also Atlantic-Pacific Constr. Co. v. NLRB*, 52 F.3d 260 (9th Cir. 1995) (group letter protesting selection of unpopular coworker as new supervisor protected); *St. Rose Dominican Hospitals*, 360 N.L.R.B. 1130 (2014) (employee who asked coworkers to support his defense against claim he had threatened another employee engaged in protected concerted activity); *Bob Evans Farms v. NLRB*, 163 F.3d 1012 (7th Cir. 1998) (walkout to protest discharge of supervisor protected when employees believed supervisor's termination would adversely affect their working conditions).

On the other hand, not all informal actions directed at improving workplace conditions are protected. For example, in *Joanna Cotton Mills Co. v. NLRB*, 176 F.2d 749 (4th Cir. 1949), the court held that circulating a petition for the removal of a supervisor was not protected because the individual was nursing a grudge against the supervisor and the petition was not truly being circulated "for mutual aid and protection." In another case, the Board found that when an employee sent an anonymous letter on behalf of several workers to their employer complaining about the work of the maintenance facilitator and falsely listed the name and address of a coworker on the envelope, he was not engaged in protected concerted activity, since the deliberate falsification of the coworker's name on the envelope posed a substantial risk to that person's reputation and employment status. *Ogihara America Corp.*, 347 N.L.R.B. 110 (2006), *enforced*, 514 F.3d 574 (6th Cir. 2008). And when an employee engages in wholly individual conduct not designed to elicit concerted behavior by coworkers, that person's behavior is likely to be found unprotected. *Summit Regional Medical Ctr.*, 357 N.L.R.B. 1614 (2011).

1. Concerted Activity on Social Media

Unfair labor practice complaints based upon employee postings on social media sites have increased dramatically in the last decade. NLRB field offices have issued charges against employers in a number of these instances. The Labor Board has found violations of § 8(a)(1) in a number of cases involving social media postings by employees and has issued guidance to employers.

In one of the earliest cases to address social media postings, *Hispanics United of Buffalo Inc.*, 359 N.L.R.B. 368 (2012), Lydia Cruz-Moore, an advocate for victims of domestic violence employed by a nonprofit Buffalo, New York, social service provider, criticized other employees for keeping clients waiting and for not doing their jobs. When Cruz-Moore announced her intention to take her complaints to the social service organization's executive director, a coworker posted a message on her personal Facebook page during off-duty time complaining about Cruz-Moore's criticisms and asking other employees how they felt. Four other employees responded in a sympathetic vein. Cruz-Moore saw the comments on Facebook and became upset. Cruz-Moore complained to the executive director, who discharged the Facebook-posting employees for violating the company's zero-tolerance policy against harassment and bullying by posting on their Facebook pages. The Board ruled that the discharges violated the Act. The Facebook postings were for the purpose of mutual aid or protection since they represented "a first step towards taking group action to defend themselves against the accusations they could reasonably believe Cruz-Moore was going to make to management." Further, they were concerted and focused on job performance, a protected subject of discussion. The employer was ordered to reinstate the terminated employees and to make them whole for loss of pay or benefits stemming from the discharges. *Accord, Triple Play Sports Bar & Grille*, 361 N.L.R.B. 308 (2014), *enforced, Three D, LLC v. NLRB*, 2015 U.S. App. LEXIS 18493 (2d Cir. 2015).

In evaluating protection for social media postings, the Board has struggled with how to handle section 7 protected activity that is intertwined with profanity or other comments that are insubordinate or disrespectful toward management. Initially, the Board assessed the section 7 activity and the profanity or insubordinate speech holistically. For example, in *Pier Sixty, LLC*, 362 N.L.R.B. 505 (2015), *enforced*, 855 F.3d 115 (2d Cir. 2017), an employee complaining about mistreatment of workers by a supervisor posted comments on Facebook during his break, stating that the supervisor was "such a NASTY MOTHER F — ER" and "f — his mother and his entire f — ing family!!! What a LOSER!!! Vote YES for the UNION!!!" He was discharged for such conduct, but the Obama Board found his termination to violate § 8(a)(3). The statements constituted protected concerted activity protesting poor supervisory treatment, and encouraged coworkers to vote for the union in a coming election to rectify this situation. The Board noted that the employer had tolerated widespread use of profanity in the workplace, and did not have a policy prohibiting offensive language by employees. *Compare Good Samaritan Med. Ctr. v. NLRB*, 858 F.3d 617 (1st Cir. 2017) (employer did not violate the NLRA when it discharged a worker complaining about a union security policy, where the termination was based upon the employee's overt rudeness rather than the substance of his complaint). Most recently, the Trump Board criticized the "totality of the circumstances" approach used in *Pier Sixty* and other social media cases involving employee speech that contains profanity or abusive language, indicating that it will henceforth apply the *Wright Line* test to determine whether an employee's conduct loses protection where discipline is imposed on an employee who has engaged in both protected conduct and abusive or profane speech. Under the *Wright Line* test, the Board General Counsel must establish that the employee engaged in section 7 activity, that the employer knew of the activity, and that the employer had animus against the activity, established by proof of a causal relationship between the discipline and the section 7 activity. *GM LLC and Charles Robinson*, 369 N.L.R.B. No. 127 (2020).

What degree of activity on Facebook should be required for §7 protection to attach? For example, if an employee posted Facebook comments containing some obscenities critical of the employer, and another worker added a post "liking" those comments, would liking the post be sufficient activity to warrant statutory protection? In *Triple Play Sports Bar & Grille*, 361 N.L.R.B. 308 (2014), the Board ruled that it would, and the Second Circuit enforced the Board's order. *Three D, LLC v. NLRB*, 2015 U.S. App. LEXIS 18493 (2d Cir. 2015).

2. Employer Work Rules and Policies Potentially Restricting § 7 Activity

Company policies limiting employee speech may violate the NLRA where employees would reasonably interpret them as limiting their exercise of § 7 rights, effectively chilling speech that might lead to formation of a union or other concerted activity. *See Lafayette Park Hotel*, 326 N.L.R.B. 824, 825 (1998), *enforced*, 203 F.3d 52 (D.C. Cir. 1999). For example, employers that use confidentiality policies that limit the right of employees to discuss their wages and employment terms among themselves are usually found in violation of § 8(a)(1) for interfering with the concerted rights of those workers. *See Cintas Corp. v. NLRB*, 482 F.3d 463 (D.C. Cir. 2007); *Double Eagle Hotel & Casino v. NLRB*, 414 F.3d 1249 (10th Cir. 2005), *cert. denied*, 546 U.S. 1170 (2006). For a comprehensive analysis of pay secrecy/confidentiality rules, see Gely & Bierman, *Pay Secrecy/Confidentiality Rules and the National Labor Relations Act*, 6 U. PA. J. LAB. & EMP. L. 121 (2003). *See also Phoenix Transit Sys.*, 337 N.L.R.B. 510 (2002) (employer violated NLRA when it enforced "confidentiality rule" prohibiting employees from discussing among themselves complaints concerning sexual harassment). Employees using email to discuss wages or working conditions are likely to be protected under § 7. *See Timekeeping Sys.*, 323 N.L.R.B. 244 (1997).

In *Lutheran Heritage Village-Livonia*, 343 N.L.R.B. 646, 647 (2004), the Board began using a two-step inquiry to evaluate employer work rules. First, it asked whether the rule *explicitly* restricted § 7 protected activities; if it did, it violated § 8(a)(1), which prohibits interference with, restraint, or coercion of employees in the exercise of § 7 rights. Under this prong of the analysis, for example, a rule that prohibited employees from discussing or denigrating the employees' terms and conditions of employment in any forum would violate § 8(a)(1), as would pay confidentiality provisions. If the company rule did not explicitly restrict § 7 protected activity, it still could have violated § 8(a)(1) if: (1) employees could reasonably construe the language to prohibit § 7 activity; (2) the rule was promulgated in response to union activity; or (3) the rule had been applied to restrict the exercise of § 7 rights. *See also Fresh & Easy Neighborhood Market*, 361 N.L.R.B. 72 (2014) (code of conduct limiting employee discussions with each other regarding their wages and employment conditions contravenes § 8(a)(1)).

Under this test, employer policies that prohibited employees from sharing or disseminating "confidential information," such as employee names, addresses, telephone numbers, email addresses, and financial data were found to infringe on section 7 rights. *MCPc, Inc.*, 360 N.L.R.B. 216 (2014) (policy prohibiting internal dissemination of confidential information invalid). If the policies contained no limiting language linking the types of confidential information to particular business purposes, they were construed against the employer and violated § 8(a)(1). *Flex Frac Logistics, LLC*, 358 N.L.R.B. 1131 (2012), *enforced*, 746 F.3d 205 (5th Cir. 2014) (confidentiality provision prohibiting disclosure of "personnel information and documents" "outside of the organization" was overbroad because employees might believe they could not discuss wages and conditions of employment with non-employee union organizers). On the other hand, company policies that advanced legitimate employer business interests such as preventing disclosure of trade secrets, prohibiting harassment, bullying, discrimination, or retaliation were not found to violate the NLRA, particularly if they provided specific illustrations of prohibited acts. *See Clearwater Paper Corp.*, No. 19-CA-64418. For example, a social media policy developed by Wal-Mart survived scrutiny by the Board's general counsel where it prohibited "inappropriate postings" including "discriminatory remarks, harassment, and threats of violence or similar inappropriate or unlawful conduct." Restrictions on tone instructing employees to "be fair and courteous" to fellow employees and suggesting that they are more likely to resolve work-related complaints by speaking directly to coworkers or by utilizing Wal-Mart's open door policy than by posting complaints on social media sites were also lawful. Board counsel found the policy gave specific examples of prohibited conduct, was aimed at egregious and unlawful conduct, and was not used to discipline § 7 activity. *See Walmart*, No. 11-CA-67171.

Many other common workplace policies violated § 8(a)(1) under the second prong of the *Lutheran Heritage Village* test because employees could reasonably understand them as prohibiting conversation critical of the company, its supervisors, and working conditions. For example, anti-disparagement rules, rules barring negativity or requiring employees to represent the employer in a positive and professional manner in the community, and no-gossip policies were found unlawful under that standard. *See Dish Network*, 359 N.L.R.B. No. 108 (2012) (policy forbidding employees from making "disparaging or defamatory comments" about the company on social media sites violated § 8(a)(1)), reaffirmed following *Noel Canning*, No. 16-CA-062433; *Hills & Dales General Hosp.*, 360 N.L.R.B. 611 (2014) (policy banning "negativity" and requiring employees to represent the employer in the community "in a positive and professional manner in every opportunity" violated § 8(a)(1)). *See also Component Bar Prods., Inc.*, 364 N.L.R.B. No. 140 (2016) (employer violated NLRA when it maintained handbook rule prohibiting "disrespectful conduct" or "other disruptive activity in the workplace," where it applied rule to discharge employee who called coworker to warn him that his job was in jeopardy since classic protected concerted activity).

More recently, in *The Boeing Co., Inc.*, 365 N.L.R.B. 634 (2017), the Board changed course and established a new test applicable to employer work rules that are facially neutral but that may, reasonably interpreted, potentially interfere with section 7 rights. The test gives more weight to business needs than the prior test, which the Board said gave too little consideration to employer interests. Under the new test, when a facially neutral rule potentially interferes with section 7 rights, the Board will consider: (1) the nature and extent of the potential impact on NLRA rights from the employees' perspective, and (2) legitimate business justifications associated with the rule's requirements, and strike the proper balance between them. Applying this test, the Board upheld the employer's "no-camera" rule banning workers from using devices to take photos or videos on job sites without permission.

The Board went on to explain that in future cases it would endeavor to provide greater clarity by establishing three categories of employment policies, rules, and handbook provisions. Category 1 would include rules that the Board designates as lawful, such as general civility policies requiring workplace harmony, since the policies would have minimal impact on workers' rights to engage in protected activity. (Such rules could, however, be unlawfully applied, for example in a discriminatory fashion). Category 2 would include rules that warrant individualized scrutiny and balancing by the Board. Category 3 would include rules that the Board designates as unlawful, such as a rule that prohibits employees from discussing wages or benefits.

Under the new *Boeing* test, the Labor Board held that employers can lawfully ban employees from discussing ongoing workplace investigations to protect the interests of the persons involved in such investigations. *Apogee Retail LLC, dba Unique Thrift Store*, 368 N.L.R.B. No. 144 (2019). In that case, the Board found that the impact of such rules on employees is "comparatively slight," so long as they are limited to ongoing investigations. If such a rule was not limited to ongoing activities, it would likely be found improper.

Problems

14. A large staffing company maintained a detailed dress code for its employees that prohibited certain types of clothing, body piercings, and tattoos. Ana, who has facial piercings, began working for the company a few months ago, and almost immediately began running afoul of its dress code. Although she was initially told that her facial piercings were not a problem, her supervisor soon told her to remove her piercings at work. Her supervisor also verbally counseled her about wearing jeans in the workplace.

A few weeks ago, the company emailed its employees about a golfing event it was sponsoring and set forth a dress requirement for the event that, among other things, required female employees to wear collared shirts and pants or non-denim shorts that were not "too short." Ana attended the golfing event wearing a collared shirt and capri pants. The following day, her supervisor issued her a written final warning for violating the dress code policy.

After work that day, Ana asked one of her coworkers, Bob, if she could get his advice on a confidential matter. Bob said yes, and Ana told him about her written warning for a dress code violation and explained why she believed it was unfair, since her pants were not denim and several other women were also wearing capri pants at the event. Ana told Bob that she was contemplating bringing the matter to the attention of higher management at an upcoming company picnic. Bob told her not to worry about it.

About a week later, though, Bob told Ana's supervisor about his conversation with her, and complained that Ana had been disrupting his work. The supervisor called Ana into his office and handed her a letter stating that she was terminated for "unprofessionalism" consisting of "attitude, dress code and negativity to other staff and corporate representatives." When pressed, her supervisor told Ana that he had heard about her conversation with Bob and that going over his head to higher management would have put him in a bad spot.

Did the staffing company commit an unfair labor practice when it fired Ana?

15. Knauz Automobile, a car dealership, hosted an "Ultimate Driving Event" to introduce a redesigned version of its high-end luxury vehicles. The sales staff met with management a day or two prior to the event to discuss what was expected of them. When the general sales manager described the food that would be served (hot dogs, bags of chips, cookies, bowls of apples and oranges, and bottles of water), sales people complained that their commissions depended upon vehicle sales, the event focused on their "bread and butter product," and that the food was substandard given the brand's luxury image. On the day of the event, a salesman, Robert, took pictures of the sales people holding hot dogs, water, and chips and posted the pictures on his social media page together with the following comment:

> I was happy to see that Knauz went "All Out" for the most important launch of a new luxury vehicle in years. A car that will generate tens of millions of dollars in revenues for Knauz over the next few years. The small 8 oz bags of chips, the $2.00 cookie plate, and the semi fresh apples and oranges were such a nice touch, but to top it all off, the Hot Dog Cart, where our clients could get an overcooked wiener on a stale bun.

Underneath the posting were comments by friends and coworkers, followed by Robert's responses. Knauz management became aware of Robert's posting, and discharged him for violation of its "workplace courtesy" policy, which prohibited the use of "disrespectful" language, profanity, or "any other language which injures the image or reputation of the Dealership."

Did Knauz Automobile commit an unfair labor practice when it fired Robert?

3. Arbitration Clauses Prohibiting Class Actions in the Nonunion Setting

Employee rights to engage in concerted activity protected under §7 of the NLRA encompass a number of activities besides union organizing and collective bargaining, and it is well-established that employers cannot require employees to waive their rights to engage in concerted activity. The Board had consistently ruled that §7 also protected the right to proceed collectively to enforce statutory or contractual employment rights, including through litigation, usually in the context of situations where employees were discharged in retaliation for bringing class claims. Accordingly, in *D.R. Horton, Inc.*, 357 N.L.R.B. 2277 (2012), the Board ruled that a predispute agreement that required arbitration of claims on an individual basis and simultaneously blocked employees from filing a lawsuit or other civil proceeding relating to employment on a class or collective basis violated §8(a)(1) of the NLRA. It found that the contractual language would lead employees reasonably to believe that they were prohibited from exercising their associational rights under §7 of the NLRA. The Board reasoned that just as the processing of a labor grievance under the arbitration machinery in a collective bargaining agreement is concerted activity (citing *NLRB v. City Disposal Systems, Inc.*, 465 U.S. 822, 836 (1984)), so, too are claims pursued in employment arbitration by two or more employees. 357 N.L.R.B. at 2278–79. According to the Board, the right to proceed concertedly was the core substantive right protected by the NLRA, regardless of the statutory or contractual basis for the underlying claim. *Id.* at 2285–86. The Fifth Circuit refused to enforce this part of the Board's order, finding that the NLRB had failed to give sufficient weight to the FAA and that the right to bring class claims is not a substantive right. *D.R Horton, Inc. v. NLRB*, 737 F.3d 344, 357 (5th Cir. 2013). Other circuits later agreed with the Board's interpretation and a circuit split developed. The Supreme Court granted certiorari in three consolidated cases and resolved the issue in the following case.

Epic Systems Corp. v. Lewis, 138 S. Ct. 1612 (2018). An employer and employee in each of the consolidated cases entered into agreements providing for individualized arbitration proceedings to resolve any employment disputes. Each employee, however, then sought to litigate claims under the Fair Labor Standards Act and related state law claims through class actions in federal court. The employees argued that although the Federal Arbitration Act requires courts to enforce arbitration agreements as written, its "savings clause" removes that obligation if the agreement violates some other federal law. In this case, the employees argued that requiring individualized proceedings violated the National Labor Relations Act, which guarantees a right to engage in concerted activity.

A five-Justice majority held that employment contracts requiring employees to resolve all employment disputes through private arbitration procedures on an individual basis and that preclude class action cases are enforceable under the Federal Arbitration Act and are not contrary to the collective action provision in the NLRA. The Court found that Congress intended the Arbitration Act to permit the enforcement of agreements requiring persons to arbitrate employment disputes on an individual basis. The Court also found that the general language set forth in Section 7 of the NLRA did not indicate a congressional intention to modify the express language set forth in the Arbitration Act, explaining:

> The notion that Section 7 confers a right to class or collective actions seems pretty unlikely when you recall that procedures like that were hardly known when the NLRA was adopted in 1935. Federal Rule of Civil Procedure 23 didn't create the modern class action until 1966; class arbitration didn't emerge until later still; and even the Fair Labor Standards Act's collective action provision postdated Section 7 by years.

The Court went on to reject the very notion that the NLRA's protection of "other concerted activities for the purposes of . . . other mutual aid or protection" could be read to include class and collective legal actions:

> [T]he term appears at the end of a detailed list of activities speaking of "self-organization," "form[ing], join[ing], or assist[ing] labor organizations,"

and "bargain[ing] collectively." 29 U.S.C. §157. And where, as here, a more general term follows more specific terms in a list, the general term is usually understood to "'embrace only objects similar in nature to those objects enumerated by the preceding specific words.'" *Circuit City Stores, Inc. v. Adams*, 532 U.S. 105, 115 (2001) (discussing *ejusdem generis* canon); *National Assn. of Mfrs. v. Department of Defense*, 583 U.S. ___, ___, (2018) (slip op., at 10). All of which suggests that the term "other concerted activities" should, like the terms that precede it, serve to protect things employees "just do" for themselves in the course of exercising their right to free association in the workplace, rather than "the highly regulated, courtroom-bound 'activities' of class and joint litigation." *Alternative Entertainment*, 858 F.3d, at 414–415 (Sutton, J., concurring in part and dissenting in part) (emphasis deleted).

This case involved claims arising under the Fair Labor Standards Act, and the Court did not have to decide whether such arbitration provisions could prevent groups of employees from raising unfair labor practice issues before the Labor Board. The four dissenting Justices strongly disagreed with the majority opinion, pointing out that such arbitration provisions precluding class claims would significantly reduce the number of small value claims affecting many employees that would traditionally be handled through class action lawsuits.

Note

The substantive rights at issue in *Epic Systems* were NLRA rights, not FLSA rights, although the employees ultimately sought to bring FLSA claims. How did the employees argue that their NLRA rights were threatened? How does the Court majority understand the scope of rights protected by §7? Do you think its reasoning is consistent with the statutory text and precedent?

As a result of the *Epic Systems Corp.* decision, the Labor Board has held that employers do not violate the NLRA when they require employees to waive their right to pursue class actions through judicial or arbitral proceedings. *Arise Virtual Solutions, Inc.*, 366 N.L.R.B. No. 163 (2018). Nevertheless, in *Prime Healthcare*, 368 N.L.R.B. No. 10 (2019), *review dismissed*, 2019 U.S. App. LEXIS 38937 (D.C. Cir. 2019), a unanimous Labor Board held that despite the *Epic Systems Corp.* decision, it would be an unfair labor practice for an employer to require employees to sign an arbitration agreement that would preclude access to the NLRB. "No legitimate justification outweighs, or could outweigh, the adverse impact of such provisions on employee rights and the administration of the Act." *Accord*, *Beena Beauty Holding, Inc.*, 2019 L.R.R.M. 386501 (2019). And finally, in *Cordua Restaurants*, 368 N.L.R.B. No. 43 (2019), the Labor Board held that an employer violated the NLRA when it discharged an employee who filed a collective action with two other workers under the Fair Labor Standards Act, since their action was clearly concerted and they had no contractual obligation to take such claims to arbitration. Nonetheless, the Board held that employers may warn workers that they may be discharged if they fail or refuse to sign mandatory arbitration agreements requiring them to resolve all of

4. Constructive Concerted Activity

NLRB v. City Disposal Systems

Supreme Court of the United States
465 U.S. 822, 104 S. Ct. 1505, 79 L. Ed. 2d 839 (1984)

JUSTICE BRENNAN delivered the opinion of the Court.

James Brown, a truck driver employed by respondent, was discharged when he refused to drive a truck that he honestly and reasonably believed to be unsafe because of faulty brakes. Article XXI of the collective-bargaining agreement between respondent and Local 247 of the International Brotherhood of Teamsters, Chauffeurs, Warehousemen and Helpers of America, which covered Brown, provides:

> [t]he Employer shall not require employees to take out on the streets or highways any vehicle that is not in safe operating condition or equipped with safety appliances prescribed by law. It shall not be a violation of the Agreement where employees refuse to operate such equipment unless such refusal is unjustified.

The question to be decided is whether Brown's honest and reasonable assertion of his right to be free of the obligation to drive unsafe trucks constituted "concerted activit[y]" within the meaning of §7 of the National Labor Relations Act (NLRA or Act), 29 U.S.C. §157. The National Labor Relations Board (NLRB or Board) held that Brown's refusal was concerted activity within §7, and that his discharge was, therefore, an unfair labor practice under §8(a)(1) of the Act, 29 U.S.C. 158(a). 256 N.L.R.B. 451 (1981). The Court of Appeals disagreed and declined enforcement. 683 F.2d 1005 (CA6 (1982)....

I

The facts are not in dispute in the current posture of this case. Respondent, City Disposal System, Inc. (City Disposal), hauls garbage for the City of Detroit....

James Brown was assigned to truck No. 245. On Saturday, May 12, 1979, Brown observed that a fellow driver had difficulty with the brakes of another truck, truck No. 244. As a result of the brake problem, truck No. 244 nearly collided with Brown's truck. After unloading their garbage at the land fill, Brown and the driver of truck No. 244 brought No. 244 to respondent's truck-repair facility, where they were told that the brakes would be repaired either over the weekend or in the morning of Monday, May 14.

Early in the morning of Monday, May 14, while transporting a load of garbage to the land fill, Brown experienced difficulty with one of the wheels of his own truck—No. 245—and brought that truck in for repair. At the repair facility, Brown was told that, because of a backlog at the facility, No. 245 could not be repaired that day.

Brown reported the situation to his supervisor, Otto Jasmund, who ordered Brown to punch out and go home. Before Brown could leave, however, Jasmund changed his mind and asked Brown to drive truck No. 244 instead. Brown refused, explaining that "there's something wrong with that truck. . . . [S]omething was wrong with the brakes . . . there was a grease seal or something leaking causing it to be affecting the brakes." Brown did not, however, explicitly refer to Article XXI of the collective-bargaining agreement or to the agreement in general. In response to Brown's refusal to drive truck No. 244, Jasmund angrily told Brown to go home. At that point, an argument ensued and Robert Madary, another supervisor, intervened, repeating Jasmund's request that Brown drive truck No. 244. Again, Brown refused, explaining that No. 244 "has got problems and I don't want to drive it." Madary replied that half the trucks had problems and that if respondent tried to fix all of them it would be unable to do business. He went on to tell Brown that "[w]e've got all this garbage out here to haul and you tell me about you don't want to drive." Brown responded, "Bob, what you going to do, put the garbage ahead of the safety of the men?" Finally, Madary went to his office and Brown went home. Later that day, Brown received word that he had been discharged. He immediately returned to work in an attempt to gain reinstatement but was unsuccessful.

On May 15, the day after the discharge, Brown filed a written grievance, pursuant to the collective-bargaining agreement, asserting that truck No. 244 was defective, that it had been improper for him to have been ordered to drive the truck, and that his discharge was therefore also improper. The union, however, found no objective merit in the grievance and declined to process it.

On September 7, 1979, Brown filed an unfair labor practice charge with the NLRB, challenging his discharge. . . .

II

Section 7 of the NLRA provides that "[e]mployees shall have the right to . . . join or assist labor organizations, to bargain collectively through representatives of their own choosing, and to engage in other concerted activities for the purpose of collective bargaining or other mutual aid or protection." 29 U.S.C. §157 (emphasis added). The NLRB's decision in this case applied the Board's longstanding "*Interboro* doctrine," under which an individual's assertion of a right grounded in a collective-bargaining agreement is recognized as "concerted activit[y]" and therefore accorded the protection of §7. *See Interboro Contractors, Inc.*, 157 N.L.R.B. 1295, 1298 (1966), enforced, 388 F.2d 495 (CA2 1967); *Bunney Bros. Construction Co.*, 139 N.L.R.B. 1516, 1519 (1962). The Board has relied on two justifications for the doctrine: First, the assertion of a right contained in a collective-bargaining agreement is an extension of the concerted action that produced the agreement, *Bunney Bros. Construction, supra*, at 1519; and second, the assertion of such a right affects the rights of all employees covered by the collective-bargaining agreement. *Interboro Contractors, supra*, at 1298. . . .

Neither the Court of Appeals nor respondent appears to question that an employee's invocation of a right derived from a collective-bargaining agreement meets §7's requirement that an employee's action be taken "for purposes of collective bargaining or other mutual aid or protection." As the Board first explained in the *Interboro* case, a single employee's invocation of such rights affects all the employees that are covered by the collective-bargaining agreement. *Interboro Contractors, Inc., supra*, at 1298. This type of generalized effect, as our cases have demonstrated, is sufficient to bring the actions of an individual employee within the "mutual aid or protection" standard, regardless of whether the employee has his own interests most immediately in mind. *See, e.g., Weingarten v. NLRB*, 420 U.S. 251, 260–261 (1974).

The term "concerted activit[y]" is not defined in the Act but it clearly enough embraces the activities of employees who have joined together in order to achieve common goals. . . .

Although one could interpret the phrase, "to engage in concerted activities," to refer to a situation in which two or more employees are working together at the same time and the same place toward a common goal, the language of §7 does not confine itself to such a narrow meaning. In fact, §7 itself defines both joining and assisting labor organizations—activities in which a single employee can engage—as concerted activities. Indeed, even the courts that have rejected the *Interboro* doctrine recognize the possibility that an individual employee may be engaged in concerted activity when he acts alone. They have limited their recognition of this type of concerted activity, however, to two situations: (1) that in which the lone employee intends to induce group activity, and (2) that in which the employee acts as a representative of at least one other employee. *See, e.g., Aro, Inc. v. NLRB*, 596 F.2d, at 713, 717 (CA6 1979); *NLRB v. Northern Metal Co.*, 440 F.2d 881, 884 (CA3 1971). . . .

The invocation of a right rooted in a collective-bargaining agreement is unquestionably an integral part of the process that gave rise to the agreement. That process—beginning with the organization of a union, continuing into the negotiation of a collective-bargaining agreement, and extending through the enforcement of the agreement—is a single, collective activity. Obviously, an employee could not invoke a right grounded in a collective-bargaining agreement were it not for the prior negotiating activities of his fellow employees. Nor would it make sense for a union to negotiate a collective-bargaining agreement if individual employees could not invoke the rights thereby created against their employer. Moreover, when an employee invokes a right grounded in the collective-bargaining agreement, he does not stand alone. Instead, he brings to bear on his employer the power and resolve of all his fellow employees. When, for instance, James Brown refused to drive a truck he believed to be unsafe, he was in effect reminding his employer that he and his fellow employees, at the time their collective-bargaining agreement was signed, had extracted a promise from City Disposal that they would not be asked to drive unsafe trucks. He was also reminding his employer that if it persisted in ordering him to drive an unsafe truck, he could reharness the power of that group to ensure the enforcement of that promise. It was just as though James Brown was reassembling his fellow union members to reenact their decision not to drive unsafe trucks. A lone employee's invocation of a right grounded in his collective-bargaining agreement is, therefore, a concerted activity in a very real sense.

Furthermore, the acts of joining and assisting a labor organization, which §7 explicitly recognizes as concerted, are related to collective action in essentially the same way that the invocation of a collectively bargained right is related to collective action. When an employee joins or assists a labor organization, his actions may be divorced in time, and in location as well, from the actions of fellow employees. Because of the integral relationship among the employees' actions, however, Congress viewed each employee as engaged in concerted activity. The lone employee could not join or assist a labor organization were it not for the related organizing activities of his fellow employees. Conversely, there would be limited utility in forming a labor organization if other employees could not join or assist the organization once it is formed. Thus, the formation of a labor organization is integrally related to the activity of joining or assisting such an organization in the same sense that the negotiation of a collective-bargaining agreement is integrally related to the invocation of a right provided for in the agreement. In each case, neither the individual activity nor the group activity would be complete without the other.[4] . . . [I]t is evident that, in enacting §7 of the NLRA, Congress sought generally to equalize the bargaining power of the employee with that of his employer by allowing employees to band together in confronting an employer regarding the terms and conditions of their employment. There is no indication that Congress intended to limit this protection to situations in which an employee's activity and that of his fellow employees combine with one another in any particular way. Nor, more specifically, does it appear that Congress intended to have this general protection withdrawn in situations in which a single employee, acting alone, participates in an integral aspect of a collective process. Instead, what emerges from the general background of §7—and what is consistent with the Act's statement of purpose—is a congressional intent to create an equality in bargaining power between the employee and the

---

4. [10] Of course, at some point an individual employee's actions may become so remotely related to the activities of fellow employees that it cannot reasonably be said that the employee is engaged in concerted activity. For instance, the Board has held that if an employer were to discharge an employee for purely personal "griping," the employee could not claim the protection of §7. *See, e.g., Capital Ornamental Concrete Specialities, Inc.*, 248 N.L.R.B. 851 (1980).

In addition, although the Board relies entirely on its interpretation of §7 as support for the *Interboro* doctrine, it bears noting that under §8(a)(1), an employer commits an unfair labor practice if he or she "interfere[s] with, [or] restrain[s]" concerted activity. It is possible, therefore, for an employer to commit an unfair labor practice by discharging an employee who is not himself involved in concerted activity, but whose actions are related to other employees' concerted activities in such a manner as to render his discharge an interference or restraint on those activities. In the context of the *Interboro* doctrine, for instance, even if an individual's invocation of rights provided for in a collective-bargaining agreement, for some reason, were not concerted activity, the discharge of that individual would still be an unfair labor practice if the result were to restrain or interfere with the concerted activity of negotiating or enforcing a collective-bargaining agreement.

employer throughout the entire process of labor organizing, collective bargaining, and enforcement of collective-bargaining agreements.

The Board's *Interboro* doctrine, based on a recognition that the potential inequality in the relationship between the employee and the employer continues beyond the point at which a collective-bargaining agreement is signed, mitigates that inequality throughout the duration of the employment relationship, and is, therefore, fully consistent with congressional intent. Moreover, by applying § 7 to the actions of individual employees invoking their rights under a collective-bargaining agreement, the *Interboro* doctrine preserves the integrity of the entire collective-bargaining process; for by invoking a right grounded in a collective-bargaining agreement, the employee makes that right a reality, and breathes life, not only into the promises contained in the collective-bargaining agreement, but also into the entire process envisioned by Congress as the means by which to achieve industrial peace.

To be sure, the principal tool by which an employee invokes the rights granted him in a collective-bargaining agreement is the processing of a grievance according to whatever procedures his collective-bargaining agreement establishes. No one doubts that the processing of a grievance in such a manner is concerted activity within the meaning of § 7. *See, e.g., NLRB v. Ford Motor Co.*, 683 F.2d 156, 159 (CA6 1982); *Crown Central Petroleum Corp. v. NLRB*, 430 F.2d 724, 729 (CA5 1970). Indeed, it would make little sense for § 7 to cover an employee's conduct while negotiating a collective-bargaining agreement, including a grievance mechanism by which to protect the rights created by the agreement, but not to cover an employee's attempt to utilize that mechanism to enforce the agreement. . . .

[A]n employee's initial statement to an employer to the effect that he believes a collectively bargained right is being violated, or the employee's initial refusal to do that which he believes he is not obligated to do, might serve as both a natural prelude to, and an efficient substitute for, the filing of a formal grievance. As long as the employee's statement or action is based on a reasonable and honest belief that he is being, or has been, asked to perform a task that he is not required to perform under his collective-bargaining agreement, and the statement or action is reasonably directed toward the enforcement of a collectively bargained right, there is no justification for overturning the Board's judgment that the employee is engaged in concerted activity, just as he would have been had he filed a formal grievance.

The fact that an activity is concerted, however, does not necessarily mean that an employee can engage in the activity with impunity. An employee may engage in concerted activity in such an abusive manner that he loses the protection of § 7. *See, e.g., Crown Central Petroleum Corp. v. NLRB*, 430 F.2d 724, 729 (CA5 1970); *Yellow Freight System, Inc.*, 247 N.L.R.B. 177, 181 (1980). *Cf. Eastex, Inc. v. NLRB*, 437 U.S. 556 (1978) (finding concerted activity nonetheless unprotected); *NLRB v. Babcock & Wilcox Co.*, 351 U.S. 105 (1956) (same). Furthermore, if an employer does not wish to tolerate certain methods by which employees invoke their collectively bargained rights, he is free to negotiate a provision in his collective-bargaining agreement that limits the availability of such methods. No-strike provisions, for instance, are a common mechanism by which employers and employees agree that the latter will not invoke their rights by refusing to work. In general, if an employee violates such a provision, his activity is unprotected even though it may be concerted. *Mastro Plastics Corp. v. NLRB*, 350 U.S. 270 (1956). Whether Brown's action in this case was unprotected, however, is not before us. . . .

III

. . . Respondent argues that Brown's action was not concerted because he did not explicitly refer to the collective-bargaining agreement as a basis for his refusal to drive the truck. The Board, however, has never held that an employee must make such an explicit reference for his actions to be covered by the *Interboro* doctrine, and we find that position reasonable. We have often recognized the importance of "the Board's special function of applying the general provisions of the Act to the complexities of industrial life." *NLRB v. Erie Resistor Corp.*, 373 U.S. 221, 236 (1963). As long as the nature of the employee's complaint is reasonably clear to the person to whom it is communicated, and the complaint does, in fact, refer to a reasonably perceived violation of the collective-bargaining agreement, the complaining employee is engaged in the process of enforcing that agreement. In the context of a workplace dispute, where the participants are likely to be unsophisticated in collective-bargaining matters, a requirement that the employee explicitly refer to the collective-bargaining agreement is likely to serve as nothing more than a trap for the unwary.

Respondent further argues that the Board erred in finding Brown's action concerted based only on Brown's reasonable and honest belief that truck No. 244 was unsafe. Respondent bases its argument on the language of the collective-bargaining agreement, which provides that an employee may refuse to drive an unsafe truck "unless such refusal is unjustified." In the view of respondent, this language allows a driver to refuse to drive a truck only if the truck is objectively unsafe. Regardless of whether respondent's interpretation of the agreement is correct, a question as to which we express no view, this argument confuses the threshold question whether Brown's conduct was concerted with the ultimate question whether that conduct was protected. The rationale of the *Interboro* doctrine compels the conclusion that an honest and reasonable invocation of a collectively bargained right constitutes concerted activity, regardless of whether the employee turns out to have been correct in his belief that his right was violated. No one would suggest, for instance, that the filing of a grievance is concerted only if the grievance turns out to be meritorious. As long as the grievance is based on an honest and reasonable belief that a right had been violated, its filing is a concerted activity because it is an integral part of the process by which the collective-bargaining agreement is enforced. The same is true of other methods by which an employee enforces the agreement. On the other hand, if the collective-bargaining agreement imposes a limitation on the means by which a right may be invoked, the concerted activity would be unprotected if it went beyond that limitation. . . .

[The case was remanded for consideration of the contention that Brown's conduct was unprotected, even if concerted.]

Justice O'Connor, with whom The Chief Justice, Justice Powell and Justice Rehnquist join, dissenting.

In my view, the fact that the right the employee asserts ultimately can be grounded in the collective bargaining agreement is not enough to make the individual's self-interested action concerted. If it could, then *every* contract claim could be the basis for an unfair labor practice complaint. But the law is clear that an employer's alleged violation of a collective agreement cannot, by itself, provide the basis for an unfair labor practice complaint. See *NLRB v. C & C Plywood*, 385 U.S. 421, 427–428 (1967). . . . When employees act together in expressing a mutual concern, contractual or otherwise, their action is "concerted" and the statute authorizes them to seek vindication through the Board's administrative processes. In contrast, when an employee acts alone in expressing a personal concern, contractual or otherwise, his action is not "concerted"; in such cases, the statute instructs him to seek vindication through his union, and where necessary, through the courts. . . . There is no evidence that employee James Brown discussed the truck's alleged safety problem with other employees, sought their support in remedying the problem, or requested their or his union's assistance in protesting to his employer. He did not seek to warn others of the problem or even initially to file a grievance through his union. He simply asserted that the truck was not safe enough for *him* to drive. James Brown was not engaging in "concerted activity" in any reasonable sense of the term.

Notes

1. *Constructive Concerted Activity and Statutory Rights*—The NLRB extended the *Interboro* "constructive concerted activity" doctrine to situations in which no collective bargaining contract existed. Thus the Board found that an employee was engaged in concerted activity when he filed a safety complaint under a state statute, even though he acted alone and his coworkers showed no support for his efforts. Absent any indication that the coworkers disavowed the employee's efforts, the Board found that the consent of the coworkers was "implied." *Alleluia Cushion Co.*, 221 N.L.R.B. 999 (1975). However, in *Meyers Indus.*, 268 N.L.R.B. 493 (1984), the Board, while distinguishing *Interboro*, overruled *Alleluia Cushion* and held that a truck driver employed in a nonunion plant not covered by any bargaining agreement who refused to drive his vehicle and who complained to a state regulatory agency about allegedly unsafe brakes was not engaged in concerted activity. The Board reaffirmed this approach in *Meyers Industries, Inc.*, 281 N.L.R.B. 882 (1986), *affirmed sum nom. Prill v. NLRB*, 835 F.2d 1481 (D.C. Cir. 1987), *cert. denied*, 487 U.S. 1205 (1988). Accord *Ewing v. NLRB*, 861 F.2d 353 (2d Cir. 1988).

2. *When Is Individual Activity Concerted?*—In *Root-Carlin, Inc.*, 92 N.L.R.B. 1313 (1951), the Board said where "one employee discusses with another the need for union organization, their action is 'concerted' . . . for it involves more than one

employee, even though one be in the role of speaker and the other of listener." Similarly, concerted activity may take place where only one person seeks to induce action by others. *See, e.g., Medeco Sec. Locks v. NLRB*, 142 F.3d 733 (4th Cir. 1998) (employee talking to coworkers about his own test scores to enlist their support regarding matter of common interest); *Salt River Valley Water Users' Ass'n v. NLRB*, 206 F.2d 325 (9th Cir. 1953) (circulating a petition for back wages); *Gatliff Coal Co. v. NLRB*, 953 F.2d 247 (6th Cir. 1992) (joint protest by two female employees regarding rumor started by coworkers concerning their alleged extramarital conduct with male employee protected, since the issue affected their working conditions).

In *Mike Yurosek & Son*, 310 N.L.R.B. 831 (1993), *affirmed*, 53 F.3d 261 (9th Cir. 1995), the Labor Board found that employees who individually declined overtime work were acting in concert, since their refusals were the "logical outgrowth" of concerns expressed earlier by a group of employees. *See also Every Woman's Place, Inc.*, 282 N.L.R.B. 413 (1986), *enforced*, 833 F.2d 1012 (6th Cir. 1987), holding that an employer unlawfully fired an employee for calling the U.S. Department of Labor to inquire about holiday pay requirements. Since the employee and two coworkers had repeatedly complained about overtime compensation to the employer, without a response, it was "immaterial that she was not following express instructions from the other employees" in telephoning. *See also NLRB v. Caval Tool Div., Chromalloy Gas Turbine Corp.*, 262 F.3d 184 (2d Cir. 2001) (statements by individual employee at group meeting assembled by employer to announce change in policy affecting working conditions protected concerted activity). *Compare Manimark Corp. v. NLRB*, 7 F.3d 547 (6th Cir. 1993) (holding that the focus of an individual employee on issues of group concern was not sufficient to generate NLRA protection, absent evidence the worker was acting on behalf of other employees). Most recently, the Labor Board limited the scope of concerted activity where an individual's complaint is made in the presence of coworkers and a supervisor. Even if the employee's remarks relate to wages or working conditions, the mere fact that the employee uses the phrase "we" in making the complaint does not transform "individual griping" into "concerted activity"; instead, the statement must either bring a truly group complaint to management's attention, or there must be a reasonable inference, in the totality of the circumstances, that the employee was seeking to initiate, induce, or prepare for group action. *See Alstate Maintenance*, 367 N.L.R.B. No. 68 (2019).

3. *Mistaken Belief*—Applying *City Disposal*, the Labor Board concluded that an employee was protected when he asserted a right to higher pay under his collective bargaining agreement where his belief that the contract covered him was mistaken, but honest and reasonable. *Omni Commercial Lighting, Inc.*, 364 N.L.R.B. No. 54 (2016). Another case, *KBO, Inc.*, 315 N.L.R.B. 570 (1994), *enforced by order*, 153 L.R.R.M. (BNA) 2512 (6th Cir. 1996), involved an employee who was suspended for telling other workers about an alleged tape recording on which the employer's operations manager supposedly said that the employer was "taking money out of the employees' profit sharing accounts to pay the lawyers to fight the union." Even though the tape recording may not have existed, the fact that the employee honestly believed the story rendered his conduct protected.

In *Whirlpool Corp. v. Marshall*, 445 U.S. 1 (1980), the Supreme Court held proper the promulgation and enforcement by the Secretary of Labor of OSHA regulations permitting employee refusals to perform unsafe work if their fear of serious injury or death is objectively reasonable. The court in *NLRB v. Modern Carpet Industries, Inc.*, 611 F.2d 811 (10th Cir. 1979), agreed with the NLRB that §7 protects employee declinations to perform work under unsafe conditions if their fear of harm is genuine, thus obviating the need for an objective assessment. *Accord Odyssey Capital Group, L.P., III*, 337 N.L.R.B. 1110 (2002).

4. *General Employee Advocacy*—In *Eastex, Inc. v. NLRB*, 437 U.S. 556 (1978) [discussed in *City Disposal Systems*], the Supreme Court held that employees are engaged in activity protected under §7 when they participate in concerted activities "in support of employees of employers other than their own," or "seek to improve their lot as employees through channels outside the immediate employer-employee relationship." Thus, the Board has held in a number of cases that employee appeals to legislators or governmental agencies are protected, as long as they relate directly to employee working conditions. Accordingly, employee advocacy has been held protected regarding issues including visas for foreign workers, the minimum wage, state right-to-work legislation, living wages and benefits, employee drug testing, and workplace and environmental safety laws. However, the *Eastex* Court was careful to add that the principle cannot be extended to protect all forms of political activity no matter how attenuated from employees' workplace interests. Thus, under current Board jurisprudence, school bus drivers who complain about working conditions are protected, but those who complain about student safety are not; similarly, nurses who complain about staffing levels are protected, but those who complain about the quality of patient care are not.

Problem

16. American Farms is a large meatpacking plant specializing in beef products. It employs close to 2,000 workers, most of whom live in a small town near the plant since there's very little housing within commuting distance. The meat-packing process is quite labor-intensive: it involves slaughtering cows, cutting the meat, packaging it, and delivering it to stores. The process also generates a large amount of wastewater, which, after some treatment, is discharged into the local river. Even after being treated, however, the wastewater still contains high levels of oxygen-depleting pollutants such as nitrogen and phosphorous that many in the town blame for the degradation of their river.

About two dozen citizens of the town, several of whom worked or had family members who worked at the plant, formed a small group and began protesting against American Farms for their role in polluting the river. They wrote letters to the editor of the local paper, put up signs on public property near the plant, and sponsored a program in a local church where environmentalists explained the science behind the issue. When American Farms management found out about the group, it investigated the movement and discharged every employee who was in the group themselves or had a family member in the group.

A few months later, the novel coronavirus pandemic came to the plant. When it hit, it hit hard: in the first week, scores of workers became sick (and two older workers eventually passed away). It turned out that conditions were ripe in meat-packing plants for virus transmission. The production process puts hundreds of workers standing shoulder to shoulder as carcasses whiz by on hooks or conveyer belts. The work is fast-paced, physically demanding, and loud — which means that the workers are often breathing heavily and have to shout to be heard.

Several of the workers asked the company to implement safety measures such as slowing down the production lines and spacing out some of the workstations. The company refused, but did begin to require workers to wear masks and submit to temperature checks at the beginning of every shift. As the number of new cases began to level out, a rumor spread throughout the plant that the company was beginning to allow workers with temperatures up to 101 degrees to work (the cutoff was supposed to be 99 degrees). For the workers in the deboning section of the plant, this was the last straw, and they walked off the job in protest of what they thought were unreasonably dangerous working conditions. The company discharged all of the workers involved in the walkout. A later investigation revealed that the 101-degree rumor was false.

Did American Farms commit an unfair labor practice when it discharged the environmental protesters, those who had family members in the protest group, or the walkouts?

5. Weingarten *Rights*

NLRB v. J. Weingarten, Inc., 420 U.S. 251, 95 S. Ct. 959, 43 L. Ed. 2d 171 (1975). A store manager and a "loss prevention specialist" summoned an employee to an interview to question her about a report from a fellow employee that she had purchased a box of chicken that sold for $2.98, but had only placed $1.00 in the cash register at the lunch counter where she worked. The store manager denied the employee's requests that a union representative be called to the interview. Although the interview revealed that the employee was innocent of the act alleged, the employee did "blurt out" that "the only thing she had ever gotten from the store without paying for it was her free lunch." Free lunches at the store were against company policy and the employee was informed that she owed the store approximately $160 for lunches.

The Supreme Court held that the employer's denial of the employee's request that her union representative be present at the investigatory interview which the employee reasonably believed might result in disciplinary action violated § 8(a)(1) of the NLRA because it interfered with the rights of the employee under § 7 of the Act. The Court agreed with the NLRB that the right to union representation at such interviews falls within the guarantee in §7 of the right of employees to act in concert for mutual aid and protection. It viewed the request for representation as concerted activity because the union representative would safeguard the interests of all unit employees against unjust disciplinary procedures and his presence would assure all employees that they could also have his assistance if called to an investigatory interview. Mr. Justice Powell, dissenting, thought that this was not concerted activity within the meaning of the Act and that the matter is better left to collective bargaining.

Notes

1. *General Considerations*—In a recent case, Bellagio called an employee suspected of misconduct into an investigatory meeting. The employee requested the presence of a union representative, and Bellagio invited him to contact the union agent himself. When he was unable to contact that person, two managers left the room and sought help from the employee relations department. They then gave the employee the option of filling out a written statement before the interview ended or leaving without such a result. No violation of his *Weingarten* rights was found, since Bellagio had effectively offered him the option of filling out the statement without a union representative present or ending the interview. *Bellagio, LLC v. NLRB*, 854 F.3d 703 (D.C. Cir. 2017). *See also Midwest Division-MMC, LLC v. NLRB*, 867 F.3d 1288 (D.C. Cir. 2017) (employer does not have to grant employee request to have union representative attend investigatory interview that might result in discipline where employer offers employee choice of attending alone or of having no interview at all).

2. *Expectation of Discipline*—The NLRB declared that in deciding whether a *Weingarten* right exists at a meeting, "what is determinative is whether discipline reasonably can be expected to follow." *Northwest Engineering Co.*, 265 N.L.R.B. 190 (1982). *See, e.g., Safeway Stores, Inc.*, 303 N.L.R.B. 989 (1991), recognizing the right of an employee to union representation when directed by a supervisor to take a drug test following a series of continued absences, since the procedure could result in discipline. *See also Ralphs Grocery Co.*, 361 N.L.R.B. 80 (2014).

In *General Die Casters Inc.*, 358 N.L.R.B. 742 (2012), the Board held that an employer violated an employee's *Weingarten* rights when it met with him to discuss discipline that had been imposed due to inaccurate time card entries and indicated that additional discipline could result; the employee could reasonably have feared that the additional discussion could generate responses by him that could be used if future discipline were imposed. On the other hand, a divided Board accepted the Ninth Circuit's holding in *NLRB v. Certified Grocers of California, Ltd.*, 587 F.2d 449 (1978), that no *Weingarten* right arises if the employer intends merely to communicate a disciplinary decision previously made. *Baton Rouge Water Works Co.*, 246 N.L.R.B. 995 (1979).

3. *The Role of the Representative*—In *Amax, Inc., Climax Molybdenum Co. Div.*, 227 N.L.R.B. 1189 (1977), a Board majority held that the right to engage in concerted activity for mutual aid or protection guarantees an employee a right to consult with

his representative prior to the investigatory interview. The Tenth Circuit, however, denied enforcement of the Board's order. 584 F.2d 360 (1978). In *Pacific Tel. & Tel. Co.*, 262 N.L.R.B. 1048 (1982), *enforced*, 711 F.2d 134 (9th Cir. 1983), a majority held that the right to prior consultation includes a right to be informed as to the subject of the interview as well. *See also United States Postal Service v. NLRB*, 969 F.2d 1064 (D.C. Cir. 1992) (sustaining right of employees to consult union stewards prior to disciplinary interviews). *See also Fry's Food Stores*, 361 N.L.R.B. 1216 (2014) (employer violated employee's *Weingarten* rights when it prevented her from calling union representative of her choice prior to investigatory interview she reasonably feared might result in discipline, prohibited her from consulting with employer-appointed representative prior to interview, and told that representative to remain silent during interview).

Although it is not clear the exact role a union representative may play during an investigatory interview, the Labor Board has held that an employer may not limit the role of a representative to that of a silent observer. *Barnard College*, 340 N.L.R.B. 934 (2003). And in *Howard Industries*, 362 N.L.R.B. 303 (2015), the Board held that an employer violated the NLRA when it threatened a union steward with suspension for using notes during an investigatory interview to assist the employee being questioned with his responses. Although the employer had the right to insist on hearing the employee's account, the steward had the right to show the interviewee his notes as part of the "active assistance" stewards may provide to employees during such encounters.

An employer is not obliged to inform an employee suspected of misconduct of his right to union representation during an investigatory interview. Even where a prospective interviewee is frightened and confused, no right to union representation attaches unless he requests such assistance. *See Montgomery Ward & Co.*, 269 N.L.R.B. 904 (1984).

An employee may request the presence of a specific union representative if that person is available (*Anheuser-Busch, Inc. v. NLRB*, 338 F.3d 267 (4th Cir. 2003), *cert. denied*, 541 U.S. 973 (2004)), but an employee may not decline to attend an investigatory interview because his or her preferred representative is not available if some other designated representative is (*Roadway Express, Inc.*, 246 N.L.R.B. 1127 (1979)). It is the union's obligation to keep employees informed of all available representatives.

The Labor Board has ruled that an employer violated Section 8(a)(1) when it refused to allow the representative union's attorney to act as a *Weingarten* representative at a disciplinary meeting. *PAE Applied Technologies, LLC*, 367 N.L.R.B. No. 105 (2019).

4. *Nonunion Situations*—The Labor Board ruled in *Materials Research Corp.*, 262 N.L.R.B. 1010 (1982), that nonunion employees are entitled to have coworkers present at management interviews they reasonably believe may result in discipline, but it subsequently overruled *Materials Research* and held that the *Weingarten* right

to be represented during investigatory interviews is an organizational right that is not available to nonunion employees. *Sears, Roebuck & Co.*, 274 N.L.R.B. 230 (1985). In *Epilepsy Found. of Northeast Ohio*, 331 N.L.R.B. 676 (2000), the Board overruled *Sears, Roebuck & Co.*, and returned to the position originally taken in *Materials Research Corp.*, as it held that nonunion employees have the *Weingarten* right to have coworkers accompany them to investigatory interviews they reasonably believe may result in discipline. In *Epilepsy Found. v. NLRB*, 268 F.3d 1095 (D.C. Cir. 2001), *cert. denied*, 536 U.S. 904 (2002), the D.C. Circuit found the Board's position to be a reasonable interpretation of the Act, noting that "the presence of a coworker gives an employee a potential witness, advisor, and advocate in an adversarial situation, and, ideally, militates against the imposition of unjust discipline by the employer. The Board's position also recognizes that even nonunion employees may have a shared interest in preventing the imposition of unjust punishment, and an employee's assertion of *Weingarten* invokes this shared interest." Nonetheless, in *IBM Corp.*, 341 N.L.R.B. 1288 (2004), the Board overturned *Epilepsy Foundation* and again held that nonunion employees do not have the statutory right to be accompanied by coworkers when they participate in investigatory interviews they think may result in discipline.

5. *Remedies* — When an employer impermissibly refuses to grant employee requests for representation during investigatory interviews, the Board will automatically issue a cease and desist order to rectify the violation. If individuals are terminated because of their invocation of their *Weingarten* right, reinstatement and back pay will also be provided. If, however, the employer's basis for the employee's discharge is unrelated to the denial of the worker's *Weingarten* right, the Board will not order reinstatement or back pay. *See Taracorp Industries, Div. of Taracorp, Inc.*, 273 N.L.R.B. 221 (1984). The *Taracorp* doctrine was judicially approved in *Communication Workers of America, Local 5008 v. NLRB*, 784 F.2d 847 (7th Cir. 1986).

6. *The Railway Labor Act* — In *Pawlowski v. Northeast Ill. Reg'l Commuter R.R. Corp.*, 186 F.3d 997 (7th Cir. 1999), *cert. denied*, 528 U.S. 1117 (2000), the court held that § 2 of the Railway Labor Act, which imposes on carriers a general duty to afford their workers the opportunity to meet and discuss grievances with union representatives, does not afford railroad employees the right to have union representatives present during investigatory interviews. The right to union representation only becomes operative once discipline has been imposed and grievance procedures have been invoked.

6. Loss of Protection Due to Unlawful Objective, Unlawful Means, or Means against Public Policy

Assuming that the activity is "concerted" and that it is for "the purpose of collective bargaining or other mutual aid or protection," it still may not be protected against employer interference (§ 8(a)(1)) and discrimination (§ 8(a)(3)). Not all concerted activities are protected by § 7. The problem is how to draw the line. In general, the activities must have a lawful objective and must be carried on in a lawful manner. But what is meant by the term "lawful" in this connection?

Fairly clear are the cases in which the concerted activities are for an objective that is outlawed by the Taft-Hartley Act itself as a union unfair labor practice. It would not effectuate the policies of the Act to afford relief against employer reprisal to employees who were themselves violating the Act. "For example, the act expressly prohibits jurisdictional strikes, secondary boycotts, and strikes for recognition in defiance of a certified union." *See International Brotherhood of Electrical Workers v. NLRB*, 202 F.2d 186, 187 (D.C. Cir. 1952). Employees who engage in recognition picketing in violation of § 8(b)(7) lose their protected status under the Act, and an employer may lawfully refuse to reinstate them. *Teamsters, Local 707 (Claremont Polychemical Corp.)*, 196 N.L.R.B. 613 (1972). A strike or a boycott to compel an employer to commit an employer unfair labor practice is similarly unprotected. *Hoover Co. v. NLRB*, 191 F.2d 380 (6th Cir. 1951); *Thompson Products, Inc. (Detroit, Mich.)*, 72 N.L.R.B. 886 (1947). Finally, even if the objective is legal, the protection of the NLRA is withdrawn if the concerted activity is tortious or criminal in nature; for example, action involving sit-down strikes (forcible seizure of property) (*NLRB v. Fansteel Metallurgical Corp.*, 306 U.S. 240 (1939)) or mutiny in violation of the federal criminal code (*Southern S.S. Co. v. NLRB*, 316 U.S. 31 (1942)).

The most difficult cases concern concerted activities that are not clearly unlawful but that are thought to be inconsistent with public policy considerations, including regard for the basic rights of employers. When concerted activity appears to be inappropriate and not the sort of conduct that the members of Congress, had they thought about it, would have intended to insulate against employer reprisals, §7 protection will be lost. In *Local 702, Int'l. Union of Electrical Wkrs. v. NLRB*, 215 F.3d 11 (7th Cir. 2000), *cert. denied*, 531 U.S. 1051 (2000), for example, the court sustained a Board decision that found that two striking workers engaged in unprotected activity during a work stoppage when they came upon a firm truck on the highway and moved their vehicles in front of the truck, blocked ordinary traffic flow, and prevented the truck from passing them. *See also Carolina Freight Carriers Corp.*, 295 N.L.R.B. 1080 (1989) (persistent refusal to carry out supervisor's direct order); *NLRB v. Brookshire Grocery Co.*, 919 F.2d 359 (5th Cir. 1990) (improper obtaining of information from confidential personnel files for dissemination to other workers).

In analyzing concerted activity that trenches on the basic rights of employers — such as the right to control property in the event of a work stoppage that occurs on the employer's premises — the Board applies a 10-factor test that assists in balancing the employer's property rights against the section 7 rights of employees. In *Quietflex Mfg. Co.*, 344 N.L.R.B. 1055 (2005), the Board listed the factors that it will consider:

> (1) The reason the employees have stopped working; (2) whether the work stoppage was peaceful; (3) whether the work stoppage interfered with production, or deprived the employer of access to its property; (4) whether employees had adequate opportunity to present grievances to management;

(5) whether employees were given any warning that they must leave the property or face discharge; (6) the duration of the work stoppage; (7) whether employees were represented or had an established grievance procedure; (8) whether employees remained on the premises beyond their shift; (9) whether the employees attempted to seize the employer's property; and (10) the reason for which the employees were ultimately discharged.

In *Wal-Mart Stores, Inc.*, 364 N.L.R.B. No. 118 (2016), the Labor Board applied *Quietflex Mfg. Co.* to a protest on company property by nonunion employees. Six employees who had received "disciplinary coachings" after engaging in an earlier work stoppage ceased work and gathered in the customer service area near the store entrance about 30 minutes before the store opened to the public at 6:00 a.m. They were joined by four nonemployee protesters when the store opened, and the group displayed an 8-by-10-foot banner reading "Stand Up, Live Better, ForRespect.org, OUR Walmart, Organization United for Respect at Walmart." The sign was initially held in front of the customer service desk, and later moved behind the desk. The protesters complied with requests to move the protest and all left the store by 6:52 a.m. The Labor Board found that nearly every factor of the *Quietflex* analysis favored a finding that the work stoppage was protected, since it was initiated in response to pressing problems including abusive treatment by a supervisor, caused little or no disruption to the company's ability to serve customers (no customers attempted to access the customer service area during the protest), the protest was brief, and the protest group left immediately when asked to do so by police. Although the employer did offer to meet with employees through its open door policy to address concerns, it was willing to do so only individually and group grievances were barred. The Board majority rejected the dissent's argument that *Quietflex* should not apply to retail settings where the potential for business disruption is greater and employers are more likely to suffer economic harm, reasoning that a permissible purpose of concerted activity is to exert economic pressure on the employer.

Similarly, in *Meyer Tool, Inc.*, 366 N.L.R.B. No. 32 (2018), *enforced*, 763 Fed. Appx. 5 (2d Cir. 2019), the Board found that an employer violated the NLRA when it indefinitely suspended an employee who refused to leave the company premises after being ordered to do so, where the employee and two coworkers went to the human resources department to complain about harassment by managers regarding protected activity. The court found that the individual had not forfeited his NLRA protection by refusing to leave the premises and was entitled to greater latitude due to the seriousness of the issues being raised by the employees involved.

Conduct that would otherwise be protected may lose that status if it presents a threat of physical violence. In *Universal Truss, Inc.*, 348 N.L.R.B. 733 (2006), the Labor Board carefully distinguished between *protected* concerted activity that might involve exuberant employee conduct that does not directly threaten physical harm and *unprotected* activity that poses a discernible threat of physical violence. The Board found that the employer violated the NLRA when it discharged an employee who had told an individual working during a strike to "come outside if you're a man, don't lock yourself in like a whore," where these remarks did not rise to the level of a physical threat. On the other hand, no violation was found when the employer discharged a striker who told a group of nonstrikers "we're going to get you all alone ... and we're going to f— you up," since these statements followed violent attacks by other strikers on nonstrikers and contained a real threat of physical harm.

Finally, concerted activities that contravene basic policies of the National Labor Relations Act, such as the promotion of stable collective bargaining relationships and the sanctity of collective agreements, have also been held to be unprotected. Examples include "wildcat" strikes in derogation of the authority of the recognized collective bargaining representative. See *NLRB v. Sunbeam Lighting Co.*, 318 F.2d 661 (7th Cir. 1963); *Harnischfeger Corp. v. NLRB*, 207 F.2d 575 (7th Cir. 1953); *NLRB v. Draper Corp.*, 145 F.2d 199 (4th Cir. 1944). See generally Gould, *The Status of Unauthorized and "Wildcat" Strikes Under the National Labor Relations Act*, 52 CORNELL L.Q. 672 (1967). See also *Emporium Capwell Co. v. Western Addition Community Organization*, 420 U.S. 50 (1975), set forth *infra*.

Elk Lumber Co.
National Labor Relations Board
91 N.L.R.B. 333 (1950)

[The General Counsel's complaint alleged that the respondent Elk Lumber Company had violated §8(a)(1) and (3) of the act by discharging five employees because they engaged in protected concerted activity to protest a change in the method of wage payment.]

The Respondent contends, and the Trial Examiner apparently found, that the five carloaders were discharged, not for having engaged in concerted activities, as alleged in the complaint, but because their production was not satisfactory. It is clear, however, that their failure to produce was the result of an agreement to slow down. In our opinion, therefore, the only question presented is whether this conduct was a form of concerted activity protected by the act. We believe, contrary to the contention of the General Counsel, that it was not.

Section 7 of the act guarantees to employees the right to engage in concerted activities for the purpose of collective bargaining or other mutual aid or protection. However, both the Board and the courts have recognized that not every form of activity that falls within the letter of this provision is protected. The test, as laid down by the Board in the *Harnischfeger Corporation* case, and referred to with apparent approval by the Supreme Court in the recent *Wisconsin* case [UAWA-AFL v. WERB, 336 U.S. 245], is whether the particular activity involved is so indefensible as to warrant the employer in discharging the participating employees. Either an unlawful objective or the adoption of improper means of achieving it may deprive employees engaged in concerted activities of the protection of the act.

Here, the objective of the carloaders' concerted activity — to induce the Respondent to increase their hourly rate of pay or to return to the piecework rate — was a lawful one. To achieve this objective, however, they adopted the plan of decreasing their production to the amount they considered adequate for the pay they were then receiving. In effect, this constituted a refusal on their part to accept the terms of employment set by their employer without engaging in a stoppage, but to continue rather to work on their own terms. The courts, in somewhat similar situations, have held that such conduct is justifiable cause for discharge. Thus, in the *Conn* case [108 F.2d 390], the Court of Appeals for the Seventh Circuit found that the employer was justified in discharging employees who refused to work overtime, saying:

> We are aware of no law or logic that gives the employee the right to work upon terms prescribed solely by him. That is plainly what was sought to be done in this instance. It is not a situation in which employees ceased work in protest against conditions imposed by the employer, but one in which the employees sought and intended to work upon their own notion of the terms which should prevail. If they had a right to fix the hours of their employment, it would follow that a similar right existed by which they could prescribe all conditions and regulations affecting their employment.

And in the *Montgomery Ward* case [157 F.2d 486], in which employees at one of the employer's plants refused to process orders from another plant where a strike was in progress, the Court of Appeals for the Eighth Circuit said:

> It was implied in the contract of hiring that these employees would do the work assigned to them in a careful and workmanlike manner; that they would comply with all reasonable orders and conduct themselves so as not to work injury to the employer's business; that they would serve faithfully and be regardful of the interests of the employer during the term of their service, and carefully discharge their duties to the extent reasonably required.... Any employee may, of course, be lawfully discharged for disobedience of the employer's directions in breach of his contract.... While these employees had the undoubted right to go on a strike and quit their employment, they could not continue to work and remain at their positions, accept the wages paid them, and at the same time select what part of their allotted tasks they cared to perform of their own volition, or refuse openly or secretly to the employer's damage, to do other work.

We believe that the principle of these decisions is applicable to the situation before us, and that, under the circumstances, the carloaders' conduct justified their discharge.

The General Counsel contends, however, that "if such activity [a slowdown] is to be condemned by the Board, it should only be done after there has been a deliberate refusal to do the Employer's bidding," and that here, "at the time of discharge there still had been no failure to comply with any command of management." In support of this contention, he asserts that "after the outset of this slowdown, the Employer obviously acquiesced in it and made no protest"; that it "did not set a definite rate [of production], nor did it make any statement as to what rate of production was considered accurate"; and that it discharged the men "without any warning or reason being given."

On the record before us, however, we find no convincing evidence that the Respondent at any time acquiesced in the slowdown....

Furthermore, although the Respondent admittedly did not tell the carloaders how many cars a day they were expected to load, and, so far as the present record shows, did not warn them that they would be discharged if they did not increase their production, it is clear that the men knew that the rate they had adopted was not satisfactory. Despite this knowledge, they continued to load fewer cars a day than they could have loaded, or than they would have loaded for more money. Under these particular circumstances, we regard it as immaterial that the Respondent had given them no express order as to the amount of work required, or any warning that they would be discharged if they failed to meet the requirement.

We therefore find that the Respondent did not violate the act by discharging the five carloaders named in the complaint. As no other unfair labor practices are alleged, we affirm and adopt the Trial Examiner's ruling dismissing the complaint in its entirety.

Notes

1. *Slowdowns, Partial Strikes, and Intermittent Strikes* — In an effort to enhance their economic clout without the need to resort to formal strikes, some unions effectively create slowdowns by having employees strictly conform to inefficient employer work rules. (The so-called "work-to-rule" strategy.) Would such tactics cause a loss of NLRA protection under the *Elk Lumber* approach? *See* Leroy, *Creating Order Out of Chaos and Other Partial and Intermittent Strikes*, 95 Nw. U. L. Rev. 221 (2000); Sharpe, *"By Any Means Necessary"— Unprotected Conduct and Decisional Discretion Under the National Labor Relations Act*, 20 Berkeley J. Emp. & Lab. L. 203 (1999); Becker, *"Better than a Strike": Protecting New Forms of Collective Work Stoppages Under the National Labor Relations Act*, 61 U. Chi. L. Rev. 351 (1994).

"Partial" strikes of various kinds have been found to constitute unprotected conduct. For example, *Yale Univ.*, 330 N.L.R.B. 246 (1999), concerned the refusal of graduate teaching fellows to submit final student grades for the fall semester to enhance their bargaining position with the university. Since the teaching fellows were willing to perform all of their other duties, including their preparation to teach spring semester courses, the Board found that their conduct constituted an unprotected "partial strike." *See also Honolulu Rapid Transit Co. Ltd.*, 110 N.L.R.B. 1806 (1954) (weekend strikes); *Pacific Telephone & Telegraph Co. (San Francisco, Cal.)*, 107 N.L.R.B. 1547 (1954) ("hit-and-run" unannounced work stoppages); *Valley City Furniture Co.*, 110 N.L.R.B. 1589 (1954), *enforced*, 230 F.2d 947 (6th Cir. 1956) (one-hour-a-day strikes).

Intermittent strikes involving a plan to strike, return to work, and strike again, are unprotected if a series of strikes are undertaken close in time and for the same goal. *Walmart Stores, Inc.*, 368 N.L.R.B. No. 24 (2019). On the other hand, strikes that respond to distinct employer actions or issues do not lose protection as intermittent strikes even if they occur close in time. The critical question is whether there is evidence of a plan to strike intermittently. *Id.* When Las Vegas was thinking of expanding the number of taxi medallions, which would have created greater competition for current taxi drivers, a group of drivers extended their regular meal breaks by one or two hours to protest this proposed action in an effort to induce their taxi employer to oppose the medallion expansion. Some were suspended for engaging in such intermittent actions, but the Labor Board found their concerted action protected due to their significant interest in the issue involved, the minimal impact upon their employer, and the fact the employer did not direct them to return to work during their protest. *Nellis Taxi Co.*, 362 N.L.R.B. 1587 (2015).

2. *Disloyalty* — In *Hoover Co. v. NLRB*, 191 F.2d 380, 389–90 (6th Cir. 1951), the court explained why some forms of protest, though concerted and for mutual aid or protection, lose their protected status, ruling that efforts by nonstriking employees to generate a consumer boycott were unprotected:

> [T]he right to strike requires that strikers who exercise it must thereby cease to work and draw their pay. *NLRB v. Montgomery Ward & Co., Inc.*, 8 Cir., 157 F.2d 486. An employee cannot work and strike at the same time. He cannot continue in his employment and openly or secretly refuse to do his work. He cannot collect wages for his employment, and, at the same time, engage in activities to injure or destroy his employer's business. . . .
>
> . . . It is a wrong done to the company for employees, while being employed and paid wages by a company, to engage in a boycott to prevent others from purchasing what their employer is engaged in selling and which is the very thing their employer is paying them to produce. An employer is not required, under the Act, to finance a boycott against himself.

See also George A. Hormel & Co. v. NLRB, 962 F.2d 1061 (D.C. Cir. 1992) (employee who participated in rally advocating consumer boycott of employer's products when no labor dispute existed could be discharged for unprotected "disloyalty").

Loss of protection for disloyalty reflects the idea that employees may not engage in concerted activities that are inconsistent with the basic rights of the employer. In one well-known case that arose during the course of a collective bargaining dispute, TV technicians, while remaining on the job, distributed handbills in their off-hours to the public. The handbills criticized the TV station for failing to purchase the equipment needed to present live programs and suggested that the company was treating "Charlotte as a second-class city" by putting on only programs that were on film. The handbills made no reference to the union, to a labor controversy, or to collective bargaining. The Court found that this "sharp, public disparaging attack upon the quality of the Company's product and its business policies, in a manner reasonably calculated to harm the Company's reputation and reduce its income," was a demonstration of such detrimental disloyalty as to provide cause for the company's refusal to continue in its employ the perpetrators of the attack. *NLRB v. Local Union No. 1229, IBEW [Jefferson Standard]*, 346 U.S. 464 (1953). (Justices Frankfurter, Black, and Douglas dissented.) *See also NLRB v. Federal Sec.*, 154 F.3d 751 (7th Cir. 1998) (spontaneous walkout by private security guards at extremely dangerous public housing project unprotected since guards left complex unattended and endangered lives of residents).

Suppose that (a) the handbill in the *Jefferson Standard* case had been distributed while the employees were on strike, and (b) the handbill had stated an appeal for public support in the union's current labor dispute with the company. Consider the Board's decision in *Patterson-Sargent Co.*, 115 N.L.R.B. 1627 (1956), where several employees were discharged for distributing the following handbill to consumers during a strike at a paint company:

Beware Paint Substitute

The employees of the Patterson-Sargent Company in Cleveland who manufacture paint under the brand of B.P.S., were forced on strike by the Company. As a result, there is not being manufactured any paint at the Patterson-Sargent Company in Cleveland by the well-trained, experienced employees who have made the paint you have always bought.

This is a warning that you should make certain that any B.P.S. paint you buy is made by the regular employees who know the formulas and the exact amount of ingredients to put into paint. If you should happen to get paint which is made by any other than the regular, well-trained experienced workers, it might not do for you what you want it to do. It could peel, crack, blister, scale or any one of many undesirable things that would cause you inconvenience, lost time and money.

Stop! Think! Is it worth your while to risk spending your good money for a product which might not be what you are accustomed to using? You will be informed when you can again buy B.P.S. paint which is made by the regular employees in Cleveland.

The NLRB split 3-2, the majority finding this conduct disloyal disparagement of the employer's product and hence unprotected under the principles of *Jefferson Standard*. They indicated that even if the handbill claims had been truthful, the disparagement of the employer's product would have still rendered the conduct unprotected. The dissenters argued that since the handbill was distributed during a strike and its contents showed a direct relation to a current labor dispute, its distribution should have been considered protected concerted activity.

Similarly, when employees publicly criticize employer services or products in ways likely to cause adverse business effects, they will usually forfeit the protection of § 7. *See Logistics N. Am., Inc.*, 347 N.L.R.B. 568 (2006) (loss of protection found where workers sent letter to employer's primary customer complaining about working conditions where letter contained maliciously false information detrimental to firm's relationship with customer). Although the Sixth Circuit agreed that a maliciously false letter sent to an employer's customers could result in a loss of statutory protection, it remanded the case to the Labor Board to reconsider whether actual malice had been shown. *Jolliff v. NLRB*, 513 F.3d 600 (6th Cir. 2008).

On the other hand, the Board concluded that an employer violated § 8(a)(1) where it discharged TV service technicians engaged in a wage dispute with an installation firm for making critical comments about their employer and DirecTV during a TV news interview. The employees explained that they were encouraged to lie to customers in order to obtain approval to make telephone connections from a satellite receiver to a landline, or suffer a charge-back for every customer who refused the connection. The employees' statements were expressly tied to their pay dispute with the installation firm and were not made with malice toward the employer or its service, distinguishing the case from *Jefferson Standard*. See *MasTec Advanced Techs.*, 357 N.L.R.B. 103 (2011), *enforced*, 837 F.3d 25 (D.C. Cir. 2016), *cert. denied*, 138 S. Ct. 92 (2017).

And where school bus drivers wrote letters to a school district urging it not to award a contract to the company for which they worked or to send the contract back for a rebid because of their concerns about the company's ability to maintain their wages and benefit levels and still provide a safe working environment given the low bid that the company had submitted during the bidding process, the activity was protected even though the statements made tended to impugn the company's reputation. Thus, the company's failure to rehire them violated § 8(a)(1). *See Five Star Transp., Inc. v. NLRB*, 522 F.3d 46 (1st Cir. 2008). See generally Finkin, *Disloyalty! Does* Jefferson Standard *Stalk Still?*, 14 BERKELEY J. EMP. & LAB. L. 541 (2007).

3. *Opprobrious Conduct*—Workers who use profanity while exercising § 7 rights may forfeit protection under the Act. In *Atlantic Steel Co.*, 245 N.L.R.B. 814 (1979), the Board developed a test for assessing whether "opprobrious conduct" during discussions with employer representatives deprives employees of statutory protection. The Board examined: (1) the location of the discussions; (2) the subject matter; (3) the nature of the employee outbursts; and (4) whether the outbursts were provoked by employer unfair labor practices. Applying this test, the Board has found that significant profanity by employees during discussions with other workers on employer premises may result in a loss of statutory protection. *See ALCOA*, 338 N.L.R.B. 20 (2002).

Nevertheless, the Board has often applied the *Atlantic Steel* test and concluded that intemperate comments that don't rise to the level of physical threats are still protected, given the understandably acrimonious and heated context in which they arise. For example, in *Kiewit Power Constructors Co. v. NLRB*, 652 F.3d 22 (D.C. Cir. 2011), the D.C. Circuit enforced the Board's decision that the employer violated the Act when it discharged two union-represented workers who reacted to discipline of a group of workers for exceeding a 15-minute break period by telling the supervisor "it's going to get ugly" and warning the supervisor to "bring [his] boxing gloves." The employees' comments were figures of speech rather than actual threats of violence, and so did not lose their protection under the Act. *See also Plaza Auto Center, Inc.*, 360 N.L.R.B. 972 (2014) (conduct of employee at meeting with manager and owner — calling employer owner "f — ing crook" and "asshole" and telling him he would regret it if he fired employee — did not lose protection of Act, where employee did not act in belligerent or physically threatening manner and was not overheard by anyone else).

The inconsistent results arising from application of *Atlantic Steel* recently persuaded the Trump Board to abandon the test, announcing that in the future these types of cases will be analyzed under the *Wright Line* standard:

> In our view, abusive conduct that occurs in the context of Section 7 activity is not analytically inseparable from the Section 7 activity itself. If the General Counsel alleges discipline was motivated by Section 7 activity and the employer contends it was motivated by abusive conduct, causation is at issue. As in any *Wright Line* case, the General Counsel must make an initial showing that (1) the employee engaged in Section 7 activity, (2) the employer knew of that activity, and (3) the employer had animus against the Section 7 activity, which must be proven with evidence sufficient to establish a causal relationship between the discipline and the Section 7 activity. If the General Counsel has made his initial case, the burden of persuasion shifts to the employer to prove it would have taken the same action even in the absence of the Section 7 activity.

GM LLC and Charles Robinson, 369 N.L.R.B. No. 127 (2020). Do you agree that application of the *Wright Line* test will produce more consistent results in these cases?

Similar considerations apply to employees who resort to sarcastic communications and even colorful "body language" to express dissatisfaction with employer actions. The Board applied a totality of the circumstances test to evaluate this conduct, which evoked diverse reactions from the Labor Board and the courts. Protection has been accorded to rolled eyes and folded arms (*Health Care & Retirement Corp.*, 306 N.L.R.B. 63 (1992), *enforcement denied on other grounds*, 987 F.2d 1256 (6th Cir. 1993)) and a cartoon T-shirt depicting a manager as a person of low intelligence (*Reef Industries, Inc. v. NLRB*, 952 F.2d 830, 839 (5th Cir. 1991)), but not to a letter mocking an employer's gift of ice cream cones (*New River Industries, Inc. v. NLRB*, 945 F.2d 1290 (4th Cir. 1991)). The Board has applied the same totality of the circumstances test to social media postings that contain profanity, and reached varying results. Generally, such postings have been protected as long as they are concerted, for mutual aid or protection, and do not entail disloyal attacks on the company. *See, e.g., Pier Sixty, LLC*, 362 N.L.R.B. 505 (2015), *enforced*, 855 F.3d 115 (2d Cir. 2017). In *GM, LLC and Charles Robinson, supra*, the Board announced that all of these contexts would also now be subject to a *Wright Line* analysis.

4. *Efforts to Affect Managerial Policy* — If employees engage in concerted activity designed to influence the "ultimate direction and managerial policies" of an employer, the activity is unprotected. In *Ampersand Publishing LLC v. NLRB*,

702 F.3d 51 (2012), the D.C. Circuit refused to enforce the Board's ruling that employees who made demands affecting editorial control of the *Santa Barbara News-Press* were engaged in protected concerted activity. Efforts to gain editorial control over the content of news coverage were essentially complaints about product quality and, as such, did not relate to wages, hours, and working conditions. Accordingly, they were outside the scope of § 7's protection.

5. *Healthcare Facilities* — Section 8(g) of the NLRA requires labor organizations representing workers at health care facilities to provide 10 days' advance notice of strikes, picketing, or other concerted refusals to work, and § 8(d) provides that "any employee . . . who engages in a strike within the appropriate period specified in subsection (g) . . . shall lose his status as an employee." In *N.Y. State Nurses Ass'n*, 334 N.L.R.B. 798 (2001), the Labor Board held that a nurses' union violated this notice provision when it failed to provide advance notice of a decision to direct its members to refuse to volunteer for overtime or to work assigned overtime, because the congressional goal of providing continued patient care justified an interpretation of § 8(g) covering such nontraditional concerted job actions. *Accord SEIU, United Healthcare Workers-West v. NLRB*, 574 F.3d 1213 (9th Cir. 2009). *Compare Mt. Clemens Gen. Hosp. v. NLRB*, 328 F.3d 837 (6th Cir. 2003) (wearing of union-distributed buttons by nurses indicating opposition to forced overtime protected activity since it did not disrupt workplace or interfere with productivity).

This provision has been applied quite strictly. *Minn. Licensed Practical Nurses Ass'n v. NLRB*, 406 F.3d 1020 (8th Cir. 2005), involved a nurses' union that gave notice that a strike would begin at 8:00 a.m. on September 10. The affected clinic made arrangements to have temporary replacement workers cover for the regular nurses beginning on the morning of September 10. The Nurses Association decided to have the regular nurses report for work that morning, so it could delay the commencement of the work stoppage for several hours. This decision caused operational difficulties for the clinic, which did not know what to do with the temporary replacements who had already arrived. Four hours later, the regular nurses began their work stoppage. The clinic decided to terminate those nurses for commencing their strike after the time set forth in the 10-day notice. Since the nurses failed to begin their strike at the time specified, the court found that they had not been engaged in protected concerted activity and could thus be discharged. The court rejected the association's claim that § 8(g) only precludes the commencement of stoppages *before* the time set forth in the strike notice but not *after* that time.

Problem

17. A home healthcare services company employs 200 home health aides, about 150 of whom are assigned to specific customers on an ongoing basis. The remaining aides form an "on call" pool of employees who perform temporary assignments. The company's customers have a wide range of physical and mental conditions ranging from depression to diabetes to post-stroke partial paralysis. The health aides report to work at the customers' homes, where they provide services such as cleaning,

shopping, bathing, reminding customers to take their medication, and observing customers for signs of immediate distress, such as dizziness or chest pains. Some customers receive care around the clock; others receive only a few hours of care per day. In order to ensure consistent service, the company maintains a rule that health aides who will not be reporting for a scheduled shift must call and notify the company in advance. While the company prefers that aides call in a day in advance, they require two hours advanced notice as a minimum.

On May 1, the union attempting to organize the health care aides notified the company that the aides would be engaging in a three-day strike starting May 12 and ending May 15. About 160 aides were scheduled to work on May 12. The week before the planned strike, the company called all of the aides scheduled to work the following week and asked whether they planned on taking any time off during the coming week. The company did not refer to the strike in calls. Fifty aides who later participated in the strike responded that they would not be working May 12 to 15. Another 20 aides participated in the strike but neither informed the company of that fact in the calls nor called in ahead of time to report that they would not be working. Several, but not all, of those aides notified the families of their customers of their intent to strike. Because of the 20 aides' failure to call in, about five clients received no services on May 12, and some others received delayed or partial services.

On May 15, the striking aides made an unconditional offer to return to work, and the company immediately reinstated the 50 aides who stated in advance that they would not be working. The remaining 20, though, were not immediately reinstated. The company informed the latter group that they had violated the call-in rule, but would not be discharged because they had been told by the union that they need not call in. At various times after May 16, all but one of the 20 aides who sought reinstatement were eventually reinstated, but not all to their pre-strike customers or with the same number of hours, and not all to regular rather than on-call positions.

Did the company commit any unfair labor practices in its response to the strike?

Mastro Plastics Corp. v. NLRB

Supreme Court of the United States
350 U.S. 270, 76 S. Ct. 349, 100 L. Ed. 309 (1956)

[The petitioners were in the plastics manufacturing business in New York, and were working under a one-year collective bargaining agreement with the Carpenters Union governing wages, hours, and working conditions. The agreement provided for arbitration of disputes and contained a clause outlawing strikes. The agreement was due to expire on November 30, 1950. The Carpenters Union gave notice of a desire to negotiate new conditions of employment on October 10, 1950. Therefore, the 60-day "cooling-off" period prescribed in §8(d)(4) would end on December 8, 1950.

During the life of this agreement the Wholesale and Warehouse Workers Union sought to displace the Carpenters as the bargaining representative of petitioner's employees. In an effort to keep the Warehouse Workers out of their plant, petitioners, not believing the Carpenters strong enough for the task, enlisted the aid of a third union, the Pulp, Sulphite and Paper Mill Workers. Petitioners unlawfully assisted the Pulp, Sulphite and Paper Mill Workers in its organizational activities, causing the Carpenters to file unfair labor practice charges with the Board. Some members of the incumbent Carpenters Union tried to counteract the influence of petitioners upon the employees, and one of these, Ciccone, was discharged for his activities on November 10.

The discharge of Ciccone, in conjunction with the antecedent employer unfair labor practices, precipitated a plant-wide strike accompanied by peaceful picketing, although neither the contract nor the 60-day waiting period had expired. The strikers made no demands relating to contract negotiations but offered to return to work if Ciccone were reinstated. The request was rejected by petitioner who notified the strikers of their discharge.

In the ensuing unfair labor practice proceedings, petitioner opposed reinstatement of the strikers upon two grounds: (1) because they had struck in breach of contract; and (2) because they lost their status as employees when they struck during the 60-day waiting period required by § 8(d) of the Taft-Hartley Act.]

Mr. Justice Burton delivered the opinion of the Court:

... In the absence of some contractual or statutory provision to the contrary, petitioners' unfair labor practices provide adequate ground for the orderly strike that occurred here. Under those circumstances, the striking employees do not lose their status and are entitled to reinstatement with back pay, even if replacements for them have been made. Failure of the Board to enjoin petitioners' illegal conduct or failure of the Board to sustain the right to strike against that conduct would seriously undermine the primary objectives of the Labor Act. See *NLRB v. [International] Rice Milling Co.*, 341 U.S. 665, 673. While we assume that the employees, by explicit contractual provision, could have waived their right to strike against such unfair labor practices and that Congress, by explicit statutory provision, could have deprived strikers, under the circumstances of this case, of their status as employees, the questions before us are whether or not such a waiver was made by the Carpenters in their 1949–1950 contract and whether or not such a deprivation of status was enacted by Congress in § 8(d) of the act, as amended in 1947.

Does the collective-bargaining contract waive the employees' right to strike against the unfair labor practices committed by their employers? The answer turns upon the proper interpretation of the particular contract before us. Like other contracts, it must be read as a whole and in the light of the law relating to it when made. . . .

On the premise of fair representation, collective-bargaining contracts frequently have included certain waivers of the employees' right to strike and of the employers' right to lockout to enforce their respective economic demands during the term of those contracts. *Provided the selection of the bargaining representative remains free,* such waivers contribute to the normal flow of commerce and to the maintenance of regular production schedules. Individuals violating such clauses appropriately lose their status as employees.

The waiver in the contract before us, upon which petitioners rely, is as follows:

> 5. The Union agrees that during the term of this agreement, there shall be no interference of any kind with the operations of the Employers, or any interruptions or slackening of production of work by any of its members. The Union further agrees to refrain from engaging in any strike or work stoppage during the term of this agreement.

That clause expresses concern for the continued operation of the plant and has a natural application to strikes and work stoppages involving the subject matter of the contract. . . .

Petitioners argue that the words "any strike" leave no room for interpretation and necessarily include all strikes, even those against unlawful practices destructive of the foundation on which collective bargaining must rest. We disagree. We believe that the contract, taken as a whole, deals solely with the economic relationship between the employers and their employees. It is a typical collective-bargaining contract dealing with terms of employment and the normal operations of the plant. It is for one year and assumes the existence of a lawfully designated bargaining representative. Its strike and lockout clauses are natural adjuncts of an operating policy aimed at avoiding interruptions of production prompted by efforts to change existing economic relationships. The main function of arbitration under the contract is to provide a mechanism for avoiding similar stoppages due to disputes over the meaning and application of the various contractual provisions.

To adopt petitioners' all-inclusive interpretation of the clause is quite a different matter. That interpretation would eliminate, for the whole year, the employees' right to strike, even if petitioners, by coercion, ousted the employees' lawful bargaining representative and, by threats of discharge, caused the employees to sign membership cards in a new union. Whatever may be said of the legality of such a waiver when explicitly stated, there is no adequate basis for implying its existence without a more compelling expression of it than appears in § 5 of this contract. . . .

II

Does § 8(d) of the National Labor Relations Act, as amended, deprive individuals of their status as employees if, within the waiting period prescribed by § 8(d)(4), they engage in a strike solely against unfair labor practices of their employers? . . .

The language in § 8(d) especially relied upon by petitioners is as follows:

> Any employee who engages in a strike within the sixty-day period specified in this subsection shall lose his status as an employee of the employer engaged in the particular labor dispute, for the purposes of §§ 8, 9, and 10 of this Act, as amended. . . .

Petitioners contend that the above words must be so read that employees who engage in any strike, regardless of its purpose, within the 60-day waiting period, thereby lose their status as employees. That interpretation would deprive Ciccone and his fellow strikers of their rights to reinstatement and would require the reversal of the judgment of the Court of Appeals. If the above words are read in complete isolation from their context in the Act, such an interpretation is possible. However, "In expounding a statute, we must not be guided by a single sentence or member of a sentence, but look to the provisions of the whole law, and its object and policy." *United States v. Boisdore's Heirs*, 8 How. 113, 122. . . .

Reading the clause in conjunction with the rest of § 8, the Board points out that "the sixty-day period" referred to is the period mentioned in paragraph (4) of § 8(d). That paragraph requires the party giving notice of a desire to *"terminate or modify"* such a contract, as part of its obligation to bargain under § 8(a)(5) or § 8(b)(3), to continue "in full force and effect, without resorting to strike or lockout, all the terms and conditions of the existing contract for a period of sixty days after such notice is given or until the expiration date of such contract, whichever occurs later." Section 8(d) thus seeks, during this natural renegotiation period, to relieve the parties from the economic pressure of a strike or lockout in relation to the subjects of negotiation. The final clause of § 8(d) also warns employees that, if they join a proscribed strike, they shall thereby lose their status as employees and, consequently, their right to reinstatement.

The Board reasons that the words which provide the key to a proper interpretation of § 8(d) with respect to this problem are "termination or modification." Since the Board expressly found that the instant strike was *not to terminate or modify* the contract, but was designed instead to protest the unfair labor practices of petitioners, the loss-of-status provision of § 8(d) is not applicable. We sustain that interpretation. Petitioners' construction would produce incongruous results. It concedes that prior to the 60-day negotiating period, employees have a right to strike against unfair labor practices designed to oust the employees' bargaining representative, yet petitioners' interpretation of § 8(d) means that if the employees give the 60-day notice of their desire to modify the contract, they are penalized for exercising that right to strike. This would deprive them of their most effective weapon at a time when their need for it is obvious. Although the employees' request to modify the contract would demonstrate their need for the services of their freely chosen representative, petitioners' interpretation would have the incongruous effect of cutting off the employees' freedom to strike against unfair labor practices aimed at that representative. This would relegate the employees to filing charges under a procedure too slow to be effective. The result would unduly favor the employers and handicap the employees during negotiation periods contrary to the purpose of the act. There also is inherent inequity in any interpretation that penalizes one party to a contract for conduct induced solely by the unlawful conduct of the other, thus giving advantage to the wrongdoer.

Petitioners contend that, unless the loss-of-status clause is applicable to unfair labor practice strikes, as well as to economic strikes, it adds nothing to the existing law relating to loss of status. Assuming that to be so, the clause is justifiable as a clarification of the law and as a warning to employees against engaging in economic strikes during the statutory waiting period. Moreover, in the face of the affirmative emphasis that is placed by the act upon freedom of concerted action and freedom of choice of representatives, any limitation on the employees' right to strike against violations of §§ 7 and 8(a), protecting those freedoms, must be more explicit and clear than it is here in order to restrict them at the very time they may be most needed. . . .

As neither the collective-bargaining contract nor § 8(d) of the National Labor Relations Act, as amended, stands in the way, the judgment of the Court of Appeals is

Affirmed.

MR. JUSTICE FRANKFURTER, whom **MR. JUSTICE MINTON** and **MR. JUSTICE HARLAN** join, dissenting.

. . . The Board and the Court of Appeals rightly held that the "no-strike" clause in the contract does not cover a work stoppage provoked by the petitioners' unfair labor practices. . . . Petitioners contend that the discharged workers lost their status as employees by reason of the 60-day "cooling-off" period provided by § 8(d) of the act. . . .

. . . Section 8 of the Wagner Act was amended [by the Taft-Hartley Act] and duties were placed upon unions. Collective action which violates any of these duties is, of course, activity unprotected by § 7. See Cox, The Right to Engage in Concerted Activities, 26 Ind. L.J. 319, 325–333 (1951). One of these new union duties, and an important one, is contained in § 8(d): unions may not strike to enforce their demands during the 60-day "cooling-off" period.

By reason of this new enactment, participating workers would not be engaged in a protected activity under § 7 by striking for the most legitimate economic reasons during the 60-day period. The strike would be in violation of the provision of that section which says that during the period there shall be no resort to a strike. The employer could discharge such strikers without violating § 8. This would be so if § 8 were without the loss-of-status provision. The Board would be powerless to order reinstatement under § 10. The loss-of-status provision in § 8(d) does not curtail the Board's power, since it did not have power to order reinstatement where a strike is resorted to for economic reasons before the 60-day period has expired. In such a situation the striker has no rights under §§ 8 and 10. Yet the Board would have us construe the loss-of-status provision as applicable only to the economic striker and qualifying a power which the Board does not have.

It is with respect to the unfair-labor-practice striker that the provision serves a purpose. This becomes clear if we assume that there were no such provision and examine the consequences of its absence. On such an assumption, a strike based on an unfair labor practice by the employer during the 60-day period may or may not be a protected activity under § 7. If it is, obviously discharged strikers would be entitled to reinstatement. The strike would not be a § 7 activity, however, if, for example, it were in breach of a no-strike clause in the contract which extends to a work stoppage provoked by an employer unfair labor practice, cf. *NLRB v. Sands Mfg. Co.*, 306 U.S. 332, 344 (1939), or if the no-strike clause in § 8(d)(4) (not to be confused with the loss-of-status provision) extends to such a work stoppage. However, even if the strike is not a § 7 activity, the Board in the unfair-labor-practice strike situation as distinguished from the economic strike situation, may in its discretion order the discharged participants reinstated. This is so because of the antecedent employer unfair practice which caused the strike, and which gave employees rights under § 8. If the Board finds that reinstatement of such strikers is a remedy that would effectuate the policies of the act, it has the power under § 10(c) to issue the necessary order.

This would not be the case, however, if the loss-of-status provision were held applicable to unfair-labor-practice strikes, because participating workers would lose their rights as "employees" for the purposes of §§ 8 and 10. Under the act only "employees" are eligible for reinstatement. The unfair-labor-practice strike, then, is the one situation where loss of status for the purposes of §§ 8 and 10 is of significance. At any rate, we have not been advised of any other situation to which the provision would apply.

We are therefore confronted with the demonstrable fact that if the provision stripping strikers of their status as employees during the 60-day period is to have any usefulness at all and not be an idle collection of words, the fact that a strike during that period is induced by the employer's unfair labor practice is immaterial.[5] Even though this might on first impression seem an undesirable result, it is so only by rejecting the important considerations in promoting peaceful industrial relations which might well have determined the action of Congress.

---

5. [1] It may be noted that the opponents of the Taft-Hartley Act objected to the loss-of-status provision for just this reason:
> [T]he section is silent as to the Board's authority to accommodate conflicting issues such as provocation on the part of the employer. Under this section an employer desirous of ridding himself either of the employees or their representative can engage in the most provocative conduct without fear of redress except by way of a lengthy hearing before the Board and a subsequent admonition to thereafter "cease and desist" from such practices. In striking contrast to the relatively delicate treatment provided for such action by an employer, employees unwilling idly to countenance abuse, who resort to self-help under the circumstances are removed from the protection of the statute and lose "employee" status. An employer is at liberty under such circumstances freely to replace any employee bold enough to insist upon justice. The provision denies to the Board the exercise of any discretion to accommodate the equitable doctrine of "clean hands." The provisions of the section are conclusive — the employee is subject to summary dismissal irrespective of the employer's conduct.

S. Rep. No. 105 (Minority), Part 2, 80th Cong., 1st Sess. 21–22 (1947).

Notes

1. *No-Strike Clauses and Unfair Labor Practice Strikes* — *Mastro Plastics* holds that a general no-strike clause does not waive the employees' right to strike in response to unfair labor practices committed by the employer. Does this mean that a strike in protest of *any* unfair labor practice is immune from a general no-strike clause? In *Arlan's Department Store of Michigan, Inc. (Local 749, Clothing Workers)*, 133 N.L.R.B. 802 (1961), a majority of a Board panel held that only strikes in protest against *serious* unfair labor practices should be held immune from general no-strike clauses. Member Fanning dissented, taking the position that all unfair labor practices are serious. See also *Dow Chemical Co.*, 244 N.L.R.B. 1060 (1979), *enforcement denied*, 636 F.2d 1352 (3d Cir. 1980), *cert. denied*, 454 U.S. 818 (1981).

2. *Disparate Discipline of Union Officers* — Following a work stoppage in violation of a no-strike provision, an employer may punish the strikers universally, randomly, or in proportion to guilt. Thus, it may discipline only the union steward if the steward instigated the stoppage. *Midwest Precision Castings Co.*, 244 N.L.R.B. 597 (1979). Should an employer be permitted to impose a more severe sanction on a union official who, while not instigating the work stoppage, makes no attempt to enforce a no-strike clause? In *Metropolitan Edison Co. v. NLRB*, 460 U.S. 693 (1983), the Supreme Court held unanimously that, in the absence of an explicit contractual duty imposed on union officials, an employer's disparate disciplining of them more severely than other employees for merely participating in a work stoppage in breach of a no-strike clause would violate § 8(a)(3) of the NLRA. The Court noted expressly that the union officials had not taken a leadership role in the unlawful strike. The Court went on to state that a union could make a "clear and unmistakable" waiver of the officials' statutory right, but concluded that the union's silence in the face of two adverse arbitration decisions under a prior labor agreement did not constitute such a waiver.

Where a collective contract requires the union to take steps to terminate any unlawful work stoppage, an employer may discipline union officials who participate in an impermissible strike more severely than other strike participants. *See Indiana & Michigan Electric Co.*, 273 N.L.R.B. 1540 (1985), *aff'd*, 786 F.2d 733 (6th Cir. 1986). *See* Note, *Selective Discipline of Union Officials After* Metropolitan Edison v. NLRB, 63 B.U. L. Rev. 473 (1983).

7. Use of Replacement Workers during Strikes

NLRB v. Mackay Radio & Telegraph Co.
Supreme Court of the United States
304 U.S. 333, 58 S. Ct. 904, 82 L. Ed. 1381 (1938)

[The Mackay Company, which was engaged in the communication business, maintained an office in San Francisco, where it employed some 60 supervisors, operators, and clerks, many of whom were members of Local No. 3 of the American Radio Telegraphists Association. In an attempt to force the company to enter into a collective agreement covering marine and point-to-point operators, the ARTA called a strike on October 4, 1935, in which Local No. 3 participated. In order to maintain service, the company brought employees from its Los Angeles and Chicago offices to fill the San Francisco strikers' places. The strike was unsuccessful, and on October 7 overtures to return to work were made in San Francisco. Company representatives advised the strikers that they could return to work, but subject to the qualification that 11 of the replacements had been promised permanent employment in San Francisco if they so desired. Accordingly, the strikers were told that they could return to work in a body, with the exception of 11 men who were told they would have to file applications for reinstatement, to be passed upon by a New York executive of the company. Thereafter, it appeared that only five of the replacements desired to remain with the company in San Francisco, and six of the 11 strikers who had been told to file formal applications for reinstatement were allowed to return to their jobs, along with the other strikers. The five strikers who were denied reinstatement were prominent in the activities of the union, and filed charges with the NLRB that the company had violated §8(1) and (3) of the original NLRA in denying them reinstatement. An NLRB complaint issued, and in due course the NLRB held the company guilty as charged, and issued a cease and desist order, and an order requiring the company to offer the five men immediate and full reinstatement. After refusal by the circuit court of appeals to enforce this order, the case was taken by the Supreme Court on certiorari. *Held*, reversed and remanded. The strikers remained "employees" under §2(3) of the Act. While there was no unfair labor practice by the company prior to or during the strike, the Board's finding of discrimination in excluding the five strikers from reinstatement was supported by the evidence.]

Mr. Justice Roberts delivered the opinion of the Court.

... Nor was it an unfair labor practice to replace the striking employees with others in an effort to carry on the business. Although §13 provides, "Nothing in this Act shall be construed so as to interfere with or impede or diminish in any way the right to strike," it does not follow that an employer, guilty of no act denounced by the statute, has lost the right to protect and continue his business by supplying places left vacant by strikers. And he is not bound to discharge those hired to fill the places of strikers, upon the election of the latter to resume their employment, in order to create places for them. The assurance by respondent to those who accepted employment during the strike that if they so desired their places might be permanent was not an unfair labor practice nor was it such to reinstate only so many of the strikers as there were vacant places to be filled. But the claim put forward is that the unfair labor practice indulged by the respondent was discrimination in reinstating striking employees by keeping out certain of them for the sole reason that they had been active in the union. As we have said, the strikers retained, under the Act, the status of employees. Any such discrimination in putting them back to work is, therefore, prohibited by § 8. . . .

As we have said, the respondent was not bound to displace men hired to take the strikers' places in order to provide positions for them. It might have refused reinstatement on the grounds of skill or ability, but the Board found that it did not do so. It might have resorted to any one of a number of methods of determining which of its striking employees would have to wait because five men had taken permanent positions during the strike, but it is found that the preparation and use of the list [*i.e.*, the list of the names of the eleven men originally selected for exclusion], and the action taken by the respondent, were with the purpose to discriminate against those most active in the union. There is evidence to support these findings.

Notes

1. *Economic Strikes* — Since the decision in the principal case, it has been recognized that where the employer is "guilty of no act denounced by the statute," it has a right, in order to keep its plant in operation, to hire permanent replacements for strikers, and thus to deprive the replaced strikers of an immediate right of reinstatement.

> If employees go out on strike for economic reasons and not because of any unfair labor practices on the part of their employer, the latter may replace them in order to keep his business running, and the strikers thereafter have no absolute right of reinstatement to their old jobs. After the termination of a strike, however, an employer may not discriminatorily refuse to reinstate or reemploy the strikers merely because of their union membership or concerted activity.

NLRB, Eighth Annual Report 32 (1943). In order to take advantage of their reinstatement rights, unreplaced economic strikers must make an unconditional application for reinstatement, either personally or through their union.

To what extent has the use of permanent replacements weakened the right to strike as guaranteed by §7? Commentators point to the dramatic decline in the number of strikes over the last several decades — the same period during which the permanent replacement of workers became more common. The number of work stoppages involving 1,000 or more workers has dropped dramatically, falling from 235 in 1979 to 187 in 1980, and declining to just 20 per year on average between 2000 and 2009. In 2020, there were only 8 work stoppages involving 1,000 or more workers and lasting at least one work shift. In comparison, the number fell below 200 only twice between 1947 and 1979. *See* Bureau of Labor Statistics, Work Stoppages Involving 1,000 or More Workers, 1947–2003, *available at* http://www.bls.gov

/news.release/wkstp.t01.htm; Bureau of Labor Statistics, Major Work Stoppages in 2020, Feb. 19, 2021, *available at* http://www.bls.gov/news.release/pdf/wkstp.pdf. One study indicated that most employers are willing to hire replacement workers to continue operations in the event of a strike, with manufacturing companies most likely to utilize permanent replacement workers. Daily Lab. Rep. (BNA) Special Supp., Jan. 24, 2003, at S-7. Does this establish the correlation between the *Mackay* rule and the decline in the incidence of strikes? What are other possible causes for the decline in strike activity? *See* J. LAMBERT, IF WORKERS TOOK A NOTION (2005) (surveying reasons); LeRoy, *Changing Paradigms in the Public Policy of Striker Replacements*, 34 B.C. L. REV. 257, 301–03 (1992–1993) (listing the declining level of union density, broader deregulation across industries, the globalization of labor, and increased job mobility as other potential contributing factors). *See generally* Getman & Kohler, *The Story of Mackay Radio*, in LABOR LAW STORIES (Cooper & Fisk eds., 2005); Pope, *How American Workers Lost the Right to Strike, and Other Tales*, 103 MICH. L. REV. 518 (2004); *see also* "*The Strike: A Contemporary Lesson from Labor History or a Historical Artifact?*", 37 LAB. STUD. J. 337 (2012) (symposium issue).

Some commentators have defended the *Mackay Radio* doctrine on the grounds that it promotes economic efficiency, helping to deter opportunistic behavior by unions and employers during strike situations. *See* Cohen & Wachter, *Replacing Striking Workers: The Law and Economics Approach*, in 43RD PROCEEDINGS OF NYU ANNUAL CONFERENCE ON LABOR 109 (1990). Professor Corbett argues that the right to hire permanent replacements during an economic strike provides a market check on the demands of the parties:

> It is reasonable to predict ... that without the possibility of permanent replacement, unions would, at least, be quicker to call strikes. To avoid such strikes and the possibly more difficult (and in some cases impossible) task of hiring temporary replacements, more employers might abandon their bargaining positions and agree to unions' demands, even if the demands are supracompetitive. In the extreme, such results would cause some employers to curtail operations, relocate assets, or perhaps eventually go out of business—harming employer and employees, the community, and consumers.

Corbett, *A Proposal for Procedural Limitations on Hiring Permanent Striker Replacements: "A Far, Far Better Thing" than the Workplace Fairness Act*, 72 N.C. L. REV. 813, 875–76 (1994). Corbett recommends limiting the doctrine, however, by instituting a temporary ban on hiring permanent replacements until it is determined that a strike is economic in nature.

The *Mackay Radio* doctrine has been the focus of several legislative proposals designed to stem the use of permanent replacements. In 1993, the House of Representatives passed the Cesar Chavez Workplace Fairness Act, which would have made it an unfair labor practice for an employer to hire or to threaten to hire permanent replacements. The Act subsequently died in the Senate. In 1995, President Clinton promulgated an Executive Order that authorized the Secretary of Labor to terminate federal contracts and to bar future contracts with any employer that anywhere in its operations permanently replaced strikers. The order was struck down by the D.C. Circuit Court on the ground that it was preempted by the NLRA as interpreted by the Court in *Mackay*. See *Chamber of Commerce of the United States v. Reich*, 74 F.3d 1322 (D.C. Cir. 1996). And, more recently, in 2020 the House of Representatives passed the Protecting the Right to Organize (PRO) Act, which, among other things, would prohibit the use of permanent replacements.

2. *Limitations on Permanent Replacements* — Although employers may hire permanent replacements for economic strikers, they must have legitimate business reasons for such action. *Sutter Roseville Med. Ctr.*, 348 N.L.R.B. 637 (2006), involved a work stoppage at a hospital. The representative union had given the hospital 10 days' notice of the intention to conduct a one-day strike, as required under §8(g), and it had accompanied that notice with a written unconditional offer for the employees to return to work at the conclusion of the one-day stoppage. The hospital made arrangements with a temporary employment service to cover for the strikers, but it entered into an agreement covering a minimum five-day period. As a result, it informed the strikers that they could not return to work until four days after their one-day strike ended. The Labor Board found that this action violated the NLRA, since the hospital did not demonstrate "substantial and legitimate business reasons" for its refusal to allow the strikers to return to work as soon as their stoppage ended.

New Eng. Health Care Emps. Union, Dist. 1199 v. NLRB, 448 F.3d 189 (2d Cir. 2006), involved an assisted living facility that filled in with managers and temporary replacements when a strike began. As the stoppage continued, however, the employer secretly began to hire permanent replacements. Once the union learned about the firm's hiring of permanent replacements, it submitted an unconditional offer for the striking employees to return to work. The employer refused to take back the strikers who had been permanently replaced before the union offer to end the strike. Even though the employer had the right to hire permanent replacements, the court found that its act of engaging in this process surreptitiously indicated that it lacked the legitimate motive of encouraging strikers to return to work and was actually motivated by a desire to break the union by getting rid of the strikers before they knew what was going on. Its refusal to take back all of the strikers thus contravened §8(a)(3).

Employers that hire permanent replacements for economic strikers on an "at-will" basis, under which they may terminate those individuals at any time, nevertheless cannot be required to displace the workers in order to reinstate the replaced strikers once the strike is settled until actual job vacancies occur. However, the employer cannot selectively fire some replacement workers in order to bring back strikers who have renounced the union, and still assert that the replacements are permanent. See *United Steel, Paper & Forestry, Rubber, Mfg., Energy, Allied Indus. & Serv. Workers Int'l Union v. NLRB*, 544 F.3d 841 (7th Cir. 2008).

In *NLRB v. International Van Lines*, 409 U.S. 48 (1972), the Supreme Court held that an employer had to offer unconditional reinstatement to striking employees whom it had discharged *before* it hired permanent replacements, since the termination of economic strikers constitutes a *per se* unfair labor practice. *Compare L.A. Water Treatment, Div. of Chromalloy American Corp. v. NLRB*, 873 F.2d 1150 (8th Cir. 1989), wherein the court disagreed with the Labor Board and held that an employer was merely informing striking employees of their permanent replacement, not their impermissible discharge, when it wrote them: "As of this date we have hired a permanent replacement for your job classification. . . . You are no longer employed."

In *River's Bend Health & Rehab. Servs.*, 350 N.L.R.B. 184 (2007), the Board held that an employer did not violate the NLRA when it informed employees prior to a scheduled work stoppage that its hiring of striker replacements would put their "continued job status in jeopardy," despite the claim that this statement suggested that strikers would lose their reinstatement rights, where the employer did not say that replaced strikers would permanently lose their jobs. *See also Pirelli Cable Corp. v. NLRB*, 141 F.3d 503 (4th Cir. 1998) (rejecting Board finding that an employer had illegally threatened employees when it gave them a pre-strike letter explaining its right to hire permanent replacements for striking employees).

3. *Rights of Permanently Replaced Employees*—In *Laidlaw Corp.*, 171 N.L.R.B. 1366 (1968), the Labor Board declared that:

> [E]conomic strikers who unconditionally apply for reinstatement at a time when their positions are filled by permanent replacements: (1) remain employees; (2) are entitled to full reinstatement upon the departure of replacements unless they have in the meantime acquired regular and substantially equivalent employment, or the employer can sustain his burden of proof that the failure to offer full reinstatement was for legitimate and substantial business reasons.

Laidlaw was enforced in 414 F.2d 99 (7th Cir. 1969), *cert. denied*, 397 U.S. 920 (1970). The Board recognized in *Rose Printing Co.*, 304 N.L.R.B. 1076 (1991), that an employer need not offer former economic strikers reinstatement to jobs that are not the same or substantially equivalent to their old jobs, even when the workers are qualified to fill them. On the other hand, an employer may not refuse to reinstate economic strikers because of its belief that replacement workers may be hostile to the returning strikers. *Diamond Walnut Growers*, 316 N.L.R.B. 36 (1995), *enforced in relevant part*, 113 F.3d 1259 (D.C. Cir. 1997) (*en banc*), *cert. denied*, 523 U.S. 1020 (1998). *See also NLRB v. Oregon Steel Mills*, 47 F.3d 1536 (9th Cir. 1995) (employer violated §8(a)(3) when it bypassed qualified strikers on a preferential rehire list in favor of temporary workers obtained through outside employment agencies, rejecting employer's contention that duty to rehire strikers only applies when firm hires new employees onto its own payroll).

In *Brooks Research & Mfg., Inc.*, 202 N.L.R.B. 634 (1973), the NLRB held that there is no time limit on an employer's obligation to reinstate economic strikers who have made an unconditional application for reinstatement. An employer may not unilaterally terminate their seniority and recall rights without bargaining with the union. An employer may, however, require unreinstated strikers to periodically indicate their continued interest in reemployment. *See Aqua-Chem, Inc., Cleaver Brooks Div.*, 288 N.L.R.B. 1108 (1988), *enforced*, 910 F.2d 1487 (7th Cir. 1990); *NLRB v. Vitronic Div. of Penn Corp.*, 630 F.2d 561 (8th Cir. 1979).

Could a union and an employer, as part of a strike settlement, place time limits on the reinstatement rights of economic strikers? In *United Aircraft Corp.*, 192 N.L.R.B. 382 (1971), *enforced in part sub nom. Lodges 743 & 1746, Int'l Ass'n of Machinists v. United Aircraft Corp.*, 534 F.2d 422 (2d Cir. 1975), the Labor Board indicated that it would accept a strike settlement agreement as determining the reinstatement rights of economic strikers, if the period fixed by the agreement for reinstatement of the strikers: (1) is not unreasonably short, (2) is not intended to be discriminatory, or misused by either party with the intent of accomplishing a discriminatory objective, (3) was not insisted upon by the employer to undermine the status of the union, and (4) was the result of good-faith bargaining.

4. *Unfair Labor Practice Strikes*—It is well established that when a strike has been called because of the employer's unfair labor practices (e.g., a refusal to bargain with a certified union), the employer is not legally free to hire permanent replacements and is obligated to reinstate the strikers upon their request. *Collins & Aikman Corp.*, 165 N.L.R.B. 678 (1967), *enforced*, 395 F.2d 277 (4th Cir. 1968).

In *Northern Wire Corp. v. NLRB*, 887 F.2d 1313 (7th Cir. 1989), the court held that union members were unfair labor practice strikers entitled to reinstatement and back pay despite their employer's contention that even without the unfair labor practices they would have struck over economic demands. It was sufficient that the stoppage was at least partially motivated by the employer's unfair labor practices. *Accord, Spurlino Materials, LLC v. NLRB*, 805 F.3d 1131 (D.C. Cir. 2015). *But see California Acrylic Indus. v. NLRB*, 150 F.3d 1095 (9th Cir. 1998) (strike motivated primarily by economic issues is economic strike despite accompanying employer unfair labor practices).

5. *Economic Strikes Converted into Unfair Labor Practice Strikes*—If the employer first commits unfair labor practices *during* the course of an ongoing economic strike, thereby prolonging it, the strike at that point becomes an unfair labor practice strike, and strikers who are replaced after that point are entitled to reinstatement upon request. *NLRB v. Pecheur Lozenge Co.*, 209 F.2d 393 (2d Cir. 1953), *cert. denied*, 347 U.S. 953 (1954); *American Cyanamid Co. v. NLRB*, 592 F.2d 356 (7th Cir. 1979). To convert an economic strike into an unfair labor practice strike, the employer's unlawful conduct must actually be found to have prolonged or intensified the work stoppage. *See F.L. Thorpe & Co. v. NLRB*, 71 F.3d 282 (8th Cir. 1995). *Compare Titan Tire Corp.*, 333 N.L.R.B. 1156 (2001) (employer that announced at press conference that if no bargaining agreement were achieved soon it would close plant and transfer equipment and jobs to other location tainted ongoing bargaining and converted economic strike into unfair labor practice stoppage).

In *Gen. Indus. Emples. Union, Local 42 v. NLRB*, 951 F.2d 1308 (D.C. Cir. 1991), the court held that an unfair labor practice strike became an economic strike when the employees continued striking for reasons that were unrelated to the unfair labor practice, even though the employer had not fully "cured" the latter.

6. *Sympathy Strikes*—In the absence of an applicable no-strike obligation, the prevailing view is that an employer may not terminate employees who honor a primary picket line at another employer's premises. Such individuals are normally treated as economic strikers. Their employer may not discipline them, but it may hire permanent replacements for them in order to maintain efficient business operations by retaining other persons who will cross the picket line. *See, e.g., Redwing Carriers, Inc. (Teamsters, Local 79)*, 137 N.L.R.B. 1545 (1962), *enforced*, 325 F.2d 1011 (D.C. Cir. 1963), *cert. denied*, 377 U.S. 905 (1964). *But see NLRB v. L. G. Everist, Inc.*, 334 F.2d 312 (8th Cir. 1964) (holding that sympathy strikers are not engaged in protected activity).

In *Brown & Root, Inc.*, 99 N.L.R.B. 1031 (1952), the Labor Board held that employees of the same company who honor the unfair labor practice strike picket line of coworkers from another department that had been adversely affected by the employer's unfair labor practices must be treated as economic sympathy strikers instead of unfair labor practice sympathy strikers, due to the fact the firm's NLRA violations had no direct effect on their employment. They could thus be permanently replaced, unlike the unfair labor practice strikers involved.

In *Indianapolis Power & Light Co.*, 273 N.L.R.B. 1715 (1985), the Labor Board overruled established precedent and held that a general no-strike clause must be read as precluding all work stoppages, including sympathy strikes. It thus sustained the right of an employer to suspend a worker who had refused to cross the picket line at the premises of another company where the applicable bargaining agreement prohibited "any strike, picketing, . . . or other curtailment of work." In *International Brotherhood of Electrical Workers, Local 387 v. NLRB*, 788 F.2d 1412 (9th Cir. 1986), however, the court held that the per se application of the Board's *Indianapolis Power & Light* doctrine was inappropriate. The Board had to consider the actual intent of the contracting parties from such evidence as their bargaining history, their past practice, and the state of the law with respect to this issue at the time they negotiated their general no-strike clause. The D.C. Circuit essentially agreed with the Ninth Circuit's view in *IBEW Local 1395 v. NLRB*, 797 F.2d 1027 (6th Cir. 1986), and remanded *Indianapolis Power & Light* for further proceedings. On remand, the Board reaffirmed the views expressed in *Indianapolis Power & Light I*, but indicated that extrinsic evidence may be used to show that the contracting parties did not intend a general no-strike clause to cover sympathy strikes. *Indianapolis Power & Light Co.*, 291 N.L.R.B. 1039 (1988), *enforced*, 898 F.2d 524 (7th Cir. 1990). Courts continue to find that general no-strike clauses do not cover sympathy strikes absent unmistakable language to the contrary. *See, e.g., Children's Hosp. Med. Ctr. v. Cal. Nurses Ass'n*, 283 F.3d 1188 (9th Cir. 2002).

7. *Picket Line Behavior*—For years, the Board applied *Clear Pine Mouldings, Inc.*, 268 N.L.R.B. 1044 (1984), to determine when conduct on the picket line was

sufficiently abusive to render it unprotected. Under that standard, employees lost protection when the conduct "'reasonably tend[ed] to coerce or intimidate employees in the exercise of rights protected under the Act.'" *Id.* at 1046 (quoting *NLRB v. W. C. McQuaide, Inc.*, 552 F.2d 519, 527 (3d Cir. 1977)). Cases applying *Clear Pine Mouldings* found that picket-line conduct lost protection only when it involved an overt or implied threat or where there was a reasonable likelihood of an imminent physical confrontation. *See, e.g., Catalytic, Inc.*, 275 N.L.R.B. 97, 98 (1985).

More recently, the Board replaced the *Clear Pine Mouldings* standard for picket-line behavior with the *Wright Line* test, discussed above, creating a uniform standard for analyzing abusive behavior on the picket line, on social media, and in workplace discussions with management. *GM LLC and Charles Robinson*, 369 N.L.R.B. No. 127 (2020). The Board believed that the *Clear Pine Mouldings* standard produced inconsistent results and, more to the point, meant that "appallingly abusive picket-line misconduct... including racially and sexually offensive language" often retained protection. *Id.* (citing examples such as *Cooper Tire & Rubber Co.*, 363 NLRB No. 194 (2016) (finding protected a white picketer saying to black replacement workers, "Hey, did you bring enough KFC for everyone?" and "Hey, anybody smell that? I smell fried chicken and watermelon."), *enforced*, 866 F.3d 885 (8th Cir. 2017), and *Nickell Moulding*, 317 NLRB 826, 828–829 (1995) (finding protected a striker carrying a sign targeted at one particular nonstriker that read: "Who is Rhonda F [with an X through the F] Sucking Today?"), *enf. denied sub nom. NMC Finishing v. NLRB*, 101 F.3d 528 (8th Cir. 1996)). Under the *Wright Line* test, once the General Counsel proves that the employer's action was based in whole or in part on anti-union animus, the employer will be found in violation unless it can prove as an affirmative defense that the adverse action would have been taken even if the employee had not been involved in protected activities. The Board believes this more familiar test will produce more consistent results and stop penalizing employers "for declining to tolerate abusive and potentially illegal conduct in the workplace." *GM LLC and Charles Robinson, supra.*

8. Inducements to Strike Crossovers and New Hires

In *NLRB v. Erie Resistor Corp.*, 373 U.S. 221 (1963), the Court reaffirmed the principle in *Mackay* that hiring replacements where necessary to continue operation of the business and offering them permanent status to reassure them that they will not be discharged to make room for returning strikers if the strike is settled is not an unfair labor practice, but established some limits on what other kinds of inducements employers might offer to striking workers to persuade them to cross the strike line and return to work. The Court struck down Erie Resistor's offer of 20 years' superseniority to new hires and strike crossovers, finding that such inducements violated §§ 8(a)(1) and 8(a)(3) because they were inherently destructive of the right to strike. The Court explained:

> ... Superseniority affects the tenure of all strikers whereas permanent replacement, proper under *Mackay*, affects only those who are, in actuality,

replaced. It is one thing to say that a striker is subject to loss of his job at the strike's end but quite another to hold that in addition to the threat of replacement, all strikers will at best return to their jobs with seniority inferior to that of the replacements and of those who left the strike.

. . . .

Unlike the replacement granted in *Mackay* which ceases to be an issue once the strike is over, the [superseniority] plan here creates a cleavage in the plant continuing long after the strike is ended. Employees are henceforth divided into two camps: those who stayed with the union and those who returned before the end of the strike and thereby gained extra seniority. This breach is reemphasized with each subsequent layoff and stands as an ever-present reminder of the dangers connected with striking and with union activities in general.

Id. at 230–31. While pressure on strikers as a group to abandon the strike does not violate the Act, inducements that create incentives for individual workers to save or improve their positions at the expense of other striking members of the bargaining unit is a divide-and-conquer tactic that jeopardizes the entire strike effort and so "strikes a fundamental blow to union . . . activity and the collective bargaining process itself." *Id.*

In *TWA v. Independent Federation of Flight Attendants*, 489 U.S. 426 (1989), flight attendants struck during collective bargaining negotiations that were stalled on wages and working conditions other than seniority. TWA announced that it would continue operations by hiring permanent replacements, by continuing to employ any flight attendant who chose not to strike, and by rehiring any striker who abandoned the strike and made an unconditional offer to return to any available vacancies. Although the collective bargaining agreement had established a complex system of bidding to ensure that flight attendants with the greatest seniority would have the best opportunity to obtain their preferred job assignments, flight schedules, and bases of operation as vacancies arose, and ensuring that flight attendants with the most seniority would be least affected by periodic furloughs, TWA informed the striking flight attendants that "any vacancies created as a result of the strike would be filled by application of the seniority bidding system to all [then] working flight attendants and that such job and domicile assignments would remain effective after the strike ended." The Court ruled that TWA's plan did not violate the Act. Even though the plan created two incentives linked to the seniority bidding system — one aimed at senior flight attendants who would be loath to give up their prior jobs and domicile assignments, and one aimed at junior flight attendants who would have an incentive to obtain more desirable job and domicile assignments previously held by more senior flight attendants — it did not deprive reinstated strikers of their seniority in absolute or relative terms. Distinguishing *Erie Resistor*, the Court observed that "resentful rifts" that persist between employees after the strike are merely a by-product of the Act's protection of both the right to strike and the right not to strike; thus, "the employer's right to hire permanent replacements in order to continue operations will inevitably also have the effect of dividing striking employees between those who, fearful of permanently losing their jobs, return to work and those who remain stalwart in the strike." *Id.* at 437. In the absence of a continuing diminution of seniority upon reinstatement at the end of the strike, then, division among employees post-strike as a result of the acceptance by some of inducements to cross the strike line is merely a "secondary effect fairly within the arsenal of economic weapons available to employers during a period of self-help." *Id.* at 438. The dissenters argued that the use of such tools unfairly burdens the right to strike, and that employers who recall workers to fill available positions at the end of a strike should be required to use principles that are neutral between employees to do so, such as seniority, rather than being permitted to discriminate on the basis of protected union activity. Per Justice Brennan, "[t]he principle of seniority is based on the notion that it is those employees who have worked longest in an enterprise and therefore have most at stake whose jobs should be most protected." *Id.* at 451.

In *Mike Yurosek & Son, Inc.*, 295 N.L.R.B. 304 (1989), a seasonal employer was permitted to recall permanent strike replacements laid off at the end of the preceding season ahead of unreinstated strikers. The Board found that the replacements had a reasonable expectation of recall, thus their seasonal layoffs did not create vacant positions. In *Delta-Macon Brick & Tile Co.*, 297 N.L.R.B. 1044 (1990), however, the Board held that an employer unlawfully recalled strike replacements who had been laid off for more than a year ahead of unreinstated economic strikers, because the lengthy layoff of the replacements had created vacancies to which the strikers were entitled to be recalled. Nonetheless, the Fifth Circuit denied enforcement of the Board order, since it found that the replacement workers still had a "reasonable expectancy" of recall and thus had continuing recall priority over the unreinstated strikers. *NLRB v. Delta-Macon Brick & Tile Co.*, 943 F.2d 567 (5th Cir. 1991). *See Aqua-Chem, Inc., Cleaver-Brooks Div. v. NLRB*, 910 F.2d 1487 (7th Cir. 1990), *reh'g denied*, 922 F.2d 403 (7th Cir.), *cert. denied*, 501 U.S. 1238 (1991) (adopting "reasonable expectation of recall" approach to determine when laid-off replacements may be recalled ahead of unreinstated strikers). *See also Waterbury Hosp. v. NLRB*, 950 F.2d 849 (2d Cir. 1991) (affirming the Board's conclusion that nonstrikers could not be considered "permanent replacements" if they were given post-strike positions different from those they occupied during the strike, unless they were in training for the positions and the positions were open during the work stoppage). When laid-off replacement workers are recalled ahead of unreinstated strikers, are the replacements effectively being granted "super seniority" similar to that prohibited in *Erie Resistor*?

Although an employer that reinstates economic strikers will generally violate the NLRA if it fails to return them to their former positions on the seniority list (*NLRB v. Bingham-Willamette Co.*, 857 F.2d 661 (9th Cir. 1988)), a labor organization may expressly waive its right to undiluted seniority in exchange for an end to the work stoppage. *See Gem City Ready Mix Co.*, 270 N.L.R.B. 1260 (1984) (sustaining validity of strike settlement agreement that unequivocally placed the three employees who continued to work during strike at top of seniority list, since waiver provision was unambiguous and returning strikers understood its application).

Aside from grants of superseniority, what other kinds of inducements might violate §§ 8(a)(1) and 8(a)(3) on the *Erie Resistor* rationale? In *Suma Corp.*, 282 N.L.R.B. 667 (1987), the Labor Board held that a hotel violated § 8(a)(3) when it gave a onetime $4,000 party for employees who had not struck or who had abandoned a strike, some three months after the strike had ended. The employer unsuccessfully tried to demonstrate as business justification that it wished to show its appreciation for "consistent loyalty" and to "cool" down the "great deal of animosity" continuing between invitees and former strikers. *See also Rubatex Corp.*, 235 N.L.R.B. 833 (1978), *enforced*, 601 F.2d 147 (4th Cir.), *cert. denied*, 444 U.S. 928 (1979) (post-strike cash bonuses to people who worked during strike not supported by valid business justification). What if, at the beginning of a strike, an employer having difficulty attracting qualified replacement workers offered cash bonuses to individuals who worked for the duration of the work stoppage?

9. Proof of Motive in Cases Involving Violations of Sections 8(a)(3) and (1)

NLRB v. Great Dane Trailers, Inc., 388 U.S. 26, 87 S. Ct. 1792, 18 L. Ed. 2d 1027 (1967). The Supreme Court further explored the extent to which *scienter* must be proved to find a violation of § 8(a)(3). In that case, an employer was held by the NLRB to have violated § 8(a)(3) when it refused to pay striking employees vacation benefits that had accrued under a terminated bargaining agreement while announcing an intent to pay such benefits to those individuals who had worked on a certain day during the strike. The court of appeals (363 F.2d 130 (5th Cir. 1966)) refused enforcement, because it found no affirmative showing of an unlawful employer motivation to discourage union membership.

The Supreme Court overturned the appeals court decision. It divided employer conduct into two categories: (1) extreme action that is "inherently destructive" of employee rights, and (2) behavior that has a "comparatively slight" effect on those rights. In both situations, "once it had been proved that the employer engaged in discriminatory conduct which could have adversely affected employee rights to some extent, the burden is upon the employer to establish that it was motivated by legitimate objectives." The court held that a violation of § 8(a)(3) can be found without proof of improper motive in unusual instances in which "inherently destructive" conduct is present even though the employer offers evidence of justification. With respect to conduct that has a "comparatively slight" effect, if the employer comes forward with exculpatory evidence that outweighs the interference with employee § 7 rights, a violation can be found only if anti-union motivation is proved.

Note

The Role of Improper Motive—Although the Supreme Court had found in *Great Dane Trailers* that an employer's refusal to pay striking employees their accrued vacation benefits constituted an unfair labor practice, the Seventh Circuit found no such violation when a company rescheduled vacations due to commence during an impending strike for all plant personnel until the end of the work stoppage. The court noted that the employer had not discriminated between striking and non-striking employees, no anti-union animus was found, the employer had a valid business reason for postponing the vacations of all workers until the strike was over, and the employer's action was not found to be "inherently destructive" of employee rights. *See Stokely-Van Camp, Inc. v. NLRB*, 722 F.2d 1324 (7th Cir. 1983). *See also Forest Products Co. v. NLRB*, 888 F.2d 72 (10th Cir. 1989), wherein the court held that an employer's failure to distribute matching contributions under a Christmas savings program to permanently replaced strikers did not violate § 8(a)(3), where the program required participants to be employed on the distribution date and the employer had previously treated persons as ineligible when they were on leave or layoff on the distribution date.

In *NLRB v. Burnup & Sims, Inc.*, 379 U.S. 21 (1964), however, the Supreme Court held that an employer violated § 8(a)(1) when it discharged two employees who were engaged in protected organizing activities, even though it had no wrongful motive. In this case, the employer terminated the two employees when it was informed they were planning to use violence during the union's organizing campaign; the information later proved to be untrue. The Court held that the policy behind § 8(a)(1) dictated the reinstatement of the employees, "[o]therwise, the protected activity would lose some of its immunity, since the example of employees who are discharged on false charges would or might have a deterrent effect on other employees." Employer good faith in the discharges was deemed irrelevant, because the false charges were inextricably intertwined with the employees' protected organizing activities.

Problem

[Under Stericycle,]

18. Southland Construction is a major supplier of construction trade labor to non-union contractors in the southern United States. Over the last several years, Southland has grown considerably, and now hires as many as several thousand employees annually. Recently, however, Southland adopted and implemented a new hiring guideline that stated: "Applicants whose most recent year of work experience is at a pay level more than 30% higher or lower than the starting wages paid on Southland assignments are not likely to be retained in the pool, and must not be hired."

The new 30% rule is based on a study of worker retention by the president of Southland. The president assumed that Southland's traditionally low employee retention rate was a result of the fact that workers who had previously earned higher wages would be less likely to continue to work for Southland. He found that to be true and, further, calculated that the wage differential breakpoint that would result in the greatest retention rate without unduly diminishing the size of the applicant pool was 30%. Although there is no evidence that Southland's 30% rule was motivated by anti-union animus, it had the effect of excluding virtually all Southland applicants who had worked for any significant period of the preceding year on a construction project where their wages were determined by a union-negotiated contract.

Does Southland's 30% rule constitute an unfair labor practice?

D. Lockouts, Plant Closings, and "Runaway Shops"

NLRB v. Truck Drivers, Local 449, International Brotherhood of Teamsters [Buffalo Linen Case]

Supreme Court of the United States
353 U.S. 87, 77 S. Ct. 643, 1 L. Ed. 2d 676 (1957)

[The union, engaged in collective bargaining on a multiemployer basis with an employers association representing eight linen supply companies in Buffalo, put into effect a "whipsaw" plan by striking one of the companies. A whipsaw strike involves striking companies in an employers association one at a time in an attempt to force the struck company to break ranks with the association and settle on terms favorable to the union. In this case, when the union struck the first of the eight linen supply companies, the other seven employers locked out their employees and ceased operating. Multiemployer negotiations continued, and, after one week, a new contract was signed and employees returned to work. The union charged the seven employers with violations of § 8(a)(1) and (3). The NLRB held no violation since the lockout was defensive. The court of appeals found a violation, holding the lockout not privileged in the absence of unusual economic hardship.]

MR. JUSTICE BRENNAN delivered the opinion of the Court.

. . . We are not concerned here with the cases in which the lockout has been held unlawful because designed to frustrate organizational efforts, to destroy or undermine bargaining representation, or to evade the duty to bargain. Nor are we called upon to define the limits of the legitimate use of the lockout.[6] The narrow question to be decided is whether a temporary lockout may lawfully be used as a defense to a union strike tactic which threatens the destruction of the employers' interest in bargaining on a group basis. . . .

Although the act protects the right of the employees to strike in support of their demands, this protection is not so absolute as to deny self-help by employers when legitimate interests of employees and employers collide. Conflict may arise, for example, between the right to strike and the interest of small employers in preserving multiemployer bargaining as a means of bargaining on an equal basis with a

---

6. [19] We thus find it unnecessary to pass upon the question whether, as a general proposition, the employer lockout is the corollary of the employees' statutory right to strike.

large union and avoiding the competitive disadvantages resulting from nonuniform contractual terms. The ultimate problem is the balancing of the conflicting legitimate interests. The function of striking that balance to effectuate national labor policy is often a difficult and delicate responsibility, which the Congress committed primarily to the National Labor Relations Board, subject to limited judicial review.

The Court of Appeals recognized that the National Labor Relations Board has legitimately balanced conflicting interests by permitting lockouts where economic hardship was shown. The court erred, however, in too narrowly confining the exercise of Board discretion to the cases of economic hardship. We hold that in the circumstances of the case the Board correctly balanced the conflicting interests in deciding that a temporary lockout to preserve the multiemployer bargaining basis from the disintegration threatened by the Union's strike action was lawful.

Reversed.

NLRB v. Brown

Supreme Court of the United States
380 U.S. 278, 85 S. Ct. 980, 13 L. Ed. 2d 839 (1965)

[The union, engaged in collective bargaining on a multiemployer basis with a group of six retail food stores in Carlsbad, New Mexico, put into effect a "whipsaw" plan by striking one of the stores, Food Jet. Food Jet continued operations with management personnel and their relatives and with a few temporary replacements. The other five stores laid off their union employees, regarding "the strike against one as a strike against all." However, in contrast to the *Buffalo Linen* situation, the five stores continued operations with management personnel, relatives, and temporary replacements, who were told that their employment would end when the "whipsaw" strike ended. Group bargaining continued; an agreement was reached after about a month; and the employers immediately released the temporary employees and recalled the strikers and locked-out employees. The NLRB (3-2) found a violation of § 8(a)(1) and (3), inferring that the employers acted not merely to protect the integrity of their multiemployer unit, but for the purpose of inhibiting a lawful strike. The court of appeals refused to enforce the Board's order.]

Mr. Justice Brennan delivered the opinion of the Court.

. . . The Board's decision does not rest upon independent evidence that the respondents acted either out of hostility toward the Local or in reprisal for the whipsaw strike. It rests upon the Board's appraisal that the respondents' conduct carried its own indicia of unlawful intent, thereby establishing, without more, that the conduct constituted an unfair labor practice. It was disagreement with this appraisal, which we share, that led the Court of Appeals to refuse to enforce the Board's order. . . .

In the circumstances of this case, we do not see how the continued operations of respondents and their use of temporary replacements any more implies hostile motivation, nor how it is inherently more destructive of employee rights, than the lockout itself. Rather, the compelling inference is that this was all part and parcel of respondents' defensive measure to preserve the multiemployer group in the face of the whipsaw strike. Since Food Jet legitimately continued business operations, it is only reasonable to regard respondents' action as evincing concern that the integrity of the employer group was threatened unless they also managed to stay open for business during the lockout. For with Food Jet open for business and respondents' stores closed, the prospect that the whipsaw strike would succeed in breaking up the employer association was not at all fanciful. The retail food industry is very competitive and repetitive patronage is highly important. Faced with the prospect of a loss of patronage to Food Jet, it is logical that respondents should have been concerned that one or more of their number might bolt the group and come to terms with the Local, thus destroying the common front essential to multiemployer bargaining. The Court of Appeals correctly pictured the respondents' dilemma in saying, "If . . . the struck employer does choose to operate with replacements and the other employers cannot replace after lockout, the economic advantage passes to the struck member, the non-struck members are deterred in exercising the defensive lockout, and the whipsaw strike . . . enjoys an almost inescapable prospect of success." 319 F.2d, at 11. Clearly respondents' continued operations with the use of temporary replacements following the lockout was wholly consistent with a legitimate business purpose.

Nor are we persuaded by the Board's argument that justification for the inference of hostile motivation appears in the respondents' use of temporary employees rather than some of the regular employees. It is not common sense, we think, to say that the regular employees were "willing to work at the employers' terms." 137 N.L.R.B., at 76. It seems probable that this "willingness" was motivated as much by their understandable desire to further the objective of the whipsaw strike—to break through the employers' united front by forcing Food Jet to accept the Local's terms—as it was by a desire to work for the employers under the existing unacceptable terms. As the Board's dissenting members put it, "These employees are willing only to receive wages while their brethren in the rest of the association-wide unit are exerting whipsaw pressure on one employer to gain benefits that will ultimately accrue to all employees in the association-wide unit, including those here locked out." 137 N.L.R.B., at 78. Moreover, the course of action to which the Board would limit the respondents would force them into the position of aiding and abetting the success of the whipsaw strike and consequently would render "largely illusory," 137 N.L.R.B., at 78–79, the right of lockout recognized by *Buffalo Linen*; the right would be meaningless if barred to non-struck stores that find it necessary to operate because the struck store does so.

The Board's finding of a §8(a)(1) violation emphasized the impact of respondents' conduct upon the effectiveness of the whipsaw strike. It is no doubt true that the collective strength of the stores to resist that strike is maintained, and even increased, when all stores stay open with temporary replacements. The pressures on the employees are necessarily greater when none of the union employees is working and the stores remain open. But these pressures are no more than the result of the Local's inability to make effective use of the whipsaw tactic. Moreover, these effects are no different from those that result from the legitimate use of any economic weapon by an employer. Continued operations with the use of temporary replacements may result in the failure of the whipsaw strike, but this does not mean that the employers' conduct is demonstrably so destructive of employee rights or so devoid of significant service to any legitimate business end that it cannot be tolerated consistently with the act. Certainly then, in the absence of evidentiary findings of hostile motive, there is no support for the conclusion that respondents violated § 8(a)(1)....

We recognize that, analogous to the determination of unfair practices under § 8(a)(1), when an employer practice is inherently destructive of employee rights and is not justified by the service of important business ends, no specific evidence of intent to discourage union membership is necessary to establish a violation of § 8(a)(3). This principle, we have said, is "but an application of the common-law rule that a man is held to intend the foreseeable consequences of his conduct." *Radio Officers Union v. NLRB, supra,* 347 U.S. at 45 (1954). For example, in *NLRB v. Erie Resistor Corp., supra,* we held that an employer's action in awarding superseniority to employees who worked during a strike was discriminatory conduct that carried with it its own indicia of improper intent. The only reasonable inference that could be drawn by the Board from the award of superseniority—balancing the prejudicial effect upon the employees against any asserted business purpose—was that it was directed against the striking employees because of their union membership; conduct so inherently destructive of employee interests could not be saved from illegality by an asserted overriding business purpose pursued in good faith. But where, as here, the tendency to discourage union membership is comparatively slight, and the employer's conduct is reasonably adapted to achieve legitimate business ends or to deal with business exigencies, we enter into an area where the improper motivation of the employer must be established by independent evidence. When so established, antiunion motivation will convert an otherwise ordinary business act into an unfair labor practice. *NLRB v. Erie Resistor Corp., supra,* 373 U.S. at 227 (1963), and cases there cited.

We agree with the Court of Appeals that respondents' conduct here clearly fits into the latter category, where actual subjective intent is determinative, and where the Board must find from evidence independent of the mere conduct involved that the conduct was primarily motivated by an antiunion animus. While the use of temporary nonunion personnel in preference to the locked-out union members is discriminatory, we think that any resulting tendency to discourage union membership is comparatively remote, and that this use of temporary personnel constitutes a measure reasonably adapted to the effectuation of a legitimate business end. Here discontent on the part of the Local's membership in all likelihood is attributable largely to the fact that the membership was locked out as a result of the Local's whipsaw stratagem. But the lockout itself is concededly within the rule of *Buffalo Linen.* We think that the added dissatisfaction and resultant pressure on membership attributable to the fact that the nonstruck employers remain in business with temporary replacements is comparatively insubstantial. First, the replacements were expressly used for the duration of the labor dispute only; thus, the displaced employees could not have looked upon the replacements as threatening their jobs. At most the union would be forced to capitulate and return its members to work on terms which, while not as desirable as hoped for, were still better than under the old contract. Second, the membership, through its control of union policy, could end the dispute and terminate the lockout at any time simply by agreeing to the employers' terms and returning to work on a regular basis. Third, in light of the union-shop provision that had been carried forward into the new contract from the old collective agreement, it would appear that a union member would have nothing to gain, and much to lose, by quitting the union. Under all these circumstances, we cannot say that the employers' conduct had any great tendency to discourage union membership. Not only was the prospect of discouragement of membership comparatively remote, but the respondents' attempt to remain open for business with the help of temporary replacements was a measure reasonably adapted to the achievement of a legitimate end — preserving the integrity of the multiemployer bargaining unit. . . .

It is argued, finally, that the Board's decision is within the area of its expert judgment and that, in setting it aside, the Courts of Appeals exceeded the authorized scope of judicial review. This proposition rests upon our statement in *Buffalo Linen* that in reconciling the conflicting interests of labor and management the Board's determination is to be subjected to "limited judicial review." 353 U.S., at 96. When we used the phrase "limited judicial review" we did not mean that the balance struck by the Board is immune from judicial examination and reversal in proper cases. Courts are expressly empowered to enforce, modify or set aside, in whole or in part, the Board's orders, except that the findings of the Board with respect to questions of fact, if supported by substantial evidence on the record considered as a whole, shall be conclusive. . . . Reviewing courts are not obliged to stand aside and rubber-stamp their affirmance of administrative decisions that they deem inconsistent with a statutory mandate or that frustrate the congressional policy underlying a statute. Not only is such review always properly within the judicial province, but courts would abdicate their responsibility if they did not fully review such administrative decisions. Of course, due deference is to be rendered to agency determinations of fact, so long as there is substantial evidence to be found in the record as a whole. But where, as here, the review is not of a question of fact, but of a judgment as to the proper balance to be struck between conflicting interests, "[t]he deference owed to an expert tribunal cannot be allowed to slip into a judicial inertia which results in the unauthorized assumption by an agency of major policy decisions properly made by Congress." *American Ship Building Co. v. NLRB*, 380 U.S. at 318 (1965).

Courts must, of course, set aside Board decisions which rest on "an erroneous legal foundation." *NLRB v. Babcock & Wilcox, supra*, 351 U.S. at 112–113. Congress has not given the Board untrammeled authority to catalogue which economic devices shall be deemed freighted with indicia of unlawful intent. *NLRB v. Insurance Agents, supra*, 361 U.S. at 498. In determining here that the respondents' conduct carried its own badge of improper motive, the Board's decision, for the reasons stated, misapplied the criteria governing the application of §§ 8(a)(1) and (3). Since the order therefore rested on "an erroneous legal foundation," the Court of Appeals properly refused to enforce it.[7]

Affirmed.

MR. JUSTICE GOLDBERG, whom THE CHIEF JUSTICE joins, concurring.

... There would be grave doubts as to whether locking out and hiring permanent replacements is justified by any legitimate interest of the nonstruck employers, for *Buffalo Linen* makes clear that the test in such a situation is not whether parity is achieved between struck and nonstruck employers, but, rather, whether the nonstruck employer's actions are necessary to counteract the whipsaw effects of the strike and to preserve the employer bargaining unit. Since in this case the nonstruck employers did nothing more than hire temporary replacements, an activity necessary to counter whipsawing by the union and to preserve the bargaining unit, I agree that, applying *Buffalo Linen*, the judgment of the Court of Appeals should be affirmed.

MR. JUSTICE WHITE, dissenting.

... This decision represents a departure from the many decisions in this Court holding that the Board has primary responsibility to weigh the interest of employees in concerted activities against that of the employer in operating his business....

The Court reasons that *Buffalo Linen* gave the nonstruck employer in a multi-employer unit a "right" to lockout whenever a member of the unit is struck so that a parity of economic advantage or disadvantage between the struck and nonstruck employers can be maintained. In order to maintain parity where the struck employer hires replacements, the nonstruck employers must also be free to hire replacements, lest the right to lockout to protect the unit be illusory. And they need not offer these jobs to the locked-out employees desiring to work, lest the parity between the struck and nonstruck employers be lost and the right to lockout be meaningless. If this reasoning is sound, the nonstruck employers can not only lock out employees who belong to the union because of their union membership but also hire permanent as well as temporary nonunion replacements whenever the struck employer hires such replacements, for parity may well so require. But I cannot accept this reasoning.

One, *Buffalo Linen* established no unqualified "right" of employers in a multiemployer unit to lockout....

Two, the threat to the integrity of the multiemployer unit, the consideration that was decisive in *Buffalo Linen*, is obviously very different where the struck employer

---

7. [16] We do not here decide whether the case would be the same had the struck employer exercised its prerogative to hire permanent replacements for the strikers under our rule in *NLRB v. Mackay Radio & Tel. Co.*, 304 U.S. 333 (1938), and the nonstruck employers had then hired permanent replacements for their locked-out employees.

continues operations with replacements; it certainly cannot be assumed that the struck employer operating with replacements is at the same disadvantage vis-à-vis the nonstruck employers as the employer in *Buffalo Linen* whose operations were totally shut down by the union. Indeed, there was no showing here that the struck employer was substantially disadvantaged at all, and the Board found that there was "no economic necessity for the other members shutting down. . . ."

Three, the disparity between the struck employer who resumes operations and the nonstruck employers who choose to lockout to maintain a united front is caused by the unilateral action of one of the employer members of the unit and not by the union's whipsawing tactic. The integrity of the multiemployer unit may be important, but surely that consideration cannot justify employer tandem action destructive of concerted activity.

Four, the Court asserts that the right of nonstruck employers to hire temporary replacements, and to refuse to hire union men, is but a concomitant of the right to lockout to preserve the multiemployer group. This sanctification of the multiemployer unit ignores the fundamental rule that an employer may not displace union members with nonunion members solely on account of union membership, the prototype of discrimination under § 8(a)(3), *NLRB v. Mackay Radio & Telegraph Co.*, 304 U.S. 333 (1938), and may not maintain operations and refuse to retain or hire nonstriking union members, notwithstanding that most of the union members and most of the workers at that very plant are on strike. The struck employer need not continue operations, but if he does, he may not give a preference to employees not affiliated with the striking union, no more than he may do so after the strike, for § 7 explicitly and unequivocally protects the right of employees to engage and not to engage in a concerted activity and § 8(a)(3) clearly prohibits discrimination which discourages union membership. . . .

Finally, I cannot agree with the Court's fundamental premise on which its balance of rights is founded: that a lockout followed by the hiring of nonunion men to operate the plant has but a "slight" tendency to discourage union membership, which includes participation in union activities, *Radio Officers' Union v. NLRB*, 347 U.S. 17 (1954), and to impinge on concerted activity generally. This proposition overturns the Board's longheld views on the effect of lockouts and dismissal of union members. Moreover, it is difficult to fathom the logic or industrial experience which on the one hand dictates that a guarantee to strike replacements that they will not be laid off after a strike is "inherently destructive of employee interests," although based on a legitimate and important business justification, *Erie Resistor*, 373 U.S. 221 (1963), and yet at the same time dictates that the dismissal of and refusal to hire nonstriking union members who desire to work because other union members working for a different employer have struck have but a slight unimportant inhibiting effect on affiliation with the union and on concerted activities. I think the Board's finding that this activity substantially burdens concerted activities and discourages union membership is far more consistent with *Erie Resistor* and industrial realities.

Notes

1. *Multiemployer Bargaining*—Unions and employers sometimes find it mutually beneficial to bargain on a multiemployer basis. Both unions and employers can save on bargaining costs, and employers benefit from the fact that they won't be undercut by competitors based on labor costs. Although employers may easily drop out of a multiemployer bargaining unit prior to the start of negotiations, their ability to do so after bargaining begins is greatly restricted—generally, they may only depart if there is mutual consent by all parties or an employer faces "unusual circumstances," which has been limited to situations involving "extreme economic difficulties" such as bankruptcy or a plant closing. *Hi-Way Billboards, Inc.*, 120 N.L.R.B. 22 (1973).

2. *Whipsaw Strikes*—If an employer struck during a whipsaw strike insists that the labor organization continue to bargain with it through the multiemployer association, a union refusal to do so may contravene § 8(b)(3), as a refusal to bargain with that employer's designated bargaining agent, and § 8(b)(1)(B), for coercing that employer in the selection of its bargaining agent. On the other hand, if the struck employer agrees to deal directly with the striking union, no violation will be found. See *Teamsters (Ind.) Local 324 (Cascade Employers Ass'n)*, 127 N.L.R.B. 488 (1960), *remanded on other grounds*, 296 F.2d 48 (9th Cir. 1961); *Ice Cream Council, Inc. (Local 717, Teamsters)*, 145 N.L.R.B. 865 (1964).

When a union strikes some members of a multiemployer bargaining unit, the other employers lockout under *Buffalo Linen*, and some employees ask to work during the lockout, may their employer tell them they can do so if they are no longer union members? In *NLRB v. Martin A. Gleason, Inc.*, 534 F.2d 466 (2d Cir. 1976), the court held yes, so long as the employer does not solicit or encourage their union resignations. The court relied on language in *Brown* indicating that an employer could use "temporary *nonunion* personnel" during a lockout. Was the *Brown* Court equating "nonunion" with "non-unit," since all bargaining unit personnel were union members pursuant to a union security clause? Does the *Martin A. Gleason* decision authorize overt anti-union discrimination in a manner that contravenes § 8(a)(3)?

American Ship Building Co. v. NLRB

Supreme Court of the United States
380 U.S. 300, 85 S. Ct. 955, 13 L. Ed. 2d 855 (1965)

[After two months of negotiating sessions, the American Ship Building Co. and a group of eight unions bargaining jointly reached an impasse on August 9, 1961. The company had made five previous contracts with the unions since 1952, each one preceded by a strike. The company operated four shipyards on the Great Lakes, most of their work coming in the winter months when the lakes are icebound. What limited business was obtained in the summer months was frequently such that speed of execution was of the utmost importance to minimize immobilization of the ships.

Despite union protestations to the contrary, the company feared a strike would be called as soon as a ship should enter the Chicago yard or that there would be a delay in negotiations into the winter to increase strike leverage. In light of the failure to reach agreement and the lack of available work, the company gradually laid off almost all employees, sending each one a notice, "Because of the labor dispute which has been unresolved . . . you are laid off until further notice." Negotiations resumed; an agreement was signed October 27; and employees were recalled the following day.

The Trial Examiner found that the employer could reasonably anticipate a strike in spite of the unions' assurances to the contrary, and concluded that the employer was economically motivated and justified in laying off its employees when it did. The Board (3-2) rejected the Trial Examiner's conclusions and found that the layoff was motivated solely by a desire to bring economic pressure and secure settlement of the dispute on favorable terms. It was agreed that the layoff had not occurred until after a bargaining impasse had been reached.]

Mr. Justice Stewart delivered the opinion of the Court.

. . . The difference between the Board and the trial examiner is thus a narrow one turning on their differing assessments of the circumstances which the employer claims gave him reason to anticipate a strike. Both the Board and the examiner assumed, within the established pattern of Board analysis, that if the employer had shut down his yard and laid off his workers solely for the purpose of bringing to bear economic pressure to break an impasse and secure more favorable contract terms, an unfair labor practice would be made out. . . .

The Board has, however, exempted certain classes of lockouts from proscription. "Accordingly, it has held that lockouts are permissible to safeguard against loss where there is reasonable ground for believing that a strike was threatened or imminent." [*Quaker State Oil Refining Co.*, 121 N.L.R.B. 334, 337.] Developing this distinction in its rulings, the Board has approved lockouts designed to prevent seizure of a plant by a sitdown strike, *Link-Belt Co.*, 26 N.L.R.B. 227; to forestall repetitive disruptions of an integrated operation by quickie strikes, *International Shoe Co.*, 93 N.L.R.B. 907; to avoid spoilage of materials which would result from a sudden work stoppage, *Duluth Bottling Ass'n*, 48 N.L.R.B. 1335; and to avert the immobilization of automobiles brought in for repair, *Betts Cadillac-Olds*, 96 N.L.R.B. 268. . . .

In analyzing the status of the bargaining lockout under §§ 8(a)(1) and 8(a)(3) of the National Labor Relations Act, it is important that the practice with which we are here concerned be distinguished from other forms of temporary separation from employment. No one would deny that an employer is free to shut down his enterprise temporarily for reasons of renovation or lack of profitable work unrelated to his collective bargaining situation. Similarly, we put to one side cases where the Board has concluded on the basis of substantial evidence that the employer has used a lockout as a means to injure a labor organization or to evade his duty to bargain collectively. *Hopwood Retinning Co.*, 4 N.L.R.B. 922; *Scott Paper Box Co.*, 81 N.L.R.B.

535. What we are here concerned with is the use of a temporary layoff of employees solely as a means to bring economic pressure to bear in support of the employer's bargaining position, after an impasse has been reached. This is the only issue before us, and all that we decide.[8]

To establish that this practice is a violation of § 8(a)(1), it must be shown that the employer has interfered with, restrained, or coerced employees in the exercise of some right protected by § 7 of the act. The Board's position is premised on the view that the lockout interferes with two of the rights guaranteed by § 7: the right to bargain collectively and the right to strike. In the Board's view, the use of the lockout "punishes" employees for the presentation of and adherence to demands made by their bargaining representatives and so coerces them in the exercise of their right to bargain collectively. It is important to note that there is here no allegation that the employer used the lockout in the service of designs inimical to the process of collective bargaining. There was no evidence and no finding that the employer was hostile to his employees banding together for collective bargaining or that the lockout was designed to discipline them for doing so. It is therefore inaccurate to say that the employer's intention was to destroy or frustrate the process of collective bargaining. What can be said is that he intended to resist the demands made of him in the negotiations and to secure modification of these demands. We cannot see that this intention is in any way inconsistent with the employees' rights to bargain collectively.

Moreover, there is no indication, either as a general matter or in this specific case, that the lockout will necessarily destroy the unions' capacity for effective and responsible representation. The unions here involved have vigorously represented the employees since 1952, and there is nothing to show that their ability to do so has been impaired by the lockout. Nor is the lockout one of those acts which is demonstrably so destructive of collective bargaining that the Board need not inquire into employer motivation, as might be the case, for example, if an employer permanently discharged his unionized staff and replaced them with employees known to be possessed of a violent antiunion animus. *Cf. NLRB v. Erie Resistor Corp.*, 373 U.S. 221 (1963). The lockout may well dissuade employees from adhering to the position which they initially adopted in the bargaining, but the right to bargain collectively does not entail any "right" to insist on one's position free from economic disadvantage. Proper analysis of the problem demands that the simple intention to support the employer's bargaining position as to compensation and the like be distinguished from a hostility to the process of collective bargaining which could suffice to render a lockout unlawful. *See NLRB v. Brown* [380 U.S. 278 (1965)].

The Board has taken the complementary view that the lockout interferes with the right to strike protected under §§ 7 and 13 of the act in that it allows the employer to

---

8. [8] Contrary to the view expressed in a concurring opinion filed in this case, we intimate no view whatever as to the consequences which would follow had the employer replaced his employees with permanent replacements or even temporary help. *Cf. NLRB v. Mackay Radio & Telegraph Co.*, 304 U.S. 333 (1938).

pre-empt the possibility of a strike and thus leave the union with "nothing to strike against." Insofar as this means that once employees are locked out, they are deprived of their right to call a strike against the employer because he is already shut down, the argument is wholly specious, for the work stoppage which would have been the object of the strike has in fact occurred. It is true that recognition of the lockout deprives the union of exclusive control of the timing and duration of work stoppages calculated to influence the result of collective bargaining negotiations, but there is nothing in the statute which would imply that the right to strike "carries with it" the right exclusively to determine the timing and duration of all work stoppages. The right to strike as commonly understood is the right to cease work — nothing more. No doubt a union's bargaining power would be enhanced if it possessed not only the simple right to strike but also the power exclusively to determine when work stoppages shall occur, but the act's provisions are not indefinitely elastic, content-free forms to be shaped in whatever manner the Board might think best conforms to the proper balance of bargaining power.

Union also argues lockout interfered w/ right to strike

Thus, we cannot see that the employer's use of a lockout solely in support of a legitimate bargaining position is in any way inconsistent with the right to bargain collectively or with the right to strike. Accordingly, we conclude that on the basis of the findings made by the Board in this case, there has been no violation of § 8(a)(1).

Section 8(a)(3) prohibits discrimination in regard to tenure or other conditions of employment to discourage union membership. Under the words of the statute there must be both discrimination and a resulting discouragement of union membership. It has long been established that a finding of violation under this section will normally turn on the employer's motivation. . . .

This is not to deny that there are some practices which are inherently so prejudicial to union interests and so devoid of significant economic justification that no specific evidence of intent to discourage union membership or other antiunion animus is required. In some cases, it may be that the employer's conduct carries with it an inference of unlawful intention so compelling that it is justifiable to disbelieve the employer's protestations of innocent purpose. *Radio Officers' Union v. NLRB, supra,* 347 U.S. at 44–45; *NLRB v. Erie Resistor Corp., supra.* Thus where many have broken a shop rule, but only union leaders have been discharged, the Board need not listen too long to the plea that shop discipline was simply being enforced. In other situations, we have described the process as the "far more delicate task . . . of weighing the interests of employees in concerted activity against the interest of the employer in operating his business in a particular manner. . . ." *NLRB v. Erie Resistor Corp., supra,* 373 U.S. at 229 (1965).

But this lockout does not fall into that category of cases arising under § 8(a)(3) in which the Board may truncate its inquiry into employer motivation. As this case well shows, use of the lockout does not carry with it any necessary implication that the employer acted to discourage union membership or otherwise discriminate against union members as such. The purpose and effect of the lockout was only to bring pressure upon the union to modify its demands. Similarly, it does not appear that the natural tendency of the lockout is severely to discourage union membership while serving no significant employer interest. In fact, it is difficult to understand what tendency to discourage union membership or otherwise discriminate against union members was perceived by the Board. There is no claim that the employer locked out only union members, or locked out any employee simply because he was a union member; nor is it alleged that the employer conditioned rehiring upon resignation from the union. It is true that the employees suffered economic disadvantage because of their union's insistence on demands unacceptable to the employer, but this is also true of many steps which an employer may take during a bargaining conflict, and the existence of an arguable possibility that someone may feel himself discouraged in his union membership or discriminated against by reason of that membership cannot suffice to label them violations of § 8(a)(3) absent some unlawful intention. The employer's permanent replacement of strikers (*NLRB v. Mackay Radio & Telegraph Co., supra*), his unilateral imposition of terms (*Labor Board v. Tex-Tan, Inc.*, 318 F.2d 472, 479–482), or his simple refusal to make a concession which would terminate a strike — all impose economic disadvantage during a bargaining conflict, but none is necessarily a violation of § 8(a)(3).

To find a violation of § 8(a)(3) then, the Board must find that the employer acted for a proscribed purpose. Indeed, the Board itself has always recognized that certain "operative" or "economic" purposes would justify a lockout. But the Board has erred in ruling that only these purposes will remove a lockout from the ambit of § 8(a)(3), for that section requires an intention to discourage union membership or otherwise discriminate against the union. There was not the slightest evidence and there was no finding, that the employer was actuated by a desire to discourage membership in the union as distinguished from a desire to affect the outcome of the particular negotiations in which he was involved. We recognize that the "union membership" which is not to be discouraged refers to more than the payment of dues and that measures taken to discourage participation in protected union activities may be found to come within the proscription. *Radio Officers' Union v. NLRB, supra*, 347 U.S. at 39–40. However, there is nothing in the act which gives employees the right to insist on their contract demands, free from the sort of economic disadvantage which frequently attends bargaining disputes. Therefore, we conclude that where the intention proven is merely to bring about a settlement of a labor dispute on favorable terms, no violation of § 8(a)(3) is shown.

The conclusions which we draw from analysis of §§ 8(a)(1) and 8(a)(3) are consonant with what little of relevance can be drawn from the balance of the statute and its legislative history. In the original version of the act, the predecessor of § 8(a)(1) declared it an unfair labor practice "[t]o attempt, by interference, influence, restraint, favor, coercion, or lockout, or by any other means, to impair the right of employees guaranteed in section 4."[9] Prominent in the criticism leveled at the bill in the Senate

---

9. [11] 1 Legislative History of the Labor Management Relations Act, 1935, 3 (hereafter L.M.R.A.). Section 4 of the bill provided:

Committee hearings was the charge that it did not accord evenhanded treatment to employers and employees because it prohibited the lockout while protecting the strike. In the face of such criticism, the Committee added a provision prohibiting employee interference with employer bargaining activities[10] and deleted the reference to the lockout.[11] A plausible inference to be drawn from this history is that the language was defeated to nullify those who saw in the bill an inequitable denial of resort to the lockout, and to remove any language which might give rise to fears that the lockout was being proscribed *per se*. It is in any event clear that the Committee was concerned with the status of the lockout and that the bill, as reported and as finally enacted, contained no prohibition on the use of the lockout as such.

Although neither § 8(a)(1) nor § 8(a)(3) refers specifically to the lockout, various other provisions of the Labor Management Relations Act do refer to the lockout, and these references can be interpreted as a recognition of the legitimacy of the device as a means of applying economic pressure in support of bargaining positions. Thus 29 U.S.C. § 158(d)(4) (1958 ed.) prohibits the use of strike or lockout unless requisite notice procedures have been complied with; 29 U.S.C. § 173(c) (1958 ed.) directs the Federal Mediation and Conciliation Service to seek voluntary resolution of labor disputes without resort to strikes or lockouts; and 29 U.S.C. §§ 176, 178 (1958 ed.), authorize procedures whereby the President can institute a board of inquiry to forestall certain strikes or lockouts. The correlative use of the terms "strike" and "lockout" in these sections contemplates that lockouts will be used in the bargaining process in some fashion. This is not to say that these provisions serve to define the permissible scope of a lockout by an employer. That, in the context of the present case, is a question ultimately to be resolved by analysis of §§ 8(a)(1) and 8(a)(3).

The Board has justified its ruling in this case and its general approach to the legality of lockouts on the basis of its special competence to weigh the competing interests of employers and employees and to accommodate these interests according to its expert judgment. "The Board has reasonably concluded that the availability

---

Employees shall have the right to organize and join labor organizations, and to engage in concerted activities, either in labor organizations or otherwise, for the purposes of organizing and bargaining collectively through representatives of their own choosing or for other purposes of mutual aid or protection.

Ibid.

10. [13] S. 2926, § 3 (2):

It shall be an unfair labor practice [f]or employees to attempt, by interference or coercion, to impair the exercise by employers of the right to join or form employer organizations and to designate representatives of their own choosing for the purpose of collective bargaining.

1 L.M.R.A. 1087.

11. [14] S. 2926, § 3 (1):

It shall be an unfair labor practice [f]or an employer to attempt, by interference or coercion, to impair the exercise by employees of the right to form or join labor organizations, to designate representatives of their own choosing, and to engage in concerted activities for the purpose of collective bargaining or other mutual aid or protection.

1 L.M.R.A. 1087.

of such a weapon would so substantially tip the scales in the employer's favor as to defeat the Congressional purpose of placing employees on a par with their adversaries at the bargaining table." To buttress its decision as to the balance struck in this particular case, the Board points out that the employer has been given other weapons to counterbalance the employees' power of strike. The employer may permanently replace workers who have gone out on strike, or by stockpiling and subcontracting, maintain his commercial operations while the strikers bear the economic brunt of the work stoppage. Similarly, the employer can institute unilaterally the working conditions which he desires once his contract with the union has expired. Given these economic weapons, it is argued, the employer has been adequately equipped with tools of economic self-help.

There is, of course, no question that the Board is entitled to the greatest deference in recognition of its special competence in dealing with labor problems. In many areas its evaluation of the competing interests of employer and employee should unquestionably be given conclusive effect in determining the application of §§ 8(a)(1), (a)(3), and (a)(5). However, we think that the Board construes its functions too expansively when it claims general authority to define national labor policy by balancing the competing interests of labor and management.

While a primary purpose of the National Labor Relations Act was to redress the perceived imbalance of economic power between labor and management, it sought to accomplish that result by conferring certain affirmative rights on employees and by placing certain enumerated restrictions on the activities of employers. . . . Having protected employee organization in countervailance to the employers' bargaining power, and having established a system of collective bargaining whereby the newly coequal adversaries might resolve their disputes, the act also contemplated resort to economic weapons should more peaceful measures not avail. Sections 8(a)(1) and 8(a)(3) do not give the Board a general authority to assess the relative economic power of the adversaries in the bargaining process and to deny weapons to one party or the other because of its assessment of that party's bargaining power. *NLRB v. Brown* [380 U.S. 278 (1965)]. In this case the Board has, in essence, denied the use of the bargaining lockout to the employer because of its conviction that use of this device would give the employer "too much power." In so doing, the Board has stretched §§ 8(a)(1) and 8(a)(3) far beyond their functions of protecting the rights of employee organization and collective bargaining. What we have recently said in a closely related context is equally applicable here:

> [W]hen the Board moves in this area . . . it is functioning as an arbiter of the sort of economic weapons the parties can use in seeking to gain acceptance of their bargaining demands. It has sought to introduce some standard of properly "balanced" bargaining power, or some new distinction of justifiable and unjustifiable, proper and "abusive" economic weapons into . . . the Act. . . . We have expressed our belief that this amounts to the Board's entrance into the substantive aspect of the bargaining process to an extent Congress has not countenanced.

NLRB v. Insurance Agents' Int'l Union, 361 U.S. 477, 497–498 (1960).

We are unable to find that any fair construction of the provisions relied on by the Board in this case can support its finding of an unfair labor practice. Indeed, the role assumed by the Board in this area is fundamentally inconsistent with the structure of the act and the function of the sections relied upon. The deference owed to an expert tribunal cannot be allowed to slip into a judicial inertia which results in the unauthorized assumption by an agency of major policy decisions properly made by Congress. Accordingly, we hold that an employer violates neither § 8(a)(1) nor § 8(a)(3) when, after a bargaining impasse has been reached, he temporarily shuts down his plant and lays off his employees for the sole purpose of bringing economic pressure to bear in support of his legitimate bargaining position.

Reversed.

Mr. Justice White, concurring in the result.

. . . In my view the issue posed in this case is whether an employer who in fact anticipates a strike may inform customers of this belief to protect his commercial relationship with customers and to safeguard their property, thereby discouraging business, and then lay off employees for whom there is no available work. I, like the trial examiner, think he may, and do not think this conduct can be impeached under §§ 8(a)(1) and 8(a)(3) by merely asserting that the employer and his customers were erroneous in believing a strike was imminent. . . .

. . . Since I think an employer's decision to lay off employees because of lack of work is not ordinarily barred by the act, and since neither the Board nor the Court properly can ignore this claim, I would reverse the Board's order, but without reaching out to decide an issue not at all presented by this case. . . .

Mr. Justice Goldberg, with whom The Chief Justice joins, concurring in the result.

I concur in the Court's conclusion that the employer's lockout in this case was not a violation of either § 8(a)(1) or § 8(a)(3) of the National Labor Relations Act, 49 Stat. 453, as amended, 29 U.S.C. §§ 158(a)(1) and (3) (1958 ed.), and I therefore join in the judgment reversing the Court of Appeals. I reach this result not for the Court's reasons, but because, from the plain facts revealed by the record, it is crystal clear that the employer's lockout here was justified. The very facts recited by the Court in its opinion show that this employer locked out his employees in the face of a threatened strike under circumstances where, had the choice of timing been left solely to the unions, the employer and his customers would have been subject to economic injury over and beyond the loss of business normally incident to a strike upon the termination of the collective bargaining agreement. A lockout under these circumstances has been recognized by the Board itself to be justifiable and not a violation of the labor statutes. *Betts Cadillac-Olds, Inc.*, 96 N.L.R.B. 268. . . .

My view of this case would make it unnecessary to deal with the broad question of whether an employer may lock out his employees solely to bring economic pressure to bear in support of his bargaining position. The question of which types of lockout are compatible with the labor statute is a complex one as this decision and the other cases decided today illustrate. *See Textile Workers Union v. Darlington Mfg. Co.*, [380 U.S.] at 263; *NLRB v. Brown*, [380 U.S.] at 278. This Court has said that the problem of the legality of certain types of strike activity must be "revealed by unfolding variant situations" and requires "an evolutionary process for its rational response, not a quick, definitive formula as a comprehensive answer." *Electrical Workers, Local 761 v. NLRB*, 366 U.S. 667, 674 (1961); *see also NLRB v. Steelworkers, supra*, 357 U.S. 362–363 (1958). The same is true of lockouts.

The types of situation in which an employer might seek to lock out his employees differ considerably one from the other. This case presents the situation of an employer with a long history of union recognition and collective bargaining, confronted with a history of past strikes, who locks out only after considerable good-faith negotiation involving agreement and compromise on numerous issues, after a bargaining impasse has been reached, more than a week after the prior contract has expired, and when faced with the threat of a strike at a time when he and the property of his customers can suffer unusual harm. Other cases in which the Board has held a lockout illegal have presented far different situations. For example, in *Quaker State Oil Refining Corp., supra*, an employer locked out his employees the day after his contract with the union expired although no impasse had been reached in the bargaining still in progress, no strike had been threatened by the unions, which had never called a sudden strike during the 13 years they had bargained with the employer, and the unions had offered to resubmit the employer's proposals to his employees for a vote. *See also Utah Plumbing and Heating Contractors Ass'n*, 126 N.L.R.B. 973. These decisions of the Labor Board properly take into account, in determining the legality of lockouts under the labor statutes, such factors as the length, character, and history of the collective bargaining relation between the union and the employer, as well as whether a bargaining impasse has been reached. Indeed, the Court itself seems to recognize that there is a difference between locking out before a bargaining impasse has been reached and locking out after collective bargaining has been exhausted, for it limits its holding to lockouts in the latter type of situation without deciding the question of the legality of locking out before bargaining is exhausted. Since the examples of different lockout situations could be multiplied, the logic of the Court's limitation of its holding should lead it to recognize that the problem of lockouts requires "an evolutionary process," not "a quick, definitive formula," for its answer.

The Court should be chary of sweeping generalizations in this complex area. When we deal with the lockout and the strike, we are dealing with weapons of industrial warfare. While the parties generally have their choice of economic weapons, *see NLRB v. Insurance Agents*, 361 U.S. 477 (1960), this choice, both with respect to the strike and the lockout, is not unrestricted. While we have recognized "the deference paid the strike weapon by the federal labor laws," *NLRB v. Erie Resistor, supra* at 235, not all forms of economically motivated strikes are protected nor even permissible under the labor statutes or the prior decisions of this Court. Moreover, a lockout prompted by an antiunion motive is plainly illegal under the National Labor Relations Act, though no similar restrictions as to motive operate to limit the legality of a strike. See *NLRB v. Somerset Shoe Co.*, 111 F.2d 681 (1st Cir. 1940); *NLRB v. Stremel*, 141 F.2d 317 (10th Cir. 1944); *NLRB v. Somerset Classics, Inc.*, 193 F.2d 613 (2d Cir. 1952). The varieties of restriction imposed upon strikes and lockouts reflect the complexities presented by variant factual situations.

The Court not only overlooks the factual diversity among different types of lockout, but its statement of the rules governing unfair labor practices under §§ 8(a)(1) and (3) does not give proper recognition to the fact that "[t]he ultimate problem [in this area] is the balancing of the conflicting legitimate interests." *NLRB v. Truck Drivers Union*, 353 U.S. 87, 96 (1957). The Court states that employer conduct, not actually motivated by antiunion bias, does not violate §§ 8(a)(1) or (3) unless it is "demonstrably so destructive of collective bargaining," or "so prejudicial to union interests and so devoid of significant economic justification," that no antiunion animus need be shown. This rule departs substantially from both the letter and the spirit of numerous prior decisions of the Court. See, e.g., *NLRB v. Truck Drivers Union, supra*, 353 U.S. at 96; *Republic Aviation Corp. v. NLRB*, 324 U.S. 793 (1945); *NLRB v. Babcock & Wilcox Co.*, 351 U.S. 105 (1956); *NLRB v. Burnup & Sims, Inc.*, 379 U.S. 21 (1964).

These decisions demonstrate that the correct test for determining whether § 8(a)(1) has been violated in cases not involving an employer antiunion motive is whether the business justification for the employer's action outweighs the interference with § 7 rights involved. In *Republic Aviation Corp. v. NLRB, supra*, for example, the Court affirmed a Board holding that a company "no-solicitation" rule was invalid as applied to prevent solicitation of employees on company property during periods when employees were free to do as they pleased, not because such a rule was "demonstrably . . . destructive of collective bargaining," but simply because there was no significant employer justification for the rule and there was a showing of union interest, though far short of a necessity, in its abolition. See also, *NLRB v. Burnup & Sims, Inc., supra*.

A similar test is applicable in § 8(a)(3) cases where no antiunion motive is shown. The Court misreads *Radio Officers' Union v. NLRB*, 347 U.S. 17, and *NLRB v. Erie Resistor Corp., supra*, in stating that the test in such cases under § 8(a)(3) is whether practices "are inherently so prejudicial to union interests and so devoid of significant economic justification that no specific evidence of intent to discourage union membership or other antiunion animus is required." *Supra*, at pp. 863, 864. *Radio Officers* did not restrict the application of § 8(a)(3) in cases devoid of antiunion motive to the extreme situations encompassed by the Court's test. Rather, in holding applicable the common-law rule that a man is presumed to intend the foreseeable consequences of his own actions, the Court extended the reach of § 8(a)(3) to all cases in which a significant antiunion effect is foreseeable regardless of the employer's motive. In such cases the Court, in *Erie Resistor Corp.*, held that conduct might be determined by the Board to violate §8(a)(3) where the Board's determination resulted from a reasonable "weighing [of] the interests of employees in concerted activity against the interests of the employer in operating his business in a particular manner and... [from] balancing in the light of the Act and its policy the intended consequences upon employee rights against the business ends to be served by the employer's conduct." 373 U.S. at 229.

These cases show that the tests as to whether an employer's conduct violates §8(a)(1) or violates §8(a)(3) without a showing of antiunion motive come down to substantially the same thing: whether the legitimate economic interests of the employer justify his interference with the rights of his employees—a test involving "the balancing of the conflicting legitimate interests." *NLRB v. Truck Drivers Union, supra*, 353 U.S. at 96. As the prior decisions of this Court have held, "[t]he function of striking... [such a] balance,... often a difficult and delicate responsibility,... Congress committed primarily to the National Labor Relations Board, subject to limited judicial review." *Ibid.*

This, of course, does not mean that reviewing courts are to abdicate their function of determining whether, giving due deference to the Board, the Board has struck the balance consistently with the language and policy of the act. *See NLRB v. Brown, supra; NLRB v. Truck Drivers Union, supra*. Nor does it mean that reviewing courts are to rubberstamp decisions of the Board where the application of principles in a particular case is irrational or not supported by substantial evidence on the record as a whole. Applying these principles to the factual situation here presented, I would accept the Board's carefully limited rule, fashioned by the Board after weighing the "conflicting legitimate interests" of employers and unions, that a lockout does not violate the act where used to "safeguard against unusual operational problems or hazards or economic loss where there is reasonable ground for believing that a strike [is] ... threatened or imminent." *Quaker State Oil Refining Corp., supra* at 337. This rule is consistent with the policies of the act and based upon the actualities of industrial relations. I would, however, reject the determination of the Board refusing to apply this rule to this case, for the undisputed facts revealed by the record bring this case clearly within the rule.

In view of the necessity for, and the desirability of, weighing the legitimate conflicting interests in variant lockout situations, there is not and cannot be any simple formula which readily demarks the permissible from the impermissible lockout. This being so, I would not reach out in this case to announce principles which are determinative of the legality of all economically motivated lockouts whether before or after a bargaining impasse has been reached. In my view both the Court and the Board, in reaching their opposite conclusions, have inadvisably and unnecessarily done so here. Rather, I would confine our decision to the simple holding, supported both by the record and the actualities of industrial relations, that the employer's fear of a strike was reasonable, and therefore, under the settled decisions of the Board, which I would approve, the lockout of his employees was justified.

Notes

1. *Offensive versus Defensive Lockouts* — Suppose two Detroit newspapers have bargained on a multiemployer basis with most of the 14 unions that represent various groups of their employees, but have each bargained separately with the Teamsters regarding their distribution workers. During negotiations with the Teamsters, the two papers conferred on three common issues, and the *News* agreed that if the Teamsters struck *The Free Press* on these issues, the *News* would not publish. *The Free Press* is struck and the *News* locks out. Teamsters President Hoffa had said that he regarded the *News'* latest proposal as a final offer, and had threatened the *News* with a strike. Is the *News'* lockout lawful? *Evening News Ass'n*, 166 N.L.R.B. 219 (1967), *aff'd*, 404 F.2d 1159 (6th Cir. 1968), *cert. denied*, 395 U.S. 923 (1969) (*Held*: Yes). The Board said:

> There is no question but that the Supreme Court's *American Ship* decision has obliterated, as a matter of law, the line previously drawn by the Board between offensive and defensive lockouts. . . . The Court stated that the test of a lockout's legality, assuming no motive to discourage union activity or to evade bargaining exists, is whether the lockout 'is inherently so prejudicial to union interest and so devoid of significant economic justification' that no evidence of intent is necessary. That test affords the basis for our determination here.

2. *Which Lockouts Are Unlawful?* — A lockout is lawful if the potential for future "quickie" strikes or intermittent work stoppages would substantially harm the employer's business. For example, in *Central Ill. Pub. Serv. Co.*, 326 N.L.R.B. 928 (1998), *aff'd*, 215 F.3d 11 (D.C. Cir.), *cert. denied*, 531 U.S. 1051 (2000), the Labor Board held that an employer did not violate the NLRA when, in response to inside game tactics of employees who were working-to-rule and refusing voluntary overtime to enhance their bargaining position, it locked out the bargaining unit members. The Board found that even if the inside game tactics constituted protected activity, the lockout was lawful because the employer had a legitimate business purpose in trying to force the union to end its inside game conduct. However, if the union agrees to refrain from such work interruptions and unconditionally offers to return to work following a one-day strike, and the employer's responses to the union's offer are vague, inconsistent, and present a "moving target," the lockout becomes unlawful as of the date the employer refuses the offer. *Dayton Newspapers, Inc. v. NLRB*, 402 F.3d 651 (6th Cir. 2005). The key to a finding that a lockout is lawful, according to the court, is that "'the employer's conduct throughout the lockout must be consistent with the advancement of its legitimate bargaining position so that the employees are able to "knowingly reevaluate their position."' . . . The employees must know at any point in the lockout what they can do to end it." (quoting *Ancor Concepts, Inc. v. Local 76B, IBEW*, 323 N.L.R.B. 742 (1997), *enforcement denied on other grounds*, 166 F.3d 55 (2d Cir. 1999)).

A preimpasse lockout to support an employer's bargaining position and to forestall a strike during its busy shipping season was held lawful in *Darling & Co.*,

171 N.L.R.B. 801 (1968). The Board stated that the absence of an impasse did not render the *American Ship* tests per se inapplicable, although "the finding of an impasse in negotiations may be a factor supporting the determination that a particular lockout is lawful." The determination must be made on a case-by-case basis. Here there had been extensive good faith bargaining on all subjects and accord on many issues, but continuing disagreement on certain key items, including a work assignment clause. Strikes had occurred during the parties' 20-year relationship, and work assignments were a major issue in a crippling strike about four years earlier. *Darling & Co.* was affirmed *sub nom. Lane v. NLRB*, 418 F.2d 1208 (D.C. Cir. 1969). On the other hand, when an employer locks out bargaining unit employees "without providing the employees with a timely, clear, and complete offer setting forth the conditions necessary to avoid the lockout," the lockout will be found unlawful absent an impasse prior to the lockout. See *Alden Leeds, Inc. v. NLRB*, 812 F.3d 159 (D.C. Cir. 2016).

3. *Replacement Workers and Subcontractors*—Suppose an employer locks out its workers and uses temporary replacements to keep the business running. Initially, the Board found a violation of § 8(a)(1) and (3) in the absence of a showing of a substantial business justification. *Oshkosh Ready-Mix Co.*, 179 N.L.R.B. 350 (1969). In enforcing the Board's order, the Seventh Circuit observed that the use of replacements by an employer during an offensive, as distinguished from a defensive, lockout "would not merely pit the employer's ability to withstand a shutdown of its business against the employees' ability to endure cessation of their jobs, but would permit the employer to impose on his employees the pressure of being out of work while obtaining for himself the returns of continued operation. Employees would be forced, at the initiative of the employer, not only to forgo their job earnings, but, in addition, to watch other workers enjoy the earning opportunities over which the locked-out employees were endeavoring to bargain." *Inland Trucking Co. v. NLRB*, 440 F.2d 562 (7th Cir.), *cert. denied*, 404 U.S. 858 (1971). Nonetheless, in *Ottawa Silica Co.*, 197 N.L.R.B. 449 (1972), *aff'd*, 482 F.2d 945 (6th Cir. 1973), and *Inter-Collegiate Press*, 199 N.L.R.B. 177 (1972), *aff'd*, 486 F.2d 837 (8th Cir. 1973), *cert. denied*, 416 U.S. 938 (1974), a Board majority found no violation where the employer showed legitimate and substantial business justification for using temporary replacements during an otherwise lawful lockout and there was no wrongful motivation.

In *Harter Equipment, Inc.*, 280 N.L.R.B. 597 (1986), *review denied*, 829 F.2d 458 (3d Cir. 1987), the Labor Board reviewed the *Inland Trucking* and *Ottawa Silica* decisions and concluded that "an employer does not violate § 8(a)(3) and (1), absent specific proof of anti-union motivation, by using temporary employees in order to engage in business operations during an otherwise lawful lockout, including a lockout initiated for the sole purpose of bringing economic pressure to bear in support of a legitimate bargaining position." The 3-1 majority found that the temporary replacement measure was "reasonably adapted to the achievement of a legitimate employer interest" and had "only a comparatively slight adverse effect on protected employee rights."

Would the result be different if the employer uses permanent replacements to keep the business running? In *Ancor Concepts, Inc.*, 323 N.L.R.B. 742 (1997), the Labor Board held that the hiring of *permanent* replacements is inconsistent with a lawful lockout and violative of §8(a)(3). Since the Second Circuit found no factual basis for the conclusion that *permanent* replacements had in fact been hired, however, it denied enforcement of the Board's decision. *NLRB v. Ancor Concepts*, 166 F.3d 55 (2d Cir. 1999), *Compare Johns-Manville Prods. Corp. v. NLRB*, 557 F.2d 1126 (5th Cir. 1977) (sabotage by employees during contract negotiations constituted in-plant "strike" that justified their lockout and subsequent *permanent* replacement).

Would it make a difference if the employer temporarily subcontracts out the work rather than hiring its own employees? *International Paper Co. v. NLRB*, 115 F.3d 1045 (D.C. Cir. 1997), involved an employer that locked out its production and maintenance workers during a bargaining dispute. The employer temporarily subcontracted the maintenance work to an outside firm. It then solicited a permanent subcontracting proposal for the maintenance work and asked the union at the bargaining table for the right to retain an outside maintenance firm on a permanent basis. When the union rejected the company's subcontracting proposal, it entered into a permanent subcontract that each party could terminate on 30 days' notice. The Labor Board found that any permanent subcontracting of the work of locked-out personnel was "inherently destructive" of employee rights and thus a violation of §8(a)(3). On appeal, the D.C. Circuit rejected the Board's analysis. It found that the employer had merely entered into a temporary subcontractual relationship when the lockout began. It then sought union permission to convert the temporary subcontracting arrangement into a permanent one. Only after bargaining over the matter to impasse did the employer establish a permanent subcontracting relationship. The court thus found no "inherently destructive" behavior, and it went on to hold that the creation of a permanent subcontracting arrangement during a lockout after good faith negotiations with the union did not contravene the NLRA.

Problem

19. Evergreen, Inc. is a lumber supply company that operates several logging camps on its extensive property holdings in the northwestern part of the country. The lumberjacks employed by Evergreen usually live and work on the property, but sometimes travel into nearby towns on the access roads that lead to the logging camps. For the last 20 years, the lumberjacks have been represented by a union. Their last contract expired about eight weeks ago and, despite an intense period of negotiation prior to the expiration, their talks with Evergreen came to a virtual standstill. Their last two contracts were secured only after protracted strikes, but union leaders have assured members that they recognize the hardship a strike would bring at the current time, and pledged to avoid one at all costs.

Six weeks ago, all of Evergreen's lumberjacks drove into a local town for the annual Paul Bunyan celebration. The celebration marks the end of the rainy season when, because of dangerous lightning and muddy roads, very little logging can be done. While at the celebration, a late season storm struck the area and washed out part of the main access road to the camp. Evergreen barricaded the access road and put up a sign saying that the road was closed. The lumberjacks remained stranded in the town, unable to get to work, for four weeks awaiting reconstruction of the road.

Unbeknownst to the lumberjacks, Evergreen had repaired the road within a few days of the flood, but, fearful of a strike, left up the barricades and sign and brought in replacement workers via a seldom-used back road who worked for a few weeks at the beginning of the busy dry season. Pressed for action by its furloughed lumberjacks, the union approached Evergreen, restarted negotiations, and came to an agreement on a new contract. At that point, Evergreen discharged the replacement workers, removed the barricades and sign, and welcomed the lumberjacks back to work.

Has Evergreen committed any unfair labor practices?

Textile Workers Union v. Darlington Mfg. Co.

Supreme Court of the United States
380 U.S. 263, 85 S. Ct. 994, 13 L. Ed. 2d 827 (1965)

Mr. Justice Harlan delivered the opinion of the Court.

We here review judgments of the Court of Appeals setting aside and refusing to enforce an order of the National Labor Relations Board which found respondent Darlington guilty of an unfair labor practice by reason of having permanently closed its plant following petitioner union's election as the bargaining representative of Darlington's employees.

Darlington Manufacturing Company was a South Carolina corporation operating one textile mill. A majority of Darlington's stock was held by Deering Milliken, a New York "selling house" marketing textiles produced by others.[12] Deering Milliken in turn was controlled by Roger Milliken, president of Darlington, and by other members of the Milliken family.[13] The National Labor Relations Board found that the Milliken family, through Deering Milliken, operated 17 textile manufacturers, including Darlington, whose products, manufactured in 27 different mills, were marketed through Deering Milliken.

In March 1956 petitioner Textile Workers Union initiated an organizational campaign at Darlington which the company resisted vigorously in various ways, including threats to close the mill if the union won a representation election.[14] On

---

12. [1] Deering Milliken & Co. owned 41% of the Darlington stock. Cotwool Manufacturing Co., another textile manufacturer, owned 18% of the stock. In 1960 Deering Milliken & Co. was merged into Cotwool, the survivor being named Deering Milliken, Inc.

13. [2] The Milliken family owned only 6% of the Darlington stock, but held a majority stock interest in both Deering Milliken & Co. and Cotwool, see note 1, *supra*.

14. [3] The Board found that Darlington had interrogated employees and threatened to close the mill if the union won the election. After the decision to liquidate was made (see *infra*), Darlington

September 6, 1956, the union won an election by a narrow margin. When Roger Milliken was advised of the union victory, he decided to call a meeting of the Darlington board of directors to consider closing the mill. Milliken testified before the Labor Board:

> I felt that as a result of the campaign that had been conducted and the promises and statements made in these letters that had been distributed [favoring unionization], that if before we had had some hope, possible hope of achieving competitive [costs] . . . by taking advantage of new machinery that was being put in, that this hope had diminished as a result of the election because a majority of the employees had voted in favor of the union. . . . [R. 457].

The board of directors met on September 12 and voted to liquidate the corporation, action which was approved by the stockholders on October 17. The plant ceased operations entirely in November, and all plant machinery and equipment was sold piecemeal at auction in December.

The union filed charges with the Labor Board claiming that Darlington had violated §§ 8(a)(1) and 8(a)(3) of the National Labor Relations Act by closing its plant, and § 8(a)(5) by refusing to bargain with the union after the election.[15] The Board, by a divided vote, found that Darlington had been closed because of the antiunion animus of Roger Milliken, and held that to be a violation of § 8(a)(3).[16] The Board also found Darlington to be part of a single integrated employer group controlled by the Milliken family through Deering Milliken; therefore Deering Milliken could be held liable for the unfair labor practices of Darlington.[17] Alternatively, since Darlington was a part of the Deering Milliken enterprise, Deering Milliken had violated the Act by closing part of its business for a discriminatory purpose. The Board ordered back pay for all Darlington employees until they obtained substantially equivalent work or were put on preferential hiring lists at the other Deering Milliken mills. Respondent Deering Milliken was ordered to bargain with the union in regard to details of compliance with the Board order. 139 N.L.R.B. 241.

---

employees were told that the decision to close was caused by the election, and they were encouraged to sign a petition disavowing the union. These practices were held to violate § 8(a)(1) of the National Labor Relations Act, and that part of the Board decision is not challenged here.

15. [5] The union asked for a bargaining conference on September 12, 1956 (the day that the board of directors voted to liquidate), but was told to await certification by the Board. The union was certified on October 24, and did meet with Darlington officials in November, but no actual bargaining took place. The Board found this to be a violation of § 8(a)(5). Such a finding was in part based on the determination that the plant closing was an unfair labor practice, and no argument is made that § 8(a)(5) requires an employer to bargain concerning a purely business decision to terminate his enterprise. Cf. Fibreboard Paper Prod. Corp. v. NLRB, 379 U.S. 203 (1964).

16. [6] Since the closing was held to be illegal, the Board found that the gradual discharges of all employees during November and December constituted § 8(a)(1) violations. The propriety of this determination depends entirely on whether the decision to close the plant violated § 8(a)(3).

17. [7] Members Leedom and Rodgers agreed with the trial examiner that Deering Milliken was not a single employer. Member Rodgers dissented in arguing that Darlington had not violated § 8(a)(3) by closing.

On review, the Court of Appeals sitting *en banc*, set aside the order and denied enforcement by a divided vote. 325 F.2d 682. The Court of Appeals held that even accepting arguendo the Board's determination that Deering Milliken had the status of a single employer, a company has the absolute right to close out a part or all of its business regardless of antiunion motives. The court therefore did not review the Board's finding that Deering Milliken was a single integrated employer.... We hold that so far as the Labor Act is concerned, an employer has the absolute right to terminate his entire business for any reason he pleases, but disagree with the Court of Appeals that such right includes the ability to close part of a business no matter what the reason. We conclude that the cause must be remanded to the Board for further proceedings.

Preliminarily it should be observed that both petitioners argue that the Darlington closing violated § 8(a)(1) as well as § 8(a)(3) of the Act. We think, however, that the Board was correct in treating the closing only under § 8(a)(3).[18] Section 8(a)(1) provides that it is an unfair labor practice for an employer "to interfere with, restrain, or coerce employees in the exercise of" § 7 rights. Naturally, certain business decisions will, to some degree, interfere with concerted activities by employees. But it is only when the interference with § 7 rights outweighs the business justification for the employer's action that § 8(a)(1) is violated. See e.g., *NLRB v. Steelworkers*, 357 U.S. 357 (1958); *Republic Aviation Corp. v. NLRB*, 324 U.S. 793 (1945). A violation of § 8(a)(1) alone therefore presupposes an act which is unlawful even absent a discriminatory motive. Whatever may be the limits of § 8(a)(1), some employer decisions are so peculiarly matters of management prerogative that they would never constitute violations of § 8(a)(1), whether or not they involved sound business judgment, unless they also violated § 8(a)(3). Thus it is not questioned in this case that an employer has the right to terminate his business, whatever the impact of such action on concerted activities, if the decision to close is motivated by other than discriminatory reasons.[19] But such action, if discriminatorily motivated, is encompassed within the literal language of § 8(a)(3). We therefore deal with the Darlington closing under that section.

I

We consider first the argument, advanced by the petitioner union but not by the Board, and rejected by the Court of Appeals, that an employer may not go completely

---

18. [8] The Board did find that Darlington's discharge of employees following the decision to close violated § 8(a)(1). See note 6, *supra*.

19. [10] It is also clear that the ambiguous act of closing a plant following the election of a union is not, absent an inquiry into the employer's motive, inherently discriminatory. We are thus not confronted with a situation where the employer "must be held to intend the very consequences which foreseeably and inescapably flow from his actions...." (*NLRB v. Erie Resistor Corp.*, 373 U.S. 221, 228 (1963)), in which the Board could find a violation of § 8(a)(3) without an examination into motive. See *Radio Officers v. NLRB*, 347 U.S. 17, 42–43 (1954); *Teamsters Local v. NLRB*, 365 U.S. 667, 674–676 (1961).

out of business without running afoul of the Labor Act if such action is prompted by a desire to avoid unionization.[20] Given the Board's findings on the issue of motive, acceptance of this contention would carry the day for the Board's conclusion that the closing of this plant was an unfair labor practice, even on the assumption that Darlington is to be regarded as an independent unrelated employer. A proposition that a single businessman cannot choose to go out of business if he wants to would represent such a startling innovation that it should not be entertained without the clearest manifestation of legislative intent or unequivocal judicial precedent so construing the Labor Act. We find neither.

So far as legislative manifestation is concerned, it is sufficient to say that there is not the slightest indication in the history of the Wagner Act or of the Taft-Hartley Act that Congress envisaged any such result under either statute.

As for judicial precedent, the Board recognized that "[t]here is no decided case directly dispositive of Darlington's claim that it had an absolute right to close its mill, irrespective of motive." 139 N.L.R.B., at 250. The only language by this Court in any way adverting to this problem is found in *Southport Petroleum Co. v. NLRB*, 315 U.S. 100, 106 (1942), where it was stated:

> Whether there was a bona fide discontinuance and a true change of ownership — which would terminate the duty of reinstatement created by the Board's order — or merely a disguised continuance of the old employer, does not clearly appear. . . .

The courts of appeals have generally assumed that a complete cessation of business will remove an employer from future coverage by the Act. Thus the Court of Appeals said in these cases: The Act "does not compel a person to become or remain an employee. It does not compel one to become or remain an employer. Either may withdraw from that status with immunity, so long as the obligations of an employment contract have been met." 325 F.2d, at 685. The Eighth Circuit, in *NLRB v. New Madrid Mfg. Co.*, 215 F.2d 908, 914 (8th Cir. 1954), was equally explicit:

> But none of this can be taken to mean that an employer does not have the absolute right, at all times, to permanently close and go out of business . . . for whatever reason he may choose, whether union animosity or anything else, and without his being thereby left subject to a remedial liability under the Labor Management Relations Act for such unfair labor practices as he may have committed in the enterprise, except up to the time that such actual and permanent closing . . . has occurred.[21]

---

20. [11] The Board predicates its argument on the finding that Deering Milliken was an integrated enterprise, and does not consider it necessary to argue that an employer may not go completely out of business for antiunion reasons. Brief for National Labor Relations Board, at 3, n. 2.

21. [12] In *New Madrid* the business was transferred to a new employer, which was held liable for the unfair labor practices committed by its predecessor before closing. The closing itself was not found to be an unfair labor practice.

The AFL-CIO suggests in its *amicus* brief that Darlington's action was similar to a discriminatory lockout, which is prohibited "'because designed to frustrate organizational efforts, to destroy or undermine bargaining representation, or to evade the duty to bargain.'" One of the purposes of the Labor Act is to prohibit the discriminatory use of the economic weapons in an effort to obtain future benefits. The discriminatory lockout designed to destroy a union like a "runaway shop," is a lever which has been used to discourage collective employee activities in the future. But a complete liquidation of a business yields no such future benefit for the employer, if the termination is bona fide.[22] It may be motivated more by spite against the union than by business reasons, but it is not the type of discrimination which is prohibited by the Act. The personal satisfaction that such an employer may derive from standing on his beliefs or the mere possibility that other employers will follow his example are surely too remote to be considered dangers at which the labor statutes were aimed.[23] Although employees may be prohibited from engaging in a strike under certain conditions, no one would consider it a violation of the Act for the same employees to quit their employment *en masse*, even if motivated by a desire to ruin the employer. The very permanence of such action would negate any future economic benefit to the employees. The employer's right to go out of business is no different.

We are not presented here with the case of a "runaway shop,"[24] whereby Darlington would transfer its work to another plant or open a new plant in another locality to replace its closed plant.[25] Nor are we concerned with a shutdown where the employees, by renouncing the union, could cause the plant to reopen.[26] Such cases would involve discriminatory employer action for the purpose of obtaining some benefit from the employees in the future.[27] We hold here only that when an employer

---

22. [14] The Darlington property and equipment could not be sold as a unit, and were eventually auctioned off piecemeal. We therefore are not confronted with a sale of a going concern, which might present different considerations under §§ 8(a)(3) and 8(a)(5). *Cf. John Wiley & Sons v. Livingston*, 376 U.S. 543 (1964); *NLRB v. Deena Artware, Inc.*, 361 U.S. 398 (1960).

23. [15] *Cf.* NLRB § 8(c), 29 U.S.C. § 158(c) (1958 ed.). Different considerations would arise were it made to appear that the closing employer was acting pursuant to some arrangement or understanding with other employers to discourage employee organizational activities in their businesses.

24. [16] *E.g., NLRB v. Preston Feed Corp.*, 309 F.2d 346 (4th Cir. 1962); *NLRB v. Wallick*, 198 F.2d 477 (3d Cir. 1952). An analogous problem is presented where a department is closed for antiunion reasons but the work is continued by independent contractors. *See, e.g., NLRB v. Kelly & Picerne, Inc.*, 298 F.2d 895 (1st Cir. 1962); *Jays Foods, Inc. v. NLRB*, 292 F.2d 317 (7th Cir. 1961); *NLRB v. R. C. Mahon Co.*, 269 F.2d 44 (6th Cir. 1959); *NLRB v. Bank of Am.*, 130 F.2d 624 (9th Cir. 1942); *Williams Motor Co. v. NLRB*, 128 F.2d 960 (8th Cir. 1942).

25. [17] After the decision to close the plant, Darlington accepted no new orders, and merely continued operations for a time to fill pending orders. 139 N.L.R.B., at 244.

26. [18] *E.g., NLRB v. Norma Mining Corp.*, 206 F.2d 38 (4th Cir. 1963). Similarly, if all employees are discharged but the work continues with new personnel, the effect is to discourage any future union activities. *See NLRB v. Waterman S.S. Corp.*, 309 U.S. 206 (1940); *NLRB v. National Garment Co.*, 166 F.2d 233 (8th Cir. 1948); *NLRB v. Stremel*, 141 F.2d 317 (10th Cir. 1944).

27. [19] All of the cases to which we have been cited involved closings found to have been motivated, at least in part, by the expectation of achieving future benefits. See cases cited notes 16, 18

closes his entire business, even if the liquidation is motivated by vindictiveness toward the union, such action is not an unfair labor practice.[28]

II

While we thus agree with the Court of Appeals that viewing Darlington as an independent employer the liquidation of its business was not an unfair labor practice, we cannot accept the lower court's view that the same conclusion necessarily follows if Darlington is regarded as an integral part of the Deering Milliken enterprise.

The closing of an entire business, even though discriminatory, ends the employer-employee relationship; the force of such a closing is entirely spent as to that business when termination of the enterprise takes place. On the other hand, a discriminatory partial closing may have repercussions on what remains of the business, affording employer leverage for discouraging the free exercise of § 7 rights among remaining employees of much the same kind as that found to exist in the "runaway shop" and "temporary closing" cases. Moreover, a possible remedy open to the Board in such a case, like the remedies available in the "runaway shop" and "temporary closing" cases, is to order reinstatement of the discharged employees in the other parts of the

---

supra. The two cases which are urged as indistinguishable from *Darlington* are *NLRB v. Savoy Laundry*, 327 F.2d 370 (9th Cir. 1956), and *NLRB v. Missouri Transit Co.*, 250 F.2d 261 (8th Cir. 1957). In *Savoy Laundry* the employer operated one laundry plant where he processed both retail laundry pickups and wholesale laundering. Once that laundry was marked, all of it was processed together. After some of the employees organized, the employer discontinued most of the wholesale service, and thereafter discharged some of his employees. There was no separate wholesale department, and the discriminatory motive was obviously to discourage unionization in the entire plant. *Missouri Transit* presents a similar situation. A bus company operated an interstate line and intrastate shuttle service connecting a military base with the interstate terminal. When the union attempted to organize all of the drivers, the shuttle service was sold and the shuttle drivers discharged. Although the two services were treated as separate departments, it is clear from the facts of the case that the union was attempting to organize all of the drivers, and the discriminatory motive of the employer was to discourage unionization in the interstate service as well as the shuttle service.

28. [20] Nothing we have said in this opinion would justify an employer interfering with employee organizational activities by threatening to close his plant, as distinguished from announcing a decision to close already reached by the board of directors or other management authority empowered to make such a decision. We recognize that this safeguard does not wholly remove the possibility that our holding may result in some deterrent effect on organizational activities independent of that arising for the closing itself. An employer may be encouraged to make a definite decision to close on the theory that its mere announcement before a representation election will discourage the employees from voting for the union, and thus his decision may not have to be implemented. Such a possibility is not likely to occur, however, except in a marginal business; a solidly successful employer is not apt to hazard the possibility that the employees will call his bluff by voting to organize. We see no practical way of eliminating this possible consequence of our holding short of allowing the Board to order an employer who chooses so to gamble with his employees not to carry out his announced intention to close. We do not consider the matter of sufficient significance in the over-all labor-management relations picture to require or justify a decision different from the one we have made.

business. No such remedy is available when an entire business has been terminated. By analogy to those cases involving a continuing enterprise we are constrained to hold, in disagreement with the Court of Appeals, that a partial closing is an unfair labor practice under § 8(a)(3) if motivated by a purpose to chill unionism in any of the remaining plants of the single employer and if the employer may reasonably have foreseen that such closing will likely have that effect.

While we have spoken in terms of a "partial closing" in the context of the Board's finding that Darlington was part of a larger single enterprise controlled by the Milliken family, we do not mean to suggest that an organizational integration of plants or corporations is a necessary prerequisite to the establishment of such a violation of § 8(a)(3). If the persons exercising control over a plant that is being closed for antiunion reasons (1) have an interest in another business, whether or not affiliated with or engaged in the same line of commercial activity as the closed plant, of sufficient substantiality to give promise of their reaping a benefit from the discouragement of unionization in that business; (2) act to close their plant with the purpose of producing such a result; and (3) occupy a relationship to the other business which makes it realistically foreseeable that its employees will fear that such business will also be closed down if they persist in organizational activities, we think that an unfair labor practice has been made out.

Although the Board's single employer finding necessarily embraced findings as to Roger Milliken and the Milliken family which, if sustained by the Court of Appeals, would satisfy the elements of "interest" and "relationship" with respect to other parts of the Deering Milliken enterprise, that and the other Board findings fall short of establishing the factors of "purpose" and "effect" which are vital requisites of the general principles that govern a case of this kind.

Thus, the Board's findings as to the purpose and foreseeable effect of the Darlington closing pertained *only* to its impact on the Darlington employees. No findings were made as to the purpose and effect of the closing with respect to the employees in the other plants comprising the Deering Milliken group. It does not suffice to establish the unfair labor practice charged here to argue that the Darlington closing necessarily had an adverse impact upon unionization in such other plants. We have heretofore observed that employer action which has a foreseeable consequence of discouraging concerted activities generally does not amount to a violation of § 8(a)(3) in the absence of a showing of motivation which is aimed at achieving the prohibited effect. See *Teamsters Local v. NLRB*, 365 U.S. 667 (1961), and the concurring opinion therein, at 677. In an area which trenches so closely upon otherwise legitimate employer prerogatives, we consider the absence of Board findings on this score a fatal defect in its decision. The Court of Appeals for its part did not deal with the question of purpose and effect at all, since it concluded that an employer's right to close down his entire business because of distaste for unionism, also embraced a partial closing so motivated.

Apart from this, the Board's holding should not be accepted or rejected without court review of its single employer finding, judged, however, in accordance with the general principles set forth above. Review of that finding, which the lower court found unnecessary on its view of the cause, now becomes necessary in light of our holding in this part of our opinion, and is a task that devolves upon the Court of Appeals in the first instance. *Universal Camera Corp. v. NLRB*, 340 U.S. 474 (1951).

In these circumstances, we think the proper disposition of this cause is to require that it be remanded to the Board so as to afford the Board the opportunity to make further findings on the issue of purpose and effect. *See, e.g., NLRB v. Virginia Elec. & Power Co.*, 314 U.S. 469, 479–480 (1941). This is particularly appropriate here since the case involve issues of first impression. If such findings are made, the cases will then be in a posture for further review by the Court of Appeals on all issues. Accordingly, without intimating any view as to how any of these matters should eventuate, we vacate the judgments of the Court of Appeals and remand the cases to that court with instructions to remand them to the Board for further proceedings consistent with this opinion.

It is so ordered.

Mr. Justice Stewart took no part in the decision of these cases.

Mr. Justice Goldberg took no part in the consideration or decision of these cases.

Notes

1. *Aftermath* — On remand, the Trial Examiner concluded that there was insufficient evidence to show a purpose to chill unionism at the other plants or a foreseeable chilling effect. The NLRB, however, disagreed and concluded that the record indicated, at least in part, an illegal "purpose" and "foreseeable effect." *Darlington Mfg. Co.*, 165 N.L.R.B. 1074 (1967), *enforced*, 397 F.2d 760 (4th Cir. 1968), *cert. denied*, 393 U.S. 1023 (1969).

Evidence the Board found telling included the following:

(a) Roger Milliken made speeches to South Carolina government and business leaders before the Darlington organization drive, indicating his intense concern with what he regarded as a threat to the Southern industrial community posed by unionism and the need to preserve "cooperation between management and labor . . . at all costs." Section 8(c) does not preclude the Board from using such speeches as evidence of motivation, the Board said, because "this Section left unrestricted the Board's right to consider employer statements for purposes for which they would be admissible in courts of law."

(b) Milliken sent officials of all other Deering Milliken mills reprints of a trade magazine article headlined, "Darlington Situation Becomes Object Lesson to All Concerned," urging the other mill officials to undertake a "public relations" program to make the community leaders understand the consequences of unionization. "The only way the community leaders could make use of this information would be by impressing upon employees the risks of unionism."

(c) The dispatch with which Milliken closed the plant and auctioned off the machinery led the Board to infer that "he saw the opportunity to convey to all his employees an object lesson of the folly of selecting the Union."

(d) There was evidence that news of the Darlington closing spread rapidly to other Deering Milliken plants and was much discussed, frequently in terms of "Mr. Milliken would not operate a plant under a union." From such evidence, the Board inferred a "foreseeable chilling effect." Proof of actual effect, according to the NLRB, is not an essential element.

2. *The Timing of Decisions to Close* — A small family-owned business did not violate § 8(a)(1) or (3) by laying off all of its employees the day after they voted for union representation where the layoff was based on the company owner's terminal medical condition and the poor financial condition of the company. The company made the decision to lay off employees prior to the election when a management team recommended that the family sell the company. On advice of counsel, the company deliberately timed the notice of layoff so that it would not interfere with the conduct of the election and likely trigger unfair labor practice charges. See *Starcraft Aero., Inc.*, 346 N.L.R.B. 1228 (2006).

On the other hand, in *Healthcare Emps. Union, Local 399 v. NLRB*, 463 F.3d 909 (9th Cir. 2006), the Ninth Circuit ruled that an employer violated § 8(a)(3) where it began considering subcontracting out work around the time that the union's organizing campaign ramped up, and implemented the decision two weeks before a representation election. The effect of the outsourcing was the disenfranchisement of 25% of the employees, 95% of whom had already expressed their desire to join the union. An inference of anti-union animus behind the decision was raised by the employer's knowledge of the organizing drive, its resistance to unionization, and the timing of the action during the period following petition filing and prior to the election. The court concluded:

> [T]he inference of anti-union animus raised by the timing of [the employer's] decision to subcontract is 'stunningly obvious,' ... [c]ourts have consistently treated an employer's adverse employment action occurring between the filing of a petition for a representation election with the Board and the ensuing election as raising a powerful inference of anti-union animus.

3. *Runaway Shops* — For an example of the "runaway shop," which the Supreme Court mentioned in *Darlington* at note 16 as an unfair labor practice, see *Garwin Corp.*, 153 N.L.R.B. 664 (1965), *enforced in part*, 374 F.2d 295 (D.C. Cir. 1967). In this case, the employer's motivation for the move was found to be anti-union hostility — not economic necessity. However, when the employer offers sufficient economic reasons for the plant removal, it may be difficult to establish wrongful purpose. *NLRB v. Rapid Bindery, Inc.*, 293 F.2d 170 (2d Cir. 1961); *NLRB v. Adkins Transfer Co.*, 226 F.2d 324 (6th Cir. 1955).

When a "runaway shop" violation is found, the Board often finds it difficult to formulate an adequate remedy. In determining the appropriateness of ordering restoration of a discriminatorily relocated operation, the Board has decided to abandon the standard of whether restoration would jeopardize the "continued viability" of the business and inquire only whether restoration would be "unduly burdensome." *Lear Siegler Inc. v. International Union United Automobile Aerospace & Agricultural Implement Workers of America*, 295 N.L.R.B. 857 (1989). *See Coronet Foods, Inc. v. NLRB*, 981 F.2d 1284 (D.C. Cir. 1993); *Mid-South Bottling Co. v. NLRB*, 876 F.2d 458 (5th Cir. 1989) (finding orders directing reopening of discriminatorily closed facilities not unduly burdensome). When restoration of eliminated operations is not feasible, the Board may order back pay, reinstatement at either the old or the new location, and reimbursement for necessary moving expenses. *Industrial Fabricating Inc.*, 119 N.L.R.B. 162 (1957), *enforced*, 272 F.2d 184 (6th Cir. 1959).

In 2011, the Board's approach to remedying runaway shops came under public scrutiny in the context of a dispute between Boeing and its union, the International Association of Machinists. Boeing and the IAM had a long-standing bargaining relationship in Washington State and in Oregon, where Boeing production and maintenance employees manufactured aircraft. IAM had engaged in strikes in 1977, 1989, 1995, 2005, and 2008. In 2009, Boeing announced that in order to address a backlog of orders for its 787 Dreamliner aircraft, it would place a production line in its facility in South Carolina, where it would produce three aircraft per month in addition to the seven per month produced in Puget Sound. The announcement came one month after employees at the South Carolina facility voted to decertify the IAM as their bargaining agent, and on the same day that the South Carolina legislature approved an economic development package aimed at providing incentives for Boeing to expand in South Carolina. In addition, company officials made multiple statements linking the plan to shift work to South Carolina to the company's experience with IAM strikes in Washington State and its concern about future work stoppages. The Board's acting General Counsel issued a complaint alleging that Boeing had illegally transferred some of its work to South Carolina in response to lawful strikes initiated by the IAM in Washington State over contract disputes with the company. Because the company's actions were illegally motivated and inherently destructive of employee rights, the GC argued that Boeing had violated §§ 8(a)(1) and 8(a)(3). Daily Lab. Rep. (BNA) No. 77, Apr. 21, 2011, at AA-1. *Compare Amglo Kemlite Laboratories, Inc.*, 360 N.L.R.B. 319 (2014) (employer violated NLRA when it decided to transfer manufacturing work to its Mexico facility in retaliation for nonunion employee work stoppage at its U.S. plant).

A media furor ensued. Much of the negative publicity surrounding the case focused on the remedy sought by the GC, which was an order requiring Boeing to have IAM-represented workers in Washington operate the company's second Dreamliner production line, using supply lines already maintained by bargaining unit employees in Washington and Oregon. Questions were also raised about whether this amounted to an unlawful transfer of work, as the GC had alleged, or simply the creation of new work through the opening of a new production line to handle historic demand for the jetliner. Daily Lab. Rep. (BNA) No. 86, May 4,

2011, at A-12, A-13. The case ultimately settled when the parties signed a new four-year labor contract; Boeing agreed to build a new line of 737 MAX jetliners in Washington State, but also continued production of its 787 Dreamliners in South Carolina. Daily Lab. Rep. (BNA) No. 237, Dec. 9, 2011, at AA-2. Eight years later (during the pandemic) Boeing ultimately ended production of its 787 Dreamliner in Washington State and consolidated its assembly operations in South Carolina. Tangel, *Boeing to Consolidate Dreamliner Production in South Carolina*, WALL ST. J., Oct. 2, 2020.

Problem

20. Luciano Blue was the owner of Blue Lighting Company, a small manufacturer of residential lighting fixtures. Blue also sat on the board of Yellow Lighting, Inc., a larger manufacturer of commercial lighting fixtures, and owned a five percent stake in the corporation. The employees at both companies were represented by the electrical workers union.

Blue had been bargaining with the union over terms of a new agreement for Blue Lighting for several months, and was getting fed up with the whole process. The two sides were still far apart on basic issues such as wage rates, but the real sticking point was the union's insistence that the agreement contain the following clause: "The Blue Lighting Company hereby agrees to employ only members in good standing of the electrical workers' union." In order to put additional pressure on Blue to accede to its demands, the union called a strike and started picketing Blue Lighting. Production came to a standstill.

Blue was enraged by the strike. He walked out to the picket line, asked the leaders of the strike to identify themselves and, once they did, fired them on the spot. He then told the rest of the striking workers that they had exactly one hour to get back on the job or they would meet with a similar fate. Most of the workers returned to work within the hour. Shortly thereafter, Blue and the union signed a new agreement without the offending clause.

A few months later, after listening to one too many union grievances, Blue decided he was fed up with dealing with unions so he closed the plant, laid off the workers, and dissolved Blue Lighting Company. Soon thereafter, he was quoted in the local trade association newsletter as saying, "Unions are a cancer on the body of free enterprise. I'd counsel anyone dealing with a recalcitrant union to do what I did: shut them down and send a message to employees everywhere."

Has Blue committed any unfair labor practices?

E. Remedial Problems

Phelps Dodge Corp. v. NLRB, 313 U.S. 177, 61 S. Ct. 845, 85 L. Ed. 1271 (1941). In this landmark case, the Supreme Court interpreted the National Labor Relations Act as giving the Board broad and flexible powers to fashion remedies to effectuate the purposes of the Act. The Court held that the Board has the power to order the hiring of applicants for employment who were discriminated against because of their union membership. The Court also indicated that the Board may order reinstatement of employees who have been discriminated against, even though they have obtained substantially equivalent employment. Finally, the Court held that, in calculating back pay, a deduction should be made, not only for actual interim earnings, but also for amounts the worker failed without excuse to earn.

Notes

1. *Duty to Mitigate* — To satisfy their duty to mitigate damages, discharged employees must conduct a reasonably diligent search for alternative employment. They need not seek employment involving working conditions substantially more onerous than their previous positions, including jobs located substantially farther from home than their original positions. *NLRB v. St. George Warehouse, Inc.*, 645 F.3d 666 (3d Cir. 2011).

In *Tubari, Ltd. v. NLRB*, 959 F.2d 451 (3d Cir. 1992), the court reversed the Labor Board determination and held that no back pay was due unlawfully discharged employees who had obtained interim jobs picketing for their union at lower pay, since they had not fulfilled their duty to mitigate damages.

In *King Soopers, Inc. v. NLRB*, 859 F.3d 23 (D.C. Cir. 2017) the court enforced the Labor Board's ruling that job search expenses incurred by unlawfully discharged employees shouldn't be offset from interim earnings, permitting the Board to order the employer to pay for job search expenses in order to make the employee whole where the employee struggles to find new work but doesn't generate any interim earnings.

Unemployment compensation benefits are not deducted from back pay. *See NLRB v. Gullett Gin Co.*, 340 U.S. 361 (1951). Does this make the employee "more than whole"? *See also NLRB v. Illinois Dep't of Employment Sec.*, 988 F.2d 735 (7th Cir. 1993) (NLRB may enjoin state effort to recoup unemployment compensation from individuals granted back pay awards under the NLRA).

2. *Undocumented Workers* — *Sure-Tan, Inc. v. NLRB*, 467 U.S. 883 (1984), concerned an employer that reported undocumented aliens to the Immigration and Naturalization Service in retaliation for their union activities. The aliens thereafter agreed to leave the country voluntarily. The Supreme Court agreed with the Labor Board that such undocumented aliens constitute "employees" within the meaning of the NLRA, and it thus found that the employer's retaliatory action had violated the Act. Recognizing the unusual nature of undocumented aliens, the Supreme Court made the Board's reinstatement and back pay order conditional on the discriminatees' legal reentry into the United States. This limitation was based upon the fact that employees "must be deemed unavailable for work (and the accrual of back pay therefore tolled) during any period when the employees were not lawfully entitled to be present and employed in the United States."

In *Hoffman Plastic Compounds, Inc. v. NLRB*, 535 U.S. 137 (2002), a five-Justice Supreme Court majority extended the remedial limitation the Court had imposed in *Sure-Tan*, as it held that the enactment of the Immigration Reform and Control Act (IRCA) in 1986 made it even clearer that the NLRB may not order the reinstatement of, or award back pay to, undocumented workers illegally discharged by employers because of their protected activities—even if those remedies are conditioned upon the lawful reentry of the discriminatees into the United States. Such persons could only have obtained employment if they falsified their employment documents or they were knowingly hired by employers in violation of IRCA provisions. The majority thus concluded that it would undermine the congressional policy underlying IRCA if back pay or reinstatement could be awarded to undocumented discriminatees. "[A]llowing the Board to award back pay to illegal aliens would unduly trench upon explicit statutory prohibitions critical to federal immigration policy, as expressed in IRCA. It would encourage the successful evasion of apprehension by immigration authorities, condone prior violations of the immigration laws, and encourage future violations." The four dissenting Justices asserted that the denial of any back pay to undocumented workers—especially those who had been knowingly or indifferently hired by employers—would reduce the cost to firms that illegally discharge employees for supporting labor organizations. Does the *Hoffman Plastics* limitation actually encourage nonunion employers to hire undocumented workers knowing that if those employees decide to organize they can be terminated at no cost? *See generally* Brudney, *Private Injuries, Public Policies: Adjusting the NLRB's Approach to Backpay Remedies*, 5 F.I.U. L. Rev. 645 (2010).

In *Mezonos Maven Bakery, Inc.*, 362 N.L.R.B. 360 (2015), the Labor Board held that where an employer knowingly employs undocumented workers and then fires them in violation of the NLRA, it may be ordered to offer those persons reinstatement on the condition they subsequently document their right for employment under the Immigration Reform and Control Act. The Board did not believe that such conditional reinstatement orders would be contrary to the *Hoffman Plastic Compounds* holding.

3. *Extraordinary Remedies*—In cases in which the Board finds "massive" unfair labor practices, it often orders novel remedies. Among these are the remedies used in the numerous cases involving J.P. Stevens & Co. The Board has ordered, and the courts have upheld, the following remedies: requiring the employer to post notice of the Board's order not only in the plant in which the unfair labor practice occurred, but in all 43 company plants, and requiring the employer to mail the order to each of the employees in the 43 plants (380 F.2d 292 (2d Cir. 1967)); requiring that the employer give the union, upon request, reasonable access to plant bulletin boards for a period of one year, and requiring the Board order to be read to employees during working time (441 F.2d 514 (5th Cir. 1971); 461 F.2d 490 (4th Cir. 1972)); requiring the employer to give a list of the names and addresses of all the employees in all its plants to the union (406 F.2d 1017 (4th Cir. 1968); 417 F.2d 533 (5th Cir. 1969)).

In finding J.P. Stevens to be in civil contempt, the court in *NLRB v. J. P. Stevens & Co.*, 464 F.2d 1326 (2d Cir. 1972), *cert. denied*, 410 U.S. 926 (1973), ordered the company to pay to the NLRB all costs and expenses, including counsel fees and salaries, incurred by the Board as a result of the contempt proceedings.

In *Beverly Cal. Corp.*, 334 N.L.R.B. 713, *enforced*, 2001 U.S. App. LEXIS 25079 (7th Cir. Nov. 20, 2001), the Board issued a corporate-wide cease and desist order against Beverly Enterprises based upon numerous flagrant violations of the Act at many facilities located in different states. A similar nationwide remedial order was sustained against Beverly Enterprises in *Beverly Health & Rehab. Servs. v. NLRB*, 317 F.3d 316 (D.C. Cir. 2003).

4. *Section 10(j) Injunctive Relief*—The Board has made more frequent use of interim §10(j) injunctive relief in recent years. For example, the Board petitioned for and was granted a §10(j) injunction against a nursing home that withdrew recognition from its union during contract negotiations based on a disaffection petition signed by a bare majority of the unit employees where the employer participated in soliciting employees to sign the petition. The employer was ordered to restore recognition to the union, resume contract negotiations, and to rescind unilateral wage increases. *See Glasser ex rel. NLRB v. Heartland—Univ. of Livonia, MI, LLC*, 632 F. Supp. 2d 659 (E.D. Mich. 2009). Similarly, the Board petitioned for and was granted a §10(j) injunction in a case involving an employer that withdrew recognition from its union based upon a disaffection petition with a number of "stale" signatures (some of which were more than a year old) and ceased bargaining without affording the union an opportunity to present its own evidence of support. The union immediately filed a complaint with the Board and brought forward a sufficient number of signatures revoking those on the petition to delegitimate the employer's withdrawal of recognition. The court ordered the employer to restore recognition and to continue bargaining. *See Norelli v. Fremont-Rideout Health Group*, 632 F. Supp. 2d 993 (E.D. Cal. 2009). *See also Reichard ex rel. NLRB v. Foster Poultry Farms*, 425 F. Supp. 2d 1090 (E.D. Cal. 2006) (granting petition for relief under §10(j) where employer withdrew recognition from the union and ceased bargaining for a first contract following the union's affiliation with the International Association of Machinists). Should the Labor Board seek §10(j) interim relief to reinstate employees who appear to have been unlawfully terminated during union organizing campaigns due to their organizing activities?

In *McKinney v. Creative Vision Res., LLC*, 783 F.3d 293 (5th Cir. 2015), the court vacated a lower court's grant of section 10(j) injunctive relief requested by the Board requiring a successor employer to bargain with its predecessor's union. The court applied its traditional two-part test and asked whether the Board had established that: (1) it had reasonable cause to believe that an unfair labor practice had occurred and (2) that injunctive relief was just and proper (i.e., that the alleged harm had not yet taken its toll so that injunctive relief could meaningfully preserve the status quo). The court noted that section 10(j) relief remains an "extraordinary remedy," and that the Board had failed to establish that the employer's alleged violations of the Act and harm to the employees or the union were concrete and egregious or otherwise exceptional.

5. *Successorship* — Suppose an employer that has been found guilty of discriminatory discharges sells its business to a bona fide purchaser (not just an alter ego of the employer) that has knowledge of the unfair labor practices. The Supreme Court concluded that such a purchaser who continues to operate the business without significant change may be held jointly and severally liable with the seller for remedying the antecedent unfair labor practices. *Golden State Bottling Co. v. NLRB*, 414 U.S. 168 (1973). *See also NLRB v. Laborers' International Union*, 882 F.2d 949 (5th Cir. 1989); *NLRB v. Local Union No. 46, Metallic Lathers & Reinforcing Iron Workers*, 727 F.2d 234 (2d Cir. 1984) (applying same rule to successor unions).

Part 3

Representation Questions

John Logan, *Consultants, Lawyers, and the "Union Free" Movement in the USA Since the 1970s*
33 Indus. Rel. J. 197, 199–201, 203–05 (2002)*

Over the past three decades, counter-organizing campaigns have formed the bulk of most consultants' "union business." Through almost daily contact with NLRB regional offices, consultants frequently know about union petitions for recognition before the targeted companies do, thus convincing management that the consultants are indeed experts on union representation. . . .

Consultants encourage the employer to think of the union campaign as a failure on its part and to view the election as a referendum on management, telling them that employees vote for or against management, not for the union. They advise employers to give the consultant complete responsibility for the running of the anti-union campaign and most comply enthusiastically. Counter-organizing campaigns range from sophisticated, lengthy and expensive campaigns conducted by several consultants, often costing thousands of dollars per day, to "quick and dirty," low-budget, packaged campaigns for employers seeking the expertise of a consultant, but unable to afford the cost of a major operation. . . .

Prior to a certification election, the union is required to submit to the NLRB authorization cards signed by at least 30% of the eligible bargaining unit. Consultants tell employers to write, publicize and enforce a clear policy against solicitation on company premises by non-employees that must be enforced against, for example, the Salvation Army as well as against the union. If a card drive does develop amongst employees, consultants encourage employers to act quickly and decisively against the campaign because "no company has ever lost an election that wasn't held," The tougher you are at the outset, the consultants advise, the better your chances at driving the union to another company that is easier to deal with. Before the union files the cards, consultants emphasize their critical importance, cautioning employees that signing an authorization card is akin to signing over power of attorney to the union or signing a blank check.

Supervisors tell employees that the card campaign is going badly and warn that union organizers are using intimidation, harassment, and pressure tactics to

---

* Copyright © 2008, John Wiley and Sons. Reprinted with permission.

force employees to sign cards, thus placing the union on the defensive and making employees wary of approaches from union supporters. They also caution employees that their cards are not necessarily confidential, as organizers have promised, because the union may provide management with copies of the cards as proof of majority support. If employees have signed cards but the union has not yet filed the cards with the labor board, management advises employees to ask the union to return their cards; and to facilitate the process, it often distributes sample letters requesting the return of cards and envelopes addressed to the NLRB. By giving the impression that some employees wish to withdraw their cards, this tactic creates doubt among employees about the level of support enjoyed by the union, especially among those who are not solid union supporters. . . .

. . . When the NLRB organizes a date for the election, the employer is required to provide the union with a list of employees' names and addresses, — the so-called "Excelsior" list. Consultants recommend that management provide the union with an incomplete, outdated and misleading list at the last moment permitted by law and tell employees that the NLRB compels them to provide this information to the union. The consequence could well be unwarranted intrusions on their privacy, such as union organizers calling on their homes. . . .

Consultants advise employers on how to object to both the size and make-up of the bargaining unit, how to pack units with anti-union employees, exclude pro-union employees, and reduce the number of employees eligible for collective bargaining. . . . Consultants often attempt to persuade the NLRB that union activists are, in fact, supervisors, thereby removing them from the union campaign and leading to possible charges that supervisors have unlawfully assisted an organizing drive. By reclassifying ordinary employees as supervisors, part-time, contingent or temporary employees, or as independent contractors, employers can reduce significantly the number of employees who are eligible for unionization. . . .

Consultants have also developed a host of complex legal maneuvers designed to delay NLRB proceedings. They stress that time is on the side of the employer and teach managers how to file frivolous complaints with the NLRB in order to delay the election process and prevent the expeditious enforcement of the law. Delays extend the duration and effectiveness of the employer campaign and undermine employee confidence in the effectiveness of both the union and the labor board. . . .

Consultants try to persuade employees that the company, not the union, is the sole source of credible information. Designed to create an atmosphere of fear, intimidation and confusion within the workplace, most "impersonal" consultant communications (letters, newsletters, videos, etc.) stress similar themes — strikes, violence, insecurity and disruption. Anti-union literature attacks both the labor movement in general and the particular union involved in organizing the campaign. . . . Consultant propaganda includes predictions of violent strikes and permanent replacements, restrictive clauses of the union constitution, salaries of union officials, union dues, allegations of corruption, charges that employees will surrender their right to deal directly with management, and warnings about the difficulty in decertifying unwanted unions. Intended to undermine the credibility of the union and its supporters, impersonal propaganda is relayed, whenever possible, through "neutral" third-party sources — press clippings, publications of government departments and research organizations, and perhaps most valuable, the testimony of former union members who are now hostile to unions....

... Consultants recommend that management organize "going out of business" discussions — especially in manufacturing plants where the threat of closure or relocation is greatest — but caution on conducting these meetings carefully, so as to avoid unfair labor charges.... The purpose of these meetings is to convince employees that, instead of voting for the union or no union, the real choice they are facing is between the union and their jobs. Employees are told that they should vote against the union "as if your jobs depended on it." Another common tactic is to distribute literature relating the story of a neighboring business that has folded, shed jobs or relocated following a union victory, even if no evidence exists linking this development to the employees' decision to unionize....

The consultant warns the employees about the potentially disastrous consequences of collective bargaining.... Employer communications frequently imply that strikes are all but inevitable if the union wins and warn that during strikes employees lose not only wages but health insurance, face the threat of permanent replacement, and have no automatic right to unemployment benefits....

Consultants also employ "interpersonal" methods — such as captive speeches and ventilation meetings — of conveying management's anti-union message. Apart from its superior financial resources, management's greatest advantage during an organizing campaign, consultants stress, lies with its exclusive and unlimited access to employees at the workplace.... They advise employers how to conduct captive audience meetings involving small groups of employees or the entire workforce, which take place on company premises on paid time.... Although speaking directly to employees legally requires consultants to report their activities and income to the Labor Department, few actually do so.... Most consultants claim that one of the few emphatic policies that they adhere to during counter-organizing campaigns is never to engage in reportable activities [by dealing directly only with supervisors and management].

Section I. Establishing Representative Status through NLRB Elections

Statutory References

RLA § 2, Fourth and Ninth; NLRA § 9

Foreword

Problems with respect to the representation of employees arise at the moment the process of organization begins and continue until a given union achieves a secure position as bargaining representative. The labor relations acts have accented these problems by according a special status to the union that succeeds in organizing a "majority" of the employees in a defined group. At the same time, the statutes have provided procedures that may be used to determine whether a given union has achieved this status. In this section we are concerned with these procedures and the questions that arise in connection with their use. Problems with respect to the use by unions of collective action for organizational purposes are to be treated in Part Four. Presumptively, the availability and use of the labor relations act procedures have tended to reduce the resort to self-help.

The procedure in representation cases has been summarized by the NLRB in its *Casehandling Manual, Part 2, Representation Proceedings* (which may be found on the NLRB website at https://www.nlrb.gov/guidance/key-reference-materials/manuals-and-guides).

NLRB, Twenty-Sixth Annual Report
3, 4 (1961)

In fiscal 1961, the National Labor Relations Board delegated its decisional powers with respect to employee collective bargaining election cases to its 28 regional directors. This was a new procedural step — and one of the most important in Board history — made possible by the 1959 amendments to the Act. The principal effect of this delegation was to permit regional directors to decide in their regions election cases that before the 1959 amendments had been ruled on only by the five-man Board in Washington.

This delegation includes decisions as to whether a question concerning representation exists, determination of appropriate bargaining unit, directions of elections to determine whether employees wish union representation for collective bargaining purposes, and rulings on other matters such as challenged ballots and objections to elections.

Announcing the delegation, Chairman McCulloch said:

> This delegation of decision making and other powers by the Board to its regional directors promises to be one of the most far-reaching steps the Board has ever taken with respect to its election cases. It should provide a

major speed up in NLRB case handling in line with the policy of President Kennedy for the independent regulatory agencies.

Actions taken by regional directors under the delegation are final, subject to discretionary review by the Board in Washington on restricted grounds. The Board's delegation covers not only employee petitions to select collective-bargaining representatives, but also employer petitions questioning representation, employee petitions to decertify unions, and petitions to rescind union-security authorizations.

In the delegation the Board provided that review of regional directors' decisions could be sought on these four grounds:

1. Where a substantial question of law or policy is raised because of (a) the absence of, or (b) the departure from, officially reported precedent.

2. Where a regional director's decision on a substantial factual issue is clearly erroneous, and such error prejudicially affects the rights of a party.

3. Where the conduct of the hearing in an election case or any ruling made in connection with the proceeding has resulted in prejudicial error.

4. Where there are compelling reasons for reconsideration of an important Board rule or policy.

NLRB, Forty-Sixth Annual Report
31 (1981)

The Act requires that an employer bargain with the representative designated by a majority of his employees in a unit appropriate for collective bargaining. But it does not require that the representative be designated by any particular procedure as long as the representative is clearly the choice of a majority of the employees. As one method for employees to select a majority representative, the Act authorizes the Board to conduct representation elections. The Board may conduct such an election after a petition has been filed by or on behalf of the employees [supported by a 30 percent "showing of interest" — usually authorization cards signed by employees in the proposed bargaining unit], or by an employer who has been confronted with a claim for recognition from an individual or a labor organization. Incident to its authority to conduct elections, the Board has the power to determine the unit of employees appropriate for collective bargaining, and formally to certify a collective-bargaining representative upon the basis of the results of the election. Once certified by the Board, the bargaining agent is the exclusive representative of all employees in the appropriate unit for collective bargaining in respect to rates of pay, wages, hours of employment, or other conditions of employment. The Act also empowers the Board to conduct elections to decertify incumbent bargaining agents which have been previously certified, or which are being currently recognized by the employer. Decertification petitions may be filed by employees, or individuals other than management representatives, or by labor organizations acting on behalf of employees.

Notes

1. *Voter Eligibility*—Employees are eligible to vote in Board representation elections if they were employed on the "voter eligibility date" (usually the payday immediately preceding the election) *and* were employed on the date of the election. Individuals on sick leave or disability leave remain eligible (*Home Care Network, Inc.*, 347 N.L.R.B. 859 (2006)), as do laid-off personnel who have a reasonable expectation of recall in the foreseeable future (*Red Arrow Freight Lines, Inc.*, 278 N.L.R.B. 965 (1986)). Undocumented aliens allegedly employed in violation of the Immigration Reform and Control Act may vote in representation elections if they are employed in the bargaining unit during the eligibility period. *See NLRB v. Kolkka*, 170 F.3d 937 (9th Cir. 1999).

2. *Temporary Employees*—In deciding whether temporary employees are eligible to vote, the Board has applied two different tests. Under the "reasonable expectation" test, temporary workers with a reasonable expectation of continued employment are allowed to vote, while under the "date certain" test, temporary employees whose terms of employment remain uncertain are permitted to vote. In *NLRB v. S.R.D.C., Inc.*, 45 F.3d 328 (9th Cir. 1995), the court decided that the "date certain" approach should generally be used to determine the voting eligibility of temporary personnel.

3. *Consent Elections*—Parties to a representation proceeding may agree to a Consent Election Agreement in which they stipulate the appropriate unit and the eligible voters and agree to have all post-election objections resolved finally by the Regional Director. They may alternatively agree to a Stipulation for Certification Election Agreement in which they similarly stipulate the unit and eligible voters, but specifically guarantee themselves the right of review by the NLRB of post-election objection rulings by the Regional Director. In 2005, the Labor Board created a new consent agreement in which the parties do not agree upon the exact unit and/or voter eligibility, but do agree to have all such pre-election issues and all post-election objections resolved finally by the Regional Director. 176 L.R.R. 172 (Jan. 31, 2005). *See* 29 C.F.R. § 102.62(a), (b), (c).

A. Bars to Conducting an Election

NLRB, THIRTY-SEVENTH ANNUAL REPORT
50–52 (1972)

In certain situations the Board, in the interest of promoting the stability of labor relations, will conclude that circumstances appropriately preclude the raising of a question concerning representation. Thus, under the Board's contract-bar rules, a present election among employees currently covered by a valid collective-bargaining agreement may, with certain exceptions, be barred by an outstanding contract. Generally, these rules require that to operate as a bar, the contract must be in writing, properly executed, and binding on the parties; it must be of definite duration and in effect for no more than 3 years; and it must also contain substantive terms and conditions of employment which in turn must be consistent with the policies of the Act.

The period during the contract term when a petition may be timely filed is ordinarily calculated from the expiration date of the agreement. A petition is timely when filed not more than 90 nor less than 60 days before the terminal date of an outstanding contract. Thus, a petition which is filed during the last 60 days of a valid contract will be considered untimely and will be dismissed. During this 60 day "insulated" period, the parties to the existing contract are free to execute a new or amended agreement without the intrusion of a rival petition, but if no agreement is reached or if the agreement which is reached does not constitute a bar itself, then a petition filed after the expiration of the old valid contract will be timely and entertained. In addition, the Board's contract-bar rules do not permit the parties to an existing collective-bargaining relationship to avoid this filing period by executing an amendment or new contract term which prematurely extends the date of expiration of that contract. In the event of such premature extension, the new contract ordinarily will not bar an election.

Notes

1. *Contracts with Automatic Renewal Clauses*—A three-year labor contract with an automatic renewal clause did function as a contract barring a rival union's election petition that was not filed during the open period, but instead three weeks after the automatic renewal date. The majority found this an unremarkable application of precedent because automatic renewal provisions have long been held adequate for contract bar purposes. The dissenting Board member complained that there was no document to which third parties could look to determine whether the contract had ended or renewed itself. *ALJUD Licensed Home Care Servs.*, 345 N.L.R.B. 1089 (2005).

2. *Contractual Defects*—A contract containing an illegal clause may not function as a bar to an election petition, especially when the offending clause touches on issues of representation or union membership. For example, in *Paragon Products Corp.*, 134 N.L.R.B. 662, 666 (1961), the Board said:

> [W]e now hold that only those contracts containing a union-security provision which is clearly unlawful on its face, or which has been found to be unlawful in an unfair labor practice proceeding, may not bar a representation petition. A clearly unlawful union-security provision for this purpose is one which by its express terms clearly and unequivocally goes beyond the limited form of union-security permitted by §8(a)(3) of the act, and is therefore incapable of a lawful interpretation. Such unlawful provisions include (1) those which expressly and unambiguously require the employer to give preference to union members (a) in hiring, (b) in laying off, or (c) for purpose of seniority; (2) those which specifically withhold from incumbent nonmembers and/or new employees the statutory 30-day grace period; and (3) those which expressly require as a condition of continued employment

the payment of sums of money other than periodic dues and initiation fees uniformly required.

A similar result may be found in *Pioneer Bus Co.*, 140 N.L.R.B. 54 (1962), where an employer met separately with representatives of white and black workers and executed separate contracts with each. Although the contractual terms were substantially the same, the Board held that this separate representational treatment along racial lines prevented the contracts from standing as a bar to a new election. The Board stated: "Consistent with clear court decisions in other contexts which condemn government sanctioning of racially separate groupings as inherently discriminatory, the Board will not permit its contract bar rules to be utilized to shield contracts such as those here involved from the challenge of otherwise appropriate election petitions."

However, in *Food Haulers, Inc.*, 136 N.L.R.B. 394 (1962), the NLRB held that a contract stands as a bar to an election, even though it contains an illegal "hot-cargo" clause. The majority reasoned that the clause, though unlawful, does not interfere with the employees' choice of bargaining representative or with any other objective of contract-bar rules, and the setting aside of the entire contract as an election bar on a finding of an unlawful hot-cargo clause constitutes a more drastic sanction in the representation proceeding than is permitted under the statute in unfair labor practice proceedings. *See* § 8(e) and the material in Part Four on "hot-cargo" contracts.

3. *Election and Certification Bars*—The statutory goal of stability in labor relations is also promoted by several restraints on elections that are tied to prior resolutions of representation questions. The Taft-Hartley Act, for example, added § 9(c)(3), which prohibits the Board from holding a new election within one year of a valid election for the same bargaining unit. This statutory "election bar" is supplemented by the long-standing, judicially approved "certification bar," where the Board's subsequent certification of a representative also serves as a bar for at least one year. This certification bar is important because certification sometimes occurs well after an election, especially when there are challenges to the election itself. In addition, when an employer frustrates the union's bargaining efforts for a significant portion of the certification year, the Board may extend the period for a commensurate time.

4. *Recognition Bars*—The Board also applies a voluntary recognition bar to elections when an employer recognizes a union based on its claim of majority support. The recognition bar period is more flexible than the election and certification bar period, but generally lasts for at least six months from the time of recognition.

In *Dana Corp.*, 351 N.L.R.B. 434 (2007), a closely divided Labor Board announced a new rule with respect to the right of employees to challenge employer grants of voluntary recognition. Employees would have 45 days after voluntary recognition has been granted to file a decertification petition challenging such action. The Board further indicated that the traditional contract bar doctrine would be suspended during this 45-day period to allow the filing of a decertification petition even if a first contract has already been negotiated. A few years later, the Labor Board overruled *Dana Corp.* in *Lamons Gasket Co.*, 357 N.L.R.B. 739 (2011), and returned to the traditional rule providing newly recognized labor organizations with a "reasonable period of time" to negotiate a first contract before it would entertain any decertification petition. More recently, however, the Labor Board issued a series of amendments to its representation election rules in which it rejected *Lamons Gasket* and reinstated the *Dana Corp.* approach that would allow employees or rival labor organizations to challenge the validity of voluntary recognitions for up to 45 days following such recognitions. 85 Fed. Reg. 18366, April 1, 2020 (effective June 1, 2020).

The Labor Board early on developed a practice of dismissing an election petition if substantial unfair labor practice charges affecting the unit have been filed and are unresolved—such charges are referred to as "blocking charges." *See U.S. Coal & Coke*, 3 N.L.R.B. 398 (1937) (dismissing decertification petition until unfair labor practice charges affecting the unit were resolved); NLRB, Casehandling Manual ¶ 11730 (2017) (describing blocking charge procedure). In 2020, however, the Labor Board amended its representation election rules to replace the blocking charge policy with either a vote-and-count or a vote-and-impound procedure. Thus, rather than delaying the election until the unfair labor practices are resolved, the election is held, the ballots are counted or impounded, and the results held until the charges are resolved. 85 Fed. Reg. 18366, April 1, 2020 (effective June 1, 2020).

B. Defining the Appropriate Unit

Blue Man Vegas, LLC v. NLRB

United States Court of Appeals for the District of Columbia Circuit
529 F.3d 417 (D.C. Cir. 2008)

GINSBURG, *Circuit Judge*:

Blue Man Vegas, LLC (BMV) petitions for review of the National Labor Relations Board's decision that it engaged in unfair labor practices by refusing to bargain with the International Alliance of Theatrical Stage Employees, Moving Picture Technicians, Artists & Allied Crafts of the United States, Its Territories & Canada, AFL-CIO (the Union), elected to represent certain of its employees. BMV argues the Board erred in holding the bargaining unit proposed by the Union was appropriate. We deny Blue Man's petition and grant the Board's cross-application for enforcement.

I. Background

BMV manages and produces the Las Vegas production of the *Blue Man Group*, a theatrical show in which men wearing blue grease paint on their faces and heads and dressed entirely in black perform a series of skits and dance routines involving music, props, and videos. On stage with the "Blue Men" are seven musicians. The Blue Men and the musicians are assisted by a stage crew comprising seven departments: audio; carpentry; electrics; properties (props); video; wardrobe; and musical instrument technicians (MITs), who maintain the musical instruments, many of which are unique to *Blue Man Group* productions. There are also a handful of so-called "swings," who BMV explains are "trained in numerous departments to provide coverage . . . as needed due to vacation or illness." During a performance, each of the seven stage crews performs its own "cue tracks," which are series of carefully planned actions. For example, a carpentry crew's cue tracks might involve placing and moving scenic backdrops at specified times.

From 2000 through most of 2005, BMV performed at the Luxor Hotel and Casino. During that time, BMV employed the MITs directly, but the Luxor employed the members of the other stage crews, as to whom it entered into a collective bargaining agreement with the Union. As a result, there were differences in the terms and conditions of employment of the MITs and of the other crews. The MITs reported to BMV's Production Manager, John McInnis, whereas the other stage crews reported to the Luxor; the MITs were paid a salary whereas the others were paid an hourly wage; and the MITs' pre-performance sign-in sheet was separate from the sign-in sheet for the others.

In September 2005, BMV left the Luxor and reopened a month later at the Venetian Hotel and Casino. Incident to the move, BMV decided to employ the entire stage crew directly. To handle its many new stage crew employees, BMV erected a new management structure. A department head would supervise the employees in each of the six departments that previously reported to the Luxor, and the "technical supervisor" would supervise the six new department heads and report to McInnis.

Although the employees in all seven stage crew departments were now employed directly by BMV, several differences between the MITs and the other crews were carried over from the Luxor to the Venetian. First, whereas the others were separated from McInnis, the production manager, by two levels of supervision (a department head and the technical supervisor), the MITs continued to report directly to McInnis. Second, the two MITs who had been with BMV at the Luxor were still paid a salary, whereas the members of the other crews were paid a wage, as they had been at the Luxor. (The four MITs hired after BMV left the Luxor were paid a wage, however.) Finally, the MITs' sign-in sheet remained separate from the sign-in sheet for the other crews.

In March 2006, the Union petitioned the Board for a representation election in a unit comprising all stage crew employees except the MITs. BMV objected that the MITs should be included in the bargaining unit. After a hearing, the Board's Regional Director (RD) determined, pursuant to § 9(b) of the National Labor Relations Act, 29 U.S.C. § 159(b), that the unit proposed by the Union was an appropriate unit and ordered a representation election. The RD found significant the differences between the MITs and the other stage crews that stemmed from the prior unit's bargaining history, namely, those relating to supervision, form of payment, and sign-in sheets. He also found significant a number of differences that cannot be attributed to BMV's time at the Luxor: The MITs have separate substitutes during days off and vacations, "skills separate from the other stage crew members," and different cue tracks; they "do not 'swing' to other stage crew positions"; and they "work in different areas" and "interact[]" primarily "with musicians, not stage crew members." The Board denied BMV's petition for review of the RD's decision.

The Union won the ensuing representation election by a vote of 20-14 and the RD duly certified the Union as the exclusive bargaining representative. About a month later, the RD issued a complaint against BMV alleging it had refused to bargain with the Union, in violation of § 8(a)(1) and (5) of the NLRA, 29 U.S.C. § 158(a)(1) & (5). BMV argued it was not required to bargain because the exclusion of the MITs rendered the unit inappropriate. Finding BMV had raised or could have raised all issues relating to representation in the prior unit determination hearing and BMV did not proffer any previously unavailable evidence, the Board granted summary judgment for the General Counsel. BMV then petitioned for review in this court and the Board cross-applied for enforcement of its decision.

II. Analysis

BMV challenges the Board's decision that its refusal to bargain was an unfair labor practice on the ground that the unit was not appropriate. . . .

BMV advances three arguments: The Board applied the wrong standard to determine whether the proposed unit was appropriate; the unit determination was not supported by substantial evidence; and the exclusion of the MITs from the proposed unit created a "disfavored residual unit." None is persuasive.

A. The Unit Determination Standard

BMV's primary argument is that the Board applied a standard for the unit determination that conflicts with the NLRA and has been, for that reason, rejected by the Fourth Circuit. BMV's position, although superficially plausible, is based upon a misapprehension of the framework governing unit determinations.

The Board's principal concern in evaluating a proposed bargaining unit is whether the employees share a "community of interest." *NLRB v. Action Auto., Inc.*, 469 U.S. 490, 494, 105 S. Ct. 984, 83 L. Ed. 2d 986 (1985); *see also Agri Processor Co., Inc. v. NLRB*, 379 U.S. App. D.C. 318, 514 F.3d 1, 8–9 (D.C. Cir. 2008). "There is no hard and fast definition or an inclusive or exclusive listing of the factors to consider [under the community-of-interest standard]. Rather, unit determinations must be made only after weighing all relevant factors on a case-by-case basis." *Country Ford Trucks*, 229 F.3d at 1190–91 (quotation marks, citations, and ellipsis omitted). Those factors include whether, in distinction from other employees, the employees in the proposed unit have "different methods of compensation, hours of work, benefits, supervision, training and skills; if their contact with other employees is infrequent; if their work functions are not integrated with those of other employees; and if they have historically been part of a distinct bargaining unit." *Trident Seafoods, Inc. v. NLRB*, 322 U.S. App. D.C. 1, 101 F.3d 111, 118 n.11 (D.C. Cir. 1996); *see also Agri Processor*, 514 F.3d at 9 (collecting factors); *NLRB v. Lundy Packing Co. (Lundy II)*, 68 F.3d 1577, 1580 (4th Cir. 1995) (listing factors). And, although the NLRA provides "the extent to which the employees have organized shall not be controlling," 29

246   3 · REPRESENTATION QUESTIONS

U.S.C. §159(c)(5), the Supreme Court has held that the extent of their organization may be "consider[ed] ... as one factor" in determining whether a proposed unit is appropriate. *NLRB v. Metro. Life Ins. Co.*, 380 U.S. 438, 442, 85 S. Ct. 1061, 13 L. Ed. 2d 951 (1965).

Decisions of the Board and of the courts in unit determination cases generally conform to a consistent analytic framework. If the employees in the proposed unit share a community of interest, then the unit is *prima facie* appropriate. In order successfully to challenge that unit, the employer must do more than show there is another appropriate unit because "more than one appropriate bargaining unit logically can be defined in any particular factual setting." *Country Ford Trucks*, 229 F.3d at 1189 (quotation marks omitted). Rather, as the Board emphasizes, the employer's burden is to show the *prima facie* appropriate unit is "truly inappropriate." *Id.* at 1189; *Dunbar Armored, Inc. v. NLRB*, 186 F.3d 844, 847 (7th Cir. 1999) ("clearly inappropriate") (quotation marks omitted); *see also Serramonte Oldsmobile, Inc. v. NLRB*, 318 U.S. App. D.C. 153, 86 F.3d 227, 236 (D.C. Cir. 1996) (the Board "need only select *an* appropriate unit, not *the most* appropriate unit") (quotation marks omitted).

A unit is truly inappropriate if, for example, there is no legitimate basis upon which to exclude certain employees from it. That the excluded employees share a community of interest with the included employees does not, however, mean there may be no legitimate basis upon which to exclude them; that follows apodictically from the proposition that there may be more than one appropriate bargaining unit. If, however, the excluded employees share an overwhelming community of interest with the included employees, then there is no legitimate basis upon which to exclude them from the bargaining unit. We held in *Trident Seafoods*, for example, the Board's unit determination was "irrational" and "unsupported by substantial evidence" because the employer had adduced unrebutted evidence showing that "the functional integration of the overwhelming similarities between the [excluded] and [included employees] are such that neither group can be said to have any separate community of interest justifying a separate bargaining unit." 101 F.3d at 120; *see also Jewish Hosp. Ass'n*, 223 N.L.R.B. 614, 617 (1976) (unit limited to service employees inappropriate because of "overwhelming community of interest" with maintenance employees); *Lodgian, Inc.*, 332 N.L.R.B. 1246, 1255 (2000) (RD required inclusion in unit of employees who "share an overwhelming community of interest with the employees whom the [union] seeks to represent").

A Venn diagram may clarify these principles. Each rectangle represents the interests of a group of identically situated employees. The region in which two or more rectangles overlap represents the degree to which those groups have common interests. In *Figure 1*, Rectangles A, B, and C all overlap because all the groups have a community of interest with each other. Consequently, any combination of the groups—AB, AC, BC, or ABC—is a *prima facie* appropriate bargaining unit. Note, however, that Rectangles A and B overlap almost completely; this indicates they have an overwhelming community of interest. Any unit that includes one but excludes the other is "truly inappropriate." Therefore, the only units that could be deemed appropriate in the face of a challenge are AB and ABC.

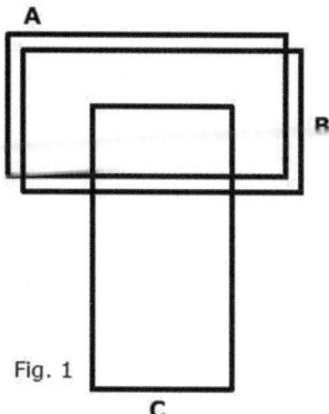

Fig. 1

BMV contends the Board applied the wrong standard in making its unit determination, effectively "accord[ing] controlling weight to the Union's extent of organization," in violation of § 9(c)(5) of the NLRA. According to BMV, the Board erred in basing its decision upon *Lundy Packing Co. (Lundy I)*, 314 N.L.R.B. 1042, 1043–44 (1994), in which the Board upheld the unit proposed by the union, thereby "fail[ing] to heed" the Fourth Circuit's subsequent refusal to enforce that decision, which BMV says rested on the ground that the overwhelming-community-of-interest standard unlawfully gives controlling weight to the union's extent of organization.

BMV's reading of *Lundy II* and of the Board's decision in this case reflect a misapprehension of the governing framework just described, as well as a misreading of the Fourth Circuit's opinion. In effect, BMV contends that, as long as the MITs had a community of interest to any degree with the other stage crews, they could not be excluded from the bargaining unit. That view is obviously at odds with the principles discussed above.

Lundy II, on the other hand, is consistent with the framework set out above. The Fourth Circuit there objected to the combination of the overwhelming-community-of-interest standard and the presumption the Board had employed in favor of the proposed unit: "By presuming the union-proposed unit proper unless there is 'an overwhelming community of interest' with excluded employees, the Board effectively accorded controlling weight to the extent of union organization." *Lundy II*, 68 F.3d at 1581. As long as the Board applies the overwhelming community-of-interest standard only after the proposed unit has been shown to be *prima facie* appropriate, the Board does not run afoul of the statutory injunction that the extent of the union's organization not be given controlling weight.

Here, the Board correctly applied the overwhelming-community-of-interest standard; it did not presume the Union's proposed unit was valid, as it had done in *Lundy I*. Rather, the RD first determined "[t]he record ... establishes that the petitioned-for unit, which excludes MITs, is an appropriate unit for collective bargaining"; indeed, he noted, "the parties have never contended" otherwise. The RD then went on to apply the overwhelming-community-of-interest standard to determine whether BMV had shown the exclusion of the MITs rendered the proposed unit truly inappropriate. As the Board says, the RD cited *Lundy I* to support the generally correct proposition that "a unit need not be an all-inclusive unit in order to be an appropriate unit," and then looked to that decision for guidance as to the "factors" to be considered in deciding whether the two groups of employees have an overwhelming community of interest. The Board's use of the overwhelming-community-of-interest standard, therefore, did not give controlling weight to the extent of the Union's organization.

B. Substantial Evidence

BMV contends the Board's finding that the proposed bargaining unit was appropriate was not supported by substantial evidence. . . .

BMV launches its challenge to the evidence upon which the Board relied by isolating the differences that "are holdovers from the Luxor," namely, the different supervisory structure, separate sign-in sheets, and salary versus wage compensation. BMV characterizes these differences as matters of "bargaining history," and then ties the bargaining history to the "extent of organization," thus: "The Regional Director reache[d] beyond the parties in this case and relie[d] on an IATSE contract with a completely different employer [i.e., the Luxor]. This bargaining history is not relevant to this analysis except to demonstrate the Union's extent of organization."

We need not decide whether BMV correctly equates bargaining history with extent of organization in the circumstances of this case because this line of argument still would fail for two reasons. First, the differences between the MITs and the other stage crew employees that are "holdovers from the Luxor" are not merely of historical interest; they are present facts the Board could reasonably conclude differentiate the employment interests of the MITs from those of the other crews. As the Board rather forcefully puts it, "the ... suggestion ... that the Board should have ignored the terms and conditions of employment that [BMV] intentionally carried over from the Luxor is absurd." Second, in light of the numerous differences that are not "holdovers from the Luxor," the Board cannot be said to have given controlling weight to bargaining history nor, if it is the same thing on the present facts, to the Union's extent of organization.

As for those differences that do not stem from the Luxor era, BMV maintains they do not distinguish the MITs from the employees in the other stage crews as a group, but rather distinguish the employees in each crew from the employees in every other crew. For example, BMV observes that, although the MITs have separate substitutes, so do the other stage crews because "[s]ubs do not work for more than one department." BMV makes a similar point with respect to the MITs' technical skills, cue tracks, use of swings, work space, and lack of interaction with other stage crew employees during the show. Thus, BMV argues, the Board acted arbitrarily by excluding the MITs from the unit on the basis of certain differences between the MITs and the other stage crews while at the same time ignoring the same types of differences among the various crews that were included in the unit.

We need not decide whether that would be an arbitrary or otherwise unlawful decision because that is not what the Board did. Rather, as discussed above, the Board recognized the MITs also differ from the employees in the other crews in ways that are "holdovers from the Luxor" and are therefore unique to the MITs, namely, in terms of supervision, form of payment, and sign-in sheets. The Board did not act arbitrarily by treating the MITs differently from the other stage crew employees in light of those differences.

Moreover, the Board's finding that the proposed unit was appropriate without the MITs was certainly reasonable and supported by substantial evidence in view of the analytic framework set out above. A unit comprising all the non-MIT stage crews is *prima facie* appropriate because, notwithstanding the differences among them, those employees share a community of interest. It may well be that a unit comprising all the stage crews, including the MITs, would also be *prima facie* appropriate because the MITs also share a community of interest with the other stage crew employees, but that does not necessarily render the unit comprising only the non-MIT stage crews "truly inappropriate." Indeed, both the differences that are unique to the MITs and the differences that can be found among all the stage crews stand in BMV's way: The MITs lack an overwhelming community of interest with the other stage crews (just as each of the non-MIT crews may lack an overwhelming community of interest with each of the other non-MIT crews).

To illustrate, in *Figure 2* Rectangle M represents the interests of the MITs, while Rectangles X and Y represent the interests of the employees in any two other departments. The shaded regions represent interests relating to subs, technical skills, cue tracks, swings, work space, and interaction with members of other stage crews during the show, that is, factors with respect to which each department has (we assume) different interests. The spotted regions represent interests relating to supervision, sign-in sheets, and form of payment, that is, factors carried over from the Luxor, which distinguish the MITs from the employees in all the other stage crew departments. The Board in effect found Unit XY appropriate. As the diagram shows, the Board was justified in doing so, though it could also have found Unit XYM appropriate because all three rectangles overlap, reflecting a community of interest among them, as represented by the cross-hatched region. Unlike Rectangles A and B in *Figure 1*, however, Rectangle M does not have a nearly complete overlap with any other rectangle, reflecting the MITs' lack of an overwhelming community of interest with any of the other stage crews. Consequently, the exclusion of Rectangle M from a unit comprising Rectangles X and Y—that is, the exclusion of the MITs from the unit comprising the other stage crew employees—does not render that unit "truly inappropriate," notwithstanding the substantial differences among the stage crew employees, as represented by the shaded and spotted regions.

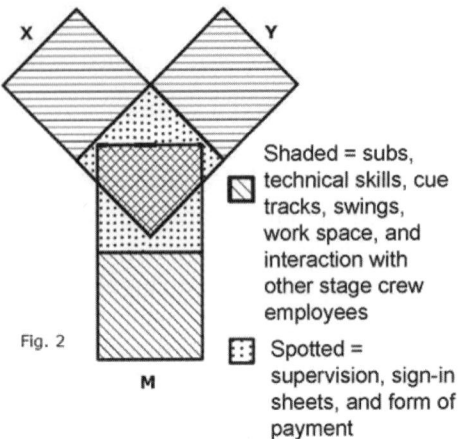

Fig. 2

Shaded = subs, technical skills, cue tracks, swings, work space, and interaction with other stage crew employees

Spotted = supervision, sign-in sheets, and form of payment

Turning from the facts to the law, BMV claims the Board's finding that the MITs do not share an overwhelming community of interest with the other stage crews conflicts with the Fourth Circuit's analysis in *Lundy II* and with the Board's analysis in *Studio 54*, 260 N.L.R.B. 1200 (1982). As BMV notes, "the Board cannot ignore its own relevant precedent but must explain why it is not controlling." *Lemoyne-Owen College v. NLRB*, 360 U.S. App. D.C. 40, 357 F.3d 55, 60 (D.C. Cir. 2004) (quotation marks omitted). We find the Board's decision consistent with both *Lundy II* and *Studio 54* because neither case involved differences as extensive as here.

. . . .

C. Residual Unit

Finally, BMV contends the Board's decision is arbitrary and capricious because it creates an allegedly "disfavored residual unit." According to BMV, a residual unit consists of excluded employees "sharing a of interest with the [included] employees." Thus, BMV argues, because the MITs "shar[e] an obvious community of interest" with the other stage crew departments, the Board improperly created a residual unit of MITs by excluding them from the unit.

BMV's supposed rule against residual units is misconceived. It implies that all employees who share a community of interest must be included in the same unit, which proposition conflicts with the principle that more than one bargaining unit may be appropriate in any particular setting. *See, e.g., Country Ford Trucks*, 229 F.3d at 1189–91 (holding that although "broader unit encompassing all parts and service department employees at both facilities" may have been appropriate, Board not " *required*" to include all such employees in unit in light of differences between facilities). In any event, the Board's residual unit policy has no bearing upon this case because it relates only to whether a proposed residual unit is appropriate, not to whether a proposed initial unit is appropriate. See *Carl Buddig & Co.*, 328 N.L.R.B. 929, 930 (1999).

III. Conclusion

In sum, we hold the Board applied the correct legal standard to determine whether the proposed bargaining unit was appropriate. The Board's determination that the MI1's may be excluded from the bargaining unit because they do not share an overwhelming community of interest with the stage crew employees included in the unit is supported by substantial evidence and does not conflict with precedent or the Board's residual unit policy. We therefore deny BMV's petition for review and grant the Board's cross-application for enforcement.

So ordered.

Notes

1. *Community of Interest Standard*—As explained by the court in *Blue Man Vegas*, the overriding inquiry in the unit determination analysis is whether the employees share a "community of interest," which is determined by weighing all relevant factors on a case-by-case basis. The factors include consideration of whether the employees in the proposed unit have different methods of compensation, hours of work, benefits, supervision, training, and skills than employees excluded from the unit; whether their contact with other employees is infrequent; whether their work functions are separated from those of other employees or integrated; and whether they have historically been part of a distinct bargaining unit. If the Board concludes that the employees share a community of interest, the unit is "*prima facie* appropriate." The employer may rebut the unit only by showing that the unit is "truly inappropriate"—merely showing that there is another appropriate bargaining unit will not suffice because more than one unit is logically possible in most settings.

2. *Acute Care Hospitals*—In 1989, the Board promulgated a rule that provides that "[e]xcept in extraordinary circumstances and in circumstances in which there are existing non-conforming units," a total of eight bargaining units "shall be appropriate units" in private acute care hospitals. The eight units are: all registered nurses; all physicians; all other professionals; all technical employees; all skilled maintenance employees; all business office clerical employees; all guards; and all nonprofessional employees except for those in the preceding four categories. The Supreme Court upheld the rule in *American Hospital Association v. NLRB*, 499 U.S. 606 (1991).

3. *Non-Acute Healthcare Facilities, Retail Settings, Universities, and Other Contexts*—In *Specialty Healthcare & Rehabilitation Ctr. of Mobile*, 357 N.L.R.B. 934 (2011), *enforced sub nom. Kindred Nursing Centers East LLC*, 727 F.3d 552 (6th Cir. 2013), the Obama Board held that the "community of interest" standard applied to determine appropriate bargaining units in non-acute healthcare facilities. Under this standard, the Board would first determine whether the employees in the petitioned-for unit are "readily identifiable as a distinct group," and whether they share a community of interest using traditional criteria. If the Board concluded that the unit sought was appropriate, the proponent of any larger unit was required to establish that the employees it proposed to include shared an "overwhelming community of interest" with the workers covered by the petition.

The *Specialty Healthcare* standard was subsequently applied in other contexts, including retail stores. In *Macy's, Inc. v. NLRB*, 824 F.3d 557 (5th Cir. 2016), *cert. denied*, 137 S. Ct. 2265 (2017), the court held that the Labor Board has broad discretion when determining the scope of bargaining units, and sustained the Board's application of its *Specialty Healthcare* test in a retail setting. The Board's certification of a unit of cosmetics and fragrances employees and its rejection of a "wall-to-wall" unit of all employees in the store or alternatively all selling employees was thus appropriate. There was little evidence of interchange between the cosmetics and fragrances employees and other selling employees at the department store in question, and the department was organized as a separate department supervised by a separate sales manager and located in a distinct area of the store. Seven other circuit courts subsequently upheld the Board's *Specialty Healthcare* test, which came to be known as the "micro unit" test. *See Rhino Northwest, LLC v. NLRB*, 867 F.3d 95 (D.C. Cir. 2017) (approving the test as a reasonable formulation drawn from Board precedent and citing decisions to the same effect from the Second, Third, Fourth, Sixth, Seventh, and Eighth Circuits). The test was also used to justify organizing of graduate students in a university on a department-by-department basis rather than university-wide. *See Yale Univ.*, N.L.R.B. No. 01-RC-183014, Jan. 17, 2017 (election order permitting graduate students in nine academic departments to organize as individual bargaining units). Even under this standard, there remained, of course, limits on the Board's discretion. *See, e.g., NLRB v. Tito Contractors, Inc.*, 847 F.3d 724 (D.C. Cir. 2017) (setting aside Board's certification of company-wide unit where the business was comprised of two discrete halves, consisting of a labor side and a recycling side, and Board failed to consider the lack of interchange between the two groups and significant differences regarding the wages, hours, and working conditions between the two groups).

However, in *PCC Structurals, Inc.*, 365 N.L.R.B. No. 160 (2017), the Trump Board overruled *Specialty Healthcare* and rejected the micro-unit standard, setting aside a regional director's decision to allow a union to limit an election to 100 welding employees at a manufacturing company with a workforce of more than 2,500. On remand, the regional director was instructed to apply the traditional community-of-interest test utilized prior to 2011, which entails considering the interests of all employees, within and without the proposed unit, without regard for whether they possess an overwhelming community of interests. In *The Boeing Company*, 368 N.L.R.B. No. 67 (2019), the Board applied and clarified the traditional community of interests test that it had announced in *PCC Structurals*. The Board will consider: (1) whether the members of the petitioned-for unit share a community of interest, (2) whether the employees excluded from the unit have meaningfully distinct interests in the collective bargaining context that outweigh their similarities with unit members, and (3) any guidelines the Board has established for appropriate unit configurations in particular industries.

4. *Joint Employers*—Over the past several decades, many firms have obtained the continued services of "perma-temps" from separate employment companies. In *Browning-Ferris Indus. of Calif.*, 362 N.L.R.B. 1599 (2015), a closely divided Labor Board decided to adopt a new test to determine when such arrangements should lead to findings of joint employer relationships requiring the borrowing and lending firms to negotiate jointly with labor organizations selected as bargaining representatives for the workers in question.

> The Board may find that two or more entities are joint employers of a single work force if they are both employers within the meaning of the common law, and if they share or codetermine those matters governing the essential terms and conditions of employment. In evaluating the allocation and exercise of control in the workplace, we will consider the various ways in which joint employers may "share" control over the terms and conditions of employment or "codetermine" them, as the Board and courts have done in the past.

Browning-Ferris obtained recycling services from Leadpoint Business Services. Although Leadpoint controlled the recruitment, hiring, disciplining, and scheduling of such persons, Browning-Ferris exercised meaningful control over the way they performed their work through directives given to Leadpoint supervisors. As a result, the three-member majority found these two firms to be joint employers of the workers in question. The two dissenting members said that the majority approach was wholly inconsistent with prior rulings finding such workers to only be employees of the firm that controlled their hiring, work, and discipline.

In late 2018, a divided D.C. Circuit upheld the Board's *Browning-Ferris Industries of Calif.* approach, but found that the Board had failed to apply those standards properly. The court held that the Board did not properly distinguish between forms of indirect control that affect "workers' essential terms and conditions" and those that are "intrinsic to ordinary third-party contracting relationships." *Browning-Ferris Industries of Calif. v. NLRB*, 911 F.3d 1195 (D.C. Cir. 2018). However, in *McDonald's USA LLC*, 368 N.L.R.B. No. 134 (2019), a closely divided Labor Board held that McDonald's USA could not be held jointly liable with several of its franchises for violations committed by those franchises, since there was no evidence that McDonald's USA exercised any "direct and immediate control" over the franchise employees. And in February 2020, the Labor Board issued a new joint employer rule requiring a firm to exercise "substantial, direct, and immediate" control over the important elements of a worker's job, like hiring, firing, and discipline, before it can be considered a joint employer with the primary company involved. 85 Fed. Reg. 11184 (Feb. 26, 2020).

5. *Professional Employees and Craft Units* — In deciding each case on its own facts, as it must do, the Board is vested with broad discretion, but its discretion in certain instances is limited by some restrictions put in place by the Taft-Hartley amendments. Some of these restrictions we've seen before — "supervisors" and "independent contractors" are expressly excluded from the definition of "employees" covered by the act, and thus may not be included in a bargaining unit. In addition, several new provisos were added to §9 that dictate conditions affecting the unit placement of particular kinds of employees. Two of those provisos address how the Board may approach the issues that arise with respect to the placement of more highly educated or skilled employees into broader units. Section 9(b)(1) prohibits the Board from including both professional and nonprofessional employees in the same unit without approval from a majority of the professional employees. In a somewhat similar vein, §9(b)(2) provides that the Board cannot find a proposed craft unit to be inappropriate because another, more inclusive unit had already been found to be appropriate unless a majority of employees in the proposed craft unit vote against separate representation.

6. *Guards* — Section 9(b)(3) provides that no labor organization shall be certified as the representative of employees in a bargaining unit of guards if it admits to membership, or is affiliated with any organization that admits to membership, employees other than guards. Although the Labor Board previously permitted such a mixed organization to intervene in a representation proceeding and be on the ballot with an all-guard petitioning union, it has rejected this approach and no longer allows a mixed organization to intervene in an election proceeding pertaining to a guard unit. *See University of Chicago*, 272 N.L.R.B. 873 (1984).

In *Loomis Armored US, Inc.*, 364 N.L.R.B. No. 23 (2016), the Labor Board held that an employer that voluntarily recognizes a "mixed guard union" must continue to recognize and bargain with that union until it has evidence the labor organization has lost its majority support. The Board majority indicated that once an employer grants voluntary recognition to a union, it must continue to recognize that organization until the union has actually lost its majority support.

In *Bellagio, LLC v. NLRB*, 863 F.3d 839 (D.C. Cir. 2017), the court held that an employer that operates a hotel and casino did not unlawfully refuse to bargain with a union certified by the Labor Board as the representative of surveillance technicians in a unit that included non-guard employees. Since the surveillance technicians maintain comprehensive camera footage of resorts and control access to all sensitive areas of casinos, they constitute "guards" under Section 9(b)(3) of the NLRA and cannot be included in units with non-guard employees.

Although armored car drivers who carry valuable customer goods and are trained to protect those goods with weapons they are authorized to carry are considered "guards" under §9(b)(3), unarmed courier-guards who merely transport customer property and who receive minimal training with respect to the protection of that property do not constitute statutory "guards." *Purolator Courier Corp.*, 300 N.L.R.B. 812 (1990).

7. *Extent of Organization* — Although § 9(c)(5) states that "the extent to which the employees have organized shall not be controlling," this does not prevent the Board from determining a unit that coincides with the extent of union organizing, if that unit is found to be appropriate when other factors are considered. It only prohibits reliance on the extent of organization as the *controlling factor*. See, e.g., Overnite Transp. Co. v. NLRB, 294 F.3d 615 (4th Cir. 2002).

1. Multiple Plant Units

NLRB, Seventeenth Annual Report
68–69 (1952)

When dealing with employees of companies which operate more than one plant, the Board must frequently determine whether an employer-wide unit, or a less comprehensive one, is appropriate. In making such determinations, the Board must take into consideration all relevant factors, but it is precluded by the act from determining the scope of the unit solely on the basis of the extent to which the company's employees have organized. This statutory limitation sometimes is invoked in opposition to a less than company-wide unit. On this point, the Board has repeatedly held that it is precluded only from giving *controlling* weight to extent of organization, but not from taking the present extent of the employees' organization into consideration together with other pertinent circumstances. In cases where extent of organization was the only basis for the proposed unit, the Board has consistently rejected the unit.

Principal factors considered in cases where multiplant units are proposed include: (1) bargaining history, (2) the extent of interchange and contacts between employees in the various plants, (3) the extent of functional integration of operations between the plants, (4) differences in the products of the plants or in the skills and types of work required, (5) the centralization, or lack of centralization, of management and supervision, particularly in regard to labor relations and the power to hire and discharge, and (6) the physical or geographical location of the plants in relation to each other.

In most cases, several of these factors are present — some pointing to the appropriateness of a multiplant unit, others pointing to the appropriateness of a narrower unit. In each case, the Board must weigh all the factors present, one against the other, in deciding the proper scope of the unit. However, in certain industries, company-wide or multiplant units are generally favored. Foremost among such industries are public utilities, such as power, telephone, and gas companies, where it has long been the Board's policy to establish system-wide or multiplant units whenever feasible. This policy is based upon the highly integrated and interdependent character of public utility operations and the high degree of coordination among the employees required by the type of service rendered.

The Board similarly favors system-wide and division-wide units of employees in the transportation industry.

Note

Single-Plant versus Multiple-Plant Units—Over the years the Board has developed a presumption in favor of single-plant or single-store units in many industries. The presumption will be relied on absent "a functional integration so severe as to negate the identity" of the one-unit facility. *NLRB v. Living & Learning Centers, Inc.*, 652 F.2d 209 (5th Cir. 1981). *See also Mass. Soc'y for the Prevention of Cruelty to Children v. NLRB*, 297 F.3d 41 (1st Cir. 2002).

Where the strong local autonomy of store managers outweighed evidence of centralized management of a grocery division of Kroger Foods (d/b/a Hilander Foods), the Labor Board found that a single-store unit sought by the union was appropriate. Evidence of standardized personnel policies, centralized administrative services, and a common budget was not sufficient to overcome the Board's presumption in favor of a single-facility unit where the local store managers interviewed and hired applicants, set wages within a prescribed range, handled scheduling and vacation, handled transfers, layoffs, and recalls, meted out discipline, and could suspend or fire employees without approval from the central administration. *Hilander Foods*, 348 N.L.R.B. 1200 (2006).

2. Multiemployer Units

NLRB, Twenty-Third Annual Report
36–37 (1958)

In dealing with requests for multi-employer units, the Board is primarily guided by the rule that a single-employer unit is presumptively appropriate and that to establish a contested claim for a broader unit a controlling history of collective bargaining on such a basis by the employers and the union involved must be shown. But no controlling weight was given to multi-employer bargaining which was preceded by a long history of single-employer bargaining, was of brief duration, did not result in a written contract of substantial duration, and was not based on any Board unit finding.

The existence of a controlling multi-employer bargaining history may also depend on whether the employer group has in fact bargained jointly or on an individual basis. Generally, the Board will find that joint bargaining is established where the employers involved have for a substantial period directly participated in joint bargaining or delegated the power to bind them in collective bargaining to a joint agent, have executed the resulting contract, and have not negotiated on an individual basis. Execution of the contract by each employer separately does not preclude a finding of a multi-employer bargaining history where the employers are clearly shown to have participated in a pattern of joint bargaining.

a. Scope of Multi-Employer Unit

A multi-employer unit may include only employers who have participated in and are bound by joint negotiations. The mere adoption of a group contract by an employer who has not participated in joint bargaining directly or through an agent, or has indicated his intention not to be bound by future group negotiations, is insufficient to permit his inclusion in a proposed multi-employer unit.

b. Withdrawal from Multi-Employer Unit

A petition for a single-employer unit, in the face of a multi-employer bargaining history, will be granted if it appears that the employer involved has effectively withdrawn from the multi-employer group and has abandoned group bargaining. In order for withdrawal from multi-employer bargaining to be effective, the withdrawing party must unequivocally indicate at an appropriate time that it desires to abandon such bargaining. Pointing out in one case that the necessary stability in bargaining relations requires reasonable limits on the time and manner for withdrawal from an established multi-employer bargaining unit, the Board held that—

> The decision to withdraw must contemplate a sincere abandonment, with relative permanency, of the multi-employer unit and the embracement of a different course of bargaining on an individual-employer basis. The element of good faith is a necessary requirement in any such decision to withdraw, because of the unstabilizing and disrupting effect on multi-employer collective bargaining which would result if such withdrawal were permitted to be lightly made.

A majority of the Board also believed that the issues raised in this case justified establishment of "specific ground rules" governing the withdrawal from multi-employer bargaining units in future cases. Noting particularly that insurance of stability in multi-employer bargaining relationships requires limitations on the timing of withdrawals, the majority announced that hereafter—

> [The Board] would ... refuse to permit the withdrawal of an employer or a union from a duly established multi-employer bargaining unit, except upon adequate written notice given prior to the date set by the contract for modification, or to the agreed-upon date to begin the multi-employer negotiations. Where actual bargaining negotiations based on the existing multi-employer unit have begun, we would not permit, except on mutual consent, an abandonment of the unit upon which each side has committed itself to the other, absent unusual circumstances. [*Retail Associates Inc. v. Retail Clerks International Association Locals Nos. 128 and 633*, 120 N.L.R.B. 388 (1958).]

Charles D. Bonanno Linen Service, Inc. v. NLRB, 454 U.S. 404, 102 S. Ct. 720, 70 L. Ed. 2d 656 (1982). Bonanno Linen Service, Inc., was a member of a linen supply association, consisting of 10 employers, that negotiated as a multiemployer unit with Teamsters Local No. 25. The union and the Association held 10 bargaining sessions during March and April 1975, attempting to come to terms on a new contract. After the union membership rejected a contract agreed to by the Association and the union, negotiations reached an impasse over the issue of the method of compensation (the union demanded the drivers be paid on commission, while the Association insisted on continuing payment at an hourly rate). When subsequent meetings failed to break the impasse, the union began a selective strike against one member of the multiemployer unit, Bonanno. The Association responded with a lockout, and Bonanno then hired permanent replacements for its strikers and gave notice to the Association and union that it was withdrawing from the multiemployer unit. When the Association and the union reached agreement, Bonanno refused to sign the contract and denied that it was bound by its terms. The union, which had not consented to Bonanno's withdrawal from the bargaining unit, filed unfair labor practice charges. The Board, adhering to its position first enunciated in *Hi-Way Billboards, Inc.*, 206 N.L.R.B. 22 (1973), that an impasse is not such an "unusual circumstance" as to justify unilateral withdrawal from the bargaining unit, ordered Bonanno to sign and implement the contract retroactively.

The Supreme Court, expressing its view that multiemployer bargaining is beneficial for industrial harmony, adopted the Board's analysis that "an impasse is not sufficiently destructive of group bargaining to justify unilateral withdrawal," since an impasse is merely a "temporary deadlock or hiatus in negotiations which in almost all cases is eventually broken either through a change of mind or the application of economic force." Speaking for the Court, Justice White declared:

> The Board's reasons for adhering to its *Hi-Way Billboards* position are telling. They are surely adequate to survive judicial review. First, it is said that strikes and interim agreements often occur in the course of negotiations prior to impasse and that neither tactic is necessarily associated with impasse. Second, it is "vital" to understand that the Board distinguishes "between interim agreements which contemplate adherence to a final unit-wide contract and are thus not antithetical to group bargaining and individual agreements which are clearly inconsistent with, and destructive of, group bargaining." 243 N.L.R.B. at 1096....
>
> On the other hand, where the union, not content with interim agreements that expire with the execution of a unit-wide contract, executes separate agreements that will survive unit negotiations, the union has so "effectively fragmented and destroyed the integrity of the bargaining unit," *id.*, as to create an "unusual circumstance" under *Retail Associates* rules. Furthermore, the Board has held that the execution of separate agreements that would permit either the union or the employer to escape the binding effect of an agreement resulting from group bargaining is a refusal to bargain and an unfair labor practice on the part of both the union and any employer executing such an agreement. *Teamsters Union Local No. 378 (Olympia Automobile Dealers Assn.)*, 243 N.L.R.B. 1086 (1979). The remaining members of the unit thus can insist that parties remain subject to unit negotiations in accordance with their original understanding.

Chief Justice Burger and Justice Rehnquist dissented in *Bonnano*, insisting the Board had struck the wrong balance in this case. They pointed out that there was no more temporary impasse at the time of the employer's withdrawal:

> [T]he negotiations had been stalemated for more than six months, a selective strike and unit-wide lockout had kept employees away from their jobs for five months, and there were no signs that the parties would return to the bargaining table. . . . Thus, with all of the members of a multiemployer group closed down or crippled by a strike or a lockout, the union is permitted to 'divide and conquer' by coming to terms with some of the employers, allowing them to resume operations with a full staff.

Notes

1. *Notice of Withdrawal* — When an employer that has sent timely notice of its withdrawal from a multiemployer association engages in subsequent conduct that is inconsistent with its stated intent to abandon group bargaining, it may find itself bound by the newly negotiated multiemployer agreement. *See NLRB v. Hartman*, 774 F.2d 1376 (9th Cir. 1985).

2. *Union Withdrawal* — Rules governing employer withdrawal are equally applicable to unions. Since the multiemployer unit depends for its existence on the continued consent of both parties, if either party indicates in a timely and unequivocal fashion a preference for bargaining on a single-employer basis, the Board gives effect to that preference. *Detroit Newspaper Publishers Ass'n v. NLRB*, 372 F.2d 569 (6th Cir. 1967); *Publishers' Ass'n of New York City v. NLRB*, 364 F.2d 293 (2d Cir.), *cert. denied*, 385 U.S. 971 (1966). Nonetheless, the Board does allow a union to withdraw from a multiemployer unit with respect to some of the employers, while continuing multiemployer bargaining with the others. *Pacific Coast Ass'n of Pulp & Paper Mfrs.*, 163 N.L.R.B. 892 (1967). The Board noted that if the employer had made a timely bid to withdraw, it would be allowed to do so, and the union may be allowed no less a right to withdraw.

Problem

21. The following three people have petitioned for a representation election:

(a) Anna, the president of Yreka Bakery Co., has petitioned for an election for a bargaining unit comprising the company's kneaders. Anna says that she has just been approached by a representative from the Bakers' Union who claimed that it represented a majority of the kneaders and showed Anna a letter signed by a majority of the kneaders to that effect. Anna did not submit the letter or any other evidence of union support with her petition. For the past 10 years, the kneaders have been represented by another union, the Brotherhood of Breadmakers. In fact, the kneaders are currently covered by a two-year collective bargaining agreement negotiated by the Brotherhood that will expire 75 days from now.

[Margin note: Not a covered dispute? Domestic workers?]

(b) Bertha, a representative from the United Federation of Homecare Workers, has petitioned for an election for a multiemployer bargaining unit. The union seeks to represent a unit consisting of the 50 home healthcare aides that work for wealthy families in Highland Park, Texas. Bertha presented the Regional Office with signed authorization cards from 40 of the aides. The aides have been represented by the Federation for 15 years. In that time, the Federation has had a good relationship with all of the families, and has successfully bargained with the families through their agent, a homeowners' association. That bargaining has produced five, three-year contracts over the last 15 years, the last of which expired a month ago.

[Margin note: Bd can hold election for decert based on rival union's petition if filed 45 days after recognition; deadline passed here (Dana Corp.)]

(c) Celia, a representative from the Auto Care Workers Union (ACWU), has petitioned for an election for a bargaining unit comprised of the 30 workers at Gleam Machine, a large car wash establishment. She brought signed union membership cards from 20 of the workers. For years, the workers were unrepresented. But about six months ago, two unions—ACWU and the Brotherhood of Auto Detailers (BAD), started organizing campaigns at the car wash. Two months ago, BAD approached the president of Gleam Machine with signed union membership cards from 16 of the workers and asked for recognition. The president voluntarily recognized BAD that very afternoon, but the president and BAD have not yet started negotiating a new contract, nor has either informed the Board or the workers of the grant of recognition.

May the Board move forward on these petitions and hold an election? What additional information might help you answer this question with respect to each petition?

C. The Conduct of Representation Elections

NLRB, Thirty-First Annual Report
59, 61–65 (1966)

Section 9(c)(1) of the act provides that if, upon a petition filed, a question of representation exists, the Board must resolve it through an election by secret ballot. The election details are left to the Board. Such matters as voting eligibility, timing of elections, and standards of election conduct are subject to rules laid down in the Board's Rules and Regulations and in its decisions. Board elections are conducted in accordance with strict standards designed to assure that the participating employees have an opportunity to determine, and to register a free and untrammeled choice in the selection of, a bargaining representative. Any party to an election who believes that the standards have not been met may file timely objections to the election with the regional director under whose supervision it was held. In that event, the regional director may, as the situation warrants, either make an administrative investigation of the objections or hold a formal hearing to develop a record as the basis for decision. If the election was held pursuant to a consent-election agreement authorizing a determination by the regional director, the regional director will then issue a decision on the objections which is final. If the election was held pursuant to a consent agreement authorizing a determination by the Board, the regional director will then issue a report on objections which is then subject to exceptions by the parties and decision by the Board. However, if the election was one directed by the Board, the regional director may (1) either make a report on the objections, subject to exceptions with the decision to be made by the Board, or (2) dispose of the issues by issuing a decision, which is then subject to limited review by the Board.

Disclosure of Names and Addresses of Eligible Employees

In fulfillment of "the Board's function to conduct elections in which employees have the opportunity to cast their ballots for or against representation under circumstances that are free not only from interference, restraint, or coercion violative of the act, but also from other elements that prevent or impede a free and reasoned choice," the Board, in the *Excelsior Underwear* case,[1] promulgated an employee name and address disclosure rule designed to facilitate campaign communications with the eligible voters and thereby assure an informed electorate. It established as a requirement applicable prospectively to all election cases[2] that within 7 days after the election has been directed or agreed upon, "the employer must file with the Regional Director an election eligibility list, containing the names and addresses of all the eligible voters. The Regional Director, in turn, shall make this information available to all parties in the case. Failure to comply with this requirement shall be grounds for setting aside the election whenever proper objections are filed." . . .

In rejecting the contention that disclosure could only be required if the union would otherwise be unable to reach the employees with its message, the Board distinguished court cases[3] which limit a union's access to employer's premises to those situations where alternative channels of communication are unavailable. It viewed those decisions as being predicated upon protection of property rights, a significant employer interest, whereas in the situation presented the employer has no such significant interest in the secrecy of employee names and addresses.

Note

The validity of the *Excelsior Underwear* "names-and-addresses" rule was sustained by the Supreme Court in *NLRB v. Wyman-Gordon Co.*, 394 U.S. 759 (1969).

---

1. [67] 156 N.L.R.B. 1236 (1966).

2. [68] The requirement not only applies to petitions for certification or decertification of representatives under §9(c)(1) of the act, but also to deauthorization elections under §9(e)(1). Due to the expedited procedure it does not apply to elections conducted pursuant to §8(b)(7)(C). It became applicable only to elections directed or consented to subsequent to 30 days from the date of the *Excelsior* decision.

3. [69] *NLRB v. Babcock & Wilcox Co.*, 351 U.S. 105 (1956); *NLRB v. United Steelworkers (NuTone, Inc.)*, 357 U.S. 357 (1958).

However, in *Bear Truss, Inc.*, 325 N.L.R.B. 1162 (1998), the Board refused to set aside an election despite 10 inaccurate addresses on an *Excelsior* list of 142 eligible voters, where the employer had prepared the list in good faith and the errors were due to the failure of employees to notify the employer of changed addresses as they were supposed to do.

NLRB, Thirty-First Annual Report
66–68 (1966)

Conduct Affecting Elections — Election Propaganda

Threats of adverse economic consequences as well as appeals to racism were alleged as a basis for objections to the election in the *Universal Mfg. Corp.* case.[4] There, the Board was called upon to evaluate the impact of antiunion election campaign propaganda originating with community groups which injected themselves into the campaign. The community members and groups, not shown to be acting as agents of the employer, were responsible for newspaper editorials, advertisements, and handbills containing appeals to racist sentiment, charges of Communist control over unions and the civil rights movement, and warnings of economic disaster to the community in the event of unionization of the plant. Applying its established standards[5] that racial propaganda will not be tolerated unless the statements are "truthful, temperate, and germane to a party's position," and do not "deliberately seek to overstress and exacerbate racial feelings by irrelevant, inflammatory appeals," the Board found that permissible bounds had been exceeded by handbills, cartoons, and newspaper editorials concerning actions and attitudes of union leaders and supporters. The matters commented on were, at best, irrelevant to the campaign and inflammatory in nature and intent. In some instances the handbills were distributed by methods which also established that "the sponsoring parties intended, not to educate or inform the employees about an issue germane to the election, but to prompt them to vote against the union 'on racial grounds alone.'"

The newspaper editorials, full-page advertisements, and handbills reiterated the themes that success of the union might cause the plant to close and would squelch any chance for industrial expansion in the area, thereby impairing employment opportunities and causing higher taxes, and in general could spell out economic hardship for employees, their families, and neighbors. The newspaper communications also contained threats of blacklisting, along with statements which linked unions, civil rights, and communism as if they were aspects of a single pernicious entity, implying that union dues would end up in Communist Party coffers. The Board found that "By appealing to the employees' sentiments as civic minded individuals, injecting the fear of personal economic loss, and playing on racial prejudice, the full-page ads, the editorials, the cartoon, and the handbill were calculated

---

4. [80] 156 N.L.R.B. 1459 (1966).
5. [81] *Sewell Mfg. Co.*, 138 N.L.R.B. 66, Twenty-Eighth Annual Report 58–59 (1963).

to convince the employees that a vote for the union meant the betrayal of the community's best interests. Faced with pressures of this sort, the employees in our opinion were inhibited from freely exercising their choice in the election." The election was therefore set aside.

Employer Talks to Employee Groups

In determining whether preelection propaganda has interfered with the holding of a free election, the Board looks not only to the content of the propaganda but also at the circumstances under which it was disseminated. One means of dissemination which may overstep permissible bounds is employer talks to groups of employees brought together in some "locus of final authority in the plant,"[6] such as a supervisor's office, under circumstances where statements made may be expected to have greater impact. In one case,[7] decided during the year, the Board overruled an objection to an election based upon the fact that the employer had held a series of meetings in the plant cafeteria attended by groups of from 10 to 14 employees to propagandize against union representation. The meetings, all held more than 24 hours before the election, were addressed by the company president and its attorney with comments limited to legitimate campaign propaganda. The Board noted that the plant cafeteria had been used for other employee meetings and activities in the past and that about 90 percent of the 400 unit employees, eligible and ineligible, were at different times called to the meetings in question. Under these circumstances, it found "insufficient basis for concluding that the Employer's action in holding group meetings constituted an isolation of a few from among the many at a locus of managerial authority in order to create an aura of special treatment to individuals, as distinguished from employees as a whole, so as to bring ... [that] conduct within the prohibition of the *General Shoe* doctrine."

Another limitation upon the circumstances under which propaganda is disseminated is the *Peerless Plywood*[8] rule prohibiting either party from making election speeches on company time to massed assemblies of employees within 24 hours before the election, even though such speeches may not be otherwise objectionable.

Notes

1. *New Election Rules* — In 2014, the Obama Board adopted new election rules by a 3-2 vote; the rules went into effect on April 14, 2015. 79 Fed. Reg. 74318. The new rules provided for the electronic filing of petitions, required employers to provide electronic copies of voter lists (including employees' personal email addresses and phone numbers), contemplated pre-election hearings held eight days after the notice of hearing is served, eliminated pre-election evidentiary hearings and requests for review, deferred decision on most issues relating to appropriateness of units and

---

6. [82] *General Shoe Corp.*, 97 N.L.R.B. 499.
7. [83] *Dempster Brothers, Inc.*, 154 N.L.R.B. 688.
8. [84] *Peerless Plywood Co.*, 107 N.L.R.B. 427, Nineteenth Annual Report 65 (1954).

voter eligibility until after the election, and required employers to provide preliminary voter eligibility lists and a statement of the employer's position the day before the hearing. Finally, the rules eliminated the mandatory 25-day waiting period between the filing of the election petition and the election. In *Associated Builders & Contractors of Texas v. NLRB*, 826 F.3d 215 (5th Cir. 2016), the court sustained the authority of the Labor Board to expedite the scheduling of representation elections by conducting such elections before considering the validity of employer objections to those elections.

The 2014 rules were designed to minimize delay, modernize and streamline procedures, and ensure transparency and fairness. Early reports from the Board suggested that the rules had significant effect: median time from petition filing to election under the new rules was 24 days, compared with 36–39 days under the old rules. Further, the Board saw a significant increase in representation case filings in the first month after the new rules went into effect — up 17% over the same period one year prior. Daily Lab. Rep. (BNA) No. 102, May 28, 2015. Union win rates overall remained nearly unchanged.

In late 2019, the Trump Board modified its procedures for representation elections by extending the deadlines that had been established during the Obama Administration. 84 Fed. Reg. 69,524 (Dec. 18, 2019). Under the new rules, the Board would suspend the holding of an election until it resolves disputes over whether a proposed bargaining unit is appropriate and it makes a determination regarding the individuals qualified to vote in the proposed election. Many aspects of the 2019 rules, however, were soon enjoined in *AFL-CIO v. NLRB*, 2020 U.S. Dist. LEXIS 99491 (D.D.C. June 7, 2020), which found that several of the more significant changes involved substantive, not procedural, rules, and thus were not exempt under the Administrative Procedure Act from the requirement that the Board go through notice-and-comment rulemaking procedures.

These continuing disputes over the Board's election procedures raise many questions. For example, many critics of the 2014 rules ask whether shortening the representation election timeframe unreasonably limits the ability of employers to exercise their §7 right to communicate anti-union messages to employees and deprive their employees of the right to hear both sides. Those rules were dubbed the "ambush" or "quickie" election rules by critics, who believe that shortening the time between the filing of an election petition and the holding of the election unfairly infringes on employers' free speech rights to communicate with workers on the pros and cons of unionization, guaranteed by §8(c). Nevertheless, early results show that despite the shortening of time to election resulting from those rules, only in the most rapid elections — those lasting two weeks or less — was a significant advantage for unions obtained. *Labor Board Rule to Speed Up Union Elections Shows Mixed Results*, Daily Lab. Rep. (BNA) No. 83, at AA-3, May 2, 2017. For a good analysis, see Hirsch, *NLRB Elections: Ambush or Anticlimax?*, 64 Emory L.J. 1647 (2015); Mastrosimone, *Limiting Information in the Information Age: The NLRB's Misguided Attempt to Squelch Employer Speech*, 52 Washburn L.J. 473 (2013).

2. *Employer Speech and Behavior*—In *Dal-Tex Optical Co.*, 137 N.L.R.B. 1782 (1962), the Board discussed its laboratory conditions standard, applicable to conduct during the campaign leading up to an election. In that case, the employer delivered speeches to employees that were found to be grounds for setting aside the election, even if they did not constitute unfair labor practices. The Board held that conduct that is violative of § 8(a)(1) generally interferes with the exercise of a free election "because the test of conduct which may interfere with the 'laboratory conditions' for an election is considerably more restrictive than the test of conduct which amounts to interference, restraint, or coercion which violates § 8(a)(1)." The Board found that "Congress specifically limited § 8(c) to the adversary proceedings involved in unfair labor practice cases and it has no application to representation cases. . . . The strictures of the first amendment, to be sure, must be considered in all cases."

Larson Tool & Stamping Co., 296 N.L.R.B. 895 (1989), involved employer letters to employees that stated: "During [an economic] strike, you could LOSE YOUR JOB TO A PERMANENT REPLACEMENT." The Board found that the employer's unqualified statement about job loss could "fairly be understood as a threat of reprisal." *Fred Wilkinson Ass'n, Inc.*, 297 N.L.R.B. 737 (1990), concerned a firm that informed employees: "The only thing [the union] can guarantee is a strike. In fact, the only thing [the union] can do to try to get the Company to agree to its demands is to call a strike." The Board found that these statements "created an atmosphere of fear" by suggesting that a strike was inevitable in any effort to obtain concessions from the employer. *Compare Fiber-Lam, Inc.*, 301 N.L.R.B. 94 (1991), wherein the Board found that an employer's statement that economic strikers could lose their jobs since a company is free to replace them did not cross the "narrow line" between the permissible warning of employees regarding the possible adverse consequences of a strike and the impermissible threat of job losses if workers elected to unionize. *See also Contech Div., SPX Corp*, 320 N.L.R.B. 219 (1995) (employer's predictions, unsupported by objective facts, that union victory would mean loss of customers invalidated election).

Just prior to a decertification election challenging the ongoing majority of the incumbent Teamsters Union among the delivery workers at a Chicago bakery, a company translator told Spanish-speaking workers they would be replaced with "legal workers" in the event of a strike. A closely divided Labor Board set aside the election, which the Union lost, based upon the belief this statement improperly suggested that the immigration status of Hispanic drivers would be questioned if they supported a work stoppage. *Labriola Baking Co.*, 361 N.L.R.B. 412 (2014).

In *Barton Nelson, Inc.*, 318 N.L.R.B. 712 (1995), supervisor distribution of antiunion hats directly to employees was held to warrant setting aside an election, even though there was no evidence of a listing of who did or did not take the hats. *See also Circuit City Stores, Inc.*, 324 N.L.R.B. 147 (1997) (store manager interfered with election when he approached individual employees prior to election and gave them coffee mugs bearing the slogans "Vote No" and "Just Vote No").

In *Sunrise Rehab. Hosp.*, 320 N.L.R.B. 212 (1995), the Board held that an employer interfered with an election by offering employees who were not scheduled to work two hours of pay to come in to vote, since those employees may have felt obliged to return the employer's favor by voting against the union. In *Seton Medical Ctr./ Seton Coastside*, 360 N.L.R.B. 302 (2014), the Board held that an employer engaged in objectionable conduct warranting a new election when it permitted the incumbent union to solicit employees during their work time and in areas of immediate patient care, but denied such activities by supporters of the outside petitioning labor organization. Overturning prior decisions, the Labor Board ruled in *Atlantic Limousine, Inc.*, 331 N.L.R.B. 1025 (2000), that employers and unions are prohibited from conducting preelection raffles if eligibility to participate is in any way tied to voting in a representation election or being at the election site on the day of the election, or if the raffle is conducted during the period beginning 24 hours prior to the opening of the polls and ending with the closing of the polls.

Election results may also be set aside when members of management assist the union. *Compare Madison Square Garden Ct, LLC*, 350 N.L.R.B. 117 (2007) (election won by union on 27 to 22 vote set aside based upon fact supervisors solicited authorization cards from employees and made pro-union statements since such conduct was inherently coercive with respect to the subordinates who were solicited), *and Harborside Healthcare, Inc.*, 343 N.L.R.B. 906 (2004) (solicitation of employees to sign authorization cards by pro-union supervisors is inherently coercive absent mitigating circumstances), *with Veritas Health Services Inc. v. NLRB*, 671 F.3d 1267 (D.C. Cir. 2012), *and Northeast Iowa Tel. Co.*, 346 N.L.R.B. 465 (2006) (union certification election victory not set aside despite pro-union acts by managers who attended and participated in union organizational meetings and openly signed authorization cards at those meetings, since such conduct did not tend to interfere with employee free choice).

Although conduct violative of § 8(a)(1) presumptively interferes with employee free choice, the Board occasionally declines to set an election aside when the unfair labor practice was isolated and too minimal to have affected the results of the election. *Caron International, Inc.*, 246 N.L.R.B. 1120 (1979). *See also Advanced Disposal Services East, Inc. v. NLRB*, 820 F.3d 592 (3d Cir. 2016) (finding that though the Labor Board endeavors to require "laboratory conditions" surrounding representation elections, the fact that perfect conditions were not maintained does not *ipso facto* result in the setting aside of election results so long as no coercive conduct poisoned the fair and free choice that employees are entitled to make).

3. *The Impact of Anti-Union Campaigns* — Do anti-union campaigns launched by employers actually reduce the likelihood of union certification? An empirical study by Professors Getman, Goldberg, and Herman suggested that employer campaigns played a limited role in employees' choice to vote for or against union representation. Employees were largely inattentive to employer campaigns and based their votes predominantly on long-standing attitudes about unions and working conditions. Even in circumstances where union supporters interpreted employer communications as threats or reprisals, they were unlikely to change their voting posture. Based on these findings, Getman et al. concluded that the Board's effort to set aside elections or find unfair labor practices based on written or oral communications was misguided. Instead, they argued, speech in representation elections should be as free from governmental restraint as speech in political elections. J. GETMAN, S. GOLDBERG & J. HERMAN, UNION REPRESENTATION ELECTIONS: LAW AND REALITY 140–46 (1976).

These conclusions were disputed in subsequent studies. Professor Weiler criticized the Getman study for its focus on the behavior of the average individual union voter rather than the ultimate election verdict. For example, in the Getman study, the authors of the study interviewed each employee before and after the employer campaign, correlated any changes in the worker's decision about union representation with the type of campaign to which he or she was exposed, and then aggregated the results across all the campaigns in order to determine the effect of the campaign on the average voter. Weiler argues that the Getman methodology resulted in miscalculating the true effect of employer campaigns on election results by ignoring how close the elections actually were and how the affected employees were distributed across different employee units. In fact, the results suggested that even a small shift of employee votes significantly impacted election outcomes in a majority rule, winner-takes-all system. Weiler, *Promises to Keep: Securing Workers' Rights to Self-Organization Under the NLRA*, 96 HARV. L. REV. 1769, 1782–86 (1983).

More recent studies show a powerful correlation between employer anti-union campaigns and union election losses. *See, e.g.*, Bronfenbrenner, *No Holds Barred: The Intensification of Employer Opposition to Organizing*, Economic Policy Institute, May 20, 2009; Bronfenbrenner, *Employer Behavior in Certification Elections and First-Contract Campaigns: Implications for Labor Law Reform*, in RESTORING THE PROMISE OF AMERICAN LABOR LAW 75 (S. Friedman et al. eds., 1994); Bronfenbrenner, *Uneasy Terrain: The Impact of Capital Mobility on Workers, Wages, and Union Organizing*, Submitted to the U.S. Trade Deficit Review Commission (Sept. 6, 2000).

4. *Union Speech and Behavior* — In *NLRB v. Savair Mfg. Co.*, 414 U.S. 270 (1973), the Court held that an election had to be set aside where a union offered to waive the initiation fee, if the union won the election, for all employees who executed pre-election authorization cards. This practice allowed the union to "buy" authorization card signatures from employees seeking to avoid having to pay the initiation fee and may have caused some card signers to feel obliged to vote for the union in the Board election. In *NLRB v. VSA, Inc.*, 24 F.3d 588 (4th Cir.), *cert. denied*, 513 U.S. 1041 (1994), the court held that a union did not act improperly when it offered to waive initiation fees for all employees if it won the election. *See also Community Options*, 359 N.L.R.B. 1534 (2013) (no reason to set aside results of decertification election favoring incumbent union where it had waived dues payments for first six months of initial contract for all unit employees). *Savair Mfg. Co.* was distinguished, since the waiver in that case was limited to employees who signed authorization cards prior

to the election. *Compare S.T.A.R., Inc.*, 347 N.L.R.B. 82 (2006), wherein the Labor Board held that a labor organization had engaged in objectionable conduct warranting the setting aside of an election victory when it gave employees a pre-election brochure stating that "[w]orkers who organize to join [the union] are exempt" from the $50 initiation fee, since the brochure language did not make it clear that employees who remained silent or opposed the union would also be exempt from the initiation fee.

Does a labor organization impermissibly influence election results when it provides prospective bargaining unit employees with free legal services in a class action wage or civil rights suit filed prior to the election? *Compare Nestle Ice Cream Co. v. NLRB*, 46 F.3d 578 (6th Cir. 1995) (yes), *with Novotel N.Y. v. Hotel & Motel Trades Council*, 321 N.L.R.B. 624 (1996) (no). *See also Freund Baking Co. v. NLRB*, 165 F.3d 928 (D.C. Cir. 1999) (union impermissibly influenced election results when it participated in a lawsuit by four employees seeking overtime payments during organizing campaign, where union described its participation in the lawsuit in its campaign literature).

Where pro-union employees threaten their coworkers with job losses if they don't support the union, must the union's close election win be set aside? Although the Labor Board held "no," the Fourth Circuit disagreed, finding the statements coercive. *NLRB v. Ky. Tenn. Clay Co.*, 295 F.3d 436 (4th Cir. 2002). *See also Associated Rubber Co. v. NLRB*, 296 F.3d 1055 (11th Cir. 2002) (overturning union election victory that took place three days after pro-union employee threatened and then retaliated against coworker who refused to accept union literature).

5. *Misleading Statements*—The NLRB has vacillated in recent years regarding its treatment of pre-election misrepresentations. In 1962, the Board indicated that it would set aside an election whenever it appeared that: (1) there had been a material misrepresentation of fact, (2) this misrepresentation came from a party who had special knowledge or was in an authoritative position to know the true facts, and (3) no other party had sufficient opportunity to correct the misrepresentations before the election. *Hollywood Ceramics Co.*, 140 N.L.R.B. 221 (1962).

In *Shopping Kart Food Market, Inc.*, 228 N.L.R.B. 1311 (1977), a 3-2 Board majority abandoned the *Hollywood Ceramics* test and stated that the Board would no longer set elections aside on the basis of misleading statements. Elections would only be set aside when a party has engaged in coercive tactics, such as threats of reprisal, or deceptive practices, such as the use of forged documents, but the Board would no longer probe the truth or falsity of campaign statements. The majority asserted that Board rules "must be based on a view of employees as mature individuals who are capable of recognizing campaign propaganda for what it is and discounting it." Although the Board briefly returned to the *Hollywood Ceramics* approach in *General Knit*, 239 N.L.R.B. 619 (1978), it quickly overruled *General Knit* and returned to the "sound rule" of *Shopping Kart*. *See Midland Nat'l Life Ins. Co.*, 263 N.L.R.B. 127 (1982). As a result, the Board no longer evaluates the veracity of campaign representations. Appellate courts have accepted the Board's *Midland Nat'l Life Ins.* approach. *See, e.g., US Ecology, Inc. v. NLRB*, 772 F.2d 1478 (9th Cir. 1985); *NLRB v. Affiliated Midwest Hospital, Inc.*, 789 F.2d 524 (7th Cir. 1986). *Compare Dayton Hudson Dep't Store Co. v. NLRB*, 79 F.3d 546 (6th Cir.), *cert. denied*, 519 U.S. 819 (1996) (union's pre-election letter that grossly exaggerated employer's profitability did not invalidate union's election victory), *with NLRB v. Hub Plastics*, 52 F.3d 608 (6th Cir. 1995) (union statements prior to election indicating that the NLRB had found the company guilty of unfair labor practice violations, when the Board had only issued a complaint against that firm, may provide a basis for setting aside the union's election victory). *See also Albertson's, Inc.*, 344 N.L.R.B. 1357 (2005), wherein the Labor Board set aside an election where a union distributed a letter forged on the employer's letterhead claiming that the employer's nonunion stores would be converted to low-priced discount stores. The union refused to inform employees about the forgery even after the employer objected, and prevailed in the election by a narrow margin. The Board found that a reasonable employee would not have been able to recognize the letter as a forgery, and that the company's response was insufficient to correct the confusion in the face of the union's silence.

Until recently, the Labor Board distinguished use of official NLRB election documents during organizing campaigns. While altered documents that clearly identified the party responsible for the additional markings would not serve as the basis to set aside elections, the circulation of altered Board documents that did not indicate the party responsible for the changes would warrant the voiding of elections. *See, e.g., Archer Services, Inc.*, 298 N.L.R.B. 312 (1990). After the NLRB revised its Notice of Election form to specifically disavow Board involvement in any defacement or alteration of Board documents and to assert NLRB neutrality in the election process, the Labor Board decided that it would no longer permit modified Board documents to provide the basis for new elections, even when it is not clear which party changed the documents in question. *See Irvington Nursing Care Servs.*, 312 N.L.R.B. 594 (1993).

The Board's 1993 amendment to its Notice of Election Form to assert its neutrality and to disavow any involvement in the alteration of official Board documents proved ineffective in ending disputes about the potential to mislead voters inherent in the use of altered sample ballots during organizing campaigns. In *Ryder Memorial Hosp.*, 351 N.L.R.B. 214 (2007), the Board announced that it would modify the wording on ballots used in representation elections to add a statement of its neutrality; parties using reproductions with marked choices in their campaign materials must duplicate the disclaimer in their ballot reproductions. The Board will no longer entertain challenges to elections based upon a party's distribution of an altered sample ballot, as long as the ballot is an accurate reproduction of the Board's ballot including the new neutrality language.

6. *Appeals to Race and Ethnicity* — For contrasting treatment of racial and ethnic slurs voiced by union supporters, compare *M & M Supermarkets, Inc. v. NLRB*, 818 F.2d 1567 (11th Cir. 1987) (anti-Semitic remarks against employer's owners by black employees so derogatory and inflammatory that they destroyed laboratory conditions necessary for a free and fair election), *and KI (USA) Corp. v. NLRB*, 35 F.3d 256 (6th Cir. 1994) (union appeals to racial and national origin prejudice sufficiently inflammatory to invalidate election results), *with Catherine's, Inc.*, 316 N.L.R.B. 186 (1995) (union comments concerning Jewish law firm representing employer and fact the few white employees in workforce would likely vote against union insufficient to warrant setting aside election), *and NLRB v. Herbert Halperin Distributing Corp.*, 826 F.2d 287 (4th Cir. 1987) (comments such as "those goddamn white boys—they won't support the blacks" did not indicate an atmosphere so inflamed by racial prejudice as to invalidate the election).

In *Family Serv. Agency San Francisco v. NLRB*, 163 F.3d 1369 (D.C. Cir. 1999), the court held that a union had not impermissibly appealed to racial prejudice during an organizing campaign when it complained about an employer policy barring employees from speaking Spanish at work and discussed the impact of that rule on Latina employees. *See also Ashland Facility Operations LLC v. NLRB*, 701 F.3d 983 (4th Cir. 2013) (sustaining union certification following representation election prior to which comments by NAACP executives criticized employer for allegedly discriminatory practices, where no showing that NAACP executives were acting as agents of union and did not involve appeals to racial prejudice). Should a union's appeal to racial or ethnic pride when organizing minority workers justify setting aside an election? *See* Crain, *Whitewashed Labor Law, Skinwalking Unions*, 23 Berkeley J. Emp. & Lab. L. 211 (2002). *See also* Crain, *Colorblind Unionism*, 49 UCLA L. Rev. 1313 (2002).

7. *Twenty-four Hours Before the Election*—The Board reviews speeches, conversations and potentially coercive actions carefully when they occur during the final 24 hours preceding an election, particularly if they are made to a captive audience (i.e., employees are required to attend because the speeches are made during working time, or messages are conveyed by the union in such a fashion that employees cannot escape). *See Peerless Plywood Co.*, 107 N.L.R.B. 427 (1954). For example, just before Board elections, some employers present employees with split paychecks—one containing the amount of periodic union dues and the other containing the remainder of their take-home pay—to remind them of the cost of unionization. In *Kalin Constr. Co.*, 321 N.L.R.B. 649 (1996), the Board established a strict rule prohibiting employers from altering the usual paycheck process during the 24 hours prior to the scheduled opening of the polls. Employers wishing to issue split paychecks must now do so more than 24 hours before elections commence. On the other hand, in *Flex Products, Inc.*, 280 N.L.R.B. 1117 (1986), the Labor Board held an employer did not interfere with an election when its president met individually with about 120 of its 164 employees in the plant manager's office during the 24 hours preceding the election. The president had previously met with employees in the manager's office; the president periodically walked around the plant and greeted employees, who called him by his first name; and his remarks at the individual meetings were temperate and noncoercive.

Unions can also violate the laboratory conditions standard and the same *Peerless Plywood* standard applies to their activities in the last 24 hours prior to an election. In *Industrial Acoustics Co. v. NLRB*, 912 F.2d 717 (4th Cir. 1990), for example, the court ruled that a union's election-eve and election-day campaign broadcasts to employees from a soundcar parked 25 to 30 yards from the main plant entrance contravened the *Peerless Plywood* 24-hour "captive audience" rule and invalidated the union's election victory. *Accord Bro-Tech Corp. v. NLRB*, 105 F.3d 890 (3d Cir. 1997). *Compare Overnite Transp. Co. v. NLRB*, 104 F.3d 109 (7th Cir. 1997) (boisterous, party-like behavior, including sign carrying, horn blowing, and flag waving, outside a truck terminal in which NLRB election was being held did not invalidate election).

8. *What Constitutes a Majority Choice?*—It has been held that the outcome of an NLRB election depends on "a majority of those voting in the election" rather than "a majority of those eligible to vote." *R.C.A. Mfg. Co.*, 2 N.L.R.B. 159 (1936). *See also Lee Mark Metal Mfg. Co.*, 85 N.L.R.B. 1299 (1949) (tie vote in decertification election results in decertification of incumbent union due to lack of continued majority support).

The Labor Board will not invalidate an election as "unrepresentative" because less than a "substantial" number of eligible voters participate. Results will be certified if there is "adequate notice and opportunity to vote and employees are not prevented from voting by the conduct of a party or by unfairness in the scheduling or mechanics of the election." *Lemco Constr., Inc.*, 283 N.L.R.B. 459 (1987).

Eligible employees must usually vote in person, with mail ballots only being used when voters are scattered over a wide geographic area, employee schedules vary so greatly that they are not at a common location at common times, or a strike or lockout is in progress. *San Diego Gas & Elec.*, 325 N.L.R.B. 1143 (1998).

For almost 85 years under the Railway Labor Act, only persons desiring representation voted at National Mediation Board-conducted elections, and a majority of eligible voters had to cast ballots for certification to be awarded. In 2010, the NMB changed this practice by including no representation as a ballot choice and simply requiring labor organizations to obtain a majority of votes cast to obtain certification. In *Air Transport Ass'n. v. National Mediation Board*, 663 F.3d 476 (D.C. Cir. 2011), the court sustained the authority of the NMB to make this change.

9. *Runoff Elections*—When two or more unions are competing for certification, and none of the labor organizations nor the "no representation" choice receives a majority of the votes cast, §9(c)(3) requires that "a run-off shall be conducted, the ballot providing for a selection between the two choices receiving the largest number of valid votes cast in the election." Thus, if 100 employees vote in the original election as follows: 45 for Union A, 30 for No Union, and 25 for Union B, the runoff will be between Union A and No Union.

10. *Eligibility to Vote during a Strike or Lockout*—During the Wagner Act period, strikers were allowed to vote, but a Taft-Hartley amendment deprived replaced economic strikers of the right to vote. Experience demonstrated that this could be used as a "union-busting" device, so Congress modified § 9(c)(3) in 1959 to provide that:

> [E]mployees engaged in an economic strike who are not entitled to reinstatement shall be eligible to vote under such regulations as the Board shall find are consistent with the purposes and provisions of the National Labor Relations Act, as amended, in any election conducted within twelve months after the commencement of the strike.

In *Pacific Tile & Porcelain Co.*, 137 N.L.R.B. 1358 (1962), the NLRB clarified its rules concerning the voting eligibility of strikers and replacements. To challenge an economic striker's vote, the challenger must affirmatively show that the striker has "no further interest in his struck job." To challenge a replacement's vote, the challenger had to show that the individual was not employed on a permanent basis. In *O.E. Butterfield, Inc.*, 319 N.L.R.B. 1004 (1995), however, the Board modified the *Pacific Tile & Porcelain Co.* rules when it held that in representation cases, as in unfair labor practice cases, the burden is on the employer to demonstrate that strike replacements are permanent employees and thus qualified to vote in an election.

In *Gulf States Paper Corp., EZ Packaging Div.*, 219 N.L.R.B. 806 (1975), the Board held that economic strikers who have been on strike for more than one year and have been permanently replaced are ineligible to vote in an NLRB election. However, unreplaced economic strikers are eligible to vote if their jobs have not been permanently eliminated, they have not found permanent employment elsewhere, and the employer has not refused to reinstate them for misconduct rendering them unsuitable for reemployment.

Harter Equipment, Inc., 293 N.L.R.B. 647 (1989), concerned the voting rights of locked-out employees and their replacements. The Board held that the five employees who had been locked out and replaced were the only persons eligible to vote on a decertification petition filed about two years after the lockout began, even though 17 employees were currently working in bargaining unit positions. The locked-out employees had not abandoned their jobs and could not be permanently replaced, thus the replacements were all temporary employees.

Problem

22. One week before a scheduled representation election, the president of Comet Electrical Co. told her employees to report back to the shop at 3:00 p.m. for a meeting (the employees' regular quitting time is 4:00 p.m.). At the meeting, which lasted from 3:00 to 5:00 p.m., the president made an anti-union speech to the assembled employees. None of the employees left the meeting or asked to leave while it was in progress.

Although the workers usually received their paychecks at the end of their shift at 4:00 p.m., on the day of the meeting they were not paid until the meeting concluded. After the meeting, some of the employees noted on their timecards that their day ended at 3:00 p.m., and discovered on payday the following week (the day of the election) that they were not paid for any time after that. Other employees claimed two hours for attending the meeting, but were only paid for one of those two hours.

The union lost the election by a vote of 16 to 12, and filed a timely objection. Should the Board set aside the election results and direct a second election?

D. Court Review of Representation Proceedings

Leedom v. Kyne
Supreme Court of the United States
358 U.S. 184, 79 S. Ct. 180, 3 L. Ed. 2d 210 (1958)

Mr. Justice Whittaker delivered the opinion of the Court.

Section 9(b)(1) of the National Labor Relations Act, §9, 49 Stat. 453, 61 Stat. 143, 29 U.S.C. §159(b)(1), provides that, in determining the unit appropriate for collective bargaining purposes, "the Board shall not (1) decide that any unit is appropriate for such purposes if such unit includes both professional employees and employees who are not professional employees unless a majority of such professional employees vote for inclusion in such unit." The Board, after refusing to take a vote among the professional employees to determine whether a majority of them would "vote for inclusion in such unit," included both professional and nonprofessional employees in the bargaining unit that it found appropriate. The sole and narrow question presented is whether a Federal District Court has jurisdiction of an original suit to vacate that determination of the Board because made in excess of its powers.

The facts are undisputed. Buffalo Section, Westinghouse Engineers Association, Engineers and Scientists of America, a voluntary unincorporated labor organization, hereafter called the Association, was created for the purpose of promoting the economic and professional status of the nonsupervisory professional employees of Westinghouse Electric Corporation at its plant in Cheektowaga, New York, through collective bargaining with their employer. In October, 1955, the Association petitioned the National Labor Relations Board for certification as the exclusive collective bargaining agent of all nonsupervisory professional employees, being then 233 in number, of the Westinghouse Company at its Cheektowaga plant, pursuant to the provisions of §9 of the act, 29 U.S.C. §159. A hearing was held by the board upon that petition. A competing labor organization was permitted by the Board to intervene. It asked the Board to expand the unit to include employees in five other categories who performed technical work and were thought by it to be "professional employees" within the meaning of §2(12) of the act, 29 U.S.C. §152(12). The Board found that they were not professional employees within the meaning of the act. However, it found that nine employees in three of those categories should nevertheless be included in the unit because they "share a close community of employment interests with [the professional employees, and their inclusion would not] destroy the predominantly professional character of such a unit." The Board, after denying the Association's request to take a vote among the professional employees to determine whether a majority of them favored "inclusion in such unit," included the 233 professional employees and the nine nonprofessional employees in the unit and directed an election to determine whether they desired to be represented by the Association, by the other labor organization, or by neither. The Association moved the Board to stay the election and to amend its decision by excluding the nonprofessional employees from the unit. The Board denied that motion and went ahead with the election at which the Association received a majority of the valid votes cast and was thereafter certified by the Board as the collective bargaining agent for the unit.

Thereafter respondent, individually, and as president of the Association, brought this suit in the District Court against the members of the Board, alleging the foregoing facts and asserting that the Board had exceeded its statutory power in including the professional employees, without their consent, in a unit with nonprofessional employees in violation of § 9(b)(1) which commands that the Board "shall not" do so, and praying, among other things, that the Board's action be set aside. The defendants, members of the Board, moved to dismiss for want of jurisdiction and, in the alternative, for a summary judgment. The plaintiff also moved for summary judgment. The trial court found that the Board had disobeyed the express command of § 9(b)(1) in including nonprofessional employees and professional employees in the same unit without the latter's consent, and in doing so had acted in excess of its powers to the injury of the professional employees, and that the court had jurisdiction to grant the relief prayed. It accordingly denied the Board's motion and granted the plaintiff's motion and entered judgment setting aside the Board's determination of the bargaining unit and also the election and the Board's certification.

On the Board's appeal it did not contest the trial court's conclusion that the Board, in commingling professional with nonprofessional employees in the unit, had acted in excess of its powers and had thereby worked injury to the statutory rights of the professional employees. Instead, it contended only that the District Court lacked jurisdiction to entertain the suit. The Court of Appeals held that the District Court did have jurisdiction and affirmed the judgment. 101 App. D.C. 398, 249 F.2d 490. . . .

Petitioners, members of the Board, concede here that the District Court had jurisdiction of the suit under § 24(8) of the Judicial Code, 28 U.S.C. § 1337, unless the review provisions of the National Labor Relations Act destroyed it. In *AFL v. NLRB*, 308 U.S. 401 (1940), this Court held that a Board order in certification proceedings under § 9 is not "a final order" and therefore is not subject to judicial review except as it may be drawn in question by a petition for enforcement or review of an order, made under § 10(c) of the act, restraining an unfair labor practice. But the Court was at pains to point out in that case "[t]he question [there presented was] distinct from . . . whether petitioners are precluded by the provisions of the Wagner Act from maintaining an independent suit in a district court to set aside the Board's action because contrary to the statute. . . ." Id. at 404. The Board argued there, as it does here, that the provisions of the act, particularly § 9(d), have foreclosed review of its action by an original suit in a District Court. This Court said: "But that question is not presented for decision by the record before us. Its answer involves a determination whether the Wagner Act, in so far as it has given legally enforceable rights, has deprived the district courts of some portion of their original jurisdiction conferred by § 24 of the Judicial Code. It can be appropriately answered only upon a showing in such a suit that unlawful action of the Board has inflicted an injury on the petitioners for which the law, *apart from the review provisions of the Wagner Act*, affords a remedy. This question can be properly and adequately considered only when it is brought to us for review upon a suitable record." *Id.* at 412. (Emphasis added.)

The record in this case squarely presents the question found not to have been presented by the record in American Federation of Labor v. NLRB, *supra*. This case, in its posture before us, involves "unlawful action of the Board [which] has inflicted an injury on the [respondent]." Does the law, "apart from the review provisions of the . . . act," afford a remedy? We think the answer surely must be yes. This suit is not one to "review," in the sense of that term as used in the act, a decision of the Board made within its jurisdiction. Rather it is one to strike down an order of the Board made in excess of its delegated powers and contrary to a specific prohibition in the act. Section 9(b)(1) is clear and mandatory. It says that, in determining the unit appropriate for the purposes of collective bargaining, "the Board *shall not* (1) decide that any unit is appropriate for such purposes if such unit includes both professional employees and employees who are not professional employees unless a majority of such professional employees vote for inclusion in such unit." (Emphasis added.) Yet, the Board included in the unit employees whom it found were not professional employees, after refusing to determine whether a majority of the professional employees would "vote for inclusion in such unit." Plainly, this was an attempted exercise of power that had been specifically withheld. It deprived the professional employees of a "right" assured to them by Congress. Surely, in these circumstances, a Federal District Court has jurisdiction of an original suit to prevent deprivation of a right so given.

In *Texas & N. O. R. Co. v. Brotherhood of R. & S.S. Clerks*, 281 U.S. 548 (1930), it was contended that, because no remedy had been expressly given for redress of the congressionally created right in suit, the act conferred "merely an abstract right which was not intended to be enforced by legal proceedings." *Id.* at 558. This Court rejected that contention. It said: "While an affirmative declaration of duty contained in a legislative enactment may be of imperfect obligation because not enforceable in terms, a definite statutory prohibition of conduct which would thwart the declared purpose of the legislation cannot be disregarded. . . . If Congress intended that the prohibition, as thus construed, should be enforced, the courts would encounter no difficulty in fulfilling its purpose. . . . The definite prohibition which Congress inserted in the act cannot therefore be overridden in the view that Congress intended it to be ignored. As the prohibition was appropriate to the aim of Congress, and is capable of enforcement, the conclusion must be that enforcement was contemplated." *Id.* at 568, 569. And compare *Virginian R. Co. v. System Federation*, 300 U.S. 515.

In *Switchmen's Union of North America v. National Mediation Board*, 320 U.S. 297, this Court held that the District Court did not have jurisdiction of an original suit to review an order of the National Mediation Board determining that all yardmen of the rail lines operated by the New York Central system constituted an appropriate bargaining unit, because the Railway Labor Board had acted within its delegated powers. But in the course of that opinion the Court announced principles that are controlling here. "If the absence of jurisdiction of the federal courts meant a sacrifice or obliteration of a right which Congress had created, the inference would be strong that Congress intended the statutory provisions governing the general jurisdiction of those courts to control. That was the purport of the decisions of this Court in *Texas & N. O. R. Co. v. Brotherhood of R. & S.S. Clerks*, 281 U.S. 548 (1930), and *Virginian R. Co. v. System Federation*, 300 U.S. 515 (1937). In those cases it was apparent that but for the general jurisdiction of the federal courts there would be no remedy to enforce the statutory commands which Congress had written into the Railway Labor Act. The result would have been that the 'right' of collective bargaining was unsupported by any legal sanction. That would have robbed the act of its vitality and thwarted its purpose." *Id.* at 300.

Here, differently from *Switchmen's* case, "absence of jurisdiction of the federal courts" would mean "a sacrifice or obliteration of a right which Congress" has given professional employees, for there is no other means within their control (*American Federation of Labor v. NLRB, supra*), to protect and enforce that right. And "the inference [is] strong that Congress intended the statutory provisions governing the general jurisdiction of those courts to control." 320 U.S. at 300. This Court cannot lightly infer that Congress does not intend judicial protection of rights it confers against agency action taken in excess of delegated powers. *Cf. Harmon v. Brucker*, 355 U.S. 579 (1958); *Stark v. Wickard*, 321 U.S. 288 (1944); *School of Magnetic Healing v. McAnnulty*, 187 U.S. 94 (1902).

Where, as here, Congress has given a "right" to the professional employees it must be held that it intended that right to be enforced, and the "courts ... encounter no difficulty in fulfilling its purpose." *Texas & New Orleans R. Co. v. Railway Clerks, supra* at 568.

The Court of Appeals was right in holding, in the circumstances of this case, that the District Court had jurisdiction of this suit, and its judgment is

Affirmed.

Mr. Justice Brennan, whom Mr. Justice Frankfurter joins, dissenting.

The legislative history of the Wagner Act, and of the Taft-Hartley amendments, shows a considered congressional purpose to restrict judicial review of National Labor Relations Board representation certifications to review in the Courts of Appeals in the circumstances specified in §9(d), 29 U.S.C. §159(d). The question was extensively debated when both acts were being considered, and on both occasions Congress concluded that, unless drastically limited, time-consuming court procedures would seriously threaten to frustrate the basic national policy of preventing industrial strife and achieving industrial peace by promoting collective bargaining....

The Court today opens a gaping hole in this congressional wall against direct resort to the courts. The Court holds that a party alleging that the Board was guilty of "unlawful action" in making an investigation and certification of representatives need not await judicial review until the situation specified in § 9(d) arises, but has a case immediately cognizable by a District Court under the "original jurisdiction" granted by 28 U.S.C. § 1337 of "any civil action or proceeding arising under any Act of Congress regulating commerce." The Court, borrowing a statement from *Switchmen's Union v. National Mediation Board*, 320 U.S. 297, 300 (1943), finds that, in such case "the inference [is] strong that Congress intended the statutory provisions governing the general jurisdiction of those [District] courts to control."...

I daresay that the ingenuity of counsel will, after today's decision, be entirely adequate to the task of finding some alleged "unlawful action," whether in statutory interpretation or otherwise, sufficient to get a foot in a District Court door under 28 U.S.C. § 1337. Even when the Board wins such a case on the merits,... while the case is dragging through the courts the threat will be ever present of the industrial strife sought to be averted by Congress in providing only drastically limited judicial review under § 9(d). Both union and management will be able to use the tactic of litigation to delay the initiation of collective bargaining when it suits their purposes....

It is no support for the Court's decision that the respondent union may suffer hardship if review under 28 U.S.C. § 1337 is not open to it. The Congress was fully aware of the disadvantages and possible unfairness which could result from the limitation on judicial review enacted in § 9(d). The House proposal for direct review of Board certifications in the Taft-Hartley amendments was based in part upon the fact that, under the Wagner Act, the operation of § 9(d) was "unfair to ... the union that loses, which has no appeal at all no matter how wrong the certification may be; [and to] the employees, who have no appeal...." Congress nevertheless continued the limited judicial review provided by § 9(d) because Congress believed the disadvantages of broader review to be more serious than the difficulties which limited review posed for the parties. Furthermore, Congress felt that the Board procedures and the limited review provided in § 9(d) were adequate to protect the parties....

I would reverse and remand the case to the District Court with instructions to dismiss the complaint for lack of jurisdiction of the subject matter.

Notes

1. *Other Applications of* Kyne — A district court may enjoin the NLRB from holding an election among seamen on foreign-flag ships even though the Board did not violate any specific prohibition in the NLRA, since the Board's assertion of power to determine representation of foreign seamen aboard foreign flag vessels had aroused vigorous protests from foreign governments and created international problems for the United States, the presence of which was a uniquely compelling justification for prompt judicial resolution of the controversy. *McCulloch v. Sociedad Nacional de Marineros de Honduras*, 372 U.S. 10 (1963).

Fay v. Douds, 172 F.2d 720 (2d Cir. 1949), indicated that direct district court intervention would be appropriate in cases involving a clear deprivation of a constitutional right that could not be adequately remedied through regular Labor Board representation procedures.

2. *Limits to the* Kyne *Exception* — In *Boire v. Greyhound Corp.*, 376 U.S. 473 (1964), the Court held that a federal district court erred when it enjoined the Board from conducting an election among maintenance and service workers at a bus company's terminals. The district court had found that the NLRB had misapplied the act in holding the bus company and the maintenance company to be joint employers.

> [W]hether Greyhound possessed sufficient indicia of control to be an "employer" is essentially a factual issue, unlike the question in *Kyne*, which depended solely upon construction of the statute. The *Kyne* exception is a narrow one, not to be extended to permit plenary district court review of Board orders in certification proceedings whenever it can be said that an erroneous assessment of the particular facts before the Board has led it to a conclusion which does not comport with the law. Judicial review in such a situation has been limited by Congress to the courts of appeals, and then only under the conditions explicitly laid down in § 9(d) of the Act.

The Ninth Circuit recently reaffirmed the narrow applicability of the *Leedom v. Kyne* exception, finding that the party seeking judicial review must not only establish that the NLRB exceeded its statutory authority, but also that the party would be "wholly deprived" of a means to vindicate its statutory rights if a court did not review the order. Where intervention in the pending unfair labor practice proceeding was a possible alternative path to challenge the Board's determination under section 10(k) resolving a dispute between rival unions over whose members should perform particular work, the Board's order was not a final decision subject to judicial review. *Pac. Mar. Ass'n v. NLRB*, 827 F.3d 1203 (9th Cir. 2016).

Section II. Establishing Representative Status through Unfair Labor Practice Proceedings

We have thus far been concerned with formal representation proceedings that result, if the union wins the secret ballot election, in certification of the union as exclusive bargaining representative. It has historically been common for collective bargaining relationships to be established simply by unions showing employers that they represent a majority of their employees, usually by "card checks" of authorization cards signed by the employees, and by voluntary employer recognition of the bargaining rights of those labor organizations.

If the employer refuses to recognize the union, another procedure by which the union can get the NLRB to order the employer to bargain with it and thus establish representative status, is to bring unfair labor practice proceedings.

NLRB v. Gissel Packing Co.

Supreme Court of the United States
395 U.S. 575, 89 S. Ct. 1918, 23 L. Ed. 2d 547 (1969)

Mr. Chief Justice Warren delivered the opinion of the Court.

These cases involve the extent of an employer's duty under the National Labor Relations Act to recognize a union that bases its claim to representative status solely on the possession of union authorization cards, and the steps an employer may take, particularly with regard to the scope and content of statements he may make, in legitimately resisting such card-based recognition. The specific questions facing us here are whether the duty to bargain can arise without a Board election under the Act; whether union authorization cards, if obtained from a majority of employees without misrepresentation or coercion, are reliable enough generally to provide a valid, alternate route to majority status; whether a bargaining order is an appropriate and authorized remedy where an employer rejects a card majority while at the same time committing unfair labor practices that tend to undermine the union's majority and make a fair election an unlikely possibility; and whether certain specific statements made by an employer to his employees constituted such an election-voiding unfair labor practice and thus fell outside the protection of the First Amendment and § 8(c) of the Act. For reasons given below, we answer each of these questions in the affirmative.

I

... In each of the cases from the Fourth Circuit, the course of action followed by the Union and the employer and the Board's response were similar. In each case, the union waged an organizational campaign, obtained authorization cards from a majority of employees in the appropriate bargaining unit, and then on the basis of the cards, demanded recognition by the employer. All three employers refused to bargain on the ground that authorization cards were inherently unreliable indicators of employee desires; and they either embarked on, or continued, vigorous antiunion campaigns that gave rise to numerous unfair labor practice charges. In *Gissel*, where the employer's campaign began almost at the outset of the Union's organizational drive, the Union (petitioner in No. 691), did not seek an election, but instead filed three unfair labor practice charges against the employer, for refusing to bargain in violation of § 8(a)(5), for coercion and intimidation of employees in violation of § 8(a)(1), and for discharge of union adherents in violation of § 8(a)(3). In *Heck's* an election sought by the Union was never held because of nearly identical unfair labor practice charges later filed by the Union as a result of the employer's antiunion campaign, initiated after the Union's recognition demand. And in *General Steel*, an election petitioned for by the Union and won by the employer was set aside by the Board because of the unfair labor practices committed by the employer in the pre-election period.

In each case, the Board's primary response was an order to bargain directed at the employers, despite the absence of an election in *Gissel* and *Heck's* and the employer's victory in *General Steel*. More specifically the Board found in each case that (1) the union had obtained valid authorization cards[9] from a majority of the employees in the bargaining unit and was thus entitled to represent the employees for collective bargaining purposes; and (2) that the employers' refusal to bargain with the unions in violation of § 8(a)(5) was motivated not by a "good faith" doubt of the unions' majority status, but by a desire to gain time to dissipate that status. The Board based its conclusion as to the lack of good faith doubt on the fact that the employers had committed substantial unfair labor practices during their antiunion campaign efforts to resist recognition. Thus, the Board found that all three employers had engaged in restraint and coercion of employees in violation of § 8(a)(1) — in *Gissel*, for coercively interrogating employees about union activities, threatening them with discharge and promising them benefits; in *Heck's*, for coercively interrogating employees, threatening reprisals, creating the appearance of surveillance, and offering benefits for opposing the Union; and in *General Steel*, for coercive interrogation and threats of reprisals, including discharge. In addition, the Board found that the employers in *Gissel* and *Heck's* had wrongfully discharged employees for engaging in union activities in violation of § 8(a)(3). And, because the employers had rejected the card-based bargaining demand in bad faith, the Board found that all three had refused to recognize the unions in violation of § 8(a)(5).

Only in *General Steel* was there any objection by an employer to the validity of the cards and the manner in which they had been solicited, and the doubt raised by the evidence was resolved in the following manner. The customary approach of the Board in dealing with allegations of misrepresentation by the union and misunderstanding by the employees of the purpose for which the cards were being solicited has been set out in *Cumberland Shoe Corp.*, 144 N.L.R.B. 1268 (1964), and reaffirmed in *Levi Strauss & Co.*, 172 N.L.R.B. No. 57, 68 L.R.R.M. 1338 (1968). Under the *Cumberland Shoe* doctrine, if the card itself is unambiguous (*i.e.*, states on its face that the signer authorizes the union to represent the employee for collective bargaining purposes and not to seek an election), it will be counted unless it is proved that the employee was told that the card was to be used *solely* for the

---

9. [4] The cards used in all four campaigns in Nos. 573 and 691 and in the one drive in No. 585 unambiguously authorized the Union to represent the signing employee for collective bargaining purposes; there was no reference to elections. Typical of the cards was the one used in the Charleston campaign in *Heck's*, and it stated in relevant part:

> Desiring to become a member of the above Union of the International Brotherhood of Teamsters, Chauffeurs, Warehousemen and Helpers of America, I hereby make application for admission to membership. I hereby authorize you, or your agents or representatives to act for me as collective bargaining agent on all matters pertaining to rates of pay, hours or any other condition of employment.

purpose of obtaining an election. In *General Steel*, the trial examiner considered the allegations of misrepresentation at length and, applying the Board's customary analysis, rejected the claims with findings that were adopted by the Board and are reprinted in the margin.

Consequently, the Board ordered the companies to cease and desist from their unfair labor practices, to offer reinstatement and back pay to the employees who had been discriminatorily discharged, to bargain with the Union on request, and to post the appropriate notices.

On appeal, the Court of Appeals for the Fourth Circuit, in *per curiam* opinions in each of the three cases (398 F.2d 336, 337, 339), sustained the Board's findings as to the §§ 8(a)(1) and (3) violations, but rejected the Board's findings that the employers' refusal to bargain violated § 8(a)(5) and declined to enforce those portions of the Board's orders directing the respondent companies to bargain in good faith. The court based its § 8(a)(5) rulings on its 1967 decisions raising the same fundamental issues, *Crawford Mfg. Co. v. NLRB*, 386 F.2d 367 (C.A. 4th Cir. 1967), *cert. denied*, 390 U.S. 1028 (1968); *NLRB v. Logan Packing Co.*, 386 F.2d 562 (C.A. 4th Cir. 1967); *NLRB v. Sehon Stevenson & Co., Inc.*, 386 F.2d 551 (C.A. 4th Cir. 1967). The court in those cases held that the 1947 Taft-Hartley amendments to the Act, which permitted the Board to resolve representation disputes by certification under § 9(c) only by secret ballot election, withdrew from the Board the authority to order an employer to bargain under § 8(a)(5) on the basis of cards, in the absence of NLRB certification, unless the employer knows independently of the cards that there is in fact no representation dispute. The court held that the cards themselves were so inherently unreliable that their use gave an employer virtually an automatic, good faith claim that such a dispute existed, for which a secret election was necessary. Thus, these rulings established that a company could not be ordered to bargain unless (1) there was no question about a union's majority status (either because the employer agreed the cards were valid or had conducted his own poll so indicating), or (2) the employer's §§ 8(a)(1) and (3) unfair labor practices committed during the representation campaign were so extensive and pervasive that a bargaining order was the only available Board remedy irrespective of a card majority. . . .

II

In urging us to reverse the Fourth Circuit and to affirm the First Circuit, the National Labor Relations Board contends that we should approve its interpretation and administration of the duties and obligations imposed by the Act in authorization card cases. The Board argues (1) that unions have never been limited under § 9(c) of either the Wagner Act or the 1947 amendments to certified elections as the sole route to attaining representative status. Unions may, the Board contends, impose a duty to bargain on the employer under § 8(a)(5) by reliance on other evidence of majority employee support, such as authorization cards. Contrary to the Fourth Circuit's holding, the Board asserts, the 1947 amendments did not eliminate the alternative routes to majority status. The Board contends (2) that the cards themselves, when solicited in accordance with Board standards which adequately insure against union misrepresentation, are sufficiently reliable indicators of employee desires to support a bargaining order against an employer who refuses to recognize a card majority in violation of § 8(a)(5). The Board argues (3) that a bargaining order is the appropriate remedy for the § 8(a)(5) violation, where the employer commits other unfair labor practices that tend to undermine union support and render a fair election improbable.

Relying on these three assertions, the Board asks us to approve its current practice, which is briefly as follows. When confronted by a recognition demand based on possession of cards allegedly signed by a majority of his employees, an employer need not grant recognition immediately, but may, unless he has knowledge independently of the cards that the union has a majority, decline the union's request and insist on an election, either by requesting the union to file an election petition or by filing such a petition himself under § 9(c)(1)(B). If, however, the employer commits independent and substantial unfair labor practices disruptive of election conditions, the Board may withhold the election or set it aside, and issue instead a bargaining order as a remedy for the various violations. A bargaining order will not issue, of course, if the union obtained the cards through misrepresentation or coercion or if the employer's unfair labor practices are unrelated generally to the representation campaign. Conversely, the employers in these cases urge us to adopt the views of the Fourth Circuit. . . .

The traditional approach utilized by the Board for many years has been known as the *Joy Silk* doctrine. *Joy Silk Mills, Inc. v. NLRB*, 85 N.L.R.B. 1263 (1949), *enforced* 185 F.2d 732, 87 U.S. App. D.C. 360 (C.A.D.C. Cir. 1950). Under that rule, an employer could lawfully refuse to bargain with a union claiming representative status through possession of authorization cards if he had a "good faith doubt" as to the union's majority status; instead of bargaining, he could insist that the union seek an election in order to test out his doubts. The Board, then, could find a lack of good faith doubt and enter a bargaining order in one of two ways. It could find (1) that the employer's independent unfair labor practices were evidence of bad faith, showing that the employer was seeking time to dissipate the union's majority. Or the Board could find (2) that the employer had come forward with no reasons for entertaining any doubt and therefore that he must have rejected the bargaining demand in bad faith. An example of the second category was *Snow & Sons*, 134 N.L.R.B. 709 (1961), *enforced* 308 F.2d 687 (C.A. 9th Cir. 1962), where the employer reneged on his agreement to bargain after a third party checked the validity of the card signatures and insisted on an election because he doubted that the employees truly desired representation. The Board entered a bargaining order with very broad language to the effect that an employer could not refuse a bargaining demand and seek an election instead "without valid ground therefor," 134 N.L.R.B. at 710–711. *See also Dixon Ford Shoe Co., Inc.*, 150 N.L.R.B. 861 (1965); *Kellogg Mills*, 147 N.L.R.B. 342, 346 (1964), *enforced* 347 F.2d 219 (C.A. 9th Cir. 1965).

The leading case codifying modifications to the *Joy Silk* doctrine was *Aaron Brothers*, 158 N.L.R.B. 1077 (1966). There the Board made it clear that it had shifted the burden to the General Counsel to show bad faith and that an employer "will not be held to have violated his bargaining obligation . . . simply because he refuses to rely on cards, rather than an election, as the method for determining the union's majority." 158 N.L.R.B., at 1078. Two significant consequences were emphasized. The Board noted (1) that not every unfair labor practice would automatically result in a finding of bad faith and therefore a bargaining order; the Board implied that it would find bad faith only if the unfair labor practice was serious enough to have the tendency to dissipate the union's majority. The Board noted (2) that an employer no longer needed to come forward with reasons for rejecting a bargaining demand. The Board pointed out, however, that a bargaining order would issue if it could prove that an employer's "course of conduct" gave indications as to the employer's bad faith. As examples of such a "course of conduct," the Board cited *Snow & Sons, supra; Dixon Ford Shoe Co., Inc., supra*, and *Kellogg Mills, supra*, thereby reaffirming *John P. Serpa, Inc.*, 155 N.L.R.B. No. 12 (1965), where the Board had limited *Snow & Sons* to its facts.

Although the Board's brief before this Court generally followed the approach as set out in *Aaron Brothers, supra*, the Board announced at oral argument that it had virtually abandoned the *Joy Silk* doctrine altogether. Under the Board's current practice, an employer's good faith doubt is largely irrelevant, and the key to the issuance of a bargaining order is the commission of serious unfair labor practices that interfere with the election processes and tend to preclude the holding of a fair election. Thus, an employer can insist that a union go to an election, regardless of his subjective motivation, so long as he is not guilty of misconduct; he need give no affirmative reasons for rejecting a recognition request, and he can demand an election with a simple "no comment" to the union. The Board pointed out, however, (1) that an employer could not refuse to bargain if he *knew*, through a personal poll for instance, that a majority of his employees supported the union, and (2) that an employer could not refuse recognition initially because of questions as to the appropriateness of the unit and then later claim, as an afterthought, that he doubted the union's strength.

The union argues here that an employer's right to insist on an election in the absence of unfair labor practices should be more circumscribed, and a union's right to rely on cards correspondingly more expanded, than the Board would have us rule. The union's contention is that an employer, when confronted with a card-based bargaining demand, can insist on an election only by filing the election petition himself immediately under § 9(c)(1)(B) and not by insisting that the union file the election petition, whereby the election can be subjected to considerable delay. If the employer does not himself petition for an election, the union argues, he must recognize the union regardless of his good or bad faith and regardless of his other unfair labor practices, and should be ordered to bargain if the cards were in fact validly obtained. And if this Court should continue to utilize the good faith doubt rule, the union contends that at the least we should put the burden on the employer to make an affirmative showing of his reasons for entertaining such doubt.

Because the employers' refusal to bargain in each of these cases was accompanied in each instance by independent unfair labor practices which tend to preclude the holding of a fair election, we need not decide whether a bargaining order is ever appropriate in cases where there is no interference with the election processes....

III

A. The first issue facing us is whether a union can establish a bargaining obligation by means other than a Board election and whether the validity of alternate routes to majority status, such as cards, was affected by the 1947 Taft-Hartley amendments. The most commonly traveled route for a union to obtain recognition as the exclusive bargaining representative of an unorganized group of employees is through the Board's election and certification procedures under §9(c) of the Act (29 U.S.C. §159(c) (1964 ed.)); it is also, from the Board's point of view, the preferred route. A union is not limited to a Board election, however, for, in addition to §9, the present Act provides in §8(a)(5)..., as did the Wagner Act in §8(5), that "it shall be an unfair labor practice for an employer... to refuse to bargain collectively with the representatives of his employees, subject to the provisions of section 9(a)." Since §9(a), in both the Wagner Act and the present Act, refers to the representative as the one "designated or selected" by a majority of the employees without specifying precisely how that representative is to be chosen, it was early recognized that an employer had a duty to bargain whenever the union representative presented "convincing evidence of majority support." Almost from the inception of the Act, then, it was recognized that a union did not have to be certified as the winner of a Board election to invoke a bargaining obligation; it could establish majority status by other means under the unfair labor practice provision of §8(a)(5) — by showing convincing support, for instance, by a union-called strike or strike vote, or, as here, by possession of cards signed by a majority of the employees authorizing the union to represent them for collective bargaining purposes....

... Indeed, the 1947 amendments weaken rather than strengthen the position taken by the employers here and the Fourth Circuit below. An early version of the bill in the House would have amended §8(5) of the Wagner Act to permit the Board to find a refusal to bargain violation only where an employer had failed to bargain with a union "currently recognized by the employer or certified as such [through an election] under section 9." Section 8(a)(5) of H.R. 3020, 80th Cong., 1st Sess. (1947). The proposed change, which would have eliminated the use of cards, was rejected in Conference (H.R. Conf. Rep. No. 510, 80th Cong., 1st Sess., 41 (1947)), however, and we cannot make a similar change in the Act simply because, as the employers assert, Congress did not expressly approve the use of cards in rejecting the House amendment. Nor can we accept the Fourth Circuit's conclusion that the change was wrought when Congress amended §9(c) to make election the sole basis for *certification* by eliminating the phrase "any other suitable method to ascertain such representatives," under which the Board had occasionally used cards as a certification basis. A certified union has the benefit of numerous special privileges which are not accorded unions recognized voluntarily or under a bargaining order and which,

Congress could determine, should not be dispensed unless a union has survived the crucible of a secret ballot election.

The employers rely finally on the addition to §9(c) of subparagraph (B), which allows an employer to petition for an election whenever "one or more individuals or labor organizations have presented to him a claim to be recognized as the representative defined in section 9(a)." That provision was not added, as the employers assert, to give them an absolute right to an election at any time; rather, it was intended, as the legislative history indicates, to allow them, after asked to bargain, to test out their doubts as to a union's majority in a secret election which they would then presumably not cause to be set aside by illegal antiunion activity. We agree with the Board's assertion here that there is no suggestion that Congress intended §9(c)(1)(B) to relieve any employer of his §8(a)(5) bargaining obligation where, without good faith, he engaged in unfair labor practices disruptive of the Board's election machinery. And we agree that the policies reflected in §9(c)(1)(B) fully support the Board's present administration of the Act . . . ; for an employer can insist on a secret ballot election, unless, in the words of the Board, he engages "in contemporaneous unfair labor practices likely to destroy the union's majority and seriously impede the election." . . .

In short, we hold that the 1947 amendments did not restrict an employer's duty to bargain under §8(a)(5) solely to those unions whose representative status is certified after a Board election.

B. We next consider the question whether authorization cards are such inherently unreliable indicators of employee desires that whatever the validity of other alternate routes to representative status, the cards themselves may never be used to determine a union's majority and to support an order to bargain. In this context, the employers urge us to take the step the 1947 amendments and their legislative history indicate Congress did not take, namely, to rule out completely the use of cards in the bargaining arena. Even if we do not unhesitatingly accept the Fourth Circuit's view in the matter, the employers argue, at the very least we should overrule the *Cumberland Shoe* doctrine . . . and establish stricter controls over the solicitation of the cards by union representatives. . . .

That the cards, though admittedly inferior to the election process, can adequately reflect employee sentiment when that process has been impeded, needs no extended discussion, for the employers' contentions cannot withstand close examination. The employers argue that their employees cannot make an informed choice because the card drive will be over before the employer has had a chance to present his side of the unionization issues. Normally, however, the union will inform the employer of its organization drive early in order to subject the employer to the unfair labor practice provisions of the Act; the union must be able to show the employer's awareness of the drive in order to prove that his contemporaneous conduct constituted unfair labor practices on which a bargaining order can be based if the drive is ultimately successful. *See, e.g., Hunt Oil Co.*, 157 N.L.R.B. 282 (1966); *Don Swart Trucking Co.*, 154 N.L.R.B. 1345 (1965). Thus, in all of the cases here but the Charleston campaign in *Heck's* the employer, whether informed by the union or not, was aware of the union's organizing drive almost at the outset and began his antiunion campaign at that time; and even in the *Heck's-Charleston* case, where the recognition demand came about a week after the solicitation began, the employer was able to deliver a speech before the union obtained a majority. Further, the employers argue that without a secret ballot an employee may, in a card drive, succumb to group pressures or sign simply to get the union "off his back" and then be unable to change his mind as he would be free to do once inside a voting booth. But the same pressures are likely to be equally present in an election, for election cases arise most often with small bargaining units where virtually every voter's sentiments can be carefully and individually canvassed. And no voter, of course, can change his mind after casting a ballot in an election even though he may think better of his choice shortly thereafter.

The employer's second complaint, that the cards are too often obtained through misrepresentation and coercion, must be rejected also in view of the Board's present rules for controlling card solicitation, which we view as adequate to the task where the cards involved state their purpose clearly and unambiguously on their face. We would be closing our eyes to obvious difficulties, of course, if we did not recognize that there have been abuses, primarily arising out of misrepresentations by union organizers as to whether the effect of signing a card was to designate the union to represent the employee for collective bargaining purposes or merely to authorize it to seek an election to determine that issue. And we would be equally blind if we did not recognize that various courts of appeals and commentators have differed significantly as to the effectiveness of the Board's *Cumberland Shoe* doctrine . . . to cure such abuses. . . .

We need make no decision as to the conflicting approaches used with regard to dual-purpose cards, for in each of the five organization campaigns in the four cases before us the cards used were single-purpose cards, stating clearly and unambiguously on their face that the signer designated the union as his representative. And even the view forcefully voiced by the Fourth Circuit below that unambiguous cards as well present too many opportunities for misrepresentation comes before us somewhat weakened in view of the fact that there were no allegations of irregularities in four of those five campaigns (*Gissel*, the two *Heck's* campaigns, and *Sinclair*). Only in *General Steel* did the employer challenge the cards on the basis of misrepresentations. There, the trial examiner, after hearing testimony from over 100 employees and applying the traditional Board approach . . . concluded that "all of these employees not only intended, but were fully aware that they were designating the union as their representative." Thus, the sole question before us, raised in only one of the four cases here, is whether the *Cumberland Shoe* doctrine is an adequate rule under the Act for assuring employee free choice.

In resolving the conflict among the circuits in favor of approving the Board's *Cumberland* rule, we think it sufficient to point out that employees should be bound by the clear language of what they sign unless that language is deliberately and clearly canceled by a union adherent with words calculated to direct the signer to disregard and forget the language above his signature. There is nothing inconsistent in handing an employee a card that says the signer authorizes the union to represent him and then telling him that the card will probably be used first to get an election. Elections have been, after all, and will continue to be, held in the vast majority of cases; the union will still have to have the signatures of 30% of the employees when an employer rejects a bargaining demand and insists that the union seek an election. We cannot agree with the employers here that employees as a rule are too unsophisticated to be bound by what they sign unless expressly told that their act of signing represents something else. In addition to approving the use of cards, of course, Congress has expressly authorized reliance on employee signatures alone in other areas of labor relations, even where criminal sanctions hang in the balance, and we should not act hastily in disregarding congressional judgments that employees can be counted on to take responsibility for their acts.

We agree, however, with the Board's own warnings in *Levi Strauss*, 172 N.L.R.B. No. 57, 68 L.R.R.M. 1338, 1341, and n.7 (1968), that in hearing testimony concerning a card challenge, trial examiners should not neglect their obligation to ensure employee free choice by a too easy mechanical application of the *Cumberland* rule. We also accept the observation that employees are more likely than not, many months after a card drive and in response to questions by company counsel, to give testimony damaging to the union, particularly where company officials have previously threatened reprisals for union activity in violation of § 8(a)(1). We therefore reject any rule that requires a probe of an employee's subjective motivations as involving an endless and unreliable inquiry....

C. Remaining before us is the propriety of a bargaining order as a remedy for a § 8(a)(5) refusal to bargain where an employer has committed independent unfair labor practices which have made the holding of a fair election unlikely or which have in fact undermined a union's majority and caused an election to be set aside. We have long held that the Board is not limited to a cease-and-desist order in such cases, but has the authority to issue a bargaining order without first requiring the union to show that it has been able to maintain its majority status. *See NLRB v. Katz*, 369 U.S. 736, 748, n.16 (1962); *NLRB v. P. Lorillard Co.*, 314 U.S. 512 (1942). And we have held that the Board has the same authority even where it is clear that the union, which once had possession of cards from a majority of the employees, represents only a minority when the bargaining order is entered. *Franks Bros. Co. v. NLRB*, 321 U.S. 702 (1943). We see no reason now to withdraw this authority from the Board. If the Board could enter only a cease-and-desist order and direct an election or a rerun, it would in effect be rewarding the employer and allowing him "to profit from [his] own wrongful refusal to bargain." *Franks Bros., supra*, at 704, while at the same time severely curtailing the employees' right freely to determine whether they desire a representative. The employer could continue to delay or disrupt the election processes and put off indefinitely his obligation to bargain; and any election held under these circumstances would not be likely to demonstrate the employees' true, undistorted desires....

Before considering whether the bargaining orders were appropriately entered in these cases, we should summarize the factors that go into such a determination. Despite our reversal of the Fourth Circuit below in Nos. 573 and 691 on all major issues, the actual area of disagreement between our position here and that of the Fourth Circuit is not large as a practical matter. While refusing to validate the general use of a bargaining order in reliance on cards, the Fourth Circuit nevertheless left open the possibility of imposing a bargaining order, without need of inquiry into majority status on the basis of cards or otherwise, in "exceptional" cases marked by "outrageous" and "pervasive" unfair labor practices. Such an order would be an appropriate remedy for those practices, the court noted, if they are of "such a nature that their coercive effects cannot be eliminated by the application of traditional remedies, with the result that a fair and reliable election cannot be had." *NLRB v. Logan Packing Co.*, 386 F.2d 562, 570 (C.A. 4th Cir. 1967); *see also NLRB v. Heck's supra*, 308 F.2d, at 338. The Board itself, we should add, has long had a similar policy of issuing a bargaining order, in the absence of a § 8(a)(5) violation or even a bargaining demand, when that was the only available, effective remedy for substantial unfair labor practices. . . .

The only effect of our holding here is to approve the Board's use of the bargaining order in less extraordinary cases marked by less pervasive practices which nonetheless still have the tendency to undermine majority strength and impede the election processes. The Board's authority to issue such an order on a lesser showing of employer misconduct is appropriate, we should reemphasize, where there is also a showing that at one point the union had a majority; in such a case, of course, effectuating ascertainable employee free choice becomes as important a goal as deterring employer misbehavior. In fashioning a remedy in the exercise of its discretion, then, the Board can properly take into consideration the extensiveness of an employer's unfair practices in terms of their past effect on election conditions and the likelihood of their recurrence in the future. If the Board finds that the possibility of erasing the effects of past practices and of ensuring a fair election (or a fair rerun) by the use of traditional remedies, though present, is slight and that employee sentiment once expressed through cards would, on balance, be better protected by a bargaining order, then such an order should issue. . . .

We emphasize that under the Board's remedial power there is still a third category of minor or less extensive unfair labor practices, which, because of their minimal impact on the election machinery, will not sustain a bargaining order. There is, the Board says, no *per se* rule that the commission of any unfair practice will automatically result in a § 8(a)(5) violation and the issuance of an order to bargain. See *Aaron Brothers, supra*.

With these considerations in mind, we turn to an examination of the orders in these cases. In *Sinclair*, No. 585, the Board made a finding, left undisturbed by the First Circuit, that the employer's threats of reprisal were so coercive that, even in the absence of a § 8(a)(5) violation, a bargaining order would have been necessary to repair the unlawful effect of those threats. The Board therefore did not have to make the determination called for in the intermediate situation above that the risks that a fair rerun election might not be possible were too great to disregard the desires of the employees already expressed through the cards....

In the three cases in Nos. 573 and 691 from the Fourth Circuit, on the other hand, the Board did not make a similar finding that a bargaining order would have been necessary in the absence of an unlawful refusal to bargain. Nor did it make a finding that, even though traditional remedies might be able to ensure a fair election, there was insufficient indication that an election (or a rerun in *General Steel*) would definitely be a more reliable test of the employees' desires than the card count taken before the unfair labor practices occurred. The employees [employers] argue that such findings would not be warranted, and the court below ruled in *General Steel* that available remedies short of a bargaining order could guarantee a fair election.... We think it possible that the requisite findings were implicit in the Board's decisions below to issue bargaining orders (and to set aside the election in *General Steel*); and we think it clearly inappropriate for the court below to make any contrary finding on its own.... Because the Board's current practice at the time required it to phrase its findings in terms of an employer's good- or bad-faith doubts (see Part II, *supra*), however, the precise analysis the Board now puts forth was not employed below, and we therefore remand these cases to the Board for proper findings.

Notes

1. *Aftermath*—On remand in *Gissel*, the Board upheld issuance of a bargaining order, since it found that the employer's unfair labor practices, both before and after the denial of the union's request for recognition on the basis of authorization cards, were sufficiently pervasive to preclude the holding of a fair election. *Gissel Packing Co.*, 180 N.L.R.B. 54 (1969), *enforced*, 76 L.R.R.M. 2175 (4th Cir. 1970).

2. *When Is a* Gissel *Order Appropriate?*—Remedial bargaining orders are most frequently issued in cases involving § 8(a)(3) discharges of union activists, threats to lay off union supporters or to close unionized facilities, and similar "hallmark" violations. In recent years, the NLRB and courts have suggested that extraordinary bargaining orders should be reserved for extreme cases. *Compare Evergreen Am. Corp. v. NLRB*, 531 F.3d 321 (4th Cir. 2008), *and Ctr. Constr. Co. v. NLRB*, 482 F.3d 425 (6th Cir. 2007) (sustaining issuance of bargaining orders where election process was marred by extensive employer unfair labor practices), *with Almet, Inc.*, 305 N.L.R.B. 626 (1991), *aff'd*, 987 F.2d 445 (7th Cir. 1993) (employer's threats to close the plant and to discharge union supporters and its suspension of one union activist not "sufficiently egregious" to warrant a bargaining order, since the conduct took place two months before the election and the employer subsequently "ameliorated" the effects of its unlawful conduct by assuring employees that it would stay open and by compensating the suspended employee for his lost time), *and Kinney Drugs v. NLRB*, 74 F.3d 1419 (2d Cir. 1996) (single hallmark violation—employer threat to discharge two union supporters unless they called meeting to discourage coworkers from voting for union—insufficient to support bargaining order).

After a union has lost a representation election, the Board will only issue a bargaining order to remedy pre-election unfair labor practices if the labor organization files both unfair labor practice charges *and* timely election objections. "We will not grant [a bargaining order] . . . unless the election be set aside on the basis of meritorious objections filed in the representation case." *Irving Air Chute Co.*, 149 N.L.R.B. 627 (1964), *enforced*, 350 F.2d 176 (2d Cir. 1965).

3. *Timing Issues* — The Labor Board believes that *Gissel* "contemplated that the propriety of a bargaining order would be judged as of the time of the commission of the unfair labor practices and not in the light of subsequent events." Otherwise, an employer could profit from its wrongdoing by preventing a union whose majority has been undermined from securing a bargaining order. *Gibson Products Co. of Washington Parish, La., Inc.*, 185 N.L.R.B. 362 (1970), *supplemented*, 199 N.L.R.B. 794 (1972), *enforcement denied*, 494 F.2d 762 (5th Cir. 1974). *Accord New Alaska Development Corp. v. NLRB*, 441 F.2d 491 (7th Cir. 1971) (bargaining order valid even though turnover of employees and their lack of knowledge of threats had changed situation so that fair election could now be had); *NLRB v. L. B. Foster Co.*, 418 F.2d 1 (9th Cir. 1969) (court cannot set aside bargaining order merely because there was possibility that not one employee remained who had been at plant during the original election). The Fifth Circuit disagreed, declaring that no bargaining order should issue unless *at the time such an order is directed* the Board "finds the electoral atmosphere unlikely to produce a fair election." *NLRB v. American Cable Systems, Inc.*, 427 F.2d 446 (5th Cir.), *cert. denied*, 400 U.S. 957 (1970).

Courts continue to differ with respect to the impact of elapsed time on the enforceability of remedial bargaining orders. *Compare NLRB v. USA Polymer Corp*, 272 F.3d 289 (5th Cir. 2001), *cert. denied*, 536 U.S. 939 (2002) (enforcing bargaining order despite 4.5-year delay between commission of unfair labor practices and entry of order, restructuring of business in the interim, and nearly 100% turnover in unit), *with Overnite Transp. Co. v. NLRB*, 280 F.3d 417 (4th Cir. 2002) (denying enforcement of bargaining order where five years had elapsed between commission of unfair labor practices and entry of remedial order, significant employee turnover had occurred, and employer had taken steps to redress prior unfair labor practices). More recently, in *Novelis Corp. v. NLRB*, 885 F.3d 100 (2d Cir. 2018), the court refused to enforce a *Gissel* bargaining order despite significant employer unfair labor practices committed prior to the Board election, where the company had complied with a § 10(j) injunction, there had been a substantial lapse of time between the representation election and the final Board order, and there had been a significant degree of employee turnover since the prior election.

Although § 9(c)(3) prohibits the holding of more than one valid election within 12 months, it does not preclude issuance of an otherwise appropriate Board bargaining order within one year of a valid election. *Camvac Int'l, Inc.*, 297 N.L.R.B. 853 (1990); *Concren, Inc. v. Retail Store Employees Union, Local 550*, 156 N.L.R.B. 592, *enforced*, 368 F.2d 173 (7th Cir. 1966), *cert. denied*, 386 U.S. 974 (1967).

In *Seeler v. Trading Port, Inc.*, 517 F.2d 33 (2d Cir. 1975), the court held that in *Gissel*-type cases, a regional director may obtain a preliminary bargaining order against an employer under § 10(j) of the NLRA, pending a final determination by the Board concerning the union's bargaining status. *Accord Scott ex rel. NLRB v Stephen Dunn & Assocs.*, 241 F.3d 652 (9th Cir. 2001).

In *Trading Port, Inc.*, 219 N.L.R.B. 298 (1975), the Board indicated that "an employer's obligation under a bargaining order remedy should commence as of the time the employer has embarked on a clear course of unlawful conduct or has engaged in sufficient unfair labor practices to undermine the union's majority status." What is the significance of a retroactive bargaining order to the affected labor organization?

4. *Remedial Bargaining Orders in Situations Where the Union Has Never Enjoyed Majority Support* — In *J.P. Stevens & Co., Gulistan Div. v. NLRB*, 441 F.2d 514 (5th Cir.), *cert. denied*, 404 U.S. 830 (1971), the court interpreted *Gissel* as authorizing the issuance of a bargaining order to a union that has never established its majority status, where an employer's unfair labor practices are so "outrageous" and "pervasive" that their coercive effects cannot be overcome by traditional remedies. Although the *Stevens* court found that the union at one point actually did represent a majority of the employees, the court said that the employer's "full scale war against unionization" made it unnecessary for the union to demonstrate its majority status. The company had discharged three leading union adherents and had engaged in a campaign of blatant surveillance, interrogation, and threats.

In *Conair Corp.*, 261 N.L.R.B. 1189 (1982), the NLRB, for the first time, found an employer's unfair labor practices sufficiently "outrageous" and "pervasive" to justify the issuance of a bargaining order in favor of a union that had never established its majority status. A panel of the D.C. Circuit denied enforcement of the Board's bargaining order, however, in *Conair Corp. v. NLRB*, 721 F.2d 1355 (1983), *cert. denied*, 467 U.S. 1241 (1984). Although agreeing that the employer's unfair labor practices were outrageous and pervasive, the majority concluded that any departure from the principle of majority rule should be left to Congress. Judge Wald dissented on the ground that the bargaining order was the only way to remedy the employer's "massive and unrelenting coercive conduct." In *Gourmet Foods, Inc.*, 270 N.L.R.B. 578 (1984), the Board indicated that it would no longer issue bargaining orders in favor of unions that have not established majority support.

In *Marie Phillips, Inc.*, 178 N.L.R.B. 340 (1969), *enforced*, 443 F.2d 667 (D.C. Cir. 1970), the Board rejected an employer's contention that 26 unequivocal authorization cards that helped establish a union's majority were invalid because the union had solicited them by misrepresenting that a majority of the employees had already signed. The Board indicated that an objective standard must be used to determine the impact of misrepresentations on the validity of authorization cards:

> Where the objective facts, as evidenced by events contemporaneous with the signing, clearly demonstrate that the misrepresentation was the decisive

factor in causing an employee to sign a card, we shall not count such a card in determining a union's majority. However, ... where the only indication of reliance is a signer's subsequent testimony as to his subjective state of mind when signing the card, such showing is insufficient to invalidate the card.

5. *Achieving Representative Status through an Employer Poll*—An employer that conducts a poll and verifies that a majority of its employees wants union representation forfeits its right to an election and subjects itself to issuance of a § 8(a)(5) bargaining order, regardless of whether the poll was lawfully conducted. *NLRB v. English Bros. Pattern & Foundry*, 679 F.2d 787 (9th Cir. 1982).

Linden Lumber Division, Summer & Co. v. NLRB
Supreme Court of the United States
419 U.S. 301, 95 S. Ct. 429, 42 L. Ed. 2d 465 (1974)

MR. JUSTICE DOUGLAS delivered the opinion of the Court.

These cases present a question expressly reserved in *National Labor Relations Board v. Gissel Packing Co.*, 395 U.S. 575, 595, 601, n. 18 (1969).

In *Linden* respondent union obtained authorization cards from a majority of petitioner's employees and demanded that it be recognized as the collective-bargaining representative of those employees. Linden said it doubted the union's claimed majority status and suggested the union petition the Board for an election. The union filed such a petition with the Board but later withdrew it when Linden declined to enter a consent election agreement or abide by an election on the ground that respondent union's organizational campaign had been improperly assisted by company supervisors. Respondent union thereupon renewed its demand for collective bargaining; and again Linden declined, saying that the union's claimed membership had been improperly influenced by supervisors. Thereupon respondent union struck for recognition as the bargaining representative and shortly filed a charge of unfair labor practice against Linden based on its refusal to bargain.

There is no charge that Linden engaged in an unfair labor practice apart from its refusal to bargain. The Board held that Linden should not be guilty of an unfair labor practice solely on the basis "of its refusal to accept evidence of majority status other than the results of a Board election." . . .

In *Wilder* there apparently were 30 employees in the plant and the union with 11 signed and two unsigned authorization cards requested recognition as the bargaining agent for the company's production and maintenance employees. Of the 30 employees 18 were in the production and maintenance unit which the Board found to be appropriate for collective bargaining. No answer was given by Wilder, and recognitional picketing began. The request was renewed when the two unsigned cards were signed, but Wilder denied recognition. Thereupon the union filed unfair labor practice charges against Wilder. A series of Board decisions and judicial decisions, not necessary to recapitulate here, consumed about seven years until the present decision by the Court of Appeals. The Board made the same ruling as respects Wilder as it did in Linden's case. . . . On petitions for review of the Court of Appeals reversed. 487 F.2d 1099 (1973). We reverse the Court of Appeals.

In *Gissel* we held that an employer who engages in "unfair" labor practices "likely to destroy the union's majority and seriously impede the election" may not insist that before it bargains the union get a secret ballot election. 395 U.S. at 600. There were no such unfair labor practices here, nor had the employer in either case agreed to a voluntary settlement of the dispute and then reneged. As noted, we reserved in *Gissel* the questions "whether, absent election interference by an employer's unfair labor practices, he may obtain an election only if he petitions for one himself; whether, if he does not, he must bargain with a card majority if the union chooses not to seek an election; and whether, in the latter situation, he is bound by the Board's ultimate determination of the card results regardless of his earlier good faith doubts, or whether he can still insist on a Union-sought election if he makes an affirmative showing of his positive reasons for believing there is a representation dispute." *Id.* at 601, n. 18.

We recognized in *Gissel* that while the election process had acknowledged superiority in ascertaining whether a union has majority support, cards may "adequately reflect employee sentiment." *Id.* at 603.

Generalizations are difficult; and it is urged by the unions that only the precise facts should dispose of concrete cases. As we said, however, in *Gissel*, the Board had largely abandoned its earlier test that the employer's refusal to bargain was warranted, if he had a good-faith doubt that the union represented a majority. . . .

In the present cases the Board found that the employers "should not be found guilty of a violation of Section 8(a)(5) solely upon the basis of [their] refusal to accept evidence of majority status other than the results of a Board election." . . . The question whether the employers had good reasons or poor reasons was not deemed relevant to the inquiry. The Court of Appeals concluded that if the employer had doubts as to a union's majority status, it could and should test out its doubts by petitioning for an election. . . .

To take the Board's position is not to say that authorization cards are wholly unreliable as an indication of employee support of the union. An employer concededly may have valid objections to recognizing a union on that basis. His objection to cards may, of course, mask his opposition to unions. On the other hand he may have rational, good-faith grounds for distrusting authorization cards in a given situation. He may be convinced that the fact that a majority of the employees strike and picket does not necessarily establish that they desire the particular union as their representative. Fear may indeed prevent some from crossing a picket line; or sympathy for strikers, not the desire to have the particular union in the saddle, may influence others. These factors make difficult an examination of the employer's motive to ascertain whether it was in good faith. To enter that domain is to reject the approval by *Gissel* of the retreat which the Board took from its "good faith" inquiries.

The union which is faced with an unwilling employer has two alternative remedies under the Board's decision in the instant case. It can file for an election; or it can press unfair labor practices against the employer under *Gissel*. The latter alternative promises to consume much time. In *Linden* the time between filing the charge and the Board's ruling was about 4½ years; in *Wilder*, about 6½ years. The Board's experience indicates that the median time in a contested case is 388 days. *Gissel*, 395 U.S. at 611, n. 30. On the other hand the median time between the filing of the petition for an election and the decision of the regional director is about 45 days. In terms of getting on with the problems of inaugurating regimes of industrial peace, the policy of encouraging secret elections under the Act is favored. The question remains — should the burden be on the union to ask for an election or should it be the responsibility of the employer?

The Court of Appeals concluded that since Congress in 1947 authorized employers to file their own representation petitions by enacting § 9(c)(1)(B), the burden was on them. But the history of that provision indicates it was aimed at eliminating the discrimination against employers which had previously existed under the Board's prior rules, permitting employers to petition for an election only when confronted with claims by two or more unions. There is no suggestion that Congress wanted to place the burden of getting a secret election on the employer.

> Today an employer is faced with this situation. A man comes into his office and says, "I represent your employees. Sign this agreement or we strike tomorrow." Such instances have occurred all over the United States. The employer has no way in which to determine whether this man really does represent his employees or does not. The bill gives him the right to go to the Board under those circumstances, and say, "I want an election. I want to know who is the bargaining agent for my employees."

93 Cong. Rec. 3838 (1947) (remarks of Senator Taft).

Our problem is not one of picking favorites but of trying to find the congressional purpose by examining the statutory and administrative interpretations that squint one way or another. Large issues ride on who takes the initiative. A common issue is, what should be the representative unit? In *Wilder* the employer at first took the position that the unit should be one of 30 employees. If it were 18, as the union claimed (or even 25 as the employer later argued), the union with its 13 authorization cards (assuming them to be valid) would have a majority. If the unit were 30, the union would be out of business.

Section 9(c)(1)(B) visualizes an employer faced with a claim by individuals or unions "to be recognized as the representative defined in § 9(a)." That question of representation is raised only by a claim that the applicant represents a majority of employees, "in a unit appropriate for such purposes." § 9(a). If there is a significant discrepancy between the unit which the employer wants and the unit for which the union asked recognition, the Board will dismiss the employer's petition. [Citing cases.] In that event the union, if it desired the smaller unit, would have to file its [10] own petition, leaving the employer free to contest the appropriateness of that unit. The Court of Appeals thought that if the employer were required to petition the Board for an election, the litigable issues would be reduced. The recurring conflict over what should be the appropriate bargaining unit coupled with the fact that if the employer asks for a unit which the union opposes, his election petition is dismissed is answer enough.

The Board has at least some expertise in these matters and its judgment is that an employer's petition for an election, though permissible, is not the required course. It points out in its brief here that an employer wanting to gain delay can draw a petition to elicit protests by the union, and the thought that an employer petition would obviate litigation over the sufficiency of the union's showing of interest is in its purview apparently not well taken. A union petition to be sure must be backed by a 30% showing of employee interest. But the sufficiency of such a showing is not litigable by the parties.

In light of the statutory scheme and the practical administrative procedural questions involved, we cannot say that the Board's decision that the union should go forward and ask for an election on the employer's refusal to recognize the authorization cards was arbitrary and capricious or an abuse of discretion.

In sum, we sustain the Board in holding that, unless an employer has engaged in an unfair labor practice that impairs the electoral process, a union with authorization cards purporting to represent a majority of the employees, which is refused recognition, has the burden of taking the next step in invoking the Board's election procedure.

Reversed.

Mr. Justice Stewart, with whom Mr. Justice White, Mr. Justice Marshall, and Mr. Justice Powell join, dissenting.

Section 9(a) expressly provides that the employees' exclusive bargaining representative shall be the union "designated or selected" by a majority of the employees in an appropriate unit. Neither § 9(a) nor § 8(a)(5), which makes it an unfair labor practice for an employer to refuse to bargain with the representative of his employees, specifies how that representative is to be chosen. The language of the Act thus seems purposefully designed to impose a duty upon an employer to bargain whenever the union representative presents convincing evidence of majority support, regardless of the method by which that support is demonstrated. And both the Board and this Court have in the past consistently interpreted §§ 8(a)(5) and 9(a) to mean exactly that. . . .

As the Court recognized in *Gissel*, the 1947 Taft-Hartley amendments strengthen this interpretation of the Act. One early version of the House bill would have

---

10. [10] We do not reach the question whether the same result obtains if the employer breaches his agreement to permit majority status to be determined by means other than a Board election. . . .

amended the Act to permit the Board to find an employer unfair labor practice for refusing to bargain with a union only if the union was "currently recognized by the employer or certified as such [through an election] under section 9." Section 8(a)(5) of H. R. 3020, 80th Cong., 1st Sess. The proposed change, which would have eliminated any method of requiring employer recognition of a union other than a Board-supervised election, was rejected in Conference. H. R. Conf. Rep. No. 510, 80th Cong., 1st Sess., 41. After rejection of the proposed House amendment, the House Conference Report explicitly stated that § 8(a)(5) was intended to follow the provisions of "existing law." *Ibid.* And "existing law" unequivocally recognized that a union could establish majority status and thereby impose a bargaining obligation on an unwilling employer by means other than petitioning for and winning a Board-supervised election. *NLRB v. Gissel Packing Co., supra*, at 596–598.

The 1947 amendments, however, did provide an alternative to immediate union recognition for an employer faced with a union demand to bargain on behalf of his employees. Section 9(c)(1)(B), added to the Act in 1947, provides that an employer, alleging that one or more individuals or labor organizations have presented a claim to be recognized as the exclusive representative of his employees, may file a petition for a Board-supervised representation election.

This section, together with §§ 8(a)(5) and 9(a), provides clear congressional direction as to the proper approach to the situation before us. When an employer is faced with a demand for recognition by a union that has presented convincing evidence of majority support, he may elect to follow one of four alternatives. First, he is free to recognize the union and thereby satisfy his § 8(a)(5) obligation to bargain with the representatives "designated or selected" by his employees. Second, he may petition for a Board-supervised election, pursuant to § 9(c)(1)(B). *NLRB v. Gissel Packing Co., supra*, at 599. Third, rather than file his own election petition, the employer can agree to be bound by the results of an expedited consent election ordered after the filing of a union election petition. See 29 CFR § 102.62. Finally, the employer can refuse to recognize the union, despite its convincing evidence of majority support, and also refuse either to petition for an election or to consent to a union-requested election. In this event, however, the Act clearly provides that the union may charge the employer with an unfair labor practice under § 8(a)(5) for refusing to bargain collectively with the representatives of his employees. If the General Counsel issues a complaint and the Board determines that the union in fact represents a majority of the employees, the Board must issue an order directing the employer to bargain with the union. *See, e.g., NLRB v. Dahlstrom Metallic Door Co.*, 112 F.2d 756; cf. *NLRB v. Gissel Packing Co.*, 395 U.S., at 595–600.

The Court offers two justifications for its approval of the new Board practice which, disregarding the clear language of §§ 8(a)(5) and 9(a), requires an employer to bargain only with a union certified as bargaining representative after a Board-supervised election conducted upon the petition of the union.

First, it is suggested that to require the Board under some circumstances to find a § 8(a)(5) violation when an employer refuses to bargain with the noncertified union supported by a majority of his employees would compel the Board to reenter the domain of subjective "good faith" inquiries. *Ante,* at slip op. 5. This fear is unwarranted....

Within broad limits imposed by the Act itself, the Board may use its understanding of the policies and practical considerations of the Act's administration to determine the circumstances under which an employer must take evidence of majority support as "convincing." *Cf. NLRB v. Insurance Agents' International Union,* 361 U.S. 477, 499; *NLRB v. Local 449, Teamsters,* 353 U.S. 87, 96. The Act in no way requires the Board to define "convincing evidence" in a manner that reintroduces a subjective test of the employer's good faith in refusing to bargain with the union. If the Board continues to believe, as it has in the recent past, that it is unworkable to adopt any standard for determining when an employer has breached his duty to bargain that incorporates a subjective element, *see NLRB v. Gissel Packing Co.,* 395 U.S. at 592–594, it may define "convincing evidence of majority support" solely by reference to objective criteria — for example, by reference to "a union-called strike or strike vote, or, as here, by possession of cards signed by a majority of the employees...." *Id.* at 597.

Even with adoption of such an objective standard for measuring "convincing evidence of majority support," the employer's "subjective" doubts would be adequately safeguarded by § 9(c)(1)(B)'s assurance of the right to file his own petition for an election. Despite the Board's broad discretion in this area, however, the Act simply does not permit the Board to adopt a rule that avoids *subjective* inquiries by eliminating entirely *all* inquiries into an employer's obligation to bargain with a noncertified union selected by a majority of his employees.

The second ground upon which the Court justifies its approval of the Board's new practice is that it serves to remove from the employer the burden of obtaining a Board-supervised election.... Although I agree with the Court that it would be improper to impose such an obligation on an employer, the Board's new policy is not necessary to eliminate such a burden.

The only employer obligation relevant to this case, apart from the requirement that the employer not commit independent unfair labor practices that would prejudice the holding of a fair election, is the one imposed by §§ 8(a)(5) and 9(a) of the Act: an employer has a duty to bargain collectively with the representative designated or selected by his employees. When an employer is confronted with "convincing evidence of majority support," he has the *option* of petitioning for an election or consenting to an expedited union-petitioned election. As the Court explains, § 9(c)(1)(B) does not require the employer to exercise this option. If he does not, however, and if he does not voluntarily recognize the union, he must take the risk that his conduct will be found by the Board to constitute a violation of his § 8(a)(5) duty to bargain. In short, petitioning for an election is not an employer obligation; it is a device created by Congress for the employer's self-protection, much as Congress gave unions the right to petition for elections to establish their majority status but deliberately chose not to require a union to seek an election before it could impose a bargaining obligation on an unwilling employer. *NLRB v. Gissel Packing Co.*, 395 U.S. at 598–599.

The language and history of the Act clearly indicate that Congress intended to impose upon an employer the duty to bargain with a union that has presented convincing evidence of majority support, even though the union has not petitioned for and won a Board-supervised election. "It is not necessary for us to justify the policy of Congress. It is enough that we find it in the statute. That policy cannot be defeated by the Board's policy." *Colgate-Palmolive-Peet Co. v. NLRB*, 338 U.S. 355, 363. Accordingly, I would affirm the judgment of the Court of Appeals remanding the case to the Board, but for further proceedings consistent with the views expressed in this opinion.

Note

In *Jefferson Smurfit Corp.*, 331 N.L.R.B. 809 (2000), the Board held that an employer presented with a union recognition demand letter accompanied by employee authorization cards and whose employee relations manager read the letter and examined the cards did not become obliged to grant recognition. The employer had no duty to accept the card count absent a clear agreement to do so.

Section III. Duration of the Duty to Bargain

Brooks v. NLRB

Supreme Court of the United States
348 U.S. 96, 75 S. Ct. 176, 99 L. Ed. 125 (1954)

Mr. Justice Frankfurter delivered the opinion of the Court.

The National Labor Relations Board conducted a representation election in petitioner's Chrysler-Plymouth agency on April 12, 1951. District Lodge No. 727, International Association of Machinists, won by a vote of eight to five, and the Labor Board certified it as the exclusive bargaining representative on April 20. A week after the election and the day before the certification, petitioner received a handwritten letter signed by nine of the 13 employees in the bargaining unit stating: "We, the undersigned majority of the employees . . . are not in favor of being represented by Union Local No. 727 as a bargaining agent."

Relying on this letter and the decision of the Court of Appeals for the Sixth Circuit in *NLRB v. Vulcan Forging Co.*, 188 F.2d 927 (6th Cir. 1951), petitioner refused to bargain with the union. The Labor Board found, 98 N.L.R.B. 976, that petitioner had thereby committed an unfair labor practice in violation of §§ 8(a)(1) and 8(a)(5) of the amended National Labor Relations Act, 61 Stat. 140–141, 29 U.S.C. §§ 158(a)(1), (a)(5), and the Court of Appeals for the Ninth Circuit enforced the Board's order to bargain, 204 F.2d 899 (9th Cir. 1953). In view of the conflict between the Circuits, we granted certiorari, 347 U.S. 916 (1954).

The issue before us is the duty of an employer toward a duly certified bargaining agent, if, shortly after the election which resulted in the certification, the union has lost, without the employer's fault, a majority of the employees from its membership.

Under the original Wagner Act, the Labor Board was given the power to certify a union as the exclusive representative of the employees in a bargaining unit when it had determined, by election or "any other suitable method," that the union commanded majority support. Section 9(c), 49 Stat. 453. In exercising this authority the Board evolved a number of working rules of which the following are relevant to our purpose:

> (a) A certification, if based on a Board-conducted election, must be honored for a "reasonable" period, ordinarily "one year," in the absence of "unusual circumstances."
>
> (b) "Unusual circumstances" were found in at least three situations: (1) The certified union dissolved or became defunct; (2) as a result of a schism, substantially all the members and officers of the certified union transferred their affiliation to a new local or international; (3) the size of the bargaining unit fluctuated radically within a short time.
>
> (c) Loss of majority support after the "reasonable" period could be questioned in two ways: (1) employer's refusal to bargain, or (2) petition by a rival union for a new election.
>
> (d) If the initial election resulted in a majority for "no union," the election—unlike a certification—did not bar a second election within a year.

The Board uniformly found an unfair labor practice where, during the so-called "certification year," an employer refused to bargain on the ground that the certified union no longer possessed a majority. While the courts in the main enforced the Board's decisions, they did not commit themselves to one year as the determinate content of reasonableness. The Board and the courts proceeded along this line of reasoning:

> (a) In the political and business spheres, the choice of the voters in an election binds them for a fixed time. This promotes a sense of responsibility in the electorate and needed coherence in administration. These considerations are equally relevant to healthy labor relations.
>
> (b) Since an election is a solemn and costly occasion, conducted under safeguards to voluntary choice, revocation of authority should occur by a procedure no less solemn than that of the initial designation. A petition or a public meeting—in which those voting for and against unionism are disclosed to management, and in which the influences of mass psychology are present—is not comparable to the privacy and independence of the voting booth.
>
> (c) A union should be given ample time for carrying out its mandate on behalf of its members, and should not be under exigent pressure to produce hot-house results or be turned out.

(d) It is scarcely conducive to bargaining in good faith for an employer to know that, if he dillydallies or subtly undermines, union strength may erode and thereby relieve him of his statutory duties at any time, while if he works conscientiously toward agreement, the rank and file may, at the last moment, repudiate their agent.

(e) In these situations, not wholly rare, where unions are competing, raiding and strife will be minimized if elections are not at the hazard of informal and short-term recall.

Certain aspects of the Labor Board's representation procedures came under scrutiny in the Congress that enacted the Taft-Hartley Act in 1947, 61 Stat. 136. Congress was mindful that, once employees had chosen a union, they could not vote to revoke its authority and refrain from union activities, while if they voted against having a union in the first place, the union could begin at once to agitate for a new election. The National Labor Relations Act was amended to provide that (a) employees could petition the Board for a decertification election, at which they would have an opportunity to choose no longer to be represented by a union, 61 Stat. 144, 29 U.S.C. §159(c)(1)(A)(ii); (b) an employer, if in doubt as to the majority claimed by a union without formal election or beset by the conflicting claims of rival unions, could likewise petition the Board for an election, 61 Stat. 144, 29 U.S.C. §159(c)(1)(B); (c) after a valid certification or decertification election had been conducted, the Board could not hold a second election in the same bargaining unit until a year had elapsed, 61 Stat. 144, 29 U.S.C. §159(c)(3); (d) Board certification could only be granted as the result of an election, 61 Stat. 144, 29 U.S.C. §159(c)(1), though an employer would presumably still be under a duty to bargain with an uncertified union that had a clear majority, see *NLRB v. Kobritz*, 193 F.2d 8 (1st Cir. 1951).

The Board continued to apply its "one-year certification" rule after the Taft-Hartley Act came into force, except that even "unusual circumstances" no longer left the Board free to order an election where one had taken place within the preceding 12 months. Conflicting views became manifest in the Court of Appeals when the Board sought to enforce orders based on a refusal to bargain in violation of its rule. Some Circuits sanctioned the Board's position. The Court of Appeals for the Sixth Circuit denied enforcement. The Court of Appeals for the Third Circuit held that a "reasonable" period depended on the facts of the particular case.

The issue is open here. No case touching the problem has directly presented it. In *Franks Bros. Co. v. NLRB*, 321 U.S. 702 (1944), we held that where a union's majority was dissipated after an employer's unfair labor practice in refusing to bargain, the Board could appropriately find that such conduct had undermined the prestige of the union and require the employer to bargain with it for a reasonable period despite the loss of majority. And in *NLRB v. Mexia Textile Mills, Inc.*, 339 U.S. 563 (1950), we held that a claim of an intervening loss of majority was no defense to a proceeding for enforcement of an order to cease and desist from certain unfair labor practices.

Petitioner contends that whenever an employer is presented with evidence that his employees have deserted their certified union, he may forthwith refuse to bargain. In effect, he seeks to vindicate the rights of his employees to select their bargaining representative. If the employees are dissatisfied with their chosen union, they may submit their own grievance to the Board. If an employer has doubts about his duty to continue bargaining, it is his responsibility to petition the Board for relief, while continuing to bargain in good faith at least until the Board has given some indication that his claim has merit. Although the Board may, if the facts warrant, revoke a certification or agree not to pursue a charge of unfair labor practice, these are matters for the Board; they do not justify the employer self-help or judicial intervention. The underlying purpose of this statute is industrial peace. To allow employers to rely on employees' rights in refusing to bargain with the formally designated union is not conducive to that end, it is inimical to it. Congress has devised a formal mode for selection and rejection of bargaining agents and has fixed the spacing of elections, with a view of furthering industrial stability and with due regard to administrative prudence.

We find wanting the arguments against these controlling considerations. In placing a nonconsenting minority under the bargaining responsibility of an agency selected by a majority of the workers, Congress has discarded common-law doctrines of agency. It is contended that since a bargaining agency may be ascertained by methods less formal than a supervised election, informal repudiation should also be sanctioned where decertification by another election is precluded. This is to make situations that are different appear the same. Finally, it is not within the power of this Court to require the Board, as is suggested, to relieve a small employer, like the one involved in this case, of the duty that may be exacted from an enterprise with many employees.

To be sure, what we have said has special pertinence only to the period during which a second election is impossible. But the Board's view that the one-year period should run from the date of certification rather than the date of election seems within the allowable area of the Board's discretion in carrying out congressional policy. *See Phelps Dodge Corp. v. NLRB*, 313 U.S. 177, 192–197 (1941); *NLRB v. Seven-Up Bottling Co.*, 344 U.S. 344 (1953). Otherwise, encouragement would be given to management or a rival union to delay certification by spurious objections to the conduct of an election and thereby diminish the duration of the duty to bargain. Furthermore, the Board has ruled that one year after certification the employer can ask for an election or, if he has fair doubts about the union's continuing majority, he may refuse to bargain further with it. This, too, is a matter appropriately determined by the Board's administrative authority.

We concluded that the judgment of the Court of Appeals enforcing the Board's order must be

Affirmed.

Notes

1. *Scope of the Certification Bar* — In *Americare-New Lexington Health Care Ctr.*, 316 N.L.R.B. 1226 (1995), *enforced*, 124 F.3d 753 (6th Cir. 1997), the Board refused to limit the certification year presumption of majority support to the year following the initial certification of unions. It held that the certification year presumption also applies to the 12-month period following election victories by incumbent unions in *decertification* elections.

Mere inaction during the certification year will not constitute a waiver of a union's bargaining rights. *See Airport Shuttle-Cincinnati, Inc. v. NLRB*, 703 F.2d 220 (6th Cir. 1983) (union did not contact employer for seven months after certification and was completely dormant during that period).

2. *Other Election Petition Bars*

a. *Voluntary Recognition* — The Labor Board traditionally recognized that an uncertified union that had been lawfully recognized on the basis of a "card check" or the settlement of refusal-to-bargain charges was entitled to retain bargaining rights for a "reasonable period of time." The NLRB would not entertain a decertification petition filed during this period, and the filing of such a petition did not constitute sufficient grounds for the employer to refuse to bargain with the union. *Universal Gear Service Corp.*, 157 N.L.R.B. 1169 (1966), *enforced*, 394 F.2d 396 (6th Cir. 1968); *NLRB v. Montgomery Ward & Co.*, 399 F.2d 409 (7th Cir. 1968). *See also Exxel/Atmos, Inc. v. NLRB*, 28 F.3d 1243 (D.C. Cir. 1994), wherein the court agreed with the NLRB that an employer violated § 8(a)(5) when it withdrew recognition from a union it had voluntarily recognized eight months earlier and demanded a representation election even though the company had some evidence that union support had declined, since an employer is not entitled to an election after voluntary recognition until the passage of a "reasonable period of time," which is generally one year. In *Mar-Jac Poultry Co.*, 136 N.L.R.B. 785 (1962), the Board held that when an employer agrees to bargain in good faith in settlement of a certified union's refusal-to-bargain charge, an election petition by the employer will be denied for 12 months following the settlement agreement. The union was said to be entitled to at least one year of actual bargaining from the date of the settlement. *Accord Va. Mason Med. Ctr. v. NLRB*, 558 F.3d 891 (9th Cir. 2009); *Van Dorn Plastic Mach. Co., Div. of Van Dorn Co.*, 300 N.L.R.B. 278 (1990), *enforced*, 939 F.2d 402 (6th Cir. 1991). And in *Americold Logistics, LLC*, 362 N.L.R.B. 493 (2015), the Board clarified that the one-year maximum bar to a petition for an ouster of a voluntarily-recognized union runs from the date of the union's first bargaining session with the employer, not from the date of its execution of a recognition agreement.

As discussed above, in *Dana Corp.*, 351 N.L.R.B. 434 (2007), a closely divided Labor Board announced a new rule with respect to the right of employees to challenge employer grants of voluntary recognition. Employees would have 45 days after voluntary recognition had been granted to file a decertification petition challenging such action. The Board further indicated that the traditional contract bar doctrine would be suspended during this 45-day period to allow the filing of a decertification petition even if a first contract had already been negotiated. Given the fact that voluntary recognition of a union lacking majority support constitutes a per se § 8(a)(2)/8(b)(1)(A) violation that can be immediately challenged through an unfair labor practice proceeding, why do you think the Board decided to postpone the usual recognition bar—and contract bar—for 45 days to allow dissatisfied unit members to challenge voluntary recognition grants through the decertification process?

In *Lamons Gasket Co.*, 357 N.L.R.B. 739 (2011), the Labor Board overruled *Dana Corp.* and returned to the traditional rule providing newly recognized labor organizations with a "reasonable period of time" to negotiate a first contract before it would entertain any decertification petition. It noted that such a reasonable period is normally no less than six months after the parties' initial bargaining session, and no more than the one-year period provided to certified unions under § 9(c)(3). Then, in March 2020, the Labor Board adopted a new rule applicable to voluntary recognition situations that rejected the *Lamons Gasket* approach and reinstated the *Dana Corp.* approach, allowing employees or rival labor organizations to challenge the validity of voluntary recognitions for up to 45 days following such recognitions. 85 Fed. Reg. 18366, April 1, 2020 (effective June 1, 2020).

b. Gissel *Bargaining Orders*—A union enjoys a presumption of majority status for a reasonable period following receipt of a *Gissel* bargaining order, with this period normally being a minimum of six months and a maximum of 12 months. *Lee Lumber & Bldg. Material Corp.*, 334 N.L.R.B. 399 (2001), *enforced*, 310 F.3d 209 (D.C. Cir. 2002).

3. *Contract Bar Periods*—An employer is obliged to bargain with an incumbent union for the period during which an existing labor contract is a bar to a Board election, despite good-faith doubts it may have about the union's continued majority support. This is so whether the union has been certified (*Hexton Furniture Co.*, 111 N.L.R.B. 342 (1955)) or has been recognized voluntarily without an election (*Shamrock Dairy, Inc.*, 119 N.L.R.B. 998 (1957)). In *Shaw's Supermarkets, Inc.*, 350 N.L.R.B. 585 (2007), the Labor Board decided that the usual presumption of majority support only exists during the first three years of longer-term contracts, allowing an employer to withdraw recognition from an incumbent union after the third year of a five-year agreement where a majority of unit employees signed a petition disavowing support for that labor organization.

4. *Successor Employers*—In *St. Elizabeth Manor, Inc.*, 329 N.L.R.B. 341 (1999), a closely divided Board overruled precedent and decided that once a successor employer becomes obliged to recognize the incumbent union of the predecessor firm based upon the fact that there has been substantial continuity in the business and the successor has hired a majority of its employees from the predecessor firm's workforce, the union must be given a "reasonable period of time" to negotiate a new contract, with the Board refusing to entertain election petitions challenging the continued majority status of that organization during the recognition-bar period. Three years later, a reconstituted Board reversed itself and returned to its earlier rule that an incumbent union in a successor employer situation is only entitled to a rebuttable presumption of continuing majority status that may be challenged by the filing of an election petition. *MV Transp.*, 337 N.L.R.B. 770 (2002). In *UGL-UNICCO Service Co.*, 357 N.L.R.B. 801 (2011), however, the Labor Board overruled *MV Transportation* and restored the *St. Elizabeth Manor* standard, ruling that the "reasonable period of time" petition bar applies to such successor employers once union recognition has been granted.

Auciello Iron Works, Inc. v. NLRB
Supreme Court of the United States
517 U.S. 781, 116 S. Ct. 1754, 135 L. Ed. 2d 64 (1996)

JUSTICE SOUTER delivered the opinion of the Court.

The question here is whether an employer may disavow a collective-bargaining agreement because of a good-faith doubt about a union's majority status at the time the contract was made, when the doubt arises from facts known to the employer before its contract offer had been accepted by the union. We hold that the National Labor Relations Board reasonably concluded that an employer challenging an agreement under these circumstances commits an unfair labor practice in violation of §§ 8(a)(1) and (5) of the National Labor Relations Act. . . .

I

Petitioner Auciello Iron Works of Hudson, Massachusetts, had 23 production and maintenance employees during the period in question. After a union election in 1977, the NLRB certified Shopmen's Local No. 501, a/w International Association of Bridge, Structural, and Ornamental Iron Workers, AFL-CIO, as the collective-bargaining representative of Auciello's employees. Over the following years, the company and the Union were able to negotiate a series of collective-bargaining agreements, one of which expired on September 25, 1988. Negotiations for a new one were unsuccessful throughout September and October 1988, however, and when Auciello and the Union had not made a new contract by October 14, 1988, the employees went on strike. Negotiations continued, nonetheless, and, on November 17, 1988, Auciello presented the Union with a complete contract proposal. On November 18, 1988, the picketing stopped, and nine days later, on a Sunday evening, the Union telegraphed its acceptance of the outstanding offer. The very next day, however, Auciello told the Union that it doubted that a majority of the bargaining unit's employees supported the Union, and for that reason disavowed the collective-bargaining agreement and denied it had any duty to continue negotiating. Auciello traced its doubt to knowledge acquired before the Union accepted the contract offer, including the facts that 9 employees had crossed the picket line, that 13 employees had given it signed forms indicating their resignation from the Union, and that 16 had expressed dissatisfaction with the Union.

In January 1989, the Board's General Counsel issued an administrative complaint charging Auciello with violation of §§ 8(a)(1) and (5) of the NLRA. An administrative law judge found that a contract existed between the parties and that Auciello's withdrawal from it violated the Act. . . . The Board affirmed the administrative law judge's decision; it treated Auciello's claim of good-faith doubt as irrelevant and ordered Auciello to reduce the collective-bargaining agreement to a formal written instrument. . . . But when the Board applied to the Court of Appeals for the First Circuit for enforcement of its order, the Court of Appeals declined on the ground that the Board had not adequately explained its refusal to consider Auciello's defense of good-faith doubt about the Union's majority status. . . . On remand, the Board issued a supplemental opinion to justify its position, . . . and the Court of Appeals thereafter enforced the order as resting on a "policy choice [both] . . . reasonable and . . . quite persuasive." 60 F.3d 24, 27 (C.A.1 1995). We granted certiorari, . . . and now affirm.

II

A

The object of the National Labor Relations Act is industrial peace and stability, fostered by collective-bargaining agreements providing for the orderly resolution of labor disputes between workers and employees. . . . *Fall River Dyeing & Finishing Corp. v. NLRB*, 482 U.S. 27, 38 (1987). To such ends, the Board has adopted various presumptions about the existence of majority support for a union within a bargaining unit, the precondition for service as its exclusive representative. Cf. *id.*, at 37–39. The first two are conclusive presumptions. A union "usually is entitled to a conclusive presumption of majority status for one year following" Board certification as such a representative. *Id.*, at 37. A union is likewise entitled under Board precedent to a conclusive presumption of majority status during the term of any collective-bargaining agreement, up to three years. See *NLRB v. Burns Int'l Security Services, Inc.*, 406 U.S. 272, 290, n. 12 (1972). . . .

There is a third presumption, though not a conclusive one. At the end of the certification year or upon expiration of the collective-bargaining agreement, the presumption of majority status becomes a rebuttable one. See *NLRB v. Curtin Matheson Scientific, Inc.*, 494 U.S. 775, 778 (1990); see n. 6, *infra*. Then, an employer may overcome the presumption (when, for example, defending against an unfair labor practice charge) "by showing that, at the time of [its] refusal to bargain, either (1) the union did not *in fact* enjoy majority support, or (2) the employer had a 'good-faith' doubt, founded on a sufficient objective basis, of the union's majority support." *Curtin Matheson, supra*, at 778 (emphasis in original). Auciello asks this Court to hold that it may raise the latter defense even after a collective-bargaining contract period has apparently begun to run upon a union's acceptance of an employer's outstanding offer.

B

The same need for repose that first prompted the Board to adopt the rule presuming the union's majority status during the term of a collective-bargaining agreement also led the Board to rule out an exception for the benefit of an employer with doubts arising from facts antedating the contract. The Board said that such an exception would allow an employer to control the timing of its assertion of good-faith doubt and thus to "'sit' on that doubt and ... raise it after the offer is accepted." 317 N.L.R.B., at 370. The Board thought that the risks associated with giving employers such "unilatera[l] control [over] a vital part of the collective-bargaining process," *ibid.*, would undermine the stability of the collective-bargaining relationship, *id.*, at 374, and thus outweigh any benefit that might in theory follow from vindicating a doubt that ultimately proved to be sound.

The Board's judgment in the matter is entitled to prevail. To affirm its rule of decision in this case, indeed, there is no need to invoke the full measure of the "considerable deference" that the Board is due, *NLRB v. Curtin Matheson Scientific, Inc., supra*, at 786, by virtue of its charge to develop national labor policy.... It might be tempting to think that Auciello's doubt was expressed so soon after the apparent contract formation that little would be lost by vindicating that doubt and wiping the contractual slate clean, if in fact the company can make a convincing case for the doubt it claims. On this view, the loss of repose would be slight. But if doubts about the union's majority status would justify repudiating a contract one day after its ostensible formation, why should the same doubt not serve as well a year into the contract's term? Auciello implicitly agrees on the need to provide some cutoff, but argues that the limit should be expressed as a "reasonable time" to repudiate the contract. That is, it seeks case-by-case determinations of the appropriate time for asserting a good-faith doubt in place of the Board's bright-line rule cutting off the opportunity at the moment of apparent contract formation. Auciello's desire is natural, but its argument fails to point up anything unreasonable in the Board's position.

The Board's approach generally allows companies an adequate chance to act on their preacceptance doubts before contract formation, just as Auciello could have acted effectively under the Board's rule in this case. Auciello knew that the picket line had been crossed and that a number of its employees had expressed dissatisfaction with the Union at least nine days before the contract's acceptance, and all of the resignation forms Auciello received were dated at least five days before the acceptance date. During the week preceding the apparent formation of the contract, Auciello had at least three alternatives to doing nothing. It could have withdrawn the outstanding offer and then, like its employees, petitioned for a representation election. See 29 U.S.C. § 159(c)(1)(A)(ii) (employee petitions); § 159(c)(1)(B) (employer petitions); *NLRB v. Financial Institution Employees*, 475 U.S. 192, 198 (1986). "[I]f the Board determines, after investigation and hearing, that a question of representation exists, it directs an election by secret ballot and certifies the result." *Ibid.* Following withdrawal, it could also have refused to bargain further on the basis of its good-faith doubt, leaving it to the Union to charge an unfair labor practice, against which it could defend on the basis of the doubt. Cf. *Curtin Matheson*, 494 U.S., at 778. And, of course, it could have withdrawn its offer to allow it time to investigate while it continued to fulfill its duty to bargain in good faith with the Union. The company thus had generous opportunities to avoid the presumption before the moment of acceptance.

There may, to be sure, be cases where the opportunity requires prompt action, but labor negotiators are not the least nimble, and the Board could reasonably have thought the price of making more time for the sluggish was too high, since it would encourage bad-faith bargaining. As Auciello would have it, any employer with genuine doubt about a union's hold on its employees would be invited to go right on bargaining, with the prospect of locking in a favorable contract that it could, if it wished, then challenge. Here, for example, if Auciello had acted before the Union's telegram by withdrawing its offer and declining further negotiation based on its doubt (or petitioning for decertification), flames would have been fanned, and if it ultimately had been obliged to bargain further, a favorable agreement would have been more difficult to obtain. But by saving its challenge until after a contract had apparently been formed, it could not end up with a worse agreement than the one it had. The Board could reasonably say that giving employers some flexibility in raising their scruples would not be worth skewing bargaining relationships by such one-sided leverage, and the fact that any collective-bargaining agreement might be vulnerable to such a post-formation challenge would hardly serve the Act's goal of achieving industrial peace by promoting stable collective-bargaining relationships. Cf. *Fall River Dyeing*, 482 U.S., at 38–39; *Franks Bros. Co. v. NLRB*, 321 U.S. 702, 705 (1944).

Nor do we find anything compelling in Auciello's contention that its employees' statutory right "to bargain collectively through representatives of their own choosing" and to refrain from doing so, 29 U.S.C. §157, compels us to reject the Board's position. Although we take seriously the Act's command to respect "the free choice of employees" as well as to "promot[e] stability in collective-bargaining relationships," *Fall River Dyeing, supra*, at 38 (internal quotation marks omitted), we have rejected the position that employers may refuse to bargain whenever presented with evidence that their employees no longer support their certified union. "To allow employers to rely on employees' rights in refusing to bargain with the formally designated union is not conducive to [industrial peace], it is inimical to it." *Brooks v. NLRB*, 348 U.S. 96, 103 (1954). The Board is accordingly entitled to suspicion when faced with an employer's benevolence as its workers' champion against their certified union, which is subject to a decertification petition from the workers if they want to file one. There is nothing unreasonable in giving a short leash to the employer as vindicator of its employees' organizational freedom.

C

Merits aside, Auciello also claims that the precedent of *Garment Workers v. NLRB*, 366 U.S. 731 (1961), compels reversal, but it does not. In *Garment Workers*, we held that a bona fide but mistaken belief in a union's majority status cannot support an employer's agreement purporting to recognize a union newly organized but as yet uncertified. We upheld the Board's rule out of concern that an employer and a union could make a deal giving the union "'a marked advantage over any other [union] in securing the adherence of employees,'" *id.*, at 738 (quoting *NLRB v. Pennsylvania Greyhound Lines, Inc.*, 303 U.S. 261, 267 (1938)), thereby distorting the process by which employees elect the bargaining agent of their choice. 366 U.S., at 738–739.

Here, in contrast, the Union continued to enjoy a rebuttable presumption of majority support, and the bargaining unit employees had ample opportunity to initiate decertification of the Union but apparently chose not to do so. With entire consistency, the Board may deny employers the power gained from recognizing a union, even when it flows from a good-faith but mistaken belief in a newly organized union's majority status, and at the same time deny them the power to disturb collective-bargaining agreements based on a doubt (without more) that its employees' bargaining agent has retained majority status. Good-faith belief can neither force a union's precipitate recognition nor destroy a recognized union's contracting authority after the fact by intentional delay. There is, indeed, a symmetry in the two positions.

* * *

We hold that the Board reasonably found an employer's precontractual, good-faith doubt inadequate to support an exception to the conclusive presumption arising at the moment a collective-bargaining contract offer has been accepted. We accordingly affirm the judgment of the Court of Appeals for the First Circuit.

It is so ordered.

Notes

1. *Standard for Challenging Majority Status*—In *Levitz Furniture Co. of the Pac., Inc.*, 333 N.L.R.B. 717 (2001), the Labor Board accepted the *Auciello Iron Works* Court's invitation to reconsider the way in which employers may challenge the continued majority status of incumbent unions. Overruling precedent, the Board indicated that it would no longer permit employers to *withdraw recognition* from incumbent unions based solely upon their reasonable belief that the unions had lost their majority support. Henceforth, "an employer may unilaterally withdraw recognition from an incumbent union only where the union has *actually lost* the support of the majority of bargaining unit employees." At the same time, the Board made it easier for employers to file representation petitions challenging the continued majority support of incumbent unions. To file such petitions, employers need only demonstrate "reasonable good-faith *uncertainty* as to incumbent unions' continued majority status."

2. *Actual Loss of Majority Status*—When an employer receives a petition signed by a majority of unit employees disavowing support for the incumbent union, it may lawfully withdraw recognition from that labor organization based on the union's apparent loss of majority support. *Unifirst Corp.*, 346 N.L.R.B. 591 (2006). The Board requires that the language of the petition be clear and unambiguous. *See Highlands Hosp. Corp.*, 347 N.L.R.B. 1404 (2006), *enforced*, 508 F.3d 28 (D.C. Cir. 2007) (finding that petition entitled "showing of interest for decertification" was insufficient to establish actual loss of majority support where extrinsic evidence existed that signatures were collected only for the purpose of obtaining an election). Employers may not rely, however, upon decertification petitions that are "tainted" by the employer's unlawful assistance.

When an employer receives a petition signed by a majority of bargaining unit members that might indicate that they no longer wish to be represented by the incumbent union, but that includes ambiguous language that does not clearly state that the signers no longer wish to be represented, the employer's withdrawal of recognition is likely to be found a § 8(a)(5) violation. *See Kauai Veterans Express*, 369 N.L.R.B. No. 59 (2020); *Liberty Bakery Kitchen, Inc.*, 366 N.L.R.B. No. 19 (2018).

In *YWCA*, 349 N.L.R.B. 762 (2007), the employer and union reached an oral agreement in bargaining and the employees voted to ratify the offer. The employer agreed to prepare the final written document setting out all the terms of the agreement, but before it could complete the task it was presented with cards signed by a majority of its employees stating that they no longer wished to be represented by the union. The cards were dated after the oral agreement but both before and after the ratification vote. The employer refused to sign the agreement and withdrew recognition from the union. No employee filed a decertification petition. The Board found a § 8(a)(5) violation, reasoning that under *Auciello Iron Works* the contract bar doctrine was triggered once the parties reached final agreement, even though the agreement was not yet incorporated in a written document. *Levitz* did not require a different result because it did not change the law as to when a lawful withdrawal of recognition could occur — only the quantum and type of evidence required to support it. *See also Polycon Indus., Inc. v. NLRB*, 821 F.3d 905 (7th Cir. 2016). In *Silvan Industries*, 367 N.L.R.B. No. 28 (2018), however, the Labor Board held that an employer did not act improperly when it filed a representation election petition challenging the majority status of a labor organization that had won a Board election a year earlier and had finally negotiated a bargaining agreement with the employer where unit employees had petitioned the employer, asking it to terminate union representation after the parties had reached an agreement but before the date the agreement was to take effect.

NLRB v. Curtin Matheson Scientific, Inc.

Supreme Court of the United States
494 U.S. 775, 110 S. Ct. 1542, 108 L. Ed. 2d 801 (1990)

Justice Marshall delivered the opinion of the Court.

This case presents the question whether the National Labor Relations Board, in evaluating an employer's claim that it had a reasonable basis for doubting a union's majority support, must presume that striker replacements oppose the union. We hold that the Board acted within its discretion in refusing to adopt a presumption of replacement opposition to the union and therefore reverse the judgment of the Court of Appeals.

I

Upon certification by the NLRB as the exclusive bargaining agent for a unit of employees, a union enjoys an irrebuttable presumption of majority support for one year. *Fall River Dyeing & Finishing Corp. v. NLRB*, 482 U.S. 27, 37 (1987). During that time, an employer's refusal to bargain with the union is per se an unfair labor practice under §§ 8(a)(1) and 8(a)(5) of the National Labor Relations Act. . . . See *Celanese Corp. of America*, 95 N.L.R.B. 664, 672 (1951); R. Gorman, Labor Law, Unionization and Collective Bargaining 109 (1976). After the first year, the presumption continues but is rebuttable. *Fall River, supra*, at 38. Under the Board's longstanding approach, an employer may rebut that presumption by showing that, at the time of the refusal to bargain, either (1) the union did not *in fact* enjoy majority support, or (2) the employer had a "good faith" doubt, founded on a sufficient objective basis, of the union's majority support. *Station KKHI*, 284 N.L.R.B. 1339 (1987), enf'd, 891 F.2d 230 (CA9 1989). The question presented in this case is whether the Board must, in determining whether an employer has presented sufficient objective evidence of a good-faith doubt, presume that striker replacements oppose the union.

The Board has long presumed that new employees hired in nonstrike circumstances support the incumbent union in the same proportion as the employees they replace. *See, e.g., National Plastic Products Co.*, 78 N.L.R.B. 699, 706 (1948). The Board's approach to evaluating the union sentiments of employees hired to replace strikers, however, has not been so consistent. Initially, the Board appeared to assume that replacements did not support the union. *See, e.g., Stoner Rubber Co.*, 123 N.L.R.B. 1440, 1444 (1959) . . . .

A 1974 decision, *Peoples Gas System, Inc.*, 214 N.L.R.B. 944 (1974), rev'd and remanded on other grounds *sub nom. Teamsters Local Union 769 v. NLRB*, 532 F.2d 1385, 1391, 174 U.S. App. D.C. 310, 316 (1976), signaled a shift in the Board's approach. The Board recognized that "it is of course possible that the replacements, who had chosen not to engage in the strike activity, might nevertheless have favored union representation." 214 N.L.R.B., at 947. Still, the Board held that "it was not unreasonable for [the employer] to infer that the degree of union support among these employees who had chosen to ignore a Union-sponsored picket line might well be somewhat weaker than the support offered by those who had vigorously engaged in concerted activity on behalf on [sic] Union-sponsored objectives." *Ibid.*

A year later, in *Cutten Supermarket*, 220 N.L.R.B. 507 (1975), the Board reversed course completely, stating that striker replacements, like new employees generally, are presumed to support the union in the same ratio as the strikers they replaced. *Id.*, at 509. The Board's initial adherence to this new approach, however, was equivocal. In *Arkay Packaging Corp.*, 227 N.L.R.B. 397 (1976), review denied *sub nom. New York Printing Pressmen & Offset Workers Union, No. 51 v. NLRB*, 575 F.2d 1045 (CA2 1978), the Board stated that "it would be wholly unwarranted and unrealistic to presume as a matter of law that, when hired, the replacements for the union employees who had gone out on strike favored representation by the Unions to the same extent as the strikers." 227 N.L.R.B., at 397–398. . . . Finally, in 1980, the Board reiterated that the presumption that new employees support the union applies equally to striker replacements. *Pennco, Inc.*, 250 N.L.R.B. 716, 717–718 (1980), enf'd, 684 F.2d 340 (CA6), *cert. denied*, 459 U.S. 994 (1982).

In 1987, after several Courts of Appeals rejected the Board's approach, the Board determined that no universal generalizations could be made about replacements' union sentiments that would justify a presumption either of support for or of opposition to the union. *Station KKHI*, 284 N.L.R.B. 1339 (1987). On the one hand, the Board found that the pro-union presumption lacked empirical foundation because "incumbent unions and strikers sometimes have shown hostility toward the permanent replacements" and "replacements are typically aware of the union's primary concern for the striker's welfare, rather than that of the replacements." *Id.*, at 1344. On the other hand, the Board found that an antiunion presumption was "equally unsupportable" factually. *Ibid.* The Board observed that a striker replacement "may be forced to work for financial reasons, or may disapprove of the strike in question but still desire union representation and would support other union initiatives." *Ibid.* Moreover, the Board found as a matter of policy that adoption of an antiunion presumption would "substantially impair the employees' right to strike by adding to the risk of replacement the risk of loss of the bargaining representative as soon as replacements equal in number to the strikers are willing to cross the picket line." *Ibid.* Accordingly, the Board held that it would not apply any presumption regarding striker replacements' union sentiments, but would determine their views on a case-by-case basis. 284 N.L.R.B., at 1344–1345.

II

We now turn to the Board's application of its *Station KKHI* no-presumption approach in this case. Respondent Curtin Matheson Scientific, Inc., buys and sells laboratory instruments and supplies. In 1970, the Board certified Teamsters Local 968, General Drivers, Warehousemen and Helpers as the collective-bargaining agent for respondent's production and maintenance employees. On May 21, 1979, the most recent bargaining agreement between respondent and the Union expired. Respondent made its final offer for a new agreement on May 25, but the Union rejected that offer. Respondent then locked out the 27 bargaining-unit employees. On June 12, respondent renewed its May 25 offer, but the Union again rejected it. The Union then commenced an economic strike. The record contains no evidence of any strike-related violence or threats of violence.

Five employees immediately crossed the picket line and reported for work. On June 25, while the strike was still in effect, respondent hired 29 permanent replacement employees to replace the 22 strikers. The Union ended its strike on July 16, offering to accept unconditionally respondent's May 25 contract offer. On July 20, respondent informed the Union that the May 25 offer was no longer available. In addition, respondent withdrew recognition from the Union and refused to bargain further, stating that it doubted that the Union was supported by a majority of the employees in the unit. Respondent subsequently refused to provide the Union with information it had requested concerning the total number of bargaining-unit employees on the payroll, and the job classification and seniority of each employee. As of July 20, the bargaining unit consisted of 19 strikers, 25 permanent replacements, and the 5 employees who had crossed the picket line at the strike's inception.

On July 30, the Union filed an unfair labor practice charge with the Board. Following an investigation, the General Counsel issued a complaint, alleging that respondent's withdrawal of recognition, refusal to execute a contract embodying the terms of the May 25 offer, and failure to provide the requested information violated §§ 8(a)(1) and 8(a)(5) of the NLRA.... In its defense to the charge, respondent claimed that it had a reasonably based, good-faith doubt of the Union's majority status. The Administrative Law Judge agreed with respondent and dismissed the complaint. The Board, however, reversed, holding that respondent lacked sufficient objective basis to doubt the Union's majority support. 287 N.L.R.B. No. 35 (1987).

First, the Board noted that the crossover of 5 of the original 27 employees did not in itself support an inference that the 5 had repudiated the Union, because their failure to join the strike may have "indicate[d] their economic concerns rather than a lack of support for the union."... Second, the Board found that the resignation from their jobs of two of the original bargaining-unit employees, including the chief shop steward, after the commencement of the strike did not indicate opposition to the Union, but merely served to reduce the size of the bargaining unit as of the date of respondent's withdrawal of recognition.... Third, the Board discounted statements made by six employees to a representative of respondent during the strike. Although some of these statements may have indicated rejection of the Union as the bargaining representative, the Board noted, others "appear[ed] ambiguous at best."... Moreover, the Board stated, "[e]ven attributing to them the meaning most favorable to the Respondent, it would merely signify that 6 employees of a total bargaining unit of approximately 50 did not desire to keep the Union as the collective-bargaining representative."...

Finally, regarding respondent's hiring of striker replacements, the Board stated that, in accordance with the *Station KKHI* approach, it would "not use any presumptions with respect to [the replacements'] union sentiments," but would instead "take a case-by-case approach [and] require additional evidence of a lack of union support on the replacements' part in evaluating the significance of this factor in the employer's showing of good faith doubt."... The Board noted that respondent's only evidence of the replacements' attitudes toward the Union was its employee relations director's account of a conversation with one of the replacements. The replacement employee reportedly told her that he had worked in union and nonunion workplaces and did not see any need for a union as long as the company treated him well; in addition, he said that he did not think the Union in this case represented the employees.... The Board did not determine whether this statement indicated the replacement employee's repudiation of the Union, but found that the statement was, in any event, an insufficient basis for "inferring the union sentiments of the replacement employees as a group."...

The Board therefore concluded that "the evidence [was] insufficient to rebut the presumption of the Union's continuing majority status."... Accordingly, the Board held that respondent had violated §§ 8(a)(1) and 8(a)(5) by withdrawing recognition from the Union, failing to furnish the requested information, and refusing to execute a contract embodying the terms respondent had offered on May 25, 1979. The Board ordered respondent to bargain with the Union on request, provide the requisite information, execute an agreement, and make the bargaining-unit employees whole for whatever losses they had suffered from respondent's failure to execute a contract.

The Court of Appeals, in a divided opinion, refused to enforce the Board's order, holding that respondent was justified in doubting the Union's majority support. 859 F.2d 362 (CA5 1988). Specifically, the court rejected the Board's decision not to apply any presumption in evaluating striker replacements' union sentiments and endorsed the so-called "Gorman presumption" that striker replacements oppose the union. We granted certiorari . . . to resolve a circuit split on the question whether the Board must presume that striker replacements oppose the union.

III

A

This Court has emphasized often that the NLRB has the primary responsibility for developing and applying national labor policy. . . . This Court therefore has accorded Board rules considerable deference. . . . We will uphold a Board rule as long as it is rational and consistent with the Act, . . . even if we would have formulated a different rule had we sat on the Board. . . .

B

Before assessing the Board's justification for rejecting the antiunion presumption, we will make clear precisely how that presumption would differ in operation from the Board's current approach. As noted above, . . . the starting point for the Board's analysis is the basic presumption that the union is supported by a majority of bargaining-unit employees. The employer bears the burden of rebutting that presumption, after the certification year, either by showing that the union in fact lacks majority support or by demonstrating a sufficient objective basis for doubting the union's majority status. Respondent here urges that in evaluating an employer's claim of a good-faith doubt, the Board must adopt a second, subsidiary presumption — that replacement employees oppose the union. Under this approach, if a majority of employees in the bargaining unit were striker replacements, the employer would not need to offer any objective evidence of the employees' union sentiments to rebut the presumption of the union's continuing majority status. The presumption of the replacements' opposition to the union would, in effect, override the presumption of continuing majority status. In contrast, under its no-presumption approach the Board "take[s] into account the particular circumstances surrounding each strike and the hiring of replacements, while retaining the long-standing requirement that the employer must come forth with some objective evidence to substantiate his doubt of continuing majority status." 859 F.2d, at 370 (Williams, J., dissenting).[11]

---

11. [8] Contrary to respondent's assertion, the Board's no-presumption approach does not constitute an unexplained abandonment of the good-faith doubt defense to a refusal to bargain charge. . . . This Court has never expressly considered the validity of the good-faith doubt standard. . . . We

C

We find the Board's no-presumption approach rational as an empirical matter. Presumptions normally arise when proof of one fact renders the existence of another fact "so probable that it is sensible and timesaving to assume the truth of [the inferred] fact... until the adversary disproves it." E. Cleary, McCormick on Evidence § 343, p. 969 (3d ed. 1984). Although replacements often may not favor the incumbent union, the Board reasonably concluded, in light of its long experience in addressing these issues, that replacements may in some circumstances desire union representation despite their willingness to cross the picket line. Economic concerns, for instance, may force a replacement employee to work for a struck employer even though he otherwise supports the union and wants the benefits of union representation. In this sense the replacement worker is no different from a striker who, feeling the financial heat of the strike on herself and her family, is forced to abandon the picket line and go back to work. *Cf. Lyng v. Automobile Workers*, 485 U.S. 360, 371 (1988) (recognizing that "a striking individual faces an immediate and often total drop in income during a strike"). In addition, a replacement, like a nonstriker or a strike crossover, may disagree with the purpose or strategy of the particular strike and refuse to support that strike, while still wanting that union's representation at the bargaining table.

Respondent insists that the interests of strikers and replacements are diametrically opposed and that unions inevitably side with the strikers. For instance, respondent argues, picket-line violence often stems directly from the hiring of replacements. Furthermore, unions often negotiate with employers for strike settlements that would return the strikers to their jobs, thereby displacing some or all of the replacements. Respondent asserts that replacements, aware of the union's loyalty to the strikers, most likely would not support the union. In a related argument, respondent contends that the Board's no-presumption approach is irreconcilable with the Board's decisions holding that employers have no duty to bargain with a striking union over replacements' employment terms because the "inherent conflict" between strikers and replacements renders the union incapable of "bargain[ing] simultaneously in the best interests of both strikers and their replacements." *Service Electric Co.*, 281 N.L.R.B. 633, 641 (1986)....

These arguments do not persuade us that the Board's position is irrational. Unions do not inevitably demand displacement of all strike replacements....

The extent to which a union demands displacement of permanent replacement workers logically will depend on the union's bargaining power. Under this Court's decision in *NLRB v. Mackay Radio & Telegraph Co.*, 304 U.S. 333 (1938), an employer is not required to discharge permanent replacements at the conclusion of an economic

---

decline to address that issue here, as both parties assume the validity of the standard, and resolution of the issue is not necessary to our decision....

strike to make room for returning strikers; rather, the employer must only reinstate strikers as vacancies arise. The strikers' only chance for immediate reinstatement, then, lies in the union's ability to force the employer to discharge the replacements as a condition for the union's ending the strike. Unions' leverage to compel such a strike settlement will vary greatly from strike to strike. If, for example, the jobs at issue do not require highly trained workers and the replacements perform as well as the strikers did, the employer will have little incentive to hire back the strikers and fire the replacements; consequently, the union will have little bargaining power. Consumers' reaction to a strike will also determine the union's bargaining position. If the employer's customers have no reluctance to cross the picket line and deal with the employer, the union will be in a poor position to bargain for a favorable settlement. Thus, a union's demands will inevitably turn on the strength of the union's hand in negotiations. A union with little bargaining leverage is unlikely to press the employer — at least not very forcefully or for very long — to discharge the replacements and reinstate all the strikers. Cognizant of the union's weak position, many if not all of the replacements justifiably may not fear that they will lose their jobs at the end of the strike. They may still want the union's representation after the strike, though, despite the union's lack of bargaining strength during the strike, because of the union's role in processing grievances, monitoring the employer's actions, and performing other non-strike roles. Because the circumstances of each strike and the leverage of each union will vary greatly, it was not irrational for the Board to reject the antiunion presumption and adopt a case-by-case approach in determining replacements' union sentiments.

Moreover, even if the interests of strikers and replacements conflict during the strike, those interests may converge after the strike, once job rights have been resolved. Thus, while the strike continues, a replacement worker whose job appears relatively secure might well want the union to continue to represent the unit regardless of the union's bargaining posture during the strike. . . .

Furthermore, the Board has not deemed picket-line violence or a union's demand that replacements be terminated irrelevant to its evaluation of replacements' attitudes toward the union. The Board's position, rather, is that "the hiring of permanent replacements who cross a picket line, *in itself*, does not support an inference that the replacements repudiate the union as collective-bargaining representative." *Station KKHI*, 284 N.L.R.B., at 1344 (emphasis added). In both *Station KKHI* and this case, the Board noted that the picket line was peaceful, *id.*, at 1345; *Curtin Matheson Scientific*, 287 N.L.R.B., at 352; and in neither case did the employer present evidence that the union was actively negotiating for ouster of the replacements. To the extent that the Board regards evidence of these factors relevant to its evaluation of replacements' union sentiments, then, respondent's contentions ring hollow. . . .

In sum, the Board recognized that the circumstances surrounding each strike and replacements' reasons for crossing a picket line vary greatly. Even if replacements often do not support the union, then, it was not irrational for the Board to conclude that the probability of replacement opposition to the union is insufficient to justify an antiunion presumption.

D

The Board's refusal to adopt an antiunion presumption is also consistent with the Act's "overriding policy" of achieving "'industrial peace.'" *Fall River*, 482 U.S., at 38 (quoting *Brooks v. NLRB*, 348 U.S. 96, 103 (1954)). In *Fall River*, the Court held that the presumption of continuing majority support for a union "further[s] this policy by 'promot[ing] stability in collective-bargaining relationships, without impairing the free choice of employees.'" *Ibid.* . . . The Court reasoned that this presumption "enable[s] a union to concentrate on obtaining and fairly administering a collective-bargaining agreement without worrying that, unless it produces immediate results, it will lose majority support." *Ibid.* (citing *Brooks v. NLRB, supra*, at 100). In addition, this presumption "remove[s] any temptation on the part of the employer to avoid good-faith bargaining in the hope that, by delaying, it will undermine the union's support among the employees." 482 U.S., at 38.

The Board's approach to determining the union views of strike replacements is directed at this same goal because it limits employers' ability to oust a union without adducing any evidence of the employees' union sentiments and encourages negotiated solutions to strikes. It was reasonable for the Board to conclude that the antiunion presumption, in contrast, could allow an employer to eliminate the union merely by hiring a sufficient number of replacement employees. That rule thus might encourage the employer to avoid good-faith bargaining over a strike settlement, and instead to use the strike as a means of removing the union altogether. . . . Restricting an employer's ability to use a strike as a means of terminating the bargaining relationship serves the policies of promoting industrial stability and negotiated settlements. . . .

Furthermore, it was reasonable for the Board to decide that the antiunion presumption might chill employees' exercise of their statutory right to engage in "concerted activities," including the right to strike. If an employer could remove a union merely by hiring a sufficient number of replacements, employees considering a strike would face not only the prospect of being permanently replaced, but also a greater risk that they would lose their bargaining representative, thereby diminishing their chance of obtaining reinstatement through a strike settlement. It was rational for the Board to conclude, then, that adoption of the antiunion presumption could chill employees' exercise of their right to strike. . . .

IV

We hold that the Board's refusal to adopt a presumption that striker replacements oppose the union is rational and consistent with the Act. We therefore reverse the judgment of the Court of Appeals and remand for further proceedings consistent with this opinion.

It is so ordered.

[The concurring opinion of CHIEF JUSTICE REHNQUIST and the dissenting opinion of JUSTICE BRENNAN are omitted.]

JUSTICE SCALIA, with whom JUSTICE O'CONNOR and JUSTICE KENNEDY join, dissenting.

The Court makes heavy weather out of what is, under well-established principles of administrative law, a straightforward case. The National Labor Relations Board... has established as one of the central factual determinations to be made in § 8(a)(5) unfair-labor-practice adjudications, whether the employer had a reasonable, good-faith doubt concerning the majority status of the union at the time it requested to bargain. The Board held in the present case that such a doubt was not established by a record showing that at the time of the union's request a majority of the bargaining unit were strike replacements, and containing no affirmative evidence that any of those replacements supported the union. The question presented is whether that factual finding is supported by substantial evidence. Since the principal employment-related interest of strike replacements (to retain their jobs) is almost invariably opposed to the principal interest of the striking union (to replace them with its striking members) it seems to me impossible to conclude on this record that the employer did not have a reasonable, good-faith doubt regarding the union's majority status. The Board's factual finding being unsupported by substantial evidence, it cannot stand. I therefore dissent from the judgment reversing the Fifth Circuit's refusal to enforce the Board's order....

[O]f the 49 employees in the bargaining unit at the time of respondent's refusal to bargain, a majority (25) were strike replacements, and another 5 were former employees who had crossed the union's picket line. It may well be doubtful whether the latter group could be thought to support the union, but it suffices to focus upon the 25 strike replacements, who must be thought to oppose the union if the Board's own policies are to be believed. There was a deep and inherent conflict between the interests of these employees and the interests of the union....

The respondent in this case, therefore, had an employee bargaining unit a majority of whose members (1) were not entitled to have their best interests considered by the complainant union, (2) would have been foolish to expect their best interests to be considered by that union, and indeed (3) in light of their status as breakers of that union's strike, would have been foolish not to expect their best interests to be subverted by that union wherever possible. There was, moreover, not a shred of affirmative evidence that any strike replacement supported, or had reason to support, the union. On those facts, any reasonable factfinder must conclude that the respondent possessed, not necessarily a certainty, but at least a reasonable, good-faith doubt, that the union did not have majority support....

Also embarrassingly wide of the mark is the Court's observation that "[u]nions do not inevitably demand displacement of all strike replacements."... It is not necessary to believe that unions inevitably demand displacement of all strike replacements in order to doubt (as any reasonable person must) that strike replacements support a union that is under no obligation to take their employment interests into account, and that is almost certain to demand displacement of as many strike replacements as is necessary to reinstate former employees. . . .

Of course the Board may choose to implement authorized law or policy in adjudication by *forbidding* a *rational* inference, just as it may do so by *requiring* a *nonrational* one (which is what a presumption of law is). And perhaps it could lawfully have reached the outcome it did here in that fashion—saying that *even though* it must reasonably be inferred that an employer has good-faith doubt of majority status when more than half of the bargaining unit are strike replacements whose job rights have not been resolved, we will not permit that inference to be made. (This would produce an effect close to a rule of law eliminating the good-faith doubt defense except for cases in which the employer can demonstrate, by employee statements, lack of support for the union.) But that is not what the agency did here. It relied on the reasoning of *Station KKHI*, which rested upon the conclusion that, as a matter of logic and reasoning, "the hiring of permanent replacements who cross a picket line, in itself, does not support an inference that the replacements repudiate the union as collective-bargaining representative." . . . That is simply false. It is bad factfinding, and must be reversed under the "substantial evidence" test.

Notes

1. *Economic Strikers*—In *Pioneer Flour Mills*, 174 N.L.R.B. 1202 (1969), *enforced*, 427 F.2d 983 (5th Cir.), *cert. denied*, 400 U.S. 942 (1970), the Board took account of the 1959 amendment to § 9(c)(3) of the NLRA, providing that replaced economic strikers are entitled to vote in any election conducted within 12 months of the commencement of the strike, as it held that economic strikers must be counted as members of the bargaining unit for the first 12 months of the strike for the purposes of determining the union's majority status in a § 8(a)(5) case.

2. *Good Faith Doubt*—The "serious doubt" that is sufficient to rebut the presumption of a union's continuing majority following expiration of the certification year has two components: (1) a reasonable basis in fact, and (2) good faith. When an employer decides to conduct a *Struksnes* poll to determine whether an incumbent representative continues to enjoy majority support, the company must be able to demonstrate that objective considerations provide it with a "reasonable doubt" concerning the union's current majority status—the same burden applicable to cases in which an employer files a petition for a certification election challenging the continued support of an incumbent union. *Allentown Mack Sales & Serv. v. NLRB*, 522 U.S. 359 (1998). As seen above, under *Levitz Furniture Co. of the Pac., Inc.*, 333 N.L.R.B. 717 (2001), an employer may only withdraw recognition from an incumbent union if that labor organization has actually lost its majority support.

3. *Section 8(f) Prehire Agreements*—Employers and unions in the construction industry may enter into pre-hire agreements defining basic employment terms

under § 8(f) without the need for a showing of majority support, with exclusive bargaining relationships developing only after the unions demonstrate majority support. Although employers may repudiate the terms of pre-hire agreements if they expire before unions achieve majority status, once majority support is established, they must recognize and bargain with the unions for a reasonable time even after the original pre-hire agreements have expired and they may not unilaterally change the existing employment conditions without bargaining with the representative labor organizations. *M&M Backhoe Serv. v. NLRB,* 469 F.3d 1047 (D.C. Cir. 2006). More recently, the Board made clear in its amendments to the representation case procedures that a voluntary recognition or a collective bargaining agreement in the building and construction industry will not bar an election petition "absent positive evidence that the union unequivocally demanded recognition as the section 9(a) exclusive bargaining representative of employees in an appropriate bargaining unit, and that the employer unequivocally accepted it as such, based on a contemporaneous showing of support from a majority of employees in an appropriate unit." 85 Fed. Reg. 18366 (April 1, 2020). The change applies to any instances of voluntary recognition or collective bargaining agreements entered into on or after June 1, 2020.

American Seating Co.
National Labor Relations Board
106 N.L.R.B. 250 (1953)

. . . .

The facts in the case are undisputed. On September 20, 1949, following an election, the Board certified International Union, Automobile, Aircraft and Agricultural Implement Workers of America (UAW-CIO), and its Local No. 135, herein called the UAW-CIO, as bargaining representative of the Respondent's production and maintenance employees. On July 1, 1950, the Respondent and the UAW-CIO entered into a three-year collective bargaining contract covering all employees in the certified unit. Shortly before the expiration of two years from the date of signing of the contract, Pattern Makers' Association of Grand Rapids, Pattern Makers' League of North America, AFL, herein called the Union, filed a representation petition seeking to sever a craft unit of patternmakers from the existing production and maintenance unit. Both the Respondent and the UAWCIO opposed the petition, contending that their three-year contract which would not expire until July 1, 1953, was a bar. In a decision issued on September 4, 1952, the Board rejected this contention. It held that, as the contract had been in existence for two years, and as the contracting parties had failed to establish that contracts for three-year terms were customary in the seating industry, the contract was not a bar during the third year of its term. Accordingly, the Board directed an election in a unit of patternmakers, which the Union won.

On October 6, 1952, the Board certified the Union as bargaining representative of the Respondent's patternmakers. Approximately ten days later, the Union submitted to the Respondent a proposed collective bargaining agreement covering terms and conditions of employment for patternmakers to be effective immediately. The Respondent replied that it recognized the Union as bargaining representative of the patternmakers and that it was willing to negotiate or discuss subjects properly open for discussion, but that the existing contract with the UAWCIO was still in full force and effect and remained binding upon all employees, including patternmakers, until its July 1, 1953, expiration date.

... The Respondent contends that the certification of the Pattern Makers merely resulted in the substitution of a new bargaining representative for patternmakers in place of the old representative, with the substantive terms of the contract remaining unchanged. In support of this position, the Respondent argues that the UAW-CIO was the agent of the patternmakers when it entered into the 1950 agreement with that organization, and that the patternmakers, as principals, are bound by that contract to the expiration date thereof, notwithstanding that they have changed their agent. The General Counsel, on the other hand, contends that the certification of the Pattern Makers resulted in making the existing contract with the UAW-CIO inoperative as to the employees in the unit of patternmakers.

The Respondent's principal-agent argument assumes that common-law principles of agency control the relationship of exclusive bargaining representative to employees in an appropriate unit. We think that this assumption is unwarranted and overlooks the unique character of that relationship under the National Labor Relations Act.

... A duly selected statutory representative is the representative of a shifting group of employees in an appropriate unit which includes not only those employees who approve such relationship, but also those who disapprove and those who have never had an opportunity to express their choice. Under agency principles, a principal has the power to terminate the authority of his agent at any time. Not so in the case of a statutory bargaining representative. Thus, in its most important aspects the relationship of statutory bargaining representative to employees in an appropriate unit resembles a political rather than a private law relationship. In any event, because of the unique character of the statutory representative, a solution for the problem presented in this case must be sought in the light of that special relationship rather than by the device of pinning labels on the various parties involved and applying without change principles of law evolved to govern entirely different situations.

... One of the problems in this connection arises from the claim that a collective bargaining contract of fixed term should bar a new election during the entire term of such contract. In solving this problem, the Board has had to balance two separate interests: The interest of employees and society in the stability that is essential to the effective encouragement of collective bargaining, and the sometimes conflicting interest of employees in being free to change their representatives at will. Reconciling these two interests in the early days of the Act, the Board decided that it would not consider a contract of unreasonable duration a bar to an election to determine a new bargaining representative. The Board further decided that a contract of more than one year was of unreasonable duration and that it would direct an election after the first year of the existence of such a contract. In 1947, in the further interest of stability, the Board extended from one to two years the period during which a valid collective bargaining contract would be considered a bar to a new determination of representatives.

... If the Respondent's contention is sound, a certified bargaining representative might be deprived of effective statutory power as to the most important subjects of collective bargaining for an unlimited number of years as the result of an agreement negotiated by an unwanted and repudiated bargaining representative. There is no provision in the statute for this kind of emasculated certified bargaining representative. Moreover, the rule urged by the Respondent seems hardly calculated to reduce "industrial strife" by encouraging the "practice and procedure of collective bargaining," the declared purpose of the National Labor Relations Act, as amended.

The purpose of the Board's rule holding a contract of unreasonable duration not a bar to a new determination of representatives is the democratic one of insuring to employees the right at reasonable intervals of reappraising and changing, if they so desire, their union representation. Bargaining representatives are thereby kept responsive to the needs and desires of their constituents; and employees dissatisfied with their representative know that they will have the opportunity of changing them by peaceful means at an election conducted by an impartial Government agency. Strikes for a change of representatives are thereby reduced and effects of employee dissatisfaction with their representatives are mitigated. But, if a newly chosen representative is to be hobbled in the way proposed by the Respondent, a great part of the benefit to be derived from the no-bar rule will be dissipated. There is little point in selecting a new bargaining representative which is unable to negotiate new terms and conditions of employment for an extended period of time.

We hold that, for the reasons which led the Board to adopt the rule that a contract of unreasonable duration is not a bar to a new determination of representatives, such a contract may not bar full statutory collective bargaining, including the reduction to writing of any agreement reached, as to any group of employees in an appropriate unit covered by such contract, upon the certification of a new collective bargaining representative for them. Accordingly, we find that by refusing on and after October 16, 1952, to bargain with the Pattern Makers concerning wages, hours, and other working conditions for employees in the unit of patternmakers, the Respondent violated §§ 8(a)(5) and (1) of the Act.

Note

Would the newly certified union in the principal case be free to strike for changes in contract terms? See § 8(d)(4) of the NLRA, which expressly indicates that the advance strike notification provisions of that section are inapplicable upon the intervening certification of a new union to supersede the incumbent labor organization. Should the employer also be entitled to demand bargaining for a new contract?

International Ladies' Garment Workers' Union Local 57 v. NLRB [Garwin Corp.], 374 F.2d 295 (D.C. Cir.), *cert. denied*, 387 U.S. 942 (1967). The employer, without consulting the union about its decision, closed its plant in New York City, discharged its employees, and moved its operations to Miami, Florida. The NLRB found the move was motivated by anti-union sentiment, not economic necessity, and held the employer in violation of § 8(a)(5), (3), and (1) of the Act. In addition to ordering reinstatement and back pay for the workers, the Board ordered the "runaway" employer to bargain with the union either at the New York plant or the new Florida location, regardless of whether the union had majority status. The court of appeals refused enforcement of the bargaining portion of the Board's order, saying "the remedy fashioned by the Board in this case imposes on the Florida workers a bargaining representative without reference to their choice." Removing the benefits of the employer's wrongdoing, "standing alone and without relationship to redressing grievances of the New York workers, who suffered the violation of their statutory rights," was not enough "to justify infringing fundamental rights of comparable magnitude vested by law in the Florida workers." On remand, the Board ordered bargaining upon proof of a union majority in Florida. *Garwin Corp.*, 169 N.L.R.B. 1030 (1968), *enforced*, 70 L.R.R.M. 2465 (D.C. Cir.), *cert. denied*, 395 U.S. 980 (1969).

Problems

23. Moonbeam Enterprises is a large manufacturer of New Age paraphernalia. About five years ago, Moonbeam voluntarily recognized the Brotherhood of Liberated, Intelligent, Savvy Socialists (BLISS), a union, as the representative of its employees. Soon after that, BLISS negotiated its first contract. That first contract expired one month ago, and Moonbeam and BLISS have been engaged in intense negotiations over the terms of a new contract.

Over the last two weeks, the president of Moonbeam overheard many comments around the plant concerning employee support of BLISS. Many of the employees said that BLISS gave them "bad vibes," others said that BLISS's negotiating tactics were "less than holistic," and one employee, a vegan, said that she didn't support the union because the negotiators kept ordering their lunches from McDonald's. The president, concluding that BLISS had probably lost majority support, withdrew from the negotiations and now refuses to recognize BLISS as the representative of Moonbeam's employees.

Did Moonbeam commit an unfair labor practice when it withdrew recognition? Did the president have any other options to assess the degree of union support?

24. The Wicked Company is a large candle manufacturer in Angel Fire, New Mexico. Wicked employs hundreds of candlemakers at its main production facility.

For years, the relationship between Wicked and its workers was very good. More recently, however, the candlemakers have become dissatisfied with their pay and working conditions—those long hours over vats of molten wax began to take their toll.

Sensing an opportunity, the Brotherhood of Butchers, Bakers, and Candlestickmakers (BBBC) began an organizing campaign. After a few weeks, they had signed union cards from more than half of the Wicked candlemakers. A BBBC representative then met with the president of Wicked, told her that BBBC represented a majority of its candlemakers, and asked her to start discussing the terms of a new collective bargaining agreement. The company president was unsure about the veracity of the claim of majority support, so she informed her employees of the situation and took a poll (by secret ballot) to determine their level of support. When the poll results came back confirming the union's claim of majority support, the president recognized the BBBC and started bargaining.

About three weeks into the bargaining, the Wicked president began to have doubts about whether the BBBC continued to have her workers' support. She heard some of the workers complain that the BBBC was only interested in collecting dues. She noticed that some of the workers were talking about filing a petition for a Board election (but they didn't know whether they could or not). And, after about 30 candlemakers quit last week, she hired replacements for them plus an additional 20 new candlemakers to prepare for the upcoming holiday season.

May the president of Wicked withdraw her grant of recognition to BBBC and cease bargaining? Would the Board entertain a petition for an election from the president or the employees?

25. The employees at Manville Pipe Manufacturing have long been represented by the Machinist Union. After expiration of their last contract, the employees went out on strike. Manville quickly hired permanent replacements and continued to operate the facility. About two weeks into the strike, the employee pool consisted of 500 employees: 230 strikers, 260 replacements, and 10 union members who refused to honor the strike and crossed the picket lines.

The strike was marked by a great deal of hostility directed toward the replacement job applicants and the non-striking workers. Strikers blocked their cars, made obscene gestures, and called them "scabs." A dummy with the words "scab" on its chest was hanged by its neck near the plant entrance. More than 50 cars owned by employees sustained some combination of smashed windows, slashed tires, or body damage. And the strikers actually assaulted applicants for replacement positions by throwing objects such as steel balls at them and making thinly veiled threats such as "I know where you live." At least some of the incidents occurred with the knowledge and participation of union officials.

As the contract negotiations continued, it became clear that the only real point of contention between Manville and the union was the job status of the replacements. The union offered to accept an earlier proposal by Manville on the condition that the replacements be discharged in adequate numbers to accommodate all of the returning strikers; Manville rejected this offer and informed the replacements of the union's demand.

The replacements, upon hearing of this demand, gathered 220 signatures on a decertification petition that they filed with the Board (the election has not yet been held because of pending unfair labor practice charges filed by the union). In addition, supervisors have reported "overwhelming sentiment" among the replacements that they oppose the union, and all of the non-striking union members have tendered their resignations from the union.

At this point, may Manville withdraw recognition from the union? Alternatively, may Manville take a poll of all the employees to gauge their level of support?

Part 4

Union Collective Action

Neil W. Chamberlain, *The Philosophy of American Management Toward Labor*, in LABOR IN A CHANGING AMERICA
181–82 (W. Haber ed., 1966)

When a businessman strives for cost reduction, quality control, an improved rate of output, he is simply conforming to the institutional role which has been written for him by the society of which he is a part. But inescapably, that role brings him into conflict with organized labor, whose own institutional role is bound up with preserving the income continuity of its members, protecting the value of their learned skills, relaxing disciplinary and production pressures. It is not a matter of one of these groups being right and the other wrong, or of one being narrowly preoccupied with money values and the other more broadly concerned with human values. It is simply that American society has written different scripts for these two sets of economic performers, and the roles in which they are respectively cast *call* for a clash of objectives on the economic stage....

Lloyd G. Reynolds, Stanley H. Masters & Colletta H. Moser, LABOR ECONOMICS AND LABOR RELATIONS
495, 497, 512 (9th ed. 1986)

... To discover [what] was responsible for a particular strike requires careful analysis of the circumstances. The union normally makes the first overt move, and the public therefore tends to regard it as the aggressor. The employer can cause a strike by doing nothing; the union has to take the positive step of calling out the workers. But all one can conclude from the fact of a strike is that there was a failure to reach agreement. The reasons for the failure can be learned from an inside knowledge of the people and issues involved....

As regards economic cost, one must distinguish between private and social cost, between cost to the parties and cost to the economy. The striking workers lose some wages and the company loses some profit. These are losses that the parties consider it worthwhile to bear rather than settle on adverse terms. The loss to the economy consists in a reduced output of goods and services available for consumption or investment....

Section I. Introduction

It is apparent that labor organizations are not mere fraternal societies conducting polite social functions. They are militant groups formed for the primary purpose of advancing the economic interests of their members, and they have not been content to rely exclusively on the art of persuasion through exhortation either in gaining members or in wresting concessions from employers. From the beginning they have also made use of economic and political action to gain their ends. Economic action has typically taken the form of the strike, the picket line, and the boycott.

A. Collective Action at Common Law

Part One contained a brief treatment of the early antecedents of American labor law and an outline of the principles that courts have used, or purportedly used, when deciding cases involving collective action by labor groups. It was suggested that the concept most frequently found in the cases was that union activities that inflict injury had to be tested by the propriety of the objective being sought and the means being used. This is the general principle that, in 1938, was articulated by Professor Shulman and his assisting experts in the *Torts Restatement* of the law of labor disputes. The rules stated in the *Restatement* were by no means universally accepted by the courts, and there is a real question whether anything purporting to be an actual "restatement" could reasonably be attempted.

We have come a long way from the views represented in the early nineteenth-century criminal conspiracy cases. The right of individuals to quit their jobs is considered to be inviolate, at least as against injunctive or other official restraint, and the peaceful strike is privileged at common law, at least as long as the objective is "proper" and it does not go beyond the "proper" area for economic action. Picketing has had more difficulty in gaining recognition as an accepted method of collective action, because it has carried in the minds of some judges connotations of violence regardless of its actual physical characteristics. Many courts have been quick to seize upon the slightest manifestation of violence or abuse (e.g., numbers of picketers, minor breaches of peace, rough-and-tumble and frequently "unnice" language) as a pretext for granting relief despite lip service to the doctrine, now generally established, that peaceful and nonfraudulent picketing for a proper objective is lawful. The boycott has fared least well, particularly when it has been found to be "secondary."

B. Anti-Injunction Statutes

An attempt was made in 1914 to get the federal courts out of the business of issuing injunctions in labor disputes by the passage of the Clayton Act. However, this legislative effort was not fully effective. One frequent basis for an injunction in the federal courts was the Sherman Antitrust Act. During the decade of the 1920s, in such cases as *Duplex Printing Press Co. v. Deering*, 254 U.S. 443 (1921), and *Bedford Cut Stone Co. v. Journeymen Stone Cutters' Ass'n*, 274 U.S. 37 (1927), the federal courts continued to issue injunctions against secondary boycotts as violations of the antitrust laws.

Public dissatisfaction with the labor injunction grew in the late 1920s and early 1930s, with agitation for reform coming not only from representatives of the labor movement, but also from persons in the legal profession who were concerned about the reputation of the judicial system. The particularized evils of the labor injunction that were highly publicized at this time are set forth in the historical introduction (Part One, *supra*). *See generally* F. FRANKFURTER & N. GREENE, THE LABOR INJUNCTION (1930).

The Norris-LaGuardia Act, enacted in 1932, operates as a restriction upon the equity jurisdiction of the federal courts in cases involving or growing out of *labor disputes* (*see* § 13). The Act is set out in *Selected Federal Statutes*. Its incidence is twofold: (1) it lays down certain definite requirements of procedure and proof (which we shall refer to as "procedural" requirements) that must be met before an injunction may issue (*see* §§ 6, 7, 8, 9, 10, 11, and 12); and (2) it removes from the federal courts all "jurisdiction" to restrain certain specified kinds of acts, even though the procedural requirements are met (*see* § 4). The Norris Act has been substantially duplicated by state legislation in a number of states, in some instances with variations designed to meet specific problems considered important.

Marine Cooks & Stewards v. Panama S.S. Co., 362 U.S. 365, 80 S. Ct. 779, 4 L. Ed. 2d 797 (1960). This case involved the picketing of a Liberian ship by an American union in the Port of Tacoma. The union did not seek to represent the foreign crew, which had no labor dispute with the ship owners. The purpose of the picketing was to protest the substandard wages and benefits received by the ship's crew that caused a loss of jobs for American seamen. Despite the lack of any direct connection between the American union and the foreign flag vessel and its foreign crew, the Court found that a labor dispute existed because of the union's interest in the employment conditions aboard the ship. As a result, the district court lacked the authority to enjoin the picketing.

> It is difficult to see how this controversy could be thought to spring from anything except one "concerning terms or conditions of employment," and hence a labor dispute within the meaning of the Norris-La Guardia Act. The protest stated by the pickets concerned "sub-standard wages or sub-standard conditions." The controversy does involve, as the Act requires, "persons who are engaged in the same industry, trade, craft or occupation." And it is immaterial under the Act that the unions and the ship and the consignees did not "stand in a proximate relation of employer and employee." This case clearly does grow out of a labor dispute within the meaning of the Norris-La Guardia Act.

The District Court held, however, that even if this case involved a labor dispute under the Norris-La Guardia Act the court had jurisdiction to issue the injunction because the picketing was an "unlawful interference with foreign commerce" and interfered "in the internal economy of a vessel registered under the flag of a friendly foreign power" and prevented "such a vessel from lawfully loading or discharging cargo at ports in the United States." The Court of Appeals adopted this position, but cited no authority for its statement that the picketing was "unlawful,"... And even if unlawful, it would not follow that the federal court would have jurisdiction to enjoin the particular conduct which §4 of the Norris-La Guardia Act declared shall not be enjoined. Nor does the language of the Norris-La Guardia Act leave room to hold that jurisdiction it denies a District Court to issue a particular type of restraining order can be restored to it by a finding that the nonenjoinable conduct may "interfere in the internal economy of a vessel registered under the flag of a friendly foreign power."

Notes

1. *Scope of a "Labor Dispute" Under the Norris-LaGuardia Act*—In *New Negro Alliance v. Sanitary Grocery Co.*, 303 U.S. 552 (1938), the Supreme Court reversed the granting of an injunction against the New Negro Alliance, an incorporated association (not a labor union) that was boycotting and picketing a grocery store, demanding that the store hire black workers. The Supreme Court applied the Norris-LaGuardia Act, reasoning that the parties in a labor dispute need not have the relationship of employer and employee, and that the Alliance had a direct interest in the labor dispute. The Court also emphasized that the Act is not concerned with the motives for the dispute. Similar reasoning would probably preclude issuance of an injunction against groups seeking to organize workers on an ethnic, gender, or alienage basis, even though the NLRA does not authorize such interest-based bargaining arrangements.

Emphasizing that the term "labor dispute" in §4 of the Norris-LaGuardia Act must not be narrowly construed, the Supreme Court held that a politically motivated refusal by longshoremen to load vessels with cargo bound for the Soviet Union could not be enjoined by the federal courts. *Jacksonville Bulk Terminals, Inc. v. International Longshoremen's Ass'n*, 457 U.S. 702 (1982). Since an employer and the union representing its employees had a dispute over the interpretation of the no-strike clause of their labor contract, the employer-employee relationship was the "matrix" of the controversy. The union's noneconomic motives did not take the dispute out of the reach of Norris-LaGuardia.

2. *Limits to the Norris-LaGuardia Act*—In *San Antonio Community Hosp. v. Southern Cal. Dist. Council of Carpenters*, 125 F.3d 1230 (9th Cir. 1997), *rehearing denied*, 137 F.3d 1090 (9th Cir. 1998), the Ninth Circuit upheld an injunction against union picketing of a hospital's maternity entrance with a banner reading, "THIS MEDICAL FACILITY IS FULL OF RATS." The union insisted the "rats" referred to a

construction contractor that was not paying prevailing union wages. The court concluded that the banner fell within the "fraud" exception to Norris-LaGuardia's anti-injunction ban, since it could deceive the public into believing the hospital was infested with rodents.

3. *NLRB Petitions for Injunctive Relief* — Under § 10(j) and (*l*) of the National Labor Relations Act, the NLRB is empowered, and in the case of some union unfair labor practices, directed, to petition federal district courts for temporary restraining orders to maintain the status quo while the cases are being litigated before the Board. Also, to enforce its orders, the NLRB is authorized under § 10(e) to petition a federal court of appeals for an enforcement order.

Accordingly, § 10(h) of the Act provides:

> (h) When granting appropriate temporary relief or a restraining order, or making and entering a decree enforcing, modifying, and enforcing as so modified, or setting aside in whole or in part an order of the Board, as provided in this section, the jurisdiction of courts sitting in equity shall not be limited by the Act entitled "An Act to amend the Judicial Code and to define and limit the jurisdiction of courts sitting in equity, and for other purposes," approved March 23, 1932 (29 U.S.C. §§ 101–15) [Norris-La Guardia Act].

Thus the Norris-LaGuardia Act does not preclude injunctions against unfair labor practices when they are sought by the NLRB. But it does prevent private parties from obtaining injunctive relief against unfair labor practices. *Bakery Sales Drivers, Local 33 v. Wagshal*, 333 U.S. 437, 442 (1948).

The Ninth Circuit has indicated that district courts must consider traditional equitable doctrines when deciding whether to issue § 10(j) injunctions sought by Labor Board attorneys. Despite the NLRB's weighing of public interest factors when deciding whether to request § 10(j) relief, courts must still evaluate: (1) the likelihood the plaintiff will ultimately prevail on the merits; (2) the possibility the plaintiff will be irreparably injured if temporary relief is not granted; (3) the extent to which the balance of hardships favors one party or the other; and (4) whether the public interest will be advanced by the granting of the preliminary relief being sought. *Miller v. California Pac. Medical Ctr.*, 991 F.2d 536 (9th Cir. 1993).

The power to initiate or maintain injunctive actions under § 10(*l*) is restricted to the NLRB. Thus, charging parties have been denied permission even to intervene in proceedings brought by a Board regional director against a union under § 10(*l*). *Solien on behalf of NLRB v. Miscellaneous Drivers & Helpers Union Local 610* [*Sears, Roebuck & Co.*], 440 F.2d 124 (8th Cir.), *cert. denied*, 403 U.S. 905 (1971). At the same time, regional director discretion under the mandatory injunction provisions of § 10(*l*) is limited, and an employer charging a union with an unlawful secondary boycott may go into federal district court for a mandamus order compelling the regional director to seek a temporary injunction against the union's activity. *Terminal Freight Handling Co. v. Solien*, 444 F.2d 699 (8th Cir. 1971), *cert. denied*, 405 U.S. 996 (1972).

Section II. Union Discipline

NLRB v. Allis-Chalmers Mfg. Co.

Supreme Court of the United States
388 U.S. 175, 87 S. Ct. 2001, 18 L. Ed. 2d 1123 (1967)

Mr. Justice Brennan delivered the opinion of the Court.

The question here is whether a union which threatened and imposed fines [of $20 to $100] and brought suit for their collection, against members who crossed the union's picket line and went to work during an authorized strike against their employer, committed the unfair labor practice under §8(b)(1)(A) of the National Labor Relations Act of engaging in conduct "to restrain or coerce" employees in the exercise of their right guaranteed by §7 to "refrain from" concerted activities....

I

... It is highly unrealistic to regard §8(b)(1), and particularly its words "restrain or coerce," as precisely and unambiguously covering the union conduct involved in this case. On its face court enforcement of fines imposed on members for violation of membership obligations is no more conduct to "restrain or coerce" satisfaction of such obligations than court enforcement of penalties imposed on citizens for violation of their obligations as citizens to pay income taxes, or court awards of damages against a contracting party for nonperformance of a contractual obligation voluntarily undertaken. But even if the inherent imprecision of the words "restrain or coerce" may be overlooked, recourse to legislative history to determine the sense in which Congress used the words is not foreclosed....

To say that Congress meant in 1947 by the §7 amendments and §8(b)(1)(A) to strip unions of the power to fine members for strikebreaking, however lawful the strike vote, and however fair the disciplinary procedures and penalty, is to say that Congress preceded the Landrum-Griffin amendments with an even more pervasive regulation of the internal affairs of unions. It is also to attribute to Congress an intent at war with the understanding of the union-membership relation which has been at the heart of its effort "to fashion a coherent labor policy" and which has been a predicate underlying action by this Court and the state courts. More importantly, it is to say that Congress limited unions in the powers necessary to the discharge of their role as exclusive statutory bargaining agents by impairing the usefulness of labor's cherished strike weapon. It is no answer that the proviso to §8(b)(1)(A) preserves to the union the power to expel the offending member. Where the union is strong and membership therefore valuable, to require expulsion of the member visits a far more severe penalty upon the member than a reasonable fine. Where the union is weak, and membership therefore of little value, the union faced with further depletion of its ranks may have no real choice except to condone the member's disobedience. Yet it is just such weak unions for which the power to execute union decisions taken for the benefit of all employees is most critical to effective discharge of its statutory function.

Congressional meaning is of course ordinarily to be discerned in the words Congress uses. But when the literal application of the imprecise words "restrain or coerce" Congress employed in § 8(b)(1)(A) produce the extraordinary results we have mentioned we should determine whether this meaning is confirmed in the legislative history of the section.

ii

The explicit wording of § 8(b)(2), which is concerned with union powers to affect a member's employment, is in sharp contrast with the imprecise words of § 8(b) (1) (A). . . . Senator Taft, in answer to protestations by Senator Pepper that § 8(b)(2) would intervene into the union's internal affairs and "deny it the right to protect itself against a man in the union who betrays the objectives of the union . . . ," stated:

> *The pending measure does not propose any limitation with respect to the internal affairs of unions.* They still will be able to fire any members they wish to fire, *and they still will be able to try any of their members.* All that they will not be able to do, after the enactment of this bill, is this: If they fire a member for some reason other than nonpayment of dues they cannot make his employer discharge him from his job and throw him out of work. That is the only result of the provision under discussion.[1] . . .

What legislative materials there are dealing with § 8(b)(1)(A) contain not a single word referring to the application of its prohibitions to traditional internal union discipline in general, or disciplinary fines in particular. On the contrary there are a number of assurances by its sponsors that the section was not meant to regulate the internal affairs of unions. . . .

It is true that there are references in the Senate debate on § 8(b)(1)(A) to an intent to impose the same prohibitions on unions that applied to employers as regards restraint and coercion of employees in their exercise of § 7 rights. However, apposite this parallel might be when applied to organizational tactics, it clearly is inapplicable to the relationship of a union member to his own union. Union membership allows the member a part in choosing the very course of action to which he refuses to adhere, but he has of course no role in employer conduct, and nonunion employees have no voice in the affairs of the union.

Cogent support for an interpretation of the body of § 8(b)(1) as not reaching the imposition of fines and attempts at court enforcement is the proviso to § 8(b)(1). . . . Senator Holland offered the proviso during debate and Senator Ball immediately accepted it, stating that it was not the intent of the sponsors in any way to regulate the internal affairs of unions. At the very least it can be said that the proviso preserves the rights of unions to impose fines, as a lesser penalty than expulsion, and to impose fines which carry the explicit or implicit threat of expulsion for nonpayment.

---

1. [13] 93 Cong. Rec. 4193, II Legislative History of the Labor Management Relations Act of 1947, 1097 (hereafter, Leg. Hist.).

Therefore, under the proviso the rule in the UAW constitution governing fines is valid and the fines themselves and expulsion for nonpayment would not be an unfair labor practice. Assuming that the proviso cannot also be read to authorize court enforcement of fines, a question we need not reach, the fact remains that to interpret the body of § 8(b)(1) to apply to the imposition and collection of fines would be to impute to Congress a concern with the permissible *means* of enforcement of union fines and to attribute to Congress a narrow and discrete interest in banning court enforcement of such fines. Yet there is not one word of the legislative history evidencing any such congressional concern. And as we have pointed out, a distinction between court enforcement and expulsion would have been anomalous for several reasons. First, Congress was operating within the context of the "contract theory" of the union-member relationship which widely prevailed at that time. The efficacy of a contract is precisely its legal enforceability. A lawsuit is and has been the ordinary way by which performance of private money obligations is compelled. Second, as we have noted, such a distinction would visit upon the member of a strong union a potentially more severe punishment than court enforcement of fines, while impairing the bargaining facility of the weak union by requiring it either to condone misconduct or deplete its ranks.

There may be concern that court enforcement may permit the collection of unreasonably large fines. However, even were there evidence that Congress shared this concern, this would not justify reading the Act also to bar court enforcement of reasonable fines.

The 1959 Landrum-Griffin amendments, thought to be the first comprehensive regulation by Congress of the conduct of internal union affairs,[2] also negate the reach given § 8(b)(1)(A) by the majority *en banc* below.... In 1959 Congress did seek to protect union members in their relationship to the union by adopting measures to insure the provision of democratic processes in the conduct of union affairs and procedural due process to members subjected to discipline. Even then, some Senators emphasized that "[I]n establishing and enforcing statutory standards great care should be taken not to undermine union self-government or weaken unions in their role as collective-bargaining agents." S. Rep. No. 187, 86th Cong., 1st Sess., 7. The Eighty-sixth Congress was thus plainly of the view that union self-government was not regulated in 1947. Indeed, that Congress expressly recognized that a union member may be "fined, suspended, expelled, or otherwise disciplined," and enacted only procedural requirements to be observed. 29 U.S.C. § 411(a)(5). Moreover, Congress added a proviso to the guarantee of freedom of speech and assembly disclaiming any intent "to impair the right of a labor organization to adopt and enforce reasonable rules as to the responsibility of every member toward the organization as an institution...." 29 U.S.C. § 411(a)(2)....

---

2. [33] In 1957, in *Machinists v. Gonzales*, 356 U.S. 617, 620, we said: "[T]he protection of union members in their rights as members from arbitrary conduct by unions and union officers has not been undertaken by federal law, and indeed the assertion of any such power has been expressly denied."

Thus this history of congressional action does not support a conclusion that the Taft-Hartley prohibitions against restraint or coercion of an employee to refrain from concerted activities included a prohibition against the imposition of fines on members who decline to honor an authorized strike and attempts to collect such fines. Rather, the contrary inference is more justified in light of the repeated refrain throughout the debates on § 8(b)(1)(A) and other sections that Congress did not propose any limitations with respect to the internal affairs of unions, aside from barring enforcement of a union's internal regulations to affect a member's employment status.

III

... The collective bargaining agreements with the locals incorporate union security clauses. Full union membership is not compelled by the clauses: an employee is required only to become and remain "a member of the union to the extent of paying his monthly dues...." The majority *en banc* below nevertheless regarded full membership to be "the result not of individual voluntary choice but of the insertion of [this] union security provision in the contract under which a substantial minority of the employees may have been forced into membership." 358 F.2d at 660. But the relevant inquiry here is not what motivated a member's full membership but whether the Taft-Hartley amendments prohibited disciplinary measures against a full member who crossed his union's picket line. It is clear that the fined employees involved in these cases enjoyed full union membership. Each executed the pledge of allegiance to the UAW constitution and took the oath of full membership. Moreover, the record of the Milwaukee County Court case against Benjamin Natzke discloses that two disciplined employees testified that they had fully participated in the proceedings leading to the strike. They attended the meetings at which the secret strike vote and the renewed strike vote were taken. It was upon this and similar evidence that the Milwaukee County Court found that Natzke "had by his actions become a member of the union for all purposes...." Allis-Chalmers offered no evidence in this proceeding that any of the fined employees enjoyed other than full union membership. We will not presume the contrary. *Cf. Machinists v. Street*, 367 U.S. 740, 774. Indeed, it is and has been Allis-Chalmers' position that the Taft-Hartley prohibitions apply whatever the nature of the membership. Whether those prohibitions would apply if the locals had imposed fines on members whose membership was in fact limited to the obligation of paying monthly dues is a question not before us and upon which we intimate no view.

The judgment of the Court of Appeals is

Reversed.

Mr. Justice White, concurring.

It is true that § 8(b)(1)(A) makes it an unfair labor practice for a union to restrain or coerce any employees in the exercise of § 7 rights, but the proviso permits the union to make its own rules with respect to acquisition and retention of membership. Hence, a union may expel to enforce its own internal rules, even though a particular rule limits the §7 rights of its members and even though expulsion to enforce it would be a clear and serious brand of "coercion" imposed in derogation of those §7 rights. Such restraint and coercion Congress permitted by adding the proviso to §8(b)(1)(A). Thus, neither the majority nor the dissent in this case questions the validity of the union rule against its members crossing picket lines during a properly called strike, nor the propriety of expulsion to enforce the rule. Section 8(b)(1)(A), therefore, does not bar *all* restraint and coercion by a union to prevent the exercise by its members of their §7 rights. "Coercive" union rules are enforceable at least by expulsion.

The dissenting opinion in this case, although not questioning the enforceability of coercive rules by expulsion from membership, questions whether fines for violating such rules are enforceable at all, by expulsion or otherwise. The dissent would at least hold court collection of fines to be an unfair labor practice, apparently for the reason that fines collectible in court may be more coercive than fines enforceable by expulsion. My Brother BRENNAN, for the Court, takes a different view, reasoning that since expulsion would in many cases — certainly in this one involving a strong union — be a far more coercive technique for enforcing a union rule and for collecting a reasonable fine than the threat of court enforcement, there is no basis for thinking that Congress, having accepted expulsion as a permissible technique to enforce a rule in derogation of §7 rights, nevertheless intended to bar enforcement by another method which may be far less coercive.

I do not mean to indicate, and I do not read the majority opinion otherwise, that every conceivable internal union rule which impinges upon the §7 rights of union members is valid and enforceable by expulsion and court action. There may well be some internal union rules which on their face are wholly invalid and unenforceable. But the Court seems unanimous in upholding the rule against crossing picket lines during a strike and its enforceability by expulsion from membership. On this premise I think the opinion written for the Court is the more persuasive and sensible construction of the statute and I therefore join it, although I am doubtful about the implications of some of its generalized statements.

MR. JUSTICE BLACK, whom MR. JUSTICE DOUGLAS, MR. JUSTICE HARLAN, and MR. JUSTICE STEWART join, dissenting. . . .

I

In determining what the Court here holds, it is helpful to note what it does not hold. Since the union resorted to the courts to enforce its fines instead of relying on its own internal sanctions such as expulsion from membership, the Court correctly assumes that the proviso to §8(b)(1)(A) cannot be read to authorize its holding. Neither does the Court attempt to sustain its holding by reference to §7 which gives employees the right to refrain from engaging in concerted activities. To be sure, the Court in characterizing the union-member relationship as "contractual" and in emphasizing that its holding is limited to situations where the employee is a "full member" of the union, implies that by joining a union an employee gives up or waives some of his §7 rights. But the Court does not say that a union member is without the §7 right to refrain from participating in such concerted activity as an economic strike called by his union. . . .

With no reliance on the proviso to §8(b)(1)(A) or on the meaning of §7, the Court's holding boils down to this: a court-enforced reasonable fine for nonparticipation in a strike does not "restrain or coerce" an employee in the exercise of his right not to participate in the strike. In holding as it does, the Court interprets the words "restrain or coerce" in a way directly opposed to their literal meaning, for the Court admits that fines are as coercive as penalties imposed on citizens for the nonpayment of taxes. Though Senator Taft, in answer to charges that these words were ambiguous, said their meaning "is perfectly clear," 93 Cong. Rec. 4021, II Leg. Hist. 1025, and though any union official with sufficient intelligence and learning to be chosen as such could hardly fail to comprehend the meaning of these plain, simple English words, the Court insists on finding an "inherent imprecision" in these words. And that characterization then allows the Court to resort to "what legislative materials there are."

. . . The real reason for the Court's decision is its policy judgment that unions, especially weak ones, need the power to impose fines on strikebreakers and to enforce those fines in court. It is not enough, says the Court, that the unions have the power to expel those members who refuse to participate in a strike or who fail to pay fines imposed on them for such failure to participate; it is essential that weak unions have the choice between expulsion and court-enforced fines, simply because the latter are more effective in the sense of being more punitive. Though the entire mood of Congress in 1947 was to curtail the power of unions, as it had previously curtailed the power of employers, in order to equalize the power of the two, the Court is unwilling to believe that Congress intended to impair "the usefulness of labor's cherished strike weapon." I cannot agree with this conclusion or subscribe to the Court's unarticulated premise that the Court has power to add a new weapon to the union's economic arsenal whenever the Court believes that the union needs that weapon. That is a job for Congress, not this Court.

II

. . . Contrary to the Court, I am not at all certain that a union's right under the proviso to prescribe rules for the retention of membership includes the right to restrain a member from working by trying him on the vague charge of "conduct unbecoming a union member" and fining him for exercising his §7 right of refusing to participate in a strike, even though the fine is only enforceable by expulsion from membership. It is one thing to say that Congress did not wish to interfere with the union's power, similar to that of any other kind of voluntary association, to prescribe specific conditions of membership. It is quite another thing to say that Congress intended to leave unions free to exercise a court-like power to try and punish members with a direct economic sanction for exercising their right to work. Just because a union might be free, under the proviso, to expel a member for crossing a picket line does not mean that Congress left unions free to threaten their members with fines. Even though a member may later discover that the threatened fine is only enforceable by expulsion, and in that sense a "lesser penalty," the direct threat of a fine, to a member normally unaware of the method the union might resort to for compelling its payment, would often be more coercive than a threat of expulsion.

Even on the assumption that § 8(b)(1)(A) permits a union to fine a member as long as the fine is only enforceable by expulsion, the fundamental error of the Court's opinion is its failure to recognize the practical and theoretical difference between a court-enforced fine, as here, and a fine enforced by expulsion or less drastic intra-union means. As the Court recognizes, expulsion for nonpayment of a fine may, especially in the case of a strong union, be more severe than judicial collection of the fine. But, if the union membership has little value and if the fine is great, then court-enforcement of the fine may be more effective punishment, and that is precisely why the Court desires to provide weak unions with this alternative to expulsion, an alternative which is similar to a criminal court's power to imprison defendants who fail to pay fines. . . .

The Court disposes of this tremendous practical difference between court-enforced and union-enforced fines by suggesting that Congress was not concerned with "the permissible means of enforcement of union fines" and that court-enforcement of fines is a necessary consequence of the "contract theory" of the union-member relationship. And then the Court cautions that its holding may only apply to court enforcement of "reasonable fines." Apparently the Court believes that these considerations somehow bring reasonable court-enforced fines within the ambit of "internal union affairs." There is no basis either historically or logically for this conclusion or the considerations upon which it is based. First, the Court says that disciplinary fines were commonplace at the time the Taft-Hartley Act was passed, and thus Congress could not have meant to prohibit these "traditional internal discipline" measures without saying so. Yet there is not one word in the authorities cited by the Court that indicates that court enforcement of fines was commonplace or traditional in 1947, and, to the contrary, until recently unions rarely resorted to court enforcement of union fines. Second, Congress' unfamiliarity in 1947 with this recent innovation and consequent failure to make any distinction between union-enforced and court-enforced fines cannot support the conclusion that Congress was unconcerned with the "means" a union uses to enforce its fines. Congress was expressly concerned with enacting "rules of the game" for unions to abide by. 93 Cong. Rec. 4436, II Leg. Hist. 1206. . . .

V

. . . The union here had a union security clause in its contract with Chalmers. That clause made it necessary for all employees, including the ones involved here, to pay dues and fees to the union. But § 8(a)(3) and § 8(b)(2) make it clear that "Congress intended to prevent utilization of union security agreements for any purpose other than to compel payment of union dues and fees." *Radio Officers' Union v. Labor Board*, 347 U.S. 17, 41. If the union uses the union security clause to compel employees to pay dues, characterizes such employees as members, and then uses such membership as a basis for imposing court-enforced fines upon those employees unwilling to participate in a union strike, then the union security clause is being used for a purpose other than "to compel payment of union dues and fees." It is being used to coerce employees to join in union activity in violation of § 8(b)(2).

The Court suggests that this problem is not present here, because the fined employees failed to prove they enjoyed other than full union membership, that their role in the union was not in fact limited to the obligation of paying dues. For several reasons, I am unable to agree with the Court's approach. Few employees forced to become "members" of the union by virtue of the union security clause will be aware of the fact that they must somehow "limit" their membership to avoid the union's court-enforced fines. Even those who are brash enough to attempt to do so may be unfamiliar with how to do it. Must they refrain from doing anything but paying dues, or will signing the routine union pledge still leave them with less than full membership? And finally, it is clear that what restrains the employee from going to work during a union strike is the union's threat that it will fine him and collect those fines from him in court. How many employees in a union shop whose names appear on the union's membership rolls will be willing to ignore that threat in the hope that they will later be able to convince the Labor Board or the state court that they were not full members of the union?

Notes

1. *Scope of Union Power to Fine* — If union discipline does not "restrain or coerce" employees within the meaning of § 8(b)(1)(A) in the circumstances of the principal case, does it make any difference *why* the penalty is imposed? In *Scofield v. NLRB*, 394 U.S. 423 (1969), the Supreme Court found no violation of § 8(b)(1)(A) when a union sued in state court to collect fines levied against members who had breached a union rule forbidding the receipt of pay for production that exceeded a set ceiling. *See United Paperworkers Int'l Union Local 5 (Int'l Paper Co.)*, 294 N.L.R.B. 1168 (1989) (union could fine members who defied ban on performance of work outside bargaining unit); *Winery, Distillery & Allied Workers Union, Local 186 (E & J Gallo Winery)*, 296 N.L.R.B. 519 (1989) (union could fine member who announced she would defy strike call and argued for ouster of union, since this was more than expression of dissenting opinion and justified union's action to maintain membership strike solidarity).

2. *Limits on Disciplinary Fines* — Union discipline that frustrates an overriding federal labor policy will be held to violate § 8(b)(1)(A). For example, a labor organization may not fine members who refuse to participate in a work stoppage that contravenes a contractual no-strike clause. *Laborers Local 135 (Bechtel Power Co.)*, 271 N.L.R.B. 777 (1984), *enforced*, 782 F.2d 1030 (3d Cir. 1986). Nor may it discipline members who refuse to honor a picket line established by a sister union, when such action would violate contractual prohibitions against sympathy strikes. *United Mine Workers, Dist. 50, Local 12419 (National Grinding Wheel Co.)*, 176 N.L.R.B. 628

(1969); *United Food & Commercial Workers Union, Local 1439 (Rosauer's Supermarkets)*, 275 N.L.R.B. 30 (1985). *See also United Ass'n of Journeymen & Apprentices of Plumbing & Pipefitting Industry, Local 444 (Hanson Plumbing)*, 277 N.L.R.B. 1231 (1985), *enforced*, 827 F.2d 579 (9th Cir. 1987) (union violated § 8(b)(1)(A) when it fined members who refused to honor primary picket line at a common situs construction project, since union impermissibly sought to exert pressure against primary general contractor through secondary subcontractor).

When a union and an employer included a "two-way" amnesty provision in their strike settlement agreement, the union violated § 8(b)(1)(A) by disciplining members for working during the strike. The policy favoring collective bargaining overrode the right of the union to regulate its internal affairs. *Operating Engineers, Local 39 (San Jose Hosp.)*, 240 N.L.R.B. 1122 (1979).

3. *Fines versus Expulsion*—Should it make any difference whether a union penalizes a member who files a decertification petition through a fine or expulsion? *See Molders, Local 125 (Blackhawk Tanning Co.)*, 178 N.L.R.B. 208 (1969), *enforced*, 442 F.2d 92 (7th Cir. 1971) (fine is punitive and forbidden, while expulsion is defensive and allowable). *See also Tri-Rivers Marine Engineers (United States Steel Corp.)*, 189 N.L.R.B. 838 (1971) (union may threaten to expel member who solicits authorization cards for rival union, but may not fine that person).

There are, however, limits to a union's ability to expel members. In *NLRB v. Industrial Union of Marine & Shipbuilding Workers*, 391 U.S. 418 (1968), for example, the Court held that a union violated § 8(b)(1)(A) by expelling a member for filing an unfair labor practice charge with the Board without first having exhausted internal union remedies. Declared the Court: "Section 8(b)(1)(A) assures a union freedom of self-regulation where its legitimate internal affairs are concerned. But where a union rule penalizes a member for filing an unfair labor practice charge with the Board other considerations of public policy come into play."

4. *Shop Stewards, Union Representatives, and Supervisor-Members*—In *Local 254, SEIU (Brandeis Univ.)*, 332 N.L.R.B. 1118 (2000), the Board found that a union's removal of a dissident member from positions as shop steward and union representative on a contractually created labor-management committee did not violate the NLRA, because this action did not directly affect that person's employment relationship and the union had a bona fide interest in limiting shop stewards and union representatives to individuals who would demonstrate undivided loyalty to union positions. *See also Office & Prof'l Employees Int'l Union, Local 251 (Scandia Corp.)*, 331 N.L.R.B. 1417 (2000) (union did not violate § 8(b)(1)(A) when it removed two elected members from union office and disciplined two other members for opposing the local president, since these were internal union sanctions that had no impact on the employment relationships of the disciplined individuals).

Union discipline imposed on supervisor-members in response to their performance of certain job functions may be found to coerce the affected employer with respect to its selection of grievance adjustment or bargaining representatives, and thus contravene §8(b)(1)(B). *Compare Florida Power & Light Co. v. International Brotherhood of Elec. Workers, Local 641*, 417 U.S. 790 (1974) (union may fine supervisor-members who perform rank-and-file work during strike), *with American Broadcasting Cos. v. Writers Guild of Am., W.*, 437 U.S. 411 (1978) (union may not fine supervisor-members for performing customary supervisory functions, including grievance adjustment), *and Mailers, Local 143 (Dow Jones & Co.)*, 181 N.L.R.B. 286 (1970), *enforced on other grounds*, 445 F.2d 730 (D.C. Cir. 1971) (union may not discipline supervisor-members because of way in which they administer labor contract). *See generally* Grissom, *Union Discipline of Supervisor-Members Under Section 8 (b)(1)(B) of the National Labor Relations Act: Drawing the Line After Florida Power*, 27 Ala. L. Rev. 575 (1975).

In *NLRB v. International Bhd. of Elec. Workers, Local 340*, 481 U.S. 573 (1987), the Supreme Court held that a union did not violate §8(b)(1)(B) by fining two supervisor-members who had breached the union constitution by working for employers that did not have contracts with the union, since those supervisors did not engage in collective bargaining or grievance adjustment. The Court expressly rejected the Board's "reservoir doctrine," under which all persons defined as §2(11) "supervisors" were considered part of a "reservoir" of workers available for future employer selection as bargaining representatives or grievance adjusters. The Court ruled that §8(b)(1)(B) only protects those supervisors who currently possess bargaining or grievance adjustment authority.

NLRB v. Boeing Co., 412 U.S. 67, 93 S. Ct. 1952, 36 L. Ed. 2d 752 (1973). During an 18-day economic strike, certain union members crossed the picket line and returned to work. Although the weekly earnings of the workers ranged from $95 to $145, the returning members were each fined $450. After the union filed state-court actions to collect the unpaid fines, charges were filed with the NLRB under §8(b)(1)(A) claiming that the excessive nature of the fines coerced and restrained the disciplined members. The Labor Board held that "Congress did not intend to give [it] authority to regulate the size of union fines or to establish standards with respect to a fine's reasonableness." The Supreme Court sustained this conclusion.

> [I]n both [*NLRB v. Allis-Chalmers Mfg. Co.*, 388 U.S. 175 (1967)] and in [*Scofield v. NLRB*, 394 U.S. 423 (1969)], the reasonableness of the fines was assumed. Being squarely presented with the issue in this case, we recede from the implications of the dicta in these earlier cases. While "unreasonable" fines may be more coercive than "reasonable" fines, all fines are coercive to a greater or lesser degree. The underlying basis for the holdings of *Allis-Chalmers* and Scofield was not that reasonable fines were noncoercive under the language of §8(b)(1)(A) of the Act, but was instead that those provisions were not intended by Congress to apply to the imposition by the union of fines not affecting the employer-employee relationship and not otherwise prohibited by the Act. The reason for this determination, in turn, was that Congress had not intended by enacting this section to regulate the

internal affairs of unions to the extent that would be required in order to base unfair labor practice charges on the levying of such fines....

Issues as to the reasonableness or unreasonableness of such fines must be decided upon the basis of the law of contracts, voluntary associations, or such other principles of law as may be applied in a forum competent to adjudicate the issue. Under our holding, state courts will be wholly free to apply state law to such issues.

Note

The NLRB has concluded that it is not to assess the fairness of the internal union procedures by which fines are imposed. *Electrical Workers, UE, Local 1012 (General Electric Co.)*, 187 N.L.R.B. 375 (1970). Procedural due process, said the Board, is irrelevant in determining the legality of fines under the NLRA. *See* Craver, *The Boeing Decision: A Blow to Federalism, Individual Rights, and Stare Decisis*, 122 U. PENN. L. REV. 556 (1974).

Pattern Makers' League of North America v. NLRB

Supreme Court of the United States
473 U.S. 95, 105 S. Ct. 3064, 87 L. Ed. 2d 68 (1985)

JUSTICE POWELL delivered the opinion of the Court.

The Pattern Makers' League of North America, AFL-CIO (the League), a labor union, provides in its constitution that resignations are not permitted during a strike or when a strike is imminent. The League fined 10 of its members who, in violation of this provision, resigned during a strike and returned to work. The National Labor Relations Board held that these fines were imposed in violation of § 8(b)(1)(A) of the National Labor Relations Act, 29 U.S.C. § 158(b)(1)(A). We granted a petition for a writ of certiorari in order to decide whether § 8(b)(1)(A) reasonably may be construed by the Board as prohibiting a union from fining members who have tendered resignations invalid under the union constitution.

I

The League is a national union composed of local associations (locals). In May 1976, its constitution was amended to provide that:

No resignation or withdrawal from an Association, or from the League, shall be accepted during a strike or lockout, or at a time when a strike or lockout appears imminent.

This amendment, known as League Law 13, became effective in October 1976, after being ratified by the League's locals. On May 5, 1977, when a collective-bargaining agreement expired, two locals began an economic strike against several manufacturing companies in Rockford, Illinois and Beloit, Wisconsin. Forty-three of the two locals' members participated. In early September 1977, after the locals formally rejected a contract offer, a striking union member submitted a letter of resignation to the Beloit association. He returned to work the following day. During the next three months, 10 more union members resigned from the Rockford and Beloit locals and returned to work. On December 19, 1977, the strike ended when the parties signed a new collective-bargaining agreement. The locals notified 10 employees who had resigned that their resignations had been rejected as violative of League Law 13.[3] The locals further informed the employees that, as union members, they were subject to sanctions for returning to work. Each was fined approximately the equivalent of his earnings during the strike.

The Rockford-Beloit Pattern Jobbers' Association (the Association) had represented the employers throughout the collective-bargaining process. It filed charges with the Board against the League and its two locals, the petitioners. Relying on § 8(b)(1)(A), the Association claimed that levying fines against employees who had resigned was an unfair labor practice. Following a hearing, an Administrative Law Judge found that the petitioners had violated § 8(b)(1)(A) by fining employees for returning to work after tendering resignations. *Pattern Makers' League of North America*, 265 N.L.R.B. 1332, 1339 (1982) (decision of G. Wacknov, ALJ). The Board agreed that § 8(b)(1)(A) prohibited the union from imposing sanctions on the 10 employees. *Pattern Makers' League of North America, supra.* In holding that League Law 13 did not justify the imposition of fines on the members who attempted to resign, the Board relied on its earlier decision in *Machinists Local 1327 (Dalmo Victor II)*, 263 N.L.R.B. 984 (1982), *enf. denied*, 725 F.2d 1212 (CA9 1984).[4]

ALJ held this was ULP, NLRB agreed

---

3. [2] Kohl, the other employee who returned to work, was expelled from the union. On January 14, 1978, the Beloit local notified Kohl's employer that because he was no longer a union member, he should be discharged pursuant to the "union shop" agreement. Two weeks later, the Beloit local informed Kohl that he could gain readmission to the union, and thus remain employed, if he paid back dues, a readmission fee, and $4,200 in "damages . . . for deserting the strike by returning to work." *Pattern Makers' League of North America*, 265 N.L.R.B. 1332, 1337 (1982) (decision of G. Wacknov, ALJ). Kohl was denied readmission to the union because he refused to pay the amounts allegedly due. Nevertheless, he was not discharged by his employer. *Ibid.*

4. [5] In *Machinists Local 1327 (Dalmo Victor II)*, 263 N.L.R.B. 984 (1982), *enf. denied*, 725 F.2d 1212 (CA9 1984), several employees resigned from a union and returned to work during a strike. The union constitution prohibited resignations during, or within 14 days preceding, strikes. As in this case, the employees' resignations were not accepted, and they were fined for aiding and abetting the employer. The Board held that fining these employees for returning to work after tendering resignations violated § 8(b)(1)(A).

Chairman Van de Water and Member Hunter stated that no restriction on the right to resign was permissible under the Act; they reasoned that such a rule allowed the union to exercise control over "external matters." Moreover, these Board members thought that restrictions on resignation impaired the congressional policy, embodied in § 8(a)(3), of voluntary unionism. Therefore, they concluded that any discipline premised on such a rule violates Section 8(b)(1)(A). 263 N.L.R.B., at 988. Members Fanning and Zimmerman asserted that a rule legitimately could restrict the right to resign for a period of 30 days. Because the rule in question restricted the right to resign indefinitely, however, they agreed that the union had violated § 8(b)(1)(A), 29 U.S.C. § 158(b)(1)(A). *Id.*, at 987.

Member Jenkins, the lone dissenter, contended that the union's restriction on resignation was protected by the proviso to § 8(b)(1)(A), which states that a union may "prescribe its own rules with respect to the acquisition or retention of membership therein." *Id.*, at 993.

The United States Court of Appeals for the Seventh Circuit enforced the Board's order. 724 F.2d 57 (1983). The Court of Appeals stated that by restricting the union members' freedom to resign, League Law 13 "frustrate[d] the overriding policy of labor law that employees be free to choose whether to engage in concerted activities." *Id.*, at 60. Noting that the "mutual reliance" theory was given little weight in *NLRB v. Textile Workers*, 409 U.S. 213 (1972), the court rejected petitioners' argument that their members, by participating in the strike vote, had "waived their Section 7 right to abandon the strike." 724 F.2d, at 60–61. Finally, the Court of Appeals reasoned that under *Scofield v. NLRB*, 394 U.S. 423 (1969), labor organizations may impose disciplinary fines against members only if they are "free to leave the union and escape the rule[s]." 724 F.2d, at 61.

We granted a petition for a writ of certiorari, 469 U.S. 814 (1984), to resolve the conflict between the Courts of Appeals over the validity of restrictions on union members' right to resign. The Board has held that such restrictions are invalid and do not justify imposing sanctions on employees who have attempted to resign from the union. Because of the Board's "special competence" in the field of labor relations, its interpretation of the Act is accorded substantial deference. *NLRB v. Weingarten, Inc.*, 420 U.S. 251, 266 (1975). The question for decision today is thus narrowed to whether the Board's construction of § 8(b)(1)(A) is reasonable. *NLRB v. City Disposal Systems, Inc.*, 465 U.S. 822, 830 (1984). We believe that § 8(b)(1)(A) properly may be construed as prohibiting the fining of employees who have tendered resignations ineffective under a restriction in the union constitution. We therefore affirm the judgment of the Court of Appeals enforcing the Board's order.

II

A. Section 7 of the Act, 29 U.S.C. § 157, grants employees the right to "refrain from any or all [concerted] . . . activities. . . ." This general right is implemented by § 8(b)(1)(A). The latter section provides that a union commits an unfair labor practice if it "restrain[s] or coerce[s] employees in the exercise" of their § 7 rights. When employee members of a union refuse to support a strike (whether or not a rule prohibits returning to work during a strike), they are refraining from "concerted activity." Therefore, imposing fines on these employees for returning to work "restrain[s]" the exercise of their § 7 rights. Indeed, if the terms "refrain" and "restrain or coerce" are interpreted literally, fining employees to enforce compliance with any union rule or policy would violate the Act.

Despite this language from the Act, the Court in *NLRB v. Allis-Chalmers*, 388 U.S. 175 (1967), held that § 8(b)(1)(A) does not prohibit labor organizations from fining current members. In *NLRB v. Textile Workers, supra*, and *Machinists & Aerospace Workers v. NLRB*, 412 U.S. 84 (1973) (per curiam), the Court found as a corollary that unions may not fine former members who have resigned lawfully. Neither *Textile Workers, supra*, nor *Machinists, supra*, however, involved a provision like League Law 13, restricting the members' right to resign. We decide today whether a union is precluded from fining employees who have attempted to resign when resignations are prohibited by the union's constitution.

B. The Court's reasoning in *Allis-Chalmers, supra*, supports the Board's conclusion that petitioners in this case violated § 8(b)(1)(A). In *Allis-Chalmers*, the Court held that imposing court-enforceable fines against current union members does not "restrain or coerce" the workers in the exercise of their § 7 rights.[5] In so concluding, the Court relied on the legislative history of the Taft-Hartley Act. It noted that the sponsor of § 8(b)(1)(A) never intended for that provision "'to interfere with the internal affairs or organization of unions,'" 388 U.S., at 187, quoting 93 Cong. Rec. 4272 (1947) (statement of Sen. Ball), and that other proponents of the measure likewise disclaimed an intent to interfere with unions' "internal affairs." 388 U.S., at 187–190. From the legislative history, the Court reasoned that Congress did not intend to prohibit unions from fining present members, as this was an internal matter. The Court has emphasized that the crux of *Allis-Chalmers'* holding was the distinction between "internal and external enforcement of union rules. . . ." *Scofield v. NLRB*, 394 U.S., at 428. *See also NLRB v. Boeing Co.*, 412 U.S. 67, 73 (1973).

The Congressional purpose to preserve unions' control over their own "internal affairs" does not suggest an intent to authorize restrictions on the right to resign. Traditionally, union members were free to resign and escape union discipline. In 1947, union constitutional provisions restricting the right to resign were uncommon, if not unknown. Therefore, allowing unions to "extend an employee's membership obligation through restrictions on resignation" would "expan[d] the definition of internal action" beyond the contours envisioned by the Taft-Hartley Congress. *International Ass'n of Machinists, Local 1414 (Neufeld Porsche-Audi, Inc.)*, 270 N.L.R.B. No. 209, p. 11 (1984).[6]

C. Language and reasoning from other opinions of this Court confirm that the Board's construction of § 8(b)(1)(A) is reasonable. In *Scofield v. NLRB*, 394 U.S. 423 (1969), the Court upheld a union rule setting a ceiling on the daily wages that members working on an incentive basis could earn. The union members' freedom to resign was critical to the Court's decision that the union rule did not "restrain or coerce" the employees within the meaning of § 8(b)(1)(A). It stated that the rule was "reasonably enforced against union members who [were] free to leave the union and escape the rule." *Id.*, at 430. The Court deemed it important that if members were unable to take full advantage of their contractual right to earn additional pay, it

---

5. [10] The proviso to § 8(b)(1)(A), 29 U.S.C. § 158(b)(1)(A) states that nothing in the section shall "impair the right of a labor organization to prescribe its own rules with respect to the acquisition or retention of membership therein." The Court in *Allis-Chalmers* assumed that the proviso could not be read to authorize the imposition of court-enforceable fines. 388 U.S., at 192. *See NLRB v. Boeing Co.*, 412 U.S. 67, 71, n. 5 (1973) ("This Court . . . , in holding that court enforcement of union fines was not an unfair labor practice in *NLRB v. Allis-Chalmers Mfg. Co.*, relied on congressional intent only with respect to the first part of this section") (citation omitted).

6. [13] In *International Assn. of Machinists, Local 1414 (Neufeld Porsche-Audi, Inc.)*, 270 N.L.R.B. No. 209 (1984), a majority of the Board held that *any* restriction on the right to resign violates the Act. This was the position taken by Chairman Van de Water and Member Hunter in *Machinists Local 1327, Dalmo Victor II*, 263 N.L.R.B. 984 (1982), *enf. denied*, 725 F.2d 1212 (CA9 1984). *See* n. 5, *supra*.

was because they had "chosen to become *and remain* union members." *Id.*, at 435 (emphasis added).

The decision in *NLRB v. Textile Workers*, 409 U.S. 213 (1972), also supports the Board's view that §8(b)(1)(A) prohibits unions from punishing members not free to resign. There, 31 employees resigned their union membership and resumed working during a strike. We held that fining these former members "restrained or coerced" them, within the meaning of §8(b)(1)(A). In reaching this conclusion, we said that "the vitality of §7 requires that the member be free to refrain in November from the actions he endorsed in May." *Id.*, at 217–218. Restrictions on the right to resign curtail the freedom that the *Textile Workers* Court deemed so important. *See also Machinists, supra.*

III

Section 8(b)(1)(A) allows unions to enforce only those rules that "impai[r] no policy Congress has imbedded in the labor laws...." *Scofield, supra,* at 430. The Board has found union restrictions on the right to resign to be inconsistent with the policy of voluntary unionism implicit in §8(a)(3). *See Neufeld Porsche-Audi*, 270 N.L.R.B. No. 209 (1984); *Machinists Local 1327 (Dalmo Victor II)*, 263 N.L.R.B., at 992 (Chairman Van de Water and Member Hunter, concurring), *enf. denied*, 725 F.2d 1212 (1984). We believe that the inconsistency between union restrictions on the right to resign and the policy of voluntary unionism supports the Board's conclusion that League Law 13 is invalid.

Closed shop agreements, legalized by the Wagner Act in 1935, became quite common in the early 1940s. Under these agreements, employers could hire and retain in their employ only union members in good standing. R. Gorman, *Labor Law*, ch. 28, §1, p. 639 (1976). Full union membership was thus compulsory in a closed shop; in order to keep their jobs, employees were required to attend union meetings, support union leaders, and otherwise adhere to union rules. Because of mounting objections to the closed shop, in 1947—after hearings and full consideration—Congress enacted the Taft-Harley Act. Section 8(a)(3) of that Act effectively eliminated compulsory union membership by outlawing the closed shop. The union security agreements permitted by §8(a)(3) require employees to pay dues, but an employee cannot be discharged for failing to abide by union rules or policies with which he disagrees.[7]

---

7. [16] Under §8(a)(3), the only aspect of union membership that can be required pursuant to a union shop agreement is the payment of dues. *See Radio Officers v. NLRB*, 347 U.S. 17, 41 (1954) (union security agreements cannot be used for "any purpose other than to compel payment of union dues and fees"). "'Membership,' as a condition of employment, is whittled down to its financial core." *NLRB v. General Motors Corp.*, 373 U.S. 734, 742 (1963). *See also* Ellis v. Railway Clerks, 466 U.S. 435 (1984) (under the Railway Labor Act, employees in a "union shop" cannot be compelled to pay dues to support certain union activities). Therefore, an employee required by a union security agreement to assume financial "membership" is not subject to union discipline. Such an employee is a "member" of the union only in the most limited sense.

Full union membership thus no longer can be a requirement of employment. If a new employee refuses formally to join a union and subject himself to its discipline, he cannot be fired. Moreover, no employee can be discharged if he initially joins a union, and subsequently resigns. We think it noteworthy that § 8(a)(3) protects the employment rights of the dissatisfied member, as well as those of the worker who never assumed full union membership. By allowing employees to resign from a union at any time, § 8(a)(3) protects the employee whose views come to diverge from those of his union.

League Law 13 curtails this freedom to resign from full union membership. Nevertheless, the petitioners contend that League Law 13 does not contravene the policy of voluntary unionism imbedded in the Act. They assert that this provision does not interfere with workers' employment rights because offending members are not discharged, but only fined. We find this argument unpersuasive, for a union has not left a "worker's employment rights inviolate when it exacts [his entire] paycheck in satisfaction of a fine imposed for working." Wellington, *Union Fines and Workers' Rights*, 85 Yale L.J. 1022, 1023 (1976). Congress in 1947 sought to eliminate completely any requirement that the employee maintain full union membership. Therefore, the Board was justified in concluding that by restricting the right of employees to resign, League Law 13 impairs the policy of voluntary unionism.

IV

We now consider specifically three arguments advanced by petitioners: (i) union rules restricting the right to resign are protected by the proviso to § 8(b)(1)(A); (ii) the legislative history of the Act shows that Congress did not intend to protect the right of union members to resign; and (iii) labor unions should be allowed to restrict the right to resign because other voluntary associations are permitted to do so.[8]

A. Petitioners first argue that the proviso to § 8(b)(1)(A) expressly allows unions to place restrictions on the right to resign. The proviso states that nothing in § 8(b)(1)(A) shall "impair the right of a labor organization to prescribe its own rules

---

8. [18] The dissent suggests that the Board's decision is inconsistent with 29 U.S.C. § 163, which provides that nothing in the Act "shall be construed so as . . . to interfere with or impede or diminish in any way the right to strike." The Board does not believe, and neither do we, that its interpretation of § 8(b)(1)(A) impedes the "right to strike." "It [will] not outlaw anybody striking who want[s] to strike. It [will] not prevent anyone using the strike in a legitimate way. . . . All it [will] do [is] . . . outlaw such restraint and coercion as would prevent people from going to work if they wished to go to work." 93 Cong. Rec. 4436 (1947) (remarks of Sen. Taft).

Moreover, we do not believe that the effectiveness of strikes will be unduly hampered by the Board's decision. An employee who voluntarily has joined a union will be reluctant to give up his membership. As Dean Wellington has said:

"In making his resignation decision, the dissident must remember that the union whose policies he finds distasteful will continue to hold substantial economic power over him as exclusive bargaining agent. By resigning, the worker surrenders his right to vote for union officials, to express himself at union meetings, and even participate in determining the amount or use of dues he may be forced to pay under a union security clause." Wellington, *Union Fines and Workers' Rights*, 85 Yale L.J. 1022, 1046 (1976).

with respect to the acquisition or retention of membership therein." 29 U.S.C. §158(b)(1)(A). Petitioners contend that because League Law 13 places restrictions on the right to withdraw from the union, it is a "rul[e] with respect to the ... retention of membership," within the meaning of the proviso.

Neither the Board nor this Court has ever interpreted the proviso as allowing unions to make rules restricting the right to resign. Rather, the Court has assumed that "rules with respect to the ... retention of membership" are those that provide for the expulsion of employees from the union. The legislative history of the Taft-Hartley Act is consistent with this interpretation. Senator Holland, the proviso's sponsor, stated that §8(b)(1)(A) should not outlaw union rules "which ha[ve] to do with the admission *or the expulsion* of members." 93 Cong. Rec. 4271 (1947) (emphasis added). Senator Taft accepted the proviso, for he likewise believed that a union should be free to "refuse [a] man admission to the union, or *expel him from the union.*" *Id.*, at 4272 (emphasis added). Furthermore, the legislative history of the Labor-Management Reporting and Disclosure Act of 1959, 29 U.S.C. §401 *et seq.*, confirms that the proviso was intended to protect union rules involving admission and expulsion. Accordingly, we find no basis for refusing to defer to the Board's conclusion that League Law 13 is not a "rule with respect to the retention of membership," within the meaning of the proviso.

B. The petitioners next argue that the legislative history of the Taft-Hartley Act shows that Congress made a considered decision not to protect union members' right to resign. Section 8(c) of the House bill contained a detailed "bill of rights" for labor union members. H.R. 3020, §8(c), 80th Cong., 1st Sess., at pp. 22–26 (1947). Included was a provision making it an unfair labor practice to "deny to any [union] member the right to resign from the organization at any time." H.R. 3020, *supra*, §8(c)(4), at 23. The Senate bill, on the other hand, did not set forth specific employee rights, but stated more generally that it was an unfair labor practice to "restrain or coerce" employees in the exercise of their §7 rights. H.R. 3020, 80th Cong., 1st Sess., §8(b)(1)(A), p. 81 (1947) (as passed Senate). The Taft-Hartley Act contains the Senate bill's general language rather than the more specific House prohibitions. *See* 29 U.S.C. §158(b)(1)(A). The petitioners contend that the omission of the House provision shows that Congress expressly decided not to protect the "right to resign."

The legislative history does not support this contention. The "right to resign" apparently was included in the original House bill to protect workers unable to resign because of "closed shop" agreements. Union constitutions limiting the right to resign were uncommon in 1947; closed shop agreements, however, often impeded union resignations. The House Report, H.R. Rep. No. 245, 80th Cong., 1st Sess. (1947), confirms that closed shop agreements provided the impetus for the inclusion of a right to resign in the House bill. The report simply states that even under the proposed legislation, employees could be required to pay dues pursuant to union security agreements. *Id.*, at 32. Because the closed shop was outlawed by the

Taft-Hartley Act, *see* § 8(a)(3), 29 U.S.C. § 158(a)(3), it is not surprising that Congress though it unnecessarily explicitly to preserve the right to resign. . . .

C. In *Textile Workers*, 409 U.S., at 216, and *Machinists*, 412 U.S., at 88 (per curiam) the Court stated that when a union constitution does not purport to restrict the right to resign, the "law which normally is reflected in our free institutions" is applicable. Relying on this quoted language, petitioners argue that League Law 13 is valid. They assert that because the common law does not prohibit restrictions on resignation, such provisions are not violative of § 8(b)(1)(A) of the Act. We find no merit in this argument. *Textile Workers*, *supra*, and *Machinists*, *supra*, held only that in the absence of restrictions on the right to resign, members are free to leave the union at any time. Although the Court noted that its decisions were consistent with the common-law rule, it did not state that the validity of restrictions on the right to resign should be determined with reference to common law.

The Court's decision in *NLRB v. Marine & Shipbuilding Workers*, 391 U.S. 418 (1968), demonstrates that many union rules, although valid under the common law of associations, run afoul of § 8(b)(1)(A) of the Act. There the union expelled a member who failed to comply with a rule requiring the "exhaust[ion of] all remedies and appeals within the Union . . . before . . . resort to any court or other tribunal outside of the Union." *Id.*, at 421. Under the common law, associations may require their members to exhaust all internal remedies. *See, e.g., Medical Soc. of Mobile Cty. v. Walker*, 245 Ala. 135, 16 So. 2d 321 (1944). Nevertheless, the *Marine Workers* Court held that "considerations of public policy" mandated a holding that the union rule requiring exhaustion violated § 8(b)(1)(A), 29 U.S.C. § 158(b)(1)(A). 391 U.S., at 424; *see also Scofield v. NLRB*, 394 U.S., at 430 (union rule is invalid under § 8(b)(1)(A) if it "impairs [a] policy Congress has imbedded in the labor laws").

The Board reasonably has concluded that League Law 13 "restrains or coerces" employees, *see* § 8(b)(1)(A), and is inconsistent with the congressional policy of voluntary unionism. Therefore, whatever may have been the common law, the Board's interpretation of the Act merits our deference.

V

The Board has the primary responsibility for applying "'the general provisions of the Act to the complexities of industrial life.'" *Ford Motor Co. v. NLRB*, 441 U.S. 488, 496 (1979), quoting *NLRB v. Erie Resistor Corp.*, 373 U.S. 221, 236 (1963), quoting, *NLRB v. Steelworkers*, 357 U.S. 357, 362–363 (1958). Where the Board's construction of the Act is reasonable, it should not be rejected "merely because the courts might prefer another view of the statute." *Ford Motor Co. v. NLRB, supra*, at 497. In this case, two factors suggest that we should be particularly reluctant to hold that the Board's interpretation of the Act is impermissible. First, in related cases this Court invariably has yielded to Board decisions on whether fines imposed by a union "restrain or coerce" employees. Second, the Board consistently has construed § 8(b)(1)(A) as prohibiting the imposition of fines on employees who have tendered resignations invalid under a union constitution.⁹ Therefore, we conclude that the Board's decision here is entitled to our deference.

VI

The Board found that by fining employees who had tendered resignations, the petitioners violated § 8(b)(1)(A) of the Act, even though League Law 13 purported to render the resignations ineffective. We defer to the Board's interpretation of the Act and so affirm the judgment of the Court of Appeals enforcing the Board's order.

It is so ordered.

Justice White, concurring.

I agree with the Court that the Board's construction of §§ 7 and 8(b)(1)(A) is a permissible one and should be upheld. The employee's rights under § 7 include, among others, the right to refrain from joining or assisting a labor organization and from engaging in concerted activities for mutual aid or protection. The right to join or not to join a labor union includes the right to resign, and § 8(b)(1)(A) forbids unions to interfere with that right except to the extent, if any, that such interference is permitted by the proviso to that section, which preserves the union's right to prescribe its own rules with respect to the acquisition or retention of membership. The proviso might be read as permitting restrictions on resignation during a strike, since they would seem to relate to the "retention" of membership. But it can also be sensibly read to refer only to the union's right to determine who shall be allowed to join and to remain in the union. The latter is the Board's interpretation. Under that view, restrictions on resignations are not saved by the proviso, and the rule at issue in this case may not be enforced....

Justice Blackmun, with whom Justice Brennan and Justice Marshall join, dissenting....

I

A. Having determined that the individual worker standing alone lacked sufficient bargaining power to achieve a fair agreement with his employer over the terms and conditions of his employment, Congress passed the NLRA in order to protect

---

9. [28] In *United Automobile, Aerospace & Agricultural Implement Workers, Local 647 (General Electric Co.)*, 197 N.L.R.B. 608 (1972), the Board held that § 8(b)(1)(A) prohibits a union from fining employees who have resigned, even when a provision in the union constitution purports to make the resignations invalid. There two employees resigned during a strike and returned to work. Their resignations were ineffective under a union constitutional provision permitting resignations only during the last ten days of the union's fiscal year. The Board nevertheless held that the employees could not be fined for crossing the picket line. It noted that imposing fines on these employees was inconsistent with *Scofield v. NLRB*, 394 U.S. 423 (1969), for they effectively were denied "a voluntary method of severing their relationship with the Union." 197 N.L.R.B., at 609. The Board reached the same conclusion in *United Automobile, Aerospace & Agricultural Implement Workers, Local 469 (Master Lock Co.)*, 221 N.L.R.B. 748 (1975). See also *Local 1384, United Automobile, Aerospace & Agricultural Implement Workers (Ex-Cell-O Corp.)*, 219 N.L.R.B. 729 (1975).

employees' rights to join together and act collectively. *See* 29 U.S.C. §151. Thus, the heart of the Act is the protection of workers' §7 rights to self-organization and to free collective bargaining, which are in turn protected by §8 of the Act. 29 U.S.C. §§157 and 158.

Because the employees' power protected in the NLRA is the power to act collectively, it has long been settled that the collective has a right to promulgate rules binding on its members, so long as the employee's decision to become a member is a voluntary one and the rules are democratically adopted. When these requirements of free association are met, the union has the right to enforce such rules "through reasonable discipline," including fines. *See NLRB v. Allis-Chalmers Mfg. Co.*, 388 U.S. 175, 181 (1967). Unless internal rules can be enforced, the union's status as bargaining representative will be eroded, and the rights of the members to act collectively will be jeopardized. *Ibid.* "Union activity, by its very nature, is group activity, and is grounded on the notion that strength can be garnered from unity, solidarity, and mutual commitment. This concept is of particular force during a strike, where the individual members of the union draw strength from the commitments of fellow members, and where the activities carried on by the union rest fundamentally on the mutual reliance that inheres in the 'pact.'" *NLRB v. Textile Workers*, 409 U.S. 213, 221 (1973) (dissenting opinion); *see Allis-Chalmers, supra*, at 181.

It is in the proviso to §8(b)(1)(A), 29 U.S.C. §158(b)(1)(A), that Congress preserved for the union the right to establish "the contractual relationship between union and member." *Textile Workers, supra*, at 217. Recognizing "the law which normally is reflected in our free institutions," *id.*, at 216, Congress in the proviso preserved a union's status as a voluntary association free to define its own membership....

League Law 13 is an internal union rule, a "rule with respect to the acquisition or retention of membership" protected by the proviso to §8(b)(1)(A). It requires that employees who freely choose to join the union promise to remain members during a strike or lockout, as well as during the time when a strike or lockout appears imminent. In other words, the rule imposes a condition upon members of the bargaining unit who would like to acquire membership rights. The rule stands for the proposition that to become a union member one must be willing to incur a certain obligation upon which others may rely; as such, it is a rule literally involving the acquisition and retention of membership. Conversely, League Law 13 does not in any way affect the relationship between the employee and the employer. An employee who violates the rule does not risk losing his job, and the union cannot seek an employer's coercive assistance in collecting any fine that is imposed. The rule neither coerces a worker to become a union member against his will, nor affects an employee's status as an employee under the Act. Thus, it clearly falls within the powers of any voluntary association to enact and enforce "the requirements and standards of membership itself," so as to permit the association effectively to pursue collective goals. 93 Cong. Rec. 4433 (1947) (remarks of Sen. Ball).

B. . . .

Moreover, Congress explicitly has rejected the Court's interpretation of §§ 7 and 8(b)(1)(A). The "right to refrain" language upon which the Court relies was contained in § 7(a) of the House version of the Act, H.R. 3020, 80th Cong., 1st Sess. (1947) (House bill). Section 7 of the House bill was divided into subsection (a), granting "employees" the right to refrain from concerted activity, and subsection (b), granting "members of any labor organization" rights concerning the "affairs of the organization." Corresponding to these provisions were § 8(b), which made it an unfair labor practice for anyone to interfere with an employee's § 7(a) rights, and § 8(c), which made it an unfair labor practice to interfere with an employee's § 7(b) rights. In particular, § 8(c) created a bill of rights for union members in their dealings with their union, establishing 10 unfair labor practices which regulated the major facets of the member-union relationship. Among these specifically enumerated rights was § 8(c)(4), which made it an unfair labor practice "to deny to any member the right to resign from the organization at any time."

Thus, the House regarded the "right to refrain" of § 7(a) as the right not to join in union activity, making it illegal for "representatives and their partisans and adherents to harass or abuse employees into joining labor organizations." H.R. Rep. No. 245, 80th Cong., 1st Sess., 30 (1947). And the House believed that § 7(b) and § 8(c) of its bill, which included a proscription of internal rules concerning a member's right to resign, regulated the member-union relationship. There is no suggestion that the House considered the right to refrain to include the right to abandon an agreed-upon undertaking at will, nor to relate to the rights against the union protected by §§ 7(b) and 8(c) of the House bill, including the right to resign at will. Rather, these distinct rights arose from separate sections of the House bill.

It is critical to an understanding of the Taft-Hartley bill, therefore, to recognize that the Senate explicitly *rejected* the House bill's §§ 7(b) and 8(c). It did so not, as the Court intimates, because it considered the specific provisions of §§ 7(b) and 8(c) to encompass the "right to refrain" language adopted from § 7(a), but because it decided that "the formulation of a code of rights for individual members of trade unions . . . should receive more extended study by a special joint congressional committee." S. Rep. No. 105, 80th Cong., 1st Sess., 2 (1947). . . .

The proviso serves a fundamentally different purpose — to make manifest that § 8 did not grant the Board the authority to impair the basic right of all membership associations to establish their own reasonable membership rules. League Law 13 is such a rule. It binds members to a reciprocal promise not to resign and return to work during a strike. It does not involve use of the employer's power or affect an individual's employment status, and so does not implicate § 8(a)(3). A member who violates the union rule may be fined, or even expelled from the union, but his employment status remains unaffected. Despite the Court's suggestions to the contrary, "voluntary unionism" does not require that an employee who has freely chosen to join a union and retain his membership therein, in full knowledge that by those decisions he has accepted specified obligations to other members, nevertheless has a federally protected right to disregard those obligations at will, regardless of the acts of others taken in reliance on them. . . .

II

Congress' decision not to intervene in the internal affairs of a union reflects Congress' understanding that membership in a union — if not a precondition for one's right to employment — is a freely chosen membership in a voluntary association. The Court therefore has looked to "the law which normally is reflected in our free institutions" to determine whether any given membership rule is lawful. *NLRB v. Textile Workers*, 409 U.S., at 216. And the common law of associations establishes that an association may place reasonable restrictions on its members' right to resign where such restrictions are designed to further a basic purpose for which the association was formed — here, where the restriction "reflects a legitimate union interest." *Scofield*, 394 U.S., at 430. The Pattern Makers evidently promulgated League Law 13 to protect the common interest in maintaining a united front during an economic strike. Such a rule protects individual union members' decisions to place their own and their families' welfare at risk in reliance on the reciprocal decisions of their fellow workers, and furthers the union's ability to bargain with the employer on equal terms, as envisioned by the Act. As such, the rule comports with the broader goals of federal labor policy, which guarantees workers the right to collective action and, in particular, the right to strike.

. . . .

JUSTICE STEVENS, dissenting.

The legislative history of the Labor-Management Relations Act of 1947 discussed in Part I-B of JUSTICE BLACKMUN's dissenting opinion, coupled with the plain language in the proviso to §8(b)(1)(A) persuades me that the "right to refrain" protected by §7 of the Act does not encompass the "right to resign." Accordingly, I respectfully dissent.

Notes

1. *Resignations* — In *International Typographical Union (Register Publishing Co.)*, 270 N.L.R.B. 1386 (1984), the Labor Board held that unions that refuse to give effect to valid member resignations violate §8(b)(1)(A). In *Carpenters Local 470 (Tacoma Boatbuilding)*, 277 N.L.R.B. 513 (1985), the Board held that a labor organization could not fine members who crossed a picket line after they sent letters to the union changing their membership status "from that of a 'full' member to that of a 'financial core' member," since "financial core" members are not subject to union disciplinary authority. *See also Teamsters Cannery Local 670 v. NLRB*, 856 F.2d 1250 (9th Cir. 1988) (§8(b)(1)(A) violation when union retaliated against "financial core" members for their strike-related activities by refusing to issue them work-registration certificates and by denying them access to union pharmacy and clinics).

The Seventh Circuit upheld the Labor Board extension of *Pattern Makers* to prohibit union rules preventing resignations in anticipation of or during the pendency of disciplinary proceedings. *NLRB v. Local 73, Sheet Metal Workers' International Ass'n*, 840 F.2d 501 (7th Cir. 1988). *Accord International Union, United Auto. Workers, Local 449 v. NLRB*, 865 F.2d 791 (6th Cir.), *cert. denied*, 493 U.S. 818 (1989).

2. *Timing Issues* — A labor organization may fine employees who return to work on the same day they mail letters of resignation to their union, where they are found to still be union members at the time they cross the picket line. *See Communications Workers of America, Local 9201 (Pacific Northwest Bell)*, 275 N.L.R.B. 1529 (1985). *But cf. NLRB v. General Teamsters Local 439*, 837 F.2d 888 (9th Cir. 1988) (resignation placed in union's after-hours deposit box on night before member crossed picket line was effective when deposited).

Although the Labor Board had previously recognized that mailed resignations took effect on the day after they were mailed or whenever the union could establish it actually received those communications, it has adopted a uniform rule presuming that all mailed resignations become effective at 12:01 a.m. local time on the day following their postmarks. *Pattern & Model Makers Ass'n (Michigan Model Mfg.)*, 310 N.L.R.B. 929 (1993).

3. *Expulsion* — Although labor organizations cannot fine individuals who resign before they return to work during a strike, the Labor Board has held (3-2) that they can expel or suspend such persons. Such a distinction between fines and membership revocation respects the right of unions under the proviso to § 8(b)(1)(A) "to prescribe [their] own rules with respect to the acquisition or retention of membership therein." *Meat Cutters Union Local 81 (MacDonald Meat Co.)*, 284 N.L.R.B. 1084 (1987).

Problem

26. Brent Burtin and Peter Cannistra, master woodworkers at a large commercial cabinet manufacturer, were represented by the United Brotherhood of Cabinetmakers (UBC). One morning, Brent noticed that a guard on one of the table saws was missing, which was a safety violation. The company rules — which were incorporated into the collective bargaining agreement — oblige any employee to report safety violations to a supervisor. Brent promptly reported the violation to his supervisor, Steve Ellis. Steve, with Brent's help, investigated the issue and determined that Peter had removed the guard. As a result, Peter was suspended for three days for the violation.

The UBC officials did not look kindly upon members "ratting out" fellow members to the employer. For that reason, Brent's role in reporting and investigating the safety violation led the UBC to file charges against him for gross disloyalty and conduct unbecoming a union member. The union fined Brent $2500 for the infractions.

Meanwhile, Peter filed a grievance over his suspension, but the UBC failed to pursue it because it thought the rules violation was so clear. Fed up with what he saw as the employer's "nitpicky rules" and the union's complicit role in their promulgation and enforcement, Peter began gathering signed cards from fellow workers asking for a new election. A few weeks later, he filed a petition with the NLRB for a decertification election. Upon hearing about the petition, the UBC fined Peter $2500, expelled him from the union, and asked the company to discharge him pursuant to a union shop clause in their contract.

Did the United Brotherhood of Cabinetmakers commit an unfair labor practice when it fined Brent? How about when it fined Peter? May the union expel Peter and, if so, may it then seek to have him discharged?

Section III. Organizational and Recognitional Picketing

NLRB v. Drivers, Chauffeurs, Helpers, Local 639 [Curtis Bros.]

Supreme Court of the United States
362 U.S. 274, 80 S. Ct. 706, 4 L. Ed. 2d 710 (1960)

[The union was certified by the Board in 1953 as the exclusive bargaining representative of Curtis Brothers' drivers, helpers, warehousemen, and furniture finishers. An impasse was reached in the resultant bargaining and the union started picketing the company's premises early in 1954. This picketing continued for about two years, during which time the company replaced the strikers.

On February 1, 1955, the company filed a representation petition, in which it questioned the union's continued majority status and asked for an election. About two weeks later, on February 16, 1955, the union filed a statement purportedly disavowing any current intention to represent the employees in their dealings with the company. Before such disclaimer, the union's picket signs read: "CURTIS BROTHERS ON STRIKE. UNFAIR TO ORGANIZED LABOR. DRIVERS, HELPERS, AND WAREHOUSEMEN OF LOCAL 639 (AF of L)." Thereafter, they read on one side "CURTIS BROS. EMPLOYS Non-Union drivers, helpers, warehousemen, etc. Unfair to Teamsters Union No. 639 AFL," and on the other side "Teamsters Union No. 639 AFL wants employees of Curtis Bros. to join them to gain union wages, hours and working conditions."

In September 1955, the Board directed an election in the representation case, finding that the union was still seeking to win immediate recognition by the company. The Board reasoned:

> "[T]hat the Union's current picketing activities cannot be reconciled with its disclaimer of interest in representing the employees in question. In the light of all the material facts of this case, including the certification of the Petitioner, the circumstances preceding the strike, the nature of the first signs carried by the pickets, the brief discontinuance of picketing, and

its early resumption, we are convinced that the current picketing is not for the sole purpose of getting employees to join the Union, as the more recent picket signs indicate, but is tantamount to a present demand that the Employer enter into a contract with the Union without regard to the question of its majority status among the employees concerned. [Citing cases.]"

Twenty-eight employees voted against Local 639, and only one for it. As stated, the union never altered its picketing activities. It is conceded that at no time after February, 1955, did the union represent a majority of the employees.

The NLRB held that the picketing violated § 8(b)(1)(A). The court of appeals set the Board's order aside.]

MR. JUSTICE BRENNAN delivered the opinion of the Court.

The question in this case is whether peaceful picketing by a union, which does not represent a majority of the employees, to compel immediate recognition as the employees' exclusive bargaining agent, is conduct of the union "to restrain or coerce" the employees in the exercise of rights guaranteed in § 7, and thus an unfair labor practice under § 8(b)(1)(A) of the Taft-Hartley Act. . . .

After we granted certiorari, the Congress enacted the Labor-Management Reporting and Disclosure Act of 1959, which, among other things, adds a new § 8(b)(7) to the National Labor Relations Act. It was stated by the Board on oral argument that if this case arose under the 1959 Act, the Board might have proceeded against the Local under § 8(b)(7). This does not, however, relegate this litigation to the status of an unimportant controversy over the meaning of a statute which has been significantly changed. For the Board contends that new § 8(b)(7) does not displace § 8(b)(1)(A) but merely "supplements the power already conferred by § 8(b)(1)(A)." It argues that the Board may proceed against peaceful "recognitional" picketing conducted by a minority union in more situations than are specified in § 8(b)(7) and without regard to the limitations of § 8(b)(7)(C). . . .

We conclude that the Board's interpretation of § 8(b)(1)(A) finds support neither in the way Congress structured § 8(b) nor in the legislative history of § 8(b)(1)(A). Rather it seems clear, and we hold, that Congress in the Taft-Hartley Act authorized the Board to regulate peaceful "recognitional" picketing only when it is employed to accomplish objectives specified in § 8(b)(4); and that § 8(b)(1)(A) is a grant of power to the Board limited to authority to proceed against union tactics involving violence, intimidation, and reprisal or threats thereof — conduct involving more than the general pressures upon persons employed by the affected employers implicit in economic strikes.

The Board's own interpretation for nearly a decade after the passage of the Taft-Hartley Act gave § 8(b)(1)(A) this limited application. . . .

We are confirmed in our view by the action of Congress in passing the Labor-Management Reporting and Disclosure Act of 1959. That act goes beyond the

Taft-Hartley Act to legislate a comprehensive code governing organizational strikes and picketing and draws no distinction between "organizational" and "recognitional" picketing. While proscribing peaceful organizational strikes in many situations, it also establishes safeguards against the Board's interference with legitimate picketing activity. See § 8(b)(7)(C). Were § 8(b)(1)(A) to have the sweep contended for by the Board, the Board might proceed against peaceful picketing in disregard of these safeguards. To be sure, what Congress did in 1959 does not establish what it meant in 1947. However, as another major step in an evolving pattern of regulation of union conduct, the 1959 Act is a relevant consideration. Courts may properly take into account the later act when asked to extend the reach of the earlier act's vague language to the limits which, read literally, the words might permit. We avoid the incongruous result implicit in the Board's construction, by reading § 8(b)(1)(A) which is only one of many interwoven sections in a complex act mindful of the manifest purpose of the Congress to fashion a coherent national labor policy.

Affirmed.

Note

Provisions of the Labor-Management Reporting and Disclosure Act of 1959 dealing with organizational and recognition picketing—As can readily be observed in the *Curtis Bros.* case, there was considerable confusion in 1958 and 1959 as to the applicability of § 8(b)(1) of the NLRA to organizational and recognition picketing. During the same period, the McClellan Committee hearings were revealing instances in which certain unions, particularly the Teamsters, were employing such economic weapons under circumstances that were widely regarded as abusive.

Congressman Griffin, in explaining the Landrum-Griffin bill to the House, described the need for legislation:

> It is intended to prohibit blackmail recognition picketing by unions which do not represent the employees. Under the National Labor Relations Act elaborate election machinery is provided for ascertaining the wishes of employees in selecting or rejecting bargaining representatives. The act contains provisions for giving employees an opportunity to vote by secret ballot. In recent years the safeguards intended by these election provisions have been thwarted by unions which have lost elections and unions which do not have enough employee support to petition for an election but yet insist upon compelling employers to sign contracts with them—irrespective of the sentiment of the employees.
>
> The customary method employed to force employers to do this is to place picket lines around their plants or shops. Such picketing, even when peaceful, will frequently cause small employers to capitulate. The picket line is a signal for truckers not to pick up or deliver goods to employees of maintenance contractors. Pickets also deter many customers from entering retail or service establishments. In the face of such tactics employees whose jobs

are in jeopardy as they see their employer's business choked off are soon coerced into joining the picketing union—even though they might prefer another union. In many such cases their employer forces them in a particular union by signing a compulsory membership agreement with the picketing union.

The NLRB has attempted to give some relief to employers and employees victimized in such situations by holding it an unfair labor practice for a union to picket for recognition after it has lost an election. While such relief seems called for, nevertheless the courts of appeal are in conflict as to whether the Board has even this limited power.

105 Cong. Rec. 14347 (1959).

International HOD Carriers Local 840 [Blinne Construction Co.]

National Labor Relations Board
135 N.L.R.B. 1153 (1962)

Supplemental Decision and Order

On February 20, 1961, the Board (Member Fanning dissenting) issued a Decision and Order in this case finding that Respondent Union had engaged in unfair labor practices in violation of Section 8(b)(7)(C) of the Act. Thereafter, on or about April 3, 1961, Respondent Union filed with the Board a motion for reconsideration and for dismissal of the complaint. . . .

I

. . . .

As indicated by its text, the thrust of Section 8(b)(7) is to deal with recognition and organization picketing, a matter not dealt with directly in the Taft-Hartley Act except to the limited extent provided in Section 8(b)(4)(C) of that Act. . . .

Even a cursory examination of the legislative history of the provisions here in issue reveals that, like the so-called "secondary boycott" provisions of the Taft-Hartley Act, Section 8(b)(7) was also "to a marked degree, the result of conflict and compromise between strong contending forces and deeply held views on the role of organized labor in the free economic life of the Nation and the appropriate balance to be struck between the uncontrolled power of management and labor to further their respective interests." *Local 1976, United Brotherhood of Carpenters and Joiners of America, AFL, et al. (Sand Door & Plywood Co.) v. N.L.R.B.*, 357 U.S. 93, 99–100. . . .

II

Before proceeding to determine the application of Section 8(b)(7)(C) to the facts of the instant case, it is essential to note the interplay of the several subsections of Section 8(b)(7), of which subparagraph (C) is only a constituent part.

The section as a whole, as is apparent from its opening phrases, prescribes limitations only on picketing for an object of "recognition" or "bargaining" (both of which terms will hereinafter be subsumed under the single term "recognition") or for an object of organization. Picketing for other objects is not proscribed by this section. Moreover, not all picketing for recognition or organization is proscribed. A "currently certified" union may picket for recognition or organization of employees for whom it is certified. And even a union which is not certified is barred from recognition or organization picketing only in three general areas. The first area, defined in subparagraph (A) of Section 8(b)(7), relates to situations where another union has been lawfully recognized and a question concerning representation cannot appropriately be raised. The second area, defined in subparagraph (B), relates to situations where, within the preceding 12 months, a "valid election" has been held.

The intent of subparagraphs (A) and (B) is fairly clear. Congress concluded that where a union has been lawfully recognized and a question concerning representation cannot appropriately be raised, or where the employees within the preceding 12 months have made known their views concerning representation, both the employer and employees are entitled to immunity from recognition or organization picketing for prescribed periods.

Congress did not stop there, however. Deeply concerned with other abuses, most particularly "blackmail" picketing, Congress concluded that it would be salutary to impose even further limitations on picketing for recognition or organization. Accordingly, subparagraph (C) provides that even where such picketing is not barred by the provisions of (A) or (B) so that picketing for recognition or organization would otherwise be permissible, such picketing is limited to a reasonable period not to exceed 30 days unless a representation petition is filed prior to the expiration of that period. Absent the filing of such a timely petition, continuation of the picketing beyond the reasonable period becomes an unfair labor practice. On the other hand, the filing of a timely petition stays the limitation and picketing may continue pending the processing of the petition. Even here, however, Congress by the addition of the first proviso to subparagraph (C) made it possible to foreshorten the period of permissible picketing by directing the holding of an expedited election pursuant to the representation petition.

The expedited election procedure is applicable, of course, only in a Section 8(b)(7)(C) proceeding, i.e., where an 8(b)(7)(C) unfair labor practice charge has been filed. Congress rejected efforts to amend the provisions of Section 9(c) of the Act so as to dispense generally with preelection hearings. Thus, in the absence of an 8(b)(7)(C) unfair labor practice charge, a union will not be enabled to obtain an expedited election by the mere device of engaging in recognition or organization picketing and filing a representation petition.[10] And on the other hand, a picketing union which files

---

10. [10] Congress plainly did not intend such a result. See Congressman Barden's statement (105 Daily Cong. Rec., A8062, September 2, 1959; 2 Legis. Hist. 1813). And the Board has ruled further that a charge filed by a picketing union or a person "fronting" for it may not be utilized to invoke an

a representation petition pursuant to the mandate of Section 8(b)(7)(C) and to avoid its sanctions will not be propelled into an expedited election, which it may not desire, merely because it has filed such a petition. In both the above situations, the normal representation procedures are applicable; the showing of a substantial interest will be required, and the preelection hearing directed in Section 9(c)(1) will be held.

This, in our considered judgment, puts the expedited election procedure prescribed in the first proviso to subparagraph (C) in its proper and intended focus. That procedure was devised to shield aggrieved employers and employees from the adverse effects of prolonged recognition or organization picketing. Absent such a grievance, it was not designed either to benefit or to handicap picketing activity. As District Judge Thornton aptly stated in *Reed v. Roumell*, 185 F. Supp. 4 (D.C., E. Mich.), "If [the first proviso] were intended to confer a primary or independent right to an expedited election entirely separated from the statutory scheme, it would seem that such intention would have manifested itself in a more forthright manner, rather than in the shy seclusion of Section 8(b)(7)(C)."

Subparagraphs (B) and (C) serve different purposes. But it is especially significant to note their interrelationship. Congress was particularly concerned, even where picketing for recognition or organization was otherwise permissible, that the question concerning representation which gave rise to the picketing be resolved as quickly as possible. It was for this reason that it provided for the filing of a petition pursuant to which the Board could direct an expedited election in which the employees could freely indicate their desires as to representation. If, in the free exercise of their choice, they designate the picketing union as their bargaining representative, that union will be certified and it will by the express terms of Section 8(b)(7) be exonerated from the strictures of that section. If, conversely, the employees reject the picketing union, that union will be barred from picketing for 12 months thereafter under the provisions of subparagraph (B).

The scheme which Congress thus devised represents what that legislative body deemed a practical accommodation between the right of a union to engage in legitimate picketing for recognition or organization and abuse of that right. One caveat must be noted in that regard. The congressional scheme is, perforce, based on the premise that the election to be conducted under the first proviso to subparagraph (C) represents the free and uncoerced choice of the employee electorate. Absent such a free and uncoerced choice, the underlying question concerning representation is not resolved and, more particularly, subparagraph (B) which turns on the holding of a "valid election" does not become operative.

There remains to be considered only the second proviso to subparagraph (C). In sum, that proviso removes the time limitation imposed upon, and preserves the legality of, recognition or organization picketing falling within the ambit of

---

expedited election. *Claussen Baking Company*, Case No. 11-RC-1329, May 5, 1960 (not published in NLRB volumes). See also *Reed v. Roumell*, cited *infra*.

subparagraph (C), where that picketing merely advises the public that an employer does not employ members of, or have a contract with, a union unless an effect of such picketing is to halt pickups or deliveries, or the performance of services. Needless to add, picketing which meets the requirements of the proviso also renders the expedited election procedure inapplicable.

Except for the final clause in Section 8(b)(7) which provides that nothing in that section shall be construed to permit any act otherwise proscribed under Section 8(b) of the Act, the foregoing sums up the limitations imposed upon recognition or organization picketing by the Landrum-Griffin amendments. However, at the risk of laboring the obvious, it is important to note that structurally, as well as grammatically, subparagraphs (A), (B), and (C) are subordinate to and controlled by the opening phrases of Section 8(b)(7). In other words, the thrust of all the Section 8(b)(7) provisions is only upon picketing for an object of recognition or organization, and not upon picketing for other objects. Similarly, both structurally and grammatically, the two provisos in subparagraphs (C) appertain only to the situation defined in the principal clause of that subparagraph.

III

Having outlined, in concededly broad strokes, the statutory framework of Section 8(b)(7) and particularly subparagraph (C) thereof, we may appropriately turn to a consideration of the instant case which presents issues going to the heart of that legislation.

The relevant facts may be briefly stated. On February 2, 1960, all three common laborers employed by Blinne at the Fort Leonard Wood jobsite signed cards designating the Union to represent them for purposes of collective bargaining. The next day the Union demanded that Blinne recognize the Union as the bargaining agent for the three laborers. Blinne not only refused recognition but told the Union it would transfer one of the laborers, Wann, in order to destroy the Union's majority. Blinne carried out this threat and transferred Wann 5 days later, on February 8. Following this refusal to recognize the Union and the transfer of Wann the Union started picketing at Fort Wood. The picketing, which began on February 8, immediately following the transfer of Wann, had three announced objectives: (1) recognition of the Union; (2) payment of the Davis-Bacon scale of wages; and (3) protest against Blinne's unfair labor practices in refusing to recognize the Union and in threatening to transfer and transferring Wann.

The picketing continued, with interruptions due to bad weather, until at least March 11, 1960, a period of more than 30 days from the date the picketing commenced. The picketing was peaceful, only one picket was on duty, and the picket sign he carried read "C.A. Blinne Construction Company, unfair." The three laborers on the job (one was the replacement for Wann) struck when the picketing started.

The Union, of course, was not the certified bargaining representative of the employees. Moreover, no representation petition was filed during the more than 30 days in which picketing was taking place. On March 1, however, about 3 weeks after the picketing commenced and well within the statutory 30-day period, the Union filed unfair labor practice charges against Blinne, alleging violations of Section 8(a)(1), (2), (3), and (5). On March 22, the Regional Director dismissed the 8(a)(2) and (5) charges, whereupon the Union forthwith filed a representation petition under Section 9(c) of the Act. Subsequently, on April 20, the Regional Director approved a unilateral settlement agreement with Blinne with respect to the Section 8(a)(1) and (3) charges which had not been dismissed. In the settlement agreement, Blinne neither admitted nor denied that it had committed unfair labor practices.

General Counsel argues that a violation of Section 8(b)(7)(C) has occurred within the literal terms of that provision because (1) the Union's picketing was concededly for an object of obtaining recognition; (2) the Union was not currently certified as the representative of the employees involved; and (3) no petition for representation was filed within 30 days of the commencement of the picketing. Inasmuch as the Union made no contention that its recognition picketing was "informational" within the meaning of the second proviso to subparagraph (C) or that it otherwise comported with the strictures of that proviso, General Counsel contends that a finding of unfair labor practice is required.

Respondent Union, for its part, points to the manifest inequity of such a finding and argues that Congress could not have intended so incongruous a result. In essence, its position is that it was entitled to recognition because it represented all the employees in the appropriate unit, that Blinne by a series of unfair labor practices deprived the Union and the employees it sought to represent of fundamental rights guaranteed by the Act, and that the impact of a finding adverse to the Union would be to punish the innocent and reward the wrongdoer. More specifically, Respondent argues that Section 8(b)(7)(C) was not intended to apply to picketing by a majority union and that, in any event, Blinne's unfair labor practices exonerated it from the statutory requirement of filing a timely representation petition. . . .

IV

. . . .

A. The contention that Section 8(b)(7)(C) does not proscribe picketing for recognition or organization by a majority union

Respondent, urging the self-evident proposition that a statute should be read as a whole, argues that Section 8(b)(7)(C) was not designed to prohibit picketing for recognition by a union enjoying majority status in an appropriate unit. Such picketing is for a lawful purpose inasmuch as Sections 8(a)(5) and 9(a) of the Act specifically impose upon an employer the duty to recognize and bargain with a union which enjoys that status. Accordingly, Respondent contends, absent express language requiring such a result, Section 8(b)(7)(C) should not be read in derogation of the duty so imposed. . . .

[W]e find [this contention] to be without merit. To be sure, the legislative history is replete with references that Congress in framing the 1959 amendments was primarily concerned with "blackmail" picketing where the picketing union represented none or few of the employees whose allegiance it sought. Legislative references susceptible to an interpretation that Congress was concerned with the evils of majority picketing are sparse. Yet it cannot be gainsaid that Section 8(b)(7) by its explicit language exempts only "currently certified" unions from its proscriptions. Cautious as we should be to avoid a mechanical reading of statutory terms in involved legislative enactments, it is difficult to avoid giving the quoted words, essentially words of art, their natural construction. Moreover, such a construction is consonant with the underlying statutory scheme which is to resolve disputed issues of majority status, whenever possible, by the machinery of a Board election. Absent unfair labor practices or preelection misconduct warranting the setting aside of the election, majority unions will presumably not be prejudiced by such resolution. On the other hand, the admitted difficulties of determining majority status without such an election are obviated by this construction. . . .

B. The contention that employer unfair labor practices are a defense to a charge of a Section 8(b)(7)(C) violation

We turn now to the second issue, namely, whether employer unfair labor practices are a defense to an 8(b)(7)(C) violation. As set forth in the original Decision and Order, the Union argues that Blinne was engaged in unfair labor practices within the meaning of Section 8(a)(1) and (3) of the Act; that it filed appropriate unfair labor practice charges against Blinne within a reasonable period of time after the commencement of the picketing; that it filed a representation petition as soon as the 8(a)(2) and (5) allegations of the charges were dismissed; that the 8(a)(1) and (3) allegations were in effect sustained and a settlement agreement was subsequently entered into with the approval of the Board; and that, therefore, this sequence of events should satisfy the requirements of Section 8(b)(7)(C).

The majority of the Board in the original Decision and Order rejected this argument. Pointing out that the representation petition was concededly filed more than 30 days after the commencement of the picketing, the majority concluded that the clear terms of Section 8(b)(7)(C) had been violated.

The majority also addressed itself specifically to the Union's contention that Section 8(b)(7)(C) could not have been intended by Congress to apply where an employer unfair labor practice had occurred. Its opinion alludes to the fact that the then Senator, now President, Kennedy had proposed statutory language to the effect that any employer unfair labor practice would be a defense to a charge of an 8(b)(7) violation both with respect to an application to the courts for a temporary restraining order and with respect to the unfair labor practice proceeding itself. The majority noted that the Congress did not adopt this proposal but instead limited itself merely to the insertion of a proviso in Section 10(*l*) prohibiting the application for a restraining order under Section 8(b)(7)(C) if there was reason to believe that a Section 8(a)(2) violation existed. Accordingly, the majority concluded that Congress had specifically rejected the very contention which Respondent urged. . . .

It seems fair to say that Congress was unwilling to write an exemption into Section 8(b)(7)(C) dispensing with the necessity for filing a representation petition wherever employer unfair labor practices were alleged. The fact that the bill as ultimately enacted by the Congress did not contain the amendment to Section 10(*l*) which the Senate had adopted in S. 1555 cogently establishes that this reluctance was not due to oversight. On the other hand, it strains credulity to believe that Congress proposed to make the rights of union and employees turn upon the results of an election which, because of the existence of unremedied unfair labor practices, is unlikely to reflect the true wishes of the employees.

We do not find ourselves impaled on the horns of this dilemma. Upon careful reappraisal of the statutory scheme we are satisfied that Congress meant to require, and did require, in an 8(b)(7)(C) situation, that a representation petition be filed within a reasonable period, not to exceed 30 days. By this device machinery can quickly be set in motion to resolve by a free and fair election the underlying question concerning representation out of which the picketing arises. This is the normal situation, and the situation which the statute is basically designed to serve.

There is legitimate concern, however, with the abnormal situation, that is, the situation where because of unremedied unfair labor practices a free and fair election cannot be held. We believe Congress anticipated this contingency also. Thus, we find no mandate in the legislative scheme to compel the holding of an election pursuant to a representation petition where, because of unremedied unfair labor practices or for other valid reason, a free and uncoerced election cannot be held. On the contrary, the interrelated provisions of subparagraphs (B) and (C), by their respective references to a "valid election" and to a "certif[ication of] results" presuppose that Congress contemplated only a fair and free election. Only after such an election could the Board certify the results and only after such an election could the salutary provisions of subparagraph (B) become operative.

In our view, therefore, Congress intended that, except to the limited extent set forth in the first proviso, the Board in 8(b)(7)(C) cases follow the tried and familiar procedures it typically follows in representation cases where unfair labor practice charges are filed. That procedure, as already set forth, is to hold the representation case in abeyance and refrain from holding an election pending the resolution of the unfair labor practice charges. Thus, the fears that the statutory requirement for filing a timely petition will compel a union which has been the victim of unfair labor practices to undergo a coerced election are groundless. No action will be taken on that petition while unfair labor practice charges are pending, and until a valid election is held pursuant to that petition, the union's right to picket under the statutory scheme is unimpaired.

On the other side of the coin, it may safely be assumed that groundless unfair labor practice charges in this area, because of the statutory priority accorded Section 8(b)(7) violations, will be quickly dismissed. Following such dismissal an election can be directed forthwith upon the subsisting petition, thereby effectuating the congressional purpose. Moreover, the fact that a timely petition is on file will protect the innocent union, which through a mistake of fact or law has filed a groundless unfair labor practice charge, from a finding of an 8(b)(7)(C) violation. Thus, the policy of the entire Act is effectuated and all rights guaranteed by its several provisions are appropriately safeguarded. *See Mastro Plastics Corp. v. N.L.R.B.*, 350 U.S. 270, 285.

The facts of the instant case may be utilized to demonstrate the practical operation of the legislative scheme. Here the union had filed unfair labor practice charges alleging violations by the employer of Section 8(a)(1), (2), (3), and (5) of the Act. General Counsel found the allegations of 8(a)(2) and (5) violations groundless. Hence had these allegations stood alone and had a timely petition been on file, an election could have been directed forthwith and the underlying question concerning representation out of which the picketing arose could have been resolved pursuant to the statutory scheme. The failure to file a timely petition frustrated that scheme.[11]

On the other hand, the Section 8(a)(1) and (3) charges were found meritorious. Under these circumstances, and again consistent with uniform practice, no election would have been directed notwithstanding the currency of a timely petition; the petition would be held in abeyance pending a satisfactory resolution of the unfair labor practice charges. The aggrieved union's right to picket would not be abated in the interim and the sole prejudice to the employer would be the delay engendered by its own unfair labor practices. The absence of a timely petition, however, precludes disposition of the underlying question concerning representation which thus remains unresolved even after the Section 8(a)(1) and (3) charges are satisfactorily disposed of. Accordingly, to condone the refusal to file a timely petition in such situations would be to condone the flouting of a legislative judgment. Moreover, and

---

11. [24] We would, however, have had a much different case here if the Section 8(a)(5) charge had been found meritorious so as to warrant issuance of a complaint. A representation petition assumes an unresolved question concerning representation. A Section 8(a)(5) charge, on the other hand, presupposes that no such question exists and that the employer is wrongfully refusing to recognize or bargain with a statutory bargaining representative. Because of this basic inconsistency, the Board has over the years uniformly refused to entertain representation petitions where a meritorious charge of refusal to bargain has been filed and, indeed, has dismissed any representation petition which may already have been on file. The same considerations apply where a meritorious Section 8(a)(5) charge is filed in a Section 8(b)(7)(C) context. Congressional acquiescence in the Board's long-standing practice prior to the enactment of Section 8(b)(7)(C) imports, in our view, congressional approval of a continuation of that practice thereafter. *Cf. Gullett Gin Co. v. N.L.R.B.*, 340 U.S. 361, 366. Accordingly, where a meritorious 8(a)(5) charge was filed in an 8(b)(7)(C) situation, the Board dismissed the representation petition. *See Robert P. Scott, Inc. v. Rothman*, 46 LRRM 2793 (D.C.D.C.); *Colony Materials, Inc. v. Rothman*, 46 LRRM 2794 (D.C.D.C.). So here, if a meritorious 8(a)(5) charge had been filed, a petition for representation would not have been required.... [T]he filing of a representation petition will not be required of a union when it has filed a meritorious 8(a)(5) charge, but will be required where it has filed other 8(a) charges. The point of the distinction — a point which our colleagues inexplicably ignore — is simply this: a meritorious 8(a)(5) case moots the question concerning representation which the petition is designed to resolve; other 8(a) charges merely delay the time when that unresolved question can be submitted to a free election by the employees....

most important, to impose a lesser requirement would fly in the face of the public interest which prompted that judgment.

Conclusion

Because we read Section 8(b)(7)(C) as requiring in the instant case the filing of a timely petition and because such a petition was admittedly not filed until more than 30 days after the commencement of the picketing, we find that Respondent violated Section 8(b)(7)(C) of the Act. As previously noted, it is undisputed that "an object" of the picketing was for recognition. It affords Respondent no comfort that its picketing was also in protest against the discriminatory transfer of an employee and against payment of wages at a rate lower than that prescribed by law. Had Respondent confined its picketing to these objectives rather than, as it did, include a demand for recognition, we believe none of the provisions of Section 8(b)(7) would be applicable.[12] Under the circumstances here, however, Section 8(b)(7)(C) is applicable.

Accordingly, having concluded as in the original decision herein that a violation of Section 8(b)(7)(C) has occurred, albeit for differing reasons, we reaffirm the Order entered therein.

[The "separate opinion" of MEMBERS ROGERS and LEEDOM and the "concurring and dissenting" opinion of MEMBER FANNING are omitted.]

Note

In *International Transp. Serv. v. NLRB*, 449 F.3d 160 (D.C. Cir. 2006), the court held that a labor organization violated § 8(b)(7)(C) when it picketed for recognition of a one-person bargaining unit since the Labor Board will not entertain petitions for certification with respect to one-person units; thus no petition could be filed within a reasonable period.

---

12. [29] As noted at the outset, Section 8(b)(7) is directed only at recognition and organization picketing and not at picketing for other objects including so-called protest picketing against unfair labor practices. There is ample legislative history to substantiate the proposition that Congress did not intend to outlaw picketing against unfair labor practices as such. *See*, for example, 105 Daily Cong. Rec. 5756, 5766, 15121, 15907, 16400, 16541; 2 Legis. Hist. 1361, 1384, 1429, 1714. Absent other evidence (such as is present in this case) of an organizational, recognition, or bargaining objective it is clear that Congress did not consider picketing against unfair labor practices as such to be also for proscribed objectives and, hence, outlawed. Parenthetically, it follows that cease-and-desist order issued against picketing in violation of Section 8(b)(7) will enjoin only picketing for recognition, bargaining, or organization and will not be a bar to protest picketing against unfair labor practices. . . .

Smitley, d/b/a Crown Cafeteria v. NLRB

United States Court of Appeals, Ninth Circuit
327 F.2d 351 (1964)

[The NLRB dismissed a complaint that the union had engaged in unlawful recognition picketing under § 8(b)(7)(C).]

DUNIWAY, CIRCUIT JUDGE. . . .

The findings of the Board as to the facts are not attacked. It found, in substance, that the unions picketed the cafeteria for more than thirty days before filing a representation petition under § 9(c) of the act (29 U.S.C. § 159(c)), that an object of the picketing was to secure recognition, that the purpose of the picketing was truthfully to advise the public that petitioners employed nonunion employees or had no contract with the unions, and that the picketing did not have the effect of inducing any stoppage of deliveries or services to the cafeteria by employees of any other employer. The matter was twice heard by the Board, which first concluded, by a majority of 3 to 2, that the picketing did violate the statute in question (130 N.L.R.B. 570), and then held, following a change in its membership, and by a majority of 3 to 2, that the picketing did not violate the statute (135 N.L.R.B. 1183). We conclude that the views of the Board, as stated after its second consideration of the matter, are correct, and that the statute has not been violated.

The Board states its interpretation of the section, including the proviso quoted above, as follows:

> Congress framed a general rule covering all organizational or recognitional picketing carried on for more than 30 days without the filing of a representation petition. Then, Congress excepted from that rule picketing which, although it had an organizational or recognitional objective, was addressed primarily to the public, was truthful in nature, and did not interfere to any significant extent with deliveries or the rendition of services by the employees of any other employer.

We think that this is the correct interpretation. It will be noted that subdivision (7) of subsection (b), § 8, quoted above, starts with the general prohibition of picketing "where an object thereof is forcing or requiring an employer to recognize or bargain with a labor organization" (This is often called recognitional picketing) ". . . or forcing or requiring the employees of an employer to accept or select such labor organization. . . ." (This is often called organizational picketing), ". . . unless such labor organization is currently certified as the representative of such employees: . . . ." This is followed by three subparagraphs, (A), (B) and (C). Each begins with the same word, "where." (A) deals with the situation "where" the employer has lawfully recognized another labor organization and a question of representation cannot be raised under § 9(c). (B) refers to the situation "where," within the preceding 12 months, a valid election under § 9(c) has been conducted. (C), with which we are concerned, refers to a situation "where" there has been no petition for an election under § 9(c) filed within a reasonable period of time, not to exceed thirty days, from the commencement of the picketing. Thus, § 8(b)(7) does not purport to prohibit all picketing having the named "object" of recognitional or organizational picketing. It limits the prohibition of such picketing to three specific situations.

There are no exceptions or provisos in subparagraphs (A) and (B), which describe two of those situations. There are, however, two provisos in subparagraph (C). The first sets up a special procedure for an expedited election under § 9(c). The second is the one with which we are concerned. It is an exception to the prohibition of "such picketing," *i.e.*, recognitional or organizational picketing, being a proviso to a prohibition of such picketing "where" certain conditions exist. It can only mean, indeed, it says, that "such picketing," which otherwise falls within subparagraph (C), is not prohibited if it falls within the terms of the proviso. That proviso says that subparagraph (C) is not to be construed to prohibit "any picketing" for "the purpose" of truthfully advising the public (including consumers) that an employer does not employ members of, or have a contract with, a labor organization. To this exception there is an exception, stated in the last "unless" clause, namely, that "such picketing," *i.e.*, picketing where "an object" is recognitional or organizational, but which has "the" excepting "purpose," would still be illegal if an effect were to induce any individual employee of other persons not to pick up, deliver, or transport any goods, or not to perform any services. Admittedly, the picketing here does not fall within the "unless" clause in the second proviso to subparagraph (C). It does, however, fall within the proviso, since it does have "the purpose" that brings it within the proviso. It also has "an object" that brings it within the first sentence of subsection (b) and the first clause of subdivision (7), and within the circumstances stated in the opening clause of subparagraph (C). If it did not have "an object" bringing it within subdivision (7), it would not be prohibited at all. Moreover, if it did have that "object," it still would not be prohibited at all, unless it occurred in circumstances described in subparagraph (A), (B) or (C). Here, neither (A) or (B) applies; (C) does. But, unlike (A) or (B), it has an excepting proviso. Unless that proviso refers to picketing having as "an object" either recognition or organization, it can have no meaning, for it would not be an exception or proviso to anything. It would be referring to conduct not prohibited in § 8(b) at all.

Petitioners urge that if the picketing has "an object" recognition or organization, then it is still illegal, even though it has "the purpose" of truthfully advising the public, etc., within the meaning of the second proviso to subparagraph (C). It seems to us, as it did to the Board, that to so construe the statute would make the proviso meaningless. The hard realities of union-employer relations are such that it is difficult, indeed almost impossible, for us to conceive of picketing falling within the terms of the proviso that did not also have as "an object" obtaining a contract with the employer. This is normally the ultimate objective of any union in relation to an employer who has employees whose jobs fall within the categories of employment that are within the jurisdiction of the union, which is admittedly the situation here.

We note that the Court of Appeals for the Second Circuit has reached a similar conclusion. In *NLRB v. Local 3, International Bhd. of Electrical Workers*, 317 F.2d 193 (2d Cir. 1963), that court considered the section at some length, and said:

> It seems, however, much more realistic to suppose that Congress framed a general rule covering the field of recognitional and organizational picketing, conducted under alternate sets of circumstances described in subparagraphs (A), (B), and (C), and then excepted from the operation of the rule, as it applied to the circumstances set forth in subparagraph (C), a comparatively innocuous species of picketing having the immediate purpose of informing or advising the public, even though its ultimate object was success in recognition and organization....
>
> One of the principal difficulties in construing and applying subparagraph (C) is that §8(b)(7) contains the partially synonymous words, "object" and "purpose," used in two distinct contexts but to which much of the same evidence is relevant. These are: "where an object thereof is forcing or requiring an employer to recognize or bargain...." and "for the purpose of truthfully advising the public...." It does not necessarily follow that, where an object of the picketing is forcing or requiring an employer to recognize or bargain, the purpose of the picketing, in the context of the second proviso, is not truthfully to advise the public, etc. The union may legitimately have a long range or strategic objective of getting the employer to bargain with or recognize the union and still the picketing may be permissive. This proviso gives the union freedom to appeal to the unorganized public for spontaneous popular pressure upon an employer; it is intended, however, to exclude the invocation of pressure by organized labor groups or members of unions, as such.
>
> The permissible picketing is, therefore, that which through the dissemination of certain allowed representations, is designed to influence members of the unorganized public, as individuals, because the impact upon the employer by way of such individuals is weaker, more indirect and less coercive.

We agree. *See also Getreu v. Bartenders and Hotel & Restaurant Employees Union Local 58*, 181 F. Supp. 738 (N.D. Ind. 1960).

Both sides have reviewed legislative history. We think this unnecessary, because we think that the meaning of the statute is clear. We also find the history inconclusive, but it seems to us to point somewhat more strongly toward the view that we here adopt than to the contrary view. Petitioners rely on language used by Senator Kennedy, who was one of the sponsors of the bill in the Senate and one of the Senate Conferees, in which he referred to the second proviso as permitting "purely informational" picketing. Counsel for petitioners frankly conceded, however, at oral argument, that most of the legislative history is against the view that he urged, and we agree. A discussion of legislative history appears in the dissent to the Board's first opinion (130 N.L.R.B. 576–77) and we therefore do not repeat it here. We think that even Senator Kennedy's comment, upon which petitioners most heavily rely, taken in context, was not intended to have the limiting effect which petitioners would give it. Senator Kennedy was more concerned, on the one hand, with the economic pressure involved in recognitional and organizational picketing, and on the other hand, with the right of labor truthfully to advise the public that the employer was nonunion, or that the employer did not have a contract with the union, than he was with whether or not, in addition to having an informational purpose described in the proviso, there was also a recognitional or organizational object. See 105 Cong. Rec. 17898 (1959). *See also* Cox, *The Landrum-Griffin Amendments to the National Labor Relations Act*, 44 Minn. L. Rev. 257, 267. Mr. Cox, now the Solicitor General, was then Senator Kennedy's chief advisor on the bill.

We think that, in substance, the effect of the second proviso to subparagraph (C) is to allow recognitional or organizational picketing to continue if it meets two important restrictions: (1) it must be addressed to the public and be truthful and (2) it must not induce other unions to stop deliveries or services. The picketing here met those criteria.

Notes

1. *What Counts as Organizational or Recognitional Picketing?*

   a. *Picketing solely to protest an employee's discharge and not for union recognition does not violate § 8(b)(7)(C). Local 259, International Union, United Automobile, Aircraft and Agricultural Implement Workers of America (Fanelli Ford Sales)*, 133 N.L.R.B. 1468 (1961).

   b. *Picketing by the incumbent union to compel the employer to comply with an existing bargaining agreement is not unlawful recognition picketing within the meaning of § 8(b)(7)(C) of the NLRA. Building & Construction Trades Council (Santa Barbara & Ventura Counties) (Sullivan Electric Co.)*, 146 N.L.R.B. 1086 (1964). *Compare Soft Drink Workers Union Local 812, Int'l Brotherhood of Teamsters v. NLRB*, 937 F.2d 684 (D.C. Cir. 1991) (recognition picketing by incumbent union after it lost representation election violated § 8(b)(7)(B) since within 12 months of valid election).

   c. In *NLRB v. International Ass'n of Bridge (Iron Workers Local 103)*, 434 U.S. 335 (1978), the Supreme Court held that it was a violation of § 8(b)(7)(C) for an uncertified union, not representing a majority of construction employees, to engage in extended picketing to enforce a § 8(f) pre-hire agreement, since such picketing was legally equivalent to picketing for organizational purposes.

2. *Threats to Picket* — Although § 8(b)(7)(C) refers to "picketing" that "has been conducted," *threats to picket* are proscribed by the same provision. While an unretracted union threat to engage in picketing if an employer does not grant union recognition does not contravene § 8(b)(7)(C) if the threatening union may lawfully seek to represent the employees in question, a similar threat by a labor organization that is barred from being certified as a collective bargaining representative of the target employees constitutes an immediate § 8(b)(7)(C) violation since such a disqualified union cannot file a valid representation petition. *Service Employees, Local 73 (A-1 Security Serv. Co.)*, 224 N.L.R.B. 434 (1976), *enforced*, 578 F.2d 361 (D.C. Cir. 1978).

3. *The Informational Picketing Proviso* — In defining the term "effect" in the proviso to § 8(b)(7)(C), the Board has looked to the "actual impact" on the employer's business, rather than to a quantitative test based solely on the number of deliveries not made or services not performed, when determining whether to remove informational picketing from the proviso's protection. The presence or absence of a violation depends on whether the picketing actually disrupted, interfered with, or curtailed the employer's business. For example, in *Retail Clerks Union Local 324 and Retail Clerks Union 770, Retail Clerks International Association, AFL-CIO (Barker Bros. Corp. and Gold's, Inc.)*, 138 N.L.R.B. 478 (1962), *enforced*, 328 F.2d 431 (9th Cir. 1964), where the union picketed 18 stores over a period of 12 weeks, taking active measures to ensure no interruption of service, the Board held that three delivery stoppages, two work delays, and several delivery delays were insufficient to constitute the "effect" contemplated by the proviso.

Houston Building & Construction Trades Council [Claude Everett Construction Co.]

National Labor Relations Board
136 N.L.R.B. 321 (1962)

... The Respondent, a council of local unions in the building and construction industry in the Houston, Texas, area, inquired on March 8, 1961, about the wage rates of Claude Everett Construction Company, a general construction contractor in that area. The Respondent's representative was told by Wilson, the Company's construction superintendent, that it operated an "open shop," and that its wage rates were lower than those negotiated in the area by the local unions which were members of the Respondent. On March 10, 1961, the Respondent wrote to the Company protesting its "substandard" wages and threatening to picket its construction site on March 13, unless "prevailing" rates were paid. When this letter had not been answered by March 16, the Respondent began picketing the Company's jobsite with a sign which read as follows:

> Houston Building and Construction Trades Council, AFL-CIO protests substandard wages and conditions being paid on this job by Claude Everett Company. Houston Building and Construction Trades Council does not intend by this picket line to induce or encourage the employees of any other employer to engage in a strike or a concerted refusal to work.

Such picketing continued for more than 30 days without the filing of a petition under § 9(c) of the act. The Respondent has never been certified as the representative of the Company's employees. The parties stipulated at the hearing that the picketing interfered with deliveries and services by inducing individuals employed by suppliers, service companies, and common carriers not to make pickups or deliveries or to perform services for the Company.

The Trial Examiner found that the Respondent picketed the Company to require it to conform its wage rates to those paid by employers having union contracts.

Relying on the original Board decision in the *Calumet Contractors* case,[13] he concluded that such picketing violated § 8(b)(7)(C) of the act. Subsequent to the issuance of his Intermediate Report, however, the Board, having reconsidered the *Calumet Contractors* case,[14] found the picketing there involved not unlawful, and stated that:

> ... Respondent's admitted objective to require the Association ... to conform standards of employment to those prevailing in the area, is not tantamount to, nor does it have an objective of, recognition or bargaining. A union may legitimately be concerned that a particular employer is undermining area standards of employment by maintaining lower standards. It may be willing to forego recognition and bargaining provided subnormal working conditions are eliminated from area considerations.

While the *Calumet Contractors* case arose under § 8(b)(4)(C) of the act, which prohibits only recognitional picketing, whereas the instant case arose under § 8(b)(7)(C), which proscribes both recognitional and organizational picketing, the language of both subsections is similar, and the rationale in that case is equally applicable herein. The Respondent in the present case did not, in its conversation with the Company, its letter to the Company, or its picket sign, claim to represent the Company's employees, request recognition by the Company, or solicit employees of the Company to become members of any of the locals which are members of the Respondent. Moreover, the undisputed testimony of Executive Secretary Graham reveals that the Respondent Union has on numerous occasions in the past made similar protests against substandard wages paid by other employers without ever requesting recognition as the bargaining representative of their employees. Thus, it is clear, from the entire record, that the objective of the Respondent's picketing was to induce the Company to raise its wage rates to the union scale prevailing in the area. We cannot, as do our dissenting colleagues, equate this attempt to maintain area wage standards with conduct "forcing or requiring an employer to recognize or bargain with a labor organization as the representative of his employees, or forcing or requiring the employees ... to accept or select such labor organization as their collective bargaining representative," the conduct proscribed by § 8(b)(7).

Nor do we agree with our dissenting colleagues that the fact that the picketing interfered with deliveries and services in itself constitutes a violation of § 8(b)(7)(C). To determine the effect of § 8(b)(7)(C), we must look at the section in its entirety, in accord with the long-established principle of statutory construction that a legislative enactment is to be read in its entirety, not in bits and pieces. It is clear that this section, read as a whole, declares picketing by an uncertified union unlawful if it has a recognitional or organizational objective and if a petition has not been filed within a reasonable time, and that the interruption-of deliveries clause does not enter into the picture unless the picketing can first be shown to have such a prohibited objective. As we stated in the *Blinne* case [135 N.L.R.B. 1153]:

---

13. [2] *Hod Carriers, Local 41 (Calumet Contractors Ass'n)*, 130 N.L.R.B. 78.
14. [3] *Hod Carriers, Local 41 (Calumet Contractors Ass'n)*, 133 N.L.R.B. 512 (Members Rodgers and Leedom dissenting).

[S]tructurally, as well as grammatically, subparagraphs (A), (B), and (C) are subordinate to and controlled by the opening phrases of § 8(b)(7). In other words, the thrust of all the § 8(b)(7) provisions is only upon picketing for an object of recognition or organization, and not upon picketing for other objects. Similarly, both structurally and grammatically, the two provisos in subparagraph (C) appertain only to the situation defined in the principal clause of that subparagraph.

Our dissenting colleagues interpret the second proviso of subparagraph (C) as though it creates a completely independent unfair labor practice, without reference to the fact that it is a subsidiary clause in a section which initially prohibits picketing with a recognitional or organizational objective. Such a reading would remove the proviso from its statutory setting, an interpretive result we feel constrained to avoid.

Accordingly, on the basis of the facts in the present case and of "the thrust of all the § 8(b)(7) provisions," we find that the Respondent's picketing did not have a recognitional or organizational objective, and, therefore, that it did not violate the act even though the picketing interfered with deliveries and services. Accordingly, we shall dismiss the complaint.

[The Board dismissed the complaint.]

[MEMBERS RODGERS and LEEDOM dissented.]

Note

The Limits of Area Standards Picketing—The line between recognitional and area standards picketing can be difficult to discern. In *Centralia Bldg. & Constr. Trades Council v. NLRB*, 363 F.2d 699 (D.C. Cir. 1966), the Board and the court held that the union's picketing was not "area standards" picketing but rather recognition picketing when the union, without inquiring whether Pacific's wages were in fact substandard, demanded that it sign an agreement to pay its employees "wages and fringe benefits equal to such allowances then being received by comparable employees working under the Union Agreement. If [the Union's] industry agreements were so negotiated as to provide increases or decreases, Pacific's total 'economic package' was to be increased or decreased by an equivalent amount." The union also demanded that its accountants be permitted to make monthly inspection of Pacific's records as to the economic benefits being paid to its employees. It was held that the net effect of this would be to establish the union as negotiator of Pacific's wages and benefits, tantamount to recognition, despite the union's disclaimers to the contrary. *See also Retail Clerks, Local 899 (State-Mart, Inc. dba Giant Food)*, 166 N.L.R.B. 818 (1967), *enforced*, 404 F.2d 855 (9th Cir. 1968) (although a union may picket for "area standards" by demanding that the nonunion employer pay its employees an economic package equal in total cost to what unionized employers pay, the picketing becomes unlawful "recognition" picketing when the union insists that the package include specific benefits, such as a welfare and pension plan).

Further, the Sixth Circuit has held that area standards picketing by nonemployees is only protected conduct when the union can demonstrate that it has meaningful evidence indicating that the target firm actually provides its employees with substandard wages and benefits. *NLRB v. Great Scot*, 39 F.3d 678 (6th Cir. 1994). *See also O'Neil's Mkts. v. NLRB*, 95 F.3d 733 (8th Cir. 1996) (union wishing to have nonemployees engage in area standards picketing must demonstrate bona fide attempt to ascertain if employer is actually paying less than area standards wage).

Problems

27. The Blue Toad is a company that produces supplies to be used in high school biology classes. Its principal live products are mice, rats, and fruit flies; its principal dead products are earthworms, red herrings, and, of course, toads. It conducts most of its business in August and September, the beginning of the school year, when schools find themselves in need of supplies.

The employees at the Blue Toad are represented by the Association of Anatomy Workers (AAW). The Blue Toad voluntarily recognized the AAW 10 years ago, and the relationship between the company and the union has been fairly harmonious (though there was one early incident in which a union representative threatened to dissect the company president, but the statute of limitations has long passed on that little problem).

On December 1, 2018, the Blue Toad and the AAW signed a three-year collective bargaining agreement. Then, two years later, on December 1, 2020, the parties signed a new three-year agreement that superseded the old agreement. The new agreement contained a union security clause that read as follows:

> Each employee covered by this agreement must, as a condition of continued employment, either (1) become and remain a member of the AAW on or after the thirtieth day following the beginning of employment or following the date of this agreement, whichever is later, or (2) pay to the union bargaining fees in amounts equal to the customary initiation fee and periodic dues required of members.

Another union, the Brotherhood of Biology Workers (BBW), has had its eye on the Blue Toad for years. The BBW believes that the AAW cut a lousy deal with the Blue Toad, and that the BBW negotiators were much more likely to get the employees the market wages that they deserved. Thus, on September 10, 2021, the BBW sent 50 of its members to picket the entrance of the Blue Toad. The picketers carried signs and passed out handbills that read as follows:

BLUE TOAD IS UNFAIR!

The BBW wants employees of Blue Toad to join them to gain better wages, hours, and working conditions.

The BBW also protests the substandard wages and benefits being paid to Blue Toad employees.

The Blue Toad immediately began losing business because many of its suppliers and customers honored the picket line. The picket line, however, did not convince any of the Blue Toad employees to join the BBW (or even honor the picket line), and so the BBW stopped picketing on September 30, 2021. The BBW never filed a petition for an election with the NLRB.

Has the Brotherhood of Biology Workers committed any unfair labor practices? What options were available to the Blue Toad once the picketing began?

28. For years, the United Foodworkers of America (UFA) has been trying to organize the workers at Sam's World Market, a nationwide chain of grocery stores. At one point, the union conducted organizational pickets and mass demonstrations against 20 stores across the country. The pickets lasted two weeks, at which point they stopped and were replaced with pickets and handbilling by an affiliated organization: United for Respect at Sam's World Market (URSWM).

The union founded and provided operating funds for URSWM in order to make broader appeals to Sam's, its workers, and the public. The union maintains that its intention is to help Sam's workers as individuals and groups in their dealings with Sam's over labor rights and standards, and in worker efforts to have Sam's publicly commit to adhering to labor rights and standards. The signs and handbills asked Sam's to take action with respect to the following:

- Pay workers a base wage of $18 an hour with appropriate raises for long-term workers.
- Provide consistent schedules and full-time hours for those who want to work more hours.
- Establish and follow a healthy sick time policy that allows workers to take time off to care for their families, because no one should be afraid to lose their job.
- Respect all workers by putting an end to discrimination, favoritism, and unjust and unlawful termination.
- Worker representation on the board of directors to ensure that that workers have a say in decisions that impact their work and their lives.

All of the signs and handbills included the directions, "Come to www.urswm.org for more information about how you can join the fight." On that URSWM homepage, the organization makes clear its relationship with the union, but specifically disavows having any intention of organizing workers or seeking recognition or bargaining rights.

Has UFA or URSWM committed any unfair labor practices. Is there any kind of additional information that would help you answer that question?

Section IV. Secondary Pressure

No problem of labor law is more complex or confusing than the attempt to restrict, within "legitimate" areas, the use by unions of the power they may exert through strikes, picketing, and boycotts. The difficulty arises from the fact that, even when conducted peacefully, these methods involve economic coercion. A strike by employees to force their employer to accede to some demand is the simplest example. When picketing goes beyond the bounds of "fair persuasion," to use the language of the *Restatement of Torts*, in the sense that it involves an attempt to induce, by economic threats, non-dealing with the employer, or when the strike is sought to be supported by "secondary" or "sympathetic" action by other labor groups or is itself secondary or sympathetic, or when the strikers or their union agents seek to enlist the support of consumers or others against their employer, the problem with which we are here concerned arises. The basic question is how far and on what principle Congress should intervene to limit such use of economic force.

This basic question involves a host of related issues. For example, should a distinction be drawn between the situation in which an embattled union simply *asks* for the support (by boycott) of other unions and of the consuming public without being able to *command* such support and that in which the union is able, by virtue of binding obligations, as through a central trades council, to command a labor boycott? It is well known that many unions, either by formulated policy or by custom, "respect" picket lines established by other unions, even non-affiliated unions. The result is that, in some cases, an employer embroiled in a dispute with its own union suddenly finds, for example, that it cannot get supplies because members of a teamsters' or drivers' union will not deliver goods across the picket line.

In 1947, the LMRA proscribed certain types of secondary activity. The Supreme Court recognized, however, that Congress had not prohibited all forms of secondary conduct:

> Whatever may have been said in Congress preceding the passage of the Taft-Hartley Act concerning the evil of all forms of "secondary boycotts" and the desirability of outlawing them, it is clear that no such sweeping prohibition was in fact enacted in § 8(b)(4)(A). The section does not speak generally of secondary boycotts. It describes and condemns specific union conduct directed to specific objectives.

Local 1976, United Brotherhood of Carpenters & Joiners v. NLRB, 357 U.S. 93, 98 (1958).

As a result of a widespread feeling that there were "loopholes" in the provisions of the LMRA dealing with secondary boycotts, and particularly as the result of the McClellan Committee's dramatization of the power of James R. Hoffa and the Teamsters Union, Congress acted in the Labor-Management Reporting and Disclosure Act amendments to tighten up the secondary boycott provisions. Some cases decided under the Taft-Hartley Act have been retained in this edition to show the background of the 1959 legislation. The chart on the following page may be of assistance in analyzing § 8(b)(4)(A) and (B) after the 1959 amendments. When reading cases decided before the 1959 amendments, it should be noted that the language that was previously set forth in § 8(b)(4)(A) became § 8(b)(4)(B).

ANALYSIS OF § 8(B)(4)(A) AND (B) AS AMENDED IN 1959

§ 8(B)(4)

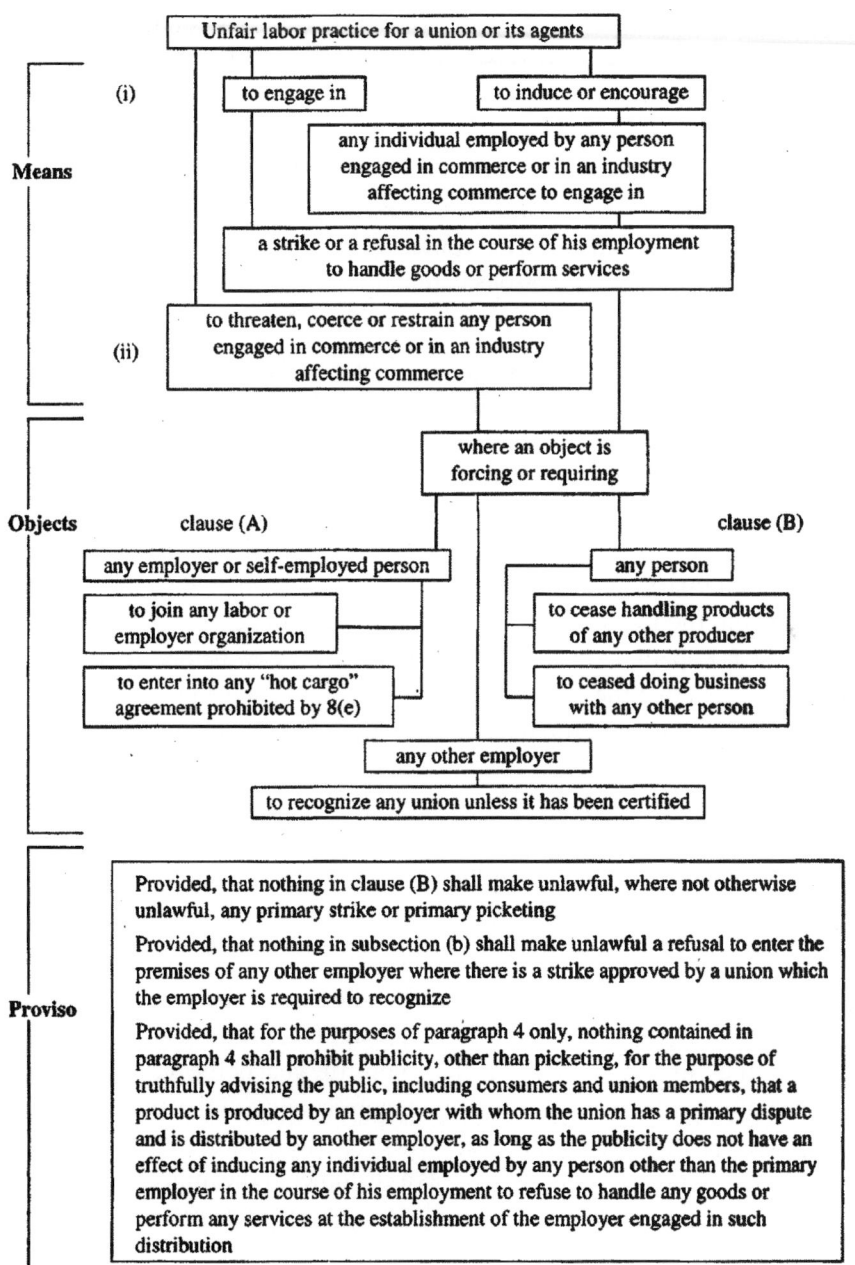

A. Primary-Secondary Distinction

NLRB v. International Rice Milling Co.

Supreme Court of the United States
341 U.S. 665, 71 S. Ct. 961, 95 L. Ed. 1277 (1951)

Mr. Justice Burton delivered the opinion of the Court.

The question presented is whether a union violated § 8(b)(4) of the National Labor Relations Act, 49 Stat. 449, 29 U.S.C. § 151, as amended by the Labor Management Relations Act, 1947, under the following circumstances: Although not certified or recognized as the representative of the employees of a certain mill engaged in interstate commerce, the agents of the union picketed the mill with the object of securing recognition of the union as the collective bargaining representative of the mill employees. In the course of their picketing, the agents sought to influence, or in the language of the statute they "encouraged," two men in charge of a truck of a neutral customer of the mill to refuse, in the course of their employment, to go to the mill for an order of goods. For the reasons hereinafter stated, we hold that such conduct did not violate § 8(b)(4). . . .

This review is confined to the single incident described in the complaint issued by the Acting Regional Director of the National Labor Relations Board against the International Brotherhood of Teamsters, Chauffeurs, Warehousemen and Helpers of America, Local 201, AFL, herein called the union. The complaint originally was based upon four charges made against the union by several rice mills engaged in interstate commerce near the center of the Louisiana rice industry. The mills included the International Rice Milling Company, Inc., which gives its name to this proceeding, and the Kaplan Rice Mills, Inc., a Louisiana corporation, which operated the mill at Kaplan, Louisiana, where the incident now before us occurred. The complaint charged that the union or its agents, by their conduct toward two employees of a neutral customer of the Kaplan Rice Mills, engaged in an unfair labor practice contrary to § 8(b)(4). The Board, with one member not participating, adopted the findings and conclusions of its trial examiner as to the facts but disagreed with his recommendation that those facts constituted a violation of § 8(b)(4)(A) or (B). The Board dismissed the complaint but attached the trial examiner's intermediate reports to its decision. 84 N.L.R.B. 360. The court of appeals set aside the dismissal and remanded the case for further proceedings. 183 F.2d 21. . . .

The findings adopted by the Board show that the incident before us occurred at the union's picket line near the Kaplan Mill, October, 1947. The pickets generally carried signs, one being "This job is unfair to" the union. The goal of the pickets was recognition of the union as the collective bargaining representative of the mill employees, but none of those employees took part in the picketing. Late one afternoon two employees of The Sales and Services House, which was a customer of the mill, came in a truck to the Kaplan Mill to obtain rice or bran for their employer. The union had no grievance against the customer and the latter was a neutral in the dispute between the union and the mill. The pickets formed a line across the road and walked toward the truck. When the truck stopped, the pickets told its occupants there was a strike on and that the truck would have to go back. Those on the truck agreed, went back to the highway and stopped. There one got out and went to the mill across the street. At that time a vice president of the Kaplan Mill came out and asked whether the truck was on its way to the mill and whether its occupants wanted to get the order they came for. The man on the truck explained that he was not the driver and that he would have to see the driver. On the driver's return, the truck proceeded, with the vice president, to the mill by a short detour. The pickets ran toward the truck and threw stones at it. The truck entered the mill, but the findings do not disclose whether the articles sought there were obtained. The Board adopted the finding that "the stopping of the Sales House truck drivers and the use of force in connection with the stoppage were within the 'scope of the employment' of the pickets as agents of the respondent [union] and that such activities are attributable to the respondent." 84 N.L.R.B. 360, 372.

[margin note: "Encouragement" involved throwing stones at customers' trucks when they approached employer's place of business]

The most that can be concluded from the foregoing, to establish a violation of § 8(b)(4), is that the union, in the course of picketing the Kaplan Mill, did encourage two employees of a neutral customer to turn back from an intended trip to the mill and thus to refuse, in the course of their employment, to transport articles or perform certain services for their employer. We may assume, without the necessity of adopting the Board's findings to that effect, that the objects of such conduct on the part of the union and its agents were (1) to force Kaplan's customer to cease handling transporting or otherwise dealing in products of the mill or to cease doing business with Kaplan, at that time and place, and (2) to add to the pressure on Kaplan to recognize the union as the bargaining representative of the mill employees.

[margin note: Even if this conduct attributable to union & even if done w/ purposes of forcing customer to cease doing business w/ employer & to add pressure on employer to recognize union, conduct was ~ "concerted" & therefore ~ violated 8(b)(4)]

A sufficient answer to this claimed violation of the section is that the union's picketing and its encouragement of the men on the truck did not amount to such an inducement or encouragement to "concerted" activity as the section proscribes. While each case must be considered in the light of its surrounding circumstances, yet the applicable proscriptions of § 8(b)(4) are expressly limited to the inducement or encouragement of *concerted* conduct by the employees of the neutral employer. That language contemplates inducement or encouragement to some concert of action greater than is evidenced by the pickets' request to a driver of a single truck to discontinue a pending trip to a picketed mill. There was no attempt by the union to induce any action by the employees of the neutral customer which would be more widespread than that already described. There were no inducements or encouragements applied elsewhere than on the picket line. The limitation of the complaint to an incident in the geographically restricted area near the mill is significant, although not necessarily conclusive. The picketing was directed at the Kaplan employees and at their employer in a manner traditional in labor disputes. Clearly, that, in itself, was not proscribed by § 8(b)(4). Insofar as the union's efforts were directed beyond that and toward the employees of anyone other than Kaplan, there is no suggestion that the union sought *concerted* conduct by such other employees. Such efforts also fall short of the proscriptions in § 8(b)(4). In this case, therefore, we need not determine the specific objects toward which a union's encouragement of concerted conduct must be directed in order to amount to an unfair labor practice under subsection (A) or (B) of § 8(b)(4). A union's inducements or encouragements reaching individual employees of neutral employers only as they happen to approach the picketed place of business generally are not aimed at concerted, as distinguished from individual, conduct by such employees. Generally, therefore, such actions do not come within the proscription of § 8(b)(4), and they do not here.

In the instant case the violence on the picket line is not material. The complaint was not based upon that violence, as such. To reach it, the complaint more properly would have relied upon § 8(b)(1)(A) or would have addressed itself to local authorities. The substitution of violent coercion in place of peaceful persuasion would not in itself bring the complained-of conduct into conflict with § 8(b)(4). It is the object of union encouragement that is proscribed by that section, rather than the means adopted to make it felt.

That Congress did not seek, by § 8(b)(4), to interfere with the ordinary strike has been indicated recently by this Court. This is emphasized in § 13 as follows:

"Nothing in this Act, except as specifically provided for herein, shall be construed so as either to interfere with or impede or diminish in any way the right to strike, or to affect the limitations or qualifications on that right." 61 Stat. 151, 29 U.S.C. (Supp. III) § 163.

By § 13, Congress has made it clear that § 8(b)(4), and all other parts of the act which otherwise might be read so as to interfere with, impede or diminish the union's traditional right to strike, may be so read only if such interference, impediment or diminution is "specifically provided for" in the act. No such specific provision in § 8(b)(4) reaches the incident here. The material legislative history supports this view.

On the single issue before us, we sustain the action of the Board and the judgment of the court of appeals, accordingly is

Reversed.

Notes

1. *Inducement of "Concerted" Activity* — The 1959 amendments removed the requirement for inducement of a "concerted" refusal to work on the part of employees of secondary employers. Congressman Griffin, in his analysis of this provision of the Landrum-Griffin bill, explained it as follows:

> As the present act forbids inducing "employees" to engage in a strike or "concerted" refusal to do their work, the courts have held that unions may induce employees one at a time to engage in secondary boycotts (citing *NLRB v. International Rice Milling Co.*, 341 U.S. 665). By changing "employees" to "any individual" and omitting the word "concerted," the proposed revision . . . closes this loophole.

105 Cong. Rec. 14347 (1959).

2. *"Primary" Picketing*—Was the fundamental basis for the decision in the *Rice Milling* case the fact that the picketing was "primary" in the sense that it was done at the primary employer's premises?

When the 1959 amendments to the LMRA were passed, the conference committee inserted a new proviso to the secondary boycott provisions of the Landrum-Griffin bill: "[N]othing contained in clause (B) of this paragraph (4) shall be construed to make unlawful, where not otherwise unlawful, any primary strike or primary picketing." The House managers explained:

> The purpose of this provision is to make it clear that the changes in § 8(b)(4) do not overrule or qualify the present rules of law permitting picketing at the site of a primary labor dispute. This provision does not eliminate, restrict, or modify the limitations on picketing at the site of a primary labor dispute that are in existing law.

H.R. Rep. No. 1147, 86th Cong., 1st Sess. 38 (1959). In *Landgrebe Motor Transp. Inc. v. Dist. 72, International Ass'n of Machinists & Aerospace Workers*, 763 F.2d 241 (7th Cir. 1985), the court held that the fact that union members who were picketing at the premises of the primary employer utilized violence to prevent a trucking company employee from entering the primary employer's facility to pick up a load did not negate the primary nature of the picketing or deprive it of the protection afforded by the primary picketing proviso to § 8(b)(4)(B). *See also Production Workers Union, Local 707 v. NLRB*, 793 F.2d 323 (D.C. Cir. 1986), holding that picketing at the premises of the primary employer is not subject to the secondary picketing proscription of § 8(b)(4)(B) merely because the labor organization is picketing on behalf of independent contractors, instead of employees.

3. *Secondary Recognitional Picketing by Certified Unions*—Were the secondary boycott provisions aimed at secondary recognitional picketing by a *certified union*—picketing a secondary employer's situs for the purpose of enforcing the Board's certification of the union as the exclusive bargaining representative of the primary employees? In *United Food & Comml. Workers, Local 1996*, 336 N.L.R.B. 421 (2001), the Board found no violation. The plain meaning of the second clause of § 8(b)(4)(B) exempts "recognition" boycotts by certified unions, and a contrary construction would render that clause superfluous.

4. *The Railway Labor Act*—The Supreme Court has held that the Railway Labor Act (RLA) contains no express or implied ban on secondary activity. As a result, the Norris-LaGuardia Act's broad prohibition against injunctions in "labor disputes" prevents a district court from enjoining picketing by a railroad workers' union even against railroads not "substantially aligned" with the railroad involved in the primary dispute. The Court noted that the union and the primary employer had exhausted the "major dispute" procedures of the RLA, and that therefore the parties were entitled to resort to self-help. *Burlington N. R.R. Co. v. Brotherhood of Maintenance of Way Employees*, 481 U.S. 429 (1987).

B. Common Situs Problems

Sailors' Union of the Pacific & Moore Dry Dock Co.

National Labor Relations Board
92 N.L.R.B. 547 (1950)

[Samsoc, a Greek-owned shipping company, made a contract with Kaiser Gypsum to carry gypsum from Mexico in the Samsoc ship *Phopho*. This meant replacement of an American crew for the Greek ship with a Greek crew. To convert the *Phopho* for this job, it was placed in the Moore Dry Dock Co. shipyard. Moore Dry Dock agreed that two weeks before completion Samsoc could put its crew on board for training purposes. In January 1950, while the boat was in the shipyard, the union learned of the arrangement. It demanded bargaining rights on the ship, but on February 16 this demand was refused. On the next day it placed pickets at the entrance to the shipyard. The union also informed the bargaining representatives of Moore's employees that the *Phopho* was "hot" and requested cooperation. On February 21, all of Moore's employees refused to work on the *Phopho*, but continued on other work.]

Section 8(b)(4)(A) is aimed at secondary boycotts and secondary strike activities. It was not intended to proscribe primary action by a union having a legitimate labor dispute with an employer. Picketing at the premises of a primary employer is traditionally recognized as primary action, even though it is "necessarily designed to induce and encourage third persons to cease doing business with the picketed employer. . . ."[15]

Hence, if Samsoc, the owner of the *S.S. Phopho*, had had a dock of its own in California to which the *Phopho* had been tied up while undergoing conversion by Moore Dry Dock employees, picketing by the Respondent at the dock site would unquestionably have constituted *primary* action even though the Respondent might have expected that the picketing would be more effective in persuading Moore employees not to work on the ship than to persuade the seamen aboard the *Phopho* to quit that vessel. The difficulty in the present case arises therefore, not because of any difference in picketing objectives,[16] but from the fact that the *Phopho* was not tied up at its own dock, but at that of Moore, while the picketing was going on in front of the Moore premises.

In the usual case, the *situs* of a labor dispute is the premises of the primary employer. Picketing of the premises is also picketing of the *situs*; the test of legality

---

15. [3] *Oil Workers Local 346 (Pure Oil Co.)* [84 N.L.R.B. 315, 318].

16. [5] "Plainly, the object of all picketing at all times is to influence third persons to withhold their business or services from the struck employer. In this respect there is no distinction between lawful primary picketing and unlawful secondary picketing proscribed by § 8(b)(4)(A)." *Teamsters Local 807 (Schultz Refrigerated Service, Inc.)* [87 N.L.R.B. 502].

of picketing is that enunciated by the Board in the *Pure Oil*[17] and *Ryan Construction*[18] cases. But in some cases the *situs* of the dispute may not be limited to a fixed location; it may be ambulatory. Thus, in the *Schultz*[19] case, a majority of the Board held that the truck upon which a truck driver worked was the *situs* of a labor dispute between him and the owner of the truck. Similarly, we hold in the present case that, as the *Phopho* was the place of employment of the seamen, it was the *situs* of the dispute between Samsoc and the Respondent over working conditions aboard the vessel.

When the *situs* is ambulatory, it may come to rest temporarily at the premises of another employer. The perplexing question is: Does the right to picket follow the *situs* while it is stationed at the premises of a secondary employer, when the only way to picket that *situs* is in front of the secondary employer's premises? Admittedly, no easy answer is possible. Essentially the problem is one of balancing the right of a union to picket at the site of its dispute as against the right of a secondary employer to be free from picketing in a controversy in which it is not directly involved.

When a secondary employer is harboring the *situs* of a dispute between a union and a primary employer, the right of neither the union to picket nor of the secondary employer to be free from picketing can be absolute. The enmeshing of premises and *situs* qualifies both rights. In the kind of situation that exists in this case, we believe that picketing of the premises of a secondary employer is primary if it meets the following conditions: (a) The picketing is strictly limited to times when the *situs* of dispute is located on the secondary employer's premises; (b) at the time of the picketing the primary employer is engaged in its normal business at the *situs*; (c) the picketing is limited to places reasonably close to the location of the *situs*; (d) the picketing discloses clearly that the dispute is with the primary employer. All these conditions were met in the present case.

(a) During the entire period of the picketing the *Phopho* was tied up at a dock in the Moore shipyard.

(b) Under its contract with Samsoc, Moore agreed to permit the former to put a crew on board the *Phopho* for training purposes during the last two weeks before the vessel's delivery to Samsoc. At the time the picketing started on February 17, 1950, 90 per cent of the conversion job had been completed, practically the entire crew had been hired, the ship's oil bunkers had been filled and other stores were shortly to be put aboard. The various members of the crew commenced work as soon as they reported aboard the *Phopho*. Those in the deck compartment did painting and cleaning up; those in the steward's department, cooking and cleaning up; and those in the engine department, oiling and cleaning up. The crew were thus getting the ship ready for sea. They were on board to serve the purposes of Samsoc, the

---

17. [7] [*Supra* note 3.]
18. [8] [United Electrical, Radio & Machine Workers (Ryan Constr. Co.), 85 N.L.R.B. 417.]
19. [9] [*Supra* note 5.]

Phopho's owners, and not Moore. The normal business of a ship does not only begin with its departure on the scheduled voyage. The multitudinous steps of preparation, including hiring and training a crew and putting stores aboard, are as much a part of the normal business of a ship as the voyage itself. We find, therefore, that the *Phopho* was engaged in its normal business.

(c) Before placing its pickets outside the entrance to the Moore shipyard, the Respondent Union asked, but was refused, permission to place its pickets at the dock where the *Phopho* was tied up. The respondent, therefore, posted its pickets at the yard entrance which, as the parties stipulated, was as close to the *Phopho* as they could get under the circumstances.

(d) Finally, by its picketing and other conduct the Respondent was scrupulously careful to indicate that its dispute was solely with the primary employer, the owners of the *Phopho*. Thus the signs carried by the pickets said only that the *Phopho* was unfair to the Respondent. The *Phopho* and not Moore was declared "hot." Similarly, in asking co-operation of other unions, the Respondent clearly revealed that its dispute was with the *Phopho*. Finally, Moore's own witnesses admitted that no attempt was made to interfere with other work in progress in the Moore yard.

We believe that our dissenting colleagues' expressions of alarm are based on a misunderstanding of our decision. We are not holding, as the dissenters seem to think, that a union which has a dispute with a shipowner over working conditions of seamen aboard a ship may lawfully picket the premises of an independent shipyard to which the shipowner has delivered his vessel for overhaul and repair. We are only holding that, if a shipyard permits the owner of a vessel to use its dock for the purpose of readying and training a crew and putting stores aboard a ship, a union representing seamen may then, within the careful limitations laid down in this decision, lawfully picket the front of the shipyard premises to advertise its dispute with the shipowner. . . .

Notes

1. *Primary Situs or Primary Employees?* — If the shipping company (primary employer with whom union had its dispute) removed all of its employees from the ship while it was in dry dock undergoing repairs, continued union picketing would usually contravene § 8(b)(4)(B). The ongoing union presence would indicate that the labor organization was endeavoring to enmesh secondary parties in its dispute with the primary employer. On the other hand, if the shipping company removed its nonsupervisory employees but kept supervisory personnel on the ship to oversee the repairs, the union would probably still be allowed to picket the dry dock, so long as its signs clearly stated that the dispute was solely with the shipping company. The continued presence of the supervisors on the ship would establish that the primary employer was still located on the dry dock premises and was engaged in normal operations. *See Seafarers Int'l Union v. NLRB*, 265 F.2d 585 (D.C. Cir. 1959). In response to the argument that "an object" of the union's continued picketing

must have been to induce employees of the dry dock company to refuse to work on the ship, the court found that since the picketing was "primary," such inducement of dry dock employees was an "incidental" effect of lawful primary picketing.

In *Carpet Service Int'l. v. Chicago Reg'l Council of Carpenters*, 698 F.3d 394 (7th Cir. 2012), *cert. denied*, 569 U.S. 920 (2013), the court held that a labor organization did not violate § 8(b)(4)(ii)(B) when the union picketed a location where primary and secondary employers shared the same construction work site, where the union limited picketing to times when it reasonably believed the primary employer was working and the union pickets clearly indicated that the picketing was solely of the primary employer. In *Fidelity Interior Constr. Inc. v. Southwestern Carpenters Reg'l Council*, 675 F.3d 1250 (11th Cir. 2012), however, the court found that a labor organization violated § 8(b)(4)(ii)(B) when it picketed a nonunion contractor's construction sites at times when the primary target was not present at those locations and used signs that did not clearly indicate that the dispute was only with the primary employer.

2. *Location*—*Local Union 501, International Brotherhood of Electrical Workers v. NLRB*, 756 F.2d 888 (D.C. Cir. 1985), involved a union engaged in an area standards dispute with a nonunion subcontractor working on a multiemployer construction project. The court indicated that the labor organization may not have violated § 8(b)(4)(B) when it picketed a gate reserved for neutral parties, since the gate designated for the exclusive use of the primary subcontractor and its employees was "effectively hidden from public view." The court directed the Labor Board to determine whether a site existed where the union could reasonably have conveyed its message to the public without involving secondary parties in its dispute. "In view of its protected interest in communicating its area standards dispute with [the primary employer] to the general public, we believe that [the union's] refusal to confine its picketing to a back entrance hidden from virtually all public view does not by itself imply an unlawful intent to enmesh neutrals." Compare *Carpenters Local 33 (CB Constr. Co.)*, 289 N.L.R.B. 528 (1988), *aff'd*, 873 F.2d 316 (D.C. Cir. 1989).

Problem

29. U.S. Tire, Inc., required certain electrical work on its premises. Lake City Electric, a nonunion contractor, bid for the work, and that bid was accepted. The job was expected to take about a week.

Lake City maintained an office in the area, where its electricians would normally report in the morning to be dispatched by truck to their jobs and then report back in the evening. But when contract work extended over a period of days, the electricians sometimes reported directly to the jobsite and went straight home at the end of the day.

On the first day of the U.S. Tire job, all four of the electricians reported to the Lake City office and then went to the jobsite. On most days after that, just two of the workers reported to the office in the morning, picked up tools and supplies, and then went to U.S. Tire. The other two workers reported directly to the jobsite. On several occasions, one or two of the electricians would return to the office during the course of the day to pick up tools or materials.

The day the contract work started, the International Brotherhood of Electrical Workers set up a picket in front of the entrance of U.S. Tire. The picket signs stated "Lake City Electric is attempting to destroy working conditions established through negotiations by the IBEW. No dispute with any other contractor." The picket stayed up during the regular working hours of the Lake City electricians and, when the electricians left for lunch or a coffee break, the picketing continued. There was no picketing at any time at Lake City's office.

Did the IBEW commit an unfair labor practice in picketing in front of U.S. Tire?

NLRB v. Denver Building & Construction Trades Council

Supreme Court of the United States
341 U.S. 675, 71 S. Ct. 943, 95 L. Ed. 1284 (1951)

Mr. Justice Burton delivered the opinion of the Court.

The principal question here is whether a labor organization committed an unfair labor practice, within the meaning of § 8(b)(4)(A) of the National Labor Relations Act, . . . as amended by the Labor Management Relations Act, 1947, by engaging in a strike, an object of which was to force the general contractor on a construction project to terminate its contract with a certain subcontractor on that project. For the reasons hereafter stated, we hold that such an unfair labor practice was committed.

In September, 1947, Doose & Lintner was the general contractor for the construction of a commercial building in Denver, Colorado. It awarded a subcontract for electrical work on the building, in an estimated amount of $2,300, to Gould & Preisner, a firm which for 20 years had employed nonunion workmen on construction work in that city. The latter's employees proved to be the only nonunion workmen on the project. Those of the general contractor and of the other subcontractors were members of unions affiliated with the respondent Denver Building and Construction Trades Council (here called the Council). In November a representative of one of those unions told Gould that he did not see how the job could progress with Gould's nonunion men on it. Gould insisted that they would complete the electrical work unless bodily put off. The representative replied that the situation would be difficult for both Gould & Preisner and Doose & Lintner.

January 8, 1948, the Council's Board of Business Agents instructed the Council's representative "to place a picket on the job stating that the job was unfair" to it. In keeping with the Council's practice, each affiliate was notified of that decision. That notice was a signal in the nature of an order to the members of the affiliated unions to leave the job and remain away until otherwise ordered. Representatives of the Council and each of the respondent unions visited the project and reminded the contractor that Gould & Preisner employed nonunion workmen and said that union men could not work on the job with nonunion men. They further advised that if Gould & Preisner's men did work on the job, the Council and its affiliates would put a picket on it to notify their members that nonunion men were working on it and that the job was unfair. All parties stood their ground.

January 9, the Council posted a picket at the project carrying a placard stating "This Job Unfair to Denver Building and Construction Trades Council." He was paid by the Council and his picketing continued from January 9 through January 22. During that time the only persons who reported for work were the nonunion electricians of Gould & Preisner. January 22, before Gould & Preisner had completed its subcontract, the general contractor notified it to get off the job so that Doose & Lintner could continue with the project. January 23, the Council removed its picket and shortly thereafter the union employees resumed work on the project. Gould & Preisner protested this treatment but its workmen were denied entrance to the job.

On charges filed by Gould & Preisner, the Regional Director of the National Labor Relations Board issued the complaint in this case against the Council and the respondent unions. It alleged that they had engaged in a strike or had caused strike action to be taken on the project by employees of the general contractor and of other subcontractors, an object of which was to force the general contractor to cease doing business with Gould & Preisner on that project.

Between the Board's receipt of the charges and the filing of the complaint based upon them, the Regional Director of the Board petitioned the United States District Court for the District of Colorado for injunctive relief. That petition was dismissed on the jurisdictional ground that the activities complained of did not affect interstate commerce. *Sperry v. Denver Building Trades Council*, 77 F. Supp. 321 (1958). Such action will be discussed later under the heading of *res judicata*. Hearings were held by the Board's trial examiner on the merits of the complaint. The Board adopted its examiner's findings, conclusions and recommendations, with minor additions and modifications not here material. It attached the examiner's intermediate report to its decision and ordered respondents to cease and desist from engaging in the activities charged. 82 N.L.R.B. 1195. Respondents petitioned the United States Court of Appeals for the District of Columbia Circuit for a review under §10(f). The Board answered and asked for enforcement of its order. That court held, with one judge dissenting, that the conduct complained of affected interstate commerce sufficiently to give the Board jurisdiction over it, but the court unanimously set aside the order of the Board and said: "Convinced that the action in the circumstances of this case is primary and not secondary we are obliged to refuse to enforce the order based on §8(b)(4)(A)." 87 App. D.C. 293, 304, 186 F.2d 326, 337. . . .

III

The Secondary Boycott. — We now reach the merits. They require a study of the objectives of the strike and a determination whether the strike came within the definition of an unfair labor practice stated in §8(b)(4)(A).

The language of that section which is here essential is as follows:

§(b)(4)(A)

> (b) It shall be an unfair labor practice for a labor organization. . . .
>
> (4) to engage in . . . a strike . . . where an object thereof is: (A) forcing or requiring . . . any employer or other person . . . to cease doing business with any other person; . . .

While §8(b)(4) does not expressly mention "primary" or "secondary" disputes, strikes or boycotts, that section often is referred to in the act's legislative history as one of the act's "secondary boycott sections." The other is §303, 61 Stat. 158, 29 U.S.C. (Supp. III) §187, which uses the same language in defining the basis for private actions for damages caused by these proscribed activities.

Senator Taft, who was the sponsor of the bill in the Senate and was the Chairman of the Senate Committee on Labor and Public Welfare in charge of the bill, said, in discussing this section:

> . . . [U]nder the provisions of the Norris-La Guardia Act, it became impossible to stop a secondary boycott or any other kind of a strike, no matter how unlawful it may have been at common law. All this provision of the bill does is to reverse the effect of the law as to secondary boycotts. It has been set forth that there are good secondary boycotts and bad secondary boycotts. Our committee heard evidence for weeks and never succeeded in having anyone tell us any difference between different kinds of secondary boycotts. So we have so broadened the provision dealing with secondary boycotts as to make them an unfair labor practice.

93 Cong. Rec. 4198.

The Conference Report to the House of Representatives said:

> Under clause (A) [of §8(b)(4)] strikes or boycotts, or attempts to induce or encourage such action, were made unfair labor practices if the purpose was to force an employer or other person to cease using, selling, handling, transporting, or otherwise dealing in the products of another, or to cease doing business with any other person. Thus it was made an unfair labor practice for a union to engage in a strike against employer A for the purpose of forcing that employer to cease doing business with employer B. Similarly it would not be lawful for a union to boycott employer A because employer A uses or otherwise deals in the goods of, or does business with, employer B.

H.R. Rep. No. 510, 80th Cong., 1st Sess. 43.

At the same time that §§7 and 13 safeguard collective bargaining, concerted activities and strikes between the primary parties to a labor dispute, §8(b)(4) restricts a labor organization and its agents in the use of economic pressure where an object of it is to force an employer or other person to boycott someone else.

A. We must first determine whether the strike in this case had a proscribed object. The conduct which the Board here condemned is readily distinguishable from that which it declined to condemn in the *Rice Milling* case, *supra* at 665. There the accused union sought merely to obtain its own recognition by the operator of a mill, and the union's pickets near the mill sought to influence two employees of a customer of the mill not to cross the picket line. In that case we supported the Board in its conclusion that such conduct was no more than was traditional and permissible in a primary strike. The union did not engage in a strike against the customer. It did not encourage concerted action by the customer's employees to force the customer to boycott the mill. It did not commit any unfair labor practice proscribed by § 8(b)(4).

In the background of the instant case there was a long-standing labor dispute between the Council and Gould & Preisner due to the latter's practice of employing nonunion workmen on construction jobs in Denver. The respondent labor organizations contend that they engaged in a primary dispute with Doose & Lintner alone, and that they sought simply to force Doose & Lintner to make the project an all-union job. If there had been no contract between Doose & Lintner and Gould & Preisner there might be substance in their contention that the dispute involved no boycott. If, for example, Doose & Lintner had been doing all the electrical work on this project through its own nonunion employees, it could have replaced them with union men and thus disposed of the dispute. However, the existence of the Gould & Preisner subcontract presented a materially different situation. The nonunion employees were employees of Gould & Preisner. The only way that respondents could attain their purpose was to force Gould & Preisner itself off the job. This, in turn, could be done only through Doose & Lintner's termination of Gould & Preisner's subcontract. The result is that the Council's strike, in order to attain its ultimate purpose, must have included among its objects that of forcing Doose & Lintner to terminate that subcontract. On that point, the Board adopted the following finding:

> That *an* object, if not the only object, of what transpired with respect to ... Doose & Lintner was to force or require them to cease doing business with Gould & Preisner seems scarcely open to question, in view of all of the facts. And it is clear, at least as to Doose & Lintner, that that purpose was achieved. (Emphasis supplied.)

82 N.L.R.B. at 1212.

We accept this crucial finding. It was an object of the strike to force the contractor to terminate Gould & Preisner's subcontract.

B. We hold also that a strike with such an object was an unfair labor practice within the meaning of § 8(b)(4)(A).

It is not necessary to find that the *sole* object of the strike was that of forcing the contractor to terminate the subcontractor's contract. This is emphasized in the legislative history of the section. See also, *NLRB v. Wine, Liquor & Distillery Workers Union*, 178 F.2d 584, 586 (2d Cir. 1949).

We agree with the Board also in its conclusion that the fact that the contractor and subcontractor were engaged on the same construction project, and that the contractor had some supervision over the subcontractor's work, did not eliminate the status of each as an independent contractor or make the employees of one the employees of the other. The business relationship between independent contractors is too well established in the law to be overridden without clear language doing so. The Board found that the relationship between Doose & Lintner and Gould & Preisner was one of "doing business" and we find no adequate reason for upsetting that conclusion.

Finally, § 8(c) safeguarding freedom of speech has no significant application to the picket's placard in this case. Section 8(c) does not apply to a mere signal by a labor organization to its members, or to the members of its affiliates, to engage in an unfair labor practice such as a strike proscribed by § 8(b)(4)(A). That the placard was merely such a signal, tantamount to a direction to strike, was found by the Board.

> ... [T]he issues in this case turn upon acts by labor organizations which are tantamount to directions and instructions to their members to engage in strike action. The protection afforded by § 8(c) of the Act to the expression of 'any views, arguments or opinion' does not pertain where, as here, the issues raised under § 8(b)(4)(A) turn on official directions or instructions to a union's own members.

82 N.L.R.B. at 1213.

The further conclusion that § 8(c) does not immunize action against the specific provisions of § 8(b)(4)(A) has been announced in other cases. *See IBEW, Local 108 v. NLRB, infra* at 694.

Not only are the findings of the Board conclusive with respect to questions of fact in this field when supported by substantial evidence on the record as a whole, but the Board's interpretation of the act and the Board's application of it in doubtful situations are entitled to weight. In the views of the Board as applied to this case we find conformity with the dual congressional objectives of preserving the right of labor organizations to bring pressure to bear on offending employers in primary labor disputes and of shielding unoffending employers and others from pressures in controversies not their own.

For these reasons we conclude that the conduct of respondents constituted an unfair labor practice within the meaning of § 8(b)(4)(A). The judgment of the Court of Appeals accordingly is reversed and the case is remanded to it for procedure not inconsistent with this opinion.

It is so ordered.

MR. JUSTICE JACKSON would affirm the judgment of the Court of Appeals.

MR. JUSTICE DOUGLAS, with whom MR. JUSTICE REED joins, dissenting.

The employment of union and nonunion men on the same job is a basic protest in trade union history. That was the protest here. The union was not out to destroy the contractor because of his antiunion attitude. The union was not pursuing the contractor to other jobs. All the union asked was that union men not be compelled to work alongside nonunion men on the same job. As Judge Rifkind stated in an analogous case, "the union was not extending its activity to a front remote from the immediate dispute but to one intimately and indeed inextricably united to it."

The picketing would undoubtedly have been legal if there had been no subcontractor involved—if the general contractor had put nonunion men on the job. The presence of a subcontractor does not alter one whit the realities of the situation; the protest of the union is precisely the same. In each the union was trying to protect the job on which union men were employed. If that is forbidden, the Taft-Hartley Act makes the right to strike, guaranteed by §13, dependent on fortuitous business arrangements that have no significance so far as the evils of the secondary boycott are concerned. I would give scope to both §8(b)(4) and §13 by reading the restrictions of §8(b)(4) to reach the case where an industrial dispute spreads from the job to another front.

Note

Limits of Denver Building & Construction Trades Council—There may be unusual circumstances under which a general contractor on a construction project assumes such substantial control over subcontractor employees that it would no longer be regarded as a neutral, but instead as a primary employer along with the subcontractors, and thus be subject to subcontractor union picketing without recourse under §8(b)(4)(B). *See Teamsters, Local 363 (Roslyn Americana Corp.)*, 214 N.L.R.B. 868 (1974).

International Union of Electrical, Radio & Machine Workers, Local 761, AFL-CIO v. NLRB [General Electric Co.]

Supreme Court of the United States
366 U.S. 667, 81 S. Ct. 1285, 6 L. Ed. 2d 592 (1961)

Mr. Justice Frankfurter delivered the opinion of the Court.

Local 761 of International Union of Electrical, Radio and Machine Workers, AFL-CIO was charged with a violation of §8(b)(4)(A) of the National Labor Relations Act, as amended by the Taft-Hartley Act, 61 Stat. 136, 141, upon the following facts.

General Electric Corporation operates a plant outside of Louisville, Kentucky, where it manufactures washers, dryers, and other electrical household appliances. The square-shaped, thousand-acre, unfenced plant is known as Appliance Park. A large drainage ditch makes ingress and egress impossible except over five roadways across culverts, designated as gates.

Since 1954, General Electric sought to confine the employees of independent contractors, described hereafter, who work on the premises of the Park, to the use of Gate 3-A and confine its use to them. The undisputed reason for doing so was to insulate General Electric employees from the frequent labor disputes in which the contractors were involved. Gate 3-A is 550 feet away from the nearest entrance available for General Electric employees, suppliers, and deliverymen. Although anyone can pass the gate without challenge, the roadway leads to a guardhouse where identification must be presented. Vehicle stickers of various shapes and colors enable a guard to check on sight whether a vehicle is authorized to use Gate 3-A. Since January 1958, a prominent sign has been posted at the gate which states: "GATE 3-A FOR EMPLOYEES OF CONTRACTORS ONLY — G. E. EMPLOYEES USE OTHER GATES." On rare occasions, it appears, a General Electric employee was allowed to pass the guardhouse, but such occurrence was in violation of company instructions. There was no proof of any unauthorized attempts to pass the gate during the strike in question.

The independent contractors are utilized for a great variety of tasks on the Appliance Park premises. Some do construction work on new buildings; some install and repair ventilation and heating equipment; some engage in retooling and rearranging operations necessary to the manufacture of new models; others do "general maintenance work." These services are contracted to outside employers either because the company's employees lack the necessary skill or manpower, or because the work can be done more economically by independent contractors. The latter reason determined the contracting of maintenance work for which the Central Maintenance department of the company bid competitively with the contractors. While some of the work done by these contractors had on occasion been previously performed by Central Maintenance, the findings do not disclose the number of employees of independent contractors who were performing these routine maintenance services, as compared with those who were doing specialized work of a capital-improvement nature.

The Union, petitioner here, is the certified bargaining representative for the production and maintenance workers who constitute approximately 7,600 of the 10,500 employees of General Electric at Appliance Park. On July 27, 1958, the Union called a strike because of 24 unsettled grievances with the company. Picketing occurred at all gates, including Gate 3-A, and continued until August 9 when an injunction was issued by a Federal District Court. The signs carried by the pickets at all gates read: "LOCAL 761 ON STRIKE — G.E. UNFAIR." Because of the picketing, almost all of the employees of independent contractors refused to enter the company premises.

Neither the legality of the strike or of the picketing at any of the gates except 3-A is in dispute, nor that the picketing was other than peaceful in nature. The sole claim was that the picketing before the gate exclusively used by employees of independent contractors was conduct proscribed by § 8(b)(4)(A).

The Trial Examiner recommended that the Board dismiss the complaint. He concluded that the limitations on picketing which the Board had prescribed in so-called "common situs" cases were not applicable to the situation before him, in that the picketing at Gate 3-A represented traditional primary action which necessarily had a secondary effect of inconveniencing those who did business with the struck employer. He reasoned that if a primary employer could limit the area of picketing around his own premises by constructing a separate gate for employees of independent contractors, such a device could also be used to isolate employees of his suppliers and customers, and that such action could not relevantly be distinguished from oral appeals made to secondary employees not to cross a picket line where only a single gate existed.

The Board rejected the Trial Examiner's conclusion, 123 N.L.R.B. 1547. It held that since only the employees of the independent contractors were allowed to use Gate

3-A, the Union's object in picketing there was "to enmesh these employees of the neutral employers in its dispute with the Company" thereby constituting a violation of § 8(b)(4)(A) because the independent employees were encouraged to engage in a concerted refusal to work "with an object of forcing the independent contractors to cease doing business with the Company."

The Court of Appeals for the District of Columbia granted enforcement of the Board's order, 107 App. D.C. 402, 278 F.2d 282. Although noting that a fine line was being drawn, it concluded that the Board was correct in finding that the objective of the Gate 3-A picketing was to encourage the independent-contractor employees to engage in a concerted refusal to perform services for their employers in order to bring pressure on General Electric. . . .

I

Section 8(b)(4)(A) . . . could not be literally construed; otherwise it would ban most strikes historically considered to be lawful, so-called primary activity. "While § 8(b)(4) does not expressly mention 'primary' or 'secondary' disputes, strikes or boycotts, that section often is referred to in the Act's legislative history as one of the Act's 'secondary boycott sections.'" *NLRB v. Denver Bldg. & Constr. Trades Council*, 341 U.S. 675, 686 (1951). "Congress did not seek by § 8(b)(4), to interfere with the ordinary strike. . . ." *NLRB v. International Rice Milling Co.*, 341 U.S. 665, 672 (1951). The impact of the section was directed toward what is known as the secondary boycott whose "sanctions bear, not upon the employer who alone is a party to the dispute, but upon some third party who has no concern in it." *IBEW, Local 501 v. NLRB*, 181 F.2d 34, 37 (2d Cir. 1950). Thus the section "left a striking labor organization free to use persuasion, including picketing, not only on the primary employer and his employees but on numerous others. Among these were secondary employers who were customers or suppliers of the primary employer and persons dealing with them . . . and even employees of secondary employers so long as the labor organization did not . . . 'induce or encourage the employees of any employer to engage, in a strike or a concerted refusal in the course of their employment' . . . ." *NLRB v. Teamsters Local 294*, 284 F.2d 887, 889 (2d Cir. 1960).

But not all so-called secondary boycotts were outlawed in § 8(b)(4)(A). "The section does not speak generally of secondary boycotts. It describes and condemns specific union conduct directed to specific objectives. . . . Employees must be induced; they must be induced to engage in a strike or concerted refusal; an object must be to force or require their employer or another person to cease doing business with a third person. Thus, much that might argumentatively be found to fall within the broad and somewhat vague concept of secondary boycott is not in terms prohibited." *Local 1976, United Brotherhood of Carpenters & Joiners v. NLRB*, 357 U.S. 93, 98 (1958). See also *United Bhd. of Carpenters (Wadsworth Bldg. Co.)*, 81 N.L.R.B. 802, 805.

Important as is the distinction between legitimate "primary activity" and banned "secondary activity," it does not present a glaringly bright line. The objectives of any picketing include a desire to influence others from withholding from the employer their services or trade. *See Sailors' Union of the Pacific (Moore Dry Dock)*, 92 N.L.R.B. 547. "[I]ntended or not, sought for or not, aimed for or not, employees of neutral employers do take action sympathetic with strikers and do put pressure on their own employers." *Seafarers Int'l Union v. NLRB*, 105 App. D.C. 211, 265 F.2d 585, 590 (1959). "It is clear that, when a union pickets an employer with whom it has a dispute, it hopes, even if it does not intend, that all persons will honor the picket line, and that hope encompasses the employees of neutral employers who may in the course of their employment (deliverymen and the like) have to enter the premises." *Id.* at page 591. "Almost all picketing, even at the situs of the primary employer and surely at that of the secondary, hopes to achieve the forbidden objective, whatever other motives there may be and however small the chances of success." Local 294, *supra*, 284 F.2d at 890. But picketing which induces secondary employees to respect a picket line is not the equivalent of picketing which has an object of inducing those employees to engage in concerted conduct against their employer in order to force him to refuse to deal with the struck employer. *NLRB v. International Rice Milling Co., supra*.

However difficult the drawing of lines more nice than obvious, the statute compels the task. Accordingly, the Board and the courts have attempted to devise reasonable criteria drawing heavily upon the means to which a union resorts in promoting its cause. Although "[n]o rigid rule which would make . . . [a] few factors conclusive is contained in or deducible from the statute," *Sales Drivers v. NLRB*, 97 App. D.C. 173, 229 F.2d 514, 517 (1955), "[I]n the absence of admissions by the union of an illegal intent, the nature of acts performed shows the intent." *Seafarers Int'l Union, supra* at 591.

The nature of the problem, as revealed by unfolding variant situations, inevitably involves an evolutionary process for its rational response, not a quick, definitive formula as a comprehensive answer. And so, it is not surprising that the Board has more or less felt its way during the fourteen years in which it has had to apply § 8(b)(4)(A), and has modified and reformed its standards on the basis of accumulating experience. . . .

II

The early decisions of the Board following the Taft-Hartley amendments involved activity which took place around the secondary employer's premises. For example, in *Wadsworth Building Co., supra*, the union set up a picket line around the situs of a builder who had contracted to purchase prefabricated houses from the primary employer. The Board found this to be illegal secondary activity. *See also Printing Specialties Union (Sealbright Pacific)*, 82 N.L.R.B. 271. In contrast, when picketing took place around the premises of the primary employer, the Board regarded this as valid primary activity. . . .

In *United Electrical Workers (Ryan Constr. Corp.)*, 85 N.L.R.B. 417, Ryan had contracted to perform construction work on a building adjacent to the Bucyrus plant and inside its fence. A separate gate was cut through the fence for Ryan's employees which no employee of Bucyrus ever used. The Board concluded that the union—on strike against Bucyrus—could picket the Ryan gate, even though an object of the picketing was to enlist the aid of Ryan employees, since Congress did not intend to outlaw primary picketing....

However, the impact of the new situations made the Board conscious of the complexity of the problem by reason of the protean forms in which it appeared. This became clear in the "common situs" cases—situations where two employers were performing separate tasks on common premises. The *Moore Dry Dock* case, *supra*, laid out the Board's new standards in this area....

In *Local 55 (PBM)*, 108 N.L.R.B. 363, the Board for the first time applied the *Dry Dock* test although the picketing occurred at premises owned by the primary employer. There, an insurance company owned a tract of land that it was developing, and also served as the general contractor. A neutral subcontractor was also doing work at the site. The union, engaged in a strike against the insurance company, picketed the entire premises, characterizing the entire job as unfair, and the employees of the subcontractor walked off. The Court of Appeals for the Tenth Circuit enforced the Board's order which found the picketing to be illegal on the ground that the picket signs did not measure up to the *Dry Dock* standard that they clearly disclose that the picketing was directed against the struck employer only. 218 F.2d 226.

The Board's application of the *Dry Dock* standards to picketing at the premises of the struck employer was made more explicit in *Retail Fruit & Vegetable Clerks (Crystal Palace Market)*, 116 N.L.R.B. 856. The owner of a large common market operated some of the shops within, and leased out others to independent sellers. The union, although given permission to picket the owner's individual stands, chose to picket outside the entire market. The Board held that this action was violative of §8(b)(4)(A) in that the union did not attempt to minimize the effect of its picketing, as required in a common-situs case, on the operations of the neutral employers utilizing the market. "We believe...that the foregoing principles should apply to all common situs picketing, including cases where, as here, the picketed premises are owned by the primary employer." 116 N.L.R.B., at 859. The *Ryan* case, *supra*, was overruled to the extent it implied the contrary. The Court of Appeals for the Ninth Circuit, in enforcing the Board's order, specifically approved its disavowal of an ownership test. 249 F.2d 591. The Board made clear that its decision did not affect situations where picketing which had effects on neutral third parties who dealt with the employer occurred at premises occupied solely by him. "In such cases, we adhere to the rule established by the Board...that more latitude be given to picketing at such separate primary premises than at premises occupied in part (or entirely) by secondary employers." 116 N.L.R.B., at 860, n. 10.

In rejecting the ownership test in situations where two employers were performing work upon a common site, the Board was naturally guided by this Court's opinion in *Rice Milling*, in which we indicated that the location of the picketing at the primary employer's premises was "not necessarily conclusive" of its legality. 341 U.S. at 671. Where the work done by the secondary employees is unrelated to the normal operations of the primary employer, it is difficult to perceive how the pressure of picketing the entire situs is any less on the neutral employer merely because the picketing takes place at property owned by the struck employer. The application of the *Dry Dock* tests to limit the picketing effects to the employees of the employer against whom the dispute is directed carries out the "dual congressional objectives of preserving the right of labor organizations to bring pressure to bear on offending employers in primary labor disputes and of shielding unoffending employers and others from pressures in controversies not their own." *NLRB v. Denver Bldg. & Constr. Trades Council, supra*, 341 U.S. at 692 (1951).

III

From this necessary survey of the course of the Board's treatment of our problem, the precise nature of the issue before us emerges. With due regard to the relation between the Board's function and the scope of judicial review of its ruling, the question is whether the Board may apply the *Dry Dock* criteria so as to make unlawful picketing at a gate utilized exclusively by employees of independent contractors who work on the struck employers' premises. The effect of such a holding would not bar the union from picketing at all gates used by the employees, suppliers, and customers of the struck employer. Of course an employer may not, by removing all his employees from the situs of the strike, bar the union from publicizing its cause, *see Automotive, Petroleum, Local 618 v. NLRB*, 249 F.2d 332 (8th Cir. 1957). The basis of the Board's decision in this case would not remotely have that effect, nor any such tendency for the future.

The Union claims that if the Board's ruling is upheld, employers will be free to erect separate gates for deliveries, customers, and replacement workers which will be immunized from picketing. This fear is baseless. The key to the problem is found in the type of work that is being performed by those who use the separate gate. It is significant that the Board has since applied its rationale, first stated in the present case, only to situations where the independent workers were performing tasks unconnected to the normal operations of the struck employer—usually construction work on his buildings. In such situations, the indicated limitations on picketing activity respect the balance of competing interests that Congress has required the Board to enforce. On the other hand, if a separate gate were devised for regular plant deliveries, the barring of picketing at that location would make a clear invasion on traditional primary activity of appealing to neutral employees whose tasks aid the employer's everyday operations. . . .

In a case similar to the one now before us, the Court of Appeals for the Second Circuit sustained the Board in its application of § 8(b)(4)(A) to a separate-gate situation. "There must be a separate gate marked and set apart from other gates; the work done by the men who use the gate must be unrelated to the normal operations of the employer, and the work must be of a kind that would not, if done when the plant were engaged in its regular operations, necessitate curtailing those operations." *United Steelworkers v. NLRB*, 289 F.2d 591, 595 (2d Cir. 1961). These seem to us controlling considerations.

IV

The foregoing course of reasoning would require that the judgment below sustaining the Board's order be affirmed but for one consideration, even though this consideration may turn out not to affect the result. The legal path by which the Board and the Court of Appeals reached their decisions did not take into account that if Gate 3-A was in fact used by employees of independent contractors who performed conventional maintenance work necessary to the normal operations of General Electric, the use of the gate would have been a mingled one outside the bar of § 8(b)(4)(A). In short, such mixed use of this portion of the struck employer's premises would not bar picketing rights of the striking employees. While the record shows some such mingled use, it sheds no light on its extent. It may well turn out to be that the instances of these maintenance tasks were so insubstantial as to be treated by the Board as *de minimis*. We cannot here guess at the quantitative aspects of this problem. It calls for Board determination. For determination of the questions thus raised, the case must be remanded by the Court of Appeals to the Board.

Reversed.

THE CHIEF JUSTICE and MR. JUSTICE BLACK concur in the result.

Notes

1. *Applications*—In *United Steelworkers of America v. NLRB (Carrier Corp.)*, 376 U.S. 492 (1964), the Supreme Court unanimously upheld a union's picketing of a gate through which a railroad entered a fenced-in area alongside the primary employer's plant, the right-of-way being owned by the railroad. The Court stated that its decision was grounded on the doctrine enunciated in the 1961 *General Electric* reserved-gate picketing case; that is, if the duties of the secondary employees were connected with the normal operations of the struck plant, then the picketing would be primary activity within the protection of the primary-picketing proviso to § 8(b)(4)(B). In noting that "the location of the picketing is an important but not decisive factor," the Court said that in the instant case the "railroad gate adjoined company property and was in fact the railroad entrance gate to the Carrier plant." Therefore, "for the purposes of § 8(b)(4) picketing at a situs so proximate and related to the employer's day-to-day operations is no more illegal than if it had occurred at a gate owned by Carrier." Moreover, the Court held that "under § 8(b)(4) the distinction between primary and secondary picketing carried on at a separate gate maintained on the premises of the primary employer does not rest upon the peaceful or violent nature of the conduct, but upon the type of work being done by the picketed secondary employees." However, the Court cautioned that this did not mean that violent primary picketing is in all respects legal but only that it is not forbidden by the secondary boycott provisions.

Santa Fe operates a rail terminal at Richmond, California. Approximately 40% of the rail freight traffic at that terminal is intermodal freight transported to and from the rail terminal in truck trailers and containers. Santa Fe awarded Piggyback a subcontract to ramp and deramp the trailers and containers at the rail terminal.

This work had previously been performed by union members for a wholly owned subsidiary of Santa Fe. When Piggyback, a nonunion firm, allegedly reneged on a promise to hire the former union workers, the union began to picket and handbill Santa Fe's Richmond terminal. To insulate itself from the dispute between the union and Piggyback, Santa Fe designated Gate 1 as the sole entrance for employees, customers, and suppliers of Piggyback, with four other "neutral" gates being reserved for the exclusive use of Santa Fe employees, customers, and suppliers. Although Piggyback employees, customers, and suppliers only used Gate 1 and the union admitted that it had no labor dispute with Santa Fe, it picketed and handbilled all four neutral gates urging employees and customers entering the Santa Fe terminal either to honor the picket line or to cease all work related to Piggyback's operations. Union-represented drivers of UPS and other Santa Fe customers honored the picket line by refusing to deliver intermodal freight to the Richmond terminal. The Board and the court rejected a union request to apply the *General Electric* "related work" doctrine, because the picketing occurred at premises that were neither owned by the primary employer (Piggyback) nor proximate to the primary employer's premises. They instead applied the *Moore Dry Dock* common situs standards, and found a §8(b)(4)(B) violation due to the union's impermissible picketing of neutral gates that were not used by employees of the primary employer. *NLRB v. General Truck Drivers, Local 315 (Atchison, Topeka & Santa Fe Ry.)*, 20 F.3d 1017 (9th Cir.), *cert. denied*, 513 U.S. 946 (1994).

If a union struck a manufacturer and picketed the single gate used by both primary employees and contractor personnel who were performing unrelated construction work on the manufacturer's premises, could the pickets appeal to the contractor employees? *See Teamsters, Chauffeurs, Warehousemen & Helpers Local, etc. v. NLRB*, 293 F.2d 881 (D.C. Cir. 1961) (finding *General Electric* "related work" doctrine limited to separate gate situations, even when picketing union could easily distinguish between primary and secondary employees).

2. *First Amendment Issues*—*NLRB v. IAB Local 229*, 941 F.3d 902 (9th Cir. 2019), involved a wage dispute between Local 229 of the International Association of Bridge and Iron Workers and Western Concrete Pumping (WCP) over a parking lot construction that generated a work stoppage by the union. When Local 229 encouraged employees of Commercial Metals Company, which worked with WCP, to also stop work on the construction project, the Labor Board found a §8(b)(4)(B) violation. Local 229 appealed the Board's decision, claiming that application of §8(b)(4)(B) to such appeals to the employees of secondary firms violated the Free Speech section of the First Amendment, and the §8(c) free speech section of the NLRA. The Ninth Circuit rejected these claims, finding that the NLRA ban "carries no unconstitutional abridgement of free speech" since even peaceful picketing can violate that ban.

Problems

30. Anchortank is in the business of unloading chemicals from ships and storing them until they are ready for further shipment. The chemicals arrive by pipe, tank truck, barge, and oceangoing vessels and are stored until Anchortank transfers the material to a conveyance of the owner's choice for further transportation.

Anchortank's main storage facility abuts a public dock on the Gulf of Mexico. The dock is leased by Anchortank and two other businesses, which take turns using it. There are two ways to access the dock by land—a private ramp leading from Anchortank's property to the dock that is used solely by Anchortank employees, and a public ramp extending from the dock to a public access road. For ships coming to the dock, a pilot licensed by the state is required to direct ships from the gulf to the dock and then take the ships back out to sea. The pilots are members of the Master Mates and Pilots Union.

The Oil and Chemical Workers Union had been engaged in an organizing campaign at Anchortank. The Board held a representation election but had withheld certification because of alleged balloting irregularities and, as a result, Anchortank had neither recognized the union nor had it been certified by the Board. At that point, the union called a strike, and began to picket the main land entrance of the Anchortank facility with signs that read "OCWU on Strike, Unfair Labor Practices."

Soon afterward, the union began to picket the public dock from both the land and the water. It picketed the land entrance to the dock with the same signs that it used at the land entrance to Anchortank's facility, but did not picket when the dock was empty or when a company other than Anchortank was using it. The union picketed from the water in a small motorboat carrying a sign that read "To the Public: OCWU on Strike against Anchortank. OCWU does not have a dispute with any other employer." As a result of the motorboat picketing, the pilots refused to assist vessels scheduled for Anchortank's use of the public dock, and all shipments from the gulf ceased.

Did the OCWU engage in unlawful secondary behavior with either of its land-based pickets? What about the motorboat picket?

31. BeauSoleil, Inc., is a general contractor that specializes in the construction and maintenance of water treatment plants in areas adjacent to bayous in southern Louisiana. It just secured a major contract for the expansion of a filtration plant owned by Vermillion Parish. BeauSoleil decided to perform most of the project with its own workers, but subcontracted the more highly specialized piledriving work out to the Zydeco Brothers.

Zydeco employs members of the piledrivers union associated with the Building & Construction Trades Council of Southern Louisiana. BeauSoleil, however, does not; in fact, the Council has been engaged in a long-standing campaign to organize the workers at BeauSoleil, which remains one of the few nonunion construction outfits in the region. When the Council heard about the Vermillion Parish expansion, it sensed opportunity.

The Vermillion Parish filtration plant is surrounded by a chain-link fence, with two gates for vehicles—one on the north side of the plant, and another on the east side. As soon as BeauSoleil began work on the project, the Council began picketing both gates. The picketing took place during normal work hours, and the number of pickets ranged from one to three individuals. The picket signs listed the rates that should be paid on the job and carried the following message: "BeauSoleil does not have a signed agreement with the Building & Construction Trades Council of Southern Louisiana." At no time did any of the Zydeco workers cross the picket lines to perform work.

About a week into the job, BeauSoleil posted a sign on the east gate, reserving it for use by subcontractors and prohibiting its use by BeauSoleil employees and suppliers. The north gate, on the other hand, was designated for exclusive use by BeauSoleil workers and suppliers. When the picketers showed up that morning, they saw the newly marked gates and pulled the picket from the east gate. As a result, the piledriving crews employed by Zydeco entered the east gate and began working. About two hours later, the picket returned to the east gate, and Zydeco workers walked off. At that point, BeauSoleil decided to remove all of its workers from the site in the hope that Zydeco would be able to complete the piledriving work. Although the Council was informed of the absence of BeauSoleil employees, the picketing continued. And when the Zydeco crew again honored the picket line, BeauSoleil recalled its employees to complete the piledriving work themselves.

Did the Building & Construction Trades Council commit an unfair labor practice? Would your answer change if BeauSoleil was engaged in a construction project on land that it owned?

C. The Ally Doctrine

NLRB v. Business Machine & Office Appliance Mechanics Conference Board, IUE, Local 459 [Royal Typewriter Co.]

United States Court of Appeals, Second Circuit
228 F.2d 553 (1955), *cert. denied*, 351 U.S. 962 (1956)

LUMBARD, CIRCUIT JUDGE.

This case arose out of a labor dispute between the Royal Typewriter Company and the Business Machine and Office Appliance Mechanics Conference Board, Local 459, IUE-CIO, the certified bargaining agent of Royal's typewriter mechanics and other service personnel. The National Labor Relations Board now seeks enforcement of an order directing the Union to cease and desist from certain picketing and to post appropriate notices.

The findings of the Board, adequately supported by the record, disclose the following facts, about which there is no significant dispute. On about March 23, 1954, the Union, being unable to reach agreement with Royal on the terms of a contract, called the Royal service personnel out on strike. The service employees customarily repair typewriters either at Royal's branch offices or at its customers' premises. Royal has several arrangements under which it is obligated to render service to its customers. First, Royal's warranty on each new machine obligates it to provide free inspection and repair for one year. Second, for a fixed periodic fee Royal contracts to service machines not under warranty. Finally, Royal is committed to repairing typewriters rented from it or loaned by it to replace machines undergoing repair. Of course, in addition Royal provides repair service on call by non-contract users.

During the strike Royal differentiated between calls from customers to whom it owed a repair obligation and others. Royal's office personnel were instructed to tell the latter to call some independent repair company listed in the telephone directory. Contract customers, however, were advised to select such an independent from the directory, to have the repair made, and to send a receipted invoice to Royal for reimbursement for reasonable repairs within their agreement with Royal. Consequently many of Royal's contract customers had repair services performed by various independent repair companies. In most instances the customer sent Royal the unpaid repair bill and Royal paid the independent company directly. Among the independent companies paid directly by Royal for repairs made for such customers were Typewriter Maintenance and Sales Company and Tytell Typewriter Company....

During May, 1954, the Union picketed four independent typewriter repair companies who had been doing work covered by Royal's contracts pursuant to the arrangement described above. The Board found this picketing unlawful with respect to Typewriter Maintenance and Tytell. Typewriter Maintenance was picketed for about three days and Tytell for several hours on one day. In each instance the picketing, which was peaceful and orderly, took place before entrances used in common by employees, deliverymen and the general public. The signs read substantially as follows (with the appropriate repair company name inserted):

Notice to the Public Only Employees of Royal Typewriter Company on Strike

Tytell Typewriter Company Employees Are Being Used as Strikebreakers

Business Machine & Office Appliance Mechanics Union, Local 459, IUE-CIO

Both before and after this picketing, which took place in mid-May, Tytell and Typewriter Maintenance did work on Royal accounts and received payment directly from Royal. Royal's records show that Typewriter Maintenance's first voucher was passed for payment by Royal on April 20, 1954, and Tytell's first voucher was passed for payment on May 3, 1954. After these dates each independent serviced various of Royal's customers on numerous occasions and received payment directly from Royal....

On the above facts the Trial Examiner and the Board found that... the repair company picketing violated § 8(b)(4) of the National Labor Relations Act, 29 U.S.C. § 158(b)(4)....

We are of the opinion that the Board's finding with respect to the repair company picketing cannot be sustained. The independent repair companies were so allied with Royal that the Union's picketing of their premises was not prohibited by § 8(b)(4)(A).

We approve the "ally" doctrine which had its origin in a well reasoned opinion by Judge Rifkind in the *Ebasco case, Douds v. Architects, Engineers, Chemists & Technicians, Local 231*, 75 F. Supp. 672 (S.D.N.Y. 1948). Ebasco, a corporation engaged in the business of providing engineering services, had a close business relationship with Project, a firm providing similar services. Ebasco subcontracted some of its work to Project and when it did so Ebasco supervised the work of Project's employees and paid Project for the time spent by Project's employees on Ebasco's work plus a factor for overhead and profit. When Ebasco's employees went on strike, Ebasco transferred a greater percentage of its work to Project, including some jobs that had already been started by Ebasco's employees. When Project refused to heed the Union's requests to stop doing Ebasco's work, the Union picketed Project and induced some of Project's employees to cease work. On these facts Judge Rifkind found that Project was not "doing business" with Ebasco within the meaning of § 8(b)(4)(A) and that the Union had therefore not committed an unfair labor practice under that Section. He reached this result by looking to the legislative history of the Taft-Hartley Act and to the history of the secondary boycotts which it sought to outlaw. He determined that Project was not a person "wholly unconcerned in the disagreement between an employer and his employees" such as § 8(b)(4)(A) was designed to protect. The result has been described as a proper interpretation of the Act by its principal sponsor, Senator Taft, 95 Cong. Rec. 8709 (1949), and President Eisenhower in his January, 1954, recommendations to Congress for revision of the Act included a suggestion which would make this rule explicit.

Here there was evidence of only one instance where Royal contacted an independent (Manhattan Typewriter Service, not named in the complaint) to see whether it could handle some of Royal's calls. Apart from that incident there is no evidence that Royal made any arrangement with an independent directly. It is obvious, however, that what the independents did would inevitably tend to break the strike. As Judge Rifkind pointed out in the *Ebasco* case:

> The economic effect on Ebasco's employees was precisely that which would flow from Ebasco's hiring strikebreakers to work on its own premises.

And at 95 Cong. Rec. 8709 (1949) Senator Taft said:

> The spirit of the Act is not intended to protect a man who in the last case I mentioned is cooperating with a primary employer and taking his work and doing the work which he is unable to do because of the strike.

President Eisenhower's recommendation referred to above was to make it explicit "that concerted action against (1) an employer who is performing 'farmed-out' work for the account of another employer whose employees are on strike . . . will not be treated as a secondary boycott." Text of President's Message to Congress on Taft-Hartley Amendments, January 11, 1954. At least one commentator has suggested that the enactment of this change would add nothing to existing law. Cushman, Secondary Boycotts and the Taft-Hartley Law, 6 Syracuse L. Rev. 109, 121 (1954). Moreover, there is evidence that the secondary strikes and boycotts sought to be outlawed by § 8(b)(4)(A) were only those which had been unlawful at common law. 93 Cong. Rec. 3950, 4323 (1947) (Senator Taft), 2 Legislative History of Labor Management Relations Act, 1947, 1006, 1106. And although secondary boycotts were generally unlawful, it has been held that the common law does not proscribe union activity designed to prevent employers from doing the farmed-out work of a struck employer. *Iron Moulders Union v. Allis-Chalmers Co.*, 166 Fed. 45, 51 (7th Cir. 1908). Thus the picketing of the independent typewriter companies was not the kind of secondary activity which § 8(b)(4)(A) of the Taft-Hartley Act was designed to outlaw. Where an employer is attempting to avoid the economic impact of a strike by securing the services of others to do his work, the striking union obviously has a great interest, and we think a proper interest, in preventing those services from being rendered. This interest is more fundamental than the interest in bringing pressure on customers of the primary employer. Nor are those who render such services completely uninvolved in the primary strike. By doing the work of the primary employer they secure benefits themselves at the same time that they aid the primary employer. The ally employer may easily extricate himself from the dispute and insulate himself from picketing by refusing to do that work. A case may arise where the ally employer is unable to determine that the work he is doing is "farmed-out." We need not decide whether the picketing of such an employer would be lawful, for that is not the situation here. The existence of the strike, the receipt of checks from Royal, and the picketing itself certainly put the independents on notice that some of the work they were doing might be work farmed-out by Royal. Wherever they worked on new Royal machines they were probably aware that such machines were covered by a Royal warranty. But in any event, before working on a Royal machine they could have inquired of the customer whether it was covered by a Royal contract and refused to work on it if it was. There is no indication that they made any effort to avoid doing Royal's work. The Union was justified in picketing them in order to induce them to make such an effort. We therefore hold that an employer is not within the protection of § 8(b)(4)(A) when he knowingly does work which would otherwise be done by the striking employees of the primary employer and where this work is paid for by the primary employer pursuant to an arrangement devised and originated by him to enable him to meet his contractual obligations. The result must be the same whether or not the primary employer makes any direct arrangement with the employers providing the services. . . .

Enforcement of the Board's order is therefore in all respects denied.

Notes

1. *The Role of Employer Knowledge*—In *Teamsters, Local 563 (Fox Valley Material Suppliers Ass'n., Inc.)*, 176 N.L.R.B. 386 (1969), *enforced*, 76 L.R.R.M. 3002 (7th Cir.), *cert. denied*, 404 U.S. 912 (1971), the Labor Board indicated that a contractor could become an ally of a primary employer by "unknowingly" performing struck work for it. An employer has "the burden of determining whether or not it is engaged in neutral or ally type work." Here, the contractor was hired directly by the primary employer, and had reason to know the latter was involved in a strike.

2. *Common Ownership*—Under what circumstances will common ownership and control bring two businesses within the "ally doctrine"? In *Miami Newspaper Pressmen's Local 46 v. NLRB*, 322 F.2d 405 (D.C. Cir. 1963), the court enforced a Board order holding that common ownership of two newspapers—each, however, owned by a different corporation—was not alone sufficient to deprive either of them of its neutral status in a labor dispute involving the other. The court emphasized that the two papers were independently managed and transacted only a negligible amount of business between each other. *See also American Federation of Television & Radio Artists v. NLRB*, 462 F.2d 887 (D.C. Cir. 1972).

In *International Brotherhood of Teamsters v. NLRB*, 543 F.2d 1373 (D.C. Cir. 1976), *cert. denied*, 430 U.S. 967 (1977), the union had a labor dispute with the Mideast division of Vulcan. It then picketed the Chattanooga division of Vulcan, inducing its employees to strike in furtherance of the union's dispute with the Mideast division. The Board found, and the Court of Appeals agreed, that Chattanooga and Mideast were separate "persons" within the meaning of § 8(b)(4), since the divisions were operated as autonomous enterprises; thus the union's picketing was illegal. *See also Local 456, Teamsters & Chauffeurs Union*, 273 N.L.R.B. 516 (1984).

3. *Consequences of Finding an Ally Relationship*—When an ally relationship is found, employees of the secondary employer may be induced to stop work entirely and not to cease working on "hot" products destined to or from the primary employer, since that party is considered an extension of the primary employer. *See Shopmen Local 501, Iron Workers (Oliver Whyte Co.)*, 120 N.L.R.B. 856 (1958).

Problems

32. Greenrock, Inc., operated a quarry and sold stone to contractors across Idaho for use in construction projects. Traditionally, it sold its stone "f.o.b. [jobsite]," which meant that the quarry handled the delivery using its own trucks and assumed responsibility for the stone until it arrived at the jobsite. Greenrock's employees, including its truck drivers, are represented by the Quarry Workers Union. That union called a strike in support of its most recent bargaining demands.

During the strike, two of the contractors who bought Greenrock's stone—Bob the Builder, LLC, and Wendy's Construction Corp.—made arrangements with independent truckers to deliver the stone to their jobsites and deducted the truck charges from the contract price of the stone. The Quarry Workers Union sent pickets to both construction sites with signs that read:

"Don't Buy Products of Greenrock.

Unfair!

This picketing is directed only at employees of Greenrock, Inc."

The pickets sent to Bob the Builder's jobsite continued for some time after the trucks had left the jobsite, with one of the union representatives telling Bob that the union would "picket the stone wherever and whenever the opportunity presented itself." The pickets at Wendy's, however, only stayed up as long as the delivery trucks were at the jobsite, though the union representative told Wendy that she "wasn't going to get any more Greenrock stone without a picket." When the pickets appeared, some of the employees of both contractors quit work and did not return for some time. There were never any employees of Greenrock at either of the jobsites.

Did the Quarry Workers Union commit any unfair labor practices in its pickets of Bob's or Wendy's jobsites?

33. The Janitors' Union (JU) had its sights set on organizing the janitors who cleaned large commercial buildings. Such workers were usually employed by commercial cleaning services. Those cleaning services, in turn, had cleaning contracts with building owners or tenants.

JU's first target was a big building in the center of town owned by the Second Bank of America (SBA). SBA used the top half of the building for its own offices, and leased the bottom half of the building to two law firms. The leases provided that, among other things, SBA would keep the floors leased by the law firms clean. SBA contracted with Perfection Cleaners (PC), a nonunion cleaning company, to provide services to the entire building.

In the first week of its organizing campaign, JU set up a picket line on the public sidewalk in front of the SBA building's main entrance. The main entrance was used by almost everyone that worked in or did business with the owners or tenants of the building, including PC employees. The union picketed overnight, from 4:00 p.m. to 8:00 a.m., which were the usual working hours of the PC employees. The picket signs read as follows: "JU Protests PC's Use of Nonunion Labor."

By the end of the first week, PC's janitors decided to support the union and refused to cross the picket lines. Soon thereafter, the building started to get dirty, and the law firms demanded that SBA make good on its lease contracts to keep the offices clean. SBA, in turn, demanded that PC make good on its contract to keep the building clean. But PC couldn't get its employees, or any replacement workers, to cross the picket lines.

SBA and PC, both of whom faced liability on their respective leases and cleaning contract, decided to cut a deal. SBA agreed to have its own maintenance staff clean the entire building. In return, PC would pay the salaries of those SBA maintenance staff members assigned to cleaning duties. In addition, because SBA was concerned about the effect the picketing was having on its business and the business of the law firms, it set up a separate, back entrance for exclusive use by the SBA maintenance staff members assigned to cleaning duties. The back entrance was clearly marked as such, and no other employees, customers, or suppliers of SBA or the law firms used it. Thus, during the second week of JU's organizing campaign, SBA's maintenance staff cleaned the building.

When JU soon heard about the agreement between SBA and PC, it immediately began picketing both the front and back entrances to the building, 24 hours a day, with signs that read as follows: "JU Protests Practices that are Unfair to Labor." As a result of this second round of picketing, many employees, customers, and suppliers of both SBA and the law firms refused to cross the picket lines. SBA and the law firms began to suffer enormous financial losses.

Did the Janitors Union commit an unfair labor practice with its first or second week of picketing?

D. Consumer Picketing

NLRB v. Retail Clerks, Local 1001 [Safeco Title Insurance Co.]

Supreme Court of the United States
447 U.S. 607, 100 S. Ct. 2372, 65 L. Ed. 2d 377 (1980)

Mr. Justice Powell delivered the opinion of the Court.

The question is whether §8(b)(4)(ii)(B) of the National Labor Relations Act, 29 U.S.C. §158(b)(4)(ii)(B), forbids secondary picketing against a struck product when such picketing predictably encourages consumers to boycott a neutral party's business.

I

Safeco Title Insurance Co. underwrites real estate title insurance in the State of Washington. It maintains close business relationships with five local title companies. The companies search land titles, perform escrow services, and sell title insurance. Over 90% of their gross incomes derives from the sale of Safeco insurance. Safeco has substantial stockholdings in each title company, and at least one Safeco officer serves on each company's board of directors. Safeco, however, has no control over the companies' daily operations. It does not direct their personnel policies, and it never exchanges employees with them.

Local 1001 of the Retail Store Employees Union became the certified bargaining representative for certain Safeco employees in 1974. When contract negotiations between Safeco and the Union reached an impasse, the employees went on strike. The Union did not confine picketing to Safeco's office in Seattle. The Union also picketed each of the five local title companies. The pickets carried signs declaring that Safeco had no contract with the Union, and they distributed handbills asking consumers to support the strike by cancelling their Safeco policies.

Safeco and one of the title companies filed complaints with the National Labor Relations Board. They charged that the Union had engaged in an unfair labor practice by picketing in order to promote a secondary boycott against the title companies. The Board agreed. 226 N.L.R.B. 754 (1976). It found the title companies to be neutral in the dispute between Safeco and the Union. The Board then concluded that the Union's picketing violated §8(b)(4)(ii)(B) of the National Labor Relations Act. The Union had directed its appeal against Safeco insurance policies. But since the sale of those policies accounted for substantially all of the title companies' business, the Board found that the Union's action was "reasonably calculated to induce customers not to patronize the neutral parties at all." The Board therefore rejected the Union's reliance upon *NLRB v. Fruit Packers (Tree Fruits)*, 377 U.S. 58 (1964), which held that §8(b)(4)(ii)(B) allows secondary picketing against a struck product. It ordered the Union to cease picketing and to take limited corrective action.

The United States Court of Appeals for the District of Columbia Circuit set aside the Board's order. 194 U.S. App. D.C. 400, 600 F.2d 280 (1979) (en banc). The court agreed that the title companies were neutral parties entitled to the benefit of §8(b)(4)(ii)(B). It held, however, that *Tree Fruits* leaves neutrals susceptible to whatever consequences may flow from secondary picketing against the consumption of products produced by an employer involved in a labor dispute. Even when product picketing predictably encourages consumers to boycott a neutral altogether, the court concluded, §8(b)(4)(ii)(B) provides no protection.

We granted a writ of certiorari to consider whether the Court of Appeals correctly understood §8(b)(4)(ii)(B) as interpreted in *Tree Fruits*. Having concluded that the Court of Appeals misapplied the statute, we now reverse and remand for enforcement of the Board's order.

II

In *Tree Fruits*, the Court held that §8(b)(4)(ii)(B) does not prohibit all peaceful picketing at secondary sites. There, a union striking certain Washington fruit packers picketed large supermarkets in order to persuade consumers not to buy Washington apples. Concerned that a broad ban against such picketing might run afoul of the First Amendment, the Court found the statute directed to an "'isolated evil.'" The evil was use of secondary picketing "to persuade the customers of the secondary employer to cease trading with him in order to force him to cease dealing with, or to put pressure upon, the primary employer." Congress intended to protect secondary parties from pressures that might embroil them in the labor disputes of others, but not to shield them from business losses caused by a campaign that successfully persuades consumers "to boycott the primary employer's goods." Thus, the Court drew a distinction between picketing "to shut off all trade with the secondary employer unless he aids the union in its dispute with the primary employer" and picketing that "only persuades his customers not to buy the struck product." The picketing in that case, which "merely follow[ed] the struck product," did not "'threaten, coerce, or restrain'" the secondary party within the meaning of § 8(b)(4)(ii)(B).

Although *Tree Fruits* suggested that secondary picketing against a struck product and secondary picketing against a neutral party were "poles apart," the courts soon discovered that product picketing could have the same effect as an illegal secondary boycott. In *Hoffman ex rel. NLRB v. Cement Masons Local 337*, 468 F.2d 1187 (CA9 1972), cert. denied, 411 U.S. 986 (1973), for example, a union embroiled with a general contractor picketed the housing subdivision that he had constructed for a real estate developer. Pickets sought to persuade prospective purchasers not to buy the contractor's houses. The picketing was held illegal because purchasers "could reasonably expect that they were being asked not to transact any business whatsoever" with the neutral developer. "[W]hen a union's interest in picketing a primary employer at a 'one product' site [directly conflicts] with the need to protect . . . neutral employers from the labor disputes of others," Congress has determined that the neutrals' interests should prevail.[20]

Cement Masons highlights the critical difference between the picketing in this case and the picketing at issue in *Tree Fruits*. The product picketed in *Tree Fruits* was but one item among the many that made up the retailer's trade. If the appeal against such a product succeeds, the Court observed, it simply induces the neutral retailer to reduce his orders for the product or "to drop the item as a poor seller." The decline in sales attributable to consumer rejection of the struck product puts pressure upon the primary employer, and the marginal injury to the neutral retailer is purely incidental to the product boycott. The neutral therefore has little reason to become involved in the labor dispute. In this case, on the other hand, the title companies sell only the primary employer's product and perform the services associated with it. Secondary picketing against consumption of the primary product leaves responsive consumers no realistic option other than to boycott the title companies altogether. If the appeal succeeds, each company "stops buying the struck product, not because of a falling demand, but in response to pressure designed to inflict injury on [its] business generally." Thus, "the union does more than merely follow the struck product; it creates a separate dispute with the secondary employer." Such an expansion of labor discord was one of the evils that Congress intended § 8(b)(4)(ii)(B) to prevent.

As long as secondary picketing only discourages consumption of a struck product, incidental injury to the neutral is a natural consequence of an effective primary boycott. But the Union's secondary appeal against the central product sold by

---

20. [7] The so-called merged product cases also involve situations where an attempt to follow the struck product inevitably encourages an illegal boycott of the neutral party. See *K & K Construction Co. v. NLRB*, 592 F.2d 1228, 1231–1234 (CA3 1979); *American Bread Co. v. NLRB*, 411 F.2d 147, 154–155 (CA6 1969); *Honolulu Typographical Union No. 37 v. NLRB*, 401 F.2d 952, 954–955 (1968); Note, *Consumer Picketing and the Single-Product Secondary Employer*, 47 U. Chi. L. Rev. 112, 132–136 (1979).

the title companies in this case is "reasonably calculated to induce customers not to patronize the neutrals at all." 226 N.L.R.B., at 757.[21] The resulting injury to their businesses is distinctly different from the injury that the Court considered in *Tree Fruits*. Product picketing that reasonably can be expected to threaten neutral parties with ruin or substantial loss simply does not square with the language or the purpose of § 8(b)(4)(ii)(B). Since successful secondary picketing would put the title companies to a choice between their survival and the severance of their ties with Safeco, the picketing plainly violates the statutory ban on the coercion of neutrals with the object of "forcing or requiring [them] to cease ... dealing in the [primary] produc[t] ... or to cease doing business with" the primary employer. § 8(b)(4)(ii)(B); see *Tree Fruits*, 377 U.S., at 68.[22]

III

The Court of Appeals suggested that application of § 8(b)(4)(ii)(B) to the picketing in this case might violate the First Amendment. We think not. Although the Court recognized in *Tree Fruits* that the Constitution might not permit "a broad ban against peaceful picketing," the Court left no doubt that Congress may prohibit secondary picketing calculated "to persuade the customers of the secondary employer to cease trading with him in order to force him to cease dealing with, or to put pressure upon, the primary employer." Such picketing spreads labor discord by coercing a neutral party to join the fray. In *Electrical Workers v. NLRB*, 341 U.S. 694, 705 (1951), this Court expressly held that a prohibition on "picketing in furtherance of [such] unlawful objectives" did not offend the First Amendment. See *American Radio Ass'n v. Mobile S.S. Ass'n*, 419 U.S. 215, 229–231 (1974); *Teamsters Union v. Vogt, Inc.*, 354 U.S. 284 (1957). We perceive no reason to depart from that well-established understanding. As applied to picketing that predictably encourages

---

21. [8] ... We do not disagree with Mr. Justice Brennan's dissenting view that successful secondary product picketing may have no greater effect upon a neutral than a legal primary boycott. But when the neutral's business depends upon the products of a particular primary employer, secondary product picketing can produce injury almost identical to the harm resulting from an illegal secondary boycott. See generally Duerr, *Developing a Standard for Secondary Consumer Picketing*, 26 Lab. L.J. 585 (1975). Congress intended § 8(b)(4)(ii)(B) to protect neutrals from that type of coercion. Mr. Justice Brennan's view that the legality of secondary picketing should depend upon whether the pickets "urge only a boycott of the primary employer's product," would provide little or no protection. No well-advised union would allow secondary pickets to carry placards urging anything other than a product boycott. Section 8(b)(4)(ii)(B) cannot bear a construction so inconsistent with the congressional intention to prevent neutrals from becoming innocent victims in contests between others.

22. [11] The picketing in *Tree Fruits* and the picketing in this case are relatively extreme examples of the spectrum of conduct that the Board and the courts will encounter in complaints charging violations of § 8(b)(4)(ii)(B). If secondary picketing were directed against a product representing a major portion of a neutral's business, but significantly less than that represented by a single dominant product, neither *Tree Fruits* nor today's decision necessarily would control. The critical question would be whether, by encouraging customers to reject the struck product, the secondary appeal is reasonably likely to threaten the neutral party with ruin or substantial loss. Resolution of the question in each case will be entrusted to the Board's expertise.

consumers to boycott a secondary business, § 8(b)(4)(ii)(B) imposes no impermissible restrictions upon constitutionally protected speech.

Accordingly, the judgment of the Court of Appeals is reversed and the case is remanded with directions to enforce the National Labor Relations Board's order.

So ordered.

Mr. Justice Blackmun, concurring in part and concurring in the result.

I join Parts I and II of the Court's opinion, but not Part III. The Court's cursory discussion of what for me are difficult First Amendment issues presented by this case fails to take account of the effect of this Court's decision in *Police Department of Chicago v. Mosley*, 408 U.S. 92 (1972), on the question whether the National Labor Relations Act's content-based ban on peaceful picketing of secondary employers is constitutional. The failure to take *Mosley* into account is particularly ironic given that the Court today reaffirms and extends the principles of that case in *Carey v. Brown, ante*.

In *NLRB v. Fruit Packers*, 377 U.S. 58, 76 (1964), Mr. Justice Black wrote a concurring opinion in which he concluded that § 8(b)(4)(ii)(B) of the National Labor Relations Act "abridges freedom of speech and press in violation of the First Amendment." He said:

> In short, we have neither a case in which picketing is banned because the picketers are asking others to do something unlawful nor a case in which *all* picketing is, for reasons of public order, banned. Instead, we have a case in which picketing, otherwise lawful, is banned only when the picketers express particular views. The result is an abridgement of the freedom of these picketers to tell a part of the public their side of a labor controversy, a subject the free discussion of which is protected by the First Amendment.

Id., at 79. (Emphasis in original).

These views, central to Mr. Justice Black's vision of the First Amendment, were, one would have supposed until today, "accepted" by the Court in *Mosley*. See 408 U.S., at 98.

I have never been fully comfortable with *Mosley*'s equating all content selectivity in affording access to picketers with censorship. See *Mosley*, 408 U.S., at 102 (concurring statement). For this reason, I join today in Mr. Justice Rehnquist's dissenting opinion in *Carey v. Brown*. I concur in the result in this case, however, only because I am reluctant to hold unconstitutional Congress' striking of the delicate balance between union freedom of expression and the ability of neutral employers, employees, and consumers to remain free from coerced participation in industrial strife. My vote should not be read as foreclosing an opposite conclusion where another statutory ban on peaceful picketing, unsupported by equally substantial governmental interests, is at issue.

Mr. Justice Stevens, concurring in part and concurring in the result.

For the reasons stated by Mr. Justice Harlan and Mr. Justice Black in their separate opinions in *Tree Fruits*, 377 U.S. 58, 76, 80, I am persuaded that Congress intended to prohibit this secondary picketing, and for the reasons stated by Mr. Justice Powell, I agree that this case is not governed by *Tree Fruits*. I therefore join Parts I and II of the Court's opinion.

The constitutional issue, however, is not quite as easy as the Court would make it seem because, as Mr. Justice Black pointed out in *Tree Fruits*, "we have a case in which picketing, otherwise lawful, is banned only when the picketers express particular views." In other words, this is another situation in which regulation of the means of expression is predicated squarely on its content. *See Consolidated Edison Co. v. Public Service Commission*, 447 U.S. 530, 546 (Stevens, J., concurring). I agree with the Court that this content-based restriction is permissible but not simply because it is in furtherance of objectives deemed unlawful by Congress. That a statute proscribes the otherwise lawful expression of views in a particular manner and at a particular location cannot in itself totally justify the restriction. Otherwise the First Amendment would place no limit on Congress' power. In my judgment, it is our responsibility to determine whether the method or manner of expression, considered in context, justifies the particular restriction.

I have little difficulty in concluding that the restriction at issue in this case is constitutional. Like so many other kinds of expression, picketing is a mixture of conduct and communication. In the labor context, it is the conduct element rather than the particular idea being expressed that often provides the most persuasive deterrent to third persons about to enter a business establishment. In his concurring opinion in *Bakery Drivers Local v. Wohl*, 315 U.S. 769, 776–777, Mr. Justice Douglas stated:

> Picketing by an organized group is more than free speech, since it involves patrol of a particular locality and since the very presence of a picket line may induce action of one kind or another, quite irrespective of the nature of the ideas which are being disseminated. Hence those aspects of picketing make it the subject of restrictive regulation.

Indeed, no doubt the principal reason why handbills containing the same message are so much less effective than labor picketing is that the former depend entirely on the persuasive force of the idea.

The statutory ban in this case affects only that aspect of the union's effort to communicate its views that calls for an automatic response to a signal, rather than a reasoned response to an idea. And the restriction on picketing is limited in geographical scope to sites of neutrals in the labor dispute. Because I believe that such restrictions on conduct are sufficiently justified by the purpose to avoid embroiling neutrals in a third party's labor dispute, I agree that the statute is consistent with the First Amendment.

Mr. Justice Brennan, with whom Mr. Justice White and Mr. Justice Marshall join, dissenting.

NLRB v. Fruit Packers, 377 U.S. 58 (1964) (*Tree Fruits*), held that it was permissible under §8(b)(4)(ii)(B) of the National Labor Relations Act (NLRA) for a union involved in a labor dispute with a primary employer to conduct peaceful picketing at a secondary site with the object of persuading consumers to boycott the primary employer's product. Today's decision stunts *Tree Fruits* by declaring that secondary site picketing is illegal when the primary employer's product at which it is aimed happens to be the only product which the secondary retailer distributes. I dissent.

The NLRA does not place the secondary site off limits to all consumer picketing over the dispute with the primary employer. The Act only forbids a labor union from picketing to "coerce" a secondary firm into joining the union's struggle against the primary employer. §8(b)(4)(ii)(B). But inasmuch as the secondary retailer is, by definition, at least partially dependent upon the sale of the primary employer's goods, the secondary firm will necessarily feel the pressure of labor activity pointed at the primary enterprise. Thus, the pivotal problem in secondary site picketing cases is determining when the pressure imposed by consumer picketing is illegitimate, and therefore deemed to "coerce" the secondary retailer.

Tree Fruits addressed this problem by focusing upon whether picketing at the secondary site is directed at the primary employer's product, or whether it more broadly exhorts customers to withhold patronage from the full range of goods carried by the secondary retailer, *including those goods originating from nonprimary sources*. The *Tree Fruits* test reflects the distinction between economic damage sustained by the secondary firm solely by virtue of its dependence upon the primary employer's goods, and injuries inflicted upon interests of the secondary firm that are unrelated to the primary dispute — injuries that are calculated to influence the secondary retailer's conduct with respect to the primary dispute.

The former sort of harm is simply the result of union success in its conflict with the primary employer. The secondary firm is hurt only insofar as it entwines its economic fate with that of the primary employer by carrying the latter's goods. To be sure, the secondary site may be a battleground; but the secondary retailer, in its own right, is not enlisted as a combatant.

The latter kind of economic harm to the secondary firm, however, does not involve merely the necessary commercial fallout from the primary dispute. Appeals to boycott nonprimary goods sold by a secondary retailer place more at stake for the retailer than the risk it has assumed by handling the primary employer's product. Four considerations indicate that this broader pressure is highly undesirable from the standpoint of labor policy. First, nonprimary product boycotts distort the strength of consumer response to the primary dispute; the secondary retailer's decision to continue purchasing the primary employer's line becomes a function of consumer reaction to the primary conflict *amplified* by the impact of the boycott upon nonprimary goods. Second, although it seems proper to compel the producer or retailer of an individual primary product to internalize the costs of labor conflict engendered in the course of the item's production, a nonprimary product boycott may unfairly impose multiple costs upon the secondary retailer who does not wish to terminate his relationship with the primary employer. Third, nonprimary product boycotts attack interests of the secondary firm that are not derivative of the interests of the primary enterprise; because the retailer thereby becomes an independent disputant, the primary labor controversy may be aggravated and complicated. Finally, by affecting the sales on nonprimary goods handled by the secondary firm, the disruptive effect of the primary dispute is felt even by those businesses that manufacture and sell nonprimary products to the secondary retailer.

These sound reasons support *Tree Fruits*' conclusion that the legality of secondary site picketing should turn upon whether the union pickets urge only a boycott of the primary employer's product.[23] Concomitantly, *Tree Fruits* expressly rejected the notion that the coerciveness of picketing should depend upon the extent of loss suffered by the secondary firm through diminished purchases of the primary product. Nevertheless, the Court has now apparently abandoned the *Tree Fruits* approach, choosing instead to identify coerciveness with the percentage of the secondary firm's business made up by the primary product.

The conceptual underpinnings of this new standard are seriously flawed. The type of economic pressure exerted upon the secondary retailer by a primary product boycott is the same whatever the percentage of its business the primary product composes—in each case, a decline in sales at the secondary outlet may well lead either to a decrease in purchases from the primary employer or to product substitution. To be sure, the damaging effect of this pressure upon individual secondary firms will vary, but it is far from clear that the harmfulness of a primary product boycott is necessarily correlated with the percentage of the secondary firm's business the product constitutes. For example, a marginally profitable large retailer may handle a multiplicity of products, yet find the decrease in sales of a single, very profitable, primary product ruinous. A small healthy single product secondary retailer, on the other hand, might be able to sustain losses during a boycott, or substitute a comparable product.

Moreover, it is odd to treat the NLRA's prohibition against coercion of neutral secondary parties as a means of protecting single product secondary firms from the effects of a successful primary product boycott. A single product retailer will always suffer a degree of harm incident to a successful primary product boycott, whether or not the retailer becomes the focus of union activity. Thus, a ban on coercion of neutral businesses is mismatched to the goal of averting that harm. Far more sensible

---

23. [2] Because a "merged product" consists in part of nonprimary products, the prohibition of "merged product" boycotts follows as a matter of logic and of policy from *Tree Fruits*' primary product boycott test. Thus, "merged product" cases, *see, e.g., American Bread Co. v. NLRB*, 411 F.2d 147, 154 (CA6 1969), do not support the Court's view that certain purely primary product boycotts are proscribed by the National Labor Relations Act. In fact, "merged product" boycotts are wholly different than primary product boycotts against single product retailers. "Merged product" boycotts need not entail a total withholding of patronage from the secondary retailer, which may carry other, nonmerged, products.

would be to read the statutory ban on coercion of neutral parties as shielding secondary firms from the injuries that ensue precisely because of union conduct aimed at them. Nonprimary product boycotts fall within this category because they are specifically targeted at the secondary retailer.

Unlike the *Tree Fruits* rule, the test formulated by the Court in this case is not rooted in the policy of maintaining secondary firm neutrality with respect to the primary dispute. There is no ground to believe that a single product secondary retailer is more prone than a multiproduct retailer to react to a primary product boycott by joining the union in its struggle against the primary employer. On the contrary, the single product secondary firm is likely to be the primary employer's strongest ally because of the alignment of their respective economic interests. Nor is it especially unfair to subject the single product retailer to a primary product boycott. Whatever the percentage of a retailer's business that is constituted by a given item, the retailer necessarily assumes the risks of interrupted supply of declining sales that follow when labor conflict embroils the manufacturer of the item.

By shifting its focus from the nature of the product boycotted to the composition of the secondary firm's business, today's decision substitutes a confusing and unsteady standard for *Tree Fruits'* clear approach to secondary site picketing. Labor unions will no longer be able to assure that their secondary site picketing is lawful by restricting advocacy of a boycott to the primary product, as ordained by *Tree Fruits*. Instead, picketers will be compelled to guess whether the primary product makes up a sufficient proportion of the retailer's business to trigger the displeasure of the courts or the Labor Relations Board. Indeed, the Court's general disapproval of "[p]roduct picketing that reasonably can be expected to threaten neutral parties with ruin or substantial loss . . . ," *ante*, at 614, leaves one wondering whether unions will also have to inspect balance sheets to determine whether the primary product they wish to picket is too profitable for the secondary firm.

I continue to "disagree . . . that the test of 'to threaten, coerce, or restrain' . . . is whether [the secondary retailer] . . . suffered or was likely to suffer economic loss." *Tree Fruits, supra*, at 72. I would adhere to the primary product test. Accordingly, I dissent.

Note

Merged Products — May a union engage in consumer picketing of nonunion bread served in a restaurant or nonunion paper bags used by a grocery store? Is the restaurant or grocery store distributing a primary product, or has that product lost its identity and become fully integrated into the "products" of the secondary retailers? *Compare Teamsters, Local 327 (American Bread Co.)*, 170 N.L.R.B. 91 (1968), *enforced*, 411 F.2d 147 (6th Cir. 1969) (bread sold to restaurant "merged" into secondary meals and thus not subject to consumer picketing), *with Paperworkers, Local 832 (Duro Paper Bag Mfg. Co.)*, 236 N.L.R.B. 1525 (1978) (paper bags used by grocery store not "merged" into secondary retail products and thus subject to consumer appeals). The Sixth Circuit set aside the Board's *Duro Paper Bag* finding, since the court viewed the bags as being "merged" into the "products" of the secondary grocery store. *Kroger Co. v. NLRB*, 647 F.2d 634 (6th Cir. 1980).

Problem

34. Juicy Juicer, Inc., is a food processing company whose primary product is orange juice concentrate. Over the last two decades, as consumers switched from juices to soft drinks, many of Juicy Juicer's customers — supermarkets and retail juice establishments — canceled their contracts with the company. But one large customer, which now accounts for more than 90% of Juicy Juicer's business, remains. That customer is Ambrosia, Inc.

Ambrosia owns more than 500 retail juice outlets, most of which are in malls or sports arenas. The company's primary product is a light, frothy juice drink made by blending orange juice concentrate with sugar, milk, vanilla, and ice. Ambrosia gets about five percent of its orange juice concentrate from Juicy Juicer; the rest it buys from other suppliers. And, despite a general downturn in the juice business, Ambrosia continues to make money hand over fist (probably because it adds sugar to its drink and can therefore compete with soft drinks).

The employees at Juicy Juicer have been represented for decades by the Food Workers' Union (FWU). Juicy Juicer informally recognized the FWU for much of that time, but three years ago another union tried to woo the employees away from the FWU, and petitioned for an election. The NLRB held an election, which the FWU won handily, and certified the FWU as the exclusive bargaining representative of the Juicy Juicer employees.

About two months ago, Juicy Juicer fired two workers for holding home meetings with new employees to explain the benefits of joining the FWU. The FWU immediately called a strike and set about picketing the Juicy Juicer plant with signs that read: "FWU on Strike to Protest Juicy Juicer's Unfair Labor Practices." The strike went on for 35 days. Juicy Juicer, by hiring temporary replacements for the striking workers, was able to maintain production and fulfill its contractual obligations with its customers.

About a month ago, the FWU decided to turn up the heat, and asked Ambrosia to accept no further shipments from Juicy Juicer until the two workers were reinstated. When Ambrosia refused, the FWU began picketing in front of about 20 Ambrosia stores in the area. The picket signs read: "Ambrosia is Unfair for Supporting Juicy Juicer."

About two weeks ago, FWU called off its first picket in front of the Ambrosia Stores, but soon thereafter started a second round of picketing with signs that read: "FWU on strike against Juicy Juicer. We request that you not purchase orange drinks here because Ambrosia uses orange juice concentrate produced by Juicy Juicer." None of the other orange juice concentrate suppliers honored this picket line but, because many customers did honor the request, all of the picketed Ambrosia stores experienced a decline in sales.

Did the FWU commit an unfair labor practice by picketing Juicy Juicer? How about the first or second picket of Ambrosia?

E. Threats and Coercion of Secondary Employers

NLRB v. Servette, Inc., 377 U.S. 46, 84 S. Ct. 1098, 12 L. Ed. 2d 121 (1964). During a strike against Servette, a wholesale food distributor, the union requested managers of retail chain stores not to handle goods from Servette and threatened to pass out handbills asking the public not to buy named items distributed by Servette. The Supreme Court held that this conduct did not contravene § 8(b)(4)(i), since the union did not seek to induce the managers to cease work. It instead sought to have them make a managerial decision not to handle goods from Servette. The Court further found that the union's behavior did not "threaten, restrain, or coerce" the retailers within the meaning of § 8(b)(4)(ii). The handbilling would be a form of publicity protected by the proviso, and a union may threaten to do that which it may legally do. Even though a wholesaler like Servette does not make anything, it is a "producer," within the meaning of the publicity proviso to § 8(b)(4). If the manager "agreed" with the union not to handle the struck products, would their accord constitute a "hot cargo" contract under § 8(e)?

Notes

1. *Picketing versus Handbilling* — In *Tree Fruits*, the Supreme Court carefully distinguished between consumer *picketing* and consumer *handbilling*:

> Peaceful consumer picketing to shut off all trade with the secondary employer unless he aids the union in its dispute with the primary employer, is poles apart from such picketing which only persuades his customers not to buy the struck product. The proviso indicates no more than that the Senate conferees' constitutional doubts led Congress to authorize publicity other than picketing which persuades the customers of a secondary employer to stop all trading with him, but not such publicity which has the effect of cutting off his deliveries or inducing his employees to cease work. On the other hand, picketing which persuades the customers of a secondary employer to stop all trading with him was also to be barred.

In *Sheet Metal Workers Local 15*, 356 N.L.R.B. 1290 (2011), the Labor Board held that a union did not violate § 8(b)(4)(B) when it displayed a 16-foot inflated rat balloon on a flatbed trailer at a hospital work site of a secondary employer and a union member stood at one of the hospital's vehicle entrances displaying a union leaflet, because there was no picketing and the conduct in question was not "coercive" within the meaning of § 8(b)(4)(ii) since there was nothing likely to frighten or disturb patients or their families or that would otherwise interfere with hospital business.

Is there a fundamental difference between picketing and handbilling? *See generally* Note, *Picketing and Publicity Under Section 8(b)(4) of the LMRA*, 73 Yale L.J. 1265 (1964).

2. *What Counts as Picketing?* — Since picketing was expressly excluded from the protection of the publicity proviso to § 8(b)(4), problems have arisen as to whether or not certain union activities should be characterized as picketing. *Service & Maint. Employees, Local 399 (William J. Burns Detective Agency)*, 136 N.L.R.B. 431 (1962), illustrates the difficulties the Board sometimes encounters. Members Rodgers and Leedom were convinced that patrolling by 20 to 70 union members in an elliptical path in front of the main entrance to a sports arena constituted "picketing" and thus violated § 8(b)(4)(ii)(B), even though the patrollers distributed handbills but carried no placards. Members Brown and Fanning held that even if the patrolling did not constitute picketing, it did exceed the limits of allowable publicity since the patrollers, by virtue of their numbers and close-knit formation, imposed some element of physical restraint upon patrons of the arena. Chairman McCulloch voted to dismiss the complaint.

Carrying of placards is not necessarily "picketing." An essential element of picketing, the Board has said, is some form of confrontation between the pickets and employees, customers, or suppliers who are trying to enter the picketed premises. Union members patrolling shopping centers and the entrances to public buildings with signs advertising a labor dispute were found to be conducting "publicity other than picketing." *Chicago Typographical Union Local 16 (Alden Press, Inc.)*, 151 N.L.R.B. 1666 (1965).

3. *Other Coercive Behavior* — A labor organization violated § 8(b)(4)(ii)(B) when it refused to enter into a pre-hire agreement with a fencing company that sought to do business with a nonunion contractor. The union contended that its refusal to enter into such an agreement was not economically coercive, since the company had no prior union affiliation and had no right to union affiliation, even though a union-only subcontracting provision in the union's multiemployer bargaining agreement meant that this company would be barred from all union projects at a time when more union than nonunion work was available. The court found that such an economic impact was sufficient to create "coercion" within the meaning of § 8(b)(4)(ii). *Laborers Dist. Council of Minnesota & N. Dakota v. NLRB*, 688 F.3d 374 (8th Cir. 2012).

Edward J. DeBartolo Corp. v. Florida Gulf Coast Building Trades Council

Supreme Court of the United States
485 U.S. 568, 108 S. Ct. 1392, 99 L. Ed. 2d 645 (1988)

JUSTICE WHITE delivered the opinion of the Court.

This case centers around the respondent union's peaceful handbilling of the businesses operating in a shopping mall in Tampa, Florida, owned by petitioner, the Edward J. DeBartolo Corporation (DeBartolo). The union's primary labor dispute was with H. J. High Construction Company (High) over alleged substandard wages and fringe benefits. High was retained by the H. J. Wilson Company (Wilson) to construct a department store in the mall, and neither DeBartolo nor any of the other 85 or so mall tenants had any contractual right to influence the selection of contractors.

The union, however, sought to obtain their influence upon Wilson and High by distributing handbills asking mall customers not to shop at any of the stores in the mall "until the Mall's owner publicly promises that all construction at the Mall will be done using contractors who pay their employees fair wages and fringe benefits."[24] The handbills' message was that "[t]he payment of substandard wages not only diminishes the working person's ability to purchase with earned, rather than borrowed, dollars, but it also undercuts the wage standard of the entire community." The handbills made clear that the union was seeking only a consumer boycott against the other mall tenants, not a secondary strike by their employees. At all four entrances to the mall for about three weeks in December 1979, the union peacefully distributed the handbills without any accompanying picketing or patrolling.

After DeBartolo failed to convince the union to alter the language of the handbills to state that its dispute did not involve DeBartolo or the mall lessees other than Wilson and to limit its distribution to the immediate vicinity of Wilson's construction site, it filed a complaint with the National Labor Relations Board (Board), charging the union with engaging in unfair labor practices under §8(b)(4) of the National Labor Relations Act.... The Board's General Counsel issued a complaint, but the Board eventually dismissed it, concluding that the handbilling was protected by

---

24. [1] The handbill read:

PLEASE *DON'T SHOP AT EAST LAKE SQUARE MALL* PLEASE

The FLA. GULF COAST BUILDING TRADES COUNCIL, AFL-CIO is requesting that you do not shop at the stores in the East Lake Square Mall because of The Mall ownership's contribution to substandard wages.

The Wilson's Department Store under construction on these premises is being built by contractors who pay substandard wages and fringe benefits. In the past, the Mall's owner, The Edward J. DeBartolo Corporation, has supported labor and our local economy by insuring that the Mall and its stores be built by contractors who pay fair wages and fringe benefits. Now, however, and for no apparent reason, the Mall owners have taken a giant step backwards by permitting our standards to be torn down. The payment of substandard wages not only diminishes the working person's ability to purchase with earned, rather than borrowed, dollars, but it also undercuts the wage standard of the entire community. Since low construction wages at this time of inflation means decreased purchasing power, do the owners of East Lake Mall intend to compensate for the decreased purchasing power of workers of the community by encouraging the stores in East Lake Mall to cut their prices and lower their profits? CUT-RATE WAGES ARE NOT FAIR UNLESS MERCHANDISE PRICES ARE ALSO CUT-RATE.

We ask for your support in our protest against substandard wages. Please do not patronize the stores in the East Lake Square Mall until the Mall's owner publicly promises that all construction at the Mall will be done using contractors who pay their employees fair wages and fringe benefits. IF YOU MUST ENTER THE MALL TO DO BUSINESS, please express to the store managers your concern over substandard wages and your support of our efforts.

We are appealing only to the public—the consumer. We are not seeking to induce any person to cease work or to refuse to make deliveries.

the publicity proviso of § 8(b)(4). *Florida Gulf Coast Bldg. & Constr. Trades Council*, 252 N.L.R.B. 702 (1980). The Court of Appeals for the Fourth Circuit affirmed the Board, 662 F.2d 264 (1981), but this Court reversed in *Edward J. DeBartolo Corp. v. NLRB*, 463 U.S. 147 (1983). There, we concluded that the handbilling did not fall within the proviso's limited scope of exempting "publicity intended to inform the public that the primary employer's product is 'distributed by' the secondary employer" because DeBartolo and the other tenants, as opposed to Wilson, did not distribute products of High. *Id.*, at 155–157. Since there had not been a determination below whether the union's handbilling fell within the prohibition of § 8(b)(4), and, if so, whether it was protected by the First Amendment, we remanded the case.

On remand, the Board held that the union's handbilling was proscribed by § 8(b)(4)(ii)(B). 273 N.L.R.B. 1431 (1985). It stated that under its prior cases "handbilling and other activity urging a consumer boycott constituted coercion." *Id.*, at 1432. The Board reasoned that "[a]ppealing to the public not to patronize secondary employers is an attempt to inflict economic harm on the secondary employers by causing them to lose business," and "such appeals constitute 'economic retaliation' and are therefore a form of coercion." *Id.*, at 1432, n. 6. It viewed the object of the handbilling as attempting "to force the mall tenants to cease doing business with DeBartolo in order to force DeBartolo and/or Wilson's not to do business with High." *Id.*, at 1432. The Board observed that it need not inquire whether the prohibition of this handbilling raised serious questions under the First Amendment, for "the statute's literal language and the applicable case law require[d]" a finding of a violation. *Ibid.* Finally, it reiterated its longstanding position that "as a congressionally created administrative agency, we will presume the constitutionality of the Act we administer." *Ibid.* . . .

We agree with the Court of Appeals and respondents that this case calls for the invocation of the *Catholic Bishop* rule, for the Board's construction of the statute, as applied in this case, poses serious questions of the validity of § 8(b)(4) under the First Amendment. The handbills involved here truthfully revealed the existence of a labor dispute and urged potential customers of the mall to follow a wholly legal course of action, namely, not to patronize the retailers doing business in the mall. The handbilling was peaceful. No picketing or patrolling was involved. On its face, this was expressive activity arguing that substandard wages should be opposed by abstaining from shopping in a mall where such wages were paid. Had the union simply been leafletting the public generally, including those entering every shopping mall in town, pursuant to an annual educational effort against substandard pay, there is little doubt that legislative proscription of such leaflets would pose a substantial issue of validity under the First Amendment. The same may well be true in this case, although here the handbills called attention to a specific situation in the mall allegedly involving the payment of unacceptably low wages by a construction contractor.

That a labor union is the leafletter and that a labor dispute was involved does not foreclose this analysis. We do not suggest that communications by labor unions are never of the commercial speech variety and thereby entitled to a lesser degree of constitutional protection. The handbills involved here, however, do not appear to be typical commercial speech such as advertising the price of a product or arguing its merits, for they pressed the benefits of unionism to the community and the dangers of inadequate wages to the economy and the standard of living of the populace. Of course, commercial speech itself is protected by the First Amendment, *Virginia Pharmacy Bd. v. Virginia Citizens Consumer Council, Inc.*, 425 U.S. 748, 762 (1976), and however these handbills are to be classified, the Court of Appeals was plainly correct in holding that the Board's construction would require deciding serious constitutional issues. . . .

The Board was urged to construe the statute in light of the asserted constitutional considerations, but thought that it was constrained by its own prior authority and cases in the courts of appeals, as well as by the express language of the Act, to hold that § 8(b)(4) must be construed to forbid the handbilling involved here. Even if this construction of the Act were thought to be a permissible one, we are quite sure that in light of the traditional rule followed in *Catholic Bishop*, we must independently inquire whether there is another interpretation, not raising these serious constitutional concerns, that may fairly be ascribed to § 8(b)(4)(ii). This the Court has done in several cases. . . .

We follow this course here and conclude, as did the Court of Appeals, that the section is open to a construction that obviates deciding whether a congressional prohibition of handbilling on the facts of this case would violate the First Amendment.

The case turns on whether handbilling such as involved here must be held to "threaten, coerce, or restrain any person" to cease doing business with another, within the meaning of § 8(b)(4)(ii)(B). We note first that "induc[ing] or encourag[ing]" employees of the secondary employer to strike is proscribed by § 8(b)(4)(i). But more than mere persuasion is necessary to prove a violation of § 8(b)(4)(ii): that section requires a showing of threats, coercion, or restraints. Those words, we have said, are "nonspecific, indeed vague," and should be interpreted with "caution" and not given a "broad sweep." *Drivers, supra*, at 290; and in applying § 8(b)(1)(A) they were not to be construed to reach peaceful recognitional picketing. Neither is there any necessity to construe such language to reach the handbills involved in this case. There is no suggestion that the leaflets had any coercive effect on customers of the mall. There was no violence, picketing, or patrolling and only an attempt to persuade customers not to shop in the mall.

The Board nevertheless found that the handbilling "coerced" mall tenants and explained in a footnote that "[a]ppealing to the public not to patronize secondary employers is an attempt to inflict economic harm on the secondary employers by causing them to lose business. As the case law makes clear, such appeals constitute 'economic retaliation' and are therefore a form of coercion." 273 N.L.R.B., at 1432, n. 6. Our decision in *Tree Fruits*, however, makes untenable the notion that *any* kind of handbilling, picketing, or other appeals to a secondary employer to cease doing business with the employer involved in the labor dispute is "coercion" within the meaning of § 8(b)(4)(ii)(B) if it has some economic impact on the neutral. In that case, the union picketed a secondary employer, a retailer, asking the public not to buy a product produced by the primary employer. We held that the impact of this picketing was not coercion within the meaning of § 8(b)(4) even though, if the appeal succeeded, the retailer would lose revenue.

NLRB v. Retail Store Employees, 447 U.S. 607 (1980) (*Safeco*), in turn, held that consumer picketing urging a general boycott of a secondary employer aimed at causing him to sever relations with the union's real antagonist was coercive and forbidden by § 8(b)(4). It is urged that *Safeco* rules this case because the union sought a general boycott of all tenants in the mall. But "picketing is qualitatively 'different from other modes of communication,'" *Babbitt v. Farm Workers*, 442 U.S. 289, 311, n. 17 (1979) (quoting *Hughes v. Superior Court*, 339 U.S. 460, 465 (1950)), and *Safeco* noted that the picketing there actually threatened the neutral with ruin or substantial loss. As JUSTICE STEVENS pointed out in his concurrence in *Safeco, supra*, at 619, picketing is "a mixture of conduct and communication" and the conduct element "often provides the most persuasive deterrent to third persons about to enter a business establishment." Handbills containing the same message, he observed, are "much less effective than labor picketing" because they "depend entirely on the persuasive force of the idea." *Ibid*. . . .

In *Tree Fruits*, we could not discern with the "requisite clarity" that Congress intended to proscribe all peaceful consumer picketing at secondary sites. There is even less reason to find in the language of § 8(b)(4)(ii), standing alone, any clear indication that handbilling, without picketing, "coerces" secondary employers. The loss of customers because they read a handbill urging them not to patronize a business, and not because they are intimidated by a line of picketers, is the result of mere persuasion, and the neutral who reacts is doing no more than what its customers honestly want it to do.

The Board argues that our first *DeBartolo* case goes far to dispose of this case because there we said that the only nonpicketing publicity "exempted from the prohibition is publicity intended to inform the public that the primary employer's product is 'distributed by' the secondary employer." 463 U.S., at 155. We also indicated that if the handbilling were protected by the proviso, the distribution requirement would be without substantial practical effect. *Id.*, at 157. But we obviously did not there conclude or indicate that the handbills were covered by § 8(b)(4)(ii), for we remanded the case on this very issue. *Id.*, at 157–158.

It is nevertheless argued that the second proviso to § 8(b)(4) makes clear that that section, as amended in 1959, was intended to proscribe nonpicketing appeals such as handbilling urging a consumer boycott of a neutral employer. . . . By its terms, the proviso protects nonpicketing communications directed at customers of a distributor of goods produced by an employer with whom the union has a labor dispute. Because handbilling and other consumer appeals not involving such a distributor are not within the proviso, the argument goes, those appeals must be considered coercive within the meaning of § 8(b)(4)(ii). Otherwise, it is said, the proviso is meaningless, for if handbilling and like communications are never coercive and within the reach of the section, there would have been no need whatsoever for the proviso.

This approach treats the proviso as establishing an exception to a prohibition that would otherwise reach the conduct excepted. But this proviso has a different ring to it. It states that § 8(b)(4) "shall not be construed" to forbid certain described nonpicketing publicity. That language need not be read as an exception. It may indicate only that without the proviso, the particular nonpicketing communication the proviso protects might have been considered to be coercive, even if other forms of publicity would not be. Section 8(b)(4), with its proviso, may thus be read as not covering nonpicketing publicity, including appeals to customers of a retailer as they approach the store, urging a complete boycott of the retailer because he handles products produced by nonunion shops.

The Board's reading of § 8(b)(4) would make an unfair labor practice out of any kind of publicity or communication to the public urging a consumer boycott of employers other than those the proviso specifically deals with. On the facts of this case, newspaper, radio, and television appeals not to patronize the mall would be prohibited; and it would be an unfair labor practice for unions in their own meetings to urge their members not to shop in the mall. Nor could a union's handbills simply urge not shopping at a department store because it is using a nonunion contractor, although the union could safely ask the store's customers not to buy there because it is selling mattresses not carrying the union label. It is difficult, to say the least, to fathom why Congress would consider appeals urging a boycott of a distributor of a nonunion product to be more deserving of protection than nonpicketing persuasion of customers of other neutral employers such as that involved in this case.

Neither do we find any clear indication in the relevant legislative history that Congress intended § 8(b)(4)(ii) to proscribe peaceful handbilling, unaccompanied by picketing, urging a consumer boycott of a neutral employer. That section was one of several amendments to the NLRA enacted in 1959 and aimed at closing what were thought to be loopholes in the protections to which secondary employers were entitled. We recounted the legislative history in *Tree Fruits* and *NLRB v. Servette, Inc.*, 377 U.S. 46 (1964), and the Court of Appeals carefully reexamined it in this case and found "no affirmative intention of Congress clearly expressed to prohibit nonpicketing labor publicity." 796 F.2d, at 1346. For the following reasons, for the most part expressed by the Court of Appeals, we agree with that conclusion.

First, among the concerns of the proponents of the provision barring threats, coercion, or restraints aimed at secondary employers was consumer boycotts of neutral employers carried out by picketing. At no time did they suggest that merely handbilling the customers of the neutral employer was one of the evils at which their proposals were aimed. Had they wanted to bar any and all nonpicketing appeals, through newspapers, radio, television, handbills or otherwise, the debates and discussions would surely have reflected this intention. Instead, when asked, Congressman Griffin, co-sponsor of the bill that passed the House, stated that the bill covered boycotts carried out by picketing neutrals but would not interfere with the constitutional right of free speech. 105 Cong. Rec. 15673, 2 Leg. Hist. 1615.

Second, the only suggestions that the ban against coercing secondary employers would forbid peaceful persuasion of customers by means other than picketing came from the opponents of any proposals to close the perceived loopholes in § 8(b)(4). Among their arguments in both the House and the Senate was that picketing and handbilling a neutral employer to force him to cease dealing in the products of an employer engaged in labor disputes, appeals which were then said to be legal, would be forbidden by the proposal that became § 8(b)(4)(ii). The prohibition, it was said, "reaches not only picketing but leaflets, radio broadcasts, and newspaper advertisements, thereby interfering with freedom of speech." 105 Cong. Rec. 15540, 2 Leg. Hist. 1576. The views of opponents of a bill with respect to its meaning, however, are not persuasive. . . .

Third, § 8(b)(4)(ii) was one of the amendments agreed upon by a House-Senate Conference on the House's Landrum-Griffin bill and the Senate's Kennedy-Ervin bill. An analysis of the Conference bill was presented in the House by Representative Griffin and in the Senate by Senator Goldwater. With respect to appeals to consumers, the summary said that the House provision prohibiting secondary consumer picketing was adopted but "with clarification that other forms of publicity are not prohibited." 105 Cong. Rec. 18706, Leg. Hist. 1454 (Sen. Goldwater); 105 Cong. Rec. 18022, Leg. Hist. 1712 (Rep. Griffin). The clarification referred to was the second proviso to § 8(b)(4). See *supra*. The Court of Appeals held that although the proviso was itself confined to advising the customers of an employer that the latter was distributing a product of another employer with whom the union had a labor dispute, the legislative history did not foreclose understanding the proviso as a clarification of the meaning of § 8(b)(4) rather than an exception to a general ban on consumer publicity. We agree with this view.

In addition to the summary presented by Senator Goldwater and Congressman Griffin, Senator Kennedy, the Chairman of the Conference Committee, in presenting the Conference Report on the Senate floor, 105 Cong. Rec. 17898–17899, 2 Leg. Hist. 1431–1432, stated that under the amendments as reported by the Conference Committee, a "union can hand out handbills at the shop, can place advertisements in newspapers, can make announcements over the radio, and can carry on all publicity short of having ambulatory picketing in front of a secondary site." And he assured Senator Goldwater that union buy-America campaigns — that is, publicity requesting that consumers not buy foreign-made products, even though there is no ongoing labor dispute with the actual producer — would not be prohibited by the section.

Senator Kennedy included in his statement, however, the following:

> Under the Landrum-Griffin Bill it would have been impossible for a union to inform the customers of a secondary employer that that employer or

store was selling goods which were made under racket conditions or sweatshop conditions, or in a plant where an economic strike was in progress. We were not able to persuade the House conferees to permit picketing in front of that secondary shop, but we were able to persuade them to agree that the union shall be free to conduct informational activity short of picketing.

105 Cong. Rec. 17898–17899, 2 Leg. Hist. 1432.

The Board relies on this part of the Senator's exposition as an authoritative interpretation of the words "threaten, coerce, or restrain" and argues that except as saved by the express language of the proviso, informational appeals to customers not to deal with secondary employers are unfair labor practices. The Senator's remarks about the meaning of § 8(b)(4)(ii) echoed his views, and that of others, expressed in opposing and defeating in the Senate any attempts to give more protection to secondary employers from consumer boycotts, whether carried out by picketing or nonpicketing means. And if the proviso added in conference were an exception rather than a clarification, it surely would not follow, as the Senator said, that under the Conference bill, unions would be free to "conduct informational activity short of picketing" and could handbill, advertise in newspapers, and carry out all publicity short of ambulatory picketing in front of a secondary site. Nor would buy-America appeals be permissible, for they do not fall within the proviso's terms. At the very least, the Kennedy-Goldwater colloquy falls far short of revealing a clear intent that all nonpicketing appeals to customers urging a secondary boycott were unfair practices unless protected by the express words of the proviso. Nor does that exchange together with the other bits of legislative history relied on by the Board rise to that level.

In our view, interpreting § 8(b)(4) as not reaching the handbilling involved in this case is not foreclosed either by the language of the section or its legislative history. That construction makes unnecessary passing on the serious constitutional questions that would be raised by the Board's understanding of the statute. Accordingly, the judgment of the Court of Appeals is

Affirmed.

JUSTICE O'CONNOR and JUSTICE SCALIA concur in the judgment.

JUSTICE KENNEDY took no part in the consideration or decision of this case.

Note

Banners—*United Bhd. of Carpenters & Joiners of Am., Local Union 1506*, 355 N. LR.B. 797 (2010), involved protest activity by a construction union at the site of several businesses at which nonunion contractors were performing construction work. The union supporters displayed large stationary banners in front of these secondary businesses protesting the substandard wages and benefits paid by the contractors who were explicitly identified as the targets of the union activity. A closely divided Labor Board found that the use of such stationary banners unaccompanied by any ambulatory or confrontational activities did not contravene §8(b)(4)(ii)(B), under the rationale of *Edward DeBartolo*, due to the lack of any "coercion." Nonetheless, if secondary union handbilling is accompanied by picketing or involves other confrontational tactics, §8(b)(4)(ii)(B) liability is likely to be found. *See Boxhorn's Big Muskego Gun Club, Inc. v. Electrical Workers Local 494*, 798 F.2d 1016 (7th Cir. 1986). The court also found impermissible the fact the handbills failed to disclose the actual relationship between the handbilled firm and the primary employer.

The Board continues to find stationary bannering to be non-coercive and analytically distinct from picketing, even where the banners are quite effective and have an economic impact similar to that of a traditional picket line. In *Carpenters & Joiners of Am. Local 1827*, 357 N.L.R.B. 415 (2011), the Board found no violation of §8(b)(4)(ii)(B) where the union displayed a large banner that proclaimed "shame" on a neutral employer during a labor dispute with the primary, a construction company. The banners were located 24 to 100 feet from building entrances and did not block access to the facility. *See also Southwest Reg'l Council of Carpenters (New Star Gen. Contractors Inc.)*, 356 N.L.R.B. 613 (2011) (finding bannering at construction site designed to shame secondary employers not violative of §8(b)(4)(i)(B) where there was no inducement directed at workers to refuse to work or to stop delivering goods at the job site).

Problem

35. It was the holiday season, but the workers at Duff Beverages, one of the largest beer companies in the country, were not in a celebratory mood. The union that represented them—the United Brewery and Distillery Workers—was in contract negotiations with Duff. And despite five straight years of record profits, the company was balking at the union's latest proposal of a three percent wage increase for each of the next four years.

The holidays were a particularly profitable time for Duff. For that reason, the union decided to turn up the heat by organizing several shopping trips to local retail establishments that sold Duff beer. In each case, the union placed a giant, inflatable Grinch drinking a Duff beer on the public sidewalk outside the designated store (the Grinch symbolized greediness during the holiday season). Union members then descended in droves upon the store and engaged in multiple rounds of penny-ante purchasing, buying small, inexpensive items such as packs of chewing gum or bags of potato chips and paying for them with large denomination bills. This led to overcrowded parking lots, congested aisles, long checkout lines, and an exodus of regular customers. While some of the group shoppers were wearing t-shirts with pictures of the Grinch and union buttons, they did not engage in any other expressive activity within the stores. All of the group shopping trips occurred in the late afternoon (a prime time in the retail store trade) on the days before Christmas.

Did any of the union's activities at the local retail stores constitute unfair labor practices?

F. Hot Cargo Agreements

United Brotherhood of Carpenters & Joiners, Local 1976 v. NLRB [Sand Door]

Supreme Court of the United States
357 U.S. 93, 78 S. Ct. 1011, 2 L. Ed. 2d 1186 (1958)

MR. JUSTICE FRANKFURTER delivered the opinion of the Court.

. . . .

[This case] arises out of a labor dispute between carpenter unions and an employer engaged in the building construction trade in Southern California. The Sand Door and Plywood Company is the exclusive distributor in Southern California of doors manufactured by the Paine Lumber Company of Oshkosh, Wisconsin. Watson and Dreps are millwork contractors who purchase doors from Sand. Havstad and Jensen are the general contractors who were at the time of the dispute involved, engaged in the construction of a hospital in Los Angeles. Havstad and Jensen are parties to a master labor agreement negotiated with the United Brotherhood of Carpenters and Joiners of America on behalf of its affiliated district councils and locals including petitioner unions. This agreement, comprehensively regulating the labor relations of Havstad and Jensen and its carpenter employees, includes a provision that, "workmen shall not be required to handle nonunion material."

In August, 1954, doors manufactured by Paine and purchased by Sand were delivered to the hospital construction site by Watson and Dreps. On the morning of August 17, Fleisher, business agent of petitioner Local 1976, came to the construction site and notified Steinert, Havstad and Jensen's foreman, that the doors were nonunion and could not be hung. Steinert therefore ordered employees to cease handling the doors. When Nicholson, Havstad, and Jensen's general superintendent, appeared on the job and asked Fleisher why the workers had been prevented from handling the doors, he stated that they had been stopped until it could be determined whether the doors were union or nonunion. Subsequent negotiations between officers of Sand and the Union failed to produce an agreement that would permit the doors to be installed. . . .

. . . The employees' action may be described as a "strike or concerted refusal," and there is a "forcing or requiring" of the employer, even though there is a hot cargo provision. The realities of coercion are not altered simply because it is said that the employer is forced to carry out a prior engagement rather than forced now to cease doing business with another. A more important consideration, and one peculiarly within the cognizance of the Board because of its closeness to and familiarity with the practicalities of the collective bargaining process, is the possibility that the contractual provision itself may well not have been the result of choice on the employer's part free from the kind of coercion Congress has condemned. It may have been forced upon him by strikes that, if used to bring about a boycott when the union is engaged in a dispute with some primary employer, would clearly be prohibited by the act. Thus, to allow the union to invoke the provision to justify conduct that in the absence of such a provision would be a violation of the statute might give it the means to transmit to the moment of boycott, through the contract, the very pressures from which Congress has determined to relieve secondary employers.

Thus inducements of employees that are prohibited under § 8(b)(4)(A) in the absence of a hot cargo provision are likewise prohibited when there is such a provision. The Board has concluded that a union may not, on the assumption that the employer will respect his contractual obligation, order its members to cease handling goods, and that any direct appeal to the employees to engage in a strike or concerted refusal to handle goods is proscribed. This conclusion was reached only after considerable experience with the difficulty of determining whether an employer has in fact acquiesced in a boycott, whether he did or did not order his employees to handle the goods, and the significance of an employer's silence. Of course if an employer does intend to observe the contract, and does truly sanction and support the boycott, there is no violation of § 8(b)(4)(A). A voluntary employer boycott does not become prohibited activity simply because a hot cargo clause exists. But there remains the question whether the employer has in fact truly sanctioned and supported the boycott, and whether he has exercised the choice contemplated by the statute. The potentiality of coercion in a situation where the union is free to approach the employees and induce them to enforce their contractual rights by self-help is very great. Faced with a concerted work stoppage already in progress, an employer may find it substantially more difficult than he otherwise would to decide that business should go on as usual and that his employees must handle the goods. His "acquiescence" in the boycott may be anything but free. In order to give effect to the statutory policy, it is not unreasonable to insist, as the Board has done, that even when there is a contractual provision the union must not appeal to the employees or induce them not to handle the goods. Such a rule expresses practical judgment on the effect of union conduct in the framework of actual labor disputes and what is necessary to preserve to the employer the freedom of choice that Congress has decreed. On such a matter the judgment of the Board must be given great weight, and we ought not set against it our estimate of the relevant factors.

There is no occasion to consider the invalidity of hot cargo provisions as such. The sole concern of the Board in the present cases was whether the contractual provision could be used by the unions as a defense to a charge of inducing employees to strike or refuse to handle goods for objectives proscribed by § 8(b)(4)(A). As we have said, it cannot be so used. But the Board has no general commission to police collective bargaining agreements and strike down contractual provisions in which there is no element of an unfair labor practice. Certainly the voluntary observance of a hot cargo provision by an employer does not constitute a violation of § 8(b)(4)(A), and its mere execution is not, contrary to the suggestion of two members of the Board in the *Genuine Parts* case, Truck Drivers, 119 N.L.R.B. No. 53, *prima facie* evidence of prohibited inducement of employees. It does not necessarily follow from the fact that the unions cannot invoke the contractual provision in the manner in which they sought to do so in the present cases that it may not, in some totally different context not now before the Court still have legal radiations affecting the relations between the parties. All we need now say is that the contract cannot be enforced by the means specifically prohibited in § 8(b)(4)(A).

Mr. Justice Douglas, with whom The Chief Justice and Mr. Justice Black concur, dissenting. . . .

The provision of the collective bargaining agreement in the *Carpenters* case is typical of those in issue here:

> Workmen shall not be required to handle non-union material.

That provision was bargained for like every other claim in the collective agreement. It was agreed to by the employer. How important it may have been to the parties—how high or low in their scale of values—we do not know. But on these records it was the product of bargaining, not of coercion. The Court concedes that its inclusion in the contracts may not be called "forcing or requiring" the employer to cease handling other products within the meaning of the act. Enforcing the collective bargaining agreement—standing by its terms—is not one of the coercive practices at which the act was aimed. Enforcement of these agreements is conducive to peace. Disregard of collective agreements—the flouting of them—is disruptive. That was the philosophy of the *Conway's Express* decision of the Labor Board, 87 N.L.R.B. 972, *aff'd sub nom. Rabouin v. NLRB*, 195 F.2d 906 (2d Cir. 1952), and I think it squares with the act.

The present decision is capricious. The boycott is lawful if the employer agrees to abide by this collective bargaining agreement. It is unlawful if the employer reneges.

The hostile attitude of labor against patronizing or handling "unfair" goods goes deep into our history. It is not peculiarly American, though it has found expression in various forms in our history from the refusal of Americans to buy British tea, to the refusal of Abolitionists to buy slave-made products, to the refusal of unions to work on convict-made or on other nonunion goods. Unions have adhered to the practice because of their principle of mutual aid and protection. Section 7 of the act, indeed, recognizes that principle in its guarantee that "Employees shall have the right . . . to engage in . . . concerted activities for the purpose of collective bargaining or other mutual aid or protection." We noticed in *Apex Hosiery Co. v. Leader*, 310 U.S. 469, 503 (1940), that the elimination of "competition from non-union made goods" was a legitimate labor objective.

The reason an employer may also agree to that phase of union policies, the reason he may acquiesce in the inclusion of such a clause in a particular collective agreement, may only be surmised. Perhaps he sees eye to eye with the union. Perhaps he receives important concessions in exchange for his assistance to the union.

Certain it is that where he voluntarily agrees to the "unfair" goods clause he is not forced or coerced in the statutory sense. . . .

We act today more like a Committee of the Congress than the Court. We strain to outlaw bargaining contracts long accepted, long used. Perhaps these particular provisions have evils in them that should be declared contrary to the public interest. They are, however, so much a part of the very fabric of collective bargaining that we should leave this policy-making to Congress and not rush in to undo what a century or more of experience has imbedded into labor-management agreements. I have not found a word of legislative history which even intimates that these "unfair" goods provisions of collective bargaining agreements are unlawful.

Notes

1. *Legislative Action*—Congress took drastic action with respect to "hot cargo" agreements in the amendments to the LMRA included in the Labor-Management Reporting and Disclosure Act of 1959. The House members of the conference committee made the following explanation:

> The Senate bill amends § 8 of the National Labor Relations Act, as amended, by adding at the end thereof a new subsection (e) which makes it an unfair labor practice for any labor organization and any employer who is a common carrier subject to part II of the Interstate Commerce Act to enter into any contract or agreement, express or implied, whereby such employer ceases or refrains or agrees to cease or refrain from handling, using, or transporting any of the products of any other employer, or to cease doing business with the same.

> The House amendment amends § 8 of the National Labor Relations Act, as amended, by adding at the end thereof a new subsection (e) to make it an unfair labor practice for any labor organization and any employer to enter into any contract or agreement, express or implied, whereby such employer ceases or refrains or agrees to cease or refrain from handling, using, selling, transporting or otherwise dealing in any of the products of any other employer, or to cease doing business with any other person. The House amendment also makes any such agreement heretofore or hereafter executed unenforcible and void.

> The conference committee adopted the House amendment but added three provisos. The first proviso specifies:

> that nothing in this subsection (e) shall apply to an agreement between a labor organization and an employer in the construction industry relating to the contracting or subcontracting of work to be done at the site of the construction, alteration, painting, or repair of a building, structure, or other work.

> It should be particularly noted that the proviso relates only and exclusively to the contracting or subcontracting of work to be done at the site of the construction. The proviso does not exempt from § 8(e) agreements

relating to supplies or other products or materials shipped or otherwise transported to and delivered on the site of the construction. The committee of conference does not intend that this proviso should be construed so as to change the present state of the law with respect to the validity of this specific type of agreement relating to work to be done at the site of the construction project or to remove the limitations which the present law imposes with respect to such agreements. Picketing to enforce such contracts would be illegal under the *Sand Door* case, *Carpenters, Local 1976, AFL v. NLRB*, 357 U.S. 93 (1958). To the extent that such agreements are legal today under § 8(b)(4) of the National Labor Relations Act, as amended, the proviso would prevent such legality from being affected by § 8(e). The proviso applies only to § 8(e) and therefore leaves unaffected the law developed under § 8(b)(4). The *Denver Building Trades* case and the *Moore Dry Dock* cases would remain in full force and effect. The proviso is not intended to limit, change, or modify the present state of the law with respect to picketing at the site of a construction project. Restrictions and limitations imposed upon such picketing under present law as interpreted, for example, in the U. S. Supreme Court decision in the *Denver Building Trades* case would remain in full force and effect. It is not intended that the proviso change the existing law with respect to judicial enforcement of these contracts or with respect to the legality of a strike to obtain such a contract.

The second proviso specifies that for the purposes of this subsection (e) and § 8(b)(4) the terms "any employer," "any person engaged in commerce or an industry affecting commerce," and "any person" when used in relation to the terms "any other producer, processor, or manufacturer," "any other employer," or "any other person" shall not include persons in the relation of a jobber, manufacturer, contractor, or subcontractor working on the goods or premises of a jobber or manufacturer or performing parts of an integrated process of production in the apparel and clothing industry. This proviso grants a limited exemption in three specific situations in the apparel and clothing industry, but in no other industry regardless of whether similar integrated processes of production may exist between jobbers, manufacturers, contractors, and subcontractors.

The third proviso applies solely to the apparel and clothing industry.

H.R. Rep. No. 1147, 86th Cong., 1st Sess. 39–40 (1959).

2. *Agreement between Union and Employer* — To find a violation of § 8(e), there must be evidence of an express or implied agreement between a labor organization and an employer. If an employer unilaterally decides to sever a relationship with a nonunion party, no violation may be found, even if the employer's decision was induced by the union's use of coercive measures. See *Am. Steel Erectors v. Local Union No. 7*, 815 F.3d 43 (1st Cir. 2016).

3. *Construction Industry Proviso* — Under the 1959 amendments to § 8(b)(4)(A), a strike to obtain a "hot cargo" clause prohibited by § 8(e) was made a union unfair labor practice. Likewise, union threats or coercion designed to induce an employer to enter into such an agreement was also prohibited.

Since the construction industry *proviso* excepts agreements "relating to the contracting or subcontracting of work to be done at the site of the construction," a construction union may picket or strike *to obtain* such a contractual restriction without violating § 8(b)(4)(A) — that is, it is not seeking an agreement prohibited by § 8(e). *Construction, Production & Maintenance Laborers Union Local 383 v. NLRB*, 323 F.2d 422 (9th Cir. 1963); *Essex County & Vicinity Dist. Council of Carpenters v. NLRB*, 332 F.2d 636 (3d Cir. 1964). As the *Sand Door* decision recognized, however, a union could not employ such coercive tactics *to enforce* such a clause, due to the absence of any exemption from § 8(b)(4)(B).

Connell Construction Co. v. Plumbers Local 100
Supreme Court of the United States
421 U.S. 616, 95 S. Ct. 1830, 44 L. Ed. 2d 418 (1975)

Mr. Justice Powell delivered the opinion of the Court....

I

Local 100 is the bargaining representative for workers in the plumbing and mechanical trades in Dallas. When this litigation began, it was party to a multiemployer bargaining agreement with the Mechanical Contractors Association of Dallas, a group of about 75 mechanical contractors. That contract contained a "most favored nation" clause, by which the union agreed that if it granted a more favorable contract to any other employer it would extend the same terms to all members of the Association.

Connell Construction Co. is a general building contractor in Dallas. It obtains jobs by competitive bidding and subcontracts all plumbing and mechanical work. Connell has followed a policy of awarding these subcontracts on the basis of competitive bids, and it has done business with both union and nonunion subcontractors. Connell's employees are represented by various building trade unions. Local 100 has never sought to represent them or to bargain with Connell on their behalf.

In November 1970, Local 100 asked Connell to agree that it would subcontract mechanical work only to firms that had a current contract with the union. It demanded that Connell sign the following agreement:

> WHEREAS, the contractor and the union are engaged in the construction industry, and
>
> WHEREAS, the contractor and the union desire to make an agreement applying in the event of subcontracting in accordance with Section 8(e) of the Labor-Management Relations Act;

WHEREAS, it is understood that by this agreement the contractor does not grant, nor does the union seek, recognition as the collective bargaining representative of any employees of the signatory contractor; and

WHEREAS, it is further understood that the subcontracting limitation provided herein applies only to mechanical work which the contractor does not perform with his own employees but uniformly subcontracts to other firms;

THEREFORE, the contractor and the union mutually agree with respect to work falling within the scope of this agreement that is to be done at the site of construction, alteration, painting or repair of any building, structure, or other works, that if the contractor should contract or subcontract any of the aforesaid work falling within the normal trade jurisdiction of the union, said contractor shall contract or subcontract such work only to firms that are parties to an executed, current collective bargaining agreement with Local Union 100 of the United Association of Journeymen and Apprentices of the Plumbing and Pipefitting Industry.

When Connell refused to sign this agreement, Local 100 stationed a single picket at one of Connell's major construction sites. About 150 workers walked off the job, and construction halted. Connell filed suit in state court to enjoin the picketing as a violation of Texas antitrust laws. Local 100 removed the case to federal court. Connell then signed the subcontracting agreement under protest. It amended its complaint to claim that the agreement violated §§ 1 and 2 of the Sherman Act ... and was therefore invalid. Connell sought a declaration to this effect and an injunction against any further efforts to force it to sign such an agreement.

By the time the case went to trial, Local 100 had submitted identical agreements to a number of other general contractors in Dallas. Five others had signed, and the union was waging a selective picketing campaign against those who resisted.

The District Court held that the subcontracting agreement was exempt from federal antitrust laws because it was authorized by the construction industry proviso to § 8(e) of the National Labor Relations Act, ... The court also held that federal labor legislation pre-empted the State's antitrust laws.... The Court of Appeals for the Fifth Circuit affirmed, 483 F.2d 1154 (1973), with one judge dissenting. It held that Local 100's goal of organizing nonunion subcontractors was a legitimate union interest and that its efforts toward that goal were therefore exempt from federal antitrust laws. On the second issue, it held that state law was pre-empted under *San Diego Building Trades Council v. Garmon*, 359 U.S. 236 (1959). We granted certiorari on Connell's petition. We reverse on the question of federal antitrust immunity and affirm the ruling on state law pre-emption.

II

The basic sources of organized labor's exemption from federal antitrust laws are §§ 6 and 20 of the Clayton Act, ... and the Norris-La Guardia Act, ... These statutes declare that labor unions are not combinations or conspiracies in restraint of trade, and exempt specific union activities, including secondary picketing and boycotts, from the operation of the antitrust laws. See *United States v. Hutcheson*, 312 U.S. 219 (1941). They do not exempt concerted action or agreements between unions and nonlabor parties. *Mine Workers v. Pennington*, 381 U.S. 657, 662 (1965). The Court has recognized, however, that a proper accommodation between the congressional policy favoring collective bargaining under the NLRA and the congressional policy favoring free competition in business markets requires that some union-employer agreements be accorded a limited nonstatutory exemption from antitrust sanctions. *Meat Cutters v. Jewel Tea Co.*, 381 U.S. 676 (1965).

The nonstatutory exemption has its source in the strong labor policy favoring the association of employees to eliminate competition over wages and working conditions. Union success in organizing workers and standardizing wages ultimately will affect price competition among employers, but the goals of federal labor law never could be achieved if this effect on business competition were held a violation of the antitrust laws. The Court therefore has acknowledged that labor policy requires tolerance for the lessening of business competition based on differences in wages and working conditions. See *Mine Workers v. Pennington, supra*, at 666; *Jewel Tea, supra*, at 692–693 (opinion of WHITE, J.). Labor policy clearly does not require, however, that a union have freedom to impose direct restraints on competition among those who employ its members. Thus, while the statutory exemption allows unions to accomplish some restraints by acting unilaterally, e.g., *Federation of Musicians v. Carroll*, 391 U.S. 99 (1968), the nonstatutory exemption offers no similar protection when a union and a nonlabor party agree to restrain competition in a business market. See *Allen Bradley Co. v. Electrical Workers*, 325 U.S. 797, 806–811 (1945); Cox, *Labor and the Antitrust Laws — A Preliminary Analysis*, 104 U. Pa. L. Rev. 252 (1955); Meltzer, *Labor Unions, Collective Bargaining, and the Antitrust Laws*, 32 U. Chi. L. Rev. 659 (1965).

In this case Local 100 used direct restraints on the business market to support its organizing campaign. The agreements with Connell and other general contractors indiscriminately excluded nonunion subcontractors from a portion of the market, even if their competitive advantages were not derived from substandard wages and working conditions but rather from more efficient operating methods. Curtailment of competition based on efficiency is neither a goal of federal labor policy nor a necessary effect of the elimination of competition among workers. Moreover, competition based on efficiency is a positive value that the antitrust laws strive to protect.

The multiemployer bargaining agreement between Local 100 and the Association, though not challenged in this suit, is relevant in determining the effect that the agreement between Local 100 and Connell would have on the business market. The "most favored nation" clause in the multi-employer agreement promised to eliminate competition between members of the Association and any other subcontractors that Local 100 might organize. By giving members of the Association a contractual right to insist on terms as favorable as those given any competitor, it guaranteed that the union would make no agreement that would give an unaffiliated contractor a competitive advantage over members of the Association. Subcontractors in the Association thus stood to benefit from any extension of Local 100's organization, but the method Local 100 chose also had the effect of sheltering them from outside competition in that portion of the market covered by subcontracting agreements between general contractors and Local 100. In that portion of the market, the restriction on subcontracting would eliminate competition on all subjects covered by the multi-employer agreement, even on subjects unrelated to wages, hours, and working conditions.

Success in exacting agreements from general contractors would also give Local 100 power to control access to the market for mechanical subcontracting work. The agreements with general contractors did not simply prohibit subcontracting to any nonunion firm; they prohibited subcontracting to any firm that did not have a contract with Local 100. The union thus had complete control over subcontract work offered by general contractors that had signed these agreements. Such control could result in significant adverse effects on the market and on consumers — effects unrelated to the union's legitimate goals of organizing workers and standardizing working conditions. For example, if the union thought the interests of its members would be served by having fewer subcontractors competing for the available work, it could refuse to sign collective-bargaining agreements with marginal firms. Cf. *Mine Workers v. Pennington, supra.* Or, since Local 100 has a well-defined geographical jurisdiction, it could exclude "traveling" subcontractors by refusing to deal with them. Local 100 thus might be able to create a geographical enclave for local contractors, similar to the closed market in *Allen Bradley, supra.*

This record contains no evidence that the union's goal was anything other than organizing as many subcontractors as possible. This goal was legal, even though a successful organizing campaign ultimately would reduce the competition that unionized employers face from nonunion firms. But the methods the union chose are not immune from antitrust sanctions simply because the goal is legal. Here Local 100, by agreement with several contractors, made nonunion subcontractors ineligible to compete for a portion of the available work. This kind of direct restraint on the business market has substantial anticompetitive effects, both actual and potential, that would not follow naturally from the elimination of competition over wages and working conditions. It contravenes antitrust policies to a degree not justified by congressional labor policy, and therefore cannot claim a nonstatutory exemption from the antitrust laws.

There can be no argument in this case, whatever its force in other contexts, that a restraint of this magnitude might be entitled to an antitrust exemption if it were included in a lawful collective-bargaining agreement. Cf. *Mine Workers v. Pennington*, 381 U.S., at 664–665; *Jewel Tea*, 381 U.S., at 689–690 (opinion of WHITE, J.); *id.*, at 709–713, 732–733 (opinion of GOLDBERG, J.). In this case, Local 100 had no interest in representing Connell's employees. The federal policy favoring collective bargaining therefore can offer no shelter for the union's coercive action against Connell or its campaign to exclude nonunion firms from the subcontracting market.

III

Local 100 nonetheless contends that the kind of agreement it obtained from Connell is explicitly allowed by the construction-industry proviso to § 8(e) and that antitrust policy therefore must defer to the NLRA. The majority in the Court of Appeals declined to decide this issue, holding that it was subject to the "exclusive jurisdiction" of the NLRB. This Court has held, however, that the federal courts may decide labor law questions that emerge as collateral issues in suits brought under independent federal remedies, including the antitrust laws. We conclude that § 8(e) does not allow this type of agreement. . . .

Section 8(e) was part of a legislative program designed to plug technical loopholes in § 8 (b)(4)'s general prohibition of secondary activities. In § 8(e) Congress broadly proscribed using contractual agreements to achieve the economic coercion prohibited by § 8 (b)(4). See *National Woodwork Mfrs. Assn., supra*, at 634. The provisos exempting the construction and garment industries were added by the Conference Committee in an apparent compromise between the House bill, which prohibited all "hot cargo" agreements, and the Senate bill, which prohibited them only in the trucking industry. Although the garment-industry proviso was supported by detailed explanations in both Houses, the construction-industry proviso was explained only by bare references to "the pattern of collective bargaining" in the industry. It seems, however, to have been adopted as a partial substitute for an attempt to overrule this Court's decision in *NLRB v. Denver Building & Construction Trades Council*, 341 U.S. 675 (1951). Discussion of "special problems" in the construction industry, applicable to both the § 8(e) proviso and the attempt to overrule *Denver Building Trades*, focused on the problems of picketing a single nonunion subcontractor on a multiemployer building project, and the close relationship between contractors and subcontractors at the jobsite. Congress limited the construction-industry proviso to that single situation, allowing subcontracting agreements only in relation to work done on a jobsite. In contrast to the latitude it provided in the garment-industry proviso, Congress did not afford construction unions an exemption from § 8 (b)(4)(B) or otherwise indicate that they were free to use subcontracting agreements as a broad organizational weapon. In keeping with these limitations, the Court has interpreted the construction-industry proviso as

> a measure designed to allow agreements pertaining to certain secondary activities on the construction site because of the close community of interests there, but to ban secondary- objective agreements concerning nonjobsite work, in which respect the construction industry is no different from any other.
>
> *National Woodwork Mfrs. Assn.*, 386 U.S., at 638–639 (footnote omitted). . . .

Local 100 does not suggest that its subcontracting agreement is related to any of these policies. It does not claim to be protecting Connell's employees from having to work alongside nonunion men. The agreement apparently was not designed to protect Local 100's members in that regard, since it was not limited to jobsites on which they were working. Moreover, the subcontracting restriction applied only to the work Local 100's members would perform themselves and allowed free subcontracting of all other work, thus leaving open a possibility that they would be employed alongside nonunion subcontractors. Nor was Local 100 trying to organize a nonunion subcontractor on the building project it picketed. The union admits that it sought the agreement solely as a way of pressuring mechanical subcontractors in the Dallas area to recognize it as the representative of their employees.

If we agreed with Local 100 that the construction-industry proviso authorizes subcontracting agreements with "stranger" contractors, not limited to any particular jobsite, our ruling would give construction unions an almost unlimited organizational weapon. The unions would be free to enlist any general contractor to bring economic pressure on nonunion subcontractors, as long as the agreement recited that it only covered work to be performed on some jobsite somewhere. The proviso's jobsite restriction then would serve only to prohibit agreements relating to subcontractors that deliver their work complete to the jobsite.

It is highly improbable that Congress intended such a result. One of the major aims of the 1959 Act was to limit "top-down" organizing campaigns, in which unions used economic weapons to force recognition from an employer regardless of the wishes of his employees. Congress accomplished this goal by enacting § 8 (b)(7), which restricts primary recognitional picketing, and by further tightening § 8 (b)(4)(B), which prohibits the use of most secondary tactics in organizational campaigns. Construction unions are fully covered by these sections. The only special consideration given them in organizational campaigns is § 8(f), which allows "prehire" agreements in the construction industry, but only under careful safeguards preserving workers' rights to decline union representation. The legislative history accompanying § 8(f) also suggests that Congress may not have intended that strikes or picketing could be used to extract prehire agreements from unwilling employers.

These careful limits on the economic pressure unions may use in aid of their organizational campaigns would be undermined seriously if the proviso to § 8(e) were construed to allow unions to seek subcontracting agreements, at large, from any general contractor vulnerable to picketing. Absent a clear indication that Congress intended to leave such a glaring loophole in its restrictions on "top-down" organizing, we are unwilling to read the construction industry proviso as broadly as Local 100 suggests. Instead, we think its authorization extends only to agreements in the context of collective-bargaining relationships and, in light of congressional references to the Denver Building Trades problem, possibly to common-situs relationships on particular jobsites as well.

Finally, Local 100 contends that even if the subcontracting agreement is not sanctioned by the construction-industry proviso and therefore is illegal under § 8(e), it cannot be the basis for antitrust liability because the remedies in the NLRA are exclusive. This argument is grounded in the legislative history of the 1947 Taft-Hartley amendments. Congress rejected attempts to regulate secondary activities by repealing the antitrust exemptions in the Clayton and Norris-LaGuardia Acts, and created special remedies under the labor law instead. It made secondary activities unfair labor practices under § 8(b)(4), and drafted special provisions for preliminary injunctions at the suit of the NLRB and for recovery of actual damages in the district courts. § 10(*l*) of the NLRA . . . and § 303 of the Labor Management Relations Act. But whatever significance this legislative choice has for antitrust suits based on those secondary activities prohibited by § 8(b)(4), it has no relevance to the question whether Congress meant to preclude antitrust suits based on the "hot cargo" agreements that it outlawed in 1959. There is no legislative history in the 1959 Congress suggesting that labor-law remedies for § 8(e) violations were intended to be exclusive, or that Congress thought allowing antitrust remedies in cases like the present one would be inconsistent with the remedial scheme of the NLRA.[25]

We therefore hold that this agreement, which is outside the context of a collective-bargaining relationship and not restricted to a particular jobsite, but which nonetheless obligates Connell to subcontract work only to firms that have a contract with Local 100, may be the basis of a federal antitrust suit because it has a potential for restraining competition in the business market in ways that would not follow naturally from elimination of competition over wages and working conditions.

IV

Although we hold that the union's agreement with Connell is subject to the federal antitrust laws, it does not follow that state antitrust law may apply as well. The Court has held repeatedly that federal law pre-empts state remedies that interfere with federal labor policy or with specific provisions of the NLRA. . . . The use of state antitrust law to regulate union activities in aid of organization must also be pre-empted because it creates a substantial risk of conflict with policies central to federal labor law.

In this area, the accommodation between federal labor and antitrust policy is delicate. Congress and this Court have carefully tailored the antitrust statutes to

---

25. [16] The dissenting opinion of MR. JUSTICE STEWART argues that § 303 provides the exclusive remedy for violations of § 8(e), thereby precluding recourse to antitrust remedies. For that proposition the dissenting opinion relies upon "considerable evidence in the legislative materials." In our view, these materials are unpersuasive. In the first place, Congress did not amend § 303 expressly to provide a remedy for violations of § 8(e). . . . . The House in 1959 did reject proposals by Representatives Hiestand, Alger, and Hoffman to repeal labor's antitrust immunity. Those proposals, however, were much broader than the issue in this case. The Hiestand-Alger proposal would have repealed antitrust immunity for any action in concert by two or more labor organizations. The Hoffman proposal apparently intended to repeal labor's antitrust immunity entirely. That the Congress rejected these extravagant proposals hardly furnishes proof that it intended to extend labor's antitrust immunity to include agreements with nonlabor parties, or that it thought antitrust liability under the existing statutes would be inconsistent with the NLRA. The bill introduced by Senator McClellan two years later provides even less support for that proposition. Like most bills introduced in Congress, it never reached a vote.

avoid conflict with the labor policy favoring lawful employee organization, not only by delineating exemptions from antitrust coverage but also by adjusting the scope of the antitrust remedies themselves. See *Apex Hosiery Co. v. Leader*, 310 U.S. 469 (1940). State antitrust laws generally have not been subjected to this process of accommodation. If they take account of labor goals at all, they may represent a totally different balance between labor and antitrust policies. Permitting state antitrust law to operate in this field could frustrate the basic federal policies favoring employee organization and allowing elimination of competition among wage earners, and interfere with the detailed system Congress has created for regulating organizational techniques.

Because employee organization is central to federal labor policy and regulation of organizational procedures is comprehensive, federal law does not admit the use of state antitrust law to regulate union activity that is closely related to organizational goals. Of course, other agreements between unions and nonlabor parties may yet be subject to state antitrust laws. See *Teamsters v. Oliver, supra*, at 295–297. The governing factor is the risk of conflict with the NLRA or with federal labor policy.

V

Neither the District Court nor the Court of Appeals decided whether the agreement between Local 100 and Connell, if subject to the antitrust laws, would constitute an agreement that restrains trade within the meaning of the Sherman Act. The issue was not briefed and argued fully in this Court. Accordingly, we remand for consideration whether the agreement violated the Sherman Act.[26]

Reversed in part, affirmed in part, and remanded.

Mr. Justice Douglas, dissenting.

While I join the opinion of Mr. Justice Stewart, I write to emphasize what is, for me, the determinative feature of the case. Throughout this litigation, Connell has maintained only that Local 100 coerced it into signing the subcontracting agreement. With the complaint so drawn, I have no difficulty in concluding that the union's conduct is regulated solely by the labor laws. The question of antitrust immunity would be far different, however, if it were alleged that Local 100 had

---

26. [19] In addition to seeking a declaratory judgment that the agreement with Local 100 violated the antitrust laws, Connell sought a permanent injunction against further picketing to coerce execution of the contract in litigation. Connell obtained a temporary restraining order against the picketing on January 21, 1971, and thereafter executed the contract — under protest — with Local 100 on March 28, 1971. So far as the record in this case reveals, there has been no further picketing at Connell's construction sites. Accordingly, there is no occasion for us to consider whether the Norris-LaGuardia Act forbids such an injunction where the specific agreement sought by the union is illegal, or to determine whether, within the meaning of the Norris-LaGuardia Act, there was a "labor dispute" between these parties. If the Norris-LaGuardia Act were applicable to this picketing, injunctive relief would not be available under the antitrust laws. See *United States v. Hutcheson*, 312 U.S. 219 (1941). If the agreement in question is held on remand to be invalid under federal antitrust laws, we cannot anticipate that Local 100 will resume picketing to obtain or enforce an illegal agreement.

conspired with mechanical subcontractors to force nonunion subcontractors from the market by entering into exclusionary agreements with general contractors like Connell. An arrangement of that character was condemned in *Allen Bradley Co. v. Local 3, IBEW*, 325 U.S. 797 . . . . Were such a conspiracy alleged, the multi-employer bargaining agreement between Local 100 and the mechanical subcontractors would unquestionably be relevant. See *United Mine Workers v. Pennington*, 381 U.S. 657, 673 (concurring opinion); *Meat Cutters v. Jewel Tea Co.*, 381 U.S. 676, 737 (dissenting opinion) . . . .

Mr. Justice Stewart, with whom Mr. Justice Douglas, Mr. Justice Brennan, and Mr. Justice Marshall join, dissenting.

As part of its effort to organize mechanical contractors in the Dallas area, the respondent Local Union No. 100 engaged in peaceful picketing to induce the petitioner Connell Construction Co., a general contractor in the building and construction industry, to agree to subcontract plumbing and mechanical work at the construction site only to firms that had signed a collective-bargaining agreement with Local 100. None of Connell's own employees were members of Local 100, and the subcontracting agreement contained the union's express disavowal of any intent to organize or represent them. The picketing at Connell's construction site was therefore secondary activity, subject to detailed and comprehensive regulation pursuant to § 8(b)(4) of the National Labor Relations Act, . . . and § 303 of the Labor Management Relations Act, ... Similarly, the subcontracting agreement under which Connell agreed to cease doing business with nonunion mechanical contractors is governed by the provisions of § 8(e) of the National Labor Relations Act, ... The relevant legislative history unmistakably demonstrates that in regulating secondary activity and "hot cargo" agreements in 1947 and 1959, Congress selected with great care the sanctions to be imposed if proscribed union activity should occur. In so doing, Congress rejected efforts to give private parties injured by union activity such as that engaged in by Local 100 the right to seek relief under federal antitrust laws. Accordingly, I would affirm the judgment before us. . . .

II

Contrary to the assertion in the Court's opinion, *ante*, the deliberate congressional decision to make § 303 the exclusive private remedy for unlawful secondary activity is clearly relevant to the question of Local 100's antitrust liability in the case before us. The Court is correct, of course, in noting that § 8(e)'s prohibition of "hot cargo" agreements was not added to the Act until 1959, and that § 303 was not then amended to cover § 8(e) violations standing alone. But as part of the 1959 amendments designed to close "technical loopholes" perceived in the Taft-Hartley Act, Congress amended § 8(b)(4) to make it an unfair labor practice for a labor organization to threaten or coerce a neutral employer, either directly or through his employees, where an object of the secondary pressure is to force the employer to enter into an agreement prohibited by § 8(e). At the same time, Congress expanded the scope of the § 303 damages remedy to allow recovery of the actual damages sustained as a result of a union's engaging in secondary activity to force an employer to sign an agreement in violation of § 8(e). In short, Congress has provided an employer like Connell with a fully effective private damages remedy for the allegedly unlawful union conduct involved in this case.

The essence of Connell's complaint is that it was coerced by Local 100's picketing into "conspiring" with the union by signing an agreement that limited its ability to subcontract mechanical work on a competitive basis. If, as the Court today holds, the subcontracting agreement is not within the construction-industry proviso to § 8(e), then Local 100's picketing to induce Connell to sign the agreement constituted a § 8(b)(4) unfair labor practice, and was therefore also unlawful under § 303(a).[27] Accordingly, Connell has the right to sue Local 100 for damages sustained as a result of Local 100's unlawful secondary activity pursuant to § 303(b). Although "limited to actual, compensatory damages," *Teamsters v. Morton*, 377 U.S., at 260, Connell would be entitled under § 303 to recover all damages to its business that resulted from the union's coercive conduct, including any provable damage caused by Connell's inability to subcontract mechanical work to nonunion firms. Similarly, any nonunion mechanical contractor who believes his business has been harmed by Local 100's having coerced Connell into signing the subcontracting agreement is entitled to sue the union for compensatory damages; for § 303 broadly grants its damages action to "[w]hoever shall be injured in his business or property" by reason of a labor organization's engaging in a § 8(b)(4) unfair labor practice.[28]

---

27. [8] If, contrary to the Court's conclusion, see *ante*, Congress intended what it said in the proviso to § 8(e), then the subcontracting agreement is valid and, under the view of the Board and those courts of appeals that have considered the question, Local 100's picketing to obtain the agreement would also be lawful.... Connell would therefore have neither a remedy under § 303 nor one with the Board.

It would seem necessary to follow that conduct specifically authorized by Congress in the National Labor Relations Act could not by itself be the basis for federal antitrust liability, unless the Court intends to return to the era when the judiciary frustrated congressional design by determining for itself "what public policy in regard to the industrial struggle demands." *Duplex Printing Press Co. v. Deering*, 254 U.S. 443, 485 (Brandeis, J., dissenting). See *United States v. Hutcheson*, 312 U.S. 219. In my view, however, even if Local 100's conduct was unlawful, Connell may not seek to invoke the sanctions of the antitrust laws. Accordingly, I find it unnecessary to decide in this case whether the subcontracting agreement entered into by Connell and Local 100 is within the ambit of the construction industry proviso to § 8(e), and, if it is, whether it was permissible for Local 100 to utilize peaceful picketing to induce Connell to sign the agreement.

28. [9] If Connell and Local 100 had entered into a purely voluntary "hot cargo" agreement in violation of § 8(e), an injured nonunion mechanical subcontractor would have no § 303 remedy because the union would not have engaged in any § 8(b)(4) unfair labor practice. The subcontractor, however, would still be able to seek the full range of Board remedies available for a § 8(e) unfair labor practice. Moreover, if Connell had truly agreed to limit its subcontracting without any coercion whatsoever on the part of Local 100, the affected subcontractor might well have a valid antitrust claim on the ground that Local 100 and Connell were engaged in the type of conspiracy aimed at third parties with which this Court dealt in *Allen Bradley Co. v. Electrical Workers*, 325 U.S. 797....

Moreover, there is considerable evidence in the legislative materials indicating that in expanding the scope of § 303 to include a remedy for secondary pressure designed to force an employer to sign an illegal "hot cargo" clause and in restricting the remedies for violation of § 8(e) itself to those available from the Board, Congress in 1959 made the same deliberate choice to exclude antitrust remedies as was made by the 1947 Congress....

The Landrum-Griffin bill, H.R. 8400, 86th Cong., 1st Sess., which, as amended, was enacted as the Labor-Management Reporting and Disclosure Act of 1959, by contrast, clearly provided that the new secondary-boycott and "hot cargo" provisions were to be enforced solely through the Board and by use of the § 303 damages remedy. *See* 105 Cong. Rec. 14347–14348, 2 Leg. Hist. of LMRDA 1522–1523. Recognizing this important difference, Representative Alger proposed to amend the Landrum-Griffin bill by adding, as an additional title, the antitrust provisions of H.R. 8003. 105 Cong. Rec. 15532–15533, 2 Leg. Hist. of LMRDA 1569. Representative Alger once again stated that his proposed amendment would make it unlawful for an individual local union to "[e]nter into any arrangement — voluntary or coerced — with any employer, groups of employers, or other unions which cause product boycotts, price fixing, or other types of restrictive trade practices." 105 Cong. Rec. 15533, 2 Leg. Hist. of LMRDA 1569.

Representative Griffin responded to Representative Alger's proposed amendment by observing that it:

> serves to point out that the substitute [the Landrum-Griffin bill] is a minimum bill. It might be well at this point to mention some provisions that are not in it.
>
> There is no antitrust law provision in this bill....

The Alger amendment was rejected, as were additional efforts to subject proscribed union activities to the antitrust laws and their sanctions. *See, e.g.*, 105 Cong. Rec. 15853, 2 Leg. Hist. of LMRDA 1685 (amendment offered by Rep. Hoffman). The House then adopted the Landrum-Griffin bill over protests that it "does not go far enough, that it needs more teeth, and that more teeth are going to come in the form of legislation to bring labor union activities under the antitrust laws." 105 Cong. Rec. 15858, 2 Leg. Hist. of LMRDA 1690 (remarks of Rep. Alger); ...

In sum, the legislative history of the 1947 and 1959 amendments and additions to national labor law clearly demonstrates that Congress did not intend to restore antitrust sanctions for secondary boycott activity such as that engaged in by Local 100 in this case, but rather intended to subject such activity only to regulation under the National Labor Relations Act and § 303 of the Labor Management Relations Act. The judicial imposition of "independent federal remedies" not intended by Congress, no less than the application of state law to union conduct that is either protected or prohibited by federal labor law, threatens "to upset the balance of power between labor and management expressed in our national labor policy." *Teamsters v. Morton*, 377 U.S., at 260 ....

Note

In *Woelke & Romero Framing v. NLRB*, 456 U.S. 645 (1982), the Supreme Court held that the construction industry proviso to § 8(e) protects union signatory subcontracting clauses sought or negotiated in the context of a collective bargaining relationship, thus resolving an issue left open in *Connell Constr. Co.* The decision involved two cases in which employers with established collective bargaining relationships challenged clauses that required them to subcontract work only to subcontractors who had agreements with a particular union. The employers contended that the proviso protected only subcontracting agreements that applied to sites and times at which union employees were working, and did not protect agreements requiring subcontractors to have agreements with particular unions. In rejecting this contention, the Court found that the proviso was added because Congress wanted to preserve the status quo regarding agreements in the construction industry. It stated: "Congress believed that broad subcontracting clauses similar to those at issue here were part of the pattern of collective-bargaining prior to 1959, and that the Board and the Courts had found them to be lawful. This perception was apparently accurate. Thus, endorsing the clauses at issue here is fully consistent with the legislative history of § 8(e) and the construction industry proviso." *Compare Iron Workers Dist. Council of Pacific Northwest v. NLRB*, 913 F.2d 1470 (9th Cir. 1990) (union violated § 8(b)(4)(A) when it picketed general contractor seeking clause limiting subcontracting to union firms, when bargaining relationship between union and general contractor had terminated prior to time of picketing).

United Rentals Highway Techs., Inc. v. Indiana Constructors, Inc., 518 F.3d 526 (7th Cir. 2008), concerned the legality of a provision in a bargaining agreement between a construction contractors' association and the Laborers International Union, prohibiting the subcontracting of work at highway construction sites to non-union firms. United Rentals is a nonunion company that controls traffic at highway construction sites by placing cones and other barricades to block or reroute traffic and installs guardrails when needed. It brought an antitrust action challenging this provision contending that it fell outside the construction industry proviso to § 8(e) on the ground its employees did not perform work on the construction sites. The Court of Appeals rejected this assertion, based upon the fact the work of United Rentals is inextricably intertwined with the highway construction work its employees work to protect.

Labor and Antitrust. As the Court indicated in the *Connell Constr. Co.* decision, organized labor enjoys two separate exemptions from the antitrust laws. The so-called *statutory exemption* set forth in § 20 of the Clayton Antitrust Act provides that individuals and labor organizations engaging in peaceful labor and employment activities are exempt from antitrust liability. In *United States v. Hutcheson*, 312 U.S. 219 (1941), the Supreme Court acknowledged that this exemption applies to workers and unions working together whether or not the party with whom they have a dispute is the direct employer of the individuals involved. As a result, worker and consumer boycotts of nonunion firms or employers with whom unions have disputes are exempt, and courts are not to evaluate the validity of union claims when determining the scope of this exemption.

> So long as a union acts in its self-interest *and does not combine with nonlabor groups*, the licit and the illicit under § 20 are not to be distinguished by any judgment regarding the wisdom or unwisdom, the rightness or wrongness, the selfishness or unselfishness of the end of which the particular union activities are the means.

312 U.S. at 232 (emphasis added).

Once a union combines with a nonlabor entity — even by entering into a bargaining agreement with a single employer, as in the *Connell Constr. Co.* case — the statutory exemption is lost and the labor organization and workers must rely upon the *nonstatutory exemption* that emanates from the general scope of the NLRA. Under this more limited exemption, courts weigh the policies of the NLRA against the policies of the antitrust statutes. When the restriction in question pertains to a mandatory subject of bargaining and does not have a predatory objective, it will generally be exempt due to the strong NLRA policy fostering agreements over such topics. On the other hand, when the restriction does not pertain to a mandatory topic and does have a meaningful impact upon the competitive market, the nonstatutory exemption is likely to be lost.

Amalgamated Meat Cutters & Butcher Workmen Local 189 v. Jewel Tea Co., 381 U.S. 676, 85 S. Ct. 1596, 14 L. Ed. 2d 640 (1965), involved a bargaining agreement clause that provided that supermarkets could only sell fresh meats between 9:00 a.m. and 6:00 p.m. This term had a direct impact upon the product market because it prevented supermarkets from competing with butcher shops through night sales. Although the specific hours employees must work is a mandatory topic for bargaining, the Court had to decide whether such a limitation — not on hours of work but on the hours stores could sell prepackaged meats — should be considered a mandatory bargaining topic. The Court decided that employees do have a sufficient interest in night sales to bring this topic into the mandatory area.

> [I]n stores where meat is sold at night, it is impractical to operate without either butchers or other employees. Someone must arrange, replenish and clean the counters and supply customer services. Operating without butchers would mean that their work would be done by others unskilled in the trade, and would involve an increase in workload in preparing for night work and cleaning the next morning.

The Court thus concluded that this contractually imposed limitation was exempt from antitrust liability, despite the impact of the provision on the ability of markets to compete with night sales, due to the direct interest of bargaining unit members on evening sales.

United Mine Workers v. Pennington, 381 U.S. 657, 85 S. Ct. 1585, 14 L. Ed. 2d 625 (1965), concerned the legality of an alleged agreement between the Mine Workers Union and a multiemployer group to impose elevated wages and benefits contained in their collective contract on other non-unit employers. The Court found this arrangement was not exempt, even though the provision concerned wages, due to fact it was not limited to the immediate bargaining unit covered by the multiemployer contract and had a significant impact on the competitive market.

> It is true that wages lie at the very heart of those subjects about which employers and unions must bargain and the law contemplates agreements on wages not only between individual employers and a union, but agreements between the union and employers in a multi-employer bargaining unit. *NLRB v. Truck Drivers Union*, 353 U.S. 87, 94–96 (1957). The union benefit from the wage scale agreed upon is direct and concrete and the effect on the product market, though clearly present, results from the elimination of competition based on wages among the employers in the bargaining unit which is not the kind of restraint Congress intended the Sharman Act to proscribe....

> [A] union may make wage agreements with a multi-employer bargaining unit and may in pursuance of its own union interests seek to obtain the same terms from other employers. No case under the antitrust laws could be made out on evidence limited to such union behavior. But we think a union forfeits its exemption from the antitrust laws when it is clearly shown that it has agreed with one set of employers to impose a certain wage scale on other bargaining units. One group of employers may not conspire to limit competitors from the industry and the union is liable with the employers if it becomes a party to the conspiracy.

Note

California ex rel. Brown v. Safeway, Inc., 615 F.3d 1171 (9th Cir. 2010), involved a group of independent grocery companies that negotiated bargaining agreements with the UFCW Union on a multiemployer basis. When they feared a possible whipsaw strike against a single firm during upcoming negotiations, the grocery companies agreed that if one was struck, the others would lock out their employees in support of the struck firm, and the stores that were able to remain open would share their increased profits with the shutdown concerns. The State of California challenged this profit-sharing arrangement as a restraint of trade that violated Section 1 of the Sherman Act, but the grocery companies claimed that it was protected by the nonstatutory labor exemption. The Ninth Circuit rejected this contention, because it held that the nonstatutory exemption only applies to labor practices that are "essential to collective bargaining," and it found that such a profit-sharing plan was not sufficiently related to the bargaining process to bring it within the nonstatutory exemption.

National Woodwork Manufacturers Ass'n v. NLRB
Supreme Court of the United States
386 U.S. 612, 87 S. Ct. 1250, 18 L. Ed. 2d 357 (1967)

MR. JUSTICE BRENNAN delivered the opinion of the Court.

Under the Landrum-Griffin Act amendments enacted in 1959, § 8(b)(4)(A) of the National Labor Relations Act became § 8(b)(4)(B) and § 8(e) was added. The questions here are whether, in the circumstances of these cases, the Metropolitan District Council of Philadelphia and Vicinity of the United Brotherhood of Carpenters and Joiners of America, AFL-CIO (hereafter the Union), committed the unfair labor practices prohibited by §§ 8(e) and 8(b)(4)(B).

Frouge Corporation, a Bridgeport, Connecticut, concern, was the general contractor on a housing project in Philadelphia. Frouge had a collective bargaining agreement with the Carpenters' International Union under which Frouge agreed to be bound by the rules and regulations agreed upon by local unions with contractors in areas in which Frouge had jobs. Frouge was therefore subject to the provisions of a collective bargaining agreement between the Union and an organization of Philadelphia contractors, the General Building Contractors Association, Inc. A sentence in a provision of that agreement entitled Rule 17 provides that ". . . No member of this District Council will handle . . . any doors . . . which have been fitted prior to being furnished on the job. . . ."[29] Frouge's Philadelphia project called for 3,600 doors. Customarily, before the doors could be hung on such projects, "blank" or "blind" doors would be mortised for the knob, routed for the hinges, and beveled to make them fit between jambs. These are tasks traditionally performed in the Philadelphia area by the carpenters employed on the jobsite. However, precut and prefitted doors ready to hang may be purchased from door manufacturers. Although Frouge's contract and job specifications did not call for premachined doors, and "blank" or "blind" doors could have been ordered, Frouge contracted for the purchase of premachined doors from a Pennsylvania door manufacturer which is a member of the National Woodwork Manufacturers Association, petitioner in No. 110 and respondent in No. 111. The Union ordered its carpenter members not to hang the doors when they arrived

---

29. [2] The full text of Rule 17 is as follows:

> No employee shall work on any job on which cabinet work, fixtures, millwork, sash, doors, trim or other detailed millwork is used unless the same is Union-made and bears the Union Label of the United Brotherhood of Carpenters and Joiners of America. No member of this District Council will handle material coming from a mill where cutting out and fitting has been done for butts, locks, letter plates, or hardware of any description, nor any doors or transoms which have been fitted prior to being furnished on job, including base, chair, rail, picture moulding, which has been previously fitted. This section to exempt partition work furnished in sections.

The National Labor Relations Board determined that the first sentence violated § 8 (e), 149 N.L.R.B. 646, 655–656, and the Union did not seek judicial review of that determination.

at the jobsite. Frouge thereupon withdrew the prefabricated doors and substituted "blank" doors which were fitted and cut by its carpenters on the jobsite.

The National Woodwork Manufacturers Association and another filed charges with the National Labor Relations Board against the Union alleging that by including the "will not handle" sentence of Rule 17 in the collective bargaining agreement the Union committed the unfair labor practice under § 8(e) of entering into an "agreement . . . whereby [the] employer . . . agrees to cease or refrain from handling . . . any of the products of any other employer . . . ," and alleging further that in enforcing the sentence against Frouge, the Union committed the unfair labor practice under § 8(b)(4)(B) of "forcing or requiring any person to cease using . . . the products of any other . . . manufacturer. . . ." The National Labor Relations Board dismissed the charges, 149 N.L.R.B. 646.[30] The Board adopted the findings of the Trial Examiner that the "will not handle" sentence in Rule 17 was language used by the parties to protect and preserve cutting out and fitting as unit work to be performed by the jobsite carpenters. The Board also adopted the holding of the Trial Examiner that both the sentence of Rule 17 itself and its maintenance against Frouge were therefore "primary" activity outside the prohibitions of §§ 8(e) and 8(b)(4)(B). . . .

The Court of Appeals for the Seventh Circuit reversed the Board in this respect. 354 F.2d 594, 599 (1965). The court held that the "will not handle" agreement violated § 8(e) without regard to any "primary" or "secondary" objective, and remanded to the Board with instructions to enter an order accordingly. . . .

The Court of Appeals sustained, however, the dismissal of the § 8(b)(4)(B) charge. The court agreed with the Board that the Union's conduct as to Frouge involved only a primary dispute with it and held that the conduct was therefore not prohibited by that section but expressly protected by the proviso "that nothing contained in this clause (B) shall be construed to make unlawful, where not otherwise unlawful, any primary strike or primary picketing. . . ." 354 F.2d, at 597.

---

30. [3] There were also charges of violation of §§ 8(e) and 8(b)(4)(B) arising from the enforcement of the Rule 17 provision against three other contractors whose contracts with the owners of the construction projects involved specified that the contractors should furnish and install precut and prefinished doors. The Union refused to permit its members to hang these doors. The Board held that this refusal violated § 8(b)(4)(B). The Board reasoned that, since these contractors (in contrast to Frouge) did not have "control" over the work that the Union sought to preserve for its members, the Union's objective was secondary — to compel the project owners to stop specifying precut doors in their contracts with the employer-contractors. 149 N.L.R.B., at 658. The Union petitioned the Court of Appeals to set aside the remedial order issued by the Board on this finding, but the court sustained the Board. 354 F.2d 594, 597 (1965). The Union did not seek review of the question here. Not before us, therefore, is the issue argued by the AFL-CIO in its brief *amicus curiae*, namely, whether the Board's "right-to-control doctrine — that employees can never strike against their own employer about a matter over which he lacks the legal power to grant their demand" — is an incorrect rule of law inconsistent with the Court's decision in *Labor Board v. Insurance Agents' International Union*, 361 U.S. 477, 497–498 (1960).

We granted certiorari on the petition of the Woodwork Manufacturers Association in No. 110 and on the petition of the Board in No. 111. 384 U.S. 968. We affirm in No. 110 and reverse in No. 111.

I

Even on the doubtful premise that the words of § 8(e) unambiguously embrace the sentence of Rule 17,[31] this does not end inquiry into Congress' purpose in enacting the section. It is a "familiar rule, that a thing may be within the letter of the statute and yet not within the statute, because not within its spirit, nor within the intention of its makers." *Holy Trinity Church v. United States*, 143 U.S. 457, 459 (1892). That principle has particular application in the construction of labor legislation which is "to a marked degree, the result of conflict and compromise between strong contending forces and deeply held views on the role of organized labor in the free economic life of the Nation and the appropriate balance to be struck between the uncontrolled power of management and labor to further their respective interests." *Carpenters, Local 1976 v. NLRB (Sand Door)*, 357 U.S. 93, 99–100 (1958). . . .

Strongly held opposing views have invariably marked controversy over labor's use of the boycott to further its aims by involving an employer in disputes not his own. But congressional action to deal with such conduct has stopped short of proscribing identical activity having the object of pressuring the employer for agreements regulating relations between him and his own employees. That Congress meant §§ 8(e) and 8(b)(4)(B) to prohibit only "secondary" objectives clearly appears from an examination of the history of congressional action on the subject. . . .

[The Court reviewed the legislative history regarding the treatment of secondary boycotts under the Sherman Act, Clayton Act, Norris-LaGuardia Act, and Taft-Hartley Act.]

Judicial decisions interpreting the broad language of § 8(b)(4)(A) of the Taft-Hartley Act uniformly limited its application to such "secondary" situations.[32] This limitation was in "conformity with the dual congressional objectives of preserving the right of labor organizations to bring pressure to bear on offending employers in primary labor disputes and of shielding unoffending employers and others from pressures in controversies not their own." *NLRB v. Denver Bldg. Trades Council*, 341 U.S. 675, 692 (1951). This Court accordingly refused to read § 8(b)(4)(A) to ban

---

31. [4] The statutory language of § 8(e) is far from unambiguous. It prohibits agreements to "cease . . . from handling . . . any of the products *of any other employer.* . . ." (Emphasis supplied.) Since both the product and its source are mentioned, the provision might be read not to prohibit an agreement relating solely to the nature of the product itself, such as a work-preservation agreement, but only to prohibit one arising from an objection to the other employers or a definable group of employers who are the source of the product, for example, their nonunion status.

32. [16] [Citations] An oft-cited definition of the conduct banned by § 8(b)(4)(A) was that of Judge Learned Hand in *I.B.E.W. v. NLRB*, 181 F.2d 34, 37 (2d Cir. 1950): "The gravamen of a secondary boycott is that its sanctions bear, not upon the employer who alone is a party to the dispute, but upon some third party who has no concern in it. Its aim is to compel him to stop business with the employer in the hope that this will induce the employer to give in to his employees' demands." . . .

traditional primary strikes and picketing having an impact on neutral employers even though the activity fell within its sweeping terms. *NLRB v. Int'l Rice Milling Co.*, 341 U.S. 665 (1951); see *IUE, Local 761 v. NLRB*, 366 U.S. 667 (1961). Thus, however severe the impact of primary activity on neutral employers, it was not thereby transformed into activity with a secondary objective.

The literal terms of § 8(b)(4)(A) also were not applied in the so-called "ally doctrine" cases, in which the union's pressure was aimed toward employers performing the work of the primary employer's striking employees. The rationale, again, was the inapplicability of the provision's central theme, the protection of neutrals against secondary pressure, where the secondary employer against whom the union's pressure is directed has entangled himself in the vortex of the primary dispute. "The union was not extending its activity to a front remote from the immediate dispute but to one intimately and indeed inextricably united to it." *Douds v. Metropolitan Federation of Architects*, 75 F. Supp. 672, 677 (S.D.N.Y. 1948); see *NLRB v. Business Machine & Office Appliance Mechanics*, 228 F.2d 553 (2d Cir. 1955). We summarized our reading of § 8(b)(4)(A) just a year before enactment of § 8(e):

> It aimed to restrict the area of industrial conflict insofar as this could be achieved by prohibiting the most obvious, widespread, and, as Congress evidently judged, dangerous practice of unions to widen that conflict: the coercion of neutral employers, themselves not concerned with a primary labor dispute, through the inducement of their employees to engage in strikes or concerted refusals to handle goods.

Carpenters, Local 1976 v. NLRB (Sand Door), 357 U.S. 93, 100 (1958). . . .

In effect Congress, in enacting § 8(b)(4)(A) of the Act, returned to the regime of *Duplex Printing Press Co. v. Deering*, 254 U.S. 443 (1921), and *Bedford Cut Stone Co. v. Stone Cutters' Ass'n*, 274 U.S. 37 (1927), and barred as a secondary boycott union activity directed against a neutral employer, including the immediate employer when in fact the activity directed against him was carried on for its effect elsewhere.

Indeed, Congress in rewriting § 8(b)(4)(A) as § 8(b)(4)(B) took pains to confirm the limited application of the section to such "secondary" conduct. The word "concerted" in former § 8(b)(4) was deleted to reach secondary conduct directed to only one individual. This was in response to the Court's holding in *NLRB v. Int'l Rice Milling Co.*, 341 U.S. 665 (1951), that "concerted" required proof of inducement of two or more employees. But to make clear that the deletion was not to be read as supporting a construction of the statute as prohibiting the incidental effects of traditional primary activity, Congress added the proviso that nothing in the amended section "shall be construed to make unlawful, where not otherwise unlawful, any primary strike or primary picketing." Many statements and examples proffered in the 1959 debates confirm this congressional acceptance of the distinction between primary and secondary activity.

II

The Landrum-Griffin Act amendments in 1959 were adopted only to close various loopholes in the application of § 8(b)(4)(A) which had been exposed in Board and court decisions. We discussed some of these loopholes, and the particular amendments adopted to close them, in *NLRB v. Servette, Inc.*, 377 U.S. 46, 51–54 (1964)....

Section 8(e) simply closed still another loophole. In *Carpenters, Local 1976 v. NLRB (Sand Door)*, 357 U.S. 93 (1958), the Court held that it was no defense to an unfair labor practice charge under § 8(b)(4)(A) that the struck employer had agreed, in a contract with the union, not to handle nonunion material. However, the Court emphasized that the mere execution of such a contract provision (known as a "hot cargo" clause because of its prevalence in Teamsters Union contracts), or its voluntary observance by the employer, was not unlawful under § 8(b)(4)(A). Section 8(e) was designed to plug this gap in the legislation by making the "hot cargo" clause itself unlawful. The *Sand Door* decision was believed by Congress not only to create the possibility of damage actions against employers for breaches of "hot cargo" clauses, but also to create a situation in which such clauses might be employed to exert subtle pressures upon employers to engage in "voluntary" boycotts. Hearings in late 1958 before the Senate Select Committee explored seven cases of "hot cargo" clauses in Teamsters Union contracts, the use of which the Committee found conscripted neutral employers in Teamsters organizational campaigns.[33]

This loophole-closing measure likewise did not expand the type of conduct which § 8(b)(4)(A) condemned. Although the language of § 8(e) is sweeping, it closely tracks that of § 8(b)(4)(A), and just as the latter and its successor § 8(b)(4)(B) did not reach employees' activity to pressure their employer to preserve for themselves work traditionally done by them, § 8(e) does not prohibit agreements made and maintained for that purpose.

The legislative history of § 8(e) confirms this conclusion....

The only mention of a broader reach for § 8(e) appears in isolated statements by opponents of that provision, expressing fears that work preservation agreements would be banned. These statements have scant probative value against the backdrop of the strong evidence to the contrary. Too, "we have often cautioned against the danger, when interpreting a statute, of reliance upon the views of its legislative opponents. In their zeal to defeat a bill, they understandably tend to overstate its reach." *NLRB v. Fruit & Vegetable Packers*, 377 U.S. 58, 66 (1964). "It is the sponsors

---

33. [24] See Final Report of the Senate Select Committee on Improper Activities in the Labor or Management Field, S. Rep. No. 1139, 86th Cong., 2d Sess., 3 (1960). The Final Report, ordered to be printed after enactment of the Landrum-Griffin Act, defined a "hot cargo" clause as "an agreement between a union and a unionized employer that his employees shall not be required to work on or handle 'hot goods' or 'hot cargo' being manufactured or transferred by another employer with whom the union has a labor dispute or whom the union considers and labels as being unfair to organized labor." *Ibid.*

that we look to when the meaning of the statutory words is in doubt." *Schwegmann Bros. v. Calvert Distillers Corp.*, 341 U.S. 384, 394–395 (1951). . . .

In addition to all else, "the silence of the sponsors of [the] amendments is pregnant with significance. . . ." *NLRB v. Fruit & Vegetable Packers, supra*, at 66. Before we may say that Congress meant to strike from workers' hands the economic weapons traditionally used against their employers' efforts to abolish their jobs, that meaning should plainly appear. "In this era of automation and onrushing technological change, no problems in the domestic economy are of greater concern than those involving job security and employment stability. Because of the potentially cruel impact upon the lives and fortunes of the working men and women of the Nation, these problems have understandably engaged the solicitous attention of government, of responsible private business, and particularly of organized labor." *Fibreboard Paper Prods. Corp. v. NLRB*, 379 U.S. 203, 225 (concurring opinion of Stewart, J.). We would expect that legislation curtailing the ability of management and labor voluntarily to negotiate for solutions to these significant and difficult problems would be preceded by extensive congressional study and debate, and consideration of voluminous economic, scientific, and statistical data. . . . It would . . . be incongruous to interpret § 8(e) to invalidate clauses over which the parties may be mandated to bargain and which have been successfully incorporated through collective bargaining in many of this Nation's major labor agreements.

. . . .

The Woodwork Manufacturers Association and amici who support its position advance several reasons, grounded in economic and technological factors, why "will not handle" clauses should be invalid in all circumstances. Those arguments are addressed to the wrong branch of government. It may be "that the time has come for a re-evaluation of the basic content of collective bargaining as contemplated by the federal legislation. But that is for Congress. . . .

III

The determination whether the "will not handle" sentence of Rule 17 and its enforcement violated § 8(e) and § 8(b)(4)(B) cannot be made without an inquiry into whether, under all the surrounding circumstances, the Union's objective was preservation of work for Frouge's employees, or whether the agreements and boycott were tactically calculated to satisfy union objectives elsewhere. Were the latter the case, Frouge, the boycotting employer, would be a neutral bystander, and the agreement or boycott would, within the intent of Congress, become secondary. There need not be an actual dispute with the boycotted employer, here the door manufacturer, for the activity to fall within this category, so long as the tactical object of the agreement and its maintenance is that employer, or benefits to other than the boycotting employees or other employees of the primary employer thus making the agreement or boycott secondary in its aim. The touchstone is whether the agreement or its maintenance is addressed to the labor relations of the contracting employer vis-à-vis his own employees. This will not always be a simple test to apply.

But "however difficult the drawing of lines more nice than obvious, the statute compels the task." *IUE, Local 761 v. NLRB*, 366 U.S. 667, 674 (1961).

That the "will not handle" provision was not an unfair labor practice in these cases is clear. The finding of the Trial Examiner, adopted by the Board, was that the objective of the sentence was preservation of work traditionally performed by the jobsite carpenters. This finding is supported by substantial evidence, and therefore the Union's making of the "will not handle" agreement was not a violation of § 8(e).

Similarly, the Union's maintenance of the provision was not a violation of § 8(b)(4)(B). The Union refused to hang prefabricated doors whether or not they bore a union label, and even refused to install prefabricated doors manufactured off the jobsite by members of the Union. This and other substantial evidence supported the finding that the conduct of the Union on the Frouge jobsite related solely to preservation of the traditional tasks of the jobsite carpenters.

The judgment is affirmed in No. 110, and reversed in No. 111.

It is so ordered.

Memorandum of Mr. Justice Harlan.

In joining the Court's opinion, I am constrained to add these few words by way of underscoring the salient factors which, in my judgment, make for the decision that has been reached in these difficult cases.

1. The facts as found by the Board and the Court of Appeals show that the contractual restrictive-product rule in question, and the boycott in support of its enforcement, had as their sole objective the protection of union members from a diminution of work flowing from changes in technology. Union members traditionally had performed the task of fitting doors on the jobsite, and there is no evidence of any motive for this contract provision and its companion boycott other than the preservation of that work. This, then, is not a case of a union seeking to restrict by contract or boycott an employer with respect to the products he uses, for the purpose of acquiring for its members work that had not previously been theirs.

. . . .

5. We are thus left with a legislative history which, on the precise point at issue, is essentially negative, which shows with fair conclusiveness only that Congress was not squarely faced with the problem these cases present. In view of Congress' deep commitment to the resolution of matters of vital importance to management and labor through the collective bargaining process, and its recognition of the boycott as a legitimate weapon in that process, it would be unfortunate were this Court to attribute to Congress, on the basis of such an opaque legislative record, a purpose to outlaw the kind of collective bargaining and conduct involved in these cases. Especially at a time when Congress is continuing to explore methods for meeting the economic problems increasingly arising in this technological age from scientific advances, this Court should not take such a step until Congress has made unmistakably clear that

it wishes wholly to exclude collective bargaining as one avenue of approach to solutions in this elusive aspect of our economy.

Mr. Justice Stewart, whom Mr. Justice Black, Mr. Justice Douglas, and Mr. Justice Clark join, dissenting. . . .

The Court undertakes a protracted review of legislative and decisional history in an effort to show that the clear words of the statute should be disregarded in these cases. But the fact is that the relevant history fully confirms that Congress meant what it said, and I therefore dissent.

The Court concludes that the Union's conduct in these cases falls outside the ambit of § 8(b)(4) because it had an ultimate purpose that the Court characterizes as "primary" in nature — the preservation of work for union members. But § 8(b)(4) is not limited to boycotts that have as their only purpose the forcing of any person to cease using the products of another; it is sufficient if that result is "an object" of the boycott. Legitimate union objectives may not be accomplished through means proscribed by the statute. See *NLRB v. Denver Bldg. Trades Council*, 341 U.S. 675, 688–689. Without question, preventing Frouge from using prefitted doors was "an object" of the Union's conduct here.

It is, of course, true that courts have distinguished "primary" and "secondary" activities, and have found the former permitted despite the literal applicability of the statutory language. See *IBEW, Local 761 v. NLRB*, 366 U.S. 667. But the Court errs in concluding that the product boycott conducted by the Union in these cases was protected primary activity. As the Court points out, a typical form of secondary boycott is the visitation of sanctions on Employer A, with whom the union has no dispute, in order to force him to cease doing business with Employer B, with whom the union does have a dispute. But this is not the only form of secondary boycott that § 8(b)(4) was intended to reach. The Court overlooks the fact that a product boycott for work preservation purposes has consistently been regarded by the courts, and by the Congress that passed the Taft-Hartley Act, as a proscribed "secondary boycott." [Citing *Allen Bradley* and earlier labor antitrust decisions.] . . .

NLRB v. International Longshoremen's Ass'n, 447 U.S. 490, 100 S. Ct. 2305, 65 L. Ed. 2d 289 (1980). Prior to the introduction of containerization, trucks carried loose, or break-bulk, cargo to and from piers, and that cargo was transferred piece-by-piece from truck tailgates to ship holds and from ship holds to trucks by longshore workers. During the 1960s, shipping companies introduced containers ranging in length from 20 to 40 feet. These were filled by producers, warehousers, or shippers, transported to the piers on trucks, and loaded onto ships by large cranes container-by-container. Incoming vessels were unloaded in a similar manner. In an effort to preserve member jobs, the ILA negotiated bargaining agreement provisions that required all containers owned or leased by shipping companies that were to be stripped (unloaded) or stuffed (loaded) within a 50-mile radius of the port to be restripped and restuffed by longshore employees on the piers before they could be loaded onto or unloaded from ships. Shipping firms claimed that these contractual provisions violated § 8(e) and that ILA efforts to enforce these rules contravened § 8(b)(4)(B). Since the Labor Board found that ILA workers had not engaged in such stripping or stuffing prior to containerization, it concluded that the challenged provisions constituted secondary "work acquisition" rather than primary "work preservation." The Supreme Court, however, rejected the Board's "simplistic" approach and directed it to engage in a more searching evaluation.

> Section 8(b)(4)(B) of the Act prohibits unions and their agents from engaging in secondary activities whose object is to force one employer to cease doing business with another. Section 8(e) makes unlawful those collective-bargaining agreements in which the employer agrees to cease doing business with any other person. Although § 8(e) does not in terms distinguish between primary and secondary activity, we have held that, as in § 8(b)(4)(B), Congress intended to reach only agreements with secondary objectives. See *NLRB v. Pipefitters*, 429 U.S. 507, 517 (1977) (hereinafter *Pipefitters*); *National Woodwork Mfgrs. Ass'n v. NLRB*, 386 U.S. 612, 620, 635 (1967) (hereinafter *National Woodwork*).
>
> Among the primary purposes protected by the Act is "the purpose of preserving for the contracting employees themselves work traditionally done by them." *Pipefitters, supra*, at 517. Whether an agreement is a lawful work preservation agreement depends on "whether, under the surrounding circumstances, the Union's objective was preservation of work for [bargaining unit] employees, or whether the [agreement was] tactically calculated to satisfy union objectives elsewhere. . . . . The touchstone is whether the agreement or its maintenance is addressed to the labor relations of the contracting employer vis-à-vis his own employees." *National Woodwork, supra*, at 644–645 (footnotes omitted). Under this approach, a lawful work preservation agreement must pass two tests: First, it must have as its objective the preservation of work traditionally performed by employees represented by the union. Second, the contracting employer must have the power to give the employees the work in question—the so-called "right of control" test of *Pipefitters, supra*. The rationale of the second test is that if the contracting employer has no power to assign the work, it is reasonable to infer that the agreement has a secondary objective, that is, to influence whoever does have such power over the work. "Were the latter the case, [the contracting employer] would be a neutral bystander, and the agreement or boycott would, within the intent of Congress, become secondary." *National Woodwork, supra*, at 644–645.
>
> In applying the work preservation doctrine, the first and most basic question is: What is the "work" that the agreement allegedly seeks to preserve? . . . [I]n many cases it is not so easy to find the starting point of the analysis. Work preservation agreements typically come into being when employees' traditional work is displaced, or threatened with displacement,

by technological innovation. The national labor policy expresses a preference for addressing "the threats to workers posed by increased technology and automation" by means of "labor-management agreements to ease these effects through collective bargaining on this most vital problem created by advanced technology." *National Woodwork, supra,* at 641, 642. In many instances, technological innovation may change the method of doing the work, instead of merely shifting the same work to a different location. One way to preserve the work of the employees represented by the union in the face of such a change is simply to insist that the innovation not be adopted and that the work continue to be done in the traditional way. The union in *National Woodwork* followed this tactic and negotiated an agreement in which the employer agreed not to use prefabricated materials. We held that agreement was lawful under §§ 8(e) and 8(b)(4)(B). But the protection Congress afforded to work preservation agreements cannot be limited solely to employees who respond to change with intransigence....

The Board's approach reflects a fundamental misconception of the work preservation doctrine as it has been applied in our previous cases. Identification of the work at issue in a complex case of technological displacement requires a careful analysis of the traditional work patterns that the parties are allegedly seeking to preserve, and of how the agreement seeks to accomplish that result under the changed circumstances created by the technological advance. The analysis must take into account "all the surrounding circumstances," *National Woodwork,* 386 U.S., at 644, including the nature of the work both before and after the innovation. In a relatively simple case, such as *National Woodwork* or *Pipefitters*, the inquiry may be of rather limited scope. Other, more complex cases will require a broader view, taking into account the transformation of several interrelated industries or types of work; this is such a case. Whatever its scope, however, the inquiry must be carefully focused: to determine whether an agreement seeks no more than to preserve the work of bargaining unit members, the Board must focus on the work of the bargaining unit employees, not on the work of other employees who may be doing the same or similar work, and examine the relationship between the work as it existed before the innovation and as the agreement proposes to preserve it....

Thus the Board's determination that the work of longshoremen has historically been the loading and unloading of ships should be only the beginning of the analysis. The next step is to look at how the contracting parties sought to preserve that work, to the extent possible, in the face of a massive technological change that largely eliminated the need for cargo handling at intermediate stages of the intermodal transportation of goods, and to evaluate the relationship between traditional longshore work and the work which the Rules attempt to assign to ILA members. This case presents a much more difficult problem than either *National Woodwork* or *Pipefitters* because the union did not simply insist on doing the work as it had always been done and try to prevent the employers from using container ships at all.... Instead, ILA permitted the great majority of containers to pass over the piers intact, reserving the right to stuff and strip only those containers that would otherwise have been stuffed or stripped locally by anyone except the beneficial owner's employees. The legality of the agreement turns, as an initial matter, on whether the historical and functional relationship between this retained work and traditional longshore work can support the conclusion that the objective of the agreement was work preservation rather than the satisfaction of union goals elsewhere.... [I]n judging the legality of a thoroughly bargained and apparently reasonable accommodation to technological change, the question is not whether the Rules represent the most rational or efficient response to innovation, but whether they are a legally permissible effort to preserve jobs.

Notes

1. *Aftermath*—On remand, the Labor Board generally sustained the validity of the ILA Rules on Containers. They were found to have a lawful work preservation objective, since they were functionally related to the traditional loading and unloading work performed by longshore workers. On the other hand, the practice of "short-stopping" (the loading and unloading of full shippers' loads) and certain warehousing practices were found to have an unlawful work acquisition objective, since these particular steps in the cargo-handling process no longer existed and the new container technology made the work of the longshore personnel wholly duplicative of the tasks performed by truckers and warehousers. *International Longshoremen's Ass'n*, 266 N.L.R.B. 230 (1983). On appeal, the Fourth Circuit rejected the Board's finding of any work acquisition objective with respect to these functions and sustained the ILA rules in their entirety. The Supreme Court affirmed the court's decision. *NLRB v. International Longshoremen's Ass'n*, 473 U.S. 61 (1985).

In *New York Shipping Ass'n v. FMC*, 854 F.2d 1338 (D.C. Cir. 1988), *cert. denied*, 488 U.S. 1041 (1989), the court sustained the authority of the Federal Maritime Commission to exclude labor policy considerations when it concluded that the "Rules on Containers" preserving the work of ILA members contravened shipping laws as being unreasonable and unjustly discriminatory vis-à-vis certain classes of shippers.

2. *What Is Primary Work Preservation?*—In *Sheet Metal Div. v. Local 38, Sheet Metal Workers Int'l Ass'n*, 208 F.3d 18 (2d Cir. 2000), the court held that a multi-employer agreement with Local 38 restricting sketching and fabrication of sheet metal work to Local 38 members was primary work preservation beyond the scope of § 8(e), because the union demonstrated that Local 38 members had traditionally performed such work. The fact that some of that work had occasionally been performed outside Local 38's geographical jurisdiction did not detract from the fact that Local 38 members had usually performed those tasks. *Accord, NLRB v. Int'l. Bhd. of Teamsters Local 251*, 691 F.3d 49 (1st Cir. 2012).

In *American Boiler Mfrs. Ass'n v. NLRB*, 404 F.2d 547 (8th Cir. 1968), *cert. denied*, 398 U.S. 960 (1970), *National Woodwork* was read as sustaining a "work *re*acquisition" clause. The employer argued unsuccessfully that the allowable preservation of "traditional work" encompassed only work that is "currently, continuously and exclusively performed by unit employees." *Compare Carrier Air Conditioning Co. v. NLRB*, 547 F.2d 1178 (2d Cir. 1976), *cert. denied*, 431 U.S. 974 (1977).

Maui Trucking v. Operating Eng'rs Local Union 3, 37 F.3d 436 (9th Cir. 1994), considered the legality of a contractual provision in an agreement between Local 3 and a general contractor association that specified the minimum wages and benefits that had to be paid to nonunion subcontractor employees performing offsite hauling work. The court indicated that this restriction would constitute a lawful primary work preservation clause if it was designed to protect the employment opportunities of general contractor employees, but would be an unlawful secondary provision if it preserved almost no general contractor jobs and was effectively designed to regulate the employment conditions of the nonunion subcontractors.

3. *Application of Pipefitters' "Right to Control" Test* — In *Local 742, United Brotherhood of Carpenters & Joiners (J.L. Simmons Co.)*, 237 N.L.R.B. 564 (1978), on remand following the *Pipefitters* case, the Board held that a union whose members refused to install premachined doors in a hospital violated § 8(b)(4). Their employer did not have the right to control use of the doors, since they were provided for in the hospital's specifications. As a result, this work stoppage was not primary since it was designed to influence the hospital.

Problem

36. For the last 30 years, a major meatpacking plant in Fort Worth, Texas, had an agreement with a local truck drivers' union requiring that deliveries of meat products to customers within the city of Fort Worth would be made by members of the union. During most of that period, the company's main plant was in Fort Worth, and thus the products almost always originated within the city for delivery to city customers. Toward the end of the last decade, however, the company began to move its primary slaughtering and processing operations outside of Fort Worth. As a result, of the 120 truck drivers employed at the beginning of the prior contract term, only 40 were employed four years later when negotiations began for a new agreement. Deliveries to customers in Fort Worth were increasingly being made by over-the-road drivers whose runs originated from the company's new facilities outside of the Fort Worth area.

In response to the new state of affairs, the union's chief objective in this round of negotiations is the recovery of jobs lost to the out-of-town truck drivers and the retention of truck driving jobs in the city. To that end, the union proposed two clauses for the new agreement:

1. A requirement that all deliveries in Fort Worth, whether originating from within the city or from without, be made by local truck drivers covered

by the agreement. Under this provision, the packing company would be required to divide their shipments from their plant outside of Fort Worth into two segments — from the plant to a terminal in the city, and then from the terminal to the customers, with the covered drivers making the latter runs.

2. A subcontracting requirement providing that any time the company did not have sufficient trucking capacity to deliver within the Fort Worth area, it could contract with any outside trucking company who employs truck drivers who are members of the local truck drivers' union.

The union has now threatened to strike in order to put pressure on the company to accede to its demands. The company has claimed that the two clauses violate the NLRA.

Are either of the two clauses problematic under the NLRA? Would a strike to obtain either of them constitute an unfair labor practice?

G. Damages for Unlawful Secondary Activity

United Mine Workers, District 28 v. Patton
United States Court of Appeals, Fourth Circuit
211 F.2d 742, *cert. denied*, 348 U.S. 824 (1954)

[Plaintiff was a partner in a mining operation in the coal fields of Western Virginia. The basis of the action was that the defendants by a strike at the mines of the Clinchfield Coal Corp. caused that corporation to cease doing business with plaintiff, resulting in the destruction of the partnership business. A jury in the trial court below awarded the partnership actual damages in the sum of $150,000 and punitive damages in the sum of $75,000 under the provisions of § 303 of the LMRA.]

PARKER, CHIEF JUDGE. . . . . The chief argument of the defendants . . . is that there is no evidence that they authorized or ratified the strikes upon which plaintiffs rely for recovery. It is true that there is no evidence of any resolution of either the United Mine Workers or District 28 authorizing or ratifying the strikes. There is evidence, however, that the strikes were called by the Field Representative of the United Mine Workers, who was employed by District 28, and that he was engaged in the organization work that was being carried on by the international union through District 28, which was a mere division of the international union. . . .

Section 301(b) of the Labor Management Relations Act, 29 U.S.C. § 185(b) expressly provides:

(b) Any labor organization which represents employees in an industry affecting commerce as defined in this chapter and any employer whose activities affect commerce as defined in this chapter shall be bound by the acts of its agents. . . .

[S]ection 301(e), 61 Stat. 156, 157, 29 U.S.C. § 185(e) . . . provides:

For the purposes of this section, in determining whether any person is acting as an "agent" of another person so as to make such other person responsible for his acts, the question of whether the specific acts performed were actually authorized or subsequently ratified shall not be controlling. . . .

In his analysis of the bill Senator Taft had the following to say, 93 Cong. Record, p. 7001, Legislative History of Labor Management Relations Act, Vol. 2, p. 1622:

Section 2(2), 2(13), and 301(e):

The conference agreement in defining the term employer struck out the vague phrase in the Wagner Act "anyone acting in the interest of an employer" and inserted in lieu thereof the word "agent." The term agent is defined in §2(13) and §301(e), since it is used throughout the unfair labor practice sections of title I and in §§301 and 303 of title III. In defining the term the conference amendment reads "the question of whether the specific acts performed were actually authorized or subsequently ratified shall not be controlling." This restores the law of agency as it has been developed at common law. . . .

[W]e think there was error in allowing the jury to award punitive damages. This is not a case brought under the diversity jurisdiction of the federal courts to enforce a common law liability, where we are governed by state decisions and would be bound on the question of punitive damages by the decision of the Supreme Court of Appeals of Virginia in *United Constr. Workers v. Laburnum Constr. Corp., supra*, 194 Va. 872, 75 S.E.2d 694 (1953). There is no diversity of citizenship and the plaintiffs are entitled to invoke the jurisdiction of the federal courts only because they sue on a cause of action created by a federal statute, *i.e.*, on the cause of action created by §303(b) of the Labor Management Relations Act, 29 U.S.C. §187(b), heretofore quoted. That section makes no provision for the recovery of punitive damages; but on the contrary provides expressly that the aggrieved party "shall recover *the damages by him sustained* and the cost of the suit." (Italics supplied.) "Punitive damages are damages beyond and above the amount which a plaintiff has really suffered, and they are awarded upon the theory that they are a punishment to the defendant, and not a mere matter of compensation for injuries sustained by plaintiff." *Washington Gas Light Co. v. Lansden*, 172 U.S. 534, 553 (1899). . . .

In the absence of anything in the act itself or in its history indicating an intention on the part of Congress to authorize the recovery of punitive damages by this highly controversial legislation, the courts would not be justified, we think, in construing it to permit such recovery. . . .

Notes

1. *Punitive Damages*—As indicated in the principal case, punitive damages cannot be awarded under §303, but such damages may be granted under applicable state law. In *Teamsters, Chauffeurs & Helpers Union Local 20 v. Morton*, 377 U.S. 252 (1964), however, the Court unanimously held that "state law has been displaced by §303 in private damage actions based on peaceful union secondary activity."

2. *Parties Plaintiff Under § 303* — Either primary or secondary employers may sue for damages under § 303. *United Brick & Clay Workers v. Deena Artware, Inc.*, 198 F.2d 637 (6th Cir.), *cert. denied*, 344 U.S. 897 (1952) (primary); *International Longshoremen's Ass'n v. Allied Int'l*, 456 U.S. 212 (1982) (secondary).

Although the literal language of § 303(b) would appear to permit anyone even remotely injured by reason of an unlawful secondary boycott to sue for damages, courts have generally extended standing only to those parties foreseeably injured in a manner intended by the labor organization involved. Where there was no evidence to suggest that the boycotting union sought to injure the employees of the neutral company whose ships its members refused to unload, the court found that an employee of that employer lacked standing to sue the union for the economic losses she suffered when her boycotted employer abolished her job. *Charvet v. International Longshoremen's Ass'n*, 736 F.2d 1572 (D.C. Cir. 1984).

3. *Nature of the Remedy* — Under § 303, a union may be sued for damages by a private party in federal district court for engaging in any of the kinds of activity defined in § 8(b)(4). This does not mean that the filing of a damage suit must await a final NLRB order stating that § 8(b)(4) was violated. An action may be brought under § 303 regardless of whether unfair practice charges are filed with the NLRB; or, if unfair practice charges have been filed with the NLRB, a damage suit may be brought at the same time. *International Longshoremen's & Warehousemen's Union v. Juneau Spruce Corp.*, 342 U.S. 237 (1952). Damages have been awarded even though there has been a finding that no unfair labor practice was committed. *See United Brick & Clay Workers v. Deena Artware, supra*. However, in several cases, a final decision of the NLRB as to an unfair labor practice under § 8(b)(4) has been treated as res judicata or collateral estoppel in a subsequent § 303 action. *Paramount Transport Systems v. Chauffeurs, Teamsters & Helpers Local 150*, 436 F.2d 1064 (9th Cir. 1971); *International Wire v. International Brotherhood of Electrical Workers Local 38*, 475 F.2d 1078 (6th Cir.), *cert. denied*, 414 U.S. 867 (1973).

Section V. Jurisdictional Disputes

NLRB, Thirty-Seventh Annual Report
121 (1972)

Section 8(b)(4)(D) prohibits a labor organization from engaging in or inducing strike action for the purpose of forcing any employer to assign particular work to "employees in a particular labor organization or in a particular trade, craft, or class rather than to employees in another labor organization or in another trade, craft, or class, unless such employer is failing to conform to an order or certification of the Board determining the bargaining representative for employees performing such work."

An unfair labor practice charge under this section, however, must be handled differently from a charge alleging any other type of unfair labor practice. Section 10(k) requires that parties to a jurisdictional dispute be given 10 days, after notice of the filing of the charges with the Board, to adjust their dispute. If at the end of that time they are unable to "submit to the Board satisfactory evidence that they have adjusted, or agreed upon methods for the voluntary adjustment of the dispute," the Board is empowered to hear the dispute and make an affirmative assignment of the disputed work.

Section 10(k) further provides that pending 8(b)(4)(D) charges shall be dismissed where the Board's determination of the underlying dispute has been complied with, or the parties have voluntarily adjusted the dispute. An 8(b)(4)(D) complaint issues if the party charged fails to comply with the Board's determination. A complaint may be also issued by the General Counsel in the event recourse to the method agreed upon to adjust the dispute fails to result in an adjustment.

NLRB v. Radio & Television Broadcast Engineers Local 1212 (CBS), 364 U.S. 573, 81 S. Ct. 330, 5 L. Ed. 2d 302 (1961). Columbia Broadcasting System (CBS) was scheduled to conduct a television broadcast from the Waldorf-Astoria Hotel, and it assigned the lighting work to individuals represented by the stage employees union. The technicians union protested this work assignment, and its members refused to operate the cameras unless the lighting work was assigned to them. After the program was cancelled, CBS filed a § 8(b)(4)(D) charge challenging the action of the technicians union. Since the parties failed to agree upon a voluntary dispute resolution process, the Board held a limited § 10(k) proceeding. The Board found that the technicians union had no right to perform the work in question under an outstanding Board certification, a prior Board work assignment order, or the applicable bargaining agreement, and it held that the union's work refusal constituted a § 8(b)(4)(D) violation. The NLRB refused to consider other factors, such as the employer's prior practices or the custom within the industry in general, due to the absence of such express authorization in § 10(k). The Supreme Court rejected the Labor Board's narrow reading of its authority under that statutory provision.

> ... Obviously, if § 8(b)(4)(D) stood alone, what this union did in the absence of a Board order or certification entitling its members to be assigned to these particular jobs would be enough to support a finding of an unfair labor practice in a normal proceeding under § 10(c) of the act. But when Congress created this new type of unfair labor practice by enacting § 8(b)(4)(D) as part of the Taft-Hartley Act in 1947, it also added § 10(k) to the act. Section 10(k) ... quite plainly emphasizes the belief of Congress that it is more important to industrial peace that jurisdictional disputes be settled permanently than it is that unfair labor practice sanctions for jurisdictional strikes be imposed upon unions. Accordingly, § 10(k) offers strong inducements to quarrelling unions to settle their differences by directing dismissal of unfair labor practice charges upon voluntary adjustment of jurisdictional disputes. And even where no voluntary adjustment is made, "the Board is empowered and directed," by § 10(k), "to hear and determine the dispute

out of which such unfair labor practice shall have arisen," and upon compliance by the disputants with the Board's decision the unfair labor practice charges must be dismissed.

. . . .

We agree with the Second, Third, and Seventh Circuits that § 10(k) requires the Board to decide jurisdictional disputes on their merits and conclude that in this case that requirement means that the board should affirmatively have decided whether the technicians or the stage employees were entitled to the disputed work. The language of § 10(k), supplementing § 8(b)(4)(D) as it does, sets up a method adopted by Congress to try to get jurisdictional disputes settled. The words "hear and determine the dispute" convey not only the idea of hearing but also the idea of deciding a controversy. . . . This language also indicates a congressional purpose to have the Board do something more than merely look at prior Board orders and certifications or a collective bargaining contract to determine whether one or the other union has a clearly defined statutory or contractual right to have the employees it represents perform certain work tasks. For, in the vast majority of cases, such a narrow determination would leave the broader problem of work assignments in the hands of the employer, exactly where it was before the enactment of § 10(k) . . . .

The Board contends, however, that this interpretation of § 10(k) should be rejected, despite the language and history of that section. In support of this contention, it . . . points out that § 10(k) sets forth no standards to guide it in determining jurisdictional disputes on their merits. . . . It is true that this forces the Board to exercise under § 10(k) powers which are broad and lacking in rigid standards to govern their application. But administrative agencies are frequently given rather loosely defined powers to cope with problems as difficult as those posed by jurisdictional disputes and strikes. It might have been better, as some persuasively argued in Congress, to intrust this matter to arbitrators. But Congress, after discussion and consideration, decided to intrust this decision to the Board. It has had long experience in hearing and disposing of similar labor problems. With this experience and a knowledge of the standards generally used by arbitrators, unions, employers, joint boards and others in wrestling with this problem, we are confident that the Board need not disclaim the power given it for lack of standards. Experience and common sense will supply the grounds for the performance of this job which Congress has assigned the Board.

Notes

1. *What Is a Jurisdictional Dispute?* — The essence of a "jurisdictional dispute" within the meaning of §§ 8(b)(4)(D) and 10(k) is the existence of "a dispute between two or more groups of employees over which is entitled to do certain work for an employer." When one of two potentially competing labor organizations expressly disclaims interest in the work at issue, no jurisdictional dispute exists, and the Labor Board lacks the authority to conduct a § 10(k) proceeding or to find a § 8(b)(4)(D) violation. *See International Longshoremen's & Warehousemen's Union, Local 62-B v. NLRB*, 781 F.2d 919 (D.C. Cir. 1986).

A jurisdictional dispute need not involve two competing unions. A union thus violated § 8(b)(4)(D) when it picketed an employer for assigning wood-chip loading work to its own nonunion employees rather than to union employees who had performed loading work for a separate company with which the employer was no longer dealing. *International Longshoremen's & Warehousemen's Union, Local 14 v. NLRB*, 85 F.3d 646 (D.C. Cir. 1996).

In *NLRB v. Plasterers' Local Union 79*, 404 U.S. 116 (1971), the Court held that employers with substantial financial stakes in the outcome of § 10(k) proceedings are "parties to the dispute" within the meaning of that section. The NLRB is thus empowered to determine jurisdictional disputes under § 10(k) when only the competing unions—but not the interested employers—have agreed upon a voluntary method of adjustment.

2. *Relationship to § 301 Suits*—In *ILWU, Local 32 v. Pacific Maritime Ass'n*, 773 F.2d 1012 (9th Cir. 1985), *cert. denied*, 476 U.S. 1158 (1986), the court found that a union violated § 8(b)(4)(D) when, after it had lost a § 10(k) proceeding to another labor organization, it filed a § 301 suit seeking to enforce an arbitral award directing the employer to make "time-in-lieu" payments for the work it had lost, since such action was without merit in light of the NLRB's § 10(k) determination and constituted "coercion" within the meaning of § 8(b)(4)(D). *See also International Longshoremen's & Warehousemen's Union v. NLRB*, 884 F.2d 1407 (D.C. Cir. 1989) (filing of grievance contrary to prior § 10(k) award constitutes "coercion" under § 8(b)(4)(D)); *T. Equip. Corp. v. Massachusetts Laborers' Dist. Council*, 166 F.3d 11 (1st Cir. 1999) (arbitral award that conflicts with Labor Board determination in § 10(k) proceeding is unenforceable).

In *Sheet Metal Workers Local 27 v. E.P. Donnelly, Inc.*, 737 F.3d 879 (3d Cir. 2013), the court enforced the Board's ruling that a labor union violated the Act when it continued to claim roofing work on a construction job after the Board had awarded the work to another union by filing an LMRA § 301 claim seeking damages and monetary relief to enforce a favorable arbitration award that it had secured pursuant to a dispute resolution system applicable to project labor agreements. The court found that continuing to pursue the § 301 lawsuit in contravention of the Board's award of work violated § 8(b)(4)(ii)(D).

3. *Factors in Awarding Disputed Work*—The factors the Board considers relevant in determining who is entitled to disputed work include: "the skills and work involved, certifications by the Board, company and industry practice, agreements between unions and between employers and unions, awards of arbitrators, joint boards, and the AFL-CIO in the same or related cases, the assignment made by the employer, and the efficient operation of the employer's business." *Machinists Lodge 1743 (J. A. Jones Construction Co.)*, 135 N.L.R.B. 1402, 1410–11 (1962).

Section VI. "Featherbedding"

American Newspaper Publishers Ass'n v. NLRB
Supreme Court of the United States
345 U.S. 100, 73 S. Ct. 552, 97 L. Ed. 852 (1953)

MR. JUSTICE BURTON delivered the opinion of the Court.

The question here is whether a labor organization engages in an unfair labor practice within the meaning of § 8(b)(6) of the National Labor Relations Act, as amended by the Labor Management Relations Act, 1947, when it insists that newspaper publishers pay printers for reproducing advertising matter for which the publishers ordinarily have no use. For the reasons hereafter stated, we hold that it does not....

When a newspaper advertisement was set up in type, it was impressed on a cardboard matrix, or "mat." These mats were used by their makers and also were reproduced and distributed, at little or no cost, to other publishers who used them as molds for metal castings from which to print the same advertisement. This procedure by-passed all compositors except those who made up the original form. Facing this loss of work, ITU secured the agreement of newspaper publishers to permit their respective compositors, at convenient times, to set up duplicate forms for all local advertisements in precisely the same manner as though the mat had not been used. For this reproduction work the printers received their regular pay. The doing of this "made work" came to be known in the trade as "setting bogus." It was a wasteful procedure. Nevertheless, it has become a recognized idiosyncrasy of the trade and a customary feature of the wage structure and work schedule of newspaper printers.... On rare occasions the reproduced compositions are used to print the advertisements when rerun, but, ordinarily, they are promptly consigned to the "hell box" and melted down.

However desirable the elimination of all industrial featherbedding practices may have appeared to Congress, the legislative history of the Taft-Hartley Act demonstrates that when the legislation was put in final form Congress decided to limit the practice but little by law....

> There is one further provision which may possibly be of interest which was not in the Senate bill. The House had rather elaborate provisions prohibiting so-called featherbedding practices and making them unlawful labor practices. The Senate conferees, while not approving of featherbedding practices, felt that it was impracticable to give to a board or a court the power to say that so many men are all right, and so many men are too many. It would require a practical application of the law by the courts in hundreds

of different industries, and a determination of facts which it seemed to me would be almost impossible. So we declined to adopt the provisions which are now in the Petrillo Act. After all, that statute applies to only one industry. Those provisions are now the subject of court procedure. Their constitutionality has been questioned. We thought that probably we had better wait and see what happened, in any event, even though we are in favor of prohibiting all featherbedding practices. However, we did accept one provision which makes it an unlawful labor practice for a union to accept money for people who do not work. That seemed to be a fairly clear case, easy to determine, and we accepted that additional unfair labor practice on the part of unions, which was not in the Senate bill.

93 Cong. Rec. 6441 [comments of Senator Taft]. *See also*, his supplementary analysis inserted in the Record June 12, 1947. 93 Cong. Rec. 6859.

As indicated above, the Taft-Hartley bill, H.R. 3020, when it passed in the House, April 17, 1947, contained in §§ 2(17) and 12(a)(3)(B) an explicit condemnation of featherbedding. Its definition of featherbedding was based upon that in the Lea Act. For example, it condemned practices which required an employer to employ "persons in excess of the number of employees reasonably required by such employer to perform actual services," as well as practices which required an employer to pay "for services . . . which are not to be performed."

The substitution of the present § 8(b)(6) for that definition compels the conclusion that § 8(b)(6) means what the court below has said it means. The Act now limits its condemnation to instances where a labor organization or its agents exact pay from an employer in return for services not performed or not to be performed. Thus, where work is done by an employee, with the employer's consent, a labor organization's demand that the employee be compensated for time spent in doing the disputed work does not become an unfair labor practice. The transaction simply does not fall within the kind of featherbedding defined in the statute. . . . Section 8(b)(6) leaves to collective bargaining the determination of what, if any, work, including bona fide "made work," shall be included as compensable services and what rate of compensation shall be paid for it.

Accordingly, the judgment of the Court of Appeals sustaining dismissal of the complaint, insofar as it was based upon § 8(b)(6), is

Affirmed.

[**The dissenting opinions of Mr. Justice Douglas and Mr. Justice Clark, with whom The Chief Justice joined, are omitted.**]

NLRB v. Gamble Enterprises, Inc., 345 U.S. 117, 73 S. Ct. 560, 97 L. Ed. 864 (1953). The Musicians' Union refused to permit out-of-town orchestras to appear in respondent's theater unless it agreed to employ local musicians for a number of independent performances having a relation to the number of traveling band appearances.

This and similar union proposals were declined by respondent on the ground that the local orchestra was neither necessary nor desired. Respondent sought a Board order based on § 8(b)(6). *Held*:

> Since we and the Board treat the union's proposals as in good faith contemplating the performance of actual services, we agree that the union has not, on this record, engaged in a practice proscribed by § 8(b)(6). It has remained for respondent to accept or reject the union's offers on their merits in the light of all material circumstances. We do not find it necessary to determine also whether such offers were 'in the nature of an exaction.' We are not dealing here with offers of mere 'token' or nominal services. The proposals before us were appropriately treated by the Board as offers in good faith of substantial performances by competent musicians. There is no reason to think that sham can be substituted for substance under § 8(b)(6) any more than under any other statute. Payments for 'standing-by,' or for the substantial equivalent of 'standing-by,' are not payments for services performed, but when an employer receives a bona fide offer of competent performance of relevant services, it remains for the employer, through free and fair negotiation, to determine whether such offer shall be accepted and what compensation shall be paid for the work done.

345 U.S. at 123–24.

Section VII. National Labor Relations Act Preemption

To what extent does federal labor legislation "preempt" the regulatory power of the states with respect to industries "affecting commerce"? In those small and local trades in which there is no direct or indirect connection with interstate commerce, state power remains unaffected by the federal preemption doctrine. However, where state law trenches upon the federal power to regulate interstate commerce and to legislate in the area of labor relations, federal law controls. *See* U.S. Const. art. I, § 8 (commerce clause); U.S. Const. art. VI (supremacy clause).

Congress has not chosen to exercise its power and to exclusively occupy the field of labor relations. As a result, interesting questions have arisen around state laws that potentially interfere with the federal scheme of regulation. Preemption questions arise around state laws that contradict federal law or that supplement federal law but provide remedies not available under federal law, and the state laws in question can assume the form of statutes or common law (called *Garmon* preemption). Preemption questions can also arise in situations where state law seeks to regulate in an area that Congress chose to leave unregulated, altering the balance of power between labor and management (*Machinists* preemption). This section addresses the doctrines applicable to those situations. Preemption questions can also arise where a collective bargaining agreement governs a situation for which an individual or group of employees are seeking redress in the state courts on a state statutory or common law claim that necessitates interpretation or application of the contract's terms (called LMRA § 301 preemption). We will cover this third strain of preemption in Part Six in connection with enforcement of the collective bargaining agreement.

A. *Garmon* Preemption

The *Garmon* strain of preemption doctrine guards against a substantive conflict between state or local law and federal labor law: the NLRA preempts state regulation of conduct that is protected or prohibited by the NLRA, or arguably protected or prohibited by the NLRA.

San Diego Building Trades Council v. Garmon
Supreme Court of the United States
359 U.S. 236, 79 S. Ct. 773, 3 L. Ed. 2d 775 (1959)

[In the *Garmon* case, which has become the leading case setting out the general principles of federal preemption, the issue on certiorari was whether the State of California had jurisdiction to award damages for a tort under state law against a union for engaging in peaceful picketing. The purpose of the picketing was in dispute, the union claiming that the only purpose was to educate the workers and persuade them to become members, and the employer claiming that the sole purpose was to compel the employer to execute a union shop agreement.]

MR. JUSTICE FRANKFURTER delivered the opinion of the Court. . . .

Administration is more than a means of regulation; administration is regulation. We have been concerned with conflict in its broadest sense; conflict with a complex and interrelated federal scheme of law, remedy, and administration. Thus, judicial concern has necessarily focused on the nature of the activities which the States have sought to regulate, rather than on the method of regulation adopted. When the exercise of state power over a particular area of activity threatened interference with the clearly indicated policy of industrial relations, it has been judicially necessary to preclude the States from acting. However, due regard for the presuppositions of our embracing federal system, including the principle of diffusion of power not as a matter of doctrinaire localism but as a promoter of democracy, has required us not to find withdrawal from the States of power to regulate where the activity regulated was a merely peripheral concern of the Labor Management Relations Act. *See IAM v. Gonzales*, 356 U.S. 617 (1958). Or where the regulated conduct touched interests so deeply rooted in local feeling and responsibility that, in the absence of compelling congressional direction, we could not infer that Congress had deprived the States of the power to act.

When it is clear or may fairly be assumed that the activities which a State purports to regulate are protected by § 7 of the Taft-Hartley Act, or constitute an unfair labor practice under § 8, due regard for the federal enactment requires that state jurisdiction must yield. To leave the States free to regulate conduct so plainly within the central aim of federal regulation involves too great a danger of conflict between power asserted by Congress and requirements imposed by state law. Nor has it mattered whether the States have acted through laws of broad general application rather than laws specifically directed towards the governance of industrial relations. Regardless of the mode adopted, to allow the States to control conduct which is the subject of national regulation would create potential frustration of national purposes.

At times it has not been clear whether the particular activity regulated by the states was governed by §7 or §8 or was, perhaps, outside both these sections. But courts are not primary tribunals to adjudicate such issues. It is essential to the administration of the Act that these determinations be left in the first instance to the National Labor Relations Board. What is outside the scope of this Court's authority cannot remain within a State's power and state jurisdiction too must yield to the exclusive primary competence of the Board. *See, e.g., Garner v. Teamsters*, 346 U.S. 485 (1953), especially at 489–491; *Weber v. AnheuserBusch, Inc.*, 348 U.S. 468 (1955).

The case before us is such a case. The adjudication in California has throughout been based on the assumption that the behavior of the petitioning unions constituted an unfair labor practice. This conclusion was derived by the California courts from the facts as well as from their view of the Act. It is not for us to decide whether the National Labor Relations Board would have, or should have, decided these questions in the same manner. When an activity is arguably subject to §7 or §8 of the Act, the States as well as the federal courts must defer to the exclusive competence of the National Labor Relations Board if the danger of state interference with national policy is to be averted.

To require the States to yield to the primary jurisdiction of the National Board does not ensure Board adjudication of the status of a disputed activity. If the Board decides, subject to appropriate federal judicial review, that conduct is protected by §7, or prohibited by §8, then the matter is at an end, and the States are ousted of all jurisdiction. Or the Board may decide that an activity is neither protected nor prohibited, and thereby raise the question whether such activity may be regulated by the States.[34] . . . In the absence of the Board's clear determination that an activity is neither protected nor prohibited or of compelling precedent applied to essentially undisputed facts, it is not for this Court to decide whether such activities are subject to state jurisdiction. . . . The governing consideration is that to allow the States to control activities that are potentially subject to federal regulation involves too great a danger of conflict with national labor policy.[35]

---

34. [4] *See UAW v. WERB*, 336 U.S. 245 (1949). The approach taken in that case, in which the Court undertook for itself to determine the status of the disputed activity, has not been followed in later decisions, and is no longer of general application.

35. [5] "When Congress has taken the particular subject matter in hand coincidence is as ineffective as opposition. . . ." *Charleston & West. Carolina R. Co. v. Varnville Furniture Co.*, 237 U.S. 597, 601 (1915).

In the light of these principles the case before us is clear. Since the National Labor Relations Board has not adjudicated the status of the conduct for which the State of California seeks to give a remedy in damages, and since such activity is arguably within the compass of § 7 or § 8 of the Act, the State's jurisdiction is displaced.

Nor is it significant that California asserted its power to give damages rather than to enjoin what the Board may restrain though it could not compensate. Our concern is with delimiting areas of conduct which must be free from state regulation if national policy is to be left unhampered. Such regulation can be as effectively exerted through an award of damages as through some form of preventive relief. The obligation to pay compensation can be, indeed is designed to be, a potent method of governing conduct and controlling policy. Even the States' salutary effort to redress private wrongs or grant compensation for past harm cannot be exerted to regulate activities that are potentially subject to the exclusive federal regulatory scheme. *See Garner v. Teamsters*, 346 U.S. 485, 492–497 (1953). It may be that an award of damages in a particular situation will not, in fact, conflict with the active assertion of federal authority. The same may be true of the incidence of a particular state injunction. To sanction either involves a conflict with federal policy in that it involves allowing two law-making sources to govern. In fact, since remedies form an ingredient of any integrated scheme of regulation, to allow the State to grant a remedy here which has been withheld from the National Labor Relations Board only accentuates the danger of conflict.

It is true that we have allowed the States to grant compensation for the consequences, as defined by the traditional law of torts, of conduct marked by violence and imminent threats to the public order. *UAW v. Russell*, 356 U.S. 634 (1958); *United Constr. Workers v. Laburnum*, 347 U.S. 656 (1954). We have also allowed the States to enjoin such conduct. *Youngdahl v. Rainfair*, 355 U.S. 131 (1957); *UAW v. WERB*, 351 U.S. 266 (1956). State jurisdiction has prevailed in these situations because the compelling state interest, in the scheme of our federalism, in the maintenance of domestic peace is not overridden in the absence of clearly expressed congressional direction. We recognize that the opinion in *United Constr. Workers v. Laburnum*, 347 U.S. 656 (1954), found support in the fact that the state remedy had no federal counterpart. But that decision was determined, as is demonstrated by the question to which review was restricted by the "type of conduct" involved, *i.e.*, "intimidation and threats of violence." In the present case there is no such compelling state interest.

[The concurring opinion of Mr. Justice Harlan, with whom Justices Clark, Whittaker, and Stewart joined, is omitted.]

Notes

1. *Interests Deeply Rooted in Local Feeling and Responsibility* — As the Court explained in *Garmon*, states retain their historic power to regulate traditionally local matters such as public safety and order, and the use of streets and highways. *Allen-Bradley*

Local v. Wisconsin Employment Relations Board, 315 U.S. 740 (1942). Thus, in *Youngdahl v. Rainfair, Inc.*, 355 U.S. 131 (1957), the Supreme Court held that a state may exercise its police power to enjoin threats of violence, obstruction of the streets and of entrances to a plant, and massed name-calling, calculated to provoke violence, but the state may not simultaneously enjoin other picketing at the plant, because regulation of peaceful picketing is within the exclusive domain of the NLRB.

2. *Scope and Review of State Court Injunctions* — When a state court issues an injunction against union collective action that appears to be within the exclusive jurisdiction of NLRB, a federal court will not entertain a union petition to enjoin enforcement of that state court injunction, since under 28 U.S.C. § 2283, "a court of the United States may not grant an injunction to stay proceedings in a State court except as expressly authorized by Act of Congress, or where necessary in aid of its jurisdiction, or to protect or effectuate its judgments." *Amalgamated Clothing Workers v. Richman Bros.*, 348 U.S. 511 (1955). The union must ordinarily appeal the injunctive order to the highest state court and then to the United States Supreme Court. A union's burden in contesting a state court injunction has been considerably eased, however, by Supreme Court decisions modifying the general rule as follows:

a. If an unfair labor practice charge has been filed with the NLRB and the Board has sought a federal court injunction, the federal court, "in aid of its jurisdiction," may enjoin the enforcement of the state court injunction. *Capital Service, Inc. v. NLRB*, 347 U.S. 501 (1954). Even in the absence of unfair labor practice charges, the NLRB may seek federal injunctive relief against preempted state court action. In *NLRB v. Nash-Finch Co.*, 404 U.S. 138 (1971), the Supreme Court sustained the power of the Board to ask a federal court to enjoin a state court injunction against peaceful picketing, despite the prohibition of 28 U.S.C. § 2283 against federal injunctions to stay state court proceedings and the failure of the affected company to file § 8(b)(4) or § 8(b)(7) charges against the union. Since the Board had no basis for requesting a § 10(j) or § 10(*l*) injunction, the express exception in § 2283 permitting a federal court to enjoin state proceedings "in aid of its jurisdiction" was not applicable. But in order "to prevent frustration of the policies of the Act," the Board was found to have "implied authority," as a federal agency, "to enjoin state action where its federal power preempts the field."

b. *ILA v. Davis*, 476 U.S. 380 (1986), held that since a preemption claim challenges the actual power of a state court to hear a particular case, that jurisdictional question must be resolved according to federal — not state — law. The Court thus rejected a state court attempt to treat a preemption issue as an "affirmative defense" that could be waived if not raised in a timely fashion. *See also Liner v. Jafco, Inc.*, 375 U.S. 301 (1964) (question whether state court injunctive order has become moot is question of federal, not state, law).

c. A state court has no power to hold a person in contempt for violating an injunction entered by a court lacking jurisdiction because of federal preemption. It is a denial of due process to convict someone of contempt without giving the person an opportunity to establish that the state court was trenching on exclusive federal domain. *In re Green*, 369 U.S. 689 (1962). *See also Ex parte George*, 371 U.S. 72 (1962). *Compare United States v. United Mine Workers*, 330 U.S. 258 (1947) (a state court may issue a temporary injunctive order that must be obeyed while it determines whether it possesses jurisdiction over the underlying controversy).

Amalgamated Ass'n of Street, Electric Railway & Motor Coach Employees of America v. Lockridge

Supreme Court of the United States
403 U.S. 274, 91 S. Ct. 1909, 29 L. Ed. 2d 473 (1971)

[Lockridge was employed by Greyhound Lines under a collective contract that contained a union security clause. The union constitution had conflicting provisions regarding the status of members who failed to tender their dues in a timely manner. One stated that members one month behind were debarred from benefits, with persons two months in arrears being suspended from membership. Another provision said that members working in shops covered by union security clauses shall be suspended from membership and terminated from employment if they fell one month behind. The union had not previously sought the discharge of delinquent members until they were two months in arrears. Nonetheless, after Lockridge fell one month behind, the union sought and obtained his termination. He then sued the union in state court, claiming that it had violated an implied promise not to seek the termination of members who were only one month in arrears. Lockridge obtained a judgment for $32,678.56 against the union on a breach of contract theory. The question whether the union had properly sought his job termination involved interpretation of both the union constitution and the collective bargaining agreement. The Supreme Court reversed the judgment on the basis of federal preemption, and the Court's opinion explains more fully the rationale of *Garmon*.]

MR. JUSTICE HARLAN delivered the opinion of the Court. . . .

II

A. . . . [I]n *San Diego Building Trades Council v. Garmon*, 359 U.S. 236, 245 (1959), we held that the National Labor Relations Act preempts the jurisdiction of state and federal courts to regulate conduct "arguably subject to § 7 or § 8 of the Act." On their face, [§§ 8(b)(2), 8(b)(1)(A), and 8(a)(3)] of the Act at least arguably either permit or forbid the union conduct dealt with by the judgment below. For the evident thrust of this aspect of the federal statutory scheme is to permit the enforcement of union security clauses, by dismissal from employment, only for failure to pay dues. Whatever other sanctions may be employed to exact compliance with those internal union rules unrelated to dues payment, the Act seems generally to exclude dismissal from employment. *See Radio Officers' Union v. National Labor Relations Bd.*, 347 U.S. 17 (1954). Indeed, in the course of rejecting petitioner's preemption argument, the Idaho Supreme Court stated that, in its opinion, the Union "did most certainly violate 8(b)(1)(A), did most certainly violate 8(b)(2) . . . and probably caused the employer to violate 8(a)(3)." 93 Idaho at 299, 460 P.2d at 724. Thus, given the broad preemption principle enunciated in *Garmon*, the want of state court power to resolve Lockridge's complaint might well seem to follow as a matter of course.

The Idaho Supreme Court, however, concluded that it nevertheless possessed jurisdiction in these circumstances. That determination, as we understand it, rested upon three separate propositions; all of which are urged here by respondent. The first is that the Union's conduct was not only an unfair labor practice, but a breach of its contract with Lockridge as well. "Preemption is not established simply by showing that the same facts will establish two different legal wrongs." 93 Idaho at 300, 460 P.2d at 725. In other words *Garmon*, the state court and respondent assert, states a principle applicable only where the state law invoked is designed specifically to regulate labor relations; it has no force where the State applies its general common law of contracts to resolve disputes between a union and its members. Secondly, it is urged that the facts that might be shown to vindicate Lockridge's claim in the Idaho state courts differ from those relevant to proceedings governed by the National Labor Relations Act. It is said that the conduct regulated by the Act is union and employer discrimination; general contract law takes into account only the correctness of competing interpretations of the language embodied in agreements. 93 Idaho at 303–304, 460 P.2d at 728–729. Finally, there recurs throughout the state court opinion, and the arguments of respondent here, the theme that the facts of the instant case render it virtually indistinguishable from *Association of Machinists v. Gonzales*, 356 U.S. 617 (1959), where this Court upheld the exercise of state court jurisdiction in an opinion written only one Term prior to *Garmon* by the author of *Garmon* and which was approvingly cited in the *Garmon* opinion itself.

We do not believe that any of these arguments suffice to overcome the plain purport of *Garmon* as applied to the facts of this case. However, we have determined to treat these considerations at some length because of the understandable confusion, perhaps in a measure attributable to the previous opinions of this Court, they reflect over the jurisprudential bases upon which the *Garmon* doctrine rests.

B. The constitutional principles of preemption, in whatever particular field of law they operate, are designed with a common end in view: to avoid conflicting regulation of conduct by various official bodies which might have some authority over the subject matter. A full understanding of the particular preemption rule set forth in *Garmon* especially requires, we think, appreciation of the precise nature and extent of the potential for injurious conflict that would inhere in a system unaffected by such a doctrine, and also the setting in which the general problem of accommodating conflicting claims of competence to resolve disputes touching upon labor relations has been presented to this Court....

The rationale for preemption, then, rests in large measure upon our determination that when it set down a federal labor policy Congress plainly meant to do more than simply to alter the then prevailing substantive law. It sought as well to restructure fundamentally the processes for effectuating that policy, deliberately placing the responsibility for applying and developing this comprehensive legal system in the hands of an expert administrative body rather than the federalized judicial system. Thus, that a local court, while adjudicating a labor dispute also within the jurisdiction of the NLRB, may purport to apply legal rules identical to those prescribed in the federal Act or may eschew the authority to define or apply principles specifically developed to regulate labor relations does not mean that all relevant potential for debilitating conflict is absent.

A second factor that has played an important role in our shaping of the preemption doctrine has been the necessity to act without specific congressional direction. The precise extent to which state law must be displaced to achieve those unifying ends sought by the national legislature has never been determined by the Congress. This has, quite frankly, left the Court with few available options. We cannot declare preempted all local regulation that touches or concerns in any way the complex interrelationships between employees, employers, and unions; obviously, much of this is left to the States. Nor can we proceed on a case-by-case basis to determine whether each particular final judicial pronouncement does, or might reasonably be thought to, conflict in some relevant manner with federal labor policy. This Court is ill-equipped to play such a role and the federal system dictates that this problem be solved with a rule capable of relatively easy application, so that lower courts may largely police themselves in this regard. Equally important, such a principle would fail to take account of the fact, as discussed above, that simple congruity of legal rules does not, in this area, prove the absence of untenable conflict. Further, it is surely not possible for this Court to treat the National Labor Relations Act section by section, committing enforcement of some of its provisions wholly to the NLRB and others to the concurrent domain of local law. Nothing in the language or underlying purposes of the Act suggests any basis for such distinctions. Finally, treating differently judicial power to deal with conduct protected by the Act from that prohibited by it would likewise be unsatisfactory. Both areas equally involve conduct whose legality is governed by federal law, the application of which Congress committed to the Board, not courts.

This is not to say, however, that these inherent limitations on this Court's ability to state a workable rule that comports reasonably with apparent congressional objectives are necessarily self-evident. In fact, varying approaches were taken by the Court in initially grappling with this preemption problem. Thus, for example, some early cases suggested the true distinction lay between judicial application of general common law, which was permissible, as opposed to state rules specifically designed to regulate labor relations, which were preempted. *See, e.g., Automobile Workers v. Russell*, 356 U.S. 634, 645 (1958). Others made preemption turn on whether the States purported to apply a remedy not provided for by the federal scheme, *e.g., Weber v. Anheuser-Busch, Inc.*, 348 U.S. 468, 479–480 (1955), while in still others the Court undertook a thorough scrutiny of the federal Act to ascertain whether the state courts had, in fact, arrived at conclusions inconsistent with its provisions, *e.g.,*

Automobile Workers v. Wisconsin Employment Relations Bd., 336 U.S. 245 (1949). For the reasons outlined above none of these approaches proved satisfactory, however, and each was ultimately abandoned. It was, in short, experience—not pure logic—which initially taught that each of these methods sacrificed important federal interests in a uniform law of labor relations centrally administered by an expert agency without yielding anything in return by way of predictability or ease of judicial application.

The failure of alternative analyses and the interplay of the foregoing policy considerations, then, led this Court to hold in *Garmon*, 359 U.S. at 244:

> When it is clear or may fairly be assumed that the activities which a State purports to regulate are protected by §7 of the National Labor Relations Act, or constitute an unfair labor practice under §8, due regard for the federal enactment requires that state jurisdiction must yield. To leave the States free to regulate conduct so plainly within the central aim of federal regulation involves too great a danger of conflict between power asserted by Congress and requirements imposed by state law.

C. Upon these premises, we think that *Garmon* rather clearly dictates reversal of the judgment below. None of the propositions asserted to support that judgment can withstand an application, in light of those factors that compelled its promulgation, of the *Garmon* rule.

Assuredly the proposition that Lockridge's complaint was not subject to the exclusive jurisdiction of the NLRB because it charged a breach of contract rather than an unfair labor practice is not tenable. Preemption, as shown above, is designed to shield the system from conflicting regulation of conduct. It is the conduct being regulated, not the formal description of governing legal standards, that is the proper focus of concern. Indeed, the notion that a relevant distinction exists for such purposes between particularized and generalized labor law was explicitly rejected in *Garmon* itself. 359 U.S. at 244.

The second argument, closely related to the first, is that the state courts in resolving this controversy, did deal with different conduct, *i.e.*, interpretation of contractual terms, than would the NLRB which would be required to decide whether the Union discriminated against Lockridge. At bottom, of course, the Union's action in procuring Lockridge's dismissal from employment is the conduct which Idaho courts have sought to regulate. Thus, this second point demonstrates at best that Idaho defines differently what sorts of such union conduct may permissibly be proscribed. This is to say either that the regulatory schemes, state and federal, conflict (in which case preemption is clearly called for) or that Idaho is dealing with conduct to which the federal Act does not speak. If the latter assertion was intended, it is not accurate. As pointed out in Part II A, *supra*, the relevant portions of the Act operate to prohibit a union from causing or attempting to cause an employer to discriminate against an employee because his membership in the union has been terminated "on some ground other than" his failure to pay those dues requisite to membership.

This has led the Board routinely and frequently to inquire into the proper construction of union regulations in order to ascertain whether the union properly found an employee to have been derelict in his dues-paying responsibilities, where his discharge was procured on the asserted grounds of nonmembership in the union. . . . That a union may in good faith have misconstrued its own rules has not been treated by the Board as a defense to a claimed violation of § 8(b)(2). In the Board's view, it is the fact of misapplication by a union of its rules, not the motivation for that discrimination, that constitutes an unfair labor practice. . . .

From the foregoing, then, it would seem that this case indeed represents one of the clearest instances where the *Garmon* principle, properly understood, should operate to oust state court jurisdiction. There being no doubt that the conduct here involved was arguably protected by § 7 or prohibited by § 8 of the Act, the full range of very substantial interests the preemption doctrine seeks to protect are directly implicated here.

However, a final strand of analysis underlies the opinion of the Idaho Supreme Court, and the position of respondent, in this case. Our decision in *Association of Machinists v. Gonzales*, 356 U.S. 617 (1958), it is argued, fully survived the subsequent reorientation of preemption doctrine effected by the *Garmon* decision, providing, in effect, an express exception for the exercise of judicial jurisdiction in cases such as this. . . .

Although it was decided only one Term subsequent to *Gonzales*, *Garmon* clearly did not fully embrace the technique of the prior case. It was precisely the realization that disparities in remedies and administration could produce substantial conflict, in the practical sense of the term, between the relevant state and federal regulatory schemes and that this Court could not effectively and responsibly superintend on a case-by-case basis the exertion of state power over matters arguably governed by the National Labor Relations Act that impelled the somewhat broader formulation of the preemption doctrine in *Garmon*. It seems evident that the full-blown rationale of *Gonzales* could not survive the rule of *Garmon*. Nevertheless, *Garmon* did not cast doubt upon the result reached in *Gonzales*, but cited it approvingly as an example of the fact that state court jurisdiction is not preempted "where the activity regulated was a merely peripheral concern of the . . . Act." 359 U.S. at 243.

Against this background, we attempted to define more precisely the reach of *Gonzales* within the more comprehensive framework *Garmon* provided in the companion cases of *Plumbers Union v. Borden*, 373 U.S. 690 (1963), and *Iron Workers v. Perko*, 373 U.S. 701 (1963).

Borden had sued his union in state courts, alleging that the union had arbitrarily refused to refer him to a particular job which he had lined up. He recovered damages, based on lost wages, on the grounds that this conduct constituted both tortious interference with his right to contract for employment and a breach of promise, implicit in his membership arrangement with the union, not to discriminate unfairly against any member or deny him the right to work. Perko had obtained a large money judgment in the Ohio courts on proof that the union had conspired, without cause, to deprive him of employment as a foreman by demanding his discharge from one such position he had held and representing to others that his foreman's rights had been suspended. We held both Perko's and Borden's judgments inconsistent with the *Garmon* rule essentially for the same reasons we have concluded that Lockridge could not, consistently with the *Garmon* decision, maintain his lawsuit in the state courts. We further held there was no necessity to "consider the present vitality of [the *Gonzales*] rationale in the light of more recent decisions," because in those cases, unlike *Gonzales*, "the crux of the action[s] . . . concerned alleged interference with the plaintiff's existing or prospective employment relations and was not directed to internal union matters." Because no specific claim for restoration of membership rights had been advanced, "there was no permissible state remedy to which the award of consequential damages for loss of earnings might be subordinated." *Perko*, 373 U.S. at 705. *See also Borden*, 373 U.S. at 697.

In sum, what distinguished *Gonzales* from *Borden* and *Perko* was that the former lawsuit "was focused on purely internal union matters," *Borden, supra*, at 697, a subject the National Labor Relations Act leaves principally to other processes of law. The possibility that, in defining the scope of the union's duty to Gonzales, the state courts would directly and consciously implicate principles of federal law was at best tangential and remote. In the instant case, however, this possibility was real and immediate. To assess the legality of his union's conduct toward Gonzales the California courts needed only to focus upon the union's constitution and by-laws. Here, however, Lockridge's entire case turned upon the construction of the applicable union security clause, a matter as to which, as shown above, federal concern is pervasive and its regulation complex. The reasons for Gonzales' deprivation of union membership had nothing to do with matters of employment, while Lockridge's cause of action and claim for damages was based solely upon the procurement of his discharge from employment. It cannot plausibly be argued, in any meaningful sense, that Lockridge's lawsuit "was focused upon purely internal matters." Although nothing said in *Garmon* necessarily suggests that States cannot regulate the general conditions which unions may impose on their membership, it surely makes crystal clear that *Gonzales* does not stand for the proposition that the resolution of any union-member conflict is within state competence so long as one of the remedies provided is restoration of union membership. This much was settled by *Borden* and *Perko*, and it is only upon such an unwarrantably broad interpretation of *Gonzales* that the judgment below could be sustained.

III

The preemption doctrine we apply today is, like any other purposefully administered legal principle, not without exception. Those same considerations that underlie *Garmon* have led this Court to permit the exercise of judicial power over conduct arguably protected or prohibited by the Act where Congress has affirmatively indicated that such power should exist, *Smith v. Evening News*, 371 U.S. 195 (1962); *Teamsters v. Morton*, 377 U.S. 252 (1964), where this Court cannot, in spite of the force of the policies *Garmon* seeks to promote, conscientiously presume that Congress meant to intrude so deeply into areas traditionally left to local law, *e.g., Linn v. Plant Guard Workers*, 383 U.S. 53 (1966); *Automobile Workers v. Russell*, 356 U.S. 634 (1958), and where the particular rule of law sought to be invoked before another tribunal is so structured and administered that, in virtually all instances, it is safe to presume that judicial supervision will not disserve the interests promoted by the federal labor statutes, *Vaca v. Sipes*, 386 U.S. 171 (1967).

In his brief before this Court, respondent has argued for the first time since this lawsuit was started that two of these exceptions to the *Garmon* principle independently justify the Idaho courts' exercise of jurisdiction over this controversy. First, Lockridge contends that his action, properly viewed, is one to enforce a collective bargaining agreement. Alternatively, he asserts the suit, in essence, was one to redress petitioner's breach of its duty of fair representation. As will be seen, these contentions are somewhat intertwined.

In § 301 of the Taft-Hartley Act, Congress authorized federal courts to exercise jurisdiction over suits brought to enforce collective bargaining agreements. We have held that such actions are judicially cognizable, even where the conduct alleged was arguably protected or prohibited by the National Labor Relations Act because the history of the enactment of § 301 reveals that "Congress deliberately chose to leave the enforcement of collective agreements 'to the usual processes of law.'" *Charles Dowd Box Co. v. Courtney*, 368 U.S. 502, 513 (1962). It is firmly established, further, that state courts retain concurrent jurisdiction to adjudicate such claims, *Charles Dowd Box Co., supra*, and that individual employees have standing to protect rights conferred upon them by such agreements, *Smith v. Evening News, supra; Humphrey v. Moore*, 375 U.S. 335 (1964).

Our cases also clearly establish that individual union members may sue their employers under § 301 for breach of a promise embedded in the collective bargaining agreement that was intended to confer a benefit upon the individual. *Smith v. Evening News, supra*. Plainly, however, this is not such a lawsuit. Lockridge specifically dropped Greyhound as a named party from his initial complaint and has never reasserted a right to redress from his former employer.

This Court has further held in *Humphrey v. Moore*, 375 U.S. 335 (1964), that § 301 will support, regardless of otherwise applicable preemption considerations, a suit in the state courts by a union member against his union that seeks to redress union interference with rights conferred on individual employees by the employer's promises in the collective-bargaining agreement, where it is proved that such interference constituted a breach of the duty of fair representation. Indeed, in *Vaca v. Sipes*, 386 U.S. 171 (1967), we held that an action seeking damages for injury inflicted by a breach of a union's duty of fair representation was judicially cognizable in any event, that is, even if the conduct complained of was arguably protected or prohibited by the National Labor Relations Act and whether or not the lawsuit was bottomed on a collective agreement. Perhaps Count One of Lockridge's second amended complaint could be construed to assert either or both of these theories of recovery. However, it is unnecessary to pass upon the extent to which *Garmon* would be inapplicable if it were shown that in these circumstances petitioner not only breached its contractual obligations to respondent, but did so in a manner that constituted a breach of the duty of fair representation. For such a claim to be made out, Lockridge must have proved "arbitrary or bad faith conduct on the part of the union." *Vaca v. Sipes, supra*, at 193. There must be "substantial evidence of fraud, deceitful action or dishonest conduct." *Humphrey v. Moore, supra*, at 348. Whether these requisite elements have been proved is a matter of federal law. Quite obviously, they were not even asserted to be relevant in the proceedings below. As the Idaho Supreme Court stated in affirming the verdict for Lockridge, "[t]his was a misinterpretation of a contract. Whatever the underlying motive for expulsion might have been, this case has been submitted and tried on the interpretation of the contract, not on a theory of discrimination." Thus, the trial judge's conclusion of law in sustaining Lockridge's claim specifically incorporates the assumption that the Union's "acts . . . were predicated solely upon the ground that [Lockridge] had failed to tender periodic dues in conformance with the requirements of the union Constitution and employment contract as they interpreted [it] . . . ." App., 66. Further, the trial court excluded as irrelevant petitioner's proffer of evidence designed to show that the Union's interpretation of the contract was reasonably based upon its understanding of prior collective bargaining agreements negotiated with Greyhound. Transcript of Trial, at 259–260. . . .

For the reasons stated above, the judgment below is

Reversed.

Mr. Justice White, with whom The Chief Justice joins, dissenting.

. . . I cannot agree with the opinion of the Court because it reaffirms the *Garmon* doctrine as applied to conduct arguably protected under §7, as well as to that arguably prohibited under §8. The essential difference, for present purposes, between activity which is arguably prohibited and that which is arguably protected is that a hearing on the latter activity is virtually impossible unless one deliberately commits an unfair labor practice. In a typical unfair practice case, by alleging conduct arguably prohibited by §8 the charging party can at least present the General Counsel with the facts, and if the General Counsel issues a complaint, the charging party can present the Board with the facts and arguments to support the claim. But for activity which is arguably protected, there is no provision for an authoritative decision by the Board in the first instance; yet the *Garmon* rule blindly preempts other tribunals. . . .

Though the most natural arena for this conflict occurs when picketers trespass on private property, *see Taggart v. Weinacker's, Inc.*, 397 U.S. 223, 227 (1970) (Burger, C.J., concurring), . . . other instances include "quickie" strikes or slowdowns, *see NLRB v. Holcombe*, 325 F.2d 508 (5th Cir. 1963), or employees' inaccurate complaints to state officials about sanitary conditions in the plant, *Walls Mfg. Co. v. NLRB*, 321 F.2d 753, 116 U.S. App. D.C. 140 (1963), or collective activity designed to persuade the employer to hire Negroes, *NLRB v. Tanner Motor Livery, Ltd.*, 349 F.2d 1 (9th Cir. 1965), or failure to participate in a union check-off, *Radio Officers' Union v. NLRB*, 347 U.S. 17, 24–28 (1954).

There seems little point in a doctrine which, in the name of national policy, encourages the commission of unfair labor practices, the evils which above all else were the object of the Act. Surely the policy of seeking uniformity in the regulation of labor practices must be given closer scrutiny when it leads to the alternative "solutions" of denying the aggrieved party a hearing or encouraging the commission of a putative unfair labor practice as the price of that hearing. . . .

Congress found the no-man's land created by *Guss* unacceptable precisely because there was no way to have rights determined. In terms of congressional intention I find it unsupportable to hold that one threatened by conduct illegal under state law may not proceed against it because it is arguably protected by federal law when he has absolutely no lawful method for determining whether that is actually, as well as arguably, the case. Particularly is this true where the dispute is between a union and its members and the latter are asserting claims under state law based on the union constitution. I would permit the state court to entertain the action and if the union defends on the ground that its conduct is protected by federal law, to pass on that claim at the outset of the proceeding. If the federal law immunizes the challenged union action, the case is terminated; but if not, the case is adjudicated under state law.

[The dissenting opinion of Mr. Justice Douglas and the dissenting statement of Mr. Justice Blackmun are omitted.]

Notes

1. *The "No-Man's-Land" and the 1959 Amendments* — As Justice White alluded to in his dissent, in *Guss v. Utah Labor Relations Bd.*, 353 U.S. 1 (1957) the Court created a legal "no-man's-land" by holding that the states were preempted from acting with respect to parties that "affected" commerce but over which the NLRB declined to exercise jurisdiction. Although the NLRB expanded its jurisdictional standards in 1958, this was only a partial solution, since about four-fifths of the cases previously consigned to the "no-man's-land" still remained there.

Congress considered several alternative proposals during its deliberations on the 1959 amendments to the NLRA. Section 14(c), which was enacted, permits states to assert jurisdiction when the Labor Board declines. It also provides, however, that the NLRB may not narrow its jurisdiction beyond the point set by the discretionary standards in effect on August 1, 1959. The bill did not say whether the states were to apply federal or state law, but Senator Kennedy, the conference chairman, was more explicit: "It was the opinion of the Senate that the Federal law should prevail with respect to interstate commerce, and, in order to compromise that feature, it was agreed that State law could prevail, but only in those areas in which the National Labor Relations Board does not now assume jurisdiction." 105 Cong. Rec. 17720

(1959). State courts have generally assumed that local law is applicable. *See, e.g., Cooper v. Nutley Sun Printing Co.*, 36 N.J. 189, 175 A.2d 639 (1961); *Kempf v. Carpenters & Joiners Local 1273*, 229 Or. 337, 367 P.2d 436 (1961).

2. *Coverage Challenges*—When is an employed person excluded from NLRA coverage and subject to state jurisdiction? In *International Ass'n of Bridge, Structural & Ornamental Iron Workers Union Local 207 v. Perko*, 373 U.S. 701 (1963), cited in *Lockridge*, a state damage action was brought against a union for allegedly conspiring to deprive a member of his job as a "foreman." The plaintiff argued against preemption on the grounds he was a "supervisor" and thus outside the NLRA's definition of "employee." The Supreme Court held that the plaintiff's duties made him at least arguably an "employee" within the meaning of the Act, thereby precluding state jurisdiction. Similarly, in *Marine Engineers Beneficial Ass'n v. Interlake S.S. Co.*, 370 U.S. 173 (1962), the Supreme Court ruled that since a union of marine engineers was arguably a "labor organization" as defined by the federal act, even though it was allegedly composed entirely of supervisors, the NLRB had exclusive primary jurisdiction to determine the union's status. As a result, a state court could not enjoin MEBA's picketing of a ship employing nonunion marine engineers. Nonetheless, once the NLRB has concluded, through the dismissal of a representation petition or unfair labor practice charges, that there is no federal jurisdiction because the union consists exclusively of supervisors, a state court may enjoin peaceful organizational picketing by the supervisors' union. *Hanna Mining Co. v. District 2, Marine Engineers Beneficial Ass'n*, 382 U.S. 181 (1965).

Sears, Roebuck & Co. v. San Diego County Dist. Council of Carpenters, 436 U.S. 180, 98 S. Ct. 1745, 56 L. Ed. 2d 209 (1978). Two Carpenters Union representatives visited the Chula Vista, California, Sears store to protest the fact that carpentry work was being performed by individuals who had not been dispatched from the union hiring hall. When the Sears store manager failed to engage a contractor that used hiring hall workers, the union established a picket line on Sears property. They picketed on privately owned walkways adjacent to the store and on the privately owned parking lot. The Sears manager demanded that the union remove the pickets from Sears property, but the union refused. Sears filed a state court action seeking an injunction against the continuing trespass. The state trial court enjoined the trespassory picketing, and the court of appeals affirmed on the ground the trespass laws fell within the long-standing preemption exception for matters of deep and traditional state concern. The California Supreme Court, however, reversed, finding that state court jurisdiction was preempted by conduct that was arguably protected by § 7 of the NLRA.

On appeal, the U.S. Supreme Court rejected the union's preemption claim. It could have followed the court of appeals' logic and held that trespass laws fall within the exception for matters of deep and traditional state concern, but it elected to engage in a more searching analysis that involved an examination of both the arguably prohibited and arguably protected preemption concepts enunciated in *San Diego Building Trades Council v. Garmon*, 359 U.S. 236 (1959), *supra*.

With respect to the arguably prohibited question, the Court noted that the focus of the state court trespass action was significantly different from NLRA concerns under §§ 8(b)(4)(D) and 8(b)(7):

> We start from the premise that the Union's picketing on Sears' property after the request to leave was continuing trespass in violation of state law. We note, however, that the scope of the controversy in the state court was limited. Sears asserted no claim that the picketing itself violated any state or federal law. It sought simply to remove the pickets from its property to the public walkways, and the injunction issued by the state court was strictly confined to the relief sought. Thus, as a matter of state law, the location of the picketing was illegal but the picketing itself was unobjectionable. . . .
>
> If an object of the picketing was to force Sears into assigning the carpentry work away from its employees to Union members dispatched from the hiring hall, the picketing may have been prohibited by 8(b)(4)(D). Alternatively, if an object of the picketing was to coerce Sears into signing a prehire or members-only type agreement with the Union, the picketing was at least arguably subject to the prohibition on recognitional picketing contained in § 8(b)(7)(C). Hence, if Sears had filed an unfair labor practice charge against the Union, the Board's concern would have been limited to the question whether the Union's picketing had an objective proscribed by the Act; the location of the picketing would have been irrelevant.

The Court thus rejected preemption under the arguably prohibited concept.

The Supreme Court then evaluated the arguably protected theory to determine whether there was any real likelihood that application of state trespass laws would undermine federal labor policies contained in §7. It first noted that Sears had expressly demanded that the union pickets leave its premises, providing the union with the opportunity to file a § 8(a)(1) charge with the NLRB and have that agency decide whether the trespassory picketing was protected conduct due to the absence of alternative means of communication:

> The primary jurisdiction rationale unquestionably requires that when the same controversy may be presented to the state court or the NLRB, it must be presented to the Board. But that rationale does not extend to cases in which an employer has no acceptable method of invoking, or inducing the Union to invoke, the jurisdiction of the Board. We are therefore persuaded that the primary jurisdiction rationale does not provide a *sufficient* justification for preempting state jurisdiction over arguably protected conduct when the party who could have presented the protection issue to the Board has not done so and the other party to the dispute has no acceptable means of doing so. . . .
>
> In *NLRB v. Babcock & Wilcox*, 351 U.S. 105, . . . the Court recognized that in certain circumstances nonemployee union organizers may have a limited right of access to an employer's premises for the purpose of engaging in

organization solicitation. And the Court has indicated that *Babock* extends to §7 rights other than organizational activity, though the "locus" of the "accommodation of §7 rights and the private property rights . . . may fall at differing points along the spectrum depending on the nature and strength of the respective §7 rights and private property rights asserted in any given context." *Hudgens v. NLRB*, 424 U.S. 507.

For purpose of analysis we must assume that the Union could have proved that its picketing was, at least in the absence of a trespass, protected by §7. The remaining question is whether under *Babcock* the trespassory nature of the picketing caused it to forfeit its protected status. Since it cannot be said with certainty that, if the Union had filed an unfair labor practice charge against Sears, the Board would have fixed the locus of the accommodation at the unprotected end of the spectrum, it is indeed "arguable" that the Union's peaceful picketing, though trespassory, was protected. Nevertheless, permitting state courts to evaluate the merits of an argument that certain trespassory activity is protected does not create an unacceptable risk of interference with conduct which the Board, and a court reviewing the board's decision, would find protected. For while there are unquestionably examples of trespassory union activity in which the question whether it is protected is fairly debatable, experience under the Act teaches that such situations are rare and that a trespass is far more likely to be unprotected than protected.

The Court thus found an absence of preemption under the arguably protected concept.

Notes

1. *Aftermath* — On remand, the California Supreme Court found the picketing lawful under state law, and held that a state anti-injunction statute required vacating the injunction. *Sears, Roebuck & Co. v. San Diego County Dist. Council of Carpenters*, 25 Cal. 3d 317, 599 P.2d 676 (1979), *cert. denied*, 447 U.S. 935 (1980).

2. *State Common Law Tort Claims* — In *Farmer v. United Brotherhood of Carpenters & Joiners*, 430 U.S. 290 (1977), the Supreme Court held that the NLRA does not preempt a state court tort action by a union member against the union and its officials seeking damages for the intentional infliction of emotional distress through "frequent public ridicule" and "incessant verbal abuse." But a verdict could not be based on evidence of discriminatory job referrals, except where such discrimination is accomplished through a "particularly abusive manner" involving outrageous conduct.

In *Linn v. United Plant Guard Workers*, 383 U.S. 53 (1966), the Supreme Court held that state libel suits based on defamatory statements made in the course of a union organizing campaign are not preempted. The Court noted the compelling state interest involved — a matter so deeply rooted in local feeling and responsibility that it cannot be assumed that Congress had deprived the states of the power to act. However, the Court limited the availability of state remedies for libel to those instances in which complainants can show that the defamatory statements were circulated with malice and caused them actual damage. "The standards enunciated in *New York Times Co. v. Sullivan*, 376 U.S. 254 (1964), are adopted by analogy rather than by constitutional compulsion. We apply the malice test to effectuate the statutory design with respect to preemption. Construing the Act to permit recovery of damages in a state cause of action only for defamatory statements published with knowledge of their falsity or with reckless disregard of whether they were true or false guards against abuse of libel actions and unwarranted intrusion upon free discussion envisioned by the Act."

In *Letter Carriers Branch 496 v. Austin*, 418 U.S. 264 (1974), decided under Executive Order No. 11491, then applicable to federal employees, the Supreme Court held that the *Linn* partial preemption doctrine requires a state court to instruct on "malice" in terms of the reckless-or-knowing falsehood test of *New York Times* rather than in common-law terms. The Court concluded that a union was protected by the federal labor laws in listing plaintiffs as scabs under a heading containing Jack London's colorful definition of "The Scab," which includes such epithets as "tumor of rotten principles" and "traitor."

Would the *Linn* standards apply to libel committed during collective bargaining sessions or grievance-adjustment meetings, or should union and employer statements in such circumstances be considered "unqualifiedly privileged"? *Compare General Motors Corp. v. Mendicki*, 367 F.2d 66 (10th Cir. 1966) ("unqualifiedly privileged"), *with Thompson v. Public Service Co.*, 800 P.2d 1299 (Colo. 1990), *cert. denied*, 502 U.S. 973 (1991) (only "qualifiedly privileged").

In *Chicago Dist. Council of Carpenters Pension Fund v. Reinke Insulation Co.*, 464 F.3d 651 (7th Cir. 2006), the court held that a company's state-law claim for tortious interference and violation of the Illinois Consumer Fraud Act, based on the union's handbill statements during a labor dispute indicating that the firm had "cheated" its workers of their medical and retirement contributions, was preempted by the NLRA under the *Garmon* doctrine; there was no evidence that the union statements were made with malice.

International Brotherhood of Teamsters, Local 24 v. Oliver, 358 U.S. 283, 79 S. Ct. 297, 3 L. Ed. 2d 312 (1959). Teamster locals entered into a collective bargaining agreement with motor carriers operating in 12 midwestern states, including Ohio. The contract included a provision prescribing the minimum rental fee and other terms of the lease when a motor vehicle was leased to a carrier by an owner who drove his own vehicle for the carrier. At the suit of one owner-driver, the Ohio courts enjoined a local and several carriers from giving effect to this provision, on the ground it violated the Ohio antitrust law as a form of price-fixing. The United States Supreme Court held that the provision in dispute dealt with a subject matter within the scope of "collective bargaining" under federal law, and that the Ohio antitrust law could not be applied to prevent the parties from carrying out their agreement on a matter "as to which federal law directs them to bargain." The Court reasoned that the purpose of the questioned clause was to protect the negotiated wage scale for employees driving carrier-owned vehicles. If owner-drivers accepted inadequate rentals for their trucks, they would have to make up the excess operating costs from their compensation as drivers. This in effect would undercut the union's wage scale, and might invite a progressive curtailment of jobs through the gradual withdrawal of carrier-owned vehicles from service. Concluded the Court: "Of course, the paramount force of federal law remains even though it is expressed in the details of a contract federal law empowers the parties to make, rather than in terms in an enactment of Congress. . . . Clearly it is immaterial that the conflict is between federal labor law and the application of what the State characterizes as an anti-trust law. . . . [T]he conflict here is between the federally sanctioned agreement and state policy which seeks specifically to adjust relationships in the world of commerce."

B. *Machinists* Preemption

In another strain of preemption analysis known as *Machinists* preemption, the Court established a rule recognizing that the NLRA leaves open a field of economic conflict that Congress intended to leave unregulated. Because state interference with this scheme alters the balance of power maintained through the "free play of economic forces," such state regulation is preempted.

Lodge 76, Int'l Ass'n of Machinists & Aerospace Workers v. Wisconsin Employment Relations Commission, 427 U.S. 132, 96 S. Ct. 2548, 49 L. Ed. 2d 396 (1976). As a bargaining tactic during negotiations for renewal of an expired collective agreement, the union refused to work overtime. The employer filed an unfair labor practice charge against the union, claiming a violation of the union's duty to bargain under § 8(b)(3) of the NLRA; but the Regional Director of the Board dismissed the charge on the ground that the conduct was not prohibited by the Act. The employer then filed a complaint before the Wisconsin Employment Relations Commission (WERC) charging that the refusal to work overtime was an unfair labor practice under state law. Finding a state law violation, the WERC issued a cease and desist order, which was sustained by the Wisconsin Supreme Court.

The U.S. Supreme Court reversed on the ground of federal preemption, expressly overruling its earlier case of *International Union, U.A.W.A. v. WERB*, 336 U.S. 245 (1949), which had held that states could regulate union conduct (intermittent, unannounced work stoppages) that Congress had neither prohibited nor protected. The Court now held that an inquiry must be made as to whether Congress intended that the conduct involved be unregulated and left to be controlled by the free play of economic forces. Stating that the use of economic pressure by the parties to a labor dispute is not a grudging exception under the NLRA but is part and parcel of the process of collective bargaining, the Court found that Wisconsin had entered into the substantive aspects of collective bargaining to an extent that Congress had not countenanced.

Chamber of Commerce of the United States v. Brown, 554 U.S. 60, 128 S. Ct. 2408, 171 L. Ed. 2d 264 (2008). A California statute prohibited employers that receive state grants or program funds in excess of $10,000 per year from using those funds "to assist, promote, or deter union organizing." The statute's preamble stated that the state's policy was "not to interfere with an employee's choice about whether to join or to be represented by a labor union." Despite the neutral ban on the use of state funds for activities designed to support *or oppose* unionization, the statute expressly exempted expenses incurred in connection with activities that facilitate unionization, including allowing a union access to the employer's property or expenses incurred in negotiating and implementing a voluntary recognition agreement with a union. The Supreme Court held that this statute was preempted under the rationale of *Machinists Lodge 76* (although the employer groups also argued that the statute was preempted under *Garmon*, the Court did not reach that question). The Court noted that Congress had amended the NLRA in 1947 through the addition of § 8(c) specifically to protect the right of employers and labor organizations to express opinions so long as such communications contain no threat of reprisal or promise of benefit. From this legislative action, the Court concluded that Congress must necessarily have intended to leave noncoercive speech unregulated and left to the "free play of economic forces." California's effort to restrict employers receiving state funds from expressing views clearly protected by § 8(c) was contrary to this congressional intent and was thus preempted, because the state law regulated within "a zone protected and reserved for market freedom."

The dissenting justices argued that the California statute's spending limitations did not "regulate" the area of noncoercive speech; all it accomplished was to refuse to provide state funding for employers' labor-related activities and speech. The dissent asked pointedly whether states that do wish to pay for employer labor-related speech could do so consistently with the NLRA.

Notes

1. *Unemployment Benefits for Strikers* — In *New York Tel. Co. v. New York State Dep't of Labor,* 440 U.S. 519 (1979), the Supreme Court held that the federal preemption doctrine did not invalidate the New York unemployment compensation statute, which gives benefits to strikers after eight weeks. Dissenting Justice Powell, joined by Chief Justice Burger and Justice Stewart, thought that such payments were preempted because they substantially altered the economic balance of free collective bargaining, contrary to the policy of the national labor laws. However, the majority found that the legislative history of the NLRA and the Social Security Act showed that Congress intended that the states be free to authorize or prohibit the payment of unemployment benefits to strikers.

The Michigan Employment Security Act specifically disqualifies from unemployment compensation employees who have provided "financing" by means other than the payment of regular union dues for any strike that causes their unemployment.

Employees who had contributed "emergency dues" to augment the UAW strike fund were laid off by General Motors (GM) as a result of UAW-financed strikes at other GM plants. The Michigan Supreme Court found that the laid-off individuals were ineligible for unemployment benefits due to their special strike fund contributions. Although such financing of local work stoppages constitutes protected activity under §7, the Supreme Court held in *Baker v. General Motors Corp.*, 478 U.S. 621 (1986), that this state disqualification determination was not preempted by the NLRA. In Title IX of the Social Security Act, Congress expressly provided states with broad discretion to decide the particular type of unemployment program they wished to establish, and no employer action impaired the §7 rights of the affected employees.

2. *Restrictions on Ability to Serve as a Union Officer* — The New Jersey Casino Control Act disqualifies individuals connected with organized crime from serving as officials and business agents of unions representing employees at Atlantic City casinos. It also provides that a labor organization may be prohibited from receiving union dues from casino employees and from administering any pension or welfare fund if any officer is a disqualified person. In *Brown v. Hotel & Restaurant Employees & Bartenders International Union Local 54*, 468 U.S. 491 (1984), a closely divided Supreme Court held that the provision preventing organized crime figures from serving as union officials was not preempted, because it does not conflict with §7 of the NLRA — which neither contains express preemptive language nor otherwise indicates a congressional intent to usurp the entire field of labor management relations. *Hill v. Florida*, 325 U.S. 538 (1945), which had struck down a Florida statute that provided for the licensing of union business agents and precluded the licensing of anyone who had not been a citizen for at least 10 years, who had been convicted of a felony, or who was not of "good moral character," on the ground it impermissibly interfered with the §7 freedom of employees to select bargaining representatives of their own choosing, was distinguished. Section 504(a) of the subsequently enacted LMRDA specifically disqualifies from union office individuals convicted of certain crimes, and the 4-3 *Brown* majority concluded that this indicated that Congress no longer views the freedom of employees to select union officers to be an unfettered right. Furthermore, §603(a) of the LMRDA explicitly disclaims any congressional intent to preempt state laws regulating the responsibility of union officials, so long as such statutes do not conflict with LMRDA provisions. The *Brown* majority thus found that Congress no longer intended to preclude all state regulations governing the qualifications of labor leaders. The Court finally noted that the New Jersey provision was designed to vindicate a legitimate and compelling state interest, and it emphasized the fact that the law "does not implicate the employees' express §7 right to select a particular labor union as their collective-bargaining representative, but only their subsidiary right to select the officials of that union organization."

Metropolitan Life Ins. Co. v. Massachusetts, 471 U.S. 724, 105 S. Ct. 2380, 85 L. Ed. 2d 728 (1985). The Supreme Court was asked to decide whether a state law, which requires certain minimum mental health care benefits to be provided in general health insurance policies and employee health care plans that cover hospital and surgical expenses, was preempted by federal law. After first determining that the Massachusetts provision was protected by an express anti-preemption section contained in ERISA that authorizes states to regulate insurance, the unanimous Supreme Court went on to find that such state-established minimum standards are not preempted by the NLRA:

> The NLRA is concerned primarily with establishing an equitable process for determining terms and conditions of employment, and not with particular substantive terms of the bargain that is struck when the parties are negotiating from relatively equal positions....
>
> The evil Congress was addressing thus was entirely unrelated to local or federal regulation establishing minimum terms of employment. Neither inequality of bargaining power nor the resultant depressed wage rates were thought to result from the choice between having terms of employment set by public law or having them set by private agreement. No incompatibility exists, therefore, between federal rules designed to restore the equality of bargaining power, and state or federal legislation that imposes minimal substantive requirements on contract terms negotiated between parties to labor agreements, at least so long as the purpose of the state legislation is not incompatible with these general goals of the NLRA.
>
> Accordingly, it never has been argued successfully that minimal labor standards imposed by other *federal* laws were not to apply to unionized employers and employees. *See, e.g., Barrentine v. Arkansas-Best Freight System, Inc.*, 450 U.S. 728, 737, 739 (1981). Nor has Congress ever seen fit to exclude unionized workers and employers from laws establishing federal minimal employment standards. We see no reason to believe that for this purpose Congress intended state minimum labor standards to be treated differently from minimum federal standards.
>
> Minimum state labor standards affect union and nonunion employees equally, and neither encourage nor discourage the collective-bargaining processes that are the subject of the NLRA. Nor do they have any but the most indirect effect on the right of self-organization established in the Act....

Notes

1. *Severance Payments* — A closely divided Supreme Court held that a Maine statute requiring a one-time severance payment for employees in the event of a plant closing was not preempted by either ERISA or the NLRA. *Fort Halifax Packing Co. v. Coyne*, 482 U.S. 1 (1987). The majority first concluded that ERISA's preemption provision applies only to "employee benefit *plans*," and that the Maine statute neither established, fostered, hindered, nor regulated such a plan. Second, the statute, like that in *Metropolitan Life*, simply created a minimum substantive labor standard that did not undercut the collective bargaining promoted by the NLRA.

2. *State Minimum Standards Legislation* — In *520 S. Mich. Ave. Assocs., Ltd. v. Shannon*, 549 F.3d 1119 (7th Cir. 2008), *cert. denied*, 130 S. Ct. 197 (2009), the court blocked a union's lawsuit alleging that the employer failed to provide rest and meal breaks to which hotel room attendants were entitled under an Illinois state law that establishes mandatory rest and meal breaks, provides for treble damages if its provisions are violated, and prohibits retaliatory action for the assertion of rights by the employee. The court found that the statute interfered with the collective bargaining processes promoted by the NLRA, and hence was preempted under *Machinists*. The court found that while state minimum labor standards laws are not generally preempted by the NLRA, the Illinois law was "much more than a mere backdrop to negotiations because it establishes terms of employment that would be very difficult for any union to bargain for." Further, the law's impact was "invasive," affecting the ability of an employer to discipline or fire employees pursuant to a labor contract, and encouraged litigation rather than grievance resolution through arbitration procedures contained in labor contracts. The court rejected the state's argument that the statute was a facially neutral minimum labor standards law, noting that since the law targeted only hotels in Illinois's largest county and had been passed in the midst of a widely publicized work stoppage at the employer's hotel following the expiration of a labor contract, it was more akin to a benefit for a bargaining unit than a minimum standards law of general application.

3. *Successorship Legislation* — Two courts have upheld against preemption challenges legislation that requires business purchasers to retain employees of the predecessor business for a period of 90 days. The employers argued that the retention of the employees would increase the likelihood that the new owner would be deemed a legal successor for purposes of its relationship with its predecessor's labor union, enhancing the union's power. *See Rhode Island Hospitality Ass'n v. City of Providence*, 667 F.3d 17 (1st Cir. 2011) (reasoning that the application of successorship doctrine under the NLRA is limited to situations where the successor makes a "conscious decision" to hire a majority of its predecessor's employees and to maintain the same business, and that it had not yet been established that the NLRB would rely upon legislatively mandated employee retention to make a successorship finding); *Cal. Grocers Ass'n v. City of Los Angeles*, 52 Cal. 4th 177, 254 P.3d 1019 (CA. S. Ct. 2011), *cert. denied*, 565 U.S. 1178 (2012) (finding that *Machinists Lodge 76*, *Metropolitan Life*, and *Fort Halifax* require preemption only in circumstances where local regulation interferes with the process of organizing and bargaining, and does not extend to local establishment of substantive employment terms, including the subject of employee hiring). Were the courts correct? Can these decisions be squared with *520 S. Mich. Ave. Assocs., Ltd. v. Shannon*?

C. Comparing *Garmon* Preemption and *Machinists* Preemption

In another important preemption case, the Court addressed both strains of preemption analysis in a particularly difficult factual context, and concluded that state common law was not preempted.

Belknap, Inc. v. Hale

Supreme Court of the United States
463 U.S. 491, 103 S. Ct. 3172, 77 L. Ed. 2d 798 (1983)

JUSTICE WHITE delivered the opinion of the Court. . . .

I

Petitioner Belknap, Inc., is a corporation engaged in the sale of hardware products and certain building materials. A bargaining unit consisting of all of Belknap's warehouse and maintenance employees selected International Brotherhood of Teamsters Local No. 89 (Union) as their collective bargaining representative. In 1975, the Union and Belknap entered into an agreement which was to expire on January 31, 1978. The two opened negotiations for a new contract shortly before the expiration of the 1975 agreement, but reached an impasse. On February 1, 1978, approximately 400 Belknap employees represented by Local 89 went out on strike. Belknap then granted a wage increase, effective February 1, for union employees who stayed on the job.

Shortly after the strike began, Belknap placed an advertisement in a local newspaper seeking applicants to "permanently replace striking warehouse and maintenance employees." A large number of people responded to the offer and were hired. After each replacement was hired, Belknap presented to the replacement the following statement for his signature:

> I, the undersigned, acknowledge and agree that I as of this date have been employed by Belknap, Inc. at its Louisville, Kentucky, facility as a regular full time permanent replacement to permanently replace _____ in the job classification of _____.

On March 7, Local 89 filed unfair labor practice charges against petitioner Belknap. The charge was based on the unilateral wage increase granted by Belknap. Belknap countered with charges of its own. On April 4, the company distributed a letter which said, in relevant part:

To All Permanent Replacement Employees

We recognize that many of you continue to be concerned about your status as an employee. The company's position on this matter has not changed nor do we expect it to change. You will continue to be permanent replacement employees so long as you conduct yourselves in accordance with the policies and practices that are in effect here at Belknap.

We continue to meet and negotiate in good faith with the Union. It is our hope and desire that a mutually acceptable agreement can be reached in the near future. However, we have made it clear to the Union that we have no intention of getting rid of the permanent replacement employees just in order to provide jobs for the replaced strikers if and when the Union calls off the strike.

On April 27, the Regional Director issued a complaint against Belknap, asserting that the unilateral increase violated §§ 8(a)(1), 8(a)(3), and 8(a)(5) of the Act. Three days later, on April 7, the company again addressed the strike replacements:

We want to make it perfectly clear, once again, that there will be no change in your employment status as a result of the charge by the National Labor Relations Board, which has been reported in this week's newspapers.

We do not believe there is any substance to the charge and we feel confident we can prove in the court's satisfaction that our intent and actions are completely within the law.

A hearing on the unfair labor practice charges was scheduled for July 19. The Regional Director convened a settlement conference shortly before the hearing was to take place. He explained that if a strike settlement could be reached, he would agree to the withdrawal and dismissal of the unfair labor practice charges and complaints against both the Company and the Union. During these discussions the parties made various concessions, leaving one major issue unresolved, the recall of the striking workers. The parties finally agreed that the Company would, at a minimum, reinstate 35 strikers per week. The settlement agreement was then reduced to writing. Petitioner laid off the replacements, including the twelve respondents, in order to make room for the returning strikers.

Respondents sued Belknap in the Jefferson County, Kentucky, Circuit Court for misrepresentation and breach of contract. Belknap, they alleged, had proclaimed that it was hiring permanent employees, knowing both that the assertion was false and that respondents would detrimentally rely on it. The alternative claim was that Belknap was liable for breaching its contracts with respondents by firing them as a result of its agreement with Local 89. Each respondent asked for $250,000 in compensatory damages, and an equal amount in punitive damages.

[Belknap claimed the replacements' causes of action were preempted by the NLRA, but a Kentucky appellate court disagreed.]

II

Our cases have announced two doctrines for determining whether state regulations or causes of action are preempted by the NLRA. Under the first, set out in *San Diego Building Trades Council v. Garmon*, 359 U.S. 236 (1959), state regulations and causes of action are presumptively preempted if they concern conduct that is actually or arguably either prohibited or protected by the Act. *Id.* at 245. The state regulation or cause of action may, however, be sustained if the behavior to be regulated is behavior that is of only peripheral concern to the federal law or touches interests deeply rooted in local feeling and responsibility. *Id.* at 243–244; *Sears, Roebuck & Co. v. Carpenters*, 436 U.S. 180, 200 (1978); *Farmer v. Carpenters*, 430 U.S. 290, 296–297 (1977). In such cases, the state's interest in controlling or remedying the effects of the conduct is balanced against both the interference with the Board's ability to adjudicate controversies committed to it by the Act, *Farmer v. Carpenters, supra* at 297; *Sears, Roebuck & Co. v. Carpenters, supra* at 200, and the risk that the state will sanction conduct that the Act protects. *Id.* at 205. The second preemption doctrine, set out in *Machinists v. Wisconsin Employment Relations Commission*, 427 U.S. 132 (1976), proscribes state regulation and state-law causes of action concerning conduct that Congress intended to be unregulated, *id.* at 140, conduct that was to remain a part of the self-help remedies left to the combatants in labor disputes, *id.* at 147–148.

Petitioner argues that the action was preempted under both *Garmon* and *Machinists*. The Board and the AFL-CIO, in *amicus* briefs, place major emphasis on *Machinists*; they argue that the Kentucky courts are attempting to impose Kentucky law with respect to areas or subjects that Congress intended to be unregulated. We address first the *Machinists* and then the *Garmon* submissions.

III

It is asserted that Congress intended the respective conduct of the Union and Belknap during the strike beginning on February 1 "'to be controlled by the free play of economic forces,'" *Machinists v. Wisconsin Employment Relations Commission, supra* at 140, *quoting NLRB v. Nash-Finch*, 404 U.S. 138, 144 (1971), and that entertaining the action against Belknap was an impermissible attempt by the Kentucky courts to regulate and burden one of the employer's primary weapons during an economic strike, that is, the right to hire permanent replacements. To permit the suit filed in this case to proceed would upset the delicate balance of forces established by the federal law. Subjecting the employer to costly suits for damages under state law for entering into settlements calling for the return of strikers would also conflict with the federal labor policy favoring the settlement of labor disputes. These arguments, it is urged, are valid whether or not a strike is an economic strike.

We are unpersuaded. It is true that the federal law permits, but does not require, the employer to hire replacements during a strike, replacements that it need not discharge in order to reinstate strikers if it hires the replacements on a "permanent" basis within the meaning of the federal labor law. But when an employer attempts to exercise this very privilege by promising the replacements that they will not be discharged to make room for returning strikers, it surely does not follow that the employer's otherwise valid promises of permanent employment are nullified by federal law and its otherwise actionable misrepresentations may not be pursued. See *J. I. Case, Co. v. NLRB*, 321 U.S. 332 (1944); *see infra*.... We find unacceptable the notion that the federal law on the one hand insists on promises of permanent employment if the employer anticipates keeping the replacements in preference to returning strikers, but on the other hand forecloses damage suits for the employer's breach of these very promises. Even more mystifying is the suggestion that the federal law shields the employer from damages suits for misrepresentations that are made during the process of securing permanent replacements and are actionable under state law.

Arguments that entertaining suits by innocent third parties for breach of contract or for misrepresentation will "burden" the employer's right to hire permanent replacements are no more than arguments that "this is war," that "anything goes," and that promises of permanent employment that under federal law the employer is free to keep, if it so chooses, are essentially meaningless. It is one thing to hold that the federal law intended to leave the employer and the union free to use their economic weapons against one another, but is quite another to hold that either the employer or the union is also free to injure innocent third parties without regard to the normal rules of law governing those relationships. We cannot agree with the dissent that Congress intended such a lawless regime.

The argument that entertaining suits like this will interfere with the asserted policy of the federal law favoring settlement of labor disputes fares no better. This is just another way of asserting that the employer need not answer for its repeated assurances of permanent employment or for its otherwise actionable misrepresentations to secure permanent replacements. We do not think that the normal contractual rights and other usual legal interests of the replacements can be so easily disposed of by broad-brush assertions that no legal rights may accrue to them during a strike because the federal law has privileged the "permanent" hiring of replacements and encourages settlement.

In defense of this position, Belknap, supported by the Board in an amicus brief, urges that permitting the state suit where employers may, after the beginning of a strike, either be ordered to reinstate strikers or find it advisable to sign agreements providing for reinstatement of strikers, will deter employers from making permanent offers of employment or at the very least force them to condition their offer by stating the circumstances under which replacements must be fired. This would considerably weaken the employer's position during the strike, it is said, because without assuring permanent employment, it would be difficult to secure sufficient replacements to keep the business operating. Indeed, as the Board interprets the law, the employer must reinstate strikers at the conclusion of even a purely economic strike unless it has hired "permanent" replacements, that is, hired in a manner that would "show that the men [and women] who replaced the strikers were regarded by themselves and the [employer] as having received their jobs on a permanent basis." *Georgia Highway Express, Inc.*, 165 NLRB 514, 516 (1967), *aff'd sub nom. Truck Drivers and Helpers Local No. 728 v. NLRB*, 403 F.2d 921 (CADC), *cert. denied*, 393 U.S. 935 (1968).

We remain unconvinced. If serious detriment will result to the employer from conditioning offers so as to avoid a breach of contract if the employer is forced by Board order to reinstate strikers or if the employer settles on terms requiring such reinstatement, much the same result would follow from Belknap's and the Board's construction of the Act. Their view is that, as a matter of federal law, an employer may terminate replacements, without liability to them, in the event of settlement or Board decision that the strike is an unfair labor practice strike. Any offer of permanent employment to replacements is thus necessarily conditional and nonpermanent. This view of the law would inevitably become widely known and would deter honest employers from making promises that they know they are not legally obligated to keep. Also, many putative replacements would know that the proffered job is, in important respects, non-permanent and may not accept employment for that reason. It is doubtful, with respect to the employer's ability to hire, that there would be a substantial difference between the effect of the Board's preferred rule and a rule that would subject the employer to damages liability unless it suitably conditions its offers of employment made to replacements.

Belknap counters that conditioning offers in such manner will render replacements non-permanent employees subject to discharge to make way for strikers at the conclusion or settlement of a purely economic strike, which would not be the case if replacements had been hired on a "permanent" basis as the Board now understands that term. The balance of power would thus be distorted if the employer is forced to condition its offers for its own protection. Under Belknap's submission, however, which is to some extent supported by the Board, Belknap's promises, although in form assuring permanent employment, would as a matter of law be non-permanent to the same extent as they would be if expressly conditioned on the eventuality of settlement requiring reinstatement of strikers and on its obligation to reinstate unfair labor practice strikers. As we have said, we cannot believe that Congress determined that the employer must be free to deceive by promising permanent employment knowing that it may choose to reinstate strikers or may be forced to do so by the Board.

An employment contract with a replacement promising permanent employment, subject only to settlement with its employees' union and to a Board unfair labor practice order directing reinstatement of strikers, would not in itself render the replacement a temporary employee subject to displacement by a striker over the employer's objection during or at the end of what is proved to be a purely economic strike. The Board suggests that such a conditional offer "might" render the replacements only temporary hires that the employer would be required to discharge at the conclusion of a purely economic strike. But the permanent-hiring requirement is designed to protect the strikers, who retain their employee status and are entitled to reinstatement unless they have been permanently replaced. That protection is unnecessary if the employer is ordered to reinstate them because of the commission of unfair labor practices. It is also meaningless if the employer settles with the union and agrees to reinstate strikers. But the protection is of great moment if the employer is not found guilty of unfair practices, does not settle with the union, or settles without a promise to reinstate. In that eventuality, the employer, although he has prevailed in the strike, may refuse reinstatement only if he has hired replacements on a permanent basis. If he has promised to keep the replacements on in such a situation, discharging them to make way for selected strikers whom he deems more experienced or more efficient would breach his contract with the replacements. Those contracts, it seems to us, create a sufficiently permanent arrangement to permit the prevailing employer to abide by its promises.[36]

We perceive no substantial impact on the availability of settlement of economic or unfair labor practice strikes if the employer is careful to protect itself against suits like this in the course of contracting with strike replacements. Its risk of liability if it discharges replacements pursuant to a settlement or to a Board order would then be minimal. We fail to understand why in such circumstances the employer would be any less willing to settle the strike than it would be under the regime proposed by Belknap and the Board, which as a matter of law, would permit it to settle without liability for misrepresentation or for breach of contract.

Belknap and its supporters, the Board and the AFL-CIO, offer no substantial case authority for the proposition that the *Machinists* rationale forecloses this suit. Surely *Machinists* did not deal with solemn promises of permanent employment, made to innocent replacements, that the employer was free to make and keep under federal law. *J. I. Case, Co. v. NLRB*, 321 U.S. 332 (1944), suggests that individual contracts of employment must give way to otherwise valid provisions of the collective bargaining contract, *id.* at 336–339 but it was careful to say that the Board "has no power to adjudicate the validity or effect of such contracts except as to their effect on matters within its jurisdiction," *id.* at 340. There, the cease-and-desist order, as modified, stated that the discontinuance of the individual contracts was "without prejudice to

---

36. [8] The refusal to fire permanent replacements because of commitments made to them in the course of an economic strike satisfies the requirement of *NLRB v. Fleetwood Trailer Co.*, 389 U.S. 375, 380 (1967), that the employer have a "legitimate and substantial justification" for his refusal to reinstate strikers. That the offer and promise of permanent employment are conditional does not render the hiring any less permanent if the conditions do not come to pass. All hirings are to some extent conditional. As the Board recognizes, Brief of the National Labor Relations Board as *Amicus Curiae* 16–17 (NLRB Br.), although respondents were hired on a permanent basis, they were subject to discharge in the event of a business slowdown. Had Belknap not settled and no unfair practices been filed, surely it would have been free to retain respondents and obligated to do so by the terms of its promises to them. The result should be the same if Belknap had promised to retain them if it did not settle with the union and if it were not ordered to reinstate strikers. The dissent and the concurrence make much of conditional offers of employment, asserting that they prevent replacements from being permanent employees. As indicated in the text, however, the Board's position is that even unconditional contracts of permanent employment are as a matter of law defeasible, first, if the strike turns out to be an unfair labor practice strike, and second, if the employer chooses to settle with the union and reinstate the strikers. If these implied conditions, including those dependent on the volitional act of settlement, do not prevent the replacements from being permanent employees, neither should express conditions which do no more than inform replacements what their legal status is in any event. The dissent and the concurrence suggest that if offers of permanent employment are not necessary to secure the manpower to keep the business operating, returning strikers must be given preference over replacements who have been hired on a permanent basis. That issue is not posed in this case, but we note that the Board has held to the contrary. . . . . *Hot Shoppes, Inc.*, 146 N.L.R.B. 802, 804 (1964). . . .

the assertion of any legal rights the employee may have acquired under such contract or to any defenses thereto by the employer." *Id.* at 342 (emphasis deleted); see *supra*. . . .

There is still another variant or refinement of the argument that the employer and the Union should be privileged to settle their dispute and provide for striker reinstatement free of burdensome law suits such as this. It is said that respondent replacements are employees within the bargaining unit, that the Union is the bargaining representative of petitioner's employees, and the replacements are thus bound by the terms of the settlement negotiated between the employer and "their" representative. The argument is not only that as a matter of federal law the employer cannot be foreclosed from discharging the replacements pursuant to a contract with a bargaining agent, but also that by virtue of the agreement with the Union it is relieved from responding in damages for its knowing breach of contract—that is, that the contracts are not only not specifically enforceable but also may be breached free from liability for damages. We need not address the former issue—the issue of specific performance—since the respondents ask only damages. As to the damages issue, as we have said above, such an argument was rejected in *J. I. Case*.

If federal law forecloses this suit, more specific and persuasive reasons than those based on *Machinists* must be identified to support any such result. Belknap insists that the rationale of the *Garmon* decision, properly construed and applied, furnishes these reasons.

IV

The complaint issued by the Regional Director alleged that on or about February 1, Belknap unilaterally put into effect a 50 cents-per-hour wage increase, that such action constituted unfair labor practices under §§ 8(a)(1), 8(a)(3) and 8(a)(5), and that the strike was prolonged by these violations. If these allegations could have been sustained, the strike would have been an unfair labor practice strike almost from the very start. From that time forward, Belknap's advertised offers of permanent employment to replacements would arguably have been unfair labor practices since they could be viewed as threats to refuse to reinstate unfair labor practice strikers. See *NLRB v. Laredo Coca Cola Bottling Co.*, 613 F.2d 1338, 1341 (CA5), *cert. denied*, 449 U.S. 889 (1980). Furthermore, if the strike had been an unfair labor practice strike, Belknap would have been forced to reinstate the strikers rather than keep replacements on the job. *Mastro Plastics Corp. v. NLRB*, 350 U.S. 270, 278 (1956). Belknap submits that its offers of permanent employment to respondents were therefore arguably unfair labor practices, the adjudication of which were within the exclusive jurisdiction of the Board, and that discharging respondents to make way for strikers was protected activity since it was no more than the federal law required in the event the unfair labor practices were proved.

Respondents do not dispute that it was the Board's exclusive business to determine, one, whether Belknap's unilateral wage increase was an unfair labor practice, which would have converted the strike into an unfair labor practice strike that [would] require the reinstatement of strikers, and, two, whether Belknap also committed unfair labor practices by offering permanent employment to respondents. They submit, however, that under our cases, properly read, their actions for fraud and breach of contract, are not preempted. We agree with respondents.

Under *Garmon*, a state may regulate conduct that is of only peripheral concern to the Act or which is so deeply rooted in local law that the courts should not assume that Congress intended to preempt the application of state law. In *Linn v. Plant Guard Workers*, 383 U.S. 53 (1966), we held that false and malicious statements in the course of a labor dispute were actionable under state law if injurious to reputation, even though such statements were in themselves unfair labor practices adjudicable by the Board. Likewise, in *Farmer v. Carpenters*, 430 U.S. 290 (1977), we held that the Act did not preempt a state action for intentionally inflicting emotional distress, even though a major part of the cause of action consisted of conduct that was arguably an unfair labor practice. Finally in *Sears, Roebuck & Co. v. Carpenters*, 436 U.S. 180 (1978), we held that a state trespass action was permissible and not preempted, since the action concerned only the location of the picketing while the arguable unfair labor practice would focus on the object of the picketing. In that case, we emphasized that a critical inquiry in applying the *Garmon* rules, where the conduct at issue in the state litigation is said to be arguably prohibited by the Act and hence within the exclusive jurisdiction of the NLRB, is whether the controversy presented to the state court is identical with that which could be presented to the Board. There the state court and Board controversies could not fairly be called identical. This is also the case here.

Belknap contends that the misrepresentation suit is preempted because it related to the offers and contracts for permanent employment, conduct that was part and a parcel of an arguable unfair labor practice. It is true that whether the strike was an unfair labor practice strike and whether the offer to replacements was the kind of offer forbidden during such a dispute were matters for the Board. The focus of these determinations, however, would be on whether the rights of strikers were being infringed. Neither controversy would have anything in common with the question whether Belknap made misrepresentations to replacements that were actionable under state law. The Board would be concerned with the impact on strikers[,] not with whether the employer deceived replacements. As in *Linn v. Plant Guard Workers*, *supra*, "the Board [will] not be ignored since its sanctions alone can adjust the equilibrium disturbed by an unfair labor practice." *Id.* at 66. The strikers cannot secure reinstatement, or indeed any relief, by suing for misrepresentation in state court. The state courts in no way offer them an alternative forum for obtaining relief that the Board can provide. The same was true in *Sears* and *Farmer*. Hence, it appears to us that maintaining the misrepresentation action would not interfere with the Board's determination of matters within its jurisdiction and that such an action is of no more than peripheral concern to the Board and the federal law. At the same time, Kentucky surely has a substantial interest in protecting its citizens from misrepresentations that have caused them grievous harm. It is no less true here than it was in *Linn v. Plant Guard Workers, supra* at 63, that "[t]he injury" remedied by the state law "has no relevance to the Board's function" and that "[t]he Board can award no damages, impose no penalty, or give any other relief to the plaintiffs in this case." The state interests involved in this case clearly outweigh any possible interference with the Board's function that may result from permitting the action for misrepresentation to proceed.

Neither can we accept the assertion that the breach of contract claim is preempted. The claimed breach is the discharge of respondents to make way for strikers, an action allegedly contrary to promises that were binding under state law. As we have said, respondents do not deny that had the strike been adjudicated an unfair labor practice strike Belknap would have been required to reinstate the strikers, an obligation that the state could not negate.[37] But respondents do assert that such an adjudication has not been made, that Belknap prevented such an adjudication by settling with the Union and voluntarily agreeing to reinstate strikers, and that, in any event, the reinstatement of strikers, even if ordered by the Board, would only prevent the specific performance of Belknap's promises to respondents, not immunize Belknap from responding in damages from its breach of its otherwise enforceable contracts.

For the most part, we agree with respondents. We have already concluded that the federal law does not expressly or impliedly privilege an employer, as part of a settlement with a union, to discharge replacements in breach of its promises of permanent employment. Also, even had there been no settlement and the Board had ordered reinstatement of what it held to be unfair labor practice strikers, the suit for damages for breach of contract could still be maintained without in any way prejudicing the jurisdiction of the Board or the interest of the federal law in insuring the replacement of strikers. The interests of the Board and the NLRA, on the one hand, and the interest of the state in providing a remedy to its citizens for breach of contract, on the other, are "discrete" concerns, cf. *Farmer v. Carpenters, supra*, at 304. We see no basis for holding that permitting the contract cause of action will conflict with the rights of either the strikers or the employer or would frustrate any policy of the federal labor laws.

V

Because neither the misrepresentation nor the breach-of-contract cause of action is preempted under *Garmon* or *Machinists*, the decision of the Kentucky Court of Appeals is

Affirmed.

[The opinion of Justice Blackmun, concurring in the judgment, is omitted.]

---

37. [13] Kentucky may not mandate specific performance of the contract between Belknap and respondents nor may it enter an injunction requiring the reinstatement of respondents as a remedy for fraud if either action necessitates the firing of a striker entitled to reinstatement. To do so would be to deprive returning strikers of jobs committed to them by the national labor laws. . . .

JUSTICE BRENNAN, with whom JUSTICE MARSHALL and JUSTICE POWELL join, dissenting. . . .

Despite the conceded difficulty of this case, I cannot agree with the Court's conclusion that neither respondents' breach of contract claim nor their misrepresentation claim is preempted by federal law. In my view these claims go to the core of federal labor policy. If respondents are allowed to pursue their claims in state court, employers will be subject to potentially conflicting state and federal regulation of their activities; the efficient administration of the National Labor Relations Act will be threatened; and the structure of the economic weapons Congress has provided to parties to a labor dispute will be altered. In short, the purposes and policies of federal law will be frustrated. I, therefore, respectfully dissent. . . .

Respondents' breach of contract claim is based on the allegation that petitioner breached his contracts with them by entering into a settlement agreement with the union that called for the gradual reinstatement of the strikers respondents had replaced. . . . The strike involved in this case, however, arguably was converted into an unfair labor practice strike almost immediately after it started. . . . If the strike was converted into an unfair labor practice strike, the striking employees were entitled to reinstatement irrespective of petitioner's decision to hire permanent replacements. . . . Under these circumstances, federal law would have required petitioner to reinstate the striking employees and to discharge the replacements. In this light, it is clear that petitioner's decision to breach its contracts with respondents was arguably *required* by federal law. . . .

In my view . . . basic principles compel a conclusion that respondents' breach of contract claim is preempted. The potential for conflicting regulation clearly exists in this case. Respondents' breach of contract claim seeks to regulate activity that may well have been required by federal law. Petitioner may have to answer in damages for taking such an action. This sort of conflicting regulation is intolerable. As the Court stated in *Motor Coach Employees v. Lockridge, supra,* if "the regulatory schemes, state and federal, conflict . . . pre-emption is clearly called for. . . ." 403 U.S. at 292. . . .

Prohibiting specific enforcement, but permitting a damages award, does nothing to eliminate the conflict between state and federal law in this context. The Court fails to recognize that "regulation can be as effectively exerted through an award of damages as through some form of preventive relief." *Garmon,* 359 U.S. at 247. "The obligation to pay compensation can be, indeed is designed to be, a potent method of governing conduct and controlling policy." *Ibid.* The force of these observations is apparent in this case. If an employer is confronted with potential liability for discharging workers he has hired to replace striking employees, he is likely to be much less willing to enter into a settlement agreement calling for the dismissal of unfair labor practice charges and for the reinstatement of strikers. Instead, he is much more likely to refuse to settle and to litigate the charges at issue while retaining the replacements. Such developments would frustrate the strong federal interest in ending strikes and in settling labor disputes. In addition, the National Labor Relations

Board has suggested that any impediment to the settlement of unfair labor practice charges would have a serious adverse effect on the Board's administration of the Act. Finally, any obstacle to strike settlement agreements clearly affects adversely the interest of striking employees in returning to work, to say nothing of the public interest in ending labor strife. Consideration of these factors leads to the clear conclusion that respondents' breach of contract claim must be preempted. . . .

Respondents' misrepresentation claim stands on a somewhat different footing than their breach of contract claim. There is no sense in which it can be said that federal law required petitioner to misrepresent to respondents the terms on which they were hired. Permitting respondents to pursue their misrepresentation claim in state court, therefore, does not present the same potential for directly conflicting regulation of employer activity as permitting respondents to pursue their breach of contract claim. Nor can it be said that petitioner's alleged misrepresentation was "arguably protected" under *Garmon*. While it is arguable that petitioner's alleged offers of permanent employment were prohibited by the Act and therefore preempted under *Garmon*, . . . careful analysis yields the conclusion that this is not a sufficient ground for preempting respondents' misrepresentation claim. In my view, however, respondents' misrepresentation claim is preempted under the analysis articulated principally in *Machinists v. Wisconsin Emp. Rel. Comm'n*, 427 U.S. 132 (1976). . . .

Machinists relied on *Garner* and *Morton* in expressly articulating a branch of labor law preemption analysis distinct from the *Garmon* line of cases. The Court in *Machinists* described this branch as "focusing upon the crucial inquiry whether Congress intended that the conduct involved be unregulated because left 'to be controlled by the free play of economic forces.'" 427 U.S. at 140 (citation omitted). While earlier cases had addressed this question within the context of union and employee activities, see *id.*, at 147, the Court noted that "self-help is . . . also the prerogative of the employer because he, too, may properly employ economic weapons Congress meant to be unregulable." *Ibid.* The Court stated: "Whether self-help economic activities are employed by employer or union, the crucial inquiry regarding preemption is the same: whether 'the exercise of plenary state authority to curtail or entirely prohibit self-help would frustrate effective implementation of the Act's processes.'" *Id.* at 147–148 (citation omitted).

As noted, . . . employers have the right to hire replacements for striking employees. This is an economic weapon that the employer may use to combat pressure brought to bear by the union. Permitting the use of this weapon is part of the balance struck by the Act between labor and management. There is no doubt that respondents' misrepresentation claim, involving as it does the potential for substantial employer liability, burdens an employer's right to resort to this weapon. This is especially apparent when one considers the fact that the character of a strike is often unclear. A strike that starts as an economic strike, during which an employer is entitled to hire permanent replacements that he need not discharge to make way for returning strikers, may be converted into an unfair labor practice strike, in which case the employer loses his right to hire permanent replacements subsequent to the date of the conversion. . . .

Based on this analysis, it is clear that permitting respondents to pursue their misrepresentation claim in state court would limit and substantially burden an employer's resort to an economic weapon available to him under federal law. This would have the inevitable effect of distorting the delicate balance struck by the Act between the rights of labor and management in labor disputes. For these reasons, respondents' misrepresentation claim must be preempted. . . .

Notes

1. *Statutes Predicated on the State's Spending Power*—In *Wisconsin Dep't of Indus., Labor & Human Relations v. Gould, Inc.*, 475 U.S. 282 (1986), the Supreme Court held that the NLRA preempted a Wisconsin statute debarring any firm violating the NLRA three times within five years from doing business with the state. To the state's argument that its scheme should escape preemption as an exercise of the spending power rather than the regulatory power, the Court responded: "But that seems to us a distinction without a difference, at least in this case, because on its face the debarment statute serves plainly as a means of enforcing the NLRA." The Court also said: "Because Wisconsin's debarment law functions unambiguously as a supplemental sanction for violations of the NLRA, it conflicts with the Board's comprehensive regulation of industrial relations in precisely the same way as would a state statute preventing repeat labor law violators from doing any business with private parties within the State." *See also Employers Ass'n v. United Steelworkers*, 32 F.3d 1297 (8th Cir. 1994) and *Midwest Motor Express v. Int'l Bhd. of Teamsters Local 120*, 512 N.W.2d 881 (Minn. 1994) (Minnesota Striker Replacement Act proscribing hiring of permanent striker replacements preempted by NLRA).

The Supreme Court sustained a Massachusetts Water Resources Authority bidding specification requiring contractors wishing to work on the $6 billion Boston Harbor cleanup project to comply with the terms of a master labor agreement, since the Court concluded that such a lawful prehire agreement requirement could be imposed by a state acting as the owner of a construction project, as opposed to a state acting in a regulatory capacity. *Bldg. & Constr. Trades Council v. Associated Builders & Contrs.*, 507 U.S. 218 (1993).

2. *State Regulatory Pressure on Parties to Reach a Collective Bargaining Agreement*—In 1980, when the Golden State Transit Corporation applied for a renewal of its taxicab license, the City of Los Angeles conditioned renewal upon Golden State's settlement of its existing bargaining dispute by a certain date. When the dispute was not resolved by that date, Los Angeles refused to renew Golden State's taxicab license. The Supreme Court was asked to determine whether the actions of Los Angeles were preempted by the NLRA.

> Congress' decision to prohibit certain forms of economic pressure while leaving others unregulated represents an intentional balance "between the

uncontrolled power of management and labor to further their respective interests." *Machinists v. Wisconsin Empl. Rels. Comm.*, 427 U.S. 132, 146 (1976). States are therefore prohibited from imposing additional restrictions on economic weapons of self-help, such as strikes or lockouts, unless such restrictions presumably were contemplated by Congress. "Whether self-help economic activities are employed by employer or union, the crucial inquiry regarding pre-emption is the same: whether the exercise of plenary state authority to curtail or entirely prohibit self-help would frustrate effective implementation of the Act's processes." *Id.* at 147–48. . . . The parties' resort to economic pressure was a legitimate part of their collective-bargaining process. But the bargaining process was thwarted when the city in effect imposed a positive durational limit on the exercise of self-help.

Golden State Transit Corp. v. Los Angeles, 475 U.S. 608 (1986).

Since the Court found that Los Angeles had "[entered] into the substantive aspects of the bargaining process to an extent Congress has not countenanced," it concluded that its actions were preempted. *Id.*

In *Metropolitan Milwaukee Ass'n of Commerce v. Milwaukee County*, 431 F.3d 277 (7th Cir. 2005), the court found preempted a county ordinance requiring employers that have contracts to provide transportation and other services to county residents to enter into "labor peace agreements" with unions desiring to organize their employees, since this law directly regulated the labor relations policies of those firms.

A New York State statute requires union approval of apprenticeship programs when there is a labor contract or agreement providing for union participation. During stalled contract negotiations with the union, an employer applied for registration of an apprenticeship program with the New York State Department of Labor. The Labor Commissioner refused to process the application due to the absence of union approval. The court found that inaction by the Labor Commissioner was preempted by the NLRA under a *Machinists* rationale, since it placed economic pressure on the employer to agree to a contract or reach impasse, thus skewing the bargaining process. *Bldg. Trades Emplrs. Educ. Ass'n v. McGowan*, 311 F.3d 501 (2d Cir. 2002).

3. *Regulating Nonlawyer Consultants* — In *Ohio State Bar Ass'n v. Burdzinski, Brinkman, Czarzasty & Landwehr, Inc.*, 112 Ohio St. 3d 107, 858 N.E.2d 372 (2006), the court held that federal labor relations statutes do not preempt the right of states to regulate the activities of nonlawyer consultants with respect to labor-related matters performed for employers subject to NLRA coverage. It went on to hold that nonlawyer consultants do not engage in the unauthorized practice of law when they represent employers in union matters or they negotiate for firms on labor issues, so long as they confine themselves to advice and services that do not require legal analysis, legal conclusions, or legal training. Although nonlawyer consultants may negotiate on behalf of employers, they may not draft collective bargaining agreements, even if copied from form books, since such work constitutes the practice of law.

Problem

37. A state recently passed a comprehensive pay equity law that, among other things, makes it an unfair employment practice for employers to prohibit their employees from discussing their own compensation or the compensation of other employees. The law also prohibits employers from requiring employees to sign a waiver that purports to deny the employee the right to disclose compensation information. There is nothing in the law that limits an employee's right to discuss the compensation of another employee even if that information has been obtained improperly and without the permission of the employee whose compensation is being discussed. The new law imposes civil penalties for employers who violate its provisions: $1,000 for the first violation; $5,000 for the second violation; and $20,000 for each subsequent violation.

Are the provisions of this new law preempted by the NLRA?

Part 5

Collective Bargaining

ALBERT REES, THE ECONOMICS OF TRADE UNIONS
74, 89–90, 186–87 (2d ed. 1977)*

Many people view trade unions as a device for increasing the worker's share in the distribution of income at the expense of capital; that is, at the expense of the receivers of rent, interest, and profits. Attempts to test this view, which is often expressed by the unions themselves, have led to a number of studies of the effect of unions on labor's share. The studies to date must be regarded as highly inconclusive; no union effect on labor's share can be discovered with any consistency....

It may seem very strange that statistical studies can find a considerable effect of unions on wages and none on labor's share. On further consideration, however, this result is quite reasonable.... [A] successful union will not necessarily raise labor's share even in its own industry. The wage bill will rise following a wage increase if the demand for labor is inelastic (that is, if the percentage reduction in employment is smaller than the percentage increase in wages) and this will raise labor's share in the short run. But as time passes the employer will tend to substitute capital for labor.... In extreme cases, total wage payments may fall as employment contracts so that they are smaller than they were before the wage increase.... It is thus entirely possible for a union simultaneously to raise the relative wages of its members and to reduce their aggregate share of income arising in their industry....

If the union is viewed solely in terms of its effect on the economy, it must in my opinion be considered an obstacle to the optimum performance of our economic system. It alters the wage structure in a way that impedes the growth of employment in sectors of the economy where productivity and income are naturally high and that leaves too much labor in low-income sectors of the economy like southern agriculture and the least skilled service trades. It benefits most those workers who would in any case be relatively well off, and while some of this gain may be at the expense of the owners of capital, most of it must be at the expense of consumers and the lower-paid workers. Unions interfere blatantly with the use of the most productive techniques in some industries, and this effect is probably not offset by the stimulus to higher productivity furnished by some other unions.

---

* Reprinted with the permission of the University of Chicago Press.

Many of my fellow economists would stop at this point and conclude that unions are harmful and that their power should be curbed. I do not agree that one can judge the value of a complex institution from so narrow a point of view. Other aspects of unions must also be considered. The protection against the abuse of managerial authority given by seniority systems and grievance procedures seems to me to be a union accomplishment of the greatest importance. So too is the organized representation in public affairs given the worker by the political activities of unions.... If the job rights won for workers by unions are not conceded by the rest of society simply because they are just, they should be conceded because they help to protect the minimum consensus that keeps our society stable. In my judgment, the economic losses imposed by unions are not too high a price to pay for their successful performance of this role.

Freeman & Medoff, *The Two Faces of Unionism*, in THE PUBLIC INTEREST
69, 76, 78–82, 85, 86 (Fall 1979)*

Since, in fact, unions have both monopoly and collective-voice/institutional response components, the key question for understanding unionism in the United States relates to the relative importance of these two faces. Are unions primarily monopolistic institutions, or are they primarily voice institutions that induce socially beneficial responses?

Most of the econometric analysis of unions has focused on the question of central concern to the monopoly view: How large is the union wage effect? In his important book, Unionism and Relative Wages, H. Gregg Lewis summarized results of this analysis through the early 1960's, concluding that, while differing over time and across settings, the union wage effect averages on the order of 10 to 15 percent.

As predicted by the monopoly wage model, the capital-labor ratio and average "quality" of labor both appear to be somewhat greater than "optimal" in union settings. However, the total loss in output due to this misallocation of resources appears to be minuscule; an analysis done by Albert Rees suggests that the loss is less than 0.3 percent of the gross national product.

One of the central tenets of the collective-voice/institutional-response model is that among workers receiving the same pay, unions reduce employee turnover and its associated costs by offering "voice" as an alternative to exit. Our own research shows that, with diverse factors (including wages) held constant, unionized workers do have significantly lower quit rates than nonunion workers who are comparable in other respects.

---

* Copyright © 1979 by The Bureau of National Affairs, Inc. Reprinted by permission of the authors and The Public Interest. Https://nationalaffairs.com/public_interest/detail/the-two-faces-of-unionism.

Our analyses of... available data on unionism and output per worker in many establishments or sectors suggests that the monopoly view of unions as a major deterrent to productivity is erroneous. In some settings, unionism leads to *higher* productivity, not only because of the greater capital intensity and higher labor quality, but also because of what can best be termed institutional-response factors.

In manufacturing, productivity in the organized sector appears to be substantially higher than in the unorganized sector, by an amount that could roughly offset the increase in total costs attributable to higher union wages.

There is limited tentative evidence that, on average, net profits are reduced somewhat by unionism, particularly in oligopolistic industries, though there are notable exceptions. At present, there is no definitive accounting of what proportion of the union wage effect comes at the expense of capital, other labor, or consumers, and what portion is offset by previously unexploited possibilities for productivity improvements.

Finally, it is important to note that despite what some critics of unions might claim, strikes do not seem to cost society a substantial amount of goods and services. For the economy as a whole, the percentage of total working time lost directly to strikes during the past two decades has never been greater than 0.5 percent and has averaged about 0.2 percent.

Under the monopoly view, the exit and entry of workers permits each individual to find a firm offering the mix of employee benefits and personnel policies that he or she prefers. In the voice view, a union provides management with information at the bargaining table concerning policies affecting its entire membership (*e.g.*, the mix of the employee-compensation package or the firm's employment practices during a downturn) which can be expected to be different from that derived from the movements of marginal workers.

Data on the remuneration of individual workers and on the expenditures for employees by firms show that the proportion of compensation allotted to fringe benefits is markedly higher for organized blue-collar workers than for similar nonunion workers. Within most industries, important fringes such as pensions, and life, accident, and health insurance are much more likely to be found in unionized establishments.

According to the monopoly model, the workers displaced from unionized firms as a result of union wage gains raise the supply of labor to nonunion firms, which can therefore be expected to reduce wages. Thus in the monopoly view unionized workers are likely to be made better off at the expense of nonunion workers. The fact that organized blue-collar workers would tend to be more skilled and higher paid than other blue-collar workers even in the absence of unionism implies further that unionism benefits "labor's elite" at the expense of those with less skill and earning power.

In fact, the collective-voice/institutional-response model suggests very different effects on equality than does the monopoly view. Given that union decisions are based on a political process, and given that the majority of union members are likely to have earnings below the mean (including white-collar workers) in any workplace, unions can be expected to seek to reduce wage inequality. Union members are also likely to favor a less-dispersed distribution of earnings for reasons of ideology and organizational solidarity. Finally, by its nature, collective bargaining reduces managerial discretion in the wage-setting process, and this should also reduce differences among similarly situated workers.

Our empirical estimates . . . show that standardization policies have substantially reduced wage inequality, and that this effect dominates the monopoly wage effect. When, for instance, the distribution of earnings for male blue-collar workers is graphed, the results for unionized workers in both the manufacturing and nonmanufacturing sectors show a much narrower distribution, compressed at the extremes and radically peaked in the middle. For nonunion workers, by contrast, the graphs show a much more dispersed pattern of earnings.

In addition to reducing earnings inequality among blue-collar workers, union wage policies contribute to the equalization of wages by decreasing the differential between covered blue-collar workers and uncovered white-collar workers. In manufacturing, though white-collar workers earn an average of 49 percent more than blue-collar workers, our estimates indicate that in unionized enterprises this premium is only 32 percent; in the nonmanufacturing sector, where white-collar workers average 31 percent more in earnings than blue-collar workers, the estimated differential is only 19 percent where there are unions.

Notes

1. *The Union Wage Premium*—Freeman & Medoff cite a union wage premium averaging between 10 and 15% by the early 1960s. Union wage premiums increased during the late 1970s and early 1980s to an estimated 21–32%. Although the wage premium has declined since then as a result of external pressures imposed by globalization, technological innovation, and demographic shifts, research suggests that a sizable gap still remains between unionized and nonunionized workers: by 2017, estimates placed the overall union wage premium at 13.2%. The wage premium was higher for African Americans and Hispanics, 14.7% and 21.8%, respectively, as compared with an 8.7% premium for whites. *See* Bivens et al., *How Today's Unions Help Working People*, Aug. 24, 2017, available at www.epi.org. A union premium also exists on other aspects of the compensation package, including health insurance (94% of union workers are covered by employer-provided health insurance, compared with 67% of nonunion workers), pension benefits (90% of union workers participate in a retirement plan, compared with 75% of nonunion workers, and 74% of union workers with pensions enjoy a traditional defined benefit retirement plan compared with 15% of nonunion workers), and paid time off (89% of private sector union workers enjoy paid vacation or holidays, compared with 75% of nonunion workers in the private sector). *Id.*

2. *Rising Income Inequality, Declining Unionization*—Income inequality in the United States has increased dramatically since the 1970s. In 1980, the richest 10% of Americans collected about one-third of the nation's income; by 2012, they were receiving one-half. The top one percent of income earners saw their share more than double between 1973 and 2011. Crain & Matheny, *Unionism, Law, and the Collective Struggle for Economic Justice*, in WORKING AND LIVING IN THE SHADOW OF ECONOMIC FRAGILITY 101 (M. Crain & M. Sherraden eds. 2014). By 2014, some estimates placed the income share accruing to the wealthiest one percent of Americans at 22 percent, making the U.S. income distribution significantly more skewed than other comparable economies. *See* J. STIGLITZ, THE GREAT DIVIDE: UNEQUAL SOCIETIES AND WHAT WE CAN DO ABOUT THEM (2015); E. PORTER, THE PRICE OF EVERYTHING: SOLVING THE MYSTERY OF WHY WE PAY WHAT WE DO (2011). What is the relationship between declining union density and increasing income inequality? As Freeman and Medoff observe, unions historically have reduced income inequality because they raise wages at the bottom and middle of the income scale and union density tends to be higher among lower-wage and middle-wage workers than at the top of the scale. Researchers have documented a correlation between rising income inequality and declining union density over the period when union membership fell most precipitously. *See* Western & Rosenfeld, *Unions, Norms, and the Rise in U.S. Wage Inequality*, 76 AM. Soc. REV. 513 (2011). A more recent study also suggests that economic mobility is correlated with whether children grow up in areas with high union density: a 10 percentage point increase in union density is associated with a 4.5% increase in the income of children from a particular geographic area. The results were particularly pronounced for children whose parents did not graduate from college. *See Union Membership Correlates with Economic Mobility, CAP Report Says*, Daily Lab. Rep. (BNA) No. 174, Sept. 9, 2015, at A-11 (summarizing results of report by the Center for American Progress).

With the decline of union density over the last several decades, are unions still effective at reducing income inequality and improving workplace conditions? For an argument that they are not, see J. ROSENFELD, WHAT UNIONS NO LONGER DO (2014) (detailing consequences of labor's decline, including curtailed advocacy for better working conditions and reduced efficacy in addressing wage gaps, particularly for African Americans and immigrants). Unions have historically contributed to increased wages and enhanced workplace benefits in two ways: directly, through collective bargaining, and indirectly, through political action, lobbying for legislation, and litigation. Is part of organized labor's decreased efficacy attributable to the blurring of the line between unions' representative role in the workplace and their political role in our democratic system? Professor Sachs proposes legal intervention designed to disentangle labor's collective bargaining function from its political function to make political organizing easier for low- and middle-income groups in a members-only form. *See* Sachs, *The Unbundled Union: Politics without Collective Bargaining*, 123 YALE L.J. 148 (2013).

3. *The Union Voice Effect* — Rees and Freeman & Medoff also allude to the function that unions serve in providing a voice for workers, both at the firm level as an alternative to exit, and at the larger political level. Unions have played an important role in lobbying for legislation protecting the rights of all workers, not just those in the unionized sector. Unions were an important political force in the enactment of Title VII, the Occupational Safety and Health Act, the Employee Retirement Income Security Act, the Worker Adjustment Retraining and Notification Act, the Family and Medical Leave Act, and other legislation conferring individual rights on workers. Unions also finance and pursue important impact litigation, including sex and race discrimination cases under Title VII, cases involving the constitutional rights of public sector employees, and cases involving the scope of minimum standards legislation such as the Fair Labor Standards Act and the Occupational Safety and Health Act. *See* Garden, *Union Made: Labor's Litigation for Social Change*, 88 Tul. L. Rev. 193 (2013).

4. *Other Benefits of Unionism* — Rees and Freeman & Medoff also point to other benefits of unionism not captured by economic analysis. For example, unions have been very successful in obtaining due process protections for workers that reduce the tyranny of the shop foreman over the workers by protecting workers against arbitrary discharge. Most labor contracts contain just-cause-for-discharge clauses that establish a system of progressive discipline, ensuring that the workplace version of capital punishment — discharge — cannot be imposed without warning and an opportunity to reform conduct. In addition, nearly every collective bargaining agreement establishes and administers a seniority system. Seniority systems serve three functions, all beneficial in a unionized environment: they protect against favoritism by supervisors, furnishing an objective method for distributing benefits and opportunities; they provide union leaders with an objective means to settle disputes between union members over job entitlement; and they offer a basis upon which workers can predict their future employment positions. At bottom, however, seniority principles are grounded in notions of equity:

> A company should not take from a man the best working years of his life and then, if times turn bad or he slows down, throw him out like so much spent machinery. A worker who has provided his employer with many years of faithful service is entitled to some protection when, no longer young, he can no longer protect himself.

Poplin, *Fair Employment in a Depressed Economy: The Layoff Problem*, 23 UCLA L. Rev. 177, 196–97 (1975); *see also* Aaron, *Reflections on the Legal Nature and Enforceability of Seniority Rights*, 75 Harv. L. Rev. 1532, 1534 (1962).

Section I. Exclusive Representation and Majority Rule

J. I. Case Co. v. NLRB
Supreme Court of the United States
321 U.S. 332, 64 S. Ct. 576, 88 L. Ed. 762 (1944)

Mr. Justice Jackson delivered the opinion of the Court.

This cause was heard by the National Labor Relations Board on stipulated facts which so far as concern present issues are as follows:

The petitioner, J.I. Case Company, at its Rock Island, Illinois, plant, from 1937 offered each employee an individual contract of employment. The contracts were uniform and for a term of one year. The Company agreed to furnish employment as steadily as conditions permitted, to pay a specified rate, which the Company might redetermine if the job changed, and to maintain certain hospital facilities. The employee agreed to accept the provisions, to serve faithfully and honestly for the term, to comply with factory rules, and that defective work should not be paid for. About 75% of the employees accepted and worked under these agreements. . . .

While the individual contracts executed August 1, 1941, were in effect, a CIO union petitioned the Board for certification as the exclusive bargaining representative of the production and maintenance employees. On December 17, 1941, a hearing was held, at which the Company urged the individual contracts as a bar to representation proceedings. The Board, however, directed an election, which was won by the union. The union was thereupon certified as the exclusive bargaining representative of the employees in question in respect to wages, hours, and other conditions of employment.

The union then asked the Company to bargain. It refused, declaring that it could not deal with the union in any manner affecting rights and obligations under the individual contracts while they remained in effect. It offered to negotiate on matters which did not affect rights under the individual contracts, and said that upon the expiration of the contracts it would bargain as to all matters. Twice the Company sent circulars to its employees asserting the validity of the individual contracts and stating the position that it took before the Board in reference to them.

The Board held that the Company had refused to bargain collectively, in violation of § 8(5) of the National Labor Relations Act. . . .

Individual contracts, no matter what the circumstances that justify their execution or what their terms, may not be availed of to defeat or delay the procedures prescribed by the National Labor Relations Act looking to collective bargaining, nor to exclude the contracting employee from a duly ascertained bargaining unit; nor may they be used to forestall bargaining or to limit or condition the terms of the collective agreement. "The Board asserts a public right vested in it as a public body, charged in the public interest with the duty of preventing unfair labor practices." *National*

Licorice Co. v. NLRB, 309 U.S. 350, 364 (1940). Wherever private contracts conflict with its functions, they obviously must yield or the Act would be reduced to a futility.

It is equally clear since the collective trade agreement is to serve the purpose contemplated by the Act, the individual contract cannot be effective as a waiver of any benefit to which the employee otherwise would be entitled under the trade agreement. The very purpose of providing by statute for the collective agreement is to supersede the terms of separate agreements of employees with terms which reflect the strength and bargaining power and serve the welfare of the group. Its benefits and advantages are open to every employee of the represented unit, whatever the type or terms of his pre-existing contract of employment.

But it is urged that some employees may lose by the collective agreement, that an individual workman may sometimes have, or be capable of getting, better terms than those obtainable by the group and that his freedom of contract must be respected on that account. We are not called upon to say that under no circumstances can an individual enforce an agreement more advantageous than a collective agreement, but we find the mere possibility that such agreements might be made no ground for holding generally that individual contracts may survive or surmount collective ones. The practice and philosophy of collective bargaining looks with suspicion on such individual advantages. Of course, where there is a great variation in circumstances of employment or capacity of employees, it is possible for the collective bargain to prescribe only minimum rates or maximum hours or expressly to leave certain areas open to individual bargaining. But except as so provided, advantages to individuals may prove as disruptive of industrial peace as disadvantages. They are a fruitful way of interfering with organization and choice of representative; increased compensation, if individually deserved, is often earned at the cost of breaking down some other standard thought to be for the welfare of the group, and always creates the suspicion of being paid at the long-range expense of the group as a whole. Such discriminations not infrequently amount to unfair labor practices. The workman is free, if he values his own bargaining position more than that of the group, to vote against representation; but the majority rules, and if it collectivizes the employment bargain, individual advantages or favors will generally in practice go in as a contribution to the collective result. We cannot except individual contracts generally from the operation of collective ones because some may be more individually advantageous. Individual contracts cannot subtract from collective ones, and whether under some circumstances they may add to them in matters covered by the collective bargain, we leave to be determined by appropriate forums under the laws of contracts applicable, and to the Labor Board if they constitute unfair labor practices.

It also is urged that such individual contracts may embody matters that are not necessarily included within the statutory scope of collective bargaining, such as stock purchase, group insurance, hospitalization, or medical attention. We know of nothing to prevent the employee's, because he is an employee, making any contract provided it is not inconsistent with a collective agreement or does not amount to or result from or is not part of an unfair labor practice. But in so doing the employer may not incidentally exact or obtain any diminution of his own obligation or any increase of those of employees in the matters covered by collective agreement. Hence we find that the contentions of the Company that the individual contracts precluded a choice of representatives and warranted refusal to bargain during their duration were properly overruled. It follows that representation to the employees by circular letter that they had such legal effect was improper and could properly be prohibited by the Board....

Notes

1. *Individual Contracts Made without Union Consultation* — In *Order of R. Telegraphers v. Railway Express Agency, Inc.*, 321 U.S. 342 (1944), the Supreme Court held that individual contracts made after the collective agreement did not supersede the collective provisions. Under the collective agreement, unexpectedly high rates were payable to a few specially situated station agents. To correct this situation, the company made individual contracts with those agents, but without getting the union's approval or modifying the collective agreement. Under the principle of exclusive representation, the Court held that the union was entitled to be consulted about "the exceptional as well as the routine rates, rules and working conditions."

2. *Individual Contracts Independent of the Collective Bargaining Agreement* — In *Caterpillar, Inc. v. Williams*, 482 U.S. 386 (1987), employees sought to enforce individual contracts — entered into while they were in management positions outside the bargaining unit — guaranteeing them employment at other facilities if the plant closed. After they returned to the bargaining unit, however, the plant closed and they were laid off with the other unit employees. Finding the individual contracts enforceable, the Court observed:

> *J.I. Case* does not stand for the proposition that all individual employment contracts are subsumed into, or eliminated by, the collective- bargaining agreement.... Thus, individual employment contracts are not inevitably superseded by any subsequent collective agreement covering an individual employee, and claims based upon them may arise under state law. [A] plaintiff covered by a collective-bargaining agreement is permitted to assert legal rights *independent* of that agreement, including state-law contract rights, so long as the contract relied upon is *not* a collective-bargaining agreement.

Id. at 396. Critical to the Court's analysis was the fact that the individual contracts at issue were negotiated while the employees were not represented by the union and so did not conflict with any term of the labor contract. Suppose instead that the plant had not closed, but only downsized, resulting in a layoff of half the unit employees. Could the claimants in *Williams* have used their individual contracts to retain their jobs even if they lacked sufficient seniority under the labor contract to avoid a layoff?

3. *Union Power to Bind Dissenting Employees* — Exclusive representation enables unions to bind dissenters, within certain limits, on the wages they will receive, the

hours they will work, and nearly every other facet of their industrial existence. Is this a far more significant encroachment on "individual rights" than the union shop, under which employees may be required to contribute to the financial support of their bargaining representative? Should the exclusivity doctrine be the proper target of those concerned about excessive union power and denial of individual employee voice? In *Janus v. AFSCME, Council 31*, 138 U.S. 1 (2018), the Supreme Court ruled that the First Amendment prohibits mandatory agency fees in the public sector, characterizing the compulsory payment of agency fees as compelled speech. In its decision, the Court alluded to the exclusivity principle, suggesting that it infringes on associational freedoms to a degree "that would not be tolerated in other contexts," and drew the line at requiring dissenting employees to financially support majority unions in the public sector. Taking these comments as an indication of the Court's hostility to the exclusivity doctrine, conservative legal groups filed a number of lawsuits in the federal courts challenging the authority of unions to speak as the exclusive representative in collective bargaining on behalf of all workers in a public sector bargaining unit. *See* Higgins, *Conservatives Take Another Swing at Public Sector Unions*, Washington Examiner, Jan. 4, 2019; Horowitz, *Ohio and Minnesota Teachers Challenge Public-Sector Union Monopoly Representation*, National Legal and Policy Center, Oct. 24, 2018; Needham, *After 'Janus': Anti-Union Forces Target Representation Structure in New Suit*, Rewire.News, Aug. 9, 2018. Although the federal circuit courts have thus far rejected these challenges and the Supreme Court refused certiorari in a post-*Janus* case raising the issue, *Uradnik v. Inter Faculty Association*, 2018 WL 4654751 (D. Minn. Sept. 27, 2018), *cert. denied*, 139 S. Ct. 1618 (2019), other cases are still pending, and it seems likely that the issue will continue to percolate in the public sector. What impact might a successful challenge in the public sector have on the NLRA's exclusivity doctrine? Is exclusive representation indispensable to the effective functioning of collective bargaining? *See generally* Crain & Matheny, *Beyond Unions, Notwithstanding Labor Law*, 4 U.C. Irvine L. Rev. 561 (2014).

4. *Exclusivity in the Global Context*—Exclusivity is unique to American and Canadian labor law regimes; other forms of worker organization and collective representation prevail in most economically advanced democracies. *See* Comparative Labour Law and Industrial Relations in Industrialized Market Economies (R. Blanpain ed., 8th ed. 2004). For example, Japanese law requires employers to bargain with any union representing at least two people; multiple unionism is common. *See* Duff, *Japanese and American Labor Law: Structural Similarities and Substantive Differences*, 9 Emp. Rel. L.J. 629 (1984); Matsuzaki, *Enterprise Unions in Japan*, 34 Indus. Rel. 617 (1992). On the other hand, in many of these countries the detailed administration of the workplace is the prerogative of a paternalistic management. There is little connection between the plant level and the industry level of workers' organizations, and their functions tend to be more social and political than economic. Does this experience shed any light on the question of exclusive representation? Is it coincidental that union density is lower in the United States and Canada than it is in industrialized countries that have rejected exclusivity?

Problems

38. Joanna is an administrative assistant at a large bank. In the last year, the bank assistants elected a union to represent them, and that union just finished negotiating its first contract, which included a standard day of 9:00 a.m. to 5:00 p.m. Joanna voted against union representation, and has since refused to join the union.

a. Joanna just found out that she needs to leave work an hour early on Tuesdays to take her kids to soccer practice, and has approached her supervisor about the issue. May Joanna's supervisor allow her to leave early on Tuesdays and make the time up Wednesday mornings without consulting the union? Would it have made a difference if Joanna had made her request after the election but before the union and bank had signed their collective bargaining agreement? Would it make a difference if Joanna had joined the union?

b. If the collective bargaining agreement establishes base pay and a 40-hour workweek for the assistants and the employer provides that base pay for the 40-hour workweek, may Joanna's supervisor make a separate arrangement with her to do work on the weekends for her at a pay rate they agree upon together?

c. During the COVID-19 pandemic, the union proposes that all assistants work virtually until a vaccine is developed. The employer refuses the proposal, saying that it plans to establish an environment with appropriate safeguards in which the assistants could work in the office. If Joanna's supervisor nevertheless gives her permission to work virtually because she is especially fearful of the virus, is there a violation of the Act? Explain.

39. The associates at a large law firm just elected a union to represent them, and that union is negotiating its first contract. Both sides recognize that there is a great demand for new associates coming out of judicial clerkships, and that the market for them is exceedingly fluid and competitive. The union would like to give the firm the ability to freely negotiate clerkship bonuses for incoming associates without union involvement. May the union agree to a term in the collective bargaining agreement that leaves clerkship bonuses up to individual negotiation?

Emporium Capwell Co. v. Western Addition Community Organization

Supreme Court of the United States
420 U.S. 50, 95 S. Ct. 977, 43 L. Ed. 2d 12 (1975)

Opinion of the Court by Mr. Justice Marshall. . . .

This litigation presents the question whether, in light of the national policy against racial discrimination in employment, the National Labor Relations Act protects concerted activity by a group of minority employees to bargain with their employer over issues of employment discrimination. The National Labor Relations Board held that the employees could not circumvent their elected representative to engage in such bargaining. The Court of Appeals for the District of Columbia

Circuit reversed and remanded, holding that in certain circumstances the activity would be protected.... We now reverse.

I

The Emporium Capwell Co. (Company) operates a department store in San Francisco. At all times relevant to this litigation it was a party to the collective bargaining agreement negotiated by the San Francisco Retailer's Council, of which it was a member, and the Department Store Employees Union (Union) which represented all stock and marking area employees of the Company. The agreement, in which the Union was recognized as the sole collective bargaining agency for all covered employees, prohibited employment discrimination by reason of race, color, creed, national origin, age, or sex, as well as union activity. It had a no-strike or lockout clause, and it established grievance and arbitration machinery for processing any claimed violation of the contract, including a violation of the anti-discrimination clause.

On April 3, 1968, a group of Company employees covered by the agreement met with the Secretary-Treasurer of the Union, Walter Johnson, to present a list of grievances including a claim that the Company was discriminating on the basis of race in making assignments and promotions. The union official agreed to take certain of the grievances and to investigate the charge of racial discrimination. He appointed an investigating committee and prepared a report on the employees' grievances, which he submitted to the Retailer's Council and which the Council in turn referred to the Company. The report described "the possibility of racial discrimination" as perhaps the most important issue raised by the employees and termed the situation at the Company as potentially explosive if corrective action were not taken....

Shortly after receiving the report, the Company's labor relations director met with Union representatives and agreed to "look into the matter" of discrimination and see what needed to be done. Apparently unsatisfied with these representations, the Union held a meeting in September attended by Union officials, Company employees, and representatives of the California Fair Employment Practices Committee (FEPC) and the local antipoverty agency. The Secretary-Treasurer of the Union announced that the Union had concluded that the Company was discriminating, and that it would process every such grievance through to arbitration if necessary. Testimony about the Company's practices was taken and transcribed by a court reporter, and the next day the Union notified the Company of its formal charge and demanded that the joint union-management Adjustment Board be convened "to hear the entire case."

At the September meeting some of the Company's employees had expressed their view that the contract procedures were inadequate to handle a systemic grievance of this sort; they suggested that the Union instead begin picketing the store in protest. Johnson explained that the collective agreement bound the Union to its processes and expressed his view that successful grievants would be helping not only themselves but all others who might be the victims of invidious discrimination as well.

The FEPC and antipoverty agency representatives offered the same advice. Nonetheless, when the Adjustment Board meeting convened on October 16, James Joseph Hollins, Tom Hawkins, and two other employees whose testimony the Union had intended to elicit refused to participate in the grievance procedure. Instead, Hollins read a statement objecting to reliance on correction of individual inequities as an approach to the problem of discrimination at the store and demanding that the president of the Company meet with the four protestants to work out a broader agreement for dealing with the issue as they saw it. The four employees then walked out of the hearing.

Hollins attempted to discuss the question of racial discrimination with the Company president shortly after the incidents of October 16. The president refused to be drawn into such a discussion but suggested to Hollins that he see the personnel director about the matter. Hollins, who had spoken to the personnel director before, made no effort to do so again. Rather, he and Hawkins and several other dissident employees held a press conference on October 22 at which they denounced the store's employment policy as racist, reiterated their desire to deal directly with "the top management" of the Company over minority employment conditions, and announced their intention to picket and institute a boycott of the store. On Saturday, November 2, Hollins, Hawkins, and at least two other employees picketed the store throughout the day and distributed at the entrance handbills urging consumers not to patronize the store.[1] Johnson encountered the picketing employees, again urged them to rely on the grievance process, and warned that they might be fired for their activities. The picketers, however, were not dissuaded, and they continued to press their demand to deal directly with the Company president.

On November 7, Hollins and Hawkins were given written warnings that a repetition of the picketing or public statements about the Company could lead to their discharge. When the conduct was repeated the following Saturday, the two employees were fired.

Respondent Western Addition Community Organization, a local civil rights association of which Hollins and Hawkins were members, filed a charge against the

---

1. [2] The full text of the handbill read:* * BEWARE * * * * BEWARE * * * * BEWARE * *EMPORIUM SHOPPERS "Boycott Is On" "Boycott Is On" "Boycott Is On"

For years at The Emporium black, brown, yellow and red people have worked at the lowest jobs at the lowest levels. Time and time again we have seen intelligent, hard working brothers and sisters denied promotions and respect.

The Emporium is a 20th Century colonial plantation. The brothers and sisters are being treated the same way as our brothers are being treated in the slave mines of Africa.

Whenever the racist pig at The Emporium injures or harms a black sister or brother, they injure and insult all black people. THE EMPORIUM MUST PAY FOR THESE INSULTS. Therefore, we encourage all of our people to take their money out of this racist store, until black people have full employment and are promoted justly through out The Emporium. We welcome the support of our brothers and sisters from the churches, unions, sororities, fraternities, social clubs, Afro-American Institute, Black Panther Party, W.A.C.O. and the Poor Peoples Institute.

Company with the National Labor Relations Board. The Board's General Counsel subsequently issued a complaint alleging that in discharging the two the Company had violated § 8 (a)(1) of the National Labor Relations Act.... After a hearing the NLRB Trial Examiner found that the discharged employees had believed in good faith that the Company was discriminating against minority employees, and that they had resorted to concerted activity on the basis of that belief. He concluded, however, that their activity was not protected by § 7 of the Act and that their discharges did not, therefore, violate § 8 (a)(1).

The Board, after oral argument, adopted the findings and conclusions of its Trial Examiner and dismissed the complaint. 192 N.L.R.B. 173. Among the findings adopted by the Board was that the discharged employees' course of conduct:

> was no mere presentation of a grievance, but nothing short of a demand that the [Company] bargain with the picketing employees for the entire group of minority employees.

The Board concluded that protection of such an attempt to bargain would undermine the statutory system of bargaining through an exclusive, elected representative, impede elected unions' efforts at bettering the working conditions of minority employees "and place on the Employer an unreasonable burden of attempting to placate self-designated representatives of minority groups while abiding by the terms of a valid bargaining agreement and attempting in good faith to meet whatever demands the bargaining representative put forth under that agreement."

On respondent's petition for review the Court of Appeals reversed and remanded. The court was of the view that concerted activity directed against racial discrimination enjoys a "unique status" by virtue of the national labor policy against discrimination, as expressed in both the NLRA, *see United Packinghouse Workers Union v. NLRB*, 416 F.2d 1126, *cert. denied*, 396 U.S. 903 (1969), and in Title VII of the Civil Rights Act of 1964, 42 U.S.C. § 2000e *et seq.*, and that the Board had not adequately taken account of the necessity to accommodate the exclusive bargaining principle of the NLRA to the national policy of protecting action taken in opposition to discrimination from employer retaliation. The court recognized that protection of the minority group concerted activity involved in this case would interfere to some extent with the orderly collective bargaining process, but it considered the disruptive effect on that process to be outweighed where protection of minority activity is necessary to full and immediate realization of the policy against discrimination. In formulating a standard for distinguishing between protected and unprotected activity, the majority held that the "Board should inquire, in cases such as this, whether the union was actually remedying the discrimination to the *fullest extent possible by the most expedient and efficacious means*. Where the union's efforts fall short of this high standard, the minority group's concerted activity cannot lose its section 7 protection." Accordingly, the court remanded the case for the Board to make this determination and, if it found in favor of the employees, to consider whether their particular tactics were so disloyal to their employer as to deprive them of § 7 protection under our decision in *NLRB v. Local Union No. 1229*, 346 U.S. 464 (1953).

II

Before turning to the central questions of labor policy raised by this case, it is important to have firmly in mind the character of the underlying conduct to which we apply them. As stated, the Trial Examiner and the Board found that the employees were discharged for attempting to bargain with the Company over the terms and conditions of employment as they affected racial minorities. Although the Court of Appeals expressly declined to set aside this finding, respondent has devoted considerable effort to attacking it in this Court, on the theory that the employees were attempting only to present a grievance to their employer within the meaning of the first proviso to § 9(a). We see no occasion to disturb the finding of the Board. *Universal Camera Corp. v. NLRB*, 340 U.S. 474, 491 (1951). The issue, then, is whether such attempts to engage in separate bargaining are protected by § 7 of the Act or proscribed by § 9(a).

A. . . . Central to the policy of fostering collective bargaining, where the employees elect that course, is the principle of majority rule. *See NLRB v. Jones & Laughlin Steel Corp.*, 301 U.S. 1 (1937). If the majority of a unit chooses union representation, the NLRA permits them to bargain with their employer to make union membership a condition of employment, thereby imposing their choice upon the minority. . . . In establishing a regime of majority rule, Congress sought to secure to all members of the unit the benefits of their collective strength and bargaining power, in full awareness that the superior strength of some individuals or groups might be subordinated to the interest of the majority. . . . As a result, "[t]he complete satisfaction of all who are represented is hardly to be expected." *Ford Motor Co. v. Huffman*, 345 U.S. 330, 338 (1953). . . .

Investing the representatives of the majority with this broad power Congress did not, of course, authorize a tyranny of the majority over minority interests. First, it confined the exercise of these powers to the context of a "unit appropriate for the purposes of collective bargaining," *i.e.*, a group of employees with a sufficient commonality of circumstances to ensure against the submergence of a minority with distinctively different interests in the terms and conditions of their employment. *See Allied Chemical Workers v. Pittsburgh Plate Glass Co.*, 404 U.S. 157, 171 (1971). Second, it undertook in the 1959 Landrum-Griffin amendments, 73 Stat. 519, to assure that minority voices are heard as they are in the functioning of a democratic institution. Third, we have held, by the very nature of the exclusive bargaining representative's status as representative of *all* unit employees, Congress implicitly imposed upon it a duty fairly and in good faith to represent the interests of minorities within the unit. *Vaca v. Sipes, supra; Wallace Corp. v. NLRB*, 323 U.S. 248 (1948); *cf. Steele v. Louisville & N. R. Co.*, 323 U.S. 192 (1944). And the Board has taken the position that a union's refusal to process grievances against racial discrimination, in violation of that duty, is an unfair labor practice. *Hughes Tool Co.*, 147 N.L.R.B. 1573 (1964); *see Miranda Fuel Co.*, 140 N.L.R.B. 181 (1962), *enforcement denied*, 326 F.2d 172 (2d Cir. 1962). Indeed, the Board has ordered a union implicated by a collective bargaining agreement in discrimination with an employer to propose specific contractual provisions to prohibit racial discrimination. *See Local Union No. 12, United Rubber Workers of America v. NLRB*, 368 F.2d 12 (5th Cir. 1966) (enforcement granted).

B. Against this background of long and consistent adherence to the principle of exclusive representation tempered by safeguards for the protection of minority interests, respondent urges this Court to fashion a limited exception to that principle: employees who seek to bargain separately with their employer as to the elimination of racially discriminatory employment practices peculiarly affecting them, should be free from the constraints of the exclusivity principle of § 9 (a). Essentially because established procedures under Title VII or, as in this case, a grievance machinery, are too time-consuming, the national labor policy against discrimination requires this exception, respondent argues, and its adoption would not unduly compromise the legitimate interests of either unions or employers.

Plainly, national labor policy embodies the principles of nondiscrimination as a matter of highest priority, *Alexander v. Gardner-Denver Co.*, 415 U.S. 36, 47 (1974), and it is a common-place that we must construe the NLRA in light of the broad national labor policy of which it is a part. *See Textile Workers v. Lincoln Mills*, 353 U.S. 448, 456–458 (1958). These general principles do not aid respondent, however, as it is far from clear that separate bargaining is necessary to help eliminate discrimination. Indeed, as the facts of this case demonstrate, the proposed remedy might have just the opposite effect. The collective bargaining agreement in this case prohibited without qualification all manner of invidious discrimination and made any claimed violation a grievable issue. The grievance procedure is directed precisely at determining whether discrimination has occurred. That orderly determination, if affirmative, could lead to an arbitral award enforceable in court. Nor is there any reason to believe that the processing of grievances is inherently limited to the correction of individual cases of discrimination. Quite apart from the essentially contractual question of whether the Union could grieve against a "pattern or practice" it deems inconsistent with the nondiscrimination clause of the contract, one would hardly expect an employer to continue in effect an employment practice that routinely results in adverse arbitral decisions.

The decision by a handful of employees to bypass the grievance procedure in favor of attempting to bargain with their employer, by contrast, may or may not be predicated upon the actual existence of discrimination. An employer confronted with bargaining demands from each of several minority groups would not necessarily, or even probably, be able to agree to remedial steps satisfactory to all at once. Competing claims on the employer's ability to accommodate each group's demands, *e.g.*, for reassignments and promotions to a limited number of positions, could only set one group against the other even if it is not the employer's intention to divide and overcome them. Having divided themselves, the minority employees will not be in position to advance their cause unless it be by recourse *seriatim* to economic coercion, which can only have the effect of further dividing them along racial or other lines. Nor is the situation materially different where, as apparently happened here, self-designated representatives purport to speak for all groups that might consider themselves to be victims of discrimination. Even if in actual bargaining the various groups did not perceive their interests as divergent and further subdivide themselves, the employer would be bound to bargain with them in a field largely preempted by the current collective bargaining agreement with the elected bargaining representatives....

What has been said here in evaluating respondent's claim that the policy against discrimination requires §7 protection for concerted efforts at minority bargaining has obvious implications for the related claim that legitimate employer and union interests would not be unduly compromised thereby. The court below minimized the impact on the Union in this case by noting that it was not working at cross-purposes with the dissidents, and that indeed it could not do so consistent with its duty of fair representation and perhaps its obligations under Title VII. As to the Company, its obligations under Title VII are cited for the proposition that it could have no legitimate objection to bargaining with the dissidents in order to achieve full compliance with that law.

This argument confuses the employees' substantive right to be free of racial discrimination with the procedures available under the NLRA for securing these rights. Whether they are thought to depend upon Title VII or have an independent source in the NLRA, they cannot be pursued at the expense of the orderly collective bargaining process contemplated by the NLRA. The elimination of discrimination and its vestiges is an appropriate subject of bargaining, and an employer may have no objection to incorporating into a collective agreement the substance of his obligation not to discriminate in personnel decisions; the Company here has done as much, making any claimed dereliction a matter subject to the grievance-arbitration machinery as well as to the processes of Title VII. But that does not mean that he may not have strong and legitimate objections to bargaining on several fronts over the implementation of the right to be free of discrimination for some of the reasons set forth above. Similarly, while a union cannot lawfully bargain for the establishment or continuation of discriminatory practices, *see Steele v. Louisville & N. R. Co., supra*, 42 U.S.C. §2000-2(c)(3), it has legitimate interest in presenting a united front on this as on other issues and in not seeing its strength dissipated and its stature denigrated by subgroups within the unit separately pursuing what they see as separate interests. When union and employer are not responsive to their legal obligations, the bargain they have struck must yield *pro tanto* to the law, whether by means of conciliation through the offices of the EEOC, or by means of federal court enforcement at the instance of either that agency or the party claiming to be aggrieved.

Accordingly, we think neither aspect of respondent's contention in support of a right to short-circuit orderly, established processes for eliminating discrimination in employment is well-founded. The policy of industrial self-determination as expressed in §7 does not require fragmentation of the bargaining unit along racial or other lines in order to consist with the national labor policy against discrimination. And in the face of such fragmentation, whatever its effect on discriminatory practices, the bargaining process that the principle of exclusive representation is meant to lubricate could not endure unhampered.

III

. . . Even assuming that § 704(a) [of Title VII] protects employees' picketing and instituting a consumer boycott of their employer, the same conduct is not necessarily entitled to affirmative protection from the NLRA. Under the scheme of that Act, conduct which is not protected concerted activity may lawfully form the basis for the participants' discharge. That does not mean that the discharge is immune from attack on other statutory grounds in an appropriate case. . . .

Reversed.

[The dissenting opinion of MR. JUSTICE DOUGLAS is omitted.]

Notes

1. *Understanding Emporium Capwell* — What was the critical factor in *Emporium Capwell*? Would it have been different if there had been no collective bargaining agreement? Suppose the employees had walked out without union authorization to protest employer action but had made no effort to take negotiations into their own hands. *See East Chicago Rehabilitation Center v. NLRB*, 710 F.2d 397 (7th Cir. 1983), *cert. denied*, 465 U.S. 1065 (1984) (spontaneous walkout to express workers' anger over change in working conditions protected under section 7). *See also* Cantor, *Dissident Worker Action, After The* Emporium, 29 RUTGERS L. REV. 35 (1975); Craver, *Minority Action versus Union Exclusivity: The Need to Harmonize NLRA and Title VII Policies*, 26 HASTINGS L.J. 1 (1974).

2. *Employee Voice and "Members-Only" Unions* — A number of scholars have observed that exclusivity and majority rule blocks voice for workers who have not selected a union by creating an all-or-nothing scenario for workers. Professor Estreicher observes that the exclusivity/majority rule doctrine contributes to a "hard in, hard out" system for deciding whether workers may exercise voice through collective representation, when what we need is an "easy in, easy out" arrangement. Estreicher, *'Easy In, Easy Out': A Future for U.S. Workplace Representation*, 98 MINN. L. REV. 1615 (2014).

While the NLRA does not preclude unions from representing less than a majority of workers in a given unit, the NLRB has long held that employers have no obligation to bargain with a representative of less than a majority of their workforces. Professor Morris has advanced an interpretation of the NLRA that would require employers to bargain collectively with unions representing a minority of the employees even if they are not represented by a union with majority status. In his book THE BLUE EAGLE AT WORK: RECLAIMING DEMOCRATIC RIGHTS IN THE AMERICAN WORKPLACE (2004), Morris documents the historical understanding that members-only, minority-union recognition and bargaining were permissible, even common, in the early years after the Wagner Act was passed. He argues that the statutory language of §§ 7 and 8(a)(5) only limits minority collective bargaining rights after an exclusive representative has been selected, and urges the Board to ground bargaining rights in §7 rather than in §9. What are the pros and cons of such a proposal, if the Board were to adopt it?

What role might "members only" unionism play in a nonunion establishment if an employer voluntarily agrees to bargain with a minority union? Following the UAW's defeat in February 2014 in a traditional union election, Volkswagen announced a new "community organization engagement policy" applicable at its Chattanooga, Tennessee, plant that established sliding-scale, members-only representation rights. The policy allowed employee groups to use company property to hold meetings and post information and announcements, and established a multilayered system of engagement with Volkswagen management based upon the percentage of workers belonging to a given employee group. Employee groups that had the support of more than 15% of employees (measured by authorization cards consistent with those used in NLRA organizing drives) could meet monthly with Volkswagen's human resources officials; groups with more than 30% support could meet quarterly with a member of the Volkswagen's executive committee; and groups with more than 45% support could meet once every two weeks with Volkswagen's executive committee. The policy was based on the European "works council" approach to employee management and representation, which reflects a commitment to a culture of codetermination. *See* Greenhouse, *Volkswagen to Allow Labor Groups to Represent Workers at Chattanooga Plant*, N.Y. TIMES, Nov. 12, 2014; Daily Lab. Rep. (BNA) No. 218, Nov. 12, 2014, at A-9. Would a policy like Volkswagen's undercut efforts to form independent unions or would it serve instead as a breeding ground for worker collective consciousness?

3. *Justifying Exclusivity/Majority Rule*—Justice Marshall suggests two justifications for exclusivity/majority rule. The first is that exclusivity is more efficient, more workable, than a system of individual bargaining or multiple representation, which would likely complicate bargaining and create leapfrogging and whipsawing problems between competing factions of employees. The second is that exclusivity shores up union strength by allowing employees to present a united front in their dealings with the employer, avoiding problems of internecine competition among workers that would ultimately undermine the collective effort. How persuasive are these justifications? Is the Court correct that separate bargaining would only further divide employees along racial or gender lines? Or does the fact pattern of *Emporium Capwell* itself provide evidence that competing subgroups, once constituted by employer discrimination, will endure? Does withholding §7 protection for the actions of the dissident employees resolve these divisions? If not, what does it accomplish?

4. *Justice Marshall's Commitment to Racial Equality*—Justice Marshall was a longtime advocate for racial equality; he directed the NAACP Legal Defense and Education Fund from 1939 to 1961 and was instrumental in litigating landmark civil rights cases, including *Brown v. Board of Educ.*, 347 U.S. 483 (1954). Is this background inconsistent with the opinion that he authored for the Court in this case? *See* Sharpe, Crain & Schiller, *The Story of* Emporium Capwell: *Civil Rights, Collective*

Action, and the Constraints of Union Power, in Labor Law Stories (L. Cooper & C. Fisk eds., Foundation Press 2005); Sharpe, *"Judging in Good Faith"—Seeing Justice Marshall's Legacy through a Labor Case*, 26 Ariz. St. L.J. 479 (1994).

What functions do majority rule and exclusivity serve in the modern workplace with its low union density, ethnically and racially diverse workforce, and individualistic ethos? Does the denial of voice to dissident workers in unionized workplaces raise particular problems in an increasingly diverse workforce? Consider the views in the following two excerpts.

Molly S. McUsic & Michael Selmi, *Postmodern Unions: Identity Politics in the Workplace*
82 Iowa L. Rev. 1339, 1353–60 (1997)*

The original notion of solidarity underlying the labor laws was that employees organized as a group would have greater power than they could obtain individually in dealing with the employer. Absent solidarity, the notion of workers operating as a community is replaced with "the feeble strength of one" or at best the feeble strength of a small group. This strength can be further diminished when the employer plays groups off each other, engaging in a version of "divide and conquer" among the various workplace groups. In the past, employers frequently used the racial and ethnic distribution of jobs and organization tasks as a deliberate managerial tactic to divide the labor force and to forestall class identification and union organization. For example, during the late nineteenth and early twentieth centuries companies regularly sought to divide workers by employing minorities and women during strikes. Corporate executives have likewise used the lower compensation of minority and female workers as a means of moderating union demands for higher rates of pay for white male employees. . . .

. . . Currently, whatever conflicts exist among the union membership are resolved by the union; although this can lead to the union favoring its primary constituency, the alternatives in a workplace comprised of multiple representative units are no less problematic. . . . [I]t might be left to the employer to mediate group conflicts. By any measure, [this] resolution seems inferior to allowing for union resolution—otherwise there would be little need for a union or employee representation in the first instance. . . .

But the danger from fragmentation includes more than a loss of power for workers through numerical dispersion. More fundamentally, the fragmentation of groups . . . prevents the forging of larger groups and prevents the creation of common bonds among workers: in such a system, employees are left emphasizing their incommensurate differences while ignoring their potential commonalities. . . .

---

* Copyright © 1997 Molly S. McUsic & Michael Selmi. Reprinted with permission.

Where difference becomes the prism through which the workplace is viewed, it becomes all too easy to lose sight of the economic battle between the workers and management....

The end result of this failure to unite effectively against the economic center of power is that all workers become relatively worse off materially.

Marion Crain & Ken Matheny, *"Labor's Divided Ranks": Privilege and the United Front Ideology*
84 Cornell L. Rev. 1542, 1620–21, 1624–25 (1999)*

[D]efenders of majority rule and exclusivity maintain that a united front strategy is necessary to create solidarity within a group of workers that lacks cohesion and faces virulent opposition from employers. Only through a united front can workers attain sufficient economic leverage through their unions in dealing with the employer. One cannot, however, create solidarity by imposing it from above; illusory and superficial at best, such solidarity will dissolve quickly when the employer attempts to undermine it.

Further, we must reexamine the assumption that coerced solidarity confers economic clout.... Majority unions do not always succeed in putting effective economic pressure on an employer. One need only consider the great difficulty that majority unions have had recently in winning strikes. Indeed, one experienced labor lawyer wrote that the odds against a union are so great that it is "insane" to go on strike. While this may be an exaggeration, the crushing defeat of unions in well-publicized strikes... grimly illustrates the trouble that even strong unions have winning strikes. Enhanced capital mobility, the ability of employers to rely on technology to continue operation during a strike, and employers' increased willingness to hire permanent replacement workers raise the distinct possibility that the strike is becoming obsolete....

... [M]ultiple representation could ultimately unify the working class by encouraging discussion and a compromise-style resolution of conflicts where they do exist. If differences do bring groups into direct conflict, even to the extent of stalling decision making and undermining the solidarity of the larger group, multiple representation would still be preferable to the situation that exists today, where the vast majority of workers—and particularly those at the bottom of the income scale—have no collective representation in their workplaces, and where those who do... may find their interests ignored by the majority union in a travesty of solidarity....

... While employers undoubtedly have taken advantage of opportunities to exacerbate the divisions within the working class in order to undermine working-class unity, the labor movement's failure to confront and recognize the divisions

---

* Copyright © 1999 Cornell University. Reprinted with permission.

that exist within the working class has contributed to the problem. One can fairly place some of the responsibility for this problem at the labor movement's door, particularly when one considers the lengthy history of feminist and antiracist critiques showing that labor has at times actively fought for the interests of white men at the expense of those of women and people of color. . . .

. . . Unfortunately, despite wishful thinking and emotional appeals to class unity, 'divisions between [workers] will not simply disappear in the magic of solidarity.' Because those divisions are based upon material conflicts of interest which lie at the heart of worker organizing and collective bargaining under labor law, they will continue to fester and grow unless they are unmasked and addressed directly. . . . [T]his attention is unlikely to occur in a system characterized by a legally coerced united front.

Notes

1. *Pros and Cons of Exclusivity/Majority Rule*—Professor Schatzki questioned the benefits of exclusivity and majority rule in an influential early article, arguing that abolishing these twin doctrines would yield a number of benefits for workers and unions. *See* Schatzki, *Majority Rule, Exclusive Representation, and the Interests of Individual Workers: Should Exclusivity Be Abolished?*, 123 U. Pa. L. Rev. 897 (1975). First, because all employees would voluntarily choose their unions, employee participation in union activities would increase, and union democracy would be enhanced. Second, competition between unions would be encouraged, with the result that unions would invest more resources in organizing and be more responsive to the concerns of their members and more aggressive in advocating for them with employers. Individual voice would be amplified, as more individual employee or minority employee views would be heard through the process of multiple representation, rather than being resolved internally inside the majority union out of the necessity to present a united front. Such solidarity as emerged out of the process of coalition-building would be voluntary, rather than legally coerced. On the legal level, duty of fair representation claims would be minimized.

On the other hand, the advantage of solidarity and presenting a united front in dealings with the employer—particularly the leverage of the strike weapon—would be lost. *Id.* at 926–32. Employees might form "undesirable" homogenous groups—perhaps by skill level, or even by race or gender—that would consolidate the power of the more privileged workers at the expense of the less privileged. *Id.* at 933–35. It would be difficult to negotiate firmwide seniority systems. Employers confronted with multiple unions with competing claims on company resources might find negotiation of agreements highly inefficient and time-consuming. *Id.* at 935–38.

Professor Schatzki ultimately concluded that majority rule and exclusivity should be abolished in favor of a representation system more heavily dependent on voluntarism. Consider the more recent excerpts from Professors McUsic & Selmi and Crain & Matheny, *supra*. Are the benefits of enhanced solidarity and market power worth the burdens on dissident workers' voice in the modern era?

2. *Labor Unionism and Sexual Harassment*—Exclusivity and majority rule have posed particularly poignant challenges around issues of discrimination and sexual harassment. During the #MeToo era, for example, organized labor was conspicuously absent from the dialogue about how to confront and prevent sexual harassment at work. Indeed, some unions were still busy addressing sexual harassment in their own ranks, including the SEIU and the AFL-CIO itself. *See* Crain & Matheny, *Sexual Harassment and Solidarity*, 87 Geo. Wash. L. Rev. 56, 65 (2019) (documenting issues). Although #MeToo prompted many union leaders to publicly denounce sexual harassment and promise to redouble union efforts to eradicate it, union leaders often simultaneously disclaimed legal responsibility for preventing and addressing sexual harassment in the workplace, reaffirming that the duty to create harassment prevention policies and to shift workplace culture is on the employer, with the union's role limited to enforcing those policies. *Id.* at 65–66. At the root of this understanding of the unions' relatively passive role are the legal doctrines of exclusivity and majority rule, which place labor unions in a Catch-22:

> Not all the blame for labor's passive stance can be laid on labor's doorstep. Unions are hamstrung by a legal structure that creates a fundamental conflict for unions that represent a workforce that includes both potential harassers and victims. The National Labor Relations Act ("NLRA") erects an employee representation system founded upon principles of majority rule and exclusivity, in which the union once elected becomes the exclusive representative with a duty to fairly represent all the workers in the bargaining unit. In this system, the majority union is envisioned as a united front, speaking with a single voice on behalf of all the workers in the bargaining unit on issues affecting their economic futures. This united front ideology suppresses conflicts arising along identity lines within the bargaining unit, channeling them instead into a statutory antidiscrimination-law track where the victims must represent themselves or seek assistance from nonlabor groups, such as the National Organization for Women's Legal Defense Fund. Meanwhile, if the employer takes disciplinary action based on the victim's complaint, the union is obligated to represent the alleged harasser and enforce the typical collective bargaining agreement's guarantee of protection against discharge without just cause—with the victim serving as the key witness for the employer. This combination of legal obligations has deterred unions with scarce resources from taking a proactive approach to sexual harassment. Unfortunately, this mix of legal obligations and union shirking has the effect of positioning employers as proactive advocates for workplace equality and pushing unions into a fundamentally reactive posture. Labor's voice is silenced in the rooms where anti–sexual harassment policies are created. All workers suffer as a result: unionized workers are deprived of a representative on an issue fundamental to safe and productive workplaces, and nonunion workers learn to see unions as largely irrelevant in the struggle to eradicate discrimination

at work — a significant strategic mistake in an increasingly diverse labor force.

Id. at 66–67. For reform proposals designed to address the tension between a legal system predicated on majority rule and exclusivity, and the identity-based interests of a race- and gender-diverse workforce, see Cobble, *The Next Unionism: Structural Innovations for a Revitalized Labor Movement*, 48 Lab. L.J. 439 (1997); Crain, *Women, Labor Unions and Hostile Work Environment Sexual Harassment: The Untold Story*, 4 Tex. J. Women & L. 9 (1995); Crain & Matheny, *Labor's Identity Crisis*, 89 Calif. L. Rev. 1767 (2001); Craver, *The Labor Movement Needs a Twenty-First Century Committee for Industrial Organization*, 23 Hofstra Lab. & Emp. L.J. 69 (2005).

3. *Identity Caucuses, Workers' Centers, and "Alt-Labor" Groups*—Unions are not the only form that worker self-organization and voice may assume. Other forms of collective identity have emerged among workers who band together around identities other than occupational commonality, and often do not seek bargaining at the firm level. Identity caucuses—informal groups of employees that come together in workplaces around shared concerns arising out of social identities that transcend the workplace—have evolved from worksite-based organizations into nationwide constituency groups, many of which are now affiliated with the AFL-CIO. Examples include the Coalition of Black Trade Unionists, the Labor Council on Latin American Advancement, the Coalition of Labor Union Women, the Asian Pacific American Labor Alliance, and Pride at Work. These groups press existing labor unions to respond to the interests of their constituencies. *See* Garcia, *New Voices at Work: Race and Gender Caucuses in the U.S. Labor Movement*, 54 Hastings L.J. 79 (2002). Identity caucuses have also played an important role in challenging workplace discrimination and changing employer practices by invoking statutory rights in litigation to advance their constituents' interests. *See* Yelnosky, *Title VII, Mediation, and Collective Action*, 1999 U. Ill. L. Rev. 583, 615–17. Because they are "members only" groups not constrained by majoritarian interests in the same way that unions are, such activities do not create the same conflicts of interest that they might in the union context. Other potential roles exist for identity caucuses as well: if afforded a formal status as workers' representatives, identity caucuses could take on the job of representing constituent workers in workplace arbitration processes, whether established unilaterally by employers or jointly by an employer and union through collective bargaining. *See* Hodges, *Trilogy Redux: Using Arbitration to Rebuild the Labor Movement*, 98 Minn. L. Rev. 1682 (2014). Currently, the exclusivity and majority rule doctrines pose significant legal barriers to this strategy. *See* Crain, *Women, Labor Unions, and Hostile Work Environment Sexual Harassment: The Untold Story*, 4 Tex. J. Women & L. 9, 61, 78–79 (1995).

Another form of collective organization is the workers' center, a nonprofit community-based membership group committed to building democratic organizations that are accountable to the interests, needs, and goals of the workers being organized. Workers' centers emphasize that the workers themselves must assume leadership roles in organizing and transform themselves from victims to advocates. Workers typically serve on the organizations' boards of directors, participate in making strategy decisions in organizing campaigns, plan demonstrations, raise funds, and speak to the press. *See* Jenkins, *Organizing, Advocacy, and Member Power: A Critical Reflection*, WORKING USA, Fall 2002, at 56, 57. They are particularly effective in immigrant communities, where workers tend to live in proximity to one another and to work in similar service jobs that systematically exploit the workers' undocumented status and lack of familiarity with U.S. laws and the English language. These organizations provide the foundation for labor union organizing, but do not themselves seek to supplant labor unionism. *See generally* J. FINE, WORKER CENTERS: ORGANIZING AT THE EDGE OF THE DREAM (2006); J. GORDON, SUBURBAN SWEATSHOPS — THE FIGHT FOR IMMIGRANT RIGHTS (2005); Gordon, *We Make the Road by Walking: Immigrant Workers, the Workplace Project, and the Struggle for Social Change*, 30 HARV. C.R.-C.L. L. REV. 407 (1995).

Workers' centers and organizations dedicated to particular occupational sectors have also evolved, particularly in the low-wage sector. Referred to generally as "alt-labor," these organizations typically seek social bargaining — bargaining at a regional, state, or community level for benefits that extend to a broad swath of workers, often defined by occupation. *See* Andrias, *The New Labor Law*, 126 YALE L.J. 2 (2016). Well-known alt-labor groups include the Domestic Workers Alliance, the New York Taxi Workers Alliance, and the Restaurant Opportunities Center (ROC) United. *See* Windham, *Why Alt-Labor Groups Are Making Employers Mighty Nervous*, AM. PROSPECT, Jan. 30, 2014, *available at* http://prospect.org/article/why-alt-labor-groups-are-making-employers-mighty-nervous; Eidelson, *Alt-Labor*, AM. PROSPECT, Jan. 29, 2013, *available at* http://prospect.org/article/alt-labor. Some of these organizations enjoy significant financial backing and organizational support from traditional unions. Perhaps the most well-publicized of these is the Fight for 15, a worker organizing effort that originated in fast-food restaurant chains and has since spread to other low-wage sectors. The Fight for 15 utilizes mass actions, political organizing, legislative advocacy at the local level, and legal strategies before the NLRB and in the courts. For more on the Fight for 15 and its relationship to unionism, see Andrias, *supra*; Oswalt, *Improvisational Unionism*, 104 CAL. L. REV. 597 (2016); Crain & Inazu, *Re-Assembling Labor*, 2015 U. ILL. L. REV. 1791 (2015).

A vexing challenge for all of these groups is how to leverage worker power to accomplish change. In some industries, particularly those in which workers are fungible or employers are mobile, workers' social power may be negligible. Although identity caucuses, workers' centers, and grassroots organizing may offer extraordinary potential to articulate workers' voice, their utility as a market power device is less certain. Traditional unions undeniably enhance wages and working conditions for unionized workers, and the collective bargaining agreements they negotiate protect workers' job security. They also play an important role in democratizing the workplace. *See* Malin, *Alt Labor? Why We Still Need Traditional Labor*, 95 Chi.-Kent L. Rev. 157, 164–66 (2020) (describing benefits of traditional unionism and arguing that it is still necessary). Can the goal of furthering workers' voice be separated from the substantive goal of economic empowerment? Are the two goals mutually exclusive? Finally, how should alt-labor groups be funded, if not through automatic dues collection? *Id.* at 171.

Section II. Fair Representation and Individual Contract Rights

Archibald Cox, *The Duty of Fair Representation*
2 Vill. L. Rev. 151, 167 (1957)

Too strict judicial or administrative supervision through the concept of fair representation would impair the flexibility and adaptability of collective bargaining while substituting governmental decisions for self-determination. Past experience with judicial intervention in labor relations gives little reason to suppose that the judges' decision would be wiser than negotiated settlements. On the other hand, so long as numerical majorities occasionally yield to selfishness or caprice, there will be somewhat the same need for judicial or administrative checks on majority rule in collective bargaining as there is for judicial review of legislative enactments. Whether courts and agencies steer a safe central course between the opposing dangers will probably depend upon their success in developing standards of "fairness."

Clyde W. Summers, *Individual Rights in Collective Agreements and Arbitration*
37 N.Y.U. L. Rev. 362, 393 (1962)

The individual's interest may more often be vitiated without vindictiveness or deliberate discrimination. Incomplete investigation of the facts, reliance on untested evidence, or colored evaluation of witnesses may lead the union to reject grievances which more objective inquiry would prove meritorious. Union officials burdened with institutional concerns may be willing to barter unrelated grievances or accept wholesale settlements if the total package is advantageous, even though some good grievances are lost. Concern for collective interests and the needs for the enterprise may dull the sense of personal injustice.

A. Judicial Enforcement of Fair Representation

Steele v. Louisville & Nashville Railroad
Supreme Court of the United States
323 U.S. 192, 65 S. Ct. 226, 89 L. Ed. 173 (1944)

Mr. Chief Justice Stone delivered the opinion of the Court.

The question is whether the Railway Labor Act . . . imposes on a labor organization, acting by authority of the statute as the exclusive bargaining representative of a craft or class of railway employees, the duty to represent all the employees in the craft without discrimination because of their race, and, if so, whether the courts have jurisdiction to protect the minority of the craft or class from the violation of such obligation.

. . . Petitioner, a Negro, is a locomotive fireman in the employ of respondent railroad, suing on his own behalf and that of his fellow employees who, like petitioner, are Negro firemen employed by the Railroad. Respondent Brotherhood, a labor organization, is as provided under Section 2, Fourth of the Railway Labor Act, the exclusive bargaining representative of the craft of firemen employed by the Railroad and is recognized as such by it and the members of the craft. The majority of the firemen employed by the Railroad are white and are members of the Brotherhood, but a substantial minority are Negroes who, by the constitution and ritual of the Brotherhood, are excluded from its membership. As the membership of the Brotherhood constitutes a majority of all firemen employed on respondent Railroad and as under Section 2, Fourth, the members, because they are the majority, have the right to choose and have chosen the Brotherhood to represent the craft, petitioner and other Negro firemen on the road have been required to accept the Brotherhood as their representative for the purposes of the Act.

On March 28, 1940, the Brotherhood, purporting to act as representative of the entire craft of firemen, without informing the Negro firemen or giving them opportunity to be heard, served a notice on respondent Railroad and on twenty other railroads operating principally in the southeastern part of the United States. The notice announced the Brotherhood's desire to amend the existing collective bargaining agreement in such manner as ultimately to exclude all Negro firemen from the service. By established practice on the several railroads so notified only white firemen can be promoted to serve as engineers, and the notice proposed that only "promotable," *i.e.*, white, men should be employed as firemen or assigned to new runs or jobs or permanent vacancies in established runs or jobs.

On February 18, 1941, the railroads and the Brotherhood, as representative of the craft, entered into a new agreement which provided that not more than 50 percent of the firemen in each class of service in each seniority district of carrier should be Negroes; that until such percentage should be reached all new runs and all vacancies should be filled by white men; and that the agreement did not sanction the employment of Negroes in any seniority district in which they were not working. . . .

If the Railway Labor Act purports to impose on petitioner and the other Negro members of the craft the legal duty to comply with the terms of a contract whereby the representative has discriminatorily restricted their employment for the benefit and advantage of the Brotherhood's own members, we must decide the constitutional questions which petitioner raises in his pleading.

But we think that Congress, in enacting the Railway Labor Act and authorizing a labor union, chosen by a majority of a craft, to represent the craft, did not intend to confer plenary power upon the union to sacrifice, for the benefit of its members, rights of the minority of the craft, without imposing on it any duty to protect the minority. Since petitioner and the other Negro members of the craft are not members of the Brotherhood or eligible for membership, the authority to act for them is derived not from their action or consent but wholly from the command of the Act....

Section 2, Second, requiring carriers to bargain with the representative so chosen, operates to exclude any other from representing a craft. *Virginian Ry. Co. v. System Federation, supra*, 300 U.S. 545 (1930). The minority members of a craft are thus deprived by the statute of the right, which they would otherwise possess, to choose a representative of their own, and its members cannot bargain individually on behalf of themselves as to matters which are properly the subject of collective bargaining....

The fair interpretation of the statutory language is that the organization chosen to represent a craft is to represent all its members, the majority as well as the minority, and it is to act for and not against those whom it represents. It is a principle of general application that the exercise of a granted power to act in behalf of others involves the assumption toward them of a duty to exercise the power in their interest and behalf, and that such a grant of power will not be deemed to dispense with all duty toward those for whom it is exercised unless so expressed.

We think that Railway Labor Act imposes upon the statutory representative of a craft at least as exacting a duty to protect equally the interests of the members of the craft as the Constitution imposes upon a legislature to give equal protection to the interests of those for whom it legislates. Congress has seen fit to clothe the bargaining representative with powers comparable to those possessed by a legislative body both to create and restrict the rights of those whom it represents, *cf. J.I. Case Co. v. NLRB, supra*, 321 U.S. 335 (1944), but it has also imposed on the representative a corresponding duty. We hold that the language of the Act which we have referred, read in the light of the purposes of the Act, expresses the aim of Congress to impose on the bargaining representative of a craft or class of employees the duty to exercise fairly the power conferred upon it in behalf of all those for whom it acts, without hostile discrimination against them.

This does not mean that the statutory representative of a craft is barred from making contracts which may have unfavorable effects on some of the members of the craft represented. Variations in the terms of the contract based on differences relevant to the authorized purposes of the contract in conditions to which they are to be applied, such as differences in seniority, the type of work performed, the competence and skill with which it is performed, are within the scope of the bargaining representation of a craft, all of whose members are not identical in their interest of merit. Without attempting to mark the allowable limits of differences in the terms of contracts based on differences of conditions to which they apply, it is enough for present purposes to say that the statutory power to represent a craft and to make contracts as to wages, hours and working conditions does not include the authority to make among members of the craft discriminations not based on such relevant differences. Here the discriminations based on race alone are obviously irrelevant and invidious. Congress plainly did not undertake to authorize the bargaining representative to make such discriminations....

The representative which thus discriminates may be enjoined from so doing, and its members may be enjoined from taking the benefit of such discriminatory action. No more is the Railroad bound by or entitled to take the benefit of a contract which the bargaining representative is prohibited by the statute from making. In both cases the right asserted, which is derived from the duty imposed by the statute on the bargaining representative, is a federal right implied from the statute and the policy which it has adopted....

So long as a labor union assumes to act as the statutory representative of a craft, it cannot rightly refuse to perform the duty, which is inseparable from the power of representation conferred upon it, to represent the entire membership of the craft. While the statute does not deny to such a bargaining labor organization the right to determine eligibility to its membership, it does require the union, in collective bargaining and in making contracts with the carrier, to represent nonunion or minority union members of the craft without hostile discrimination, fairly, impartially, and in good faith. Wherever necessary to that end, the union is required to consider requests of non-union members of the craft and expression of their views with respect to collective bargaining with the employer and to give to them notice of an opportunity for hearing upon its proposed action....

We conclude that the duty which the statute imposes on a union representative of a craft to represent the interests of all its members stands on no different footing and that the statute contemplates resort to the usual judicial remedies of injunction and award of damages when appropriate for breach of that duty.

The judgment is accordingly reversed and remanded for further proceedings not inconsistent with this opinion.

Reversed.

Mr. Justice Black concurs in the result.

Mr. Justice Murphy, concurring.

The economic discrimination against Negroes practiced by the Brotherhood and the railroad under color of Congressional authority raises a grave constitutional issue that should be squarely faced....

The constitutional problem inherent in this instance is clear. Congress, through the Railway Labor Act, has conferred upon the union selected by a majority of a craft or class of railway workers the power to represent the entire craft or class in all collective bargaining matters. While such a union is essentially a private organization, its power to represent and bind all members of a class or craft is derived solely from Congress. The Act contains no language which directs the manner in which the bargaining representative shall perform its duties. But it cannot be assumed that Congress meant to authorize the bargaining representative to act so as to ignore rights guaranteed by the Constitution. Otherwise the Act would bear the stigma of unconstitutionality under the Fifth Amendment in this respect. For that reason I am willing to read the statute as not permitting or allowing any action by the bargaining representative in the exercise of its delegated powers which would in effect violate the constitutional rights of individuals.

Notes

1. *Nature of the Duty*—The existence of a duty of fair representation under the NLRA, as well as under the RLA, was established in *Syres v. Oil Workers Int'l Union*, 350 U.S. 892 (1955) (per curiam). On the standard of fairness, the Supreme Court said at a relatively early point in this line of decisions:

> Inevitably differences arise in the manner and degree to which the terms of any negotiated agreement affect individual employees and classes of employees. The mere existence of such differences does not make them invalid. The complete satisfaction of all who are represented is hardly to be expected. A wide range of reasonableness must be allowed a statutory bargaining representative in serving the unit it represents, subject always to complete good faith and honesty of purpose in the exercise of its discretion.

Ford Motor Co. v. Huffman, 345 U.S. 330, 338 (1953).

2. *Union Duty to Eliminate an Employer's Discriminatory Practices*—Does the duty of fair representation impose on a union the affirmative obligation to seek the elimination of an employer's discriminatory employment practices? If so, how far must a union go to discharge its obligation? Is it sufficient to process a grievance or to raise the question in contract negotiations?

Problem

40. James Woods, an African American worker in a manufacturing plant, was covered by a collective bargaining agreement that contained an explicit clause prohibiting discrimination based on race. But little good that did him. Over a period of months, Woods was targeted by his coworkers and subjected to racial epithets, taunting, and graphic cartoons on his locker. He complained to his union shop steward, who in fact worked 100 feet away from him in the plant and had overheard many of the comments and witnessed the cartoons being placed on the locker, and done nothing. If the shop steward refuses to file a grievance on the basis that it is the employer's duty to police the working environment, has the union violated its duty of fair representation? Suppose that the shop steward has filed grievances on Woods' behalf for disciplinary actions by the employer that were allegedly based on race — does that make a difference?

1. Defining the Duty

Vaca v. Sipes
Supreme Court of the United States
386 U.S. 171, 87 S. Ct. 903, 17 L. Ed. 2d 842 (1967)

[Owens, a long-time high blood pressure patient, returned from a half-year sick leave to resume his heavy work in a meat-packing plant of Swift & Company. Although Owens' family physician and another outside doctor certified his fitness, the company doctor concluded Owens' blood pressure was too high to permit reinstatement and he was permanently discharged. Owens' union processed a grievance through to the fourth step of the procedure established by the collective bargaining agreement. The union then sent Owens to a new doctor at union expense to "get some better medical evidence so that we could go to arbitration." When this examination did not support Owens' position, the union's executive board voted not to take the grievance to arbitration. Union officers suggested that Owens accept Swift's offer of referral to a rehabilitation center, but Owens declined and demanded arbitration. The union stood by its refusal. Owens thereupon brought a class action in a Missouri state court against petitioners as officers and representatives of the union, alleging that the union had "arbitrarily, [and] capriciously" failed to take his case to arbitration. A jury verdict in his favor was sustained by the Missouri Supreme Court in the amount of $7,000 compensatory and $3,000 punitive damages.]

Mr. Justice White delivered the opinion of the Court.

... Although we conclude that state courts have jurisdiction in this type of case, we hold that federal law governs, that the governing federal standards were not applied here, and that the judgment of the Supreme Court of Missouri must accordingly be reversed....

II

Petitioners challenge the jurisdiction of the Missouri courts on the ground that the alleged conduct of the Union was arguably an unfair labor practice and within the exclusive jurisdiction of the NLRB. Petitioners rely on *Miranda Fuel Co.*, 140 N.L.R.B. 181 (1962), enforcement denied, 326 F.2d 172 (2d Cir. 1963), where a sharply divided Board held for the first time that a union's breach of its statutory duty of fair representation violates NLRA § 8(b), as amended. With the NLRB's adoption of *Miranda Fuel*, petitioners argue, the broad pre-emption doctrine defined in *San Diego Building Trades Council v. Garmon*, 359 U.S. 236 (1959), becomes applicable. For the reasons which follow, we reject this argument.

It is now well established that, as the exclusive bargaining representative of the employees in Owens' bargaining unit, the Union had a statutory duty fairly to represent all of those employees, both in its collective bargaining with Swift, *see Ford Motor Co. v. Huffman*, 345 U.S. 330 (1953); *Syres v. Oil Workers*, 350 U.S. 892 (1955), and in its enforcement of the resulting collective bargaining agreement, see *Humphrey v. Moore*, 375 U.S. 335 (1964). The statutory duty of fair representation was developed over 20 years ago in a series of cases involving alleged racial discrimination by unions certified as exclusive bargaining representatives under the Railway Labor Act, *see Steele v. Louisville & N.R.R.*, 323 U.S. 192 (1944); *Tunstall v. Brotherhood of Locomotive Firemen*, 323 U.S. 210 (1944), and was soon extended to unions certified under the NLRA, *see Ford Motor Co. v. Huffman, supra*. Under this doctrine, the exclusive agent's statutory authority to represent all members of a designated unit includes a statutory obligation to serve the interests of all members without hostility or discrimination toward any, to exercise its discretion with complete good faith and honesty, and to avoid arbitrary conduct. *Humphrey v. Moore*, 375 U.S. at 342 (1964). It is obvious that Owens' complaint alleged a breach by the Union of a duty grounded in federal statutes, and that federal law therefore governs his cause of action. *E.g., Ford Motor Co. v. Huffman, supra.*

Although NLRA § 8(b) was enacted in 1947, the NLRB did not until *Miranda Fuel* interpret a breach of a union's duty of fair representation as an unfair labor practice. . . .

A. In *Garmon*, this Court recognized that the broad powers conferred by Congress upon the National Labor Relations Board to interpret and to enforce the complex Labor Management Relations Act necessarily imply that potentially conflicting "rules of law, of remedy, and of administration" cannot be permitted to operate. 359 U.S. at 242. . . . Consequently, as a general rule, neither state nor federal courts have jurisdiction over suits directly involving "activity [which] is arguably subject to § 7 or 8 of the Act." *San Diego Building Trades Council v. Garmon*, 359 U.S. at 245.

This pre-emption doctrine, however, has never been rigidly applied to cases where it could not fairly be inferred that Congress intended exclusive jurisdiction to lie with the NLRB. . . .

A primary justification for the pre-emption doctrine — the need to avoid conflicting rules of substantive law in the labor relations area and the desirability of leaving the development of such rules to the administrative agency created by Congress for that purpose — is not applicable to cases involving alleged breaches of the union duty of fair representation. The doctrine was judicially developed in *Steele* and its progeny, and suits alleging breach of the duty remained judicially cognizable long after the NLRB was given unfair labor practice jurisdiction over union activities by the LMRA. Moreover, when the Board declared in *Miranda Fuel* that a union's breach of its duty of fair representation would henceforth be treated as an unfair labor practice, the board adopted and applied the doctrine as it had been developed by the federal courts. Finally, as the dissenting Board members in *Miranda Fuel* have pointed out, fair representation duty suits often require review of the substantive positions taken and policies pursued by a union in its negotiation of a collective bargaining agreement and its handling of the grievance machinery; as these matters are not normally within the Board's unfair labor practice jurisdiction, it can be doubted whether the Board brings substantially greater expertise to bear on these problems than do the courts, which have been engaged in this type of review since the *Steele* decision.

In addition to the above considerations, the unique interests served by the duty of fair representation doctrine have a profound effect, in our opinion, on the applicability of the pre-emption rule to this class of cases.... This Court recognized in *Steele* that the congressional grant of power to a union to act as exclusive collective bargaining representative, with its corresponding reduction in the individual rights of the employees so represented, would raise grave constitutional problems if unions were free to exercise this power to further racial discrimination.... Since that landmark decision, the duty of fair representation has stood as a bulwark to prevent arbitrary union conduct against individuals stripped of traditional forms of redress by the provisions of federal labor law. Were we to hold, as petitioners and the government urge, that the courts are pre-empted by the NLRB's *Miranda Fuel* decision of this traditional supervisory jurisdiction, the individual employee injured by arbitrary or discriminatory union conduct could no longer be assured of impartial review of his complaint, since the Board's General Counsel has unreviewable discretion to refuse to institute an unfair labor practice complaint.... For these reasons, we cannot assume from the NLRB's tardy assumption of jurisdiction in these cases that Congress, when it enacted NLRA § 8(b) in 1947, intended to oust the courts of their traditional jurisdiction to curb arbitrary conduct by the individual employee's statutory representative.

B. There are also some intensely practical considerations which foreclose preemption of judicial cognizance of fair representation duty suits, considerations which emerge from the intricate relationship between the duty of fair representation and the enforcement of collective bargaining contracts. For the fact is that the question of whether a union has breached its duty of fair representation will in many cases be a critical issue in a suit under LMRA § 301 charging an employer with a breach of contract. To illustrate, let us assume a collective bargaining agreement that limits discharges to those for good cause and that contains no grievance, arbitration or other provisions purporting to restrict access to the courts. If an employee is discharged without cause, either the union or the employee may sue the employer under LMRA § 301. Under this section, courts have jurisdiction over suits to enforce collective bargaining agreements even though the conduct of the employer which is challenged as a breach of contract is also arguably an unfair labor practice within the jurisdiction of the NLRB. *Garmon* and like cases have no application § 301 suits. *Smith v. Evening News Ass'n*, 371 U.S. 195 (1962).

The rule is the same with regard to pre-emption where the bargaining agreement contains grievance and arbitration provisions which are intended to provide the exclusive remedy for breach of contract claims. If an employee is discharged without cause in violation of such an agreement, that the employer's conduct may be an unfair labor practice does not preclude a suit by the union against the employer to compel arbitration of the employee's grievance; the adjudication of the claim by the arbitrator; or a suit to enforce the resulting arbitration award. *See, e.g., Steelworkers v. American Mfg. Co.*, 363 U.S. 564 (1960).

However, if the wrongfully discharged employee himself resorts to the courts before the grievance procedures have been fully exhausted, the employer may well defend on the ground that the exclusive remedies provided by such a contract have not been exhausted. Since the employee's claim is based upon breach of the collective bargaining agreement, he is bound by terms of that agreement which govern the manner in which contractual rights may be enforced. For this reason, it is settled that the employee must at least attempt to exhaust exclusive grievance and arbitration procedures established by the bargaining agreement. *Republic Steel Corp. v. Maddox*, 379 U.S. 650 (1965). However, because these contractual remedies have been devised and are often controlled by the union and the employer, they may well prove unsatisfactory or unworkable for the individual grievant. The problem then is to determine under what circumstances the individual employee may obtain judicial review of his breach-of-contract claim despite his failure to secure relief through the contractual remedial procedures. . . .

[W]e think the wrongfully discharged employee may bring an action against his employer in the face of a defense based upon the failure to exhaust contractual remedies, provided the employee can prove that the union as bargaining agent breached its duty of fair representation in its handling of the employee's grievance. We may assume for present purposes that such a breach of duty by the union is an unfair labor practice, as the NLRB and the Fifth Circuit have held. The employee's suit against the employer, however, remains a § 301 suit, and the jurisdiction of the courts is no more destroyed by the fact that the employee, as part and parcel of his § 301 action, finds it necessary to prove an unfair labor practice by the union, than it is by the fact that the suit may involve an unfair labor practice by the employer himself. The court is free to determine whether the employee is barred by the actions of his union representative, and, if not, to proceed with the case. And if, to facilitate his case, the employee joins the union as defendant, the situation is not substantially changed. The action is still a § 301 suit, and the jurisdiction of the courts is not preempted under the *Garmon* principle. This, at the very least, is the holding of *Humphrey v. Moore* with respect to pre-emption, as petitioners recognize in their brief. And, insofar as adjudication of the union's breach of duty is concerned, the result should be no different if the employee, as Owens did here, sues the employer and the union in separate actions. There would be very little to commend a rule which would permit the Missouri courts to adjudicate the Union's conduct in an action against Swift but not in an action against the Union itself.

For the above reasons, it is obvious that the courts will be compelled to pass upon whether there has been a breach of the duty of fair representation in the context of many § 301 breach-of-contract actions. If a breach of duty by the union and a breach of contract by the employer are proven, the court must fashion an appropriate remedy. Presumably, in at least some cases, the union's breach of duty will have enhanced or contributed to the employee's injury. What possible sense could there be in a rule which would permit a court that has litigated the fault of employer and union to fashion a remedy only with respect to the employer? Under such a rule, either the employer would be compelled by the court to pay for the union's wrong — slight deterrence indeed, to future union misconduct — or the injured employee would be forced to go to two tribunals to repair a single injury. Moreover, the Board would be compelled in many cases either to remedy injuries arising out of a breach of contract, a task which Congress has not assigned to it, or to leave the individual employee without remedy for the union's wrong. Given the strong reasons for not pre-empting duty of fair representation suits in general, and the fact that the courts in many § 301 suits must adjudicate whether the union has breached its duty, we conclude that the courts may also fashion remedies for such a breach of duty....

III

Petitioners contend, as they did in their motion for judgment notwithstanding the jury's verdict, that Owens failed to prove that the Union breached its duty of fair representation in its handling of Owens' grievance. Petitioners also argue that the Supreme Court of Missouri, in rejecting this contention, applied a standard that is inconsistent with governing principles of federal law with respect to the Union's duty to an individual employee in its processing of grievances under the collective bargaining agreement with Swift. We agree with both contentions.

A.... Quite obviously, the question which the Missouri Supreme Court thought dispositive of the issue of liability was whether the evidence supported Owens' assertion that he had been wrongfully discharged by Swift, regardless of the Union's good faith in reaching a contrary conclusion. This was also the major concern of the plaintiff at trial: the bulk of Owens' evidence was directed at whether he was medically fit at the time of discharge and whether he had performed heavy work after that discharge.

A breach of the statutory duty of fair representation occurs only when a union's conduct toward a member of the collective bargaining unit is arbitrary, discriminatory, or in bad faith. *See Humphrey v. Moore, supra; Ford Motor Co. v. Huffman, supra*. There has been considerable debate over the extent of this duty in the context of a union's enforcement of the grievance and arbitration procedures in a collective bargaining agreement.... Some have suggested that every individual employee should have the right to have his grievance taken to arbitration. Others have urged that the Union be given substantial discretion (if the collective bargaining agreement so provides) to decide whether a grievance should be taken to arbitration, subject only to the duty to refrain from patently wrongful conduct such as racial discrimination or personal hostility.

Though we accept the proposition that a union may not arbitrarily ignore a meritorious grievance or process it in perfunctory fashion, we do not agree that the individual employee has an absolute right to have his grievance taken to arbitration regardless of the provisions of the applicable collective bargaining agreement.... In providing for a grievance and arbitration procedure which gives the union discretion to supervise the grievance machinery and to invoke arbitration, the employer and the union contemplate that each will endeavor in good faith to settle grievances short of arbitration. Through this settlement process, frivolous grievances are ended prior to the most costly and time-consuming step in the grievance procedures. Moreover, both sides are assured that similar complaints will be treated consistently, and major problem areas in the interpretation of the collective bargaining contract can be isolated and perhaps resolved. And finally, the settlement process furthers the interest of the union as statutory agent and as coauthor of the bargaining agreement in representing the employees in the enforcement of that agreement....

For these same reasons, the standard applied here by the Missouri Supreme Court cannot be sustained. For if a union's decision that a particular grievance lacks sufficient merit to justify arbitration would constitute a breach of the duty of fair representation because a judge or jury later found the grievance meritorious, the union's incentive to settle such grievances short of arbitration would be seriously reduced. The dampening effect on the entire grievance procedure of this reduction of the union's freedom to settle claims in good faith would surely be substantial. Since the union's statutory duty of fair representation protects the individual employee from arbitrary abuses of the settlement device by providing him with recourse against both employer (in a §301 suit) and union, this severe limitation on the power to settle grievances is neither necessary nor desirable....

B. Applying the proper standard of union liability to the facts of this case, we cannot uphold the jury's award, for we conclude that as a matter of federal law the evidence does not support a verdict that the Union breached its duty of fair representation....

In administering the grievance and arbitration machinery as statutory agent of the employees, a union must in good faith and in a nonarbitrary manner, make decisions as to the merits of particular grievances. *See Humphrey v. Moore*, 375 U.S. 335, 349–350 (1964); *Ford Motor Co. v. Huffman*, 345 U.S. 330, 337–339 (1953). In a case such as this, when Owens supplied the Union with medical evidence supporting his position, the Union might well have breached its duty had it ignored Owens' complaint or had it processed the grievance in a perfunctory manner. *See* Cox, *Rights under a Labor Agreement*, 69 Harv. L. Rev., at 632–634. But here the Union processed the grievance into the fourth step, attempted to gather sufficient evidence to prove Owens' case, attempted to secure for Owens less vigorous work at the plant, and joined in the employer's efforts to have Owens rehabilitated. Only when these efforts all proved unsuccessful did the Union conclude both that arbitration would be fruitless and that the grievance should be dismissed. There was no evidence that any Union officer was personally hostile to Owens or that the Union acted at any time other than in good faith. Having concluded that the individual employee has no absolute right to have his grievance arbitrated under the collective bargaining agreement at issue, and that a breach of the duty of fair representation is not established merely by proof that the underlying grievance was meritorious, we must conclude that that duty was not breached here.

IV

In our opinion, there is another important reason why the judgment of the Missouri Supreme Court cannot stand. Owens' suit against the Union was grounded on his claim that Swift had discharged him in violation of the applicable collective bargaining agreement....

The appropriate remedy for a breach of a union's duty of fair representation must vary with the circumstances of the particular breach. In this case, the employee's complaint was that the Union wrongfully failed to afford him the arbitration remedy against his employer established by the collective bargaining agreement. But the damages sought by Owens were primarily those suffered because of the employer's alleged breach of contract. Assuming for the moment that Owens had been wrongfully discharged, Swift's only defense to a direct action for breach of contract would have been the Union's failure to resort to arbitration, *compare Republic Steel Corp. v. Maddox*, 379 U.S. 650 (1965), *with Smith v. Evening News Ass'n*, 371 U.S. 195 (1962), and if that failure was itself a violation of the Union's statutory duty to the employee, there is no reason to exempt the employer from contractual damages which he would otherwise have had to pay.... The difficulty lies in fashioning an appropriate scheme of remedies.

Petitioners urge that an employee be restricted in such circumstances to a decree compelling the employer and the union to arbitrate the underlying grievance. It is true that the employee's action is based on the employer's alleged breach of contract plus the union's alleged wrongful failure to afford him his contractual remedy of arbitration. For this reason, an order compelling arbitration should be viewed as one of the available remedies when a breach of the union's duty is proved. But we see no reason inflexibly to require arbitration in all cases....

A more difficult question is, what portion of the employee's damages may be charged to the union: in particular, may an award against a union include, as it did here, damages attributable solely to the employer's breach of contract? We think not. Though the union has violated a statutory duty in failing to press the grievance, it is the employer's unrelated breach of contract which triggered the controversy and which caused this portion of the employee's damages. The employee should have no difficulty recovering these damages from the employer, who cannot, as we have explained, hide behind the union's wrongful failure to act; in fact, the employer may be (and probably should be) joined as a defendant in the fair representation suit, as in *Humphrey v. Moore, supra*. It could be a real hardship on the union to pay these damages, even if the union were given a right of indemnification against the employer. With the employee assured of direct recovery from the employer, we see no merit in requiring the union to pay the employer's share of the damages.

The governing principle, then, is to apportion liability between the employer and the union according to the damage caused by the fault of each. Thus, damages attributable solely to the employer's breach of contract should not be charged to the union, but increases if any in those damages caused by the union's refusal to process the grievance should not be charged to the employer. In this case, even if the Union had breached its duty, all or almost all of Owens' damages would still be attributable to his allegedly wrongful discharge by Swift. For these reasons, even if the Union here had properly been found liable for a breach of duty, it is clear that the damage award was improper.

Reversed.

Mr. Justice Fortas, with whom The Chief Justice and Mr. Justice Harlan join, concurring in the result.

1. In my view, a complaint by an employee that the union has breached its duty of fair representation is subject to the exclusive jurisdiction of the NLRB. It is a charge of unfair labor practice. See *Miranda Fuel Co.*, 140 N.L.R.B. 181 (1962); *Rubber Workers Local 12*, 150 N.L.R.B. 312, *enforced*, 368 F.2d 12 (5th Cir. 1966). As is the case with most other unfair labor practices, the Board's jurisdiction is pre-emptive. . . . There is no basis for failure to apply the preemption principles in the present case, and, as I shall discuss, strong reason for its application. The relationship between the union and the individual employee with respect to the processing of claims to employment rights under the collective bargaining agreement is fundamental to the design and operation of federal labor law. It is not "merely peripheral," as the Court's opinion states. It "presents difficult problems of definition of status, problems which we have held are precisely 'of a kind most wisely entrusted initially to the agency charged with the day-today administration of the Act as a whole.'" *Iron Workers v. Perko*, 373 U.S. at 706. Accordingly, the judgment of the Supreme Court of Missouri should be reversed and the complaint dismissed for this reason and on this basis. I agree, however, that if it were assumed that jurisdiction of the subject matter exists, the judgment would still have to be reversed because of the use by the Missouri court of an improper standard for measuring the union's duty, and the absence of evidence to establish that the union refused further to process Owens' grievance because of bad faith or arbitrarily.

2. I regret the elaborate discussion in the Court's opinion of problems which are irrelevant. This is not an action by the employee against the employer, and the discussion of the requisites of such an action is, in my judgment, unnecessary. The Court argues that the employee could sue the employer under LMRA § 301; and that to maintain such an action the employee would have to show that he has exhausted his remedies under the collective bargaining agreement, or alternatively that he was prevented from doing so because the union breached its duty to him by failure completely to process his claim. That may be; or maybe all he would have to show to maintain an action against the employer for wrongful discharge is that he demanded that the union process his claim to exhaustion of available remedies, and that it refused to do so. I see no need for the Court to pass upon that question, which

is not presented here, and which, with all respect, lends no support to the Court's argument. The Court seems to use its discussion of the employee-employer litigation as somehow analogous to or supportive of its conclusion that the employee may maintain a court action against the union. But I do not believe that this follows. I agree that the NLRB's unfair labor practice jurisdiction does not preclude an action under § 301 against the employer for wrongful discharge from employment. *Smith v. Evening News Ass'n*, 371 U.S. 195 (1962). Therefore, Owens might maintain an action against his employer in the present case. This would be an action to enforce the collective bargaining agreement, and Congress has authorized the courts to entertain actions of this type. But his claim against the union is quite different in character, as the Court itself recognizes. The Court holds — and I think correctly if the issue is to be reached — that the union could not be required to pay damages measured by the breach of the employment contract, because it was not the union but the employer that breached the contract. I agree; but I suggest that this reveals the point for which I contend: that the employee's claim against the union is not a claim under the collective bargaining agreement, but a claim that the union has breached its statutory duty of fair representation. This claim, I submit, is a claim of unfair labor practice and it is within the exclusive jurisdiction of the NLRB....

3. If we look beyond logic and precedent to the policy of the labor relations design which Congress has provided, court jurisdiction of this type of action seems anomalous and ill-advised. We are not dealing here with the interpretation of a contract or with an alleged breach of an employment agreement. As the Court in effect acknowledges, we are concerned with the subtleties of a union's statutory duty faithfully to represent employees in the unit, including those who may not be members of the union. The Court — regrettably, in my opinion — ventures to state judgments as to the metes and bounds of the reciprocal duties involved in the relationship between the union and the employee. In my opinion, this is precisely and especially the kind of judgment that Congress intended to entrust to the Board and which is well within the pre-emption doctrine that this Court has prudently stated.... The nuances of union-employee and union-employer relationships are infinite and consequential, particularly when the issue is as amorphous as whether the union was proved guilty of "arbitrary or bad-faith conduct" which the Court states as the standard applicable here. In all reason and in all good judgment, this jurisdiction should be left with the Board and not be placed in the courts, especially with the complex and necessarily confusing guidebook that the Court now publishes.

[The dissenting opinion of MR. JUSTICE BLACK is omitted.]

Notes

1. *Who "Owns" the Grievance?* — Prior to the principal case, the lower courts had developed at least two main approaches to an individual employee's right to take a grievance to arbitration. Under one line of cases, illustrated by *Donnelly v. United Fruit Co.*, 40 N.J. 61, 190 A.2d 825 (1963), an employee was regarded as having a "statutorily vested right" under § 9(a) to invoke the grievance procedure, including

the final step of arbitration, if the union failed to press the claim. Under a second group of decisions, represented by *Black-Clawson Co. Paper Machine Div. v. International Ass'n of Machinists*, 313 F.2d 179 (2d Cir. 1962), an individual employee could not compel the employer to arbitrate a grievance unless the contract specifically so provided; § 9(a) was deemed merely to permit but not require an employer to hear and adjust employee grievances.

2. *Negligence versus Perfunctory Grievance Handling*—The Supreme Court ended a long debate over whether a union's negligence alone could constitute unfair representation when it declared in *United Steelworkers of America v. Rawson*, 495 U.S. 362, 372–73 (1990): "The courts have in general assumed that mere negligence, even in the enforcement of a collective bargaining agreement, would not state a claim for breach of the duty of fair representation, and we endorse that view today." Courts are also generally reluctant to second-guess union handling of the grievance process. *See, e.g., Badkin v. Lockheed Martin Corp.*, 2020 WL 5117950 (9th Cir. 2020) (no breach of duty where union decided not to pursue employee's grievance and did not timely inform the employee of its decision); *Inechien v. Nichols Aluminum, LLC*, 728 F.3d 816 (8th Cir. 2013) (no breach of duty where union could have handled investigation in more professional manner); *Emmanuel v. Int'l Bhd. of Teamsters, Local 25*, 426 F.3d 416 (1st Cir. 2005), *cert. denied*, 547 U.S. 1055 (2006) (no breach of duty where union business agent actively investigated charge, pursued a procedural claim rather than the substantive theory that the grievant advanced, and lost grievance); *see also Baxter v. United Paperworkers Int'l Union, Local 7370*, 140 F.3d 745 (8th Cir. 1998) (denying grievants the right to be represented by their own private attorneys in discharge arbitration proceedings is not *ipso facto* arbitrary nor a breach of the union's duty of fair representation).

Nevertheless, unions may breach the duty of fair representation when they engage in perfunctory or irrational grievance handling. Courts of appeals have imposed liability on unions for breach of the duty of fair representation where union officials with access to relevant employer information prevented employees from filing nonfrivolous grievances, missed contractual filing deadlines, or failed to conduct even cursory investigations of employee grievances. *See, e.g., Pauley v. CF Entm't*, 773 Fed. App'x. 357 (9th Cir. 2019) (claim for breach of duty could proceed where union failed to timely file grievance despite reaching a $1.4 million settlement with employer purportedly covering all outstanding grievances); *Rollins v. Cmty. Hosp. of San Bernardino*, 839 F.3d 1181 (9th Cir. 2016) (claim for breach of duty survived summary judgment where union did not seriously consider grievant's claim and improperly lumped her claim into a class action grievance with non-similarly situated employees); *Beck v. UFCW, Local 99*, 506 F.3d 874 (9th Cir. 2007) (union breached duty where it failed to timely file a grievance after agreeing to file it; not filing in time was failure to perform a ministerial function, not exercise of judgment); *Cruz v. Local 3 of the IBEW*, 34 F.3d 1148 (2d Cir. 1994) (union breached duty by failing to investigate employees' complaints despite having information to do so). *But cf. Saunders v. Ford Motor Co,*, 879 F.3d 742 (6th Cir. 2018) (court refused to second-guess union's judgment in withdrawing grievance after it had filed, investigated, argued, and appealed the grievance); *Matthews v. Milwaukee Area Local Postal Workers Union, AFL-CIO*, 495 F.3d 438 (7th Cir. 2007) (no breach where union waited 31 days to file grievance under contract containing 14-day filing period, where employer did not challenge timeliness of grievance and rejected it instead on the merits).

What is the difference between negligence or poor judgment and actionable perfunctory or irrational grievance handling? *See Taha v. Teamsters Local 781*, 947 F.3d 464 (7th Cir. 2020) (no breach of duty where union chose not to allow grievant to testify and did not introduce certain exhibits in grievance process; union's choice was not irrational); *Blesedell v. Chillicothe Telephone Co.*, 811 F.3d 211 (6th Cir. 2016) (observing that a union only acts arbitrarily when its conduct is so far outside a wide range of reasonableness that it can be considered to be irrational or arbitrary; union that investigated an employee's grievance challenging his discharge, processed it through several stages, and then decided the claim lacked merit and declined to take it to arbitration did not breach its fair representation duty); *Int'l. Union, United Automobile v. NLRB*, 844 F.3d 590 (6th Cir. 2016) (union did not breach duty of fair representation when shop steward processing a terminated employee's grievance made adverse statements against the grievant during the employer's investigation and did not recuse herself from the case or disclose the adverse statements to the grievant). On the other hand, the court in *Rupcich v. Food & Commercial Workers Local 881*, 833 F.3d 847 (7th Cir. 2016) allowed a 25-year employee with a good work record who had been fired for theft after what turned out to be an inadvertent work mistake (taking a bag of birdseed in a cart past the supermarket's last checkout point) to proceed with a duty of fair representation claim where the union failed to complete the first three steps of a grievance procedure mandated by the collective agreement and declined to take the case to arbitration, and the grievant demonstrated that the union had taken other substantively similar claims to arbitration.

3. *Calculating Damages for Breach*—The Supreme Court elaborated on its *Vaca* rule for calculating damages against a union guilty of unfair representation in *Czosek v. O'Mara*, 397 U.S. 25 (1970). Said the Court:

> Assuming a wrongful discharge by the employer independent of any discriminatory conduct by the union and a subsequent discriminatory refusal by the union to process grievances based on the discharge, damages against the union for loss of employment are unrecoverable except to the extent that its refusal to handle the grievances added to the difficulty and expense of collecting from the employer.

But in *Bowen v. United States Postal Service*, 459 U.S. 212 (1983), a sharply divided (5-4) Supreme Court limited to Railway Labor Act cases the *Czosek v. O'Mara* formula for calculating damages against unions that breach their duty of fair representation. When an employer subject to the NLRA wrongfully discharges an employee and the union aggravates the harm by improperly declining to arbitrate the case, damages must be apportioned between the parties. The union will be liable to the extent it increased the employee's losses. For example, the union may be responsible for the back pay that accrues after the date of the hypothetical arbitration decision that would have reinstated the employee. *Czosek* was distinguished on the basis that the RLA provides employees with an alternative statutory remedy if the union refuses to process their grievance. *See* VanderVelde, *Making Good on* Vaca's *Promise: Apportioning Back Pay to Achieve Remedial Goals*, 32 UCLA L. Rev. 302 (1984).

4. *Jurisdiction over Fair Representation Cases*—The Supreme Court held in *Breininger v. Sheet Metal Workers Int'l Ass'n Local 6*, 493 U.S. 67 (1989), that the NLRB did not have exclusive jurisdiction over a union member's claim that his union violated its duty of fair representation by discriminating against him in job referrals through a union hiring hall. The Court noted that "[t]he duty of fair representation is not intended to mirror the contours of §8(b); rather, it arises independently from the grant under §9(a) of the NLRA of the union's exclusive power to represent all employees in a particular bargaining unit." Barring federal jurisdiction because of specialized Board expertise, said the Court, "would remove an unacceptably large number of fair representation claims from federal courts."

Air Line Pilots Ass'n, Int'l v. O'Neill, 499 U.S. 65, 111 S. Ct. 1127, 113 L. Ed. 2d 51 (1991). The Air Line Pilots settled a bitter two-year strike against Continental Airlines by an agreement that gave striking pilots three different options. By hindsight it appeared that the deal arranged by the union was worse than if the strike had simply been terminated and the pilots left to seek reemployment in the order of seniority. A group of former strikers sued ALPA for breach of the duty of fair representation. The Supreme Court first held that the tripartite standard of unfair representation established in *Vaca v. Sipes*—"arbitrary, discriminatory, or in bad faith"—applies to union contract negotiation as well as to contract administration. The Court then reversed a court of appeals' ruling against ALPA, declaring that "the final product of the bargaining process may constitute evidence of a breach of duty only if it can be fairly characterized as so far outside a 'wide range of reasonableness' . . . that it is wholly 'irrational' or 'arbitrary.'"

Notes

1. *Individual versus Collective Interests*—To what extent should a union, even if acting in accordance with its honest judgment, be allowed to sacrifice individual interests for the sake of the group? Should grievance "horsetrading" constitute a breach of the union's duty of fair representation? Consistent with the broad latitude extended to unions in grievance processing, most courts extend similar wide latitude to unions seeking to negotiate the best deal for the majority, even at the expense of individual contract rights. *See, e.g., Danylchuk v. Des Moines Register & Tribune Co.*, 128 F.3d 653 (8th Cir. 1997) (sustaining right of union to agree to drop pending discharge grievance as condition for achieving new bargaining agreement); *Cleveland v. Porca Co.*, 38 F.3d 289 (7th Cir. 1994) (union that obtained an arbitral award finding that employer violated its bargaining agreement by failing to require the purchaser of the business to assume the existing contract did not breach

its duty of fair representation by negotiating a settlement agreement that permitted the termination of some workers); *Burkevich v. Air Line Pilots Ass'n, Int'l*, 894 F.2d 346 (9th Cir. 1990) (union did not breach duty of fair representation when it waived the shutdown damage claims of pilots "as a group" against a bankrupt airline and refused to press the demands of individual pilots, since it received a quid pro quo in the employer's agreement to resume limited flight operations); *but see Bishop v. ALPA, Int'l*, 900 F.3d 388 (7th Cir. 2018) (retroactive pay settlement negotiated by union disfavored pilot instructors, who constituted a small minority of the bargaining unit, and in so doing breached duty of fair representation); *Aguinaga v. United Food & Commercial Workers Int'l Union*, 993 F.2d 1463 (10th Cir. 1993) (union wrongfully "bartered away" employees' contract rights for extraneous institutional or political reasons), *cert. denied*, 510 U.S. 1072 (1994).

2. *Differential Impact Based on Seniority*—In an era of declining union strength, unions have found it increasingly difficult to resist pressure at the bargaining table from employers seeking to cut labor costs. In order to preserve jobs, a union may agree to a "two-tiered" system in which employees hired after the labor contract's effective date receive lower wages and benefits than current employees. Would this arrangement violate the union's duty of fair representation? Does the union owe a duty to not-yet-hired workers?

What, if any, issues might such a pay structure ultimately create for union solidarity? In 2007, the UAW agreed to a two-tiered wage structure at Fiat Chrysler, GM, and Ford in order to help the automakers lower labor costs without sharply cutting wages and benefits for longtime employees. By 2015, nearly half of Fiat Chrysler's workers were earning second tier wages of around $16 to $19 per hour; meanwhile, veteran workers earned $28 per hour. Daily Lab. Rep. (BNA) No. 178, Sept. 15, 2015, at A-5, A-6. In its 2015 contract negotiations the union vowed to bring second-tier workers up to the wages earned by Tier 1 workers. The union reached a tentative agreement on a new contract with the first of the Big Three to enter negotiations on a contract, Fiat Chrysler, creating a "pathway" to higher wages for entry-level workers, bringing them up to $22 to $25 per hour while raising veteran wages to $30 per hour. Complaining that the union had not fulfilled its promise to eliminate the two-tier system, workers voted to reject the proposed contract and threatened a strike. Daily Lab. Rep. (BNA) No. 179, Sept. 16, 2015, at A-4, A-5; Daily Lab. Rep. (BNA) No. 184, Sept. 23, 2015, at A-7; Daily Lab. Rep. (BNA) No. 190, Oct. 1, 2015, at A-11, A-12; Scheiber, *UAW Contract Vote at Fiat Chrysler Takes a Populist Tone*, N.Y. Times, Oct. 1, 2015; Vlasic, *UAW Warns Fiat Chrysler to Make Deal or Face Strike*, N.Y. Times, Oct. 6, 2015. Why do you think the workers rejected the advice of union leadership and voted to strike despite a proposed contract that was quite favorable? The union and the company reached a contract shortly thereafter that provided larger raises for entry-level workers, moving them to $29 per hour—nearly on par with veteran workers who would earn a little less than $30 per hour by the end of the contract. Vlasic & Chapman, *Fiat Chrysler and UAW Reach Deal, with Bigger Raise at Entry Level*, N.Y. Times,

Oct. 8, 2015. Nevertheless, the two-tier bargaining practice later became an anti-union talking point at Volkswagen and Nissan plants in the south, undermining the UAW's efforts to market itself as an advocate for all the workers. Press, *How Two-Tier Unions Turn Workers Against One Another*, WASH. POST, Aug. 29, 2018. And because two-tiered contracts drive a wedge between union members, ending or resisting two-tiered arrangements has become an important rallying cry in a number of recent labor disputes. *See id.* (describing UPS negotiations that included a demand for a two-tiered contract); Cohen, *Ending GM's Two-Tiered Labor System is UAW Members' Top Demand—and Part of a Bigger Fight Against Worker Misclassification*, THE INTERCEPT, Sept. 26, 2019 (reporting on GM workers' strike against two-tiered system).

Alternatively, suppose the union negotiates for a pension or seniority system that negatively impacts workers with greater seniority, who may be on the verge of retirement. Would that violate the duty of fair representation? Absent proof of union animus or discriminatory intent based on age, courts quite consistently rule that the mere fact that some employees are impacted more harshly than others by the union's stance does not establish a breach of the union's duty of fair representation. *See, e.g., Demitris v. Transport Workers Union*, 862 F.3d 799 (9th Cir. 2017) (no breach of duty of fair representation where, during employer's Chapter 11 bankruptcy proceedings, union negotiated an equity distribution scheme that excluded members who took advantage of an early separation program; plaintiffs did not provide evidence of discrimination or bad faith by union); *Vaughn v. Air Line Pilots, Ass'n, Int'l*, 604 F.3d 703 (2d Cir. 2010) (where airline had filed for bankruptcy under Chapter 11, union's failure to conduct audit to assess financial health of defined benefit plan prior to agreeing to replace it with a defined contribution plan did not constitute breach of duty of fair representation, even where pilots at or approaching mandatory retirement age were impacted more harshly by modification); *Merritt v. Int'l Ass'n of Machinists & Aero. Workers*, 613 F.3d 609 (6th Cir. 2010) (no breach of duty of fair representation where union negotiated a different seniority-based pay scale for quality service agents than for the rest of its membership in the context of airline's bankruptcy; union had a legitimate reason for the distinction); *Jeffreys v. Communication Workers*, 354 F.3d 270 (4th Cir. 2003) (no breach of duty of fair representation where union weighed values of seniority and stability when pressed by financial crisis created by tragic events of September 11 and backed a furlough system and job bidding program that resulted in the smallest number of displacements system-wide, but negatively impacted senior employees who would have benefited from alternative system involving "ricochet" bidding).

3. *To Whom Does the Union Owe a Duty?*—Mergers and bankruptcies in the airline industry have provided fertile ground for judicial interpretation of the extent of the union's duty. For example, *Addington v. U.S. Air Line Pilots Ass'n, Int'l*, 791 F.3d 967 (9th Cir. 2015), involved a merger between America West and US Airways. The newly formed union presented a seniority proposal that disadvantaged the former America West pilots and favored pilots at pre-merger US Airways, who were in the majority and tended to be more senior than the America West pilots. The Ninth Circuit concluded that the union breached its duty to fairly represent the former America West pilots in seniority list integration negotiations, pointing to the union's "manifest disregard for the interests of the [America] West pilots and its discriminatory conduct towards them," and criticizing the union for violating "the most elementary principle of the duty of fair representation — to serve the interests of all of its members, not just the pilots who voted for the union." Similarly, *Bernard v. Air Line Pilots Ass'n, Int'l*, 873 F.2d 213 (9th Cir. 1989), involved a merger between union and nonunion airlines. The labor organization that represented the pilots of the unionized carrier was found to owe a duty of fair representation to the pilots of the nonunion carrier when it negotiated a seniority integration agreement affecting the employment rights of the pilots from both carriers. *See also Ramey v. Dist. 141 Int'l Ass'n of Machinists & Aerospace Workers*, 378 F.3d 269 (2d Cir. 2004) (union breached duty of fair representation by failing to bargain for full seniority for airline mechanics employed by shuttle service that was acquired by US Airways; evidence established that union was motivated by retaliatory animus against mechanics who were previously represented by rival union).

On the other hand, in *McNamara-Blad v. Ass'n of Prof'l Flight Attendants*, 275 F.3d 1165 (9th Cir. 2002), APFA represented American Airlines' flight attendants prior to a merger of American Airlines with another air carrier, Reno Air. The flight attendants at Reno Air were represented by the Teamsters. Before the merger was completed, American Airlines negotiated an agreement with APFA that created a combined seniority list and placed the Reno Air flight attendants at the bottom of the list. Following the merger, American implemented the combined seniority list. The Reno flight attendants sued APFA for breach of the duty of fair representation. The court found that because the workforces of the two airlines did not become a single bargaining unit until after the merger, APFA owed no duty to the Reno flight attendants prior to the merger, at the time the combined seniority list was negotiated. Nor were the Reno flight attendants "de facto" members of the eventual bargaining unit at American Air as of the date on which the seniority list was negotiated. Accordingly, APFA's decision to subordinate the seniority of the Reno flight attendants to that of the American flight attendants was a bona fide economic decision designed to protect the interests of those flight attendants that it did represent. Similarly, the Seventh Circuit found no breach of the duty of fair representation in an airline merger where the union negotiated an agreement that slotted pre-merger United Airlines pilots into an integrated longevity table below a group of former Continental Airlines pilots, affecting pilot pay rates. Because the United pilots were not credited with longevity for prior furloughs, they alleged that they were systematically disadvantaged. Observing that "[c]ombining work forces following an airline merger is not for the faint-hearted," the court praised the union for its efforts to accommodate interests and found no evidence of discrimination by the union. Citing *ALPA v. O'Neill*, the court underscored its review of the union's performance as "highly deferential" to the union's rational adjustment of the pilots' competing interests. *Cunningham v. Air Line Pilots' Ass'n.*, 769 F.3d 539 (7th Cir. 2014). *See also Flight Attendants in Reunion v. Am. Airlines, Inc.*, 813 F.3d 468 (2d Cir. 2016), *cert. denied*, 137 S. Ct. 313 (2016) (no breach of the duty of fair representation where a union negotiated and implemented an integrated seniority list of flight attendants following the merger of American Airlines with US Airways, even though union did not reorder existing American Airlines seniority list to give American flight attendants credit for time worked at Trans World Airlines, thus keeping them near the bottom of the merged seniority list; union's decision was not arbitrary, irrational, or discriminatory).

4. *Union Conduct during Contract Ratification Vote.* Is union conduct during a contract ratification vote subject to the duty of fair representation? In *International Longshoreman's Ass'n, Local 1575*, 332 N.L.R.B. 1336 (2000), during a ratification meeting on a newly negotiated contract, 80 percent of the members rose from their chairs to indicate their disapproval of a particular contract term. The local union president announced that all members in favor of ratifying the new agreement should stand up, and then proclaimed that the contract was ratified based upon the number of union members still standing to protest the objectionable provision. The Labor Board found no fair representation breach by this somewhat devious maneuver because the contract ratification process is an internal union matter not covered by the duty of fair representation.

Problems

41. A fast-food restaurant with 12 employees suffered unexplained losses of food and money and suspected that one or more of its workers was committing theft. The employer threatened to fire the entire crew. Rather than have that happen, the union representing the workers acquiesced in the employer's trial layoff of five employees. The thefts came to a stop, and the five workers were permanently discharged. One of the discharged workers filed a grievance claiming (correctly) that there was no direct proof of her dishonesty. Did the union breach its duty of fair representation when it refused to process her grievance? What if the union had refused to process her discharge grievance in exchange for the restaurant's agreement to a new collective bargaining agreement?

42. The Teamsters Union seeks to organize workers at a Kansas City trucking company that is critical to the union's effort to expand its footprint in the Midwest. Achieving representative status there will allow the union to more effectively wield its strike and boycott power to leverage gains at the bargaining table for all truckers. The union persuades the employer to agree to a neutrality pledge and not contest the organizing drive focused on truckers, in exchange for the union's promise not to organize the pink collar administrative and clerical staff in the office. Has the union violated its duty of fair representation? Should it matter if there are more truckers benefited than clerical workers disadvantaged? Does it matter what the gender composition of the respective job categories is?

2. Relationship to Contract Breach

Hines v. Anchor Motor Freight, Inc.

Supreme Court of the United States
424 U.S. 554, 96 S. Ct. 1048, 47 L. Ed. 2d 231 (1976)

MR. JUSTICE WHITE delivered the opinion of the Court.

The issue here is whether a suit against an employer by employees asserting breach of a collective bargaining contract was properly dismissed where the accompanying complaint against the Union for breach of duty of fair representation has withstood the Union's motion for summary judgment and remains to be tried.

I

Petitioners, who were formerly employed as truck drivers by respondent Anchor Motor Freight, Inc. (Anchor), were discharged on June 5, 1967. The applicable collective bargaining contract forbade discharges without just cause. The company charged dishonesty. The practice at Anchor was to reimburse drivers for money spent for lodging while the drivers were on the road overnight. Anchor's assertion was that petitioners had sought reimbursement for motel expenses in excess of the actual charges sustained by them. At a meeting between the company and the union, Local 377, International Brotherhood of Teamsters (the Union), which was also attended by petitioners, Anchor presented motel receipts previously submitted by petitioners which were in excess of the charges shown on the motel's registration cards; a notarized statement of the motel clerk asserting the accuracy of the registration cards; and an affidavit of the motel owner affirming that the registration cards were accurate and that inflated receipts had been furnished petitioners. The Union claimed petitioners were innocent and opposed the discharges. It was then agreed that the matter would be presented to the joint arbitration committee for the area, to which the collective-bargaining contract permitted either party to submit an unresolved grievance.[2]

Pending this hearing, petitioners were reinstated. Their suggestion that the motel be investigated was answered by the Union representatives' assurances that "there was nothing to worry about" and that they need not hire their own attorney.

---

2. [2] The contractual grievance procedure is set out in Art. 7 of the Central Conference Area Supplement to the National Master Agreement. App. 226–233. Grievances were to be taken up by the employee involved and if no settlement was reached, were then to be considered by the business agent of the local union and the employer representative. If the dispute remained unresolved, either party had the right to present the case for decision to the appropriate joint area arbitration committee. These committees are organized on a geographical area basis and hear grievances in panels made up of an equal number of representatives of the parties to the collective-bargaining agreement. Cases that deadlocked before the joint area committee could be taken to a panel of the national joint arbitration committee, composed like the area committee panels of an equal number of representatives of the parties to the agreement. If unresolved there, they would be resolved by a panel including an impartial arbitrator. The joint arbitration committee for the Detroit area is involved in this case.

A hearing before the joint area committee was held on July 26, 1967. Anchor presented its case. Both the Union and petitioners were afforded an opportunity to present their case and to be heard. Petitioners denied their dishonesty, but neither they nor the Union presented any other evidence contradicting the documents presented by the company. The committee sustained the discharges. Petitioners then retained an attorney and sought rehearing based on a statement by the motel owner that he had no personal knowledge of the events, but that the discrepancy between the receipts and the registration cards could have been attributable to the motel clerk's recording on the cards less than was actually paid and retaining for himself the difference between the amount receipted and the amount recorded. The committee, after hearing, unanimously denied rehearing "because there was no new evidence presented which would justify reopening this case."

There were later indications that the motel clerk was in fact the culprit; and the present suit was filed in June 1969, against Anchor, the Union and its International. The complaint alleged that the charges of dishonesty made against petitioners by Anchor were false, that there was no just cause for discharge and that the discharges had been in breach of contract. It was also asserted that the falsity of the charges could have been discovered with a minimum of investigation, that the Union had made no effort to ascertain the truth of the charges and that the Union had violated its duty of fair representation by arbitrarily and in bad faith depriving petitioners of their employment and permitting their discharge without sufficient proof.

The Union denied the charges and relied on the decision of the joint area committee. Anchor asserted that petitioners had been properly discharged for just cause. It also defended on the ground that petitioners, diligently and in good faith represented by the Union, had unsuccessfully resorted to the grievance and arbitration machinery provided by the contract and that the adverse decision of the joint arbitration committee was binding upon the Union and petitioners under the contractual provision declaring that "[a] decision by a majority of a Panel of any of the Committees shall be final and binding on all parties, including the employee and/or employees affected." Discovery followed, including a deposition of the motel clerk revealing that he had falsified the records and that it was he who had pocketed the difference between the sums shown on the receipts and the registration cards. Motions for summary judgment filed by Anchor and the Unions were granted by the District Court on the ground that the decision of the arbitration committee was final and binding on the employees and "for failure to show facts comprising bad faith, arbitrariness or perfunctoriness on the part of the Unions." Although indicating that the acts of the Union "may not meet professional standards of competency, and while it might have been advisable for the Union to further investigate the charges . . . ," the District Court concluded that the facts demonstrated at most bad judgment on the part of the Union, which was insufficient to prove a breach of duty or make out a prima facie case against it. . . .

After reviewing the allegations and the record before it, the court of appeals concluded that there were sufficient facts from which bad faith or arbitrary conduct on the part of the local Union could be inferred by the trier of fact and that petitioners should have been afforded an opportunity to prove their charges.[3] To this extent the judgment of the district court was reversed. The Court of Appeals affirmed the judgment in favor of Anchor and the International. . . .

It is this judgment of the court of appeals with respect to Anchor that is now before us on our limited grant of the employees' petition for writ of certiorari. . . . We reverse that judgment. . . .

III

Even though under *Vaca* the employer may not insist on exhaustion of grievance procedures when the union has breached its representation duty, it is urged that when the procedures have been followed and a decision favorable to the employer announced, the employer must be protected from relitigation by the express contractual provision declaring a decision to be final and binding. We disagree. The union's breach of duty relieves the employee of an express or implied requirement that disputes be settled through contractual grievance procedures; if it seriously undermines the integrity of the arbitral process the union's breach also removes the bar of the finality provisions of the contract. . . .

Anchor would have it that petitioners are foreclosed from judicial relief unless some blameworthy conduct on its part disentitles it to rely on the finality rule. But it was Anchor that originated the discharges for dishonesty. If those charges were in error, Anchor has surely played its part in precipitating this dispute. Of course, both courts below held there were no facts suggesting that Anchor either knowingly or negligently relied on false evidence. As far as the record reveals it also prevailed before the joint committee after presenting its case in accordance with what were ostensibly wholly fair procedures. Nevertheless there remains the question whether the contractual protection against relitigating an arbitral decision binds employees who assert that the process has fundamentally malfunctioned by reason of the bad-faith performance of the union, their statutorily imposed collective bargaining agent.

Under the rule announced by the court of appeals, unless the employer is implicated in the Union's malfeasance or has otherwise caused the arbitral process to err, petitioners would have no remedy against Anchor even though they

---

3. [5] As summarized by the Court of Appeals, the allegations relied on were:
    They consist of the motel clerk's admission, made a year after the discharge was upheld in arbitration, that he, not plaintiffs, pocketed the money; the claim of the union's failure to investigate the motel clerk's original story implicating plaintiffs despite their requests; the account of the union officials' assurances to plaintiffs that 'they had nothing to worry about' and 'that there was no need for them to investigate'; the contention that no exculpatory evidence was presented at the hearing; and the assertion that there existed political antagonism between local union officials and plaintiffs because of a wildcat strike led by some of the plaintiffs and a dispute over the appointment of a steward, resulting in denunciation of plaintiffs as 'hillbillies' by Angelo, the union president.

506 F.2d 1153, 1156 (6th Cir. 1974).

are successful in proving the Union's bad faith, the falsity of the charges against them and the breach of contract by Anchor by discharging without cause. This rule would apparently govern even in circumstances where it is shown that a union has manufactured the evidence and knows from the start that it is false; or even if, unbeknownst to the employer, the union has corrupted the arbitrator to the detriment of disfavored Union members. As is the case where there has been a failure to exhaust, however, we cannot believe that Congress intended to foreclose the employee from his § 301 remedy otherwise available against the employer if the contractual processes have been seriously flawed by the union's breach of its duty to represent employees honestly and in good faith and without invidious discrimination or arbitrary conduct.

It is urged that the reversal of the court of appeals will undermine not only the finality rule but the entire collective bargaining process. Employers, it is said, will be far less willing to give up their untrammeled right to discharge without cause and to agree to private settlement procedures. But the burden on employees will remain a substantial one, far too heavy in the opinion of some. To prevail against either the company or the Union, petitioners must show not only that their discharge was contrary to the contract but must also carry the burden of demonstrating breach of duty by the Union. As the District Court indicated, this involves more than demonstrating mere errors in judgment.

Petitioners are not entitled to relitigate their discharge merely because they offer newly discovered evidence that the charges against them were false and that in fact they were fired without cause. The grievance processes cannot be expected to be error-free. The finality provision has sufficient force to surmount occasional instances of mistake. But it is quite another matter to suggest that erroneous arbitration decisions must stand even though the employee's representation by the union has been dishonest, in bad faith or discriminatory; for in that event error and injustice of the grossest sort would multiply. The contractual system would then cease to qualify as an adequate mechanism to secure individual redress for damaging failure of the employer to abide by the contract. Congress has put its blessing on private dispute settlement arrangements provided in collective agreements, but it was anticipated, we are sure, that the contractual machinery would operate within some minimum levels of integrity. In our view, enforcement of the finality provision where the arbitrator has erred is conditioned upon the Union's having satisfied its statutory duty fairly to represent the employee in connection with the arbitration proceedings. Wrongfully discharged employees would be left without jobs and without a fair opportunity to secure an adequate remedy.

Except for this case the courts of appeals have arrived at similar conclusions. As the Court of Appeals for the Ninth Circuit put it in *Margetta v. Pam Corp.*, 501 F.2d 179, 180 (1974): "To us, it makes little difference whether the union subverts the arbitration process by refusing to proceed as in *Vaca* or follows the arbitration trail to the end, but in doing so subverts the arbitration process by failing to fairly represent the employee. In neither case does the employee receive fair representation."

Petitioners, if they prove an erroneous discharge and the Union's breach of duty tainting the decision of the joint committee, are entitled to an appropriate remedy against the employer as well as the Union. It was error to affirm the district court's final dismissal of petitioners' action against Anchor. To this extent the judgment of the court of appeals is reversed.

So ordered.

MR. JUSTICE STEVENS took no part in the consideration or decision of this case.

[The concurring opinion of MR. JUSTICE STEWART and the dissenting opinion of MR. JUSTICE REHNQUIST, with whom THE CHIEF JUSTICE joined, are omitted.]

Notes

1. *Claims Resolution in Hybrid Section 301 Cases* — In subsequent cases, courts of appeals have made it clear that hybrid claims need not be addressed in any particular order. Thus, if the court finds that the employee has failed to establish a breach of the labor contract, it need not rule on the fair representation claim: it may dismiss the suit if either claim fails. *Bliesner v. Commun. Workers of Am.*, 464 F.3d 910 (9th Cir. 2006), *cert. denied*, 551 U.S. 1144 (2007); *see also Cole v. Int'l Union, UAW*, 533 F.3d 932 (8th Cir. 2008).

2. *Ethical Obligations of Union Lawyers* — The duty of a union lawyer to the union and to individual employee-members where the two sets of interests conflict raises complex ethical issues. Who is the union lawyer's client? Is it the union, the bargaining unit member, the union and the bargaining unit member, or one of the two as primary client and the other as derivative client? Is it significant that the union furnishes and pays for the lawyer? How can ethical obligations be harmonized with labor law's vision of unions as the exclusive representative of the collective of workers? Should a union attorney be immune from legal malpractice liability for failing to represent an individual employee adequately? (Hint: what is the individual liability of union agents under *Atkinson v. Sinclair Ref. Co.* (*supra* at *Complete Auto Transit, Inc. v. Reis* discussion)?) *See Arnold v. Air Midwest*, 100 F.3d 857 (10th Cir. 1996). *See generally* Fisk, *Union Lawyers and Employment Law*, 23 BERKELEY J. EMP. & LAB. L. 57 (2002); Pearce, *The Union Lawyer's Obligations to Bargaining Unit Members: A Case Study of the Interdependence of Legal Ethics and Substantive Law*, 37 S. TEX. L. REV. 1095 (1996).

A related question involves the lawyer's duty of confidentiality — to which client(s) does the lawyer's duty run? A panel of the New York State Bar Association's Ethics Committee determined that when an employee is a party to a grievance arbitration, the union lawyer represents the employee and owes a duty of confidentiality to the individual union member, and therefore may not disseminate copies of an arbitration decision without the member's permission. This is so even if the union supplies and pays for the lawyer. However, when the lawyer represents the union as a party to the grievance proceedings, the union is the lawyer's client. The lawyer must disclose to the member that she or he represents only the union and that information may be shared with the union and disseminated at the union's discretion to other members. *New York State Bar Ass'n Comm. on Professional Ethics, Op. 743*, May 25, 2001.

3. *Right to Jury Trial*—An individual who seeks compensatory damages for lost wages and benefits in a fair representation suit prosecuted against a labor organization is entitled to a jury trial under the Seventh Amendment, since such monetary relief is of a legal, rather than a restitutionary, nature. *Chauffeurs, Teamsters & Helpers, Local 391 v. Terry*, 494 U.S. 558 (1990). The same jury privilege applies to both the contractual and fair representation issues in a *Vaca v. Sipes* suit against an employer and representative union when a plaintiff seeks both equitable and legal relief. The jury must determine the common legal issues before the trial court considers the equitable questions. *See Black v. Ryder/P.I.E. Nationwide*, 930 F.2d 505 (6th Cir. 1991); *Brownlee v. Yellow Freight System, Inc.*, 921 F.2d 745 (8th Cir. 1990).

4. *Damages*—The Supreme Court has held, apparently as a blanket rule, that punitive damages are not available against unions for breach of the duty of fair representation in processing grievances. *International Brotherhood of Electrical Workers v. Foust*, 442 U.S. 42 (1979). The Court reasoned that the strong interest in protecting the collective interests of union members and preserving their limited funds and the interest in promoting "responsible decisionmaking essential to peaceful labor relations" counseled against allowing recovery of punitive damages. Some state courts, however, have permitted punitive damages. *See, e.g., Akins v. USW, Local 187*, 237 P.3d 744 (N.M. 2010) (permitting punitive damage recovery and observing that several other states also provide for punitive damages in duty of fair representation cases).

5. *Statute of Limitations*—In *DelCostello v. Int'l Bhd. of Teamsters*, 462 U.S. 151 (1983), the Supreme Court ruled that the NLRA's §10(b) six-month statute of limitations governs an employee's *Vaca-Sipes* or *Hines-Anchor Motor Freight* suit against both employer and union, alleging employer breach of contract under §301 of Taft-Hartley and union breach of the duty of fair representation. The Court concluded that "state limitations periods for vacating arbitration awards fail to provide an aggrieved employee with a satisfactory opportunity to vindicate his rights under §301 and the fair representation doctrine." *UAW v. Hoosier-Cardinal Corp., supra*, was distinguished as a "straightforward breach of contract suit under §301" brought by a union, while *DelCostello* was a "hybrid §301/fair representation claim" having "no close analogy in ordinary state law." The six-month limitations period has also been held applicable to a fair representation suit against a union alone. *Johnson v. Graphic Communications Int'l Union*, 930 F.2d 1178 (7th Cir.), *cert. denied*, 502 U.S. 862 (1991). *Cf. Cephas v. MVM, Inc.*, 520 F.3d 480 (D.C. Cir. 2008) (six-month limitations period does not apply unless suit includes potential duty of fair representation claim; thus, where the claimed breach was not subject to the contractual arbitration and grievance procedures, the limitations period was inapposite). The claim accrues when the plaintiffs knew, or should have known, of the alleged wrongful acts. *Adorno v. Crowley Towing & Transp. Co.*, 443 F.3d 122 (1st Cir. 2006).

Clayton v. International Union, United Automobile Workers, 451 U.S. 679, 101 S. Ct. 2088, 68 L. Ed. 2d 538 (1981). The UAW withdrew its request for the arbitration of an employee's discharge. Although the union's constitution required aggrieved members to exhaust internal appeals procedures before seeking redress from a court, the employee immediately sued the union under § 301 of the LMRA, alleging breach of the duty of fair representation. The Supreme Court held that exhaustion of internal remedies will not be required when a union appeals procedure cannot result in reactivation of the employee grievance or an award of complete relief. The latter might include reinstatement as well as back pay. Even though the union could provide full monetary relief, only the employer could grant reinstatement.

Notes

1. *Aftermath* — Shortly after *Clayton* was decided, the UAW secured the agreement of a number of the employers with which it bargains that they would permit the reactivation of employees' grievances in situations where the Public Review Board, the International Executive Board, or the Convention Appeals Committee found the union had breached its duty of fair representation. *See, e.g.*, GM-UAW 1982 National Agreement, p. 321; *see also Monroe v. International Union, UAW*, 723 F.2d 22 (6th Cir. 1983) (requiring exhaustion of such internal union procedures).

2. *Limitations Periods and the Exhaustion Requirement* — Where an employee is required to exhaust internal union procedures before seeking judicial redress, the six-month statute of limitations period will be tolled until the internal union procedures have concluded. *See Frandsen v. Brotherhood of Ry., etc.*, 782 F.2d 674 (7th Cir. 1986). But the First Circuit has held that the pendency of arbitration proceedings did not toll the statute in a hybrid § 301 action when employees were not obliged to exhaust contractual grievance procedures or internal union appeals. *Arriaga-Zayas v. International Ladies' Garment Workers' Union-Puerto Rico Council*, 835 F.2d 11 (1st Cir. 1987), *cert. denied*, 486 U.S. 1033 (1988). What is necessary to "exhaust" intra-union procedures? *See, e.g., Stafford v. Ford Motor Co.*, 835 F.2d 1227 (8th Cir. 1987) (sufficient for member to send letter to international president requesting a "new trial").

3. *When the Exhaustion Requirement Applies* — The Sixth Circuit clarified some confusion in its precedents between the exhaustion requirements as they apply to grievance procedures in labor contracts, and to appeals processes under union constitutions. Although union members do not have to exhaust the grievance procedure available under their labor contract where they allege breach of the duty of fair representation against their unions in hybrid § 301 claims (*Hines v. Anchor Motor Freight*), under *Clayton v. Int'l Union, UAW* they generally must exhaust internal appeals required by a union constitution prior to bringing suit for breach of the duty of fair representation unless union officials are so hostile that a fair hearing on the claim is hopeless, the internal appeals procedures would be inadequate to reactivate the grievance or to award the employee the full relief that he seeks, or where exhaustion would unreasonably delay the opportunity to obtain a judicial hearing on the merits. *Chapman v. United Auto Workers Local 1005*, 670 F.3d 677 (6th Cir. 2012) (*en banc*), *cert. denied*, 568 U.S. 943 (2012).

Glover v. St. Louis-San Francisco R. Co., 393 U.S. 324, 89 S. Ct. 548, 21 L. Ed. 2d 519 (1969). Black and white railroad employees sued their union and employer, claiming that racial discrimination practiced by the railroad with the sub rosa agreement of certain union officials kept the plaintiffs from securing higher-paying jobs. The defendants moved to dismiss on the ground that the plaintiffs had not exhausted their administrative remedies under the contract grievance procedure, in the union constitution, or before the National Railroad Adjustment Board. Plaintiffs responded that they had tried in vain to present their grievances to union and company officials. The Supreme Court held that since the union and the employer were allegedly scheming together to bar the black employees from promotion, the employees should not be required to pursue further any relief administered by the union, the company, or both. Even though the Railroad Adjustment Board ordinarily has exclusive jurisdiction under § 3 First (i) of the Railway Labor Act to interpret collective bargaining agreements, it too was suspect here since its membership is largely chosen by the railroads and the brotherhoods.

Notes

1. *Availability of the* Clayton *and* Glover *Exceptions* — In *Bell v. DaimlerChrysler Corp.*, 547 F.3d 796 (7th Cir. 2008), the court entered summary judgment in favor of the employer where the plaintiff auto workers failed to file a timely appeal of a union official's decision not to pursue a grievance over the company's failure to recall laid-off workers. Citing *Clayton, supra*, the court explained that:

> [A] member will not be heard to complain in court that his union breached his duty of fair representation unless he has first presented his grievance to the union and, if rebuffed, exhausted any and all of the internal union appeals available to him — *so long as* such appeals could result either in granting him complete relief or in the reinstatement of his grievance.

The court reasoned that if the plaintiffs had pursued an internal union appeal, the UAW might have revived their grievance and presented it to the employer. Nor did a UAW official's comment that the layoff grievance was a "dead" issue establish futility where union hostility did not permeate every step of the internal appeals process. Finally, rejecting the plaintiffs' argument that they were unaware of the right to appeal, the court placed the responsibility to learn about the remedies available squarely on the workers. The court stated that a union member "must make himself aware of the remedies that are available to him even when he has been told by a union officer that nothing more can be done." Does this narrow reading of the exceptions created by *Clayton* and *Glover* seem warranted?

2. *The Right to Strike and § 301 Claims* — The contract in *Groves v. Ring Screw Works, Ferndale Fastener Div.*, 498 U.S. 168 (1990), contained a grievance procedure that did not culminate in binding arbitration. If a grievance was not mutually resolved, the union retained the right to strike. Several workers were discharged, and they exhausted the available grievance procedures without success. They then commenced a § 301 breach of contract action against their employer. A unanimous Supreme Court held that they could prosecute their § 301 suit against the employer. The Court refused to find that the contract provision preserving the union's right to resort to economic weapons divested the courts of jurisdiction to hear unresolved contract claims.

B. Unfair Representation as an Unfair Labor Practice

Teamsters (Ind.) Local 553 (Miranda Fuel Co., Inc.), 140 N.L.R.B. 181 (1962). During a fuel company's slack season, from April 15 to October 15, employees subject to unsteady employment were entitled under a collective bargaining agreement to a leave of absence without loss of seniority. One employee, Lopuch, obtained the employer's permission to leave at the end of work on April 12, a Friday. Lopuch became ill in mid-October and did not return until October 30. He had a doctor's certificate, however, and the company excused the late return. At the urging of other employees, the union demanded that Lopuch be reduced from the middle to the bottom of the seniority list for violating the contract by his lateness. When the union learned about the excused illness, it changed its claim and relied instead on Lopuch's early departure. The employer reluctantly acquiesced in the seniority reduction even though the contract did not call for it. The Board held (3–2) that the demotion was due to "irrelevant, unfair or invidious reasons," and that it violated the union's duty of fair representation under § 9(a) of the NLRA. Moreover, although Lopuch was a union member himself, the Board majority found that the union had violated § 8(b)(1)(A) and (b)(2). It reasoned that the union's duty to represent all employees fairly and impartially under § 9(a) is incorporated into employees' § 7 rights "to bargain collectively through representatives of their own choosing." Unfair representation, whether or not influenced by an employee's union activities, violates § 8(b)(1)(A), and attempts to secure employer participation violates § 8(b)(2). Employer complicity is in turn violative of § 8(a)(3) and (a)(1).

Notes

1. *Aftermath* — The Second Circuit refused to enforce the Board's ruling in *NLRB v. Miranda Fuel Co.*, 326 F.2d 172 (2d Cir. 1963). Judge Medina agreed with the Board's dissenting members that "discrimination for reasons wholly unrelated to 'union membership, loyalty . . . or the performance of union obligations' is not sufficient to support findings of violations of [§ 8] of the Act." Judge Lumbard concurred, finding insufficient evidence of any breach of the union's duty of fair representation, and thus he did not have to consider its status as a possible § 8(b)(1) violation. Judge

Friendly dissented, but also avoided the unfair representation issue. He read "discrimination" broadly as any distinction made without a proper basis, and argued that any demonstration of union power causing an employer to discriminate was sufficient "encouragement of union membership" to be grounds for finding violations of § 8(b)(2) and (a)(3).

Despite the rebuff by the Second Circuit in *Miranda*, the NLRB has persisted in treating unfair representation as an unfair labor practice, and other courts have proved more receptive to its view. In a racial discrimination case, the Fifth Circuit upheld the Board's theory that union unfair representation is a violation of § 8(b)(1)(A) of the NLRA, but did not pass on the Board's contention that it is also a violation of § 8(b)(2) and (b)(3). *United Rubber, Cork, Linoleum & Plastic Workers Local 12 v. NLRB*, 368 F.2d 12 (5th Cir. 1966), *cert. denied*, 389 U.S. 837 (1967). *Accord NLRB v. Glass Bottle Blowers Ass'n*, 520 F.2d 693 (6th Cir. 1975) (sexually segregated locals); *Truck Drivers & Helpers, Teamsters Local 568 v. NLRB*, 379 F.2d 137 (D.C. Cir. 1967) (involving a nonracial situation). Although the Supreme Court has never squarely ruled on the question, its tacit acceptance of the Labor Board's unfair representation doctrine in *Vaca v. Sipes*, *supra*, has tended to still further debate.

2. *The Board's Role in Oversight of the Labor Contract*—Does the Board's view of unfair representation as an unfair labor practice create tension with its general hands-off approach to the substance of collective bargaining? In *Independent Metal Workers, Locals 1 & 2 (Hughes Tool Co.)*, 147 N.L.R.B. 1573 (1964), the NLRB held that a union's outright rejection of an employee's grievance for racial reasons violated § 8(b)(1)(A), (b)(2), and (b)(3), and that the joint certification issued to a white local and a black local should be rescinded because they had entered into racially discriminatory contracts. Chairman McCulloch and Member Fanning, who had dissented in *Miranda*, concurred in the rescission of the certification and in the finding of a § 8(b)(1)(A) violation, the latter on the narrow ground that the black employee had been discriminated against because he was not a member of the white local. In rejecting once again the concept of unfair representation as an unfair labor practice, McCulloch and Fanning elaborated on the rationale for their *Miranda* dissent:

> The purpose of the Act is primarily to protect the organizational rights of employees. But apart from the obligation to bargain in good faith, "Congress intended that the parties would have wide latitude in their negotiations, unrestricted by any governmental power to regulate the substantive solution of their differences." Before *Miranda*, it was assumed that contract or grievance decisions by employers and unions were immune from examination by the Board unless they were influenced by union considerations. But, under the underlying reasoning of the *Miranda* majority and that of the present decision, the Board is now constituted a tribunal to which every employee who feels aggrieved by a bargaining representative's action, whether in contract negotiations or in grievance handling, may appeal, regardless of whether the decision has been influenced in whole or in part

by considerations of union membership, loyalty, or activity. The Board must determine on such appeal, without statutory standards, whether the representative's decision was motivated by "unfair or irrelevant or invidious" considerations and therefore to be set aside, or was within the "wide range of reasonableness . . . allowed a statutory representative in serving the unit it represents . . ." and to be sustained. Inevitably, the Board will have to sit in judgment on the substantive matters of collective bargaining, the very thing the Supreme Court has said the Board must not do, and in which it has no special experience or competence.

Id. at 1588–91.

3. *Race Discrimination as an Employer Unfair Labor Practice* — In an unprecedented decision, a court of appeals held that racial discrimination by an employer acting on its own violates § 8(a)(1) where it has the effect of "producing a docility in its victims which inhibits the exercise of their § 7 rights." *United Packinghouse, Food & Allied Workers International Union v. NLRB*, 416 F.2d 1126 (D.C. Cir.), *cert. denied*, 396 U.S. 903 (1969). For the case on remand, see *Farmers' Cooperative Compress*, 194 N.L.R.B. 85 (1971).

4. *Sex Discrimination as an Unfair Labor Practice* — Sex discrimination by a union is also unfair representation in violation of § 8(b)(1)(A) and (b)(2), and a participating employer violates § 8(a)(3) and (a)(1). *Pacific Maritime Ass'n (Longshoremen & Warehousemen, Local 52)*, 209 N.L.R.B. 519 (1974). But an employer's unilateral sex discrimination is not an unfair labor practice. *Jubilee Mfg. Co.*, 202 N.L.R.B. 272 (1973), *aff'd*, 504 F.2d 271 (D.C. Cir. 1974).

5. *Other Situations* — For Board findings of union unfair representation in situations not involving race or sex discrimination, see UFCW Local 540, 366 N.L.R.B. No. 105 (2018) (union committed unfair labor practice when it told a bargaining unit member that it would not file a grievance on his behalf because he was not a union member); *Teamsters Local 727*, 360 N.L.R.B. 65 (2013) (where business merged two different facilities and union demanded that seniority lists from the two locations be end-tailed, instead of dove-tailed, effect was to place workers at the facility previously represented by the union for many years ahead of the individuals from the other facility that had been represented by the local union for a much shorter time, causing employees from the disfavored location to be laid off ahead of those from the favored location; Board ruled that a discriminatory system based solely upon the time the workers had been represented by the local union breached the duty of fair representation and violated § 8(b)(1)(A) and (b)(2)); *Roadway Express, Inc.*, 355 N.L.R.B. 197 (2010) (union breached duty of fair representation under § 8(b)(1)(A) where business agent who represented grievant in arbitration proceeding deliberately misled the arbitration panel and virtually ensured that the grievance would be denied; grievant and business agent were long-time political rivals within the union), *enforced*, 2011 U.S. App. LEXIS 10832 (11th Cir. May 27, 2011); *but cf. Nat'l Ass'n of Letter Carriers*, 347 N.L.R.B. 289 (2006) (no violation of union's duty of fair representation where union relied in good faith upon advice of legal counsel in distributing proceeds from class action pay grievance settlement unequally between retirees and current employees).

6. *Exclusive Hiring Halls* — When a labor organization operates an exclusive hiring hall, does it breach the fair representation duty owed to all members if it negligently refers lower-priority candidates to job opportunities ahead of a higher priority candidate? In *Steamfitters Local 342*, 329 N.L.R.B. 688 (1999), the Labor Board initially said "no," noting that mere negligence with respect to the representation of bargaining unit personnel does not normally constitute a fair representation breach. Some evidence of personal hostility or arbitrary or capricious conduct is required. On appeal, however, the D.C. Circuit concluded that unions operating exclusive hiring halls owe a higher duty of care to members than is owed during the traditional representation function. The court remanded the case, instructing the Board to reevaluate the union's conduct based on the heightened duty standard. *Jacoby v. NLRB*, 233 F.3d 611 (D.C. Cir. 2000) (*Jacoby I*).

On remand, the Board concluded that even under the heightened duty standard, simple negligence is insufficient to support a duty of fair representation claim; deliberate wrongdoing is required. The Board reaffirmed its previous conclusion that the union's error in referring lower-priority workers ahead of a higher-priority worker because of an inadvertent clerical mistake did not breach the duty of fair representation. *Steamfitters Local 342*, 336 N.L.R.B. 549 (2001). The Board reasoned that inadvertent errors do not signal the union's power to affect the livelihoods of hiring hall users in the same way that deliberate conduct does, and thus do not enhance the union's power to recruit applicants to membership through coercion. Moreover, as a matter of public policy it is vital that the standard not require perfect operation of hiring halls lest unions be discouraged from performing a valuable service for employers and employees. A union must, however, provide access to the job referral lists so that individuals may determine whether or not their referral rights are being protected. *Operating Eng'rs Local 627*, 361 N.L.R.B. 908 (2014), *enforced*, 635 Fed. App'x 480 (10th Cir. 2015). The D.C. Circuit upheld the Board's ruling in *Steamfitters Local 342*, deferring to its interpretation of the duty of fair representation standard as "eminently reasonable." *Jacoby v. NLRB*, 325 F.3d 301 (D.C. Cir. 2003) (*Jacoby II*).

7. *Nonexclusive Hiring Halls* — A union operating a nonexclusive hiring hall owes no duty of fair representation, since in such an arrangement workers can also apply directly to employers. In the absence of exclusive bargaining representative status, there is no justification for imposing a duty of fair representation. Nor is there any obligation on the union in this context to furnish information regarding worker referrals to union members who request it, unless there exists evidence of union retaliation against the charging party on the basis of §7 protected activity. *Local 370, United Bhd. of Carpenters & Joiners*, 332 N.L.R.B. 174 (2000).

In *Lydon v. Electrical Workers IBEW Local 103*, 770 F.3d 48 (1st Cir. 2014), the IBEW adopted a preferred referral system that required local unions to run exclusive hiring halls. A local union chose not to follow that system and turned its exclusive, seniority-based referral hiring hall into a nonexclusive hiring hall that allowed members to solicit work directly from local employers, disadvantaging some union members. The court found no breach of the duty of fair representation, citing the wide range of reasonableness the union enjoys in striking a balance between competing interests. Because the local's new solicitation system was open to every member and members could choose whether or not to use it, there was no discrimination. Nor was the decision to adopt the system arbitrary or irrational.

8. *Remedies*—In *Iron Workers Local 377,* 326 N.L.R.B. 375 (1998), the Board ruled that an employee is entitled to make-whole monetary relief from a union for breach of its duty of fair representation only if the Board General Counsel proves that the grievance was meritorious. Further, a union that fails to pursue such a grievance is liable only for the increase in damages caused by its breach, and not the damages caused by the employer's violation of the labor contract. The Board abandoned its previous approach in *United Rubber Workers, Local 250,* 290 N.L.R.B. 817 (1988)—allowing a make-whole remedy if the General Counsel showed that the employee's grievance was not "clearly frivolous"—because it risked "imposing essentially punitive liability on the union and granting a windfall to the grievant." Such an allocation of evidentiary burdens, the Board concluded, conflicted with "the essentially remedial character of the Act."

When a union fails to represent an employee fairly in grievance handling, it may be required to pay for outside legal counsel to process the case through arbitration. *See Nat'l Ass'n of Letter Carriers, AFL-CIO, Branch 3126 v. NLRB*, 281 F.3d 235 (D.C. Cir. 2002) (where union stewards prevented an employee who was not a union member from filing a nonfrivolous grievance about missed overtime opportunities, the D.C. Circuit enforced the Board's order finding a § 8(b)(1)(A) violation and requiring the union to allow the employee to proceed with his grievance and to pay his attorneys' fees; Board was within its discretion in concluding that the union stewards' mistreatment of a nonmember rendered independent counsel necessary).

Problem

43. An electrical workers' union operates an exclusive hiring hall for journeyman and apprentice electricians. Under the collective bargaining agreement, electricians register themselves on the union's "books," where they are placed in order based on their seniority. The cardinal rule of the hiring hall is first in, first out: a referral must be offered first to the highest-listed registrant present in the hall. The only exception to the rule is for jobs requiring special skills, when the referral must be offered to the highest-listed applicant who possesses the skill requested by the contractor.

The union maintains a "salting" program that sends union members to nonunion contractors in order to organize their employees. As part of that program, the union departs from the rules governing its hiring hall and gives salts preferential treatment—it effectively moves them to the top of the list—when one of their targeted contractors requests an electrician. Does this preferential treatment of salts breach the union's duty of fair representation?

Section III. Union Representation and Antidiscrimination Law

Beginning in the 1960s, Congress enacted a series of statutes prohibiting discrimination in employment. Protection was first extended to employees who suffered discrimination on the basis of race, color, religion, sex, or national origin. *See* Title VII of the Civil Rights Act of 1964, 42 U.S.C. § 2000 *et seq* (Title VII). Subsequently, Congress enacted separate statutes affording employees protection against age discrimination, *see* Age Discrimination in Employment Act, 29 U.S.C. §§ 621–634 (1967) (ADEA), and disability discrimination, *see* Rehabilitation Act of 1973, 29 U.S.C. §§ 701–796 (Rehabilitation Act), and The Americans with Disabilities Act of 1990, 42 U.S.C. §§ 12101–12213 (ADA). Issues surrounding the tension between collective and individual rights find their sharpest focus in cases where claims under antidiscrimination statutes clash with labor law policy. Accordingly, we treat them briefly here.

A. An Overview of Title VII

Title VII of the Civil Rights Act of 1964 is the centerpiece of federal antidiscrimination law. It prohibits discrimination on the basis of "race, color, religion, sex, or national origin" by employers, labor organizations, and employment agencies. It is an unlawful employment practice for an employer to "fail or refuse to hire or to discharge any individual, or otherwise to discriminate against any individual with respect to . . . compensation, terms, conditions, or privileges of employment," or "to limit, segregate, or classify . . . employees or applicants for employment in any way which would deprive or tend to deprive any individual of employment opportunities or otherwise adversely affect [his/her] status as an employee, because of the individual's race, color, religion, sex, or national origin." (§ 703(a).) It is an unlawful employment practice for a labor organization to "exclude or to expel from its membership, or otherwise to discriminate against, any individual," "limit, segregate or classify its membership or applicants for membership, or to classify or fail or refuse to refer for employment any individual, in any way which would deprive or tend to deprive any individual of employment opportunities, or . . . limit such employment opportunities or otherwise adversely affect [his/her] status as an employee or an applicant," or "to cause or attempt to cause an employer to discriminate against an individual . . . because of an individual's race, color, religion, sex, or national origin." (§ 703(c).) Title VII was amended significantly by the Civil Rights Act of 1991, Pub. L. No. 102-66, 105 Stat. 1071, primarily on the issues of remedies available and methods/burdens of proof. In 2015, President Obama amended Executive Order 11246 to add sexual orientation and gender identity to the antidiscrimination rules applicable to federal contractors. In 2020, the Supreme Court ruled in *Bostock v. Clayton County*, 140 S. Ct. 1731 (2020), that Title VII's prohibition on sex discrimination includes discrimination on the basis of sexual orientation or transgender status.

Title VII's "because of sex" language also encompasses sexual harassment, whether by a member of the same sex or the opposite sex as the victim, where members of one sex are exposed to disadvantageous terms of conditions of employment to which members of the other sex are not exposed, resulting in a hostile or abusive work environment. *Meritor Sav. Bank, FSB v. Vinson*, 477 U.S. 57 (1986); *Oncale v. Sundowner Offshore Servs.*, 523 U.S. 75 (1998). To ground a claim of hostile work environment sexual harassment, the conduct: (1) must be "severe or pervasive enough to create an objectively hostile or abusive work environment—an environment that a reasonable person would find hostile or abusive"; and (2) must "actually alter . . . the conditions of the victim's employment" in that the victim "subjectively perceive[s] the environment to be abusive." It is not necessary, however, that the conduct "seriously affect employees' psychological well-being." The determination depends on all the circumstances, including the frequency and severity of the conduct, whether it is physically threatening or humiliating or is merely an offensive utterance, and whether it interferes unreasonably with an employee's work performance. *Harris v. Forklift Sys.*, 510 U.S. 17 (1993). Title VII also prohibits workplace harassment on the basis of race, color, national origin, and religion.

B. The Age Discrimination in Employment Act (ADEA)

The ADEA was enacted in 1967, and prohibits discrimination in employment on the basis of age. The heart of the prohibition against discrimination is contained in § 4(a), and it is parallel to the Title VII prohibition except for the substitution of the word "age" as the prohibited basis of discrimination. The covered class of employees protected under this statute is limited to those who are 40 years of age or older (§ 12(a)). There is no action for reverse age discrimination against the young (unlike the reverse sex and race discrimination claims available under Title VII). Thus, employer policies (including collectively bargained two-tiered arrangements or benefits to future retirees which extend only to those over age 50) do not violate the Act. *Gen. Dynamics Land Sys. v. Cline*, 540 U.S. 581 (2004). However, if a person in the protected class is replaced with another person in the same class (e.g., 56-year-old replaced by 40-year-old) an action will lie, at least if the replacement is "substantially younger" and the plaintiff can demonstrate that the reason for his loss of employment is because of his age. *O'Connor v. Consolidated Coin Caterers Corp.*, 517 U.S. 308 (1996). In addition, the Older Workers Benefit Protection Act, Pub. L. No. 101-433, 104 Stat. 978 (1990), prohibits age discrimination with respect to employee benefit plans.

C. The Americans with Disabilities Act (ADA)

The Americans with Disabilities Act of 1990, 42 U.S.C. § 12101 *et seq.*, prohibits discrimination in employment against qualified individuals because of their physical or mental disabilities. Employers are obliged to make reasonable accommodations for disabilities when that can be accomplished without undue hardship to the operation of the business. The ADA mirrors the Rehabilitation Act of 1973, which applies to federal departments, agencies, and other executive instrumentalities. The ADA expands the antidiscrimination concept expressed in the Rehabilitation Act into the private sector. The ADA also applies to labor unions, state and local government employers, and the U.S. Congress. Federal employees remain covered by the Rehabilitation Act.

The ADA prohibits discrimination in employment (job application procedures, hiring, advancement, discharge, compensation, job training, and other terms, conditions, and privileges of employment) against a "qualified individual" with a "disability," because of the disability (§ 102(a)). Discrimination is defined to include "not making reasonable accommodations to the known physical or mental limitations of an otherwise qualified individual with a disability," unless "the accommodation would impose an undue hardship on the operation of the business." (§ 102(b)(5)(A).) Both intentional and unintentional discrimination are prohibited. *See Alexander v. Choate*, 469 U.S. 287 (1985). In 2008, the Act was amended to clarify and broaden the definition of a qualified individual with a disability covered by the Act, making it easier for claimants to demonstrate either that their conditions severely limit a major life activity, or that they are regarded as disabled. *See* ADA Amendments Act of 2008, Pub. L. No. 110-325, 122 Stat. 3553.

D. Areas of Tension between Labor Law and Antidiscrimination Law

1. Sexual and Racial Harassment by Coworkers

The tension between majority rights protected under the labor laws and individual rights against discrimination conferred by antidiscrimination laws has often arisen in the context of race and sex discrimination that is either furthered by union practice or perpetrated by union members, albeit with the tolerance of the employer.

Most courts have ruled that Title VII does not obligate unions to adopt an aggressive stance toward eradicating workplace discrimination. Courts reason that absent some affirmative act of discrimination by a union, employers, not unions, are liable for discrimination occurring in the workplace, either recognizing the potential role strain for unions or unions' lack of control over the workplace and the workforce. Accordingly, passive acquiescence in workplace discrimination, including harassment, will not ground union liability unless the union has responsibility for the particular workplace conditions affected and is aware of the situation. *See Buford v. Laborers' Int'l Union Local 269,* 787 Fed. App'x 341 (7th Cir. 2019) (union not liable for member's use of racial slur toward coworker because there was no evidence that union leaders knew of or condoned the slur); *EEOC v. Pipefitters Ass'n Local Union 597,* 334 F.3d 656 (7th Cir. 2003) (union not liable for failing to prevent display of graffiti in the workplace; unions that "merely fail . . . to effectuate change in the workplace" are not liable under Title VII); *Thorn v. Amalgamated Transit Union,* 305 F.3d 826 (8th Cir. 2002) (no union liability under Title VII for passive acquiescence in sexual harassment by coworkers and supervisors; imposing an affirmative duty on unions would place them in an untenable position when one member accuses another member of causing the employer to discriminate, since union has duty to fairly represent both workers in disciplinary proceedings). *But cf. Maalik v. Int'l Union of Elevator Constructors, Local 2*, 437 F.3d 650 (7th Cir. 2006) (union liable for discrimination in the administration of training and apprenticeship program where union "made a conscious decision to do nothing" to address mechanics' refusal to provide on-the-job training to African American woman; union was responsible for operation of training and apprenticeship programs and consciously chose not to utilize intra-union remedies such as fines, suspension, or expulsion at its disposal); *Dowd v. United Steelworkers of Am., Local No. 286*, 253 F.3d 1093 (8th Cir. 2001) (union liable for racial epithets and threats of violence by union leader and union members on the picket line during a union-sponsored strike). Nor are unions responsible for the discriminatory acts of their members; thus, most courts state that unions have no duty to take remedial action absent proof that the union, as an organization, instigated or actively supported the discriminatory acts. *See, e.g., Eliserio v. USW, Local 310*, 398 F.3d 1071 (8th Cir. 2005).

On the other hand, active ratification of harassment, discriminatory refusals to investigate or press grievances, or discrimination against women or minorities in membership policies generally does violate Title VII. *See Goodman v. Lukens Steel Co.*, 482 U.S. 656 (1987) (union refusal to grieve race discrimination complaints by African American members violated Title VII); *Beck v. UFCW, Local 99*, 506 F.3d 874 (9th Cir. 2007) (finding union liability under Title VII and for breach of duty of fair representation where union provided more aggressive representation for men than for women in contract enforcement, and failed to file a grievance on behalf of female plaintiff); *Eliserio v. USW, Local 310*, 398 F.3d 1071 (8th Cir. 2005) (union liable for harassment where it supported graffiti campaign involving ethnic slurs); *Woods v. Graphic Communications*, 925 F.2d 1195 (9th Cir. 1991) (union may be liable for acquiescing in a racially discriminatory work environment through deliberate choice not to process grievances); *Greenier v. Pace, Local No. 1188*, 201 F. Supp. 2d 172 (D. Me. 2002) (worker may proceed on ADA claim against union based on the union's "deliberate acquiescence" with the potentially illegal actions of the employer, where union took no action to enforce arbitration decision in employee's favor on harassment and termination claim, joked about his disability with human resources officials, and failed to advance his interest during a second arbitration following his subsequent termination). Some courts require proof that the union breached its duty to fairly represent employees and that its actions were motivated by discriminatory animus as a necessary element of proving a Title VII claim against a union. *See, e.g., McIntyre v. Longwood Cent. Sch. Dist.*, 2010 U.S. App. LEXIS 11393 (2d Cir. June 4, 2010).

In addition, unions have an affirmative duty to take corrective steps to prevent the perpetuation of past discrimination by pressing at the bargaining table for an end to institutionalized discriminatory practices, at least where they stem from prior negotiations in collective bargaining. Thus, unions that fail to challenge discriminatory seniority systems or testing schemes face potential Title VII liability. *Howard v. Int'l Molders & Allied Workers Union, etc., Local No. 100*, 779 F.3d 1546 (11th Cir.), *cert. denied*, 476 U.S. 1174 (1986). Although it may be easier for an employee to establish a discrimination claim against her union under the civil rights laws where she can also show that the union has breached its duty of fair representation, it is not always essential. The Sixth, Seventh, and Ninth Circuits permit employees to proceed directly against their unions in cases under Title VII or the ADA even if they are unable to establish a breach of the duty of fair representation. *See Peeples v. City of Detroit*, 891 F.3d 622 (6th Cir. 2018) (Title VII); *Garity v. APWU Nat'l Labor Org.*, 828 F.3d 848 (9th Cir. 2016) (ADA claim); *Green v. Am. Fed'n of Teachers/Ill. Fed. of Teachers Local 604*, 740 F.3d 1104 (7th Cir. 2014) (Title VII).

What role should the union play in cases involving hostile work environment racial or sexual harassment perpetrated by union members against their peers? Traditionally, unions have conceptualized themselves as defenders of employees' class interests and focused their efforts on defending job security of members who have been disciplined or terminated by the employer because they have violated work rules. Thus, unions have been most visible as the defenders of accused harassers in the grievance process. *See, e.g., Ellison v. Brady*, 924 F.2d 872 (9th Cir. 1991) (union represented harasser in grievance against company for involuntary transfer following sexual harassment complaints by female coworker). Indeed, failure to pursue grievances on behalf of workers disciplined or discharged by the employer will expose the union to a claim for breach of the duty of fair representation — or at least, require it to incur costs to defend against such a claim. *Cf. Mulvihill v. Top-Flite Golf Co.*, 335 F.3d 15 (1st Cir. 2003) (finding no union liability on hybrid § 301/breach of duty of fair representation claim where evidence against alleged sexual harasser was so convincing that union was justified in not pursuing arbitration on his behalf).

Unfortunately, this reactive approach neglects the job security of the victims of harassment, who may suffer a constructive discharge or manifest other problems in response to the harassment (such as absenteeism, illness, or inefficiency at work) that affect job performance and ultimately result in discharge for cause. *See* Crain, *Women, Labor Unions, and Hostile Work Environment Sexual Harassment: The Untold Story*, 4 Tex. J. Women & L. 9 (1995). Alternatively, unions that fail to take a proactive role in mediating between members' interests may find themselves dealing with court-ordered programs designed to remedy the effects of discrimination and harassment that in turn impact members' job security. *See Robinson v. Jacksonville Shipyards, Inc.*, 760 F. Supp. 1486 (M.D. Fla. 1991) (woman employee challenging hostile work environment was represented by the National Organization for Women's Legal Defense Fund, while the union defended the right of its male members to have pornography in the workplace, telling management that it would grieve any rule barring such pornography from the shipyards on the grounds that such a rule would burden its male members' rights to free expression; court ordered employer to implement a sexual harassment policy drafted by NOWLDF). How should the union resolve these dilemmas? *See generally* Crain & Matheny, *"Labor's Divided Ranks": Privilege and the United Front Ideology*, 84 CORNELL L. REV. 1542 (1999); Crain, *Women, Labor Unions, and Hostile Work Environment Sexual Harassment: The Untold Story*, 4 TEX. J. WOMEN & L. 9 (1995); Hodges, *Strategies for Combating Sexual Harassment: The Role of Labor Unions*, 15 TEX. J. WOMEN & L. 183 (2006); O'Melveny, *Negotiating the Minefields: Selected Issues for Labor Unions Addressing Sexual Harassment Complaints by Represented Employees*, 15 LAB. LAW. 321 (2000).

Suppose a union has obtained procedural protections in the collective bargaining agreement pertaining to employer disciplinary action. May employers raise such provisions as defenses in harassment cases? *EEOC v. Ind. Bell Tel. Co.*, 256 F.3d 516 (7th Cir. 2001) (*en banc*), concerned the propriety of a $635,000 jury verdict against the company on sexual harassment claims brought by 18 female employees who claimed victimization by a "serial harasser" coworker over a 20-year period. The Seventh Circuit found that although the EEOC had produced sufficient evidence to support the verdict and compensatory damage award, the trial court had committed reversible error with respect to the punitive damage portion of the award by excluding evidence of bargaining agreement provisions that imposed time limitations on the employer, preventing it from firing the harasser sooner. According to the court, the company's obligations under Title VII and under its collective contract must both be presented to the jury, so that the reasonableness of its response to the allegations of sexual harassment could be assessed to determine whether the company's actions had evidenced malice or a reckless indifference to the plaintiff's rights.

2. Individual Requests for Accommodation Under the ADA

Another vexing problem stemming from the tension between majority rights protected under a collective bargaining agreement and individual minority rights protected by employment discrimination statutes has arisen in the context of individual employee requests for employer accommodation under the Americans with Disabilities Act. The question in these cases is whether seniority rights guaranteed under the collective bargaining agreement trump statutorily created individual rights. A majority of the courts that have confronted this issue have concluded that an accommodation that violates a collective bargaining agreement is per se unreasonable. In *Eckles v. CONRAIL*, 94 F.3d 1041 (7th Cir. 1996), *cert. denied*, 520 U.S. 1146 (1997), the Seventh Circuit confronted the potential conflict between the ADA and the operation of collectively bargained seniority systems under the RLA. The employee had requested accommodations to his epilepsy under the ADA (a transfer and a preference in scheduling that would have entailed bumping a senior employee from the desired job) that infringed on the seniority rights of the other employees guaranteed in the collective bargaining agreement between the employer and the union. Relying on cases decided under the Rehabilitation Act of 1973 (on which the ADA was modeled), and case law dealing with the requirement of reasonable accommodation to employee religion under Title VII, the court concluded that the ADA does not require disabled employees to be accommodated by sacrificing the collectively bargained seniority rights of other employees; such seniority rights have "preexisting special status in the law." *Accord Willis v. Pac. Mar. Ass'n*, 244 F.3d 675 (9th Cir. 2001); *Boersig v. Union Elec. Co.*, 219 F.3d 816 (8th Cir. 2000), *cert. denied*, 531 U.S. 1113 (2001); *Davis v. Florida Power & Light Co.*, 205 F.3d 1301 (11th Cir.), *cert. denied*, 531 U.S. 927 (2000); *Benson v. Northwest Airlines*, 62 F.3d 1108 (8th Cir. 1995). *See also Daugherty v. City of El Paso*, 56 F.3d 695 (5th Cir. 1995), *cert. denied*, 516 U.S. 1172 (1996); *Milton v. Scrivner, Inc.*, 53 F.3d 1118 (10th Cir. 1995) (refusing to uphold individual employee requests for accommodations under the ADA where collectively bargained seniority rights would be sacrificed, but stopping short of adopting a per se rule). *But cf. Aka v. Washington Hosp. Ctr.*, 116 F.3d 876 (D.C. Cir.) (ruling that majority rights do not automatically trump the interests of the disabled; instead, the court must make an individual determination "in light of the specific nature of the requested determinations in each case, including — but not limited to — the degree to which the accommodation might disrupt the workforce by upsetting settled expectations under the collective bargaining agreement, or by undermining the operational structure instituted by the agreement"), *vacated and reh'g en banc granted*, 124 F.3d 1302 (1997), *op. reinstated in part on reh'g*, 156 F.3d 1284 (1998) (declining to rule on whether a per se or a balancing approach is more appropriate, and remanding for a determination whether the proposed accommodation actually conflicted with the seniority system).

Interesting developments have occurred in the nonunion context that may affect the tension between rights created under collective bargaining agreements and those conferred by the ADA. In *US Airways, Inc. v. Barnett*, 535 U.S. 391 (2002), the Court adopted a middle ground approach in a context where the employee's ADA accommodation rights conflict was unilaterally created by the employer rather than being a product of union-employer negotiations codified in a labor contract. The Court rejected the employer's argument that a proposed accommodation that conflicted with an employer-established seniority system was per se unreasonable, and also rejected the argument that the accommodation's conflict with seniority rules constituted an undue hardship. Instead, it held that employers are entitled to a rebuttable presumption that the accommodation is unreasonable where it conflicts with the employer's established seniority system. Justice Breyer, writing for the majority, suggested that although the seniority system will prevail "in the run of cases," the employee may rebut the presumption by showing special circumstances: for example, that the employer changes the system fairly frequently, or that the system already contemplates a number of exceptions.

Relatedly, one court has held that the EEOC may enforce a subpoena to obtain staffing information from employers with labor contracts, in order to determine whether a reasonable accommodation under the ADA was available. In *EEOC v. Dillon Cos.*, 310 F.3d 1271 (10th Cir. 2002), the court ruled that the employer's statement that there were no positions available due to the seniority system established in the collective bargaining agreement was insufficient to block the EEOC's investigation on an employee's ADA claim. Although the court acknowledged that the employer might rely upon its collectively bargained seniority system as a defense, it could not raise it as an affirmative bar to an investigation. The court cited *U.S. Airways v. Barnett* in support of its refusal to accept the per se position advanced by the employer.

Problem

44. For decades, an industrial valve manufacturer had used a mechanical comprehension test as a condition for promotion within the firm. Ten years ago, black employees started complaining to both the firm and the union that they thought the test screened out disproportionate numbers of black employees and that it tested skills unrelated to their actual work. The union, however, did not raise the issue in its last several rounds of contract negotiations, and, pursuant to its obligations under the series of resulting contracts, the company continued using the test.

A few years ago, several of the black employees, fed up with the inaction, sued both the employer and the union under Title VII of the Civil Rights Act. The court will be ruling against the employer, finding that the test had disparate impact on the basis of race and could not be justified as job related and consistent with business necessity. How should the court rule on the union's liability under Title VII?

E. Union Waiver of Individual Statutory Forum Rights

As unions have undertaken representation of increasingly diverse workforces and to negotiate contractual protections tailored to their concerns about discrimination, a new wrinkle has emerged: under what conditions might a union be deemed to have waived its members' rights to proceed individually in court on statute-based discrimination claims? The Court has addressed this question in a line of cases.

Alexander v. Gardner-Denver Co., 415 U.S. 36, 94 S. Ct. 1011, 39 L. Ed. 2d 147 (1974). A black employee who had been discharged for allegedly poor work performance processed a claim through the contractual grievance-arbitration procedures. At the arbitration hearing, he testified that the employer's action was racially motivated in violation of the bargaining agreement's antidiscrimination provision and informed the arbitrator that he had filed a charge with the Colorado Civil Rights Commission (which in turn referred the complaint to the EEOC) because he "could not rely on the union." The arbitrator ruled that the employee had been terminated for "just cause." He did not specifically address the grievant's discrimination claim. Following his exhaustion of EEOC procedures, the discharged worker commenced a Title VII action in federal district court. Although the employer asserted that the previous arbitral decision should preclude judicial consideration of the plaintiff's Title VII suit, based upon collateral estoppel, res judicata, election of remedies, and waiver theories, the Supreme Court rejected these contentions.

The Court reasoned that Title VII evinced a legislative intent to authorize parallel and overlapping remedies for discrimination in employment. The Court explained that two independent sources of rights existed, even if they arose out of the same factual setting. Grievance arbitration under a collective bargaining agreement seeks to vindicate contractual rights, while lawsuits under federal antidiscrimination statutes assert independent statutory rights. The Court concluded:

> We are . . . unable to accept the proposition that petitioner waived his cause of action under Title VII [by proceeding in arbitration]. To begin, we think it clear that there can be no prospective waiver of an employee's rights under Title VII. It is true, of course, that a union may waive certain statutory rights related to collective activity, such as the right to strike. . . . These rights are conferred on employees collectively to foster the processes of bargaining and properly may be exercised or relinquished by the union as collective-bargaining agent to obtain economic benefits for union members. Title VII, on the other hand, stands on plainly different ground; it concerns not majoritarian processes, but an individual's right to equal employment opportunities. Title VII's strictures are absolute and represent a congressional command that each employee be free from discriminatory practices. Of necessity, the rights conferred can form no part of the collective-bargaining process since waiver of these rights would defeat the paramount congressional purpose behind Title VII.

Id. at 51–52. In addition, the Court observed, the role of the arbitrator in grievance resolution under a collective bargaining agreement is completely different from that of a court enforcing statutory rights. The arbitrator — often himself not a lawyer — derives his authority solely from the labor contract, and sits as the proctor of the parties' bargain, seeking to effectuate their intent. He has no authority to invoke public laws that might conflict with the contract's provisions: indeed, if he grounds his award on what he believes is required by statute, his award can be set aside on the grounds that he has exceeded the scope of his authority. *Id.* at 53–54.

The Court also rejected the employer's argument that federal courts should defer to arbitral decisions on discrimination claims where the collective bargaining agreement contains an antidiscrimination clause tracking the language of the statutory right. The Court explained:

> Arbitral procedures, while well suited to the resolution of contractual disputes, make arbitration a comparatively inappropriate forum for the final resolution of rights created by Title VII. This conclusion rests first on the special role of the arbitrator, whose task is to effectuate the intent of the parties rather than the requirements of enacted legislation. . . .
>
> Moreover, the fact-finding process in arbitration usually is not equivalent to judicial fact-finding. The record of the arbitration proceedings is not as complete; the usual rules of evidence do not apply; and rights and procedures common to civil trials, such as discovery, compulsory process, cross-examination, and testimony under oath, are often severely limited or unavailable. And as this Court has recognized, "arbitrators have no obligation to the court to give their reasons for an award." *United Steelworkers*

of America v. Enterprise Wheel & Car Corp., 363 U.S., at 598. Indeed, it is the informality of arbitral procedure that enables it to function as an efficient, inexpensive, and expeditious means for dispute resolution. This same characteristic, however, makes arbitration a less appropriate forum for final resolution of Title VII issues than the federal courts.

Id. at 56–58. The Court added in a footnote an additional argument against deferral stemming from the union's exclusive control over the manner and extent to which any individual grievance is processed. Because the union's role is to represent the interests of all the employees in the bargaining unit, individual interests are subordinated to collective interests and the union may make decisions that are adverse to the individual's interests. The Court took judicial notice of the fact that conflicts of interest among workers are particularly likely where a claim of race discrimination is made, alluding to the legacy of racial discrimination by some unions. The Court observed that it could be difficult for an individual employee to establish a breach of the union's duty of fair representation, and noted that Congress thought it necessary to afford Title VII protections against unions as well as against employers. Id. at 58 n.19.

The Court concluded:

> We think, therefore, that the federal policy favoring arbitration of labor disputes and the federal policy against discriminatory employment practices can best be accommodated by permitting an employee to pursue fully both his remedy under the grievance-arbitration clause of a collective-bargaining agreement and his cause of action under Title VII. The federal court should consider the employee's claim *de novo*. The arbitral decision may be admitted as evidence and accorded such weight as the court deems appropriate.

Id. at 59–60.

Notes

1. *Aftermath* — On remand, the district court's decision that the discharge was nondiscriminatory was affirmed. *Alexander v. Gardner-Denver Co.*, 519 F.2d 503 (10th Cir. 1975), *cert. denied*, 423 U.S. 1058 (1976).

2. *Finality of Arbitrator's Factual Findings* — If an arbitrator determines that an employee has been discharged for just cause under a collective bargaining agreement, without dealing with any question of discrimination under Title VII, should a federal court in a subsequent Title VII action accord finality to the factual findings underlying the arbitration decision, while reserving to itself the statutory issue of discrimination? In *Collins v. N.Y. City Transit Auth.*, 305 F.3d 113 (2d Cir. 2002), the court found that although a negative arbitration decision rendered pursuant to a collective bargaining agreement did not bar a Title VII action by a discharged employee, the arbitration decision did constitute evidence of a lack of discriminatory motive by the employer. Thus, the employee could survive a summary judgment motion only by establishing that the decision was wrong as a matter of fact,

based either on new evidence or a showing that the arbitration tribunal was not impartial. On the other hand, in *Coleman v. Donahoe*, 667 F.3d 835 (7th Cir. 2012), the court held that an arbitrator's decision that the Postal Service lacked just cause to terminate an employee did not have preclusive effect in her subsequent Title VII claim, where the issue before the arbitrator was whether the employee posed a threat to others in the workplace, while the issue before the court was whether the employer's motive for termination was a pretext for race and sex discrimination.

Would it make any difference if the employee had presented the question of racial, religious, or sex discrimination to the arbitrator? Would it make any difference if the employee had previously challenged the arbitration award in federal court under §301 and had lost? *Compare Becton v. Detroit Terminal of Consol. Freightways*, 687 F.2d 140 (6th Cir. 1982) (plaintiff must be allowed to present the evidence that was used to challenge discharge in arbitration to support statutory claim of discrimination in court), *cert. denied*, 460 U.S. 1040 (1983), *with Aleem v. General Felt Industries, Inc.*, 661 F.2d 135 (9th Cir. 1981) (plaintiff may try Title VII claim *de novo* despite prior court decision upholding arbitrator's ruling that plaintiff was fired for cause rather than for discriminatory reasons).

An employee whose claim of discriminatory discharge has been rejected by the NLRB may still be able to litigate a charge of racial discrimination based on the same incidents under Title VII. *Tipler v. E. I. Du Pont de Nemours & Co.*, 443 F.2d 125 (6th Cir. 1971). Although there is an overlap in the application of the NLRA and the Civil Rights Act, the same issue is not necessarily presented in proceedings under the two statutes.

3. *Waiver of Other Statutory Rights* — What about other statutory individual rights claims — are they waivable by the union? In *Barrentine v. Arkansas-Best Freight System, Inc.*, 450 U.S. 728 (1981), the Court ruled (7-2) that claims by employees under the Fair Labor Standards Act for compensation for time spent in vehicle maintenance procedures mandated by the employer were not barred even though they had been previously adjudicated adversely to the plaintiffs under contractual dispute-resolution procedures. Drawing an analogy between the FLSA rights asserted here and the Title VII rights at the heart of its decision in *Gardner-Denver*, the Court stated: "In sum, the FLSA rights petitioners seek to assert in this action are independent of the collective bargaining process. They devolve on petitioners as individual workers, not as members of a collective organization. They are not waivable." *See also Bernard v. IBP, Inc.*, 154 F.3d 259 (5th Cir. 1998) (following *Barrentine* and noting the differences in the remedies available under the FLSA and arbitration).

The use of arbitration to resolve employment disputes in nonunion workplaces has become an increasingly popular practice, encouraged by the proliferation of statutes and common-law causes of action (such as wrongful discharge) protecting individual employee rights. Employers now routinely ask prospective employees to sign predispute arbitration agreements waiving their statutory forum rights and any claims they may have at common law before the courts in exchange for private arbitration. In the following case, the Court addressed the enforceability of such agreements in the nonunion context. As we shall see, the case had dramatic implications for the union context as well.

Gilmer v. Interstate/Johnson Lane Corp., 500 U.S. 20, 111 S. Ct. 1647, 114 L. Ed. 2d 26 (1991). An individual employed as a financial services manager at a brokerage firm, not covered by a collective bargaining agreement, was required by the rules of the New York Stock Exchange to arbitrate all controversies arising out of his employment. When he was discharged, he brought an action in federal court alleging a violation of the Age Discrimination in Employment Act (ADEA). The employer moved to compel arbitration. The Supreme Court held (7-2) that the predispute arbitration agreement was enforceable and that he was obliged to arbitrate his ADEA claim. The Court distinguished *Gardner-Denver* on three grounds. First, *Gardner-Denver* had involved an agreement to arbitrate contractual claims that did not extend to statutory claims; the arbitrator was authorized only to determine private rights under the collective bargaining agreement. By contrast, the Stock Exchange's arbitral rules specifically empowered arbitrators to resolve external statutory issues. Second, the *Gardner-Denver* situation had involved the grievance and arbitration machinery in a labor contract that could be enforced only by the union, not by the individual employee. A potential conflict of interest thus existed between the union's role as enforcer of majority rights under the contract and the individual employee's statutory rights. Third, the claim in *Gilmer* arose under the Federal Arbitration Act, which reflects a liberal policy favoring arbitration agreements, while the *Gardner-Denver* claim had arisen under a collective bargaining agreement.

Notes

1. *Broad Applicability of the FAA's Pro-Arbitration Policy* — Ten years after *Gilmer*, the Court resolved one question left open in *Gilmer*: whether the Federal Arbitration Act of 1925 (FAA) applies to private contracts of employment. Section 1 of the FAA excludes from coverage "contracts of employment of seamen, railroad employees, or any other class of workers engaged in foreign or interstate commerce." Although some courts had decided that this exclusionary language exempted all individual employment contracts of workers employed by employers "engaged in commerce," the Court ruled 5-4 that the FAA's exclusion only applies to employment contracts involving transportation workers. *Circuit City Stores, Inc. v. Adams*, 532 U.S. 105 (2001). The Court's narrow reading of the exemption was based upon a strict textual analysis of the statute. The Court justified its interpretation with a strong defense of arbitration in the employment context, noting that many employers had adopted alternative dispute resolution procedures in the wake of *Gilmer* and expressing reluctance to cast doubt upon the enforceability of those agreements. The Court remanded the case to the Ninth Circuit to apply the FAA to the plaintiff's sexual harassment claim under the California Fair Employment and Housing Act. The dissenting Justices argued that both legislative history and historical context supported

the opposite reading of the FAA's exclusion, such that all contracts of employment would be exempted.

2. *Limitations on the Enforceability of Predispute Employment Arbitration Agreements*—In the wake of *Gilmer*, the circuit courts developed standards of fairness limiting the enforceability of predispute arbitration agreements outside the collective bargaining context. For example, on remand in *Circuit City* the Ninth Circuit concluded that the Circuit City arbitration agreement was nonetheless unenforceable because it was a contract of adhesion between parties of unequal bargaining power that conferred asymmetrical rights on employees and the employer and limited damages, and thus was both procedurally and substantively unconscionable under California state law. *Circuit City Stores v. Adams*, 279 F.3d 889 (9th Cir.), *cert. denied*, 535 U.S. 1112 (2002). In two subsequent cases, the Ninth Circuit continued to refuse on grounds of unconscionability to compel arbitration under revised Circuit City arbitration clauses, and the Supreme Court denied *certiorari* in both cases. See *Ingle v. Circuit City Stores, Inc.*, 328 F.3d 1165 (9th Cir. 2003), *cert. denied*, 540 U.S. 1160 (2004) (refusing to compel arbitration pursuant to agreement that one-sidedly limited employee's right to bring suit, imposed one-year statute of limitations on claims, prohibited consolidation of employee claims, imposed filing fees, required cost-splitting, limited remedies, and allowed employer to unilaterally modify the agreement); *Circuit City Stores, Inc. v. Mantor*, 335 F.3d 1101 (9th Cir. 2003), *cert. denied*, 540 U.S. 1160 (2004) (refusing to compel arbitration under agreement that still contained statute of limitations, prohibition on class actions, requirement of filing fee, cost-splitting provisions, and vested employer with unilateral power to terminate or modify the agreement). See also *Alexander v. Anthony Int'l, L.P.*, 341 F.3d 256 (3d Cir. 2003) (laying out two-tiered framework for unconscionability analysis that includes inquiry into procedural and substantive unconscionability); *Hooters of Am., Inc. v. Phillips*, 173 F.3d 933 (4th Cir. 1999) (striking down employer's unilaterally established "one-sided" arbitration procedures); *Cole v. Burns Int'l Sec. Servs.*, 105 F.3d 1465 (D.C. Cir. 1997) (refusing to enforce arbitration agreements requiring employees to pay costs for which they would not be responsible in court).

The evolving standards for assessing fairness or unconscionability in arbitration agreements apply to unions functioning as employers. In *Murray v. UFCW Int'l Union, Local 400*, 289 F.3d 297 (4th Cir. 2002), the union sought to enforce a predispute arbitration agreement against one of its union organizers that contained a provision for a single arbitrator chosen from a list provided by the local union president. According to the Fourth Circuit, such an arbitration agreement is unconscionable and therefore unenforceable.

3. *A Role for Unions?*—Some have suggested a role for unions in solving the problem of inequality in bargaining power and the resulting lopsided individual employee arbitration agreements. The AFL-CIO has experimented with establishing a category of membership called "associate membership," which allows nonunion workers access to limited union benefits such as group health or life insurance, discounts on legal services, and educational programs. Associate memberships are designed

to market union membership to workers, particularly in newly targeted industries or labor sectors, by providing information about what unions do and demonstrating their value. *See* Wial, *The Emerging Organizational Structure of Unionism in Low-Wage Services*, 45 RUTGERS L. REV. 671, 701 n.90 (1993). Might associate memberships be expanded to include a package of services pertaining to advising and representing nonunion workers covered by predispute arbitration agreements?

Alternatively, unions might use the prevalence of mandatory arbitration programs in nonunion shops as a basis for organizing employees into unions that could negotiate traditional grievance and arbitration machinery through collective bargaining. *See* Crain & Matheny, *Labor's Identity Crisis*, 89 CAL. L. REV. 1767, 1845–46 (2001); Green, *Opposing Excessive Use of Employer Bargaining Power in Mandatory Arbitration Agreements Through Collective Employee Actions*, 10 TEX. WESLEYAN L. REV. 77, 105–06 (2003); Hodges, *Trilogy Redux: Using Arbitration to Rebuild the Labor Movement*, 98 MINN. L. REV. 1682 (2014). So far, such possibilities do not seem to be "on the radar screen" for unions. Why not? Should they be?

4. *Judicial Review of Arbitration*—What relationship do these important developments in the nonunion sector bear to the standards for judicial review of arbitration awards in the collective bargaining context? Historically, judicial review of arbitration awards in the labor context has been very narrow. *See infra* Part Six, Section III. In *Oxford Health Plans, LLC v. Sutter*, 569 U.S. 564 (2013), the Court summarized its decisions from the collective bargaining context and applied them to arbitration decisions governed by the FAA. Reasoning that the parties to an employment arbitration agreement bargained for the arbitrator's construction of their agreement, the Court ruled that an arbitral decision "even arguably construing or applying the contract" must stand, regardless of a court's view of its merits, unless the arbitrator strays outside the scope of his contractually delegated authority and issues an award reflecting his own notions of economic justice. Is it reasonable to apply a doctrine developed in a context where a union negotiates for an arbitration and grievance process, plays a central role in selecting the arbitrator, and frames the case before the arbitrator to a situation where an individual nonunion employee is covered by a predispute arbitration agreement?

Wright v. Universal Maritime Serv. Corp., 525 U.S. 70, 119 S. Ct. 391, 142 L. Ed. 2d 361 (1998). A longshoreman represented by a union who had obtained employment through a union hiring hall arrangement governed by a collective bargaining agreement was injured at work and was unable to work for three years. He received Social Security disability benefits and workers' compensation benefits while he was unemployed. When he returned to the union hiring hall and pursued jobs to which he was referred by the union, he was told by the employers that his status as "permanently disabled" disqualified him from performing stevedoring work under the collective bargaining agreement. The union urged Wright to hire a lawyer and to pursue a claim under the Americans with Disabilities Act. When Wright did so, the court dismissed his case for failure to exhaust the grievance procedure available to him under the collective bargaining agreement. The Fourth Circuit affirmed, applying *Gilmer* to union-negotiated grievance and arbitration provisions.

The Supreme Court acknowledged the tension between *Gardner-Denver* and *Gilmer*, observing that *Gilmer* could be understood to either: (1) distinguish between union-negotiated waivers and individually executed contracts, permitting waiver of statutory rights by individuals but not by unions, or (2) completely overrule the *Gardner-Denver* line of cases in favor of a policy enforcing contractual waiver of federal forum rights in exchange for arbitration, whether agreed to by the individual or by the union. The Court implied that unions could waive individual employee rights conferred by statutory schemes in favor of arbitration under the collective bargaining agreement as long as the waiver was "clear and unmistakable," but refused to decide the question or to resolve the tension in the case before it, since the alleged waiver in the case at bar fell short of the clear and unmistakable standard: the labor contract contained only a general arbitration clause that did not explicitly bar discrimination or incorporate the provisions of the antidiscrimination statutes by reference, and lacked a nondiscrimination provision of any kind. The Court vacated the Fourth Circuit's judgment and remanded the case, explicitly reserving the issue of whether union-negotiated waivers that *are* clear and unmistakable would be enforceable. The Court concluded: "*Gardner-Denver* at least stands for the proposition that the right to a federal judicial forum is of sufficient importance to be protected against less-than-explicit union waiver" in a collective bargaining agreement. *Id.* at 80.

14 Penn Plaza LLC v. Pyett

United States Supreme Court
556 U.S. 247, 129 S. Ct. 1456, 173 L. Ed. 2d 398 (2009)

[With the union's consent, the employer contracted with a unionized security services contractor to provide licensed security guards to staff the lobby and entrances of its building. This resulted in the displacement of employees who worked as night lobby watchmen. The employer reassigned them to positions as light duty cleaners and night porters, which were less desirable jobs that entailed a loss of income and status for the security guards. At the employees' request, the union challenged the job reassignments by filing grievances under the collective bargaining agreement. The union's grievances alleged that the reassignments (1) violated the labor contract's ban on age discrimination, (2) breached seniority rules that required a different reassignment to a more desirable position, and (3) failed to equitably rotate overtime. The union pursued the grievances to arbitration, but ultimately withdrew the age discrimination grievances because it had consented to the contract for new security personnel that led to the reassignments. It continued to arbitrate the seniority and overtime claims, which were ultimately denied. After the union withdrew the age discrimination claims, the employees filed a complaint with the EEOC alleging violations of the ADEA. The agency issued a right to sue letter, and the employees filed suit in federal district court. The employer moved to compel arbitration, the district court denied the motion, and the Second Circuit affirmed, applying *Gardner-Denver*.]

JUSTICE THOMAS delivered the opinion of the Court.

. . . .

I

. . . .

The Court of Appeals attempted to reconcile *Gardner-Denver* and *Gilmer* by holding that arbitration provisions in a collective-bargaining agreement, "which purport to waive employees' rights to a federal forum with respect to statutory claims, are unenforceable." 498 F.3d, at 93–94. As a result, an individual employee would be free to choose compulsory arbitration under *Gilmer*, but a labor union could not collectively bargain for arbitration on behalf of its members. We granted certiorari, 552 U.S. 1178, 128 S. Ct. 1223 (2008), to address the issue left unresolved in *Wright*, which continues to divide the Courts of Appeals, and now reverse.

II

A

The NLRA governs federal labor-relations law. As permitted by that statute, respondents designated the Union as their "exclusive representativ[e] . . . for the purposes of collective bargaining in respect to rates of pay, wages, hours of employment, or other conditions of employment." 29 U.S.C. § 159(a). As the employees' exclusive bargaining representative, the Union "enjoys broad authority . . . in the negotiation and administration of [the] collective bargaining contract." *Communications Workers v. Beck*, 487 U.S. 735, 739 (1988) (internal quotation marks omitted). But this broad authority "is accompanied by a responsibility of equal scope, the responsibility and duty of fair representation." *Humphrey v. Moore*, 375 U.S. 335, 342 (1964). The employer has a corresponding duty under the NLRA to bargain in good faith "with the representatives of his employees" on wages, hours, and conditions of employment. 29 U.S.C. § 158(a)(5); see also § 158(d).

In this instance, the Union and the [employer] collectively bargained in good faith and agreed that employment-related discrimination claims, including claims brought under the ADEA, would be resolved in arbitration. This freely negotiated term between the Union and the [employer] easily qualifies as a "conditio[n] of employment" that is subject to mandatory bargaining under § 159(a). . . . The decision to fashion a CBA to require arbitration of employment-discrimination claims is no different from the many other decisions made by parties in designing grievance machinery.[4]

---

4. [5] Justice SOUTER claims that this understanding is "impossible to square with our conclusion in [*Alexander v.*] *Gardner-Denver [Co.*, 415 U.S. 36 (1974)] that 'Title VII . . . stands on plainly different ground' from 'statutory rights related to collective activity': 'it concerns not majoritarian

Respondents, however, contend that the arbitration clause here is outside the permissible scope of the collective-bargaining process because it affects the "employees' individual, non-economic statutory rights." . . . We disagree. Parties generally favor arbitration precisely because of the economics of dispute resolution. See *Circuit City Stores, Inc. v. Adams*, 532 U.S. 105, 123 (2001) ("Arbitration agreements allow parties to avoid the costs of litigation, a benefit that may be of particular importance in employment litigation, which often involves smaller sums of money than disputes concerning commercial contracts"). As in any contractual negotiation, a union may agree to the inclusion of an arbitration provision in a collective-bargaining agreement in return for other concessions from the employer. Courts generally may not interfere in this bargained-for exchange. "Judicial nullification of contractual concessions . . . is contrary to what the Court has recognized as one of the fundamental policies of the National Labor Relations Act — freedom of contract." *NLRB v. Magnavox Co.*, 415 U.S. 322, 328 (1974) (STEWART, J., concurring in part and dissenting in part).

As a result, the CBA's arbitration provision must be honored unless the ADEA itself removes this particular class of grievances from the NLRA's broad sweep. See *Mitsubishi Motors Corp. v. Soler Chrysler-Plymouth, Inc.*, 473 U.S. 614, 628 (1985). It does not. This Court has squarely held that the ADEA does not preclude arbitration of claims brought under the statute. See *Gilmer*, 500 U.S., at 26–33.

In *Gilmer*, the Court explained that "[a]lthough all statutory claims may not be appropriate for arbitration, 'having made the bargain to arbitrate, the party should be held to it unless Congress itself has evinced an intention to preclude a waiver of judicial remedies for the statutory rights at issue.'" *Id.*, at 26. . . . The Court determined that "nothing in the text of the ADEA or its legislative history explicitly precludes arbitration." *Id.*, at 26–27. The Court also concluded that arbitrating ADEA disputes would not undermine the statute's "remedial and deterrent function." *Id.*, at 28. . . .

The *Gilmer* Court's interpretation of the ADEA fully applies in the collective-bargaining context. Nothing in the law suggests a distinction between the status of arbitration agreements signed by an individual employee and those agreed to by a union representative. This Court has required only that an agreement to arbitrate statutory antidiscrimination claims be "explicitly stated" in the collective-bargaining agreement. *Wright*, 525 U.S., at 80. The CBA under review here meets that obligation. Respondents incorrectly counter that an individual employee must personally "waive" a "[substantive] right" to proceed in court for a waiver to

---

processes, but an individual's right to equal employment opportunities.'" *Post*, at 1479 (dissenting opinion) (quoting *Gardner-Denver*, 415 U.S., at 51). As explained below, however, Justice SOUTER repeats the key analytical mistake made in *Gardner-Denver*'s dicta by equating the decision to arbitrate Title VII and ADEA claims to a decision to forgo these substantive guarantees against workplace discrimination. See *infra*, at 1468–1470. The right to a judicial forum is not the nonwaivable "substantive" right protected by the ADEA. See *infra*, at 1465, 1474. . . .

be "knowing and voluntary" under the ADEA. 29 U.S.C. § 626(f)(1). As explained below, however, the agreement to arbitrate ADEA claims is not the waiver of a "substantive right" as that term is employed in the ADEA. . . .

Examination of the two federal statutes at issue in this case, therefore, yields a straightforward answer to the question presented: The NLRA provided the Union and the [employer] with statutory authority to collectively bargain for arbitration of workplace discrimination claims, and Congress did not terminate that authority with respect to federal age-discrimination claims in the ADEA. Accordingly, there is no legal basis for the Court to strike down the arbitration clause in this CBA, which was freely negotiated by the Union and the [employer], and which clearly and unmistakably requires respondents to arbitrate the age-discrimination claims at issue in this appeal. Congress has chosen to allow arbitration of ADEA claims. The Judiciary must respect that choice.

B

The CBA's arbitration provision is also fully enforceable under the *Gardner-Denver* line of cases. Respondents interpret *Gardner-Denver* and its progeny to hold that "a union cannot waive an employee's right to a judicial forum under the federal antidiscrimination statutes" because "allowing the union to waive this right would substitute the union's interests for the employee's antidiscrimination rights." The "combination of union control over the process and inherent conflict of interest with respect to discrimination claims," they argue, "provided the foundation for the Court's holding [in *Gardner-Denver*] that arbitration under a collective-bargaining agreement could not preclude an individual employee's right to bring a lawsuit in court to vindicate a statutory discrimination claim." *Id.*, at 15. We disagree.

1

The holding of *Gardner-Denver* is not as broad as respondents suggest. . . .

. . . .

. . . [I]n *Gilmer*, this Court made clear that the *Gardner-Denver* line of cases "did not involve the issue of the enforceability of an agreement to arbitrate statutory claims." 500 U.S., at 35. Th[e] decisions instead "involved the quite different issue whether arbitration of contract-based claims precluded subsequent judicial resolution of statutory claims. Since the employees there had not agreed to arbitrate their statutory claims, and the labor arbitrators were not authorized to resolve such claims, the arbitration in those cases understandably was held not to preclude subsequent statutory actions." *Ibid.*; see also *Wright*, 525 U.S., at 76. *Gardner-Denver* and its progeny thus do not control the outcome where, as is the case here, the collective-bargaining agreement's arbitration provision expressly covers both statutory and contractual discrimination claims.[5]

---

5. [8] Because today's decision does not contradict the holding of *Gardner-Denver*, we need not resolve the *stare decisis* concerns raised by the dissenting opinions. See *post*, at 1478, 1481 (opinion

2

We recognize that apart from their narrow holdings, the *Gardner-Denver* line of cases included broad *dicta* that was highly critical of the use of arbitration for the vindication of statutory antidiscrimination rights. That skepticism, however, rested on a misconceived view of arbitration that this Court has since abandoned.

First, the Court in *Gardner-Denver* erroneously assumed that an agreement to submit statutory discrimination claims to arbitration was tantamount to a waiver of those rights. For this reason, the Court stated, "the rights conferred [by Title VII] can form no part of the collective-bargaining process since waiver of these rights would defeat the paramount congressional purpose behind Title VII." *Ibid.*; see also *id.*, at 56 ("we have long recognized that 'the choice of forums inevitably affects the scope of the substantive right to be vindicated.'").

The Court was correct in concluding that federal antidiscrimination rights may not be prospectively waived, see 29 U.S.C. §626(f)(1)(C); but it confused an agreement to arbitrate those statutory claims with a prospective waiver of the substantive right. The decision to resolve ADEA claims by way of arbitration instead of litigation does not waive the statutory right to be free from workplace age discrimination; it waives only the right to seek relief from a court in the first instance. See *Gilmer, supra*, at 26 ("'[B]y agreeing to arbitrate a statutory claim, a party does not forgo the substantive rights afforded by the statute; it only submits to their resolution in an arbitral, rather than a judicial, forum'" (quoting *Mitsubishi Motors Corp.*, 473 U.S., at 628)). This "Court has been quite specific in holding that arbitration agreements can be enforced under the FAA without contravening the policies of congressional enactments giving employees specific protection against discrimination prohibited by federal law." *Circuit City Stores, Inc.*, 532 U.S., at 123. The suggestion in *Gardner-Denver* that the decision to arbitrate statutory discrimination claims was tantamount to a substantive waiver of those rights, therefore, reveals a distorted understanding of the compromise made when an employee agrees to compulsory arbitration.

. . . .

Second, *Gardner-Denver* mistakenly suggested that certain features of arbitration made it a forum "well suited to the resolution of contractual disputes," but "a comparatively inappropriate forum for the final resolution of rights created by Title VII." 415 U.S., at 56. According to the Court, the "factfinding process in arbitration" is "not equivalent to judicial factfinding" and the "informality of arbitral procedure . . . makes arbitration a less appropriate forum for final resolution of Title VII issues than the federal courts." *Id.*, at 57, 58. The Court also questioned the

---

of SOUTER, J.). . . . But given the development of this Court's arbitration jurisprudence in the intervening years, see *infra*, at 1469–1471, *Gardner-Denver* would appear to be a strong candidate for overruling if the dissents' broad view of its holding, see *post*, at 1479–1480 (opinion of SOUTER, J.), were correct. . . .

competence of arbitrators to decide federal statutory claims. See *id.*, at 57 ("[T]he specialized competence of arbitrators pertains primarily to the law of the shop, not the law of the land"). . . . In the Court's view, "the resolution of statutory or constitutional issues is a primary responsibility of courts, and judicial construction has proved especially necessary with respect to Title VII, whose broad language frequently can be given meaning only by reference to public law concepts." *Gardner-Denver, supra*, at 57 . . . .

These misconceptions have been corrected. For example, the Court has "recognized that arbitral tribunals are readily capable of handling the factual and legal complexities of antitrust claims, notwithstanding the absence of judicial instruction and supervision" and that "there is no reason to assume at the outset that arbitrators will not follow the law." [*Shearson/American Express Inc. v.*] *McMahon* [482 U.S. 220, 232 (1987)]. . . . An arbitrator's capacity to resolve complex questions of fact and law extends with equal force to discrimination claims brought under the ADEA. Moreover, the recognition that arbitration procedures are more streamlined than federal litigation is not a basis for finding the forum somehow inadequate; the relative informality of arbitration is one of the chief reasons that parties select arbitration. Parties "trad[e] the procedures and opportunity for review of the courtroom for the simplicity, informality, and expedition of arbitration." [*Mitsubishi Motors Corp.*, 473 U.S., at 628]. . . . At bottom, objections centered on the nature of arbitration do not offer a credible basis for discrediting the choice of that forum to resolve statutory antidiscrimination claims.

Third, the Court in *Gardner-Denver* raised in a footnote a "further concern" regarding "the union's exclusive control over the manner and extent to which an individual grievance is presented." 415 U.S., at 58, n. 19. The Court suggested that in arbitration, as in the collective-bargaining process, a union may subordinate the interests of an individual employee to the collective interests of all employees in the bargaining unit. *Ibid.*

We cannot rely on this judicial policy concern as a source of authority for introducing a qualification into the ADEA that is not found in its text. Absent a constitutional barrier, "it is not for us to substitute our view of . . . policy for the legislation which has been passed by Congress." *Florida Dept. of Revenue v. Piccadilly Cafeterias, Inc.*, 554 U.S. 33, 52, 128 S.Ct. 2326, 2338–2339 (2008). Congress is fully equipped "to identify any category of claims as to which agreements to arbitrate will be held unenforceable." *Mitsubishi Motors Corp., supra*, at 627. Until Congress amends the ADEA to meet the conflict-of-interest concern identified in the *Gardner-Denver* dicta, and seized on by respondents here, there is "no reason to color the lens through which the arbitration clause is read" simply because of an alleged conflict of interest between a union and its members. *Mitsubishi Motors Corp., supra*, at 628. This is a "battl[e] that should be fought among the political branches and the industry. Those parties should not seek to amend the statute by appeal to the Judicial Branch." *Barnhart v. Sigmon Coal Co.*, 534 U.S. 438, 462 (2002).

The conflict-of-interest argument also proves too much. Labor unions certainly balance the economic interests of some employees against the needs of the larger work force as they negotiate collective-bargain agreements and implement them on a daily basis. But this attribute of organized labor does not justify singling out an arbitration provision for disfavored treatment. This "principle of majority rule" to which respondents object is in fact the central premise of the NLRA. *Emporium Capwell Co. v. Western Addition Community Organization*, 420 U.S. 50, 62 (1975). "In establishing a regime of majority rule, Congress sought to secure to all members of the unit the benefits of their collective strength and bargaining power, in full awareness that the superior strength of some individuals or groups might be subordinated to the interest of the majority." *Ibid.*; see also *Ford Motor Co. v. Huffman*, 345 U.S. 330, 338 (1953) ("The complete satisfaction of all who are represented is hardly to be expected").... It was Congress' verdict that the benefits of organized labor outweigh the sacrifice of individual liberty that this system necessarily demands. Respondents' argument that they were deprived of the right to pursue their ADEA claims in federal court by a labor union with a conflict of interest is therefore unsustainable; it amounts to a collateral attack on the NLRA.

In any event, Congress has accounted for this conflict of interest in several ways. As indicated above, the NLRA has been interpreted to impose a "duty of fair representation" on labor unions, which a union breaches "when its conduct toward a member of the bargaining unit is arbitrary, discriminatory, or in bad faith." *Marquez v. Screen Actors*, 525 U.S. 33, 44 (1998). This duty extends to "challenges leveled not only at a union's contract administration and enforcement efforts but at its negotiation activities as well." *Beck*, 487 U.S., at 743. Thus, a union is subject to liability under the NLRA if it illegally discriminates against older workers in either the formation or governance of the collective-bargaining agreement, such as by deciding not to pursue a grievance on behalf of one of its members for discriminatory reasons. See *Vaca v. Sipes*, 386 U.S. 171, 177 (1967) (describing the duty of fair representation as the "statutory obligation to serve the interests of *all* members without hostility or discrimination toward any, to exercise its discretion with complete good faith and honesty, and to avoid arbitrary conduct"). Respondents in fact brought a fair representation suit against the Union based on its withdrawal of support for their age-discrimination claims. Given this avenue that Congress has made available to redress a union's violation of its duty to its members, it is particularly inappropriate to ask this Court to impose an artificial limitation on the collective-bargaining process.

In addition, a union is subject to liability under the ADEA if the union itself discriminates against its members on the basis of age. See 29 U.S.C. § 623(d).... Union members may also file age-discrimination claims with the EEOC and the National Labor Relations Board, which may then seek judicial intervention under this Court's precedent. See *EEOC v. Waffle House, Inc.*, 534 U.S. 279, 295–296 (2002). In sum, Congress has provided remedies for the situation where a labor union is less than vigorous in defense of its members' claims of discrimination under the ADEA....

[The Court also rejected the respondents' contractual argument that the collective bargaining agreement in this case did not clearly and unmistakably require arbitration of their ADEA claims, noting that the employees failed to raise their arguments in the courts below, and in fact conceded that the provision requiring arbitration was sufficiently explicit to constitute a waiver.]

We hold that a collective-bargaining agreement that clearly and unmistakably requires union members to arbitrate ADEA claims is enforceable as a matter of federal law. The judgment of the Court of Appeals is reversed, and the case is remanded for further proceedings consistent with this opinion.

It is so ordered.

[**The dissenting opinion of JUSTICE STEVENS is omitted**].

JUSTICE SOUTER, with whom JUSTICE STEVENS, JUSTICE GINSBURG, and JUSTICE BREYER join, dissenting.

The issue here is whether employees subject to a collective-bargaining agreement (CBA) providing for conclusive arbitration of all grievances, including claimed breaches of the Age Discrimination in Employment Act of 1967 (ADEA), 29 U.S.C. § 621 *et seq.*, lose their statutory right to bring an ADEA claim in court, § 626(c). Under the 35-year-old holding in *Alexander v. Gardner-Denver Co.*, 415 U.S. 36 (1974), they do not, and I would adhere to *stare decisis* and so hold today.

I

... *Gardner-Denver* considered the effect of a CBA's arbitration clause on an employee's right to sue under Title VII. One of the employer's arguments was that the CBA entered into by the union had waived individual employees' statutory cause of action subject to a judicial remedy for discrimination in violation of Title VII. Although Title VII, like the ADEA, "does not speak expressly to the relationship between federal courts and the grievance-arbitration machinery of collective-bargaining agreements," 415 U.S., at 47, we unanimously held that "the rights conferred" by Title VII (with no exception for the right to a judicial forum) cannot be waived as "part of the collective bargaining process," *id.*, at 51. We stressed the contrast between two categories of rights in labor and employment law. There were "statutory rights related to collective activity," which "are conferred on employees collectively to foster the processes of bargaining [, which] properly may be exercised or relinquished by the union as collective-bargaining agent to obtain economic benefits for union members." *Ibid.* But "Title VII ... stands on plainly different [categorical] ground; it concerns not majoritarian processes, but an individual's right to equal employment opportunities." *Ibid.* Thus, as the Court previously realized, *Gardner-Denver* imposed a "seemingly absolute prohibition of union waiver of employees' federal forum rights." *Wright v. Universal Maritime Service Corp.*, 525 U.S. 70, 80.

We supported the judgment with several other lines of complementary reasoning. First, we explained that antidiscrimination statutes "have long evinced a general intent to accord parallel or overlapping remedies against discrimination," and Title VII's statutory scheme carried "no suggestion . . . that a prior arbitral decision either forecloses an individual's right to sue or divests federal courts of jurisdiction." *Gardner-Denver*, 415 U.S., at 47. We accordingly concluded that "an individual does not forfeit his private cause of action if he first pursues his grievance to final arbitration under the nondiscrimination clause of a collective-bargaining agreement." *Id.*, at 49.

Second, we rejected the District Court's view that simply participating in the arbitration amounted to electing the arbitration remedy and waiving the plaintiff's right to sue. We said that the arbitration agreement at issue covered only a contractual right under the CBA to be free from discrimination, not the "independent statutory rights accorded by Congress" in Title VII. *Id.*, at 49–50. Third, we rebuffed the employer's argument that federal courts should defer to arbitral rulings. We declined to make the "assumption that arbitral processes are commensurate with judicial processes," *id.*, at 56, and described arbitration as "a less appropriate forum for final resolution of Title VII issues than the federal courts," *id.*, at 58.

Finally, we took note that "[i]n arbitration, as in the collective bargaining process, the interests of the individual employee may be subordinated to the collective interests of all employees in the bargaining unit," *ibid.*, n. 19, a result we deemed unacceptable when it came to Title VII claims. In sum, *Gardner-Denver* held that an individual's statutory right of freedom from discrimination and access to court for enforcement were beyond a union's power to waive.

Our analysis of Title VII in *Gardner-Denver* is just as pertinent to the ADEA in this case. The "interpretation of Title VII . . . applies with equal force in the context of age discrimination, for the substantive provisions of the ADEA 'were derived *in haec verba* from Title VII,'" and indeed neither petitioners nor the Court points to any relevant distinction between the two statutes. Given the unquestionable applicability of the *Gardner-Denver* rule to this ADEA issue, the argument that its precedent be followed in this case of statutory interpretation is equally unquestionable. "Principles of *stare decisis* . . . demand respect for precedent whether judicial methods of interpretation change or stay the same. Were that not so, those principles would fail to achieve the legal stability that they seek and upon which the rule of law depends." *CBOCS West, Inc. v. Humphries*, 553 U.S. 442, 457, 128 S.Ct. 1951, 1961 (2008). . . . There is no argument for abandoning precedent here, and *Gardner-Denver* controls.

II

The majority evades the precedent of *Gardner-Denver* as long as it can simply by ignoring it. The Court never mentions the case before concluding that the ADEA and the National Labor Relations Act, 29 U.S.C. §151 *et seq.*, "yiel[d] a straightforward answer to the question presented," *ante*, at 1466, that is, that unions can bargain away individual rights to a federal forum for antidiscrimination claims. If this were a case of first impression, it would at least be possible to consider that conclusion, but the issue is settled and the time is too late by 35 years to make the bald assertion that "[n]othing in the law suggests a distinction between the status of arbitration agreements signed by an individual employee and those agreed to by a union representative." *Ante*, at 1465. In fact, we recently and unanimously said that the principle that "federal forum rights cannot be waived in union-negotiated CBAs even if they can be waived in individually executed contracts . . . assuredly finds support in" our case law, *Wright*, 525 U.S., at 77 . . . .

Equally at odds with existing law is the majority's statement that "[t]he decision to fashion a CBA to require arbitration of employment-discrimination claims is no different from the many other decisions made by parties in designing grievance machinery." *Ante*, at 1464. That is simply impossible to square with our conclusion in *Gardner-Denver* that "Title VII . . . stands on plainly different ground" from "statutory rights related to collective activity": "it concerns not majoritarian processes, but an individual's right to equal employment opportunities." 415 U.S., at 51. . . .

When the majority does speak to *Gardner-Denver*, it misreads the case in claiming that it turned solely "on the narrow ground that the arbitration was not preclusive because the collective-bargaining agreement did not cover statutory claims." *Ante*, at 1467. That, however, was merely one of several reasons given in support of the decision, see *Gardner-Denver*, 415 U.S., at 47–59, and we raised it to explain why the District Court made a mistake in thinking that the employee lost his Title VII rights by electing to pursue the contractual arbitration remedy, see *id.*, at 49–50. One need only read *Gardner-Denver* itself to know that it was not at all so narrowly reasoned. . . . Indeed, if the Court can read *Gardner-Denver* as resting on nothing more than a contractual failure to reach as far as statutory claims, it must think the Court has been wreaking havoc on the truth for years, since (as noted) we have unanimously described the case as raising a "seemingly absolute prohibition of union waiver of employees' federal forum rights." *Wright, supra*, at 80.[6] Human ingenuity is not equal to the task of reconciling statements like this with the majority's representation that *Gardner-Denver* held only that "the arbitration was not preclusive because the collective-bargaining agreement did not cover statutory claims." *Ante*, at 1467 . . . .

Nor, finally, does the majority have any better chance of being rid of another of *Gardner-Denver*'s statements supporting its rule of decision, set out and repeated in previous quotations: "in arbitration, as in the collective-bargaining process, a union may subordinate the interests of an individual employee to the collective interests of all employees in the bargaining unit," *ante*, at 1472 (citing 415 U.S., at 58, n. 19),

---

6. [2] The majority seems inexplicably to think that the statutory right to a federal forum is not a right, or that *Gardner-Denver* failed to recognize it because it is not "substantive." *Ante*, at 1464, n. 5. But *Gardner-Denver* forbade union waiver of employees' federal forum rights in large part because of the importance of such rights and a fear that unions would too easily give them up to benefit the many at the expense of the few, a far less salient concern when only economic interests are at stake. See, *e.g.*, *Barrentine v. Arkansas-Best Freight System, Inc.*, 450 U.S. 728, 737 (1981).

an unacceptable result when it comes to "an individual's right to equal employment opportunities," *id.*, at 51. The majority tries to diminish this reasoning, and the previously stated holding it supported, by making the remarkable rejoinder that "[w]e cannot rely on this judicial policy concern as a source of authority for introducing a qualification into the ADEA that is not found in its text." *Ante*, at 1472.[7] It is enough to recall that respondents are not seeking to "introduc[e] a qualification into" the law; they are justifiably relying on statutory-interpretation precedent decades old, never overruled, and serially reaffirmed over the years). See, *e.g.*, *McDonald v. West Branch*, 466 U.S. 284, 291 (1984); *Barrentine, supra*, at 742. With that precedent on the books, it makes no sense for the majority to claim that "judicial policy concern[s]" about unions sacrificing individual antidiscrimination rights should be left to Congress.

For that matter, Congress has unsurprisingly understood *Gardner-Denver* the way we have repeatedly explained it and has operated on the assumption that a CBA cannot waive employees' rights to a judicial forum to enforce antidiscrimination statutes. See, *e.g.*, H.R.Rep. No. 102-40, pt. 1, p. 97 (1991) (stating that, "consistent with the Supreme Court's interpretation of Title VII in *[Gardner-Denver]*," "any agreement to submit disputed issues to arbitration . . . in the context of a collective bargaining agreement . . . does not preclude the affected person from seeking relief under the enforcement provisions of Title VII"). And Congress apparently does not share the Court's demotion of *Gardner-Denver*'s holding to a suspect judicial policy concern: "Congress has had [over] 30 years in which it could have corrected our decision . . . if it disagreed with it, and has chosen not to do so. We should accord weight to this continued acceptance of our earlier holding." *Hilton*, 502 U.S., at 202.

III

On one level, the majority opinion may have little effect, for it explicitly reserves the question whether a CBA's waiver of a judicial forum is enforceable when the union controls access to and presentation of employees' claims in arbitration, *ante*, at 1473–1474, which "is usually the case," *McDonald, supra*, at 291. But as a treatment of precedent in statutory interpretation, the majority's opinion cannot be reconciled

---

7. [4] The majority says it would be "particularly inappropriate" to consider *Gardner-Denver*'s conflict-of-interest rationale because "Congress has made available" another "avenue" to protect workers against union discrimination, namely, a duty of fair representation claim. *Ante*, at 1472–1473. This answer misunderstands the law, for unions may decline for a variety of reasons to pursue potentially meritorious discrimination claims without succumbing to a member's suit for failure of fair representation. See, *e.g.*, *Barrentine*, 450 U.S., at 742 ("[E]ven if the employee's claim were meritorious, his union might, without breaching its duty of fair representation, reasonably and in good faith decide not to support the claim vigorously in arbitration"). More importantly, we have rejected precisely this argument in the past, making this yet another occasion where the majority ignores precedent. See, *e.g.*, *ibid.*; *Gardner-Denver, supra*, at 58, n. 19 (noting that a duty of fair representation claim would often "prove difficult to establish"). And we were wise to reject it. When the Court construes statutes to allow a union to eliminate a statutory right to sue in favor of arbitration in which the union cannot represent the employee because it agreed to the employer's challenged action, it is not very consoling to add that the employee can sue the union for being unfair.

with the *Gardner-Denver* Court's own view of its holding, repeated over the years and generally understood, and I respectfully dissent.

Notes

1. *Harmonizing* Gardner-Denver *and* Pyett—Is the Court's effort to distinguish and limit *Gardner-Denver* persuasive, or did the Court effectively overrule *Gardner-Denver*? Are there any distinctions remaining in this area between unionized and nonunionized employees?

2. *Which Waivers Will Be Enforceable?*—Justice Souter's dissent predicts that the reach of *Pyett* may be narrow. First, the custom and practice of the union in this case was apparently to turn over claims to the individuals if the union opted not to pursue them. Employees then had the option to hire a private attorney or to arbitrate the claim themselves. *Supreme Court Considers Enforceability of Arbitration Provision Covering EEO Claims*, Daily Lab. Rep. (BNA) No. 231, Dec. 2, 2008, at AA-1, AA-2. Thus, the Court did not resolve the question whether the presence of a contractual provision affording the union exclusive control over the grievance process—a common feature of collective bargaining agreements—would alter the analysis. Some courts have since concluded that it would. *See, e.g., Kravar v. Triangle Servs.*, 2009 U.S. Dist. LEXIS 42944 (S.D.N.Y. May 12, 2009) (refusing to compel arbitration of employee's claim under the Americans with Disabilities Act where the labor contract gave the union control over arbitration of an employee's claims; the court reasoned that this amounted to a substantive waiver of her statutory rights under the ADA in any forum and was thus unenforceable, citing *Pyett*).

Second, the collective bargaining agreement in *Pyett* contained an unusually clear provision committing all antidiscrimination claims to arbitration under the collective bargaining agreement. The contract provided:

> § 30 NO DISCRIMINATION. There shall be no discrimination against any present or future employee by reason of race, creed, color, age, disability, national origin, sex, union membership, or any other characteristic protected by law, including, but not limited to, claims made pursuant to Title VII of the Civil Rights Act, the Americans with Disabilities Act, the Age Discrimination in Employment Act, the New York State Human Rights Law, the New York City Human Rights Code, . . . or any other similar laws, rules, or regulations. All such claims shall be subject to the grievance and arbitration procedures (Articles V and VI) as the sole and exclusive remedy for violations. Arbitrators shall apply appropriate law in rendering decisions based upon claims of discrimination.

556 U.S. at 252.

Finally, the Court did not establish standards for determining whether a particular waiver is clear and unmistakable, an issue that has divided the lower courts since *Wright*. Some circuits have developed bright-line standards for clear and unmistakable waiver, finding waiver only where the collective bargaining agreement explicitly lists the relevant statute containing employee rights, *see, e.g., Abdullayeva v. Attending Homecare Servs.*, LLC, 928 F.3d 218 (2d Cir. 2019); *Cavallaro v. UMass Mem'l Healthcare, Inc.*, 678 F.3d 1 (1st Cir. 2012); *Aleman v. Chugach Support Servs., Inc.*, 485 F.3d 206 (4th Cir. 2007); *Bratten v. SSI Servs., Inc.*, 185 F.3d 625 (6th Cir. 1999), or a general arbitration clause is accompanied by an explicit incorporation of statutory antidiscrimination requirements elsewhere in the contract, *see, e.g., Ibarra v. United Parcel Serv.*, 695 F.3d 354 (5th Cir. 2012). Others have adopted a contract interpretation approach more susceptible to finding waiver even if the arbitration clause is more general. *See, e.g., Darrington v. Milton Hershey School*, 958 F.3d 188 (3d Cir. 2020) (finding waiver where the collective bargaining agreement defined a grievance subject to arbitration as "any dispute alleging discrimination against any [Union members] based upon membership in any protected categories under federal or state law . . . ," and the union waived "any right to institute or maintain any private lawsuit alleging employment discrimination in any state or federal court regarding the matters encompassed within this grievance procedure.").

3. *"A Collateral Attack on the NLRA"* — Justice Thomas describes the employees' argument that the union-negotiated antidiscrimination clause in the collective bargaining agreement deprived them of their statutory rights to pursue their ADEA claims in court as "a collateral attack on the NLRA." 556 U.S. at 271. He points specifically to the principle of majority rule, a core feature of the NLRA, which subordinates the interests of individual employees to that of the collective for purposes of the advancement of workers' economic rights. What safeguards exist for the protection of minority interests in the collective bargaining system? Are they sufficient?

The dissent in *Pyett* complained that the union's duty of fair representation provides inadequate protection for individual employees whose statutory forum rights are subordinated to the majority's interests. *See id.* at 285 n.4 (Souter, J., dissenting). On the other hand, might the Court's ruling in *Pyett* be read to broaden the duty of fair representation owed by unions to individual employees? If a union negotiates a waiver of employees' Title VII rights, for example, might the union also owe a duty to negotiate arbitration processes that provide parallel protections to those available in litigation, and perhaps subsidize lawyers for employees who wish to pursue antidiscrimination claims through arbitration?

4. *Winners and Losers in* Pyett — The employees in *Pyett* lost the case, but is the ruling necessarily bad news for unions or for workers as a class? Some employers may be eager to negotiate antidiscrimination provisions that cover bargaining unit employees in order to limit liability and avoid litigation expenses associated with statutory resolution of antidiscrimination claims. The Court's decision in *Pyett* potentially confers significant bargaining leverage on unions. Might employers be willing to offer unions an "enticing quid pro quo" in exchange for the inclusion of such provisions in collective bargaining agreements? *See* St. Antoine, Gilmer *in the Collective Bargaining Context*, 16 Ohio St. J. on Disp. Resol. 491 (2001). Are there independent reasons why unions might desire antidiscrimination clauses that include waivers of statutory forum rights beyond the use of such rights as bargaining chips? From a

worker perspective, might the availability of a union-negotiated arbitral forum with union representation be a boon for low-waged workers who have difficulty vindicating their antidiscrimination claims in court because of lack of access to legal counsel? Which workers are most likely to lose rights as a result of *Pyett*?

To appreciate the tradeoffs here, consider how employers might have responded had the Court applied *Gardner-Denver* and ruled that union waivers of antidiscrimination forum rights were *unenforceable*. Such a ruling would likely have rendered predispute arbitration agreements non-mandatory subjects of bargaining (since the union could not legally bind employees to them), thus allowing employers to bypass the union and deal directly with individual employees, requiring them to sign such agreements as a condition of employment. The D.C. Circuit took this position prior to *Pyett*. See *Air Line Pilots Ass'n, Int'l v. Northwest Airlines, Inc.*, 199 F.3d 477 (D.C. Cir. 1999), *enforced on reh'g en banc*, 211 F.3d 1312 (D.C. Cir.), *cert. denied*, 531 U.S. 1011 (2000). Which rule is better for workers as a class: a rule that the union *can* waive their statutory forum rights or a rule that the union *cannot*? Consider the following analysis:

> A number of commentators have argued quite forcefully that the arbitration of employment discrimination claims is not a fair substitute for litigation, at least when the arbitration agreements are imposed upon individual workers who lack union representation. Yet when workers are represented by unions, arbitration processes may be a fair and pragmatic substitute for litigation. While the informality of arbitration risks creating a "second class" justice [system] because rules of law (substantive as well as evidentiary) do not necessarily apply or because their application cannot be effectively reviewed, this need not be the case where a union negotiates the parameters of the system.
>
> ... After *Gilmer* ... employers are free to impose arbitration on employees as a substitute for litigation of statutory rights. Under [the D.C. Circuit's decision in *Air Line Pilots Ass'n*] employers may do so even when a union represents the workers. Thus, the question is not whether to utilize arbitration as an alternative dispute resolution mechanism, it is who will negotiate its substantive coverage and procedural protections, and whether employees will have representation in the process. Overruling *Gardner-Denver* would transform the employer's ability to require waiver of an individual worker's statutory discrimination rights into a powerful incentive for workers to join unions. Unions are likely to be far more effective than individual employees in negotiating for procedural and substantive protections in an arbitration system, [including written opinions, scope of arbitral authority, expanded remedies, precedential effect of decisions, and choice of arbitrators—all protections rarely found in individual predispute arbitration agreements unilaterally imposed on workers by employers]....

Crain & Matheny, *Labor's Identity Crisis*, 89 Cal. L. Rev. 1767, 1842–43 (2001).

How should unions desiring to represent an increasingly diverse workforce respond? Should they continue to negotiate for such clauses in order to advance antidiscrimination protections through collective bargaining and grievance arbitration? Is discrimination an individual injury or a collective injury? If collective, would it not be best redressed through collective action and collective bargaining? What are the problems with committing it to the grievance processes available under the collective bargaining agreement?

Section IV. The Nature of the Duty to Bargain

The obligation to "bargain collectively" is generally, though not universally, included in federal and state labor relations acts. The original NLRA imposed the duty on the employer as a means of implementing the right to organize and to bargain collectively, which was declared in §7. The "Wagner Act" type of statute exacted no requirements of unions. The later "Taft-Hartley" type of statute made the bargaining obligation mutual.

The legal duty created by the original NLRA and the RLA was not defined by Congress. Section 2, First, of the RLA requires that the parties exert "every reasonable effort to make and maintain agreements concerning rates of pay, rules, and working conditions," and Section 2, Ninth, obligates the carrier to "treat with" the duly certified employee representative. These provisions, together with the duty "to bargain collectively" specified in the Wagner Act, and corresponding provisions of state acts, had to be given meaning by the courts and the enforcement agencies. *See generally* C. REHMUS, THE RAILWAY LABOR ACT AT FIFTY (1976); Thoms & Dooley, *Collective Bargaining Under the Railway Labor Act*, 20 TRANSP. L.J. 275 (1992).

In the first case to come before the Supreme Court under the RLA, the Court declared that the statute "does not undertake to compel agreement between the employer and employees, but it does command those preliminary steps without which no agreement can be reached," including "reasonable efforts to compose differences." *Virginian R. Co. v. System Federation*, 300 U.S. 515, 548 (1937). Even prior to this decision there had been some development of the concept of bargaining by the National Labor Board and the old National Labor Relations Board, which had been given advisory adjudicative responsibility regarding §7a of the National Industrial Recovery Act of 1933. In the much-cited *Houde Eng'g Corp.* case, 1 N.L.R.B. (Old) 35 (1934), the old NLRB interpreted the decisions of the NLB as having established the "incontestably sound principle that the employer is obligated by the statute to negotiate in good faith with his employees' representatives; to match their proposals, if unacceptable, with counter-proposals; and to make every reasonable effort to reach an agreement." In applying §8(5) of the NLRA of 1935, the NLRB adopted this principle with the full support of the courts. The duty to bargain encompassed an obligation to enter into negotiations with "an open and fair mind" and "a sincere purpose to find a basis of agreement." *See, e.g., NLRB v. Boss Mfg. Co.*, 118 F.2d 187,

189 (7th Cir. 1941); *Globe Cotton Mills v. NLRB*, 103 F.2d 91, 94 (5th Cir. 1939); *Highland Park Mfg. Co.*, 12 N.L.R.B. 1238, 1248–49 (1939), *enforced*, 110 F.2d 632 (4th Cir. 1940).

Section 8(5) of the NLRA had its origin in a Senate bill (S. 2926) introduced by Senator Wagner in March 1934. One provision, obviously patterned on the Railway Labor Act counterpart, read as follows:

> It shall be an unfair labor practice ... to refuse to recognize and/or deal with representatives of his [the employer's] employees, or to fail to exert every reasonable effort to make and maintain agreements with such representatives concerning wages, hours, and other conditions of employment.

At the committee hearings on the bill, Dr. Slichter of Harvard University argued for deletion of the requirement of a "reasonable effort to make and maintain agreements," and so forth, as "merely the expression of a pious wish": "You cannot make it a definite duty of a man to try to agree. . . . You might almost enact that the lions and lambs shall not fail to exert every reasonable effort to lie down together." Dr. Leiserson, then Chairman of the Petroleum Labor Policy Board, disagreed: "Now, I think it is exceedingly important that it should stay in the bill. It should not be thrown out on the theory, 'Well, you cannot enforce that anyway.' If we can say, . . . to an employer, 'Now, you really haven't tried to agree with them, so that we will avoid a strike. They have elected their representatives. Now sit down and make an earnest effort, the way the law says.' You will avoid many disputes in that way." Smith, *The Evolution of the "Duty to Bargain" Concept in American Law*, 39 MICH. L. REV. 1065, 1083–84 (1941).

The Senate Committee on Education and Labor, reporting in 1935 on the Wagner-Connery Bill, said regarding § 8(5):

> The committee wishes to dispel any possible false impression that this bill is designed to compel the making of agreements or to permit governmental supervision of their terms. It must be stressed that the duty to bargain collectively does not carry with it the duty to reach an agreement, because the essence of collective bargaining is that either party shall be free to decide whether proposals made to it are satisfactory.

Id. at 1085.

Senator Walsh, Chairman of the Committee on Education and Labor, summed up one prominent legislative attitude in these terms:

> The bill indicates the method and manner in which employees may organize, the method and manner of selecting their representatives or spokesmen, and leads them to the office door of their employer with the legal authority to negotiate for their fellow employees. The bill does not go beyond the office door. It leaves the discussion between the employer and the employee, and the agreements which they may or may not make, voluntary and with that sacredness and solemnity to a voluntary agreement with which both parties to an agreement should be enshrouded.

Id. at 1087. *See also* Latham, *Legislative Purpose and Administrative Policy Under the National Labor Relations Act*, 4 Geo. Wash. L. Rev. 433 (1936). For contrasting views, see W. Spencer, The National Labor Relations Act 24 (1935); Rheinstein, *Methods of Wage Policy*, 6 U. Chi. L. Rev. 552, 576 (1939).

When Congress passed the LMRA in 1947, §8(d) was written into the law, spelling out to some extent the duty to bargain collectively. The Senate bill (S. 1126), in its proposed amendment of the NLRA, included a §8(d) substantially similar to this section as eventually enacted, but lacking its final paragraph. The Senate Committee on Labor and Public Welfare stated, S. Rep. No. 105, 80th Cong., 1st Sess. 24 (1947):

> Section 8(d) contains a definition of the duty to bargain collectively and, consequently, relates both to the duties of employers to bargain and labor organizations to bargain under Sections 8(a)(5) and 8(b)(3), respectively. The definition makes it clear that the duty to bargain collectively does not require either party to agree to a particular demand or to make a concession. It should be noted that the word "concession" was used rather than "counterproposal" to meet an objection raised by the Chairman of the Board to a corresponding provision in one of the early drafts of the bill.

The Conference Committee reported concerning the version of §8(d) as finally enacted, H.R. Rep. No. 510, 80th Cong., 1st Sess. 34 (1947):

> This mutual obligation was not to compel either party to agree to a proposal or require the making of any concession. Hence, the Senate amendment, while it did not prescribe a purely objective test of what constituted collective bargaining, as did the House bill, had, to a very substantial extent, the same effect as the House bill in this regard, since it rejected, as a factor in determining good faith, the test of making a concession and thus prevented the Board from determining the merits of the positions of the parties.

A. Good Faith

Labor Study Group,[*] The Public Interest in National Labor Policy
82 (Committee for Economic Development 1961)

Parties have been told that they must bargain in good faith, and elaborate tests have been devised in an attempt to determine "objectively" whether the proper subjective attitude prevails. The limitations and artificiality of such tests are apparent, and the possibilities of evasion are almost limitless.... Basically, it is unrealistic to expect that, by legislation, "good faith" can be brought to the bargaining table. Indeed, the provisions designed to bring "good faith" have become a tactical weapon used in many situations as a means of harassment.

---

[*] The members of the Study Group were Clark Kerr, Douglass V. Brown, David L. Cole, John T. Dunlop, William Y. Elliott, Albert Rees, Robert M. Solow, Philip Taft, and George W. Taylor.

The Labor Board wrestled with the meaning of good faith bargaining in the well-known case summarized below. The first excerpt provides the Board's ruling; the second excerpt is the Second Circuit's decision and reasoning on appeal.

General Electric Co.
National Labor Relations Board
150 N.L.R.B. 192 (1964)

The Trial Examiner found that Respondent had not bargained in good faith with the Union, thereby violating § 8(a)(5) and (1) of the Act. . . .

In challenging the Trial Examiner's finding that it violated § 8(a)(5), Respondent argues that an employer cannot be found guilty of having violated its statutory bargaining duty where it is desirous of entering into a collective bargaining agreement, where it has met and conferred with the bargaining representative on all required subjects of bargaining as prescribed by statute and has not taken unlawful unilateral action, and where it has not demanded the inclusion in the collective bargaining contract of any illegal clauses or insisted to an impasse upon any non-mandatory bargaining provisions. Given compliance with the above, Respondent further argues that an employer's technique of bargaining is not subject to approval or disapproval by the Board.

Respondent reads the statutory requirements for bargaining collectively too narrowly. It is true that an employer does violate § 8(a)(5) where it enters into bargaining negotiations with a desire not to reach an agreement with the union, or has taken unilateral action with respect to a term or condition of employment, or has adamantly demanded the inclusion of illegal or nonmandatory clauses in the collective bargaining contract. But, having refrained from any of the foregoing conduct, an employer may still have failed to discharge its statutory obligation to bargain in good faith. As the Supreme Court has said:[8]

> . . . the Board is authorized to order the cessation of behavior which is in effect a refusal to negotiate, *or* which directly obstructs or inhibits the actual process of discussion, *or* which reflects a cast of mind against reaching agreement. [Emphasis supplied.]

Thus, a party who enters into bargaining negotiations with a "take-it-or-leave-it" attitude violates its duty to bargain although it goes through the forms of bargaining, does not insist on any illegal or nonmandatory bargaining proposals, and wants to sign an agreement.[9] For good-faith bargaining means more than "going through

---

8. [8] *NLRB v. Bennie Katz, etc., d/b/a Williamsburg Steel Prod. Co., supra* [369 U.S. 736] at 747 (1962).
9. [9] *NLRB v. Insurance Agents' Union, AFL-CIO (Prudential Ins. Co.),* 361 U.S. 477, 487 (1960).

the motions of negotiating."[10] ". . . [T]he essential thing is rather the serious intent to adjust differences and to reach an acceptable common ground. . . ."[11]

Good-faith bargaining thus involves both a procedure for meeting and negotiating, which may be called the externals of collecting bargaining, and a bona fide intention, the presence or absence of which must be discerned from the record. It requires recognition by both parties, not merely formal but real, that "collective bargaining" is a shared process in which each party, labor union and employer, has the right to play an active role. On the part of the employer, it requires at a minimum recognition that the statutory representative is the one with whom it must deal in conducting bargaining negotiations, and that it can no longer bargain directly or indirectly with the employees. It is inconsistent with this obligation for an employer to mount a campaign, as Respondent did, both before and during negotiations, for the purpose of disparaging and discrediting the statutory representative in the eyes of its employee constituents, to seek to persuade the employees to exert pressure on the representative to submit to the will of the employer, and to create the impression that the employer rather than the union is the true protector of the employees' interests. As the Trial Examiner phrased it, the employer's statutory obligation is to deal with the employees through the union, and not with the union through the employees.

We do not rely solely on Respondent's campaign among its employees for our finding that it did not deal in good faith with the Union. Respondent's policy of disparaging the Union by means of the communications campaign as fully detailed in the Trial Examiner's Intermediate Report, was implemented and furthered by its conduct at the bargaining table. Thus, the negotiations themselves, although maintaining the form of "collective bargaining," fell short, in a realistic sense, of the concept of meaningful and fruitful "negotiation" envisaged by the Act. As the record in the case reflects, Respondent regards itself as a sort of administrative body which has the unilateral responsibility for determining wages and working conditions for employees, and it regards the union's role as merely that of a kind of advisor for an interested group — the employees. Thus, according to its professed philosophy of "bargaining," Respondent on the basis of its own research and evaluation of union demands, determines what is "right" for its employees, and then makes a "fair and firm offer" to the unions without holding anything back for later trading or compromising. It professes a willingness to make prompt adjustments in its offer, but only if new information or a change in facts indicates that its initial offer is no longer "right." It believes that if its research has been done properly there will be no need to change its offer unless something entirely unforeseen has developed in the meantime. Simultaneously, Respondent emphasizes, especially to employees, that as a matter of policy it will not be

---

10. [10] *NLRB v. Truitt Mfg. Co.*, 351 U.S. 149, 155 (1956) (Frankfurter, J.).

11. [11] First Annual Report of the National Labor Relations Board, at 85, quoted with approval by the Supreme Court in *NLRB v. Insurance Agents' Union, AFL-CIO (Prudential Ins. Co.), supra* at 485.

induced by a strike or a threat of a strike to make any change in its proposals which it believes to be "wrong." This "bargaining" approach undoubtedly eliminates the "ask-and-bid" or "auction" form of bargaining, but in the process devitalizes negotiations and collective bargaining and robs them of their commonly accepted meaning. "Collective bargaining" as thus practiced is tantamount to mere formality and serves to transform the role of the statutory representative from a joint participant in the bargaining process to that of an advisor. In practical effect, Respondent's "bargaining" position is akin to that of a party who enters into negotiations "with a predetermined resolve not to budge from an initial position," an attitude inconsistent with good-faith bargaining. In fact Respondent here went even further. It consciously placed itself in a position where it could not give unfettered consideration to the merits of any proposals the Union might offer. Thus, Respondent pointed out to the Union, after Respondent's communications to the employees and its "fair and firm offer" to the Union, that "everything we think we should do is in the proposal and we told our employees that, and we would look ridiculous if we changed now."

In short, both major facets of Respondent's 1960 "bargaining" technique, its campaign among the employees and its conduct at the bargaining table, complementing each other, were calculated to disparage the Union and to impose without substantial alteration Respondent's "fair and firm" proposal, rather than to satisfy the true standards of good-faith collective bargaining required by the statute. A course of conduct whose major purpose is so directed scarcely evinces a sincere desire to resolve differences and reach a common ground. For the above reasons, as well as those elaborated at greater length by the Trial Examiner in his Intermediate Report, we adopt his conclusion that Respondent did not bargain in good faith with the Union, thereby violating § 8(a)(5) and (1) of the Act....

Nothing in our decision bans fact-gathering or any specific methods of formulating proposals. We prescribe no timetable for negotiators. We lay down no rules as to any required substance or content of agreements. Our decision rests rather upon a consideration of the totality of Respondent's conduct....

Member Leedom, dissenting in part:

.... On the issue as to Respondent's overall good or bad faith it should be conceded that there are various approaches to, and tactics in, negotiations that are wholly consistent with the bargaining obligation imposed by the Act; and it seems to me that both management and labor should not be discouraged from seeking new techniques in dealing with the constantly evolving problems with which they are faced across the bargaining table. Consequently we should take care not to create the impression that we view with suspicion novel approaches to, and techniques of, collective bargaining....

No matter how much we may disclaim any intent to compel bargaining to proceed in some set form, the fact that we closely scrutinize what goes on at the bargaining table will necessarily have the effect of directing bargaining into channels which we have in the past approved, for in such channels will lie security in bargaining, if not success. Whether the substitution of our judgment as to the proper forms and content of bargaining be made directly or indirectly is a difference of no consequence insofar as it interferes with free bargaining and tends to discourage innovation both in tactics and proposals which, as I believe, could be of benefit not only to the parties but to the public as well. Consequently, good policy suggests that we leave the parties to their own devices at the bargaining table unless some compelling facts force us into the area of bargaining. . . .

I do not mean to suggest that the issue of good or bad faith has any clear cut answer here. My position is not dictated so much by strong conviction as by uncertainty. I am not persuaded by the reasons that the majority state for their finding of bad-faith bargaining; and the finding itself and the supporting rationale leave me in the dark as to their practical efficacy. But I am particularly disturbed by the treatment accorded Respondent's communications. Surely the Respondent can lawfully communicate with its employees. Yet here, although the communications are held to be some evidence of bad faith, the majority neither in its decision nor in adopting the Trial Examiner's Recommended Order provides the Respondent with any guides by which it can with reasonable certainty determine what it can lawfully say to its employees. In areas such as this bordering on § 8(c) of the Act and free speech, I believe that the Respondent is entitled to something more by way of clarification than the vague proscription implied in the general bargaining order. But I doubt if the facts and findings indicate what specific limitations can properly be laid down. In any event, the situation with respect to the bad-faith finding is at best ambiguous, and I would, therefore, find that the General Counsel has failed to prove by a preponderance of the evidence that the Respondent did not bargain in good faith during the 1960 negotiations with the Union.

[The concurring opinion of MEMBER JENKINS is omitted.]

Note

The bargaining technique employed by General Electric in the 1960 negotiations is commonly known as "Boulwarism," after Lemuel R. Boulware, a former GE vice president who first devised it in the late 1940s. It is discussed in detail by its leading academic exponent in H. NORTHRUP, BOULWARISM (1964). *See also* L. BOULWARE, THE TRUTH ABOUT BOULWARISM: TRYING TO DO RIGHT VOLUNTARILY (1969); Cooper, *Boulwarism and the Duty to Bargain in Good Faith*, 20 RUTGERS L. REV. 653 (1966); Gross, Cullen & Hanslowe, *Good Faith in Labor Negotiations: Tests and Remedies*, 53 CORNELL L. REV. 1009 (1968).

"Almost ten years after the events that gave rise to this controversy," as the court put it, the Second Circuit in a 2-to-1 decision sustained the Labor Board's condemnation of "Boulwarism." Three judges wrote opinions totaling some 40 pages. Reproduced below are severely edited excerpts from the majority and minority opinions, with the emphasis on those portions dealing with General Electric's "overall approach to bargaining."

NLRB v. General Electric Co.
United States Court of Appeals, Second Circuit
418 F.2d 736 (1969), *cert. denied*, 397 U.S. 965 (1970)

IRVING R. KAUFMAN, CIRCUIT JUDGE. . . .

The new plan ["Boulwarism"] was threefold. GE began by soliciting comments from its local management personnel on the desires of the work force, and the type and level of benefits that they expected. These were then translated into specific proposals, and their cost and effectiveness researched, in order to formulate a "product" that would be attractive to the employees, and within the Company's means. The last step was the most important, most innovative, and most often criticized. GE took its "product" — now a series of fully-formed bargaining proposals — and "sold" it to its employees and the general public. Through a veritable avalanche of publicity, reaching awesome proportions prior to and during negotiations, GE sought to tell its side of the issues to its employees. It described its proposals as a "fair, firm offer," characteristic of its desire to "do right voluntarily," without the need for any union pressure or strike. In negotiations, GE announced that it would have nothing to do with the "blood-and-threat-and-thunder" approach, in which each side presented patently unreasonable demands, and finally chose a middle ground that both knew would be the probable outcome even before the beginning of the bargaining. The Company believed that such tactics diminished the company's credibility in the eyes of its employees, and at the same time appeared to give the union credit for wringing from the Company what it had been willing to offer all along. Henceforth GE would hold nothing back when it made its offer to the Union; it would take all the facts into consideration, and make that offer it thought right under all the circumstances. Though willing to accept Union suggestions based on facts the Company might have overlooked, once the basic outlines of the proposal had been set, the mere fact that the Union disagreed would be no ground for change. When GE said firm, it meant firm, and it denounced the traditional give and take of the so-called auction bargaining as "flea bitten eastern type of cunning and dishonest but pointless haggling."

To bring its position home to its employees, GE utilized a vast network of plant newspapers, bulletins, letters, television and radio announcements, and personal contacts through management personnel. . . .

. . . [T]he Board found that GE's bargaining stance and conduct, considered as a whole, were designed to derogate the Union in the eyes of its members and the public at large. This plan had two major facets: first, a take-it- or-leave-it approach ("firm, fair offer") to negotiations in general which emphasized both the powerlessness and uselessness of the Union to its members, and second, a communications program that pictured the Company as the true defender of the employees' interests, further denigrating the Union, and sharply curbing the Company's ability to change its own position. . . .

[A]cts not in themselves unfair labor practices may support an inference that a party is acting in bad faith. *See NLRB v. Insurance Agents' Union*, 361 U.S. 477, 506 (1960) (Frankfurter, J., concurring). While GE may have believed that it was acting within its "rights" in offering a take-it-or-leave-it proposal, doing so may still be some evidence of lack of good faith. Here there was no substantial justification offered for refusing to discuss the matter, other than a niggling — and incorrect — view of the contract and the statute. *Cf. NLRB v. Reed & Prince Mfg. Co.*, 205 F.2d 131 (1st Cir.) (Magruder, J.) ("must make *some* reasonable effort in *some* direction"), *cert. denied*, 346 U.S. 887 (1953). Given the effects of take-it-or-leave-it proposals on the Union, . . . the Board could appropriately infer the presence of anti-Union animus, and in conjunction with other similar conduct could reasonably discern a pattern of illegal activity designed primarily to subvert the Union.

. . . . GE's attitude . . . was characterized by a pettifogging insistence on doing not one whit more than the law absolutely required, an insistence that eventually strayed over into doing considerably less. GE's conduct, as the Board's opinion points out, was all of a piece. It negotiated, to the greatest possible extent by ignoring the legitimacy and relevance of the Union's position as statutory representative of its members. Thus it is hardly surprising that IUE requests for information were met (at least once negotiations had begun) with less than enthusiasm, for they reflect the Union's contrary belief that it had to know the worth of the Company proposals in order to evaluate them for its members. . . .

When the last act was virtually played out and it had become apparent that the Union would have to end its abortive strike and concede to GE's terms, the Company continued to display a stiff and unbending patriarchal posture hardly consistent with "common willingness among the parties to discuss freely and fully their respective claims and demands and, when these are opposed, to justify them on reason." *NLRB v. George P. Pilling & Son Co.*, 119 F.2d 32, 37 (3d Cir. 1941). With the Union, as it were, "on the ropes," the Company insisted that IUE choose the options that it preferred, and assent to the contract unconditionally, without ever seeing the final contract language. When the Union protested that the memorandum proposed for its signature was too vague, the Company refused to submit more definite language. Four days later, the Union capitulated completely and signed the short form memorandum, still without having seen the final contract to which it was agreeing. . . .

The Company's stand, however, would be utterly inexplicable without the background of its publicity program. Only when viewed in that context does it become meaningful. We have already indicated that one of the central tenets of "the Boulware approach" is that the "product" or "firm, fair offer" must be marketed vigorously to the "consumers" or employees, to convince them that the Company, and not the Union, is their true representative. GE, the Trial Examiner found, chose to rely "entirely" on its communications program to the virtual exclusion of genuine negotiations, which it sought to evade by any means possible. Bypassing the national negotiators in favor of direct settlement dealings with employees and local officials forms another consistent thread in this pattern. The aim, in a word, was to deal with the Union through the employees, rather than with the employees through the Union.

The Company's refusal to withhold publicizing its offer until the Union had had an opportunity to propose suggested modifications is indicative of this attitude. Here two interests diverged. The command of the Boulware approach was clear: employees and the general public must be barraged with communications that emphasized the generosity of the offer, and restated the firmness of GE's position. A genuine desire to reach a mutual accommodation might, on the other hand, have called for GE to await Union comments before taking a stand from which it would be difficult to retreat. GE hardly hesitated. It released the offer the next day without waiting for Union comments on the specific portions.

The most telling effect of GE's marketing campaign was not on the Union, but on GE itself. Having told its employees that it had made a "firm, fair offer," that there was "nothing more to come," and that it would not change its position in the face of "threats" of a strike, GE had in effect rested all on the expectation that it could institute its offer without significant modification. Properly viewed, then, its communications approach determined its take-it-or-leave-it bargaining strategy. Each was the natural complement of the other; if either were substantially changed, the other would in all probability have to be modified as well. . . .

The Company, having created a view of the bargaining process that admitted of no compromise, was trapped by its own creation. It could no longer seek peace without total victory, for it had by its own words and actions branded any compromise a defeat.

GE urges that § 8(c) . . . prohibits the Board from considering its publicity efforts in passing on the legality of its bargaining conduct. . . . GE would have us read that section as a bar to the Board's use of any communications, in any manner, unless the communication itself contained a threat or a promise of benefit. The legislative history, past decisions, and the logic of the statutory framework, however, indicate a contrary conclusion.

The bald prohibition of § 8(c) invited comment when it was enacted, as well as later. Senator Taft replied to some of the criticism of the bill that bears his name:

> It should be noted that this subsection is limited to "views, arguments, or opinions" and does not cover instructions, directions, or other statements that would ordinarily be deemed relevant and admissible in courts of law.

I Legislative History of the LMRA 1947, at 1541. The key word is "relevant." The evil at which the section was aimed was the alleged practice of the Board in inferring the existence of an unfair labor practice from a totally unrelated speech or opinion delivered by an employer. Senator Taft later indicated, for example, in the context of a § 8(a)(3) discriminatory firing, that prior statements of the employer would have to be shown to "tie in" with the specific unfair labor practice. I Legislative History of the LMRA 1947, at 1545. Later references to the section described the barred statements as those which were "severable or unrelated," and "irrelevant or immaterial." II Legislative History of the LMRA 1947, at 429 (Senate Report), 549 (House Conference Report). The objective of §8(c) then, was to impose a rule of relevancy on the Board in evaluating the legality of statements by parties to a labor dispute. Its purpose was hardly to eliminate all communications from the Board's purview, for to do so would be to emasculate a statute whose structure depends heavily on evaluation of motive and intent. . . .

While it is clear that the Board is not to control the substantive terms of a collective bargaining contract, nonetheless the parties must do more than meet. Our brother Friendly makes much of the point that General Electric did bargain and reach an "agreement" with the Union. . . . The statute does not say that any "agreement" reached will validate whatever tactics have been employed to exact it. To imply such a Congressional purpose would be to encourage parties to make their violation so blatant that it would be impossible for the other side to continue to exist without signing. Instead the statute clearly contemplates that to the end of encouraging productive bargaining, the parties must make "a serious attempt to resolve differences and reach a common ground," *NLRB v. Insurance Agents' Int'l Union*, 361 U.S. 477, 486, 487, 488 (1960), an effort inconsistent with a "predetermined resolve not to budge from an initial position." *NLRB v. Truitt Mfg. Co.*, 351 U.S. 149, 154–155 (1956) (Frankfurter, J., concurring). . . .

The Company and the dissenting opinion seem to take the novel position that the holding in *Insurance Agents'*—that the Board might not forbid a partial strike during bargaining—ousts the Board's control over bargaining tactics. But in *NLRB v. Katz*, 369 U.S. 736 (1962), the Court held that at least one tactic—instituting unilateral changes during bargaining—was forbidden, for it put a bargainable topic outside the reach of the bargaining process. GE has done no less; it has, if anything, done more. By its communications and bargaining strategy it in effect painted itself into a corner on *all* bargainable matters. . . .

We do not today hold that an employer may not communicate with his employees during negotiations. Nor are we deciding that the "best offer first" bargaining technique is forbidden. Moreover, we do not require an employer to engage in "auction bargaining," or, as the dissent seems to suggest, compel him to make concessions, "minor" or otherwise. . . .

We hold that an employer may not so combine "take-it-or-leave-it" bargaining methods with a widely publicized stance of unbending firmness that he is himself unable to alter a position once taken. It is this specific conduct that GE must avoid in order to comply with the Board's order, and not a carbon copy of every underlying event relied upon by the Board to support its findings. Such conduct, we find, constitutes a refusal to bargain "in fact." *NLRB v. Katz*, 369 U.S. 736, 743 (1962). It also constitutes, as the facts of this action demonstrate, an absence of subjective good faith, for it implies that the Company can deliberately bargain and communicate as though the Union did not exist, in clear derogation of the Union's status as exclusive representative of its members under §9(a). . . .

Friendly, Circuit Judge (concurring and dissenting)....

The danger of collision with § 8(c) or (d) arises only when the Board makes a finding of violation although the parties have sat down with each other and have not engaged in any proscribed tactic. Still I have no difficulty with the Board's making a finding of bad faith based on an entire course of conduct so long as the standard of bad faith is, in Judge Magruder's well-known phrase, a "desire not to reach an agreement with the Union." *NLRB v. Reed & Prince Mfg. Co.*, 205 F.2d 131, 134 (1st Cir.), *cert. denied*, 346 U.S. 887 (1953)....

While the lead opinion makes much use of the "take-it-or-leave-it" phrase, it never defines this. I should suppose it meant a resolve to adhere to a position without even listening to and considering the views of the other side. To go further and say that a party, whether employer or union, who, after listening to and considering such proposals, violates § 8(a)(5) if he rejects them because of confidence in his own bargaining power, would ignore the explicit command of § 8(d)....

It surely cannot be, for example, that a union intent on imposing area standards violates § 8(b)(3) if it refuses to heed the well-documented presentation of an employer who insists that acceptance of them will drive him out of business. Neither can it be that a union violates § 8(b)(3) if it insists on its demands because it knows the employer simply cannot stand a strike. It must be equally true that an employer is not to be condemned for "take-it-or-leave-it" bargaining when, after discussing the union's proposals and supporting arguments, he formulates what he considers a sufficiently attractive offer and refuses to alter it unless convinced an alteration is "right."...

Once we rid ourselves of the prejudice inevitably engendered by this catch-phrase, we reach the argument that a party violates § 8(a)(5) if he gets himself into a situation where he is "unable to alter a position once taken," even though he would otherwise be willing to do so.

While this sounds fair enough, as does the Board's somewhat similar remark about the continuing duty to give "unfettered consideration," it would seemingly outlaw practices that no one has considered illegal up to this time. A union that has won a favorable contract from one employer and has broadcast that it will take no less from others seems to me to be quite as "unable to alter a position once taken" as GE was here, yet I should not have supposed this violated the Act. So also with an employer who has negotiated a contract with one union and has proclaimed that he will do no better for others. To say that taking such positions violates § 8(b)(3) or 8(a)(5) is steering a collision course with § 8(d)....

An essential element to the Board's conclusion of GE's offending was the Company's publicity campaign. "The disparagement of the Union as bargaining representative" is item (5) in the Board's bill of particulars...

I find no warrant for such a holding in the language of the statute, its legislative history or decisions construing it. GE's communications fit snugly under the phrase "views, argument, or opinion" in § 8(c). The very archetypes of what Congress had in mind were communications by an employer to his workers designed to influence their decisions contrary to union views, and communications by unions to workers designed to influence their decisions contrary to employer views. The statute draws no distinctions between communications by an employer in an effort to head off organization and communications after organization intended to show that he is doing right by his employees and will do no more under the threat of a strike. Congress had enough faith in the common sense of the American working man to believe he did not need — or want — to be shielded by a government agency from hearing whatever arguments employers or unions desired to make to him. Freedom of choice by employees after hearing all relevant arguments is the cornerstone of the National Labor Relations Act. . . .

The Examiner coined a phrase, echoed both by the Board and in the lead opinion, . . . namely, that GE's communications program was an attempt "to deal with the Union through the employees rather than with the employees through the Union." . . . Picturesque characterizations of this sort, at such sharp variance with the record, scarcely aid the quest for a right result. Members of Congress would probably be surprised to learn that being "exclusive representatives" means that interested parties may not go to constituents in an endeavor to influence the representatives to depart from positions they have taken. There can be nothing wrong in an employer's urging employees to communicate with their representatives simply because the communication is one the representatives do not want to hear. I thus find it impossible to accept the proposition that, by exercising its § 8(c) right to persuade the employees and by encouraging them to exercise their right to persuade their representatives, GE was somehow "ignoring the legitimacy and relevance of the Union's position as statutory representative of its members." . . .

Notes

1. *Hard Bargaining versus Surface Bargaining* — "Hard bargaining" by an employer is not in itself unlawful. *See Arlington Metals Corp.*, 368 N.L.R.B. No. 74 (2019) (employer did not violate § 8(a)(5) even though it made only minor concessions over 37 sessions of hard bargaining spanning several years). At some juncture in the negotiations an employer clearly may make a firm and final offer. *See, e.g., Carey, Philip, Mfg. Co. (Automobile Workers, Local 689)*, 140 N.L.R.B. 1103 (1963), *enforced in part*, 331 F.2d 720 (6th Cir.), *cert. denied*, 379 U.S. 888 (1964) (finding no violation of § 8(a)(5) when employer made a final offer at the eleventh meeting in a series of give-and-take bargaining sessions). Generally, an employer who meets with the union's bargaining committee, explains its bargaining position, makes some concessions, reaches agreement on some issues, and does not engage in regressive bargaining will not violate § 8(a)(5), even if other conduct such as away-from-the-table comments, delay, or reluctance to provide information are also present. *St. George Warehouse, Inc.*, 341 N.L.R.B. 904 (2004), *enforced*, 420 F.3d 294 (3d Cir. 2005). The Board and the courts do not always see eye-to-eye, however, on the legality of

particular instances of hard bargaining. *See* Brown, *Hard Bargaining: The Board Says No, the Court Says Yes*, 8 Employee Rel. L.J. 37 (1982).

2. *Substantive Proposals as Evidence of Bad Faith Bargaining*—Occasionally, an employer's substantive proposals have been treated as evidence of bad faith, especially when combined with other conduct such as delaying tactics. So classified were an insistence on an "open shop" and absolute employer control over wage rates, *NLRB v. Wright Motors, Inc.*, 603 F.2d 604 (7th Cir. 1979); an offer of little or no wage increase during a period of double-digit inflation, *K-Mart Corp. v. NLRB*, 626 F.2d 704 (9th Cir. 1980); an uncompromising management rights proposal that was "obviously unpalatable" to the union, *Sparks Nugget, Inc. v. NLRB*, 968 F.2d 991 (9th Cir. 1992); and a no-strike clause that prohibited handbilling or "protest[s] regardless of the reason," *Altura Communication Solutions*, 369 N.L.R.B. No. 85 (2020).

In a few instances a finding of bad faith has been predicated in part on the employer's rejection of proposals submitted by the union. The proposals at issue included a clause embodying a right guaranteed to the employees by the labor relations statute, *Montgomery Ward & Co., Inc. (Portland, Or.)*, 37 N.L.R.B. 100 (1941), *enforced*, 133 F.2d 676 (9th Cir. 1943); permission for the union to use the company bulletin board, an accepted practice in the industry, *Reed & Prince Mfg. Co.*, 96 N.L.R.B. 850 (1951), *enforced*, 205 F.2d 131 (1st Cir.), *cert. denied*, 346 U.S. 887 (1953); and a dues checkoff provision, *H.K. Porter, Inc.*, 153 N.L.R.B. 1370 (1965), *enforced*, 363 F.2d 272 (D.C. Cir.), *cert. denied*, 385 U.S. 851 (1966). In such cases, the Board and courts typically conclude that employer intransigence is aimed at undermining the union and is lacking in any legitimate business purpose. *See, e.g., Universal Fuel, Inc.*, 358 N.L.R.B. 150 (2012) (bad faith bargaining shown where employer opposed union proposal on union security for purely "philosophical" reasons, refusing to advance any legitimate business justification, and insisted on negotiating over amount of fees to be paid under proposed agency shop arrangement, a permissive bargaining subject), *vacated due to lack of a Board quorum, Noel Canning v. NLRB*.

3. *Regressive Proposals*—Regressive proposals are not necessarily indicative of bad faith. According to the Board, the good faith/bad faith line is drawn where the cumulative effect of the employer's proposals negates the union's ability to act as representative of the employees or leaves the employees in a worse position than they were prior to bargaining. *See Public Serv. Co. v. NLRB*, 318 F.3d 1173 (10th Cir. 2003) (finding bad faith where employer's proposals as a whole undermined union's ability to function as employees' bargaining representative, even though no individual proposal was illegal). So, for example, if the employer's proposals require the waiver of statutory rights without making any economic concessions or offering to accept limits on employer rights, bad faith may be inferred. *See Hydrotherm, Inc.*, 302 N.L.R.B. 990 (1991). Similarly, an employer who made a series of regressive bargaining proposals that would freeze wages, reduce vacation leave, and eliminate overtime, bonuses, and a 401(k) retirement savings plan, while unilaterally changing health insurance providers and altering benefits and wage rates violated § 8(a)(5).

Statements by supervisors outside of bargaining indicated that the employer had no intention of reaching agreement on a contract and planned to seek a decertification election, supporting the Board's finding of surface bargaining against the backdrop of a larger plan to oust the union. *NLRB v. Hardesty Co.*, 308 F.3d 859 (8th Cir. 2002).

However, proposals to reduce the status quo by eliminating a union security clause, reducing wages and benefits, and insisting on at-will employment are not indicative of bad faith bargaining if the employer has a legitimate business reason for its proposal. *See KFMB Stations*, 349 N.L.R.B. 373 (2007), *review denied*, *AFTRA v. NLRB*, 2008 U.S. App. LEXIS 26636 (9th Cir. 2008) (employer proposal to remove union security clause present in prior contracts did not constitute bad faith where employer offered reasonable business justification of not wanting to remove on-the-air talent for nonpayment of union dues); *Mgmt. & Training Corp.*, 366 N.L.R.B. No. 134 (2018) (employer's regressive proposal to eliminate arbitration was justified by employer's proffered reason that union had not responded to earlier proposals and had filed frivolous grievances; employer also requested continuing negotiation); *S & F Enters.*, 312 N.L.R.B. 770 (1993) (employer's rigidity on at-will employment and refusal to agree to arbitration was justified by its "undisputedly precarious financial condition"); *Optica Lee Borinquen, Inc.*, 307 N.L.R.B. 705 (1992), *enforced*, 991 F.2d 786 (1st Cir. 1993) (deep reductions sought in allegedly noncompetitive existing benefits not evidence of bad faith). Further, a regressive proposal that does not completely foreclose bargaining is not by itself an indication of bad faith; substantial evidence must be offered to link the proposal to the goal of frustrating bargaining. *Carey Salt Co. v. NLRB*, 736 F.3d 405 (5th Cir. 2013).

4. *Style of Bargaining* — How much of the good faith inquiry is based on the form that bargaining takes rather than its substance? In *NLRB v. Montgomery Ward & Co.*, 133 F.2d 676, 687 (9th Cir. 1943), the court said: "Wards was not bound to offer a counterproposal . . . but when one is asked for, it ought to be made, although not indispensable. [I]t is not incumbent upon the employees continually to present new contracts until ultimately one meets the approval of the company." Could one say there is a duty to make counterproposals but no duty to make concessions? What would that mean? *See TNT Logistics N. Am., Inc.*, 346 N.L.R.B. 1301 (2006), *enforced*, 2007 U.S. App. LEXIS 16235 (4th Cir. 2007) (finding §8(a)(5) violation where employer held only one bargaining session, refused to respond to union's request for additional sessions, did not specify terms that would elicit its agreement, and failed to offer counterproposal); *Print Fulfillment Servs., LLC*, 361 N.L.R.B. 1243 (2014) (finding §8(a)(5) violation where employer merely "went through the motions" of bargaining and refused to engage in any form of meaningful dialogue).

5. *Totality of the Circumstances* — Ordinarily, the good faith of the employer is to be judged by the NLRB on the basis of all the circumstances, including conduct away from the bargaining table. Delaying tactics, the nature of the employer's bargaining demands, unilateral changes in mandatory subjects of bargaining, efforts to bypass the union, or failure to designate an agent with sufficient bargaining authority may raise an inference of bad faith. The test is whether the "totality of the employer's conduct ... manifests a mindset at odds with reaching an agreement." *Bethea Baptist Home*, 310 N.L.R.B. 156 (1993). Thus, an employer's pre-election speeches concerning its intentions in negotiations may be evidence of unlawful "surface bargaining." *NLRB v. Overnite Transp. Co.*, 938 F.2d 815 (7th Cir. 1991). Similarly, an employer's statements at the bargaining table that it "would not mind" if its proposals prompted a strike, and that the General Manager "wanted a strike so that he could replace the employees and get rid of the unions," combined with "regressive and confrontational proposals" (wage reduction, elimination of the pension plan, and institution of an inferior health plan) evidenced egregious surface bargaining and a desire to frustrate agreement. *Unbelievable, Inc.*, 318 N.L.R.B. 857 (1995), *enforced in part*, 118 F.3d 795 (D.C. Cir. 1997).

A party's withdrawal without good cause of a bargaining proposal upon which the parties have tentatively agreed can evidence lack of good-faith bargaining. Consideration of such a factor is consistent with the Board's totality of the circumstances inquiry when taken in combination with contextual factors, including the suddenness of the withdrawal and lack of convincing rationale for it, the importance of the proposal to the agreement as a whole, and the fact that the agreement was nearly completed at the time of the withdrawal. *NLRB v. Suffield Acad.*, 322 F.3d 196 (2d Cir. 2003); *see also Leader Communications, Inc.*, 361 N.L.R.B. 243 (2014) (employer violated § 8(a)(5) by repudiating a tentative agreement with the union without good cause); *Graham Auto., Inc.*, 347 N.L.R.B. 615 (2006) (employer violated § 8(a)(5) by failing to execute a collective bargaining agreement after the parties had arrived at a meeting of the minds); *Gen. Teamsters Union Local 662*, 339 N.L.R.B. 893 (2003) (union violated § 8(b)(3) by refusing to execute agreement).

6. *Direct Employer-Employee Communication* — The Labor Board has indicated that an employer has a fundamental First Amendment right to communicate directly with employees to publicize its bargaining position, so long as it does not endeavor to deal directly with the employees or to bypass the workers' chosen bargaining agent, and the communication is accomplished in a noncoercive manner. *See United Technologies Corp.*, 274 N.L.R.B. 1069 (1985), *enforced*, 789 F.2d 121 (2d Cir. 1986); *El Paso Elec. Co.*, 355 N.L.R.B. 544 (2010). There is no requirement that the union be given a meaningful opportunity to consider a proposal before the employer disseminates information to employees. *Americare Pine Lodge Nursing & Rehabilitation Ctr. v. NLRB*, 164 F.3d 867 (4th Cir. 1999). Thus, requests or proposals made directly to employees that do not offer the employees different terms than the employer has previously offered the union are permissible. *See Boehringer Ingleheim VetMedica, Inc.*, 350 N.L.R.B. 678 (2007) (employer's request that locked-out employees who showed up to work following a union strike sign a no-strike promise did not violate the Act where the employer advised employees to talk to their union representatives before signing and offered nothing more than what it had previously offered the union in bargaining).

On the other hand, direct dealing that undermines the union's efficacy as bargaining agent is unlawful. For example, an employer violated § 8(a)(5) when it dealt directly with bargaining unit members instead of going through the representative union, encouraging the unit employees to accept its 401(k) plan instead of the union pension program. *Certco Distrib. Ctrs.*, 346 N.L.R.B. 1214 (2006), *enforced*, 722 F.3d 1097 (7th Cir. 2013). Similarly, an employer engaged in prohibited direct dealing with employees when it allowed two clerical assistants to work virtually after rejecting the union's proposal to allow all clerical assistants affected by closures of physical offices to work virtually. *YP Advertising & Publishing LLC*, 366 N.L.R.B. No. 89 (2018). However, no violation occurred when the employer informed employees directly of its proposal for a new compensation plan when the information was paired with assurances that the employer would bargain with the union over the proposal. *Id.* See also *Mercy Health Partners*, 358 N.L.R.B. 566 (2012) (employer violated § 8(a)(5) by meeting directly with employees and bypassing the union on issues relating to effects of business decision that entailed relocating their jobs to a nonunion facility; further, evidence suggested that the employer intended to undercut the union's role as bargaining agent).

Problems

45. The workers at Alpine Meadows, Inc., the area's largest supplier of landscape rock, gravel, and sand, recently elected the Crushed Stone Workers Union to represent them. The company and the union just began negotiating their first contract, but things were not going well. There were two sticking points. First, the union asked Alpine to agree to a clause under which it would withhold dues and remit them directly to the union. With respect to this request, the company told the union it could "go pound sand," and that it would never garnish employee wages for such a purpose because of the administrative burden. Their payroll system, Alpine claimed, was not set up to handle it, and overhauling it would cost millions. Second, as the negotiations continued, it became clear that Alpine was going to insist on incorporating into the collective agreement its pre-election employee handbook, which establishes basic terms and conditions of employment and is unilaterally modifiable by the employer at any time.

Does Alpine's refusal to agree to the clause about withholding dues constitute evidence of bad faith bargaining? What about its insistence on incorporating the employee handbook?

46. Uniformity of labor standards in an industry or geographical area is a traditional goal of many unions. After a union has come to terms with the principal employer association in a given area, would it violate § 8(b)(3) for the union to require an identical contract with every independent employer, resorting to a strike to compel agreement if necessary?

Is there any difference between the union's "take-it-or-leave-it" attitude in such circumstances and GE's in the 1960 negotiations with the IUE? Even if the union engaged in the usual give-and-take bargaining with the employer association, what good is this to an independent employer confronted by a peremptory demand to sign the standard labor agreement?

NLRB v. American National Insurance Co.
Supreme Court of the United States
343 U.S. 395, 72 S. Ct. 824, 96 L. Ed. 1027 (1952)

Mr. Chief Justice Vinson delivered the opinion of the Court.

This case arises out of a complaint that respondent refused to bargain collectively with the representatives of its employees as required under the National Labor Relations Act, as amended.

The Office Employees International Union, AFL, Local No. 27, certified by the National Labor Relations Board as the exclusive bargaining representative of respondent's office employees, requested a meeting with respondent for the purpose of negotiating an agreement governing employment relations. At the first meetings, beginning on November 30, 1948, the Union submitted a proposed contract covering wages, hours, promotions, vacations and other provisions commonly found in collective bargaining agreements, including a clause establishing a procedure for settling grievances arising under the contract by successive appeals to management with ultimate resort to an arbitrator.

On January 10, 1949, following a recess for study of the Union's contract proposals, respondent objected to the provisions calling for unlimited arbitration. To meet this objection, respondent proposed a so-called management functions clause listing matters such as promotions, discipline and work scheduling as the responsibility of management and excluding such matters from arbitration. The Union's representative took the position "as soon as [he] heard [the proposed clause]" that the Union would not agree to such a clause so long as it covered matters subject to the duty to bargain collectively under the Labor Act.

Several further bargaining sessions were held without reaching agreement on the Union's proposal or respondent's counter-proposal to unlimited arbitration. As a result, the management functions clause was "by-passed" for bargaining on other terms of the Union's contract proposal. On January 17, 1949, respondent stated in writing its agreement with some of the terms proposed by the Union and, where there was disagreement, respondent offered counterproposals, including a clause entitled "Functions and Prerogatives of Management" along the lines suggested at the meeting of January 10th. The Union objected to the portion of the clause providing:

> The right to select and hire, to promote to a better position, to discharge, demote or discipline for cause, and to maintain discipline and efficiency of employees and to determine the schedules of work is recognized by both union and company as the proper responsibility and prerogative of management to be held and exercised by the company, and while it is agreed that an employee feeling himself to have been aggrieved by any decision of the company in respect to such matters, or the union in his behalf, shall have the right to have such decision reviewed by top management officials

of the company under the grievance machinery hereinafter set forth, it is further agreed that the final decision of the company made by such top management officials shall not be further reviewable by arbitration.

At this stage of the negotiations, the National Labor Relations Board filed a complaint against respondent based on the Union's charge that respondent had refused to bargain as required by the Labor Act and was thereby guilty of interfering with the rights of its employees guaranteed by § 7 of the Act and of unfair labor practices under §§ 8(a)(1) and 8(a)(5) of the Act. While the proceeding was pending, negotiations between the Union and respondent continued with the management functions clause remaining an obstacle to agreement. . . .

On May 19, 1949, a Union representative offered a second contract proposal which included a management functions clause containing much of the language found in respondent's second counterproposal, quoted above, with the vital difference that questions arising under the Union's proposed clause would be subject to arbitration as in the case of other grievances. Finally, on January 13, 1950, after the Trial Examiner had issued his report but before decision by the Board, an agreement between the Union and respondent was signed. The agreement contained a management functions clause that rendered nonarbitrable matters of discipline, work schedules and other matters covered by the clause. The subject of promotions and demotions was deleted from the clause and made the subject of a special clause establishing a union-management committee to pass upon promotion matters.

While these negotiations were in progress, the Board's Trial Examiner conducted hearings on the Union's complaint. The Examiner held that respondent had a right to bargain for inclusion of a management functions clause in a contract. However, upon review of the entire negotiations, including respondent's unilateral action in changing working conditions during the bargaining, the Examiner found that from and after November 30, 1948, respondent had refused to bargain in a good faith effort to reach agreement. The Examiner recommended that respondent be ordered in general terms to bargain collectively with the Union.

The Board agreed with the Trial Examiner that respondent had not bargained in a good faith effort to reach an agreement with the Union. But the Board rejected the Examiner's views on an employer's right to bargain for a management functions clause and held that respondent's action in bargaining for inclusion of any such clause "constituted, quite [apart from] Respondent's demonstrated bad faith, per se violations of § 8(a)(5) and (1)." Accordingly, the Board not only ordered respondent in general terms to bargain collectively with the Union (par. 2 (a)), but also included in its order a paragraph designed to prohibit bargaining for any management functions clause covering a condition of employment. (Par. 1(a)). 89 N.L.R.B. 185. . . .

First. The National Labor Relations Act is designed to promote industrial peace by encouraging the making of voluntary agreements governing relations between unions and employers. The Act does not compel any agreement whatsoever between employees and employers. Nor does the Act regulate the substantive terms governing wages, hours and working conditions which are incorporated in an agreement. The theory of the Act is that the making of voluntary labor agreements is encouraged by protecting employees' rights to organize for collective bargaining and by imposing on labor and management the mutual obligation to bargain collectively.

Enforcement of the obligation to bargain collectively is crucial to the statutory scheme. And, as has long been recognized, performance of the duty to bargain requires more than a willingness to enter upon a sterile discussion of union-management differences. Before the enactment of the National Labor Relations Act, it was held that the duty of an employer to bargain collectively required the employer "to negotiate in good faith with his employees' representatives; to match their proposals, if unacceptable, with counterproposals; and to make every reasonable effort to reach an agreement." The duty to bargain collectively, implicit in the Wagner Act as introduced in Congress, was made express by the insertion of the fifth employer unfair labor practice accompanied by an explanation of the purpose and meaning of the phrase "bargain collectively in a good faith effort to reach an agreement." This understanding of the duty to bargain collectively has been accepted and applied throughout the administration of the Wagner Act by the National Labor Relations Board and the Courts of Appeal.

In 1947, the fear was expressed in Congress that the Board "has gone very far, in the guise of determining whether or not employers had bargained in good faith, in setting itself up as the judge of what concessions an employer must make and of the proposals and counterproposals that he may or may not make." Accordingly, the Hartley Bill, passed by the House, eliminated the good faith test and expressly provided that the duty to bargain collectively did not require submission of counterproposals. As amended in the Senate and passed as the Taft-Hartley Act, the good faith test of bargaining was retained and written into § 8(d) of the National Labor Relations Act. That section contains the express provision that the obligation to bargain collectively does not compel either party to agree to a proposal or require the making of a concession.

Thus it is now apparent from the statute itself that the Act does not encourage a party to engage in fruitless marathon discussions at the expense of frank statement and support of his position. And it is equally clear that the Board may not, either directly or indirectly, compel concessions or otherwise sit in judgment upon the substantive terms of collective bargaining agreements.

Second. The Board offers in support of the portion of its order before this Court a theory quite apart from the test of good faith bargaining prescribed in § 8(d) of the Act, a theory that respondent's bargaining for a management functions clause as a counterproposal to the Union's demand for unlimited arbitration was, *"per se,"* a violation of the Act.

Counsel for the Board do not contend that a management functions clause covering some conditions of employment is an illegal contract term. As a matter of fact, a review of typical contract clauses collected for convenience in drafting labor agreements shows that management functions clauses similar in essential detail to the clause proposed by respondent have been included in contracts negotiated by national unions with many employers. The National War Labor Board, empowered during the last war "[t]o decide the dispute, and provide by order the wages and hours and all other terms and conditions (customarily included in collective bargaining agreements)," ordered management functions clauses included in a number of agreements. Several such clauses ordered by the War Labor Board provided for arbitration in case of union dissatisfaction with the exercise of management functions, while others, as in the clause proposed by respondent in this case, provided that management decisions would be final. Without intimating any opinion as to the form of management function clause proposed by respondent in this case or the desirability of including any such clause in a labor agreement, it is manifest that bargaining for management functions clauses is common collective bargaining practice.

If the Board is correct, an employer violates the Act by bargaining for a management functions clause touching any condition of employment without regard to the traditions of bargaining in the particular industry or such other evidence of good faith as the fact in this case that respondent's clause was offered as a counterproposal to the Union's demand for unlimited arbitration. The Board's argument is a technical one for it is conceded that respondent would not be guilty of an unfair labor practice if, instead of proposing a clause that removed some matters from arbitration, it simply refused in good faith to agree to the Union proposal for unlimited arbitration. The argument starts with a finding, not challenged by the court below or by respondent, that at least some of the matters covered by the management functions clause proposed by respondent are "conditions of employment" which are appropriate subjects of collective bargaining under §§ 8(a)(5), 8(d) and 9(a) of the Act. The Board considers that employer bargaining for a clause under which management retains initial responsibility for work scheduling, a "condition of employment," for the duration of the contract is an unfair labor practice because it is "in derogation of" employees' statutory rights to bargain collectively as to conditions of employment.[12]

Conceding that there is nothing unlawful in including a management functions clause in a labor agreement, the Board would permit an employer to "propose" such a clause. But the Board would forbid bargaining for any such clause when the Union declines to accept the proposal, even where the clause is offered as a counterproposal to a Union demand for unlimited arbitration. Ignoring the nature of the

---

12. [22] The Board's argument would seem to prevent an employer from bargaining for a "no-strike" clause, commonly found in labor agreements, requiring a union to forego for the duration of the contract the right to strike expressly granted by § 7 of the Act. However, the Board has permitted an employer to bargain in good faith for such a clause. *Shell Oil Co.*, 77 N.L.R.B. 1306 (1948). This result is explained by referring to the "salutary objective" of such a clause. *Bethlehem Steel Co.*, 89 N.L.R.B. 341, 345 (1950).

Union's demand in this case, the board takes the position that employers subject to the Act must agree to include in any labor agreement provisions establishing fixed standards for work schedules or any other condition of employment. An employer would be permitted to bargain as to the content of the standard so long as he agrees to freeze a standard into a contract. Bargaining for more flexible treatment of such matters would be denied employers even though the result may be contrary to common collective bargaining practice in the industry. The Board was not empowered so to disrupt collective bargaining practices. On the contrary, the term "bargain collectively" as used in the Act "has been considered to absorb and give statutory approval to the philosophy of bargaining as worked out in the labor movement in the United States." *Order of Railroad Telegraphers v. Railway Express Agency*, 321 U.S. 342 (1944).

Congress provided expressly that the Board should not pass upon the desirability of the substantive terms of labor agreements. Whether a contract should contain a clause fixing standards for such matters as work scheduling or should provide for more flexible treatment of such matters is an issue for determination across the bargaining table, not by the Board. If the latter approach is agreed upon, the extent of union and management participation in the administration of such matters is itself a condition of employment to be settled by bargaining.

Accordingly, we reject the Board's holding that bargaining for the management functions clause proposed by respondent was, *per se*, an unfair labor practice. Any fears the Board may entertain that use of management functions clauses will lead to evasion of an employer's duty to bargain collectively as to "rates of pay, wages, hours and conditions of employment" do not justify condemning all bargaining for management functions clauses covering any "condition of employment" as *per se* violations of the Act. The duty to bargain collectively is to be enforced by application of the good faith bargaining standards of § 8(d) to the facts of each case rather than by prohibiting all employers in every industry from bargaining for management functions clauses altogether. . . .

Accepting as we do the finding of the Court below that respondent bargained in good faith for the management functions clause proposed by it, we hold that respondent was not in that respect guilty of refusing to bargain collectively as required by the National Labor Relations Act. Accordingly, enforcement of paragraph 1(a) of the Board's order was properly denied.

Affirmed.

Mr. Justice Minton, with whom Mr. Justice Black and Mr. Justice Douglas join, dissenting:

I do not see how this case is solved by telling the National Labor Relations Board that since *some* "management functions" clauses are valid (which the Board freely admits), respondent was not guilty of an unfair labor practice *in this case*. The record is replete with evidence that respondent insisted on a clause which would classify the control over certain conditions of employment as a management prerogative, and that the insistence took the form of a refusal to reach a settlement unless the union accepted the clause. The Court of Appeals agreed that the respondent was "steadfast" in this demand.

Therefore, *this case* is one where the employer came into the bargaining room with a demand that certain topics upon which it had a duty to bargain were to be removed from the agenda — that was the price the union had to pay to gain a contract. There is all the difference between the hypothetical "management functions" clauses envisioned by the majority and this "management functions" clause as there is between waiver and coercion. No one suggests that an employer is guilty of an unfair labor practice when it proposes that it be given unilateral control over certain working conditions and the union accepts the proposal in return for various other benefits. But where, as here, the employer tells the union that the only way to obtain a contract as to wages is to agree not to bargain about certain other working conditions, the employer has refused to bargain about those other working conditions. There is more than a semantic difference between a proposal that the union waive certain rights and a demand that the union give up those rights as a condition precedent to enjoying other rights.

I need not and do not take issue with the Court of Appeals' conclusion that there was no absence of good faith. Where there is a refusal to bargain, the Act does not require an inquiry as to whether that refusal was in good faith or bad faith. The duty to bargain about certain subjects is made absolute by the Act. The majority seems to suggest that an employer could be found guilty of bad faith if it used a "management functions" clause to close off bargaining about all topics of discussion. Whether the employer closes off all bargaining or, as in this case, only a certain area of bargaining, he has refused to bargain as to whatever he has closed off, and any discussion of his good faith is pointless.

That portion of § 8(d) of the Act which declares that an employer need not agree to a proposal or make concessions does not dispose of this case. Certainly the Board lacks power to compel concessions as to the substantive terms of labor agreements. But the Board in this case was seeking to compel the employer to bargain about subjects properly within the scope of collective bargaining. That the employer has such a duty to bargain and that the Board is empowered to enforce the duty is clear.

An employer may not stake out an area which is a proper subject for bargaining and say, "As to this we will not bargain." To do so is a plain refusal to bargain in violation of § 8(a)(5) of the Act. If employees' bargaining rights can be cut away so easily, they are indeed illusory. I would reverse.

Problem

47. Following several back-and-forth bargaining sessions, an employer made the following final offer as to the management rights clause it insisted must be included in the collective agreement before it would sign a contract: "The management-rights

clause must provide the employer the right to unilaterally make and implement management decisions regarding the operation of its business and the management of its employees, limited only by the express and specific terms of the agreement, including determining whether employees covered by the CBA or other workers would produce goods or services. Further, the exercise of management's rights would be excluded from the grievance procedure except where specifically and clearly limited by the agreement's express terms." As part of its proposal, management also insisted on the following provisions:

1. A broad "zipper" clause that waived the Union's right to bargain regarding any subject arising during the course of the contract.

2. Work-jurisdiction provisions placing no restrictions on the employer's use of non-unit employees for work that had been exclusively or regularly performed by the unit.

3. A broad no-strike clause prohibiting protests for any reason.

4. An arbitration clause limiting arbitrators' authority to specific alleged violations.

5. Layoff provisions that give the employer broad discretion to eliminate seniority as a consideration, and conditioning severance benefits on waivers.

Are any of these clauses, by themselves, violative of the Act? Has the employer nevertheless violated the Act by failing to bargain in good faith?

NLRB v. Insurance Agents' International Union, 361 U.S. 477, 80 S. Ct. 419, 4 L. Ed. 2d 454 (1960). In order to put economic pressure on an employer to yield to bargaining demands, a union of insurance agents engaged in concerted on-the-job activities designed to harass the company. These included refusal for a time to solicit new business, refusal to follow reporting procedures, late arrival at work and early departure, failure to attend meetings, and picketing of company offices. Although the union continued to negotiate with the employer in an effort to reach agreement on a new contract, the National Labor Relations Board held that its harassing tactics constituted a refusal to bargain in good faith as required by § 8(b)(3) of the NLRA. The Supreme Court disagreed. Pointing out that Congress did not intend the NLRB to regulate the substantive terms of labor agreements, the Court stated: "[I]f the Board could regulate the choice of economic weapons that may be used as part of collective bargaining, it would be in a position to exercise considerable influence upon the substantive terms on which the parties contract." Even on the assumption the employees' conduct was unprotected, and they could have been discharged for it, it was not inconsistent with good-faith bargaining.

General Electric Co. v. NLRB, 412 F.2d 512 (2d Cir. 1969). The IUE and seven other unions representing General Electric workers, concerned about the company's technique of presenting a separate "fair, firm offer" to each union almost simultaneously and then whipsawing one against the other, formed a Committee on Collective Bargaining (CCB) to coordinate bargaining in 1966 with GE and its major competitor, Westinghouse. After GE rejected the CCB's request for informal joint discussions, the company and the IUE set a date to begin individual negotiations. But the GE representatives walked out when they discovered that the IUE bargaining committee had been enlarged by one person from each of the other seven unions comprising the CCB, even though the IUE insisted the seven new committee members had no vote and were present only to assist the IUE and not to represent their own unions. The NLRB found the company had violated § 8(a)(5) in its refusal to confer and the Second Circuit agreed. The court observed that the right of both employees and employers "to choose whomever they wish to represent them in formal labor negotiations is fundamental to the statutory scheme." The rare exceptions to the rule of free choice of representatives are situations where personal ill will or conflicts of interest create a "clear and present" danger to the collective bargaining process. Furthermore, there was no showing that the CCB was attempting to use the augmented negotiating committee to impose joint bargaining on the company or that the IUE was committed not to accept any GE offer unless the other unions agreed. The company was therefore obligated to test the IUE's good faith.

Notes

1. *Employer Insistence on Joint Negotiations* — An employer may not insist upon joint negotiations with two unions representing separate units of the company's employees. To carry such a demand to impasse is a violation of § 8(a)(5), since only the employees or their representatives have the right to select the members of the union's bargaining team. *Woolworth, F.W., Co.*, 179 N.L.R.B. 748 (1969).

2. *Employer Influence Over Union's Choice of Bargaining Representative* — Under what circumstances may an employer influence the employees' choice of representative at the bargaining table? An employer's refusal to negotiate with a union business agent who was an ex-employee terminated four years previously for threatening and violent conduct did not violate § 8(a)(5). In light of the employer's history with the agent — whose actions had in the past jeopardized the safety of others — his presence at the bargaining table might preclude good faith bargaining by suppressing the vigorous exchange of positions unencumbered by fear of one's adversary's violent reaction. *See King Soopers, Inc.*, 338 N.L.R.B. 269 (2002); *see also Pan Am. Grain Co.*, 343 N.L.R.B. 205 (2004) (employer who declined to meet with union president after the union president made threatening comments to a supervisor and invited him outside to fight did not violate § 8(a)(5); obligation to deal with the other party's chosen representatives in bargaining ceases when a particular representative's presence would render collective bargaining impossible or futile). On the other hand, a § 8(a)(5) violation was found where an employer denied unpaid leaves of absence to union bargaining committee members, insisted that they use their accrued "Personal Days Off" leave that was of finite duration, and refused to negotiate during nonwork hours, since this would chill participation by committee members with family or other personal obligations. *Ceridian Corp. v. NLRB*, 435 F.3d 352 (D.C. Cir. 2006).

3. *Union Insistence on Joint Negotiations* — Should labor organizations representing different bargaining units of the same employer be entitled to insist upon joint negotiations? In *AFL-CIO Joint Negotiating Committee (Phelps Dodge Corp.)*, 184 N.L.R.B. 976 (1970), the Labor Board held that a group of unions violated § 8(b)(3) by insisting in effect on company-wide bargaining. The unions demanded the simultaneous and satisfactory settlement of contracts in other bargaining units of the company, and struck in support of their demands. The Board said that the integrity of a bargaining unit, whether established by certification or by voluntary agreement of the parties, may not be unilaterally attacked. Enforcement was denied in *AFL-CIO Joint Negotiating Committee for Phelps Dodge v. NLRB*, 470 F.2d 722 (3d Cir.), *cert. denied*, 409 U.S. 1059 (1972). The court of appeals pointed out that all the union demands were mandatory subjects of bargaining, and that the parallel action of the units in going to impasse was not evidence of an attempt to merge the bargaining of separate units. "The fact that a demand may have extra-unit effects does not alter its status as a mandatory subject of bargaining." *But cf. United Paperworkers Int'l Union Eriez Local Union No. 620*, 309 N.L.R.B. 44 (1992) (union demand for pooled voting among all units in ratifying agreement was unlawful; agreement in one unit may not be conditioned upon the satisfactory conclusion of negotiations for another unit); *see* Getman & Marshall, *Industrial Relations in Transition: The Paper Industry Example*, 102 YALE L.J. 1803 (1993) (criticizing *Paperworkers* decision and doctrine).

4. *Obligation to Meet and Confer* — Section 8(d) requires the parties "to meet at reasonable times and confer in good faith" with respect to mandatory subjects of bargaining. Where an employer only agreed to one or two dates a month during the certification year, restricted meetings to times other than normal business hours, often canceled scheduled sessions, and refused to meet on weekends and many week nights, the Board was warranted in finding a § 8(a)(5) violation. *Lancaster Nissan, Inc. v. NLRB*, 344 N.L.R.B. 225 (2005), *enforced*, 2007 U.S. App. LEXIS 7747 (3d Cir. 2007). *See also Prof'l Transp., Inc.*, 362 N.L.R.B. 534 (2015) (employer that canceled seven consecutive bargaining sessions and conditioned further bargaining on the outcome of *NLRB v. Noel Canning* evidenced pattern of dilatory conduct that violated § 8(a)(5)); *Camelot Terrace*, 357 N.L.R.B. 1934 (2011) (employer that imposed arbitrary limits on the length of bargaining sessions and repeatedly canceled sessions violated § 8(a)(5)); *Garden Ridge Mgmt.*, 347 N.L.R.B. 131 (2006) (employer's refusal of union's requests for more frequent bargaining sessions during initial contract negotiations violated § 8(a)(5)).

Nor may an employer condition meeting with the union upon advance submission of a detailed bargaining agenda and bargaining proposals, *see Vanguard Fire & Supply Co.*, 345 N.L.R.B. 1016 (2005), *enforced*, 468 F.3d 952 (6th Cir. 2006); upon the presence of a court reporter, *see Bartlett Collins Co.*, 237 N.L.R.B. 770 (1978), *enforced*, 639 F.2d 652 (10th Cir.), *cert. denied*, 452 U.S. 961 (1981); or upon the assistance of a mediator in negotiations held in separate rooms, *see Success Vill. Apartments, Inc.*, 347 N.L.R.B. 1065 (2006).

Problem

48. A nurse's union was in the middle of negotiating its next contract with a hospital when the COVID-19 pandemic struck. The hospital proposed conducting future bargaining sessions via videoconferencing, using Zoom. The union objected, arguing that face-to-face negotiations are critical and that precautions can be taken to ensure safety of the negotiating teams. If the hospital refuses the face-to-face negotiation, has it violated the Act's requirement that the parties meet and confer?

Charles D. Bonanno Linen Service, Inc. v. NLRB, 454 U.S. 404, 102 S. Ct. 720, 70 L. Ed. 2d 656 (1982). For several years, Bonanno was a member of the Linen Supply Association, a group of 10 employers formed to negotiate with a Teamsters local as a multiemployer unit. In February 1975, Bonanno authorized the Association to represent it in the forthcoming negotiations. The union and the Association held 10 bargaining sessions during March and April. On April 30, the negotiators reached a tentative agreement but the union members rejected it. By May 15, bargaining had come to an impasse over the method of compensation. On June 23, the union selectively struck Bonanno and in response most other Association members locked out their drivers. The stalemate continued over the summer despite sporadic meetings. Bonanno permanently replaced all its striking drivers and on November 21 announced its withdrawal from the Association because of the "ongoing impasse." Shortly thereafter, the Association ended its lockout and resumed negotiations, without Bonanno. A new contract was agreed upon in April 1976 but Bonanno refused to be bound by its terms.

The Supreme Court accepted the NLRB's recognition of the voluntary nature of multiemployer bargaining, and the notion that both unions and employers may withdraw by giving timely, unequivocal notice prior to negotiations. Absent unusual circumstances, however, the policy of promoting labor peace supports the rule that no party can unilaterally withdraw during negotiations. A 5-4 majority of the Court concluded that it should defer to the Board's judgment that an impasse, standing alone, was not such an unusual circumstance or so destructive of group bargaining as to justify a unilateral withdrawal. Even the possibility that a union might sign interim agreements with certain employers, pending the execution of a unitwide contract, would not destroy the integrity of the multiemployer unit.

Chief Justice Burger and Justice Rehnquist dissented in *Bonanno,* arguing that the Court's majority was too deferential to the NLRB's flat rule that an impasse does not justify an employer's withdrawal from multiemployer bargaining, regardless of the severity and length of the impasse and the presence of interim agreements with some employers. Those dissenters contended that a rule permitting unilateral withdrawal upon impasse was more consistent with the goal of industrial peace and less likely to force the parties into "escalated economic warfare." Justices O'Connor and Powell, dissenting, would avoid the "absolute positions" of both the majority and the Chief Justice. Instead, they would require an examination into the particular circumstances of any impasse. For example, when there is a "complete breakdown in negotiations," not just a "temporary impasse," they would allow an employer to withdraw.

Notes

1. *Withdrawal from a Multiemployer Bargaining Unit* — Withdrawal from multiemployer bargaining is always permissible upon the "mutual consent" of the union and the association. *Retail Associates Inc. v. Retail Clerks International Association Locals Nos. 128 and 633*, 120 N.L.R.B. 388 (1958); *see also CTS, Inc.*, 340 N.L.R.B. 904 (2003) (Board found consent by union to employer's withdrawal from association based on totality of union's conduct). An employer may withdraw during bargaining if negotiations were initiated prematurely. *Action Elec., Inc. v. Local Union No. 292, International Brotherhood of Electrical Workers*, 856 F.2d 1062 (8th Cir. 1988). If impasse alone does not justify unilateral withdrawal after multiemployer negotiations have begun, what circumstances would? What about a sharp decline in a company's business—would this constitute "unusual circumstances," permitting a unilateral withdrawal from multiemployer negotiations? *See Serv-All Co., Inc.*, 199 N.L.R.B. 1131 (1972), *enforcement denied*, 491 F.2d 1273 (10th Cir. 1974). *See generally* Bock, *Multiemployer Bargaining and Withdrawing from the Association After Bargaining Has Begun: 38 Years of "Unusual Circumstances" Under Retail Associates*, 13 Hofstra Lab. L.J. 519 (1996).

2. *Section 8(f) Pre-Hire Bargaining Relationships* — The rules for post-impasse withdrawal from a multiemployer bargaining group enunciated in *Retail Associates* do not apply to pre-hire bargaining relationships established by construction industry parties under §8(f). As a result, a continuing obligation to participate in negotiations for a new agreement does not apply to employers with §8(f) relationships. *Madison Indus.*, 349 N.L.R.B. 1306 (2007).

B. Bargaining Remedies

H. K. Porter Co. v. NLRB

Supreme Court of the United States
397 U.S. 99, 90 S. Ct. 821, 26 L. Ed. 2d 146 (1970)

Mr. Justice Black delivered the opinion of the Court.

After an election respondent United Steelworkers Union was, on October 5, 1961, certified by the National Labor Relations Board as the bargaining agent for the employees at the Danville, Virginia, plant of the petitioner, H.K. Porter Co. Thereafter negotiations commenced for a collective bargaining agreement. Since that time the controversy has seesawed between the Board, the Court of Appeals for the District of Columbia Circuit, and this Court. This delay of over eight years is not because the case is exceedingly complex, but appears to have occurred chiefly because of the skill of the company's negotiators in taking advantage of every opportunity for delay in an Act more noticeable for its generality than for its precise prescriptions. The entire lengthy dispute mainly revolves around the union's desire to have the company agree to "check off" the dues owed to the union by its members, that is, to deduct those dues periodically from the company's wage payments to the employees. The record shows, as the Board found, that the company's objection to a checkoff was not due to any general principle or policy against making deductions from employees' wages. The company does deduct charges for things like insurance, taxes, and contributions to charities, and at some other plants it has a checkoff arrangement for union dues.

The evidence shows, and the court below found, that the company's objection was not because of inconvenience, but solely on the ground that the company was "not going to aid and comfort the union." Efforts by the union to obtain some kind of compromise on the checkoff request were all met with the same staccato response to the effect that the collection of union dues was the "union's business" and the company was not going to provide any assistance. Based on this and other evidence the Board found, and the Court of Appeals approved the finding, that the refusal of the company to bargain about the checkoff was not made in good faith, but was done solely to frustrate the making of any collective bargaining agreement. In May 1966, the Court of Appeals upheld the Board's order requiring the company to cease and desist from refusing to bargain in good faith and directing it to engage in further collective bargaining, if requested by the union to do so, over the checkoff. *United Steelworkers v. NLRB*, 363 F.2d 272, *cert. denied*, 385 U.S. 851.

In the course of that opinion, the Court of Appeals intimated that the Board conceivably might have required petitioner to agree to a checkoff provision as a remedy for the prior bad-faith bargaining, although the order enforced at that time did not contain any such provision. 363 F.2d at 275–276, n. 16. In the ensuing negotiations the company offered to discuss alternative arrangements for collecting the union's dues, but the union insisted that the company was required to agree to the checkoff proposal without modification. Because of this disagreement over the proper interpretation of the court's opinion, the union, in February 1967, filed a motion for clarification of the 1966 opinion. The motion was denied by the court on March 22, 1967, in an order suggesting that contempt proceedings before the Board would be the proper avenue for testing the employer's compliance with the original order. A request for the institution of such proceedings was made by the union, and in June 1967, the Regional Director of the Board declined to prosecute a contempt charge, finding that the employer had "satisfactorily complied with the affirmative requirements of the Order." . . . The union then filed in the Court of Appeals a motion for reconsideration of the earlier motion to clarify the 1966 opinion. The court granted that motion and issued a new opinion in which it held that in certain circumstances a "checkoff may be imposed as a remedy for bad-faith bargaining." *United Steelworkers v. NLRB*, 389 F.2d 295, 298 (1967). The case was then remanded to the Board and on July 3, 1968, the Board issued a supplemental order requiring the petitioner to "[g]rant to the Union a contract clause providing for the checkoff of union dues." 172 N.L.R.B. 966. The Court of Appeals affirmed this order, *H.K. Porter Co. v. NLRB*, 414 F.2d 1123 (1969). We granted certiorari to consider whether the Board in these circumstances had the power to remedy the unfair labor practice by requiring the company to agree to check off the dues of the workers. . . . For reasons to be stated we hold that while the Board does have power under the Labor Management Relations Act . . . to require employers and employees to negotiate, it is without power to compel a company or a union to agree to any substantive contractual provision of a collective bargaining agreement.

Since 1935 the story of labor relations in this country has largely been a history of governmental regulation of the process of collective bargaining. In that year Congress decided that disturbances in the area of labor relations led to undesirable burdens on and obstructions of interstate commerce, and passed the National Labor Relations Act. . . . Without spelling out the details, the Act provided that it was an unfair labor practice for an employer to refuse to bargain. Thus a general process was established which would ensure that employees as a group could express their opinions and exert their combined influence over the terms and conditions of their employment. The Board would act to see that the process worked.

The object of this Act was not to allow governmental regulation of the terms and conditions of employment, but rather to ensure that employers and their employees could work together to establish mutually satisfactory conditions. The basic theme of the Act was that through collective bargaining the passions, arguments, and struggles of prior years would be channeled into constructive, open discussions leading, hopefully, to mutual agreement. But it was recognized from the beginning that agreement might in some cases be impossible, and it was never intended that the Government would in such cases step in, become a party to the negotiations and impose its own views of a desirable settlement. This fundamental limitation was made abundantly clear in the legislative reports accompanying the 1935 Act. . . . The discussions on the floor of Congress consistently reflect this same understanding.

The Act was passed at a time in our Nation's history when there was considerable legal debate over the constitutionality of any law that required employers to conform their business behavior to any governmentally imposed standards. It was seriously contended that Congress could not constitutionally compel an employer to recognize a union and allow his employees to participate in setting the terms and conditions of employment. In *NLRB v. Jones & Laughlin Steel Corp.*, 301 U.S. 1 (1937), this Court, in a 5-to-4 decision, held that Congress was within the limits of its constitutional powers in passing the Act. In the course of that decision the Court said:

> The Act does not compel agreements between employers and employees. It does not compel any agreement whatever. . . . The theory of the Act is that free opportunity for negotiation with accredited representatives of

employees is likely to promote industrial peace and may bring about the adjustments and agreements which the Act in itself does not attempt to compel.

Id. at 45.

In 1947 Congress reviewed the experience under the Act and concluded that certain amendments were in order. In the House committee report accompanying what eventually became the Labor Management Relations Act of 1947, the committee referred to the above quoted language in *Jones & Laughlin* and said:

> "Notwithstanding this language of the Court, the present Board has gone very far, in the guise of determining whether or not employers had bargained in good faith, in setting itself up as the judge of what concessions an employer must make and of the proposals and counterproposals that he may or may not make.
>
> . . .
>
> "[U]nless Congress writes into the law guides for the Board to follow, the Board may attempt to carry this process still further and seek to control more and more the terms of collective bargaining agreements."[13]

Accordingly Congress amended the provisions defining unfair labor practices and said in § 8(d) that: "*. . . such obligation [to bargain collectively] does not compel either party to agree to a proposal or require the making of a concession.*"

In discussing the effect of that amendment, this Court said it is "clear that the Board may not, either directly or indirectly, compel concessions or otherwise sit in judgment upon the substantive terms of collective bargaining agreements." *NLRB v. American Ins. Co.*, 343 U.S. 395, 404 (1952). Later this Court affirmed that view stating that "it remains clear that § 8(d) was an attempt by Congress to prevent the Board from controlling the settling of the terms of collective bargaining agreements." *NLRB v. Insurance Agents*, 361 U.S. 477, 487 (1960). The parties to the instant case are agreed that this is the first time in the 35-year history of the Act that the Board has ordered either an employer or a union to agree to a substantive term of a collective bargaining agreement.

Recognizing the fundamental principle "that the National Labor Relations Act is grounded on the premise of freedom of contract," 389 F.2d at 300, the Court of Appeals in this case concluded that nevertheless in the circumstances presented here the Board could properly compel the employer to agree to a proposed checkoff clause. The Board had found that the refusal was based on a desire to frustrate agreement and not on any legitimate business reason. On the basis of that finding the Court of Appeals approved the further finding that the employer had not bargained in good faith, and the validity of that finding is not now before us. Where

---

13. [3] H.R. Rep. No. 245, 80th Cong., 1st Sess. 19–20 (1947).

the record thus revealed repeated refusals by the employer to bargain in good faith on this issue, the Court of Appeals concluded that ordering agreement to the check-off clause "may be the only means of assuring the Board, and the court, that [the employer] no longer harbors an illegal intent." 389 F.2d at 299.

In reaching this conclusion the Court of Appeals held that § 8(d) did not forbid the Board from compelling agreement. That court felt that "[s]ection 8(d) defines collective bargaining and relates to a determination of *whether* a . . . violation has occurred and not to the *scope* of the remedy which may be necessary to cure violations which have already occurred." 389 F.2d at 299. We may agree with the Court of Appeals that as a matter of strict, literal interpretation of that section it refers only to deciding when a violation has occurred, but we do not agree that that observation justifies the conclusion that the remedial powers of the Board are not also limited by the same considerations that led Congress to enact § 8(d). It is implicit in the entire structure of the Act that the Board acts to oversee and referee the process of collective bargaining, leaving the results of the contest to the bargaining strengths of the parties. It would be anomalous indeed to hold that while § 8(d) prohibits the Board from relying on a refusal to agree as the sole evidence of bad faith bargaining, the Act permits the Board to compel agreement in that same dispute. The Board's remedial powers under § 10 of the Act are broad, but they are limited to carrying out the policies of the Act itself. One of these fundamental policies is freedom of contract. While the parties' freedom of contract is not absolute under the Act, allowing the Board to compel agreement when the parties themselves are unable to do so would violate the fundamental premise on which the Act is based — private bargaining under governmental supervision of the procedure alone, without any official compulsion over the actual terms of the contract.

In reaching its decision the Court of Appeals relied extensively on the equally important policy of the Act that workers' rights to collective bargaining are to be secured. In this case the Court apparently felt that the employer was trying effectively to destroy the union by refusing to agree to what the union may have considered its most important demand. Perhaps the court, fearing that the parties might resort to economic combat, was also trying to maintain the industrial peace which the Act is designed to further. But the Act as presently drawn does not contemplate that unions will always be secure and able to achieve agreement even when their economic position is weak, nor that strikes and lockouts will never result from a bargaining to impasse. It cannot be said that the Act forbids an employer or a union to rely ultimately on its economic strength to try to secure what it cannot obtain through bargaining. It may well be true, as the Court of Appeals felt, that the present remedial powers of the Board are insufficiently broad to cope with important labor problems. But it is the job of Congress, not the Board or the courts, to decide when and if it is necessary to allow governmental review of proposals for collective bargaining agreements and compulsory submission to one side's demands. The present Act does not envision such a process.

The judgment is reversed and the case is remanded to the Court of Appeals for further action consistent with this opinion.

Reversed and remanded.

Mr. Justice White took no part in the decision of this case.

Mr. Justice Marshall took no part in the consideration or decision of this case.

[The concurring opinion of Mr. Justice Harlan and the dissenting opinion of Mr. Justice Douglas, in which Mr. Justice Stewart concurred, are omitted.]

Notes

1. *Reconciling* H.K. Porter *and* General Electric — Does *H.K. Porter* undercut the anti-Boulwarism stance of the NLRB and the Second Circuit in the *General Electric* decisions, *supra*? The Board has ruled that even where an employer signals a refusal to compromise, makes no effort to reach agreement, and offers a status quo proposal that amounts to bad-faith bargaining in violation of § 8(a)(5), the employer cannot be ordered to cease and desist from making such a proposal because "no party can be required to agree to any particular substantive bargaining provision." *See J & C Towing Co.*, 307 N.L.R.B. 198 (1992); *see also* Goldstein, *When and Where Should Be the Limits of NLRB Intervention? in* N.Y.U. Twenty-Third Annual Conference on Labor 55 (1970).

2. *Refusal to Execute a Contract After Negotiations are Complete* — *Ivaldi v. NLRB*, 48 F.3d 444 (9th Cir. 1995), involved an employer that refused to execute a collective contract with a union that had accepted the firm's "last, best and final offer" four months after the offer was made. Although the employer argued that its offer had lapsed when the union failed to accept it within a reasonable period of time, the Labor Board found no indication that the offer had been withdrawn before union acceptance. The court affirmed the Board's finding that the employer's refusal to execute the accepted agreement contravened § 8(a)(5) and enforced the remedial order directing the company to execute that contract.

3. *Extension of Certification Year* — Where an employer commits numerous violations of the Act and repeatedly refuses to bargain with a certified union, the Board may order an extension of the union's certification year. Duration of the extension varies with the nature of the violations and their impact on the bargaining process, but can extend to a full year. *See, e.g., Fallbrook Hosp. Corp. v. NLRB*, 785 F.3d 729 (D.C. Cir. 2015) (enforcing Board order extending certification period by one year and requiring reimbursement of union's negotiating expenses); *Frankl ex rel. NLRB v. HTH Corp.*, 693 F.3d 1051 (9th Cir. 2012) (finding Board's extension of certification period by one full year reasonable); *Mercy, Inc.*, 346 N.L.R.B. 1004 (2006) (three-month extension).

Ex-Cell-O Corp.
National Labor Relations Board
185 N.L.R.B. 107 (1970)

This case began with the UAW's request for recognition on August 3, 1964. Ex-Cell-O refused the Union's request on August 10, 1964, and the Union immediately filed a petition for Certification of Representative. After a hearing the Regional Director ordered an election, which was held on October 22, 1964, and a majority of the employees voted for the Union. The Company, however, filed objections to the conduct of the election, alleging that the Union made certain misrepresentations which assertedly interfered therewith, but the Acting Regional Director, in a Supplemental Decision of December 29, 1964, overruled them. The Company then requested review of that decision, which the Board granted, and a hearing was held on May 18 and 19, 1965. The Hearing Officer issued his Report on Objections on July 15, 1965, and recommended that the objections be overruled. The Company filed exceptions thereto, but on October 28, 1965, the Board adopted the Hearing Officer's findings and recommendations and affirmed the Regional Director's certification of the Union.

The day after the Board's certification was issued, the Company advised the Union that it would refuse to bargain in order to secure a court review of the Board's action and later reiterated this position after receiving the Union's request for a bargaining meeting. The Union thereupon filed the 8(a)(1) and (5) charge in this case and the complaint was issued on November 23, 1965. The Respondent's answer admitted the factual allegations of the complaint but denied the violation on the ground that the Board's certification was invalid. The hearing herein, originally scheduled for February 15, 1966, commenced on June 1, 1966; it was adjourned until June 29, 1966, to permit the Union to offer evidence supporting its request for a compensatory remedy for the alleged refusal to bargain; the hearing was postponed again until July 28, 1966. The Company also petitioned the United States District Court for an injunction against the Regional Director and the Trial Examiner to restrain the latter from closing the hearing until the Regional Director had produced the investigative records in the representation case. The court issued a summary judgment denying the injunction on December 13, 1966, and on December 21, 1966, the Trial Examiner formally closed his hearing. On March 2, 1967, the Trial Examiner issued his Decision, finding that the Company had unlawfully refused to bargain in violation of Section 8(a)(5) and (1) of the Act and recommended the standard bargaining order as a remedy. In addition the Trial Examiner ordered the Company to compensate its employees for monetary losses incurred as a result of its unlawful conduct.

It is not disputed that Respondent refused to bargain with the Union, and we hereby affirm the Trial Examiner's conclusion that Respondent thereby violated Section 8(a)(1) and (5) of the Act. The compensatory remedy which he recommends, however, raises important issues concerning the Board's powers and duties to fashion appropriate remedies in its efforts to effectuate the policies of the National Labor Relations Act.

It is argued that such a remedy exceeds the Board's general statutory powers. In addition, it is contended that it cannot be granted because the amount of employee loss, if any, is so speculative that an order to make employees whole would amount to the imposition of a penalty. And the position is advanced that the adoption of this remedy would amount to the writing of a contract for the parties, which is prohibited by Section 8(d).

We have given most serious consideration to the Trial Examiner's recommended financial reparations order, and are in complete agreement with his finding that current remedies of the Board designed to cure violations of Section 8(a)(5) are inadequate. A mere affirmative order that an employer bargain upon request does not eradicate the effects of an unlawful delay of 2 or more years in the fulfillment of a statutory bargaining obligation. It does not put the employees in the position of bargaining strength they would have enjoyed if their employer had immediately recognized and bargained with their chosen representative. It does not dissolve the inevitable employee frustration or protect the Union from a loss of employee support attributable to such delay. The inadequacy of the remedy is all the more egregious where, as in the recent *NLRB v. Tiidee Products*[14] case, the court found that the employer had raised "frivolous" issues in order to postpone or avoid its lawful obligation to bargain. We have weighed these considerations most carefully. For the reasons stated below, however, we have reluctantly concluded that we cannot approve the Trial Examiner's Recommended Order that Respondent compensate its employees for monetary losses incurred as a consequence of Respondent's determination to refuse to bargain until it had tested in court the validity of the Board's certification.

Section 10(c) of the Act directs the Board to order a person found to have committed an unfair labor practice to cease and desist and "to take such affirmative action including reinstatement of employees with or without back pay, as will effectuate the policies of this Act." This authority, as our colleagues note with full documentation, is extremely broad and was so intended by Congress. It is not so broad, however, as to permit the punishment of a particular respondent or a class of respondents. Nor is the statutory direction to the Board so compelling that the Board is without discretion in exercising the full sweep of its power, for it would defeat the purposes of the Act if the Board imposed an otherwise proper remedy that resulted in irreparable harm to a particular respondent and hampered rather than promoted meaningful collective bargaining. Moreover, as the Supreme Court recently emphasized, the Board's grant of power does not extend to compelling agreement. (*H.K. Porter Co., Inc. v. NLRB*, 397 U.S. 99.) It is with respect to these three limitations upon the Board's power to remedy a violation of Section 8(a)(5) that we examine the UAW's requested remedy in this case.

---

14. [6] 426 F.2d 1243 [(D.C. Cir. 1970), *cert. denied*, 400 U.S. 950 (1970)].

The Trial Examiner concluded that the proposed remedy was not punitive, that it merely made the employees partially whole for losses occasioned by the Respondent's refusal to bargain, and was much less harsh than a backpay order for discharged employees, which might require the Respondent to pay wages to these employees as well as their replacements. Viewed solely in the context of an assumption of employee monetary losses resulting directly from the Respondent's violation of Section 8(a)(5), as finally determined in court, the Trial Examiner's conclusion appears reasonable. There are, however, other factors in this case which provide counter weights to that rationale. In the first place, there is no contention that this Respondent acted in a manner flagrantly in defiance of the statutory policy. On the contrary, the record indicates that this Respondent responsibly fulfills its legally established collective bargaining obligations. It is clear that Respondent merely sought judicial affirmance of the Board's decision that the election of October 22, 1964, should not be set aside on the Respondent's objections. In the past whenever an employer has sought court intervention in a representation proceeding the Board has argued forcefully that court intervention would be premature, that the employer had an unquestioned right under the statute to seek court review of any Board order before its bargaining obligation became final. Should this procedural right in 8(a)(5) cases be tempered by a large monetary liability in the event the employer's position in the representation case is ultimately found to be without merit? Of course, an employer or a union, which engages in conduct later found in violation of the Act, does so at the peril of ultimate conviction and responsibility for a make-whole remedy.

But the validity of a particular Board election tried in an unfair labor practice case is not, in our opinion, an issue on the same plane as the discharge of employees for union activity or other conduct in flagrant disregard of employee rights. There are wrongdoers and wrongdoers. Where the wrong in refusing to bargain is, at most, a debatable question, though ultimately found a wrong, the imposition of a large financial obligation on such a respondent may come close to a form of punishment for having elected to pursue a representation question beyond the Board and to the courts. The desirability of a compensatory remedy in a case remarkably similar to the instant case was recently considered by the Court of Appeals for the District of Columbia in *United Steelworkers [Quality Rubber Manufacturing Company, Inc.] v. NLRB*, [430 F.2d 519] (July 10, 1970). There the court, distinguishing *Tiidee Products, supra*, indicated that the Board was warranted in refusing to grant such a remedy in an 8(a)(5) case where the employer "desired only to obtain an authoritative determination of the validity of the Board's decision." It is not clear whether the court was of the opinion that the requested remedy was within the Board's discretion or whether it would have struck down such a remedy as punitive in view of the technical nature of the respondent's unfair labor practice. In any event, we find ourselves in disagreement with the Trial Examiner's view that a compensatory remedy as applied to the Respondent in the instant case is not punitive "in any sense of the word."

In *Tiidee Products* the court suggested that the Board need not follow a uniform policy in the application of a compensatory remedy in 8(a)(5) cases. Indeed, the court noted that such uniformity in this area of the law would be unfair when applied "to unlike cases." The court was of the opinion that the remedy was proper where the employer had engaged in a "manifestly unjustifiable refusal to bargain" and where its position was "palpably without merit." As in *Quality Rubber*, the court in *Tiidee Products* distinguished those cases in which the employer's failure to bargain rested on a "debatable question." With due respect for the opinion of the Court of Appeals for the District of Columbia, we cannot agree that the application of a compensatory remedy in 8(a)(5) cases can be fashioned on the subjective determination that the position of one respondent is "debatable" while that of another is "frivolous." What is debatable to the Board may appear frivolous to a court, and vice versa. Thus, the debatability of the employer's position in an 8(a)(5) case would itself become a matter of intense litigation.

We do not believe that the critical question of the employer's motivation in delaying bargaining should depend so largely on the expertise of counsel, the accident of circumstances, and the exigencies of the moment.

In our opinion, however, the crucial question to be determined in this case relates to the policies which the requested order would effectuate. The statutory policy as embodied in Section 8(a)(5) and (d) of the Act was considered at some length by the Supreme Court in *H.K. Porter Co., Inc. v. NLRB, supra*. . . .

It is argued that the instant case is distinguishable from *H.K. Porter* in that here the requested remedy merely would require an employer to compensate employees for losses they incurred as a consequence of their employer's failure to agree to a contract he would have agreed to if he had bargained in good faith. In our view, the distinction is more illusory than real. The remedy in *H.K. Porter* operates prospectively to bind an employer to a specific contractual term. The remedy in the instant case operates retroactively to impose financial liability upon an employer flowing from a presumed contractual agreement. The Board infers that the latter contract, though it never existed and does not and need not exist, was denied existence by the employer because of his refusal to bargain. In either case the employer has not agreed to the contractual provision for which he must accept full responsibility as though he had agreed to it. Our colleagues contend that a compensatory remedy is not the "writing of a contract" because it does not "specify new or continuing terms of employment and does not prohibit changes in existing terms and conditions." But there is no basis for such a remedy unless the Board finds, as a matter of fact, that a contract would have resulted from bargaining. The fact that the contract, so to speak, is "written in the air" does not diminish its financial impact upon the recalcitrant employer who, willy-nilly, is forced to accede to terms never mutually established by the parties. Despite the admonition of the Supreme Court that Section 8(d) was intended to mean what it says, *i.e.*, that the obligation to bargain "does not compel either party to agree to a proposal or require the making of a concession," one of the parties under this remedy is forced by the Government to submit to the other side's demands.

It does not help to argue that the remedy could not be applied unless there was substantial evidence that the employer would have yielded to these demands during bargaining negotiations. Who is to say in a specific case how much an employer is prepared to give and how much a union is willing to take? Who is to say that a favorable contract would, in any event, result from the negotiations? And it is only the employer of such good will as to whom the Board might conclude that he, at least, would have given his employees a fair increase, who can be made subject to a financial reparations order; should such an employer be singled out for the imposition of such an order? To answer these questions the Board would be required to engage in the most general, if not entirely speculative, inferences to reach the conclusion that employees were deprived of specific benefits as a consequence of their employer's refusal to bargain.

Much as we appreciate the need for more adequate remedies in 8(a)(5) cases, we believe that, as the law now stands, the proposed remedy is a matter for Congress, not the Board. In our opinion, however, substantial relief may be obtained immediately through procedural reform, giving the highest possible priority to 8(a)(5) cases combined with full resort to the injunctive relief provisions of Section 10(j) and (e) of the Act.

MEMBERS MCCULLOCH and BROWN, dissenting in part:

Although concurring in all other respects in the Decision and Order of the Board, we part company with our colleagues on the majority in that we would grant the compensatory remedy recommended by the Trial Examiner. Unlike our colleagues, we believe that the Board has the statutory authority to direct such relief and that it would effectuate the policies of the Act to do so in this case.

Section 10(c) of the Act directs the Board to remedy unfair labor practices by ordering the persons committing them to cease and desist from their unlawful conduct "and to take such affirmative action including reinstatement of employees with or without back pay, as will effectuate the policies of this Act...." The phrase "affirmative action" is nowhere qualified in the statute, except that such action must "effectuate the policies of this Act," and indicates the intent of Congress to vest the Board with remedial powers coextensive with the underlying policies of the law which is to be enforced. The provision "did not pass the Wagner Act Congress without objection to the uncontrolled breadth of this power."

But the broad language survived the challenge....

Deprivation of an employee's statutory rights is often accompanied by serious financial injury to him. Where this is so, an order which only guarantees the exercise of his rights in the future often falls far short of expunging the effects of the unlawful conduct involved. Therefore, one of the Board's most effective and well-established affirmative remedies for unlawful conduct is an order to make employees financially whole for losses resulting from violations of the Act. Various types of compensatory orders have been upheld by the Supreme Court in the belief that "Making the workers whole for losses suffered on account of an unfair practice is part of the vindication of the public policy which the Board enforces." The most familiar of these is the backpay order used to remedy the effect of employee discharges found to be in violation of Section 8(a)(3) of the Act....

It is clear from the Act that the Board's compensatory remedies need not be limited to the above situations, and the courts have always interpreted the phrase "with or without back pay" as being merely an illustrative example of the general grant of power to award affirmative relief....

The Board has already recognized in certain refusal-to-bargain situations that the usual bargaining order is not sufficient to expunge the effects of an employer's unlawful and protracted denial of its employees' right to bargain. Though the bargaining order serves to remedy the loss of the legal right and protect its exercise in the future, it does not remedy the financial injury which may also have been suffered. In a number of situations the Board has ordered the employer who unlawfully refused to bargain to compensate its employees for their resultant financial losses. Thus, some employers unlawfully refuse to sign after an agreement. The Board has in these cases ordered the employer to execute the agreement previously reached and, according to its terms, to make whole the employees for the monetary losses suffered because of the unlawful delay in its effectuation....

The question now before us is whether a reimbursement order is an appropriate remedy for other types of unlawful refusals to bargain. On the basis of the foregoing analysis regarding Section 10(c), we believe that the Board has the power to order this type of relief. Further, for the reasons set forth herein, we are of the view that the compensatory remedy is appropriate and necessary in this case to effectuate the policies of the Act....

The present remedies for unlawful refusals to bargain often fall short, as in the present case, of adequately protecting the employees' right to bargain. Recent court decisions, congressional investigations, and scholarly studies have concluded that, in the present remedial framework, justice delayed is often justice denied.

In *NLRB v. Tiidee Products, Inc.*, the Court of Appeals for the District of Columbia Circuit recently stated that:

> While [the Board's usual bargaining] remedy may provide some bargaining from the date of the order's enforcement, it operates in a real sense so as to be counterproductive, and actually to reward an employer's refusal to bargain during the critical period following a union's organization of his plant. The obligation of collective bargaining is the core of the Act, and the primary means fashioned by Congress for securing industrial peace....
>
> ...Employee interest in a union can wane quickly as working conditions remain apparently unaffected by the union or collective bargaining.

When the company is finally ordered to bargain with the union some years later, the union may find that it represents only a small fraction of the employees.... Thus the employer may reap a second benefit from his original refusal to comply with the law: He may continue to enjoy lower labor expenses after the order to bargain either because the union is gone or because it is too weak to bargain effectively....

The present case is but another example of a situation where a bargaining order by itself is not really adequate to remedy the effects of an unlawful refusal to bargain. The Union herein requested recognition on August 3, 1964, and proved that it represented a majority of employees 2-1/2 months later in a Board-conducted election. Nonetheless, since October 1965 the employer, by unlawfully refusing to bargain with the Union, had deprived its employees of their legal right to collective bargaining through their certified bargaining representative. While a bargaining order at this time, operating prospectively, may insure the exercise of that right in the future, it clearly does not repair the injury to the employees here, caused by the Respondent's denial of their rights during the past 5 years.

In these refusal-to-bargain cases there is at least a legal injury.... [W]here the legal injury is accompanied by financial loss, the employees should be compensated for it. The compensatory period would normally run from the date of the employer's unlawful refusal to bargain until it commences to negotiate in good faith, or upon the failure of the Union to commence negotiations within 5 days of the receipt of the Respondent's notice of its desire to bargain with the Union, although here a later starting date could be used because this remedy would be a substantial departure from past practices. Further, the Board could follow its usual procedure of providing a general reimbursement order with the amount, if any, to be determined as part of the compliance procedure.

This type of compensatory remedy is in no way forbidden by section 8(d). It would be designed to compensate employees for injuries incurred by them by virtue of the unfair labor practices and would not require the employer to accept the measure of compensation as a term of any contract which might result from subsequent collective bargaining. The remedy contemplated in no way "writes a contract" between the employer and the union, for it would not specify new or continuing terms of employment and would not prohibit changes in existing terms and conditions. All of these would be left to the outcome of bargaining, the commencement of which would terminate Respondent's liability.

Furthermore, this compensatory remedy is not a punitive measure. It would be designed to do no more than reimburse the employees for the loss occasioned by the deprivation of their right to be represented by their collective bargaining agent during the period of the violation. The amount to be awarded would be only that which would reasonably reflect and be measured by the loss caused by the unlawful denial of the opportunity for collective bargaining. Thus, employees would be compensated for the injury suffered as a result of their employer's unlawful refusal to bargain, and the employer would thereby be prohibited from enjoying the fruits of its forbidden conduct to the end, as embodied in the Act, that collective bargaining be encouraged and the rights of injured employees be protected. . . . [W]here the defendant's wrongful act prevents exact determination of the amount of damage, he cannot plead such uncertainty in order to deny relief to the injured person, but rather must bear the risk of the uncertainty which was created by his own wrong. The Board is often faced with the task of determining the precise amount of a make-whole order where the criteria are less than ideal, and has successfully resolved the questions presented. . . .

A showing at the compliance stage by the General Counsel or Charging Party by acceptable and demonstrable means that the employees could have reasonably expected to gain a certain amount of compensation by bargaining would establish a prima facie loss, and the Respondent would then be afforded an opportunity to rebut such a showing. This might be accomplished, for example by adducing evidence to show that a contract would probably not have been reached, or that there would have been less or no increase in compensation as a result of any contract which might have been signed.

Accordingly, uncertainty as to the amount of loss does not preclude a make-whole order proposed here, and some reasonable method or basis of computation can be worked out as part of the compliance procedure. . . . Thus, if the particular employer and union involved have contracts covering other plants of the employer, possibly in the same or a relevant area, the terms of such agreements may serve to show what the employees could probably have obtained by bargaining. The parties could also make comparisons with compensation patterns achieved through collective bargaining by other employees in the same geographic area and industry. Or the parties might employ the national average percentage changes in straight time hourly wages computed by the Bureau of Labor Statistics. . . .

Notes

1. *Efficacy of Cease and Desist Orders*—The conventional Board remedy for an employer violation of § 8(a)(5) is a cease and desist order and an affirmative order for the employer to bargain collectively with the majority representative of its employees. Since the Board cannot compel agreement, is an order to bargain anything more than a pious exhortation? Empirical studies traditionally indicated that it was. Thus, one survey revealed that successful bargaining relationships were eventually established in 75% of the cases sampled that went through to a final Board order, and in 90% of the cases that were voluntarily adjusted after the issuance of a complaint. *See* P. Ross, The Government as a Source of Union Power 180–230 (1965); McCulloch, *The Development of Administrative Remedies*, 14 Lab. L.J. 339, 348 (1963).

The picture has shifted, however, as employer resistance to unionization has grown. Professor Paul Weiler estimated in 1984 that unions forced to rely on a *Gissel* order to compel bargaining by the employer would obtain a first contract less than 20% of the time. *See* Weiler, *Striking a New Balance: Freedom of Contract and the Prospects for Union Representation*, 98 Harv. L. Rev. 351 n.31 (1984). Employer resistance is especially likely where a union is seeking to negotiate its first contract. Between 2002 and 2005, nearly 50% of all charges alleging refusals to bargain occurred in first contract negotiation situations. In 2007, the Board's General Counsel issued a memorandum recommending that officials in the Board's regional offices consider additional remedies in first contract negotiation cases characterized by "high-impact" unfair labor practices that could seriously damage the employer-union relationship and make attainment of good faith bargaining more difficult. Such remedies might include injunctive relief under §10(j), posting of notices, extension of the union's certification year, bargaining on a prescribed or compressed schedule, and reimbursement of bargaining costs. "High-impact" ULPs include outright refusals to bargain, refusals to meet at reasonable times, unlawful unilateral changes, and discriminatory discharges of union supporters. *See NLRB Office of General Counsel Memorandum GC 07–08*, May 29, 2007. In May 2008, the General Counsel announced that preliminary statistics appeared to show reductions in charges alleging employer refusals to bargain for first contracts (only 25% occurred in first contract situations between 2006 and 2007) and in the merit rate of these charges (which dropped from a merit rate of 44.4% to 37.2% in 2007), suggesting that the Board's commitment to pursuing special remedies in first contract failure-to-bargain cases might be having some impact. *See NLRB General Counsel Meisburg's Report on First-Contract Bargaining Cases, Memorandum GC 08–08*, May 15, 2008. In February 2011, the Board's acting General Counsel gave regional offices greater authority to seek additional remedies in unfair labor practice cases arising out of first-contract bargaining. These remedies include requirements that notices intended to remedy unfair labor practices be read to employees by a responsible management official, extensions of the union's certification year in situations of bad faith or surface bargaining, and requiring employers who engage in dilatory tactics to conduct negotiations on a specific bargaining schedule (usually 24 hours per month and for at least six hours per session). *See NLRB Acting General Counsel Solomon's First Contract Bargaining Cases: Regional Authorization to Seek Additional Remedies and Submissions to Division of Advice, Memorandum GC 11-06,* Feb. 18, 2011. The Trump Board's General Counsel has continued to utilize injunctive relief under §10(j) in first contract negotiations, and in a recent case involving significant employer unfair labor practices in a first contract situation the Board implemented many of these remedies, including extending the certification year and ordering reimbursement of the union's bargaining costs. *See Bemis Co.,* 370 N.L.R.B. No. 7 (2020).

The courts of appeals have not always been sympathetic to the NLRB's efforts, however. In *Gimrock Constr., Inc.,* 356 N.L.R.B. 529 (2011), the employer continued to refuse to bargain even after the Board's bargaining order was enforced by a federal court of appeals. The Board ordered the employer to bargain for a minimum of 16 hours a week and to submit monthly progress reports to the Board's regional director until an agreement was reached, the parties agreed to a hiatus, or a lawful impasse occurred. The Eleventh Circuit denied enforcement, reasoning that the

Board should have petitioned the court for an order requiring the employer to show cause why it should not be held in civil contempt for refusing to comply. Where traditional means of obtaining compliance with an injunctive order had not been exhausted, extraordinary remedies were not warranted. *NLRB v. Gimrock Constr., Inc.*, 695 F.3d 1188 (11th Cir. 2012).

The proposed Protecting the Right to Organize Act of 2019, H.R. 2474, contained provisions establishing a process for reaching a first contract, utilizing mediation, and if the employer and union cannot agree, submission to binding arbitration over the substantive terms to be included in the collective agreement. This kind of arbitration, known as "interest arbitration," is commonly used to resolve public sector labor disputes. The arbitrator is typically charged with determining what the parties should have agreed upon, considering questions of fairness, policy, and practicality. What are the arguments in favor of increased government intervention in first contract situations? What are the arguments against it? *See* Johnson, *First Contract Arbitration: Effects on Bargaining and Work Stoppages*, 63 IND. & LAB. REL. REV. 585 (2010) (analyzing the influence of first contract arbitration based upon the Canadian experience under similar legislation).

2. *Injunctive Relief Under § 10(j)* — Recently, the Board has more frequently utilized § 10(j) to avert the impact of an employer's violation of its bargaining obligation under § 8(a)(5). Section 10(j) affords the Board the right to petition the district court for interim judicial relief in order to maintain the status quo and prevent the continuing commission of unfair labor practices "upon the issuance of a [Board] complaint." Courts are divided on the standard for relief. Most circuits require a two-step proof process: the General Counsel must show reasonable cause that the alleged violations occurred, and that the relief sought is "just and proper." *See, e.g., NLRB v. Hartman & Tyner, Inc.*, 714 F.3d 1244 (11th Cir. 2013); *Chester ex rel. NLRB v. Grane Healthcare Co.*, 666 F.3d 87 (3d Cir. 2011). A few have adopted a hybrid approach that retains the "reasonable cause" requirement but incorporates traditional balancing factors into the "just and proper" determination. *See, e.g., Hoffman v. Inn Credible Caterers, Ltd.*, 247 F.3d 360 (2d Cir. 2001). Still others have constructed new tests designed to rein in the Board's power. *See, e.g., McKinney v. Southern Bakeries, LLC*, 786 F.3d 1119 (8th Cir. 2015) (applying four-factor inquiry involving the threat of irreparable harm to the moving party, the balance of harms, the likelihood of success on the merits, and the public interest, and vacating § 10(j) injunction ordering employer to bargain with union where no showing was made that this was "the rare case when a preliminary injunction is necessary to preserve the effectiveness of the ordinary adjudicatory process," or that "allowing the ordinary adjudicatory process to run its course would significantly undermine the board's ability to remedy the alleged unfair labor practices."); *accord, Henderson v. Bluefield Hosp. Co.*, 902 F.3d 434 (4th Cir. 2018) (applying four-factor test and denying injunctive relief).

The purpose of § 10(j) injunctive relief is to protect the Board's remedial powers during the pendency of the underlying unfair labor practice proceeding, not to substitute for it. Accordingly, Board delay in seeking § 10(j) relief past the point where the harm has occurred and the status quo can no longer be restored is relevant, *see Schaub v. Detroit Newspaper Agency*, 154 F.3d 276 (6th Cir. 1998), and orders to recognize and bargain with the union may be limited in duration so as to incentivize prompt resolution of the Board's unfair labor practice proceedings. *See, e.g., Glasser ex rel. NLRB v. Heartland — Univ. of Livonia, MI, LLC*, 632 F. Supp. 2d 659 (E.D. Mich. 2009) (four months).

On the General Counsel's prosecutorial powers, see Ellement, *Labor Law in 3(d): Reexamining the General Counsel of the NLRB as an Independent Prosecutor of Labor Violations*, 29 ABA J. Lab. & Emp. L. 477 (2014).

3. *Make-Whole Relief for Employees in First-Contract Contexts* — As indicated in the *Ex-Cell-O* opinions, the D.C. Circuit had ruled (2-1) in *International Union of Electrical, etc. v. NLRB*, 426 F.2d 1243 (D.C. Cir.), *cert. denied*, 400 U.S. 950 (1970) (*Tiidee I*) that the usual cease and desist order is inadequate to remedy an employer's "clear and flagrant" violation of its bargaining duty, and that the Board had the power to award make-whole compensation for the period of such an employer's unlawful refusal to bargain. The *Tiidee I* court remanded the case to the Board for further consideration of an appropriate remedy, including back pay to compensate the employees for the benefits denied them by the employer's refusal to bargain. The majority stressed that the remand was limited to consideration of past damages, and not to compulsion of a future contract term, thus distinguishing the case from the Supreme Court's decision in *H.K. Porter*. As the *Ex-Cell-O* Board noted, however, the same court had ruled in *United Steelworkers of America v. NLRB*, 430 F.2d 519 (D.C. Cir. 1970), that the Board had not abused its discretion in refusing to grant make-whole relief where an employer declines to bargain in good faith and challenges a union's certification or raises other concerns about its status as the employees' representative.

On appeal in *Ex-Cell-O*, the D.C. Circuit initially reversed the Board's decision. Citing *Tiidee I*, the court remanded the case to the Board to make a determination whether the employer's attack on the election proceedings was based on "frivolous" legal objections (potentially warranting make-whole relief) or whether it was based on a legal position that was "fairly debatable." *International Union, United Auto., etc. v. NLRB*, 449 F.2d 1046 (D.C. Cir. 1971). The court quickly reversed course, however, when the proceedings of the full record before the Board were filed with the court in connection with another motion. The court ruled that notwithstanding the Board's legal error, the order of remand should be vacated because the company's objections to the union's certification fell into the "fairly debatable" category rather than into the "frivolous" category. *Ex-Cell-O Corp. v. NLRB*, 449 F.2d 1058 (D.C. Cir. 1971).

The saga continued in *Tiidee Products, Inc.*, 194 N.L.R.B. 1234 (1972), *enforced*, 502 F.2d 349 (D.C. Cir. 1974), *cert. denied*, 421 U.S. 991 (1975) (*Tiidee II*). On remand following *Tiidee I*, a unanimous Board rejected a reimbursement order, even where the employer's refusal to bargain was a "clear and flagrant" violation of law. Nonetheless, the Board thought such a violation did warrant a remedy going beyond the customary cease and desist order. It therefore required the employer to reimburse both the NLRB and the union for their litigation expenses, to mail copies of the NLRB's notice to each employee's home, to keep the union supplied with an employee name-and-address list for one year, and to give the union reasonable access to company bulletin boards. The D.C. Circuit enforced the award in *Tiidee II*, bowing to the Board's expertise in concluding it was incapable of calculating an appropriate make-whole remedy, but eliminated the award of litigation expenses to the Board. *Cf. NLRB v. Food Store Employees Union*, 417 U.S. 1 (1974) (ruling that court of appeals exceeded its authority in ordering an employer guilty of "aggravated and pervasive" unfair labor practices to pay a union's litigation expenses and excess organizational costs, since the NLRB had ruled against such a remedy, proper procedure was a remand to the Board for reconsideration in light of its 1972 *Tiidee* decision).

4. *Extraordinary Remedies for Pervasive Unfair Labor Practices*—The Board has imposed a variety of extraordinary remedies in cases involving pervasive and outrageous unfair labor practices that occur during the organizing and election phase, but the courts have restricted its ability to remedy even the most flagrant violations of the duty to bargain when the remedy involves compulsion of future contract terms there, as well. For example, when an employer had committed more than 100 unfair labor practices during a union organizing campaign, a divided court of appeals sustained an extensive list of Board remedies, including union access to nonwork areas during employees' nonwork time and the opportunity to deliver a 30-minute speech to employees on working time prior to a new election. But the court by another 2-1 vote refused to require the employer to extend to union employees a pay increase granted to nonunion employees. *Fieldcrest Cannon v. NLRB*, 97 F.3d 65 (4th Cir. 1996). *See also Sysco Grand Rapids, LLC*, 367 N.L.R.B. No. 111 (2019) (Board ordered special remedies for severe unfair labor practices including a broad cease and desist order, a public reading of the order, and union access to the employer's facilities and employees), but the Sixth Circuit denied enforcement of the special remedies, *Sysco Grant Rapids, LLC v. NLRB*, 2020 WL 5269821 (6th Cir. Sept. 4, 2020).

Similarly, the Fourth Circuit agreed to extend the NLRB's remedy of litigation and organizing expenses, usually awarded only when an employer raises "frivolous" defenses, to an employer's "arguably non-frivolous" but ultimately unsuccessful litigation where there was "flagrant, aggravated, persistent, and pervasive employer misconduct." *J.P. Stevens & Co. v. NLRB*, 668 F.2d 767, 777 (4th Cir. 1982). The Supreme Court vacated and remanded on the award of attorneys' fees, however, 458 U.S. 1118 (1982), foreshadowing what was to come (*see* note 5, *infra*).

5. *Awards of Costs and Attorneys' Fees to Unions and the Labor Board*—The Board's remedial orders involving make-whole awards to the union and the Board for investigation and negotiation expenses in failure-to-bargain cases have fared better than its efforts to make employees whole. For example, an employer that persisted in a flat refusal to bargain with a newly certified union or to supply the union with relevant information was ordered to pay all the costs incurred by the union and the Board in investigating, preparing, and litigating the case against the employer. *Care Manor*, 318 N.L.R.B. 330 (1995); *see also Regency Serv. Carts, Inc.*, 345 N.L.R.B. 671 (2005)

(employer's bad-faith surface bargaining in negotiations justified reimbursing union for its negotiation expenses). The Board generally awards bargaining expenses as a part of its make-whole awards in § 8(a)(5) cases where the employer's conduct has "infected" the core of the bargaining process to the extent that traditional remedies are inadequate. *See, e.g., Fallbrook Hosp. Corp.*, 360 N.L.R.B. 644 (2014) (employer that repeatedly failed to bargain in good faith with union representing its registered nurses, set conditions on contract talks, refused to supply relevant information, and stopped responding to requests to bargain, "deliberately act[ing] to prevent any meaningful progress during bargaining sessions that were held," was required to reimburse the union for negotiating expenses during six months of contract negotiations because its actions frustrated good-faith bargaining), *enforced, Fallbrook Hosp. Corp. v. NLRB*, 785 F.3d 729 (D.C. Cir. 2015); *HTH Corp.*, 356 N.L.R.B. 1397 (2011) (employer that threatened closure, discharged and discriminated against employees who served on the bargaining committee, bargained in bad faith, refused to provide requested information, and withdrew recognition of the union required to reimburse union for negotiating expenses), *enforced, Frankl ex rel. NLRB v. HTH Corp.*, 693 F.3d 1051 (9th Cir. 2012).

Awards of attorneys' fees, however, can be problematic. Since 1973, the D.C. Circuit Court of Appeals had taken the position that the Board had the authority to award attorneys' fees where the employer engaged in frivolous litigation. *See Food Store Employees Union, etc. v. NLRB*, 476 F.2d 546 (D.C. Cir. 1973), *rev'd on other grounds*, 417 U.S. 1 (1974). In *Unbelievable, Inc. v. NLRB*, 118 F.3d 795 (D.C. Cir. 1997), the D.C. Circuit overturned its own precedent, ruling that the Board lacks authority to award attorneys' fees absent a statute clearly indicating congressional intent to permit an exception to the traditional American rule that each side must bear its own litigation expenses. In *HTH Corp. v. NLRB*, 823 F.3d 668 (D.C. Cir. 2016), the court reaffirmed the rule enunciated in *Unbelievable*, holding that the Labor Board lacks the statutory authority to require even pervasive NLRA violators to pay charging party and NLRB attorney fees.

6. *Awards of Costs and Attorneys' Fees to Employers* — In *Teamsters Local Union No. 122*, 334 N.L.R.B. 1190 (2001), the Board found that the union had violated § 8(b)(3) by delaying contract negotiations for a new collective bargaining agreement while simultaneously mounting a consumer boycott to force the distributor to sell the business to a more union-friendly entity. The union insisted that bargaining for two units that had previously been handled jointly be conducted separately; bargained for only short periods of time; engaged in detailed bargaining and storytelling to prolong negotiations, and refused to furnish information requested by the employer over a two-year period. The union then utilized the litigation process as a further tool of delay, raising frivolous defenses and conducting a 10-day "abusive" cross-examination of the general manager. The Board ordered the union to pay the employer's negotiating expenses and both the employer's and the Board's litigation costs. Similarly, in *Heartland Plymouth Court MI, LLC v. NLRB*, 838 F.3d 16 (D.C. Cir. 2016), the D.C. Circuit ordered the Labor Board to reimburse an employer

for attorneys' fees it incurred in successfully challenging the Board's unfair labor practice ruling in a situation where the NLRB had followed its policy of nonacquiescence and resisted a result that it knew would follow as a result of circuit precedent, amounting to bad faith litigation. The court faulted the Board for allowing the employers to file for judicial review in a circuit with adverse precedent rather than seeking enforcement of its own order in another circuit where its preferred policy had been accepted.

C. Unilateral Action

NLRB v. Katz
Supreme Court of the United States
369 U.S. 736, 82 S. Ct. 1107, 8 L. Ed. 230 (1962)

MR. JUSTICE BRENNAN delivered the opinion of the Court.

Is it a violation of the duty "to bargain collectively" imposed by § 8(a)(5) of the National Labor Relations Act for an employer, without first consulting a union with which it is carrying on bona fide contract negotiations, to institute changes regarding matters which are subjects of mandatory bargaining under § 8(d) and which are in fact under discussion? The National Labor Relations Board answered the question affirmatively in this case, in a decision which expressly disclaimed any finding that the totality of the respondents' conduct manifested bad faith in the pending negotiations. 126 N.L.R.B. 288. A divided panel of the Court of Appeals for the Second Circuit denied enforcement of the Board's cease-and-desist order, finding in our decision in *NLRB v. Insurance Agents*, 361 U.S. 477 (1960), a broad rule that the statutory duty to bargain cannot be held to be violated, when bargaining is in fact being carried on, without a finding of the respondent's subjective bad faith in negotiating. 289 F.2d 700. . . . We granted certiorari, 368 U.S. 811, in order to consider whether the Board's decision and order were contrary to *Insurance Agents*. We find nothing in the Board's decision inconsistent with *Insurance Agents* and hold that the Court of Appeals erred in refusing to enforce the Board's order. . . .

As amended and amplified at the hearing and construed by the Board, the complaint's charge of unfair labor practices particularly referred to three acts by the company: Unilaterally granting numerous merit increases in October 1956 and January 1957; unilaterally announcing a change in sick-leave policy in March 1957; and unilaterally instituting a new system of automatic wage increases during April 1957. As the ensuing litigation has developed, the company has defended against the charges along two fronts: First, it asserts that the unilateral changes occurred after a bargaining impasse had developed through the union's fault in adopting obstructive tactics. According to the Board, however, "the evidence is clear that the Respondent undertook its unilateral actions before negotiations were discontinued in May 1957, or before, as we find on the record, the existence of any possible impasse." 126 N.L.R.B. at 289–290. There is ample support in the record considered as a whole for this finding of fact, which is consistent with the Examiner's Intermediate Report, 126 N.L.R.B. at 295–296, and which the Court of Appeals did not question.

The second line of defense was that the Board could not hinge a conclusion that § 8(a)(5) had been violated on unilateral actions alone, without making a finding of the employer's subjective bad faith at the bargaining table; and that the unilateral actions were merely evidence relevant to the issue of subjective good faith. This argument prevailed in the Court of Appeals. . . .

The duty "to bargain collectively" enjoined by § 8(a)(5) is defined by § 8(d) as the duty to "meet . . . and confer in good faith with respect to wages, hours, and other terms and conditions of employment." Clearly, the duty thus defined may be violated without a general failure of subjective good faith; for there is no occasion to consider the issue of good faith if a party has refused even to negotiate *in fact*—"to meet . . . and confer"—about any of the mandatory subjects. A refusal to negotiate *in fact* as to any subject which is within § 8(d), and about which the union seeks to negotiate, violates § 8(a)(5) though the employer has every desire to reach agreement with the union upon an over-all collective agreement and earnestly and in all good faith bargains to that end. We hold that an employer's unilateral change in conditions of employment under negotiation is similarly a violation of § 8(a)(5), for it is a circumvention of the duty to negotiate which frustrates the objectives of § 8(a)(5) much as does a flat refusal.[15]

The unilateral actions of the respondent illustrate the policy and practical considerations which support our conclusion.

We consider first the matter of sick leave. A sick-leave plan had been in effect since May 1956, under which employees were allowed ten paid sick-leave days annually and could accumulate half the unused days, or up to five days each year. Changes in the plan were sought and proposals and counterproposals had come up at three bargaining conferences. In March 1957, the company, without first notifying or consulting the union, announced changes in the plan, which reduced from ten to five the number of paid sick-leave days per year, but allowed accumulation of twice the

---

15. [11] *Compare Medo Corp. v. Labor Board*, 321 U.S. 678 (1944); *May Department Stores v. NLRB*, 326 U.S. 376 (1945); *NLRB v. Crompton-Highland Mills*, 337 U.S. 217 (1949).

In *Medo*, the Court held that the employer interfered with his employees' right to bargain collectively through a chosen representative, in violation of § 8(1), 49 Stat. 452 (now § 8(a)(1)), when it treated directly with employees and granted them a wage increase in return for their promise to repudiate the union they had designated as their representative. It further held that the employer violated the statutory duty to bargain when he refused to negotiate with the union after the employees had carried out their promise.

May held that the employer violated § 8(1) when, after having unequivocally refused to bargain with a certified union on the ground that the unit was inappropriate, it announced that it had applied to the War Labor Board for permission to grant a wage increase to all its employees except those whose wages had been fixed by "closed shop agreements." *Crompton-Highland Mills* sustained the Board's conclusion that the employer's unilateral grant of a wage increase substantially greater than any it had offered to the union during negotiations which had ended in impasse clearly manifested bad faith and violated the employer's duty to bargain.

unused days, thus increasing to ten the number of days which might be carried over. This action plainly frustrated the statutory objective of establishing working conditions through bargaining. Some employees might view the change to be a diminution of benefits. Others, more interested in accumulating sick-leave days, might regard the change as an improvement. If one view or the other clearly prevailed among the employees, the unilateral action might well mean that the employer had either uselessly dissipated trading material or aggravated the sick-leave issue. On the other hand, if the employees were more evenly divided on the merits of the company's changes, the union negotiators, beset by conflicting factions, might be led to adopt a protective vagueness on the issue of sick leave, which also would inhibit the useful discussion contemplated by Congress in imposing the specific obligation to bargain collectively.

Other considerations appear from consideration of the respondents' unilateral action in increasing wages. At the April 4, 1957, meeting the employers offered, and the union rejected, a three-year contract with an immediate across-the-board increase of $7.50 per week, to be followed at the end of the first year and again at the end of the second by further increases of $5 for employees earning less than $90 at those times. Shortly thereafter, without having advised or consulted with the union, the company announced a new system of automatic wage increases whereby there would be an increase of $5 every three months up to $74.99 per week; an increase of $5 every six months between $75 and $90 per week; and a merit review every six months for employees earning over $90 per week. It is clear at a glance that the automatic wage increase system which was instituted unilaterally was considerably more generous than that which had shortly theretofore been offered to and rejected by the union. Such action conclusively manifested bad faith in the negotiations, *NLRB v. Crompton-Highland Mills*, 337 U.S. 217 (1949), and so would have violated § 8(a)(5) even on the Court of Appeals' interpretation, though no additional evidence of bad faith appeared. An employer is not required to lead with his best offer; he is free to bargain. But even after an impasse is reached he has no license to grant wage increases greater than any he has ever offered the union at the bargaining table, for such action is necessarily inconsistent with a sincere desire to conclude an agreement with the union.[16]

The respondents' third unilateral action related to merit increases, which are also a subject of mandatory bargaining. *NLRB v. Allison & Co.*, 165 F.2d 766 (6th Cir. 1948). The matter of merit increases had been raised at three of the conferences during 1956 but no final understanding had been reached. In January 1957, the company, without notice to the union, granted merit increases to 20 employees out of the approximately 50 in the unit, the increases ranging between $2 and $10. This action too must be viewed as tantamount to an outright refusal to negotiate on that subject,

---

16. [12] Of course, there is no resemblance between this situation and one wherein an employer, after notice and consultation, "unilaterally" institutes a wage increase identical with one which the union has rejected as too low. . . .

and therefore as a violation of § 8(a)(5), unless the fact that the January raises were in line with the company's long-standing practice of granting quarterly or semiannual merit reviews — in effect, were a mere continuation of the status quo — differentiates them from the wage increases and the changes in the sick-leave plan. We do not think it does. Whatever might be the case as to so-called "merit raises" which are in fact simply automatic increases to which the employer has already committed himself, the raises here in question were in no sense automatic, but were informed by a large measure of discretion. There simply is no way in such case for a union to know whether or not there has been a substantial departure from past practice, and therefore the union may properly insist that the company negotiate as to the procedures and criteria for determining such increases.

It is apparent from what we have said why we see nothing in *Insurance Agents* contrary to the Board's decision. The union in that case had not in any way whatever foreclosed discussion of any issue, by unilateral actions or otherwise. The conduct complained of consisted of partial-strike tactics designed to put pressure on the employer to come to terms with the union negotiators. We held that Congress had not, in § 8(b)(3), the counterpart of § 8(a)(5), empowered the Board to pass judgment on the legitimacy of any particular economic weapon used in support of genuine negotiations. But the Board *is* authorized to order the cessation of behavior which is in effect a refusal to negotiate, or which directly obstructs or inhibits the actual process of discussion, or which reflects a cast of mind against reaching agreement. Unilateral action by an employer without prior discussion with the union does amount to a refusal to negotiate about the affected conditions of employment under negotiation, and must of necessity obstruct bargaining, contrary to the congressional policy. It will often disclose an unwillingness to agree with the union. It will rarely be justified by any reason of substance. It follows that the Board may hold such unilateral action to be an unfair labor practice in violation of § 8(a)(5), without also finding the employer guilty of over-all subjective bad faith. While we do not foreclose the possibility that there might be circumstances which the Board could or should accept as excusing or justifying unilateral action, no such case is presented here.

The judgment of the Court of Appeals is reversed and the case is remanded with direction to the court to enforce the Board's order.

It is so ordered.

Mr. Justice Frankfurter took no part in the decision of this case.

Mr. Justice White took no part in the consideration or decision of this case.

Notes

1. *Understanding Katz* — To what extent does *Katz* make an employer's unilateral change in working conditions a refusal to bargain per se?

2. *Substantial and Material Changes* — For a unilateral change in working conditions to violate § 8(a)(5), it must constitute a "substantial and material" change. *See,*

e.g., Parsons Elec., LLC v. NLRB, 812 F.3d 716 (8th Cir. 2016) (change in employee break policy contained in an employee handbook maintained pursuant to the management rights clause in the collective agreement violated § 8(a)(5) where policy was material to employees and union was not given notice or opportunity to bargain); *Chemical Solvents, Inc.*, 362 N.L.R.B. 1469 (2015) (change in policy regarding mobile phone use while driving constituted "material, substantial and significant" change, and announcing policy without first giving union opportunity to bargain violated § 8(a)(5)); *United Rentals, Inc.*, 350 N.L.R.B. 951 (2007) (changes in equipment rental, uniform, and call-in policies constituted "material, substantial, and significant" changes, and thus § 8(a)(5) violations); *Ferguson Enters.*, 349 N.L.R.B. 617 (2007) (policy prohibiting employees from taking home their truck keys constituted a "substantial and material change," but a policy preventing them from taking home their company-issued cell phones did not); *see also Salem Hosp. Corp.*, 360 N.L.R.B. 768 (2014) (unilateral change in employee dress code violated § 8(a)(5) where it had significant financial impact on unit employees who would have to purchase new uniforms, including outerwear, sweatshirts and jackets, and imposed more stringent discipline for non-compliance than the previous dress code), *enforced*, 669 Fed. Appx. 80 (3d Cir. 2016).

Where the Board finds an unlawful unilateral change to the detriment of employees, the proper remedy is to make employees whole for losses sustained, even if the union does not seek a remedy requiring a contractual return to the status quo ante. In cases where the unilateral change benefits employees, however, the employer is ordered to rescind the change only upon the union's request. *Goya Foods of Fla.*, 356 N.L.R.B. 1461 (2011).

3. *Unilateral Implementation After Impasse*—Employers may declare an impasse when there is no realistic possibility that continuing negotiations would be fruitful. Upon impasse, an employer may implement a final offer that: (1) is a product of good faith negotiations untainted by unfair labor practices; (2) has been presented to, and rejected by, the union, and (3) is implemented in a fashion that does not disparage the union in its capacity as bargaining representative, or the collective bargaining process itself. The theory behind allowing implementation of final offers is that unilateral implementation—at least when accompanied by these safeguards—can function as an aid in breaking impasse, "a controlled escape route to put a stalemated relationship onto a new, more positive path." Dannin, *Legislative Intent and Impasse Resolution Under the National Labor Relations Act: Does Law Matter?*, 15 HOFSTRA LAB. & EMP. L.J. 11, 26 (1997).

Whether impasse has been reached in a particular case is a difficult question. In *Beverly Farm Found. v. NLRB*, 144 F.3d 1048 (7th Cir. 1998), the Seventh Circuit enforced a Board order finding that the employer had violated §§ 8(a)(1) and 8(a)(5) of the NLRA by prematurely declaring an impasse, unilaterally implementing its final offer, and withdrawing union recognition. Rejecting Beverly's contention that impasse had occurred where the parties had met 19 times over a one-year period and were still far apart, the Board noted that the parties had only discussed economic issues on three occasions of the 19, the union's bargaining posture was flexible, and the union had assured the employer that no strike was likely. The Board ordered a 10-month extension on the union's certification period, dating from resumption of bargaining; the court enforced the order. The Board is particularly likely to find a violation where the employer declares impasse but has failed to provide requested information relevant to the core issues separating the parties at the bargaining table. *See Colorado Symphony Ass'n*, 366 N.L.R.B. No. 122 (2018); *E.I. du Pont de Nemours & Co. v. NLRB*, 489 F.3d 1310 (D.C. Cir. 2007).

On the other hand, in *TruServ Corp. v. NLRB*, 254 F.3d 1105, *as amended*, 168 L.R.R.M. 2036 (D.C. Cir. 2001), *cert. denied*, 534 U.S. 1130 (2002), the D.C. Circuit refused to enforce the Board's conclusion that an employer had prematurely declared impasse and hence violated § 8(a)(5) by unilaterally implementing new work rules and disciplining employees for violating the rules. The Board had concluded that the employer had made an abrupt final offer after only eight days of bargaining, and a pattern of demonstrated flexibility in significant issues during the final days of bargaining, as well as the union's surprise at the termination of bargaining and request for further negotiations, suggested that the parties were not yet at impasse. While acknowledging that the Board was better suited than the courts to evaluate the bargaining process, the court found no substantial evidence to support the Board's conclusion since nothing in the record refuted the employer's categorization of its last offer as "final." According to the court, "the parties remain in control of their negotiations, and each party, not the Board, determines at what point it ceases to be willing to compromise." The court also noted the lengthy bargaining relationship between the parties and the experience of the negotiators as factors pointing toward impasse. *See also Dish Network Corp. v. NLRB*, 953 F.3d 370 (5th Cir. 2020) (employer permissibly declared impasse after four years of hard bargaining and one year of silence even though the union later presented a concessionary counterproposal).

Critical to a finding of impasse is pre-impasse bargaining conducted in good faith. *Compare Laurel Bay Health & Rehab. Ctr. v. NLRB*, 666 F.3d 1365 (D.C. Cir. 2012) (employer did not violate § 8(a)(5) when it unilaterally increased employee wages during negotiations over new contract where parties had strong disagreement over cost of employee healthcare and court found that parties had reached good faith impasse) *and New NGC Inc., d/b/a National Gypsum Co.*, 359 N.L.R.B. 1058 (2013) (impasse reached and thus lockout lawful where the company held firmly to its retirement benefit proposals and made clear that it was unwilling to accept concessions on other issues, and the union made equally clear that it would not accept the retirement proposals), *with Carey Salt Co. v. NLRB*, 736 F.3d 405 (5th Cir. 2013) (post-impasse change in employment terms violated § 8(a)(5) where impasse had been generated by bad-faith bargaining by employer, who sought to engineer a premature impasse and implement its proposal).

Further, an employer generally may not make unilateral changes in working conditions during collective bargaining until there is an overall impasse as to the agreement as a whole; impasses as to an individual topic will not suffice. *Duffy Tool & Stamping, L.L.C. v. NLRB*, 233 F.3d 995 (7th Cir. 2000); Visiting *Nurse Servs. v. NLRB*, 177 F.3d 52 (1st Cir. 1999), *cert. denied*, 528 U.S. 1074 (2000); *Richfield Hospitality, Inc.*, 369 N.L.R.B. No. 111 (2020). *But cf. TXU Elec. Co.*, 343 N.L.R.B. 1404 (2004) (where employees' wages are scheduled for review on a certain date and employer has a past practice of annually reviewing and adjusting those rates, employer may set wages unilaterally even if parties have not reached overall impasse or agreement in bargaining by that date).

4. *Limits on Unilateral Implementation After Impasse* — Unilateral changes made after a bargaining impasse must be "reasonably comprehended" within the employer's final pre-impasse offer, and cannot be more favorable than the proposals made to the union. Accordingly, an employer who implements *less* favorable terms following rejection by the union membership of a more favorable bargaining proposal does not violate the Act. *See Telescope Casual Furniture*, 326 N.L.R.B. 588 (1998) (employer who implemented less favorable alternative of two offered simultaneously in bargaining, a "final offer" and a "less favorable alternative," did not violate §8(a)(5) because the less favorable alternative was encompassed within final offer and was utilized to pressure the union to come to agreement rather than to frustrate bargaining). *Cf. Loral Defense Systems-Akron v. NLRB*, 200 F.3d 436 (6th Cir. 1999) (post-impasse implementation of health plan was not merely modification of existing plan discussed during negotiations but rather replacement of existing plan with wholly different system of health insurance).

An exception to the rule of implementation following impasse was outlined in *McClatchy Newspapers*, 321 N.L.R.B. 1386 (1996). A 2-1 majority of the NLRB held that an employer could not unilaterally change wages after bargaining to impasse on a proposal to institute a merit-pay plan that effectively gave the employer unfettered discretion over future wage increases, reasoning that such unlimited managerial authority would be "*inherently* destructive of the fundamental principles of collective bargaining." Although the D.C. Circuit found the question difficult, it deferred to the Board's statutory interpretation and enforced its decision, noting that the Board's holding was limited to cases in which the employer refused to state any "definable objective procedures and criteria" for determining merit. Unilateral implementation of such a merit-pay plan undermines the union's authority as the representative of the employees by depriving it of information necessary to bargain knowledgeably in subsequent sessions, thus preventing it from having any impact on the determination of wage rates. *McClatchy Newspapers v. NLRB*, 131 F.3d 1026 (D.C. Cir. 1997), *cert. denied*, 524 U.S. 937 (1998); *Cf. E.I. du Pont de Nemours & Co. v. NLRB*, 489 F.3d 1310 (D.C. Cir. 2007) (following impasse, employer may implement plan to gradually equalize health care costs where plan conferred only limited discretion on employer); *Detroit Typographical Union No. 18 v. NLRB*, 216 F.3d 109 (D.C. Cir. 2000) (employer may implement merit-pay system that includes sufficient standards to constrict its discretion over wages following good faith bargaining impasse). Under *McClatchy*, then, an employer is permitted to make one set of unilateral changes per impasse; however, such changes may not have continuing effect so that the employer avoids its bargaining obligation indefinitely and the union is made to appear impotent to its members over time. *See Edward S. Quirk Co. v. NLRB*, 241 F.3d 41 (1st Cir. 2001) (vacating and remanding Board's ruling that employer violated § 8(a)(5) by unilaterally implementing a merit wage increase plan that provided standards for merit increases), *on remand*, 340 N.L.R.B. 301 (2003) (finding wage incentive plan allowing company to choose between unspecified market rate and fixed per-hour rate left employer with total discretion to make recurring unilateral decisions about wage increases, and affirming its earlier ruling).

The D.C. Circuit subsequently limited the *McClatchy* exception to unilateral employer actions aimed primarily at wages, because they are a core focus of collective bargaining. Actions that have a business purpose and an incidental effect on wages do not fall within the exception. Thus, where the employer sought to restructure its operations in response to shifting business conditions by unilaterally relocating a transportation relay point after the parties reached impasse on the issue, no § 8(a)(5) violation occurred even though the change negatively impacted some drivers' wages. *See Mail Contrs. of Am. v. NLRB*, 514 F.3d 27 (D.C. Cir. 2008) (reasoning that placement of a relay point is a "quintessentially managerial decision" because "its location presumably will affect the efficiency of the company's operations but it will have no material effect upon the company's wage bill").

Finally, § 8(d)(3) requires a party proposing changes in an existing collective bargaining agreement to provide notice regarding its intended changes to the FMCS and any state conciliation service 30 days prior to the expiration date of the contract. If a party that fails to comply with this requirement makes any unilateral changes in an expired contract—even after a bargaining impasse has been reached—it will be found guilty of an 8(a)(5) or 8(b)(3) violation. *American Water Works Co.*, 361 N.L.R.B. 64 (2014).

5. *Duration of Impasse*—Even where impasse has been reached and the employer has unilaterally implemented its proposals, external events that spur the union to reopen negotiations may end the impasse. In *Raven Servs. Corp. v. NLRB*, 315 F.3d 499 (5th Cir. 2002), the employer made unilateral changes in job classifications pursuant to a management rights clause that it had unilaterally implemented after a bargaining impasse. However, the impasse was broken when the union elected a new unit leader and economic circumstances changed (including the expiration of a government contract and rumors of wage cuts to accompany any new contract). The employer's refusal to supply the union upon request with information regarding employee benefit plans, job classifications, pay rates, and work schedules, and its unilateral changes in job classifications, violated § 8(a)(5). "Impasses cannot continue forever, as they are by definition temporary," said the court. *See also Atrium of Princeton, LLC v. NLRB*, 684 F.3d 1310 (D.C. Cir. 2012) (employer violated § 8(a)(5) by unilaterally implementing a replacement plan for health insurance following an impasse over the costs of employee health benefits, where subsequent action by the employee benefit fund that had provided health insurance under the contract "changed the backdrop of negotiations and created the possibility of productive bargaining," thus breaking the impasse).

Determining the date of unilateral implementation has sometimes proved troublesome in connection with impasses that are broken. In *Comau, Inc. v. NLRB*, 671 F.3d 1232 (D.C. Cir. 2012), the D.C. Circuit disagreed with the Board and found that a unilateral change can be considered implemented when it is announced rather than when it occurs. Thus, even though a change in its health care plan had not yet been applied to any employee, and the employer had not reached a point of no return committing it to making the change, the employer's announcement of the change at a point when impasse had been reached in negotiations and preparation for it in the period following the announcement was lawful where impasse had been broken by the time the change became effective.

6. *Other Bases for Unilateral Changes: Business Necessity*—Even in the absence of an impasse, economic exigency may enable an employer to institute unilateral changes. See *Eagle Transport Corp.*, 338 N.L.R.B. 489 (2002). The burden is very difficult to meet: the employer must show occurrence of an extraordinary unforeseen event having a major economic impact and requiring immediate company action. Labor market competitive pressures or precarious financial conditions are not sufficient. *Pleasantview Nursing Home, Inc. v. NLRB*, 351 F.3d 747 (6th Cir. 2003). See, e.g., *Seaport Printing & AD Specialties, Inc.*, 351 N.L.R.B. 1269 (2007), enforced, 589 F.3d 812 (5th Cir. 2009) (hurricane that forced plant shutdown was economic exigency justifying employer's failure to bargain over decision to lay off employees).

In circumstances falling short of economic exigency but still calling for prompt action, an employer may act unilaterally if the union waives an opportunity to bargain. Traditionally, the Board required the waiver to be "clear and unmistakable," an exacting standard that required a finding that the parties "unequivocally and specifically express their mutual intention to permit unilateral employer action with respect to a particular employment term, notwithstanding the statutory duty to bargain that would otherwise apply." *Provena Hosps.*, 350 N.L.R.B. 808, 811 (2007). The Trump Board rejected the "clear and unmistakable" standard in cases where the issue is whether a management rights clause in a labor contract waives the duty to bargain over changes in mandatory bargaining subjects. The Trump Board adopted a "contract coverage" analysis in which the Board looks to see whether the plain language of the contract can be interpreted as providing the employer with the right to act unilaterally in that area. See *MV Transportation*, 368 N.L.R.B. No. 66 (2019); *Huber Specialty Hydrates*, 369 N.L.R.B. No. 32 (2020).

7. *Unilateral Changes against a Backdrop of Past Practice*—Suppose that the unilateral change involves a shift in a practice rather than a change that implicates a particular provision of the collective bargaining agreement. What types of employer actions would constitute a change in working conditions triggering an obligation to bargain? Generally, if the change pertains to a mandatory subject of bargaining, the employer must bargain to impasse before implementing the change. Overruling a line of cases going back over 20 years, the Board held in *Millwrights, Conveyors*

& Mach. Erectors Local Union No. 1031, 321 N.L.R.B. 30 (1996) that an employer's unilateral change of the work hours of a single employee could violate the duty to bargain where the past practice was clear.

Changes in past practice present complex issues where the past practice relates to a regularly recurring event. *See Posadas De Puerto Rico Assocs. v. NLRB*, 243 F.3d 87 (1st Cir. 2001) (employer with 20-year practice of withholding cost of group insurance premiums from employee pay checks violated § 8(a)(5) when it unilaterally discontinued withholding practice without bargaining to impasse over change, since practice pertained to insurance programs and constituted mandatory subject of bargaining); *Bonnell/Tredegar Indus. v. NLRB*, 46 F.3d 339 (4th Cir. 1995) (employer violated § 8(a)(5) when it unilaterally modified the method of calculating a contractually required Christmas bonus, even though the contract did not specify the method of calculation, because the bonus formula had become an implied term of employment that could not be unilaterally altered); *NLRB v. Plainville Ready Mix Concrete Co.*, 44 F.3d 1320 (6th Cir.), *cert. denied*, 516 U.S. 974 (1995) (employer violated § 8(a)(5) when it dropped existing gain sharing and incentive pay from its post-impasse wage plan without implementing increases in the hourly wage rates, because the employer had consistently treated the proposed hourly wage increases as the quid pro quo for the elimination of gain sharing and incentive pay).

Suppose that the employer justifies the change by pointing to the management rights clause. Outcomes in these cases have varied. *Compare Baptist Hosp.*, 351 N.L.R.B. 71 (2007) (no § 8(a)(5) violation by employer who unilaterally implemented change in shift-work scheduling where management rights clause reserved right to determine start and end times, assign employees, and change method and means of operation) *and Chicago Tribune Co. v. NLRB*, 974 F.2d 933 (7th Cir. 1992) (clause allowing employer to impose "reasonable rules relating to employee conduct" permitted unilateral establishment of drug-testing policy that authorized discipline for off-the-job drug-related conduct that could affect job performance or workplace safety), *with Hi-Tech Corp.*, 309 N.L.R.B. 3 (1992), *enforced*, 25 F.3d 1044 (5th Cir. 1994) (provision authorizing employer to "make, change, and enforce reasonable rules for efficiency, cleanliness, safety, attendance, conduct and working conditions" did not allow unilateral establishment of no-tobacco rule). In *E.I. du Pont de Nemours*, 364 N.L.R.B. No. 113 (2016), the Obama Board ruled that even actions *consistent* with past practice constitute a change requiring the employer to bargain with the union if the past practice was created under a management rights clause in a collective agreement that has expired, or where the disputed actions involved employer discretion. The Trump Board overruled *DuPont* and restored pre-*Dupont* precedent in *Raytheon Centric Network Systems*, 365 N.L.R.B. No. 161 (2017), finding that the employer's changes to employee healthcare benefits were a continuation of a past practice of unilateral changes every year for the preceding 12 years. Because the changes were similar in kind and in degree to the previous established practice, notice to the union and an opportunity to bargain were not required prior to implementation. Further, the Board noted that the principle will apply even where no collective agreement containing a management rights clause authorizing unilateral action was in effect at the point when the past practice was created or when the disputed actions were taken.

8. *Unilateral Implementation during First Contract Negotiations*—During first contract negotiations, the employer must maintain the status quo until impasse is reached, with one exception: the employer may lawfully implement a change on a discrete recurring event (such as an annual COLA) scheduled to occur during bargaining if it provides the union with reasonable advance notice and an opportunity to bargain about the change. *See Neighborhood House Ass'n*, 347 N.L.R.B. 553 (2006) (employer that conditioned implementation of regularly scheduled COLA wage increase upon union waiver of right to bargain for additional COLA increases did not violate § 8(a)(5)).

9. *Changes in Mandatory Subjects of Bargaining After Contract Expires*—Mandatory subjects of bargaining continue as terms and conditions of employment after a labor contract expires and cannot be altered unilaterally prior to a bargaining impasse. Thus, provisions relating to wages, pension and welfare benefits, hours, and working conditions survive the expiration of the agreement until a new agreement or impasse is reached. *Mike-Sell's Potato Chip Co. v. NLRB*, 807 F.3d 318 (D.C. Cir. 2015); *Prime Healthcare Services-Encino LLC v. NLRB*, 890 F.3d 286 (D.C. Cir. 2018). Nevertheless, where wage or benefit increases are specified only during the term of a contract, the obligation to continue them ceases when the contract expires. *See Finley Hospital v. NLRB*, 827 F.3d 720 (8th Cir. 2016) (one year collective agreement did not establish a status quo of annual compounded raises, so employer has no obligation to continue them during post-expiration bargaining); *see also Pittsburgh Post-Gazette*, 368 N.L.R.B. No. 41 (2019) (where collective agreement provided for annual contributions to a union health insurance fund and set percentage increases in fund contributions for each year covered by the contract, employer did not violate any contractual or statutory duty by refusing to pay additional percentage increase after contract had expired; the employer's contribution rate at the end of the contract established the status quo that must be maintained after the contract's expiration). On the other hand, matters not tied to employment itself and uniquely contractual in nature—such as union security clauses, no-strike and no-lockout clauses, and arbitration agreements—do not survive the expiration of the agreement absent express language to the contrary. *Litton Fin. Printing Div. v. NLRB*, 501 U.S. 190 (1991).

Dues checkoff clauses have been the subject of considerable flip-flopping. The Board originally held that dues checkoff clauses did not survive the expiration of a collective bargaining agreement. *See Bethlehem Steel Co.*, 136 N.L.R.B. 1500 (1962) (approved by the Supreme Court in *Litton Fin. Printing Div. v. NLRB*, 501 U.S. 190 (1991), *supra*). In *Local Joint Exec. Bd. of Las Vegas v. NLRB*, 657 F.3d 865 (9th Cir. 2011), however, the Ninth Circuit ruled that dues checkoff clauses survive the expiration of collective bargaining agreements in right-to-work states where they are not linked to lawful union security agreements, and thus employers may not unilaterally cease withholding contributions from employees and remitting them to the union.

The Board initially responded to this prompt in *WKYC-TV, Inc.*, 359 N.L.R.B. 286 (2012), reversing its long-standing precedent and reasoning that dues checkoff and union security arrangements are analytically distinct; even where a union security clause does not survive contract expiration, the dues checkoff clause does. The ruling was vacated, however, by *Noel Canning v. NLRB*. A properly constituted full Board reiterated its position that dues checkoff clauses survive the expiration of collective bargaining agreements in a 3-2 decision, *Lincoln Lutheran of Racine*, 362 N.L.R.B. 1655 (2015). The Board majority reasoned that requiring employers to honor dues checkoff arrangements after a contract expires serves the Act's goal of promoting collective bargaining and is consistent with the prohibition of post-contract unilateral changes in mandatory subjects of bargaining, citing *Katz*. The majority worried that unilateral cancellation of dues checkoff upon contract expiration would undermine the union's status as the employees' collective bargaining representative, distract the union from focusing on bargaining on other issues, and send a "powerful message" that the employer is "free to interfere with the financial lifeline between the employees and the union." The Board explained that dues checkoff clauses are different from union security clauses, arbitration clauses, no-strike clauses and management rights clauses, which don't survive contract expiration even though they are mandatory bargaining subjects, because those clauses involve waivers of statutory or nonstatutory rights that would exist absent the contract, and the waivers do not survive contract expiration. On the other hand, dues checkoff provisions are voluntary agreements that do not involve the contractual surrender of statutory or nonstatutory rights, and are provided solely as a matter of administrative convenience; therefore, they do survive contract expiration. Nevertheless, in *Valley Hosp. Med. Ctr., Inc.*, 368 N.L.R.B. No. 139 (2019), the Trump Board overruled *Lincoln Lutheran of Racine* and returned to its *Bethlehem Steel* rule, holding that dues checkoff clauses are exclusively creatures of contract, not statute, and thus do not survive the expiration of the labor contract.

10. *Changes in Employee Medical Benefits and Pension Plans* — Unilateral changes in the benefits available under employee medical and pension plans have presented special problems. Where the collective agreement contains a reservation-of-rights clause permitting the employer to make changes, unilateral alterations are permissible. *See, e.g., S. Nuclear Operating Co. v. NLRB*, 524 F.3d 1350 (D.C. Cir. 2008). Absent such a clause, however, the employer's unilateral change will violate § 8(a)(5). *See, e.g., Caterpillar, Inc.*, 355 N.L.R.B. 521 (2010) (employer violated § 8(a)(5) by unilaterally implementing changes in employee prescription drug plans); *see also Barton v. Constellium Rolled Products*, 856 F.3d 348 (4th Cir. 2017) (where collective agreement made it clear that employer could not reduce pension benefits of retired workers after contract expiration but contained no such language relative to retiree health care coverage, employer's unilateral reduction in retiree health care coverage after contract expired was lawful).

11. *Unilateral Action by a Union* — Could a union violate § 8(b)(3) by unilateral action? How? *See Painters Dist. Council 9 (Westgate Painting & Decorating Corp.)*,

186 N.L.R.B. 964 (1970), *enforced*, 453 F.2d 783 (2d Cir. 1971), *cert. denied*, 408 U.S. 930 (1972) (union committed an unfair labor practice by unilaterally implementing a maximum production quota). *But cf. Scofield v. NLRB*, 394 U.S. 423 (1969) (union could permissibly enforce properly adopted rules against its members limiting the amount of piecework production for which they could seek immediate payment).

Problems

49. Following a back-and-forth exchange with the union over the employer's proposal to alter the employees' health insurance benefits, the employer proposed the following clause:

> A committee comprised of up to five (5) bargaining unit members, as may be designated by the union, will meet with management, prior to any changes being made in the group health insurance plan, to discuss whether to keep the current group health insurance plan in lieu of the other options which may be available at that time.

When the union refused to agree to the clause, the company declared impasse and unilaterally implemented this procedure. Has the company violated the Act? Explain.

50. During the summer of 2020, in the midst of the COVID-19 pandemic, a unionized restaurant in New York City unilaterally eliminated its contribution to the employees' health insurance plans and its contribution to their retirement plans, without bargaining with the union. It also gave notice that it would be laying off employees in the near future unless the Governor and Mayor relaxed the reopening requirements for restaurants in New York City before that point. It declined the union's request for bargaining over the decision to lay off, and the effects of the decision. Did the restaurant violate the Act? Explain.

D. Supplying Information

NLRB v. Truitt Manufacturing Co.

Supreme Court of the United States
351 U.S. 149, 76 S. Ct. 753, 100 L. Ed. 1027 (1956)

Mr. Justice Black delivered the opinion of the Court.

The National Labor Relations Act makes it an unfair labor practice for an employer to refuse to bargain in good faith with the representative of his employees. The question presented by this case is whether the National Labor Relations Board may find that an employer has not bargained in good faith where the employer claims it cannot afford to pay higher wages but refuses requests to produce information substantiating its claim.

The dispute here arose when a union representing certain of respondent's employees asked for a wage increase of 10 cents per hour. The company answered that it could not afford to pay such an increase, it was undercapitalized, had never paid dividends, and that an increase of more than 2-1/2 cents per hour would put it out of business. The union asked the company to produce some evidence substantiating these statements, requesting permission to have a certified public accountant examine the company's books, financial data, etc. This request being denied, the union asked that the company submit "full and complete information with respect to its financial standing and profits," insisting that such information was pertinent and essential for the employees to determine whether or not they should continue to press their demand for a wage increase. A union official testified before the trial examiner that "[W]e were wanting anything relating to the Company's position, any records or what have you, books, accounting sheets, cost expenditures, what not, anything to back the Company's position that they were unable to give any more money." The company refused all the requests, relying solely on the statement that "the information . . . is not pertinent to this discussion and the company declines to give you such information; You have no legal right to such."

On the basis of these facts the National Labor Relations Board found that the company had "failed to bargain in good faith with respect to wages in violation of Section 8(a)(5) of the Act." 110 N.L.R.B. 856. The Board ordered the company to supply the union with such information as would "substantiate the Respondent's position of its economic inability to pay the requested wage increase." The Court of Appeals refused to enforce the Board's order, agreeing with respondent that it could not be held guilty of an unfair labor practice because of its refusal to furnish the information requested by the union. 224 F.2d 869 (4th Cir. 1955). In *NLRB v. Jacobs Mfg. Co.*, 196 F.2d 680 (2d Cir. 1952), the Second Circuit upheld a Board finding of bad-faith bargaining based on an employer's refusal to supply financial information under circumstances similar to those here. Because of the conflict and the importance of the question we granted certiorari. . . .

The company raised no objection to the Board's order on the ground that the scope of information required was too broad or that disclosure would put an undue burden on the company. Its major argument throughout has been that the information requested was irrelevant to the bargaining process and related to matters exclusively within the province of management. Thus we lay to one side the suggestion by the company here that the Board's order might be unduly burdensome or injurious to its business. In any event, the Board has heretofore taken the position in cases such as this that "It is sufficient if the information is made available in a manner not so burdensome or time-consuming as to impede the process of bargaining." And in this case the Board has held substantiation of the company's position requires no more than "reasonable proof."

We think that in determining whether the obligation of good-faith bargaining has been met the Board has a right to consider an employer's refusal to give information about its financial status. While Congress did not compel agreement between employers and bargaining representatives, it did require collective bargaining in the hope that agreements would result. Section 204(a)(1) of the Act admonishes both employers and employees to "exert every reasonable effort to make and maintain agreements concerning rates of pay, hours, and working conditions...." In their effort to reach an agreement here both the union and the company treated the company's ability to pay increased wages as highly relevant. The ability of an employer to increase wages without injury to his business is a commonly considered factor in wage negotiations. Claims for increased wages have sometimes been abandoned because of an employer's unsatisfactory business condition; employees have even voted to accept wage decreases because of such conditions.

Good-faith bargaining necessarily requires that claims made by either bargainer should be honest claims. This is true about an asserted inability to pay an increase in wages. If such an argument is important enough to present in the give and take of bargaining, it is important enough to require some sort of proof of its accuracy. And it would certainly not be farfetched for a trier of fact to reach the conclusion that bargaining lacks good faith when an employer mechanically repeats a claim of inability to pay without making the slightest effort to substantiate the claim. Such has been the holding of the Labor Board since shortly after the passage of the Wagner Act. In *Pioneer Pearl Button Co.*, decided in 1936, where the employer's representative relied on the company's asserted "poor financial condition," the Board said: "He did no more than take refuge in the assertion that the respondent's financial condition was poor; he refused either to prove his statement, or to permit independent verification. This is not collective bargaining." 1 N.L.R.B. 837, 842–843. This was the position of the Board when the Taft-Hartley Act was passed in 1947 and has been its position ever since. We agree with the Board that a refusal to attempt to substantiate a claim of inability to pay increased wages may support a finding of a failure to bargain in good faith.

The Board concluded that under the facts and circumstances of this case the respondent was guilty of an unfair labor practice in failing to bargain in good faith. We see no reason to disturb the findings of the Board. We do not hold, however, that in every case in which economic inability is raised as an argument against increased wages it automatically follows that the employees are entitled to substantiating evidence. Each case must turn upon its particular facts. The inquiry must always be whether or not under the circumstances of the particular case the statutory obligation to bargain in good faith has been met. Since we conclude that there is support in the record for the conclusion of the Board here that respondent did not bargain in good faith, it was error for the Court of Appeals to set aside the Board's order and deny enforcement.

Reversed.

[**Mr. Justice Frankfurter**, whom **Mr. Justice Clark** and **Mr. Justice Harlan** joined, concurred in part and dissented in part in an opinion that is omitted.]

NLRB v. Acme Indus. Co., 385 U.S. 432, 87 S. Ct. 565, 17 L. Ed. 2d 495 (1967). A collective bargaining agreement provided that if plant equipment was moved to another location, employees subject to layoff or reduction in grade as a result could transfer under certain conditions to the new location. The contract also contained a grievance procedure culminating in binding arbitration. When the union discovered that certain machinery was being removed from the employer's plant, it filed contract grievances and requested information about the dates of the move, the destination of the equipment, the amount of machinery involved, the reason for the transfer, and the new use to be made of the equipment. The employer replied it had no duty to furnish this information since no layoffs or reductions had occurred within the five-day time limit for filing grievances. The NLRB ruled the employer had refused to bargain in good faith, observing that the information sought was "necessary in order to enable the Union to evaluate intelligently the grievances filed" and pointing out that the agreement contained no "clause by which the Union waives its statutory right to such information." The Supreme Court upheld the Board's order. The "duty to bargain unquestionably extends beyond the period of contract negotiations and applies to labor-management relations during the term of an agreement." Moreover, the Board did not have to await an arbitrator's determination of the relevancy of the information before enforcing the union's statutory rights under § 8(a)(5). The Board "was not making a binding construction of the labor contract. It was only acting upon the probability that the desired information was relevant, and that it would be of use to the union in carrying out its statutory duties and responsibilities. . . . Thus, the assertion of jurisdiction by the Board in this case in no way threatens the power which the parties have given the arbitrator to make binding interpretations of the labor agreement."

Notes

1. *Implications of the Duty to Supply Information*—Under *Truitt* and *Acme*, is an employer's failure to supply relevant information a refusal to bargain per se? Should it be? What is the relationship between *Truitt*'s honesty-in-bargaining policy, the good faith bargaining obligation, and the duty to disclose relevant information upon which bargaining positions are predicated? *See generally* Dau-Schmidt, *The Story of* NLRB v. Truitt Manufacturing Co. *and* NLRB v. Insurance Agents' International Union: *The Duty to Bargain in Good Faith, in* LABOR LAW STORIES (Cooper & Fisk eds., 2005).

2. *Union Must Request Information*—In order to trigger the duty to furnish information, the union must make an explicit request. A company that provided oral information concerning its plans to close one of its facilities, lay off employees, and reassign work to other facilities during a telephone call with the local union president satisfied its obligation to respond to the union's information request. The union made no renewed request for information and did not pursue the matter with higher-level management as the union president had promised to do, and its filing of unfair labor practice charges four days later was not sufficient to put the employer on notice that the union sought further information. *AT&T Corp.*, 337 N.L.R.B. 689 (2002).

3. *Wage and Financial Data* — An employer must furnish all information necessary and relevant to the performance of the union's collective bargaining responsibilities. This applies to the administration as well as the negotiation of the labor agreement. In determining relevance, the Labor Board and the courts have distinguished between wage data and financial data.

Wage data, including information concerning all the factors that enter into the computation of wages or other forms of compensation, is presumptively relevant. Examples of wage data that must be furnished are: hours worked, rates of pay, and job classifications, *Marquis-Stevens, Inc.*, 334 N.L.R.B. No. 35 (2001); information regarding overtime distribution among employees, *Pavilion at Forrestal Nursing & Rehab.*, 346 N.L.R.B. 458 (2006); information regarding employee training programs, *S. Cal. Gas Co.*, 346 N.L.R.B. 449 (2006); time study data, *NLRB v. Otis Elevator Co.*, 208 F.2d 176 (2d Cir. 1953); information about the labor costs for employment of contract and outside agency employees, *Mt. Clemens Gen. Hosp. & RN Staff Council, Office*, 335 N.L.R.B. 48 (2001), *enforced*, 328 F.3d 837 (6th Cir. 2003); pricing information affecting labor costs, *Earthgrains Baking Cos., Inc.*, 327 N.L.R.B. 605 (1999); merit increases, *Otis Elevator Co.*, 170 N.L.R.B. 395 (1968); pension information, *Union Carbide Corp., Carbon Products Div.*, 197 N.L.R.B. 717 (1972); and group insurance data, *Stowe-Woodward, Inc.*, 123 N.L.R.B. 287 (1959).

Financial data include sales and production figures and other information concerning the employer's ability to meet the union's economic demands. Generally, an employer need not divulge such information unless it makes its financial position an issue in the negotiations. The employer may be required to substantiate its claims at the table by disclosing specific support for its assertions, *see Caldwell Mfg. Co.*, 346 N.L.R.B. 1159 (2006), but it need not open its books to the union unless it claims that it cannot afford to pay. The Board distinguishes between an employer claim of present inability to pay (which triggers the duty to supply financial information) and an "employer's projections of its future inability to compete" (which do not trigger the duty to supply financial information). *Nielsen Lithographing Co.*, 305 N.L.R.B. 697 (1991), *enforced sub nom. GCIU Local 508 v. NLRB*, 977 F.2d 1168 (7th Cir. 1992). According to the Board, the critical distinction between the two is this:

> The employer who claims a present inability to pay, or a prospective inability to pay during the life of the contract being negotiated, is claiming essentially that it *cannot* pay. By contrast, the employer who claims only economic difficulties or business losses or the prospect of layoffs is simply saying that it does not *want* to pay.

305 N.L.R.B. at 700. Thus, employers demanding concessions to enable them to compete more effectively are not required to honor union requests to see their financial records, since they are not asserting an inability to satisfy the proposed contract terms. *See N. Star Steel Co.*, 347 N.L.R.B. 1364 (2006) (claims that "'extremely low' future orders were 'a cause of great concern,'" "several competitors were 'effectively bankrupt,'" and that "business was really going south in a hurry" constituted claims of competitive disadvantage); *AMF Trucking & Warehousing, Inc.*, 342 N.L.R.B.

1125 (2004) (company was making claims of competitive disadvantage rather than inability to pay where it made statements indicating that it was in financial distress and was "fighting to [stay] alive"; therefore, no obligation to provide financial data arose).

The Board has struggled to draw the line between claims of inability to pay and claims of competitive disadvantage. *Compare Wayron, LLC*, 364 N.L.R.B. No. 60 (2016) (employer's claim that union concessions were essential in order to remain competitive triggered duty to furnish information in support of claims where employer stated that it had been unprofitable with existing labor costs for several years, that it had no corporate parent able to sustain losses, and that the bank providing its line of credit would no longer fund its losses without significant cost reductions), *and KLB Indus.*, 357 N.L.R.B. 127 (2011), *enforced, KLB Indus., Inc. v. NLRB*, 700 F.3d 551 (D.C. Cir. 2012) (requiring employer to provide union with information about customers and pricing to support employer's generic representations at the bargaining table that pressures to "remain competitive in both global and domestic markets" required it to seek wage reductions from the employees) *with Media Gen. Operations*, 345 N.L.R.B. 195 (2005) (employer did not violate § 8(a)(5) by unilaterally canceling annual bonus, claiming that it was "unable to pay" and denying union's request for financial information; the phrase "unable to pay" described an effort to maintain a strong cash flow rather than a measure upon which the company's survival depended).

The courts, particularly the D.C. Circuit, have been less than supportive in this struggle. For example, in *ConAgra, Inc. v. NLRB*, 117 F.3d 1435 (D.C. Cir. 1997), the employer sought steep wage cuts and made statements during bargaining that sales volume had declined sharply, that "we need to be competitive," and that "we want the company to continue." The Board found these comments sufficient to trigger an obligation to provide the union with financial information. The D.C. Circuit reversed, holding that the Board's ruling was inconsistent with its *Nielsen Lithographing* doctrine. Judge Wald filed a separate concurrence suggesting that the Board review its *Nielsen Lithographing* rationale in search of an approach that would more tightly link disclosure obligations to the union's need to evaluate the accuracy of factual claims made by the employer. *See also Lakeland Bus Lines, Inc. v. NLRB*, 347 F.3d 955 (D.C. Cir. 2003) (reversing Board order requiring disclosure of financial data where employer made its financial condition a central issue in contract negotiations, characterized its proposal to freeze wages and reduce overtime pay as essential to retain employees and to "bring the bottom line back into the black," and told the union that the "future of [this company] depends upon it"; court interpreted employer's references to lost patronage and revenue as claims of short-term business losses and competitive disadvantage distinguishable from claims of inability to pay); *SDBC Holdings, Inc. v. NLRB*, 711 F.3d 281 (2d Cir. 2013) (refusing to enforce Board's ruling where employer allowed union to inspect a 19-page financial statement in support of employer's statements at the bargaining table that it had sustained operating losses, "was not in the business to sustain losses," and "had to reduce the costs of the labor agreement in order . . . to stay in business," but did not allow the union to retain a copy of the document because of concerns that the report might fall into the hands of competitors; company's statements indicated unwillingness to meet the union's demands rather than inability to pay, and thus triggered no duty to provide information).

What statements would amount to a claim of inability to pay obligating the employer to provide financial information? According to the Board, the distinction between a claimed inability to pay and unwillingness to pay must be made in context. Thus, even where an employer uses the phrase "unable to pay" during negotiations, no duty to furnish financial information arises where the context otherwise indicates that the refusal is a result of unwillingness to pay rather than financial exigency. *See Media General Operations, Inc., supra*. Further, an employer who promptly and truthfully retracts a claim of inability to pay when the union seeks financial data may avoid a violation of § 8(a)(5), but the retraction must be "unmistakably clear." In *Am. Polystyrene Corp.*, 341 N.L.R.B. 508 (2004), the company complained at the bargaining table of inability to pay, made pleas of poverty by email, and justified bargaining proposals to reduce benefits with statements that "things were tough." When the union negotiator asked the company general manager, "Are you saying that you can't afford the union's proposals?," the manager replied "No, I can't. I'd go broke." The Board refused to require the disclosure of financial information, finding that the company's statements were made in the heat of bargaining, and that its subsequent retraction of a claim of inability to pay made the next day simultaneously with its denial of the union's request for financial data was effective. The Ninth Circuit refused to enforce the Board's order. *Int'l Chem. Workers Union Council v. NLRB*, 467 F.3d 742 (9th Cir. 2006). *See also IATSE Local 15 v. NLRB*, 2020 U.S. App. LEXIS 13739 (9th Cir. 2020) (employer that initially claimed inability to afford union demands but then quickly switched to unwillingness to do so was not required to disclose its financial data).

Is the difference in the treatment of wage data and financial data justified in the first place? Could anything be more "relevant" to a union in formulating its demands in preparation for collective bargaining than knowledge of the employer's capacity to pay? *See* Bloch, *The Disclosure of Profits in the Normal Course of Collective Bargaining*, 2 Lab. Law. 47 (1986); Robbins, *Rethinking Financial Information Disclosure Under the National Labor Relations Act*, 47 Vand. L. Rev. 1905 (1994). Finally, can wages legitimately be distinguished from other relatively fixed "cost pressures" that are verifiable by reviewing third-party contracts? *See Amersig Graphics, Inc.*, 334 N.L.R.B. 880 (2001) (Board allowed union access to documents pertaining to sale of company assets); *United States Testing Co. v. NLRB*, 160 F.3d 14 (1998) (employer required to provide union with information concerning individual claims histories of employees when it proposes cutting health benefits); *Taylor Hosp.*, 317 N.L.R.B. 991 (1995), *enforced*, 82 F.3d 406 (3d Cir. 1996) (Board allowed union access to insurance contracts).

4. *Employee Privacy* — The employer's good-faith bargaining obligation also includes the duty to provide information relevant and necessary for the union's performance of its representative function in administering and policing the contract, communicating with unit members, and preserving their work. *NLRB v. Acme Indus. Co.*, 385 U.S. 432 (1967). Suppose that the information sought is confidential and providing it would invade employees' privacy. Should the employer be permitted to resist providing it? In *Detroit Edison Co. v. NLRB*, 440 U.S. 301 (1979), the Supreme Court balanced the employer's interests against the union's interests and concluded that an employer had a sufficient interest in the secrecy of psychological aptitude test questions and answers to refuse disclosure and condition disclosure of individual scores on the employees' consent, even where the union desired the information to prepare for an arbitration.

Employer assurances of confidentiality to employees will not necessarily justify the employer's resistance to disclosure where the union demonstrates a legitimate need for the information. In a dispute involving the criteria used to fill new bargaining unit positions, the First Circuit refused to enforce a Board order requiring the employer to furnish the union with employees' psychological aptitude test scores, noting that confidentiality assurances had been made to employees by the employer. The court directed the Board to reexamine the balancing of interests required by *Detroit Edison*. *NLRB v. USPS*, 660 F.3d 65 (1st Cir. 2011). On remand the Board again ordered the employer to provide the test scores, finding that the union's need for the requested information outweighed the employees' privacy interests: because of the impact of the test scores in determining seniority, lack of access would make it impossible for the union to determine whether the Postal Service was complying with the parties' agreement regarding unit employees' relative seniority standing. Indeed, the Board concluded that the union's need for test scores and seniority-related information was even greater than in *Detroit Edison*. The Board did, however, limit the required disclosure by specifying that the scores and hiring dates be disclosed without identifying the employees by name. *USPS*, 359 N.L.R.B. 1052 (2013). *See also Metropolitan Edison Co.*, 330 N.L.R.B. 107 (1999) (employer was required to supply union with information regarding informants who had told the company that a particular worker was stealing food from the cafeteria, where union offered evidence that employer had targeted the employee because of his protected activities; employer's asserted confidentiality interest and desire to protect informants against retaliation was insufficient to justify a blanket refusal to provide any information).

Similarly, in *Piedmont Gardens*, 359 N.L.R.B. 499 (2012), *vacated due to lack of a quorum*, 2014 N.L.R.B. LEXIS 494, the Board reversed its long-standing "bright-line" rule that witness statements obtained during an employer's investigation of employee misconduct pursuant to a promise of confidentiality need not be provided to the union. Instead, such requests will be evaluated under the balancing test established in *Detroit Edison*: the Board must balance the union's need for the information against the confidentiality interests established by the employer, including the potential for harassment and coercion. A majority of the full Board reaffirmed the *Piedmont Gardens* ruling in *American Baptist Homes of the West*, 362 N.L.R.B. 1135 (2015). Acknowledging its departure from precedent, the Board made its new rule applicable prospectively only. What effect might the *Piedmont Gardens* rule have on employers' ability to conduct investigations into allegations of workplace misconduct by employees and respond appropriately? The Board has since signaled its willingness to reconsider the *Piedmont Gardens* doctrine. *American Medical Response West*, 366 N.L.R.B. No. 146, n.4 (2018).

Names, classifications, hire dates, telephone numbers, addresses, pay rates, and disciplinary records of unit employees are presumptively relevant to the union's performance of its duties as employee representative and must be furnished to the union. *River Oak Ctr. for Children, Inc.*, 345 N.L.R.B. 1335 (2005), *enforced*, 2008 U.S. App. LEXIS 9017 (9th Cir. Apr. 16, 2008). Health insurance claims experience of unit employees is also presumptively relevant to the union's representative function, *see North American Soccer League*, 245 N.L.R.B. 1301 (1979), although federal privacy laws pertaining to medical information require the employer to redact individual identifying information associated with such claims. *See Goodyear Atomic Corp.*, 266 N.L.R.B. 890 (1983), *enforced*, 738 F.2d 155 (6th Cir. 1984). Further, when an employer's accommodation of an individual's disability elevates the disabled employee to a job ahead of coworkers with greater seniority, the union is entitled to the relevant medical information supporting the employer's accommodation decision. This is to enable the union to evaluate grievances pertaining to alleged violations of the contractual seniority provisions filed by more senior personnel who were passed over in favor of the disabled employee. *See Roseburg Forest Prods. Co.*, 331 N.L.R.B. 999 (2000).

5. *Managerial Prerogative and Trade Secrets* — Employers are often reluctant to turn over confidential information containing trade secrets, customer lists, or other proprietary business information absent assurances that it will be kept confidential. If the union refuses to bargain over how to protect the employer's legitimate confidential business interests, the employer need not provide the information. *Oncor Electric Delivery, LLC*, 369 N.L.R.B. No. 40 (2020).

Suppose that a company commissions reports from a state occupational safety and health inspector who has indicated that he is likely to issue citations following an inspection of the worksite. May the employer refuse to disclose the reports to the union on the basis of attorney-client privilege, since they are integral to weighing the costs and benefits of litigation? Yes, said the Labor Board in *BP Exploration (Alaska), Inc.*, 337 N.L.R.B. 887 (2002). Assuming that the *Detroit Edison* balancing test applies to lawyer-client communications, the Board found that the employer's interest in maintaining attorney-client privilege outweighed the union's need for the reports, and the employer discharged its obligations to the union by offering the union certain information contained in the reports (an accommodation which the union rejected).

Employers that regularly use toxic substances have been required to provide unions with information concerning their generic names, morbidity and mortality tables, toxicological studies, insurance claims, radiation levels, etc., but not the medical records of identified individuals. Bargaining was ordered to establish appropriate safeguards to protect the employers' proprietary interests in trade secrets. *Oil, Chem. & Atomic Workers Local Union No. 6-418 v. NLRB*, 711 F.2d 348 (D.C. Cir. 1983). Unions are also entitled to copies of environmental audits. In *Detroit Newspaper Agency*, 317 N.L.R.B. 1071 (1995), the Board ruled against an employer who refused to provide the union with an unredacted copy of an environmental audit of the workplace. Even if the employer had a legitimate claim of confidentiality, that was outweighed by the union's interest in health and safety when the audit was a routine annual report and not prepared in response to a specific health and safety problem.

Finally, union agents must generally be allowed to enter plant premises when necessary to monitor health and safety conditions. *NLRB v. American Nat'l Can Co.*, 924 F.2d 518 (4th Cir. 1991). Thus, an employer that denied the union's request to send an accident investigator into its manufacturing plant following a workplace fatality violated § 8(a)(5). The company's argument that it needed to protect confidential information covering its plant processes was not credible since it allowed tours of the plant during working hours for customers, dealers, technical groups, and students. *Caterpillar, Inc.*, 361 N.L.R.B. 846 (2014*), enforced*, 803 F.3d 360 (7th Cir. 2015).

6. *Information Impacting Union's Ability to Enforce Contract during Its Term* — How much information must the employer provide to the union in order to assist the union in serving as an effective advocate and representative of the employees? An employer is not obliged to provide a union with requested information that might be relevant to enforcement of a bargaining agreement when compliance would be burdensome and the union's predominant purpose in requesting the information is to harass the employer and force it to forgo a right it has under the collective contract. *NLRB v. Wachter Constr.*, 23 F.3d 1378 (8th Cir. 1994); *see also Detroit Edison Co.*, 314 N.L.R.B. 1273 (1994) (employer not required to furnish requested information that has no apparent connection to contract enforcement). Nevertheless, an employer cannot refuse to supply relevant information just because the union may use it for purposes the employer finds objectionable. For example, in *Nestle Purina Petcare Co.*, 347 N.L.R.B. 891 (2006), the Labor Board found that an employer violated § 8(a)(5) when it denied the union access to its facility to enable it to conduct a time-and-motion study relevant to a grievance the union had filed seeking an upgrade for drivers. And in *Medstar Washington Hosp. Ctr.*, 360 N.L.R.B. 846 (2014), the Board required the employer to turn over its staffing matrix, tracking tools and data used to calculate nursing staff to patient ratios, and employee survey results on the patient safety culture in the hospital despite the employer's fears of embarrassment and adverse publicity as a result of dissemination of the results. Similarly, a company had to furnish the names, addresses, and wage rates of employees even though the union might solicit them to join an FLSA suit. *NLRB v. CJC Holdings*, 97 F.3d 114 (5th Cir. 1996). *But see S. Cal. Gas Co.*, 342 N.L.R.B. 613 (2004) (no obligation on employer to provide information on maintenance work done on equipment in employer's gas transmission and storage units to support class action grievance union was considering filing with the state public utilities commission regarding safety issues that might impact employees, since union did not reference labor contract or relationship of information to its role as employee representative in the workplace). Employers do not have an obligation, however, to furnish information that the union seeks to help prove pending unfair labor practice charges, because Board procedures do not include pretrial discovery. *Saginaw Control & Eng'g, Inc.*, 339 N.L.R.B. 541 (2003).

When a union seeks information that is presumptively relevant to its representation of employees during a grievance process, an employer who refuses to respond or delays in providing the information violates § 8(a)(5) — even if the information requested ultimately turns out to be irrelevant. *See Public Service Co. of New Mexico v. NLRB*, 843 F.3d 999 (D.C. Cir. 2016) (employer violated § 8(a)(5) where it failed to provide the union with information about non-bargaining-unit employees that the union sought in connection with grievances alleging disparate treatment of bargaining unit and non-bargaining unit employees under company-wide policies). A timely response in which the employer gives the reasons for its belief that requested information is irrelevant is required to demonstrate the good faith effort that the statute mandates. *Iron Tiger Logistics, Inc.*, 359 N.L.R.B. 236 (2012), *vacated due to the lack of a quorum*, 2014 U.S. App. LEXIS 14896 (D.C. Cir. 2014), *reaffirmed*, 362 N.L.R.B. 324 (2015), *enforced in relevant part*, 823 F.3d 696 (D.C. Cir. 2016). Further, a union that sought payroll information (employee names, wages, hours worked, etc.) to support a class pay grievance filed under the collective bargaining agreement was entitled to receive it, even where the employer claimed that there was no authority for processing "class" grievances under the labor contract. The Board explained that NLRB precedent requires an employer to provide relevant requested information regardless of the potential merits of the dispute. *Endo Painting Serv.*, 360 N.L.R.B. 485 (2014), *enforced*, 679 Fed Appx. 614 (9th Cir. 2017).

Similarly, unions seeking to challenge discriminatory hiring practices may obtain employer information concerning the race, national origin, and gender of job applicants, but only if the union is able to show facts supporting a reasonable basis for a belief that discrimination is occurring and further inquiry is justified. In *Hertz Corp.*, 319 N.L.R.B. 597 (1995), the Board held that a car rental company must provide this information to the union where its labor agreement contained a nondiscrimination clause, since it was relevant to the union's function as bargaining agent. The Third Circuit denied enforcement because the union had failed to communicate to Hertz any facts to support its suspicion of hiring discrimination. *Hertz Corp. v. NLRB*, 105 F.3d 868 (3d Cir. 1997).

Non-bargaining unit data, such as subcontracting costs, is not presumptively relevant, and the union therefore bears an initial burden of establishing relevance before the employer must comply. A "bare assertion" of relevance falls short of this standard. *Sara Lee Bakery Group, Inc. v. NLRB*, 514 F.3d 422 (5th Cir. 2008). Thus, in *W. Penn Power Co. v. NLRB*, 394 F.3d 233 (4th Cir. 2005), the court enforced the Board's ruling that a company had violated § 8(a)(5) by refusing to turn over information about subcontractors where the labor contract permitted subcontracting but also contained a clause explicitly requiring the employer to keep a force of regular employees sufficient to take care of its "expected work," as well as a "resource-sharing" provision establishing a preferential order for employee assignment to other work sites, with contractors to be used only if insufficient numbers of regular employees were available. The court found that the information requested was directly relevant to the union's ability to fulfill its duty to police the contract. Similarly, in *Monmouth Care Ctr. v. NLRB*, 672 F.3d 1085 (D.C. Cir. 2012), the court sustained a Labor Board finding that an employer violated § 8(a)(5) when it failed to provide, or only partially produced, information regarding its use of temporary agency employees, including names and rates of pay where the information was relevant to central bargaining issues, including the percentage of union versus temporary employees utilized by the employer. See also *New York & Presbyterian Hosp. v. NLRB*, 649 F.3d 723 (D.C. Cir. 2011) (employer violated § 8(a)(5), where it failed to produce information sought by the union about the status of non-unit workers allegedly performing bargaining unit work during grievance processing); *NLRB v. Waymouth Farms, Inc.*, 172 F.3d 598 (8th Cir. 1999) (employer that failed to provide the union with truthful information about a planned relocation violated § 8(a)(5); employer's failure to provide the union with truthful information regarding the planned relocation undermined the union's ability to bargain intelligently about the rights of the workers whose jobs were being eliminated at the old plant).

By contrast, the Board found no violation when an employer failed to provide requested information concerning subcontracting where the labor contract permitted the employer to subcontract so long as it did not result in a termination, layoff, or a failure to recall unit employees from a layoff. The union's "suspicion" that subcontractors were being hired in violation of the contract was not sufficient to require disclosure given the contract's terms, and the union was unable to provide a reason for its request that would lead to a viable claim under the labor contract. The dissent complained that the majority had set the bar too high by requiring the union to provide objective evidence that a contract violation has occurred before information must be produced. *Disneyland Park*, 350 N.L.R.B. 1256 (2007).

7. *Information Concerning Replacement Workers during a Strike*—Although an employer is generally not obliged to bargain about the employment conditions of individuals hired as replacement workers during an economic strike, it must bargain over their terms of employment after the stoppage has ended. As a result, an employer's failure to provide the representative union with the names and addresses of replacement workers during a strike violated § 8(a)(5) when the union requested the information while it was bargaining over the terms that would apply to all unit personnel once the labor dispute ended. See *Grinnell Fire Prot. Sys. Co.*, 332 N.L.R.B.

1257 (2000). On appeal, the Eighth Circuit agreed that the employer's refusal to provide the names of strike replacements was a § 8(a)(5) violation, but its refusal to provide home addresses was not. The union had access to the employees at work, and the employees' privacy interest in protecting information about their residences outweighed the union's interest in soliciting them for membership. *Grinnell Fire Protection Sys. v. NLRB*, 272 F.3d 1028 (8th Cir. 2001); *see also Chicago Tribune Co. v. NLRB*, 79 F.3d 604 (7th Cir. 1996) (employer need not furnish union with the names and addresses of strike replacements when there had been violence against replacements in the past, applying a "totality of the circumstances" approach). *Cf. Contract Carriers Corp.*, 339 N.L.R.B. 851 (2003) (names, classifications, and wage rates of temporary employees performing bargaining unit work are presumptively relevant and must be produced).

8. *Form of Disclosure* — The employer is not obliged to supply information in the exact form requested so long as it is submitted in a form that is not unduly burdensome to interpret. *Westinghouse Elec. Corp.*, 129 N.L.R.B. 850 (1960); *McLean-Arkansas Lumber Co., Inc.*, 109 N.L.R.B. 1022 (1954). Nonetheless, it is reasonable for the union to request that the information be provided in electronic form if that is how the employer stores it. *See Bouille Clark Plumbing, Heating, & Elec., Inc.*, 337 N.L.R.B. 743 (2002), *enforced*, 2003 U.S. App. LEXIS 23800 (2d Cir. 2003). Suppose the union requests access to company premises to gather particular information. Does the duty to provide information to facilitate bargaining justify such access? One court of appeals has indicated that the NLRB may balance the employer's property rights against the employees' right to effective representation. *See Brown Shoe Co. v. NLRB*, 33 F.3d 1019 (8th Cir. 1994). Is this approach consistent with the doctrine articulated in *Lechmere* with respect to nonemployee access for organizing purposes?

9. *Union Disclosure* — Unions may also have an obligation to furnish information requested by employers. *See, e.g., UNITE HERE Local 1*, 369 N.L.R.B. No. 65 (2020) (union must furnish additional details in response to employer's request for information about grievances filed where information provided in first stage of process was inadequate to allow employer to prepare response); *SEIU, Local 715*, 355 N.L.R.B. 353 (2010) (where employer had conflicting information about the union to which it owed a bargaining obligation following a change in the union's identity, union was required to disclose information about identity of officers, union assets, and other relevant information); *International Bhd. of Firemen & Oilers, Local 288*, 302 N.L.R.B. 1008 (1991) (employee medical records needed to support excuse from work).

Problems

51. The union was initially certified at the employer's Illinois steel processing facility in 2007. By 2013, the parties attended more than 35 bargaining sessions, but no collective bargaining agreement was reached. The employer, twice claiming good faith impasse was reached, unilaterally implemented economic terms and conditions of employment in 2009 and 2012. During bargaining sessions in 2013, the employer responded to the union's economic proposals with the following statements:

"Economic conditions had weakened," and the employer was "doing the best it could and had kept everyone employed."

"Production volume was down" and the employer "faced increased costs, increased taxes, and downward pressure on pricing."

Competitors were "attempting to take business away" and "business was moving."

The employer "had hoped conditions would improve" but "business had softened" and "[b]oth volume and price were down."

The "'iceberg'" the employer was on "[was] 'melting'" and the "business had changed."

Based on these statements, the union requested financial information, including a report on business conditions, four years of audited financial reports, income statements, balance sheets, cash-flow statements, sales listed by customer, and federal and state income tax returns. The employer refused to provide any of the requested information. Then, in 2014, the employer withdrew recognition from the union after receiving a decertification petition signed by a majority of the bargaining unit employees.

Has the employer violated the Act? Explain.

52. A unionized hospital responded to a nurse's error in dispensing medication to a patient by suspending the nurse without pay for two months, following guidance from its peer review process, which is designed to improve the quality of care and to reduce health insurance premiums. The nurse filed a grievance with his union. The union requested access to the hospital's archives of "incident reports" concerning patients in order to defend its member, seeking to ascertain whether similar discipline was administered in cases involving similar errors in giving medication. The hospital consults you for advice, concerned about the confidentiality of its peer review process. May the hospital refuse the union access to this information?

Section V. The Subject Matter of Collective Bargaining

NLRB v. Wooster Division of Borg-Warner Corp.

Supreme Court of the United States
356 U.S. 342, 78 S. Ct. 718, 2 L. Ed. 2d 823 (1958)

Mr. Justice Burton delivered the opinion of the Court.

In these cases an employer insisted that its collective-bargaining contract with certain of its employees include: (1) a "ballot" clause calling for a prestrike secret vote of those employees (union and non-union) as to the employer's last offer, and (2) a "recognition" clause which excluded, as a party to the contract, the International Union which had been certified by the National Labor Relations Board as the employees' exclusive bargaining agent, and substituted for it the agent's uncertified local affiliate. The Board held that the employer's insistence upon either of such clauses amounted to a refusal to bargain, in violation of §8(a)(5) of the National Labor Relations Act, as amended. The issue turns on whether either of these clauses comes within the scope of mandatory collective bargaining as defined in §8(d) of the Act. For the reasons hereafter stated, we agree with the Board that neither clause comes within that definition. Therefore, we sustain the Board's order directing the employer to cease insisting upon either clause as a condition precedent to accepting any collective- bargaining contract. . . .

[T]he "ballot" clause . . . provided that, as to all nonarbitrable issues (which eventually included modification, amendment or termination of the contract), there would be a 30-day negotiation period after which, before the union could strike, there would have to be a secret ballot taken among all employees in the unit (union and non-union) on the company's last offer. In the event a majority of the employees rejected the company's last offer, the company would have an opportunity, within 72 hours, of making a new proposal and having a vote on it prior to any strike. The union's negotiators announced they would not accept this clause "under any conditions."

From the time that the company first proposed these clauses, the employees' representatives thus made it clear that each was wholly unacceptable. The company's representatives made it equally clear that no agreement would be entered into by it unless the agreement contained both clauses. In view of this impasse, there was little further discussion of the clauses, although the parties continued to bargain as to other matters. The company submitted a "package" proposal covering economic issues but made the offer contingent upon the satisfactory settlement of "all other issues. . . ." The "package" included both of the controversial clauses. On March 15, 1953, the unions rejected that proposal and the membership voted to strike on March 20 unless a settlement were reached by then. None was reached and the unions struck. Negotiations, nevertheless, continued. . . .

Read together, [§§ 8(a)(5) and 8(d)] establish the obligation of the employer and the representative of its employees to bargain with each other in good faith with respect to "wages, hours, and other terms and conditions of employment. . . ." The duty is limited to those subjects, and within that area neither party is legally obligated to yield. *NLRB v. American National Insurance Co.*, 343 U.S. 395. As to other matters, however, each party is free to bargain or not to bargain, and to agree or not to agree.

The company's good faith has met the requirements of the statute as to the subjects of mandatory bargaining. But that good faith does not license the employer to refuse to enter into agreements on the ground that they do not include some proposal which is not a mandatory subject of bargaining. We agree with the Board that such conduct is, in substance, a refusal to bargain about the subjects that are within the scope of mandatory bargaining. This does not mean that bargaining is to be confined to the statutory subjects. Each of the two controversial clauses is lawful in itself. Each would be enforceable if agreed to by the unions. But it does not follow that, because the company may propose these clauses, it can lawfully insist upon them as a condition to any agreement.

Since it is lawful to insist upon matters within the scope of mandatory bargaining and unlawful to insist upon matters without, the issue here is whether either the "ballot" or the "recognition" clause is a subject within the phrase "wages, hours, and other terms and conditions of employment" which defines mandatory bargaining. The "ballot" clause is not within that definition. It relates only to the procedure to be followed by the employees among themselves before their representative may call a strike or refuse a final offer. It settles no term or condition of employment—it merely calls for an advisory vote of the employees. It is not a partial "no-strike" clause. A "no-strike" clause prohibits the employees from striking during the life of the contract. It regulates the relations between the employer and the employees. *See NLRB v. American National Insurance Co.*, supra at 408, n.22. The "ballot" clause, on the other hand, deals only with relations between the employees and their unions. It substantially modifies the collective bargaining system provided for in the statute by weakening the independence of the "representative" chosen by the employees. It enables the employer, in effect, to deal with its employees rather than with their statutory representative. *Cf. Medo Photo Supply Corp. v. NLRB*, 321 U.S. 678 (1944).

The "recognition" clause likewise does not come within the definition of mandatory bargaining. The statute requires the company to bargain with the certified representative of its employees. It is an evasion of that duty to insist that the certified agent not be a party to the collective bargaining contract. The Act does not prohibit the voluntary addition of a party, but that does not authorize the employer to exclude the certified representative from the contract. . . .

Mr. Justice Frankfurter joins this opinion insofar as it holds that insistence by the company on the "recognition" clause, in conflict with the provisions of the Act requiring an employer to bargain with the representative of his employees, constituted an unfair labor practice. He agrees with the views of **Mr. Justice Harlan** regarding the "ballot" clause. The subject matter of that clause is not so clearly outside the reasonable range of industrial bargaining as to establish a refusal to bargain in good faith, and is not prohibited simply because not deemed to be within the rather vague scope of the obligatory provisions of § 8(d).

Mr. Justice Harlan, whom Mr. Justice Clark and Mr. Justice Whittaker join, concurring in part and dissenting in part. . . .

The legislative history behind the Wagner and Taft-Hartley Acts persuasively indicates that the Board was never intended to have power to prevent good faith bargaining as to any subject not violative of the provisions or policies of those Acts. . . .

[E]arly intrusions of the Board into the substantive aspects of the bargaining process became a matter of concern to Congress, and in the 1947 Taft-Hartley amendments to the Wagner Act, Congress took steps to curtail them by writing into § 8(d) the particular fields as to which it considered bargaining *should* be required. . . .

The decision of this Court in 1952 in *NLRB v. American National Insurance Co., supra*, was fully in accord with this legislative background in holding that the Board lacked power to order an employer to cease bargaining over a particular clause because such bargaining under the Board's view, entirely apart from a showing of bad faith, constituted *per se* an unfair labor practice. . . .

I therefore cannot escape the view that today's decision is deeply inconsistent with legislative intention and this Court's precedents. The Act sought to compel management and labor to meet and bargain in good faith as to certain topics. This is the *affirmative* requirement of § 8(d) which the Board is specifically empowered to enforce, but I see no warrant for inferring from it any power in the Board to *prohibit* bargaining in good faith as to lawful matters not included in § 8(d). The Court reasons that such conduct on the part of the employer, when carried to the point of insistence, is in substance equivalent to a refusal to bargain as to the statutory subjects, but I cannot understand how this can be said over the Trial Examiner's unequivocal finding that the employer did in fact bargain in "good faith," not only over the disputed clauses but also over the statutory subjects. . . .

The most cursory view of decisions of the Board and the circuit courts under the National Labor Relations Act reveals the unsettled and evolving character of collective bargaining agreements. Provisions which two decades ago might have been thought to be the exclusive concern of labor or management are today commonplace in such agreements. The bargaining process should be left fluid, free from intervention of the Board leading to premature crystallization of labor agreements into any one pattern of contract provisions, so that these agreements can be adapted through collective bargaining to the changing needs of our society and to the changing concepts of the responsibilities of labor and management. What the Court does today may impede this evolutionary process. Under the facts of this case, an employer is precluded from attempting to limit the likelihood of a strike. But by the same token it would seem to follow that unions which bargain in good faith would be precluded from insisting upon contract clauses which might not be deemed statutory subjects within § 8(d).

As unqualifiedly stated in *American National Insurance Co., supra*, . . . it is through the "good faith" requirement of § 8(d) that the Board is to enforce the bargaining provisions of § 8. A determination that a party bargained as to statutory or non-statutory subjects in good or bad faith must depend upon an evaluation of the total circumstances surrounding any given situation. I do not deny that there may be instances where unyielding insistence on a particular item may be a relevant consideration in the overall picture in determining "good faith," for the demands of a party might in the context of a particular industry be so extreme as to constitute some evidence of an unwillingness to bargain. But no such situation is presented in this instance by the "ballot" clause. "No strike" clauses, and other provisions analogous to the "ballot" clause limiting the right to strike, are hardly novel to labor agreements. And in any event the uncontested finding of "good faith" by the Trial Examiner forecloses that issue here.

Of course, an employer or union cannot insist upon a clause which would be illegal under the Act's provisions, *NLRB v. National Maritime Union*, 175 F.2d 686 (2d Cir. 1949), or conduct itself so as to contravene specific requirements of the Act. *Medo Photo Supply Corp. v. NLRB*, 321 U.S. 678 (1944). But here the Court recognizes, as it must, that the clause is lawful under the Act, and I think it clear that the company's insistence upon it violated no statutory duty to which it was subject. . . .

The company's insistence on the "recognition" clause, which had the effect of excluding the International Union as a party signatory to agreement and making Local 1239 the sole contracting party on the union side, presents a different problem. In my opinion the company's action in this regard did constitute an unfair labor practice since it contravened specific requirements of the Act. . . .

Notes

1. *Who Is Empowered by the Mandatory/Permissive Subject Dichotomy?* — Which party benefits most from the mandatory/permissive subject distinction — unions or employers? Which would have benefited more if the Court had ruled in *Borg-Warner* that *all* lawful provisions are "mandatory" subjects on which bargaining is required and which may be forced to an impasse? Does *Borg-Warner* give the Board too much power to freeze or expand the list of topics on which unions and employers must bargain? Would it have been preferable to analyze the problem simply in terms of the parties' "good faith"?

2. *Strategic Considerations: What Is "Insisting"?* — A party that insists upon a nonmandatory subject for bargaining as a precondition to agreement on mandatory topics violates the duty to bargain. This is so even if the party otherwise pursues this strategy in good faith. *NLRB v. Greensburg Coca-Cola Bottling Co.*, 40 F.3d 669 (3d Cir. 1994). Suppose a union accepts an employer's total package proposal with the exception of a single nonmandatory item: a grievance settlement. Would the employer's subsequent refusal to execute the agreement necessarily constitute an unlawful insistence on a permissive subject? Would the issue turn entirely on whether an impasse had been reached? *See Good GMC, Inc.*, 267 N.L.R.B. 583 (1983) (employer's refusal to sign the agreement was not unlawful because no impasse was reached and acceptance of portions of a package proposal does not constitute a final agreement). What if a party insists upon a mandatory subject but suggests possible leeway with respect to that topic if the other side is willing to make concessions on a nonmandatory issue?

3. *Wages* — Employee compensation in a wide variety of forms has been held to be "wages" or "other conditions of employment," and thus a mandatory subject of bargaining. *See, e.g., United Rentals, Inc.*, 349 N.L.R.B. 853 (2007) (merit wage increases calculated pursuant to "merit matrix" with predominant nondiscretionary aspects); *Champion Int'l Corp.*, 339 N.L.R.B. 672 (2003) (severance pay); *Guard Publ'g Co.*, 339 N.L.R.B. 353 (2003) (sales commissions); *Inland Steel Co. v. NLRB*, 170 F.2d 247 (7th Cir. 1948), *cert. denied*, 336 U.S. 960 (1949) (pensions); *NLRB v. Mining Specialists, Inc.*, 326 F.3d 602 (4th Cir. 2003) (bonus plans tied to employee production); *Central Illinois Public Service Co.*, 139 N.L.R.B. 1407 (1962), *enforced*, 324 F.2d 916 (7th Cir. 1963) (employee discounts); *Getty Refining & Marketing Co.*, 279 N.L.R.B. 924 (1986) (recreation fund); *Bituminous Roadways*, 314 N.L.R.B. 1010 (1994) (discontinuance of dental and vision care program); *Loral Defense Systems-Akron*, 320 N.L.R.B. 755 (1996) (transfer to new delivery system for health insurance); *Posadas De Puerto Rico Assocs. v. NLRB*, 243 F.3d 87 (1st Cir. 2001) (alteration of employer's 20-year-old practice of withholding the cost of group cancer and life insurance premiums from employee paychecks). Rental fees in company-owned housing provided for employees who want it may be a mandatory topic of bargaining, depending on such circumstances as the distance to, and the availability of, other accommodations. *American Smelting & Refining Co. v. NLRB*, 406 F.2d 552 (9th Cir.), *cert. denied*, 395 U.S. 935 (1969); *but cf. Success Vill. Apts., Inc.*, 350 N.L.R.B. 908 (2007) (apartment cooperative that unilaterally changed past practice of permitting employees to purchase apartments in the complex did not violate §8(a)(5) where employees paid market rates for the apartments and enjoyed no advantage vis-à-vis the general public in purchasing them, since housing policy did not affect employees' terms and conditions of employment).

What about employee stock option purchase plans? Although the Board has ruled that stock option purchase plans are mandatory subjects where they operate akin to a retirement benefit (i.e., the employer makes matching contributions to the plan and employees do not receive stock until they retire, *see Richfield Oil Corp. (Los Angeles, Cal.)*, 110 N.L.R.B. 356 (1954)), such programs are permissive subjects where the program does not include a matching contribution from the employer, affords the employee no extension of credit to make the purchase, does not lock in a share-price below market value, and does not operate as a retirement plan (cannot be retained once the employment relationship is severed) since the employees receive no "emolument of value." *See Pieper Elec., Inc.*, 339 N.L.R.B. 1232 (2003) (no duty to furnish information concerning employee stock option purchase plan since it is a nonmandatory subject of bargaining); *see also UNITE HERE v. NLRB*, 546 F.3d 239 (2d Cir. 2008) (no duty to afford the union notice or opportunity to bargain where employer gave each regular employee 100 shares of stock valued at $1450 in connection with an initial public stock offering, where award was a "gift" unconnected to employee remuneration, the size of the award had no connection to employment-related factors, each employee received the same amount of stock, and award was a one-time event). The Board has also observed that any stock option purchase plan whose purposes are to convert employees into owners through the cumulative effect of stock ownership in an ESOP trust and to give them a controlling interest in their employer's parent corporation would be a nonmandatory subject because it would advance employees' interests as entrepreneurs rather than as workers, citing *Harrah's Lake Tahoe Resort Casino*, 307 N.L.R.B. 182 (1992).

4. *Employer Efforts to Detect and Deter Employee Misconduct* — In *Ford Motor Co. (Chicago Stamping Plant) v. NLRB*, 441 U.S. 488 (1979), the Supreme Court described mandatory subjects of bargaining as those that are "plainly germane to the working environment" and are "not among those managerial decisions which lie at the core of entrepreneurial control." Applying this test, the Board has found that a wide variety of employer investigatory tools or methods used to detect employee misconduct or violations of work rules are mandatory subjects of bargaining, since they have the potential to affect the continued employment of employees through discipline up to and including discharge and are neither entrepreneurial in character nor fundamental to the basic direction of the enterprise. *See Lockheed Shipbuilding & Constr. Co.*, 273 N.L.R.B. 171 (1984) (physical examinations); *Austin-Berryhill, Inc.*, 246 N.L.R.B. 1139 (1979) (polygraph testing); *Johnson-Bateman Co.*, 295 N.L.R.B. 180 (1989) (mandatory drug testing); *W-I Forest Prods. Co.*, 304 N.L.R.B. 957 (1991) (plant-wide ban on smoking). Drug testing of job applicants, however, is not a mandatory subject of bargaining. *Star Tribune, Div. of Cowles Media Co.*, 295 N.L.R.B. 543 (1989). *See generally* Kim, *Collective and Individual Approaches to Protecting Employee Privacy: The Experience with Workplace Drug Testing*, 66 La. L. Rev. 1009 (2006); Marcus & Smolla, Symposium, *Drug Testing in the Workplace*, 33 Wm. & Mary L. Rev. 1 (1991); Crain, *Expanded Employee Drug-Detection Programs and the Public Good: Big Brother at the Bargaining Table*, 64 N.Y.U. L. Rev. 1286 (1989). On the intersection between worker privacy interests and the NLRA, see Craver, *Privacy Issues Affecting Employers, Employees, and Labor Organizations*, 66 La. L. Rev. 1057 (2006); Levinson, *Industrial Justice: Privacy Protection for the Employed*, 18 Cornell J. L. & Pub. Pol'y 609 (2009).

What should the remedy be where the fruits of illegally obtained detection or surveillance are used in disciplinary actions against the employees? In *Brewers & Maltsters, Local Union No. 6 v. NLRB*, 414 F.3d 36 (D.C. Cir. 2005), the court enforced the Board's ruling that an employer violated § 8(a)(5), when, without offering to bargain with the union, it installed hidden surveillance cameras in designated break areas in an effort to detect illegal drug use among unit employees, since the use of hidden cameras constitutes a mandatory subject of bargaining. The Board had refused to order make-whole relief for the employees who were disciplined as a result of the illegal surveillance, however, reasoning that the employees' conduct violated plant rules and the discipline was based on their conduct, for which they should not be rewarded. The D.C. Circuit sent this part of the case back to the Board to reconsider its remedy. On remand, the Board again ruled that the employees were not entitled to reinstatement and back pay, reasoning that § 10(c) precludes reinstatement where the employees' discipline was "for cause." *Anheuser-Busch, Inc.*, 351 N.L.R.B. 644 (2007), *enforced*, 2008 U.S. App. LEXIS 24774 (D.C. Cir. 2008).

What steps must an employer take before imposing discretionary discipline on a union-represented employee where there is no collective bargaining agreement yet in force? In *Alan Ritchey, Inc.*, 359 N.L.R.B. 396 (2012), the Obama Board departed from precedent, ruling that where disciplinary action involves suspension, demotion, or discharge, the employer must give the newly elected union an opportunity to bargain before imposing discipline that would have an immediate impact on the employee's tenure, status, or earnings, including suspension, demotion, or discharge. Although the decision was voluntarily dismissed without prejudice due to the Labor Board's lack of a quorum, *Alan Ritchey, Inc.*, 32-CA-018149 (2013), a properly constituted quorum of the Board subsequently reaffirmed its decision in *Total Security Management Illinois 1, LLC*, 364 N.L.R.B. No. 106 (2016). In 2020, the Trump Board overturned *Total Security Management* and returned to precedent: employers have no duty to bargain prior to issuing serious discipline when a contract is not in force where they are applying preexisting disciplinary policies, since no material change in working conditions has occurred. *800 River Road Operating Co., LLC*, 369 N.L.R.B. No. 109 (2020).

5. *Other Mandatory Subjects*—Other provisions governing the employment relation that have been ruled subject to mandatory bargaining include: a dispute resolution system designed to provide an outlet for complaints and employee concerns regarding equal employment opportunities or corporate ethics and fairness issues, including demotion, discipline, and discharge, *Ga. Power Co. v. NLRB*, 427 F.3d 1354 (11th Cir. 2005); a no-strike clause covering both union and nonunion members of the bargaining unit, *Fry, Lloyd A., Roofing Co. (Houston, Tex.)*, 123 N.L.R.B. 647 (1959); a nondiscriminatory exclusive hiring hall arrangement in a right-to-work state, *Houston Chapter, Associated General Contractors of America, Inc. (Local 18, Hod Carriers)*, 143 N.L.R.B. 409 (1963), *enforced*, 349 F.2d 449 (5th Cir. 1965), *cert. denied*, 382 U.S. 1026 (1966); a change in a union's work jurisdiction, as distinguished from the scope of the bargaining unit, *IATSE Local 666, International Alliance of Theatrical Stage Employees etc. v. NLRB*, 904 F.2d 47 (D.C. Cir. 1990); the method by which a recall process for laid-off workers will be implemented, *Toma Metals, Inc.*, 342 N.L.R.B. 787 (2004); and changes in the employer's dress code, *Crittenton Hosp.*, 342 N.L.R.B. 686 (2004). Finally, the Congressional Research Service issued a report noting that employer-provided wellness programs set up under the Patient Protection and Affordable Care Act would be considered a mandatory subject of bargaining in unionized workplaces. See *Wellness Plans Would Be Subject to Antibias Law, Tax Codes, CRS Says*, Daily Lab. Rep. (BNA) No. 177, Sept. 14, 2010, at A-7.

6. *Permissive Subjects*—On the other hand, matters considered too remote from the employment relationship, or deemed a peculiar prerogative of employer or union, are not mandatory subjects of bargaining. If lawful, such matters are permissive subjects, and neither side may insist on a proposal to an impasse. Examples of permissive topics are negotiation ground rules, *UPS Supply Chain Solutions, Inc.*, 366 N.L.R.B. No. 111 (2018) (employer violated 8(a)(5) by insisting as a condition of continuing bargaining that the union translate its proposals to English); the scope of the bargaining unit, *Reichhold Chemicals, Inc.*, 301 N.L.R.B. 1228 (1991), *enforced*, 953 F.2d 594 (11th Cir. 1992); and the process of setting above-scale wages through direct dealing, as distinguished from the actual wage rates themselves, *Midwest TV, Inc.*, 343 N.L.R.B. 748 (2004).

7. *The Employer's Ability to Negotiate Directly with Individual Employees* — Personal service contracts between an employer and particularly talented or sought-after employees that establish above-scale wages and benefits constitute a permissive subject of bargaining where the collective contract sets minimum levels of benefits; thus, the employer may deal directly with individual employees. *KFMB Stations*, 349 N.L.R.B. 373 (2007), *review denied*, 2008 U.S. App. LEXIS 26636 (9th Cir. 2008); *but cf. Silverman ex rel. NLRB v. Major League Baseball Player Relations Comm.*, 67 F.3d 1054 (2d Cir. 1995) (free agency in baseball is mandatory subject of bargaining; ruling is unique to professional sports because of limited rights of players to sell talent to circumscribed group of owners who possess monopoly power in the sport).

Problems

53. Informed by the COVID-19 pandemic, may a rehabilitation facility unilaterally implement a policy for all of its employees that requires: (1) the wearing of face masks, (2) annual proof of inoculation with the flu vaccine, and (3) compulsory antiviral medication for employees who refuse immunization?

54. The New Yorker Union represents writers at the Conde Nast-owned publication, *The New Yorker*. During negotiations over a first contract, Conde Nast walked away from the bargaining table in response to the union's proposal for a just cause standard for discipline or termination of employees. The Union filed an unfair labor practice charge. Conde Nast defends its decision to walk away, arguing that it must insist that its editorial standards are not subject to the determinations of an outside arbitrator, as they would be in a grievance process under the just cause provision. Has Conde Nast violated the Act?

55. Furnace Refraction, Inc. sells the application of its proprietary refractory materials for the walls of furnaces used in the steel-making process. In 2012, the company's employees were represented by the International Union of Operating Engineers and covered by a collective bargaining agreement (CBA). The relevant CBA contained a management rights provision stating in part:

> Except as expressly modified or restricted by a specific provision of this Agreement, all statutory and inherent managerial rights, prerogatives, and functions are retained and vested exclusively in the Company, including, but not limited to, the rights: . . . to control and regulate the use of machinery, facilities, equipment, and other property of the Company; to introduce new or improved research, production, service, distribution, and maintenance methods, materials, machinery, and equipment; to issue, amend and revise work rules and Standards of Conduct, discipline steps, policies and practices; and to take whatever action is either necessary or advisable to manage and fulfill the mission of the Company and to direct the Company's employees.

The CBA also states:

> An employee who has never accrued seniority under this Agreement or an employee rehired shall be in probationary status until completion of six (6) months of employment.... The discipline, layoff or discharge of an employee who is in probationary status shall not be a violation of this Agreement.

Pursuant to the CBA, the company can discharge or discipline probationary employees without just cause or recourse to the grievance and arbitration process.

Without bargaining or giving notice to the union, the company began requiring new employees to sign a Noncompete and Confidentiality Agreement [NCCA] that prohibits employees from working for the company's competitors for 18 months following their employment and prohibits the disclosure of confidential or proprietary information. Another section, titled "Inventions," requires employees to assign to the company the rights to any inventions or "related know-how" developed during their employment with Furnace Refraction, Inc. The agreement also included sections titled "Interference with Relationships" and "At-Will Employee[s]." These sections provide:

> Interference with Relationships. During the Restricted Period Employee shall not, directly or indirectly, as employee, agent, consultant, stockholder, director, partner or in any other individual or representative capacity intentionally solicit or encourage any present or future customer or supplier of the Company to terminate or otherwise alter his, her or its relationship with the Company in an adverse manner.

> At-Will Employee. Employee acknowledges that this Agreement does not affect Employee's status as an employee at-will and that no additional right is provided herein which changes such status.

The company did not bargain with the Union before implementing the NCCA. Has the company violated the Act?

56. In which of the following situations may a union or an employer insist to impasse during collective bargaining without violating the NLRA?

> **a.** The union proposes a clause requiring all employees to become union members or pay a fee covering union activities associated with collective bargaining or contract administration, within 30 days from the date of hire.

> **b.** The union proposes a clause setting the amount of the union activity fee at 85 percent of the fee that members pay.

> **c.** The employer proposes a clause requiring that a supermajority of the union's members ratify the collective bargaining agreement before it becomes effective.

Allied Chemical & Alkali Workers Local 1 v. Pittsburgh Plate Glass Co.

Supreme Court of the United States
404 U.S. 157, 92 S. Ct. 383, 30 L. Ed. 2d 341 (1971)

Mr. Justice Brennan delivered the opinion of the Court. . . .

I

Since 1949, Local 1, Allied Chemical and Alkali Workers of America, has been the exclusive bargaining representative for the employees "working" on hourly rates of pay at the Barberton, Ohio, facilities of the respondent, Pittsburgh Plate Glass Company. In 1950, the Union and the Company negotiated an employee group health insurance plan, in which, it was orally agreed, retired employees could participate by contributing the required premiums, to be deducted from their pension benefits. This program continued unchanged until 1962, except for an improvement unilaterally instituted by the Company in 1954 and another improvement negotiated in 1959.

In 1962 the Company agreed to contribute two dollars per month toward the cost of insurance premiums of employees who retired in the future and elected to participate in the medical plan. The parties also agreed at this time to make 65 the mandatory retirement age. In 1964 insurance benefits were again negotiated, and the company agreed to increase its monthly contribution from two to four dollars, applicable to employees retiring after that date and also to pensioners who had retired since the effective date of the 1962 contract. It was agreed, however, that the Company might discontinue paying the two-dollar increase if Congress enacted a national health program.

In November 1965, Medicare, a national health program, was enacted. 79 Stat. 291, 42 U.S.C. §1395 *et. seq.* The 1964 contract was still in effect, and the Union sought mid-term bargaining to renegotiate insurance benefits for retired employees. The Company responded in March 1966 that, in its view, Medicare rendered the health insurance program useless because of a nonduplication of benefits provision in the Company's insurance policy, and stated, without negotiating any change, that it was planning to (a) reclaim the additional two-dollar monthly contribution as of the effective date of Medicare; (b) cancel the program for retirees; and (c) substitute the payment of the three dollar monthly subscription fee for supplemental Medicare coverage for each retired employee.

The Union acknowledged that the Company had the contractual right to reduce its monthly contribution, but challenged its proposal unilaterally to substitute supplemental Medicare coverage for the negotiated health plan. The Company, as it had done during the 1959 negotiations without pressing the point, disputed the Union's right to bargain in behalf of retired employees, but advised the Union that upon further consideration it had decided not to terminate the health plan for pensioners.

The Company stated instead that it would write each retired employee, offering to pay the supplemental Medicare premium if the employee would withdraw from the negotiated plan. Despite the Union's objections the Company did circulate its proposal to the retired employees, and 15 of 190 retirees elected to accept it. The Union thereupon filed unfair labor practice charges. . . .

II

. . . This obligation [to bargain under §§ 1, 8(a)(5), 8(d), and 9(a)] extends only to the "terms and conditions of employment" of the employer's "employees" in the "unit appropriate for such purposes" which the union represents. . . . The Board found that benefits of already retired employees fell within these constraints on alternative theories. First, it held that pensioners are themselves "employees" and members of the bargaining unit, so that their benefits are a "term and condition" of their employment. . . .

First. . . . In this cause we hold that the Board's decision is not supported by the law. The Act, after all, as § 1 makes clear, is concerned with the disruption to commerce that arises from interference with the organization and collective bargaining rights of "workers"—not those who have retired from the work force. The inequality of bargaining power that Congress sought to remedy was that of the "working" man, and the labor disputes that it ordered to be subjected to collective bargaining were those of employers and their active employees. Nowhere in the history of the National Labor Relations Act is there any evidence that retired workers are to be considered as within the ambit of the collective bargaining obligations of the statute.

To the contrary, the legislative history of § 2(3) itself indicates that the term "employee" is not to be stretched beyond its plain meaning embracing only those who work for another for hire. . . . In doubtful cases resort must still be had to economic and policy considerations to infuse § 2(3) with meaning. But, as the House comments . . . demonstrate, this is not a doubtful case. The ordinary meaning of "employee" does not include retired workers; retired employees have ceased to work for another for hire.

The decisions on which the Board relied in construing § 2(3) to the contrary are wide of the mark. The Board enumerated "unfair labor practice situations where the statute has been applied to persons who have not been initially hired by an employer or whose employment has terminated." . . . Yet all of these cases involved people who, unlike the pensioners here, were members of the active work force available for hire and at least in that sense could be identified as "employees." No decision under the Act is cited, and none to our knowledge exists, in which an individual who has ceased work without expectation of further employment has been held to be an "employee." . . .

Second. Section 9(a) of the Labor Relations Act accords representative status only to the labor organization selected or designated by the majority of employees in a "unit appropriate" "for the purposes of collective bargaining." . . .

In this case, in addition to holding that pensioners are not "employees" within the meaning of the collective bargaining obligations of the Act, we hold that they were not and could not be "employees" included in the bargaining unit. The unit determined by the Board to be appropriate was composed of "employees of the Employer's plant . . . working on hourly rates, including group leaders who work on hourly rates of pay. . . ." Apart from whether retirees could be considered "employees" within this language, they obviously were not employees "working" or "who work" on hourly rates of pay. Although those terms may include persons on temporary or limited absence from work, such as employees on military duty, it would utterly destroy the function of language to read them as embracing those whose work has ceased with no expectation of return. . . .

Here, even if, as the Board found, active and retired employees have a common concern in assuring that the latter's benefits remain adequate, they plainly do not share a community of interests broad enough to justify inclusion of the retirees in the bargaining unit. Pensioners' interests extend only to retirement benefits, to the exclusion of wage rates, hours, working conditions, and all other terms of active employment. Incorporation of such a limited-purpose constituency in the bargaining unit would create the potential for severe internal conflicts which would impair the unit's ability to function and would disrupt the processes of collective bargaining. Moreover, the risk cannot be overlooked that union representatives on occasion might see fit to bargain for improved wages or other conditions favoring active employees at the expense of retirees' benefits. . . .

Third. The Board found that bargaining over pensioners' rights has become an established industrial practice. But industrial practice cannot alter the conclusions that retirees are neither "employees" nor bargaining unit members. The parties dispute whether a practice of bargaining over pensioners' benefits exists and, if so, whether it reflects the views of labor and management that the subject is not merely a convenient but a mandatory topic of negotiation. But even if industry commonly regards retirees' benefits as a statutory subject of bargaining, that would at most, as we suggested in *Fibreboard Corp. v. NLRB*, 379 U.S. 203, 211 (1964), reflect the interests of employers and employees in the subject matter as well as its amenability to the collective bargaining process; it would not be determinative. Common practice cannot change the law and make into bargaining unit "employees" those who are not.

III

Even if pensioners are not bargaining unit "employees," are their benefits, nonetheless, a mandatory subject of collective bargaining as "terms and conditions of employment" of the active employees who remain in the unit? The Board held, alternatively, that they are, on the ground that they "vitally" affect the "terms and conditions of employment" of active employees principally by influencing the value of both their current and future benefits. . . .

Section 8(d) of the Act, of course, does not immutably fix a list of subjects for mandatory bargaining. . . . But it does establish a limitation against which proposed topics must be measured. In general terms, the limitation includes only issues which settle an aspect of the relationship between the employer and employees. *See, e.g., NLRB v. Borg-Warner Corp.*, [356 U.S. 342 (1958)]. Although normally matters involving individuals outside the employment relationship do not fall within that category, they are not wholly excluded. In *Teamsters Union v. Oliver*, 358 U.S. 283 (1959), for example, an agreement had been negotiated in the trucking industry, establishing a minimum rental which carriers would pay to truck owners who drove their own vehicles in the carriers' service in place of the latter's employees. Without determining whether the owner-drivers were themselves "employees," we held that the minimum rental was a mandatory subject of bargaining, and hence immune from state antitrust laws, because the term "was integral to the establishment of a stable wage structure for clearly covered employee-drivers." *United States v. Drum*, 368 U.S. 370, 382–383, n.26 (1962). Similarly, in *Fibreboard Corp. v. NLRB, supra* at 215, we held that "the type of 'contracting out' involved in this case—the replacement of employees in the existing bargaining unit with those of an independent contractor to do the same work under similar conditions of employment—is a statutory subject of collective bargaining...."

The Board urges that *Oliver* and *Fibreboard* provide the principle governing this case. The Company, on the other hand, would distinguish those decisions on the ground that the unions there sought to protect employees from outside threats, not to represent the interests of third parties. We agree with the Board that the principle of *Oliver* and *Fibreboard* is relevant here; in each case the question is not whether the third-party concern is antagonistic to or compatible with the interests of bargaining unit employees, but whether it vitally affects the "terms and conditions" of their employment. But we disagree with the Board's assessment of the significance of a change in retirees' benefits to the "terms and conditions of employment" of active employees.

The benefits which active workers may reap by including retired employees under the same health insurance contract are speculative and insubstantial at best. As the Board itself acknowledges in its brief, the relationship between the inclusion of retirees and the overall insurance rate is uncertain. Adding individuals increases the group experience and thereby generally tends to lower the rate, but including pensioners, who are likely to have higher medical expenses, may more than offset that effect. In any event, the impact one way or the other on the "terms and conditions of employment" of active employees is hardly comparable to the loss of jobs threatened in *Oliver* and *Fibreboard*.... The inclusion of retirees in the same insurance contract surely has even less an impact on the "terms and conditions of employment" of active employees than some of the contracting activities which we excepted from our holding in *Fibreboard*.

The mitigation of future uncertainty and the facilitation of agreement on active employees' retirement plans which the Board said would follow from the union's representation of pensioners are equally problematical.... Under the Board's theory, active employees undertake to represent pensioners in order to protect their own retirement benefits, just as if they were bargaining for, say, a cost-of-living escalation clause. But there is a crucial difference. Having once found it advantageous to bargain for improvements to pensioners' benefits, active workers are not forever thereafter bound to that view or obliged to negotiate in behalf of retirees again. To the contrary, they are free to decide, for example, that current income is preferable to greater certainty in their own retirement benefits or, indeed, to their retirement benefits altogether. By advancing pensioners' interests now, active employees, therefore, have no assurance that they will be the beneficiaries of similar representation when they retire. . . .

We recognize that "classification of bargaining subjects as 'terms [and] conditions of employment' is a matter concerning which the Board has special expertise." *Meat Cutters v. Jewel Tea*, 381 U.S. 676, 685–686 (1965). The Board's holding in this case, however, depends on the application of law to facts, and the legal standard to be applied is ultimately for the courts to decide and enforce. We think that in holding the "terms and conditions of employment" of active employees to be *vitally* affected by pensioners' benefits, the Board here simply neglected to give the adverb its ordinary meaning. *Cf. NLRB v. Brown*, 380 U.S. 278, 292 (1965).

IV

The question remains whether the Company committed an unfair labor practice by offering retirees an exchange for their withdrawal from the already negotiated health insurance plan. . . . We need not resolve, however, whether there was a "modification" within the meaning of § 8(d), because we hold that even if there was, a "modification" is a prohibited unfair labor practice only when it changes a term that is a mandatory rather than a permissive subject of bargaining.

Paragraph (4) of § 8(d), of course, requires that a party proposing a modification continue "in full force and effect . . . all the terms and conditions of the existing contract" until its expiration. Viewed in isolation from the rest of the provision, that language would preclude any distinction between contract obligations that are "terms and conditions of employment" and those that are not. But in construing § 8(d), "'we must not be guided by a single sentence or member of a sentence, but look to the provisions of the whole law, and to its object and policy.'" *Mastro Plastics Corp. v. NLRB*, 350 U.S. 270, 285 (1956). . . . Seen in that light, § 8(d) embraces only mandatory topics of bargaining. The provision begins by defining "to bargain collectively" as meeting and conferring "with respect to wages, hours, and other terms and conditions of employment." It then goes on to state that "the duty to bargain collectively shall also mean" that mid-term unilateral modifications and terminations are prohibited. Although this part of the section is introduced by a "proviso" clause, . . . it quite plainly is to be construed *in pari materia* with the preceding definition. Accordingly, just as § 8(d) defines the obligation to bargain to be with respect to mandatory terms alone, so it prescribes the duty to maintain only mandatory terms without unilateral modification for the duration of the collective bargaining agreement. . . .

The structure and language of § 8(d) point to a more specialized purpose than merely promoting general contract compliance. The conditions for a modification or termination set out in paragraphs (1) through (4) plainly are designed to regulate modifications and terminations so as to facilitate agreement in place of economic warfare. . . .

If that is correct, the distinction that we draw between mandatory and permissive terms of bargaining fits the statutory purpose. By once bargaining and agreeing on a permissive subject, the parties, naturally, do not make the subject a mandatory topic of future bargaining. When a proposed modification is to a permissive term, therefore, the purpose of facilitating accord on the proposal is not at all in point, since the parties are not required under the statute to bargain with respect to it. The irrelevance of the purpose is demonstrated by the irrelevance of the procedures themselves of § 8(d). Paragraph (2), for example, requires an offer "to meet and confer with the other party for the purpose of negotiating a new contract or a contract containing the proposed modifications." But such an offer is meaningless if a party is statutorily free to refuse to negotiate on the proposed change to the permissive term. The notification to mediation and conciliation services referred to in paragraph (3) would be equally meaningless, if required at all. We think it would be no less beside the point to read paragraph (4) of § 8(d) as requiring continued adherence to permissive as well as mandatory terms. The remedy for a unilateral mid-term modification to a permissive term lies in an action for breach of contract, . . . not in an unfair-labor-practice proceeding.

As a unilateral mid-term modification of a permissive term such as retirees' benefits does not, therefore, violate § 8(d), the judgment of the Court of Appeals is

Affirmed.

Mr. Justice Douglas dissents.

Notes

1. *Understanding Pittsburgh Plate Glass*—Do you understand the Court to be assuming, in Part IV of *Pittsburgh Plate Glass*, that there is an exact correspondence between the kind of subject matter over which an employer must bargain at the request of the union, and the kind of subject matter as to which an employer may not institute unilateral changes without prior bargaining? Is such parallelism logically necessary? Is it desirable?

2. *Converting Permissive into Mandatory Subjects by Agreement*—Has the Supreme Court foreclosed an employer and a union from converting a permissive bargaining subject into a mandatory one, even for the life of a contract? If so, would this be a sound result? In *M&G Polymers USA, LLC v. Tackett*, 574 U.S. 427 (2015), the Court intimated in dicta that such conversion was possible. *M&G Polymers* involved the subject of retiree health benefits. Despite the permissive status of retiree health benefits, the Court observed that parties "can and do voluntarily agree to make retiree benefits a subject of mandatory collective bargaining," and noted with approval that the employer and union had entered into such an agreement in the case before it. *Id.* at 936. If the parties can convert a permissive subject to a mandatory subject, what remains of the *Borg-Warner* mandatory/permissive subject dichotomy?

3. *Third-Party Effects*—The "vitally affects" test of the principal case only comes into play when the demand relates to persons outside the bargaining unit. This stiffer standard does not apply when the issue involves some immediate aspect of the relationship between an employer and its own unit employees. *See Ford Motor Co. (Chicago Stamping Plant) v. NLRB*, 441 U.S. 488 (1979) (food prices in cafeteria and vending machines operated by a third party). Suppose an employer unilaterally ceases its long-standing practice of paying employees for work time spent participating in blood donation drives. Would this amount to unilateral action on a mandatory subject of bargaining? Yes, said the Board in *Verizon N.Y., Inc.*, 339 N.L.R.B. 30 (2003), *enforced*, 360 F.3d 206 (D.C. Cir. 2004). What about an employer's change in a health insurance plan for non-bargaining unit employees that affects the spouses of employees in the bargaining unit—does this vitally affect the terms and conditions of employment of the unit employees? *See Torrington Co., Subsidiary of Ingersoll Rand Co.*, 305 N.L.R.B. 938 (1991), *reconsideration denied*, 307 N.L.R.B. 485 (1992) (no—any adverse impact is incidental). What about proposals to add or alter child care benefits? *See* Crain, *Feminizing Unions: Challenging the Gendered Structure of Wage Labor*, 89 Mich. L. Rev. 1155, 1218–19 n.355 (1991).

4. *Retirees' Vested Contract Rights*—Benefits for current retirees are not mandatory subjects of bargaining, so the employer is not required to negotiate with the union prior to altering benefits. Suppose a collective bargaining agreement guarantees "lifetime" healthcare coverage to employees. When the contract expires, may the employer eliminate or cut back company-paid healthcare coverage for employees who subsequently retire? The rising cost of health care has prompted many employers to do so. The employers argue that "lifetime" coverage means the lifetime of the contract, not the retiree. *See* Schultz, *Companies Sue Union Retirees to Cut Promised Health Benefits*, Wall St. J., Nov. 10, 2004, at A1. The answer turns on whether the benefits are vested. Where the terms of the contract or extrinsic evidence from medical or pension insurance plan documents make it clear that the parties intended that the health benefits be vested, the employer who terminates them will be liable for a breach of the collective bargaining agreement. If the benefits are not vested, the employer may terminate the plan once the collective bargaining agreement expires.

The circuit courts have struggled with the standard for determining whether retirees' contract rights to medical benefits are vested. The Sixth Circuit has been historically receptive to claims that retiree health benefits are vested. Initially it adopted an inference that retiree healthcare benefits were vested for life and required specific language in a plan document or collective bargaining agreement to overcome the inference. *See Int'l Union, United Auto Workers v. Yard-Man, Inc.*, 716 F.2d 1476 (6th Cir. 1983). Most other circuits were relatively unsympathetic to vesting claims and required stronger language or extrinsic evidence to infer vesting. *See, e.g., Pacheco v. Honeywell International, Inc.*, 918 F.3d 961 (8th Cir. 2019) (finding that early retiree health care benefits did not vest where provisions at issue limited them to duration of the collective agreement); *Bidlack v. Wheelabrator Corp.*, 993 F.2d 603 (7th Cir. 1993) (adopting default presumption against vesting rights for employees; where labor contract is ambiguous, employees must present extrinsic evidence to overcome the presumption); *but see Kelly v. Honeywell Int'l*, 933 F.3d 173 (2d Cir. 2019) (finding retiree benefits vested where effects bargaining agreement contained "unambiguous language vesting welfare benefits" and agreement was incorporated into broader collective bargaining agreement); *Alday v. Raytheon Co.*, 693 F.3d 772 (9th Cir. 2012) (confirming upon rehearing that company was obligated to provide health insurance benefits to retirees despite reservation of rights clause in plan documents where such provisions were not incorporated into the collective bargaining agreement).

In *M&G Polymers USA, LLC v. Tackett*, 574 U.S. 427 (2015), the Supreme Court provided guidance on the applicable standard for determining vesting in a case where the Sixth Circuit had invoked the *Yard-Man* inference. M&G had a collective bargaining agreement that provided that certain retirees who had a vested lifetime right to a monthly pension "will receive" health care benefits; that the retirees would receive "a full Company contribution towards the cost of [health care] benefits," and that the benefits would be provided "for the duration of [the] Agreement," which extended for three years. After the initial contract had expired, M&G announced that it would begin requiring retirees to contribute to the cost of their health benefits. The retirees sued to enforce their rights to free lifetime benefits. The Court issued a unanimous ruling invalidating the *Yard-Man* rule and instructing courts to apply "ordinary contract principles not inconsistent with federal labor policy." The Court remanded the case to the Sixth Circuit for further consideration. The Sixth Circuit responded by shifting course, and now aligns more closely with others. *See Cooper v. Honeywell International, Inc.*, 884 F.3d 612 (6th Cir. 2018) (finding that retiree health benefits were not vested despite language providing that retires under age 65 "will continue to be covered . . . until age 65" because general durational clause in collective agreement dictates when benefits expire absent an alternative specific end date); *Gallo v. Moen, Inc.*, 813 F.3d 265 (6th Cir.), *cert. denied*, 137 S. Ct. 375 (2016) (applying ordinary contract principles and ruling that retirees' "lifetime" health care benefits were not vested where collective bargaining agreements under which retirees claimed entitlement did not explicitly guarantee lifetime benefits; the use of future tense—e.g., that the benefits would continue as indicated under the 2005 collective bargaining agreement—without more did not suffice to guarantee the benefits beyond the three-year term of the contract). The inquiry is fact-specific and dependent on the language of particular collective agreements and side letters, however, and extrinsic evidence may be considered to resolve ambiguities in language.

5. *The Union's Role* — What role can unions play in continuing to advocate for retiree health benefits in light of *Pittsburgh Plate Glass*? Clearly, an employer may not unilaterally modify the retirement benefits of current bargaining unit employees without offering to bargain with the union, even if the changes pertain to pension benefits that have not yet vested. *S. Nuclear Operating Co. v. NLRB*, 524 F.3d 1350 (D.C. Cir. 2008). And it remains settled law that unions owe no duty to represent retirees. *See Eller v. National Football Players Ass'n*, 872 F. Supp. 2d 823 (D. Minn. 2012) (dismissing tortious interference with contract claim by retired NFL players against player's union that negotiated sub-par pension, retirement, and disability benefits for retired players), *affirmed*, 731 F.3d 752 (8th Cir. 2013). Nevertheless, several circuits have ruled that unions have standing to represent retirees in arbitration in disputes over retirement benefits conferred by a labor contract, and some have required arbitration under the labor contract rather than permitting litigation. In *United Steelworkers v. Cookson Am., Inc.*, 710 F.3d 470 (2d Cir. 2013), for example, the court found that the union had standing to bring an action to enforce the rights of retired employees to health benefits even though the employees were no longer covered by the collective bargaining agreement because the union had been a signatory to the document that established the benefits in conjunction with the closing of a facility. Even though the employees were no longer part of the bargaining unit, the employer was still contractually obligated to pay retirement benefits and refusal to comply would deprive the union of the benefit of its bargain. Further, because the plant had closed, there was no potential conflict of interest between the retirees and the current employees. *See also Van Pamel v. TRW Vehicle Safety Sys., Inc.*, 723 F.3d 664 (6th Cir. 2013) (where union bargained for retirees' health care benefits, retirees' claim was based upon the contract, and contract's arbitration clause did not exclude such disputes, dispute must be submitted to arbitration rather than litigated in court); *Exelon Generation Co., LLC v. Local 15*, 540 F.3d 640 (7th Cir. 2008) (applying presumption of arbitrability to retiree grievances absent express language in the labor contract excluding them from arbitration or limiting to current employees, and concluding that union has standing to represent retirees in arbitration); *Newspaper Guild of St. Louis v. St. Louis Post Dispatch*, 641 F.3d 263 (8th Cir. 2011) (applying presumption of arbitrability to vested employee rights). Some circuits require the retirees' consent to compel arbitration, *see, e.g., Int'l Ass'n of Machinists and Aero. Workers Local Lodge 2121 v. Goodrich Corp.*, 410 F.3d 204 (5th Cir. 2005); *Rosetto v. Pabst Brewing Co.*, 128 F.3d 538 (7th Cir. 1997), while others reason that the union has standing to vindicate its own contractual rights even without the consent of the affected retirees, *see, e.g., IBEW, AFL-CIO Local 1245 v. Citizens Telcoms. Co.*, 549 F.3d 781 (9th Cir. 2008).

6. *Neutrality Agreements*—Neutrality agreements, in which employers agree to remain neutral during union organizing campaigns, to permit increased union access to employer premises for organizing purposes, or to expedite bargaining if employees choose union representation, are becoming an increasingly useful tool for union organizing. Such agreements impact the rights of third parties and accordingly are subject to the "vitally affects" test.

In *Pall Biomedical Prods. Corp., a Div. of Pall Corp.*, 331 N.L.R.B. 1674 (2000), the Board ruled that an employer violated the Act by repudiating an agreement promising to extend recognition to the union at one of its new facilities if one or more workers there were performing bargaining unit work. Even though the agreement was silent on whether the union had to demonstrate majority support at the new facility prior to recognition, the agreement vitally affected the terms and conditions of employment of existing unit members, whose concern that bargaining unit work would be transferred to the new facility had prompted the agreement. The D.C. Circuit refused to enforce the Board's order, finding that while the transfer of bargaining work to a new facility would vitally affect the rights of bargaining unit employees, the recognition clause was not a "direct frontal attack" on the problem since it neither prevented work from being transferred nor extended the labor contract to apply anti-union: it merely allowed for union recognition at the new facility. *Pall Corp. v. NLRB*, 275 F.3d 116 (D.C. Cir. 2002). In *Supervalu, Inc.*, 351 N.L.R.B. 948 (2007), the Board ruled that an "additional stores" provision that required the employer to adhere to the terms of the labor contract at newly acquired grocery stores if the union presented signed authorization cards from a majority of the employees at each of the stores was not a mandatory subject of bargaining because it did not "vitally affect" unit employees. There was no evidence that the employees at the newly acquired stores would become part of the existing bargaining unit, and no evidence that employees at the existing unionized store were concerned about the potential for work transfer to a nonunion store. Thus, the employer did not violate § 8(a)(5) by refusing to grant card check recognition at those stores.

In *UNITE HERE Local 355 v. Mulhall*, 570 U.S. 915 (2013), the Court granted *certiorari* in a case in which it was expected to pass on the legality of neutrality agreements that set the ground rules for union organizing campaigns and provide for card-check recognition. The National Right to Work Legal Defense Foundation, an anti-union advocacy organization, brought suit against the union and the employer, arguing that a neutrality agreement negotiated by the employer in exchange for the union's support on a ballot proposition to license casino gaming violated § 302 of the Labor Management Relations Act, which prohibits unions and employers from exchanging "money or other thing[s] of value." The Court dismissed the petition for certiorari as improvidently granted, however. *UNITE HERE Local 355 v. Mulhall*, 571 U.S. 83 (2013). The dismissal leaves intact the Eleventh Circuit's decision finding that the neutrality agreement could be a basis for an LMRA § 302 violation if the parties had a "corrupting intent" rendering otherwise innocuous ground rules an improper payment. Whether something qualifies as an improper payment does not depend on its monetary value or its tangibility, but whether or not it is offered with the intent to gain benefit or influence the union. *Mulhall v. UNITE HERE Local 355*, 667 F.3d 1211 (11th Cir. 2012). Courts elsewhere will likely continue to uphold neutrality agreements. *See, e.g., Hotel Employees & Restaurant Employees Union, Local 57 v. Sage Hospitality Resources, LLC*, 390 F.3d 206 (3d Cir. 2004) (finding neutrality agreement not a "thing of value" within scope of LMRA § 302); *Adcock v. Freightliner, LLC*, 550 F.3d 369 (4th Cir. 2008) (neutrality agreement not a "thing of value" because it lacks "ascertainable value").

On the interesting questions posed by the increasing prevalence of neutrality and card check agreements under which employers agree to allow unions access to employer premises, to remain silent during the union's organizing campaigns at after-acquired stores, and to expedite bargaining procedures if the union obtains a majority card count, see Brudney, *Neutrality Agreements and Card Check Recognition: Prospects for Changing Paradigms*, 90 Iowa L. Rev. 819 (2005); Cooper, *Privatizing Labor Law: Neutrality/Card Check Agreements and the Role of the Arbitrator*, 83 Ind. L.J. 1589 (2008). Even if neutrality agreements do not violate LMRA § 302, might some provisions violate § 8(a)(2)? The Trump Board's General Counsel believes they do. *See* Robb, *Guidance Memorandum on Employer Assistance in Union Organizing*, Memorandum GC 20-13, Sept. 4, 2020 (acknowledging that pre-recognition neutrality agreements are generally lawful, but opining that employers that agree to provide more than ministerial aid to unions during organizing campaigns violate § 8(a)(2)).

Problem

57. Elite University's libraries staff are represented by Local 210 of the SEIU. Elite University is located in Los Angeles, which lacks a strong public transit system. Most of the employees commute long distances to work, and use their personal cars. The university leases parking lots from various businesses adjacent to campus for its employees, and covers the parking fees. One of the businesses from which Elite leases space, Capstar, doubled its leasing fee this year, and Elite has decided to terminate its lease with Capstar as a result. The closest parking lot that is comparable in price is located a mile away from campus. Elite signed a lease with the owner of that lot, and provided a commuter bus that runs every 20 minutes to ferry employees to and from campus—about a 10-minute ride to campus in traffic. The libraries staff are furious, arguing that this decision adds anywhere from 15 to 25 minutes onto their commute (depending upon whether they arrive at the parking lot in time to make the bus that is currently there, how long it takes to load the bus, and whether there is space on the bus for them). Did Elite violate the Act? If you were counsel to Elite, what would you have advised?

Fibreboard Paper Products Corp. v. NLRB

Supreme Court of the United States
379 U.S. 203, 85 S. Ct. 398, 13 L. Ed. 2d 233 (1964)

Mr. Chief Justice Warren delivered the opinion of the Court.

This case involves the obligation of an employer and the representative of his employees under §§ 8(a)(5), 8(d) and 9(a) of the National Labor Relations Act to "confer in good faith with respect to wages, hours, and other terms and conditions of employment." The primary issue is whether the "contracting out" of work being performed by employees in the bargaining unit is a statutory subject of collective bargaining under those sections.

Petitioner, Fibreboard Paper Products Corporation (the Company), has a manufacturing plant in Emeryville, California. Since 1937 the East Bay Union Machinists, Local 1304, United Steelworkers of America, AFL-CIO (the Union) has been the exclusive bargaining representative for a unit of the Company's maintenance employees. In September 1958, the Union and the Company entered the latest of a series of collective bargaining agreements which was to expire on July 31, 1959. . . . On May 26, 1959, the Union gave timely notice of its desire to modify the contract and sought to arrange a bargaining session with Company representatives. . . . Efforts by the Union to schedule a bargaining session met with no success until July 27, four days before the expiration of the contract, when the Company notified the Union of its desire to meet. . . .

At the July 27 meeting, the Company informed the Union that it had determined that substantial savings could be effected by contracting out the work upon expiration of its collective bargaining agreements with the various labor organizations representing its maintenance employees. The Company delivered to the Union representatives a letter which stated in pertinent part:

> For some time we have been seriously considering the question of letting out our Emeryville maintenance work to an independent contractor, and have now reached a definite decision to do so effective August 1, 1959.
>
> In these circumstances, we are sure you will realize that negotiation of a new contract would be pointless. However, if you have any questions, we will be glad to discuss them with you. . . .

By July 30, the Company had selected Fluor Maintenance, Inc., to do the maintenance work. Fluor had assured the Company that maintenance costs could be curtailed by reducing the work force, decreasing fringe benefits and overtime payments, and by preplanning and scheduling the services to be performed. The contract provided that Fluor would: "furnish all labor, supervision and office help required for the performance of maintenance work . . . at the Emeryville plant of Owner as Owner shall from time to time assign to Contractor during the period of this contract; and shall also furnish such tools, supplies and equipment in connection therewith as Owner shall order from Contractor, it being understood, however, that Owner shall ordinarily do its own purchasing of tools, supplies and equipment."

The contract further provided that the Company would pay Fluor the costs of the operation plus a fixed fee of $2,250 per month. . . .

On July 31, the employment of the maintenance employees represented by the Union was terminated and Fluor employees took over. That evening the Union established a picket line at the Company's plant.

The Union filed unfair labor practice charges against the Company, alleging violations of §§ 8(a)(1), 8(a)(3) and 8(a)(5). After hearings were held upon a complaint issued by the National Labor Relations Board's Regional Director, the Trial Examiner filed an Intermediate Report recommending dismissal of the complaint. The Board accepted the recommendation and dismissed the complaint. 130 N.L.R.B. 1558.

Petitions for reconsideration, filed by the General Counsel and the Union, were granted. Upon reconsideration, the Board adhered to the Trial Examiner's finding that the Company's motive in contracting out its maintenance work was economic rather than antiunion but found nonetheless that the Company's "failure to negotiate with ... [the Union] concerning its decision to subcontract its maintenance work constituted a violation of Section 8(a)(5) of the Act." ...

The Board ordered the Company to reinstitute the maintenance operation previously performed by the employees represented by the Union, to reinstate the employees to their former or substantially equivalent positions with back pay computed from the date of the Board's supplemental decision, and to fulfill its statutory obligation to bargain.

On appeal, the Court of Appeals for the District of Columbia Circuit granted the Board's petition for enforcement. 322 F.2d 411. ...

I

... Because of the limited grant of certiorari, we are concerned here only with whether the subject upon which the employer allegedly refused to bargain — contracting out of plant maintenance work previously performed by employees in the bargaining unit, which the employees were capable of continuing to perform — is covered by the phrase "terms and conditions of employment" within the meaning of § 8(d).

The subject matter of the present dispute is well within the literal meaning of the phrase "terms and conditions of employment." *See Order of Railroad Telegraphers v. Chicago & N.W.R. Co.*, 362 U.S. 330 (1960). A stipulation with respect to the contracting out of work performed by members of the bargaining unit might appropriately be called a "condition of employment." The words even more plainly cover termination of employment which, as the facts of this case indicate, necessarily results from the contracting out of work performed by members of the established bargaining unit.

The inclusion of "contracting out" within the statutory scope of collective bargaining also seems well designed to effectuate the purposes of the National Labor Relations Act. One of the primary purposes of the Act is to promote the peaceful settlement of industrial disputes by subjecting labor-management controversies to the mediatory influence of negotiation. The Act was framed with an awareness that refusals to confer and negotiate had been one of the most prolific causes of industrial strife. *NLRB v. Jones & Laughlin Steel Corp.*, 301 U.S. 1, 42–43 (1937). To hold, as the Board has done, that contracting out is a mandatory subject of collective bargaining would promote the fundamental purpose of the Act by bringing a problem of vital concern to labor and management within the framework established by Congress as most conducive to industrial peace.

The conclusion that "contracting out" is a statutory subject of collective bargaining is further reinforced by industrial practices in this country. While not determinative, it is appropriate to look to industrial bargaining practices in appraising the propriety of including a particular subject within the scope of mandatory bargaining. *NLRB v. American Nat'l Ins. Co.*, 343 U.S. 395, 408 (1952). Industrial experience is not only reflective of the interests of labor and management in the subject matter but is also indicative of the amenability of such subjects to the collective bargaining process. Experience illustrates that contracting out in one form or another has been brought, widely and successfully, within the collective bargaining framework.[17] Provisions relating to contracting out exist in numerous collective bargaining agreements,[18] and "[c]ontracting out work is the basis of many grievances; and that type of claim is grist in the mills of the arbitrators." *United Steelworkers v. Warrior & Gulf Nav. Co.*, 363 U.S. 574, 584 (1960).

The situation here is not unlike that presented in *Teamsters Union, Local 24 v. Oliver*, 358 U.S. 283 (1959), where we held that conditions imposed upon contracting out work to prevent possible curtailment of jobs and the undermining of conditions of employment for members of the bargaining unit constituted a statutory subject of collective bargaining. The issue in that case was whether state antitrust laws could be applied to a provision of a collective bargaining agreement which fixed the minimum rental to be paid by the employer motor carrier who leased vehicles to be driven by their owners rather than the carrier's employees. We held that the agreement was upon a subject matter as to which federal law directed the parties to bargain and hence that state antitrust laws could not be applied to prevent the effectuation of the agreement. . . .

The facts of the present case illustrate the propriety of submitting the dispute to collective negotiation. The Company's decision to contract out the maintenance work did not alter the Company's basic operation. The maintenance work still had to be performed in the plant. No capital investment was contemplated; the Company merely replaced existing employees with those of an independent contractor to do the same work under similar conditions of employment. Therefore, to require the employer to bargain about the matter would not significantly abridge his freedom to manage the business.

The Company was concerned with the high cost of its maintenance operation. It was induced to contract out the work by assurances from independent contractors that economies could be derived by reducing the work force, decreasing fringe benefits, and eliminating overtime payments. These have long been regarded as matters peculiarly suitable for resolution within the collective bargaining framework, and industrial experience demonstrates that collective negotiation has been highly successful in achieving peaceful accommodation of the conflicting interests. Yet, it is contended that when an employer can effect cost savings in these respects by contracting the work out, there is no need to attempt to achieve similar economies through negotiation with existing employees or to provide them with an opportunity

---

17. [6] *See* Lunden, *Subcontracting Clauses in Major Contracts*, 84 Monthly Lab. Rev. 579, 715 (1961).

18. [7] A Department of Labor study analyzed 1,687 collective bargaining agreements, which applied to approximately 7,500,000 workers (about one-half of the estimated work force covered by collective bargaining agreements). Among the agreements studied, approximately one-fourth (378) contained some form of a limitation on subcontracting. Lunden, *supra* at 581.

to negotiate a mutually acceptable alternative. The short answer is that, although it is not possible to say whether a satisfactory solution could be reached, national labor policy is founded upon the congressional determination that the chances are good enough to warrant subjecting such issues to the process of collective negotiation.

The appropriateness of the collective bargaining process for resolving such issues was apparently recognized by the Company. In explaining its decision to contract out the maintenance work, the Company pointed out that in the same plant other unions "had joined hands with management in an effort to bring about an economical and efficient operation," but "we had not been able to attain that in our discussions with this particular Local." Accordingly, based on past bargaining experience with this union, the Company unilaterally contracted out the work. While "the Act does not encourage a party to engage in fruitless marathon discussions at the expense of frank statement and support of his position," *NLRB v. American Nat'l Ins. Co.*, 343 U.S. 395, 404 (1958), it at least demands that the issue be submitted to the mediatory influence of collective negotiations. As the Court of Appeals pointed out, "it is not necessary that it be likely or probable that the union will yield or supply a feasible solution but rather that the union be afforded an opportunity to meet management's legitimate complaints that its maintenance was unduly costly."

We are thus not expanding the scope of mandatory bargaining to hold, as we do now, that the type of "contracting out" involved in this case—the replacement of employees in the existing bargaining unit with those of an independent contractor to do the same work under similar conditions of employment—is a statutory subject of collective bargaining under § 8(d). Our decision need not and does not encompass other forms of "contracting out" or "subcontracting" which arise daily in our complex economy.[19]

II

The only question remaining is whether, upon a finding that the Company had refused to bargain about a matter which is a statutory subject of collective bargaining, the Board was empowered to order the resumption of maintenance operations and reinstatement with back pay. We believe that it was so empowered. . . .

[Section 10(c)] "charges the Board with the task of devising remedies to effectuate the policies of the Act." *NLRB v. Seven-Up Bottling Co.*, 344 U.S. 344, 346 (1953). The Board's power is a broad discretionary one, subject to limited judicial review. *Ibid.* "[T]he relation of remedy to policy is peculiarly a matter for administrative competence. . . ." *Phelps Dodge Corp. v. NLRB*, 313 U.S. 177, 194 (1941). "In fashioning remedies to undo the effects of violations of the Act, the Board must draw on

---

19. [8] As the Solicitor General points out, the terms "contracting out" and "subcontracting" have no precise meaning. They are used to describe a variety of business arrangements altogether different from that involved in this case. For a discussion of the various types of "contracting out" or "subcontracting" arrangements, see Brief for Respondent, pp. 13–17; Brief for Electronic Industries Association as *amicus curiae*, pp. 5–10.

enlightenment gained from experience." *NLRB v. SevenUp Bottling Co.*, 344 U.S. 344, 346 (1953). The Board's order will not be disturbed "unless it can be shown that the order is a patent attempt to achieve ends other than those which can fairly be said to effectuate the policies of the Act." *Virginia Elec. & Power Co. v. NLRB*, 319 U.S. 533, 540 (1943). Such a showing has not been made in this case.

There has been no showing that the Board's order restoring the status quo ante to insure meaningful bargaining is not well designed to promote the policies of the Act. Nor is there evidence which would justify disturbing the Board's conclusion that the order would not impose an undue or unfair burden on the Company.[20]

It is argued, nonetheless, that the award exceeds the Board's powers under § 10(c) in that it infringes the provision that "[n]o order of the Board shall require the reinstatement of any individual as an employee who has been suspended or discharged, or the payment to him of any back pay, if such individual was suspended or discharged for cause. . . ." The legislative history of that provision indicates that it was designed to preclude the Board from reinstating an individual who had been discharged because of misconduct. There is no indication, however, that it was designed to curtail the Board's power in fashioning remedies when the loss of employment stems directly from an unfair labor practice as in the case at hand.

The judgment of the Court of Appeals is

Affirmed.

Mr. Justice Goldberg took no part in the consideration or decision of this case.

Mr. Justice Stewart, with whom **Mr. Justice Douglas** and **Mr. Justice Harlan** join, concurring.

. . . .

The question posed is whether the particular decision sought to be made unilaterally by the employer in this case is a subject of mandatory collective bargaining within the statutory phrase "terms and conditions of employment." That is all the Court decides. The Court most assuredly does not decide that every managerial decision which necessarily terminates an individual's employment is subject to the duty to bargain. Nor does the Court decide that subcontracting decisions are as a general matter subject to that duty. The Court holds no more than that this employer's decision to subcontract this work, involving "the replacement of employees in the existing bargaining unit with those of an independent contractor to do the same work under similar conditions of employment" is subject to the duty to bargain collectively. Within the narrow limitations implicit in the specific facts of this case, I agree with the Court's decision. . . .

---

20. [10] The Board stated: "We do not believe that requirement [restoring the *status quo ante*] imposes an undue or unfair burden on Respondent. The record shows that the maintenance operation is still being performed in much the same manner as it was prior to the subcontracting arrangement. Respondent has a continuing need for the services of maintenance employees; and Respondent's subcontract is terminable at any time upon 60 days' notice." 138 N.L.R.B. at 555, n. 19.

While employment security has thus properly been recognized in various circumstances as a condition of employment, it surely does not follow that every decision which may affect job security is a subject of compulsory collective bargaining. Many decisions made by management affect the job security of employees. Decisions concerning the volume and kind of advertising expenditures, product design, the manner of financing, and of sales, all may bear upon the security of the workers' jobs. Yet it is hardly conceivable that such decisions so involve "conditions of employment" that they must be negotiated with the employees' bargaining representative.

In many of these areas the impact of a particular management decision upon job security may be extremely indirect and uncertain, and this alone may be sufficient reason to conclude that such decisions are not "with respect to ... conditions of employment." Yet there are other areas where decisions by management may quite clearly imperil job security, or indeed terminate employment entirely. An enterprise may decide to invest in labor-saving machinery. Another may resolve to liquidate its assets and go out of business. Nothing the Court holds today should be understood as imposing a duty to bargain collectively regarding such managerial decisions, which lie at the core of entrepreneurial control....

Applying these concepts to the case at hand, I do not believe that an employer's subcontracting practices are, as a general matter, in themselves conditions of employment. Upon any definition of the statutory terms short of the most expansive, such practices are not conditions—tangible or intangible—of any person's employment. The question remains whether this particular kind of subcontracting decision comes within the employer's duty to bargain. On the facts of this case, I join the Court's judgment, because all that is involved is the substitution of one group of workers for another to perform the same task in the same plant under the ultimate control of the same employer. The question whether the employer may discharge one group of workers and substitute another for them is closely analogous to many other situations within the traditional framework of collective bargaining. Compulsory retirement, layoffs according to seniority, assignment of work among potentially eligible groups within the plant—all involve similar questions of discharge and work assignment, and all have been recognized as subjects of compulsory collective bargaining....

This kind of subcontracting falls short of such larger entrepreneurial questions as what shall be produced, how capital shall be invested in fixed assets, or what the basic scope of the enterprise shall be. In my view, the Court's decision in this case has nothing to do with whether any aspects of those larger issues could under any circumstances be considered subjects of compulsory collective bargaining under the present law....

Notes

1. *The Board's Evolving Approach to Subcontracting Decisions*—Prior to the Court's decision in *Fibreboard*, the NLRB for a long time held that in the absence of antiunion animus, management did not have to bargain about decisions to subcontract,

relocate operations, or introduce technological improvements, although it did have to bargain about the *effects* of such decisions on the employees displaced. Layoff schedules, severance pay, and transfer rights were thus bargainable, but the basic decision to discontinue an operation was not. See, e.g., *Brown-McLaren Mfg. Co.*, 34 N.L.R.B. 984 (1941); *Brown-Dunkin Co.*, 125 N.L.R.B. 1379 (1959), *enforced*, 287 F.2d 17 (10th Cir. 1961).

Under the so-called Kennedy Board, however, a whole range of managerial decisions were reclassified as mandatory subjects of bargaining. These included decisions to terminate a department and subcontract its work, *Town & Country Mfg. Co., Inc.*, 136 N.L.R.B. 1022 (1962), *enforced*, 316 F.2d 846 (5th Cir. 1963); to consolidate operations through technological innovations, *Renton News Record*, 136 N.L.R.B. 1294 (1962); and to close one plant of a multi-plant enterprise, *Ozark Trailers, Inc.*, 161 N.L.R.B. 561 (1966). The direction and rationale of the Board during this period were indicated in *Westinghouse Elec. Corp.*, 150 N.L.R.B. 1574 (1965), when it stated that the unilateral contracting out of unit work would violate §8(a)(5) where it "involved a departure from previously established operating practices, effected a change in conditions of employment, or resulted in a significant impairment of job tenure, employment security, or reasonably anticipated work opportunities for those in the bargaining unit."

In the modern era, the Board continues to require bargaining over issues involving subcontracting out of unit work in the absence of a clear shift in the nature and direction of the employer's overall enterprise. See, e.g., *Rigid Pak Corp.*, 366 N.L.R.B. No. 137 (2018) (employer must bargain over decision to subcontract its injection molding work where it continued to be involved in the manufacture of injection-molded products, but not required to bargain over decision to close blow-mold division where it abandoned blow-molding manufacturing); *Mi Pueblo Foods*, 360 N.L.R.B. 1097 (2014) (employer violated §8(a)(5) by subcontracting out delivery driving jobs that had previously been performed by unit drivers; even if no layoffs occur and there is no "significant negative impact" on immediate wages and hours, potential to reduce the size of the bargaining unit and dilute union strength creates adverse effect on bargaining unit); *Spurlino Materials, LLC v. N.L.R.B.*, 645 F.3d 870 (7th Cir. 2011) (finding that substantial evidence supported the Board's conclusion that employer unlawfully failed to bargain when it created new driver positions, instituted a new employee evaluation system applicable to the positions, and hired subcontractors and employees who were not members of the bargaining unit to staff a warehouse project).

2. *Relocation of Work and the Partial Closing Doctrine*—*Fibreboard* was decided in 1964, and was followed closely by the Court's decision in *Textile Workers Union v. Darlington Mfg. Co.*, 380 U.S. 263 (1965) (holding that employer decisions to close a plant lie within the core of entrepreneurial functions not subject to bargaining duties, but that partial closing decisions motivated by a purpose to chill unionism at remaining plants of a single employer violate the Act), *supra* Part Two, Section III.D Beginning in the Nixon-Ford era, the NLRB seemed to back away from some of the rulings of the Kennedy Board. This was exemplified by *Summit Tooling Co.*, 195 N.L.R.B. 479 (1972), *enforced*, 474 F.2d 1352 (7th Cir. 1973), where an employer closed the manufacturing portion of its operations without prior bargaining. Even though the shutdown could be characterized as a partial plant closing, a 2-1 Board majority held that the employer did not violate § 8(a)(5) by its failure to bargain concerning its decision to terminate the manufacturing division. To require bargaining "would significantly abridge Respondent's freedom to manage its own affairs." *See also General Motors Corp.*, 191 N.L.R.B. 951 (1971) (sale of dealership; two Board members dissenting), *aff'd sub nom. International Union, United Auto. Aerospace & Agricultural Implement Workers v. NLRB*, 470 F.2d 422 (D.C. Cir. 1972) (one judge dissenting). Under the Kennedy Board as well as its successors, there was uncertainty about an employer's obligation to bargain over an economically motivated decision to relocate a plant or certain operations. *See Garwin Corp.*, 153 N.L.R.B. 664, 665, 680 (1965), *enforced in part*, 374 F.2d 295 (D.C. Cir.), *cert. denied*, 387 U.S. 942 (1967); *Cooper Thermometer Co.*, 160 N.L.R.B. 1902 (1966), *enforced*, 376 F.2d 684 (2d Cir. 1967); *Westinghouse Electric Corp.*, 174 N.L.R.B. 636 (1969). A critical factor in relocation cases may be the severity of any adverse impact on unit jobs. But clearly there is no duty to bargain about a decision to go completely out of business. *See Textile Workers Union v. Darlington Mfg. Co., supra*. Meanwhile, the courts of appeals had become hopelessly divided in their reaction to the Labor Board's "partial closing" doctrine, thus paving the way for the Supreme Court decision in the principal case that follows next. For a good account of these judicial meanderings, see *Brockway Motor Trucks, Div. of Mack Trucks, Inc. v. NLRB*, 582 F.2d 720, 727–31 (3d Cir. 1978).

3. *Remedies* — What remedy should the Board provide when an employer institutes job changes without fulfilling its duty to bargain? Should it always order resumption of the discontinued operations, as in *Fibreboard*? What if this will cause the employer severe financial loss, or prevent it from competing economically in the market? On the other hand, if the status quo ante is not restored, how can the union engage in meaningful bargaining even about the effects of the changes on the employees?

Restoration of an employer's operation was held improper under § 10(j)'s temporary injunction provision, even though the NLRB had met its "relatively insubstantial" burden of showing reasonable cause to believe that the employer had unlawfully subcontracted bargaining unit work and laid off the employees, since it would impose undue hardship on the employer and was not necessary to preserve the Board's ultimate remedial authority. *Calatrello ex rel. v. "Automatic" Sprinkler Corp. of Am.*, 55 F.3d 208 (6th Cir. 1995). On the other hand, the Third Circuit granted the Board's request for a § 10(j) injunction to block the sale of a unionized plant pending the Board's final resolution of unfair labor practice charges based on the employer's threat to close the plant in the event of a strike. *See Hirsch v. Dorsey Trailers, Inc.*, 147 F.3d 243 (3d Cir. 1998). Because sale of the plant would have rendered the Board powerless to order the work returned to the plant, a remedy that the

ALJ hearing the case had already concluded was appropriate, any negative financial impact on the company was of its own making, and injunctive relief was justified.

If an employer unlawfully moves a plant without prior bargaining, may the Board order it to bargain at the new location despite the union's lack of a majority status there? How would this affect the rights of the employees at the new plant? *See Garwin Corp.*, 153 N.L.R.B. 664 (1965), *enforced in part*, 374 F.2d 295 (D.C. Cir.), *cert. denied*, 387 U.S. 942 (1967) (ordering employer to bargain with the union at its new location but declaring a shortened contract bar period if the union is unable to establish majority status). Where an employer unlawfully failed to bargain over the *effects* of closing one of its plants, the NLRB ordered it to pay terminated employees their normal wages until: (1) the parties bargained to agreement, (2) an impasse occurred, (3) the union failed to request bargaining within a stipulated period, or (4) the union failed to bargain in good faith. No employee was to be paid, however, beyond the date he secured equivalent employment elsewhere or beyond the date the employer went out of business entirely. *Royal Plating & Polishing Co., Inc.*, 160 N.L.R.B. 990 (1966). This remedy has come to be known as the "Transmarine" remedy, after the same remedy as employed in *Transmarine Navigation Corp.*, 170 N.L.R.B. 389 (1968). It is in common use today in plant closure situations, *see, e.g., Edward Hotel Michigan, LLC,* 369 N.L.R.B. No. 86 (2020); *Rigid Pak Corp.*, 366 N.L.R.B. No. 137 (2018), and in other contexts, *see, e.g., Rochester Gas & Elec. Corp.*, 355 N.L.R.B. 507 (2010), *enforced, sub nom. Local Union 36, IBEW, AFL-CIO v. NLRB*, 706 F.3d 73 (2d Cir. 2013), *cert. denied*, 573 U.S. 958 (2014) (back pay awarded for effects of discontinuing practice of allowing employees to drive company-issued vehicles to and from work).

First National Maintenance Corp. v. NLRB

Supreme Court of the United States
452 U.S. 666, 101 S. Ct. 2573, 69 L. Ed. 2d 318 (1981)

JUSTICE BLACKMUN delivered the opinion of the Court.

Must an employer, under its duty to bargain in good faith "with respect to wages, hours, and other terms and conditions of employment," §§ 8(d) and 8(a)(5) of the National Labor Relations Act, as amended, negotiate with the certified representative of its employees over its decision to close a part of its business? In this case, the National Labor Relations Board (the Board) imposed such a duty on petitioner with respect to its decision to terminate a contract with a customer, and the United States Court of Appeals, although differing over the appropriate rationale, enforced its order.

I

Petitioner, First National Maintenance Corporation (FNM), is a New York corporation engaged in the business of providing housekeeping, cleaning, maintenance, and related services for commercial customers in the New York City area. It supplies each of its customers, at the customer's premises, contracted-for labor force and supervision in return for reimbursement of its labor costs (gross salaries, FICA and FUTA taxes, and insurance) and payment of a set fee. It contracts for and hires personnel separately for each customer, and it does not transfer employees between locations.

During the Spring of 1977, petitioner was performing maintenance work for the Greenpark Care Center, a nursing home in Brooklyn. Its written agreement dated April 28, 1976, with Greenpark specified that Greenpark "shall furnish all tools, equipment [sic], materials, and supplies," and would pay petitioner weekly "the sum of five hundred dollars plus the gross weekly payroll and fringe benefits." Its weekly fee, however, had been reduced to $250 effective November 1, 1976. The contract prohibited Greenpark from hiring any of petitioner's employees during the term of the contract and for 90 days thereafter. Petitioner employed approximately 35 workers in its Greenpark operation.

Petitioner's business relationship with Greenpark, seemingly, was not very remunerative or smooth.... On June 30, [1977], by telephone, it asked that its weekly fee be restored at the $500 figure and, on July 6, it informed Greenpark in writing that it would discontinue its operations there on August 1 unless the increase were granted. By telegram on July 25, petitioner gave final notice of termination.

While FNM was experiencing these difficulties, District 1199, National Union of Hospital and Health Care Employees, Retail, Wholesale and Department Store Union, AFL-CIO (the union), was conducting an organization campaign among petitioner's Greenpark employees. On March 31, 1977, at a Board-conducted election, a majority of the employees selected the union as their bargaining agent. On July 12, the union's vice president, Edward Wecker, wrote petitioner, notifying it of the certification and of the union's right to bargain, and stating: "We look forward to meeting with you or your representative for that purpose. Please advise when it will be convenient." Petitioner neither responded nor sought to consult with the union.

On July 28, petitioner notified its Greenpark employees that they would be discharged 3 days later. Wecker immediately telephoned petitioner's secretary-treasurer, Leonard Marsh, to request a delay for the purpose of bargaining. Marsh refused the offer to bargain and told Wecker that the termination of the Greenpark operation was purely a matter of money, and final, and that the 30-days' notice provision of the Greenpark contract made staying on beyond August 1 prohibitively expensive.... With nothing but perfunctory further discussion, petitioner on July 31 discontinued its Greenpark operation and discharged the employees.

The union filed an unfair labor practice charge against petitioner, alleging violations of the Act's §§ 8(a)(1) and (5). After a hearing held upon the Regional Director's complaint, the administrative law judge made findings in the union's favor. Relying on *Ozark Trailers, Inc.*, 161 N.L.R.B. 561 (1966), he ruled that petitioner had failed to satisfy its duty to bargain concerning both the decision to terminate the Greenpark contract and the effect of that change upon the unit employees.... The National

Labor Relations Board adopted the administrative law judge's findings without further analysis. . . .

The United States Court of Appeals for the Second Circuit, with one judge dissenting in part, enforced the Board's order, although it adopted an analysis different from that espoused by the Board. 627 F.2d 596 (1980). The Court of Appeals reasoned that no *per se* rule could be formulated to govern an employer's decision to close part of its business. Rather, the court said, § 8(d) creates a *presumption* in favor of mandatory bargaining over such a decision, a presumption that is rebuttable "by showing that the purposes of the statute would not be furthered by imposition of a duty to bargain," for example, by demonstrating that "bargaining over the decision would be futile," or that the decision was due to "emergency financial circumstances," or that the "custom of the industry, shown by the absence of such an obligation from typical collective bargaining agreements, is not to bargain over such decisions." *Id.*, at 601–602.

The Court of Appeals' decision in this case appears to be at odds with decisions of other Courts of Appeals, some of which decline to require bargaining over any management decision involving "a major commitment of capital investment" or a "basic operational change" in the scope or direction of an enterprise, and some of which indicate that bargaining is not mandated unless a violation of § 8(a)(3) (a partial closing motivated by antiunion animus) is involved. The Court of Appeals for the Fifth Circuit has imposed a duty to bargain over partial closing decisions. See *NLRB v. Winn-Dixie Stores, Inc.*, 361 F.2d 512, *cert. denied*, 385 U.S. 935 (1966). The Board itself has not been fully consistent in its rulings applicable to this type of management decision. . . .

II

Although parties are free to bargain about any legal subject, Congress has limited the mandate or duty to bargain to matters of "wages, hours, and other terms and conditions of employment." A unilateral change as to a subject within this category violates the statutory duty to bargain and is subject to the Board's remedial order. *NLRB v. Katz*, 369 U.S. 736 (1962). Conversely, both employer and union may bargain to impasse over these matters and use the economic weapons at their disposal to attempt to secure their respective aims. *NLRB v. American National Ins. Co.*, 343 U.S. 395 (1952).[21] Congress deliberately left the words "wages, hours, and other terms and conditions of employment" without further definition, for it did not intend to deprive the Board of the power further to define those terms in light of specific industrial practices.[22]

---

21. [13] A matter that is not a mandatory subject of bargaining, unless it is illegal, may be raised at the bargaining table to be discussed in good faith, and the parties may incorporate it into an enforceable collective bargaining agreement. Labor and management may not, however, insist on it to the point of impasse. *NLRB v. Borg-Warner Corp.*, 356 U.S. 342 (1958).

22. [14] In enacting the Labor Management Relations Act, 1947, Congress rejected a proposal in the House to limit the subjects of bargaining to "(i) [w]age rates, hours of employment, and

Nonetheless, in establishing what issues must be submitted to the process of bargaining, Congress had no expectation that the elected union representative would become an equal partner in the running of the business enterprise in which the union's members are employed. Despite the deliberate open-endedness of the statutory language, there is an undeniable limit to the subjects about which bargaining must take place. . . .

Some management decisions, such as choice of advertising and promotion, product type and design, and financing arrangements, have only an indirect and attenuated impact on the employment relationship. *See Fibreboard,* 379 U.S., at 223 (STEWART, J., concurring). Other management decisions, such as the order of succession of layoffs and recalls, production quotas, and work rules, are almost exclusively "an aspect of the relationship" between employer and employee. *Chemical Workers,* 404 U.S., at 178. The present case concerns a third type of management decision, one that had a direct impact on employment, since jobs were inexorably eliminated by the termination, but had as its focus only the economic profitability of the contract with Greenpark, a concern under these facts wholly apart from the employment relationship. This decision, involving a change in the scope and direction of the enterprise, is akin to the decision whether to be in business at all, "not in [itself] primarily about conditions of employment, though the effect of the decision may be necessarily to terminate employment." *Fibreboard,* 379 U.S., at 223 (STEWART, J., concurring). *Cf. Textile Workers v. Darlington Co.,* 380 U.S. 263, 268 (1965) ("an employer has the absolute right to terminate its entire business for any reason it pleases"). At the same time, this decision touches on a matter of central and pressing concern to the union and its member employees: the possibility of continued employment and the retention of the employees' very jobs. *See Brockway Motor Trucks, Etc. v. NLRB,* 582 F.2d 720, 735–736 (CA3 1978); *Ozark Trailers, Inc.,* 161 N.L.R.B. 561, 566–568 (1966).

---

work requirements; (ii) procedures and practices relating to discharge, suspension, lay-off, recall, seniority, and discipline, or to promotion, demotion, transfer and assignment within the bargaining unit; (iii) conditions, procedures, and practices governing safety, sanitation, and protection of health at the place of employment; (iv) vacations and leaves of absence; and (v) administrative and procedural provisions relating to the foregoing subjects." H.R. 3020 § 2(11), 80th Cong., 1st Sess. (1947).

The adoption, instead, of the general phrase now part of § 8(d) was clearly meant to preserve future interpretation by the Board. *See* H.R. Rep. No. 245, 80th Cong., 1st Sess., 71 (1947) (minority report) ("The appropriate scope of collective bargaining cannot be determined by a formula; it will inevitably depend upon the traditions of an industry, the social and political climate at any given time, the needs of employers and employees, and many related factors. What are proper subject matters for collective bargaining should be left in the first instance to employers and trade unions, and in the second place, to any administrative agency skilled in the field and competent to devote the necessary time to a study of industrial practices and traditions in each industry or area of the country, subject to review by the courts. It cannot and should not be strait-jacketed by legislative enactment."); H.R. Conf. Rep. No. 510, 80th Cong., 1st Sess., 34–35 (1947). Specific references in the legislative history to plant closings, however, are inconclusive. See 79 Cong. Rec. 7673, 9682 (1935) (comments of Sen. Walsh and Rep. Griswold).

Petitioner contends it had no duty to bargain about its decision to terminate its operations at Greenpark. This contention requires that we determine whether the decision itself should be considered part of petitioner's retained freedom to manage its affairs unrelated to employment.[23] The aim of labeling a matter a mandatory subject of bargaining, rather than simply permitting, but not requiring, bargaining, is to "promote the fundamental purpose of the Act by bringing a problem of vital concern to labor and management within the framework established by Congress as most conducive to industrial peace," *Fibreboard*, 379 U.S., at 211. The concept of mandatory bargaining is premised on the belief that collective discussions backed by the parties' economic weapons will result in decisions that are better for both management and labor and for society as a whole. *Ford Motor Co.*, 441 U.S., at 500–501; *Borg-Warner*, 356 U.S., at 350 (condemning employer's proposal of "ballot" clause as weakening the collective-bargaining process). This will be true, however, only if the subject proposed for discussion is amenable to resolution through the bargaining process. Management must be free from the constraints of the bargaining process[24] to the extent essential for the running of a profitable business. It also must have some degree of certainty beforehand as to when it may proceed to reach decisions without fear of later evaluations labeling its conduct an unfair labor practice. Congress did not explicitly state what issues of mutual concern to union and management it intended to exclude from mandatory bargaining. Nonetheless, in view of an employer's need for unencumbered decision-making, bargaining over management decisions that have a substantial impact on the continued availability of employment should be required only if the benefit, for labor-management relations and the collective bargaining process, outweighs the burden placed on the conduct of the business.

The Court in *Fibreboard* implicitly engaged in this analysis with regard to a decision to subcontract for maintenance work previously done by unit employees. Holding the employer's decision a subject of mandatory bargaining, the Court relied not only on the "literal meaning" of the statutory words, but also reasoned:

> The Company's decision to contract out the maintenance work did not alter the Company's basic operation. The maintenance work still had to be performed in the plant. No capital investment was contemplated; the Company merely replaced existing employees with those of an independent contractor to do the same work under similar conditions of employment. Therefore,

---

23. [15] There is no doubt that petitioner was under a duty to bargain about the results or effects of its decision to stop the work at Greenpark, or that it violated that duty. Petitioner consented to enforcement of the Board's order concerning bargaining over the effects of the closing and has reached agreement with the union on severance pay.

24. [17] The employer has no obligation to abandon its intentions or to agree with union proposals. On proper subjects, it must meet with the union, provide information necessary to the union's understanding of the problem, and in good faith consider any proposals the union advances. In concluding to reject a union's position as to a mandatory subject, however, it must face the union's possible use of strike power. . . .

to require the employer to bargain about the matter would not significantly abridge his freedom to manage the business. 379 U.S. at 213.

The Court also emphasized that a desire to reduce labor costs, which it considered a matter "peculiarly suitable for resolution within the collective bargaining framework," was at the base of the employer's decision to subcontract. The prevalence of bargaining over "contracting out" as a matter of industrial practice generally was taken as further proof of the "amenability of such subjects to the collective bargaining process."

With this approach in mind, we turn to the specific issue at hand: an economically-motivated decision to shut down part of a business.

III

A. Both union and management regard control of the decision to shut down an operation with the utmost seriousness. As has been noted, however, the Act is not intended to serve either party's individual interest, but to foster in a neutral manner a system in which the conflict between these interests may be resolved. It seems particularly important, therefore, to consider whether requiring bargaining over this sort of decision will advance the neutral purposes of the Act.

A union's interest in participating in the decision to close a particular facility or part of an employer's operations springs from its legitimate concern over job security. The Court has observed: "The words of [§ 8(d)] . . . plainly cover termination of employment which . . . necessarily results" from closing an operation. *Fibreboard*, 379 U.S. at 210. The union's practical purpose in participating, however, will be largely uniform: it will seek to delay or halt the closing. No doubt it will be impelled, in seeking these ends, to offer concessions, information, and alternatives that might be helpful to management or forestall or prevent the termination of jobs.[25] It is unlikely, however, that requiring bargaining over the decision itself, as well as its effects, will augment this flow of information and suggestions. There is no dispute that the union must be given a significant opportunity to bargain about these matters of job security as part of the "effects" bargaining mandated by § 8(a)(5). And, under § 8(a)(5), bargaining over the effects of a decision must be conducted in a meaningful manner and at a meaningful time, and the Board may impose sanctions to insure its adequacy. A union, by pursuing such bargaining rights, may achieve

---

25. [19] We are aware of past instances where unions have aided employers in saving failing businesses by lending technical assistance, reducing wages and benefits or increasing production, and even loaning part of earned wages to forestall closures. *See* S. Slichter, J. Healy & E. Livernash, The Impact of Collective Bargaining on Management 845–851 (1960); C. Golden & H. Rutenberg, The Dynamics of Industrial Democracy 263–291 (1942). *See also United Steel Workers, Etc. v. U.S. Steel Corp.*, 492 F. Supp. 1 (ND Ohio), *aff'd in part and vacated in part*, 631 F.2d 1264 (CA6 1980) (union sought to purchase failing plant); 104 Lab. Rel. Rep. 239 (1980) (employee ownership plan instituted to save company); *id.*, at 267–268 (union accepted pay cuts to reduce plant's financial problems). These have come about without the intervention of the Board enforcing a statutory requirement to bargain.

valuable concessions from an employer engaged in a partial closing. It also may secure in contract negotiations provisions implementing rights to notice, information, and fair bargaining.

Moreover, the union's legitimate interest in fair dealing is protected by § 8(a)(3) which prohibits partial closings motivated by anti-union animus, when done to gain an unfair advantage. *Textile Workers v. Darlington Co.*, 380 U.S. 263 (1965). Under § 8(a)(3) the Board may inquire into the motivations behind a partial closing. An employer may not simply shut down part of its business and mask its desire to weaken and circumvent the union by labeling its decision "purely economic."

Thus, although the union has a natural concern that a partial closing decision not be hastily or unnecessarily entered into, it has some control over the effects of the decision and indirectly may ensure that the decision itself is deliberately considered. It also has direct protection against a partial closing decision that is motivated by an intent to harm a union.

Management's interest in whether it should discuss a decision of this kind is much more complex and varies with the particular circumstances. If labor costs are an important factor in a failing operation and the decision to close, management will have an incentive to confer voluntarily with the union to seek concessions that may make continuing the business profitable. At other times, management may have great need for speed, flexibility, and secrecy in meeting business opportunities and exigencies. It may face significant tax or securities consequences that hinge on confidentiality, the timing of a plant closing, or a reorganization of the corporate structure. The publicity incident to the normal process of bargaining may injure the possibility of a successful transition or increase the economic damage to the business. The employer also may have no feasible alternative to the closing, and even good-faith bargaining over it may be both futile and cause the employer additional loss.

There is an important difference, also, between permitted bargaining and mandated bargaining. Labeling this type of decision mandatory could afford a union a powerful tool for achieving delay, a power that might be used to thwart management's intentions in a manner unrelated to any feasible solution the union might propose. In addition, many of the cases before the Board have involved, as this one did, not simply a refusal to bargain over the decision, but a refusal to bargain at all, often coupled with other unfair labor practices. In these cases, the employer's action gave the Board reason to order remedial relief apart from access to the decision-making process. It is not clear that a union would be equally dissatisfied if an employer performed all its bargaining obligations apart from the additional remedy sought here.

While evidence of current labor practice is only an indication of what is feasible through collective bargaining, and not a binding guide, *see Chemical Workers*, 404 U.S., at 176, that evidence supports the apparent imbalance weighing against mandatory bargaining. We note that provisions giving unions a right to participate in the decision-making process concerning alteration of the scope of an enterprise appear to be relatively rare. Provisions concerning notice and "effects" bargaining are more prevalent.

Further, the presumption analysis adopted by the court of appeals seems ill suited to advance harmonious relations between employer and employee. An employer would have difficulty determining beforehand whether it was faced with a situation requiring bargaining or one that involved economic necessity sufficiently compelling to obviate the duty to bargain. If it should decide to risk not bargaining, it might be faced ultimately with harsh remedies forcing it to pay large amounts of backpay to employees who likely would have been discharged regardless of bargaining, or even to consider reopening a failing operation. Also, labor costs may not be a crucial circumstance in a particular economically-based partial termination. And in those cases, the Board's traditional remedies may well be futile. If the employer intended to try to fulfill a court's direction to bargain, it would have difficulty determining exactly at what stage of its deliberations the duty to bargain would arise and what amount of bargaining would suffice before it could implement its decision. If an employer engaged in some discussion, but did not yield to the union's demands, the Board might conclude that the employer had engaged in "surface bargaining," a violation of its good faith. A union, too, would have difficulty determining the limits of its prerogatives, whether and when it could use its economic powers to try to alter an employer's decision, or whether, in doing so, it would trigger sanctions from the Board.

We conclude that the harm likely to be done to an employer's need to operate freely in deciding whether to shut down part of its business purely for economic reasons outweighs the incremental benefit that might be gained through the union's participation in making the decision,[26] and we hold that the decision itself is *not* part of § 8(d)'s "terms and conditions," over which Congress has mandated bargaining.[27]

---

26. [22] In this opinion we of course intimate no view as to other types of management decisions, such as plant relocations, sales, other kinds of subcontracting, automation, etc., which are to be considered on their particular facts.

27. [23] Despite the contentions of *amicus* AFL-CIO our decision in *Order of Railroad Telegraphers v. Chicago & N.W.R. Co.*, 362 U.S. 330 (1960), does not require that we find bargaining over this partial closing decision mandatory.... Although the Court in part relied on an expansive interpretation of § 2, First, which requires railroads to "exert every reasonable effort to make and maintain agreements concerning rates of pay, rules, and working conditions," and § 13(c) the Norris-LaGuardia Act, 29 U.S.C. § 113(c), defining "labor dispute" as "any controversy concerning terms or conditions of employment," its decision also rested on the particular aims of the Railway Labor Act and national transportation policy. *See* 362 U.S., at 336–338. The mandatory scope of bargaining under the Railway Labor Act and the extent of the prohibition against injunctive relief contained in Norris-LaGuardia are not coextensive with the National Labor Relations Act and the Board's jurisdiction over unfair labor practices. *See Chicago & N.W.R. Co. v. Transportation Union*, 402 U.S. 570, 579, n. 11 (1971) ("parallels between the duty to bargain in good faith and the duty to exert every reasonable effort, like all parallels between the NLRA and the Railway Labor Act, should be drawn with the utmost care and with full awareness of the differences between the statutory schemes").

B. In order to illustrate the limits of our holding, we turn again to the specific facts of this case. First, we note that when petitioner decided to terminate its Greenpark contract, it had no intention to replace the discharged employees or to move that operation elsewhere. Petitioner's sole purpose was to reduce its economic loss, and the union made no claim of anti-union animus. In addition, petitioner's dispute with Greenpark was solely over the size of the management fee Greenpark was willing to pay. The union had no control or authority over that fee. The most that the union could have offered would have been advice and concessions that Greenpark, the third party upon whom rested the success or failure of the contract, had no duty even to consider. These facts in particular distinguish this case from the subcontracting issue presented in *Fibreboard*. Further, the union was not selected as the bargaining representative or certified until well after petitioner's economic difficulties at Greenpark had begun. We thus are not faced with an employer's abrogation of ongoing negotiations or an existing bargaining agreement. Finally, while petitioner's business enterprise did not involve the investment of large amounts of capital in single locations, we do not believe that the absence of "significant investment or withdrawal of capital" is crucial. The decision to halt work at this specific location represented a significant change in petitioner's operations, a change not unlike opening a new line of business or going out of business entirely.

The judgment of the court of appeals, accordingly, is reversed and the case is remanded to that court for further proceedings consistent with this opinion.

JUSTICE BRENNAN, with whom JUSTICE MARSHALL joins, dissenting.

. . . .

I respectfully dissent.

The Court bases its decision on a balancing test. It states that "bargaining over management decisions that have a substantial impact on the continued availability of employment should be required only if the benefit, for labor management relations and the collective-bargaining process, outweighs the burden placed on the conduct of the business." I cannot agree with this test, because it takes into account only the interests of *management;* it fails to consider the legitimate employment interests of the workers and their Union. Cf. *Brockway Motor Trucks v. NLRB*, 582 F.2d 720, 734–740 (CA3 1978) (balancing of interests of workers in retaining their jobs against interests of employers in maintaining unhindered control over corporate direction). This one-sided approach hardly serves "to foster in a neutral manner" a system for resolution of these serious, two-sided controversies.

Even if the Court's statement of the test were accurate, I could not join in its application, which is based solely on speculation. Apparently, the Court concludes that the benefit to labor-management relations and the collective bargaining process from negotiation over partial closings is minimal, but it provides no evidence to that effect. The Court acknowledges that the Union might be able to offer concessions, information, and alternatives that might obviate or forestall the closing, but it then asserts that "[i]t is unlikely, however, that requiring bargaining over the decision . . . will augment this flow of information and suggestions." Recent experience, however, suggests the contrary. Most conspicuous, perhaps, were the negotiations between Chrysler Corporation and the United Auto Workers, which led to significant adjustments in compensation and benefits, contributing to Chrysler's ability to remain afloat. Even where labor costs are not the direct cause of a company's financial difficulties, employee concessions can often enable the company to continue in operation — if the employees have the opportunity to offer such concessions.

The Court further presumes that management's need for "speed, flexibility, and secrecy" in making partial closing decisions would be frustrated by a requirement to bargain. In some cases the Court might be correct. In others, however, the decision will be made openly and deliberately, and considerations of "speed, flexibility, and secrecy" will be inapposite. Indeed, in view of management's admitted duty to bargain over the effects of a closing, it is difficult to understand why additional bargaining over the closing itself would necessarily unduly delay or publicize the decision.

I am not in a position to judge whether mandatory bargaining over partial closings *in all cases* is consistent with our national labor policy, and neither is the Court. The primary responsibility to determine the scope of the statutory duty to bargain has been entrusted to the NLRB, which should not be reversed by the courts merely because they might prefer another view of the statute. I therefore agree with the Court of Appeals that employers presumptively have a duty to bargain over a decision to close an operation, and that this presumption can be rebutted by a showing that bargaining would be futile, that the closing was due to emergency financial circumstances, or that, for some other reason, bargaining would not further the purposes of the National Labor Relations Act.

Dubuque Packing Co., 303 N.L.R.B. 386 (1991), *enforced sub nom. United Food & Commercial Workers Int'l Union, Local No. 150-A v. NLRB*, 1 F.3d 24 (D.C. Cir. 1993), *cert. dismissed*, 511 U.S. 1138 (1994). An employer was held to have violated § 8(a)(5) by failing to bargain with the union over the relocation of its hog slaughtering operations from its home plant in Dubuque, Iowa, to a new plant in Rochelle, Illinois. In its analysis, the Labor Board noted the uncertainty created by the different tests set forth in a famous earlier plurality decision, *Otis Elevator Co.*, 269 N.L.R.B. 891 (1984), to determine when an employer must bargain about a decision to relocate work from one facility to another. A unanimous NLRB first reviewed the principles of *Fibreboard* and *First National Maintenance*. The Board noted that relocation decisions have a direct impact upon employment. It then indicated that such decisions are more analogous to subcontracting cases than to plant closure situations, since the employer usually plans to continue the same basic operations at the new location. Based upon these considerations, the Board formulated new standards to be applied to determine when an employer has to bargain about a relocation decision:

Initially, the burden is on the General Counsel to establish that the employer's decision involved a relocation of unit work unaccompanied by a basic change in the nature of the employer's operation. If the General Counsel successfully carries his burden in this regard, he will have established prima facie that the employer's relocation decision is a mandatory subject of bargaining. At this juncture, the employer may produce evidence rebutting the prima facie case by establishing that the work performed at the new location varies significantly from the work performed at the former plant, establishing that the work performed at the former plant is to be discontinued entirely and not moved to the new location, or establishing that the employer's decision involves a change in the scope and direction of the enterprise. Alternatively, the employer may proffer a defense to show by a preponderance of the evidence: (1) that labor costs (direct and/or indirect) were not a factor in the decision or (2) that even if labor costs were a factor in the decision, the union would not have offered labor cost concessions that could have changed the employer's decision to relocate.

The first prong of the employer's burden is self-explanatory. If the employer shows that labor costs were irrelevant to the decision to relocate unit work, bargaining over the decision will not be required because the decision would not be amenable to resolution through the bargaining process.

Under the second prong, an employer would have no bargaining obligation if it showed that, although labor costs were a consideration in the decision to relocate unit work, it would not remain at the present plant because, for example, the costs for modernization of equipment or environmental controls were greater than any labor cost concessions the union could offer. On the other hand, an employer would have a bargaining obligation if the union could and would offer concessions that approximate, meet, or exceed the anticipated costs or benefits that prompted the relocation decision, since the decision then would be amenable to resolution through the bargaining process. . . .

[A]n employer would enhance its chances of establishing this defense by describing the reasons for relocating to the union, fully explaining the underlying cost or benefit considerations, and asking whether the union could offer labor cost reductions that would enable the employer to meet its profit objectives.

The Board noted that there may be unusual situations requiring an expedited employer relocation decision, and it indicated that such exigent circumstances might, in appropriate cases, relieve an employer of the duty to notify the union and provide it with an opportunity to bargain over such a decision.

Notes

1. *When Does* Dubuque *Apply?* — The *Dubuque Packing* test does not apply to subcontracting decisions in which "virtually all that is changed through the

subcontracting is the identity of the employees doing the work," or to cases in which the employer consolidates jobs and lays off unit employees, continuing to do the same work with fewer employees. Such decisions continue to be governed by *Fibreboard*. See, e.g., *Finch, Pruyn & Co.*, 349 N.L.R.B. 270 (2007) (*Dubuque* did not apply to subcontracting decision "because there was no relocation of unit work here"). It is not always clear, however, which cases require application of the *Dubuque* analysis. *Furniture Rentors of Am. v. NLRB*, 36 F.3d 1240 (3d Cir. 1994), involved an employer that encountered serious problems with its delivery personnel. The theft of $10,000 worth of furniture resulted in the arrest and resignation of several employees. The firm experienced problems with respect to packing and handling that caused damage to furniture. Delivery teams averaged three deliveries per day compared to the industry standard of four or five. When two employees and a supervisor were apprehended as part of a plot to steal furniture, the company unilaterally decided to close its delivery department and hire a contractor to perform the required delivery work. Since the Labor Board concluded that the factors that led to the employer's subcontracting decision were amenable to resolution through the bargaining process, it found the firm's failure to bargain about this decision violative of § 8(a)(5). The Third Circuit found the Board's rote application of the *Dubuque Packing* test overly simplistic in a case involving such complex managerial considerations, and it remanded the case to the NLRB for a more searching analysis. Even if the Board were to determine that the subcontracting decision had been based on factors amenable to resolution through the bargaining process, it must then decide whether the likelihood and degree of benefit, if any, to be derived from bargaining in a situation of this kind would outweigh the employer's obvious need for prompt action. On remand, the Board applied *Fibreboard* and *First National Maintenance* and found no § 8(a)(5) violation. 318 N.L.R.B. 602 (1995). *See also Rigid Pak Corp.*, 366 N.L.R.B. No. 137 (2018) (employer that utilized employees interchangeably between its blow molding and injection molding business was required to bargain over decision to subcontract out work for its injection molding business, but not over decision to subcontract out its blow-mold production where it had decided to abandon the blow-mold production operation); *Sea Mar Cmty. Health Ctrs.*, 345 N.L.R.B. 947 (2005) (employer not required to bargain over closure of dental laboratory where laboratory was created by person who lacked authority to do so, without employer's knowledge, and in direct contradiction to employer's order). *But cf. Rock-Tenn Co. v. NLRB*, 101 F.3d 1441 (D.C. Cir. 1996) (requiring bargaining on subcontracting of trucking operations done for the purpose of avoiding liability risks of maintaining a truck fleet, despite employer's contention that subcontractor's labor costs were so low that employer's own drivers would have to take a $25,000 per year pay cut and thus bargaining would be futile).

On the other hand, in *Torrington Industries,* 307 N.L.R.B. 809 (1992), the Board held that when one group of employees is substituted for another to perform the same work under the same employer, no balancing test is required and bargaining is required unless the employer can show that subcontracting the work was a "core entrepreneurial decision or dictated by emergency." Further, in *O.G.S. Technologies, Inc.*, 356 N.L.R.B. 642 (2011), a divided Labor Board ruled that OGS violated § 8(a)(5) when it unilaterally outsourced the last of its die-making business to subcontractors. The Board rejected OGS's argument that it made a core entrepreneurial decision involving the scope and direction of the business when it shifted work to subcontractors, finding the action merely a "modest change" in operations rather than the abandonment of a line of business or even a contraction of the existing business. The Board ordered bargaining over the issue, reinstatement of employees laid off as a result of the changes and back pay for losses sustained.

2. *Employer Motivation*—What is the role of employer motivation? Where the employer's relocation decision is motivated by anti-union animus or a desire to break the union, the Board and courts will find a violation of §§ 8(a)(1), 8(a)(3), and 8(a)(5) and order a resumption of operations to enforce the duty to bargain over the decision and/or its effects. *See Vico Prods. Co. v. NLRB*, 333 F.3d 198 (D.C. Cir. 2003) (Michigan employer that relocated part of its operations to Kentucky a few months after the union was certified without bargaining over the relocation decision or its effects committed unfair labor practices where the relocation of the unit work was unaccompanied by a basic change in the nature of the employer's operations and motivated by the desire to reduce labor costs, rendering it a mandatory subject of bargaining; "the haphazardness, the timing, and the secretive nature of the hasty relocation decision" made so quickly after the union won the election persuaded the Board and the court that the decision was made out of anti-union animus).

The Board's traditional remedy for such violations — an order to resume operations in the original location — has sometimes caused consternation in the courts. *See, e.g., Dorsey Trailers, Inc. v. NLRB*, 233 F.3d 831 (4th Cir. 2000) (employer that transferred work to a new plant following union's strike made a business decision that was not a mandatory subject of bargaining; Board's restoration order exceeded its authority).

In 2011, the Board brought § 8(a)(1) and § 8(a)(3) charges against the Boeing company, claiming that Boeing's decision to relocate assembly operations for its new 787 Dreamliner from union-friendly Washington State to South Carolina was made in retaliation for its unionized employees' historical use of the strike weapon during collective bargaining negotiations. The remedy sought was an order to locate the new assembly line in Washington State. *The Boeing Co.*, NLRB No. 19-CA-32431 (2011). Considerable media attention, congressional investigations and hearings ensued. The charges were ultimately withdrawn by the Board's General Counsel at the union's request after the parties reached a new collective bargaining agreement in which Boeing agreed to protect the workers' job security and to increase wages and benefits in exchange for the union's agreement not to strike for a fixed period of time. Why do you think the public reaction to a traditional labor law doctrine was so intense? *See* Getman, *Boeing, the IAM, and the NLRB: Why U.S. Labor Law Is Failing*, 98 Minn. L. Rev. 1651 (2014); Getman, *The Boeing Case: Creating Outrage Out of Very Little*, 27 A.B.A. J. Lab. & Emp. L. 99 (2011); Storm, *Boeing and the*

NLRB—A Sixty-Four-Year-Old Time Bomb Explodes, 68 NAT'L LAW. GUILD REV. 109 (2011). Despite $2.2 billion in state aid and $100 million in tax breaks from Washington to try to induce the company to continue production of the Dreamliner in Seattle, eight years later (during the pandemic) Boeing ended production of its 787 Dreamliner in Washington State and consolidated its assembly operations in South Carolina. Tangel, *Boeing to Consolidate Dreamliner Production in South Carolina*, WALL ST. J., Oct. 2, 2020.

3. *Management Rights Clauses and Union Waivers*—To what extent may a management rights clause waive a union's right to bargain over an employer's decision to subcontract or relocate work? *Compare Reece Corp.*, 294 N.L.R.B. 448 (1989), *with Batavia Newspapers Corp.*, 311 N.L.R.B. 477 (1993). The D.C. Circuit draws a distinction between a union's waiver of the right to bargain and a provision that covers a particular issue, thus fixing the parties' rights and foreclosing further mandatory bargaining. *United Mine Workers 1974 Pension v. Pittston Co.*, 984 F.2d 469 (D.C. Cir.), *cert. denied*, 509 U.S. 924 (1993).

To what extent might unions protect themselves by negotiating for job security mechanisms that give the union the right to obtain advance information from the employer about outsourcing decisions, the right to discuss alternatives with management, the right to compete by bringing subcontracted work in-house, or establish skills training programs designed to assist displaced workers in finding other positions? What about provisions in which the employer promises to invest specified funds in retooling and maintaining existing plants, or promises not to close particular plants for the life of the contract? The United Auto Workers' Union has successfully negotiated such provisions in its contracts with automakers, but how many other unions will have sufficient bargaining leverage to obtain them?

4. *Effects Bargaining*—Whether or not an employer must bargain over the actual decision to relocate operations, failure to inform the union prior to beginning the move may violate the duty to bargain over the effects of the decision. Timely notice is necessary to give the union an opportunity to negotiate while it still represents employees at work and thus retains some bargaining leverage for the existing employees. *Dodge of Naperville, Inc. v. NLRB*, 796 F.3d 31 (D.C. Cir. 2015); *Berklee College of Music*, 362 N.L.R.B. 1517 (2015). The critical factor is that notice must be given at a point sufficient to allow for meaningful bargaining. *El Paso Elec. Co. v. NLRB*, 681 F.3d 651 (5th Cir. 2012).

The duty to bargain over effects applies even where the bargaining unit is altered by the employer's decision. When Wal-Mart decided to eliminate its separate meat departments and sell only prepackaged meat, and then reassigned its meat department employees from meat cutting to the stocking of shelves with prepackaged meat, it did not have to bargain with the newly certified union of meat department employees over this managerial decision since the meat departments no longer constituted appropriate separate bargaining units, but it was obligated to negotiate over the effects of the decision to close out its meat departments. *UFCW, AFL-CIO, Local 540 v. NLRB*, 519 F.3d 490 (D.C. Cir. 2008). *See also AG Commun. Sys. Corp.*,

350 N.L.R.B. 168 (2007), *enforced*, 563 F.3d 418 (9th Cir. 2009) (company violated § 8(a)(5) where it refused to bargain over effects of decision to move telephone equipment installers into larger bargaining unit represented by a different union).

5. *Duty to Bargain over Effects of a Sale?*—Should the same or a different standard apply to an employer's duty to bargain about the effects of the sale of a business? *See NLRB v. Compact Video Servs.*, 121 F.3d 478 (9th Cir. 1997) (unionized firm whose parent corporation decides to sell its assets to another company risks violating § 8(a)(5) if it fails to notify the union of the proposed sale and provide it with the opportunity to bargain over the *effects* of the transaction on unit members). *See also Providence Hosp. v. NLRB*, 93 F.3d 1012 (1st Cir. 1996) (hospitals violated § 8(a)(5) by refusing to provide union with information about a proposed merger with a competing health care system; despite hospitals' contention that bargaining would have to await consummation of the merger, the union was entitled to information at an earlier date in order to prepare for bargaining over the effects of the merger and the structural attributes of the new system); *Reidel Int'l*, 300 N.L.R.B. 282 (1990) (union entitled to as much notice of closing as "needed for meaningful bargaining at a meaningful time").

6. *The WARN Act*—The Worker Adjustment and Retraining Notification Act (1988), 29 U.S.C. § 2101 (WARN Act), requires employers with 100 or more employees to give 60 days' advance notice of shutdowns affecting at least 50 workers and of layoffs lasting more than six months and affecting one-third of the workers at a site. Provisions in earlier bills that would have required good faith consultations with any bargaining representative regarding possible alternatives to the proposed closing or layoff were omitted in the Act as passed. *See generally* Yost, *The Worker Adjustment and Retraining Notification Act of 1988: Advance Notice Required?*, 38 Cath. U. L. Rev. 675 (1989). The Supreme Court has held unanimously that a union may sue on behalf of its members for the damages caused by an employer's violation of the WARN Act. *United Food & Commer. Workers Union Local 751 v. Brown Group*, 517 U.S. 544 (1996).

Problems

58. In March 2020, Zippers Unlimited began producing zipper chains and parts for the sliders that open and close zippers. Zippers Unlimited had several departments, including the sewing department, the finishing department, the weaving department, and the slider department. Between November 5 and 10, 2020, 59 of the approximately 86 employees signed union authorization cards seeking representation by UNITE Local 151. When the Union requested bargaining rights, management refused. The Union filed for an election. Zippers Unlimited hired an anti-union consultant and began an anti-union campaign, which included interrogations and threats aimed at those who had not yet signed union authorization cards, including threats to close. Nevertheless, all five employees in the slider department signed union cards. On December 8, the company told those five employees that the department was being closed because the operating costs for the small department were excessive and the sliders produced were not of acceptable quality. Zippers Unlimited immediately sought bids from other companies for a contract to produce sliders to complete its zippers.

On December 15, the Union won the election and demanded bargaining over, among other topics, the company's decision to close the slider department. The company refused. If you are assigned this case as NLRB counsel, what charges will you file, what arguments will you make, and what remedies will you seek? Has the company violated the Act?

59. A typical movie theater employs a staff consisting of managers, assistant managers, concessionists, box office employees, ushers, and projectionists. Where unionized, projectionists tend to be organized in a separate bargaining unit as professionals. Over the past 10 years, the general trend in the theater industry has been to eliminate the projectionist position and to convert to manager-operated theaters. Today, the duties of a projectionist generally include the following tasks: "threading" the film through the projector at the beginning of each showing and disengaging the film at each showing's end; monitoring the film's focus and volume at the outset of each showing; preparing new films for the projector's continuous film platter by splicing together the film's multiple reels; performing the "breakdown" of older movies that are no longer being shown; changing movie trailers when necessary; fixing minor projector problems, such as broken belts and loose splices; and cleaning both the projection equipment and the projection booth.

Not surprisingly, technological advances have greatly simplified the projection process and have thus eliminated many of the job duties originally performed by projectionists. For example, projectionists no longer need to change reels during a showing. In addition, a computerized projection system now opens the curtains, changes the lighting, operates the sound system, and automatically rewinds the film.

In an effort to cut costs when theaters began reopening in the wake of the COVID-19 pandemic, Regal Cinemas converted its movie theaters to "manager-operated" theaters. In a manager-operated theater, managers and assistant managers operate the projection equipment as part of their regular duties, thereby eliminating the need to employ dedicated projectionists. Regal hired assistant managers to perform most of the work previously done by the projectionists, and invested in media to automate other aspects of the projectionists' work. Regal did not bargain over this decision with the union that represented its projectionists, arguing that its decision was within the scope of entrepreneurial control, and that the union had waived the right to bargain over the automation of work—pointing to a management rights clause in the collective bargaining agreement that provided:

> The COMPANY shall have the right to introduce new or improved work methods, facilities, equipment, machinery, processes and procedures of work and to change or eliminate existing methods, facilities, equipment,

machinery, processes and procedures or work . . . and to automate. The COM-
PANY agrees to negotiate the effects [of such decisions] on the employees.

If the union files an unfair labor practice charge, how should the Board rule? Explain.

Section VI. The Duty to Bargain during a Contract's Term

The Jacobs Manufacturing Co.
National Labor Relations Board
94 N.L.R.B. 1214 (1951)

. . . In July 1948, the Respondent and the Union executed a two-year bargaining contract which, by its terms, could be reopened one year after its execution date for discussion of "wage rates." In July, 1949, the Union invoked the reopening clause of the 1948 contract, and thereafter gave the Respondent written notice of its "wage demands." In addition to a request for a wage increase, these demands included a request that the Respondent undertake the entire cost of an existing group insurance program, and another request for the establishment of a pension plan for the Respondent's employees. When the parties met thereafter to consider the Union's demands, the Respondent refused to discuss the Union's pension and insurance requests on the ground that they were not appropriate items of discussion under the reopening clause of the 1948 contract.

The group insurance program to which the Union alluded in its demands was established by the Respondent before 1948. It was underwritten by an insurance company, and provided life, accident, health, surgical, and hospital protection. All the Respondent's employees were eligible to participate in the program, and the employees shared its costs with the Respondent. When the 1948 contract was being negotiated, the Respondent and the Union had discussed changes in this *insurance program*, and had agreed to increase certain of the benefits as well as the costs. However, neither the changes thereby effected, nor the insurance program itself, was mentioned in the 1948 contract.

As indicated by the Union's request, there was no pension plan for the Respondent's employees in existence in 1949. The subject of *pensions*, moreover, had not been discussed during the 1948 negotiations; and, like insurance, that subject is not mentioned in the 1948 contract.

a. For the reasons stated below, Chairman Herzog and Members Huston and Styles agree with the Trial Examiner's conclusion that the Respondent violated § 8(a)(5) of the Act by refusing to discuss the matter of *pensions* with the Union. . . .

We are satisfied . . . that the 1948 contract did not in itself impose on the Respondent any obligation to discuss *pensions* or insurance. The reopening clause of that contract refers to *wage rates*, and thus its intention appears to have been narrowly limited to matters directly related to the amount and matter of compensation for work. For that reason, a requirement to discuss *pensions* or insurance cannot be predicated on the language of the contract.

On the other hand, a majority of the Board believes that, regardless of the character of the reopening clause, the Act itself imposed upon the Respondent the duty to discuss *pensions* with the Union during the period in question.

It is now established as a principle of law that the matter of *pensions* is a subject which falls within the area where the statute requires bargaining. And, as noted above, the 1948 contract between the Respondent and the Union was silent with respect to the subject of *pensions*; indeed, the matter had never been raised or discussed by the parties. The issue raised, therefore, is whether the Respondent was absolved of the obligation to discuss *pensions* because of the limitation contained in § 8(d) of the amended Act dealing with the duty to discuss or agree to the modification of an existing bargaining contract. . . .

The crucial point at issue here . . . is the construction to be given the phrase "terms and conditions *contained in* a contract." (Emphasis supplied.) The Board in the *Tide Water* [85 N.L.R.B. 1096] case, concluded that the pertinent portion of § 8(d):

> *refers to terms and conditions which have been integrated and embodied into a writing.* Conversely it does not have reference to matters relating to wages, hours and other terms and conditions of employment, which have not been reduced to writing. As to the written terms of the contract either party may refuse to bargain further about them, under the limitations set forth in the paragraph, without committing an unfair labor practice. With respect to unwritten terms dealing with wages, hours and other terms and conditions of employment, the obligation remains on both parties to bargain continuously.

Thus, as already construed by this Board in the *Tide Water* case, § 8(d) does not itself license a party to a bargaining contract to refuse, during the life of the contract, to discuss a bargainable subject unless it has been made part of the agreement itself. Applied here, therefore, the *Tide Water* construction of § 8(d) means that the Respondent was obligated to discuss the Union's pension demand.

Members Huston and Styles have carefully re-examined the Board's construction of § 8(d) in the *Tide Water* case, and are persuaded that the view the Board adopted in the *Tide Water* case best effectuates the declared policy of the Act. Chairman Herzog, while joining in the result with respect to the obligation to bargain here concerning *pensions*—never previously discussed by the parties—joins in the rationale herein *only* to the extent that it is consistent with his views separately recited below, concerning the insurance program.

By making mandatory the discussion of bargainable subjects not already covered by a contract, the parties to the contract are encouraged to arrive at joint decisions with respect to bargainable matters, that, at least to the party requesting discussion, appear at the time to be of some importance. The Act's policy of "encouraging the practice and procedure of collective bargaining" is consequently furthered. A different construction of § 8(d) in the circumstances — one that would permit a party to a bargaining contract to avoid discussion when it was sought on subject matters not contained in the contract — would serve, at its best, only to dissipate whatever the good will that had been engendered by the previous bargaining negotiations that led to the execution of a bargaining contract; at its worst, it could bring about the industrial strife and the production interruptions that the policy of the Act also seeks to avert.

The significance of this point cannot be overemphasized. It goes to the heart of our disagreement with our dissenting colleague, Member Reynolds. His dissent stresses the need for "contract stability," and asserts that the furtherance of sound collective bargaining requires that the collective bargaining agreement be viewed as fixing, for the term of the contract, all aspects of the employer-employee relationship, and as absolving either party of the obligation to discuss, during that term, even those matters which had never been raised, or discussed in the past. We could hardly take issue with the virtue of "contract stability," at least in the abstract, and we would certainly agree that everyone is better off when, in negotiating an agreement, the parties have been able to foresee what all the future problems may be, to discuss those problems, and either to embody a resolution of them in the contract, or to provide that they may not be raised again during the contract. But we are here concerned with the kind of case in which, for one reason or another, this has *not* been done, and the question is what best effectuates the policies of the Act in *such* a case.

In this connection we cannot ignore the fact that to say that a party to an agreement is absolved by § 8(d) of an obligation to discuss a subject not contained in a contract does not mean that the other party is prohibited from taking economic action to compel bargaining on that subject. The portion of § 8(d) we are here considering does no more than provide a *defense* to a charge of a refusal to bargain under § 8(a)(5) or § 8(b)(3) of the Act. It does not render unlawful economic action aimed at securing lawful objectives.[28] That being so, the view urged by Member Reynolds achieves "contract stability" but only at the price of industrial strife, and that is a result which now more than ever we must avoid. The basic policy of this Act to further collective bargaining is founded on the proposition — amply demonstrated by experience — that collective bargaining provides an escape valve for the pressures which otherwise result in industrial strife. With this policy in mind, we

---

28. [10] We must note, however, contrary to the assertion of Member Reynolds, that nothing in this decision is to be construed as a determination of the issue of whether a union may strike to compel bargaining on a modification of a contract which seeks to add a matter not contained in the contract without complying with the procedural requirements of § 8(d). Our decision here is limited to a construction of the language "modification of the terms and conditions *contained in* a contract." The issue raised by our dissenting colleague is not before us in this case, and we in no way pass upon it.

are loath to narrow the area of mandatory bargaining, except where the amended statute, in the clearest terms, requires that we do so.

The construction of § 8(d) adopted by the Board in the *Tide Water* case serves also to simplify, and thus to speed, the bargaining process. It eliminates the pressure upon the parties at the time when a contract is being negotiated to raise those subjects that may not then be of controlling importance, but which might in the future assume a more significant status. It also assures to both unions and employers that, if future conditions require some agreement as to matters about which the parties have not sought, or have not been able to obtain agreement, then some discussion of those matters will be forthcoming when necessary.

We cannot believe that Congress was unaware of the foregoing considerations when it amended the Act by inserting § 8(d), or that it sought, by the provision in question, to freeze the bargaining relationship by eliminating any mandatory discussion that might lead to the addition of new subject matter to an existing contract. What § 8(d) does do is to reject the pronouncements contained in some pre1947 Board and court decisions—sometimes *dicta*, sometimes necessary to the holding—to the effect that the duty to bargain continues even as to those matters upon which the parties have reached agreement and which are set forth in the terms of a written contract. But we believe it does no more. Those bargainable issues which have never been discussed by the parties, and which are in no way treated in the contract, remain matters which both the union and the employer are obliged to discuss at any time.

In so holding, we emphasize that under this rule, no less than in any other circumstance, the duty to bargain implies only an obligation to *discuss* the matter in question in good faith with a sincere purpose of reaching some agreement. It does not require that either side agree, or make concessions. And if the parties originally desire to avoid later discussion with respect to matters not specifically covered in the terms of an executed contract, they need only so specify in the terms of the contract itself. Nothing in our construction of § 8(d) precludes such an agreement, entered into in good faith, from foreclosing future discussion of matters not contained in the agreement.[29]

---

29. [13] For an example of a contract in which such a provision was incorporated, *see the contract between United Automobile Workers of America and General Motors Corp., set forth in Labor Relations Manual* (BNA), vol. 26, p. 63, 91, which states:
> (154) The parties acknowledge that during the negotiations which resulted in this agreement, each had the unlimited right and opportunity to make demands and proposals with respect to any subject or matter not removed by law from the area of collective bargaining, and that the understandings and agreements arrived at by the parties after the exercise of that right and opportunity are set forth in this agreement. Therefore, the Corporation and the Union, for the life of this agreement, each voluntarily and unqualifiedly waives the right, and each agrees that the other shall not be obligated, to bargain collectively with respect to any subject or matter not specifically referred to or covered in this agreement, even though such subjects or matter may not have been within the knowledge

b. Chairman Herzog, for reasons set forth in his separate opinion, believes that — unlike the *pensions* issue — the Respondent was under no obligation to bargain concerning the *group insurance program.* However, Members Huston and Styles — a minority of the Board on this issue — are of the further opinion that the considerations discussed above leading to the conclusion that the Respondent was obligated to discuss the matter of pensions, also impel the conclusion that the Respondent was obligated to discuss the Union's group insurance demand. Like pensions, the matter of group insurance benefits is a subject which has been held to be within the area of compulsory bargaining; and like pensions, the Respondent's group insurance program was not mentioned in the terms of the 1948 contract. Members Huston and Styles therefore believe that so far as the controlling facts are concerned the ultimate issues presented by the Union's pension and group insurance demands are identical....

Members Huston and Styles believe, moreover, that the view adopted by Chairman Herzog on the insurance issue is subject to the same basic criticism as is the view of Member Reynolds — it exalts "contract stability" over industrial peace; it eliminates mandatory collective bargaining on subjects about which one of the parties *now* wants discussion, and concerning which it may well be willing to take economic action if discussion is denied, solely because the matter has once been discussed in a manner which may warrant an inference that the failure to mention that subject in the contract was part of the bargain. Members Huston and Styles are constrained to reject the view of Chairman Herzog for the further reason that it would establish a rule which is administratively unworkable, and would inject dangerous uncertainty into the process of collective bargaining. Apart from the extremely difficult problems of proof — illustrated in this very case — which would constantly confront the Board in cases of this type, the parties to collective bargaining negotiations would always be faced with this question after a subject has been *discussed* — "Have we really *negotiated*, or are we under an obligation to discuss the subject further if asked to?" To this query the rule of the *Tide Water* case gives a clear and concise answer: "You are obligated to discuss any bargaining subject upon request unless you have reduced your agreement on that subject to writing or unless you have agreed in writing not to bargain about it during the term of the contract." Members Huston and Styles would apply that rule without deviation....

CHAIRMAN HERZOG, concurring in part:

I believe that this Respondent was *not* under a duty to discuss the Union's *group insurance* demand. The individual views which lead me, by a different road, to the result reached on this issue by Members Reynolds and Murdock, are as follows:

Unlike the issue of pensions, concerning which the contract is silent and the parties did not negotiate at all in 1948, the subject of group insurance was fully discussed

---

or contemplation of either or both of the parties at the time that they negotiated or signed this agreement.

while the Respondent and the Union were negotiating the agreement. True, that agreement is silent on the subject, so it cannot literally be said that there is a term "contained in" the 1948 contract relating to the group insurance program. The fact remains that during the negotiations which preceded its execution, the issue was consciously explored. The record reveals that the Union expressly requested that the preexisting program be changed so that the Respondent would assume its entire cost, the very proposal that was again made as part of the 1949 midterm demand which gave rise to this case. The Respondent rejected the basic proposal on this first occasion, but agreement was then reached—although outside the written contract—to increase certain benefits under the group insurance program.

In my opinion, it is only reasonable to assume that rejection of the Union's basic proposal, coupled in this particular instance with enhancement of the substantive benefits, constituted a part of the contemporaneous "bargain" which the parties made when they negotiated the entire 1948 contract. In the face of this record as to what the parties discussed and did, I believe that it would be an abuse of this Board's mandate to throw the weight of Government sanction behind the Union's attempt to disturb, in midterm, a bargain sealed when the original agreement was reached.

To hold otherwise would encourage a labor organization—or, in a § 8(b)(3) case, an employer—to come back, time without number, during the term of a contract, to demand resumed discussion of issues which, although perhaps not always incorporated in the written agreement, the other party had every good reason to believe were put at rest for a definite period. I do not think that the doctrine of the *Tide Water* case was ever intended to go so far as to extend to facts like these, or that it should be so extended. Without regard to the niceties of construing the words of § 8(d) of the amended Act, I am satisfied that it would be both inequitable and unwise to impose a statutory obligation to bargain in situations of this sort. That would serve only to stimulate uncertainty and evasion of commitments at a time when stability should be the order of the day.

MEMBER REYNOLDS, concurring separately and dissenting in part: . . .

[I]t is my opinion that § 8(d) imposes no obligation on either party to a contract to bargain on any matter during the term of the contract except as the express provisions of the contract may demand. This is a result reasonably compatible with the particular § 8(d) language involved, as well as with § 8(d) as a whole. Moreover, not only does the result accord stability and dignity to collective bargaining agreements, but it also gives substance to the practice and procedure of collective bargaining.

It is well established that the function of collective bargaining agreements is to contribute stability, so essential to sound industrial relations. Contractually stabilized industrial relations enable employers, because of fixed labor costs, to engage in sound long-range production planning, and employees, because of fixed wage, seniority, promotion, and grievance provisions, to anticipate secure employment tenure. Hence when an employer and a labor organization have through the processes of collective bargaining negotiated an agreement containing the terms and conditions of employment for a definite period of time, their total rights and obligations emanating from the employer-employee relationship should remain fixed for that time. Stabilized therefore are the rights and obligations of the parties with respect to all bargainable subjects whether the subjects are or are not specifically set forth in the contract. To hold otherwise and prescribe bargaining on unmentioned subjects would result in continued alteration of the total rights and obligations under the contract, thus rendering meaningless the concept of contract stability.

That a collective bargaining agreement stabilizes all rights and conditions of employment is consonant with the generally accepted concept of the nature of such an agreement. The basic terms and conditions of employment existing at the time the collective bargaining agreement is executed, and which are not specifically altered by, or mentioned in, the agreement, are part of the *status quo* which the parties, by implication, consider as being adopted as an essential element of the agreement. This view is termed "reasonable and logical," and its widespread endorsement as sound industrial relations practice makes it a general rule followed in the arbitration of disputes arising during the term of a contract. The reasonableness of the approach is apparent upon an understanding of collective bargaining techniques. Many items are not mentioned in a collective bargaining agreement either because of concessions at the bargaining table or because one of the parties may have considered it propitious to forego raising one subject in the hope of securing a more advantageous deal on another. Subjects traded off or foregone should, under these circumstances, be as irrevocably settled as those specifically covered and settled by the agreement. To require bargaining on such subjects during midterm debases initial contract negotiations....

MEMBER MURDOCK, dissenting in part:

I am unable to agree with my colleagues of the majority that by refusing to discuss pensions and insurance with the Union under the particular circumstances of this case, the Respondent violated § 8(a)(5) of the Act.

Despite the fact that the reopening clause in the contract which the Union here invoked was limited to "wage rates," the Union included insurance and pensions in its demands thereunder in addition to a wage increase. In my view the Respondent properly took the position that the parties were meeting pursuant to the reopening provision of the contract to discuss wage rates and that pensions and insurance were not negotiable thereunder and would not be discussed at that time....

Notes

1. *Aftermath* — The Board majority's position that *pensions* were a bargainable issue since they were neither discussed in negotiations nor embodied in the contract received judicial support in *NLRB v. Jacobs Mfg. Co.*, 196 F.2d 680 (2d Cir. 1952). The differences among the Board members in the *Jacobs* case may well have resulted from the critical comments of Professors Cox and Dunlop in *Regulation of Collective Bargaining by the National Labor Relations Board*, 63 HARV. L. REV. 389 (1950),

and *The Duty to Bargain Collectively During the Term of an Existing Agreement*, 63 Harv. L. Rev. 1097 (1950). For a vigorous defense of the Board, see Findling & Colby, *Regulation of Collective Bargaining by the National Labor Relations Board — Another View*, 51 Colum. L. Rev. 170 (1951).

2. *Union Waiver as to Matters Fully Discussed or Consciously Explored* — What must be said during negotiations to give rise to the inference that a particular matter was intended to be left in the employer's hands for the period of the contract? How reliable is the evidence likely to be? *Compare NLRB v. Nash-Finch Co.*, 211 F.2d 622 (8th Cir. 1954) *and Speidel Corp.*, 120 N.L.R.B. 733 (1958), *with Beacon Piece Dyeing & Finishing Co., Inc.*, 121 N.L.R.B. 953 (1958) *and Cloverleaf Division, Adams Dairy Co.*, 147 N.L.R.B. 1410 (1964). In *Proctor Mfg. Corp.*, 131 N.L.R.B. 1166, 1169 (1961), the Board declared:

> The Board's rule, applicable to negotiations during the contract term with respect to a subject which has been discussed in pre-contract negotiations but which has not been specifically covered in the resulting contract, is that the employer violates Section 8(a)(5) if, during the contract term, he refuses to bargain or takes unilateral action with respect to the particular subject, unless it can be said from an evaluation of the prior negotiations that the matter was 'fully discussed' or 'consciously explored' and that the Union 'consciously yielded' or clearly and unmistakably waived its interest in the matter.

See also Daniel I. Burk Enters., 313 N.L.R.B. 1263 (1994) (no union waiver of right to bargain over economically motivated closing and termination of employees even where parties' current and past labor contracts anticipated layoffs during economic downturns). The Board's clear and unmistakable waiver standard was approved by the Supreme Court in *NLRB v. C & C Plywood*, 385 U.S. 421 (1967).

Waiver cases involving a change in past practice tend to be fact-specific. In such cases, the Board examines the nature of the unilateral change, past practice, and negotiating history, as well as the contract itself for evidence of waiver. *Compare Cal. Offset Printers, Inc.*, 349 N.L.R.B. 732 (2007) (employer violated § 8(a)(5) by unilaterally implementing a requirement that employees be reachable at all hours by phone; contract did not address the issue, and general management rights clause was not sufficient as a waiver given the significant new burden that the employer's policy imposed on employees).

3. *Waiver by Inaction* — A union can waive its bargaining rights during the term of a contract by conduct or by inaction. For example, in *Allen v. McWane Inc.*, 593 F.3d 449 (5th Cir. 2010), collective bargaining agreement negotiations never included the issue of compensability for time spent donning and doffing protective gear, even though employees were entitled to such pay under the Fair Labor Standards Act. When employees sought to enforce their rights in a collective action under the FLSA, the employer moved for summary judgment on the basis of FLSA § 203(o), which provides that "time spent changing clothes or washing at the beginning or end of each workday" is not compensable if excluded by "the express terms of or by custom or practice under a bona fide collective-bargaining agreement." The court found that the union officials' lack of knowledge of such rights did not justify an exception to the well-established principle that plant custom or practice becomes an implied term of the contract through a prolonged period of acquiescence; the union was deemed to have acquiesced in the custom or practice of non-compensation for donning and doffing time. Courts reason that if the labor contract does not provide for compensation for donning and doffing time, the union and employer must have intended that in exchange for other concessions; plaintiffs cannot upend the deal struck by their union. *See, e.g., Mitchell v. JCG Indus., Inc.*, 753 F.3d 695 (7th Cir. 2014); *see also Sandifer v. U.S. Steel Corp.*, 571 U.S. 220 (2014) (confirming that "changing clothes" includes the donning and doffing of protective gear that is integral and indispensable to performance of workers' jobs, and invoking FLSA § 203(o) to bar union-represented employees from bringing FLSA claims).

Further, the union must act with due diligence and pursue its bargaining rights promptly once informed of a proposed change by the employer. *See AT&T Corp.*, 337 N.L.R.B. 689 (2002) (union waived right to bargain where employer announced impending layoffs in 60 days and union did not demand bargaining); *but cf. NLRB v. Roll & Hold Warehouse & Distrib. Corp.*, 162 F.3d 513 (7th Cir. 1998) (no union waiver where company unilaterally changed its attendance policy and presented the new plan directly to employees, undermining the negotiating role of the union). For contrasting rulings on the requirements for a union waiver of the right to bargain over management decisions or their effects, compare *American Diamond Tool, Inc.*, 306 N.L.R.B. 570 (1992) (union waiver of bargaining rights regarding layoffs when union failed without excuse to use opportunity to request bargaining over layoffs and "signalled" willingness to permit such unilateral conduct in the future), with *Porta-King Bldg. Sys.*, 310 N.L.R.B. 539 (1993), *enforced*, 14 F.3d 1258 (8th Cir. 1994) (no waiver regarding layoffs when employer failed to notify union before laying off employees, despite employer's prior practice of unilateral layoffs at former, discontinued unionized operation).

4. *The Contract Coverage Standard* — The Board applies a "contract coverage" standard in lieu of a waiver analysis where the employer has a "sound arguable basis" for its interpretation of the contract — such as a management rights clause that encompasses the change made by the employer — reasoning that the union has already had an opportunity to bargain over the subject and the alleged change in terms and conditions of employment is thus not a contract modification at all. In *M.V. Transportation*, 368 N.L.R.B. No. 66 (2019), the Labor Board abandoned the "clear and unmistakable waiver" standard, which only allowed unilateral changes in employment conditions if the applicable contract specifically and unequivocally waived the union's statutory right to bargain over those particular issues, and adopted the "contract coverage" test to determine whether mid-contract unilateral changes violate an employer's duty to bargain. Under the "contract coverage" approach, the Board

will examine the plain language of bargaining agreements to determine whether applicable provisions allow employers to make changes in employment terms without bargaining with the representative unions. The contract coverage standard originated in the D.C. Circuit and was subsequently adopted by the First and Seventh Circuits. *See NLRB v. United States Postal Serv.*, 8 F.3d 832 (D.C. Cir. 1993); *Bath Marine Draftsmen's Ass'n v. NLRB*, 475 F.3d 14 (1st Cir. 2007); *Chicago Tribune Co. v. NLRB*, 974 F.2d 933 (7th Cir. 1992); *see also Enloe Med. Ctr. v. NLRB*, 433 F.3d 834 (D.C. Cir. 2005) (finding that hospital's adoption of mandatory on-call policy for nurses and coaching strategy to address negative effects of on-call policy on nurse morale was covered by collective bargaining agreement).

The contract coverage standard for employer unilateral changes does not outlive the collective agreement, however, unless the management rights clause explicitly grants rights extending beyond the contract's expiration date. *Nexstar Broadcasting*, 369 N.L.R.B. No. 61 (2020). However, an employer may unilaterally implement changes that are consistent with past practice, even if that practice was established under a management rights clause in a collective agreement that has since expired. *Raytheon Network Centric Sys.*, 365 N.L.R.B. No. 161 (2017).

NLRB v. Lion Oil Co., 352 U.S. 282, 77 S. Ct. 330, 1 L. Ed. 2d 331 (1957). A union and an employer entered into a collective bargaining agreement to remain in effect for one year and thereafter until canceled. The agreement provided that either party could propose amendments by notifying the other party any time after the first 10 months of the contract. If agreement could not be reached on amendment of the contract during the 60-day period following this notification, either party could thereafter terminate the agreement by giving a 60-day written notice to the other. At the end of the first 10 months, the union duly served notice of its desire to modify the contract. The union never gave the further notice to terminate, and thus the contract remained in effect. Nonetheless, some eight months after its initial modification notice, the union went on strike to back up its demands for amendment. Subsequently, the employer defended against unfair labor practices allegedly committed by it during the strike by asserting that the workers had lost their status as employees under the Act by striking in violation of §8(d)(4). Section 8(d)(4) provides that a party wishing to modify or terminate a contract must not resort to a strike or lockout "for a period of sixty days after . . . notice is given or until the expiration date of such contract, whichever occurs later." The Supreme Court held that when a contract is subject to reopening in midterm, the phrase "expiration date" as used in §8(d)(4) should be construed to mean both the final termination date and the first date on which the agreement is subject to amendment. Otherwise, an obvious restriction would be imposed on employees' concerted activities, and long-term bargaining relationships would be discouraged. The Court therefore concluded that the union had fully satisfied the notice and waiting requirements of §8(d), and the strikers had not lost their status as employees.

Notes

1. *Actions during Reopener Period*—Just as the union has the right to strike during the reopener period, the employer may unilaterally implement its final proposal following a valid impasse in negotiations under a reopener clause, assuming that it provides the requisite § 8(d) notices. *See Speedrack Inc.*, 293 N.L.R.B. 1054 (1989); *see also Hydrologics, Inc.*, 293 N.L.R.B. 1060 (1989) (unless the contract states otherwise, the assumption is that the parties intend to make the same economic weapons available in the reopener context as are available at termination of the contract).

2. *Section 8(d) "Cooling Off" Provisions*—The "cooling off" provisions of § 8(d) apply only to strikes to compel a modification or termination of the collective agreement. They do not apply to a strike to protest an employer's unfair labor practice, *Mastro Plastics Corp. v. NLRB*, 350 U.S. 270 (1956), or to a walkout caused by dangerous working conditions, *NLRB v. Knight Morley Corp.*, 251 F.2d 753 (6th Cir. 1957), *cert. denied*, 357 U.S. 927 (1958). The strike-notice provisions of § 8(d) are also inapplicable to a strike over an issue not covered by the contract, since such a strike would not amount to a strike to change or end the agreement. *United Mine Workers v. NLRB*, 258 F.2d 146 (D.C. Cir. 1958); *Cheney California Lumber Co. v. NLRB*, 319 F.2d 375 (9th Cir. 1963).

A union that strikes without complying with the 60-day notice requirement has been said to "forfeit" its rights as collective bargaining agent, and the strikers lose their status as employees. *Boeing Airplane Co. v. NLRB*, 174 F.2d 988 (D.C. Cir. 1949). An employer's duty to bargain is also suspended during the period of such a strike. *Wholesale, Retail, Office & Processing Union, District 65 (Melville Shoe Corp.)*, 187 N.L.R.B. 716 (1971). When an employer egged on a union to strike, however, it waived the loss of NLRA protections for employees when the union struck during the 60-day "cooling off" period. *ABC Automotive Prods. Corp.*, 307 N.L.R.B. 248 (1992), *supplemented by* 319 N.L.R.B. 874 (1995). Similarly, an employer who locked out employees prior to the passage of 60 days following the union's untimely notice of intent to terminate their agreement violated § 8(d)(4). *Drew Div. of Ashland Chem. Co.*, 336 N.L.R.B. 477 (2001).

Problem

60. H & H Enterprises distributes plumbing fixtures and heating and air-conditioning systems throughout the United States. Its drivers are each permanently assigned to a company-owned truck, and they are allowed to take the truck keys (but not the truck) home each night. This practice shortens the amount of time needed for required safety inspections each morning since the drivers are familiar with their trucks, know where they are parked, and can park their personal cars in the spot where the truck was parked when they arrive at the worksite. Drivers are also allowed to take home their company cell phones, which facilitates contact with customers to set up deliveries before and after working hours. Finally, drivers are required to acknowledge receipt of any documents (including, for example, orders from customers, notices of discipline from the employer, and changes to the employee handbook) by signing the document itself or a separate acknowledgment form if the document is not available in hard copy.

H & H's drivers recently voted to be represented by the Teamsters Union. During negotiations over a first contract, the drivers went out on a two-day strike over pension benefits. When the company agreed to a union proposal, the drivers returned. Upon their return to work, H & H announced that drivers would no longer be permanently assigned to a truck and instead would receive their truck assignments on a daily basis. They would also be required to turn in their keys and company cell phones each evening. Finally, in order to monitor overtime work more closely, H & H announced a new policy requiring employees to sign a receipt for any overtime schedule they received from a supervisor. Two days later, H & H issued a written warning to driver Scott Baker for failing to comply with the truck key turn-in policy and the cell phone turn-in policy. H & H also issued a written warning to Sally Strickland for failing to sign a receipt for an overtime schedule she claimed to have received.

H & H did not give the Union notice or opportunity to bargain about these changes. Did any of H & H's new policies violate the Act?

Part 6

The Collective Agreement

Section I. The Legal Status of the Collective Agreement

The expected outcome of the parties' fulfillment of their bargaining obligations is the execution of a collective labor agreement. In 2020, 14.3 million wage and salary workers in the United States were represented by a labor union, although not all of them were covered by a collective bargaining agreement. BLS News Release USDL-2010081 (2021), *available at* https://www.bls.gov/news.release/union2.nr0.htm. Although labor contracts vary widely according to the nature, size, and complexity of the particular industry or company involved that no single agreement can be called typical, most of them cover relatively standard subjects. The Institute for Research on Labor and Employment at the University of California-Berkeley maintains a website that serves as a clearinghouse for union contracts that are digitized and can be searched online for examples of typical clauses. *See* https://irle.berkeley.edu/digital-collection/bargaining/. Cornell University's School of Industrial and Labor Relations also maintains a database. *See* https://digitalcommons.ilr.cornell.edu/cba/. A sample collective agreement is also included in *Selected Federal Statutes*. The sample agreement should be read thoroughly at this point in order to gain some acquaintance with its contents.

Traditionally, collective bargaining agreements were seldom involved in litigation. Court actions were regarded as detrimental to healthy labor-management relations. The paucity of suits for enforcement of collective agreements may be one of the reasons for the delayed and rather sketchy development of theories as to the nature of these instruments.

Early common-law decisions advanced at least three separate theories to explain the legal nature of the collective agreement:

1. The labor agreement establishes local customs or usages, which are then incorporated into the individual employee's contract of hire. This seems to have been the orthodox view of the American courts, at least prior to the era of the labor relations acts. *See* Rice, *Collective Labor Agreements in American Law*, 44 Harv. L. Rev. 572, 582 (1931). For historical overview, see Symposium, *Origins of the Union Contract*, 33 Lab. L.J. 512 (1982). Under the original form of this theory, the collective agreement itself was not regarded as a contract. It had legal effect only as its terms were absorbed into individual employment contracts. Somewhat similar is the traditional English concept that collective agreements are merely "gentlemen's agreements" or

moral obligations not enforceable by the courts. *Young v. Canadian N. Ry.*, [1931] A.C. 83 (P.C.); WEDDERBURN OF CHARLTON, THE WORKER AND THE LAW 318–22 (3d ed. 1986). Some American scholars also have voiced an occasional plea that court litigation over collective agreements should be rejected as detrimental to the parties' continuing relationship. *See* Shulman, *Reason, Contract, and Law in Labor Relations*, 68 HARV. L. REV. 999 (1955). Nevertheless, judicial enforcement at the behest of either employers or unions became generally accepted in this country well before the passage of the LMRA in 1947 and was confirmed by that Act.

2. The collective agreement is a contract that is negotiated by the union as the agent for the employees, who become the principals on the agreement. *A. R. Barnes & Co. v. Berry*, 169 F. 225 (6th Cir. 1909); *Maisel v. Sigman*, 123 Misc. 714, 205 N.Y.S. 807 (Sup. Ct. N.Y. County 1924). This so-called agency theory was adopted by a few courts that could not rationalize the enforceability of an instrument executed by an unincorporated association lacking juristic personality. Suits between individual employees and employers were maintainable, however, on the theory the union had merely served as the employees' agent in negotiations.

3. The collective agreement is a third-party beneficiary contract, with the employer and union cast as the mutual promisors and promisees, and the employees the beneficiaries. *Marranzano v. Riggs Nat'l Bank*, 184 F.2d 349 (D.C. Cir. 1950); *Yazoo & M. V. R. Co. v. Sideboard*, 161 Miss. 4, 133 So. 669 (1931); *H. Blum & Co. v. Landau*, 23 Ohio App. 426, 155 N.E. 154 (1926). Despite arguable shortcomings (is the employer to be left without recourse against the employee beneficiary, who has made no promises?), the third-party beneficiary theory became rather widely accepted as the best explanation of the collective agreement in terms of traditional common-law concepts. *See* C. GREGORY & H. KATZ, LABOR AND THE LAW 481 (3d ed. 1979).

Today, collective bargaining agreements in industries affecting commerce are enforced as a matter of federal law under § 301 of the LMRA. This means that the Supreme Court's views on the nature of the labor contract are now of primary concern. Two characteristics of the Court's thinking stand out. First, the Court is eclectic in its approach to common-law doctrines; it refuses to confine itself to any single theory, but draws upon whatever elements may be helpful in a variety of theories. Second, the Court has emphasized what may be described as the "constitutional" or "governmental" quality of the labor agreement. Thus, the collective agreement has been described as "not an ordinary contract" but rather a "generalized code" for "a system of industrial self-government." *See John Wiley & Sons, Inc. v. Livingston*, 376 U.S. 543, 550 (1964); *United Steelworkers of America v. Warrior & Gulf Navigation Co.*, 363 U.S. 574, 578–80 (1960).

The Supreme Court's eclectic approach to the nature of the labor contract is reflected in the following well-known comments by Mr. Justice Jackson in *J. I. Case Co. v. NLRB*, 321 U.S. 332, 334–35 (1944):

Collective bargaining between employer and the representatives of a unit, usually a union, results in an accord as to terms which will govern hiring and work and pay in that unit. The result is not, however, a contract of employment except in rare cases; no one has a job by reason of it and no obligation to any individual ordinarily comes into existence from it alone. The negotiations between union and management result in what often has been called a trade agreement, rather than in a contract of employment. Without pushing the analogy too far, the agreement may be likened to the tariffs established by a carrier, to standard provisions prescribed by supervising authorities for insurance policies, or to utility schedules of rates and rules for service, which do not of themselves establish any relationships but which do govern the terms of the shipper or insurer or customer relationship whenever and with whomever it may be established. . . .

[H]owever engaged, an employee becomes entitled by virtue of the Labor Relations Act somewhat as a third party beneficiary to all benefits of the collective trade agreement, even if on his own he would yield to less favorable terms. The individual hiring contract is subsidiary to the terms of the trade agreement and may not waive any of its benefits, any more than a shipper can contract away the benefit of filed tariffs, the insurer the benefit of standard provisions, or the utility customer the benefit of legally established rates.

Section II. Enforcement of the Collective Agreement through the Grievance and Arbitration Process

Labor Study Group, The Public Interest in National Labor Policy
32 (Committee for Economic Development 1961)

A major achievement of collective bargaining, perhaps its most significant contribution to the American workplace, is the creation of a system of industrial jurisprudence, a system under which employer and employee rights are set forth in contractual form and disputes over the meaning of the contract are settled through a rational grievance process usually ending, in the case of unresolved disputes, with arbitration. The gains from this system are especially noteworthy because of their effect on the recognition and dignity of the individual worker. The system helps prevent arbitrary action on questions of discipline, layoff, promotion, and transfer, and sets up orderly procedures for the handling of grievances. Wildcat strikes and other disorderly means of protest have been curtailed and an effective work discipline generally established. In many situations, cooperative relationships marked by mutual respect between management and labor stand as an example of what can be done.

A. The Grievance Procedure

The great mass of day-to-day disputes arising during the term of a collective agreement are settled, in actual practice, through the procedure established and administered by the parties themselves. Where satisfactory industrial relations exist under collective bargaining, only a minute percentage of such disputes will even have to go to arbitration. And of those that do, it is extraordinary for the courts to get involved, either in compelling arbitration or in requiring compliance with awards. Since we will be dealing mostly with these exceptional cases, their relatively small role in the total industrial relations picture should be kept in proper perspective.

The grievance procedure is one of the most universal and important provisions in the collective agreement. Perhaps the most common provision is a grievance and arbitration procedure to resolve disputes over contract interpretation. Bureau of Nat'l Affairs, Basic Patterns in Union Contracts 37 (14th ed. 1995) (noting that 99% of labor contracts contained such a clause). The grievance procedure has been referred to as the "core of the collective bargaining agreement." L. Hill & C. Hook, Management at the Bargaining Table 199 (1945). As the Supreme Court has explained:

> Arbitration is the means of solving the unforeseeable by molding a system of private law for all the problems which may arise and to provide for their solution in a way which will generally accord with the variant needs and desires of the parties. The processing of disputes through the grievance machinery is actually a vehicle by which meaning and content are given to the collective bargaining agreement.

United Steelworkers of America v. Warrior & Gulf Navigation Co., 363 U.S. 574, 581 (1960), excerpted and discussed *infra*. The grievance and arbitration system thus represents the acceptance in labor-management relations of the fundamental notions of due process, and of the virtues of an orderly method of adjusting disputes. The decisions rendered through the established procedure tend to become the industrial case law for the plant. The use of arbitration as the terminal step in the procedure has produced a mass of decisions through which an "industrial jurisprudence" is developing, outside the established judicial system, much as the rules governing negotiable instruments first evolved as part of the "law merchant," and the principles of unfair competition originated with the medieval merchant guilds.

B. Voluntary Arbitration

Voluntary arbitration has been defined as "a contractual proceeding whereby the parties to any dispute or controversy, in order to obtain a speedy and inexpensive final disposition of the matter involved, select a judge of their own choice and by consent submit their controversy to him for determination." *Gates v. Arizona Brewing Co.*, 54 Ariz. 266, 269, 95 P.2d 49 (1939). *See also* F. Elkouri & E. Elkouri,

How Arbitration Works, ch. 1, 1–3 (8th ed. 2016); C. Updegraff, Arbitration and Labor Relations 3 (1971). The Supreme Court has observed that while commercial arbitration is a substitute for litigation, labor arbitration is a substitute for industrial strife. *United Steelworkers of America v. Warrior & Gulf Navigation Co.*, 363 U.S. 574, 578 (1960). For the view that labor arbitration is a substitute for both strikes and litigation ("but in the sense in which a transport airplane is a substitute for a stagecoach"), see Shulman, *Reason, Contract, and Law in Labor Relations*, 68 Harv. L. Rev. 999, 1024 (1955). The increasing use of arbitration in the settlement of labor disputes is a strong indication of a higher degree of maturity in industrial relations. Today, thousands of disputes are settled in voluntary arbitration proceedings without resort to economic pressure or appeals to the sympathy of the public. St. Antoine, *ADR in Labor and Employment Law During the Past Quarter Century*, 25 ABA J. Lab. & Emp. L. 411 (2010).

Probably the greatest stimulus toward the use of arbitration to settle industrial grievances was provided by the National War Labor Board during World War II. The Board was given power to settle most types of labor disputes, and it quite regularly ordered the inclusion of arbitration clauses in new contracts whenever the parties were not able to agree upon their grievance procedure. *See generally* Symposium, *An Oral History of the National War Labor Board and Critical Issues in the Development of Modern Grievance Arbitration*, 39 Case W. Res. L. Rev. 501 (1988–89); Freidin & Ulman, *Arbitration and the National War Labor Board*, 58 Harv. L. Rev. 309 (1945). Although less than 10% of the labor agreements in effect in the early 1930s provided for arbitration, by 1944 the figure had grown to 73%. S. Slichter, J. Healy & E. Livernash, The Impact of Collective Bargaining on Management 739 (1960). *See also* Nolan & Abrams, *American Labor Arbitration: The Early Years, The Maturing Years*, 35 U. Fla. L. Rev. 373, 557 (1983). An overwhelming majority of both union and management representatives agree that the ideal grievance procedure should have arbitration as the terminal point. Jones & Smith, *Management and Labor Appraisals and Criticisms of the Arbitration Process: A Report with Comments*, 62 Mich. L. Rev. 1115, 1116–17 (1964).

Court procedures are ordinarily ill-adapted to the needs of modern labor-management relations, and in addition are costly, prolonged, and technical. *See, e.g.*, F. Elkouri & E. Elkouri, How Arbitration Works, ch. 2, 12–13 (8th ed. 2016). One significant deficiency of litigation as a solution to industrial disputes was described by Professor Harry Shulman in this way: "[L]itigation results in . . . a decision . . . which disposes of the particular controversy, but which does not affirmatively act to advance the parties' cooperative effort, [and] does not affirmatively act to affect their attitudes in their relations with one another. Arbitration can be made to do that." *Quoted in* F. Elkouri & E. Elkouri, How Arbitration Works 7 (rev. ed. 1960). Arbitration permits self-regulation by business and labor since it is a private rather than a governmental proceeding.

There are two distinct categories of labor-management arbitration: interest arbitration and grievance arbitration.

1. Interest Arbitration

Interest arbitration (or the arbitration of interests) refers to the arbitration of disputes over the substantive terms to be included in a collective agreement. When parties fail to conclude a contract through the usual negotiating sessions, they may agree to break the deadlock by submitting the issues for determination by an arbitrator. The task of the arbitrator in an arbitration of interests was well stated by arbitrator Whitley P. McCoy:

> Arbitration of contract terms ... calls for a determination, upon considerations of policy, fairness, and expediency, of what the contract rights ought to be. In submitting this case to arbitration, the parties have merely extended their negotiations — they have left it to this board to determine what they should, by negotiation, have agreed upon. We take it that the fundamental inquiry, as to each issue, is: What should the parties themselves, as reasonable men, have voluntarily agreed to?

Twin City Rapid Transit Co., 7 Lab. Arb. Rep. 845, 848 (1947).

Today, there is a fairly substantial amount of this kind of arbitration, particularly in the public sector. Twenty-three states, the District of Columbia, and the federal government utilize interest arbitration to resolve public sector labor disputes, and 13 of these have enacted statutes mandating binding interest arbitration for public sector labor disputes. *See* W. Gould, A Primer on American Labor Law (6th ed. 2019) (listing states); F. Elkouri & E. Elkouri, How Arbitration Works (8th ed. 2016) (surveying dispute resolution mechanisms in state public interest statutes). Only rarely, however, will private sector unions and employers commit themselves in advance to the arbitration of a new contract by including a provision in their labor agreement that, upon its expiration, arbitration may be invoked to resolve disputes over the terms of a renewal. Interest arbitration received a temporary boost in the private sector when the Steelworkers and the major steel producers agreed in 1973 to settle unresolved disputes about the terms of their 1974 contracts through final and binding arbitration. Labor Relations Year Book — 1973 at 32–37 (1974); *see also* Feller, *The Impetus to Contract Arbitration in the Private Area*, in N.Y.U. Twenty-Fourth Annual Conference on Labor 79 (1972). However, the provisions concerning arbitration of future contract terms were never invoked by either the industry or the unions, and when they expired in the 1980s, they were not renewed. *See* Broderdorf, *Overcoming the First Contract Hurdle: Finding a Role for Mandatory Interest Arbitration in the Private Sector*, 23 Lab. Law. 323, 330 (2008). Neither side wanted to leave the decisions concerning new contract terms in the hands of an arbitrator. *Id.*; Gottesman, *In Despair, Starting Over: Imaging a Labor Law for Unorganized Workers*, 69 Chi.-Kent L. Rev. 59, 95–96 (1993).

As the steel industry experience illustrates, the American rejection of interest arbitration in the private sector is based in part on the view that it would entail an unacceptable intrusion of the government into the workplace. The NLRA is committed to a system of "free collective bargaining" and "private ordering of the workplace" in which government's only role is to ensure that the process of collective bargaining is observed while the terms of the bargain are left to the parties. Is this view of collective bargaining supportable in the current context of heavy governmental regulation of the employment relationship and the workplace? *See* Crain, *Expanded Employee Drug Detection Programs and the Public Good: Big Brother at the Bargaining Table*, 64 N.Y.U. L. REV. 1286 (1989); Klare, *Workplace Democracy and Market Reconstruction: An Agenda for Legal Reform*, 38 CATH. U. L. REV. 1 (1988).

Nevertheless, a number of writers have suggested that interest arbitration might be used in the private sector to expand the utility of collective bargaining, further labor-management cooperation, avoid strikes, and facilitate first contract negotiations. *See* W. GOULD, AGENDA FOR REFORM: THE FUTURE OF EMPLOYMENT RELATIONSHIPS AND THE LAW 230 (1993); Black & Hosea, *First Contract Legislation in Manitoba: A Model for the United States*, 45 LAB. L.J. 33 (1994); Harper, *A Framework for the Rejuvenation of the American Labor Movement*, 76 IND. L.J. 103 (2001); Matheny & Crain, *Making Labor's Rhetoric Reality*, 5 GREEN BAG 2d 17 (2001).

Unsuccessful efforts to pass a version of the Employee Free Choice Act increased discussion of interest arbitration in first contract negotiations as a possible solution to the difficulties unions face in achieving a first contract following an election. According to one survey of NLRB elections from 2003, only 48% of newly certified unions achieve a first contract within one year of winning the election. *See* K. BRONFENBRENNER, NO HOLDS BARRED: THE INTENSIFICATION OF EMPLOYER OPPOSITION TO ORGANIZING 22 (2009). Among other provisions, EFCA would have amended the NLRA to permit either party to demand mediation by the Federal Mediation and Conciliation Service after 90 days of failed negotiations. If the parties could not reach agreement after 30 days of mediation, the FMCS would refer the dispute to binding arbitration. Employee Free Choice Act § 3 (2009). More recently, the Protecting the Right to Organize (PRO) Act, introduced in Congress in 2019, also looked to interest arbitration in first contract negotiations to assist the parties in negotiating a collective agreement. *See generally* https://www.epi.org/blog/the-pro-act-giving-workers-more-bargaining-power-on-the-job/.

Would first-contract interest arbitration necessarily be pro-labor? Some commentators have argued that although it has been framed as pro-labor in the present political and economic context, first contract arbitration could benefit employers if labor were strong. *See* Fisk & Pulver, *First Contract Arbitration and the Employee Free Choice Act*, 70 LA. L. REV. 47 (2009); *see also* Gould, *New Law Reform Variations on an Old Theme: Is the Employee Free Choice Act the Answer?*, 70 LA L. REV. 1 (2009). Alternatively, might first-contract interest arbitration provisions work in tandem with Supreme Court jurisprudence lauding the role of arbitration as a dispute resolution mechanism to limit judicial and Board oversight of first contract negotiations? *See* Minda & Klein, *The New Arbitral Paradigm in the Law of Work: How the Proposed Employee Free Choice Act Reinforces Supreme Court Arbitration Decisions in Denying Free Choice in the Workplace*, 2010 MICH. ST. L. REV. 51.

Opposition to interest arbitration reflects a widespread belief that contract terms directed by a third party will often be unworkable or unrealistic, and that agreement of the parties themselves is ordinarily more effective. F. ELKOURI & E. ELKOURI, HOW ARBITRATION WORKS, ch. 22, 5–6 (8th ed. 2016). Furthermore, an absence of definite standards in the arbitration of "interest" disputes is thought to make the arbitral task more difficult. Injudicious use of arbitration in contract negotiation disputes may also impede the development of mature labor-management relationships through collective bargaining. On the other hand, all but two Canadian jurisdictions provide for arbitration to resolve disputes regarding first contract terms. *See* Estreicher, *Labor and Employment Law Initiatives and Proposals Under the Obama Administration, in* PROCEEDINGS OF THE NEW YORK UNIVERSITY 62ND ANNUAL CONFERENCE ON LABOR 448 (2011); Johnson, *First Contract Arbitration: Effects on Bargaining and Work Stoppages,* 63 INDUS. & LAB. REL. REV. 585 (2010). Experience in those jurisdictions suggests that the primary influence of first contract arbitration is its threat effect. Such arbitration is used infrequently, and rarely is a first contract imposed in whole or in part. Nevertheless, one study found that first contract arbitration reduces the incidence of work stoppages by 50%. *See* Johnson, *supra.* Supporters of the first contract arbitration provisions in EFCA have referred to Canada's experiences with it in arguing for the introduction of similar principles into American labor law. *See, e.g.*, Hoh, *Interest Arbitration Under the Proposed Employee Free Choice Act: What We Can Learn from the American and Canadian Experiences,* 64 DISP. RESOL. J. 50 (2010); Slinn & Hurd, *Fairness and Opportunity for Choice: The Employee Free Choice Act and the Canadian Model,* 15 JUST LAB. 104, 111 (2009).

2. Grievance Arbitration

The other main category of labor-management arbitration is that commonly known as "grievance" arbitration, or, in contradistinction to "interest" arbitration, as the arbitration of "rights." This is the type of arbitration that is customarily provided as the terminal point in contract grievance procedures. It deals with disputes arising during the life of an agreement. The function of the arbitrator in the arbitration of "rights" is quasi-judicial. The arbitrator interprets and applies the provisions of the contract; generally he or she is precluded from adding to or detracting from its terms. Nonetheless, over the years arbitrators have developed somewhat divergent attitudes about the proper approach to the collective agreement.

Under a "residual rights" or "reserved rights" theory the employer retains sole discretion to make managerial decisions affecting employees except as limited, more or less expressly, by the contract. T. ST. ANTOINE, THE COMMON LAW OF THE WORKPLACE: THE VIEWS OF ARBITRATORS 100–109 (2d ed. 2005); R. SCHOONHOVEN, FAIRWEATHER'S PRACTICE AND PROCEDURE IN ARBITRATION 299–301 (4th ed. 1999); Summers, *Employment at Will in the United States: The Divine Right of Employers,* 3 U. PA. J. LAB. & EMP. L. 65, 81–84 (2000). Under an "implied limitations" or "implied obligations" theory, on the other hand, a union may acquire certain rights as a matter of reasonable inference from different clauses or from the instrument as a whole. T. St. Antoine, The Common Law of the Workplace: The Views of Arbitrators 100–109 (2d ed. 2005); Cox, *The Legal Nature of Collective Bargaining Agreements*, 57 Mich. L. Rev. 1, 28–36 (1958). Views vary under both theories about the weight the arbitrator should give to past practice and bargaining history between the parties, or to notions of essential justice.

Arbitration tribunals take several forms: temporary (*ad hoc*) or permanent arbitrators, tripartite boards, boards composed only of neutral or impartial members, or a single arbitrator. F. Elkouri & E. Elkouri, How Arbitration Works, ch. 4, 2–10 (8th ed. 2016); *see also* Nolan & Abrams, *The Labor Arbitrator's Several Roles*, 44 Md. L. Rev. 873 (1985). Apart from private arrangements made by the parties directly with arbitrators, two important sources of *ad hoc* arbitrators are the American Arbitration Association and the Federal Mediation and Conciliation Service. *See* http://www.adr.org/ and http://www.fmcs.gov/internet/. Both organizations maintain panels of qualified and available arbitrators. The parties then make a selection from lists supplied upon request by the AAA or the FMCS.

As arbitration has matured, it has suffered certain aging pains. Then-Professor Harry T. Edwards declared some years ago that the process had become "too slow and too expensive," with too much "uniformity" and "codification" and an overly "legalistic" approach to day-to-day problems. Costs, already a concern 40 years ago, have risen dramatically. A normal case heard by the FMCS cost $511 on average in 1969; now, they are well over 10 times this amount, with per diem costs for arbitrators ranging between $1000 and $2000 per day. For more detailed information, see the websites maintained by the Federal Mediation and Conciliation Services, Arbitration Services, available at https://www.fmcs.gov/services/arbitration/ and the American Arbitration Association, available at https://www.adr.org/sites/default/files/Labor_Arbitration_Fee_Schedule.pdf; *see also* Kilberg, *The FMCS and Arbitration: Problems and Prospects*, 94 Monthly Lab. Rev. 40, 41 (1971). The average total time to obtain a resolution from arbitration is 8.6 months. Weatherspoon, *Incorporating Mandatory Arbitration Clauses into Collective Bargaining Agreements: Challenges and Benefits to the Employer and the Union*, 38 Del. J. Corp. L. 1025 (2014). Of course, the costs and delays suffered by employers and unions as a result of litigation or strikes may be greater still.

These problems may be aggravated by the reluctance of many parties to use new arbitrators. It has been estimated that 90% of arbitration cases are heard by 10% of the available arbitrators. Labor Relations Year Book — 1977, at 206 (1978). Furthermore, the arbitral ranks are not particularly diverse; the profession is largely white and male. In 1994, it was estimated that only four to six percent of labor arbitrators were women. Steen et al., *A Reexamination of Gender Bias in Arbitration Decisions*, 45 Lab. L.J. 298 (1994). A study of decisions rendered in the period 1987–1994 found that 90% of arbitrators rendering awards were male. F. Elkouri & E. Elkouri, How Arbitration Works, ch. 4, 2–10 (8th ed. 2016). *See generally* Stallworth & Malin, *Workforce Diversity: A Continuing Challenge for ADR*, Disp. Resol.

J., June 1994, at 35. A number of studies have attempted to measure the factors that affect the decision making of labor arbitrators, with varying results. *See, e.g.*, Bachar, *Does Alternative Dispute Resolution Facilitate Prejudice and Bias? We Still Don't Know*, 70 SMU L. Rev. 817 (2017); Cooper, *Discipline and Discharge of Public Sector Employees: An Empirical Study of Arbitration Awards*, 27 ABA J. Lab. & Emp. L. 195 (2012); Malin & Biernat, *Do Cognitive Biases Affect Adjudication? A Study of Labor Arbitrators*, 11 U. Pa. J. Bus. L. 175 (2008).

C. Arbitration Under the Railway Labor Act

The Railway Labor Act creates special machinery to deal with the various kinds of labor disputes. The National Mediation Board functions as a mediating agency in what we have described as "interests" disputes, and the National Railroad Adjustment Board handles disputes concerning "rights." The Mediation Board has the responsibility as to disputes within its cognizance that do not concern representation; first, to use its good offices in an attempt to secure an agreement between the parties, and second, failing in such attempt, to induce the parties to submit their dispute to arbitration under the procedures of §7 of the RLA.

Arbitration under §7 is entirely voluntary, in that both parties must agree to submit an "interests" dispute to a board of arbitration. The Board's award, however, is enforceable in federal district court.

Adjudication of grievance disputes or disputes concerning "rights" by the Adjustment Board under §3 is voluntary in the sense that appeal to the Board is apparently optional. But if either party does refer the case, the Board's jurisdiction attaches and it is directed to dispose of the matter. Upon failure of the carrier to abide by an award, an appeal may be made to the appropriate district court where the award will be enforced or set aside. In the district court, "the findings and order of the division of the Adjustment Board shall be conclusive on the parties," except for failure to comply with legal requirements or for fraud or corruption.

In setting up the National Railroad Adjustment Board, Congress proceeded on the basis of 50 years of experience with efforts to provide effective methods for settling labor disputes in the railroad industry. The Board is divided into four jurisdictional divisions, of which two have 10 members each, one has eight, and the fourth has six. The members are appointed one-half by the carriers and one-half by the brotherhoods, and are compensated by the parties whom they represent. Because of the even division of members, deadlocks are common. In the event of deadlock, the division may select a referee, but if it fails to do so, the National Mediation Board designates the referee. The referee sits with the division as one of its members and hears the case. The award is written by the referee and must receive a majority vote, including the vote of the referee, for adoption by the division.

The airlines are covered by all the provisions of the Railway Labor Act except §3. Title II of the Act provides for the establishment of special boards of adjustment and a four-member National Air Transport Adjustment Board to handle grievances and disputes between air carriers and their employees over the interpretation or application of the parties' agreements. The powers and duties of the National Air Transport Adjustment Board were to be similar to those of the National Railroad Adjustment Board but it has never been established.

Section III. Judicial Enforcement of the Collective Agreement

A. Federal Oversight: Section 301 of the Labor Management Relations Act

Textile Workers Union v. Lincoln Mills
Supreme Court of the United States
353 U.S. 448, 77 S. Ct. 912, 1 L. Ed. 2d 972 (1957)

Mr. Justice Douglas delivered the opinion of the Court.

Petitioner-union entered into a collective bargaining agreement in 1953 with respondent-employer, the agreement to run one year and from year to year thereafter, unless terminated on specified notices. The agreement provided that there would be no strikes or work stoppages and that grievances would be handled pursuant to a specified procedure. The last step in the grievance procedure—a step that could be taken by either party—was arbitration.

This controversy involves several grievances that concern work loads and work assignments. The grievances were processed through the various steps in the grievance procedure and were finally denied by the employer. The union requested arbitration, and the employer refused. Thereupon the union brought this suit in the District Court to compel arbitration.

The District Court concluded that it had jurisdiction and ordered the employer to comply with the grievance arbitration provisions of the collective bargaining agreement. The Court of Appeals reversed by a divided vote. 230 F.2d 81....

The starting point of our inquiry is § 301 of the Labor Management Relations Act of 1947....

There has been considerable litigation involving § 301 and courts have construed it differently. There is one view that § 301(a) merely gives federal district courts jurisdiction in controversies that involve labor organizations in industries affecting commerce, without regard to diversity of citizenship or the amount in controversy. Under that view § 301(a) would not be the source of substantive law; it would neither supply federal law to resolve these controversies nor turn the federal judges to state law for answers to the questions. Other courts—the overwhelming number of them — hold that § 301(a) is more than jurisdictional — that it authorizes federal courts to fashion a body of federal law for the enforcement of these collective bargaining agreements and includes within that federal law specific performance of promises to arbitrate grievances under collective bargaining agreements. Perhaps the leading decision representing that point of view is the one rendered by Judge Wyzanski in *Textile Workers Union v. American Thread Co.*, 113 F. Supp. 137 (1953). That is our construction of § 301(a), which means that the agreement to arbitrate grievance disputes, contained in this collective bargaining agreement, should be specifically enforced.

From the face of the Act it is apparent that § 301(a) and § 301(b) supplement one another. Section 301(b) makes it possible for a labor organization, representing employees in an industry affecting commerce, to sue and be sued as an entity in the federal courts. Section 301(b) in other words provides the procedural remedy lacking at common law. Section 301(a) certainly does something more than that. Plainly, it supplies the basis upon which the federal district courts may take jurisdiction and apply the procedural rule of § 301(b). The question is whether § 301(a) is more than jurisdictional.

The legislative history of § 301 is somewhat cloudy and confusing. But there are a few shafts of light that illuminate our problem.

The bills, as they passed the House and the Senate, contained provisions which would have made the failure to abide by an agreement to arbitrate an unfair labor practice. S. Rep. No. 105, 80th Cong., 1st Sess., pp. 20–21, 23; H.R. Rep. No. 245, 80th Cong., 1st Sess., p. 21. This feature of the law was dropped in Conference. As the Conference Report stated, "Once parties have made a collective bargaining contract, the enforcement of that contract should be left to the usual processes of the law and not to the National Labor Relations Board." H.R. Conf. Rep. No. 510, 80th Cong., 1st Sess., p. 42.

Both the Senate and the House took pains to provide for "the usual processes of the law" by provisions which were the substantial equivalent of § 301(a) in its present form. Both the Senate Report and the House Report indicate a primary concern that unions as well as employers should be bound to collective bargaining contracts. But there was also a broader concern — a concern with a procedure for making such agreements enforceable in the courts by either party. At one point the Senate Report, *supra* at 15, states, "We feel that the aggrieved party should also have a right of action in the Federal courts. Such a policy is completely in accord with the purpose of the Wagner Act which the Supreme Court declared was 'to compel employers to bargain collectively with their employees to the end that an employment contract, binding on both parties, should be made...."

Congress was also interested in promoting collective bargaining that ended with agreements not to strike....

Thus collective bargaining contracts were made "equally binding and enforceable on both parties." *Id.* at 15. As stated in the House Report, *supra* at 6, the new provision "makes labor organizations equally responsible with employers for contract violations and provides for suit by either against the other in the United States district courts." To repeat, the Senate Report, *supra* at 17, summed up the philosophy of § 301 as follows: "Statutory recognition of the collective agreement as a valid, binding, and enforceable contract is a logical and necessary step. It will promote a higher degree of responsibility upon the parties to such agreements, and will thereby promote industrial peace."

Plainly the agreement to arbitrate grievance disputes is the *quid pro quo* for an agreement not to strike. Viewed in this light, the legislation does more than confer jurisdiction in the federal courts over labor organizations. It expresses a federal policy that federal courts should enforce these agreements on behalf of or against labor organizations and that industrial peace can be best obtained only in that way.

To be sure there is a great medley of ideas reflected in the hearings, reports, and debates on this Act. Yet, to repeat, the entire tenor of the history indicates that the agreement to arbitrate grievance disputes was considered as *quid pro quo* of a no strike agreement. And when in the House the debate narrowed to the question whether § 301 was more than jurisdictional, it became abundantly clear that the purpose of the section was to provide the necessary legal remedies. Section 302 of the House bill, the substantial equivalent of the present § 301, was being described by Mr. Hartley, the sponsor of the bill in the House:

> "Mr. Barden. Mr. Chairman, I take this time for the purpose of asking the Chairman a question, and in asking the question I want it understood that it is intended to make a part of the record that may hereafter be referred to as history of the legislation."
>
> "It is my understanding that Section 302, the section dealing with equal responsibility under collective bargaining contracts in strike actions and proceedings in district courts contemplates not only the ordinary lawsuits for damages but also such other remedial proceedings, both legal and equitable, as might be appropriate in the circumstances; in other words, proceedings could, for example, be brought by the employers, the labor organizations, or interested individual employees under the Declaratory Judgments Act in order to secure declarations from the Court of legal rights under the contract."
>
> "Mr. Hartley. The interpretation the gentlemen has just given of that section is absolutely correct." 93 Cong. Rec. 3656–3657.

It seems, therefore, clear to us that Congress adopted a policy which placed sanctions behind agreements to arbitrate grievance disputes,[1] by implication rejecting the common law rule discussed in *Red Cross Line v. Atlantic Fruit Co.*, 264 U.S. 109

---

1. [6] *Association of Westinghouse Salaried Employees v. Westinghouse Corp.*, 348 U.S. 437 (1955), is quite a different case. There the union sued to recover unpaid wages on behalf of some 4,000 employees. The basic question concerned the standing of the union to sue and recover on those

(1924), against enforcement of executory agreements to arbitrate. We would undercut the Act and defeat its policy if we read § 301 narrowly as only conferring jurisdiction over labor organizations.

The question then is, what is the substantive law to be applied in suits under § 301(a)? We conclude that the substantive law to apply in suits under § 301(a) is federal law which the courts must fashion from the policy of our national labor laws. *See* Mendelsohn, *Enforceability of Arbitration Agreements Under Taft-Hartley Section 301*, 66 Yale L.J. 167. The Labor Management Relations Act expressly furnishes some substantive law. It points out what the parties may or may not do in certain situations. Other problems will lie in the penumbra of express statutory mandates. Some will lack express statutory sanction but will be solved by looking at the policy of the legislation and fashioning a remedy that will effectuate that policy. The range of judicial inventiveness will be determined by the nature of the problem. *See Board of Commissioners v. United States*, 308 U.S. 343, 351 (1939). Federal interpretation of the federal law will govern, not state law. *Cf. Jerome v. United States*, 318 U.S. 101, 104 (1943). But state law, if compatible with the purpose of § 301, may be resorted to in order to find the rule that will best effectuate the federal policy. *See Board of Commissioners v. United States, supra* at 351–352. Any state law applied, however, will be absorbed as federal law and will not be an independent source of private rights.

It is not uncommon for federal courts to fashion federal law where federal rights are concerned. *See Clearfield Trust Co. v. United States*, 318 U.S. 363, 366–367 (1943); *National Metropolitan Bank v. United States*, 323 U.S. 454 (1945). Congress has indicated by § 301(a) the purpose to follow that course here. There is no constitutional difficulty. Article III, § 2 extends the judicial power to cases "arising under . . . the Laws of the United States. . . ." The power of Congress to regulate these labor-management controversies under the Commerce Clause is plain. *Houston Texas R. Co. v. United States*, 234 U.S. 342 (1914); *NLRB v. Jones & Laughlin Corp.*, 301 U.S. 1 (1936). A case or controversy arising under § 301(a) is, therefore, one within the purview of judicial power as defined in Article III.

The question remains whether jurisdiction to compel arbitration of grievance disputes is withdrawn by the Norris-La Guardia Act. . . . Section 7 of that Act prescribes stiff procedural requirements for issuing an injunction in a labor dispute. The kinds of acts which had given rise to abuse of the power to enjoin are listed in § 4. The failure to arbitrate was not a part and parcel of the abuses against which the Act was aimed. Section 8 of the Norris-La Guardia Act does, indeed, indicate a congressional policy toward settlement of labor disputes by arbitration, for it denies injunctive relief to any person who has failed to make "every reasonable effort" to settle the dispute by negotiation, mediation, or "voluntary arbitration." Though a literal reading might bring the dispute within the terms of the Act (*see* Cox, *Grievance*

---

individual employment contracts. The question here concerns the right of the union to enforce the agreement to arbitrate which it has made with the employer.

Arbitration in the Federal Courts, 67 Harv. L. Rev. 591, 602–604), we see no justification in policy for restricting § 301(a) to damage suits, leaving specific performance of a contract to arbitrate grievance disputes to the inapposite procedural requirements of that Act. Moreover, we held in *Virginia R. Co. v. System Federation*, 300 U.S. 515 (1937), and in *Graham v. Brotherhood of Firemen*, 338 U.S. 232, 237 (1949), that the Norris-La Guardia Act does not deprive Federal courts of jurisdiction to compel compliance with the mandates of the Railway Labor Act.... The mandates there involved concerned racial discrimination. Yet those decisions were not based on any peculiarities of the Railway Labor Act. We followed the same course in *Syres v. Oil Workers*, 350 U.S. 892 (1955), which was governed by the National Labor Relations Act.... There an injunction was sought against racial discrimination in application of a collective bargaining agreement; and we allowed the injunction to issue. The congressional policy in favor of the enforcement of agreements to arbitrate grievance disputes being clear, there is no reason to submit them to the requirements of § 7 of the Norris-La Guardia Act....

Reversed.

Mr. Justice Black took no part in the consideration or decision of this case.

Mr. Justice Burton, whom **Mr. Justice Harlan** joins, concurring in the result.

This suit was brought in a United States District Court under § 301 of the Labor Management Relations Act of 1947, ... seeking specific enforcement of the arbitration provisions of a collective bargaining contract. The District Court had jurisdiction over the action since it involved an obligation running to a union — a union controversy — and not uniquely personal rights of employees sought to be enforced by a union. *Cf. Association of Westinghouse Salaried Employees v. Westinghouse Elec. Corp.*, 348 U.S. 437 (1955). Having jurisdiction over the suit, the court was not powerless to fashion an appropriate federal remedy. The power to decree specific performance of a collectively bargained agreement to arbitrate finds its source in § 301 itself, and in a Federal District Court's inherent equitable powers, nurtured by a congressional policy to encourage and enforce labor arbitration in industries affecting commerce.

I do not subscribe to the conclusion of the Court that the substantive law to be applied in a suit under § 301 is federal law. At the same time, I agree with Judge Magruder in *International Brotherhood v. W. L. Mead, Inc.*, 230 F.2d 576 (1st Cir. 1956), that some federal rights may necessarily be involved in a § 301 case, and hence that the constitutionality of § 301 can be upheld as a congressional grant to Federal District Courts of what has been called "protective jurisdiction."

[**Mr. Justice Frankfurter** dissented in a rather unusual 86-page opinion, including the entire relevant legislative history of § 301 of the Taft-Hartley Act and its predecessor bill, the Case bill, in order to prove the point which he had made in *Westinghouse* — that § 301 did not create substantive rights but was only procedural.]

Teamsters, Chauffeurs, Warehousemen & Helpers, Local 174 v. Lucas Flour Co.

Supreme Court of the United States
369 U.S. 95, 82 S. Ct. 571, 7 L. Ed. 2d 593 (1962)

MR. JUSTICE STEWART delivered the opinion of the Court.

The petitioner and the respondent (which we shall call the union and the employer) were parties to a collective bargaining contract within the purview of the National Labor Relations Act. The contract contained the following provisions, among others:

Article II

The Employer reserves the right to discharge any man in his employ if his work is not satisfactory. . . .

Article XIV

Should any difference as to the true interpretation of this agreement arise, same shall be submitted to a Board of Arbitration of two members, one representing the firm, and one representing the Union. If said members cannot agree, a third member, who must be a disinterested party shall be selected, and the decision of the said Board of Arbitration shall be binding. It is further agreed by both parties hereto that during such arbitration, there shall be no suspension of work.

Should any difference arise between the employer and the employee, same shall be submitted to arbitration by both parties. Failing to agree, they shall mutually appoint a third person whose decision shall be final and binding.

In May of 1958, an employee named Welsch was discharged by the employer after he had damaged a new fork lift truck by running it off a loading platform and onto some railroad tracks. When a business agent of the union protested, he was told by a representative of the employer that Welsch had been discharged because of unsatisfactory work. The union thereupon called a strike to force the employer to rehire Welsch. The strike lasted eight days. After the strike was over, the issue of Welsch's discharge was submitted to arbitration. Some five months later the Board of Arbitration rendered a decision, ruling that Welsch's work had been unsatisfactory, that his unsatisfactory work had been the reason for his discharge, and that he was not entitled to reinstatement as an employee.

In the meantime, the employer had brought this suit against the union in the Superior Court of King County, Washington, asking damages for business losses caused by the strike. After a trial that court entered a judgment in favor of the employer in the amount of $6,501.60. On appeal the judgment was affirmed by Department One of the Supreme Court of Washington. 57 Wash. 2d 95, 356 P.2d 1 (1960). The reviewing court held that the preemption doctrine of *San Diego Bldg. Trades Council v. Garmon*, 359 U.S. 236 (1959), did not deprive it of jurisdiction over the controversy. The court further held that § 301 of the Labor Management Relations Act of 1947, 29 U.S.C. § 185, could not "reasonably be interpreted as preempting state jurisdiction, or as affecting it by limiting the substantive law to be applied." 57 Wash. 2d, at 102, 356 P.2d, at 5. Expressly applying principles of state law, the court reasoned that the strike was a violation of the collective bargaining contract, because it was an attempt to coerce the employer to forego his contractual right to discharge an employee for unsatisfactory work. . . .

One of [the] issues — whether § 301(a) of the Labor Management Relations Act of 1947 deprives state courts of jurisdiction over litigation such as this — we have decided this Term in *Charles Dowd Box Co. v. Courtney*, 368 U.S. 502 (1962).[2] For the reasons stated in our opinion in that case, we hold that the Washington Supreme Court was correct in ruling that it had jurisdiction over this controversy. There remain for consideration two other issues, one of them implicated but not specifically decided in *Dowd Box*. Was the Washington court free, as it thought, to decide this controversy within the limited horizon of its local law? If not, does applicable federal law require a result in this case different from that reached by the state court? . . .

It was apparently the theory of the Washington court that, although *Textile Workers v. Lincoln Mills*, 353 U.S. 448 (1957), requires the federal courts to fashion, from the policy of our national labor laws, a body of federal law for the enforcement of collective bargaining agreements, nonetheless, the courts of the states remain free to apply individualized local rules when called upon to enforce such agreements. This view cannot be accepted. The dimensions of § 301 require the conclusion that substantive principles of federal labor law must be paramount in the area covered by the statute. Comprehensiveness is inherent in the process by which the law is to be formulated under the mandate of *Lincoln Mills*, requiring issues raised in suits of a kind covered by § 301 to be decided according to the precepts of federal labor policy.

More important, the subject matter of § 301(a) "is peculiarly one that calls for uniform law." *Pennsylvania R. Co. v. Public Service Comm.*, 250 U.S. 566, 569 (1919). . . . The possibility that individual contract terms might have different meanings under state and federal law would inevitably exert a disruptive influence upon both the negotiation and administration of collective agreements. Because neither

---

2. [9] Since this was a suit for violation of a collective bargaining contract within the purview of § 301(a) of the Labor Management Relations Act of 1947, the preemptive doctrine of cases such as *San Diego Building Trades Council v. Garmon*, 359 U.S. 236 (1959), based upon the exclusive jurisdiction of the National Labor Relations Board, is not relevant. . . . As pointed out in *Charles Dowd Box Co. v. Courtney*, 368 U.S. at 513, Congress "deliberately chose to leave the enforcement of collective agreements 'to the usual processes of law.'" See also H.R. Conf. Rep. No. 510, 80th Cong., 1st Sess. at 52. It is, of course, true that conduct which is a violation of a contractual obligation may also be conduct constituting an unfair labor practice, and what has been said is not to imply that enforcement by a court of a contract obligation affects the jurisdiction of the N.L.R.B. to remedy unfair labor practices, as such. *See generally* Dunau, *Contractual Prohibition of Unfair Labor Practices: Jurisdictional Problems*, 57 Colum. L. Rev. 52 (1957).

party could be certain of the rights which it had obtained or conceded, the process of negotiating an agreement would be made immeasurably more difficult by the necessity of trying to formulate contract provisions in such a way as to contain the same meaning under two or more systems of law which might someday be invoked in enforcing the contract. Once the collective bargain was made, the possibility of conflicting substantive interpretation under competing legal systems would tend to stimulate and prolong disputes as to its interpretation. Indeed, the existence of possibly conflicting legal concepts might substantially impede the parties' willingness to agree to contract terms providing for final arbitral or judicial resolution of disputes.

The importance of the area which would be affected by separate systems of substantive law makes the need for a single body of federal law particularly compelling. The ordering and adjusting of competing interests through a process of free and voluntary collective bargaining is the keystone of the federal scheme to promote industrial peace. State law which frustrates the effort of Congress to stimulate the smooth functioning of that process thus strikes at the very core of federal labor policy. With due regard to the many factors which bear upon competing state and federal interests in this area, . . . we cannot but conclude that in enacting § 301 Congress intended doctrines of federal labor law uniformly to prevail over inconsistent local rules.

Whether, as a matter of federal law, the strike which the union called was a violation of the collective bargaining contract is thus the ultimate issue which this case presents. It is argued that there could be no violation in the absence of a no-strike clause in the contract explicitly covering the subject of the dispute over which the strike was called. We disagree.

The collective bargaining contract expressly imposed upon both parties the duty of submitting the dispute in question to final and binding arbitration. In a consistent course of decisions the Courts of Appeals of at least five Federal Circuits have held that a strike to settle a dispute which a collective bargaining agreement provides shall be settled exclusively and finally by compulsory arbitration constitutes a violation of the agreement. The National Labor Relations Board has reached the same conclusion. *W.L. Mead, Inc.*, 113 N.L.R.B. 1040. We approve that doctrine. To hold otherwise would obviously do violence to accepted principles of traditional contract law. Even more in point, a contrary view would be completely at odds with the basic policy of national labor legislation to promote the arbitral process as a substitute for economic warfare. See *United Steelworkers v. Warrior & Gulf Nav. Co.*, 363 U.S. 574 (1960).

What has been said is not to suggest that a no-strike agreement is to be implied beyond the area which it has been agreed will be exclusively covered by compulsory terminal arbitration. Nor is it to suggest that there may not arise problems in specific cases as to whether compulsory and binding arbitration has been agreed upon, and, if so, as to what disputes have been made arbitrable. But no such problems are present in this case. The grievance over which the union struck was, as it concedes, one which it had expressly agreed to settle by submission to final and binding arbitration proceedings. The strike which it called was a violation of that contractual obligation.

Affirmed.

[The dissenting opinion of MR. JUSTICE BLACK is omitted.]

Notes

1. *Concurrent State and Federal Jurisdiction, Uniform Federal Common Law of Collective Agreements* — Prior to *Lincoln Mills*, the federal circuit courts viewed § 301 as authorizing subject matter jurisdiction over suits for breach of the collective agreement in the federal courts. The Court in *Lincoln Mills* conferred on the federal courts a much broader jurisdiction under § 301 to fashion from the policy of the national labor laws the substance of the law to be applied. Soon thereafter, the Court ensured that the emerging federal labor policy would be uniformly enforced, while simultaneously conferring concurrent jurisdiction on state and federal courts to hear claims. In *Charles Dowd Box Co. v. Courtney*, 368 U.S. 502 (1962), discussed in *Lucas Flour*, the Supreme Court held that § 301 of the Taft-Hartley Act did not divest state courts of jurisdiction over a suit for violation of contract between an employer and a labor organization. To the argument that concurrent state court jurisdiction would lead to a disharmony of result incompatible with the *Lincoln Mills* concept of an all-embracing body of federal law, the Court replied:

> The legislative history of the enactment nowhere suggests that, contrary to the clear import of the statutory language, Congress intended in enacting § 301(a) to deprive a party to a collective bargaining contract of the right to seek redress for its violation in an appropriate state tribunal.... The legislative history makes clear that the basic purpose of § 301(a) was not to limit, but to expand, the availability of forums for the enforcement of contracts made by labor organizations.

Id. at 511.

2. *Suits by Unions to Enforce Employees' Contract Rights* — In *Association of Westinghouse Salaried Employees v. Westinghouse Electric Corp.*, 348 U.S. 437 (1955), the Supreme Court avoided the constitutional question reached and decided *Lincoln Mills* by holding that § 301 was not intended to authorize a union to sue on behalf of employees for accrued wage claims, which were described as "uniquely personal rights." Five years after *Lincoln Mills*, in *Smith v. Evening News Ass'n*, 371 U.S. 195, 199 (1962), *infra*, the Court declared that *Westinghouse* was "no longer authoritative as a precedent." The lower federal courts have accordingly allowed unions to maintain actions to enforce the rights of employees in a distribution of the assets of a negotiated pension fund, *Int'l Union, United Auto. v. Textron, Inc.*, 312 F.2d 688 (6th Cir. 1963); to secure for employees wages due under a cost-of-living adjustment clause in a labor contract, *Retail Clerks Union v. Alfred M. Lewis, Inc.*, 327 F.2d 442 (9th Cir. 1964); and to enforce the rights of retirees to lump-sum compensation for

sick leave, *Siu de Puerto Rico, Caribe Y Latinoamerica v. Virgin Islands Port Auth.*, 42 F.3d 801 (3d Cir. 1994).

3. *Suits Regarding Validity of a Collective Agreement*—In *Textron Lycoming Reciprocating Engine Div. v. United Auto., Aero. & Agric. Implement Workers*, 523 U.S. 653 (1998), the Supreme Court held that a federal court lacked jurisdiction over a union's suit seeking to have a collective bargaining agreement declared void as a result of alleged fraudulent inducement by the employer. During negotiations leading to a new bargaining agreement, the union repeatedly asked the employer to provide it with any information it possessed regarding plans to contract out unit work. Although the company had already drawn up a subcontracting plan, it said nothing to the union. After the new agreement was concluded, the firm announced plans to contract out half of the bargaining unit jobs. The Court held that § 301 jurisdiction is limited to actions over "suits for violation of contracts" and does not apply to suits seeking to have collective contracts declared void. The Court distinguished the situation where a party brings suit to enforce a bargaining agreement and the defendant raises an affirmative defense questioning the legality of the existing agreement. Since such a suit would initially be to enforce the terms of the contract, § 301 jurisdiction would be available, but not where the initial action merely seeks to have the contract declared invalid.

4. *Statute of Limitations Applicable to Section 301 Suits*—In *UAW v. Hoosier Cardinal Corp.*, 383 U.S. 696, 699–700 (1966), the Supreme Court held that § 301 suits are governed by state statutes of limitations. The Court subsequently held, however, that suits by individual employees against their employer for breach of contract and against their labor organization for breach of the duty of fair representation are subject to the six-month limitations period specified in § 10(b) of the NLRA for unfair labor practice cases. *See DelCostello v. Int'l Bhd. of Teamsters*, 462 U.S. 151 (1983). Should union- and employer-initiated suits to compel arbitration and to obtain the enforcement of arbitral awards be similarly governed by the § 10(b) limitations period, instead of by the different state statutory periods? The Circuits are split on the question. *Compare International Bhd. of Teamsters, Local 245 v. Kansas City Piggy Back*, 88 F.3d 659 (8th Cir. 1996) ("No"); *International Longshoremen's Ass'n v. Cataneo, Inc.*, 990 F.2d 794 (4th Cir. 1993) ("No"); *Service Employees Int'l Union Local 36 v. City Cleaning Co.*, 982 F.2d 89 (3rd Cir. 1992) ("No"); *Plumbers' Pension Fund, Local 130 v. Domas Mechanical Contractors, Inc.*, 778 F.2d 1266 (7th Cir. 1985) ("No"); *Derwin v. General Dynamics Corp.*, 719 F.2d 484 (1st Cir. 1983) ("No"); *Int'l Union of Electrical, etc. v. Ingram Mfg. Co.*, 715 F.2d 886 (5th Cir. 1983) ("No"), *with Communications Workers v. American Tel. & Tel. Co.*, 10 F.3d 887 (D.C. Cir. 1993) ("Yes"); *Cummings v. John Morrell & Co.*, 36 F.3d 499 (6th Cir. 1994) ("Yes"); *Cantrell v. International Bhd. of Elec. Workers, Local 2021*, 32 F.3d 465 (10th Cir. 1994) ("Yes").

5. *A Federal Policy Favoring Arbitration of Labor Disputes*— In *Lucas Flour*, the Court embraced a federal policy favoring arbitration as a means of resolving labor disputes, holding that a collective agreement that contains an arbitration clause will be read to include a promise not to strike, whether such an agreement is explicit or not. Because the arbitration machinery is viewed as the quid pro quo for the promise not to strike, the scope of the arbitration agreement determines the scope of the implied promise not to strike, with strikes being barred only as to labor disputes that are subject to binding arbitration. Justice Black, dissenting in *Lucas Flour*, argued that the majority was adding a clause to the contract, on the basis of its own notions of sound policy, that the parties themselves had refused to include. Do you agree? Can this be squared with *H.K. Porter* and the idea that the NLRA is grounded upon the premise of freedom of contract, such that the parties cannot be compelled to agree to any particular clause?

The vast majority of labor contracts that contain grievance and arbitration procedures also prohibit strikes and lockouts over arbitrable issues. One major survey found that 94% of the contracts surveyed contained no-strike pledges, with 63% including unconditional pledges and 31% including conditional pledges (permitting strikes under certain specific circumstances). BUREAU OF NATIONAL AFFAIRS, BASIC PATTERNS IN UNION CONTRACTS 91 (1995). Are these statistics a by-product of the Court's ruling in *Lucas Flour*, or a justification for it? Eighty-nine percent of the contracts contained no-lockout pledges, with 70% of contracts including unconditional pledges and 19%including conditional pledges. *Id.* at 92.

Retail Clerks International Ass'n v. Lion Dry Goods, Inc., 369 U.S. 17, 82 S. Ct. 541, 7 L. Ed. 2d 503 (1962). The union and the employers settled a long strike with a "statement of understanding" in which the union conceded it was not then a majority representative entitled to exclusive recognition. The employers agreed to continue wage schedules and other working conditions in effect, and to arbitrate grievances arising under the statement. Subsequently, the employers refused to abide by arbitration awards disposing of two grievances in favor of the union. The union sued for enforcement under § 301. The employers argued the strike settlement agreement was not a "contract" within the meaning of the statute. On certiorari, the Supreme Court held that the union's action could be maintained under § 301 since "[a] federal forum was provided for actions on other labor contracts besides collective bargaining contracts." Section 301 speaks of "contracts," not collective agreements, the Court observed, and the settlement agreement was a contract, even if not a collective agreement. In addition, the Court held that § 301 was not limited to suits by majority representatives, but extended to actions on the legitimate agreements of minority unions.

Note

In *Plumbers v. Plumbers Local 334*, 452 U.S. 615 (1981), the Supreme Court held that a local union was entitled to maintain an action under § 301 for an alleged violation of the union constitution by the international union in forcing consolidation of several locals. International union constitutions were held to be contracts between labor organizations, and the federal courts have jurisdiction to resolve disputes arising under them. Arguments advanced before the Court that such matters were "internal union affairs" beyond the scope of the Taft-Hartley Act were rejected by the majority as "wide of the mark." Noting an "obvious and important difference" between substantive regulation by the NLRB of internal union affairs and enforcement by the federal courts of "freely entered into agreements between separate labor organizations," the Court found no impediment to federal judicial action in the latter category. In *Wooddell v. International Bhd. of Elec. Workers, Local 71*, 502 U.S. 93 (1991), the Court extended its holding in *Plumbers*, ruling that a union member may sue his or her local under § 301 for a violation of the international constitution. Federal substantive law governed. *See also Shea v. McCarthy*, 953 F.2d 29 (2d Cir. 1992) (holding that § 301 authorizes suits by individual union members against union officials responsible for violations of a union constitution). *Compare SEIU v. Nat'l Union of Healthcare Workers*, 598 F.3d 1061 (9th Cir. 2010) (holding that § 301 supports suit for equitable relief by international union against former members of a local union), *with Korzen v. Local Union 705, Int'l Bhd. of Teamsters*, 75 F.3d 285 (7th Cir. 1996) (distinguishing claims for breach of local union constitutions as actions on contracts between a labor organization and its members from actions on international constitutions, which are agreements among labor organizations). *See also Int'l Longshoremen's Ass'n, Local 333 v. Int'l Longshoremen's Ass'n*, 687 Fed. Appx. 315 (4th Cir. 2017) (holding that nonmembers claiming that the union's failure to admit them to membership violated the union constitution did not have standing because they were not intended beneficiaries).

B. Arbitrability

United Steelworkers v. Warrior & Gulf Navigation Co.
Supreme Court of the United States
363 U.S. 574, 80 S. Ct. 1347, 4 L. Ed. 2d 1409 (1960)

Mr. Justice Douglas delivered the opinion of the Court.

Respondent transports steel and steel products by barge and maintains a terminal at Chickasaw, Alabama, where it performs maintenance and repair work on its barges. The employees at that terminal constitute a bargaining unit covered by a collective bargaining agreement negotiated by petitioner union. Respondent between 1956 and 1958 laid off some employees, reducing the bargaining unit from 42 to 23 men. This reduction was due in part to respondent contracting maintenance work, previously done by its employees, to other companies. The latter used respondent's supervisors to lay out the work and hired some of the laid-off employees of respondent (at reduced wages). Some were in fact assigned to work on respondent's barges. A number of employees signed a grievance which petitioner presented to respondent, the grievance reading:

> We are hereby protesting the Company's actions, of arbitrarily and unreasonably contracting out work to other concerns, that could and previously has been performed by Company employees.

> This practice becomes unreasonable, unjust and discriminatory in lieu [sic] of the fact that at present there are a number of employees that have been laid off for about 1 and 1/2 years or more for allegedly lack of work.
>
> Confronted with these facts we charge that the Company is in violation of the contract by inducing a partial lockout, of a number of the employees who would otherwise be working were it not for this unfair practice.

The collective agreement had both a "no strike" and a "no lockout" provision. It also had a grievance procedure which provided in relevant part as follows:

> Issues which conflict with any Federal statute in its application as established by Court procedure or matters which are strictly a function of management shall not be subject to arbitration under this section.
>
> Should differences arise between the Company and the Union or its members employed by the Company as to the meaning and application of the provisions of this Agreement, or should any local trouble of any kind arise, there shall be no suspension of work on account of such differences but an earnest effort shall be made to settle such differences immediately in the following manner:
>
> A. For Maintenance Employees:
>
> First, between the aggrieved employees, and the Foreman involved;
>
> Second, between a member or members of the Grievance Committee designated by the Union, and the Foreman and Master Mechanic.
>
> . . . .
>
> Fifth, if agreement has not been reached the matter shall be referred to an impartial umpire for decision. The parties shall meet to decide on an umpire acceptable to both. If no agreement on selection of an umpire is reached, the parties shall jointly petition the United States Conciliation Service for suggestion of a list of umpires from which selection will be made. The decision of the umpire shall be final.

Settlement of this grievance was not had and respondent refused arbitration. This suit was then commenced by the union to compel it.

The District Court granted respondent's motion to dismiss the complaint. 168 F. Supp. 702. It held after hearing evidence, much of which went to the merits of the grievance, that the agreement did not "confide in an arbitrator the right to review the defendant's business judgment in contracting out work." *Id.* at 705. It further held that "the contracting out of repair and maintenance work, as well as construction work, is strictly a function of management not limited in any respect by the labor agreement involved here." *Ibid.* The Court of Appeals affirmed by a divided vote, 269 F.2d 633, the majority holding that the collective agreement had withdrawn from the grievance procedure "matters which are strictly a function of management" and that contracting out fell in that exception. . . .

We held in *Textile Workers v. Lincoln Mills*, 353 U.S. 448, that a grievance arbitration provision in a collective agreement could be enforced by reason of § 301(a) of the Labor Management Relations Act and that the policy to be applied in enforcing this type of arbitration was that reflected in our national labor laws. *Id.* at 456–457. The present federal policy is to promote industrial stabilization through the collective bargaining agreement. *Id.* At 453–454. A major factor in achieving industrial peace is the inclusion of a provision for arbitration of grievances in the collective bargaining agreement.[3]

Thus the run of arbitration cases, illustrated by *Wilko v. Swan*, 346 U.S. 427, becomes irrelevant to our problem. There the choice is between the adjudication of cases or controversies in courts with established procedures or even special statutory safeguards on the one hand and the settlement of them in the more informal arbitration tribunal on the other. In the commercial case, arbitration is the substitute for litigation. Here arbitration is the substitute for industrial strife. Since arbitration of labor disputes has quite different functions from arbitration under an ordinary commercial agreement, the hostility evinced by courts toward arbitration of commercial agreements has no place here. For arbitration of labor disputes under collective bargaining agreements is part and parcel of the collective bargaining process itself.

The collective bargaining agreement states the rights and duties of the parties. It is more than a contract; it is a generalized code to govern a myriad of cases which the draftsmen cannot wholly anticipate. *See* Shulman, *Reason, Contract, and Law in Labor Relations*, 68 Harv. L. Rev. 999, 1004–1005. The collective agreement covers the whole employment relationship. It calls into being a new common law — the common law of a particular industry or of a particular plant. As one observer has put it:[4]

> ... [I]t is not unqualifiedly true that a collective bargaining agreement is simply a document by which the union and employees have imposed upon management limited, express restrictions of its otherwise absolute right to manage the enterprise, so that an employee's claim must fail unless he can point to a specific contract provision upon which the claim is founded. There are too many people, too many problems, too many unforeseeable contingencies to make the words of the contract the exclusive source of rights and duties. One cannot reduce all the rules governing a community like an industrial plant to fifteen or even fifty pages. Within the sphere of collective bargaining, the institutional characteristics and the governmental nature of the collective bargaining process demand a common law of

---

3. [4] Complete effectuation of the federal policy is achieved when the agreement contains both an arbitration provision for all unresolved grievances and an absolute prohibition of strikes, the arbitration agreement being the "*quid pro quo*" for the agreement not to strike. *Textile Workers v. Lincoln Mills*, 353 U.S. 448, 455.

4. [6] Cox, *Reflections Upon Labor Arbitration*, 72 Harv. L. Rev. 1482, 1498–1499 (1959).

the shop which implements and furnishes the context of the agreement. We must assume that intelligent negotiators acknowledged so plain a need unless they stated a contrary rule in plain words.

A collective bargaining agreement is an effort to erect a system of industrial self-government. When most parties enter into contractual relationship they do so voluntarily, in the sense that there is no real compulsion to deal with one another, as opposed to dealing with other parties. This is not true of the labor agreement. The choice is generally not between entering or refusing to enter into a relationship, for that in all probability preexists the negotiations. Rather it is between having that relationship governed by an agreed-upon rule of law or leaving each and every matter subject to a temporary resolution dependent solely upon the relative strength, at any given moment, of the contending forces. The mature labor agreement may attempt to regulate all aspects of the complicated relationship, from the most crucial to the most minute over an extended period of time. Because of the compulsion to reach agreement and the breadth of the matters covered, as well as the need for a fairly concise and readable instrument, the product of negotiations (the written document) is, in the words of the late Dean Shulman, "a compilation of diverse provisions: some provide objective criteria almost automatically applicable; some provide more or less specific standards which require reason and judgment in their application; and some do little more than leave problems to future consideration with an expression of hope and good faith." Shulman, *supra* at 1005. Gaps may be left to be filled in by reference to the practices of the particular industry and of the various shops covered by the agreement. Many of the specific practices which underlie the agreement may be unknown, except in hazy form, even to the negotiators. Courts and arbitration in the context of most commercial contracts are resorted to because there has been a breakdown in the working relationship of the parties; such resort is the unwanted exception. But the grievance machinery under a collective bargaining agreement is at the very heart of the system of industrial self-government. Arbitration is the means of solving the unforeseeable by molding a system of private law for all the problems which may arise and to provide for their solution in a way which will generally accord with the variant needs and desires of the parties. The processing of disputes through the grievance machinery is actually a vehicle by which meaning and content are given to the collective bargaining agreement.

Apart from matters that the parties specifically exclude, all of the questions on which the parties disagree must therefore come within the scope of the grievance and arbitration provisions of the collective agreement. The grievance procedure is, in other words, a part of the continuous collective bargaining process. It, rather than a strike, is the terminal point of a disagreement. . . .

> A proper conception of the arbitrator's function is basic. He is not a public tribunal imposed upon the parties by superior authority which the parties are obliged to accept. He has no general charter to administer justice for a community which transcends the parties. He is rather part of a system of self-government created by and confined to the parties. . . .

Shulman, *supra* at 1016.

The labor arbitrator's source of law is not confined to the express provisions of the contract, as the industrial common law—the practices of the industry and the shop—is equally a part of the collective bargaining agreement although not expressed in it. The labor arbitrator is usually chosen because of the parties' confidence in his knowledge of the common law of the shop and their trust in his personal judgment to bring to bear considerations which are not expressed in the contract as criteria for judgment. The parties expect that his judgment of a particular grievance will reflect not only what the contract says but, insofar as the collective bargaining agreement permits, such factors as the effect upon productivity of a particular result, its consequence to the morale of the shop, his judgment whether tensions will be heightened or diminished. For the parties' objective in using the arbitration process is primarily to further their common goal of uninterrupted production under the agreement, to make the agreement serve their specialized needs. The ablest judge cannot be expected to bring the same experience and competence to bear upon the determination of a grievance, because he cannot be similarly informed.

The Congress, however, has by §301 of the Labor Management Relations Act, assigned the courts the duty of determining whether the reluctant party has breached his promise to arbitrate. For arbitration is a matter of contract and a party cannot be required to submit to arbitration any dispute which he has not agreed so to submit. Yet, to be consistent with congressional policy in favor of settlement of disputes by the parties through the machinery of arbitration, the judicial inquiry under §301 must be strictly confined to the question whether the reluctant party did agree to arbitrate the grievance or did agree to give the arbitrator power to make the award he made. An order to arbitrate the particular grievance should not be denied unless it may be said with positive assurance that the arbitration clause is not susceptible of an interpretation that covers the asserted dispute. Doubts should be resolved in favor of coverage.[5]

We do not agree with the lower courts that contracting-out grievances were necessarily excepted from the grievance procedure of this agreement. To be sure, the agreement provides that "matters which are strictly a function of management shall not be subject to arbitration." But it goes on to say that if "differences" arise or if "any local trouble of any kind" arises, the grievance procedure shall be applicable.

Collective bargaining agreements regulate or restrict the exercise of management functions; they do not oust management from the performance of them. Management hires and fires, pays and promotes, supervises and plans. All these are part of

---

5. [7] It is clear that under both the agreement in this case and that involved in *American Mfg. Co., supra* at 564, the question of arbitrability is for the courts to decide. *Cf.* Cox, *Reflections Upon Labor Arbitration*, 72 Harv. L. Rev. 1482, 1508–1509 (1959). Where the assertion by the claimant is that the parties excluded from court determination not merely the decision of the merits of the grievance but also the question of its arbitrability, vesting power to make both decisions in the arbitrator, the claimant must bear the burden of a clear demonstration of that purpose.

its function, and absent a collective bargaining agreement, it may be exercised freely except as limited by public law and by the willingness of employees to work under the particular, unilaterally imposed conditions. A collective bargaining agreement may treat only with certain specific practices, leaving the rest to management but subject to the possibility of work stoppages. When, however, an absolute no-strike clause is included in the agreement, then in a very real sense everything that management does is subject to the agreement, for either management is prohibited or limited in the action it takes, or if not, it is protected from interference by strikes. This comprehensive reach of the collective bargaining agreement does not mean, however, that the language, "strictly a function of management," has no meaning.

"Strictly a function of management" might be thought to refer to any practice of management in which, under particular circumstances prescribed by the agreement, it is permitted to indulge. But if courts, in order to determine arbitrability, were allowed to determine what is permitted and what is not, the arbitration clause would be swallowed up by the exception. Every grievance in a sense involves a claim that management has violated some provision of the agreement.

Accordingly, "strictly a function of management" must be interpreted as referring only to that over which the contract gives management complete control and unfettered discretion. Respondent claims that the contracting out of work falls within this category. Contracting out work is the basis of many grievances; and that type of claim is grist in the mills of the arbitrators. A specific collective bargaining agreement may exclude contracting out from the grievance procedure. Or a written collateral agreement may make clear that contracting out was not a matter for arbitration. In such a case a grievance based solely on contracting out would not be arbitrable. Here, however, there is no such provision. Nor is there any showing that the parties designed the phrase "strictly a function of management" to encompass any and all forms of contracting out. In the absence of any express provision excluding a particular grievance from arbitration, we think only the most forceful evidence of a purpose to exclude the claim from arbitration can prevail, particularly where, as here, the exclusion clause is vague and the arbitration clause quite broad. Since any attempt by a court to infer such a purpose necessarily comprehends the merits, the court should view with suspicion an attempt to persuade it to become entangled in the construction of the substantive provisions of a labor agreement, even through the back door of interpreting the arbitration clause, when the alternative is to utilize the services of an arbitrator.

The grievance alleged that the contracting out was a violation of the collective bargaining agreement. There was, therefore, a dispute "as to the meaning and application of the provisions of this Agreement" which the parties had agreed would be determined by arbitration.

The judiciary sits in these cases to bring into operation an arbitral process which substitutes a regime of peaceful settlement for the older regime of industrial conflict. Whether contracting out in the present case violated the agreement is the question. It is a question for the arbiter, not for the courts.

Reversed.

MR. JUSTICE FRANKFURTER concurs in the result.

MR. JUSTICE BLACK took no part in the consideration or decision of this case....

MR. JUSTICE BRENNAN, with whom MR. JUSTICE HARLAN joins, concurring....

The issue in the *Warrior* case is essentially no different from that in *American* [*infra*], that is, it is whether the company agreed to arbitrate a particular grievance. In contrast to *American*, however, the arbitration promise here excludes a particular area from arbitration — "matters which are strictly a function of management." Because the arbitration promise is different, the scope of the court's inquiry may be broader. Here, a court may be required to examine the substantive provisions of the contract to ascertain whether the parties have provided that contracting out shall be a "function of management." If a court may delve into the merits to the extent of inquiring whether the parties have expressly agreed whether or not contracting out was a "function of management," why was it error for the lower court here to evaluate the evidence of bargaining history for the same purpose? Neat logical distinctions do not provide the answer. The Court rightly concludes that appropriate regard for the national labor policy and the special factors relevant to the labor arbitral process, admonish that judicial inquiry into the merits of this grievance should be limited to the search for an explicit provision which brings the grievance under the cover of the exclusion clause since "the exclusion clause is vague and arbitration clause quite broad." The hazard of going further into the merits is amply demonstrated by what the courts below did. On the basis of inconclusive evidence, those courts found that Warrior was in no way limited by any implied covenants of good faith and fair dealing from contracting out as it pleased — which would necessarily mean that Warrior was free completely to destroy the collective bargaining agreement by contracting out all the work.

The very ambiguity of the *Warrior* exclusion clause suggests that the parties were generally more concerned with having an arbitrator render decisions as to the meaning of the contract than they were in restricting the arbitrator's jurisdiction. The case might of course be otherwise were the arbitration clause very narrow, or the exclusion clause quite specific, for the inference might then be permissible that the parties had manifested a greater interest in confining the arbitrator; the presumption of arbitrability would then not have the same force and the Court would be somewhat freer to examine into the merits.

The Court makes reference to an arbitration clause being the *quid pro quo* for a no-strike clause. I do not understand the Court to mean that the application of the principles announced today depends upon the presence of a no-strike clause in the agreement.

MR. JUSTICE FRANKFURTER joins these observations.

[The dissenting opinion of MR. JUSTICE WHITTAKER is omitted.]

United Steelworkers v. American Mfg. Co., 363 U.S. 564, 80 S. Ct. 1343, 4 L. Ed. 2d 1403 (1960). A collective bargaining agreement contained a "standard" arbitration clause covering "any disputes" between the parties "as to the meaning, interpretation and application of the provisions of this agreement." The union agreed not to strike unless the employer refused to abide by a decision of the arbitrator. The contract reserved to management the power to suspend or discipline any employee "for cause." It also provided that the employer would employ and promote employees on "the principle of seniority . . . where ability and efficiency are equal." An employee left work due to an injury and later settled a worker's compensation claim against the company on the basis he was permanently partially disabled. Thereafter the union filed a grievance charging that the employee was entitled to return to his job under the seniority provision. The employer refused to arbitrate and the union sued. The Supreme Court held that arbitration should have been ordered. Declared the Court:

> The function of the court is very limited when the parties have agreed to submit all questions of contract interpretation to the arbitrator. It is confined to ascertaining whether the party seeking arbitration is making a claim which on its face is governed by the contract. Whether the moving party is right or wrong is a question of contract interpretation for the arbitrator. . . . The courts, therefore, have no business weighing the merits of the grievance. . . . The processing of even frivolous claims may have therapeutic values of which those who are not a part of the plant environment may be quite unaware.

Note

The two preceding cases, together with *Enterprise Wheel, infra*, are familiarly known as the *Steelworkers Trilogy*. Together, these cases mandate both judicial determination of arbitrability and a broad presumption of arbitrability. Federal courts continue to apply these principles quite consistently. *See, e.g., Bakery, Confectionary, Tobacco Workers and Grain Millers, Int'l Union AFL-CIO v. Kellogg Co.*, 904 F.3d 435 (6th Cir. 2018) (arbitration of dispute over whether casual employees were entitled to a ratification bonus under the collective agreement was required under a broad arbitration clause where provision excluding certain disputes from arbitration was ambiguous); *IBEW Local 2150 v. NextEra Energy Point Breach, LLC*, 762 F.3d 592 (7th Cir. 2014), *cert. denied*, 574 U.S. 1121 (2015) (arbitration of discharge decision required even where discharge arguably not disciplinary and arbitration clause referenced "claims of disciplinary action or discharge"); *UNITE HERE Local 217 v. Sage Hospitality Res.*, 642 F.3d 255 (1st Cir. 2011) (despite ambiguous language in the duration clause of a neutrality agreement between the employer and the union, arbitration required where agreement included broad arbitration provision applicable to disputes concerning construction of the contract).

Even a dispute arising under a side agreement or an oral understanding is arbitrable if the dispute is sufficiently connected to the labor contract's arbitration clause. *See Teamsters Local Union No. 89 v. Kroger Co.*, 617 F.3d 899 (6th Cir. 2010); *see generally* Bales, *The Arbitrability of Side and Settlement Agreements in the Collective Bargaining Context*, 105 W. Va. L. Rev. 575 (2003). However, the circuits are divided on the proper test to apply to determine whether such an agreement is subject to arbitration. Some circuits employ a "scope" test, under which an agreement is arbitrable if the agreement covers subjects within the scope of the arbitration clause, and the parties have not specifically disclaimed arbitrability of side agreements. Others employ a "collateral" test, under which an agreement is arbitrable only if it addresses subjects sufficiently related to those covered by the agreement containing the arbitration clause. *Compare Teamsters Local Union No. 783 v. Anheuser-Busch, Inc.*, 626 F.3d 256 (6th Cir. 2010) ("scope" test), *Inlandboatmen's Union of the Pac. v. Dutra Group*, 279 F.3d 1075 (9th Cir. 2002) ("scope" test), *Niro v. Fearn International, Inc.*, 827 F.2d 173 (7th Cir. 1987) ("scope" test), *and L.O. Koven & Bro., Inc. v. United Steelworkers of America*, 381 F.2d 196 (3d Cir. 1967) ("scope" test), *with USW, AFL-CIO-CLC v. Duluth Clinic, Ltd.*, 413 F.3d 786 (8th Cir. 2005) ("collateral" test), *Louis Dreyfus Negoce S.A. v. Blystad Shipping & Trading, Inc.*, 252 F.3d 218 (2d Cir. 2001) ("collateral" test), *and Adkins v. Times-World Corp.*, 771 F.2d 829 (4th Cir. 1985) ("collateral" test), *cert. denied*, 474 U.S. 1109 (1986).

AT&T Technologies, Inc. v. Communications Workers of America, 475 U.S. 643, 106 S. Ct. 1415, 89 L. Ed. 2d 648 (1986). A contractual provision prescribed the order in which employees were to be laid off "[w]hen lack of work necessitates Layoff." The CWA sought arbitration over layoffs that it claimed were not caused by a "lack of work." AT&T refused to arbitrate, claiming that it had made its reduction-in-force determination pursuant to the authority it possessed under a broad management-rights provision that expressly excluded matters of managerial prerogative from arbitral consideration. The district court, after finding that the union's suggested contractual interpretation was at least "arguable," held that it was for the arbitrator — not the court — to decide whether that interpretation was in fact meritorious. It thus directed the parties to have the arbitrator decide the arbitrability dispute. The Seventh Circuit affirmed this approach. The Supreme Court, however, unanimously rejected this view of the judicial function in such cases. The Supreme Court reaffirmed the principles set forth in the *Steelworkers Trilogy*, and emphasized that district courts, and not arbitrators, are required to resolve substantive arbitrability questions:

> [T]he question of arbitrability — whether a collective-bargaining agreement creates a duty for the parties to arbitrate the particular grievance — is undeniably an issue for judicial determination. Unless the parties clearly and unmistakably provide otherwise, the question of whether the parties agreed to arbitrate is to be decided by the court, not the arbitrator. . . . It is the court's duty to interpret the agreement and to determine whether the parties intended to arbitrate grievances concerning layoffs predicated

on a "lack of work" determination by the Company. If the court determines that the agreement so provides, then it is for the arbitrator to determine the relative merits of the parties' substantive interpretations of the agreement.

Granite Rock Co. v. Int'l Bhd. of Teamsters, 561 U.S. 287, 130 S. Ct. 2847, 177 L. Ed.2d 567 (2010). A supplier of building materials and a union had negotiated a collective bargaining agreement following a strike that included a no-strike provision, but the union went on strike again when the company refused to agree to a back-to-work provision that would have shielded the union and its members from liability for damages from the previous strike. The company sued to enforce the no-strike provision, and amended its complaint to add claims for economic damages arising from breach of the contract after the union held a vote to ratify the agreement and called off the strike. The parties disagreed on whether the agreement had been in force prior to the second strike or only after the later ratification vote. The district court held that the question of when the contract was signed was for the court to decide, concluded that the agreement had been ratified before the strike, and ordered arbitration of the employer's claims concerning economic damages arising from the strike. The Ninth Circuit reversed, basing its decision on two principles: first, that when both parties concede that they agreed to an arbitration clause, any ambiguities regarding its scope should be resolved in favor of arbitration, and second, that the "presumption of arbitrability applies even to disputes about the enforceability of the entire contract containing the arbitration clause."

The Supreme Court reversed, ruling that the principle that courts must resolve disputes over whether the parties had agreed to arbitration extends to disputes concerning when an agreement was formed as well as its scope. The Court stressed that only when both parties have consented to arbitration may the courts require that a party submit to arbitration on that issue, and reiterated that courts have a duty to determine whether the parties agreed to arbitration in the first instance. The Court explained:

> These unusual facts require us to reemphasize the proper framework for deciding when disputes are arbitrable under our precedents. Under that framework, a court may order arbitration of a particular dispute only where the court is satisfied that the parties agreed to arbitrate *that dispute*. *AT&T Technologies, supra*, at 648–649, 106 S. Ct. 1415, 89 L. Ed. 2d 648. [citations omitted] To satisfy itself that such agreement exists, the court must resolve any issue that calls into question the formation or applicability of the specific arbitration clause that a party seeks to have the court enforce. (citation omitted). Where there is no provision validly committing them to an arbitrator ... these issues typically concern the scope of the arbitration clause and its enforceability. In addition, these issues always include whether the clause was agreed to, and may include when that agreement was formed.

The parties agree that it was proper for the District Court to decide whether their ratification dispute was arbitrable. They disagree about whether the District Court answered the question correctly. Local contends that the District Court erred in holding that the CBA's ratification date was an issue for the court to decide. The Court of Appeals agreed, holding that the District Court's refusal to send that dispute to arbitration violated [the] principles of arbitrability set forth in our precedents. See 546 F.3d at 1177–1178. . . .

Local contends that our precedents, particularly those applying the "'federal policy favoring arbitration of labor disputes,'" permit no other result. Brief for Respondent Local, p. 15 (quoting *Gateway Coal Co.* v. *Mine Workers*, 414 U.S. 368, 377, 94 S. Ct. 629, 38 L. Ed. 2d 583 (1974)). . . . Local, like the Court of Appeals, overreads our precedents. The language and holdings on which Local and the Court of Appeals rely cannot be divorced from the first principle that underscores all of our arbitration decisions: Arbitration is strictly "a matter of consent," and thus "is a way to resolve those disputes—*but only those disputes*—that the parties have agreed to submit to arbitration." (citations omitted). Applying this principle, our precedents hold that courts should order arbitration of a dispute only where the court is satisfied that neither the formation of the parties' arbitration agreement *nor* (absent a valid provision specifically committing such disputes to an arbitrator) its enforceability or applicability to the dispute is in issue. Where a party contests either or both matters, "the court" must resolve the disagreement.

Local nonetheless interprets some of our opinions to depart from this framework and to require arbitration of certain disputes, particularly labor disputes, based on policy grounds even where evidence of the parties' agreement to arbitrate the dispute in question is lacking. See Brief for Respondent Local, p. 16 (citing cases emphasizing the policy favoring arbitration generally and the "impressive policy considerations favoring arbitration" in LMRA cases (internal quotation marks omitted)). That is not a fair reading of the opinions, all of which compelled arbitration of a dispute only after the Court was persuaded that the parties' arbitration agreement was validly formed and that it covered the dispute in question and was legally enforceable. . . .

. . . .

Our cases invoking the federal "policy favoring arbitration" of commercial and labor disputes apply the same framework. They recognize that, except where "the parties clearly and unmistakably provide otherwise," *AT&T Technologies*, 475 U.S., at 649, 106 S. Ct. 1415, 89 L. Ed. 2d 648, it is "the court's duty to interpret the agreement and to determine whether the parties intended to arbitrate grievances concerning" a particular matter, *id.*, at 651, 106 S. Ct. 1415, 89 L. Ed. 2d 648. They then discharge this duty by: (1) applying the presumption of arbitrability only where a validly formed and enforceable arbitration agreement is ambiguous about whether it covers the dispute at hand; and (2) adhering to the presumption and ordering arbitration only where the presumption is not rebutted. (citations omitted).

To the union's argument that the Court's analysis contravened *United Steelworkers v. Warrior & Gulf Navigation, supra*, the Court responded:

> Local is...wrong to suggest that the presumption of arbitrability we sometimes apply takes courts outside our settled framework [under *Warrior & Gulf*] for deciding arbitrability. The presumption simply assists in resolving arbitrability disputes within that framework. Confining the presumption to this role reflects its foundation in "the federal policy favoring arbitration."... We have applied the presumption favoring arbitration, in FAA and in labor cases, only where it reflects, and derives its legitimacy from, a judicial conclusion that arbitration of a particular dispute is what the parties intended because their express agreement to arbitrate was validly formed and (absent a provision clearly and validly committing such issues to an arbitrator) is legally enforceable and best construed to encompass the dispute. (citations omitted). This simple framework compels reversal of the Court of Appeals' judgment because it requires judicial resolution of two questions central to Local's arbitration demand: when the CBA was formed, and whether its arbitration clause covers the matters Local wishes to arbitrate.

On remand, the Ninth Circuit ruled that because the employer had asserted a legal claim for monetary damages for breach of the no-strike clause in the collective bargaining contract, it was entitled to a jury trial under § 301 of the Labor Management Relations Act. The court also held that the employer was not estopped from asserting in that proceeding its argument that the union ratified the contract on a specific date. *Granite Rock Co. v. Int'l Bhd. of Teamsters Local 287*, 649 F.3d 1067 (9th Cir. 2011), *cert. denied*, 565 U.S. 1087 (2011).

Notes

1. *Presumption of Arbitrability*—Cases from the circuit courts reaffirm the principle that arbitrability is for the courts to decide, with "doubts [being] resolved in favor of coverage." *See Local Joint Exec. Bd. v. Mirage Casino-Hotel, Inc.*, 911 F.3d 588 (9th Cir. 2018) (arbitrator exceeded authority by determining that union's grievance over casino's failure to pay accrued vacation time was not arbitrable and union did not implicitly authorize arbitrator to determine arbitrability by agreeing to arbitrate substantive issues and failing to halt arbitration proceedings); *Int'l Ass'n of Machinists & Aero. Workers v. AK Steel Corp.*, 615 F.3d 706 (6th Cir. 2010) (in absence of clear and unmistakable provision that substantive arbitrability should be decided by arbitrator, issue of substantive arbitrability of grievances under a transition agreement was for courts to decide); *see also Smith v. Transport Workers Union of Am.*, 374 F.3d 372 (5th Cir. 2004) (arbitration panel lacked authority to modify its own award; question whether panel could do so was for court to decide).

Even though specific issues are expressly excluded from arbitral coverage, courts will order arbitration when the challenged conduct may have contravened other contractual provisions subject to arbitral resolution, so long as it is not unequivocally clear that the parties intended to exclude these disputes entirely from arbitral coverage. *International Brotherhood of Electrical Workers, Local No. 4 v. KTVI-TV, Inc.*, 985 F.2d 415 (8th Cir. 1993). *But cf. General Drivers, Local Union No. 509 v. Ethyl Corp.*, 68 F.3d 80 (4th Cir. 1995) (no arbitration of union's grievance that job-promotion tests discriminated on the basis of race and age where collective bargaining agreement excluded from arbitration "matters affecting wages and rates of pay," because tests in effect determined pay rates); *International Bhd. of Teamsters, Local 371 v. Logistics Support Group*, 999 F.2d 227 (7th Cir. 1993) (no arbitration of discharge in absence of "just cause" provision when contract limited arbitration to express provisions).

2. *Who Decides Procedural Issues?* — Should the question whether a union's request to arbitrate certain grievances is timely under a time limit specified in the collective bargaining agreement be decided by the arbitrator or the courts? Most courts consider this a procedural matter for the arbitrator rather than a substantive question concerning whether the parties have agreed to arbitrate the particular dispute under a valid and binding contract — even if, as a practical matter, the procedural questions control whether the underlying disagreement will be arbitrated. *See Brown & Pipkins, LLC v. SEIU*, 846 F.3d 716 (4th Cir. 2017) (arbitrator acted within his authority in applying a continuing violation theory to find timely a grievance filed outside the time limits prescribed by the collective agreement, because issue was procedural); *Teamsters Local Union 480 v. UPS*, 748 F.3d 281 (6th Cir. 2014) (attacks on the validity of a collective bargaining agreement concerning procedural requirements for arbitrating a case should be resolved by the arbitrator); *Local 38N Graphic Communs. Conference/IBT v. St. Louis Post-Dispatch, LLC*, 638 F.3d 824 (8th Cir. 2011) (issues of procedural arbitrability are within an arbitrator's discretion, including waiver, delay, or similar defenses to arbitrability). Does the Court's decision in *Granite Rock*, *supra*, affect these rulings? *Cf. UNITE HERE Local 217 v. Sage Hospitality Res.*, 642 F.3d 255 (1st Cir. 2011) (distinguishing *Granite Rock* in a case involving a dispute over the contract termination date, which is a procedural matter for arbitrator distinct from questions concerning the formation of the agreement, its enforceability or applicability to the dispute, which are for the court).

3. *Overlap with NLRB Jurisdiction* — Does a district court have jurisdiction to compel an employer to arbitrate a union grievance despite the employer's contention that the dispute constituted a representational matter within the exclusive jurisdiction of the Labor Board? *See IBEW, Local 71 v. Trafftech, Inc.*, 461 F.3d 690 (6th Cir. 2006) (ruling that district court had jurisdiction to compel arbitration of claim challenging employer's assignment of bargaining unit work to members of a different labor organization, since grievance alleged violations of specific provisions of operative bargaining agreement).

4. *Failure to Exhaust Grievance Procedure — When Justified* — Where an employer refuses to arbitrate a grievance pursuant to a collective bargaining agreement,

the union may proceed directly under LMRA §301 with a breach of contract suit against the employer. In *Sidhu v. Flecto Co.*, 279 F.3d 896 (9th Cir. 2002), the employer refused to permit a laid-off employee to return to work following a medical leave. The union filed a grievance, but the employer declined to arbitrate on the basis that the grievance was not arbitrable. The union then brought an action under §301 in the individual employee's name, seeking to enforce his contractual rights. Although the district court dismissed the case because the union had failed to exhaust the grievance procedure by not seeking to compel arbitration, the Ninth Circuit reversed, ruling that the company's refusal to arbitrate excused noncompliance with the usual exhaustion requirement. The company had effectively repudiated the grievance procedures as to this employee's claim, and hence a direct §301 claim was available.

C. Arbitration Under Lapsed Collective Bargaining Agreements

Nolde Bros. v. Bakery & Confectionery Workers Local 358, 430 U.S. 243, 97 S. Ct. 1067, 51 L. Ed. 2d 300 (1977). A union and an employer had a contract providing that "any grievance" between the parties was subject to binding arbitration. After negotiating for three months for a contract renewal, the union exercised its option to cancel the existing agreement by giving a seven-day termination notice. Negotiations continued for four days past the effective date of the termination. Then the company, faced by a threatened strike, informed the union that it was permanently closing its plant. The company paid the employees their accrued wages and vacation pay but rejected the union's demand for severance pay called for in the labor agreement. The employer also declined to arbitrate the severance pay claims on the ground its duty to arbitrate terminated with the contract. The union sued under §301 to compel arbitration. The Supreme Court, per Chief Justice Burger, held that the issue was arbitrable. "The dispute ... although arising *after* the expiration of the collective bargaining agreement, clearly arises *under* that contract.... [N]othing in the arbitration clause ... expressly excludes ... a dispute which arises under the contract, but which is based on events that occur after its termination.... By their contract the parties clearly expressed their preference for an arbitral, rather than a judicial interpretation of their obligations...." Justices Stewart and Rehnquist dissented, arguing: "The closing of the [plant] necessarily meant that there was no continuing relationship to protect or preserve.... And the Union's termination of the contract, thereby releasing it from its obligation not to strike, foreclosed any reason for implying a continuing duty on the part of the employer to arbitrate as a *quid pro quo*."

Notes

1. *Disputes "Arising Under the Contract"* — In *Litton Fin. Printing Div. v. NLRB*, 501 U.S. 190 (1991), an employer unilaterally modified its operations and laid off some of its most senior employees 10 to 11 months after the expiration of a contract calling for layoffs on the basis of seniority. The NLRB found a §8(a)(5) violation and directed bargaining but refused to order arbitration. A 5-4 Supreme Court majority agreed that under *Nolde* post-expiration arbitration is required only with respect to "disputes arising under the contract." That would involve facts occurring before the contract expired or involving "accrued or vested rights." The four dissenting Justices believed that the majority had improperly examined the merits of the contractual dispute in the guise of determining arbitrability. *Compare Local 38N Graphic Communications Conference/IBT v. St. Louis Post-Dispatch, LLC*, 638 F.3d 824 (8th Cir. 2011) (dispute based upon facts occurring after the expiration date of the labor contract was beyond the scope of arbitration clause that expressly excluded grievances based upon events occurring after the contract expired), *with Detroit Typographical Union, Local 18 v. Detroit Newspaper Agency*, 283 F.3d 779 (6th Cir.), *cert. denied*, 537 U.S. 824 (2002) (upholding arbitrator's decision on whether employee's conduct in staging sit-down strike constituted just cause for discharge under expired labor contract that guaranteed a vested right to lifetime employment, citing *Litton*; disputes regarding such vested benefits must be resolved pursuant to the arbitration provisions of the expired contract).

2. *Timing Issues*—A possible difficulty arises under *Litton* when some facts occur before the expiration of the contract and some after. In *South Cent. Power Co. v. IBEW, Local 2359*, 186 F.3d 733 (6th Cir. 1999), the Sixth Circuit concluded that a dispute arose under the contract "when a *majority* of the *material* facts and occurrences arose before the expiration of the collective bargaining agreement." *See also Operating Eng'rs Local 3 v. Newmont Mining Corp.*, 476 F.3d 690 (9th Cir. 2007) (adopting the Sixth Circuit's logic, but concluding that the standard was not merely adding up the number of facts, or even the number of "important" facts, but rather those facts that the parties had agreed to submit to arbitration). *But cf. Trinidad Corp. v. National Maritime Union, Dist. No. 4*, 81 F.3d 769 (8th Cir. 1996) (concluding that the court's role was limited to determining whether "any" of the facts had occurred prior to termination).

3. *Reconciling Nolde Bros. and Litton*—In *Luden's Inc. v. Local 6 of the Bakery, Confectionery & Tobacco Workers Int'l Union*, 28 F.3d 347 (3d Cir. 1994), the court sought to harmonize the seemingly conflicting Supreme Court holdings in *Nolde Bros.* and *Litton Fin. Printing Div.* While *Nolde Bros.* seemed to create a judicial presumption in favor of arbitration with respect to disputes arising under lapsed contracts, *Litton Fin. Printing Div.* suggested that courts have a duty to review the merits of grievance claims to determine if the lapsed agreements actually created the rights being asserted. The Third Circuit decided that it preferred the *Nolde Bros.* approach, as it held that courts determining the arbitrability of grievances arising under lapsed contracts should not reach the merits of the underlying controversies. They should merely decide if the lapsed contracts "arguably" created the obligations the grievants seek to enforce. Since the *Luden's* court found an implied-in-fact collective contract that appeared to continue the grievance-arbitration procedures during the period

between formal agreements, it directed arbitration of the grievance in question. Similarly, in *United Steel, Paper and Forestry, Rubber, Mfg., Energy, Allied Indus. & Serv. Workers Int'l Union v. Trimas Corp.*, 531 F.3d 531 (7th Cir. 2008), the court ruled that the scope of a neutrality and card check agreement negotiated between the employer's parent company and the union was for the arbitrator, not the court. The court refused to consider evidence of oral side agreements that the company claimed operated to modify the intended scope of the neutrality agreement, which it called "extrinsic attacks" on the contract that contained the arbitration clause. The court reasoned that allowing this argument would require interpretation of the substantive terms of the agreement and entangle the court in the merits of the dispute, denying the parties the benefit of the bargain that they made to have an arbitrator rather than a court interpret their contract. Because "on its face" the union's claim was governed by the neutrality agreement, the court compelled the parties to arbitrate.

Other courts, however, have reached the opposite conclusion. *See, e.g., Rite Aid of Pennsylvania, Inc. v. UFCW, Local 1776*, 595 F.3d 128 (3d Cir. 2010) ("where the merits and arbitrability questions are inextricably intertwined, a court's arbitrability decision may, of necessity, touch incidentally on the merits"); *see also United Steel Workers Local 850L v. Cont'l Tire North Am., Inc.*, 568 F.3d 158 (4th Cir. 2009) (concluding that "courts are permitted some latitude to interpret provisions of a bargaining agreement," but that they should avoid ruling on the merits as much as possible); *Crown Cork & Seal Co. v. International Ass'n of Machinists and Aero. Workers*, 501 F.3d 912 (8th Cir. 2007) (concluding that, while the union had cited to some cases that "managed to decide the question of arbitrability without getting to the merits," other cases had "addressed the merits of an underlying dispute in order to determine arbitrability," and the court saw "no way to avoid examining and interpreting language" to determine if employee benefits at issue had vested); *Stevens Constr. Corp. v. Chi. Reg'l Council of Carpenters*, 464 F.3d 682 (7th Cir. 2006) (district court did not err in ruling on the merits of question whether company had terminated 1999 agreement when doing so was necessary in determining whether grievance was arbitrable under 2004 agreement).

4. *Contractual Disputes Over Union Security Provisions*—The First Circuit confirmed that a party's obligation to resolve grievances survives the expiration of the collective bargaining agreement in a case involving union security and dues checkoff provisions that contained an "evergreen clause." The clause provided that the union security provisions would be in force until expiration of the succeeding collective bargaining agreement. The dues checkoff clause contained a provision requiring revocation by the employee rather than by the employer. The court found that the presumption favoring arbitration controls. *Providence Journal Co. v. Providence Newspaper Guild*, 308 F.3d 129 (1st Cir. 2002). Similarly, in *Newspaper Guild/CWA of Albany v. Hearst Corp.*, 645 F.3d 527 (2d Cir. 2011), the court held that a dues checkoff provision survived the expiration of the collective bargaining agreement and the employer's discontinuation of dues checkoff was therefore subject to arbitration, where the authorizations signed by individual employees stated that they "continue[d] until revoked by the employee and [were] automatically renewed and irrevocable in certain circumstances" and the labor contract was ambiguous regarding the continuation of dues checkoff obligations beyond the contract's expiration date. *See also Office & Prof Employees Int'l Union, Local 95 v. Wood County Tel. Co.*, 408 F.3d 314 (7th Cir. 2005) (reading *Litton* as distinguishing arbitration clauses on the basis that they require mutual agreement, unlike provisions that the employer could unilaterally adopt; since the employer had continued to remit dues to the union under a dues checkoff clause in the collective bargaining agreement, the employer had "manifested a belief" that it had the assent of the employees to do so, and hence a belief that the agreement, including the employer's promise to arbitrate, had not been terminated).

5. *Effect of No-Strike Clauses After Contract Expiration* — If an employer's obligation to arbitrate survives the expiration of the contract in certain circumstances, what about the union's obligation not to strike? A court of appeals has held that a no-strike clause did not bar a union's post-contract economic strike, but that the employer remained bound to arbitrate. *United Steelworkers v. Ft. Pitt Steel Casting Division-Conval-Penn, Inc.*, 635 F.2d 1071 (3d Cir. 1980), *cert. denied*, 451 U.S. 985 (1981). *But see District No. 1-Marine Eng'rs Benefit Ass'n v. GFC Crane Consultants, Inc.*, 331 F.3d 1287 (11th Cir. 2003) ("Post-termination, a party may alter the method of dispute resolution, at least as to those claims arising post-termination. A party may refuse to abide by the strike or lockout provisions in the agreement, to the same extent that other terms of dispute resolution are not continued.")

D. Judicial Enforcement of Arbitration Awards

United Steelworkers v. Enterprise Wheel & Car Corp., 363 U.S. 593, 80 S. Ct. 1358, 4 L. Ed. 2d 1424 (1960). A collective bargaining agreement provided for "final and binding" arbitration of any differences about the "meaning and application" of the contract. If a discharge violated the agreement, the company was to "reinstate the employee and pay full compensation." Several workers were dismissed for leaving their jobs to protest the discharge of another employee. An arbitrator found that only a 10-day suspension was warranted. Even though the collective agreement had expired in the meantime, the arbitrator awarded reinstatement and full back pay, with a deduction of 10 days' pay and any sums received from other employment. A court of appeals refused to enforce the reinstatement or the award of back pay beyond the date of the contract's termination. The Supreme Court reversed this ruling, declaring: "The refusal of courts to review the merits of an arbitration award is the proper approach to arbitration under collective bargaining agreements." Speaking through Justice Douglas, the Court went on to say:

> When an arbitrator is commissioned to interpret and apply the collective bargaining agreement, he is to bring his informed judgment to bear in order to reach a fair solution of a problem. This is especially true when it comes to

formulating remedies.... Nevertheless, an arbitrator is confined to interpretation and application of the collective bargaining agreement; he does not sit to dispense his own brand of industrial justice. He may of course look for guidance from many sources, yet his award is legitimate only so long as it draws its essence from the collective bargaining agreement. When the arbitrator's words manifest an infidelity to this obligation, courts have no choice but to refuse enforcement of the award.

The opinion of the arbitrator in this case, as it bears upon the award of back pay beyond the date of the agreement's expiration and reinstatement, is ambiguous. It may be read as based solely upon the arbitrator's view of the requirements of enacted legislation, which would mean that he exceeded the scope of the submission. Or it may be read as embodying a construction of the agreement itself, perhaps with the arbitrator looking to "the law" for help in determining the sense of the agreement. A mere ambiguity in the opinion accompanying an award, which permits the inference that the arbitrator may have exceeded his authority, is not a reason for refusing to enforce the award. Arbitrators have no obligation to the court to give their reasons for an award....

Respondent's major argument seems to be that by applying correct principles of law to the interpretation of the collective bargaining agreement it can be determined that the agreement did not ... provide [for reinstatement and full back pay], and that therefore the arbitrator's decision was not based upon the contract.... This plenary review by a court of the merits would make meaningless the provisions that the arbitrator's decision is final, for in reality it would almost never be final.... It is the arbitrator's construction which was bargained for; and so far as the arbitrator's decision concerns construction of the contract, the courts have no business overruling him because their interpretation of the contract is different from his.

Note

The first two cases of the *Steelworkers Trilogy* dealt with judicial enforcement of executory agreements to arbitrate; *Enterprise Wheel* dealt with judicial enforcement of an arbitral award. Should a court apply different standards in examining the arbitrator's "jurisdiction" in these two situations? Is there, in any event, a difference between the arbitrator's "jurisdiction" to hear a dispute and her "authority" to render a particular award?

Should a party's submission to the arbitration process constitute consent to the arbitrator's exercise of jurisdiction? In *National Gypsum Co. v. Oil, Chem., & Atomic Workers Int'l Union*, 147 F.3d 399 (5th Cir. 1998), the union grieved the company's unilateral announcement of a change in the workweek that resulted in a loss of overtime pay for employees. The arbitrator ruled in favor of the union, reasoning that the change in workweek was actually a wage change, and since the contract required negotiations over wage changes, the employer had violated the contract by instituting the program unilaterally. The court enforced the award, holding that the company's submission to arbitration in spite of the fact that the parties were unable to stipulate to the issue to be resolved constituted implied consent to the arbitrator's jurisdiction, allowing the arbitrator to frame the issue under consideration. Since the arbitrator's interpretation of the contract was rational and consistent with the employer's obligations under the NLRA, it was a valid exercise of arbitral authority. *See also Pacesetter Constr. Co. v. Carpenters 46, N. Cal. Counties Conf. Bd.*, 116 F.3d 436 (9th Cir.), *cert. denied*, 522 U.S. 1014 (1997) (refusing to apply to collective bargaining context the rule stated in *First Options v. Kaplan*, 514 U.S. 938 (1995), that courts should not assume that parties to a commercial arbitration agreement agreed to arbitrate the issue of arbitrability merely by arguing that issue to the arbitration panel).

Major League Baseball Players Ass'n v. Garvey, 532 U.S. 504, 121 S. Ct. 1724, 149 L. Ed. 2d 740 (2001). A former major league baseball player claimed that his contract had not been extended at the end of his career because of owner collusion against free agents. Despite a letter to the player from the team owner indicating that his contract would have been extended but for collusion, the arbitrator ruled against the player, relying on earlier testimony by the same team owner denying any collusion. The Ninth Circuit found that the arbitrator had acted irrationally in not crediting the more recent owner letter, and it directed the arbitrator to enter an award for the player and to pay Garvey's claim. In a *per curiam* decision, the Supreme Court summarily reversed the Ninth Circuit, finding that the appellate judges had overturned the arbitrator because they disagreed with his factual findings, particularly with respect to credibility. Reaffirming the *Trilogy* principles, the Court observed that judicial disagreement with an arbitrator's interpretation of the contract is not a basis for setting aside an arbitral award; even "serious error" by the arbitrator will not justify vacating the award as long as he or she acts honestly and within the scope of his or her contractual authority. The Ninth Circuit's substitution of its judgment on credibility questions for that of the arbitrator was improper:

> Judicial review of a labor arbitration decision pursuant to [a collective bargaining agreement] is very limited. Courts are not authorized to review the arbitrator's decision on the merits despite allegations that the decision rests on factual errors or misinterprets the parties' agreement. *Paperworkers v. Misco, Inc.*, 484 U.S. 29, 36 (1987). We recently reiterated that if an "'arbitrator is even arguably construing or applying the contract and acting within the scope of his authority,' the fact that 'a court is convinced he committed serious error does not suffice to overturn his decision.'" *Eastern Associated Coal Corp. v. Mine Workers*, 531 U.S. 57, 62 (2000) (quoting *Misco, supra*, at 38). It is only when the arbitrator strays from interpretation and application of the agreement and effectively "dispense[s] his own brand of industrial justice" that his decision may be unenforceable. *Steelworkers v. Enterprise Wheel & Car Corp.*, 363 U.S. 593, 597 (1960). When an arbitrator

resolves disputes regarding the application of a contract, and no dishonesty is alleged, the arbitrator's "improvident, even silly, factfinding" does not provide a basis for a reviewing court to refuse to enforce the award. *Misco*, 484 U.S., at 39. In discussing the courts' limited role in reviewing the merits of arbitration awards, we have stated that "'courts . . . have no business weighing the merits of the grievance [or] considering whether there is equity in a particular claim.'" *Id.* at 37 (quoting *Steelworkers v. American Mfg. Co.*, 363 U.S. 564 (1960)). When the judiciary does so, "it usurps a function which . . . is entrusted to the arbitration tribunal." *Id.* at 569. Consistent with this limited role, we said in *Misco* that "[e]ven in the very rare instances where an arbitrator's procedural aberrations rise to the level of affirmative misconduct, as a rule the court must not foreclose further proceedings by settling the merits according to its own judgment of the appropriate result." 484 U.S., at 40–41, n. 10. That step, we explained, "would improperly substitute a judicial determination for the arbitrator's decision that the parties bargained for" in their agreement. *Ibid.* Instead, the court should "simply vacate the award, thus leaving open the possibility of further proceedings if they are permitted under the terms of the agreement."

Id. 532 U.S., at 509–10.

Notes

1. *Standard of Review for Arbitral Awards* — A key aspect of the federal preference for arbitration as a means of resolving labor disputes is the narrow standard of review applicable to arbitral awards rendered pursuant to an arbitration clause in a collective agreement. Under *Enterprise Wheel*, courts must enforce the arbitrator's award as long as it "draws its essence from the agreement." Arbitration is seen as a continuation of the collective bargaining process, and courts are loath to interfere with the arbitrator's interpretation of the agreement where the parties bargained for exactly that. *See, e.g., CenterPoint Energy Res. Corp. v. Gas Workers Union, Local No. 340*, 920 F.3d 1163 (8th Cir. 2019) (upholding arbitrator's decision interpreting a provision outlining offenses that constitute "absolute cause" as encompassing a right to impose discipline for those offenses but not necessarily the right to select discharge as the penalty, because arbitrator was at least arguably construing the contract); *ASARCO LLC v. United Steel, Paper and Forestry, Rubber, Mfg., Energy, Allied Ind'l and Serv. Workers Int'l Union*, 910 F.3d 485 (9th Cir. 2018) (upholding arbitrator's award amending the collective agreement based on a finding of mutual mistake despite a "no-add" provision, because award drew its essence from agreement and did not violate public policy); *National Postal Mail Handlers Union v. Am. Postal Workers Union*, 589 F.3d 437 (D.C. Cir. 2009) (upholding arbitrator's decision in a contractual dispute between two unions even though the court "would have followed the plain terms of the agreement and ruled" for the other union; the arbitrator had "at least arguably" construed the agreement); *United States Postal Serv. v. American Postal Workers Union*, 553 F.3d 686 (D.C. Cir. 2009) (upholding arbitrator's decision, even though it was "confusing" and "arguably dubious on the merits," when the arbitrator based decision on his interpretation of the agreement).

A cogent explanation for the philosophy behind such respect was articulated in *Hawaii Teamsters and Allied Workers Union, Local 996 v. UPS*, 241 F.3d 1177 (9th Cir. 2001), where the court upheld an arbitral award that sustained discharge of an employee for swearing even though swearing and insubordination were not included on a contractual list of offenses for which employees could be summarily fired. The arbitrator relied on the agreement and on previous arbitration decisions interpreting it. The court explained:

> Fundamental to an understanding of our task here is the fact that we are to view an award not as a potentially erroneous result of the arbitrator's contract interpretation, but rather as the contract itself. . . . 'Since the labor arbitrator is designed to function in essence as the parties' surrogate, he cannot "misinterpret" a collective bargaining agreement.' As Professor St. Antoine observes, "[i]n the absence of fraud or an overreaching of authority on the part of the arbitrator, he is speaking for the parties, and his award is their contract," [quoting Theodore J. St. Antoine, *Judicial Review of Labor Arbitration Awards: A Second Look at Enterprise Wheel and Its Progeny*, 75 Mich. L. Rev. 1137 (1977)]. Thus, what courts do when they review an arbitrator's award is more akin to the review of a contract than of the decision of an inferior tribunal: the award, just as a contract, is the expression of the parties' will and must be enforced as expressed unless illegal or otherwise void. Judicial "reinterpretation," no less than judicial reformation of a contract against the wishes of all the parties to it, is ordinarily an invalid exercise of our power. (quoting *Stead Motors v. Auto Machinists Lodge No. 1173*, 886 F.2d 1200 (9th Cir. 1989) (*en banc*).

See also *Kraft Foods, Inc. v. Office & Professional Employees Int'l Union, Local 1295*, 203 F.3d 98 (1st Cir. 2000) (upholding arbitrator's award ordering employer to pay back wages as a remedy for its selective violation of a contract provision requiring temporary "break-in" wages for all new employees, even though such an award effectively amounted to an order to violate the collective bargaining agreement a second time in order to remedy the first violation; arbitrator has broad authority to fashion remedies to redress contractual breach).

2. *Narrow Scope of Judicial Review*—The scope of judicial review of arbitration awards is "among the narrowest known to law." *PPG Indus. v. Int'l Chem. Workers Union Council of the United Food & Commer. Workers*, 587 F.3d 648 (4th Cir. 2009). Thus, even an arbitration award containing serious errors of contract interpretation may be upheld. In *Brentwood Med. Assocs. v. UMW*, 396 F.3d 237 (3d Cir. 2005), the court upheld an arbitral award that quoted and relied upon language in the labor contract that did not exist. The case involved a grievance filed by an employee who requested that another worker with less seniority be bumped so that she could return to a position that she had held previously. The court found that the arbitrator's conclusion that seniority bumping rights should be read into the contract rested upon a clear basis for a seniority preference unit-wide, and thus was sufficient to pass what the court called the "minimum rationality threshold." *See also Akers Nat'l Roll Co. v. United Steel, Paper and Forestry, Rubber, Mfg., Energy, Allied Indus. & Serv. Workers Int'l Union*, 712 F.3d 155 (3d Cir. 2013) (upholding arbitration award where arbitrator found employer had violated established past practice, even where language of collective bargaining agreement was ambiguous and arguably conflicted with this finding).

In *Mich. Family Res., Inc. v. SEIU Local 517M*, 475 F.3d 746 (6th Cir.) (*en banc*), *cert. denied*, 551 U.S. 1132 (2007), the Sixth Circuit affirmed the principle that judicial review of arbitrators' decisions is extremely limited. The court read the Supreme Court's decisions in *Garvey* and *Misco* as limiting the scope of judicial review even beyond that permitted under *Enterprise Wheel*. The court established a new framework for review of arbitral decisions in which the reviewing court need only ask three questions: "Did the arbitrator act 'outside his authority' by resolving a dispute not committed to arbitration? Did the arbitrator commit fraud, have a conflict of interest or otherwise act dishonestly in issuing the award? And in resolving any legal or factual disputes in the case, was the arbitrator 'arguably construing or applying the contract'?" If the answers to the first two questions were in the negative, the court should affirm the arbitrator's decision—even if the arbitrator makes "serious," "improvident," or "silly" errors in resolving the dispute.

Even under this narrow view of a court's authority to vacate an arbitrator's award, however, the arbitrator must still "address questions committed to him by the parties" and not "dispense his own brand of industrial justice." *See, e.g., Monongahela Valley Hosp. Inc. v. United Steel Paper and Forestry Rubber Mfg. Allied Indus. and Serv. Workers Int'l Union AFL-CIO*, 946 F.3d 195 (3d Cir. 2019) (vacating arbitrator's award where arbitrator disregarded plain language of the collective agreement granting the employer the "final," "exclusive," and "unilateral" right to schedule vacation time, and dispensed his own brand of justice by imposing a requirement that denial of vacation time must be based on "operating need"); *U.S. Soccer Fed'n, Inc. v. U.S. Nat'l Soccer Team Players Ass'n*, 838 F.3d 826 (7th Cir. 2016) (finding arbitrator exceeded his authority by looking to the Federation's past practice of seeking the union's advance approval for advertisements where the collective agreement was not silent on the issue of print advertisements); *Reyco Granning LLC v. Teamsters Local 245*, 735 F.3d 1018 (8th Cir. 2013) (refusing to enforce an arbitrator's order to employer to pay holiday pay to employee who was 45 minutes late to work because of a flat tire on the last work day before the holiday, where collective bargaining agreement was unambiguous in conferring discretion on the employer on how to handle such infractions; rather than construing ambiguous contract term, arbitrator effectively imposed a new obligation on the employer based on testimony about contract negotiations); *Anheuser-Busch, Inc. v. Beer Drivers, Local 744, Int'l Bhd. of Teamsters*, 280 F.3d 1133 (7th Cir.), *cert. denied*, 537 U.S. 885 (2002) (arbitrator exceeded his contractual authority when he relied on past practice and ordered company to pay its driver-salespeople at a commission rate in excess of that contained in the newly negotiated labor contract, where contract provided that the written agreement superseded any agreement or practices not "specifically preserved in the contract," and an arbitration clause divested the arbitrator of authority "to add to, subtract from, modify, or change" the contract).

3. *Extraordinary Arbitral Remedies* — Courts generally afford broad deference to the remedial aspects of arbitral awards as well. *See, e.g., CenterPoint Energy Res. Corp. v. Gas Workers Union, Local No. 340*, 920 F.3d 1163 (8th Cir. 2019) (enforcing arbitration award reinstating employee without back pay where employee was discharged for falsifying time sheets and neglect of duty and "dishonesty" and "neglect of duty" each constituted "absolute cause" for termination under the collective agreement); *Unite Here Local 1 v. Hyatt Corp.*, 862 F.3d 588 (7th Cir. 2017) (enforcing arbitrator's award of back pay at overtime rate along with prospective "cease and desist" order to remedy employer's repeated violation of the collective agreement involving managers performing bargaining unit work); *PSC Custom, LP v. Steelworkers*, 756 F.3d 627 (8th Cir. 2014) (enforcing arbitration award reducing employee's discharge to 30-day suspension even though contract provided that discharge was the penalty for insubordination, since award drew its essence from the contract's just cause for discharge clause; arbitrator found that employee's conduct was merely negligent, not the type of insubordination for which the contract required discharge); *Air Methods Corp. v. Office & Prof'l Emps.*, 737 F.3d 660 (10th Cir. 2013) (enforcing arbitration award reinstating after a six-month suspension without pay a helicopter pilot who was fired for allowing an uncertified trainee to fly the aircraft, damaging the helicopter; arbitrator acknowledged that the employee had engaged in conduct justifying discipline, but found that employer lacked just cause for termination, relying on contract's just cause provision, its commitment to a system of progressive discipline, and its provision prescribing penalties for "serious misconduct"); *Clear Channel Outdoor, Inc. v. Int'l Unions of Painters & Allied Trades, Local 770*, 558 F.3d 670 (7th Cir. 2009) (upholding arbitrator's decision that employer lacked cause to discharge employee who violated workplace safety regulation despite provision that employees "may be immediately discharged" for violating such regulations; court concluded arbitrator's award "drew its essence" from the agreement in that the term "may" could be interpreted as implying that a lesser penalty could be appropriate under some circumstances). *See also Synergy Gas Co. v. Sasso*, 853 F.2d 59 (2d Cir.), *cert. denied*, 488 U.S. 994 (1988) (arbitrator could order attorney fees, union dues, and pension fund contributions, in addition to back pay); *but see Island Creek Coal Co. v. District 28, United Mine Workers*, 29 F.3d 126 (4th Cir.), *cert. denied*, 513 U.S. 1019 (1994) (voiding unauthorized arbitral award of punitive damages). For an analysis suggesting that the number of arbitral awards containing punitive provisions has increased since 1995, but finding that courts are more likely to approve punitive remedies in employment law arbitration contexts than in the labor law context, see LeRoy & Feuille, *Reinventing the* Enterprise Wheel*: Court*

Review of Punitive Awards in Labor and Employment Arbitrations, 11 HARV. NEGO. L. REV. 199 (2006).

Courts have upheld arbitral awards even when they impact the working conditions of employees not represented by the union involved in the dispute. *See, e.g., LID Elec., Inc. v. IBEW, Local 134*, 362 F.3d 940 (7th Cir. 2004) (arbitrator did not exceed the scope of his authority in deciding that employer was obligated under agreement with union to conduct drug testing of all of its employees, not just those represented by union); *Eisenmann Corp. v. Sheet Metal Workers Int'l Ass'n Local 24*, 323 F.3d 375 (6th Cir. 2003) (arbitrator's award enforcing agreement's terms as to offsite employees did not impose union representation on those employees, but rather protected interests of on-site employees by providing disincentive to outsourcing).

Would an arbitrator be authorized to "remand" a case to the parties for further negotiations? *Compare AP Parts Co. v. International Union, United Auto. Aerospace & Agricultural Implement Workers*, 923 F.2d 488 (6th Cir. 1991) (finding that arbitrator exceeded his authority by directing the employer and union to renegotiate an issue that had already been bargained over) *with Phoenix Newspapers, Inc. v. Phoenix Mailers Union Local 752, Int'l Bhd. of Teamsters*, 989 F.2d 1077 (9th Cir. 1993) (denying enforcement of arbitrator's remedy ordering the employer and union to negotiate an issue because it created new bargaining obligations beyond the collective agreement and that violated both the agreement and the NLRA). *See generally* Feller, *The Remedy Power in Grievance Arbitration*, 5 INDUS. REL. L.J. 128 (1982); Fleming, *Arbitrators and the Remedy Power*, 48 VA. L. REV. 1199 (1962); M. HILL & A. SINICROPI, REMEDIES IN ARBITRATION (2d ed. 1991).

4. *Limits on Arbitral Remedies*—On the other hand, some courts have refused to enforce arbitral awards modifying penalties imposed upon workers who have violated company rules where they contravene express contractual provisions authorizing the punishment imposed. *See, e.g., Northern States Power Co. v. Int'l Bhd. of Elec. Workers, Local 160*, 711 F.3d 900 (8th Cir. 2013) (arbitrator exceeded his authority when he ordered reinstatement without back pay of an employee after determining that the company had just cause to discharge employee; even if arbitrator believed the penalty of discharge was too harsh, labor contract gave him no authority to award relief if the charges against the employee were sustained); *Pol. Spring Corp. v. UFCW*, 314 F.3d 29 (1st Cir. 2002), *cert. denied*, 540 U.S. 818 (2003) (arbitrator who reinstated an employee properly terminated for insubordination exceeded his authority under the contract, since contract contained a clause providing that insubordination "shall" constitute just cause for discipline and did not list insubordination as one of the offenses warranting a lower level of discipline prior to discharge; once arbitrator determined that the employee's conduct was insubordinate, he was barred from further inquiry or consideration of mitigating factors); *see also CITGO Asphalt Ref. Co. v. Paper, Allied-Industrial, Chem., & Energy Workers Int'l Union Local 2-991*, 385 F.3d 809 (3d Cir. 2004) (arbitrator exceeded authority by ruling that company's zero-tolerance substance abuse policy was unreasonable;

award did not draw its essence from the labor contract, but instead comported with the arbitrator's own view of fairness).

E. The Public Policy Exception

A court will not enforce an arbitral award that directly violates enacted law. *See Ace Elec. Contrs. v. IBEW, Local Union 292*, 414 F.3d 896 (8th Cir. 2005) (vacating arbitration award enforcing provision of agreement requiring that every fifth employee must be over 50 when that provision violated the Minnesota Human Relations Act's prohibition against age discrimination in employment). How should an arbitrator handle a conflict between "the law" and the parties' contract? For contrasting views on the question, see Edwards, *Labor Arbitration at the Crossroads: The "Common Law of the Shop" v. External Law*, 32 ARB. J. 65 (1977); Howlett, *The Arbitrator, the NLRB, and the Courts*, in NATIONAL ACADEMY OF ARBITRATORS, THE ARBITRATOR, THE NLRB, AND THE COURTS, PROCEEDINGS OF THE TWENTIETH ANNUAL MEETING 67 (1967); Malin, *Revisiting the Meltzer-Howlett Debate on External Law in Labor Arbitration: Is It Time for Courts to Declare Howlett the Winner?*, 24 THE LAB. LAW. 1 (2008); Mittenthal, *The Role of Law in Arbitration*, in NATIONAL ACADEMY OF ARBITRATORS, DEVELOPMENTS IN AMERICAN AND FOREIGN ARBITRATION, PROCEEDINGS OF THE TWENTY-FIRST ANNUAL MEETING 42 (1968); Ratner, *Observations on Some Current Issues in Labor Arbitration*, 32 LAB. L.J. 114 (1981). The following cases shed additional light on this question.

United Paperworkers International Union v. Misco, Inc., 484 U.S. 29, 108 S. Ct. 364, 98 L. Ed. 2d 286 (1987). Cooper, an employee who had been reprimanded twice for deficient performance in the operation of a slitter-rewinder machine that uses sharp blades to cut rolling coils of paper, was also under observation by police for suspected drug possession. Following a search of Cooper's home pursuant to a warrant and the discovery of a substantial amount of marijuana, police observed him at the company's parking lot during working hours and apprehended him in the back seat of another employee's car with marijuana smoke in the air and a lighted marijuana cigarette in the front-seat ashtray. The police then searched Cooper's car and found drug paraphernalia and marijuana gleanings. Cooper was arrested and charged with marijuana possession. When the company learned of the marijuana cigarette incident, it discharged Cooper for violating a company rule against possession or consumption of drugs on plant property. The company's decision to discharge was based solely upon the incident involving the smoldering marijuana cigarette; it was not aware contemporaneously of the marijuana found in Cooper's car. The arbitrator ordered the company to reinstate Cooper with back pay and full seniority, finding that the company had not demonstrated just cause for discharge based on the information available at the time the sanction was imposed; the evidence was insufficient to establish possession or use of drugs on company property. The district court vacated the award as contrary to public policy, finding that it undermined safety concerns arising from the operation of dangerous machinery while under the influence of drugs, as well as state criminal laws against drug possession. The Court of Appeals affirmed. The Supreme Court reversed, again emphasizing the limited role for courts when asked to review arbitral decisions pursuant to a collective bargaining agreement. The Court offered the following guidance:

> A court's refusal to enforce an arbitrator's award under a collective-bargaining agreement because it is contrary to public policy is a specific application of the more general doctrine, rooted in the common law, that a court may refuse to enforce contracts that violate law or public policy. *W.R. Grace & Co. v. Rubber Workers*, 461 U.S. 757, 766 (1983); *Hurd v. Hodge*, 334 U.S. 24, 34–35 (1948). That doctrine derives from the basic notion that no court will lend its aid to one who founds a cause of action upon an immoral or illegal act, and is further justified by the observation that the public's interests in confining the scope of private agreements to which it is not a party will go unrepresented unless the judiciary takes account of those interests when it considers whether to enforce such agreements. In the common law of contracts, this doctrine has served as the foundation for occasional exercises of judicial power to abrogate private agreements.
>
> In *W.R. Grace*, we recognized that "a court may not enforce a collective-bargaining agreement that is contrary to public policy," and stated that "the question of public policy is ultimately one for resolution by the courts." 461 U.S., at 766. We cautioned, however, that a court's refusal to enforce an arbitrator's *interpretation* of such contracts is limited to situations where the contract as interpreted would violate "some explicit public policy" that is "well defined and dominant, and is to be ascertained 'by reference to the laws and legal precedents and not from general considerations of supposed public interests.'" *Ibid.* (quoting *Muschany v. United States*, 324 U.S. 49, 66 (1945)). . . . Two points follow from our decision in *W.R. Grace*. First, a court may refuse to enforce a collective-bargaining agreement when the specific terms contained in that agreement violate public policy. Second, it is apparent that our decision in that case does not otherwise sanction a broad judicial power to set aside arbitration awards as against public policy. . . .
>
> The Court of Appeals made no attempt to review existing laws and legal precedents in order to demonstrate that they establish a "well defined and dominant" policy against the operation of dangerous machinery while under the influence of drugs. Although certainly such a judgment is firmly rooted in common sense, we explicitly held in *W.R. Grace* that a formulation of public policy based only on "general considerations of supposed public interests" is not the sort that permits a court to set aside an arbitration award that was entered in accordance with a valid collective-bargaining agreement. . . .

484 U.S., at 43–44.

Finally, the Court concluded that even if a well-defined and dominant public policy had been identified, the arbitrator's decision did not necessarily violate public policy. The evidentiary connection between the marijuana gleanings found in Cooper's car and his actual use of drugs in the workplace was "tenuous at best," and the Court of Appeals had improperly usurped the role of the arbitrator by drawing the inference that Cooper would operate dangerous machinery under the influence of drugs. The Court found it unnecessary to resolve the question whether the public policy basis for vacating arbitration awards was limited to situations where the award itself violates positive law or compels conduct by the employer that would violate positive law. *Id.* at 45 n.12.

Notes

1. *Aftermath* — After *Misco*, the lower courts continued to struggle with the interaction between public policy and the terms of particular contracts when reviewing arbitration awards. On remand for reconsideration in light of *Misco*, the First Circuit in *S.D. Warren Co., Div. of Scott Paper Co. v. United Paperworkers' International Union, Local 1069*, 845 F.2d 3 (1st Cir. 1988) reaffirmed its holding that an arbitrator exceeded her authority in setting aside three employees' discharges for violating a rule against drugs on company property. The court pointed out that the contract gave the employer the "sole right" to discharge for "proper cause" and stated that violations of the rule against drugs were "considered causes for discharge." *Misco* was also distinguished in *Delta Air Lines, Inc. v. Air Line Pilots Ass'n, International*, 861 F.2d 665 (11th Cir. 1988), *cert. denied*, 493 U.S. 871 (1989) (arbitral award reinstating alcoholic pilot who flew commercial flight while intoxicated contravened state and federal policies prohibiting operation of aircraft while drunk); *Iowa Electric Light & Power Co. v. Local Union 204 of International Brotherhood of Electrical Workers*, 834 F.2d 1424 (8th Cir. 1987) (public policy embodied in federally mandated safety regulations at a nuclear power plant required vacation of an arbitration award reinstating employee discharged for opening a safety door so he could take a shortcut to lunch). On the other hand, subsequent to *Misco*, the Third Circuit held that public policy did not bar an arbitral reinstatement of a postal employee who had fired two bullets through his supervisor's car windshield. *United Postal Service v. National Ass'n of Letter Carriers*, 839 F.2d 146 (3d Cir. 1988). See also *Florida Power Corp. v. International Brotherhood of Electrical Workers, etc., Local Union 433*, 847 F.2d 680 (11th Cir. 1988) (sustaining reinstatement of employee arrested for cocaine possession and drunk driving); *United States Postal Service v. National Ass'n of Letter Carriers*, 810 F.2d 1239 (D.C. Cir. 1987), *cert. dismissed*, 485 U.S. 680 (1988) (sustaining reinstatement of letter carrier who had failed to deliver thousands of pieces of mail); *Northwest Airlines, Inc. v. Air Line Pilots Ass'n, International*, 808 F.2d 76 (D.C. Cir. 1987), *cert. denied*, 486 U.S. 1014 (1988) (sustaining reinstatement of alcoholic pilot).

2. *Focus on the Arbitral Remedy* — Should a court let stand an arbitration award that results in the reinstatement of an employee who has flagrantly violated external law?

Under *Misco*, the test is not whether the employee activity itself undermines public policy, but whether the arbitral award — i.e., the reinstatement — offends public policy. One way to think about this is to ask whether the employer could have reinstated the employee without violating public policy. If so, then the arbitrator's award accomplishing the same result will not offend public policy. *See* St. Antoine, *The Changing Role of Labor Arbitration*, 76 Ind. L.J. 83, 97 (2001). The following case and notes shed further light on this question.

Eastern Associated Coal Corp. v. United Mine Workers District 17

Supreme Court of the United States
531 U.S. 57, 121 S. Ct. 462, 148 L. Ed. 2d 354 (2000)

Justice Breyer delivered the opinion of the Court.

A labor arbitrator ordered an employer to reinstate an employee truck driver who had twice tested positive for marijuana. The question before us is whether considerations of public policy require courts to refuse to enforce that arbitration award. We conclude that they do not. The courts may enforce the award. And the employer must reinstate, rather than discharge, the employee.

I

Petitioner, Eastern Associated Coal Corp., and respondent, United Mine Workers of America, are parties to a collective-bargaining agreement with arbitration provisions. The agreement specifies that, in arbitration, in order to discharge an employee, Eastern must prove it has "just cause." Otherwise the arbitrator will order the employee reinstated. The arbitrator's decision is final.

James Smith worked for Eastern as a member of a road crew, a job that required him to drive heavy trucklike vehicles on public highways. As a truck driver, Smith was subject to Department of Transportation (DOT) regulations requiring random drug testing of workers engaged in "safety-sensitive" tasks. 49 CFR §§ 382.301, 382.305 (1999). In March 1996, Smith tested positive for marijuana. Eastern sought to discharge Smith. The union went to arbitration, and the arbitrator concluded that Smith's positive drug test did not amount to "just cause" for discharge. Instead the arbitrator ordered Smith's reinstatement, provided that Smith (1) accept a suspension of 30 days without pay, (2) participate in a substance-abuse program, and (3) undergo drug tests at the discretion of Eastern (or an approved substance-abuse professional) for the next five years.

Between April 1996 and January 1997, Smith passed four random drug tests. But in July 1997 he again tested positive for marijuana. Eastern again sought to discharge Smith. The union again went to arbitration, and the arbitrator again concluded that Smith's use of marijuana did not amount to "just cause" for discharge, in light of two mitigating circumstances. First, Smith had been a good employee for 17 years. And, second, Smith had made a credible and "very personal appeal under oath . . . concerning a personal/family problem which caused this one time lapse in drug usage."

The arbitrator ordered Smith's reinstatement provided that Smith (1) accept a new suspension without pay, this time for slightly more than three months; (2) reimburse Eastern and the union for the costs of both arbitration proceedings; (3) continue to participate in a substance-abuse program; (4) continue to undergo random drug testing; and (5) provide Eastern with a signed, undated letter of resignation, to take effect if Smith again tested positive within the next five years.

Eastern brought suit in federal court seeking to have the arbitrator's award vacated, arguing that the award contravened a public policy against the operation of dangerous machinery by workers who test positive for drugs. 66 F. Supp. 2d 796 (S.D. WV 1998). The District Court, while recognizing a strong regulation-based public policy against drug use by workers who perform safety-sensitive functions, held that Smith's conditional reinstatement did not violate that policy. *Id.* at 804–805. And it ordered the award's enforcement.

The Court of Appeals for the Fourth Circuit affirmed on the reasoning of the District Court. 188 F.3d 501 (1999) (unpublished). We granted certiorari in light of disagreement among the Circuits. Compare *id.* at **1 (holding that public policy does not prohibit "reinstatement of employees who have used illegal drugs in the past"), with, *e.g., Exxon Corp. v. Esso Workers' Union, Inc.*, 118 F.3d 841, 852 (CA 1 1997) (holding that public policy prohibits enforcement of a similar arbitration award). We now affirm the Fourth Circuit's determination.

II

Eastern claims that considerations of public policy make the arbitration award unenforceable. In considering this claim, we must assume that the collective-bargaining agreement itself calls for Smith's reinstatement. That is because both employer and union have granted to the arbitrator the authority to interpret the meaning of their contract's language, including such words as "just cause." See *Steelworkers v. Enterprise Wheel & Car Corp.*, 363 U.S. 593, 599 (1960). They have "bargained for" the "arbitrator's construction" of their agreement. *Ibid.* And courts will set aside the arbitrator's interpretation of what their agreement means only in rare instances. *Id.* at 596. Of course, an arbitrator's award "must draw its essence from the contract and cannot simply reflect the arbitrator's own notions of industrial justice." *Paperworkers v. Misco, Inc.*, 484 U.S. 29, 38 (1987). "But as long as [an honest] arbitrator is even arguably construing or applying the contract and acting within the scope of his authority," the fact that "a court is convinced he committed serious error does not suffice to overturn his decision." *Ibid.*; see also *Enterprise Wheel, supra*, at 596 (the "proper" judicial approach to a labor arbitration award is to "refuse . . . to review the merits"). Eastern does not claim here that the arbitrator acted outside the scope of his contractually delegated authority. Hence we must treat the arbitrator's award as if it represented an agreement between Eastern and the union as to the proper meaning of the contract's words "just cause." See St. Antoine, *Judicial Review of Labor Arbitration Awards: A Second Look at Enterprise Wheel and Its Progeny*, 75 Mich. L. Rev. 1137, 1155 (1977). For present purposes, the award is not distinguishable from the contractual agreement.

We must then decide whether a contractual reinstatement requirement would fall within the legal exception that makes unenforceable "a collective bargaining agreement that is contrary to public policy." *W. R. Grace & Co. v. Rubber Workers*, 461 U.S. 757, 766 (1983). The Court has made clear that any such public policy must be "explicit," "well defined," and "dominant." *Ibid.* It must be "ascertained 'by reference to the laws and legal precedents and not from general considerations of supposed public interests.'" *Ibid.* (quoting *Muschany v. United States*, 324 U.S. 49, 66 (1945)); accord, *Misco, supra*, at 43. And, of course, the question to be answered is not whether Smith's drug use itself violates public policy, but whether the agreement to reinstate him does so. To put the question more specifically, does a contractual agreement to reinstate Smith with specified conditions, run contrary to an explicit, well-defined, and dominant public policy, as ascertained by reference to positive law and not from general considerations of supposed public interests? See *Misco, supra*, at 43.

III

Eastern initially argues that the District Court erred by asking, not whether the award is "contrary to" public policy "as ascertained by reference" to positive law, but whether the award "violates" positive law, a standard Eastern says is too narrow. We believe, however, that the District Court correctly articulated the standard set out in *W. R. Grace* and *Misco*, see 66 F. Supp. 2d at 803 (quoting *Misco, supra*, at 43), and applied that standard to reach the right result.

We agree, in principle, that courts' authority to invoke the public policy exception is not limited solely to instances where the arbitration award itself violates positive law. Nevertheless, the public policy exception is narrow and must satisfy the principles set forth in *W. R. Grace* and *Misco*. Moreover, in a case like the one before us, where two political branches have created a detailed regulatory regime in a specific field, courts should approach with particular caution pleas to divine further public policy in that area.

Eastern asserts that a public policy against reinstatement of workers who use drugs can be discerned from an examination of that regulatory regime, which consists of the Omnibus Transportation Employee Testing Act of 1991 and DOT's implementing regulations. The Testing Act embodies a congressional finding that "the greatest efforts must be expended to eliminate the... use of illegal drugs, whether on or off duty, by those individuals who are involved in [certain safety-sensitive positions, including] the operation of... trucks." Pub. L. 102-143, § 2(3), 105 Stat. 953. The Act adds that "increased testing" is the "most effective deterrent" to "use of illegal drugs." § 2(5). It requires the Secretary of Transportation to promulgate regulations requiring "testing of operators of commercial motor vehicles for the use of a controlled substance." 49 U.S.C. § 31306(b)(1)(A) (1994 ed., Supp. III). It mandates suspension of those operators who have driven a commercial motor vehicle while under the influence of drugs. 49 U.S.C. § 31310(b)(1)(A) (requiring suspension of at least one year for a first offense); § 31310(c)(2) (requiring suspension of at least 10 years for a second offense). And DOT's implementing regulations set forth sanctions applicable to those who test positive for illegal drugs. 49 CFR § 382.605 (1999).

In Eastern's view, these provisions embody a strong public policy against drug use by transportation workers in safety-sensitive positions and in favor of random drug testing in order to detect that use. Eastern argues that reinstatement of a driver who has twice failed random drug tests would undermine that policy — to the point where a judge must set aside an employer-union agreement requiring reinstatement.

Eastern's argument, however, loses much of its force when one considers further provisions of the Act that make clear that the Act's remedial aims are complex. The Act says that "rehabilitation is a critical component of any testing program," § 2(7), 105 Stat. 953, that rehabilitation "should be made available to individuals, as appropriate," *ibid.*, and that DOT must promulgate regulations for "rehabilitation programs," 49 U.S.C. § 31306(e). The DOT regulations specifically state that a driver who has tested positive for drugs cannot return to a safety-sensitive position until (1) the driver has been evaluated by a "substance abuse professional" to determine if treatment is needed, 49 CFR § 382.605(b) (1999); (2) the substance-abuse professional has certified that the driver has followed any rehabilitation program prescribed, § 382.605(c)(2)(i); and (3) the driver has passed a return-to-duty drug test, § 382.605(c)(1). In addition, (4) the driver must be subject to at least six random drug tests during the first year after returning to the job. § 382.605(c)(2)(ii). Neither the Act nor the regulations forbid an employer to reinstate in a safety-sensitive position an employee who fails a random drug test once or twice. The congressional and regulatory directives require only that the above-stated prerequisites to reinstatement be met.

Moreover, when promulgating these regulations, DOT decided not to require employers either to provide rehabilitation or to "hold a job open for a driver" who has tested positive, on the basis that such decisions "should be left to management/ driver negotiation." 59 Fed. Reg. 7502 (1994). That determination reflects basic background labor law principles, which caution against interference with labor-management agreements about appropriate employee discipline. *See, e.g., California Brewers Assn. v. Bryant*, 444 U.S. 598, 608 (1980) (noting that it is "this Nation's longstanding labor policy" to give "employers and employees the freedom through collective bargaining to establish conditions of employment").

We believe that these expressions of positive law embody several relevant policies. As Eastern points out, these policies include Testing Act policies against drug use by employees in safety-sensitive transportation positions and in favor of drug testing. They also include a Testing Act policy favoring rehabilitation of employees who use drugs. And the relevant statutory and regulatory provisions must be read in light of background labor law policy that favors determination of disciplinary questions through arbitration when chosen as a result of labor-management negotiation.

The award before us is not contrary to these several policies, taken together. The award does not condone Smith's conduct or ignore the risk to public safety that drug use by truck drivers may pose. Rather, the award punishes Smith by suspending him for three months, thereby depriving him of nearly $9,000 in lost wages; it requires him to pay the arbitration costs of both sides; it insists upon further substance-abuse treatment and testing; and it makes clear (by requiring Smith to provide a signed letter of resignation) that one more failed test means discharge.

The award violates no specific provision of any law or regulation. It is consistent with DOT rules requiring completion of substance-abuse treatment before returning to work, see 49 CFR § 382.605(c)(2)(i) (1999), for it does not preclude Eastern from assigning Smith to a non-safety-sensitive position until Smith completes the prescribed treatment program. It is consistent with the Testing Act's 1-year and 10-year driving license suspension requirements, for those requirements apply only to drivers who, unlike Smith, actually operated vehicles under the influence of drugs. See 49 U.S.C. § 31310(b), (c). The award is also consistent with the Act's rehabilitative concerns, for it requires substance-abuse treatment and testing before Smith can return to work.

The fact that Smith is a recidivist — that he has failed drug tests twice — is not sufficient to tip the balance in Eastern's favor. The award punishes Smith more severely for his second lapse. And that more severe punishment, which included a 90-day suspension, would have satisfied even a "recidivist" rule that DOT once proposed but did not adopt — a rule that would have punished two failed drug tests, not with discharge, but with a driving suspension of 60 days. 57 Fed. Reg. 59585 (1992). Eastern argues that DOT's withdrawal of its proposed rule leaves open the possibility that discharge is the appropriate penalty for repeat offenders. That argument fails, however, because DOT based its withdrawal, not upon a determination that a more severe penalty was needed, but upon a determination to leave in place, as the "only driving prohibition period for a controlled substances violation," the "completion of rehabilitation requirements and a return-to-duty test with a negative result." 59 Fed. Reg. 7493 (1994).

Regarding drug use by persons in safety-sensitive positions, then, Congress has enacted a detailed statute. And Congress has delegated to the Secretary of Transportation authority to issue further detailed regulations on that subject. Upon careful consideration, including public notice and comment, the Secretary has done so. Neither Congress nor the Secretary has seen fit to mandate the discharge of a worker who twice tests positive for drugs. We hesitate to infer a public policy in this area that goes beyond the careful and detailed scheme Congress and the Secretary have created.

We recognize that reasonable people can differ as to whether reinstatement or discharge is the more appropriate remedy here. But both employer and union have agreed to entrust this remedial decision to an arbitrator. We cannot find in the Act, the regulations, or any other law or legal precedent an "explicit," "well defined," "dominant" public policy to which the arbitrator's decision "runs contrary." *Misco*, 484 U.S. at 43; *W. R. Grace*, 461 U.S. at 766. We conclude that the lower courts correctly rejected Eastern's public policy claim. The judgment of the Court of Appeals is

Affirmed.

Justice Scalia, with whom Justice Thomas joins, concurring in the judgment.

I concur in the Court's judgment, because I agree that no public policy prevents the reinstatement of James Smith to his position as a truck driver, so long as he complies with the arbitrator's decision, and with those requirements set out in the Department of Transportation's regulations. I do not endorse, however, the Court's statement that "we agree, in principle, that courts' authority to invoke the public policy exception is not limited solely to instances where the arbitration award itself violates positive law." No case is cited to support that proposition, and none could be. There is not a single decision, since this Court washed its hands of general common-lawmaking authority, see *Erie R. Co. v. Tompkins*, 304 U.S. 64 (1938), in which we have refused to enforce on "public policy" grounds an agreement that did not violate, or provide for the violation of, some positive law. *See, e.g., Hurd v. Hodge*, 334 U.S. 24 (1948) (refusing to enforce under the public policy doctrine a restrictive covenant that violated Rev. Stat. § 1978, at 42 U.S.C. § 1982).

Note

The Court's decision in *Eastern Associated Coal* made it clear that the public policy grounds for refusing to enforce arbitration awards in the labor context are very narrow. Subsequent cases reflect the lower courts' increased acceptance of this principle, even where public safety is implicated. *See, e.g., Entergy Operations, Inc. v. United Gov't Sec. Officers of Am. Int'l Union*, 856 F.3d 561 (8th Cir. 2017) (arbitrator's award reinstating nuclear plant security officer whose folliculitis hindered his ability to properly wear a respirator did not violate public policy because employer could provide a posting that did not require a respirator without violating federal law); *Va. Mason Hosp. v. Wash. State Nurses Ass'n*, 511 F.3d 908 (9th Cir. 2007) (arbitrator's award requiring employer to bargain before instituting mandatory influenza vaccination of nurses did not violate public policy even though the immunization would "enhance aggressive infection control procedures" and support federal and state standards requiring hospitals to develop infection control programs); *Boston Med. Ctr. v. SEIU, Local 285*, 260 F.3d 16 (1st Cir. 2001), *cert. denied*, 534 U.S. 1083 (2002) (finding no public policy violation where arbitrator ordered reinstatement of a nurse who gave substandard care to an infant who died on her shift; there was no evidence that her continued employment would endanger patient safety in the state); *see also Cont'l Airlines, Inc. v. Air Line Pilots Ass'n, Int'l*, 555 F.3d 399 (5th Cir. 2009) (reinstatement of pilot who refused to submit to no-notice alcohol test as required under last-chance agreement did not violate dominant and well-defined public policy, but condition of reinstatement requiring pilot to participate in airline's employee assistance program for two years both failed to draw its essence from the agreement and ran counter to public policy in federal Department of Transportation regulations vesting discretion in DOT's substance abuse professionals to make treatment evaluations of employees who violate DOT drug and alcohol regulations).

Overall, the Supreme Court's powerful message to lower courts regarding deference to arbitration awards appears to have had considerable impact. A study of 281 federal court decisions concluded that the courts affirmed 77.6% of the awards that came before them, an increase of approximately seven percentage points compared to previous studies measuring confirmation rates from 1960 to 2001. LeRoy & Feuille, *As the* Enterprise Wheel *Turns: New Evidence on the Finality of Labor Arbitration Awards*, 18 STAN. L. & POL'Y REV. 191 (2007).

Problem

61. Ronnie Bizer was discharged from his position as a forklift operator by All-American Motors Corporation after he sexually assaulted a female coworker, Ann Lafont. The facts are undisputed. During a telephone conversation, Bizer put down the telephone receiver and approached Lafont from behind and grabbed her breasts as she inspected a door panel nearby, within plain view of other workers. He then returned to the telephone and stated, "Yup, they're real." Pursuant to All-American's collective bargaining agreement with the Union, Allied Industrial Workers of America, the Union filed a grievance protesting Bizer's discharge. All-American denied the grievance and the matter proceeded to arbitration. The collective bargaining agreement provided that employees could be discharged for "just cause" and that the arbitrator had authority to decide questions as to the meaning and application of the agreement terms. Although All-American presented evidence that Bizer had committed four other incidents in which he intentionally grabbed and/or pinched female coworkers, the arbitrator found that All-American acquired this information after the discharge became public (which is apparently when they first were reported by other coworkers) and no disciplinary penalties had been applied; therefore the arbitrator refused to consider it. Other than these infractions, Bizer's 25-year work record was impeccable. The arbitrator also found that the evidence upon which Bizer's discharge was based did not indicate that he could not be rehabilitated. The arbitrator concluded that severe discipline short of discharge would be adequate to deter him from further misconduct and to demonstrate to all employees All-American's opposition to sexual harassment. The arbitrator determined that Bizer was not discharged for "just cause" and reduced the penalty to a 90-day suspension without pay, and directed All-American to reinstate Bizer with back pay from the date when his suspension would have ended.

All-American asks the district court to set aside the arbitration award on the basis that the decision of the arbitrator is contrary to the public policy against sexual harassment in the workplace established by Title VII of the Civil Rights Act of 1964. What arguments do you expect each side to make, and how should the court rule? Would it make any difference if you learn that Lafont, a 16-year employee and survivor of childhood sexual abuse, suffered considerable psychological harm from the incident and quit her job thereafter, unable to face her coworkers because she felt humiliated?

Section IV. The Enforcement of Strike Bans and the Effect of Norris-La Guardia

As you may recall, the Norris-LaGuardia Act of 1932 prohibited courts from issuing injunctions in labor disputes. Norris-LaGuardia Act of 1932, 29 U.S.C. § 101 (1932). The Act was passed in response to the widespread use of injunctions in labor cases to block concerted activity by workers who sought to advance legitimate employment concerns. Even the temporary suspension of a strike in response to an injunction had the practical effect of defeating the strike, since timing is often the most important element of an impactful strike. F. Frankfurter & N. Greene, The Labor Injunction 36–37 (1930). When Congress enacted § 301 of the Labor Management Relations Act of 1947, equipping courts with the authority to determine disputes under collective bargaining agreements, the question arose whether Norris-LaGuardia still blocked injunctive relief to remedy a breach of the collective bargaining agreement. The following cases address this question.

Boys Markets, Inc. v. Retail Clerks Local 770
Supreme Court of the United States
398 U.S. 235, 90 S. Ct. 1583, 26 L. Ed. 2d 199 (1970)

Mr. Justice Brennan delivered the opinion of the Court.

In this case we re-examine the holding of *Sinclair Refining Co. v. Atkinson*, 370 U.S. 195 (1962), that the anti-injunction provisions of the Norris-LaGuardia Act preclude a federal district court from enjoining a strike in breach of a no-strike obligation under a collective bargaining agreement, even though that agreement contains provisions, enforceable under § 301(a) of the Labor-Management Relations Act for binding arbitration of the grievance dispute concerning which the strike was called. The Court of Appeals for the Ninth Circuit, considering itself bound by *Sinclair*, reversed the grant by the District Court for the Central District of California of petitioner's prayer for injunctive relief. 416 F.2d 368 (1969). We granted certiorari. . . . Having concluded that *Sinclair* was erroneously decided and that subsequent events have undermined its continuing validity, we overrule that decision and reverse the judgment of the Court of Appeals.

I

In February 1969, at the time of the incidents that produced this litigation, petitioner and respondent were parties to a collective bargaining agreement which provided, *inter alia*, that all controversies concerning its interpretation or application should be resolved by adjustment and arbitration procedures set forth therein and that, during the life of the contract, there should be "no cessation or stoppage of work, lock-out, picketing or boycotts. . . ." The dispute arose when petitioner's frozen foods supervisor and certain members of his crew who were not members of the bargaining unit began to rearrange merchandise in the frozen food cases of one of petitioner's supermarkets. A union representative insisted that the food cases be stripped of all merchandise and be restocked by union personnel. When petitioner did not accede to the union's demand, a strike was called and the union began to picket petitioner's establishment. Thereupon petitioner demanded that the union cease the work stoppage and picketing and sought to invoke the grievance and arbitration procedures specified in the contract.

The following day, since the strike had not been terminated, petitioner filed a complaint in California Superior Court seeking a temporary restraining order, a preliminary and permanent injunction, and specific performance of the contractual arbitration provision. The state court issued a temporary restraining order forbidding continuation of the strike and also an order to show cause why a preliminary injunction should not be granted. Shortly thereafter, the union removed the case to the federal district court and there made a motion to quash the state court's temporary restraining order. In opposition, petitioner moved for an order compelling arbitration and enjoining continuation of the strike. Concluding that the dispute was subject to arbitration under the collective bargaining agreement and that the strike was in violation of the contract, the District Court ordered the parties to arbitrate the underlying dispute and simultaneously enjoined the strike, all picketing in the vicinity of petitioner's supermarket, and any attempts by the union to induce the employees to strike or to refuse to perform their services.

II

At the outset, we are met with respondent's contention that *Sinclair* ought not to be disturbed because the decision turned on a question of statutory construction which Congress can alter at any time. Since Congress has not modified our conclusions in *Sinclair*, even though it has been urged to do so, respondent argues that principles of *stare decisis* should govern the present case.

[The Court initially discussed the *stare decisis* doctrine, the *Lincoln Mills* holding that the Norris-LaGuardia Act did not preclude specific performance of an employer's promise to arbitrate grievance, and the *Steelworkers Trilogy* preference for arbitration as a dispute resolution technique.]

III

. . . .

Subsequent to the decision in *Sinclair*, we held in *Avco Corp. v. Aero Lodge No. 735*, [390 U.S. 557 (1968)], that §301(a) suits initially brought in state courts may be removed to the designated federal forum under the federal question removal jurisdiction delineated in 28 U.S.C. §1441. In so holding, however, the Court expressly left open the questions whether state courts are bound by the anti-injunction proscriptions of the Norris-LaGuardia Act and whether federal courts, after removal of a §301(a) action, are required to dissolve any injunctive relief previously granted by the state courts. *See generally General Electric Co. v. Local Union 191*, 413 F.2d 964 (5th Cir. 1969) (dissolution of state injunction required). Three Justices who concurred expressed the view that *Sinclair* should be reconsidered "upon an appropriate future occasion." 390 U.S. at 562 (STEWART, J., concurring).

The decision in *Avco*, viewed in the context of *Lincoln Mills* and its progeny, has produced an anomalous situation which, in our view, makes urgent the reconsideration of *Sinclair*. The principal practical effect of *Avco* and *Sinclair* taken together is nothing less than to oust state courts of jurisdiction in § 301(a) suits where injunctive relief is sought for breach of a no-strike obligation. Union defendants can, as a matter of course, obtain removal to a federal court, and there is obviously a compelling incentive for them to do so in order to gain the advantage of the strictures upon injunctive relief which *Sinclair* imposes on federal courts. The sanctioning of this practice, however, is wholly inconsistent with our conclusion in *Dowd Box* that the congressional purpose embodied in § 301(a) was to *supplement*, and not to encroach upon, the pre-existing jurisdiction of the state courts. It is ironic indeed that the very provision which Congress clearly intended to provide additional remedies for breach of collective bargaining agreements has been employed to displace previously existing state remedies. We are not at liberty thus to depart from the clearly expressed congressional policy to the contrary.

On the other hand, to the extent that widely disparate remedies theoretically remain available in state, as opposed to federal courts, the federal policy of labor law uniformity elaborated in *Lucas Flour Co.*, is seriously offended. This policy, of course, could hardly require, as a practical matter, that labor law be administered identically in all courts, for undoubtedly a certain diversity exists among the state and federal systems in matters of procedural and remedial detail, a fact which Congress evidently took into account in deciding not to disturb the traditional jurisdiction of the States. The injunction, however, is so important a remedial device, particularly in the arbitration context, that its availability or nonavailability in various courts will not only produce rampant forum-shopping and maneuvering from one court to another but will also greatly frustrate any relative uniformity in the enforcement of arbitration agreements.

Furthermore, the existing scheme, with the injunction remedy technically available in the state courts but rendered inefficacious by the removal device, assigns to removal proceedings a totally unintended function. While the underlying purposes of Congress in providing for federal question removal jurisdiction remain somewhat obscure, there has never been a serious contention that Congress intended that the removal mechanism be utilized to foreclose completely remedies otherwise available in the state courts. Although federal question removal jurisdiction may well have been intended to provide a forum for the protection of federal rights where such protection was deemed necessary or to encourage the development of expertise by the federal courts in the interpretation of federal law, there is no indication that Congress intended by the removal mechanism to effect a wholesale dislocation in the allocation of judicial business between the state and federal courts. . . .

It is undoubtedly true that each of the foregoing objections to *Sinclair-Avco* could be remedied either by overruling *Sinclair* or by extending that decision to the States. While some commentators have suggested that the solution to the present unsatisfactory situation does lie in the extension of the *Sinclair* prohibition to state court proceedings, we agree with Chief Justice Traynor of the California Supreme Court that "whether or not Congress could deprive state courts of the power to give such [injunctive] remedies when enforcing collective bargaining agreements, it has not attempted to do so either in the Norris-LaGuardia Act or section 301." *McCarroll v. Los Angeles County Dist. Council of Carpenters*, 49 Cal. 2d 45, 61, 315 P.2d 322, 332 (1957), *cert. denied*, 355 U.S. 932 (1958)....

An additional reason for not resolving the existing dilemma by extending *Sinclair* to the States is the devastating implications for the enforceability of arbitration agreements and their accompanying no-strike obligations if equitable remedies were not available. As we have previously indicated, a no-strike obligation, express or implied, is the *quid pro quo* for an undertaking by the employer to submit grievance disputes to the process of arbitration. *See Textile Workers Union v. Lincoln Mills*, supra at 455. Any incentive for employers to enter into such an arrangement is necessarily dissipated if the principal and most expeditious method by which the no-strike obligation can be enforced is eliminated. While it is of course true, as respondent contends, that other avenues of redress, such as an action for damages, would remain open to an aggrieved employer, an award of damages after a dispute has been settled is no substitute for an immediate halt to an illegal strike. Furthermore, an action for damages prosecuted during or after a labor dispute would only tend to aggravate industrial strife and delay an early resolution of the difficulties between employer and union.

Even if management is not encouraged by the unavailability of the injunction remedy to resist arbitration agreements, the fact remains that the effectiveness of such agreements would be greatly reduced if injunctive relief were withheld. Indeed, the very purpose of arbitration procedures is to provide a mechanism for the expeditious settlement of industrial disputes without resort to strikes, lockouts, or other self-help measures. This basic purpose is obviously largely undercut if there is no immediate, effective remedy for those very tactics which arbitration is designed to obviate. Thus, because *Sinclair*, in the aftermath of *Avco*, casts serious doubt upon the effective enforcement of a vital element of stable labor-management relations — arbitration agreements with their attendant no-strike obligations — we conclude that *Sinclair* does not make a viable contribution to federal labor policy.

IV

We have also determined that the dissenting opinion in *Sinclair* states the correct principles concerning the accommodation necessary between the seemingly absolute terms of the Norris-LaGuardia Act and the policy considerations underlying § 301(a). 370 U.S. at 215. Although we need not repeat all that was there said, a few points should be emphasized at this time.

The literal terms of § 4 of the Norris-LaGuardia Act must be accommodated to the subsequently enacted provisions of § 301(a) of the Labor-Management Relations Act and the purposes of arbitration. Statutory interpretation requires more than concentration upon isolated words; rather, consideration must be given to the total corpus of pertinent law and the policies which inspired ostensibly inconsistent provisions. *See Richards v. United States*, 369 U.S. 1, 11 (1962); *Mastro Plastics Corp. v. NLRB*, 350 U.S. 270, 285 (1956); *United States v. Hutcheson*, 312 U.S. 219, 235 (1941).

The Norris-LaGuardia Act was responsive to a situation totally different from that which exists today. In the early part of this century, the federal courts generally were regarded as allies of management in its attempt to prevent the organization and strengthening of labor unions; and in this industrial struggle the injunction became a potent weapon which was wielded against the activities of labor groups. The result was a large number of sweeping decrees, often issued *ex parte*, drawn on an *ad hoc* basis without regard to any systematic elaboration of national labor policy. *See Drivers' Union v. Lake Valley Co.*, 311 U.S. 91, 102 (1940).

In 1932 Congress attempted to bring some order out of the industrial chaos that had developed and to correct the abuses which had resulted from the interjection of the federal judiciary into union-management disputes on the behalf of management. See Declaration of Public Policy, Norris-LaGuardia Act, § 2.... Congress, therefore, determined initially to limit severely the power of the federal courts to issue injunctions "in any case involving or growing out of any labor dispute...." § 4.... Even as initially enacted, however, the prohibition against federal injunctions was by no means absolute. *See* Norris-LaGuardia Act, § 7, 8, 9.... Shortly thereafter Congress passed the Wagner Act, designed to curb various management activities which tended to discourage employee participation in collective action.

As labor organizations grew in strength and developed toward maturity, congressional emphasis shifted from protection of the nascent labor movement to the encouragement of collective bargaining and to administrative techniques for the peaceful resolution of industrial disputes. This shift in emphasis was accomplished, however, without extensive revision of many of the older enactments, including the anti-injunction section of the Norris-LaGuardia Act. Thus it became the task of the courts to accommodate, to reconcile the older statutes with the more recent ones.

A leading example of this accommodation process is *Brotherhood of R.R. Trainmen v. Chicago River & Ind. R.R.*, 353 U.S. 30 (1957). There we were confronted with a peaceful strike which violated the statutory duty to arbitrate imposed by the Railway Labor Act. The Court concluded that a strike in violation of a statutory arbitration duty was not the type of situation to which the Norris-LaGuardia Act was responsive, that an important federal policy was involved in the peaceful settlement of disputes through the statutorily mandated arbitration procedure, that this important policy was imperiled if equitable remedies were not available to implement it, and hence that Norris-LaGuardia's policy of nonintervention by the federal courts should yield to the overriding interest in the successful implementation of the arbitration process.

The principles elaborated in *Chicago River* are equally applicable to the present case. To be sure, *Chicago River* involved arbitration procedures established by statute. However, we have frequently noted, in such cases as *Lincoln Mills*, the *Steelworkers*

Trilogy, and *Lucas Flour*, the importance which Congress has attached generally to the voluntary settlement of labor disputes without resort to self-help and more particularly to arbitration as a means to this end. Indeed, it has been stated that *Lincoln Mills*, in its exposition of § 301(a), "went a long way towards making arbitration the central institution in the administration of collective bargaining contracts."

The *Sinclair* decision, however, seriously undermined the effectiveness of the arbitration technique as a method peacefully to resolve industrial disputes without resort to strikes, lockouts, and similar devices. Clearly employers will be wary of assuming obligations to arbitrate specifically enforceable against them when no similarly efficacious remedy is available to enforce the concomitant undertaking of the union to refrain from striking. On the other hand, the central purpose of the Norris-LaGuardia Act to foster the growth and viability of labor organizations is hardly retarded—if anything, this goal is advanced—by a remedial device which merely enforces the obligation that the union freely undertook under a specifically enforceable agreement to submit disputes to arbitration. We conclude, therefore, that the unavailability of equitable relief in the arbitration context presents a serious impediment to the congressional policy favoring the voluntary establishment of a mechanism for the peaceful resolution of labor disputes, that the core purpose of the Norris-LaGuardia Act is not sacrificed by the limited use of equitable remedies to further this important policy, and consequently that the Norris-LaGuardia Act does not bar the granting of injunctive relief in the circumstances of the instant case.

V

Our holding in the present case is a narrow one. We do not undermine the vitality of the Norris-LaGuardia Act. We deal only with the situation in which a collective bargaining contract contains a mandatory grievance adjustment or arbitration procedure. Nor does it follow from what we have said that injunctive relief is appropriate as a matter of course in every case of a strike over an arbitrable grievance. The dissenting opinion in *Sinclair* suggested the following principles for the guidance of the district courts in determining whether to grant injunctive relief—principles which we now adopt:

> A District Court entertaining an action under § 301 may not grant injunctive relief against concerted activity unless and until it decides that the case is one in which an injunction would be appropriate despite the Norris-LaGuardia Act. When a strike is sought to be enjoined because it is over a grievance which both parties are contractually bound to arbitrate, the District Court may issue no injunctive order until it first holds that the contract *does* have that effect; and the employer should be ordered to arbitrate, as a condition of his obtaining an injunction against the strike. Beyond this, the District Court must, of course, consider whether issuance of an injunction would be warranted under ordinary principles of equity—whether breaches are occurring and will continue, or have been threatened and will be committed; whether they have caused or will cause irreparable injury to

the employer; and whether the employer will suffer more from the denial of an injunction than will the union from its issuance.

370 U.S. at 228. (Emphasis in original.)

In the present case there is no dispute that the grievance in question was subject to adjustment and arbitration under the collective bargaining agreement and that the petitioner was ready to proceed with arbitration at the time an injunction against the strike was sought and obtained. The District Court also concluded that, by reason of respondent's violations of its no-strike obligation, petitioner "has suffered irreparable injury and will continue to suffer irreparable injury." Since we now overrule *Sinclair*, the holding of the Court of Appeals in reliance on *Sinclair* must be reversed. Accordingly, we reverse the judgment of the Court of Appeals and remand the case with directions to enter a judgment affirming the order of the District Court.

It is so ordered.

MR. JUSTICE MARSHALL took no part in the decision of this case.

MR. JUSTICE BLACK, dissenting. . . .

Although Congress has been urged to overrule our holding in *Sinclair*, it has steadfastly refused to do so. Nothing in the language or history of the two Acts has changed. Nothing at all has changed, in fact, except the membership of the Court and the personal views of one Justice. I remain of the opinion that *Sinclair* was correctly decided, and, moreover, that the prohibition of the Norris-LaGuardia Act is close to the heart of the entire federal system of labor regulation. In my view *Sinclair* should control the disposition of this case.

Even if the majority were correct, however, in saying that *Sinclair* misinterpreted the Taft-Hartley and Norris-LaGuardia Acts, I should be compelled to dissent. I believe that both the making and the changing of laws which affect the substantial rights of the people are primarily for Congress, not this Court. Most especially is this so when the law involved is the focus of strongly held views of powerful but antagonistic political and economic interests. The Court's function in the application and interpretation of such laws must be carefully limited to avoid encroaching on the power of Congress to determine policies and make laws to carry them out. . . .

[The concurring opinion of MR. JUSTICE STEWART is omitted. MR. JUSTICE WHITE dissented "for the reasons stated in the majority opinion in *Sinclair Refining Co. v. Atkinson*."]

Notes

1. *The Limits of Injunctive Relief*—Even when an injunction to halt a strike is appropriate under the test laid out by the Court in *Boys Markets*, the court's order must fall within the contours of the arbitration agreement. In *Otis Elevator Co. v. Int'l Union of Elevator Constructors, Local 4*, 408 F.3d 1 (1st Cir. 2005), the First Circuit concluded that while the district court had correctly enjoined the strike at issue and

ordered the parties to submit the dispute to arbitration, it had exceeded its authority by requiring that the parties submit to expedited arbitration, by restraining the employer from disciplining striking employees, and by barring the employer from "requesting further equitable relief from the court unless [it] first extend[ed] an offer to [the union] to arbitrate the dispute pursuant to a procedure other than the one outlined in the Agreement." The court reasoned that the district court violated the principles of *Boys Markets* and *Lincoln Mills, supra,* by requiring the parties to "submit to an arbitration regime different than what was contractually bargained for."

What if the contract contains an express no-strike clause, but no final and binding arbitration clause? What if it contains a final and binding arbitration clause, but no no-strike clause? If both are present, should they be read as coterminous? *Compare Delaware Coca-Cola Bottling Co. v. General Teamster Local Union 326*, 624 F.2d 1182 (3d Cir. 1980) (Yes), *with Ryder Truck Lines, Inc. v. Teamsters Freight Local Union 480*, 727 F.2d 594 (6th Cir.), *cert. denied*, 469 U.S. 825 (1984). What about a work stoppage over a dispute that could be submitted to grievance procedures but not to arbitration? *See American Tel. & Tel. Co. v. Communications Workers of America*, 985 F.2d 855 (6th Cir. 1993). *See generally* Axelrod, *The Application of the* Boys Markets *Decision in the Federal Courts*, 16 B.C. Ind. & Com. L. Rev. 893 (1975); Gould, *On Labor Injunctions, Unions, and the Judges: the* Boys Markets *Case*, 1970 Sup. Ct. Rev. 215; Vladeck, Boys Markets *and National Labor Policy*, 24 Vand. L. Rev. 93 (1970).

2. *Standards for* Boys Markets *Injunctions*—A disagreement has developed among the circuits concerning the standard a court deciding whether to issue a *Boys Markets* injunction should apply when determining whether a mandatory arbitration provision covers the dispute provoking a strike. Under the standard employed in the Sixth Circuit, a court cannot issue a *Boys Markets* injunction if the union has made a "colorable claim" that the strike did not concern an arbitrable issue, an approach that avoids evaluating the merits of the dispute at that stage. *Allied Sys. Ltd. v. Teamsters Nat'l Auto. Transporters Indus. Negotiating Comm., Local Union 327*, 179 F.3d 982 (6th Cir. 1999). However, under the rule employed in the Second and Eighth Circuits, courts must conduct a "preliminary interpretation" of the collective agreement at issue. *Elevator Mfrs' Ass'n v. International Union of Elevator Constructors*, 689 F.2d 382 (2d Cir. 1982); *National Rejectors Indus. v. United Steelworkers*, 562 F.2d 1069 (8th Cir. 1977). The Seventh Circuit requires a court to "resolve the arbitrability issue if that can be done purely as a matter of law," and conduct the test employed by the Second and Eighth Circuits "[i]f there are contractual ambiguities that would require further proceedings." *Chi. Dist. Council of Carpenters Pension Fund v. K & I Constr.*, 270 F.3d 1060 (7th Cir. 2001). What difference does it make which standard is applied?

3. *Strikes against Dangerous Conditions in the Workplace*—In *Gateway Coal Co. v. United Mine Workers*, 414 U.S. 368 (1974), the Supreme Court held that even a strike against allegedly unsafe conditions could be enjoined, when the union could have arbitrated its grievance that a mining company was retaining foremen who

had falsified air flow records. Section 502 of the LMRA, which provides that work stoppages because of abnormally dangerous conditions are not "strikes," does not apply in the absence of "ascertainable, objective evidence" of such unsafe conditions. What would constitute "abnormally dangerous" conditions justifying a work stoppage? *See Oil, Chem. & Atomic Workers Int'l Union v. NLRB*, 46 F.3d 82 (D.C. Cir.), *cert. denied*, 516 U.S. 821 (1995). On remand from the D.C. Circuit, the NLRB held that a work stoppage by employees who worked for a manufacturer of ammunition made from depleted uranium was protected by § 502, where the employees believed in good faith that their working conditions had become abnormally dangerous and their good faith belief was supported by objective evidence indicating that further exposure to the conditions in question could cause serious illness. *TNS, Inc.*, 329 N.L.R.B. 602 (1999). On a subsequent appeal, the Sixth Circuit agreed with the Board that § 502 applies whether or not the workers are bound by a no-strike provision, that the workers need only show a good faith belief supported by objective evidence that abnormally dangerous conditions exist, and that the employer may not hire permanent replacements during such a work stoppage. However, the court vacated the Board's decision, finding no substantial evidence to support the Board's finding that the workers had an objective basis for their belief of abnormal danger. The court also considered it unreasonable to hold the company responsible for damages accruing over the 20-year period of litigation occasioned by the Board's inexcusable delay, especially since the employer's structure and business operation had changed in the interim. *TNS, Inc. v. NLRB*, 296 F.3d 384 (6th Cir. 2002), *cert. denied sub nom. Paper, Allied-Indus., Chem. & Energy Workers Int'l Union v. TNS, Inc.*, 537 U.S. 1106 (2003). *See generally* Atleson, *Threats to Health and Safety: Employee Self-Help Under the NLRA*, 59 MINN. L. REV. 647 (1975).

4. *Boys Markets Injunctions against Employers*—*Boys Markets* injunctions are available against employer as well as union breaches of labor contracts that threaten the arbitral process. Thus, unions have obtained injunctions against employers who sought to impose unilateral changes prior to arbitration—if maintenance of the status quo was necessary to preserve the union's arbitral remedy. *See Aeronautical Indus. Dist. Lodge 91 v. United Techs. Corp.*, 230 F.3d 569 (2d Cir. 2000); *Newspaper & Periodical Drivers' & Helpers Local 921 v. San Francisco Newspaper Agency*, 89 F.3d 629 (9th Cir. 1996); *Local 884, United Rubber, Cork, Linoleum & Plastic Workers v. Bridgestone/Firestone*, 61 F.3d 1347 (8th Cir. 1995). Generally, however, unions have been unsuccessful in obtaining injunctions to bar unilateral imposition of drug-testing programs. *See Niagara Hooker Employees Union v. Occidental Chemical Corp.*, 935 F.2d 1370 (2d Cir. 1991); *Local 733 of Int'l Brotherhood of Electrical Workers v. Ingalls Shipbuilding Div., Litton Systems, Inc.*, 906 F.2d 149 (5th Cir. 1990); *but see Oil, Chemical & Atomic Workers Int'l Union, Local 2-286 v. Amoco Oil Co.*, 885 F.2d 697 (10th Cir. 1989).

5. *Injunctions to Halt Arbitration of Labor Disputes*—Can a party obtain a district court injunction against arbitration of a labor dispute concerning alleged violations

of a collective bargaining agreement? The Eleventh Circuit has joined the First, Third, Seventh, Ninth, and D.C. Circuits in refusing to extend *Boys Markets* to permit injunctions to halt arbitration of labor disputes. *See Triangle Constr. & Maint. Corp. v. Our V.I. Labor Union*, 425 F.3d 938 (11th Cir. 2005).

6. *Strike Injunctions Under the Railway Labor Act* — In *Brotherhood of R. Trainmen v. Chicago R. & I. R. Co.*, 353 U.S. 30 (1957), discussed in *Boys Markets*, the Supreme Court held that the Norris-LaGuardia Act does not prevent an injunction against a strike in a so-called "minor dispute," i.e., one involving a grievance under an existing collective agreement that is subject to statutory arbitration before the National Railroad Adjustment Board. On the other hand, the Court made clear in *Brotherhood of R. Trainmen v. Toledo, P. & W. Railroad*, 321 U.S. 50 (1944), that Norris-LaGuardia does prevent an injunction in a "major dispute" — one concerning future terms of employment. *See generally* Kroner, *Interim Injunctive Relief Under the Railway Labor Act: Some Problems and Suggestions*, in N.Y.U. Eighteenth Annual Conference on Labor 179 (1966).

Problem

62. In the fall of 2020, as the country struggled to contain the COVID-19 pandemic, colleges and universities struggled with the decision whether to resume classes in person or to shift to an online modality for the 2020–21 school year. Binnings College, a private liberal arts college located in North Carolina near Chapel Hill, determined that it would forge ahead and bring all students back to campus and to the residence halls. Although Binnings followed some COVID-19 protocols, including recommending mask-wearing and urging social distancing, it did nothing to facilitate that within its residence halls, instead assigning students as usual to share rooms and bathrooms. It also did not make changes to its classroom spaces or hallways, relying instead on encouragement to students to "do the right thing" and socially distance. The teachers at Binnings are represented by the United Teachers Union and have a collective bargaining agreement that includes both a no-strike clause and a broad arbitration clause. The agreement also includes a provision requiring Binnings to maintain a safe workplace, a provision previously understood to address protections against assaults or thefts on campus property or student protests that turn violent. In response to Binnings' decision to reopen rather than to continue with online teaching, the Union called a strike. The teachers view in-person instruction as a clear threat — not only to the health and safety of the students and the surrounding community, but to own their health: the median age of teachers at Binnings is 55, and many have preexisting conditions (ranging from pregnancy to high blood pressure and autoimmune disorders) that would make exposure to COVID-19 extremely dangerous. Can Binnings obtain a *Boys Markets* injunction to stop the strike and force the UTU to arbitrate the grievance? Could the UTU have filed a grievance instead and obtained a *Boys Markets* injunction to force Binnings to implement safety measures to preserve the status quo?

Buffalo Forge Co. v. United Steelworkers

Supreme Court of the United States
428 U.S. 397, 96 S. Ct. 3141, 49 L. Ed. 2d 1022 (1976)

[The Buffalo Forge Company operates three separate plant and office facilities in the Buffalo, New York area. The Steelworkers Union has represented the production and maintenance (P&M) employees at these plants for some years. Other locals of the Steelworkers were certified in 1974 to represent the office clerical-technical (O&T) employees of Buffalo Forge at the same three plants. On November 16, 1974, after several months of negotiations looking toward their first collective bargaining agreement, the O&T employees struck and established picket lines at all three locations. The P&M employees honored the picket lines and stopped work.]

[The company sued the union under § 301 of the Taft-Hartley Act in Federal District Court for breach of the no-strike clause in the P&M collective agreement, seeking an injunction against the work stoppage. The collective agreement provided for arbitration as follows: "Should differences arise . . . as to the meaning and application of the provisions of this Agreement, or should any trouble of any kind arise in the plant, there shall be no suspension of work on account of such differences, but an earnest effort shall be made to settle such differences immediately. . . . In the event the grievance involves a question as to the meaning and application of this Agreement, and has not been previously satisfactorily adjusted, it may be submitted to arbitration upon written notice of the Union or the Company." The District Court found that the P&M employees had engaged in a sympathy action in support of the O&T employees, but held itself forbidden to enjoin it by the Norris-LaGuardia Act. The Court of Appeals affirmed, and the Supreme Court granted certiorari.]

Mr. Justice White delivered the opinion of the Court.

The issue for decision is whether a federal court may enjoin a sympathy strike pending the arbitrator's decision as to whether the strike is forbidden by the express no-strike clause contained in the collective bargaining contract to which the striking union is a party. . . .

. . . .

II

As a preliminary matter, certain elements in this case are not in dispute. The Union has gone on strike not by reason of any dispute it or any of its members has with the employer but in support of other local unions, of the same international organization, that were negotiating a contract with the employer and were out on strike. The parties involved here are bound by a collective bargaining contract containing a no-strike clause which the Union claims does not forbid sympathy strikes. The employer has the other view, its complaint in the District Court asserting that the work stoppage violated the no-strike clause. The contract between the parties also has an arbitration clause broad enough to reach not only disputes between the Union and the employer about other provisions in the contract but also as to the meaning and application of the no-strike clause itself. Whether the sympathy strike the Union called violated the no-strike clause, and the appropriate remedies if it did, are subject to the agreed-upon dispute-settlement procedures of the contract and are ultimately issues for the arbitrator. [Citing the *Steelworkers Trilogy*.] The employer thus was entitled to invoke the arbitral process to determine the legality of the sympathy strike and to obtain a court order requiring the Union to arbitrate if the Union refused to do so. *Gateway Coal Co. v. United Mine Workers*, 414 U.S. 368 (1974). Furthermore, were the issue arbitrated and the strike found illegal, the relevant federal statutes as construed in our cases would permit an injunction to enforce the arbitral decision. *United Steelworkers of America v. Enterprise Wheel & Car Corp.* [363 U.S. 593 (1960)].

The issue in this case arises because the employer not only asked for an order directing the Union to arbitrate but prayed that the strike itself be enjoined pending arbitration and the arbitrator's decision whether the strike was permissible under the no-strike clause. . . .

The holding in *Boys Markets* was said to be a "narrow one," dealing only with the situation in which the collective bargaining contract contained mandatory grievance and arbitration procedures. 398 U.S. at 253. . . . The driving force behind *Boys Markets* was to implement the strong congressional preference for the private dispute settlement mechanisms agreed upon by the parties. Only to that extent was it held necessary to accommodate §4 of the Norris-LaGuardia Act to §301 of the Labor Management Relations Act and to lift the former's ban against the issuance of injunctions in labor disputes. Striking over an arbitrable dispute would interfere with and frustrate the arbitral processes by which the parties had chosen to settle a dispute. The *quid pro quo* for the employer's promise to arbitrate was the union's obligation not to strike over issues that were subject to the arbitration machinery. Even in the absence of an express no-strike clause, an undertaking not to strike would be implied where the strike was over an otherwise arbitrable dispute. *Gateway Coal Co. v. United Mine Workers, supra; Teamsters Local v. Lucas Flour Co.*, 369 U.S. 95 (1962). Otherwise, the employer would be deprived of his bargain and the policy of the labor statutes to implement private resolution of disputes in a manner agreed upon would seriously suffer.

Boys Markets plainly does not control this case. The District Court found, and it is not now disputed, that the strike was not *over* any dispute between the Union and the employer that was even remotely subject to the arbitration provisions of the contract. The strike at issue was a sympathy strike in support of sister unions negotiating with the employer; neither its causes nor the issue underlying it were subject to the settlement procedures provided by the contract between the employer and respondents. The strike had neither the purpose nor the effect of denying or evading an obligation to arbitrate or of depriving the employer of his bargain. Thus, had the contract not contained a no-strike clause or had the clause expressly excluded sympathy strikes, there would have been no possible basis for implying from the existence of an arbitration clause a promise not to strike that could have been violated by the sympathy strike in this case. *Gateway Coal Co. v. Mine Workers, supra* at 382.[6]

Nor was the injunction authorized solely because it was alleged that the sympathy strike called by the Union violated the express no-strike provision of the contract. Section 301 of the Act assigns a major role to the courts in enforcing collective bargaining agreements, but aside from the enforcement of the arbitration provisions of such contracts, within the limits permitted by *Boys Markets*, the Court has never indicated that the courts may enjoin actual or threatened contract violations despite the Norris-LaGuardia Act. In the course of enacting the Taft-Hartley Act, Congress rejected the proposal that the Norris-LaGuardia Act's prohibition against labor-dispute injunctions be lifted to the extent necessary to make injunctive remedies available in federal courts for the purpose of enforcing collective bargaining agreements. . . . The allegation of the complaint that the Union was breaching its obligation not to strike did not in itself warrant an injunction. . . .

Here the Union struck, and the parties were in dispute whether the sympathy strike violated the Union's no-strike undertaking. Concededly, that issue was arbitrable. It was for the arbitrator to determine whether there was a breach, as well as the remedy for any breach, and the employer was entitled to an order requiring the Union to arbitrate if it refused to do so. But the Union does not deny its duty to arbitrate; in fact, it denies that the employer ever demanded arbitration. However that may be, it does not follow that the District Court was empowered not only to order arbitration but to enjoin the strike pending the decision of the arbitrator, despite the express prohibition of § 4(a) of the Norris-LaGuardia Act against injunctions prohibiting any person "from ceasing or refusing to perform any work or to remain in any relation of employment." If an injunction could issue against the strike in this case, so in proper circumstances could a court enjoin any other alleged breach of contract pending the exhaustion of the applicable grievance and arbitration provisions even though the injunction would otherwise violate one of the express prohibitions of § 104. The court in such cases would be permitted, if the dispute was arbitrable, to hold hearings, make findings of fact, interpret the applicable provisions of the contract and issue injunctions so as to restore the *status quo ante* or to otherwise regulate the relationship of the parties pending exhaustion of the arbitration process. This would cut deeply into the policy of the Norris-LaGuardia Act and make the courts potential participants in a wide range of arbitrable disputes under the many existing and future collective bargaining contracts, not just for the purpose of enforcing promises to arbitrate, which was the limit of *Boys Markets*, but for the purpose of preliminarily dealing with the merits of the factual and legal issues that are subjects for the arbitrator and of issuing injunctions that would otherwise be forbidden by the Norris-LaGuardia Act.

---

6. [10] To the extent that the Court of Appeals, 517 F.2d, at 1211, and other courts . . . have assumed that a mandatory arbitration clause implies a commitment not to engage in sympathy strikes, they are wrong.

This is not what the parties have bargained for. Surely it cannot be concluded here, as it was in *Boys Markets*, that such injunctions pending arbitration are essential to carry out promises to arbitrate and to implement the private arrangements for the administration of the contract. As is typical, the agreement in this case outlines the pre-arbitration settlement procedures and provides that if the grievance "has not been . . . satisfactorily adjusted," arbitration may be had. Nowhere does it provide for coercive action of any kind, let alone judicial injunctions, short of the terminal decision of the arbitrator. The parties have agreed to grieve and arbitrate, not to litigate. They have not contracted for a judicial preview of the facts and the law. Had they anticipated additional regulation of their relationships pending arbitration, it seems very doubtful that they would have resorted to litigation rather than to private arrangements. The unmistakable policy of Congress stated in 29 U.S.C. §173 (d), 61 Stat. 153, is that "Final adjustment by a method agreed upon by the parties is declared to be the desirable method for settlement of grievance disputes arising over the application or interpretation of an existing collective bargaining agreement." *Gateway Coal Co. v. United Mine Workers, supra* at 377. But the parties' agreement to adjust or to arbitrate their differences themselves would be eviscerated if the courts for all practical purposes were to try and decide contractual disputes at the preliminary injunction stage.

The dissent suggests that injunctions should be authorized in cases such as this at least where the violation, in the court's view, is clear and the court is sufficiently sure that the parties seeking the injunction will win before the arbitrator. But this would still involve hearings, findings and judicial interpretations of collective bargaining contracts. It is incredible to believe that the courts would always view the facts and the contract as the arbitrator would; and it is difficult to believe that the arbitrator would not be heavily influenced or wholly preempted by judicial views of the facts and the meaning of contracts if this procedure is to be permitted. Injunctions against strikes, even temporary injunctions, very often permanently settle the issue; and in other contexts time and expense would be discouraging factors to the losing party in court in considering whether to relitigate the issue before the arbitrator.

With these considerations in mind, we are far from concluding that the arbitration process will be frustrated unless the courts have the power to issue interlocutory injunctions pending arbitration in cases such as this or in others in which an arbitrable dispute awaits decision. We agree with the Court of Appeals that there is no necessity here, such as was found to be the case in *Boys Markets*, to accommodate the policies of the Norris-LaGuardia Act to the requirements of §301 by empowering the District Court to issue the injunction sought by the employer.

The judgment of the Court of Appeals is affirmed.

So ordered.

Mr. Justice Stevens, with whom **Mr. Justice Brennan, Mr. Justice Marshall,** and **Mr. Justice Powell** join, dissenting. . . .

The Court today holds that only a part of the union's *quid pro quo* is enforceable by injunction.[7] The principal bases for the holding are (1) the Court's literal interpretation of the Norris-LaGuardia Act; and (2) its fear that the federal judiciary would otherwise make a "massive" entry into the business of contract interpretation heretofore reserved for arbitrators. The first argument has been rejected repeatedly in cases in which the central concerns of the Norris-LaGuardia Act were not implicated. The second is wholly unrealistic and was implicitly rejected in *Gateway Coal* when the Court held that "a substantial question of contractual interpretation" was a sufficient basis for federal equity jurisdiction. 414 U.S. at 384. That case held that an employer might enforce a somewhat ambiguous *quid pro quo*; today the Court holds that a portion of the *quid pro quo* is unenforceable no matter how unambiguous it may be. With all respect, I am persuaded that a correct application of the reasoning underlying the landmark decision in *Boys Markets, Inc. v. Clerks Union*, 398 U.S. 235, requires a different result.

. . . .

[There follows a detailed review of the rationale in *Boys Markets*.]

The *Boys Markets* decision protects the arbitration process. A court is authorized to enjoin a strike over a grievance which the parties are contractually bound to arbitrate, but that authority is conditioned upon a finding that the contract does so provide, that the strike is in violation of the agreement, and further that the issuance of an injunction is warranted by ordinary principles of equity. These conditions plainly stated in *Boys Markets* demonstrate that the interest in protecting the arbitration process is not simply an end in itself which exists at large and apart from other fundamental aspects of our national labor policy.

On the one hand, an absolute precondition of any *Boys Markets* injunction is a contractual obligation. A court may not order arbitration unless the parties have agreed to that process; nor can the court require the parties to accept an arbitrator's decision unless they have agreed to be bound by it. If the union reserves the right to resort to self-help at the conclusion of the arbitration process, that agreement must be respected. The court's power is limited by the contours of the agreement between the parties.[8]

On the other hand, the arbitration procedure is not merely an exercise; it performs the important purpose of determining what the underlying agreement

---

7. [2] The enforceable part of the no-strike agreement is the part relating to a strike "over an arbitrable dispute." In *Gateway Coal*, however, my Brethren held that the district court had properly entered an injunction that not only terminated a strike pending an arbitrator's decision of an underlying safety dispute, but also "prospectively required both parties to abide by his resolution of the controversy." *Id.* at 373. A strike in defiance of an arbitrator's award would not be "over an arbitrable dispute"; nevertheless, the Court today recognizes the propriety of an injunction against such a strike.

8. [17] In particular, an implied no-strike clause does not extend to sympathy strikes. See *ante* at n.10.

actually means as applied to a specific setting. If the parties have agreed to be bound by the arbitrator's decision, the reasons which justify an injunction against a strike that would impair his ability to reach a decision must equally justify an injunction requiring the parties to abide by a decision that a strike is in violation of the no-strike clause.[9] The arbitration mechanism would hardly retain its respect as a method of resolving disputes if the end product of the process had less significance than the process itself. . . .

In this case, the question whether the sympathy strike violates the no-strike clause is an arbitrable issue. If the court had the benefit of an arbitrator's resolution of the issue in favor of the employer, it could enforce that decision just as it could require the parties to submit the issue to arbitration. And if the agreement were so plainly unambiguous that there could be no bona fide issue to submit to the arbitrator, there must be the same authority to enforce the parties' bargain pending the arbitrator's final decision.

The Union advances three arguments against this conclusion: (1) that interpretation of the collective bargaining agreement is the exclusive province of the arbitrator; (2) that an injunction erroneously entered pending arbitration will effectively deprive the union of the right to strike before the arbitrator can render his decision; and (3) that it is the core purpose of the Norris-LaGuardia Act to eliminate the risk of an injunction against a lawful strike. Although I acknowledge the force of these arguments, I think they are insufficient to take this case outside the rationale of *Boys Markets*.

The *Steelworkers Trilogy* establishes that a collective bargaining agreement submitting all questions of contract interpretation to the arbitrator deprives the courts of almost all power to interpret the agreement to prevent submission of a dispute to arbitration or to refuse enforcement of an arbitrator's award. *Boys Markets* itself repeated the warning that it was not for the courts to usurp the functions of the arbitrator. And *Gateway Coal* held that an injunction may issue to protect the arbitration process even if a "substantial question of contractual interpretation" must be answered to determine whether the strike is over an arbitrable grievance. In each of these cases, however, the choice was between interpretation of the agreement by the court or interpretation by the arbitrator; a decision that the dispute was not arbitrable, or not properly arbitrated, would have precluded an interpretation of the agreement according to the contractual grievance procedure. In the present case, an interim determination of the no-strike question by the court neither usurps nor precludes a decision by the arbitrator. By definition, issuance of an injunction pending the arbitrator's decision does not supplant a decision that he otherwise would have made. Indeed, it is the ineffectiveness of the damage remedy for strikes pending arbitration that lends force to the employer's argument for an injunction. The

---

9. [18] The Court recognizes that an injunction may issue to enforce an arbitrator's decision that a strike is in violation of the no-strike clause. . . .

court does not oust the arbitrator of his proper function but fulfills a role that he never served.

The Union's second point, however, is that the arbitrator will rarely render his decision quickly enough to prevent an erroneously issued injunction from effectively depriving the union of its right to strike. The Union relies particularly upon decisions of this Court that recognize that even a temporary injunction can quickly end a strike. But this argument demonstrates only that arbitration, to be effective, must be prompt, not that the federal courts must be deprived entirely of jurisdiction to grant equitable relief. Denial of an injunction when a strike violates the agreement may have effects just as devastating to an employer as the issuance of an injunction may have to the union when the strike does not violate the agreement. Furthermore, a sympathy strike does not directly further the economic interests of the members of the striking local or contribute to the resolution of any dispute between that local, or its members, and the employer. On the contrary, it is the source of a new dispute which, if the strike goes forward, will impose costs on the strikers, the employer, and the public without prospect of any direct benefit to any of these parties. A rule that authorizes postponement of a sympathy strike pending an arbitrator's clarification of the no-strike clause will not critically impair the vital interests of the striking local even if the right to strike is upheld, and will avoid the costs of interrupted production if the arbitrator concludes that the no-strike clause applies.

Finally, the Norris-LaGuardia Act cannot be interpreted to immunize the union from all risk of an erroneously issued injunction. *Boys Markets* itself subjected the union to the risk of an injunction entered upon a judge's erroneous conclusion that the dispute was arbitrable and that the strike was in violation of the no-strike clause. *Gateway Coal* subjected the union to a still greater risk, for the court there entered an injunction to enforce an implied no-strike clause despite the fact that the arbitrability of the dispute, and hence the legality of the strike over the dispute, presented a "substantial question of contractual interpretation." The strict reading that the Union would give the Norris-LaGuardia Act would not have permitted this result.

These considerations, however, do not support the conclusion that a sympathy strike should be temporarily enjoined whenever a collective bargaining agreement contains a no-strike clause and an arbitration clause. The accommodation between the Norris-LaGuardia Act and §301(a) of the Labor Management Relations Act allows the judge to apply "the usual processes of the law" but not to take the place of the arbitrator. Because of the risk that a federal judge, less expert in labor matters than an arbitrator, may misconstrue general contract language, I would agree that no injunction or temporary restraining order should issue without first giving the union an adequate opportunity to present evidence and argument, particularly upon the proper interpretation of the collective bargaining agreement; the judge should not issue an injunction without convincing evidence that the strike is clearly within the no-strike clause.[10] Furthermore, to protect the efficacy of arbitration, any such injunction should require the parties to submit the issue immediately to the contractual grievance procedure, and if the union so requests, at the last stage and upon an expedited schedule that assures a decision by the arbitrator as soon as practicable. Such stringent conditions would insure that only strikes in violation of the agreement would be enjoined and that the union's access to the arbitration process would not be foreclosed by the combined effect of a temporary injunction and protected grievance procedures. Finally, as in *Boys Markets*, the normal conditions of equitable relief would have to be met.

Like the decision in *Boys Markets*, this opinion reflects, on the one hand, my confidence that experience during the decades since the Norris-LaGuardia Act was passed has dissipated any legitimate concern about the impartiality of federal judges in disputes between labor and management, and on the other, my continued recognition of the fact that judges have less familiarity and expertise than arbitrators and administrators who regularly work in this specialized area. The decision in *Boys Markets* requires an accommodation between the Norris-LaGuardia Act and the Labor Management Relations Act. I would hold only that the terms of that accommodation do not entirely deprive the federal courts of all power to grant any relief to an employer, threatened with irreparable injury from a sympathy strike clearly in violation of a collective bargaining agreement, regardless of the equities of his claim for injunctive relief pending arbitration. . . .

Notes

1. *Reconciling* Buffalo Forge *with* Boys Markets — Doesn't *Buffalo Forge* clearly flout the *Boys Markets* policy of substituting arbitration for strikes? On the other hand, if a Justice was uneasy that *Boys Markets* itself may have come close to flouting the congressional policy expressed in Norris-LaGuardia (*see* Justice Black's majority opinion in *Sinclair Ref.*, quoted *supra*), might he or she not feel more comfortable in limiting federal injunctions so that the enjoinable no-strike *quid* is coextensive with the arbitration *quo*? See, e.g., *Westmoreland Coal Co. v. International Union, United Mine Workers*, 910 F.2d 130 (4th Cir. 1990) (affirming injunction against a work stoppage protesting the employer's discipline of sympathy strikers because issue was arbitrable). In any event, how can the Court justify under a strict *Boys Markets-Buffalo Forge* analysis the federal courts' willingness to "specifically enforce" an arbitrator's order that a union cease striking over an issue not itself subject to arbitration? See, e.g., *New Orleans S.S. Ass'n v. General Longshore Workers*, 389 F.2d 369 (5th Cir.), cert. denied, 393 U.S. 828 (1968); *Pacific Maritime Ass'n*

---

10. [27] Of course, it is possible that an arbitrator would disagree with the court even when the latter finds the strike to be clearly prohibited. But in that case, the arbitrator's determination would govern, provided it withstands the ordinary standard of review for arbitrator's awards. *See United Steelworkers of America v. Enterprise Wheel & Car Corp.*, 363 U.S. 593, 597–599.

v. International Longshoremen's & Warehousemen's Union, 454 F.2d 262 (9th Cir. 1971).

2. *Political Protests*—Applying *Buffalo Forge*, the Supreme Court held (6-3) that a *Boys Markets* injunction was unavailable against a longshoremen's union that, despite a no-strike clause, refused to handle cargo destined for the Soviet Union as a political protest against the Russian invasion of Afghanistan. The underlying political dispute was considered "plainly not arbitrable under the collective bargaining agreement." *Jacksonville Bulk Terminals, Inc. v. International Longshoremen's Ass'n*, 457 U.S. 702 (1982). *See* Rasnic, *Boys Markets and the Labor Injunction Revisited:* Jacksonville Bulk Terminals, 33 Lab. L.J. 704 (1982). However, a union cannot evade an injunction by characterizing its dispute as a political protest as opposed to a strike when the dispute either grows out of a major dispute subject to the RLA, or was over a nonmandatory subject of collective bargaining within the discretion of management. *AMTRAK v. Transp. Workers Union*, 373 F.3d 121 (D.C. Cir. 2004).

3. *Sympathy Strikes*—A general no-strike clause in a labor contract does not bar a union from engaging in sympathy strikes on behalf of other unions at the company. In order for a union to waive the employees' §7 right to engage in sympathy strikes, the waiver must be clear and unmistakable, so that union members are aware that the right is being bargained away. *Children's Hosp. Med. Ctr. v. Cal. Nurses Ass'n*, 283 F.3d 1188 (9th Cir. 2002) (citing and applying *Wright v. Universal Maritime Service Corp.*, discussed *supra*). The same standard applies to a sympathy strike mounted in support of another bargaining unit of the same union: §7 does not distinguish between sympathy strikes in support of sister unions and those in support of other units of the same union. *See Std. Concrete Prods. v. General Truck Drivers, Office, Food & Warehouse Union, Local 952*, 353 F.3d 668 (9th Cir. 2003) (finding no-strike clause not a clear and unmistakable waiver of right to engage in sympathy strike in support of another unit of the same union).

4. *Wildcat Sympathy Strikes*—In *Cedar Coal Co. v. United Mine Workers*, 560 F.2d 1153 (4th Cir. 1977), *cert. denied*, 434 U.S. 1047 (1978), the court ruled that some wildcat sympathy strikes in the coal industry may be subject to injunctive relief, despite the Supreme Court's holding in *Buffalo Forge*. Where "the purpose of the strike of Local [A] was to compel [the company] to concede an arbitrable issue to Local [B], with the same employer, the same collective bargaining agreement, the same bargaining unit, and the cause of Local [B] made its own, the *Buffalo Forge* exception to *Boys Markets* should not apply." *Cf. United States Steel Corp. v. United Mine Workers*, 593 F.2d 201 (3d Cir. 1979).

Problem

63. The players in the National Basketball Association are represented by the NBA Players' Association. Both the NBA and the Players' Association have been in the vanguard on a variety of civil rights issues over the years. That said, both the

association and the union recognize the need to maintain the broad appeal enjoyed by the league in order to maximize ticket and television advertising revenue.

The most recent collective bargaining agreement contains a no-strike clause, a broad arbitration provision, and provisions authorizing discharge or discipline of players for failing to attend practices or games. And, in response to the recent publicity surrounding a number of football players in the National Football League kneeling during the playing of the national anthem to highlight the issue of police brutality against black men, the NBA agreement contains a provision requiring players to remain standing during the anthem but allowing them to wear a black band on the top of their jersey or on their shoes to show support for any (noncommercial) cause.

In response to news coverage of a particularly egregious instance of police brutality, the players on one of the teams decide to ignore the anthem restriction and take a knee during the playing of the national anthem. They vow to continue doing so as long as black men disproportionately bear the brunt of police brutality in society.

The players on another team take the protest a step farther, and refuse to play in scheduled games. They argue that police brutality affects their lives and their families' lives, impacting their physical ability to play for the League. These players vow to continue their action until the League commits to funding social justice initiatives and police reform initiatives in support of the Black Lives Matter movement, including funding advertising spots that would air during televised games.

The NBA Players' Association did not approve the actions taken by the players on either team. Can the League obtain an injunction to stop the kneeling action or the strike? What other remedies are available?

Complete Auto Transit, Inc. v. Reis, 451 U.S. 401, 101 S. Ct. 1836, 68 L. Ed. 2d 248 (1981). Believing their union was not properly representing them in contract negotiations, a group of employees engaged in a "wildcat" or unauthorized strike in violation of a no-strike clause in the collective bargaining agreement between their employers and the union. Previously, in *Atkinson v. Sinclair Refining Co.*, 370 U.S. 238 (1962), the Supreme Court had held that § 301 did not authorize a damage action against individual union officers and members when their union was liable for violating a no-strike provision. Now a majority of the Court extended that immunity to situations where the individuals striking in breach of contract were not acting on behalf of the union but in their "personal and nonunion capacity." Justice Brennan, for the Court, recognized that § 301(b) by its terms only "forbids a money judgment entered against a union from being enforced against individual union members." But he declared that "the legislative history of § 301 clearly reveals Congress' intent to shield individual employees from liability for damages arising from their breach of the no-strike clause of a collective bargaining agreement, whether or not the union participated in or authorized the illegality." This was so, he added, "even though it might leave the employer unable to recover for his losses." The Court thought that employer or union discipline of wildcatting workers would constitute a sufficient sanction. It expressly left open the question of whether a *Boys Markets* injunction would be available against wildcatters. Chief Justice Burger and Justice Rehnquist dissented on the grounds that § 301(b) merely "affords individual union members protection against individual liability for collective action," and did not change "the common law rule of contract law of *individual* liability for *individual* conduct." The dissenters regarded such measures as employer discharge or union discipline of wildcat strikers as "no answer; they may be too little and they surely come too late."

Notes

1. Boys Markets *Injunctions against Wildcat Strikers* — Would a *Boys Markets* injunction have been available against the individual wildcat strikers in *Complete Auto Transit*? Generally, the answer is no, since § 301 of the Labor Management Relations Act does not authorize suits against individual members of a union, nor does *Boys Markets*' exception to the Norris-LaGuardia Act prohibition of injunctions in labor disputes provide for the pursuit of injunctive relief against individuals. However, where the individuals are officers of the union, the question is more difficult. *See Hobet Mining v. Local 5817, United Mine Workers*, 143 L.R.R.M. 2302 (S.D.W. Va. 1993) (refusing to impose liability on union officers and evaluating arguments pro and con). *See also* Coulson, *Justice Brennan on Wheels:* Complete Auto Transit, Best Freight *and* Clayton v. UAW, *in* N.Y.U. THIRTY-FOURTH ANNUAL CONFERENCE ON LABOR 139 (1981).

2. *Liability of International Unions for the Actions of their Locals* — The Supreme Court held in *Carbon Fuel Co. v. United Mine Workers*, 444 U.S. 212 (1979), that an international union that "neither instigates, supports, ratifies, or encourages" wildcat strikes engaged in by local unions in violation of a collective bargaining agreement is not liable in damages to affected employers even if the international union "did not use all reasonable means available to it to prevent the strikes or bring about their termination." Why was a judgment against the international union in *Carbon Fuel* so important to the plaintiffs in view of the fact that they had a very substantial judgment against the local unions? Briefs for the coal operators alleged that the "local assets are negligible" and "most Local Unions of the UMWA are, for all practical purposes, judgment proof."

Courts have employed the principles articulated in *Carbon Fuel* to determine the liability of international unions for the actions of local unions in a variety of legal contexts. *See, e.g., Laughon v. Int'l Alliance of Theatrical Stage Emples.*, 248 F.3d 931 (9th Cir. 2001) (employing *Carbon Fuel* principles in a sex discrimination suit under Title VII); *Alexander v. Local 496, Laborers' Int'l Union*, 177 F.3d 394 (6th Cir. 1999) (employing *Carbon Fuel* principles in a race discrimination suit under Title VII); *Brenner v. United Bhd. of Carpenters & Joiners*, 927 F.2d 1283 (3d Cir. 1991) (employing *Carbon Fuel* principles in a suit regarding alleged discriminatory treatment of local union members in retaliation for internal union activities); *Berger v. Iron Workers Reinforced Rodmen Local 201*, 843 F.2d 1395 (D.C. Cir. 1988) (employing *Carbon Fuel* principles in a race discrimination suit under Title VII).

3. *Mass Action Theory*—At the trial of the *Carbon Fuel* case, the locals were held responsible for the wildcat action of their members on a "mass action" theory—that "large groups of men do not act collectively without leadership and a functioning union must be held responsible for the mass action of its members. However, responsibility for wildcat strikes under this theory will ordinarily be limited to the local union." 582 F.2d 1346 (4th Cir. 1978). Supreme Court review of the judgment against the local was not sought and so *Carbon Fuel* did not afford an opportunity for the Supreme Court to consider the "mass action" theory. Its continuing vitality was accepted in *Consolidation Coal Co. v. Local 1702 United Mine Workers*, 709 F.2d 882 (4th Cir.), *cert. denied*, 464 U.S. 993 (1983), and *North River Energy Corp. v. United Mine Workers*, 664 F.2d 1184 (11th Cir. 1981), but rejected in *Fry v. Airline Pilots Ass'n*, 88 F.3d 831 (10th Cir. 1996) ("union liability under §6 for tortious acts cannot be established by an inference drawn solely from the fact that union members are committing unlawful acts, even in groups and even over a substantial period of time"). *See also* Cureton & Kisch, *Union Liability for Illegal Strikes: The Mass Action Theory Redefined*, 87 W. Va. L. Rev. 57 (1984–85).

4. *Liability of Union Officers*—While the *Complete Auto Transit* Court determined that union members are shielded from liability in their individual capacities for violation of no-strike clauses, a union officer may be held liable in his or her individual capacity for a violation of the union constitution. *See, e.g., SEIU v. Nat'l Union of Healthcare Workers*, 598 F.3d 1061 (9th Cir. 2010); *Shea v. McCarthy*, 953 F.2d 29 (2d Cir. 1992); *International Union of Elec., Salaried, Mach. & Furniture Workers v. Statham*, 97 F.3d 1416 (11th Cir. 1996). Nor are union officers immune under §301(b) from state-law claims that do not relate to collective bargaining agreements covered by §301(a). *Northwestern Ohio Adm'rs, Inc. v. Walcher & Fox, Inc.*, 270 F.3d 1018 (6th Cir. 2001); *Felice v. Sever*, 985 F.2d 1221, 1230 (3d Cir. 1993). On the other hand, citing *Atkinson* and *Complete Auto Transit*, courts have ruled that §301(b) immunizes a union attorney from suit by a union member for alleged legal malpractice committed while performing services related to a collective bargaining agreement. *See Carino v. Stefan*, 376 F.3d 156 (3rd Cir. 2004); *Waterman v. Transport Workers' Union Local 100*, 176 F.3d 150 (2d Cir. 1999); *Arnold v. Air Midwest*, 100 F.3d 857 (10th Cir. 1996); *Breda v. Scott*, 1 F.3d 908 (9th Cir. 1993); *Montplaisir v. Leighton*, 875 F.2d 1 (1st Cir. 1989); *Peterson v. Kennedy*, 771 F.2d 1244 (9th Cir. 1985).

5. *Arbitration and Injunctive Relief*—If the employer as well as the union is entitled to refer a matter to arbitration, the union can get a stay of a court suit for damages by the employer, pending arbitration, even though the union has allegedly struck in violation of the contract. *Drake Bakeries, Inc. v. American Bakery & Confectionery Workers International*, 370 U.S. 254 (1962). Declared the Court: "We can enforce both the no-strike clause and the agreement to arbitrate by granting a stay until the claim for damages is presented to an arbitrator." In response to the employer's argument that the parties could not have intended to arbitrate "so fundamental a matter as a union strike in breach of contract," the Court said:

> Arbitration provisions, which themselves have not been repudiated, are meant to survive breaches of contract, in many contexts, even total breach.... We do not decide in this case that in no circumstances would a strike in violation of the no-strike clause contained in this or other contracts entitle the employer to rescind or abandon the entire contract or to declare its promise to arbitrate forever discharged.

The union's right to arbitrate may survive even a prolonged strike. *United Packinghouse, Food & Allied Workers Local 721 v. Needham Packing Co.*, 376 U.S. 247 (1964). *But cf. Jim Walter Res., Inc. v. United Mine Workers of Am. Local 2397*, 663 F.3d 1322, 1324 (11th Cir. 2011) (distinguishing *Drake Bakeries* and ruling that an employer was not required to arbitrate its claim for monetary damages stemming from a work stoppage allegedly conducted in breach of an implied no-strike obligation in the labor contract because the employee-oriented grievance and arbitration clauses contemplated disputes arising out of employee complaints, significantly limiting the scope of claims subject to arbitration under the agreement).

Has the Supreme Court in *Drake* and *Needham* effectively read the "substantial breach" doctrine out of the federal labor contract law being developed under §301? *See* Summers, *Collective Agreements and the Law of Contracts*, 78 YALE L.J. 525 (1969). *Cf. United Steelworkers v. NLRB*, 530 F.2d 266 (3d Cir.), *cert. denied*, 429 U.S. 834 (1976). *See Mastro Plastics Corp. v. NLRB, supra*, and accompanying notes.

6. *Availability of Damages for Strikes in Breach of No-Strike Clauses*—Some years ago a committee of the American Bar Association echoed a common sentiment when it said, "We feel that damage suits are generally not good medicine for labor relations." *See* Fulda, *The No-Strike Clause*, 21 GEO. WASH. L. REV. 127, 144 (1952) (Report of the Committee on Improvement of Administration of Union-Employer Contracts, ABA Section of Labor Relations Law). Later, however, there appeared to be a trend toward attempting to secure damages for breach of unions' no-strike pledges. *See, e.g.*, Fairweather, *Employer Actions and Options in Response to Strikes in Breach of Contract*, in N.Y.U. EIGHTEENTH ANNUAL CONFERENCE ON LABOR 129 (1966); Bartlett, Newman & Mauro, *Strikes in Violation of the Contract: A Management View; A Union View*, in N.Y.U. THIRTY-FIRST ANNUAL CONFERENCE ON LABOR 117 (1978) (two separate papers); Stewart, *No-Strike Clauses in the Federal Courts*, 59 MICH. L. REV. 673 (1961). One district court awarded punitive as well as compensatory damages under §301 for a strike in breach of contract. *See Sidney Wanzer & Sons, Inc. v. Milk Drivers Union, etc.*, 249 F. Supp. 664 (N.D. Ill. 1966). But a court of appeals refused to uphold punitive damages under §301 when an employer violated a contract through a runaway shop. *United Shoe Workers v. Brooks Shoe Mfg. Co.*, 298 F.2d 277 (3d Cir. 1962), and others have since followed suit, *see Moore v. Local 569 of Int'l Bhd. of Elec. Workers*, 989 F.2d 1534 (9th Cir. 1993); *United Steelworkers v. Connors Steel Co.*, 855 F.2d 1499 (11th Cir. 1988).

Section V. Section 301 Preemption and State Claims

Lingle v. Norge Division of Magic Chef, Inc.
Supreme Court of the United States
486 U.S. 399, 108 S. Ct. 1877, 100 L. Ed. 2d 410 (1988)

JUSTICE STEVENS delivered the opinion of the Court.

In Illinois an employee who is discharged for filing a worker's compensation claim may recover compensatory and punitive damages from her employer. The question presented in this case is whether an employee covered by a collective-bargaining agreement that provides her with a contractual remedy for discharge without just cause may enforce her state law remedy for retaliatory discharge. The Court of Appeals held that the application of the state tort remedy was preempted by § 301 of the Labor Management Relations Act of 1947.... 823 F.2d 1031 (CA7 1987) (en banc). We disagree.

I

Petitioner was employed in respondent's manufacturing plant in Herrin, Illinois. On December 5, 1984, she notified respondent that she had been injured in the course of her employment and requested compensation for her medical expenses pursuant to the Illinois Workers' Compensation Act. On December 11, 1984, respondent discharged her for filing a "false worker's compensation claim." *Id.*, at 1033.

The union representing petitioner promptly filed a grievance pursuant to the collective-bargaining agreement that covered all production and maintenance employees in the Herrin plant. The agreement protected those employees, including petitioner, from discharge except for "proper" or "just" cause, and established a procedure for the arbitration of grievances. The term grievance was broadly defined to encompass "any dispute between ... the Employer and any employee, concerning the effect, interpretation, application, claim of breach or violation of this Agreement." Ultimately, an arbitrator ruled in petitioner's favor and ordered respondent to reinstate her with full back pay.

Meanwhile, on July 9, 1985, petitioner commenced this action against respondent by filing a complaint in the Illinois Circuit Court for Williamson County, alleging that she had been discharged for exercising her rights under the Illinois worker's compensation laws. *See Kelsay v. Motorola, Inc.*, 74 Ill. 2d 172, 384 N.E.2d 353 (1978); *Midgett v. Sackett-Chicago, Inc.*, 105 Ill. 2d 143, 473 N.E.2d 1280 (1984); *see also* Ill. Rev. Stat., ch. 48, ∂ 138.4(h) (1987). Respondent removed the case to the Federal District Court on the basis of diversity of citizenship, and then filed a motion praying that the Court either dismiss the case on pre-emption grounds or stay further proceedings pending the completion of the arbitration. Relying on our decision in *Allis-Chalmers Corp. v. Lueck*, 471 U.S. 202 (1985), the District Court dismissed the complaint. It concluded that the "claim for retaliatory discharge is 'inextricably intertwined' with the collective bargaining provision prohibiting wrongful discharge or discharge without just cause" and that allowing the state-law action to proceed would undermine the arbitration procedures set forth in the parties' contract. 618 F. Supp. 1448, 1449 (S.D. Ill. 1985).

The Court of Appeals agreed that the state-law claim was pre-empted by § 301. In an en banc opinion, over the dissent of two judges, it rejected petitioner's argument that the tort action was not "inextricably intertwined" with the collective-bargaining agreement because the disposition of a retaliatory discharge claim in Illinois does not depend upon an interpretation of the agreement; on the contrary, the Court concluded that "the same analysis of the facts" was implicated under both procedures. 823 F.2d, at 1046. It took note of, and declined to follow, contrary decisions in the Tenth, Third, and Second Circuits. We granted certiorari to resolve the conflict in the Circuits. . . .

II

. . . In *Textile Workers v. Lincoln Mills*, 353 U.S. 448 (1957), we held that § 301 not only provides federal-court jurisdiction over controversies involving collective-bargaining agreements, but also "authorizes federal courts to fashion a body of federal law for the enforcement of these collective bargaining agreements." *Id.*, at 451.

In *Teamsters v. Lucas Flour Co.*, 369 U.S. 95 (1962), we were confronted with a straightforward question of contract interpretation: whether a collective-bargaining agreement implicitly prohibited a strike that had been called by the union. The Washington Supreme Court had answered that question by applying state-law rules of contract interpretation. We rejected that approach, and held that § 301 mandated resort to federal rules of law in order to ensure uniform interpretation to collective-bargaining agreements, and thus to promote the peaceable, consistent resolution of labor-management disputes.

In *Allis-Chalmers Corp. v. Lueck*, 471 U.S. 202 (1985), we considered whether the Wisconsin tort remedy for bad-faith handling of an insurance claim could be applied to the handling of a claim for disability benefits that were authorized by a collective-bargaining agreement. We began by examining the collective-bargaining agreement, and determined that it provided the basis not only for the benefits, but also for the right to have payments made in a timely manner. *Id.*, at 213–216. We then analyzed the Wisconsin tort remedy, explaining that it "exists for breach of a 'duty devolv[ed] upon the insurer by reasonable implication from the express terms of the contract,' the scope of which, crucially, is 'ascertained from a consideration of the contract itself.'" *Id.*, at 216 (quoting *Hilker v. Western Automobile Ins. Co.*, 204 Wis. 1, 16, 235 N.W. 413, 415 (1931)). Since the "parties' agreement as to the manner in which a benefit claim would be handled [would] necessarily [have been] relevant to any allegation that the claim was handled in a dilatory manner," 471 U.S., at 218, we concluded that § 301 preempted the application of the Wisconsin tort remedy in this setting.

Thus, *Lueck* faithfully applied the principle of § 301 pre-emption developed in *Lucas Flour*: if the resolution of a state-law claim depends upon the meaning of a collective-bargaining agreement, the application of state law (which might lead to inconsistent results since there could be as many state-law principles as there are States) is pre-empted and federal labor-law principles — necessarily uniform throughout the nation — must be employed to resolve the dispute.

III

Illinois courts have recognized the tort of retaliatory discharge for filing a worker's compensation claim, *Kelsay v. Motorola, Inc.*, 74 Ill. 2d 172, 384 N.E.2d 353 (1978), and have held that it is applicable to employees covered by union contracts, *Midgett v. Sackett-Chicago, Inc.*, 105 Ill. 2d 143, 473 N.E.2d 1280 (1984), *cert. denied*, 474 U.S. 909 (1985). "[T]o show retaliatory discharge, the plaintiff must set forth sufficient facts from which it can be inferred that (1) he was discharged or threatened with discharge and (2) the employer's motive in discharging or threatening to discharge him was to deter him from exercising his rights under the Act or to interfere with his exercise of those rights." *Horton v. Miller Chemical Co.*, 776 F.2d 1351, 1356 (CA7 1985) (summarizing Illinois state court decisions), *cert. denied*, 475 U.S. 1122 (1986); see *Gonzalez v. Prestress Engineering Corp.*, 115 Ill. 2d 1, 503 N.E.2d 308 (1986). Each of these purely factual questions pertains to the conduct of the employee and the conduct and motivation of the employer. Neither of the elements requires a court to interpret any term of a collective-bargaining agreement. To defend against a retaliatory discharge claim, an employer must show that it had a nonretaliatory reason for the discharge, *cf. Loyola University of Chicago v. Illinois Human Rights Comm'n*, 149 Ill. App. 3d 8, 500 N.E.2d 639 (1986); this purely factual inquiry likewise does not turn on the meaning of any provision of a collective-bargaining agreement. Thus, the state-law remedy in this case is "independent" of the collective-bargaining agreement in the sense of "independent" that matters for § 301 pre-emption purposes: resolution of the state-law claim does not require construing the collective-bargaining agreement.

The Court of Appeals seems to have relied upon a different way in which a state-law claim may be considered "independent" of a collective-bargaining agreement. The court wrote that "the just cause provision in the collective bargaining agreement may well prohibit such retaliatory discharge," and went on to say that if the state-law cause of action could go forward, "a state court would be deciding precisely the *same issue* as would an arbitrator: whether there was 'just cause' to discharge the worker." 823 F.2d, at 1046 (emphasis added). The Court concluded, "the state tort of retaliatory discharge is inextricably intertwined with the collective-bargaining agreements here, because it implicates the *same analysis of the facts* as would an inquiry under the just cause provisions of the agreements." *Ibid.* (emphasis added). We agree with the Court's explanation that the state-law analysis might well involve attention to the same factual considerations as the contractual determination of whether Lingle was fired for just cause. But we disagree with the Court's conclusion that such parallelism renders the state-law analysis dependent upon the contractual analysis. For while there may be instances in which the National Labor Relations Act pre-empts state law on the basis of the subject matter of the law in question, § 301 pre-emption merely ensures that federal law will be the basis for interpreting collective-bargaining agreements, and says nothing about the substantive rights a State may provide to workers when adjudication of those rights does not depend upon the interpretation of such agreements.[11] In other words, even if dispute resolution pursuant to a collective-bargaining agreement, on the one hand, and state law, on the other, would require addressing precisely the same set of facts, as long as the state-law claim can be resolved without interpreting the agreement itself, the claim is "independent" of the agreement for § 301 pre-emption purposes.

IV

The result we reach today is consistent both with the policy of fostering uniform, certain adjudication of disputes over the meaning of collective-bargaining agreements and with cases that have permitted separate fonts of substantive rights to remain un-pre-empted by other federal labor-law statutes.

First, as we explained in *Lueck*, "[t]he need to preserve the effectiveness of arbitration was one of the central reasons that underlay the Court's holding in *Lucas Flour*." 471 U.S., at 219. Today's decision should make clear that interpretation of collective-bargaining agreements remains firmly in the arbitral realm; judges can determine questions of state law involving labor-management relations only if such questions do not require construing collective-bargaining agreements.

Second, there is nothing novel about recognizing that substantive rights in the labor relations context can exist without interpreting collective-bargaining agreements.

> This Court has, on numerous occasions, declined to hold that individual employees are, because of the availability of arbitration, barred from bringing claims under federal statutes. *See, e.g., McDonald v. West Branch*, 466 U.S. 284 (1984); *Barrentine v. Arkansas-Best Freight System, Inc.*, 450 U.S. 728 (1981); *Alexander v. Gardner-Denver Co.*, 415 U.S. 36 (1974). Although the analysis of the question under each statute is quite distinct, the theory running through these cases is that notwithstanding the strong policies encouraging arbitration, "different considerations apply *where the employee's claim is based on rights arising out of a statute designed to provide minimum substantive guarantees to individual workers.*" *Barrentine, supra*, 450 U.S., at 737.

---

11. [9] Whether a union may *waive* its members' individual, non-pre-empted state-law rights, is, likewise, a question distinct from that of whether a claim is pre-empted under § 301, and is another issue we need not resolve today. We note that under Illinois law, the parties to a collective-bargaining agreement may not waive the prohibition against retaliatory discharge nor may they alter a worker's rights under the state worker's compensation scheme. *Byrd v. Aetna Casualty & Surety Co.*, 152 Ill. App. 3d 292, 298, 504 N.E.2d 216, 221, *app. denied*, 115 Ill. 2d 539, 511 N.E.2d 426 (1987). Before deciding whether such a state law bar to waiver could be preempted under federal law by the parties to a collective-bargaining agreement, we would require "clear and unmistakable" evidence, see *Metropolitan Edison Co. v. NLRB*, 460 U.S. 693, 708 (1983), in order to conclude that such a waiver had been intended. No such evidence is available in this case.

Atchison, T. & S. F. R. Co. v. Buell, 480 U.S. 557, 565 (1987) (emphasis added).

Although our comments in *Buell*, construing the scope of Railway Labor Act pre-emption, referred to independent *federal* statutory rights, we subsequently rejected a claim that federal labor law pre-empted a *state* statute providing a onetime severance benefit to employees in the event of a plant closing. In *Fort Halifax Packing Co. v. Coyne*, 482 U.S. 1, 21 (1987), we emphasized that "preemption should not be lightly inferred in this area, since the establishment of labor standards falls within the traditional police power of the State." We specifically held that the Maine law in question was not pre-empted by the NLRA, "since its establishment of a minimum labor standard does not impermissibly intrude upon the collective-bargaining process." *Id.*, at 23.

The Court of Appeals "recognize[d] that § 301 does not pre-empt state antidiscrimination laws, even though a suit under these laws, like a suit alleging retaliatory discharge, requires a state court to determine whether just cause existed to justify the discharge." 823 F.2d, at 1046, n. 17. The court distinguished those laws because Congress has affirmatively endorsed state antidiscrimination remedies in Title VII of the Civil Rights Act of 1964, 78 Stat. 241, see 42 U.S.C. §§ 2000e-5(c) and 2000e-7, whereas there is not such explicit endorsement of state worker's compensation laws. As should be plain from our discussion in Part III, *supra*, this distinction is unnecessary for determining whether § 301 preempts the state law in question. The operation of the anti-discrimination laws does, however, illustrate the relevant point for § 301 pre-emption analysis that the mere fact that a broad contractual protection against discriminatory—or retaliatory—discharge may provide a remedy for conduct that coincidentally violates state law does not make the existence or the contours of the state-law violation dependent upon the terms of the private contract. For even if an arbitrator should conclude that the contract does not prohibit a particular discriminatory or retaliatory discharge, that conclusion might or might not be consistent with a proper interpretation of state law. In the typical case a state tribunal could resolve either a discriminatory or retaliatory discharge claim without interpreting the "just cause" language of a collective-bargaining agreement.

V

In sum, we hold that an application of state law is pre-empted by § 301 of the Labor Management Relations Act of 1947 only if such application requires the interpretation of a collective-bargaining agreement.[12]

---

12. [12] A collective-bargaining agreement may, of course, contain information such as rate of pay and other economic benefits that might be helpful in determining the damages to which a worker prevailing in a state law suit is entitled. *See Baldracchi v. Pratt & Whitney Aircraft Div., United Technologies Corp.*, 814 F.2d 102, 106 (CA2 1987). Although federal law would govern the interpretation of the agreement to determine the proper damages, the underlying state law claim, not otherwise pre-empted, would stand. Thus, as a general proposition, a state law claim may depend for its resolution upon both the interpretation of a collective-bargaining agreement and a separate state law analysis that does not turn on the agreement. In such a case, federal law would govern

The judgment of the Court of Appeals is reversed.

It is so ordered.

Notes

1. *Tort Claims* — It is not easy to distinguish between cases governed by *Lingle*, in which a state tort claim or discrimination claim is not preempted by § 301 because it exists independently of any collective bargaining agreement and requires no interpretation of the labor contract for its enforcement, and cases governed by *Lueck*, in which the supposed state claim is preempted because the existence and scope of the claim would have to be determined by resort to the applicable collective agreement. Some courts apply the § 301 preemption doctrine in an expansive manner. For example, *DeCoe v. GMC*, 32 F.3d 212 (6th Cir. 1994), involved a union official's state court defamation and tortious interference claims against his employer and several employees who had allegedly made and discussed false sexual harassment charges regarding the plaintiff. The court found these claims preempted, because resolution of both would involve interpretation and application of bargaining agreement provisions. The collective contract imposed a duty on the employer and individual employees to identify and resolve sexual harassment complaints, and the trial court would have to interpret this section of the contract when it sought to decide whether the individuals who filed charges against the plaintiff had engaged in protected conduct. The tortious interference claim was based on the economic relationship created by the bargaining agreement, and thus the trial court would have to examine that contract to determine what economic relationship existed. *See also Johnson v. Humphreys*, 949 F.3d 413 (8th Cir. 2020) (discharged delivery driver's state law race discrimination claim preempted, because proving the element that he was meeting the expectations of the employer required determining whether dropping a pallet from the truck was permitted by the collective agreement or incorporated policies); *Haggins v. Verizon New England Inc.*, 648 F.3d 50 (1st Cir. 2011) (§ 301 preempts state law privacy claim of unionized telephone installers alleging that their employer violated their privacy rights by requiring them to carry cell phones with GPS software while working where suit would require court to interpret scope of management rights clause in bargaining agreement); *Foy v. Giant Food, Inc.*, 298 F.3d 284 (4th Cir. 2002) (discharged employee's claim for intentional infliction of emotional distress preempted where claim arose out of the employee's role in a workplace altercation with a coworker, necessitating interpretation of the just cause and management rights clauses of the contract); *Baker v. Farmers Elec. Coop.*, 34 F.3d 274 (5th Cir. 1994) (claim that employer intentionally inflicted emotional distress by reassigning custodian to journeyman lineman position in retaliation against his participation in prior arbitral proceeding preempted, since resolution of question regarding

---

the interpretation of the agreement, but the separate state law analysis would not be thereby preempted. As we said in *Allis-Chalmers Corp. v. Lueck*, 471 U.S., at 211, "not every dispute ... tangentially involving a provision of a collective-bargaining agreement is preempted by § 301 . . . ."

outrageousness of employer's conduct would involve interpretation of management rights clause of contract); *In re Amoco Petroleum Additives Co.*, 964 F.2d 706 (7th Cir. 1992) (state claims for invasion of privacy and intentional infliction of emotional distress based on employer's installation of video camera near entrance to women's locker room preempted, since surveillance was arguably authorized by management rights clause in labor contract, so that interpretation of collective agreement would be required), *dismissal of action aff'd*, 6 F.3d 1176 (7th Cir. 1993).

Other courts are more willing to allow such claims where reference to the labor contract—but not interpretation of it—is required. For example, in *Carlson v. Arrowhead Concrete Works, Inc.*, 445 F.3d 1046 (8th Cir. 2006), the court allowed an employee to proceed with retaliatory discharge and failure to recall claims stemming from his efforts to report suspected safety violations in the workplace. The employee alleged violations of Minnesota's Whistleblower Act and Occupational Safety and Health Act, but also referenced and quoted the seniority provisions in the collective bargaining agreement in support of his retaliation claim. Acknowledging that adjudication of the claim might require "more than reference to" the labor agreement, the court nonetheless allowed it to proceed because it would not entail interpretation of the contract. *See also Matson v. United Parcel Serv., Inc.*, 840 F.3d 1126 (9th Cir. 2016) (state law hostile work environment sex discrimination claim based in part on employer's assignment of extra work inconsistent with seniority not preempted, because multi-factor, fact-based inquiry could be completed without interpretation of collective agreement; any provisions alleged to be in dispute had already been resolved through grievance settlements, so court need only reference the settlements, not interpret them); *McKnight v. Dresser Inc.*, 676 F.3d 426 (5th Cir. 2012) (no preemption of state law tort claims of employees who allegedly sustained long-term hearing losses in industrial manufacturing facility because employer failed to properly monitor and mitigate their exposure to loud noise, even though bargaining agreement required employer to provide safe work environment, where state tort law places duty on employers to provide safe work environments and expressly forbids contractual waiver of that duty); *CNH Am. LLC v. Int'l Union, United Auto., Aerospace & Agr. Implement Workers of Am. (UAW)*, 645 F.3d 785 (6th Cir. 2011) (no preemption of state law tort claims arising out of union's conduct in collective bargaining negotiations, including breach of implied warranty of authority, negligent misrepresentation and intentional misrepresentation, since pre-contractual conduct is independent of collective bargaining agreement, even if damage calculations require reference to the agreement); *Wynn v. AC Rochester*, 273 F.3d 153 (2d Cir. 2001) (employee's fraud claim against employer based on misrepresentations about the availability of unemployment benefits and recall rights, options conferred by the labor contract, held not preempted because fraud claim requires only consultation of the contract, not interpretation of it).

2. *Breach of Contract Claims*—In *Caterpillar, Inc. v. Williams*, 482 U.S. 386 (1987), a unanimous Supreme Court held that § 301 did not completely preempt a state-law complaint for breach of individual employment contracts and thus did not support removal to federal court. In this instance several employees had left the bargaining unit to become managerial or salaried employees and, in this capacity, had received employer assurances of job security in the event their plant closed. Later, after they had returned to unionized positions, they were notified that the plant was closing and they would be laid off. The Court concluded their complaint was not substantially dependent on an interpretation of the collective bargaining agreement. Similarly, the court in *Loewen Group Int'l v. Haberichter*, 65 F.3d 1417 (7th Cir. 1995), found no preemption of a state claim against a former employee for violating a covenant not to compete contained in an individual employment contract, even though the employee was also subject to a collective bargaining agreement; merely examining the labor contract to see whether any conflict existed was held not to be "interpreting" it for §301 preemption purposes. *Trans Penn Wax Corp. v. McCandless*, 50 F.3d 217 (3d Cir. 1995), concerned an employer that had allegedly made promises to employees of continued job security on the eve of a decertification election. After the incumbent union was decertified, the employer terminated six employees. The court found that their suit for breach of contract and misrepresentation was not preempted by §301, because resolution of their claims would not require the interpretation of any bargaining agreement provisions.

On the other hand, the Ninth Circuit found §301 preemption of a breach of contract claim based on an individual employment contract pertaining to a job covered by a collective bargaining agreement. In *Beals v. Kiewit Pacific Co.*, 114 F.3d 892 (9th Cir. 1997), *cert. denied*, 522 U.S. 1108 (1998), the employee was offered an opportunity to relocate from Southern California to Hawaii to work on a project that was covered by a union contract. After accepting the offer (which included moving expenses), the employee moved to Hawaii and began work on the job. Five months later he was terminated. Beals sued the employer for breach of contract and negligent misrepresentation. According to the court, the employer's offer was effective only as part of the labor contract and therefore was preempted because it required interpretation of the collective bargaining agreement, which gave the employer the right to terminate Beals at any time. The negligent misrepresentation claim, however, was not preempted because it was based primarily upon the employer's oral representations, which did not require interpretation of the labor contract (though it did entail comparison of the labor contract's terms to the employer's oral representations in order to assess whether Beals' reliance on the representations was justified). Similar reasons justified preemption in two other contract claims in the same circuit. *See Aguilera v. Pirelli Armstrong Tire Corp.*, 223 F.3d 1010 (9th Cir. 2000) (suit by laid-off striker replacements based on alleged breach of independent contracts of employment preempted, because resolution would require interpretation of layoff and recall provisions of bargaining agreement); *Firestone v. S. Cal. Gas Co.*, 219 F.3d 1063 (9th Cir. 2000), *cert. denied*, 536 U.S. 958 (2002) (gas company meter readers' state-law claim for time-and-one-half for all hours worked beyond eight in a day and 40 in a week preempted, since state law exempts from overtime requirements workers covered by bargaining agreements that provide for "premium wage rates" for overtime work and resolution of state-law claim would necessitate interpretation of collective contract's overtime provisions). *See also Barton v. House of Raeford Farms, Inc.*, 745 F.3d 95 (4th Cir. 2014), *cert. denied*, 574 U.S. 825 (2014) (workers' claims under state wage and hour law held preempted where employees sought payment for the time between clocking in and beginning work on the production line, as well as time between ceasing work and clocking out, because claims were nothing more than a disagreement over how to calculate "hours worked" under the labor contract, which included provisions on work hours and pay rates but was silent as to how compensable time would be calculated; the claims necessarily implicated interpretation of the contract because company had a long-standing past practice of paying workers only for time on the production line, and not for time spent donning, doffing, washing protective gear, and walking to and from the production area); *Trs. of the Twin City Bricklayers Fringe Benefit Funds v. Superior Waterproofing, Inc.*, 450 F.3d 324 (8th Cir. 2006) (claims by a third-party company and its owner that a union had fraudulently and negligently induced it to enter into a multiemployer fringe benefit plan based upon alleged promises of eligibility to bid on certain union-only projects were preempted, since court would have to interpret the relevant portions of the labor contract to determine whether they were sufficiently ambiguous that the owner could have justifiably relied upon the union's alleged misrepresentations).

3. *State Claims Based on the Union's Performance of Its Duty as Employee Representative*—In *International Bhd. of Elec. Workers v. Hechler*, 481 U.S. 851 (1987), a unanimous Supreme Court held that an employee's state-law tort claim was preempted when she alleged the union was negligent in failing to provide her with a safe place to work. Eight Justices concluded that the existence and scope of any duty of care on the union's part would have to be determined by resort to the applicable collective bargaining agreement. Thus, plaintiff's state claim was not "sufficiently independent . . . to withstand the preemptive force of §301." Justice Stevens concurred on the grounds plaintiff had alleged "nothing more than a breach of the union's federal duty of fair representation." More recent cases have pressed this issue further, with the same result. In *Sayre v. United Steelworkers*, 2010 U.S. Dist. LEXIS 101235 (S.D.W. Va. Sept. 23, 2010), retirees' claims for negligence and negligent misrepresentation against their union based upon the union's negotiation of a collective bargaining agreement that eliminated their lifetime no-cost health benefits were preempted because the claims were dependent upon the existence, interpretation, and application of rights arising out of the collective agreement. And in *BIW Deceived v. Local S6, Indus. Union of Marine & Shipbuilding Workers*, 132 F.3d 824 (1st Cir. 1997), the First Circuit ruled that §301 preemption blocked a state court action that implicitly asserted that the union had breached its duty of fair representation. The employees' complaint alleged negligence, fraudulent misrepresentation, fraud in inducement, infliction of emotional distress, loss of consortium, intentional nondisclosure, and unjust enrichment against the union, which had (pursuant to its labor contract with the employer) participated in job interviews with the employer and assured employees that they would be employed until expiration of the current union contract, and probably much longer; in reliance upon these assurances, the employees accepted offers of employment, left other jobs, and relocated to Maine to work for the employer—only to be laid off shortly thereafter. According to the court, removal to federal court was appropriate where the complaint, "though garbed in state-law raiment, sufficiently asserts a claim implicating the duty of fair representation," a matter governed completely by federal law. On the other hand, in *Figueroa v. Foster*, 864 F.3d 222 (2d Cir. 2017), the court ruled that the duty of fair representation imposed on unions by the NLRA does not preempt the New York State Human Rights Law's prohibition on discrimination by unions, since the Act's imposition of a duty of fair representation does not amount to total field preemption or pose a conflict so incompatible with federal labor law that all of its provisions must fall.

In *United Steelworkers of America v. Rawson*, 495 U.S. 362 (1990), a 6-3 majority of the Supreme Court held that a state-law wrongful-death action brought against a miners' union by the survivors of miners killed in an underground fire was preempted by §301. The complaint included allegations that the union had been negligent in its inspection activities. The Court reasoned that if the union violated any duty owed the miners in the course of the inspections, the duty arose out of the collective bargaining agreement, and was not a duty of care owed by the union to society at large. Furthermore, the survivors' action could not be based on the union's duty of fair representation, since mere negligence, even in the performance of a labor contract, would not ground a claim for breach of that duty. Three Justices, dissenting, agreed with the Supreme Court of Idaho that the survivors' case could be characterized as resting on allegations of the union's active negligence in a voluntary undertaking, as defined in the *Restatement (Second) of Torts* §323, not on the union's contractual obligations.

Suppose the negligence claim is alleged against the employer, rather than the union. Some subsequent cases have distinguished *Rawson* and found no preemption where the negligence claim is based on a duty of care arising from state common law. *See, e.g., Ward v. Circus Circus Casinos, Inc.*, 473 F.3d 994 (9th Cir. 2007) (negligence claims by workers injured when the employer's security personnel used restraint, physical force, and threats to break up a union meeting on the employer's premises arose from the employer's duty of care in hiring, training, and supervising its security guards, which did not arise from the labor contract).

Problem

64. Football is a dangerous game, causing injuries to players that are, ultimately, not only career-ending (the average length of an NFL player's career is three years) but entail long-term effects that linger for a lifetime. During games, team doctors and trainers routinely prescribe and administer pain medications in an effort to return players to the field as quickly as possible. The medications are highly effective, often returning players to the game despite torn ligaments and even broken bones. Players are also not informed of the risks associated with the pain medications or their long-term use. More than 1,000 players filed a class action against the NFL and their individual teams, alleging that team doctors and trainers negligently and fraudulently administered and prescribed pain medications in ways that violated federal and state drug laws "in efforts to return players to the game, rather than allow them to rest and heal properly." The result caused the plaintiffs to suffer "debilitating" long-term physical and mental injuries including "nerve, knee, and elbow injuries that never healed properly, heart disease, renal failure, and drug addiction." The complaint included claims for negligence per se, negligent misrepresentation, negligent hiring and retention, and fraudulent concealment. The collective bargaining agreement is silent on the question of administration of pain medications, but it does include a provision requiring the League to provide the players access to board-certified orthopedic medical care and requires the players to submit to drug testing by the League. Should the district court dismiss the claim as preempted? Why or why not?

Lividas v. Bradshaw, 512 U.S. 107, 114 S. Ct. 2068, 129 L. Ed. 2d 93 (1994). A unionized grocery clerk filed a complaint under the California Labor Code seeking penalties for the delay in payment of wages due upon her discharge. California law requires employers to pay all wages due immediately upon an employee's discharge, imposes a penalty for refusal to pay promptly, precludes any private contractual waiver of these minimum labor standards, and places responsibility for enforcing these provisions on the State Commissioner of Labor, ostensibly for the benefit of all employees. The Labor Commissioner construed state law as barring enforcement of these wage and penalty claims on behalf of individuals whose terms and conditions of employment were governed by a collective-bargaining agreement containing an arbitration clause. Lividas was covered by a collective bargaining agreement that provided that "disputes as to the interpretation or application of the agreement," including grievances arising from allegedly unjust discharge or suspension, would be subject to binding arbitration. The Commissioner refused to take action on Lividas' complaint on the basis that it would be necessary to look to and apply the collective bargaining agreement to determine what wage rate must be paid. Lividas brought an action in federal district court under 42 U.S.C. §1983, alleging that the Commissioner's nonenforcement policy was preempted by §7 of the NLRA because the policy placed a penalty on the exercise of her statutory right to bargain collectively with her employer. She stressed that there was no dispute about the amount owed and that neither she nor her employer had begun any grievance proceeding over the penalty.

The Court ruled that the NLRA preempted the Commissioner's policy, reasoning that a state rule conditioning benefits on refraining from conduct protected by the NLRA (the right to bargain collectively and the desirability of resolving contract disputes through arbitration) risked interference with congressional purpose in enacting the NLRA. To the Commissioner's argument that resolution of her claim in state court would entail the interpretation or application of a collective bargaining agreement and trench onto territory exclusively reserved to arbitrators under LMRA § 301, the Court responded:

> This reasoning... mistakes both the functions § 301 serves in our national labor law and our prior decisions according that provision pre-emptive effect. To be sure, we have read the text of § 301 not only to grant federal courts jurisdiction over claims asserting breach of collective-bargaining agreements but also to authorize the development of federal common-law rules of decision, in large part to assure that agreements to arbitrate grievances would be enforced, regardless of the vagaries of state law and lingering hostility toward extra-judicial dispute resolution, see *Textile Workers v. Lincoln Mills*, 353 U.S. 448, 455–456 (1957); see also *Steelworkers v. Warrior and Gulf Navigation Co.*, 363 U.S. 574 (1960); *Avco Corp. v. Machinists*, 390 U.S. 557, 559 (1968) ("§ 301... was fashioned by Congress to place sanctions behind agreements to arbitrate grievance disputes"). And in *Teamsters v. Lucas Flour Co.*, 369 U.S. 95 (1962), we recognized an important corollary to the *Lincoln Mills* rule: while § 301 does not preclude state courts from taking jurisdiction over cases arising from disputes over the interpretation of collective-bargaining agreements, state contract law must yield to the developing federal common law, lest common terms in bargaining agreements be given different and potentially inconsistent interpretations in different jurisdictions. See 369 U.S., at 103–104.
>
> And while this sensible "acorn" of § 301 pre-emption recognized in *Lucas Flour*, has sprouted modestly in more recent decisions of this Court, *see, e.g., Lueck, supra*, at 210 ("If the policies that animate § 301 are to be given their proper range... the pre-emptive effect of § 301 must extend beyond suits alleging contract violations"), it has not yet become, nor may it, a sufficiently "mighty oak," see *Golden State I*, 475 U.S., at 622 (REHNQUIST, J., dissenting), to supply the cover the Commissioner seeks here. To the contrary, the preemption rule has been applied only to assure that the purposes animating § 301 will be frustrated neither by state laws purporting to determine "questions relating to what the parties to a labor agreement agreed, and what legal consequences were intended to flow from breaches of that agreement," *Lueck*, 471 U.S., at 211, nor by parties' efforts to renege on their arbitration promises by "relabeling" as tort suits actions simply alleging breaches of duties assumed in collective-bargaining agreements, *id.*, at 219.
>
> In *Lueck* and in *Lingle v. Norge Division of Magic Chef, Inc.*, 486 U.S. 399 (1988), we underscored the point that § 301 cannot be read broadly to preempt nonnegotiable rights conferred on individual employees as a matter of state law, and we stressed that it is the legal character of a claim, as "independent" of rights under the collective-bargaining agreement, *Lueck, supra*, at 213 (and not whether a grievance arising from "precisely the same set of facts" could be pursued, *Lingle, supra*, at 410) that decides whether a state cause of action may go forward. Finally, we were clear that when

the meaning of contract terms is not the subject of dispute, the bare fact that a collective-bargaining agreement will be consulted in the course of state-law litigation plainly does not require the claim to be extinguished, see *Lingle*, 486 U.S., at 413, n.12 ("A collective-bargaining agreement may, of course, contain information such as rate of pay ... that might be helpful in determining the damages to which a worker prevailing in a state-law suit is entitled").

These principles foreclose even a colorable argument that a claim under Labor Code § 203 was pre-empted here. As the District Court aptly observed, the primary text for deciding whether Livadas was entitled to a penalty was not the Food Store Contract, but a calendar. The only issue raised by Livadas's claim, whether Safeway "willfully failed to pay" her wages promptly upon severance, Cal. Lab. Code Ann. § 203 (West 1989), was a question of state law, entirely independent of any understanding embodied in the collective-bargaining agreement between the union and the employer. There is no indication that there was a "dispute" in this case over the amount of the penalty to which Livadas would be entitled, and *Lingle* makes plain in so many words that when liability is governed by independent state law, the mere need to "look to" the collective-bargaining agreement for damage computation is no reason to hold the state law claim defeated by § 301. See 486 U.S., at 413, n. 12.

Notes

1. *When Does a State Law Claim Require Interpretation of the Collective Agreement?*—In *Associated Builders. & Contrs. v. Local 302, IBEW*, 109 F.3d 1353 (9th Cir. 1997), the Ninth Circuit ruled that § 301 does not preempt a state-law challenge by nonunion contractors to the legality of a construction union job-targeting program embodied in written agreements between the union-signatory contractors and the unions. Under the job-targeting programs operated by six IBEW locals, the locals set aside part of the hourly wage from workers employed on public works projects in a fund and then distributed them as subsidies to other union-signatory contractors who bid on "targeted" projects, reducing their labor costs on projects where they faced nonunion competition. The nonunion contractors' lawsuit alleged that the targeting programs were unlawful under the state's prevailing wage laws. Where the only controversy in the case was the legality under state law of the job-targeting language in the labor agreements, the court found that there was no need to "interpret" the labor contract in order to resolve the nonunion contractors' state-law claims. To rule otherwise would allow parties who wished "to immunize themselves from suit under state-laws of general applicability" to do so "by simply including their unlawful behavior in a labor contract," which "clearly exceeds the scope of section 301 preemption intended by Congress." See also *Jones v. Does 1-10 & SCO Silver Care Ops., LLC*, 57 F.3d 508 (3d Cir. 2017) (employees seeking unpaid overtime under federal and state laws could litigate claims rather than submitting them to arbitration, since

claims don't depend upon interpretation of union contract and contract contains no clear and unmistakable waiver of employees' rights to go to court); *Burnside v. Kiewit Pac. Corp.*, 491 F.3d 1053 (9th Cir. 2007) (employees' overtime-pay claims arising under state wage and hour law not preempted; even though court may be required to "look to" the labor contract to ascertain work rules and wage rates and determine the amount of damages owed, right to compensation for travel time was predicated on state law).

On the other hand, a union employee's claim under the Montana wrongful discharge statute was held preempted on the ground that it would impose a just cause term on the parties, thus "meddling at the heart of the employer-employee relationship." The employee was fired for harassing a coworker after a collective bargaining agreement expired but before negotiations reached an impasse. *Barnes v. Stone Container Corp.*, 942 F.2d 689 (9th Cir. 1991).

2. *Claims Based on State Anti-Discrimination Law*—In *Reece v. Houston Lighting & Power Co.*, 79 F.3d 485 (5th Cir.), *cert. denied*, 519 U.S. 864 (1996), the court ruled that §301 barred a state claim for racial discrimination in promotion and training, since provisions of a collective bargaining agreement governing promotions, seniority, and assignment to training would have to be interpreted. *See also Oberkramer v. IBEW-NECA Serv. Ctr.*, 151 F.3d 752 (8th Cir. 1998) (state claims based on municipal ordinance prohibiting sexual orientation discrimination were preempted where a collective bargaining agreement contained a nondiscrimination clause; since state ordinance did not provide for a private cause of action, resolution of the claims would be completely dependent on the anti-discrimination clause in the collective bargaining agreement).

On the other hand, in *Humble v. Boeing Co.*, 305 F.3d 1004 (9th Cir. 2002), the Ninth Circuit found a worker's state-law disability claim for reasonable accommodation not preempted by §301. The court noted that "defensive reliance on the terms of the CBA, mere consultation of the CBA's terms, or a speculative reliance on the CBA will not suffice to preempt a state law claim." Thus, the mere fact that the CBA provided for alternative job bidding rights for employees returning from medical leaves of absence, or that seniority provisions may confer job transfer rights to a light-duty job, did not limit the worker to a claim based on the contract. Her request for a reasonable accommodation under state disability law was not limited to a job transfer. Her intentional infliction of emotional distress and negligent infliction of emotional distress claims were preempted, however, since they were based upon the employer's conduct of repeatedly placing the employee in a job that she could not medically perform, conduct that was addressed by a provision of the labor contract imposing an obligation on the employer to consider the employee for other open positions that she was able to perform. Nor was the failure to accommodate the employee inherently outrageous, so these claims could not be tacked onto the employee's disability claim. *See also Paul v. Kaiser Found. Health Plan of Ohio*, 701 F.3d 514 (6th Cir. 2012) (employee's state law claim that the employer had failed to accommodate her disability and retaliated against her held not preempted even where the employer argued that her request infringed upon the seniority rights of other employees established pursuant to a collective bargaining agreement, since the argument was raised only as a defense and employee did not reference or rely upon any provision of the agreement); *Detabali v. St. Luke's Hospital*, 482 F.3d 1199 (9th Cir. 2007) (finding employee's state-law discrimination and retaliation claims not preempted by § 301 despite need to refer to the labor agreement to determine whether retaliation had occurred, because resolution of core claim — whether employee was discriminated against in applying the labor contract's terms — did not depend on interpretation of the labor agreement). *Cf. Watts v. United Parcel Serv., Inc.*, 701 F.3d 188 (6th Cir. 2012) (employee's federal discrimination claim under the Americans with Disabilities Act was not preempted, since § 301 preemption analysis does not apply to a federal discrimination claim).

Problem

65. Concerned about illegal drug use by its drivers, Freightways, Inc. installed concealed video and audio recording devices behind two-way mirrors in the restroom facilities of its truck terminal. When a restroom mirror fell off the wall, employees discovered the devices. The union filed a grievance under the collective bargaining agreement, which addresses the use of surveillance equipment directed at drivers (historically utilized through GPS equipment on trucks) and prohibits and provides penalties for drug use. A group of employees also brought claims in state court for invasion of privacy and intentional infliction of emotional distress, aided by a California penal law prohibiting the installation or maintenance of a two-way mirror in a restroom. The law makes it a misdemeanor to install a two-way mirror in a bathroom, criminalizes the viewing of the interior of a bathroom while it is occupied, and makes it illegal to eavesdrop by means of electronic recording devices. The company removed the state court action to federal court, alleging preemption of the state-law claims under § 301. How should the district court rule on the preemption argument, and why?

Section VI. Contract Rights and Statutory Rights — Overlapping Law and Forums

In enacting § 301 of the LMRA, Congress chose not to make breaches of the collective agreement unfair labor practices subject to the jurisdiction of the NLRB; instead, it left the enforcement of the labor contract to "the usual processes of the law." H.R. Conf. Rep. No. 510, 80th Cong., 1st Sess. 42 (1947). Nonetheless, the parties to a labor agreement may include a provision paralleling § 8(a)(3) by forbidding discrimination against employees because of union activity. The parties may also provide for arbitration of disputes about the scope of the bargaining unit. At the same time, the Board regards an employer's unilateral change in working conditions, without bargaining, as a violation of § 8(a)(5) — and where a collective agreement is in existence, that agreement is obviously the standard of many if not all working conditions in a unit. Moreover, § 8(d) makes it part of the duty to bargain to refrain from a strike or lockout to "terminate or modify" a contract prior to its expiration date. The inevitable result of all this is the possibility of overlap, or even conflict, between contractual rights and duties and statutory rights and duties.

The practical implications of this overlap may appear in several contexts: (1) before the NLRB, the respondent may claim (a) the allegation in the charge has already been the subject of an arbitral award in the respondent's favor, which the Board should "honor," or (b) the allegation could be the subject of a grievance under the parties' own contract, and the Board should therefore "defer" to arbitration; or (2) before a court (or arbitrator), the defendant may argue the matter involves an unfair labor practice or representational question subject to the exclusive primary jurisdiction of the Labor Board. The materials to follow deal with these various situations.

Analogous but even more sensitive problems arise in the relationship between contract administration and the enforcement of civil rights legislation. *See supra* Part Five, Section III.

A. Unilateral Contract Modification Cases — Bargaining during the Term of the Agreement

NLRB v. C & C Plywood Corp.
Supreme Court of the United States
385 U.S. 421, 87 S. Ct. 559, 17 L. Ed. 2d 486 (1967)

Mr. Justice Stewart delivered the opinion of the Court.

The respondent employer was brought before the National Labor Relations Board to answer a complaint that its inauguration of a premium pay plan during the term of a collective agreement, without prior consultation with the union representing its employees, violated the duties imposed by § 8(a)(5) and (1) of the National Labor Relations Act. The Board issued a cease-and-desist order, rejecting the claim that the respondent's action was authorized by the collective agreement. . . . [13]

In August 1962, the Plywood, Lumber, and Saw Mill Workers Local No. 2405 was certified as the bargaining representative of the respondent's production and maintenance employees. The agreement which resulted from collective bargaining contained the following provision:

---

13. [2] The NLRB's order directed respondent to bargain with the union upon the latter's request and similarly to rescind any payment plan which it had unilaterally instituted.

Article XVII

Wages

A. A classified wage scale has been agreed upon by the Employer and Union, and has been signed by the parties and thereby made a part of the written agreement. The Employer reserves the right to pay a premium rate over and above the contractual classified wage rate to reward any particular employee for some special fitness, skill, aptitude or the like. The payment of such a premium rate shall not be considered a permanent increase in the rate of that position and may, at the sole option of the Employer, be reduced to the contractual rate. . . .

The agreement also stipulated that wages should be "closed" during the period it was effective and that neither party should be obligated to bargain collectively with respect to any matter not specifically referred to in the contract. Grievance machinery was established, but no ultimate arbitration of grievances or other disputes was provided.

Less than three weeks after this agreement was signed, the respondent posted a notice that all members of the "glue spreader" crews would be paid $2.50 per hour if their crews met specified biweekly (and later weekly) production standards, although under the "classified wage scale" referred to in the above quoted Art. XVII of the agreement, the members of these crews were to be paid hourly wages ranging from $2.15 to $2.29, depending upon their function within the crew. When the union learned of this premium pay plan through one of its members, it immediately asked for a conference with the respondent. During the meetings between the parties which followed this request, the employer indicated a willingness to discuss the terms of the plan, but refused to rescind it pending those discussions.

It was this refusal which prompted the union to charge the respondent with an unfair labor practice in violation of §§ 8(a)(5) and (1). The trial examiner found that the respondent had instituted the premium-pay program in good-faith reliance upon the right reserved to it in the collective agreement. He, therefore, dismissed the complaint. The Board reversed. Giving consideration to the history of negotiations between the parties, as well as the express provisions of the collective agreement, the Board ruled the union had not ceded power to the employer unilaterally to change the wage system as it had. For while the agreement specified different hourly pay for different members of the glue spreader crews and allowed for merit increases for "particular employee[s]," the employer had placed all the members of these crews on the same wage scale and had made it a function of the production output of the crew as a whole.

In refusing to enforce the Board's order, the Court of Appeals did not decide that the premium-pay provision of the labor agreement had been misinterpreted by the Board. Instead, it held the Board did not have jurisdiction to find the respondent had violated § 8(a) of the Labor Act, because the "existence . . . of an unfair labor practice [did] not turn entirely upon the provisions of the Act, but arguably upon a good-faith dispute as to the correct meaning of the provisions of the collective bargaining agreement...." 351 F.2d at 228.

The respondent does not question the proposition that an employer may not unilaterally institute merit increases during the term of a collective agreement unless some provision of the contract authorizes him to do so. See *NLRB v. J.H. Allison & Co.*, 165 F.2d 766 (6th Cir. 1948), *cert. denied*, 335 U.S. 814 (1948). *Cf. Beacon Pierce Dyeing Co.*, 121 N.L.R.B. 953 (1958). The argument is, rather, that since the contract contained a provision which *might* have allowed the respondent to institute the wage plan in question, the Board was powerless to determine whether that provision *did* authorize the respondent's action, because the question was one for a state or federal court under § 301 of the Act.

In evaluating this contention, it is important first to point out that the collective bargaining agreement contained no arbitration clause.[14] The contract did provide grievance procedures, but the end result of those procedures, if differences between the parties remained unresolved, was economic warfare, not "the therapy of arbitration." *Carey v. Westinghouse Corp.*, 375 U.S. 261, 272 (1964). Thus, the Board's action in this case was in no way inconsistent with its previous recognition of arbitration as "an instrument of national labor policy for composing contractual differences." *International Harvester Co.*, 138 N.L.R.B. 923, 926 (1962), *aff'd sub nom., Ramsey v. NLRB*, 327 F.2d 784 (7th Cir. 1964), *cert. denied*, 377 U.S. 1003 (1964).

The respondent's argument rests primarily upon the legislative history of the 1947 amendments to the National Labor Relations Act. It is said that the rejection by Congress of a bill which would have given the Board unfair labor practice jurisdiction over all breaches of collective bargaining agreements shows that the Board is without power to decide any case involving the interpretation of a labor contract. We do not draw that inference from this legislative history.

When Congress determined that the Board should not have general jurisdiction over all alleged violations of collective bargaining agreements and that such matters should be placed within the jurisdiction of the courts, it was acting upon a principle which this Court had already recognized:

> The Railway Labor Act, like the National Labor Relations Act, does not undertake governmental regulation of wages, hours, or working conditions. Instead it seeks to provide a means by which agreement may be reached with respect to them.

Terminal Railroad Ass'n v. Brotherhood of Railroad Trainmen, 318 U.S. 1, 6 (1943). To have conferred upon the National Labor Relations Board generalized power to determine the rights of parties under all collective agreements would have been a

---

14. [9] The Court of Appeals in this case relied upon its previous decision in *Square D Co. v. NLRB*, 332 F.2d 360 (9th Cir. 1964). But *Square D* involved a collective agreement that provided for arbitration. *See* Note, *Use of Arbitration Clause*, 41 Ind. L.J. 455, 469 (1966).

step toward governmental regulation of the terms of those agreements. We view Congress' decision not to give the Board that broad power as a refusal to take this step.

But in this case the Board has not construed a labor agreement to determine the extent of the contractual rights which were given the union by the employer. It has not imposed its own view of what the terms and conditions of the labor agreement should be. It has done no more than merely enforce a statutory right which Congress considered necessary to allow labor and management to get on with the process of reaching fair terms and conditions of employment — "to provide a means by which agreement may be reached." The Board's interpretation went only so far as was necessary to determine that the union did not agree to give up these statutory safeguards. Thus, the Board, in necessarily construing a labor agreement to decide this unfair labor practice case, has not exceeded the jurisdiction laid out for it by Congress.

This conclusion is re-enforced by previous judicial recognition that a contractual defense does not divest the Labor Board of jurisdiction. For example, in *Mastro Plastics Corp. v. NLRB*, 350 U.S. 270 (1956), the legality of an employer's refusal to reinstate strikers was based upon the Board's construction of a "no strike" clause in the labor agreement, which the employer contended allowed him to refuse to take back workers who had walked out in protest over his unfair labor practice. . . .

If the Board in a case like this had no jurisdiction to consider a collective agreement prior to an authoritative construction by the courts, labor organizations would face inordinate delays in obtaining vindication of their statutory rights. Where, as here, the parties have not provided for arbitration, the union would have to institute a court action to determine the applicability of the premium pay provision of the collective bargaining agreement.[15] If it succeeded in court, the union would then have to go back to the Labor Board to begin an unfair labor practice proceeding. It is not unlikely that this would add years to the already lengthy period required to gain relief from the Board. Congress cannot have intended to place such obstacles in the way of the Board's effective enforcement of statutory duties. For in the labor field, as in few others, time is crucially important in obtaining relief. . . .

The legislative history of the Labor Act, the precedent interpreting it, and the interest of its efficient administration thus all lead to the conclusion that the Board had jurisdiction to deal with the unfair labor practice charge in this case. We hold that the Court of Appeals was in error in deciding to the contrary.

The remaining question, not reached by the Court of Appeals, is whether the Board was wrong in concluding that the contested provision in the collective

---

15. [15] The precise nature of the union's case in court is not readily apparent. If damages for breach of contract were sought, the union would have difficulty in establishing the amount of injury caused by respondent's action. For the real injury in this case is to the union's status as bargaining representative, and it would be difficult to translate such damage into dollars and cents. . . .

agreement gave the respondent no unilateral right to institute its premium pay plan. In reaching this conclusion, the Board relied upon its experience with labor relations and the Act's clear emphasis upon the protection of free collective bargaining. We cannot disapprove of the Board's approach. For the law of labor agreements cannot be based upon abstract definitions unrelated to the context in which the parties bargained and the basic regulatory scheme underlying that context. *See* Cox, *The Legal Nature of Collective Bargaining Agreements*, 57 Mich. L. Rev. 1 (1958). Nor can we say that the Board was wrong in holding that the union had not foregone its statutory right to bargain about the pay plan inaugurated by the respondent. For the disputed contract provision referred to increases for "particular employee[s]," not groups of workers. And there was nothing in it to suggest that the carefully worked out wage differentials for various members of the glue spreader crew would be invalidated by the respondent's decision to pay all members of the crew the same wage.

Reversed and remanded.

Notes

1. *The Role of an Agreement to Arbitrate*—Would the result in the principal case have been different if the collective bargaining agreement had contained a provision for final and binding arbitration? If so, on what theory? Does an arbitration clause constitute an agreement to channel collective bargaining in a particular way, or a waiver of a statutory right to bargain? *See, e.g., Timken Roller Bearing Co. v. NLRB*, 161 F.2d 949 (6th Cir. 1947) (duty to bargain may be channeled through arbitration by contractual agreement); *Square D Co. v. NLRB*, 332 F.2d 360 (9th Cir. 1964) (whether the union contractually waived duty to bargain was a contract interpretation question for the arbitrator). If so, why wasn't a similar agreement or waiver found in the contract in the principal case, which provided for a grievance procedure and, presumably, permitted a court suit if necessary to resolve disputes? In *NLRB v. Huttig Sash & Door Co.*, 377 F.2d 964 (8th Cir. 1967), a court of appeals, relying on *C & C Plywood*, upheld the Board's jurisdiction to find an employer guilty of an unfair labor practice in unilaterally reducing wages, even though the contract contained an arbitration clause.

2. *Zipper Clauses*—The contract in the principal case included a "zipper clause" stating that the subject of wages was closed during the period of the contract absent a specific reference in the contract, and that neither party was obligated to bargain over them during that period. Why didn't the zipper clause play a significant part in the Court's thinking? Is there a difference between a union's waiver of the right to demand bargaining over a change in working conditions proposed by the union, and a union's waiver of the right to object to, or demand bargaining over, a change in working conditions proposed (or imposed) by the employer? Can the "residual rights" theory of the labor contract be squared with the principal case? *See, e.g., Ciba-Geigy Pharmaceuticals Div. v. NLRB*, 722 F.2d 1120 (3d Cir. 1983).

3. *Breach of the Duty to Bargain, or Substantive Breach of Contract?* — Would C & C Plywood Corp. have avoided violating § 8(a)(5) if it had bargained with the union before instituting the premium pay rates? Would that depend on whether or not the unilateral granting of premium pay was a breach of contract? What if the union had been offered and had rejected an opportunity to bargain? *See C & S Industries, Inc.*, 158 N.L.R.B. 454 (1966) (employer's unilateral establishment of an incentive wage system violated § 8(a)(5) because even though the union declined to discuss the issue, the labor agreement forbade any change in the method of paying employees without the union's consent and contract disputes were subject to arbitration).

4. *The Board's Remedial Role* — Although a breach of contract as such is not an unfair labor practice, *C & S Industries, supra*, the NLRB will direct a party to "honor" a repudiated contract, *Hyde's Supermarket*, 145 N.L.R.B. 1252, *enforced*, 339 F.2d 568 (9th Cir. 1964); *Crescent Bed Co., Inc.*, 157 N.L.R.B. 296 (1966). Remedies have included orders to pay any fringe benefits that would have accrued to employees under a contract the employer unlawfully refused to sign, *NLRB v. Strong*, 393 U.S. 357 (1969), and to compensate employees for losses incurred because of a unilaterally imposed rider to an insurance policy, *Scam Instrument Corp.*, 163 N.L.R.B. 284 (1967), *enforced*, 394 F.2d 884 (7th Cir.), *cert. denied*, 393 U.S. 980 (1968). Is it still meaningful to say that the enforcement of collective bargaining agreements is a matter for the courts and not for the NLRB? What policy considerations support the enlargement of the Board's role? Can this be reconciled with the congressional decision not to make breaches of contract unfair labor practices but to subject them to court jurisdiction under § 301 of the LMRA?

Is there a meaningful line between contract breaches that are and are not also § 8(a)(5) violations? *Compare Am. Elec. Power*, 362 N.L.R.B. 803 (2015) (no § 8(a)(5) violation where employer unilaterally terminated a retiree health benefit during the term of the collective bargaining agreement, because employer had a "sound arguable basis" for its interpretation of the contract consistent with past practice; thus, dispute was "solely one of contract interpretation" devoid of evidence of "animus, bad faith, or an intent to undermine the union"), *and Velan Valve Corp.*, 316 N.L.R.B. 1273 (1995) (employer's refusal to arbitrate a grievance protesting the subcontracting of unit work did not violate § 8(a)(5), since it was not a "wholesale repudiation" of the contractual arbitration procedure), *with Oakland Physicians Med. Ctr., LLC*, 362 N.L.R.B. 1220 (2015) (employer violated § 8(a)(5) by making unilateral changes in employee health care coverage during term of labor contract where agreement gave management the right to make some changes in health plan design and selection of insurance carrier, but precluded changing the premium shares paid by employees; deferral was therefore inappropriate) *and Rangaire Acquisition Corp.*, 309 N.L.R.B. 1043 (1992), *enforced*, 9 F.3d 104 (5th Cir. 1993) (employer violated § 8(a)(5) by denying extra 15 minutes for lunch break on Thanksgiving, since it constituted a "material, substantial, and significant" change in terms of employment).

Milwaukee Spring Division of Illinois Coil Spring Co.

National Labor Relations Board
268 N.L.R.B. 601 (1984), *aff'd sub nom.* UAW v. NLRB,
765 F.2d 175 (D.C. Cir. 1985)

On 22 October 1982 the ... Board held that Respondent violated the Act [§ 8(a)(1), (3), and (5)] by deciding without the Union's consent to transfer its assembly operations from its unionized Milwaukee Spring facility to its unorganized McHenry Spring facility during the term of a collective-bargaining agreement because of the comparatively higher labor costs under the agreement, and to lay off unit employees as a consequence of that decision....

The Board has reconsidered its Decision and Order in light of the entire record and the oral arguments and has decided to reverse that decision and dismiss the complaint.

I. Factual Background

Illinois Coil Spring Company consists of three divisions—Holly Spring, McHenry Spring, and Respondent (Milwaukee Spring). The parties stipulated that, although collectively the four entities are a single employer, each location constitutes a separate bargaining unit.

Respondent, at material times, employed about 99 bargaining unit employees. These employees worked in eight departments, including an assembly operations department and a molding operations department.

The Union has represented Respondent's bargaining unit employees for a number of years. The most recent contract became effective on 1 April 1980, and remained in effect until at least 31 March 1983. The contract contains specific wage and benefits provisions. The contract also provides that the Company "recognizes the Union as the sole and exclusive collective bargaining agent for all production and maintenance employees in the Company's plant at Milwaukee, Wisconsin."

On 26 January 1982 Respondent asked the Union to forgo a scheduled wage increase and to grant other contract concessions. In March, because Respondent lost a major customer, it proposed to the Union relocating its assembly operations in the nonunionized McHenry facility, located in McHenry, Illinois, to obtain relief from the comparatively higher assembly labor costs at Milwaukee Spring. Respondent also advised the Union that it needed wage and benefit concessions to keep its molding operations in Milwaukee viable. On 23 March the Union rejected the proposed reduction in wages and benefits. On 29 March Respondent submitted to the Union a document entitled "Terms Upon Which Milwaukee Assembly Operations Will Be Retained in Milwaukee." On 4 April the Union rejected the Company's proposal for alternatives to relocation and declined to bargain further over the Company's decision to transfer its assembly operations. The Company then announced its decision to relocate the Milwaukee assembly operations to the McHenry facility.

The parties stipulated that the relocation decision was economically motivated and was not the result of union animus. The parties also stipulated that Respondent has satisfied its obligation to bargain with the Union over the decision to relocate the assembly operations and has been willing to engage in effects bargaining with the Union.[16]

II. Midterm Modification of Contracts Under Section 8(d)

A. . . . Generally, an employer may not unilaterally institute changes regarding these mandatory subjects before reaching a good-faith impasse in bargaining. Section 8(d) imposes an additional requirement when a collective-bargaining agreement is in effect and an employer seeks to "modif[y] . . . the terms and conditions contained in" the contract: the employer must obtain the union's consent before implementing the change. If the employment conditions the employer seeks to change are not "contained in" the contract, however, the employer's obligation remains the general one of bargaining in good faith to impasse over the subject before instituting the proposed change. Applying these principles to the instant case, before the Board may hold that Respondent violated Section 8(d), the Board first must identify a specific term "contained in" the contract that the Company's decision to relocate modified. In *Milwaukee Spring I*, the Board never specified the contract term that was modified by Respondent's decision to relocate the assembly operations. The Board's failure to do so is not surprising, for we have searched the contract in vain for a provision requiring bargaining unit work to remain in Milwaukee.

Milwaukee Spring I suggests, however, that the Board may have concluded that Respondent's relocation decision, because it was motivated by a desire to obtain relief from the Milwaukee contract's labor costs, modified that contract's wage and benefits provision. We believe this reasoning is flawed. While it is true that the Company proposed modifying the wage and benefits provision of the contract, the Union rejected the proposals. Following its failure to obtain the Union's consent, Respondent, in accord with Section 8(d), abandoned the proposals to modify the contract's wage and benefits provisions. Instead, Respondent decided to transfer the assembly operations to a different plant where different workers (who were not subject to the contract) would perform the work. In short, Respondent did not disturb the wages and benefits at its Milwaukee facility, and consequently did not violate Section 8(d) by modifying, without the Union's consent, the wage and benefits provisions contained in the contract.[17]

---

16. [5] The parties' stipulation and the manner in which they briefed this case treat Respondent's relocation decision as a mandatory subject of bargaining. The dissent nevertheless insists on discussing at length what it terms the "threshold issue" of whether Respondent had a duty to bargain over its decision. Based on the facts before us, we find no reason to enter this discussion. We do not find it necessary to decide whether the work relocation here was a mandatory subject of bargaining under the Supreme Court's decision in *First National Maintenance Corp. v. NLRB*, 452 U.S. 666 (1981).

17. [9] *Oak Cliff-Golman* illustrates a midterm modification of wage provisions. In that case, the contract contained wage rates that the respondent unilaterally reduced during the life of the

Nor do we find that Respondent's relocation decision modified the contract's recognition clause. In two previous cases, the Board construed recognition clauses to encompass the duties performed by bargaining unit employees and held that employers' reassignment of work modified those clauses. In both instances, reviewing courts found no basis for reading jurisdictional rights into standard clauses that merely recognized the contracts' coverage of specified employees. *Boeing Co.*, 230 NLRB 696 (1977), *cert. denied* 581 F.2d 793 (9th Cir. 1978); *University of Chicago*, 210 NLRB 190 (1974), *cert. denied* 514 F.2d 942 (7th Cir. 1975). We agree with the courts' reasoning.

Language recognizing the Union as the bargaining agent "for all production and maintenance employees in the Company's plant at Milwaukee, Wisconsin," does not state that the functions that the unit performs must remain in Milwaukee. No doubt parties could draft such a clause; indeed, work-preservation clauses are commonplace. It is not for the Board, however, to create an implied work-preservation clause in every American labor agreement based on wage and benefits or recognition provisions, and we expressly decline to do so.[18]

In sum, we find in the instant case that neither wage and benefits provisions nor the recognition clause contained in the collective-bargaining agreement preserves bargaining unit work at the Milwaukee facility for the duration of the contract, and that Respondent did not modify these contract terms when it decided to relocate its assembly operations. Further, we find that no other term contained in the contract restricts Respondent's decision-making regarding relocation.

B.[19] Our dissenting colleague and the decision in *Milwaukee Spring I* fail to recognize that decision's substantial departure from NLRB textbook law that an employer need not obtain a union's consent on a matter not contained in the body of a collective-bargaining agreement even though the subject is a mandatory subject of bargaining. *See, e.g., Ozark Trailers*, 161 NLRB 561 (1966). Although the Board found a violation in *Ozark*, it did so grounded on the employer's failure to bargain over its decision to close a part of its operation during the collective-bargaining agreement, transfer equipment to another of its plants, and subcontract out work which had

---

contract. Respondent in the instant case, having unsuccessfully sought the Union's consent to modify the contractual wages and benefits, left those provisions intact. . . .

18. [10] In *Boeing*, the court stated:

Since the purpose of the Act is to encourage labor/management peace by resolving differences through collective-bargaining and to stabilize *agreed upon* conditions during the term of a [contract], *Steelworkers v. Warrior and Gulf Co.*, 363 U.S. 574, 578 . . . (1960), a rejection of the Board's position here would seem to further the purpose of the Act. Rather than stretching the meaning of a Recognition Clause "impliedly," "implicitly," or "in effect" to cover "functions" (as did the Board), a decision against the Board would encourage the parties affirmatively to negotiate an explicit "Jurisdictional Clause" to be included in the next [contract]. [581 F.2d at 798. Emphasis in original.]

19. [11] In agreeing with her colleagues that *Milwaukee Spring I* represented a substantial departure from well-established Board precedent, Member Dennis relies on part III of the decision, and finds it unnecessary to reach the matters discussed in Part II, B.

been performed at the Ozark plant. Even though the Board's ultimate conclusion in that case may not here survive the Supreme Court's analysis in *First National Maintenance*, it is instructive to note the Board's recognition that the employer's obligation, absent a specific provision in the contract restricting its rights, was to *bargain* with the union over its decision:

> In the first place, however, as we have pointed out time and time again, an employer's obligation to bargain does not include the obligation to agree, but solely to engage in a full and frank discussion with the collective- bargaining representative in which a bona fide effort will be made to explore possible alternatives, if any, that may achieve a mutually satisfactory accommodation of the interests of both the employer and the employees. If such efforts fail, the employer is wholly free to make and effectuate his decision. [161 NLRB at 568. Footnote omitted.] . . . .

The rationale of our dissenting colleague adds to the collective-bargaining agreement terms not agreed to by the parties and forecloses the exercise of rational economic discussion and decision-making which ultimately accrue to the benefit of all parties.

C. Accordingly, we conclude that Respondent's decision to relocate did not modify the collective-bargaining agreement in violation of Section 8(d). In view of the parties' stipulation that Respondent satisfied its obligation to bargain over the decision, we also conclude that Respondent did not violate Section 8(a)(5).[20] The dissent claims that Respondent's work relocation decision would indirectly modify contractual wage rates. Thus, the dissent would imply a work-preservation clause from the mere fact that an employer and a union have agreed on a wage scale. This revolutionary concept, if adopted, would affect virtually every American collective-bargaining agreement and would undoubtedly come as a surprise to parties that have labored at the bargaining table over work preservation proposals. An agreed-upon wage scale, standing by itself, means only that the employer will pay the stated wages to the extent that the employer assigns work to the covered employees.

III. The Los Angeles Marine Case

In reaching a result contrary to that reached here, *Milwaukee Spring* I relied on *Los Angeles Marine Hardware Co.*, 235 NLRB 720 (1978), affd. 602 F.2d 1302 (9th Cir. 1979). . . . In holding that, after bargaining to impasse, the respondent was not free to relocate work from one location to another location during the contract term without union consent, *Los Angeles Marine* relied on *Boeing*, which in turn cited *University of Chicago*. . . .

---

20. [13] The dissent's references to "contract avoidance" and "do[ing] indirectly what cannot be done directly" are misleading and deflect the reader's attention from the language of Sec. 8(d). Respondent's action is branded unlawful, even though the dissent fails to identify any term or condition contained in the contract that Respondent modified. . . .

As we stated in part II, A, of this decision, however, we agree with the appellate courts, and not the Board, in the *University of Chicago* and *Boeing* cases. We are also not persuaded that work reassignment decisions and relocation decisions should be treated differently for purposes of determining whether there has been a midcontract modification within the meaning of Section 8(d). Rather, we believe that the same standard applies in both instances, and that the Seventh Circuit correctly stated the governing principles in *University of Chicago*, as follows:

> [U]nless transfers are specifically prohibited by the bargaining agreement, an employer is free to transfer work out of the bargaining unit if: (1) the employer complies with *Fibreboard Paper Products v. NLRB*, 379 U.S. 203 . . . (1964), by bargaining in good faith to impasse; and (2) the employer is not motivated by anti-union animus, *Textile Workers v. Darlington Mfg. Co.*, 380 U.S. 263 . . . (1965). [514 F.2d at 949.][21]

Consistent with our decision today, we hereby overrule *University of Chicago*, *Boeing*, and the portion of *Los Angeles Marine* that held that the respondent's transfer of work from one location to another location violated Sections 8(a)(5) and 8(d).

IV. The Section 8(a)(3) Issue

In *Milwaukee Spring I*, the Board also found that Respondent's laying off employees as a consequence of its relocation decision violated Section 8(a)(3) notwithstanding that the parties stipulated there was no union animus. Invoking the "inherently destructive" doctrine of *Great Dane Trailers*, the Board apparently held that the 8(a)(3) violation flowed from the finding that the relocation decision violated Section 8(a)(5). Accepting this logic for the purposes of our decision only, we conclude that, having found that Respondent complied with its statutory obligation before deciding to relocate and did not violate Section 8(a)(5), there is no factual or legal basis for finding that the consequent layoff of employees violated Section 8(a)(3).

V. Realistic and Meaningful Collective Bargaining

Los Angeles Marine and *Milwaukee Spring I* discourage truthful midterm bargaining over decisions to transfer unit work. Under those decisions, an employer contemplating a plant relocation for several reasons, one of which is labor costs, would be likely to admit only the reasons unrelated to labor costs in order to avoid granting the union veto power over the decision. The union, unaware that labor costs were a factor in the employer's decision, would be unlikely to volunteer wage or other appropriate concessions. Even if the union offered to consider wage concessions, the employer might hesitate to discuss such suggestions for fear that bargaining with the union over the union's proposals would be used as evidence that labor costs had motivated the relocation decision.

---

21. [14] The Seventh Circuit decided *University of Chicago* before the Supreme Court decided *First National Maintenance Corp.* We do not here consider the effect of *First National Maintenance* on *Fibreboard*. . . .

We believe our holding today avoids this dilemma and will encourage the realistic and meaningful collective bargaining that the Act contemplates. Under our decision, an employer does not risk giving a union veto power over its decision regarding relocation and should therefore be willing to disclose all factors affecting its decision. Consequently, the union will be in a better position to evaluate whether to make concessions. Because both parties will not longer have an incentive to refrain from frank bargaining, the likelihood that they will be able to resolve their differences is greatly enhanced.

VI. Conclusion

Accordingly, for all of the foregoing reasons, we reverse our original Decision and Order and dismiss the complaint.

MEMBER ZIMMERMAN, dissenting:

. . . .

There are two issues which must be decided in each plant relocation case. The first issue is whether an employer has a duty to bargain with a union over its relocation decision, or, in other words, whether the relocation decision is a mandatory subject of bargaining. As explained below, I would find such decision to be mandatory where the decision is amenable to resolution through collective bargaining. Here, I would find Respondent's decision to relocate its assembly work from Milwaukee to McHenry amenable to resolution through bargaining and thus a mandatory subject of bargaining. The second issue is whether under Section 8(d) an employer may implement its relocation decision after an impasse in bargaining during the term of the collective-bargaining agreement. As explained below, I would find that Section 8(d) prohibits such a relocation of bargaining unit work in the absence of an agreement with the union, but only where the employer's relocation decision is motivated solely or predominantly by a desire to avoid terms of the collective-bargaining agreement. My colleagues and I apparently agree that if a collective-bargaining agreement contains an applicable work-preservation clause, Section 8(d) requires the employer to obtain the union's consent prior to any transfer of work regardless of the reasons underlying the transfer. The difference, then, between my colleagues and myself is that I find Section 8(d) applicable to other contractual terms. Here, as Respondent's decision was motivated solely by its desire to avoid the wage provisions of the contract, I would find that Respondent is prohibited from implementing its decision without the Union's consent during the term of the collective-bargaining agreement. . . .

. . . Section 8(d) of the Act prohibits midterm changes in any provision of a collective-bargaining agreement relating to mandatory subjects of bargaining without first obtaining the union's consent. It is well settled, and my colleagues agree, that an employer acts in derogation of its bargaining obligations under Section 8(d), and thereby violates Section 8(a)(5), when it makes any midterm change in the contractual wage rate even though the employer's action is compelled by economic necessity or the employer has offered to bargain with the union over the change and the union has refused. Obviously then, my colleagues and I would agree that had Respondent in this case decided to reduce the wages paid to the assembly employees while continuing to perform the assembly work in Milwaukee, Respondent's decision would violate Section 8(a)(5). Respondent's decision to relocate the assembly work to McHenry would achieve the same result, albeit indirectly: its employees would continue to perform assembly work but at reduced wage rates. The issue then is whether the fact that Respondent decided to relocate the work takes Respondent's decision outside the prescriptions of Section 8(d), or in the words of the administrative law judge in *Los Angeles Marine Hardware Co.*, whether the act allows Respondent "to achieve by indirection that which [it could not] achieve by direct means under Section 8(d) of the Act." . . .

In my view the determinative factor in deciding whether an employer's midterm relocation decision is proscribed under Section 8(d) is the employer's motive. Where, as here, the decision is controlled by a desire to avoid a contractual term with regard to a mandatory subject of bargaining, such as wages, then the decision is violative under Sections 8(d) and 8(a)(5), and the employer may not implement the decision during the term of the contract without the union's consent. But where the decision is motivated by reasons unrelated to contract avoidance, then the employer may unilaterally implement its decision after bargaining to impasse with the union.

Note

In affirming *Milwaukee Spring*, the D.C. Circuit (per Edwards, J.) regarded the employer's work removal as sanctioned either by the management rights clause or by implied management-reserved rights. Perhaps most significant was the court's novel treatment of the "zipper" clause, whereby each party waived all further bargaining rights. In effect, the court equated this with a "maintenance of standards" clause, precluding the employer from instituting any unilateral changes during the term of the contract (except under a management-rights theory), regardless of whether it had bargained to impasse. If the employer was not authorized by a union's express or implied waiver to make midterm unilateral changes in a mandatory subject, it would first have to bargain to impasse over the matter. But if by a zipper clause the employer had relinquished the capacity to fulfill the condition precedent to the change, it could never make the change without the union's consent. *UAW v. NLRB*, 765 F.2d 175, 180 (D.C. Cir. 1985). *See also Mead Corp., Fine Paper Div.*, 318 N.L.R.B. 201 (1995) (zipper clause barred employer's implementation of a retirement incentive plan without the union's consent).

B. Deference to Arbitration

In the leading case of *Spielberg Mfg. Co.*, 112 N.L.R.B. 1080 (1955), the Board set forth three general conditions under which it would accord "recognition" to an arbitrator's award: "[T]he proceedings appear to have been fair and regular, all parties had agreed to be bound, and the decision of the arbitration panel is not clearly repugnant to the purposes and policies of the Act." The application (and limitations) of this formula will be considered next.

Collyer Insulated Wire
National Labor Relations Board
192 N.L.R.B. 837 (1971)

The complaint alleges and the General Counsel contends that Respondent violated Section 8(a)(5) and (1) of the National Labor Relations Act, as amended, by making assertedly unilateral changes in certain wages and working conditions. Respondent contends that its authority to make those changes was sanctioned by the collective bargaining contract between the parties and their course of dealing under that contract. Respondent further contends that any of its actions in excess of contractual authorization should properly have been remedied by grievance and arbitration proceeding, as provided in the contract. We agree with Respondent's contention that this dispute is essentially a dispute over the terms and meaning of the contract between the Union and the Respondent. For that reason, we find merit in Respondent's exceptions that the dispute should have been resolved pursuant to the contract and we shall dismiss the complaint.

I. The Alleged Unilateral Changes

Respondent manufactures insulated electrical wiring at its plant in Lincoln, Rhode Island. The Union has represented Respondent's production and maintenance employees under successive contracts since 1937. The contract in effect when this dispute arose resulted from lengthy negotiations commencing in December 1968 and concluding with the execution of the contract of September 16, 1969. The contract was made effective from April 1, 1969, until July 2, 1971.

Respondent's production employees have historically been compensated on an incentive basis. The contract provides for a job evaluation plan and for the adjustment of rates, subject to the grievance procedure, during the term of the contract. Throughout the bargaining relationship, Respondent has routinely made adjustments in incentive rates to accommodate new or changed production methods. The contract establishes non-incentive rates for skilled maintenance tradesmen but provides for changes in those rates, also, pursuant to the job evaluation plan, upon changes in or additions to the duties of the classifications. The central issue here is whether these contract provisions permitted certain mid-contract wage rate changes which Respondent made in November 1969.

A. *The Rate Increase for Skilled Maintenance Tradesmen:* Since early 1968, Respondent's wage rates for skilled tradesmen have not been sufficiently high to attract and retain the numbers of skilled maintenance mechanics and electricians required for the efficient operation of the plant. The record clearly establishes, and the Trial Examiner found, that other employers in the same region paid "substantially higher rates than those paid by Respondent." In consequence, the number of skilled maintenance workers had declined from about 40 in January 1968 to about

30 in mid-1969, and Respondent had been unable to attract employees to fill the resulting vacancies.

During negotiations, Respondent several times proposed wage raises for maintenance employees over and above those being negotiated for the production and maintenance unit generally. The Union rejected those proposals and the contract did not include any provision for such raises. It is clear, nevertheless, that the matter of the skill factor increase was left open, in *some* measure, for further negotiations after the execution of the agreement. The parties sharply dispute, however, the extent to which the matter remained open and the conditions which were to surround further discussions. The Union asserts, and the Trial Examiner found, that the Union was willing, and made known its willingness, to negotiate further wage adjustments only on a plantwide basis, consistent with the job evaluation system. Respondent insists that it understood the Union's position to be that wage increases for maintenance employees only might still be agreed to by the Union after the signing of the contract, if such increases could be justified under the job evaluation system.

At monthly meetings following conclusion of the contract negotiations, Respondent and the Union continued to discuss the Respondent's desire to raise the rates for maintenance employees. Finally, on November 12, 1969, Respondent informed the Union that five days thence, on November 17, Respondent would institute an upward adjustment of 20 cents per hour. The Union protested and restated its desire for a reevaluation of all jobs in the plant. Respondent's representative agreed to consider such an evaluation on a plantwide basis, upon union agreement to the increase for the skilled tradesmen. The Trial Examiner found that the Union did not agree. The rate increase became effective November 17, 1969.

B. *Reassignment of Job Duties:* One of the production steps, the application of insulating material to conductor, is accomplished through the operation of extruder machines. The insulating material, in bulk, is forced to and through the extruder die by a large worm gear. Each change in the type of insulation used on an extruder requires that the worm gear be removed and cleaned of insulation remaining from the previous production run. The removal, cleaning, and replacement of the worm gear is performed approximately once each week and requires approximately 40 minutes to one hour for each operation. Prior to November 12, 1969, the worm gear removal and cleaning had been performed by a team of two maintenance machinists. On November 12, Respondent directed that future worm gear removals would be performed by a single maintenance machinist with the assistance of the extruder machine operator and helper.

C. *Rate Increases for Extruder Operators:* Respondent's third change, also effective November 17, 1969, produced a rate increase for extruder operators. It had been Respondent's practice to adjust the straight time earnings of extruder operators by a factor representing the amount of time during an eight-hour shift when the extruder was in continuous operation. Under that system, for example, an operator who maintained his machine in continuous operation for eight hours was paid for 10 hours' work. This incentive factor has never been fixed by the contract and Respondent had, in the past, changed the rate for various reasons....

II. Relevant Contract Provisions

The contract now in effect between the parties makes provision for adjustment by Respondent in the wages of its employees during the contract term. Those provisions appear to contemplate changes in rates in both incentive and non-incentive jobs. Thus, article IX, section 2, provides:

> "The Corporation agrees to establish rates and differentials of pay for all employees according to their skill, experience and hazards of employment, and to review rates and differentials from time to time.... However, no change in the general scale of pay now in existence shall be made during the term of this Agreement. This Article IX is applicable to the general wage scale, but shall not be deemed to prevent adjustments in individual rates from time to time to remove inequalities or for other proper reasons."

Further evidence of the contractual intent to permit Respondent to modify job rates subject to review through the grievance and arbitration procedures is found in article XIII, section 3, paragraph b, covering new or changed jobs. That paragraph provides that the Union shall have seven days to consider any new rating established by the Company and to submit objections. Thereafter, even absent Union agreement, it vests in the Company authority to institute a new pay rate. The Union, if dissatisfied, may then challenge the propriety of the rate by invoking the grievance procedure which culminates in arbitration.

Finally, the breadth of the arbitration provision makes clear that the parties intended to make the grievance and arbitration machinery the exclusive forum for resolving contract disputes.... [Part III of the Board's opinion is omitted here]

IV. Discussion

We find merit in Respondent's exceptions that because this dispute in its entirety arises from the contract between the parties, and from the parties' relationship under the contract, it ought to be resolved in the manner which that contract prescribes. We conclude that the Board is vested with authority to withhold its processes in this case, and that the contract here made available a quick and fair means for the resolution of this dispute including, if appropriate, a fully effective remedy for any breach of contract which occurred. We conclude, in sum, that our obligation to advance the purposes of the Act is best discharged by the dismissal of this complaint.

In our view, disputes such as these can better be resolved by arbitrators with special skill and experience in deciding matters arising under established bargaining relationships than by the application by this Board of a particular provision of our statute. The necessity for such special skill and expertise is apparent upon examination of the issues arising from Respondent's actions with respect to the operators' rates, the skill factor increase, and the reassignment of duties relating to the worm gear removal. Those issues include, specifically: (a) the extent to which these actions were intended to be reserved to the management, subject to later adjustment by grievance and arbitration; (b) the extent to which the skill factor increase should properly be construed, under article IX of the agreement, as a "change in the general scale of pay" or, conversely, as "adjustments in individual rates . . . to remove inequalities or for other proper reason"; (c) the extent, if any, to which the procedures of article XIII governing new or changed jobs and job rates should have been made applicable to the skill factor increase here; and (d) the extent to which any of these issues may be affected by the long course of dealing between the parties. . . .

The Board's authority, in its discretion, to defer to the arbitration process has never been questioned by the courts of appeals, or by the Supreme Court. Although Section 10(a) of the Act clearly vests the Board with jurisdiction over conduct which constitutes a violation of the provisions of Section 8, notwithstanding the existence of methods of "adjustment or prevention that might be established by agreement," nothing in the Act intimates that the Board must exercise jurisdiction where such methods exist. On the contrary in *Carey v. Westinghouse Electric Corporation*, 375 U.S. 261, 271 (1964), the Court indicated that it favors our deference to such agreed methods. . . .

The policy favoring voluntary settlement of labor disputes through arbitral processes finds specific expression in Section 203(d) of the LMRA. . . .

And of course disputes under Section 301 of the LMRA called forth from the Supreme Court the celebrated affirmation of that national policy in the *Steelworkers Trilogy*.

Admittedly neither Section 203 nor Section 301 applies specifically to the Board. However labor law as administered by the Board does not operate in a vacuum isolated from other parts of the Act, or, indeed, from other acts of Congress. In fact the legislative history suggests that at the time the Taft-Hartley amendments were being considered, Congress anticipated that the Board would "develop by rules and regulations, a policy of entertaining under these provisions only such cases . . . as cannot be settled by resort to the machinery established by the contract itself, voluntary arbitration. . . ."[22]

The question whether the Board should withhold its process arises, of course, only when a set of facts may present not only an alleged violation of the Act but also an alleged breach of the collective bargaining agreement subject to arbitration. Thus, this case like each such case compels an accommodation between, on the one hand, the statutory policy favoring the fullest use of collective bargaining and the arbitral process and, on the other, the statutory policy reflected by Congress' grant to the Board of exclusive jurisdiction to prevent unfair labor practices.

---

22. [7] S. Rep. No. 105, 80th Cong., 1st Sess. 23 (1947).

We address the accommodations required here with the benefit of the Board's full history of such accommodations in similar cases. From the start the Board has, case by case, both asserted jurisdiction and declined, as the balance was struck on particular facts and at various stages in the long ascent of collective bargaining to its present state of wide acceptance. Those cases reveal that the Board has honored the distinction between two broad but distinct classes of cases, those in which there has been an arbitral award, and those in which there has not.

In the former class of cases the Board has long given hospitable acceptance to the arbitral process.... The Board's policy was refined in *Spielberg Manufacturing Company*,[23] where the Board established the now settled rule that it would limit its inquiry, in the presence of an arbitrator's award, to whether the procedures were fair and the result not repugnant to the Act.

In those cases in which no award had issued, the Board's guidelines have been less clear. At times the Board has dealt with the unfair labor practice, and at other times it has left the parties to their contract remedies....

Jos. Schlitz Brewing Co.[24] is the most significant recent case in which the Board has exercised its discretion to defer. The underlying dispute in *Schlitz* was strikingly similar to the one now before us. In *Schlitz* the respondent employer decided to halt its production line during employee breaks. That decision was a departure from an established practice of maintaining extra employees, relief men, to fill in for regular employees during breaktime. The change resulted in, among other things, elimination of the relief man job classification. The change elicited a union protest leading to an unfair labor practice proceeding in which the Board ruled that the case should be "left for resolution within the framework of the agreed upon settlement procedures." The majority there explained its decision in these words:

> Thus, we believe that where, as here, the contract clearly provides for grievance and arbitration machinery, where the unilateral action taken is not designed to undermine the Union and is not patently erroneous but rather is based on a substantial claim of contractual privilege, and it appears that the arbitral interpretation of the contract will resolve both the unfair labor practice issue and the contract interpretation issue in a manner compatible with the purposes of the Act, then the Board should defer to the arbitration clause conceived by the parties....

The circumstances of this case, no less than those in *Schlitz*, weigh heavily in favor of deferral. Here, as in *Schlitz*, this dispute arises within the confines of a long and productive collective bargaining relationship. The parties before us have, for 35 years, mutually and voluntarily resolved the conflicts which inhere in collective bargaining. Here, as there, no claim is made of enmity by Respondent to employees'

---

23. [10] 112 N.L.R.B. 1080, 1082 (1955).
24. [12] 175 N.L.R.B. No. 23 (1969).

exercise of protected rights. Respondent here has credibly asserted its willingness to resort to arbitration under a clause providing for arbitration in a very broad range of disputes and unquestionably broad enough to embrace this dispute.

Finally, here, as in *Schlitz*, the dispute is one eminently well suited to resolution by arbitration. The contract and its meaning in present circumstances lie at the center of this dispute. In contrast, the Act and its policies become involved only if it is determined that the agreement between the parties, examined in the light of its negotiating history and the practices of the parties thereunder, did not sanction Respondent's right to make the disputed changes, subject to review if sought by the Union, under the contractually prescribed procedure. That threshold determination is clearly within the expertise of a mutually agreed upon arbitrator. In this regard we note especially that here, as in *Schlitz*, the dispute between these parties is the very stuff of labor contract arbitration. The competence of a mutually selected arbitrator to decide the issue and fashion an appropriate remedy, if needed, can no longer be gainsaid.

We find no basis for the assertion of our dissenting colleagues that our decision here modifies the standards established in *Spielberg* for judging the acceptability of an arbitrator's award. . . .

It is true, manifestly, that we cannot judge the regularity or statutory acceptability of the result in an arbitration proceeding which has not occurred. However, we are unwilling to adopt the presumption that such a proceeding will be invalid under *Spielberg* and to exercise our decisional authority at this juncture on the basis of a mere possibility that such a proceeding might be unacceptable under *Spielberg* standards. That risk is far better accommodated, we believe, by the result reached here of retaining jurisdiction against an event which years of experience with labor arbitration have now made clear is a remote hazard.

Member Fanning's dissenting opinion incorrectly characterizes this decision as instituting "compulsory arbitration" and as creating an opportunity for employers and unions to "strip parties of statutory rights."

We are not compelling any party to agree to arbitrate disputes arising during a contract term, but are merely giving full effect to their own voluntary agreements to submit all such disputes to arbitration, rather than permitting such agreements to be sidestepped and permitting the substitution of our processes, a forum not contemplated by their own agreement.

Nor are we "stripping" any party of "statutory rights." The courts have long recognized that an industrial relations dispute may involve conduct which, at least arguably, may contravene both the collective agreement and our statute. When the parties have contractually committed themselves to mutually agreeable procedures for resolving their disputes during the period of the contract, we are of the view that those procedures should be afforded full opportunity to function. The long and successful functioning of grievance and arbitration procedures suggests to us that in the overwhelming majority of cases, the utilization of such means will resolve the underlying dispute and make it unnecessary for either party to follow the more formal, and sometimes lengthy, combination of administrative and judicial litigation provided for under our statute. At the same time, by our reservation of jurisdiction, *infra*, we guarantee that there will be no sacrifice of statutory rights if the parties' own processes fail to function in a manner consistent with the dictates of our law. . . .

V. Remedy

Without prejudice to any party and without deciding the merits of the controversy, we shall order that the complaint herein be dismissed, but we shall retain jurisdiction for a limited purpose. Our decision represents a developmental step in the Board's treatment of these problems and the controversy here arose at a time when the Board decisions may have led the parties to conclude that the Board approved dual litigation of this controversy before the Board and before an arbitrator. We are also aware that the parties herein have not resolved their dispute by the contractual grievance and arbitration procedure and that, therefore, we cannot now inquire whether resolution of the dispute will comport with the standards set forth in *Spielberg, supra*. In order to eliminate the risk of prejudice to any party we shall retain jurisdiction over this dispute solely for the purpose of entertaining an appropriate and timely motion for further consideration upon a proper showing that either (a) the dispute has not, with reasonable promptness after the issuance of this decision, either been resolved by amicable settlement in the grievance procedure or submitted promptly to arbitration, or (b) the grievance or arbitration procedures have not been fair and regular or have reached a result which is repugnant to the Act.

[The concurring opinion of MEMBER BROWN is omitted.]

MEMBER FANNING (dissenting). . . .

Clearly . . . the effect of the majority's decision is a direction to the parties to arbitrate a grievance which is no longer contractually arbitrable. The complaint is dismissed, but jurisdiction is retained, presumably to give the Union an opportunity to file a grievance under a time-expired contractual provision, with the implicit threat to the Respondent that the Board will assert jurisdiction, upon a proper motion, if Respondent is unwilling now to submit to arbitration. The majority's insistence that the parties' statutory rights cannot be adjudicated in this case except through the authority of an arbitrator verges on the practice of compulsory arbitration. Historically, in this country voluntarism has been the essence of private arbitration of labor disputes. Neither Congress nor the courts have attempted to coerce the parties in collective bargaining to resolve their grievances through arbitration. Compulsory arbitration has been regarded by some as contrary to a free, democratic society. Collective bargaining agreements, such as the one in the instant case, give aggrieved parties the *right* to file grievances and to present their disputes to an arbitrator. The element of compulsion has been deliberately omitted. To establish the principle, as a matter of labor law, that the parties to a collective bargaining agreement must, in part, surrender their protection under this statute as a consequence of agreeing to a provision for binding arbitration of grievances will, in my view, discourage rather than encourage the arbitral process in this country. Many may decide they cannot afford the luxury of such "voluntary" arbitration. . . .

The effect of the majority's decision in the instant case is clearly a reversal of the established *Spielberg* line of cases. In the future applicable standards for review of arbitration awards will not be followed. Neither the existence of an actual award, the fairness of the arbitrator's opinion or its impingement upon the policies of the Act will be considered by the Board in dismissing complaints of this nature. Under the majority's accommodation theory even consideration of the nature and scope of the alleged unfair labor practices, as set forth in . . . *Joseph Schlitz, supra*, will not receive the Board's attention. The impact of the majority's decision may be said to go beyond compulsory arbitration. For it means that in the future the Board will not concern itself with the *fact* or the *regularity* of the arbitral process, but will strip the parties of statutory rights merely on the *availability* of such a procedure.

The majority does not frame the primary issue in this case in terms calculated to resolve a particular dispute in a particular case. Rather, a new standard for the non-assertion of jurisdiction is announced, embracing a whole class of employers who have entered into contracts with unions containing a grievance-arbitration clause. In the future, complaints based upon such disputes, without regard to the seriousness of the alleged unfair labor practices, may not be litigated before this Board. . . .

Congress has said that arbitration and the voluntary settlement of disputes are the preferred method of dealing with certain kinds of industrial unrest. Congress has also said that the power of this Board to dispose of unfair labor practices is not to be affected by any other method of adjustment. Whatever these two statements mean, they do not mean that this Board can abdicate its authority wholesale. Clearly there is an accommodation to be made. The majority is so anxious to accommodate arbitration that it forgets that the first duty of this Board is to provide a forum for the adjudication of unfair labor practices. We have not been told that arbitration is the only method; it is one method.

We have recently been told by the Supreme Court that preemption in favor of this Board still exists. It is therefore inappropriate, to say the least, for us to cede our jurisdiction in all cases involving arbitration to a tribunal that may, and often does, provide only a partial remedy.

[The dissenting opinion of MEMBER JENKINS is omitted.]

Notes

1. Collyer *Deferral in Section 8(a)(5) Cases* — The D.C. Circuit subsequently reaffirmed the *Collyer* deferral doctrine in another § 8(a)(5) case, refusing to enforce a Board order against an employer who stopped providing holiday pay to employees on workers' compensation leave, and chastising the Board for failing to defer to arbitration processes available under the parties' labor contract. In *Burns Int'l Sec. Servs. v. NLRB*, 146 F.3d 873 (D.C. Cir. 1998), Judge Edwards wrote for the court:

> The relevant inquiry... is whether Burns acted on a viable claim or right under the parties' CBA in eliminating the holiday pay practice. So long as the employer plausibly claims contractual justification for its actions under the express or implied terms of the CBA, and the matter in dispute is subject to arbitration, then the Board should leave the parties to their contract remedies unless the employer refuses to go to arbitration.

Accordingly, the court overturned the Board's finding that the employees' strike in response to the employer's action was an unfair labor practice strike, eliminating the basis for the Board's ruling that the employer had violated the Act by failing to reinstate the strikers once they made an unconditional offer to return to work. *See also Caritas Good Samaritan Med. Ctr.*, 340 N.L.R.B. 61 (2003) (dismissing complaint and deferring to arbitration a dispute stemming from an employer's unilateral change in health insurance benefits where the employer "plausibly argue[d]" that the dispute was governed by a clause in the labor contract). However, when the arbitral resolution of the underlying contractual dispute may not fully resolve the relevant unfair labor practice issue, the Board will refuse to defer the controversy to arbitration. *See, e.g., Dennison*, 330 N.L.R.B. 389 (1999) (refusing to defer to arbitration where issues regarding decision to transfer work were inextricably related to issues reserved to Board, including withdrawal of recognition, termination of labor contract, and changes in terms and conditions of employment).

2. *Harmonizing Collyer and C & C Plywood* — Does *Collyer* reflect a shift in direction from *C & C Plywood, supra*? What factors must be weighed in assessing the deferral policy? What if the arbitrator's remedial authority is severely limited by the labor contract? *Compare Hoffman Air & Filtration Sys.*, 312 N.L.R.B. 349 (1993) (declining to defer § 8(a)(1) and related § 8(a)(3) issues to arbitration where the contract prevented the arbitrator from making "any recommendation for future action by the Company or the Union," effectively preventing the imposition of the equivalent of a Board cease-and-desist remedy), *with Roswil, Inc.*, 314 N.L.R.B. 9 (1994) (refusing to defer discharge case to arbitration where the labor contract limited back-pay awards to 20 days), *rev'd, NLRB v. Roswil, Inc.*, 55 F.3d 382 (8th Cir. 1995) (scope of remedies available to the arbitrator is relevant, but not dispositive of deferral issue). Whether the Board will defer in cases involving alleged statutory violations also depends upon the existence of a question of contract interpretation. In *Public Serv. Co.*, 319 N.L.R.B. 984 (1995), the Board held that it would defer to arbitration the question of whether an employer unlawfully bypassed a union, the recognized bargaining agent under the parties' contract, and dealt directly with the employees, even though the direct dealing was not accompanied by any unilateral change in the terms of employment. The dissent maintained there was no real issue of contract interpretation for the arbitrator to decide; it was essentially a matter of bargaining relationships. Nevertheless, because the arbitrator had the authority to order the employer to honor its contractual obligation to deal with the recognized union rather than with the employees, an adequate remedy existed at arbitration.

What if the arbitrator did not believe the issue was arbitrable, but persuaded by a party's arguments, reached a conclusion on the merits anyhow? In *Doerfer Eng'g v. NLRB*, 79 F.3d 101 (8th Cir. 1996), the court held that the Board had abused its discretion in not honoring an arbitrator's award that an employer could terminate a long-standing practice of allowing employees to use company tools and equipment for personal projects. The NLRB had refused to defer to the arbitrator's decision, relying on the first and last sentences of the arbitrator's opinion, which intimated that the grievance was not arbitrable. The court concluded, however, that the arbitrator had actually adjudicated the merits of the dispute. Although the employer had argued to the arbitrator against arbitrability, the union had taken the position before the arbitrator that the matter was arbitrable, and had agreed to be bound by the arbitrator's decision. According to the Eighth Circuit, the union "cannot ... change its position simply because the arbitrator reached an unfavorable conclusion on the merits. . . . A contrary decision would encourage parties to renege upon their agreement to be bound by an arbitrator's decision and to circumvent the grievance procedure by filing an unfair labor practice charge whenever they felt they had a better chance for favorable resolution before the Board."

3. *Nondeferral Involving Allegations of Failure to Provide Information Necessary for Grievance-Processing*—The Board does not defer to arbitration of disputes that include allegations of a failure to provide information necessary for grievance processing. The Board reasons that the employer's production of information is a necessary prerequisite to the union's ability to perform its statutory obligation to represent bargaining unit members during the term of a collective bargaining agreement, and that nondeferral in this context facilitates arbitration by permitting the parties to analyze the respective merits of their cases prior to committing resources to arbitration. See *Shaw's Supermarkets, Inc.*, 339 N.L.R.B. 871 (2003). Only where the union has clearly and unmistakably waived its statutory rights will *Collyer* deferral be appropriate. The mere existence of grievance machinery that includes an information provision is not sufficient to constitute a clear and unmistakable waiver of the union's statutory right to receive information. *DaimlerChrysler Corp. v. NLRB*, 288 F.3d 434 (D.C. Cir. 2002) (reviewing and approving Board's application of nondeferral policy in information disputes).

4. *Deference Accorded to Prior Arbitral Determinations*—Should the NLRB honor an arbitrator's award as a whole, or merely any findings of fact or interpretations of contractual provisions that happen also to be essential parts of the unfair labor practice case? What about an issue that the parties failed to place before the arbitrator despite the opportunity to do so? In *Olin Corp.*, 268 N.L.R.B. 573 (1984), the Labor Board announced standards to be applied when deciding whether to honor a prior arbitral decision under the *Spielberg* doctrine:

> We would find that an arbitrator has adequately considered the unfair labor practice if (1) the contractual issue is factually parallel to the unfair labor practice issue, and (2) the arbitrator was presented generally with the facts

relevant to resolving the unfair labor practice. In the [*sic*] respect, differences, if any, between the contractual and statutory standards of review should be weighed by the Board as part of its determination under the *Spielberg* standards of whether an award is "clearly repugnant" to the Act. And, with regard to the inquiry into the "clearly repugnant" standard, we would not require an arbitrator's award to be totally consistent with Board precedent. Unless the award is "palpably wrong." *i.e.*, unless the arbitrator's decision is not susceptible to an interpretation consistent with the Act, we will defer.

Finally, we would require that the party seeking to have the Board reject deferral and consider the merits of a given case show that the above standards for deferral have not been met. Thus, the party seeking to have the Board ignore the determination of an arbitrator has the burden of affirmatively demonstrating the defects in the arbitral process or award.

In *Babcock & Wilcox Constr. Co.*, 361 N.L.R.B. 1127 (2014), however, a closely divided Labor Board significantly modified the *Olin Corp.* standards, ruling that it would only defer to prior arbitral awards if the party seeking Board deferral can show that: (1) the arbitrator was explicitly authorized to decide the unfair labor practice issue; (2) that the arbitrator was presented with and considered the statutory issue, or was prevented from doing so by the party opposing deferral; and (3) Board law reasonably permits the award. The *Babcock & Wilcox* majority criticized *Olin Corp.*'s expansive deferral policy, which it said "amounts to a conclusive presumption that the arbitrator 'adequately considered' the statutory issue if the arbitrator was merely presented with facts relevant to both an alleged contract violation and an alleged unfair labor practice." Because the *Olin* standard did not appropriately balance protection for workers' rights under federal labor law with the national policy of encouraging arbitration to resolve disputes over the interpretation or application of labor contracts, the majority required clear evidence that the arbitrator was expressly authorized to decide the underlying unfair labor practice question and actually did so. The two dissenting Board members noted that most bargaining agreements only authorize arbitrators to interpret and apply the express terms of the collective contract and do not authorize them to decide external statutory matters. Under the *Babcock & Wilcox* standard, relatively few cases were subject to deferral.

The Trump Board overturned *Babcock & Wilcox* in 2019, returning to the previous *Spielberg* and *Olin Corp.* standards: the Board will defer to the arbitrator's decision only if: (1) the arbitral proceedings were fair and regular; (2) all parties agreed to be bound; (3) the contractual issue was factually parallel to the unfair labor practice issue; (4) the arbitrator was presented generally with the facts relevant to resolving the unfair labor practice issue; and (5) the arbitrator's decision was not clearly repugnant to the purposes and policies of the Act. *United Parcel Service*, 369 N.L.R.B. No. 1 (2019). Which standard do you believe better effectuates the goals of the NLRA, *Spielberg/Olin Corp.* or *Babcock & Wilcox*?

5. *Board Deference to Grievance Settlements*—The Board defers to prior labor-management grievance settlements made pursuant to the collective bargaining agreement in the same manner in which it defers to prior arbitral awards under the *Spielberg* doctrine. *See Alpha Beta Co.*, 273 N.L.R.B. 1546 (1985), *aff'd sub nom. Mahon v. NLRB*, 808 F.2d 1342 (9th Cir. 1987). Suppose the employer and the union agree to settle a grievance without the affected employee's consent—should the Board defer if the conduct might also have been the subject of an unfair labor practice charge?

6. *Extension of* Collyer *to § 8(a)(3) Cases*—The *Collyer* deferral doctrine was extended to § 8(a)(3) discrimination cases in *National Radio Co.*, 198 N.L.R.B. 527 (1972), another 3-2 decision. In *General Am. Transp. Corp.*, 228 N.L.R.B. 808 (1977), however, then-Chair Betty Murphy voted with Members Fanning and Jenkins to trim back *Collyer* to its original § 8(a)(5) dimensions and to refuse to defer to arbitration in cases alleging discrimination against individual employees. She reasoned:

> In cases alleging violations of Section 8(a)(5) and 8(b)(3), based upon conduct assertedly in derogation of the contract, the principal issue is whether the complained-of conduct is permitted by the parties' contract. Such issues are eminently suited to the arbitral process, and resolution of the contract issue by an arbitrator will, as a rule, dispose of the unfair labor practice issue. On the other hand, in cases alleging violations of Section 8(a)(1), 8(a)(3), 8(b)(1)(A), and 8(b)(2), although arguably also involving a contract violation, the determinative issue is not whether the conduct is permitted by the contract, but whether the conduct was unlawfully motivated or whether it otherwise interfered with, restrained, or coerced employees in the exercise of the rights guaranteed them by Section 7 of the Act. In these situations, an arbitrator's resolution of the contract issue will not dispose of the unfair labor practice allegation. Nor is the arbitration process suited for resolving employee complaints of discrimination under Section 7.

Nevertheless, in *United Technologies Corp.*, 268 N.L.R.B. 557 (1984), with Board members reiterating the same arguments, a 3-1 majority overruled *General American Transportation* and revitalized the *National Radio* doctrine favoring deferral in §§ 8(a)(1), 8(a)(3), 8(b)(1)(A), and 8(b)(2) cases. The D.C. Circuit accepted the *United Technologies* approach in *Hammontree v. NLRB*, 925 F.2d 1486 (D.C. Cir. 1991) (en banc). The Board recently reaffirmed its commitment to the *United Technologies Corp.* standards regarding pre-arbitral deferral in *United Parcel Service*, 369 N.L.R.B. No. 1 (2019).

Does the extension of *Collyer* to the § 8(a)(3) context seem appropriate? Is the *Collyer* doctrine adequate to protect individual employees' statutory rights under §§ 8(a)(1), 8(a)(3), 8(b)(1)(A), and 8(b)(2)? *See generally* Edwards, *Deferral to Arbitration and Waiver of the Duty to Bargain: A Possible Way Out of Everlasting Confusion at the NLRB*, 46 Ohio St. L.J. 23 (1985); Harper, *Union Waiver of Employee Rights Under the NLRA: Part II*, 4 Indus. Rel. L.J. 680 (1981); Lynch, *Deferral, Waiver, and Arbitration Under the NLRA: From Status to Contract and Back Again*, 44 U. Miami L. Rev. 237 (1989).

7. *Arbitration in the Nonunion Context* — How might the increasing use of alternative dispute resolution mechanisms in the nonunion context impact application of the *Collyer* and *Spielberg* doctrines? For example, when a nonunion employer conditions employment on the signing of predispute waivers of all statutory forum rights pertaining to employment, would those agreements divest the NLRB of jurisdiction to hear unfair labor practice claims filed by the agreement signers? In *Prime Healthcare Paradise Valley, LLC*, 368 N.L.R.B. No. 10 (2019), the Board applied the balancing test from *The Boeing Co.*, 365 N.L.R.B. No. 154 (2017), and concluded that arbitration agreements that are facially neutral but could reasonably be interpreted to block the filing of charges with the NLRB fall within category 3 and violate employees' §7 rights. *Accord, Countrywide Fin. Corp.*, 369 N.L.R.B. No. 12 (2020). On the other hand, what are the incentives for employers to seek alternative dispute resolution of NLRA claims, given that the NLRA does not allow compensatory or punitive damages for jury trials? Should the Board defer to arbitration awards of employment disputes in nonunion settings where the disputes also involve alleged unfair labor practices? *Compare* Perez, *Too Many Arbitrators Do Spoil the Soup: NLRB Charges Filed by Non-Unionized Employees Should Not be Subject to Mandatory Pre-Dispute Arbitration Agreements*, 23 Lab. Law. 285 (2008), *with* Thompson, *Arbitrators — Unlike Too Many Cooks — Do Not Spoil the Soup! Making the Case for Allowing Pre-Dispute Mandatory Arbitration of Unfair Labor Practice Charges in Nonunion Workforces*, 23 Lab. Law. 301 (2008).

Problem

66. A unionized package delivery service fired Joe McFadden for violating the employer's package delivery procedures by leaving a package on a recipient's porch rather than requiring a signature. McFadden was a union steward who had opposed the ratification of collective agreements by the union in the past, and unsuccessfully ran for local union office against Sherry Stengle, a longtime business agent. McFadden filed a grievance and was represented at the hearing before the arbitration panel by Stengle, the same business agent he had challenged in the election. The panel (a joint panel with union and management representatives) upheld the discipline, and McFadden then filed an unfair labor practice charge with the Board. The ALJ rejected the employer's argument that the Board should defer to the arbitral panel's decision, and found McFadden's dismissal unlawful. How should the Board rule under the current legal standard? Would it make a difference if the Board had changed membership under a new presidential administration and applied the Obama Board's standard (*Babcock & Wilcox*)? Are there additional facts you would need to know to answer these questions?

C. Deferral Where Labor Board Has Primary Jurisdiction — Representational Issues

Carey v. Westinghouse Electric Corp., 375 U.S. 261, 84 S. Ct. 401, 11 L. Ed. 2d 320 (1964). The IUE sought arbitration with Westinghouse regarding its contractual claim to jurisdiction over work being performed by employees represented by another union. Westinghouse refused to arbitrate on the ground that the controversy concerned a representational matter for the NLRB. Although the IUE could not compel the other labor organization to participate in its arbitral proceeding, the Supreme Court concluded that the lower court should have ordered the requested arbitration.

> Grievance arbitration is one method of settling disputes over work assignments; and it is commonly used, we are told. To be sure, only one of the two unions involved in the controversy has moved the state courts to compel arbitration. So unless the other union intervenes, an adjudication of the arbiter might not put an end to the dispute. Yet the arbitration may as a practical matter end the controversy or put into movement forces that will resolve it. . . .

The Court recognized that the Labor Board might still be asked to consider the jurisdictional question following the arbitrator's determination. "Should the Board disagree with the arbiter, by ruling, for example, that the employees involved in the controversy are members of one bargaining unit or another, the Board's ruling would, of course, take precedence."

Notes

1. *Aftermath.* Arbitration took place following the decision in the *Carey* case — The NLRB subsequently concluded, however, that the ultimate issue of representation could not be decided by the arbitrator through an interpretation of the contract, but could be resolved only through the use of Board criteria for unit determination. While giving "some consideration to the award," the Board proceeded to make a different unit allocation. *Westinghouse Electric Corp.*, 162 N.L.R.B. 768 (1967).

2. *Representation Cases* — Although the Board will not defer to arbitral determinations that primarily concern issues of representation and statutory policy, arbitration awards will generally be honored where the primary focus of the dispute is contractual. See *Appollo Sys., Inc.*, 360 N.L.R.B. 687 (2014) (Board refused to use its unit clarification proceedings to resolve a bargaining unit composition dispute arising under a § 8(f) agreement in the construction industry; issues in the case involved the existence of a valid agreement on the composition of the bargaining unit and whether the employer had breached it, a dispute presenting "classic questions of contract" appropriate for arbitration); *IBEW, Local 71 v. Trafftech, Inc.*, 461 F.3d 690 (6th Cir. 2006) (compelling arbitration of union grievance challenging employer's assignment of bargaining unit work to members of another union where union alleged violations of specific contractual provisions); *SEIU v.*

St. Vincent Med. Ctr., 344 F.3d 977 (9th Cir. 2003), *cert. denied*, 541 U.S. 973 (2004) (compelling arbitration and refusing to defer to NLRB's primary jurisdiction in dispute over whether employer violated the parties' agreement covering conduct during an organizing campaign; issue was primarily contractual in nature rather than primarily representational, since it turned on whether agreement's arbitration provision covered the dispute and did not require designation of a bargaining representative or identification of a bargaining unit). *But see Part Time Faculty Ass'n at Columbia Coll. Chicago v. Columbia Coll.*, 892 F.3d 860 (7th Cir. 2018) (refusing to enforce arbitral award determining the scope of an existing bargaining agreement where award directly conflicted with a prior unit determination made by the NLRB's Regional Director, reasoning that award was "unenforceable as a matter of law.")

3. *Deferral in Multi-Union Representational Settings* — The courts and the Board seem more willing to defer to arbitration entailing resolution of representation issues where only a single union claims the work. *See, e.g., Paper, Allied-Industrial, Chem. & Energy Workers Int'l Union, Local 5-0550 v. Air Products & Chems., Inc.*, 300 F.3d 667 (6th Cir. 2002) (dispute over seniority rights for employees who wanted to bid on new jobs at a newly constructed power plant adjacent to the original facility was primarily a matter of contractual interpretation governed on its face by the collective bargaining agreement, not a representational issue within the Board's exclusive jurisdiction, distinguishing cases involving competing unions); *Verizon Info. Sys.*, 335 N.L.R.B. 558 (2001) (holding a union representation petition in abeyance pending the outcome of arbitration over the appropriate scope of a bargaining unit pursuant to an agreement regarding employer neutrality and card check recognition, where only one union was involved). Although parties may waive the right to submit representational disputes to election, such waivers must be clear and unmistakable. *See Cent. Parking Sys.*, 335 N.L.R.B. 390 (2001) (deferring to arbitration in a case involving an "after-acquired stores" clause in a collective agreement; employer had waived its right to an election and the acquired company must therefore be added to the existing bargaining unit upon proof of majority employee support for the union).

Smith v. Evening News Ass'n, 371 U.S. 195, 83 S. Ct. 267, 9 L. Ed. 2d 246 (1962). Petitioner, a union member, sued his employer in state court for damages, alleging breach of a provision in the collective contract that there would be no discrimination against any employee because of union activity. The state courts dismissed on the ground that the subject matter was within the exclusive jurisdiction of the NLRB. The Supreme Court reversed. The Court first declared that the authority of the Board to deal with unfair labor practices that also violate collective agreements "is not exclusive and does not destroy the jurisdiction of the courts in suits under § 301." The Court then concluded that an action by an individual employee to collect wages in the form of damages is among those "suits for violation of contracts between an employer and a labor organization" arising under § 301.

Notes

1. *Factual Context*—In *Smith*, the employee filed his claim on behalf of himself and 49 other union members who were not permitted to work during a strike by another union at the employer's site, while nonunion employees were permitted to work. There was no grievance and arbitration clause so the employees could not advance their claims through arbitration. Although they could have filed an unfair labor practice charge with the NLRB, the six-month statute of limitations had expired. It was clear under *Lincoln Mills* that the union could have brought suit on their behalf, but it did not do so. Thus, the only possible recourse for the employees against the employer was a § 301 suit in court.

2. *Overlapping State Court Jurisdiction*—In *William E. Arnold Co. v. Carpenters Dist. Council*, 417 U.S. 12 (1974), the Supreme Court held that a state court had jurisdiction to enjoin a union's breach of a no-strike clause, even though the breach arguably involved a violation of § 8(b)(4)(D)'s jurisdictional dispute provisions.

D. Contract Rejection in Bankruptcy

NLRB v. Bildisco & Bildisco, 465 U.S. 513, 104 S. Ct. 1188, 79 L. Ed. 2d 482 (1984). In April 1980 the employer, a partnership in the building supplies business, filed for reorganization under Chapter 11 of the Bankruptcy Act. About half of its employees were covered by a three-year collective bargaining agreement, which was due to expire in April 1982. Beginning in January 1980 the employer defaulted on certain obligations under the contract to pay health and pension benefits and to transmit union dues, and in May 1980 it refused to pay required wage increases. In December 1980 Bildisco, as debtor-in-possession (similar to a trustee in bankruptcy) requested the bankruptcy court for permission to reject the labor agreement, and permission was granted in January 1981. Meanwhile, in mid-summer 1980 the union filed refusal-to-bargain charges against Bildisco for its unilateral actions, and the NLRB found that the employer had violated § 8(a)(5) of the NLRA. With both the bankruptcy and unfair labor practice rulings before it, the Supreme Court held unanimously that a collective bargaining agreement is an "executory contract" subject to rejection under § 365(a) of the Bankruptcy Code. The standard for rejection is that the agreement "burdens the estate" and that "the equities balance in favor of rejecting the labor contract." A divided (5-4) Court further held that a debtor-in-possession does not violate § 8(a)(5) of the NLRA by unilaterally changing the terms of the collective agreement between the date the employer filed the bankruptcy petition and the date the bankruptcy court authorized the rejection.

Notes

1. *Legislative Aftermath*—Congress responded swiftly to *Bildisco*. Pub. L. No. 98–353 (1984), 11 U.S.C. § 1113, permits the rejection or modification of a bargaining agreement only when: (1) the employer has made a proposal to the union containing those contractual modifications that are necessary to permit the reorganization of the

debtor while treating all interested parties equitably; (2) the employer has offered "to confer in good faith in attempting to reach mutually satisfactory modifications"; (3) the bankruptcy court finds that the union has rejected the employer's proposed changes "without good cause"; and (4) the court concludes that "the balance of the equities clearly favors rejection" of the bargaining agreement. The court is obliged to hold a hearing on the employer's petition within 14 days and to issue its determination within 30 days thereafter.

This 1984 amendment to the Bankruptcy Code has, at least partially, restricted the ability of employers to utilize bankruptcy proceedings to abrogate bargaining agreement obligations. An employer seeking the protection of the Bankruptcy Code is not free to modify its bargaining agreement or to ignore its grievance-arbitration obligations until it obtains bankruptcy court approval. Such an employer is not allowed to take advantage of the automatic stay provision of the Bankruptcy Code (§ 362(a)), since the express requirements of § 1113 must be satisfied before a petitioning company may avoid contractual duties. *See In re Ionosphere Clubs*, 922 F.2d 984 (2d Cir. 1990), *cert. denied sub nom. Air Line Pilots Ass'n, Int'l v. Shugrue*, 502 U.S. 808 (1991). *See also Plabell Rubber Prods., Inc.*, 307 N.L.R.B. 1197 (1992).

In *Wheeling-Pittsburgh Steel Corp. v. United Steelworkers*, 791 F.2d 1074 (3d Cir. 1986), the court ruled that a bankruptcy court erred when it allowed Wheeling-Pittsburgh to void its bargaining agreement, since the record did not clearly indicate that the employer-requested concessions were "necessary" for successful reorganization under Chapter 11 and were "fair and equitable" to all the parties. The bankruptcy judge "failed to give any persuasive rationale for the disproportionate treatment of the employees who were being asked to take a five-year agreement under a worst-case scenario without any possibility for restoration or share in the event of a better-than-anticipated recovery." The court also faulted Wheeling-Pittsburgh's failure to include a "snap back" clause in its proposed agreement that would increase wages if corporate finances improved. *But cf. Truck Drivers Local 807, etc. v. Carey Transp., Inc.*, 816 F.2d 82 (2d Cir. 1987) (rejection of collective bargaining agreement was "necessary" and "fair and equitable" when unionized labor costs were 60% above industry average, even though managers and nonunion employees would incur lesser cuts, since compensation of the latter persons was "barely competitive" and their responsibilities had increased).

A recent study found that although federal bankruptcy courts have been less likely to grant motions by companies seeking to reject their collective bargaining agreements in bankruptcy since the 1984 amendments, the "true rejection rate" (which includes cases in which assets of a firm in Chapter 11 bankruptcy were sold to a third party under Bankruptcy Code section 363, effectively nullifying the labor agreement under the successorship doctrine, *see infra* part E) has actually increased. Between 1984 and 2008, courts granted about 58% of debtors' motions to reject labor contracts (down from 67% during 1975–1984, before the enactment of § 1113). However, § 363 sales subsequently occurred in some of the cases in which rejection was denied, resulting in a true rejection rate of 71% — higher than that applicable prior to the enactment of § 1113. *See "True Rejection Rate" of Contracts Rose After 1984, Bankruptcy Case Study Finds*, Daily Lab. Rep. (BNA) No. 215, Nov. 10, 2009 (reporting on study by Christopher Cameron at Southwestern University Law School).

2. *Employer Duties Stemming from an Expired Collective Agreement*—Employers may also reject their duties pursuant to expired collective bargaining agreements in bankruptcy, proceeding in the same fashion as if the agreement were still in force: they must file a motion to reject the expired labor contract with the bankruptcy court, which will conduct the proper balancing of equities. *See In re Trump Entertainment Resorts, UNITE HERE Local 54*, 810 F.3d 161 (3d Cir. 2016) (finding that section 1113 of the federal bankruptcy code authorizes a bankruptcy court to permit a Chapter 11 debtor-employer to reject or modify continuing labor obligations established in a collective agreement even where the agreement expired before the bankruptcy filing, reasoning that it is better to preserve jobs through a rejection of the labor contract than to lose them permanently by requiring the debtor to continue to comply with the terms of a financially burdensome labor contract). Until the bankruptcy court approves rejection, the employer must maintain the status quo and continue to bargain to impasse with the union before making changes in mandatory subjects of bargaining.

3. *Unfair Labor Practice Proceedings in Bankruptcy*—In *NLRB v. Superior Forwarding, Inc.*, 762 F.2d 695 (8th Cir. 1985), the court held that a bankruptcy court possesses the authority to enjoin an NLRB unfair labor practice proceeding pertaining to a debtor-employer's rejection of its bargaining agreement where the Labor Board proceeding would threaten the debtor-employer's estate and interfere with bankruptcy court jurisdiction.

4. *Union Leverage*—What leverage does a union have when it learns that the employer plans to enter Chapter 11 proceedings and seek to reject its labor agreement? According to union activists, union leverage is limited unless the union can make a credible strike threat. Nevertheless, unions are highly motivated to avoid having a bankruptcy court void a contract, and collective bargaining may allow the union to limit the "devastation and carnage" of bankruptcy. *See Union Negotiators Describe Small Victories in Talks with Bankrupt Airlines, Steel Firms*, Daily Lab. Rep. (BNA) No. 5, Jan. 9, 2006. A 2007 ruling by the Second Circuit further limited union leverage in the RLA context. In *Northwest Airlines Corp. v. Ass'n of Flight Attendants-CWA (In re Northwest Airlines Corp.)*, 483 F.3d 160 (2d Cir. 2007), the court blocked a strike by flight attendants following the airline's cuts in wages, benefits, and other terms through Chapter 11 bankruptcy proceedings. After the bankruptcy court granted Northwest's petition to reject its labor agreement, the Flight Attendants threatened to strike over negotiations concerning future terms of employment. Acknowledging that the bankruptcy court's negation of the collective contract may have rendered the contractual no-strike clause inoperative, the Second Circuit nonetheless found that the union still had to comply with the provisions of the Railway Labor Act that prohibit work stoppages in labor disputes until the procedural prerequisites set forth in that statute are exhausted. The court observed that unions must exert "every reasonable effort" to negotiate to reach a new agreement, and work to persuade union members of the need to "face[] up to economic reality" prior to conducting a work stoppage.

Labor advocates have proposed legislation to amend § 1113 to better protect union leverage, including allowing unions to strike upon rejection of their collective bargaining agreements in bankruptcy. *See* Protecting Employees and Retirees in Business Bankruptcies Act of 2007, S. 2092/H.R. 3652. Attorneys for management argue that unions may strike under the NLRA if their contracts are rejected in bankruptcy proceedings, and that even under the RLA the strike right is only delayed, not denied: unions may strike after they are released by the National Mediation Board following the failure to reach agreement through negotiations. *See Management, Union Attorneys Debate Extent of Labor Safeguards in Bankruptcy Cases,* Daily Lab. Rep. (BNA) No. 214, Nov. 5, 2008.

Section VII. Successor Employers' Contractual and Bargaining Obligations

John Wiley & Sons, Inc. v. Livingston, 376 U.S. 543, 84 S. Ct. 909, 11 L. Ed. 2d 898 (1964). Retail, Wholesale and Department Store District 65 had a collective bargaining agreement with Interscience Publishers that was to expire in January 1962. Interscience had about 80 employees, 40 of whom were covered by the contract. In October 1961, Interscience merged with John Wiley & Sons, a much larger publisher with about 300 employees, all nonunion. Wiley took over essentially the whole Interscience workforce, and Interscience ceased to exist as a separate entity. Although the Interscience-District 65 agreement had no successorship clause, the union claimed Wiley was bound to recognize certain "vested" rights of the Interscience employees under their contract. These included seniority, severance pay, and pension fund payments. When Wiley refused these demands, the union sued it to compel arbitration a week before the Interscience contract expired. The Supreme Court unanimously held that "the disappearance by merger of a corporate employer which has entered into a collective bargaining agreement with a union does not automatically terminate all rights of the employees covered by the agreement, and . . . in appropriate circumstances, present here, the successor employer may be required to arbitrate." The Court emphasized the "central role of arbitration in effectuating national labor policy" and observed that "a collective bargaining agreement is not an ordinary contract. . . . [I]t is not in any real sense the simple product of a consensual relationship." The Court acknowledged, however, that the "lack of any substantial continuity of identity in the business enterprise before and after a change" in ownership or corporate structure would eliminate the duty to arbitrate. The Court further held that questions of "procedural arbitrability," that is, whether the steps prerequisite to the duty to arbitrate under the contract have been met, must be decided by the arbitrator and not by the courts.

Notes

1. *Substantive and Procedural Arbitrability*—*Wiley* is significant not only for its teachings on successorship, but also for its distinction between "substantive" and "procedural" arbitrability. Extending *Wiley*, the Supreme Court has held that whether a union grievance is barred by "laches" is a question for the arbitrator to decide under a broad arbitration agreement applicable to "any difference" not settled by the parties within 48 hours of occurrence, even if the claim of laches is "extrinsic" to the procedures under the agreement. *International Union of Operating Eng'rs v. Flair Builders, Inc.*, 406 U.S. 487 (1972).

2. *Section 8(a)(5) Obligations of the Merged Entity*—The obligation to arbitrate grievances pertaining to a company's takeover and arising under a labor contract may be enforced through § 8(a)(5) where the new employer's conduct in refusing to arbitrate amounts to a complete repudiation and unilateral modification of the collective agreement. *See Exxon Chem. Co. v. NLRB*, 386 F.3d 1160 (D.C. Cir. 2004). The surviving entity in a merger can also be required to continue to bargain with the union representing the workers at the subsidiary merged entity where they are doing the same work at the same location and with the same tools and equipment as they had previously. *See International Longshore & Warehouse Union v. NLRB*, 890 F.3d 1100 (D.C. Cir. 2018).

NLRB v. Burns International Security Services, Inc.

Supreme Court of the United States
406 U.S. 272, 92 S. Ct. 1571, 32 L. Ed. 2d 61 (1972)

MR. JUSTICE WHITE delivered the opinion of the Court.

Burns International Security Services, Inc. (Burns), replaced another employer, the Wackenhut Corporation (Wackenhut), which had previously provided plant protection services for the Lockheed Aircraft Service Company (Lockheed) located at the Ontario International Airport in California. When Burns began providing security service, it employed 42 guards; 27 of them had been employed by Wackenhut. Burns refused, however, to bargain with the United Plant Guard Workers of America (the union) which had been certified after an NLRB election as the exclusive bargaining representative of Wackenhut's employees less than four months earlier. The issues presented in this case are whether Burns refused to bargain with a union representing a majority of employees in an appropriate unit and whether the National Labor Relations Board could order Burns to observe the terms of a collective bargaining contract signed by the union and Wackenhut which Burns had not voluntarily assumed. Resolution turns to a great extent on the precise facts involved here.

I

The Wackenhut Corporation provided protection services at the Lockheed plant for five years before Burns took over this task. On February 28, 1967, a few months before the change-over of guard employers, a majority of the Wackenhut guards selected the union as their exclusive bargaining representative in a Board election after Wackenhut and the union had agreed that the Lockheed plant was the appropriate bargaining unit. On March 8, the Regional Director certified the union as the exclusive bargaining representative for these employees, and on April 29, Wackenhut and the union entered into a three-year collective bargaining contract.

Meanwhile, since Wackenhut's one-year service agreement to provide security protection was due to expire on June 30, Lockheed had called for bids from various companies supplying these services, and both Burns and Wackenhut submitted estimates. At a pre-bid conference attended by Burns on May 15, a representative of Lockheed informed the bidders that Wackenhut's guards were represented by the union, that the union had recently won a Board election and been certified, and that there was in existence a collective bargaining contract between Wackenhut and the union. Lockheed then accepted Burns' bid, and on May 31, Wackenhut was notified that Burns would assume responsibility for protection services on July 1. Burns chose to retain 27 of the Wackenhut guards, and it brought in 15 of its own guards from other Burns locations.

During June, when Burns hired the 27 Wackenhut guards, it supplied them with membership cards of the American Federation of Guards (AFG), another union with whom Burns had collective bargaining contracts at other locations, and informed them that they must become AFG members to work for Bums, that they would not receive uniforms otherwise, and that Burns "could not live with" the existing contract between Wackenhut and the union. On June 29, Burns recognized the AFG on the theory that it had obtained a card majority. On July 12, however, the UPG demanded that Burns recognize it as the bargaining representative of Burns' employees at Lockheed and that Burns honor the collective bargaining agreement between it and Wackenhut. When Burns refused, the UPG filed unfair labor practice charges, and Burns responded by challenging the appropriateness of the unit and by denying its obligation to bargain.

The Board, adopting the trial examiner's findings and conclusions, found the Lockheed plant an appropriate unit and held that Burns had violated §§ 8(a)(2) and 8(a)(1) of the Act . . . by unlawfully recognizing and assisting the AFG, a rival of the UPG; that it had violated §§ 8(a)(5) and 8(a)(1) . . . by failing to recognize and bargain with the UPG and by refusing to honor the collective bargaining agreement which had been negotiated between Wackenhut and UPG.

Burns did not challenge the § 8(a)(2) unlawful assistance finding in the Court of Appeals but sought review of the unit determination and the order to bargain and observe the pre-existing collective bargaining contract. The Court of Appeals accepted the Board's unit determination and enforced the Board's order insofar as it related to the finding of unlawful assistance of a rival union and the refusal to bargain, but it held that the Board had exceeded its powers in ordering Burns to honor the contract executed by Wackenhut. Both Burns and the Board petitioned for certiorari, Burns challenging the unit determination and the bargaining order and the Board maintaining its position that Burns was bound by the Wackenhut contract, and we granted both petitions, though we declined to review the propriety of the bargaining unit. . . .

II

We address first Burns' alleged duty to bargain with the union. . . . Because the Act itself imposes a duty to bargain with the representative of a majority of the employees in an appropriate unit, the initial issue before the Board was whether the charging union was such a bargaining representative. . . .

. . . In an election held but a few months before, the union had been designated bargaining agent for the employees in the unit and a majority of these employees had been hired by Burns for work in an identical unit. It is undisputed that Burns knew all the relevant facts in this regard and was aware of the certification and of the existence of a collective bargaining contract. In these circumstances, it was not unreasonable for the Board to conclude that the union certified to represent all employees in the unit still represented a majority of the employees and that Burns could not reasonably have entertained a good-faith doubt about that fact. Burns' obligation to bargain with the union over terms and conditions of employment stems from its hiring of Wackenhut's employees and from the recent election and Board certification. It has been consistently held that a mere change of employers or of ownership in the employing industry is not such an "unusual circumstance" as to affect the force of the Board's certification within the normal operative period if a majority of employees after the change of ownership or management were employed by the preceding employer. . . .

It goes without saying, of course, that Burns was not entitled to upset what it should have accepted as an established union majority by soliciting representation cards for another union and thereby committing the unfair labor practice of which it was found guilty by the Board. That holding was not challenged here and makes it imperative that the situation be viewed as it was when Burns hired its employees for the guard unit, a majority of whom were represented by a Board-certified union. *See NLRB v. Gissel Packing Co.*, 395 U.S. 575, 609, 610–616 (1969).

It would be a wholly different case if the Board had determined that because Burns' operational structure and practices differed from those of Wackenhut, the Lockheed bargaining unit was no longer an appropriate one. Likewise, it would be different if Burns had not hired employees already represented by a union certified as a bargaining agent, and the Board recognized as much at oral argument. But where the bargaining unit remains unchanged and a majority of the employees hired by the new employer are represented by a recently certified bargaining agent there is little basis for faulting the Board's implementation of the express mandates of § 8(a)(5) and § 9(a) by ordering the employer to bargain with the incumbent union. This is the view of several courts of appeal and we agree with those courts. . . .

III

It does not follow, however, from Burns' duty to bargain that it was bound to observe the substantive terms of the collective bargaining contract the union had negotiated with Wackenhut and to which Burns had in no way agreed. Section 8(d) of the Act expressly provides that the existence of such bargaining obligation "does not compel either party to agree to a proposal or require the making of a concession." Congress has consistently declined to interfere with free collective bargaining and has preferred that device, or voluntary arbitration, to the imposition of compulsory terms as a means of avoiding or terminating labor disputes. . . .

This history was reviewed in detail and given controlling effect in *H.K. Porter Co. v. NLRB*, 397 U.S. 99 (1970) . . . .

These considerations, evident from the explicit language and legislative history of the labor laws, underlay the Board's prior decisions which until now have consistently held that although successor employers may be bound to recognize and bargain with the union, they are not bound by the substantive provisions of a collective bargaining contract negotiated by their predecessors but not agreed to or assumed by them. . . .

The Board, however, has now departed from this view and argues that the same policies which mandate a continuity of bargaining obligation also require that successor employers be bound to the terms of a predecessor's collective bargaining contract. It asserts that the stability of labor relations will be jeopardized and that employees will face uncertainty and a gap in the bargained for terms and conditions of employment, as well as the possible loss of advantages gained by prior negotiations, unless the new employer is held to have assumed, as a matter of federal labor law, the obligations under the contract entered into by the former employer. Recognizing that under normal contract principles a party would not be bound to a contract in the absence of consent, the Board notes that in *John Wiley & Sons, Inc. v. Livingston*, 376 U.S. 543, 550 (1964), the Court declared that "a collective bargaining agreement is not an ordinary contract" but is rather an outline of the common law of a particular plant or industry. . . . The Board contends that the same factors which the Court emphasized in *Wiley*, the peaceful settlement of industrial conflicts and "protection [of] the employees [against] a sudden change in the employment relationship," *Id.* at 549, require that Burns be treated under the collective bargaining contract exactly as Wackenhut would have been if it had continued protecting the Lockheed plant.

We do not find *Wiley* controlling in the circumstances here. *Wiley* arose in the context of a § 301 suit to compel arbitration, not in the context of an unfair labor practice proceeding where the Board is expressly limited by the provisions of § 8(d). That decision emphasized "the preference of national labor policy for arbitration as a substitute for tests of strength between contending forces" and held only that the agreement to arbitrate, "construed in the context of national labor law," survived the merger and left to the arbitrator, subject to judicial review, the ultimate question of the extent to which, if any, the surviving company was bound by other provisions of the contract. *Id.* at 549, 551.

Wiley's limited accommodation between the legislative endorsement of freedom of contract and the judicial preference for peaceful arbitral settlement of labor disputes does not warrant the Board's holding that the employer commits an unfair labor practice unless he honors the substantive terms of the pre-existing contract. The present case does not involve a § 301 suit; nor does it involve the duty to arbitrate. Rather, the claim is that Burns must be held bound by the contract executed by Wackenhut, whether Burns has agreed to it or not and even though Burns made it perfectly clear that it had no intention of assuming that contract. *Wiley* suggests no such open-ended obligation. Its narrower holding dealt with a merger occurring against a background of state law which embodied the general rule that in merger situations the surviving corporation is liable for the obligations of the disappearing corporation. *See* N.Y. Stock Corporation Law § 90 (1951); 15 W. Fletcher, Private Corporations § 7121 (1961 rev. ed.). Here there was no merger, no sale of assets, no dealings whatsoever between Wackenhut and Burns. On the contrary, they were competitors for the same work, each bidding for the service contract at Lockheed. Burns purchased nothing from Wackenhut and became liable for none of its financial obligations. Burns merely hired enough of Wackenhut's employees to require it to bargain with the union as commanded by § 8(a)(5) and § 9(a). But this consideration is a wholly insufficient basis for implying either in fact or in law that Burns had agreed or must be held to have agreed to honor Wackenhut's collective bargaining contract. . . .

We also agree with the Court of Appeals that holding either the union or the new employer bound to the substantive terms of an old collective bargaining contract may result in serious inequities. A potential employer may be willing to take over a moribund business only if he can make changes in corporate structure, composition of the labor force, work location, task assignment, and nature of supervision. Saddling such an employer with the terms and conditions of employment contained in the old collective bargaining contract may make these changes impossible and may discourage and inhibit the transfer of capital. On the other hand, a union may have made concessions to a small or failing employer that it would be unwilling to make to a large or economically successful firm. The congressional policy manifest in the Act is to enable the parties to negotiate for any protection either deems appropriate, but to allow the balance of bargaining advantage to be set by economic power realities. Strife is bound to occur if the concessions which must be honored do not correspond to the relative economic strength of the parties.

The Board's position would also raise new problems, for the successor employer would be circumscribed in exactly the same way as the predecessor under the collective bargaining contract. It would seemingly follow that employees of the predecessor would be deemed employees of the successor, dischargeable only in accordance with provisions of the contract and subject to the grievance and arbitration provisions thereof. Burns would not have been free to replace Wackenhut's guards with its own except as the contract permitted. Given the continuity of employment relationship, the pre-existing contract's provisions with respect to wages, seniority rights, vacation privileges, pension and retirement fund benefits, job security provisions, work assignments and the like would devolve on the successor....

IV

... [T]he Board's opinion stated that "[t]he obligation to bargain imposed on a successor-employer includes the negative injunction to refrain from unilaterally changing wages and other benefits established by a prior collective bargaining agreement even though that agreement had expired. In this respect the successor-employer's obligations are the same as those imposed upon employers generally during the period between collective bargaining agreements." ... This statement by the Board is consistent with its prior and subsequent cases which hold that whether or not a successor employer is bound by its predecessor's contract, it must not institute terms and conditions of employment different from those provided in its predecessor's contract, at least without first bargaining with the employees' representative.... Thus, if Burns, without bargaining to impasse with the union, had paid its employees on and after July 1, at a rate lower than Wackenhut had paid under its contract or otherwise provided terms and conditions of employment different from those provided in the Wackenhut collective bargaining agreement, under the Board's view, Burns would have committed a § 8(a)(5) unfair labor practice and would be subject to an order to restore to employees what they had lost by this so-called unilateral change....

Although Burns had an obligation to bargain with the union concerning wages and other conditions of employment when the union requested it to do so, this case is not like a § 8(a)(5) violation where an employer unilaterally changes a condition of employment without consulting a bargaining representative. It is difficult to understand how Burns could be said to have *changed* unilaterally any pre-existing term or condition of employment without bargaining when it had no previous relationship whatsoever to the bargaining unit and, prior to July 1, no outstanding terms and conditions of employment from which a change could be inferred. The terms on which Burns hired employees for service after July 1 may have differed from the terms extended by Wackenhut and required by the collective bargaining contract, but it does not follow that Burns changed *its* terms and conditions of employment when it specified the initial basis on which employees were hired on July 1.

Although a successor employer is ordinarily free to set initial terms on which it will hire the employees of a predecessor, there will be instances in which it is perfectly clear that the new employer plans to retain all of the employees in the unit and in which it will be appropriate to have him initially consult with the employees' bargaining representative before he fixes terms. In other situations, however, it may not be clear until the successor employer has hired his full complement of employees that he has a duty to bargain with a union, since it will not be evident until then that the bargaining representative represents a majority of the employees in the union as required by § 9(a) of the Act.... Here, for example, Burns' obligation to bargain with the union did not mature until it had selected its force of guards late in June. The Board quite properly found that Burns refused to bargain on July 12 when it rejected the overtures of the union. It is true that the wages it paid when it began protecting the Lockheed plant on July 1 differed from those specified in the Wackenhut collective bargaining agreement, but there is no evidence that Burns ever unilaterally changed the terms and conditions of employment it had offered to potential employees in June after its obligation to bargain with the union became apparent. If the union had made a request to bargain after Burns had completed its hiring and if Burns had negotiated in good faith and had made offers to the union which the union rejected, Burns could have unilaterally initiated such proposals as the opening terms and conditions of employment on July 1 without committing an unfair labor practice. *Cf. NLRB v. Katz*, 369 U.S. 736, 745 n.12 (1962).... The Board's order requiring Burns to make whole its employees for any losses suffered by reason of Burns' refusal to honor and enforce the contract, cannot therefore be sustained on the ground that Burns unilaterally changed existing terms and conditions of employment, thereby committing an unfair labor practice which required monetary restitution in these circumstances.

Affirmed.

MR. JUSTICE REHNQUIST, with whom THE CHIEF JUSTICE, MR. JUSTICE BRENNAN, and MR. JUSTICE POWELL join, concurring in No. 71-124 and dissenting in No. 71-198.

Although the Court studiously avoids using the term "successorship" in concluding that Burns did have a statutory obligation to bargain with the union, it affirms the conclusions of the Board and the Court of Appeals to that effect which were based entirely on the successorship doctrine. Because I believe that the Board and the Court of Appeals stretched that concept beyond the limits of its proper application, I would enforce neither the Board's bargaining order nor its order imposing upon Burns the terms of the contract between the union and Wackenhut. I therefore concur in No. 71-123 and dissent in No. 71-198....

The rigid imposition of a prior-existing labor relations environment on a new employer whose only connection with the old employer is the hiring of some of the latter's employees and the performance of some of the work which was previously performed by the latter, might well tend to produce industrial peace of a sort. But industrial peace in such a case would be produced at a sacrifice of the determination by the Board of the appropriateness of bargaining agents and of the wishes of the majority of the employees which the Act was designed to preserve. These latter principles caution us against extending successorship, under the banner of industrial peace, step by step to a point where the only connection between the two employing entities is a naked transfer of employees....

Burns acquired not a single asset, tangible or intangible, by negotiation or transfer from Wackenhut. It succeeded to the contractual rights and duties of the plant protection service contract with Lockheed not by reason of Wackenhut's assignment or consent, but over Wackenhut's vigorous opposition. I think the only permissible conclusion is that Burns is not a successor to Wackenhut....

To conclude that Burns was a successor to Wackenhut in this situation, with its attendant consequences under the Board's order imposing a duty to bargain with the bargaining representative of Wackenhut's employees, would import unwarranted rigidity into labor-management relations. The fortunes of competing employers inevitably ebb and flow, and an employer who has currently gained production orders at the expense of another may well wish to hire employees away from that other. There is no reason to think that the best interests of the employees, the employers, and ultimately of the free market are not served by such movement. Yet inherent in the expanded doctrine of successorship which the Board urges in this case is the notion that somehow the "labor relations environment" comes with the new employees if the new employer has but obtained orders or business which previously belonged to the old employer. The fact that the employees in the instant case continue to perform their work at the same situs, while not irrelevant to analysis, cannot be deemed controlling.... Where the relation between the first employer and the second is as attenuated as it is here, and the reasonable expectations of the employees equally attenuated, the application of the successorship doctrine is not authorized by the Labor Management Relations Act.

This is not to say that Burns would be unilaterally free to mesh into its previously recognized Los Angeles County bargaining unit a group of employees such as were involved here who already have designated a collective bargaining representative in their previous employment. Burns' actions in this regard would be subject to the commands of the Labor Management Relations Act, and to the regulation of the Board under proper application of governing principles.... Had the Board made the appropriate factual inquiry and determinations required by the Act, such inquiry might have justified the conclusion that Burns was obligated to recognize and bargain with the union as a representative for its employees at the Lockheed facility.

But the Board, instead of applying this type of analysis to the union's complaints here, concluded that because Burns was a "successor" it was absolutely bound to the mold which had been fashioned by Wackenhut and its employees at Lockheed. Burns was thereby precluded from challenging the designation of Lockheed as an appropriate bargaining unit for a year after the original certification....

I am unwilling to follow the Board this far down the successorship road, since I believe to do so would substantially undercut the principle of free choice of bargaining representatives by the employees and designation of the appropriate bargaining unit by the Board which are guaranteed by the Act.

Howard Johnson Co. v. Detroit Local Joint Executive Board, 417 U.S. 249, 94 S. Ct. 2236, 41 L. Ed. 2d 46 (1974). The Grissom family operated a restaurant and motor lodge under franchise from Howard Johnson. Howard Johnson purchased the personal property used in the restaurant and motor lodge from the Grissoms, and leased the realty. After hiring only nine of its predecessor's 53 employees, Howard Johnson commenced operation of the establishment with a complement of 45. It refused to recognize the union that had bargained collectively with the Grissoms, and it refused to assume any obligations under the existing labor agreements. The union sued both the Grissoms and Howard Johnson under § 301 to require them to arbitrate the extent of their obligations to the Grissom employees. The Grissoms admitted a duty to arbitrate, but Howard Johnson denied any such duty. The Supreme Court applied *Burns*, even though it dealt with a § 8(a)(5) refusal-to-bargain charge rather than a § 301 suit for arbitration, and sustained Howard Johnson's refusal to arbitrate. The Court distinguished *Wiley* on the ground it "involved a merger, as a result of which the initial employing entity completely disappeared.... Even more important, in *Wiley* the surviving corporation hired *all* of the employees of the disappearing corporation." The Court stressed that "there was plainly no substantial continuity of identity in the work force hired by Howard Johnson with that of the Grissoms, and no express or implied assumption of the agreement to arbitrate." The question of "successorship" was declared "simply not meaningful in the abstract.... The answer to this inquiry requires analysis of the interests of the new employer and the employees and of the policies of the labor laws in light of the facts of each case and the particular legal obligation which is at issue, whether it be the duty to recognize and bargain with the union, the duty to remedy unfair labor practices, the duty to arbitrate, etc."

Notes

1. *Reconciling* Burns *and* Howard Johnson *with* Wiley — Do *Burns* and *Howard Johnson* sound the death knell of *Wiley*, or are the three cases genuinely distinguishable? If so, on what basis? Because of the different relationships between the various employers? *Cf. Local 348-S, UFCW, AFL-CIO v. Meridian Mgmt. Corp.*, 583 F.3d 65 (2d Cir. 2009) (applying *Wiley* and requiring building management company that terminated subcontract with janitorial services company but hired most of its union-represented employees at that location to arbitrate whether and to what extent it was bound by the substantive terms of the subcontractor's labor agreement; workers were essentially working for Meridian and subcontractor "was simply the middleman between Meridian and those workers").

Alternatively, is the distinction in legal outcome attributable to the differences in the proportions of the predecessor's and the successor's employees involved? Would it make sense to say that in refusal-to-bargain cases, the critical factor is the percentage (a majority?) of the successor's employees coming *from* the predecessor, while in suits to compel arbitration of the predecessor's contract, the critical factor is the percentage of the predecessor's employees going *to* the successor? *See Boeing Co. v. International Ass'n of Machinists & Aerospace Workers*, 504 F.2d 307 (5th Cir. 1974), *cert. denied*, 421 U.S. 913 (1975) (new contractor's obligation to arbitrate under predecessor's collective agreement is determined in part by what percentage of the predecessor's employees it hired, though majority is not necessarily required); *see also Publi-Inversiones de P.R., Inc. v. NLRB*, 886 F.3d 142 (D.C. Cir. 2018) (company that acquired assets of a bankrupt firm through a public sale is successor employer obligated to recognize and bargain with the union that represented the prior firm's employees if a majority of its workforce used to work for the predecessor). Consider the implications of *Golden State Bottling Co. v. NLRB*, 414 U.S. 168 (1973) (successor employer may be jointly and severally liable with predecessor for remedying unfair labor practices); *cf. Peters v. NLRB*, 153 F.3d 289 (6th Cir. 1998) (distinguishing *Golden State Bottling* and ruling that successor employer is not responsible for unfair labor practices committed by predecessor where the sale of assets occurred through receivership, preventing the successor from negotiating for indemnity or for a price that would compensate for the risk of unfair labor practices liability).

2. *"Perfectly Clear" Successors*—*Burns* indicated that when it is "perfectly clear" that a new employer is going to retain its predecessor's employees, it may have to "consult" with the union before setting new terms of employment. The courts and the Board have distinguished between "mere" successors, who are generally free to set initial terms of employment for the predecessor's employees without first bargaining with the incumbent union, and "perfectly clear" successors (where it is "perfectly clear" that the new employer intends to retain the unionized employees of its predecessor as a majority of its own workforce), who must first bargain with the union.

Shortly after the Court's decision in *Burns*, the Board announced that the "perfectly clear" category would apply to "circumstances where the new employer has either actively or, by tacit inference, misled employees into believing that they would all be retained without change in their wages, hours, or conditions of employment, or at least to circumstances where the new employer has failed to clearly announce its intent to establish a new set of conditions prior to inviting former employees to accept employment." *Spruce Up Corp.*, 209 N.L.R.B. 194, 195 (1974), *enforced per curiam*, 529 F.2d 516 (4th Cir. 1975). *See, e.g., Paragon Systems, Inc.*, 362 N.L.R.B 1385 (2015) (company that took over a government contract from a unionized firm was free to set initial terms without first negotiating with the union where it announced before taking over the work that it had the right to establish wages, benefits, and working conditions, and job applicants signed forms warning they would have to conform to the company's policies); *S & F Mkt. St. Healthcare LLC v. NLRB*, 570 F.3d 354 (D.C. Cir. 2009) (refusing to enforce Board's order characterizing company as "perfectly clear" successor where successor gave predecessor's employees "every indication" through application forms, job interviews, and letters offering temporary employment that the company planned to institute new forms of employment; the "perfectly clear" category applies only to cases where the successor leads the predecessor's employees to believe that their employment status will continue unchanged after accepting employment with the successor). *But see First Student, Inc. v. NLRB*, 935 F.3d 604 (D.C. Cir. 2019) (employer violated §§ 8(a)(1) and 8(a)(5) by announcing that it intended to make changes to terms and conditions of employment *after* it made the statements that produced the finding that it was a perfectly clear successor); *Nexeo Solutions, LLC*, 364 N.L.R.B. No. 44 (2016) (purchasing employer was a "perfectly clear" successor with obligation to bargain and to maintain the conditions established by its predecessor where purchase agreement contained a provision promising to offer all the employees jobs, and predecessor communicated successor's intent to employees in an email and did not disavow the message, thereby ratifying it).

But what if the matter is not "perfectly clear" because the purchaser is still trying to decide whether or not to purchase the business? May a prospective purchaser of a company whose workers are represented by a union engage in pre-acquisition discussions with the union in order to better estimate its labor costs? In *Majestic Weaving Co., Inc. of New York*, 147 N.L.R.B. 859 (1964), *enforcement denied on other grounds*, 355 F.2d 854 (2d Cir. 1966), the Board ruled that a company violated § 8(a)(2) by recognizing a union and negotiating a bargaining agreement even though signing was conditioned upon the union achieving majority support. Would *Majestic Weaving* block pre-acquisition discussions where the purchaser and the union are both willing participants and there is no other union on the horizon? The Board has signaled that such strategic discussions might be distinguishable from the *Majestic Weaving* scenario, but the question remains open. *See Dana Corp.*, 356 N.L.R.B. 256 (2010) (dismissing § 8(a)(2) complaint based upon Letter of Agreement between union and employer prior to the union attaining majority support, and noting that "[w]e leave for another day the adoption of a general standard for regulating pre-recognition negotiations between unions and employer"), *review denied, Montague v. NLRB*, 698 F.3d 307 (6th Cir. 2012).

3. *Refusing to Hire Predecessor's Unionized Employees to Avoid Successorship Obligations* — It is a violation of § 8(a)(3) for a purchasing employer to refuse to hire its predecessor's union-represented employees because it wishes to avoid triggering a bargaining obligation. The same action may also violate § 8(a)(5). *Planned Bldg. Servs.*, 347 N.L.R.B. 670 (2006) (employer violates § 8(a)(5) where it unilaterally sets the initial terms of employment for the persons it hires, where it is clear it would have hired all of the predecessor's employees in the absence of such discrimination calculated to avoid successorship obligations). These doctrines may be simple to state, but they are not always easy to apply. For example, in *Waterbury Hotel Mgmt., LLC v. NLRB*, 314 F.3d 645 (D.C. Cir. 2003), the successor employer hired 20 out of 82 employees when it purchased a bankrupt union-represented hotel. In refusing to hire the other employees, the successor's president stated that he had been advised by counsel "to be concerned about who he hired and how he hired," and indicated that "there were certain hiring parameters that he couldn't exceed." The Board also found that the hiring criteria used by the employer were a departure from its usual practice and a pretext for weeding out union employees, and the court agreed. Because the refusal to hire was based on anti-union animus and the employer then refused to bargain and unilaterally established terms and conditions of employment

for its employees, the employer also violated § 8(a)(5). *See also Pace Indus. v. NLRB*, 118 F.3d 585 (8th Cir. 1997), *cert. denied*, 523 U.S. 1020 (1998) (Board may properly infer unlawful motivation where successor employer implements elaborate hiring process involving a 19-pronged application and a battery of verbal, numerical, and dexterity tests, resulting in the rehiring of 22 out of 103 of the former employees).

Recently, the Trump Board further clarified and narrowed the scope of the "perfectly clear" successorship doctrine in cases involving discriminatory hiring. In *Ridgewood Health Care Center, Inc.*, 367 N.L.R.B. No. 110 (2019), the Board held that an employer violated § 8(a)(3) when it declined to hire four of the predecessor's unionized employees in order to avoid its duty to bargain as a successor employer. Hiring those four employees would have resulted in 53 of the 101 persons hired by the successor coming from the predecessor entity, so the successor also violated § 8(a)(5) by refusing to recognize the union as the representative of its own employees. Nevertheless, the Board overturned several of its prior decisions, which had held that such employers were also "perfectly clear" successors obligated to maintain the status quo until bargaining reached impasse or agreement; since the discrimination affected only four employees and the successor's hiring would have totaled a number that was barely more than half of the former unionized employees, it was not "perfectly clear" that the new employer would have hired all or substantially all of the former employer's employees. The Board ruled that only where it is clear that the successor firm would have hired the vast majority of its workforce from the predecessor's workforce but for its discriminatory hiring practices will the employer be obligated to bargain with the union before setting initial terms and conditions of employment.

4. *Statements Designed to Chill Unionism* — Suppose that the successor employer makes statements designed to chill unionism among applicants from the predecessor's workforce before it has completed its hiring. Would this constitute a separate violation of § 8(a)(1)? *See NLRB v. CNN America*, 865 F.3d 740 (D.C. Cir. 2017) (separate unfair labor practice for successor to tell predecessor employees hired by its companies that they will not have union representation at the new firm if hiring is still ongoing and successor cannot know at that point whether it will have an obligation to bargain with the union or not); *TCB Sys.*, 355 N.L.R.B. 883 (2010) (employer violated Act by threatening not to hire predecessor's employees), *aff'd*, *TCB Sys. v. NLRB*, 2011 U.S. App. LEXIS 25014 (11th Cir. Dec. 16, 2011); *see also NLRB v. Advanced Stretchforming Int'l, Inc.*, 233 F.3d 1176 (9th Cir. 2000) (employer forfeited its right to set initial terms when it made the statement that there would be "no union" at the company). *But see Brown & Root, Inc. v. NLRB*, 333 F.3d 628 (5th Cir. 2003) (refusing to enforce Board order requiring nonunion employer to hire all employees of predecessor, recognize union, and adopt terms and conditions of employment in existence when it took over operation of existing department of unionized company; manager's statement that unionized employees could apply for employment with new company but that new company "was a non-union company and was going to stay that way" was lawful expression of opinion, not threat, and neither § 8(a)(1) nor § 8(a)(3) was violated).

What about a successor employer who seeks to avoid a bargaining obligation by hiring a majority of its predecessor's employees but asserts a good faith reasonable doubt regarding whether a majority of the employees it has inherited continue to support the union? *See Allentown Mack Sales & Serv. v. NLRB*, 522 U.S. 359 (1998), *supra*, Part Three, Section III.

5. *Arbitration in Non-Merger Situations*—Prior to *Burns* and *Howard Johnson*, courts of appeals had applied *Wiley* to compel arbitration in non-merger situations, e.g., where the successor was a purchaser. *See United Steelworkers of Am. v. Reliance Universal, Inc.*, 335 F.2d 891 (3d Cir. 1964) (finding arbitration of grievances under prior collective agreement against successor purchaser appropriate, but arbitrator may take into account the changed circumstances of the transfer); *cf. Wackenhut Corp. v. Int'l Union, United Plant Guard Workers*, 332 F.2d 954 (9th Cir. 1964) (corporation that purchased assets of a limited partnership and accepted substantially all employees was bound to arbitrate grievances under the partnership's collective agreement). Are these decisions still supportable? What if the successor has lawfully recognized and contracted with a union different from the one representing the predecessor's employees? *See McGuire v. Humble Oil & Refining Co.*, 355 F.2d 352 (2d Cir.) (purchasing company was not required to arbitrate grievances under seller's collective agreement where buyer and seller each had an agreement with a different union and the Board determined the buyer's new employees were part of its bargaining unit), *cert. denied*, 384 U.S. 988 (1966); *Int'l Ass'n of Machinists v. Howmet Corp.*, 466 F.2d 1249 (9th Cir. 1972) (finding that it would be inequitable to require a unionized company that purchased and then closed a plant from another company and is bound by that plant's prior collective agreement to arbitrate issues of job transfers and preferential hiring at other plants, because it would have implications for employer's obligations under its collective agreements at other plants). Suppose the successor expressly disavows any intent to be bound by the predecessor's contract during conversations with the union and in the purchase agreement. Should it nevertheless be required to arbitrate grievances devolving from vested rights in the predecessor's contract? *See AmeriSteel Corp. v. Int'l Bhd. of Teamsters*, 267 F.3d 264 (3d Cir. 2001) (refusing to compel arbitration because the successor employer was not bound by the substantive terms of the agreement).

Should it make any difference whether the transfer is a stock purchase or a purchase of physical assets? *See* Jenero & Mennel, *Pitfalls and Opportunities: NLRA and Contractual Considerations When Purchasing a Unionized Company*, 22 Emp. Rel. L.J. 141 (1996); Krupman & Kaplan, *The Stock Purchaser After* Burns: *Must He Buy the Union Contract?*, 31 Lab. L.J. 328 (1980). *See also Stotter Div. of Graduate Plastics Co. v. District 65, United Auto Workers*, 991 F.2d 997 (2d Cir. 1993) (foreclosure sale). What about the lease of a manufacturing facility—can a lessee be a successor? *See Harter Tomato Prods. Co. v. NLRB*, 133 F.3d 934 (D.C. Cir. 1998) (yes).

6. *Successorship Clauses in Labor Contracts*—In *Lone Star Steel Co. v. NLRB*, 639 F.2d 545 (10th Cir. 1980), *cert. denied*, 450 U.S. 911 (1981), a successorship clause was held mandatory as a bargaining topic, and the union's insistence to impasse was permissible. Since it went to the effect of the employer's decision to transfer its assets, rather than the decision itself, the court found the "vitally affects" test met as to the terms and conditions of the employment of unit members, where the effect of the clause was to ensure the continuing application of the agreed terms. But if the union cannot enforce the clause directly against the successor, why would it negotiate for such a clause? In what contexts might the clause be enforceable against the predecessor? *See Equitable Res., Inc. v. United Steel, Local 8-512*, 621 F.3d 538 (6th Cir. 2010) (upholding arbitrator's award requiring parent company that dissolved a subsidiary and reorganized its operations to abide by a successorship clause in the subsidiary's labor contract where arbitrator found an alter ego relationship); *UMWA v. Rag Am. Coal Co.*, 392 F.3d 1233 (10th Cir. 2004) (finding coal company liable under §301 for selling a coal preparation plant without requiring the purchaser to assume the company's obligations pursuant to a successorship clause in the labor contract); *Wheelabrator Envirotech Operating Servs. v. Massachusetts Laborers Dist. Council Local 1144*, 88 F.3d 40 (1st Cir. 1996) (enforcing arbitrator's award that a successorship clause bound a contractor to compel the contractor's successor to assume the parties' collective bargaining agreement, even though the contractor and the successor were not in privity and the successor had outbid the contractor for a job); *Zady Natey, Inc. v. United Food & Commercial Workers Int'l Union, Local 27*, 995 F.2d 496 (4th Cir.), *cert. denied*, 510 U.S. 977 (1993) (sustaining arbitral award of damages to employees when seller failed to bind buyer in accordance with successorship clause); *Local Joint Executive Bd., etc., Local 226 v. Royal Center, Inc.*, 796 F.2d 1159 (9th Cir. 1986), *cert. denied*, 479 U.S. 1033 (1987) (employer that closed business and then sold it several months later was obligated under its collective bargaining agreement to arbitrate the union's grievance concerning alleged breach of the successorship clause, where contract contained a broad grievance-arbitration clause and a provision that required Royal to obtain a commitment from any purchaser obliging it to honor the terms of the collective contract). *See generally* Crain-Mountney, *The Unenforceable Successorship Clause: A Departure from National Labor Policy*, 30 UCLA L. Rev. 1249 (1983); Crystal, *Successors and Assigns Clauses: Do They Actually Require that a Purchaser Adopt the Seller's Contract?*, 33 Lab. L.J. 581 (1982).

7. *Alter Ego Companies*—Seemingly distinct business entities may be bound by the same bargaining or contractual obligations not only on the basis that one is the "successor" of the other but also on the basis that one is the "alter ego" of the other or that they are actually a "single employer." In determining whether two companies are alter egos for the purpose of imposing bargaining and contractual obligations, the Board examines several factors: whether the two enterprises have substantially identical ownership, management, business purpose, operation, equipment, and customers, and whether there exists anti-union animus. *See Trs. of Operating Eng'rs*

Local 324 Pension Fund v. Bourdow Contracting, Inc., 919 F.3d 368 (6th Cir. 2019) (alter ego status found where new company was formed while original company was financially failing due to pension withdrawal liability, and overlap existed between the two companies' ownership, workforce, customers, and business purposes); *Island Architectural Woodwork, Inc. v. NLRB*, 892 F.3d 362 (D.C. Cir. 2018) (alter ego status found where company created a new entity that used the company's building and equipment for free, collaborated extensively with company, utilized the same process, and made the same product in a nonunion shop in order to better compete with nonunion manufacturers); *Trafford Distrib. Ctr. v. NLRB*, 478 F.3d 172 (3d Cir.), *cert. denied*, 552 U.S. 818 (2007) (alter ego status found where company acquired assets of predecessor firm following bankruptcy but transfer was designed to avoid obligations under labor contract, successor was owned by spouse of predecessor's owner, most of the new company's managers came from the prior entity, most of the customers were the same, and new company performed same tasks on same equipment).

Where the reason for the creation of the new company does not entail anti-union animus, however, not all courts are willing to apply the alter ego doctrine. As one court put it, the doctrine is "a *tool* to be employed when the corporate shield, if respected, would inequitably prevent a party from receiving what is otherwise due and owing from the person or persons who created the shield." *Mass. Carpenters Cent. Collection Agency v. A.A. Bldg. Erectors, Inc.*, 343 F.3d 18 (1st Cir. 2003) (finding that alter ego doctrine did not obligate nonunion employer to make pension fund contributions where the second company was created to cater to customers who preferred union labor, rather than to avoid obligations under labor law). *Compare NLRB v. Allcoast Transfer, Inc.*, 780 F.2d 576 (6th Cir. 1986) (finding of employer anti-union animus not essential to imposition of alter ego status) *and Grane Health Care v. NLRB*, 712 F.3d 145 (3d Cir. 2013) (enforcing Board ruling that two private companies that acquired the assets of a county hospital were obligated to recognize and bargain with the incumbent union, since the two companies operated as an integrated entity with centralized control and hired a majority of their new employees from the county's union-represented workforce; purpose of successorship doctrine is to encourage stability during business transitions, and Board's application of successorship doctrine to a public-to-private transition was thus consistent with the Act), *with Alkire v. NLRB*, 716 F.2d 1014 (4th Cir. 1983) (imposing alter ego status where creation of new business entity results in an expected or reasonably foreseeable benefit to the original employer that relates to avoidance of its obligations under a labor contract). In one unique case, a nonunion company formed a separate company and contracted with the union to pay union-scale wages and benefits in order to have access to bidding opportunities open only to union contractors. The Ninth Circuit rejected a "reverse alter ego" argument by the union, which sought to bind the nonunion contractor to the labor contract. The court reasoned that "[t]he alter ego doctrine was never intended to coerce a nonunion company into becoming a union company by requiring its compliance with a collective bargaining agreement it never signed, with a union its employees never authorized to represent them," and concluded that there was no evidence that joint operations by the two contractors were designed to avoid the union company's obligations under its labor contract. *S. Cal. Painters & Allied Trades v. Rodin & Co., Inc.*, 558 F.3d 1028 (9th Cir. 2009). For a discussion of the role of employer anti-union animus in alter ego doctrine, see Willis & Bales, *Narrowing Successorship: The Alter Ego Doctrine and the Role of Intent*, 8 DePaul Bus. & Comm. L. J. 151 (2010).

8. *State Regulation* — May states regulate in the successorship area? *Compare United Steelworkers v. St. Gabriel's Hosp.*, 871 F. Supp. 335 (D. Minn. 1994) (Minnesota law imposing existing collective contracts on successor employers preempted by federal labor law), *and Commonwealth Edison Co. v. IBEW, Local Union No. 15*, 961 F. Supp. 1169 (N.D. Ill. 1997) (Illinois law requiring successor to hire predecessor's employees and comply with successorship clause in predecessor's collective bargaining agreement preempted), *with Rhode Island Hospitality Ass'n v. City of Providence*, 667 F.3d 17 (1st Cir. 2011) (local ordinance requiring successor hospitality employer to retain predecessor's employees for a three-month period not preempted by NLRA under either *Garmon* or *Machinists* analysis) *and California Grocers' Ass'n v. City of Los Angeles*, 254 P.3d 1019 (Cal. 2011) (ordinance requiring successor grocery store employers to retain staff for 90-day period not preempted by NLRA under *Machinists* analysis, because ordinance simply established local substantive employment terms).

Problem

67. Goody Shoes hired the vast majority of its predecessor's employees, recognized the union and continued the same rates of pay for those employees, but unilaterally established a separate pay system that applied only to employees hired after the acquisition. For those newly hired employees, the pay rate fell within a specified pay band but each individual employee's wage rate was left to Goody's discretion; under this system, the wage rate offered to each new applicant was based upon the applicant's qualifications and market conditions in the area for the job. Once the new hires became part of the workforce, subsequent changes in compensation were bargainable, and any new contract negotiated by the union and Goody would cover the new hires as well as the hires from the predecessor. Why might the union be especially concerned about this practice? As a successor employer, did Goody violate the Act?

Fall River Dyeing & Finishing Corp. v. NLRB

Supreme Court of the United States
482 U.S. 27, 107 S. Ct. 2225, 96 L. Ed. 2d 22 (1987)

JUSTICE BLACKMUN delivered the opinion of the Court.[25]

In this case we are confronted with the issue whether the National Labor Relations Board's decision is consistent with *NLRB v. Burns International Security Services, Inc.*, 406 U.S. 272 (1972). In *Burns*, this Court ruled that the new employer, succeeding to the business of another, had an obligation to bargain with the union representing the predecessor's employees. We first must decide whether *Burns* is limited to a situation where the union only recently was certified before the transition in employers, or whether that decision also applies where the union is entitled to a presumption of majority support. Our inquiry then proceeds to three questions that concern rules the Labor Board has developed in the successorship context. First, we must determine whether there is substantial record evidence to support the Board's conclusion that petitioner was a "successor" to Sterlingwale Corp., its business predecessor. Second, we must decide whether the Board's "substantial and representative complement" rule, designed to identify the date when a successor's obligation to bargain with the predecessor's employees' union arises, is consistent with *Burns*, is reasonable, and was applied properly in this case. Finally, we must examine the Board's "continuing demand" principle to the effect that, if a union has presented to a successor a premature demand for bargaining, this demand continues in effect until the successor acquires the "substantial and representative complement" of employees that triggers its obligation to bargain.

I

For over 30 years before 1982, Sterlingwale operated a textile dyeing and finishing plant in Fall River, Mass. Its business consisted basically of two types of dyeing, called, respectively, "converting" and "commission." Under the converting process, which in 1981 accounted for 60% to 70% of its business, Sterlingwale bought unfinished fabrics for its own account, dyed and finished them, and then sold them to apparel manufacturers. In commission dyeing, which accounted for the remainder of its business, Sterlingwale dyed and finished fabrics owned by customers according to their specifications. The financing and marketing aspects of converting and commission dyeing are different. Converting requires capital to purchase fabrics and a sales force to promote the finished products. The production process, however, is the same for both converting and commission dyeing.

In the late 1970's the textile-dyeing business, including Sterlingwale's, began to suffer from adverse economic conditions and foreign competition. . . . Finally, in February 1982, Sterlingwale laid off all its production employees, primarily because it no longer had the capital to continue the converting business. It retained a skeleton

---

25. [*] JUSTICE WHITE joins only Parts I and III of this opinion.

crew of workers and supervisors to ship out the goods remaining on order and to maintain the corporation's building and machinery. In the months following the layoff, Leonard Ansin, Sterlingwale's president, liquidated the inventory of the corporation and, at the same time, looked for a business partner with whom he could "resurrect the business." . . .

For almost as long as Sterlingwale had been in existence, its production and maintenance employees had been represented by the United Textile Workers of America, AFL-CIO, Local 292 (Union). The most recent collective-bargaining agreement before Sterlingwale's demise had been negotiated in 1978 and was due to expire in 1981. By an agreement dated October 1980, however, in response to the financial difficulties suffered by Sterlingwale, the Union agreed to amend the 1978 agreement to extend its expiration date by one year, until April 1, 1982, without any wage increase and with an agreement to improve labor productivity. . . .

In late summer 1982, however, Sterlingwale finally went out of business. It made an assignment for the benefit of its creditors. . . .

During this same period, a former Sterlingwale employee and officer, Herbert Chace, and Arthur Friedman, president of one of Sterlingwale's major customers, Marcamy Sales Corporation (Marcamy), formed petitioner Fall River Dyeing & Finishing Corp. Chace, who had resigned from Sterlingwale in February 1982, had worked there for 27 years, had been vice-president in charge of sales at the time of his departure, and had participated in collective bargaining with the Union during his tenure at Sterlingwale. Chace and Friedman formed petitioner with the intention of engaging strictly in the commission- dyeing business and of taking advantage of the availability of Sterlingwale's assets and workforce. Accordingly, Friedman had Marcamy acquire from [the creditors] Sterlingwale's plant, real property, and equipment, and convey them to petitioner. Petitioner also obtained some of Sterlingwale's remaining inventory at the liquidator's auction. Chace became petitioner's vice-president in charge of operations and Friedman became its president.

In September 1982, petitioner began operating out of Sterlingwale's former facilities and began hiring employees. It advertised for workers and supervisors in a local newspaper, and Chace personally got in touch with several prospective supervisors. Petitioner hired 12 supervisors, of whom 8 had been supervisors with Sterlingwale and 3 had been production employees there. In its hiring decisions for production employees, petitioner took into consideration recommendations from these supervisors and a prospective employee's former employment with Sterlingwale. Petitioner's initial hiring goal was to attain one full shift of workers, which meant from 55 to 60 employees. Petitioner planned to "see how business would be" after this initial goal had been met and, if business permitted, to expand to two shifts. The employees who were hired first spent approximately four to six weeks in start-up operations and an additional month in experimental production.

By letter dated October 19, 1982, the Union requested petitioner to recognize it as the bargaining agent for petitioner's employees and to begin collective bargaining.

Petitioner refused the request, stating that, in its view, the request had "no legal basis." At that time, 18 of petitioner's 21 employees were former employees of Sterlingwale. By November of that year, petitioner had employees in a complete range of jobs, had its production process in operation, and was handling customer orders; by mid-January 1983, it had attained its initial goal of one shift of workers. Of the 55 workers in this initial shift, a number that represented over half the workers petitioner would eventually hire, 36 were former Sterlingwale employees. Petitioner continued to expand its workforce, and by mid-April 1983 it had reached two full shifts. For the first time, ex-Sterlingwale employees were in the minority but just barely so (52 or 53 out of 107 employees).

Although petitioner engaged exclusively in commission dyeing, the employees experienced the same conditions they had when they were working for Sterlingwale. The production process was unchanged and the employees worked on the same machines, in the same building, with the same job classifications, under virtually the same supervisors. Over half the volume of petitioner's business came from former Sterlingwale customers, and, in particular, Marcamy.

On November 1, 1982, the Union filed an unfair labor practice charge with the Board, alleging that in its refusal to bargain petitioner had violated §§ 8(a)(1) and (5) of the National Labor Relations Act. After a hearing, the Administrative Law Judge (ALJ) decided that, on the facts of the case, petitioner was a successor to Sterlingwale.... Thus, in the view of the ALJ, petitioner's duty to bargain arose in mid-January because former Sterlingwale employees then were in the majority and because the Union's October demand was still in effect. Petitioner thus committed an unfair labor practice in refusing to bargain. In a brief decision and order, the Board, with one member dissenting, affirmed this decision.

The Court of Appeals for the First Circuit, also by a divided vote, enforced the order. 775 F.2d 425 (1985) . . . .

Because of the importance of the successorship issue in labor law, and because of our interest in the rules developed by the Board for successorship cases, we granted certiorari.

II

Fifteen years ago in *NLRB v. Burns International Security Services, Inc.*, 406 U.S. 272 (1972), this Court first dealt with the issue of a successor employer's obligation to bargain with a union that had represented the employees of its predecessor. [The Court discussed *Burns*.]

These presumptions [of majority support] are based not so much on an absolute certainty that the union's majority status will not erode following certification, as on a particular policy decision. The overriding policy of the NLRA is "industrial peace." *Brooks v. NLRB*, 348 U.S. [96] 103. The presumptions of majority support further this policy by "promot[ing] stability in collective bargaining relationships, without impairing the free choice of employees." *Terrell Machine Co.*, 173 N.L.R.B.

1480, 1480 (1969), *aff'd*, 427 F.2d 1088 (CA4), *cert. denied*, 398 U.S. 929 (1970). In essence, they enable a union to concentrate on obtaining and fairly administering a collective-bargaining agreement without worrying that, unless it produces immediate results, it will lose majority support and will be decertified.... The presumptions also remove any temptation on the part of the employer to avoid good-faith bargaining in the hope that, by delaying, it will undermine the union's support among the employees....

The rationale behind the presumptions is particularly pertinent in the successorship situation and so it is understandable that the Court in *Burns* referred to them. During a transition between employers, a union is in a peculiarly vulnerable position. It has no formal and established bargaining relationship with the new employer, is uncertain about the new employer's plans, and cannot be sure if or when the new employer must bargain with it. While being concerned with the future of its members with the new employer, the union also must protect whatever rights still exist for its members under the collective-bargaining agreement with the predecessor employer. Accordingly, during this unsettling transition period, the union needs the presumptions of majority status to which it is entitled to safeguard its members' rights and to develop a relationship with the successor.

The position of the employees also supports the application of the presumptions in the successorship situation. If the employees find themselves in a new enterprise that substantially resembles the old, but without their chosen bargaining representative, they may well feel that their choice of a union is subject to the vagaries of an enterprise's transformation. This feeling is not conducive to industrial peace. In addition, after being hired by a new company following a layoff from the old, employees initially will be concerned primarily with maintaining their new jobs. In fact, they might be inclined to shun support for their former union, especially if they believe that such support will jeopardize their jobs with the successor or if they are inclined to blame the union for their layoff and problems associated with it. Without the presumptions of majority support and with the wide variety of corporate transformations possible, an employer could use a successor enterprise as a way of getting rid of a labor contract and of exploiting the employees' hesitant attitude towards the union to eliminate its continuing presence.

In addition to recognizing the traditional presumptions of union majority status, however, the Court in *Burns* was careful to safeguard "'the rightful prerogative of owners independently to rearrange their businesses.'" *Golden State Bottling Co. v. NLRB*, 414 U.S. 168, 182 (1973), quoting *John Wiley & Sons, Inc. v. Livingston*, 376 U.S. 543, 549 (1964).... Thus, to a substantial extent the applicability of *Burns* rests in the hands of the successor. If the new employer makes a conscious decision to maintain generally the same business and to hire a majority of its employees from the predecessor, then the bargaining obligation of § 8(a)(5) is activated. This makes sense when one considers that the employer *intends* to take advantage of the trained workforce of its predecessor.

Accordingly, in *Burns* we acknowledged the interest of the successor in its freedom to structure its business and the interest of the employees in continued representation by the union. We now hold that a successor's obligation to bargain is not limited to a situation where the union in question has been recently certified. Where, as here, the union has a rebuttable presumption of majority status, this status continues despite the change in employers. And the new employer has an obligation to bargain with that union so long as the new employer is in fact a successor of the old employer and the majority of its employees were employed by its predecessor.

III

We turn now to the three rules, as well as to their application to the facts of this case, that the Board has adopted for the successorship situation. The Board, of course, is given considerable authority to interpret the provisions of the NLRA. . . .

A. In *Burns* we approved the approach taken by the Board and accepted by courts with respect to determining whether a new company was indeed the successor to the old. This approach, which is primarily factual in nature and is based upon the totality of the circumstances of a given situation, requires that the Board focus on whether the new company has "acquired substantial assets of its predecessor and continued, without interruption or substantial change, the predecessor's business operations." *Golden State Bottling Co. v. NLRB*, 414 U.S., at 184. Hence, the focus is on whether there is "substantial continuity" between the enterprises. Under this approach, the Board examines a number of factors: whether the business of both employers is essentially the same; whether the employees of the new company are doing the same jobs in the same working conditions under the same supervisors; and whether the new entity has the same production process, produces the same products, and basically has the same body of customers. . . .

In conducting the analysis, the Board keeps in mind the question whether "those employees who have been retained will understandably view their job situations as essentially unaltered." See *Golden State Bottling Co.*, 414 U.S., at 184; *NLRB v. Jeffries Lithograph Co.*, 752 F.2d 459, 464 (CA9 1985). This emphasis on the employees' perspective furthers the Act's policy of industrial peace. If the employees find themselves in essentially the same jobs after the employer transition and if their legitimate expectations in continued representation by their union are thwarted, their dissatisfaction may lead to labor unrest. See *Golden State Bottling Co.*, 414 U.S., at 184.

. . . [W]e find that the Board's determination that there was "substantial continuity" between Sterlingwale and petitioner and that petitioner was Sterlingwale's successor is supported by substantial evidence in the record. Petitioner acquired most of Sterlingwale's real property, its machinery and equipment, and much of its inventory and materials. It introduced no new product line. Of particular significance is the fact that, from the perspective of the employees, their jobs did not change. Although petitioner abandoned converting dyeing in exclusive favor of commission dyeing, this change did not alter the essential nature of the employees' jobs, because both types of dyeing involved the same production process. The job classifications of petitioner were the same as those of Sterlingwale; petitioners' employees worked on the same machines under the direction of supervisors most of whom were former supervisors of Sterlingwale. The record, in fact, is clear that petitioner acquired Sterlingwale's assets with the express purpose of taking advantage of its predecessor's workforce.

We do not find determinative of the successorship question the fact that there was a 7-month hiatus between Sterlingwale's demise and petitioner's start-up. Petitioner argues that this hiatus, coupled with the fact that its employees were hired through newspaper advertisements — not through Sterlingwale employment records, which were not transferred to it — resolves in its favor the "substantial continuity" question.... Yet such a hiatus is only one factor in the "substantial continuity" calculus and thus is relevant only when there are other indicia of discontinuity.... Conversely, if other factors indicate a continuity between the enterprises, and the hiatus is a normal start-up period, the "totality of the circumstances" will suggest that these circumstances present a successorship situation....

For the reasons given above, this is a case where the other factors suggest "substantial continuity" between the companies despite the 7-month hiatus. Here, moreover, the extent of the hiatus between the demise of Sterlingwale and the start-up of petitioner is somewhat less than certain. After the February layoff, Sterlingwale retained a skeleton crew of supervisors and employees that continued to ship goods to customers and to maintain the plant. In addition, until the assignment for the benefit of the creditors late in the summer, Ansin was seeking to resurrect the business or to find a buyer for Sterlingwale. The Union was aware of these efforts. Viewed from the employees' perspective, therefore, the hiatus may have been much less than seven months. Although petitioner hired the employees through advertisements, it often relied on recommendations from supervisors, themselves formerly employed by Sterlingwale, and intended the advertisements to reach the former Sterlingwale workforce.

Accordingly, we hold that, under settled law, petitioner was a successor to Sterlingwale. We thus must consider if and when petitioner's duty to bargain arose.

B. In *Burns*, the Court determined that the successor had an obligation to bargain with the union because a majority of its employees had been employed by Wackenhut. The "triggering" fact for the bargaining obligation was this composition of the successor's workforce.[26] The Court, however, did not have to consider the question

---

26. [12] After *Burns*, there was some initial confusion concerning this Court's holding. It was unclear if workforce continuity would turn on whether a majority of the successor's employees were those of the predecessor or on whether the successor had hired a majority of the predecessor's employees. *Compare* 406 U.S., at 281 ("a majority of the employees hired by the new employer are represented by a recently certified bargaining agent"), *with id.*, at 278 ("the union had been designated bargaining agent for the employees in the unit and a majority of these employees had been hired by Burns"). *See also Howard Johnson Co. v. Hotel Employees*, 417 U.S., at 263 ("successor

when the successor's obligation to bargain arose: Wackenhut's contract expired on June 30 and Burns began its services with a majority of former Wackenhut guards on July 1. In other situations, as in the present case, there is a start-up period by the new employer while it gradually builds its operations and hires employees. In these situations, the Board, with the approval of the Courts of Appeals, has adopted the "substantial and representative complement" rule for fixing the moment when the determination as to the composition of the successor's workforce is to be made. If, at this particular moment, a majority of the successor's employees had been employed by its predecessor, then the successor has an obligation to bargain with the union that represented these employees.

This rule represents an effort to balance "'the objective of insuring maximum employee participation in the selection of a bargaining agent against the goal of permitting employees to be represented as quickly as possible.'" 775 F.2d, at 430–431, quoting *NLRB v. Pre-Engineered Building Products, Inc.*, 603 F.2d 134, 136 (CA10 1979). In deciding when a "substantial and representative complement" exists in a particular employer transition, the Board examines a number of factors. It studies "whether the job classifications designated for the operation were filled or substantially filled and whether the operation was in normal or substantially normal production." See *Premium Foods, Inc. v. NLRB*, 709 F.2d 623, 628 (CA9 1983). In addition, it takes into consideration "the size of the complement on that date and the time expected to elapse before a substantially larger complement would be at work . . . as well as the relative certainty of the employer's expected expansion." *Ibid.*

Petitioner contends that the Board's representative complement rule is unreasonable, given that it injures the representation rights of many of the successor's employees and that it places significant burdens upon the successor, which is unsure whether and when the bargaining obligation will arise. . . . According to petitioner, if majority status is determined at the "full complement" stage, all the employees will have a voice in the selection of their bargaining representative, and this will reveal if the union truly has the support of most of the successor's employees. This approach, however, focuses only on the interest in having a bargaining representative selected by the majority of the employees. It fails to take into account the significant interest of employees in being represented as soon as possible. The latter interest is especially heightened in a situation where many of the successor's employees, who were formerly represented by a union, find themselves after the employer transition in essentially the same enterprise, but without their bargaining representative. Having the new employer refuse to bargain with the chosen representative of these

---

employer hires a majority of the predecessor's employees"); *Golden State Bottling Co. v. NLRB*, 414 U.S., at 184, n. 6 (same). The Board, with the approval of the Courts of Appeals, has adopted the former interpretation. *See Spruce Up Corp.*, 209 N.L.R.B. 194, 196 (1974), aff'd, 529 F.2d 516 (CA4 1975); *United Maintenance & Mfg. Co.*, 214 N.L.R.B. 529, 532–534 (1974); *Saks & Co. v. NLRB*, 634 F.2d 681, 684–686, and nn. 2 and 3 (CA2 1980) (and cases cited therein); *see also* Note, *Appropriate Standards of Successor Employer Obligations under Wiley, Howard Johnson, and Burns*, 25 Wayne L. Rev. 1279, 1299 (1979). This issue is not presented by the instant case.

employees "disrupts the employees' morale, deters their organizational activities, and discourages their membership in unions." *Franks Bros. Co. v. NLRB*, 321 U.S. 702, 704 (1944). Accordingly, petitioner's "full complement" proposal must fail.

Nor do we believe that this "substantial and representative complement" rule places an unreasonable burden on the employer. It is true that, if an employer refuses to bargain with the employees once the representative complement has been attained, it risks violating § 8(a)(5). Furthermore, if an employer recognizes the union before this complement has been reached, this recognition could constitute a violation of § 8(a)(2), which makes it an unfair labor practice for an employer to support a labor organization.... And, unlike the initial election situation,... here the employer, not the Board, applies this rule.

We conclude, however, that in this situation the successor is in the best position to follow a rule the criteria of which are straightforward. The employer generally will know with tolerable certainty when all its job classifications have been filled or substantially filled, when it has hired a majority of the employees it intends to hire, and when it has begun normal production. Moreover, the "full complement" standard advocated by petitioner is not *necessarily* easier for a successor to apply than is the "substantial and representative complement." In fact, given the expansionist dreams of many new entrepreneurs, it might well be more difficult for a successor to identify the moment when the "full complement" has been attained, which is when the business will reach the limits of the new employer's initial hopes, than it would be for this same employer to acknowledge the time when its business has begun normal production—the moment identified by the "substantial and representative complement" rule.

We therefore hold that the Board's "substantial and representative complement" rule is reasonable in the successorship context. Moreover, its application to the facts of this case is supported by substantial record evidence. The Court of Appeals observed that by mid-January petitioner "had hired employees in virtually all job classifications, had hired at least fifty percent of those it would ultimately employ in the majority of those classifications, and it employed a majority of the employees it would eventually employ when it reached full complement." 775 F.2d, at 431–432. At that time petitioner had begun normal production. Although petitioner intended to expand to two shifts, and, in fact, reached this goal by mid-April, that expansion was contingent expressly upon the growth of the business. Accordingly, as found by the Board and approved by the Court of Appeals, mid-January was the period when petitioner reached its "substantial and representative complement." Because at that time the majority of petitioner's employees were former Sterlingwale employees, petitioner had an obligation to bargain with the Union then.

C. We also hold that the Board's "continuing demand" rule is reasonable in the successorship situation. The successor's duty to bargain at the "substantial and representative complement" date is triggered only when the union has made a bargaining demand. Under the "continuing demand" rule, when a union has made a premature demand that has been rejected by the employer, this demand remains in force until the moment when the employer attains the "substantial and representative complement." *See, e.g., Aircraft Magnesium*, 265 N.L.R.B., at 1345, n. 9; *Spruce Up Corp.*, 209 N.L.R.B., at 197.

Such a rule, particularly when considered along with the "substantial and representative complement" rule, places a minimal burden on the successor and makes sense in light of the union's position. Once the employer has concluded that it has reached the appropriate complement, then, in order to determine whether its duty to bargain will be triggered, it has only to see whether the union already has made a demand for bargaining. Because the union has no established relationship with the successor and because it is unaware of the successor's plans for its operations and hiring, it is likely that, in many cases, a union's bargaining demand will be premature. It makes no sense to require the union repeatedly to renew its bargaining demand in the hope of having it correspond with the "substantial and representative complement" date, when, with little trouble, the employer can regard a previous demand as a continuing one. . . .

The judgment of the Court of Appeals is affirmed.

It is so ordered.

JUSTICE POWELL, with whom THE CHIEF JUSTICE and JUSTICE O'CONNOR join, dissenting. . . .

I

. . .

B. . . . The critical question in determining successorship is whether there is "substantial continuity" between the two businesses. *Aircraft Magnesium, a Division of Grico Corp.*, 265 N.L.R.B. 1344, 1345 (1982), *aff'd* 730 F.2d 767 (CA9 1984). *See also NLRB v. Burns International Security Services, Inc.*, 406 U.S. 272, 279–281 (1972). Here the Board concluded that there was sufficient continuity between petitioner and Sterlingwale, primarily because the workers did the same finishing work on the same equipment for petitioner as they had for their former employer. . . . In reaching this conclusion, however, the Board, and now the Court, give virtually no weight to the evidence of *dis*continuity, that I think is overwhelming.

In this case the undisputed evidence shows that petitioner is a completely separate entity from Sterlingwale. There was a clear break between the time Sterlingwale ceased normal business operations in February 1982 and when petitioner came into existence at the end of August. In addition, it is apparent that there was no direct contractual or other business relationship between petitioner and Sterlingwale. Although petitioner bought some of Sterlingwale's inventory, it did so by outbidding several other buyers on the open market. Also, the purchases at the public sale involved only tangible assets. Petitioner did not buy Sterlingwale's trade name or good will, nor did it assume any of its liabilities. And while over half of petitioner's business (measured in dollars) came from former Sterlingwale customers, apparently this was due to the new company's skill in marketing its services. There was no sale or transfer of customer lists, and given the 9-month interval between the time that Sterlingwale ended production and petitioner commenced its operations in November, the natural conclusion is that the new business attracted customers through its own efforts. No other explanation was offered.... Any one of these facts standing alone may be insufficient to defeat a finding of successorship, but together they persuasively demonstrate that the Board's finding of "substantial continuity" was incorrect.

The Court nevertheless is unpersuaded. It views these distinctions as not directly affecting the employees' expectations about their job status or the status of the union as their representative, even though the CBA with the defunct corporation had long since expired.... Yet even from the employees' perspective, there was little objective evidence that the jobs with petitioner were simply a continuation of those at Sterlingwale. When all of the production employees were laid off indefinitely in February 1982, there could have been little hope — and certainly no reasonable expectation — that Sterlingwale would ever reopen. Nor was it reasonable for the employees to expect that Sterlingwale's failed textile operations would be resumed by a corporation not then in existence. The CBA had expired in April with no serious effort to renegotiate it, and with several of the employees' benefits left unpaid. The possibility of further employment with Sterlingwale then disappeared entirely in August 1982 when the company liquidated its remaining assets. *Cf. Textile Workers Union v. Darlington Mfg. Co.*, 380 U.S. 263, 274 (1965) (the "closing of an entire business ... ends the employer-employee relationship"). After petitioner was organized, it advertised for workers in the newspaper, a move that hardly could have suggested to the old workers that they would be reinstated to their former positions. The sum of these facts inevitably would have had a negative "effect on the employees' expectations of rehire." See *Aircraft Magnesium*, 265 N.L.R.B., at 1346.... The former employees engaged by petitioner found that the new plant was smaller, and that there would be fewer workers, fewer shifts, and more hours per shift than at their prior job. Moreover, as petitioner did not acquire Sterlingwale's personnel records, the benefits of having a favorable work record presumably were lost to these employees.

In deferring to the NLRB's decision, the Court today extends the successorship doctrine in a manner that could not have been anticipated by either the employer or the employees. I would hold that the successorship doctrine has no application when the break in continuity between enterprises is as complete and extensive as it was here.

II

Even if the evidence of genuine continuity were substantial, I could not agree with the Court's decision. As we have noted in the past, if the presumption of majority support for a union is to survive a change in ownership, it must be shown that there is both a continuity of conditions *and* a continuity of work force. *Howard Johnson Co. v. Hotel Employees*, 417 U.S. 249, 263 (1974). This means that unless a majority of the new company's workers had been employed by the former company, there is no justification for assuming that the new employees wish to be represented by the former union, or by any union at all. . . .

In my view, the Board's decision to measure the composition of the petitioner work force in mid-January is unsupportable. The substantial and representative complement test can serve a useful role when the hiring process is sporadic, or the future expansion of the work force is speculative. But as the Court recognized in *NLRB v. Burns Security Services, Inc.*, in some cases "it may not be clear until the successor employer has hired his full complement of employees that he has a duty to bargain with a union, since it will not be evident until then that the bargaining representative represents a majority of the employees in the unit." 406 U.S., at 295. Indeed, where it is feasible to wait and examine the full complement — as it was here — it clearly is fairer to both employer and employees to do so. The substantial complement test provides no more than an *estimate* of the percentage of employees from the old company that eventually will be part of the new business, and thus often will be an imperfect measure of continuing union support. The risks of relying on such an estimate are obvious. If the "substantial complement" examined by the Board at a particular time contains a disproportionate number of workers from the old company, the result either might be that the full work force is deprived of union representation that a majority favors, or is required to accept representation that a majority does not want. Accordingly, unless the delay or uncertainty of future expansion would frustrate the employees' legitimate interest in early representation — a situation not shown to exist here — there is every reason to wait until the full anticipated work force has been employed. . . .

In prior decisions, courts and the Board have looked not only to the *number* of workers hired and positions filled on a particular date, but also to "the time expected to elapse before a substantially larger complement would be at work . . . as well as the relative certainty of the employer's expected expansion." *Premium Foods, Inc. v. NLRB*, 709 F.2d 623, 628 (CA9 1983). See also *St. John of God Hospital, Inc.*, 260 N.L.R.B. 905 (1982). Here the anticipated expansion was both imminent and reasonably definite. The record shows that in January petitioner both expected to, and in fact subsequently did, hire a significant number of new employees to staff its second shift. Although the Court finds that the growth of the work force was "contingent" on business conditions, neither the Administrative Law Judge nor the NLRB made such a finding.[27] In fact, they both noted that by January 15, the second shift already had begun limited operations. . . . In fact, less than three months after the duty to bargain allegedly arose, petitioner had nearly doubled the size of its mid-January work force by hiring the remaining 50-odd workers it needed to reach full production. This expansion was not unexpected; instead, it closely tracked petitioner's original forecast for growth during its first few months in business. Thus there

---

27. [7] The evidence shows that in the textile industry, two shifts are necessary for proper finishing work. *See* 775 F.2d 425, 428 (CA1 1985). Thus, it was clear in mid-January that petitioner would need more employees in the immediate future.

was no reasonable basis for selecting mid-January as the time that petitioner should have known that it should commence bargaining. . . .

In an effort to ensure that some employees will not be deprived of representation for even a short time, the Court requires petitioner to recognize a union that has never been elected or accepted by a majority of its workers. For the reasons stated, I think that the Court's decision is unfair both to petitioner, who hardly could have anticipated the date chosen by the Board, and to most of petitioner's employees, who were denied the opportunity to choose their union. I dissent.

Notes

1. *"Substantial Continuity" between the Enterprises*—In *Pa. Transformer Tech., Inc. v. NLRB*, 254 F.3d 217 (D.C. Cir. 2001), the court outlined the requirements for determining when there exists "substantial continuity" in operation and in employment sufficient to justify imposition of a bargaining obligation on the new entity employer as a "successor." Substantial continuity is found where the business of both employers is essentially the same, the employees of the new company are doing substantially the same jobs in the same working conditions under the same supervision, and the new entity has the same production process, produces the same products, and has the same customers. Accordingly, despite a two-year hiatus in operations following the closing of the predecessor's business and the fact that the new operation had a smaller workforce, a purchasing company should have recognized and bargained with the union representing the previous company's employees, since substantial continuity existed and a majority of its employees had worked for the old company. *See also Publi-Inversiones De Puerto Rico, Inc. v. NLRB*, 886 F.3d 142 (D.C. Cir. 2018) (successorship found where employer purchased the equipment and intellectual property of bankrupt newspaper and hired some of its employees); *Dean Transp. v. NLRB*, 551 F.3d 1055 (D.C. Cir. 2009) (successorship found where school district outsourced transportation services previously performed by unit workers); *Cmty. Hosps. of Cent. Cal. v. NLRB*, 335 F.3d 1079 (D.C. Cir. 2003) (public hospital taken over by a private nonprofit company that instituted new management structure remained obligated to bargain with predecessor's union where it continued to function as full-service acute-care hospital in which same employees did same work for same patient population); *Systems Mgt. v. NLRB*, 901 F.2d 297 (3d Cir. 1990) (to negate successorship, there must be a "fundamental change" in the nature of the business; altering shift hours from full-time to part-time not enough).

On the other hand, the D.C. Circuit rejected the Board's conclusion that a successorship situation existed in *CitiSteel USA v. NLRB*, 53 F.3d 350 (D.C. Cir. 1995). The Phoenix Steel Corporation began the shutdown of its Claymont, Delaware, plant in late 1986. By January 1987, all production had ceased, and by March, the remaining employees had been terminated. In December 1987, a Hong Kong investor purchased the mill for $13 million. It formed CitiSteel and spent $25 million to refurbish the facility. It began operations in February of 1989 with 124 employees—substantially fewer workers than the 1,000 who had been previously employed by Phoenix Steel.

CitiSteel had restructured job classifications and required formal cross-training for its employees. The D.C. Circuit found a lack of substantial continuity between Phoenix Steel and CitiSteel.

The mere passage of time between the termination of predecessor operations and the commencement of successor operations, however, is insufficient to defeat a successorship finding. *See Straight Creek Mining v. NLRB*, 164 F.3d 292 (6th Cir. 1998) (54-month hiatus); *Nephi Rubber Prods. Corp v NLRB*, 976 F.2d 1361 (10th Cir. 1992) (16-month hiatus); *Coastal Derby Refining Co. v. NLRB*, 915 F.2d 1448 (10th Cir. 1990) (one-year hiatus); *Tree-Free Fiber Co.*, 328 N.L.R.B. 389 (1999) (16-month hiatus). *See generally* Tenenbaum, Comment, Fall River: *The NLRB's Expansive Successorship Doctrine*, 50 Ohio St. L.J. 181 (1989).

2. *Timing of Successorship Determination* — The determination of successor status is made at the point where the employer has hired a substantial and representative complement of its workforce and has resumed operations. The Board looks at whether the job classifications for the operation have been filled, whether the operation is in normal production, the size of the workforce on the date of normal production, the time expected to elapse before a substantially larger complement would be at work, and the relative certainty and timing of expansion plans by the new employer. The Board generally finds that a substantial and representative complement of the workforce has been hired when the current workers make up at least 30% of the projected workforce and hold at least 50% of the job classifications in the expected workforce. *NLRB v. Deutsche Post Global Mail, Ltd.*, 315 F.3d 813 (7th Cir. 2003).

3. *Requirement of Bargaining Demand* — While a bargaining demand by the incumbent union was required in *Fall River Dyeing* before the successor was obligated to bargain, no demand is necessary when the new employer hires its full complement at once, including a clear majority from the former employer's workforce. The *Fall River* rule applies to the gradual hiring of employees during a startup period or the hiring of employees after a prolonged delay between the closing and reopening of a business. *Creative Vision Resources, LLC v. NLRB*, 882 F.3d 510 (5th Cir. 2018) (no bargaining demand necessary where successorship is "perfectly clear," since employer can easily discern from the outset that it will be obligated to bargain with the union).

4. *Route by Which Union Obtained Representative Status* — Should it matter in determining the successor's obligation to bargain with the predecessor whether the predecessor's union obtained its representative status through an NLRB election or through voluntary recognition by the predecessor? Three circuit courts that have addressed the question say no — the D.C. Circuit, the Sixth Circuit, and the Seventh Circuit; the same presumption of majority status arises regardless. *See, e.g., 3750 Orange Place L.P. v. NLRB*, 333 F.3d 646 (6th Cir. 2003).

5. *Duration of Bargaining Obligation* — The Board has vacillated on the issue of the duration of the bargaining obligation applicable to successor employers. In *Southern

Moldings, Inc., 219 N.L.R.B. 119 (1975), the Board ruled that a rebuttable presumption of continuing majority status applies during the period of bargaining following a successorship transition. Decertification petitions, petitions by rival unions, employer petitions, or other valid challenges to the union's majority status may be maintained. In *St. Elizabeth Manor, Inc.*, 329 N.L.R.B. 341 (1999), however, the Board departed from its previous stance and adopted a successor bar rule: once a successor employer becomes obliged to recognize the incumbent union of its predecessor, that union is entitled to a "reasonable period of time" to negotiate a new contract with the successor firm during which time the Board will not allow any challenges to the union's continued majority status. Three years later, the Board overruled the successor bar doctrine established in *St. Elizabeth Manor* and returned to its *Southern Moldings* rule, reasoning that the successor bar doctrine favored maintaining "the stability of bargaining relationships to the exclusion of the employees' §7 rights to choose their bargaining representative." *MV Transp.*, 337 N.L.R.B. 770 (2002).

Most recently, the successor bar doctrine was restored in *UGL-UNICCO Service Co.*, 357 N.L.R.B. 801 (2011), overruling *MV Transportation*, and *UGL-UNICCO Service Co.* was endorsed by the First Circuit in *NLRB v. Lily Transp. Corp.*, 853 F.3d 31 (1st Cir. 2017) (rejecting challenges that the successor bar doctrine interferes with employees' §7 rights to select their representative). A federal district court has applied *UGL-UNICCO* to an employer that purchased the assets of a unionized firm, continued operations with the same production and maintenance workers, and acknowledged its status as a successor employer, holding that even where a majority of employees sign a petition indicating that they no longer desire union representation, the successor cannot withdraw recognition from the predecessor's union for a reasonable period, which the court defined as at least six months from the date of first bargaining between the employer and the union. *Lineback v. SMI/Div'n of DCX-CHOL Enters., Inc.*, 2014 U.S. Dist. LEXIS 158136 (N.D. Ind. Nov. 7, 2014).

What policy justifications might be advanced for these shifts? Do the shifts represent "principled philosophical debate" or "partisan discourse"? For contrasting views, see Dichner, MV Transportation: *Once Again the Board Revisits the Issue of Whether an Incumbent Union Is Entitled to an Irrebuttable Presumption of Continuing Majority Status in Successorship Situations*, 19 Lab. Law. 1 (2003); Siebert, *The Brief Career of* St. Elizabeth Manor: *Once Again an Incumbent Union Is Entitled Only to a Rebuttable Presumption of Continuing Majority Status in Successorship Situations*, 19 Lab. Law. 17 (2003).

Part 7

Internal Union Affairs

Organizing employees and representing them in collective bargaining have traditionally been the primary functions of labor unions, and unions, as institutions, have been built up around these functions. Like other institutions, however, labor organizations tend to develop both external and internal relationships and problems that, while necessarily colored by their main functions, are nevertheless distinct. These relationships and problems are the subject of this brief survey in Part Seven.

Labor unions combine the features of a democratic organization and a militaristic entity. To flex their economic muscles in a strike or boycott action, unions must have buy-in from a majority of their membership and be capable of mobilizing workers to present a united front against the employers with whom they deal. The union must be able to command something like the "solidarity, discipline, and capacity for swift striking that an army has." At the same time, however, members elect their own "generals" and vote on "the declaration of war and on the terms of armistice and peace." *See* A.J. Muste, *Factional Fights in Trade Unions, in* AMERICAN LABOR DYNAMICS 332–33 (J. Hardman ed., 1928).

A reasonable question, then, arises as to whether workers gain any real freedom by substituting for the arbitrary authority of the employer or its managers a union that exercises the power to tax and to conscript. What, exactly, does the "industrial democracy" envisioned by the NLRA's architects mean, and why does it matter? How can we be sure that unions maintain their commitment to democratic principles given the pressures to produce material gains for workers and the militaristic control that unions must exercise?

Archibald Cox, *Internal Affairs of Labor Unions Under the Labor Reform Act of 1959*
58 MICH. L. REV. 819, 830 (1960)

An autocratic union may serve the material demands of its members by bargaining effectively for higher wages and increased benefits. It may establish a measure of job security. None except a democratic union, however, can achieve the idealistic aspirations which justify labor organizations. Collective bargaining may limit the employer's power by substituting a negotiated agreement for arbitrary tyranny of the boss, but it scarcely extends the rule of law to substitute an autocratic union. Only in a democratic union can workers, through chosen representatives, participate jointly with management in the government of their industrial lives even as all of us may participate, through elected representatives, in political government.

In the earlier days of the labor movement, the law took a largely "hands-off" position with regard to the internal functioning of unions; legislatures were unconcerned, and the courts interfered in union affairs as little as possible. The often iterated dogma were these: the union is not a legal entity and can therefore neither sue nor be sued in its common name; property may not be held by the union as an entity separate from its members; disputes between unions and their members are ordinarily best left to settlement within the union structure; and exhaustion of intra-union remedies must precede resort to the courts.

Before long, however, most of these common-law doctrines were well-peppered with exceptions, or, in some instances, discarded entirely. The courts began to see that the growth of unions in numbers and power made anomalous a view that would classify them with social and benevolent societies and fraternal organizations, and that would consider their affairs as of little public concern. Then came the labor relations acts, which established the broad right of a union selected by the majority of employees in a bargaining unit to represent all employees in the unit, whether or not they belong to the union. This enlargement of power, more than any other circumstance, tended to focus attention upon the subject of union responsibilities and duties.

In 1959, Congress took a substantial step toward comprehensive regulation of internal union affairs in the enactment of the Labor Management Reporting and Disclosure Act (the "Landrum-Griffin Act"). Pressure for the legislation came to a head as the result of the disclosures of the McClellan Committee between 1957 and 1959. One of the recommendations of the McClellan Committee was that measures should be taken to encourage more "democracy" in internal union affairs. The bill (S. 1555) reported out by the Senate Labor Committee in 1959 contained provisions requiring reporting and disclosure by unions to their members and regulating union elections. However, Senator McClellan introduced an amendment to the committee bill providing explicitly a "Bill of Rights" for members of labor organizations, and this was adopted, with modifications, becoming Title I of the Labor-Management Reporting and Disclosure Act of 1959 ("LMRDA," reproduced in *Selected Federal Statutes*). Most noteworthy in this Act is the emphasis upon the analogy between the rights of union members and the rights of citizens in a political democracy, protected by constitutional freedoms. The dominant idea in the Eighty-Sixth Congress was that labor unions are of such great public importance that legislation to protect union members in the exercise of basic liberties in the democratic process is essential—a far cry indeed from the concept of a labor union as a private voluntary association like a social club.

For an argument against union democracy regulation, see Estreicher, *Deregulating Union Democracy*, 21 J. Lab. Res. 247 (2000). Professor Estreicher argues that union democracy regulation is ineffectual because union members do not make the investment in information and attendance at meetings necessary to exercise an informed choice or to participate in a way that would ensure effective influence. Moreover, the right to vote on critical matters is limited to full union members, who must subject themselves to the risk of union discipline as the price of participation in union decision making. Finally, the pursuit of union democracy imposes compliance costs on unions and requires the bargaining unit to assume a certain organizational form. Consequently, internal union affairs are controlled by incumbents or challengers who lack the broad support of the membership. In short, unions have become one-party states. As an alternative, Estreicher advocates a system where the law is indifferent to the form the bargaining agent takes, as long as employees in the bargaining unit (whether or not they are union members) have low-cost opportunities to cast secret ballot votes on economic decisions of critical importance to them. These decisions should include authorization of the exclusive bargaining representative; reauthorization at periodic intervals; the employer's final contract offer; strike authorization votes; contract ratification; and the level of union dues.

As new organizational models for worker representation evolve—such as workers' centers, members-only worker advocacy organizations, and coalitions striving for higher wages across an industry or sector—how (if at all) should law regulate their governance? Could the LMRDA serve as a blueprint, or is a different structure needed? *See* Fisk, *Workplace Democracy and Democratic Worker Organizations: Notes on Worker Centers and Members-Only Unions*, 17 THEORETICAL INQUIRIES IN L. 101 (2016); Griffith, *Worker Centers and Labor Law Protections: Why Aren't They Having Their Cake?*, 36 BERKELEY J. EMP. & LAB. L. 331 (2015).

Section I. The Bill of Rights

Title I is fairly characterized as the heart of the LMRDA. Title I guarantees the following rights to individual union members: the right to nominate candidates, vote in elections, and attend and participate in union meetings (§ 101(a)(1)); freedom of speech and assembly (including the right to criticize union officials, speak at local union meetings, distribute literature at the union hall, and hold independent meetings) (§ 101(a)(2)); the right to secret ballot votes on rates of dues, initiation fees, and assessments (§ 101(a)(3)); the right to sue the union (§ 101(a)(4)); and due process safeguards in matters of internal union discipline (§ 101(a)(5)). Section 102 authorizes enforcement of these rights in federal district court. Two provisions of Title I require the union to inform members of their rights. Section 104 obligates the union to make available copies of the collective bargaining agreement to any union member upon request. Section 105 requires unions to inform members of their statutory rights under the LMRDA.

Clyde W. Summers, *The Impact of Landrum-Griffin in State Courts*, in N.Y.U. THIRTEENTH ANNUAL CONFERENCE ON LABOR
333, 335 (1960)

All of the elaborate arguments that union democracy was unnecessary, unworkable, or even unfortunate have been deliberately rejected. Financial integrity is not enough; the decisions as to dues and expenditures must be democratically made. Officers must be more than honest and responsible; they must be chosen by the members in an open election after free debate. Union members are guaranteed equal rights, freedom of speech and assembly, and due process within the union. Although the statute leaves undefined the exact amount of individual right to be protected, and cannot guarantee the full realization of the democratic process, the policy thrust of the statute is clear and strong. The public has an interest in union democracy.

Directors Guild of America, Inc. v. Superior Court of Los Angeles County
409 P.2d 934 (Cal. 1966)

. . . .

[M]embership in the union means more than mere personal or social accommodation. Such membership affords to the employee not only the opportunity to participate in the negotiation of the contract governing his employment but also the chance to engage in the institutional life of the union. Although in the case which involves interstate commerce the union must legally give fair representation to all the appropriate employees, whether or not they are members of the union, the union official, in the nature of political realities, will in all likelihood more diligently represent union members, who can vote him out of office, than employees whom he must serve only as a matter of abstract law.

Our decisions further recognize that the union functions as the medium for the exercise of industrial franchise. As Summers puts it, "The right to join a union involves the right to an economic ballot." (*The Right to Join a Union* (1947) 47 COLUM. L. REV. 33.) Participation in the union's affairs by the workman compares to the participation of the citizen in the affairs of his community. The union, as a kind of public service institution, affords to its members the opportunity to record themselves upon all matters affecting their relationships with the employer; it serves likewise as a vehicle for the expression of the membership's position on political and community issues. The shadowy right to "fair representation" by the union, accorded by the Act, is by no means the same as the hard concrete ability to vote and to participate in the affairs of the union.

In another parallel between the constitutional rights of citizens in a democracy vis-à-vis the state and the rights of union members under the LMRDA vis-à-vis the union, the Fourth Circuit held that a union member's free speech and retaliation claims under LMRDA § 101(a)(2) were not cognizable unless her speech met standards developed in the First Amendment context for public sector employees challenging retaliatory discipline for speech, namely that the speech be on a matter of public concern. The court ruled that union members' expression of views, arguments, or opinions is only protected under the LMRDA if it addresses a matter of "union concern," relating to "the general interests of the union membership at large." *Trail v. Local 2850 UAW United Def. Workers of Am.*, 710 F.3d 541 (4th Cir. 2013), *cert. denied*, 571 U.S. 1126 (2014). *See also Kazolias v. IBEWLU 363*, 806 F.3d 45 (2d Cir. 2015) (finding that Title I's protections are limited to speech of significant concern to the membership as a whole).

Section II. Reporting and Disclosure Provisions

Despite its name, the LMRDA is far more than a disclosure measure. Nevertheless, reporting provisions remain a central feature of the Act. Title II prescribes five different types of reports: (1) union organizational reports; (2) union financial reports; (3) "conflict of interest" reports by union officers and employees; (4) employer reports on such matters as payments to union representatives and payments to influence employees in the exercise of their collective rights; and (5) reports by labor relations consultants on agreements to influence employees, or to inform employers about employee or union activities in a labor dispute. The reporting obligations are subject to criminal sanctions and to a civil suit by the Secretary of Labor for an injunction or other appropriate remedy.

The information contained in union organizational and financial reports must be made available to the members of the union. LMRDA § 201(c) requires labor organizations to permit members with "just cause to examine any books, records, and accounts" upon request to verify financial reports filed with the Secretary of Labor.

The so-called "goldfish bowl" philosophy underlying the union reporting requirements is reflected in the following statement.

House Committee on Education and Labor
H.R. Rep. No. 741 on H.R. 8342, 86th Cong., 1st Sess. 7–9 (1959)

The members of a labor organization are the real owners of the money and property of such organizations and are entitled to a full accounting of all transactions involving such money and property. Because union funds belong to the members they should be expended only in furtherance of their common interest. A union treasury should not be managed as though it were the private property of the union officers, however well intentioned such officers might be, but as a fund governed by fiduciary standards....

... [T]he rules governing the conduct of the union's business, such as dues and assessments payable by members, membership rights, disciplinary procedures, election of officers, provisions governing the calling of regular and special meetings—all should be known to the members. Without such information freely available it is impossible that labor organizations can be truly responsive to their members.

It is the purpose of this bill to insure that full information concerning the financial and internal administrative practices and procedures of labor organizations shall be, in the first instance available to the members of such organizations. In addition, this information is to be made available to the Government, and through the Secretary of Labor, is to be open to inspection by the general public. By such disclosure, and by relying on voluntary action by members of labor organizations, it is hoped that a deterrent to abuses will be established. . . .

The committee believes that union members armed with adequate information and having the benefit of secret elections, as provided for in title IV of this bill, will be greatly strengthened in their efforts to rid themselves of untrustworthy or corrupt officers. In addition, the exposure to public scrutiny of all vital information concerning their operation of trade unions will help deter repetition of the financial abuses disclosed by the McClellan committee. Where union financial and other practices do not meet reasonable standards, although not willfully dishonest, this bill would have a remedial effect. Under provisions of the committee bill, both labor organizations and their officers are under obligation to make full and accurate reports, subject to criminal penalties.

LMRDA § 201(b) requires unions to file financial reports containing information on assets and liabilities, receipts, salaries and benefits to union officers and employees, and loans. The provision states that information should be provided "in such categories as the Secretary may prescribe."

In October 2003, the Labor Department announced controversial changes to the annual financial forms filed by unions under the LMRDA, the first major revision of the financial reporting rules since they were issued in 1960. The new rules required unions with annual receipts of $250,000 or more to provide more detailed disclosure of financial expenditures, obligating them to break expenses into functional categories, including political activities and lobbying, union administration, strike benefits, and representational activities (including contract negotiation and administration, and organizing). The Bush administration justified the revisions in terms of "transparency" and "accountability" to rank-and-file members, arguing that the changes would allow union members to play a more knowledgeable role in the governance of their unions. The National Right to Work Committee argued that the new reporting requirements did not go far enough, particularly in allowing expenditures for organizing to be mixed with contract negotiation and administration expenses. Daily Lab. Rep. (BNA) No. 201, Oct. 17, 2003, at A-7. Organized labor, however, characterized the new rules as a politically motivated attempt to diminish the influence of unions. The AFL-CIO complained that the extensive new reporting requirements would involve filling out huge numbers of forms, taking time away from contract negotiations, organizing, and other core union activities. Daily Lab. Rep. (BNA) No. 193, Oct. 6, 2003, at AA-1.

The new rules were slated to take effect on January 1, 2004. In November 2003, however, the AFL-CIO filed suit in federal court seeking a preliminary injunction to block implementation of the changes. In addition, the AFL-CIO sought a declaratory judgment that the Labor Department's new rules violated the Administrative Procedure Act, alleging the rules exceeded the agency's authority under LMRDA. A federal judge upheld the newly revised regulations, but delayed implementation in order to ease the burden on unions. *AFL-CIO v. Chao*, 298 F. Supp. 2d 104 (D.D.C. 2004). On appeal, the D.C. Circuit upheld the new rules requiring an itemized accounting of major transactions rather than the aggregate reporting of past years. *AFL-CIO v. Chao*, 409 F.3d 377 (D.C. Cir. 2005).

Section 203 requires that consultants and employers report expenditures made in connection with persuading employees to exercise or not to exercise rights to organize and bargain under the labor laws. Failure to report is a criminal violation. Section 203(c) provides an exemption for reporting requirements if the activity involves "giving or agreeing to give advice" to an employer or representing the employer before a court, agency, or arbitrator or in collective bargaining negotiations. Since the statute's enactment, the Department of Labor has interpreted "advice" in § 203(c) broadly, to include preparation of material such as videotapes, speeches, or documents designed to persuade employees, as long as the employer was free to accept or reject the material. This interpretation rendered the scope of the exemption very broad; essentially, anything other than direct contact between the consultant and the employees was exempt from the reporting requirement. The D.C. Circuit has approved this interpretation. *See International Union, United Auto., etc. v. Dole*, 869 F.2d 616 (D.C. Cir. 1989).

In the final days of the Clinton administration, however, the Department of Labor reacted to evidence suggesting a dramatic increase in employer use of labor relations consultants to combat union organizing by narrowing the LMRDA exemption that shields consultants from the law's reporting requirements. The Department of Labor's new interpretation of the exemption would have required reporting expenditures whenever persuading employees is an object, directly or indirectly, of a person's activity pursuant to an agreement with the employer. Preparing materials for use in an anti-union campaign would have been outside the exemption, but advice rendered in the form of reviewing or revising persuasive materials prepared by the employer or counseling the employer as to its permissible range of speech would have continued to be excluded. Daily Lab. Rep. (BNA), Jan. 11, 2001, at AA-1. The Bush administration rescinded the Department of Labor's revised interpretation before it could take effect and restored the previous broad interpretation of the exemption. Daily Lab. Rep. (BNA), Apr. 11, 2001, at AA-1.

Under the Obama administration, the DOL again proposed the interpretation it had suggested in 2001, significantly narrowing the scope of the exemption and resulting in a broader obligation to report. The DOL's Press Release explained:

> Under the proposal, an agreement would be reportable in any case where the consultant engages in persuader activities that go beyond the plain meaning of "advice." Reportable persuader activities would include those in which a consultant engages in any actions, conduct or communications on behalf of an employer that would directly or indirectly persuade workers concerning their rights to organize and bargain collectively, regardless of whether or not the consultant has direct contact with workers. An agreement also would be reportable in any case in which a consultant engages in specific persuader actions, conduct or communications regardless of whether advice is given, such as when a consultant plans or orchestrates a campaign or program to avoid or counter a union organizing or collective bargaining effort.

http://www.dol.gov/opa/media/press/olms/olms20110924.htm. A new rule was issued in 2016 but never went into effect because it was enjoined nationwide by a federal district court. *See National Federation of Independent Business v. Perez*, 2016 WL 8193279 (N.D. Tex.). In 2018, the Trump administration's Department of Labor formally rescinded the 2016 persuader rule, reasoning that it interfered with lawyer-client privilege. *See* 83 Fed. Reg. No. 138, 33826, July 18, 2018, available at https://www.federalregister.gov/documents/2018/07/18/2018-14948/rescission-of-rule-interpreting-advice-exemption-in-section-203c-of-the-labor-management-reporting.

Why has the persuader rule and its exemption been so controversial? For an overview of the interests at stake in the Act's employer and consultant reporting provisions, see Beaird, *Reporting Requirements for Employers and Labor Relations Consultants in the Labor Management Reporting and Disclosure Act of 1959*, 53 GEO. L.J. 267 (1965). On lawyer consultants in particular, see Craver, *The Application of the LMRDA "Labor Consultant" Reporting Requirements to Management Attorneys: Benign Neglect Personified*, 73 NW. U. L. REV. 605 (1978).

Section III. Trusteeships and Parent-Local Relations

A trusteeship is a method of supervision or control by which a national or international union suspends the autonomy of a subordinate local union, depriving it of its powers pursuant to its constitution or bylaws. During the McClellan Committee hearings it was disclosed that national unions sometimes used the power to impose trusteeship to "milk" local union treasuries or to manipulate electoral support for national union officers. *See* SECRETARY OF LABOR, UNION TRUSTEESHIPS: REPORT TO THE CONGRESS UPON THE OPERATION OF TITLE III OF THE

Labor-Management Reporting and Disclosure Act 5 (1962). Accordingly, the LMRDA as enacted prescribed conditions under which trusteeships could be established and continued, mandated reporting and public disclosure of their stewardship, made it a crime to count the votes of delegates of the trusteed union unless they were democratically elected or to transfer funds from the subordinate to the parent, and provided redress for the subordinate body either directly in court or through the Secretary of Labor. *Id.*

Section IV. The Regulation of Racketeering and Communist Activity

Section 302 of the LMRA addresses the problem of corruption of collective bargaining through bribery of employee representatives by employers, prohibiting unions and employers from exchanging "money or other thing[s] of value." Section 302(a) applies to the employer's side of such a transaction, and § 302(b) applies to the recipient's side.

In *UNITE HERE Local 355 v. Mulhall*, 570 U.S. 915 (2013), the Court granted certiorari in a case in which it was expected to pass on the legality under § 302 of neutrality agreements that set the ground rules for union organizing campaigns and provided for card-check recognition. The case involved an agreement between UNITE/HERE and a dog track owner under which the employer promised to: (1) provide union representatives with access to nonpublic premises to engage in organizing activities during employee nonwork time; (2) provide union representatives with the names, classifications, and addresses of employees; and (3) remain neutral during the organizing campaign. In return for these promises, the union agreed to lend financial support for a ballot initiative regarding casino gaming, for which it spent more than $100,000. The union also agreed that it would refrain from picketing, boycotting, or striking the employer. The Court dismissed the petition for certiorari as improvidently granted, however. *UNITE HERE Local 355 v. Mulhall*, 571 U.S. 83 (2013). The dismissal leaves intact the Eleventh Circuit's decision finding that the neutrality agreement could be a basis for an LMRA § 302 violation if the parties had a "corrupting intent" rendering otherwise innocuous ground rules an improper payment. According to the Eleventh Circuit, whether something qualifies as an improper payment does not depend on its monetary value or its tangibility, but on whether or not it is offered with the intent to gain benefit or influence the union. *Mulhall v. UNITE HERE Local 355*, 667 F.3d 1211 (11th Cir. 2012). Courts elsewhere have upheld neutrality agreements. *See, e.g., Hotel Employees & Restaurant Employees Union, Local 57 v. Sage Hospitality Resources, LLC*, 390 F.3d 206 (3d Cir. 2004) (finding neutrality agreement not a "thing of value" within scope of LMRA § 302); *Adcock v. Freightliner, LLC*, 550 F.3d 369 (4th Cir. 2008) (neutrality agreement not a "thing of value" because it lacks "ascertainable value"). *Compare Seton Medical Ctr./Seton Coastside*, 360 N.L.R.B. 302 (2014) (employer engaged in objectionable conduct warranting new election where it permitted incumbent union, but not petitioning union, to solicit employees during work time in immediate patient care areas of medical center).

Section 302(c) establishes an exception for funds paid by employers to employees "as compensation for, or by reason of, . . . service as an employee." Thus, § 302 is not violated when union committee members and grievance chairs take leaves without losing wages or benefits to devote their full time to union business. *See, e.g., Int'l Ass'n of Machinists & Aero. Workers, Local Lodge 964 v. BF Goodrich Aero. Aerostructures Group*, 387 F.3d 1046 (9th Cir. 2004) (collective bargaining provisions requiring employer to pay salary and benefits to union steward do not violate LMRDA § 302(a)).

Section 302(c) also exempts certain payments to union trust funds established for the exclusive benefit of employees and their families and dependents. Subsection (c) has become quite unwieldy with the addition of individual exceptions — for example, to authorize scholarships, child care centers, and prepaid legal services plans. Does this seem an appropriate approach or does it suggest a fundamental defect in the structure of § 302? *See generally* Goetz, *Developing Federal Labor Law of Welfare and Pension Funds*, 55 Cornell L. Rev. 911 (1970).

When a court finds mobster domination of a labor organization in violation of the Racketeer Influenced and Corrupt Organizations Act, 18 U.S.C. § 1961, it may impose a judicial trusteeship and direct the removal of the culpable union officials. *See, e.g., United States v. Local 560 of Int'l Bhd. of Teamsters*, 780 F.2d 267 (3d Cir. 1985), *cert. denied*, 476 U.S. 1140 (1986); *id.*, 974 F.2d 315 (3d Cir. 1992).

Under § 504(a) of the LMRDA, no person may be a union officer or employee for a maximum period of 13 years from the time he or she was convicted of, or held membership in the Communist Party, or from the time he or she was convicted of, or was imprisoned for, any of several specified crimes. Violation of § 504 is a criminal offense. In *NLRB v. Brown*, 380 U.S. 278 (1965), the Supreme Court held, with four Justices dissenting, that § 504 was unconstitutional as a bill of attainder insofar as it applied to Communist Party members. Although the Court made no reference to § 504's similar disqualification of persons convicted of various enumerated offenses, the emphasis on the evils of proscribing anyone simply on the basis of membership in a "political group" suggests that *Brown* would not be dispositive of the constitutionality of the section's anti-convict ban. Furthermore, § 504 would apparently not be vulnerable to attack as *ex post facto* legislation in its application to persons committing crimes prior to the passage of the LMRDA. In *De Veau v. Braisted*, 363 U.S. 144 (1960), the Supreme Court upheld a somewhat similar New York law, reasoning that it was designed primarily to safeguard unions against future abuses and not to punish the disqualified officials for past offenses.

Section 803 of the Comprehensive Crime Control Act of 1984, 98 Stat. 1976, 2133 (1984), amended § 504(a) of the LMRDA to add more disqualifying offenses for union personnel and to extend the disbarment period from five to thirteen years, and amended § 504(b) to increase the maximum penalty for willful violations from one year to five years. Section 504(c) was modified to require union officials convicted of labor racketeering activities to leave their union posts immediately without being permitted to await the outcome of post-conviction appeals. The 1984 Act also amended § 302(d) of the LMRA to provide that willful violations involving labor bribery or unlawful payoffs in excess of $1000 shall constitute felonies punishable by fines of up to $15,000 and/or imprisonment for up to five years. *See generally* Panter, *The Changes Accomplished by the Labor Racketeering Amendments of the Comprehensive Crime Control Act of 1984*, 36 Lab. L.J. 744 (1985).

Index

[References are to Part and Section numbers.]

A

AFL-CIO
Development of...Pt 1: Sec.I [C][3]

Age Discrimination in Employment Act (ADEA)
Generally...Pt 5: Sec.III [B]

Americans with Disabilities Act (ADA)
Generally...Pt 5: Sec.III [C]
Accommodation, requests for...Pt 5: Sec.III [D][2]

Arbitration
Generally...Pt 6: Sec.II [B]
Arbitrability...Pt 6: Sec.III [B]
Awards, Judicial enforcement of...Pt 6: Sec.III [D]
Concerted activities, clauses prohibiting...Pt 2: Sec.III [C][1]
Contractual claims overlapping with statutory rights...Pt 6: Sec.VI
Costs associated with...Pt 6: Sec.II [B][2]
Deference to arbitration...Pt 6: Sec.VI [B
Discrimination claims...Pt 6: Sec.VI, Pt 5: Sec.III [E]
Enforcement mechanisms
   Contractual claims overlapping with statutory rights...Pt 6: Sec.VI
   Discrimination claims...Pt 6: Sec.VI
   Federal statutes...Pt 6: Sec.VI
Judicial review...Pt 6: Sec.III [A]
Labor Management Relations Act, Section 301...Pt 6: Sec.III [A], Pt 6: Sec.V, Pt 6: Sec.VI [A]
Grievance procedure...Pt 6: Sec.II [A], Pt 6: Sec.II [B][2]
Interest arbitration...Pt 6: Sec.II [B][1]
Issues subject to arbitration...Pt 5: Sec.V; Pt 6: Sec.II, Pt 6: Sec.II [B][1]
Judicial enforcement of arbitration awards...Pt 6: Sec.III [D]
Labor Management Relations Act, Section 301...Pt 6: Sec.III [A], Pt 6: Sec.V, Pt 6: Sec.VI [A]
Lapsed collective bargaining agreements, arbitration under...Pt 6: Sec.III [C]
Mandatory subjects of collective bargaining...Pt 5: Sec.V
Mergers, duty to arbitrate...Pt 6: Sec.VII
Permissive subjects of collective bargaining...Pt 5: Sec.V
Railway Labor Act...Pt 6: Sec.II [C]
Successor employers, duty to arbitrate...Pt 6: Sec.VII
Takeovers, duty to arbitrate...Pt 6: Sec.VII
Tribunals...Pt 6: Sec.II [B][2]
Voluntary arbitration...Pt 6: Sec.II [B]

At-Will Employment Doctrine
Generally...Pt 1: Intro

B

Bankruptcy
Collective bargaining agreements...Pt 6: Sec.VI [D]

Boycotts (See Strikes, Boycotts and Picketing)

C

Cease and Desist Orders
NLRB actions...Pt 1: Sec.II [B]

Collective Bargaining
Agreements (See Collective Bargaining Agreements)
Concerted activities, protection of (See Concerted Activities)
Duration of duty to bargain...Pt 3: Sec.III; Pt 5: Sec.VI
Exclusive representation
  Generally...Pt 3: Sec.I; Pt 5: Sec.I
Fair representation
  Duty of...Pt 5: Sec.II [A][1]
  Individual contract rights, judicial enforcement of...Pt 5: Sec.II
  Labor Management Reporting and Disclosure Act...Pt 7: Sec. II
  Unfair representation
    Breach of contract actions...Pt 5: Sec.II [A][2]
    Discriminatory practices...Pt 5: Sec.II [B]
    Unfair labor practice, action as...Pt 5: Sec.II [B]
Financial disclosure...Pt 5: Sec.IV [D]
Good faith bargaining...Pt 5: Sec. IV [A]
Information requests by bargaining unit...Pt 5: Sec.IV [D]
Injunctive relief for refusal to bargain collectively...Pt 5: Sec. IV [B]
Majority rule...Pt 3: Sec.I; Pt 5: Sec.I
Mandatory subjects of collective bargaining...Pt 5: Sec.V
Monopoly wage model...Pt 5: Intro
Permissive subjects of collective bargaining...Pt 5: Sec.V
Release of company financial information, requests for...Pt 5: Sec.IV [D]
Remedies for refusal to bargain collectively...Pt 5: Sec.IV [B]
Subject matter of negotiations...Pt 5: Sec.V; Pt 6: Sec.II, Pt 6: Sec.II [B][1]
Successor employers...Pt 6: Sec.VII
Unfair labor practice proceedings for refusal to bargain collectively...Pt 3: Sec.II
Unilateral actions due to impasse...Pt 5: Sec.IV [C]
Units
  Appropriate bargaining unit
    Defined...Pt 3: Sec.I [B]
    Judicial review......Pt 3: Sec.I [D]
  Certification...Pt 3: Sec.I
  Elections
    Generally...Pt 3: Sec.I, Pt 3: Sec.I [C]
    Bars to conducting...Pt 3: Sec.I [A]
  Exclusive representation...Pt 3: Sec.I; Pt 5: Sec.I
  Formation of...Pt 3: Sec.I
  Labor Management Reporting and Disclosure Act...Pt 7: Sec.II
  Multiemployer units...Pt 3: Sec.I [B][2]
  Multiple plant units...Pt 3: Sec.I [B][1]
  Representative status...Pt 3: Sec.I; Pt 5: Sec.I

Collective Bargaining Agreements
Agency theory...Pt 6: Sec.I
Arbitration (See Arbitration)
Bankruptcy...Pt 6: Sec.VI [D]

Enforcement of
    Arbitration (See Arbitration)
    Grievance procedure...Pt 6: Sec.II [A], Pt 6: Sec.II [B][2]
    Judicial...Pt 6: Sec.III
Exclusive representation...Pt 5: Sec.I
Grievance procedure...Pt 6: Sec.II [A], Pt 6: Sec.II [B][2]
Judicial enforcement of...Pt 6: Sec. III
    Arbitrability...Pt 6: Sec.III [B]
    Arbitration awards, Judicial enforcement of...Pt 6: Sec.III [D]
    Federal oversight...Pt 6: Sec.III [A]
    Lapsed collective bargaining agreements, arbitration under...Pt 6: Sec.III [C]
    Public policy exception...Pt 6: Sec.III [E]
    Section 301 of the Labor Management Relations Act...Pt 6: Sec.III [A]
Legal status...Pt 6: Sec.I
Local customs or usages...Pt 6: Sec.I
Midterm modifications of agreements...Pt 6: Sec.VI [A]
Modification of...Pt 6: Sec.VI [A]
Overview...Pt 6: Sec.I
"Zipper" clauses...Pt 6: Sec.VI [A]

Common Law

Actions under...Pt 4: Sec.I [A]

Concerted Activities

Arbitration clauses prohibiting class actions in the nonunion setting...Pt 2: Sec.III [C][3]
Constructive...Pt 2: Sec.III [C][4]
Crossovers, inducements to strike...Pt 2: Sec.III [C][8]
Employer policies potentially restricting Section 7 activity...Pt 2: Sec.III [C][2]
Loss of protection
    due to means against public policy...Pt 2: Sec.III [C][6]
    due to unlawful means...Pt 2: Sec.III [C][6]
    due to unlawful objective...Pt 2: Sec.III [C][6]
New hires, inducement to strike...Pt 2: Sec.III [C][8]
Nonunion setting, arbitration clauses prohibiting class actions in...Pt 2: Sec.III [C][3]
Replacement workers, use of during strikes...Pt 2: Sec.III [C][7]
Social media, on...Pt 2: Sec.III [C][1]
Violations of Sections 8(a)(3) and (1), proof of motive...Pt 2: Sec.III [C][9]
Weingarten rights...Pt 2: Sec.III [C][5]
Work rules potentially restricting Section 7 activity...Pt 2: Sec.III [C][2]

Contracts

Breach of contract actions...Pt 5: Sec.II [A][2]
Contractual claims overlapping with statutory rights...Pt 6: Sec.VI
Individual contract rights, judicial enforcement of...Pt 5: Sec.II [A][1]
Successor employers' liability to honor contractual obligations...Pt 6: Sec.VII
Unilateral modification cases...Pt 6: Sec.VI [A]
Union contracts under collective bargaining agreements (See Collective Bargaining Agreements)

D

Deregulation

Historical perspective...Pt 1: Intro

Discharge
Retaliatory discharge for union activities...Pt 2: Sec.III [E]; Pt 6: Sec.V

Discrimination
Age Discrimination in Employment Act (ADEA)...Pt 5: Sec.III [B]
Americans with Disabilities Act (ADA)
  Generally...Pt 5: Sec.III [C]
  Accommodation, requests for...Pt 5: Sec.III [D][2]
  Arbitration of claims...Pt 5: Sec.III [E]
  Federal remedies...Pt 5: Sec.III [E]
Free rider problem, First Amendment and...Pt 2: Sec.III [B][3]
Hiring halls...Pt 2: Sec.III [B][1]; Pt 5: Sec.II [B]
Nonunion employees, discrimination against...Pt 2: Sec.III [B][1]
Racial harassment...Pt 5: Sec.III [D][1]
Representation in collective bargaining...Pt 5: Sec.II [B]
Retaliation for union involvement
  Discharge...Pt 2: Sec.III [E]; Pt 6: Sec.V
  Discrimination to discourage union activity...Pt 2: Sec.III [A]
  Union activity, discrimination to discourage...Pt 2: Sec.III [A]
Sexual harassment...Pt 5: Sec.III [D][1]
Title VII under Civil Rights Act...Pt 5: Sec.III [A]
Unfair representation in collective bargaining...Pt 5: Sec.II [B]
Union activity, to discourage...Pt 2: Sec.III [A]
Union membership, to encourage...Pt 2: Sec.III [B]

Diversity in the Workplace
Generally...Pt 1: Intro

E

Employee
Defined...Pt 1: Sec.II [A][3][a]

Employee Free Choice Act
Generally...Pt 1: Sec.I [C][6], Pt 6: Sec.II [B][1]

Employee Involvement (EI) Programs
Generally...Pt 2: Sec.II

Employer
Defined...Pt 2: Sec.I [F]

F

Featherbedding
Unfair labor practice actions...Pt 4: Sec.VI

Federal Preemption
Exercising...Pt 4: Sec.VII
Garmon preeemption...Pt 4: Sec.VII [A]
  Compared with *Machinists* preemption...Pt 4: Sec.VII [C]
Machinists preemption......Pt 4: Sec.VII [B]
  Compared with *Garmon* preemption...Pt 4: Sec.VII [C]

First Amendment
Antiunion speeches and publications...Pt 2: Sec.I [B]
Free rider problem and...Pt 2: Sec.III [B][3]
Organizing union movements...Pt 2: Intro

G

Grievance Procedure
Generally...Pt 6: Sec.II [A], Pt 6: Sec.II [B][2]

H

Historical Background
AFL-CIO...Pt 1: Sec.I [C][3]
"Business unionism" movement...Pt 1: Intro

Common law...Pt 4: Sec.I [A]
Injunctions...Pt 1: Sec.I [B][2]
Labor Management Relations Act (Taft-Hartley Act)...Pt 1: Sec.I [C][4]
Labor Management Reporting and Disclosure Act...Pt 1: Sec.I [C][5]
New Deal era
   National Industrial Recovery Act (NIRA)...Pt 1: Sec.I [C][1]
   National Labor Relations Act (Wagner Act)...Pt 1: Sec.I [C][2]
1900–1933...Pt 1: Sec.I [B][3]
1970s to present...Pt 1: Sec.I [C][6]
Norris-La Guardia Act...Pt 4: Sec.I [B]
Post-Civil War period
   Anti-union tactics...Pt 1: Sec.I [B][1]
   Growth of national unions...Pt 1: Sec.I [B][1]
   Judicial restraints against unionism...Pt 1: Sec.I [B][2]
   Strikes and labor unrest...Pt 1: Sec.I [B][1]
Pre-Civil War period
   Apprenticeship era...Pt 1: Sec.I [A][1]
   Criminal conspiracy doctrine...Pt 1: Sec.I [A][2]
Taft-Hartley Act...Pt 1: Sec.I [C][4]
Wagner, Robert (Senator) as sponsor of NLRA...Pt 1: Intro; Pt 1: Sec.I [C][2]

I

Immigrants
Immigration Reform and Control Act...Pt 1: Intro
Undocumented workers...Pt 1: Intro

Independent Contractors
Employee versus independent contractor status...Pt 1: Sec.II [A][3][a]
Exclusion under NLRA...Pt 1: Sec.II [A][3][a]

Injunctions
Historical use of...Pt 1: Sec.I [B][2]
NLRB actions...Pt 1: Sec.II [B][2]
Refusal to bargain collectively, as relief for...Pt 5: Sec.IV [B]
Right-to-work laws...Pt 2: Sec.III [B][4]
Strikes
   Generally...Pt 6: Sec.IV
   Anti-injunction statutes against boycotts or picketing...Pt 4: Sec.I [B]
   Norris-La Guardia Act, effect of...Pt 6: Sec.IV

Investors
Policies and practices, effect on...Pt 1: Intro

J

Jurisdictional Disputes
Generally...Pt 4: Sec.V

L

Labor Management Relations Act (LMRA)
Generally...Pt 1: Sec.I [C][4]
Arbitration...Pt 6: Sec.III [A], Pt 6: Sec.IV, Pt 6: Sec.V
Judicial enforcement of arbitration awards...Pt 6: Sec.III [D]
Preemption of state tort law claims...Pt 6: Sec.V

Labor Management Reporting and Disclosure Act (LMRDA)
Generally...Pt 1: Sec.I [C][5]
Bill of rights for union members...Pt 7: Sec.I
Bribery...Pt 7: Sec.IV
Communist activity, regulation of...Pt 7: Sec.IV
Corruption...Pt 7: Sec.IV

Historical background...Pt 1: Sec.I [C][5]
Racketeering...Pt 7: Sec. IV
Reporting and disclosure provisions...Pt 7: Sec.II
Trusteeships and parent-local relations...Pt 7: Sec.III

Landrum-Griffin Act (See Labor Management Reporting and Disclosure Act (LMRDA))

M

Management
Employment contracts...Pt 1: Intro
Exclusion from coverage under NLRA...Pt 1: Sec.II [A][3][e]
Responsibility for unfair labor practices...Pt 2: Sec.I [F]

Mergers
Union contracts...Pt 6: Sec.VII

N

National Labor Relations Act (NLRA)
Coverage under Act
   "Affecting commerce"...Pt 1: Sec.II [A][1]
   Exclusions from coverage
      Agricultural laborers...Pt 1: Sec.II [A][3][e][1]
      Church-operated schools and universities...Pt 1: Sec.II [A][3][e][iv]
      Confidential employees...Pt 1: Sec.II [A][3][d]
      Domestic servants...Pt 1: Sec.II [A][3][e][1]
      Employees of businesses operated by Native American tribes...Pt 1: Sec.II [A][3][e][v]
      Health care employees...Pt 1: Sec.II [A][3][e][iv]
      Independent contractors...Pt 1: Sec.II [A][3][a]
      Managerial employees...Pt 1: Sec.II [A][3][c]
      Residents and interns...Pt 1: Sec.II [A][3][e][ii]
      Students...Pt 1: Sec.II [A][3][e][ii]
      Supervisory employees...Pt 1: Sec.II [A][3][b]
   NLRB exercise of jurisdiction...Pt 1: Sec.II [A][2]
   Undocumented workers...Pt 1: Sec.II [A][3][e][iii]
Historical background...Pt 1: Sec.I [C][2]
Preemption powers of...Pt 4: Sec.VII
Unfair labor practices, protections against
   Coercion...Pt 2: Sec.I [B], Pt 2: Sec.I [D]
   Complaint proceedings...Pt 1: Sec.II [B][1]
   Concerted activities (See Concerted Activities)
   "C" proceedings...Pt 1: Sec.II [B][1]
   Discharge...Pt 2: Sec.III [E]
   Discrimination (See Discrimination)
   Economic coercion or inducement...Pt 2: Sec.I [D]; Pt 2: Sec.I [E]
   Employer responsibility for antiunion conduct of subordinates...Pt 2: Sec.I [F]
   Espionage...Pt 2: Sec.I [E]
   Featherbedding...Pt 4: Sec.VI
   First Amendment (free speech) principle
      Antiunion speeches and publications...Pt 2: Sec.I [B]
      Organizing union movements...Pt 2: Intro
   Interference by employer
      Generally...Pt 2: Sec.I

Administration of labor organization, involvement in... Pt 2: Sec.II
Antiunion speeches and publications... Pt 2: Sec.I [B]
Domination by employer... Pt 2: Sec.II
Financial intervention... Pt 2: Sec.II
Formation of labor organization, involvement in... Pt 2: Sec.II
Lockouts... Pt 2: Sec.III [D]
Supporting union organization... Pt 2: Sec.II
Interrogation of employees regarding union activity... Pt 2: Sec.I [C]
Intimidation... Pt 2: Sec.I [E]
Limiting organizational activities on employer's premises
Generally... Pt 2: Sec.I [A]
Discriminatory policies... Pt 2: Sec.I [A]
Email use by employees... Pt 2: Sec.I [A]
Off-duty employees access to employer's premises... Pt 2: Sec.I [A]
Solicitation and distribution of literature at workplace... Pt 2: Sec.I [A]
Lockouts... Pt 2: Sec.III [D]
Plant shutdowns... Pt 2: Sec.III [D]
Refusal to bargain collectively, recourse for... Pt 3: Sec.II
Representation proceedings... Pt 1: Sec.II [B][1]
Reprisals against employees (See Concerted Activities)
Restraint by employer... Pt 2: Sec.I
Retaliatory discharge... Pt 2: Sec.III [E]
"R" proceedings... Pt 1: Sec.II [B][1]
"Runaway shops"... Pt 2: Sec.III [D]
Surveillance... Pt 2: Sec.I [E]
"Temporary closing" cases... Pt 2: Sec.III [D]
Unfair representation... Pt 5: Sec.II [B]
Violence... Pt 2: Sec.I [E]

National Labor Relations Board (NLRB)
Appeals of decisions... Pt 1: Sec.II [B]
Cease and desist orders... Pt 1: Sec.II [B]
Complaint proceedings... Pt 1: Sec.II [B][1]
General counsel... Pt 1: Sec.II [B][1]
Jurisdiction, exercising... Pt 1: Sec.II [A][2]
Organization of... Pt 1: Sec.II [B][1]
Procedures for filing and handling complaints... Pt 1: Sec.II [B][2]
Reinstatement orders... Pt 1: Sec.II [B]; Pt 2: Sec.III [E]
Rulemaking authority... Pt 1: Sec.II [C]

Norris-La Guardia Act
Right to peacefully picket, boycott or strike... Pt 4: Sec.I [B]; Pt 6: Sec.IV

P

Picketing (See Strikes, Boycotts and Picketing)

R

Railway Labor Act
Arbitration under... Pt 6: Sec.II [C]

Reinstatement
NLRB actions... Pt 1: Sec.II [B][2]; Pt 2: Sec.III [E]

Retaliatory Discharge
Union involvement... Pt 2: Sec.III [E]

Right-to-Work Laws
Generally...Pt 2: Sec.III [B][4]
Crossing picket lines...Pt 4: Sec.II

S

Social Media
Concerted activities on...Pt 2: Sec. III [C][1]

Strikes, Boycotts and Picketing
Generally...Pt 5: Intro; Pt 4: Sec.I [B]
Anti-injunction statutes...Pt 4: Sec.I [B]
Byrnes Act protections against employer interference...Pt 2: Sec.I [E]
Concerted activities generally (See Concerted Activities)
Consumer boycotts...Pt 4: Sec.IV [D], Pt 4: Sec.IV [E]
Crossing picket line...Pt 4: Sec.II
Injunctions
    Generally...Pt 6: Sec.IV
    Anti-injunction statutes against boycotts or picketing...Pt 4: Sec.I [B]
    Norris-La Guardia Act, effect of...Pt 6: Sec.IV
Lockouts...Pt 2: Sec.III [D]
Norris-La Guardia Act...Pt 4: Sec.I [B]; Pt 6: Sec.IV
No-strike clauses...Pt 6: Sec.IV
"Organizational" picketing...Pt 4: Sec.III
Plant shutdowns...Pt 2: Sec.III [D]
"Recognitional" picketing...Pt 4: Sec.III
Replacement workers
    Use of during strikes...Pt 2: Sec. III [C][7]
Secondary activities
    Ally doctrine...Pt 4: Sec.IV [C]
    Common situs problems...Pt 4: Sec.IV [B]
    Consumer boycotts or picketing...Pt 4: Sec.IV [D], [E]
    Damages for unlawful secondary activity...Pt 4: Sec.IV [G]
    Handbilling...Pt 4: Sec.IV [E]
    Hot cargo agreements...Pt 4: Sec. IV [F]
    "Organizational" picketing...Pt 4: Sec.III
    Primary-secondary distinction...Pt 4: Sec.IV [A]
    "Recognitional" picketing...Pt 4: Sec.III
    Threats and coercion of secondary employers...Pt 4: Sec.IV [E]
    Unfair labor practice violation, as...Pt 5: Sec.II [B]
Sympathy strikes...Pt 6: Sec.IV
"Temporary closing" cases...Pt 2: Sec.III [D]
Union benefits...Pt 2: Sec.III [B][2]

T

Taft-Hartley Act
Generally...Pt 1: Sec.I [C][4]

Technological Changes in the Workplace
Globalization and...Pt 1: Intro

Torts
Actions for...Pt 4: Sec.I [A]
Labor Management Relations Act, Section 301 preemption of state law...Pt 6: Sec.V

U

Unfair Labor Practices
NLRA protections against (See National Labor Relations Act (NLRA))

Unions
Collective bargaining (See Collective Bargaining)

Discrimination claims (See Discrimination)

Dues
    Labor Management Reporting and Disclosure Act...Pt 7: Sec. II
    Membership...Pt 2: Sec.III [B][2]
    Right to challenge expenditures...Pt 2: Sec.III [B][2]
    Strike benefits...Pt 2: Sec.III [B][2]

Elections
    Generally...Pt 3: Sec.I, Pt 3: Sec.I [C]
    Bars to conducting...Pt 3: Sec.I [A]
    Labor Management Reporting and Disclosure Act...Pt 7: Sec. II
    "R" (representation) complaint proceedings...Pt 1: Sec.II [B][1]

Hiring halls...Pt 2: Sec.III [B][1]; Pt 5: Sec.II [B]

Internal affairs
    Autonomy...Pt 7 Intro
    Bill of rights for union members...Pt 7
    Discipline of members...Pt 4: Sec. II
    Labor Management Reporting and Disclosure Act (See Labor Management Reporting and Disclosure Act (LMRDA))

Membership and organization
    Bill of rights for members...Pt 7: Sec.I
        Checkoff...Pt 2: Sec.III [B][2]
        Closed shops...Pt 2: Sec.III [B][2]
    Collective bargaining units (See Collective Bargaining, subhead: Units)
    Discrimination actions against employees for union activities (See Discrimination)
    Employee Free Choice Act...Pt 1: Sec.I [C][6], Pt 6: Sec.II [B][1]
    Resign, right to...Pt 4: Sec.II
    "Right-to-work" legislation...Pt 2: Sec.III [B][4]

Monopoly wage model...Pt 5: Intro

Representation
    Collective bargaining units (See Collective Bargaining)
    Refusal to bargain collectively, proceedings for...Pt 1: Sec.II [B]; Pt 4: Sec.II

Resign, right to...Pt 4: Sec.II

Security agreements...Pt 2: Sec.III [B][2]

Unfair labor practices, protection against (See National Labor Relations Act (NLRA))

W

Wagner Act (See National Labor Relations Act (NLRA))

Weingarten Rights
Generally...Pt 2: Sec.III [C][5]

Work Stoppages (See Strikes, Boycotts And Picketing)

Wrongful Discharge
Retaliatory discharge...Pt 2: Sec.III [E]; Pt 6: Sec.V